Routing, Flow, and Capacity Design in Communication and Computer Networks

The Morgan Kaufmann Series in Networking
Series Editor, David Clark, M.I.T.

Routing, Flow, and Capacity Design in Communication and Computer Networks
Michal Pióro and Deepankar Medhi

Wireless Sensor Networks: An Information Processing Approach
Feng Zhao and Leonidas Guibas

Network Recovery: Protection and Restoration of Optical, SONET-SDH, IP, and MPLS
Jean Philippe Vasseur, Mario Pickavet, and Piet Demeester

Communication Networking: An Analytical Approach
Anurag Kumar, D. Manjunath, and Joy Kuri

The Internet and Its Protocols: A Comparative Approach
Adrian Farrel

Modern Cable Television Technology: Video, Voice, and Data Communications, 2e
Walter Ciciora, James Farmer, David Large, and Michael Adams

Bluetooth Application Programming with the Java APIs
C Bala Kumar, Paul J. Kline, and Timothy J. Thompson

Policy-Based Network Management: Solutions for the Next Generation
John Strassner

Computer Networks: A Systems Approach, 3e
Larry L. Peterson and Bruce S. Davie

Network Architecture, Analysis, and Design, 2e
James D. McCabe

MPLS Network Management: MIBs, Tools, and Techniques
Thomas D. Nadeau

Developing IP-Based Services: Solutions for Service Providers and Vendors
Monique Morrow and Kateel Vijayananda

Telecommunications Law in the Internet Age
Sharon K. Black

Optical Networks: A Practical Perspective, 2e
Rajiv Ramaswami and Kumar N. Sivarajan

Internet QoS: Architectures and Mechanisms
Zheng Wang

TCP/IP Sockets in Java: Practical Guide for Programmers
Michael J. Donahoo and Kenneth L. Calvert

TCP/IP Sockets in C: Practical Guide for Programmers
Kenneth L. Calvert and Michael J. Donahoo

Multicast Communication: Protocols, Programming, and Applications
Ralph Wittmann and Martina Zitterbart

MPLS: Technology and Applications
Bruce Davie and Yakov Rekhter

High-Performance Communication Networks, 2e
Jean Walrand and Pravin Varaiya

Internetworking Multimedia
Jon Crowcroft, Mark Handley, and Ian Wakeman

Understanding Networked Applications: A First Course
David G. Messerschmitt

Integrated Management of Networked Systems: Concepts, Architectures, and their Operational Application
Heinz-Gerd Hegering, Sebastian Abeck, and Bernhard Neumair

Virtual Private Networks: Making the Right Connection
Dennis Fowler

Networked Applications: A Guide to the New Computing Infrastructure
David G. Messerschmitt

Wide Area Network Design: Concepts and Tools for Optimization
Robert S. Cahn

For further information on these books and for a list of forthcoming titles, please visit our website at http://www.mkp.com

Routing, Flow, and Capacity Design in Communication and Computer Networks

Michał Pióro

Warsaw University of Technology, Warsaw, Poland

Lund University, Lund, Sweden

Deepankar Medhi

University of Missouri-Kansas City

Kansas City, Missouri, USA

ELSEVIER

AMSTERDAM • BOSTON • HEIDELBERG • LONDON
NEW YORK • OXFORD • PARIS • SAN DIEGO
SAN FRANCISCO • SINGAPORE • SYDNEY • TOKYO
MORGAN KAUFMANN PUBLISHERS IS AN IMPRINT OF ELSEVIER

MORGAN KAUFMANN PUBLISHERS

Senior Editor	Rick Adams
Publishing Services Manager	André Cuello
Project Manager	Anne B. McGee
Associate Editor	Karyn Johnson
Cover Design	Eric DeCicco
Composition	Kolam, Inc.
Copyeditor	Kolam USA
Proofreader	Kolam USA
Indexer	Kolam USA
Interior Printer	Maple-Vail Book Manufacturing Group
Cover Printer	Phoenix Color Corp.

Morgan Kaufmann Publishers is an imprint of Elsevier.
500 Sansome Street, Suite 400, San Francisco, CA 94111

This book is printed on acid-free paper.

Library of Congress Cataloging-in-Publication Data
Application submitted.

ISBN: 0-12-557189-5

For information on all Morgan Kaufmann publications, visit our website at *www.mkp.com*.

Printed and bound by CPI Group (UK) Ltd, Croydon, CR0 4YY

Transferred to Digital Print 2011

To our parents

Lilianna and the memory of Michał Pióro
Preeti and Jyotiprasad Medhi

CONTENTS

APPENDICES

FOREWORD

Debasis Mitra
Vice President, Mathematical Sciences Research,
Bell Laboratories, Lucent Technologies

Michał Pióro and Deepankar Medhi have written a book that will be welcomed by members of the networking community who have an interest in network design. Network design has traditionally played an important, perhaps even a central, role in telecommunications. There are several reasons for this, and one is that network design is the bridge between demand estimates and capital investments in network infrastructure. Its reach also extends to the design of network operations. Thus, network design has much to contribute in optimizing a service provider's capital expenditure (CAPEX) and operational expenditure (OPEX). The span of the book splendidly captures the breadth of the role of network design. For instance, major portions deal with least cost network design, which is aimed at CAPEX reduction, while other parts of the book address issues of restoration, routing, and provisioning, which affect OPEX.

The definitions of problems in network design and the algorithms for their solutions have evolved over time to keep up with the changes in technologies and their roles in telecommunications. Importantly, this book reflects the all-important dynamism of networking. The reader will find in it, for instance, the essentials of design of circuit-switched networks, the mainstay of telephony for many decades, as well as the design issues in more recent technologies, such as IP and optical networking. The book provides the reader with a kaleidoscopic view of technologies and protocols seen through the lens of network design.

The heart of the book is its treatment of modeling and algorithms. It is also the unifying force. The authors have wisely chosen to focus on a multi-commodity flow-based approach. While the inclusion of multiple approaches, such as probabilistic modeling and performance evaluation, must have appealed, the cost would have been a loss of focus and depth. As it is, the book provides an in-depth treatment of an important segment of network design algorithms, including their theoretical bases and role in design tools.

The reader will find many unique insights and pointers to research and problem solving in this book. The following topics will serve to illustrate this point. The authors bring a special perspective to the design for protection and restoration of optical and MPLS networks. The treatment of multi-layer network design, such as IP over SONET, is also quite special. Fairness in networks is, of course, a topic that has an extensive literature, but the book's thorough coverage of the implications on design represents another special feature. The design of weights for OSPF routing in IP networking is yet another example of a special feature found in the book.

Researchers, students, and practitioners of network design will warmly welcome the book to their shelves. It will serve as a beacon and be consulted for many years to come.

PREFACE

Modeling and design of large communication and computer networks has always been an important area to both researchers and practitioners. The interest in developing efficient design models and optimization methods has been stimulated by high deployment and maintenance costs of networks, which make good network design potentially capable of securing considerable savings. For many decades, the area of network design had been relatively stable and followed the development of telephone networks and their smooth transition from analog to digital systems. In the past decade, however, the networks have undergone a substantial change caused by the emergence and rapid development of new technologies and services, an enormous growth of traffic, demand for service availability and continuity, and attempts to integrate new networking and system techniques and different types of services in one network. As a consequence, today's network designers face new problems associated with diverse technologies, complicated network architectures, and advanced resource and service protection mechanisms. In the context of this book, these problems can be broadly divided into three classes: 1) developing adequate design models specific for different technologies such as transmission control protocol/Internet protocol (TCP/IP), digital telephony (i.e., integrated digital network—IDN), multi-protocol label switching (MPLS), asynchronous transfer mode (ATM), synchronous optical network/synchronous digital hierarchy (SONET/SDH), and wavelength division multiplexing (WDM); 2) proper multi-layer modeling across the network layers using different technologies (such as IP over ATM over SONET, IP over WDM, or IDN over SONET); and 3) considering restoration design, accounting for recovery from failures (such as cable cuts and switch breakdowns) of large capacity transport links and transit nodes.

As reflected in the title of the book, by network design we broadly refer to the optimal determination of traffic routing, traffic flow, and capacity of links and nodes in one or several resource layers of an expanding network, taking into account different network states related to failures and time-dependent traffic matrices. The number of papers and books on network design has constantly increased over the past decades. As a result of the collective effort, a considerable knowledge has been built, covering virtually all aspects of the field for all types of networks. Still, in general, there is a large gap between what is achievable through existing mathematical methods and what is actually used in practice for network design. The use of mathematical modeling and the application of efficient optimization algorithms to those models has not been fully utilized—in practice one often observes simplified approaches leading to too costly solutions. At the same time, it is important to recognize that much valuable theoretical work related to network design available in the existing literature may not be applicable in practice. Certainly, the relation between theory and practice of network design is not simple. In a sense, network design is a kind of art; the designer has to make selective use of various available theoretical models and approximations using his abilities, skills, and knowledge. At the same time, implementable solutions need to take into account various practical constraints which are difficult to consider in more general and abstract models. In effect, the designer is required to apply and tailor theoretical models in a way leading to solutions which can be then made useful in practice. We are convinced that in this process available mathematical developments play an important role and must be well understood. Clearly, one way to achieve this is by providing a dedicated systematic presentation of the knowledge on the network design optimization models and methods gathered in one place. This can substantially help not only a novice reader, but also an expert and a practitioner, understand where to begin, develop, and refresh their knowledge, if one were to study network design. Needless to say, our aim is at providing such an exposition in this book.

PURPOSE OF THIS BOOK

The main purpose of this book is to present basic principles and methods for developing optimization models for contemporary communication and computer network design. The book is focused on optimization problems and methods for traffic routing, flow, and resource capacity optimization. We aim at developing a general framework applicable to such technologies as IP, IDN, MPLS, ATM, SONET/SDH, and WDM, and capable to cope with new network technologies that will emerge in the future. The design models and methods considered here are mainly for backbone or core networks[1] as these are among the most challenging due to their scale, complexity, and cost. Certainly, some of the methods presented in this book can be used, after some modification, for other types of networks, e.g., access and local networks.

The current situation in network design is significantly different from that of the 1960s and 1970s, when the design methodology for the then dominant telephone networks was very well understood, described in manuals, and applied in practice. Today, with a great variety of network technologies and services, the knowledge on network design is spread over a large number of papers and books. There are many fine works that contain excellent models and methods; still, in most cases, their comprehension requires solid background in modeling and optimization, which is not common among network designers. In fact, it is hard to find works that present the material in a manner so that both beginners and experts can read and understand how different modeling and optimization techniques can be employed. Our book attempts to explain the principles and methods of network modeling and optimization in a comprehensive, unified, generic, and precise manner. To achieve this goal we present the problems on a level of abstraction that avoids unnecessary and tedious technological details, aiming at helping students, new employees, practitioners, and network designers to understand the basics, developments, and recent advances in network design.

[1]By backbone or core networks, we refer to networks, spread over a wide geographical area and carrying large volumes of traffic, that interconnect access or local networks.

Network design problems (NDPs) require mathematical formulations to become unambiguous and understandable to others; also, once the problem at hand is stated in a formal way, it reveals what optimization methods are applicable and appropriate. In our experience, most problems of routing, flow, and capacity design studied in this book are directly related to, and best tractable by the branch of optimization known as multi-commodity flow networks, extensively studied in the operations research and optimization literature for many different applications, including communication and computer networks. In fact, the multi-commodity flow network approach, with its flexibility in problem modeling and solid optimization background, is virtually the only way for achieving our target: providing general, precise, and effective means for efficient optimization-oriented modeling of the (enormously rich) family of valid NDPs.

Network designers usually have excellent knowledge of networking technologies (including communication and computer systems technologies, networking techniques, protocols, service implementation, traffic characterization, and so on), but may not have extensive background in optimization. On the other hand, specialists in optimization/operations research may not posses sufficient technological knowledge to develop and validate models for particular networks. With this in mind, our book tries to bridge the gap between the two "parallel" worlds: the people involved in networking technology and the people devoted to system modeling and optimization. In the process, when discussing the multi-commodity flow network concepts in Chapter 2, we have introduced a uniform notation and provided several problem-modeling examples. Symmetrically, in Chapter 3, we have formulated a number of problems related to specific network technologies to explain how to use the generic multi-commodity flow network modeling approaches for communication and computer networks. The subsequent chapters, devoted mostly to the presentation and development of the modeling and optimization methods for network design, are illustrated with further technology-related examples.

In an attempt to cover the major issues in the design of contemporary communication backbone networks, we have used a "three-dimensional" approach discussing the three main broad directions in network design: 1) modeling techniques for developing and formulating various design problems; 2) multi-layer modeling of networks comprising different technologies (and functionalities); and 3) incorporating network protection and restoration mechanisms. While dealing with these three dimensions, the book conveys techniques for precise modeling and formulating of valid design problems, optimization methods and algorithms applicable for the elaborated problems, and examples illustrating the efficiency of the resulting optimization models. Although the book does not attempt to answer questions whether one technology should be used instead of another for the best network design, the models and methods presented in this book can be useful in developing tools for answering such questions.

This book assumes a background in calculus and linear algebra on a level of a student with undergraduate degree in electrical engineering or computer science. Certainly, some knowledge of networking and telecommunications technology will be helpful in understanding the reasons for various modeling details.

To conclude, our attempt was to write a book that can be useful for graduate students in telecommunications, electrical engineering, computer science, and operations research, as well as for researchers in academia and industry in exploring the sometimes difficult area of contemporary communication and computer network design through mathematical optimization-oriented modeling. The topics covered in this book can hopefully be of interest to scientists and doctoral students in identifying fruitful areas for original theoretical research. Our aim was also to reach out to practitioners by illustrating various modeling techniques through technology-oriented examples. At the same time we believe that this book may be useful for the practitioners in their efforts to make advances in the area of network design through systemizing and deepening their theoretical background. For that matter, we cannot think of a better way for a network designer to extend his basic background knowledge than to study principles of the models and methods of multi-commodity flow networks, to which this book is mostly devoted.

CONTENTS AND ORGANIZATION

The book is divided into three parts. Part I—Introductory Network Design—is composed of three chapters and serves as the Introduction. Chapter 1 introduces the basic notions and concepts of network modeling and design by providing an analogy to airline networks and explaining these concepts through simple examples. In Chapter 2, we discuss and introduce the multi-commodity flow network notation used throughout the book, and illustrate the principles of building network models using representative examples, further developed in Parts II and III. Finally, in Chapter 3, we present a set of specific technology-related examples, showing how to apply multi-commodity flow network modeling techniques to selected up-to-date networks based on different technologies, such as IP, IDN, MPLS, ATM, SONET/SDH, WDM, and IP over SONET.

Part II—Design Modeling and Methods—consists of five chapters and is devoted to the most common case of designing single-layer networks for the normal state[2]. Chapter 4 presents various important general multi-commodity flow network models, starting with simple examples, and gradually extending them, showing how different types of constraints and variables can be used to express different desired characteristics of the models, such as single-path routing or modular link capacity. We discuss specific types of multi-commodity formulations, such as the node-link and the link-path formulation. In Chapter 5, we present various basic optimization approaches applicable to design problems formulated in Chapter 4 and in subsequent chapters. We discuss linear programming (including the simplex method and interior point approaches), branch-and-bound and branch-and-cut for mixed integer programming, decomposition methods for linear and mixed integer programming (Lagrangian relaxation, column generation, and Benders' decomposition), stochastic metaheuristics (simulated annealing, evolutionary algorithms, and others), and special methods for convex and concave problems. These methods are used and illustrated in the subsequent chapters. The remaining three chapters of Part II are devoted to three important classes of design models not considered in Chapter 4. Each of these chapters develops relevant design models, applies appropriate optimization methods, and shows numerical examples. Chapter 6 considers a class of design problems related to location and topological design which take into account the installation cost of links and nodes. Then we move to recent

[2]By the normal state of network operation, we mean the situation when all resources are available and fully operative, and when the demand matrix is fixed. A single-layer network is the network that utilizes one technology.

design problems and present material on designing networks with the "open shortest path first" (OSPF) type shortest-path routing in Chapter 7, discussing the state-of-the-art in this recent Internet-related network design area. Finally, in Chapter 8, we proceed to another recent issue of fair networks with elastic (e.g., IP best-effort) traffic.

Part III—Advanced Models—also contains five chapters, and explains more complicated types of problems involving multi-state and multi-layer network modeling. Chapter 9 begins by discussing protection and restoration design problems in single-layer networks, and various problem formulations corresponding to different protection mechanisms with their applicability to different technologies. Then, in Chapter 10, we present appropriate solution methods, including decomposition methods and meta-heuristics, thoroughly explaining how to apply them to different restoration problems in large networks. In Chapter 11, we discuss models for multi-hour and multi-period, single-layer network design, together with selected algorithmic approaches. We then proceed to the next group of problems, related to the important issue of multi-layer modeling and normal/restorartion design of contemporary networks (Chapter 12), including multi-layer restoration design for fair networks (Chapter 13).

Additionally, the book contains four useful appendices/refreshers (Appendices A through D), each of a value on its own, devoted respectively to the basics of optimization theory, to the notion of computational complexity and $\mathcal{NP}$-completeness, to the shortest paths algorithms, and to the use of optimization tools. This is followed by a list of acronyms used throughout the book. Each chapter (except Chapter 1) contains a list of exercises with different levels of difficulty; solutions to selected exercises are also included. An exhaustive list of the referenced and related publications is included at the end of the book. Naming and numbering conventions, as well as special separators used in proofs, remarks, and examples are described in Section 1.9 of Chapter 1.

HOW TO USE THIS BOOK

At the university level the book can be used for several different types of courses. For example:

- one-semester introductory course on network design covering Chapters 1 through 4, and some selected material from Chapter 5;
- one-semester modeling-oriented course concentrating primarily on chapters and sections on modeling (Chapters 1 through 4, parts of Chapters 6 through 8, Chapter 9, parts of Chapters 11 and 12), and skipping the chapters on optimization algorithms (Chapters 5, most of Chapter 8, Chapter 10, and most of Chapter 13);
- a more in-depth two-semester graduate course containing a fair balance between material on modeling and optimization algorithms (Chapters 1 through 8, Chapter 9, and parts of Chapters 10 through 12);
- an advanced one-semester doctoral course on selected models and advanced optimization methods, with a focus on integer programming models (Chapters 1 through 8);
- an advanced two-semester doctoral course based on the entire material covered by this book.

A companion web site is available at the publisher's address (http://www.mkp.com), which contains related materials for use with this book. For example, complete solutions to exercises can be found at the book web site for instructors; Powerpoint versions of the figures and material will also be provided for instructional use. We plan to gradually add new exercises (and solutions) as they appear, as well as to update the list of references. Furthermore, new technology-related examples and new problem formulations will be gradually added to the web site, as soon as we find them mature and appropriate.

We have tried to structure the book in such a way that it can be a valuable aid for practitioners. For example, with our introductory approach on illustrating NDPs (Chapter 2), followed by technology-oriented examples (Chapter 3), in-depth explanation of modeling issues such as how to use different types of constraints and variables (Chapter 4), and algorithmic background (Chapter 5), a practitioner should be able to understand and use this material in real-life applications.

Finally, this book can be used as a reference material by researchers and designers, where they can find a broad set of basic, as well as more advanced modeling and optimization techniques, results, and examples, and see how these techniques can be tailored and used for particular applications.

ACKNOWLEDGMENTS

The impetus for this book came about during the first author's visit to the University of Missouri–Kansas City (UMKC) as a visiting scholar and professor in the Fall 2002 semester. During a casual conversion, both authors thought that such a book would be useful to explore. This casual discussion eventually led to a draft of some early chapters and a book proposal. We thank UMKC for making this visit possible; otherwise, this book probably would not have ever materialized. During the main writing phase of this book, an invitation by Lund University to the second author during the Summer of 2003 allowed several critical pieces of this book to be discussed and completed.

Detailed reviews of various chapters by Zbigniew Dziong, Jeffrey Kennington, Bernard Liau, and Włodzimierz Ogryczak, along with their extensive comments, were extremely beneficial in improving the technical content and organization of this book and in avoiding many mistakes. In addition, many people read one or more chapters (or sections) and provided valuable comments; we thank Supratik Bhattacharyya, Robert Doverspike, David Gay, Jacek Gondzio, Bjarne Helvik, Michał Jarociński, Sławomir Kula, Józef Lubacz, Dritan Nace, Pål Nilsson, Jim Pearce, Mirosław Slomiński, Howard Thompson, David Tipper, Artur Tomaszewski, and Di Yuan for their help in this regard.

Our doctoral students from Warsaw University of Technology (Poland), UMKC (U.S.), and Lund University (Sweden) helped in many ways to make this book happen; hence, many thanks go to Gaurav Agrawal, Mateusz Dzida, Piotr Gajowniczek, Dijiang Huang, Piotr Karaś, Stanisław Kozdrowski, Balaji Krithikaivasan, Eligijus Kubilinskas, Andrzej Mysłek, Pål Nilsson, Amit Sinha, Shekhar Srivastava, Michał Szcześniak, Tomasz Szymański, and Michał Zagożdżon. Also, help from János Harmatos, Alpár Jüttner, Anusha Madhavan, and Vamsi Valluri is kindly acknowledged.

Furthermore, we thank Appie van de Liefvoort for writing Appendix B, and Mateusz Dzida, Shekhar Srivastava, and Michał Zagożdżon for their valuable contribution in writing Appendix C.

To a significant extent this book has been made possible because of the extensive research work of its authors. Over the years, while being with Warsaw University of Technology and with Lund University, the first author has lead (and participated in) many research projects on communication and computer network design for such partners as Alcatel SESA (Madrid), Ericsson (Stockholm and Budapest), International Telecommunication Union (Geneva), NUTEK (Stockholm), Polish Committee of Scientific Research (Warsaw), Telekomunikacja Polska S.A. (Warsaw), ERA GSM (Warsaw), and others. The second author started his career working for AT&T Bell Laboratories and then joined UMKC, where receiving research funding from National Science Foundation, Defense Advanced Research Project Agency, University of Missouri Research Board, and Sprint Corporation helped him explore work on survivable network design and management as well as multi-layer networking.

For many years the authors have taught courses on network design to masters and doctoral students at Warsaw University of Technology, UMKC, and Lund University; the material used in many parts of this book has evolved and been tested through delivery of these courses, giving a good sense of how to present its contents and help students understand network design.

The first author wishes to express his gratitude to such people as Åke Arvidsson, Jerry Ash, Les Berry, Prosper Chemouil, Tibor Cinkler, Zbigniew Dziong, Janusz Filipiak, Gábor Fodor, Len Forys, Richard Gibbens, André Girard, Richard Harris, Villy Bæk Iversen, Andrzej Jajszczyk, Michał Jarociński, Laszlo Jereb, Frank Kelly, Peter Key, Ulf Körner, Sławomir Kukliński, Józef Lubacz, Lorne Mason, Andrzej Pach, Harry Perros, Lars Reneby, Jim Roberts, Brunilde Sanso, Oscar González-Soto, Ignat Stanev, Áron Szentesi, Artur Tomaszewski, Bengt Wallström, Roland Wessäly, and Thomas Wickberg for valuable and clarifying discussions on network design issues carried out for over 20 years.

The second author is grateful to Jerry Ash, Fu Chang, Reynold Chen, Robert Cotter, Pete Dollard, Robert Doverspike, Brion Feinberg, André Girard, Götz Gräfe, Wayne Grover, Jeff Horen, Wen-Jung Hsin, Villy Bæk Iversen, Richard Jessup, Mukesh Kacker, Renee Keffer, John Klincewicz, Jean-François Labourdette, David Lynch, Olvi Mangasarian, Robert Meyer, Amarnath Mukherjee, Toshikane Oda, Jim Pearce, Steve Robinson, Adam Rosenberg, Eric Rosenberg, Keith Ross, Iraj Saniee, Brunilde Sansò, Val Shkolnikov, Jerry Stach, John Strand, Srinivasa Thirumalasetty, Mikkel Thorup, David Tipper, Appie van de Liefvoort, Yufei Wang, and Di Yuan for many enlightening discussion and interactions during the past two decades. Special thanks go to my siblings and cc76batch—you know who you are. Last, but not least, over the years the second author has had many conversations with his wife, Karen, whose expertise in transport network design was invaluable in helping clarify the connection between traffic and transport networks in order to address a variety of NDPs.

We also received help in many ways from several people at crucial moments during the preparation of this book. We thank Ulf Körner, Józef Lubacz and William Osborne for their support and help.

We thank Debasis Mitra for writing the foreword for this book.

During the preparation of this book, it has been a pleasure to work with Rick Adams and Karyn Johnson of Morgan Kaufmann Publishers. At various stages of the book, they provided guidance in numerous different ways. Certainly, they showed enough patience with us during the final stages of the manuscript preparation. During the final production cycle of this book, we appreciate receiving numerous help from our project manager, Christine Brandt.

Writing a book is much more work than we have ever imagined. Our families perhaps suffered the most during our long hours of working on this book. We thank our wives—Alicja Pióro and Karen Medhi—and our children—Krzysztof and Ewa Pióro, and Neiloy and Robby Medhi—for their support, love, and understanding during the preparation of this book.

Micha l Pawe l Pióro and Deepankar ''Deep'' Medhi

Warsaw, Lund, and Kansas City

I

INTRODUCTORY NETWORK DESIGN

Part I consists of three chapters. The goal of this part is to acquaint the reader with the basic ideas in network design, to introduce the proper notation for network modeling, and to show how to formulate basic design problems, first in a general way, and then for selected, technology-related cases.

In Chapter 1, we start with an overview of communication and computer networks, showing why traffic (demand) is different for different networks and describing its role in network design. We then show simple examples to illustrate how routing can influence network design. We also discuss the architecture of networks and the network management cycle and discuss their relation to network design.

Chapter 2 starts with a discussion of different notational conventions for modeling and formulating network design problem and introduces the notation adopted for this book. Next, basic types of general network design problems are introduced through simple illustrative examples. For this purpose, we have covered such problems as network dimensioning problems for normal state, shortest-path routing design, fair bandwidth assignment, topological design, restoration design, and multi-layer design. In the process, we have explained in detail the notation used, how to model different design requirements, and how to generalize the introduced formulations.

Chapter 3 takes a different route as our interest in this chapter is to give you a set of specific technology-related examples where various network design problems appear, and more importantly, how these problems can be appropriately formulated, taking into account specific, technology-driven requirements and constraints.

CHAPTER 1

Overview

Communication networks[1] were born more than 100 years ago the moment Alexander Graham Bell made his now famous call to Thomas A. Watson and said "Watson come here, I want you!" on March 10, 1876. Almost a century later, another form of communication emerged when ARPAnet's first two nodes were connected between the SDS Sigma 7 host computer at the University of California-Los Angeles and the SDS 940 host computer at the Stanford Research Institute, and the first message sent "Lo!" on October 29, 1969, crashed [Kle]! As we know, the famous phone call essentially gave birth to the development of the global switched telephone network, and the initial data message was the starting point of the eventually explosive growth of the Internet in the past quarter century. Many scientists and engineers contributed to the process of reaching where we are today.

Today, the case of routing a phone call from one user to another user needs to go through a series of telephone switches, such as central offices and toll switches, to reach the destination (Figure 1.1a). Similarly, to access a web page over the Internet, a transport layer virtual connection is established from a user's computer to the web server where data packets created by this request need to traverse from this user's computer through a hub and/or through routers (sometimes many of them) to the server at the destination (Figure 1.1b).

The views presented in Figures 1.1a and 1.1b can be best labeled as a single user's view. But there are millions of connections going on for phone calls and for web transfer; certainly, they do not and can not all go through the same set of switches (for telephone calls) and routers (for Internet). This would not be possible. Intuitively, a phone call from the second author in Kansas City, U.S., to the first author in Warsaw, Poland, would go through a different set of telephone switches than a call from the second author in Kansas City to the first author in Lund, Sweden;[2] certainly, it is possible that there are some common sets of switches along the way. Similarly, the first author, sitting in his office at the Warsaw University of Technology, Poland, and accessing the second author's web page at the University of Missouri–Kansas City would go through a set of hubs and routers which would be different than those used if he tries to access the same web page from his other office at the Lund University, Sweden; again, as in the case of the telephone calls, a subset of hubs and routers for the web transfer can be common. Now, try to imagine millions of phone calls that go between different parts of the world, or millions of web servers accessed

[1] To set the record straight, Samuel Morse sent the first telegram with the message "What hath God wrought?" from Washington, D.C., to Baltimore on May 24, 1844.

[2] Yes, the first author maintains two offices, one in Warsaw, Poland, and the other in Lund, Sweden.

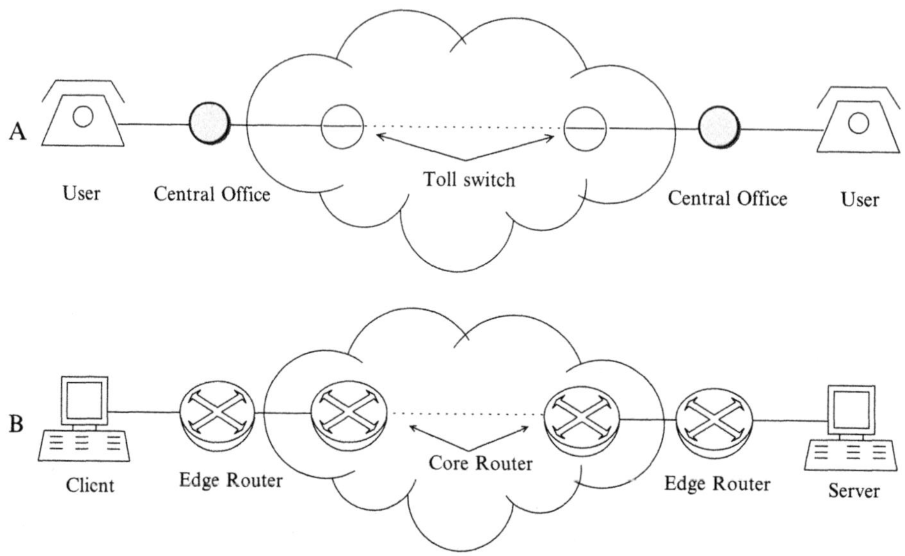

FIGURE 1.1 A Simple Example: (A) Telephone Call and (B) Internet Web Transfer

by numerous users across the networks from all over the world. The picture is actually quite different than the myopic depiction in Figures 1.1a and 1.1b; a high level view of many users involved depicting a more accurate view is shown in Figure 1.2a for telephone calls and Figure 1.2b for web transfers.

1.1 A NETWORK ANALOGY

This is where a simple analogy to air travel is perhaps helpful. Suppose that the second author wants to fly from Kansas City to Warsaw; he will need to go from his home to the Kansas City airport by car or taxi and take several airplanes hopping through many airports (and many hours of travel!) before arriving at Warsaw, and then finally reaching the first author in Warsaw. Now, if we consider the part that is confined to the airports only (i.e., leave out how the second author reached the airport in Kansas City and finally from Warsaw airport to the first author's office), then we can envision a network of airports that are connected by links (i.e., direct, non-stop flights) to go from one place to another. In this example, if the second author flies from Kansas City to Detroit, USA, to Amsterdam to Warsaw, then the network in use consists of four airports connected by three links: 1) Kansas City to Detroit, 2) Detroit to Amsterdam, and 3) Amsterdam to Warsaw. On the other hand, if the second author wants to visit the first author in Lund, then actual air travel is really from Kansas City to Detroit to Amsterdam to Copenhagen (Denmark). From Copenhagen's Kastrup airport, a train that connects to Malmö, Sweden, is taken in order to reach Lund. There are a couple of important points to make from this analogy: 1) there are multiple transportation mechanisms that may be involved for the completion of the entire travel—car, airplane and, sometimes, train; 2) the mechanism to reach the airport on one end and to reach the eventual destination on the other

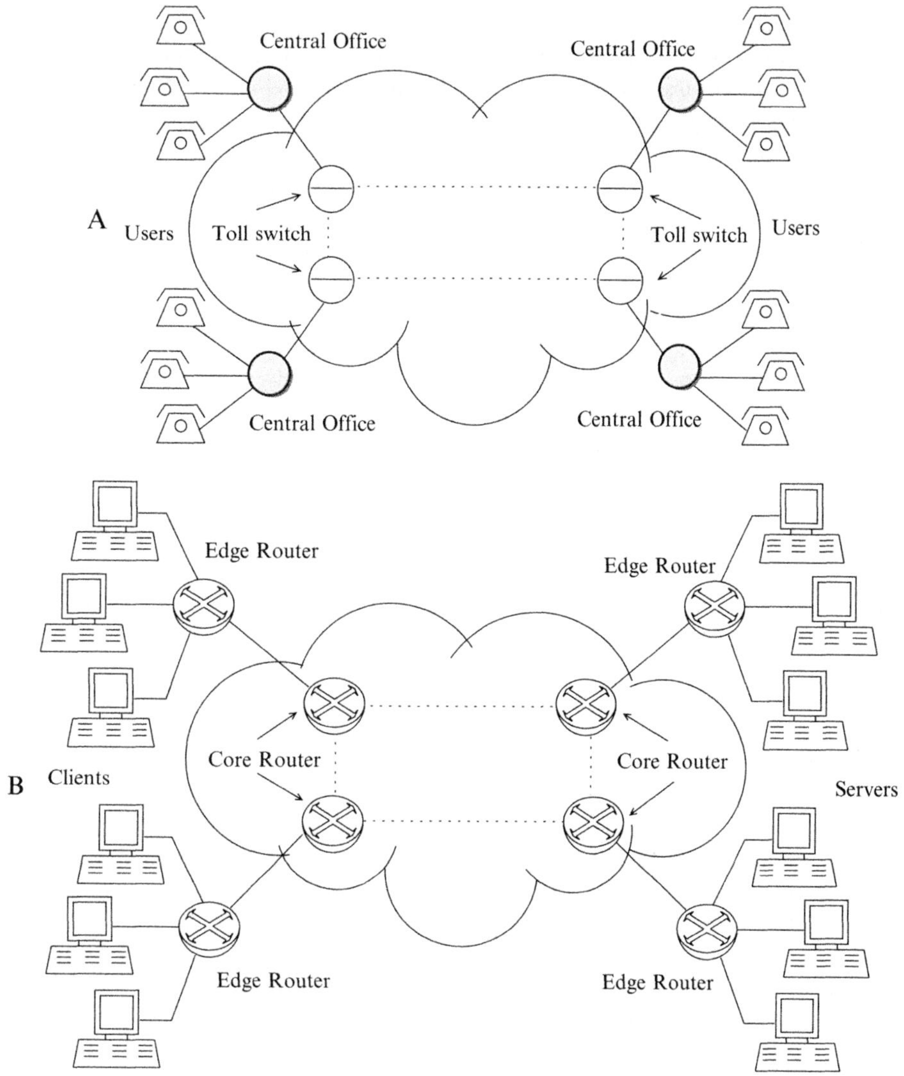

FIGURE 1.2 Many Users: (A) Telephone Networks and (B) Internet

end requires a form of *access* mechanism—car and train in this example; and 3) the core of the travel is the air travel. Thus, if we confine ourselves only to the air travel part, what we have is a collection of airports that form a core network.

In essence what we see, in the case of telephone and the Internet as well, is a topology in the form of *networks* that connect different *points* or *nodes* for requests made by numerous users as shown in Figures 1.2a and 1.2b; in fact, this is closer to reality than the simple point-to-point view shown earlier in Figures 1.1a and 1.1b. In a nutshell, the role of this book primarily concerns the *middle* part, i.e., the *core* or *backbone network*, (similar to the air travel part) which is made of routers and switches, after an end request leaves one end device (or user) and before it reaches the other end device. Generally, access links have *ingress traffic* (if traffic is entering the core) and *egress traffic* (if traffic is exiting from the core).

Consider again the air travel example. It is conceivable to have a direct, non-stop flight from Kansas City to Warsaw. In this case, a link between Kansas City and Warsaw would be in this network.[3] There are many reasons why such a direct flight between Kansas City and Warsaw may not be desirable–perhaps the most important reason is that there is not enough *traffic* between Kansas City and Warsaw to justify such a direct link (i.e., a non-stop flight); therefore, it is much more economical to let users connect or *hop* through different airports than to create such a direct flight. Certainly, users may change airline carriers at an airport to reach their destination. Similarly, there are peering points for communication networks where traffic is handed over from one network provider to another.

We have just mentioned the term *traffic* which many people understand from airline travel (and often from road travel as well). In fact, traffic is key to the telephone network and the Internet as well, and is strongly connected to the theme of this book. In Section 1.3, we will discuss what traffic really means and a brief overview of how it is estimated. Obviously, traffic changes over time, whether by the microsecond, second, minute, hour, day, month, or year; this usually depends on traffic dynamics. For now, we will assume that traffic is a fixed number, as in a fixed number of users wanting to fly, a fixed number of phone calls, or a fixed number of Internet sessions (and amount of data transfer).

The next important item is that we can use economies of scale to combine traffic between different points. For example, there could be air travelers (traffic) from St. Louis, U.S., to Copenhagen, which could possibly be routed from St. Louis to Detroit to Amsterdam to Copenhagen. The link, Detroit to Amsterdam, is common for Kansas City to Warsaw traffic and for St. Louis to Copenhagen traffic. Thus, you could imagine that bigger planes might serve better between Detroit and Amsterdam, due to high-volume common traffic which can take advantage of economies of scale.

Interestingly, communication and computer networks are not too different from the air traffic example we have discussed thus far. Refer to the example of a phone call between Kansas City and Warsaw, and the Internet web transfer. Analogous to the air travel example, a call needs to be connected through a series of switches (like airports); similarly, for accessing the second author's web page located in Kansas City from Warsaw, the request is directed through a series of routers.

As in the need to handle ensemble air travel traffic from Detroit to Amsterdam compared to other segments of travel through use of bigger airplanes (i.e., higher capacity), communication and computer networks also use links of different *capacity* (or *bandwidth*) for different parts of the network. Note also that if an airplane is full (i.e., the capacity is already saturated), no additional passenger can be admitted (unless a traveler wants to fly at a different time or date); a similar situation can happen in the telephone network if a

[3]The distance between Kansas City and Warsaw is 4,373 nautical miles. Currently, there are direct, non-stop flights longer than this distance, for example, between Hong Kong and Los Angeles; thus, a Kansas City to Warsaw flight is technically feasible [Ros03b].

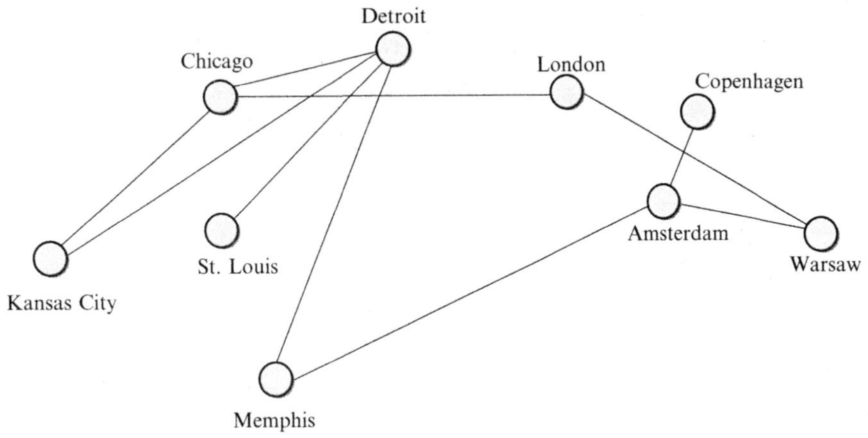

FIGURE 1.3 Possible Routes between Kansas City and Warsaw, and other Segments

link has no capacity left at a particular point in time—in which case, a call may not be admitted.

Suppose now that the airplane was actually full only for the Kansas City to Detroit link. You might still want to know if there is another way to go from Kansas City to Warsaw (at about the same time). It is indeed possible to do that either going from Kansas City to Memphis to Amsterdam to Warsaw or from Kansas City to Chicago to London to Warsaw. In other words, we have at least two other possible routes from Kansas City to Warsaw[4] (Figure 1.3). While in the case of air travel, a user is often required to *try* (or find) another path themselves (unless a travel agency is used); in the case of the telephone network, it is possible that the network itself can *try* these alternate paths from the originating point, before informing the user that the call could not be admitted to the network.[5] This is an example where the air travel network is different from the telephone network, partly due to reservation-based nature for air travel versus the real-time automated nature of call routing. Regardless, there is a set of possible paths between two end cities, which is also the case in communication networks. If a particular traffic type requires quality-of-service (QoS), e.g., in terms of bounded delay, then these possible paths can be accordingly adjusted. In terms of air travel, this would be analogous to say that you want to consider routes between two points where your travel time is less than a certain value.

Now, where and how is the Internet similar to the air travel scenario? In air travel, once you have a reservation, you are required to go from one airport to another airport before reaching your destination; in the process, you need to *wait* or halt for sometime at the intermediate airport. When you think about it, your air travel looks as if you are *stored* at an intermediate airport, before you are *forwarded*—this behavior of operation is often referred to as the *store-and-forward* paradigm. In fact, on the Internet, this paradigm holds. There is one difference. When you make a request to download a web page, the content (i.e.,

[4]These are indeed routes of different major airline carriers.

[5]In another form of telephone call routing, switches along the way determine if capacity is available on the next outgoing link.

the web page) is broken into small *chunks*, often called *data packets* or, simply, *packets*, which are transmitted through the network. Each data packet, like the user, is sent from one router to another router where it is momentarily stored before being forwarded to the next router. Thus, the Internet essentially works on the store-and-forward paradigm while the *store* part is almost instantaneous (for human perception), and fortunately not as bad as waiting at an airport. This paradigm, in the case of a packet network, is referred to as *packet switching*.

The actual routing on the Internet also has an analogy to air travel. It is possible that the second author was told in Kansas City that the path from Kansas City to Detroit to Amsterdam to Warsaw is fine; after arriving in Detroit the second author finds out that the plane from Detroit to Amsterdam is overbooked, and passengers are given the option of taking the Detroit to Memphis to Amsterdam to Warsaw route. In other words, the route *can* change while at a transit node (hop). This would be equivalent to saying that the routing is based on a *hop-by-hop*. In effect, routing in the Internet, by default, is based on this hop-by-hop notion.

Certainly, there are fundamental differences between the air travel scenario and the current Internet. We will discuss a couple of differences for the purpose of illustration: contrary to air travel where a traveler needs to make a reservation before flying (at least in most cases), a data packet currently does not need to make a reservation ahead of time to traverse the Internet; since many packets could conceivably be arriving at a router at about the same time, there is still a (minimal) delay between consecutive packets to reach the destination due to one-by-one packet processing while for air travel all travelers arrive at the same time.[6]

To summarize, a communication network needs to carry traffic where the network has different links of different capacity (bandwidth); the traffic may be routed via different paths to the destination. We need to have enough bandwidth in the network to carry the traffic while reducing the percentage of calls denied admission, or reducing the average data packet traversal delay on the Internet. In the process, we need to ask ourselves: 1) can we find better routes, 2) where should we add more bandwidth, 3) where and when should we add new nodes (and links) in the network, 4) how the inherent property of a network technology or protocol can affect our decision making, and 5) what level of abstraction is appropriate for a particular network for modeling purpose so that meaningful results can be obtained? Note that we can draw an analogy to the air travel network as well. For example, how big of a fleet is needed between Detroit and Amsterdam (and between other cities) so that traffic can be accommodated without denying access to many customers. Simply put, we ask ourselves *how to design* cost-effective core/backbone networks taking into consideration properties of the network, or in short, how to do *network design*. Interestingly, many of the problems posed here can be formulated into mathematical models and efficient optimization procedures (or algorithms) can be developed to solve these problems. In essence, this is what this book is all about.

In the next several sections, we present some basic details about networks, traffic, routing, and management to set the stage for the scope of this book (in Section 1.8).

---

[6]Note that packet processing looks similar to the road transportation network in which cars are analogous to data packets.

1.2 COMMUNICATION AND COMPUTER NETWORKS, AND NETWORK PROVIDERS

We start with additional information about networks that we will be considering in this book. For simplicity, we will continue to use the Kansas City to Warsaw example where we now assume the environment to be a communication network instead of an air travel network. We will discuss this separately for the telephone network and for the Internet.

In the case of the telephone network, consider the call originating in Kansas City from the second author's office; this will first enter the central office (a specialized name for a telephone switch) of the local telephone carrier. After that, based on determining the dialed digits and identifying the long-distance provider, the local carrier relays the call to the switch of the long-distance/international carrier, who, in turn, will carry this call through several switches in its network including the international gateway switch to make the transatlantic transfer. Eventually, the call will be delivered to the telecommunication carrier in Poland which will carry the call in its own network for delivery to the first author's office in Warsaw. The important point to note here is that a call is carried by different network providers, also called network operators, for different segments of the call. The call connection process in the telephone network uses a form of switching, known as *circuit switching* where a dedicated circuit is set for each telephone call, for example, for the call from the second author to the first author. By dedicated, we mean that no other phone call can use this circuit and the capacity required for this circuit.

In the case of the web request from the first author to the second author's web site, the request traverses through a series of different network providers (usually referred to as Internet service providers, or ISPs) as follows: WUT-net → pol34-net → geant-net (DANTE) → ucaid-net → greatplains-net → more-net → UMKC-net. In technical terms, each ISP's network is an autonomous system, or AS (although it is possible that an ISP is made of multiples ASs). This scenario is somewhat analogous to the telephone call scenario in the sense that different providers are involved in different segments to carry the data traffic for completing the actual web transfer. The data packets generated as a response to this request (i.e., acknowledgement packets) would also traverse in the same reverse direction (this is the common situation, unless there is a different routing exchange policy in place in the intermediate networks). In either direction, packet switching is used for routing packets through the network.

An important point to observe from both of these examples is that a request (a call or a web transfer) goes through a *series* of networks maintained by different providers (see Figure 1.4 where each network is depicted using a cloud); note that these providers would need to have cooperative arrangement among themselves for carrying out such a request. This cooperation between neigboring providers is often referred to as the *peering* arrangement. Now, each of these networks have their own switches or routers (depending on the request type); at the *border* or *gateway*, transfer from one network to another is accomplished. This means that it is completely up to each such network on how they want to route their traffic *within* their network and/or how many routers/switches they might want to use to accomplish this. From this practical setup, it should be clear that network design problems are essentially confined *within* each network, or its *administrative domain*

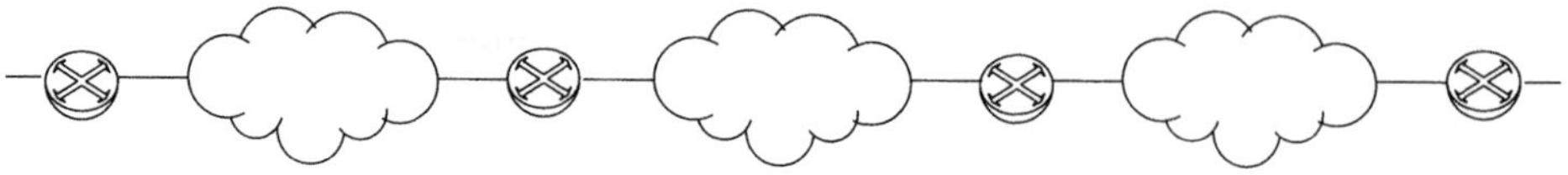

FIGURE 1.4 A Series of Networks

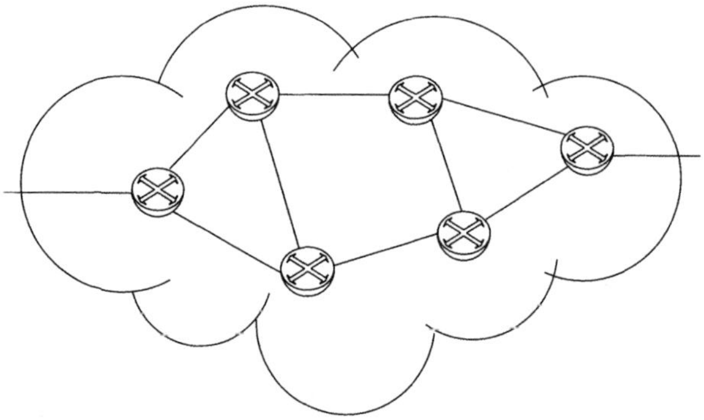

FIGURE 1.5 General Domain of Network Design Problems (Backbone Network)

as shown in Figure 1.5. For example, each domain optimizes their own routes irrespective of how other domains connected to it may be doing.

To summarize, in each network, we have a set of nodes connected by links. In the case of the telephone network, the nodes are telephone switches and the links are referred to as *trunks* (or trunk groups, or inter-machine trunks). In the case of Internet, nodes are routers, and the links are sometimes referred to as *interfaces*, *links*, or *trunks*. More specifically, the *middle* part consists of a series of networks,[7] where each network is administered by a different provider and each provider is responsible for proper design of its own network. Such providers' networks are often referred to as *backbone networks*.

Besides the telephone network and the Internet, there are actually other communication networks and infrastructure. To help distinguish, we will commonly refer to the telephone network or the Internet as *application service networks* or *traffic networks*. For example, there are private communication networks that are set up (as opposed to public networks, such as the Internet or the telephone network) for large companies and corporations to carry their own voice, data, and video services. While in such private networks companies maintain their own routing/switching devices, they actually *lease* the physical facility from other network providers; in other words, these companies are "customers" of the *physical facility network* providers.

Such physical facility providers for *transporting* application traffic for different *customers* networks are usually large telecommunication network providers. Again, for better economy of scale, a telecommunication network provider may combine traffic demand

[7]This is somewhat similar to using different airline carriers for your travel from one place to another.

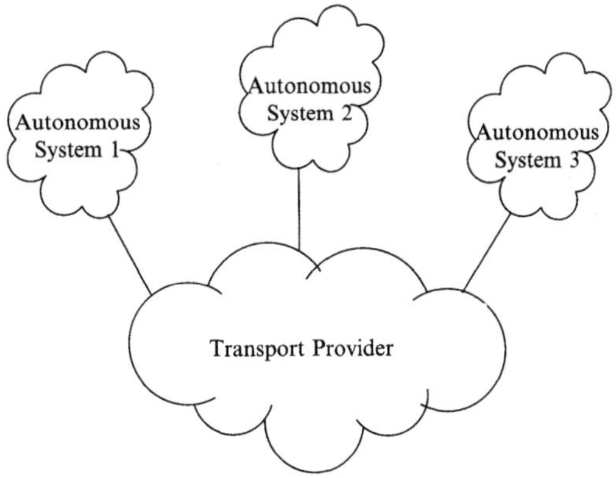

FIGURE 1.6 Three Different Administrative Domains Using the Same Transport Provider

from various private lines into one network. In general, these physical facilities networks are referred to as *transport* or *transmission* networks which may in practice consist of many different technologies, such as synchronous optical network (SONET), synchronous digital hierarchy, wavelength division multiplexing technology, and so on. Note that transport networks also have switching equipment, often referred to as cross-connects, which are used for setting up leased circuits/trunks semi-permanently or permanently.

Thus, within the context of the transport network, we can see that a transport network provider has its own domain to meet the demand requirement through transport node equipment and transport network links. It is important to point out that three different ISPs could conceivably use a single transport network provider as shown in Figure 1.6, or an ISP network may be carried by multiple transport network providers as shown in Figure 1.7. Furthermore, it is possible that a transport network provider would carry customer requirements for Internet, telephone network, or private-line customers' networks (as shown in Figure 1.8). Regardless, note that the network design within its own network remains the responsibility of each provider, be it an ISP, a telephone service provider, a private-line network provider, or a transport network provider; for simplicity, we will use the generic term *network provider* to refer to any of these providers.

It is becoming apparent that the overall conglomerate of these various networks give rise to a *multi-layer network* environment where each layer has its own definition of traffic, link capacity, and node gears (i.e., functionalities provided by the equipment in a node). In the next sections, we will give a more detailed view of these aspects.

1.3 NOTION OF TRAFFIC AND TRAFFIC DEMAND

A network provider has control over design and management of the network that is under its own administrative domain; thus, in order to do that, an important need for each provider would be to determine traffic demand in its own network. Considering all such points (or nodes) in the network, we can imagine that the traffic volume between any two such points

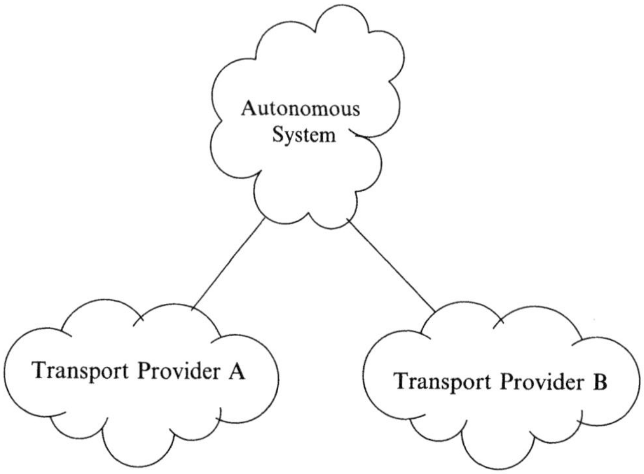

FIGURE 1.7 An Administrative Domain Using Multiple Transport Providers

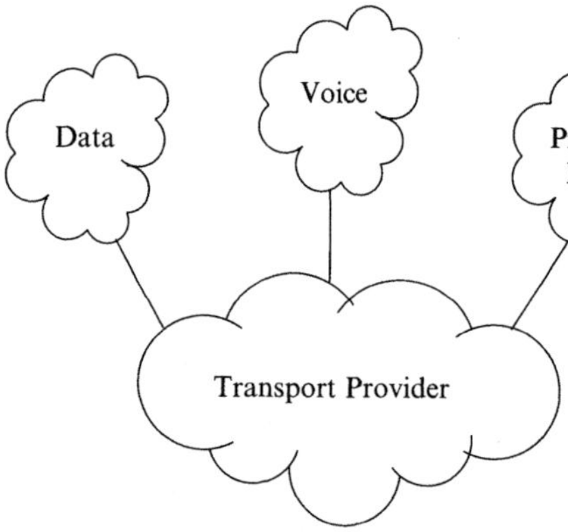

FIGURE 1.8 Multiple Service Networks Over One Transport Provider

which forms a *traffic volume matrix* or a *demand volume matrix*[8] must be determined. For ease of discussion, in this section we will consider a single-link network where the end points have traffic. We will discuss the notion of traffic for the Internet, the telephone network and then for transport (or transmission) networks.

1.3.1 Traffic in the Internet

When a user employs applications such as email, the message generated is broken down into smaller data packets for transporting over the Internet. A large portion of applications

[8] In this book, we will use these two terms interchangeably along with shorter terms: traffic matrix and demand matrix.

on the Internet uses the TCP/IP (Transmission Control Protocol/Internet Protocol) stack. The end computers are responsible for breaking an application's messages (e.g., web pages, email) into smaller packets on one end and then re-assembling them in the right order at the other end before handing it over to the application; in the process, the two end computers need to ensure that if a packet is by chance lost somewhere, they need to work together to ensure notification of the lost packet and retransmission so that the message content is correctly delivered to the application. For more details on how the TCP/IP protocol works, refer to books such as [Com00], [KR02], [PD03], and [Tan03]. The network's job is to route these packets from one end to another and, in fact, to do so without considering reliability in delivery as per TCP/IP protocol. The packets are also known as *IP datagrams*.

There are many reasons why an IP datagram may not be delivered at the other end; for example, a physical transmission error may have corrupted the datagram along the way making it meaningless to forward it any further or, due to congestion, a router in transit has run out of buffer space at the instant this particular datagram arrived. Unlike congested road networks where you are queued and delayed, in the Internet this delay can be addressed only to the extent that buffer capacity is still available and is subject to the capacity of the buffer at the arriving router as well. Going by the basic principle of the TCP/IP protocol stack, based on routing decision, a router's job is to forward packets towards the destination without necessarily taking into consideration whether there is any buffer space left at the arriving router; this is perfectly acceptable since the protocol rule allows for the end computers to re-generate any lost packets. While the protocol allows the rate to be adjusted due to congestion at the end system, any packet already in transit can still possibly be dropped.

Let us recap a couple of items from this discussion thus far. Traffic congestion can occur in a network (or in parts of a network); delay is possible; and packets may be dropped. Thus, the job of a network designer, a skilled technical professional, is to design a network that keeps delay to some acceptable minimum, and to minimize the loss of packets at routers (due to congestion). Note that congestion is a fact of life; it is impossible to avoid it completely since traffic can be unpredictable at times. However, we can design a network in such a way that the congestion does not happen *all* the time, or, rather, happens only infrequently. Essentially, our situation would be equivalent to stating the following: in a particular highway in the road network, the delay is really bad; we need more lanes constructed. Precisely the same way, in the Internet, we need to have enough *lanes* (bandwidth or capacity) so that we can give an acceptable level of service; in addition, we need router buffers in place with sufficient memory to deal with traffic burst and real-time traffic so that packet dropping is minimized.

The entire picture actually becomes a bit more complicated. To illustrate this, we need to consider the notion of traffic and traffic demand. First, we do not know ahead of time *when* a user is going to log on to their computer and whether they would be requesting a web page (from where?) or sending an email. So, from the point view of the network, we have no choice but to consider that such a request or demand arrives *randomly*, not necessarily in a deterministic fashion. Now, imagine millions of users randomly deciding to use the web or send an email. Thus, we need to resort to a statistical approach to see if such random behavior can be modeled through a statistical distribution. It has been observed in recent years that Internet data traffic has a statistical property that can be best described as *self-similar traffic* and can have *heavy tail distribution* ([WP98], [WTE96]), unlike the commonly known distributions, such as normal distribution or exponential distribution. Thus, modeling the behavior of traffic is a very complex problem (and would take a separate book to discuss it!). Thus, we refer the reader to books such as [PW00] for these details, and limit our discussion herein to issues that are relevant to network design.

To reiterate, we need to remember that requests arrive at random; in turn, this means that datagram arrival in the network is random. Thus, measurement systems need to be in place in a network to capture statistics so that traffic arrival distribution and traffic volume can be estimated. There are some recent works that address this issue; for example, see [FGL⁺00] for details on traffic estimates in backbone IP networks. One of the measurements we can obtain from such systems is to determine the average arrival rate of IP datagrams; we emphasize that this is *not* a fixed or deterministic rate. Furthermore, from measurement, we also need to obtain the average size of a packet; we will assume the average packet size to be 1 kilobyte (KB).[9] Now suppose that the average packet arrival rate is 100 packets per second (pps) offered to a single-link network of bandwidth 1.54 Megabits per second (Mbps).[10] If the average packet size is 1 kilobyte (i.e., 8 kilobits or 8 Kb), then the packet service rate of the link is 1.54 Mbps/8 Kb $\approx$ 190 pps.

Assume for the moment that packet arrival follows the Poisson process, that the packet size is exponentially distributed, and the system can be thought of as the famous *M/M/*1 queueing system (for details about Poisson process, exponential distribution, and the *M/M/*1 queueing system, for example, see [Med02]); then, there happens to be a nice analytical formula for computing the average packet delay due to queueing phenomenon. Specifically, if the average packet size is denoted by K_p bits, and the link capacity (speed) is given by C bits per second (e.g., T1-rate: 1.54 Mbps), then the average service rate of the link is $\mu_p = C/K_p$ pps. If the average arrival rate is denoted by λ_p pps, then the average delay (in seconds), $\mathcal{D}(\lambda_p, \mu_p)$, is given by:[11]

$$\mathcal{D}(\lambda_p, \mu_p) = \frac{1}{\mu_p - \lambda_p}. \tag{1.3.1}$$

This simple relation can provide ample insightful information. First, we can certainly assess the average delay; for example, for an arrival rate of 100 pps and service rate of 190 pps, the average delay would be $1/(190 - 100)$ seconds, i.e., 11.11 millisecond (ms). If the average arrival rate increases to 150 pps, then this average delay increases to 25 ms. It is usually helpful to also look at the average utilization of the system, ρ, which is given by λ_p/μ_p, i.e., the average arrival rate divided by the average service rate ($\rho = 100/190 = 0.555...$ in the considered case). To illustrate the typical delay behavior, we have plotted the

[9] In practice, datagram sizes are found to have tri-model behavior; that is, packet sizes in general cluster around either small (40/44 bytes), medium (552/576 bytes), or large (1,500 bytes) packets [CMT98].

[10] This data rate is the capacity of a North American T1-link.

[11] For our convention on equation numbering, see Section 1.9.

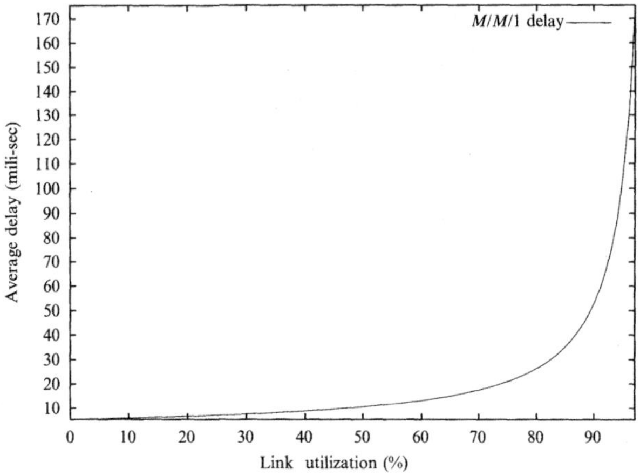

FIGURE 1.9 Average Delay Using *M/M/*1 Delay Formula

average delay function with utilization, ρ, in the x-axis and the average delay in the y-axis, keeping service rate fixed at 190 pps (Figure 1.9).

Now, when you see a number such as 11.11 ms, you might wonder why such a minor delay would be of any interest or concern. There are a couple of ways to answer this question: 1) this delay is only due to a queue related delay (other delays such as propagation and node processing will add to this number), and 2) this value is only for a single-link case (for end-to-end delay, a packet could be required to traverse many links through the Internet).

We now illustrate the second answer further by returning to the web page access example from Warsaw to Kansas City. Beyond networks in different domains visited, which we have discussed earlier, it actually goes through several routers *within* each network. Specifically, in this case, we found that the path goes through 18 hops or routers.[12] To simplify the illustration, assume that each link between two adjacent routers has the average delay of 11.11 ms. Then the end-to-end delay will be at least $11.11 \times 19 \approx 200$ ms! It is evident that when we consider the end-to-end delay, the delay components do add up due to the instantaneous store-and-forward nature of the Internet routing. Thus, it is important to keep the average delay on each link/network as low as possible.

Returning to the plot (Figure 1.9), notice that the average delay drastically increases as the average arrival rate is closer to the average service rate of the link. Thus, the average delay is a highly non-linear phenomenon which becomes worse when the utilization, ρ, is closer to 1 (i.e., 100% link utilization). This graph can be used in another way by asking: what is the acceptable delay that we would like users to tolerate for a good quality service? If we know this number, this graph (or the formula) can be used to determine what is the acceptable level of link utilization. Suppose, the acceptable average delay is 15 ms; then, we can determine that the acceptable average utilization is to be no more

[12]This information is determined using *traceroute* tool.

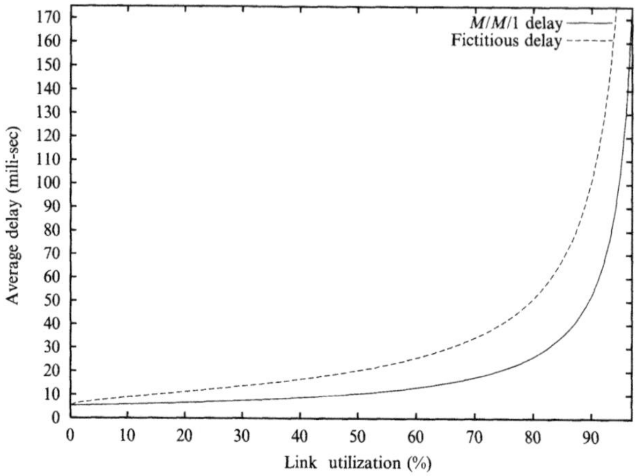

FIGURE 1.10 Average Delay Using *M/M/*1 Delay Formula and a Fictitious Delay Formula

than 64.5% on the link. The good news is that at least for the purpose of network design considerations, it may be acceptable to use a maximum link utilization as an alternative criterion to the delay criterion. However, we need to take into account another factor that we have assumed thus far, i.e., that the packet arrival rate behavior follows the Poisson process. Unfortunately, measurements from the Internet indicate that the arrival process does not follow the Poisson process and the delay is *worse* than the one calculated using the Poisson assumption. This simply means that the delay curve is above the *M/M/*1 delay curve; to illustrate this, we have plotted such a delay curve in addition to the *M/M/*1 curve in Figure 1.10. There are important network design implications that arise from the discrepancy. The idea that the 64.5% average utilization would be acceptable at 15 ms of average delay is perhaps an overestimate; in reality, we might need to hold the average utilization even lower, perhaps at about 50% on average to achieve the 15 ms delay requirement.

We now consider another important design issue referred to as the *scaling* (or packing) factor. Our *M/M/*1 illustration so far has been shown for a service rate of 190 pps (corresponding to T1-link rate). Now consider a link with 10 times the capacity of T1-link,[13] and an arrival rate 10 times more, i.e., with the average rate of 1,900 pps. Reflecting back to the average delay function (Section 1.3.1), with a ten-fold increase in both the average service rate and the average arrival rate (i.e., while the utilization remains the same), the average delay *reduces* to one-tenth of the previous value since $1/(10\mu_p - 10\lambda_p) = 0.1/(\mu_p - \lambda_p)$. Thus, it is better to have one higher-speed link instead of having 10 parallel lower-speed links to carry the same amount of total traffic. This statement is valid without taking into consideration the cost of the link; in general, while taking the typical cost structure of links into consideration, the gain resulting from using high

[13]There is no actual communication link speed at this rate; this is used just for illustration.

capacity links is even more profound.[14] This is often referred to as the *statistical multiplexing* gain. Similar phenomena also occur with air travel network where big aircraft (fleets) are used in many segments to reduce cost by better packing.

Regardless, what we need to know from the measurement is whether the utilization is observed to be higher than the acceptable threshold for a particular link type; if so, it is probably time to add bandwidth/capacity to the network. Certainly, this problem is trivial if we were to have just a single-link network since we can measure the arrival rate, observe the utilization, and determine if bandwidth needs to be increased if the utilization is, for example, more than 50% on average. In large networks (rather than just a set of serial links) where the utilization can be further impacted by routing of traffic *flows*, the network design problem of adding bandwidth is much more complex than this simple single-link network example—this will be covered extensively in this book, and we will illustrate a simple design example later in Section 1.4.

In any case, an important lesson learned from the above discussion is that determining the average arrival rate in pps (based on measurements) is required since this really refers to the traffic *volume* or demand in a particular measuring unit for the Internet; further, we need this information between different nodes in the network, somewhat similar to the air travel example where we need similar information between Kansas City and Warsaw, between Chicago and Detroit, and so on. In summary, we certainly and *minimally* need the traffic demand volume as an input for all our network design problems.

Note that we have characterized traffic only in terms of pps since we have hidden the packet size information while discussing the unit of data traffic. Actually, the average packet size could have been taken into account and the demand for data traffic could be given in Mbps instead of pps[15]—thus, both pps and Mbps are valid units for data traffic demand as long as the link capacity is used in the appropriate context. It may be noted that many ISPs in fact use Mbps (or Gigabits per second, Gbps) as the unit for traffic demand volume for the purpose of routing optimization and network design.

1.3.2 Traffic in the Telephone Network

Similar to the Internet, the telephone network also faces the random arrival pattern. In this case, the arrival is in terms of calls. Obviously, we do not know when a user wants to place a phone call and to where. Thus, again we face the issue of stochastic arrival. From the discussion of Internet, it may immediately seem that analogous to the average packet arrival rate, we need to consider measuring average call arrival rate to determine demand volume. But this is a bit different for the telephone traffic.

An important aspect about the telephone network is that when you place a call and you are connected through the network, the voice circuit is dedicated to you *until* you

---

[14]Typically, the cost of a higher data rate link is less expensive (unit cost wise) than the cost of a lower data speed link. For example, while the bandwidth of a T3-link is 28 times the bandwidth of a T1-link, the cost of a T3-link is much less than 28 times the cost of a T1-link.

[15]To see the relation in regard to delay, observe that $\mathcal{D}(\lambda_p, \mu_p) = K_p/(\mu_p K_p - \lambda_p K_p) = K_p\, \mathcal{D}(\lambda_p K_p, C)$. Now, $\lambda_p K_p$ is demand in bits per second while C is the raw link data rate.

hang up due to the circuit switching functionality. In other words, the circuits along your connection path are not released for use by another person until you are done. To make this simple, we will assume temporarily that calls arrive in a deterministic fashion and that we are considering only a single voice circuit. Suppose that a call arrives at the start of an hour and the user talks exactly for an hour. Thus, this user occupies the circuit for an hour and no one else can use it. Now suppose the user talks only for 10 minutes and then hangs up. The circuit is free for others to use for the rest of the hour. In fact, if another user arrives at that instant and occupies the circuit for, say, 10 more minutes, then a third user can start using the circuits 20 minutes into the hour. Thus, if we slice the length of the calls to fixed 10 minute windows, we can accommodate six calls; this means we can have six arrivals per hour (using 10 minutes each) as opposed to one arrival per user (using for the full hour for talking) while in either case we just needed one circuit! Simply put, this intuitively says that increase in the call arrival rate does not necessarily mean that we need more circuit (or in general bandwidth) since the average call duration time matters.

Thus, the determination of the traffic demand in the telephone network needs more than just the average call arrival rate. From the example of calls of 10 minutes each as opposed to an hour-long call, it is clear that the traffic demand somehow also needs to take into account the (average) duration of a call. Hence, going back to the average call arrival rate and the average duration of a call, a good way to capture the demand volume is to consider the product of these two terms, rather than just the average call arrival rate. Thus, if λ_t is the average call arrival rate, and τ_t is the average duration of a call, then the traffic demand, referred to as *offered load* or *offered traffic* in telephony, is given by

$$a = \lambda_t \tau_t. \tag{1.3.2}$$

This dimensionless quantity is given the unit name *Erlang* (or *Erl* in short), named after the Danish mathematician A. K. Erlang who in the early 20th century developed the foundations of the theory of telephone traffic while working for the Danish Telephone Company in Copenhagen (surely, Copenhagen comes back to the picture!).

Earlier in our example, we have temporarily assumed that calls arrive in a deterministic fashion, which is obviously not true in reality. That is, it is important to note that traffic demand in *Erl* is actually an average measure (traffic arrival rate and the call duration in reality are stochastic). In the case of telephone traffic, it has been found that the call arrival closely follows the Poisson process and the call duration is exponentially distributed [Gir90]. Analogous to the delay as the performance factor for data traffic, we also have an important factor for telephone traffic. In the case of telephone calls, we face the situation of whether there is a circuit available to connect an arriving call. The relevant interest here is to determine the probability of acceptance of calls. In other words, what is the blocking probability of calls? The good news is that we can actually compute call blocking analytically for a given offered load and link capacity. This is, in fact, a result originally derived by A.K. Erlang. Thus, if c is the capacity of a link in terms of number of voice circuits, then call blocking for offered load a is given by the following *Erlang-B loss formula*[16]:

$$\mathcal{B}(a, c) = \frac{a^c/c!}{\sum_{k=0}^{c} a^k/k!}. \tag{1.3.3}$$

Let us now consider an example. Suppose we again have a T1-link (1.54 Mpbs) where calls are offered. Since each digitized voice circuit requires 64 Kilobits per second (Kbps) (= K_t), we can easily see that the bandwidth in terms of number of circuits is $c = C/K_t$ where C is the raw data rate of the link; in the case of T1-link, we have $c = 24$ voice circuits. Suppose now, a load of 20 *Erl* is offered to this link; then, using equation (1.3.3) the call blocking probability[17] is determined to be 6.6%. There are important things to note: 1) similar to the delay formula for data traffic, the blocking formula is nonlinear, i.e., blocking changes non-linearly with increase in traffic; 2) it is possible to offer a load higher than 24 *Erl* to a link of capacity 24 since this is a *loss* system, and there is still a chance that some calls will go through; in fact, the call blocking probability, for offered load of 24 *Erl*, is 14.6%; and 3) blocking also benefits from scaling/packing factor (similar to data traffic); for example, if we increase the capacity 10 times to 240 circuits and the load 10 times to 240 *Erl*, then the blocking drops to 4.9% (from 14.6%).

Finally, we need to relate offered load to measuring call traffic. In actuality, *carried* load (or, carried traffic) is easier to measure since a system can count busy/idle state of circuits *only if* a call is admitted. So, a natural question arises: how do we determine the offered load from the carried load? First, this requires understanding what carried load means—this is really the average number of busy circuits. Suppose we determine, by monitoring a link of 24 circuits, that the average number of busy circuits results in 15 *Erl* of load.[18] The relation between offered and carried load, $\hat{a}$, is given by the following relation:

$$\hat{a} = a\,(1 - \mathcal{B}(a, c)).$$

For our example, $\hat{a} = 15$ and $c = 24$. Thus, given $\hat{a}$ and c, this equation is required to be solved in order to determine the offered load, a (question: how would you solve this equation?).

To summarize, we need an estimate of the average traffic generated by call arrival intensity and the average call duration, i.e., offered load given in *Erl*. Interestingly, we can draw a connection between call traffic and packet traffic: λ_t corresponds to λ_p, and the average duration, τ_t, to average packet length, K_p. In any case, whether it is the telephone traffic or data traffic, the quality of service certainly plays a major role which can be translated to acceptable utilization of a link for the purpose of network design.

Finally, this is a good place to discuss differences between circuit switching and packet switching. In circuit switching, a call receives a dedicated path and the capacity (i.e.,

---

[16] Incidently, the Erlang-B loss formula is insensitive to the statistical distribution of the call duration time.

[17] An online Erlang calculator can be found at http://www.erlang.com.

[18] Typically, circuits are checked for busy/idle state every 100 seconds resulting in the measure, centi-call second (CCS). It may be noted that 1 *Erl* = 36 CCS. Thus obtaining a measure of 540 CCSs over 24 trunks during an hour translates to 15 *Erl* of carried load.

64 Kbps) needed for the call is allocated to it. Thus, if a network link does not have any capacity left, an incoming call request is blocked; the user is required to redial. Note that there is no delay associated with a call once the call is set up. In the case of packet switching, packets for different applications (e.g., web, email) are mixed together on a network link and every packet is allowed to enter the network (somewhat similar to road transportation networks where cars can be allowed to enter a highway); however, delay can occur for packets that have *already* entered a network if a particular link along the route does not have enough capacity to handle all packets trying to use the link at that instant. Certainly, sometimes a router can drop packets if the router does not have enough packet buffer space to accommodate all delayed packets.

1.3.3 Demand in the Transport Network

So far, we have discussed traffic demand that comes from the stochastic nature of call and packet traffic. There is another set of demands possible in telecommunication networks. This is partly to do with the hierarchical structure or "layering" of the network *resources*, as well as to cater to user/customer groups who may want leasing circuit or capacity to serve their own network.

As you may recall, from traffic demand for data packet traffic, we needed to consider certain criteria (such as delay or utilization) to determine how much bandwidth is needed. This could be obtained in, for example, T1-capacity units. For example, we may require 15 T1s worth of capacity to carry Internet traffic from one router to another, especially over a geographical distance, for example, between Kansas City and St. Louis. Similarly, for voice calls, based on traffic demand and quality of service, it may be determined that 10 T1s are needed between Kansas City and St. Louis. We can also conceive of the situation where a corporation has offices both in Kansas City and St. Louis for which they manage their own devices and have determined that they would require 2 T1s worth of bandwidth between these two cities. Thus, to actually install a total of 27 units of T1-capacity, we may need *another* form of *capacity* between Kansas City and St. Louis and if they can be bundled together in a cost-effective manner. Thus, *output* bandwidth requirement for each of Internet, telephone and private-line service from service networks, is *input* demand to the layer beneath it!

In fact, there are node gears in a transport network that can combine these demand units into other forms of demand and capacity units while considering economies of scale. For example, another popular link rate in U.S. is T3-rate (45 Mbps) which can multiplex 28 T1-units. As we can see in the example considered above, we have accumulated 27 T1-units which would easily fit into a T3-link. In order to do that, we need to have node gears that can do *grooming* and multiplex from one unit to another at one end, and de-multiplex at the other end; in this case, from T1 to T3 at one end, and from T3 to T1 at the other end.[19] The closest (yet unrealistic) analogy we can give in relation to the air travel example is to imagine that we have to fit multiple smaller aircrafts on to a bigger aircraft for flying

[19]Certainly, grooming can be performed on link segments along the path; this will depend on demand and and the network design objective. Grooming is discussed in Section 12.7.

TABLE 1.1 **Modular Data Rates**

Signal Name	**Bit Rate (Mbps)**
DS0 (voice circuit)	0.064
T1 (DS-1)	1.54
E1	2.04
T3 (DS-3)	45.00
E3	34.36
STS-1	51.84
OC-3/STS-3/STM-1	155.52
OC-12/STS-12/STM-4	622.08
OC-48/STS-48/STM-16	2,488.32
OC-192/STS-192/STM-64	9,953.28

between two cities without the users knowing it. At the same time, for the provider of bigger aircraft services, what they need to know (as far as demand is concerned) is how many smaller aircraft demand units to account for so that the right size of a bigger aircraft can be planned, instead of worrying about how many actual travelers are flying on each of the smaller aircrafts.

Beyond T1 rate, with the advent of fiber optic networks in the past 10 to 15 years, we have seen standardization of new high data rate standards[20] with technologies such as SONET (Table 1.1). Thus, a form of multiplexing hierarchy for resources can be formed. Essentially, what we can see is that one network's capacity requirement becomes the (traffic) demand volume for another network which can go on for several layers (see Section 1.6 for further explanation). However, there is one important difference between traffic demand at the top level, such as Internet packet traffic or telephone call traffic, and the "transport" layer. At the service level, in actuality, traffic arrival is stochastic in nature; from this, traffic is forecasted (along with assessment from marketing department) into the future to determine a bandwidth requirement for that network; while this bandwidth requirement becomes an input to the next layer as *demand*, the fundamental difference is that such requests are done periodically over time, for example, once a month (or once a quarter or so on). Thus, when all is said and done, the demand input in the lower layer is essentially deterministic or precise in nature (showing up at a particular update time cycle) although this demand can be projected over multiple time periods (i.e., we need 5 T1s in month-one, 10 T1s in month-two, and so on). There is certainly a sense of quality of service in this layer as well. For example, if a customer wants 5 T1s by a certain date, the transport network provider must be able to connect these on time, instead of waiting another month to get it in the next cycle. In essence, there is a domino effect of needing to meet service guarantee that goes from one layer of the network to the next

[20]Terminologies such as STS-1, OC-3, and STM-1 are explained later in Section 3.5.

layer. This, thus, means that lower layer capacity planning in a timely manner is important as well.

1.3.4 Distinction between Traffic and Transport Network

There is however an emerging trend where high-date rate on-demand switched services are being conceived of that can be provided just like a telephone call and for a short duration. Many vendors and service providers are working on such capability even at OC-3 and higher rates (Table 1.1). Thus, we need to make an important distinction and clarification between traffic and transport networks (and services).

A traffic network is where demand is stochastic in nature irrespective of the data rate of the service (whether it is a packet, 64 Kbps voice call, or an OC-3 on-demand circuit) and has the switching/routing capability to handle short-lived requests on demand. A transport network provides high-data rate services that are required to be set up on a semi-permanent or permanent basis, and requests for those services are set up on a periodic basis.

1.3.5 Generic Naming for Demand Volume and Capacity

Now that we have covered more about the notion of traffic and traffic demand in different networks, we are in a position to introduce two generic terms to be used throughout this book: *demand volume unit* (DVU), and *link capacity units* (LCU). Each demand is characterized by the demand volume *demand volume unit* (DVU). For example, a DVU can be in pps, or *Erl*, or modular data rate, depending on the network we are interested in designing. Similarly, an LCU is the capacity unit of a link which can take a different form depending on the layer of the transport network; for example, it could be a T1 (or an E1 in Europe, which is about 2 Mbps), T3, OC-3, or so on (see Table 1.1). Again, this depends on the network layer we are designing and the modular values of link capacity that are applicable. If we now consider the hierarchical nature of network resources between traffic and transport networks, we can see that traffic demand in DVUs is translated to LCUs through network design of traffic network which, in turn, becomes DVUs for the next transport network.

The advantage of using the generic naming convention is that in many cases, you will see that the mathematical representation of design models are quite similar from one network type to another—the only thing that differs is the proper DVU and LCU that are applicable (and, certainly, routing rules). When and where differences arise as we progress through the book, we will introduce and discuss variations in models.

1.4 A SIMPLE DESIGN EXAMPLE

By now, we are more firm on the notion of traffic or demand, especially for a single-link. Prior to this, we have discussed a more complex network environment when presenting air travel network and when discussing the call or Internet packet traversal scenario between Warsaw and Kansas City.

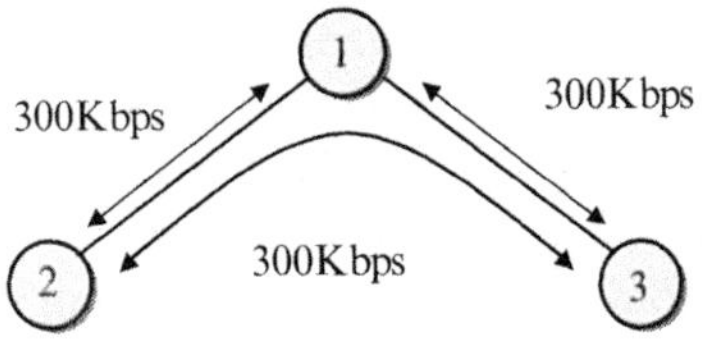

FIGURE 1.11 Three Node Example with Two Links Installed

In reality, we have many source-destination (egress-ingress) traffic demands between various points (nodes) in the network (which needs to be estimated, forecasted, or determined by other means such as marketing); thus we have a traffic/demand matrix as input to network design. Then, we need to determine a network with enough capacity and connectivity to route this traffic so that acceptable service guarantees can be provided.

Let us now consider a simple network design example. Earlier, we may have given the impression that if we know the traffic between two points, we can use an acceptable link utilization threshold to determine the link capacity needed—this is certainly true if we have just a single-link network. To address the role of network design, consider a three-node network where the traffic demand between each node is on average 300 Kbps. Thus, in this case, DVU is in Kbps. For quality of service requirements, if we are required to maintain a utilization threshold of no more than 60% for any link and we are allowed to use links of T1-capacity unit size (T1 = 1.54 Mbps), the intuitive answer could be to put three T1 links, one between each pair of nodes to satisfy the demand and the utilization requirement; in this case, the link utilization, 300 Kpbs/1.54 Mbps $\approx$ 19.5%, is below the acceptable threshold, i.e., service guarantee is met.

On a closer look, we can see that only two T1-links are needed to meet the traffic demand and stay under the utilization threshold requirement. To illustrate this, see Figure 1.11 with nodes labeled 1, 2, and 3 where we design a network with a link between 1 and 2, and another between 1 and 3, each with T1-capacity units (with no link between nodes 2 and 3). In this network, we route the traffic demand between 2 and 3 through node 1. This would result in each link (between 1 and 2, and between 1 and 3) to exhibit utilization of (300 + 300) Kbps/1.54 Mbps = 39%, which is still under the acceptable link utilization threshold for service guarantee. We also note that the sum of flows in DCU can be translated into LCU (which is given here in Mbps).

More importantly, we have accomplished this with two-third of the cost compared to the scenario where T1-links would be placed between each demand point (i.e., three links). This gives us a general idea about what network design can accomplish while meeting demand and utilization requirement. As you can see, the design may depend also on routing capabilities. In the next section, we cover certain basics about routing and flows that are pertinent to network design.

1.5 NOTION OF ROUTING AND FLOWS

When we have traffic from one point to another, it makes sense to set up a direct link as long as it is economically and traffic-wise feasible (think back about the three-node example).

This would be equivalent to the example of having a direct, non-stop flight from Kansas City to Warsaw. Since we saw several ways to go from Kansas City to Warsaw by changing an airplane at intermediate hops, it is clear that it is not always necessary to have a direct flight (or a direct link in the case of a network).

We also see another interesting scenario from the case where, on a *hop* basis, a person starting from Kansas City needs to change flights out of Detroit to go via Memphis instead of Detroit to Amsterdam. Trying to think from a call or a packet point of view in a communication and computer network, such a path is still possible. If we expect enough traffic to get diverted that way, we can still consider Kansas City-Detroit-Memphis-Amsterdam-Warsaw as a possible path in *ensemble*, no matter the number of users taking this route.

As can be seen from the air travel case, there are two possible ways to use the term *route*: 1) how a specific person might travel (i.e., a specific instance) from one point to another, and 2) how, in general, ensemble traffic may be routed between the same two points. In the same vein, we can use the word *route* or *routing* in two different ways in communication and computer networks: 1) to indicate what happens in terms of routing a particular packet or a call, and 2) in terms of if a certain amount of traffic (calls or packets) is likely to be routed on a certain path. It is important to note that our use of the route or the path is in the context of the *latter* description, i.e., how would in general traffic be routed on a particular path.[21] This is especially important since in considering design of a network how an actual packet or call is specifically routed is not necessarily important as long as the *functionality* of the network/technology/protocol to provide this call/data travel is captured appropriately; furthermore, we do not want to completely rule out a *plausible* path or route. Thus, in this book, we will use the notion of *candidate path list* to indicate possible paths that can be taken by traffic demand volume between two points. If a particular path is chosen as a valid path by network design, we will designate this as a *route*. The other aspect we need to pay attention to is how much of the total demand between two points are routed ("travel") on a certain route. Thus, the amount of traffic associated with a route can be thought of as a *flow*,[22] which is of critical importance along with a route in this book.

There is also another use of the term routing that is relevant in this book. This comes from traditional transport networks, rather than traffic networks. In transport network, we are required to route demand volume on a particular (physical) path on a permanent or semi-permanent basis. This routing is traditionally referred to as *circuit routing* (for example, see [Rey83, p. 136]) which is not to be confused with packet or call routing. Circuit routing is also referred to as transport network routing. In this book, this routing is important as we will be discussing models for transport network routing and design, by often referring to it as *flow allocation* (for example, see Chapters 3, 9, and 11).

---

[21] The first case, i.e., the specific instance, then involves having the appropriate protocol and hardware/software mechanism at a routing/switching device to do this function.

[22] We note that the term *flow* is used in many different ways in networking literature. We will use *flow* on a path to mean the amount of demand volume that is routed on a path between two nodes.

1.6 ARCHITECTURE OF NETWORKS: MULTI-LAYER NETWORKS

So far, we have discussed traffic/demand and how they are different for traffic and transport networks. Furthermore, we have highlighted how routing can impact network design. While we have brought out the fact that traffic and transport networks are different networks with different properties, in this section we elaborate further by considering the architectural aspects and intricate relationships between different pieces in a layered manner.

To put it simply, the architecture of communication networks can be complicated: this is transpired by not only the large number of nodes that can form a particular network, but also due to the traffic and the transport network concept we have introduced earlier. In essence, a network (or layer) rides on another, i.e., a traffic network needs a transport network to connect the links needed for the traffic network; then, within the transport network, multiple-layers are possible due to different data rates. From a service point of view, a user of a traffic network does not "see" the dependency on the transport network. Can an analogy be drawn to air travel? Not easily. A closer yet unrealistic analogy would be to say that a user is taking a small sized aircraft that is fitted into a larger aircraft without the user knowing it!

We will now illustrate a simple network example to draw the distinction between different layers in a network topological architecture and highlight the relationship. Consider a four node network environment for an IP network within an administrative domain. For this network, we have four routers that are connected as shown in Figure 1.12 (top); links (trunks) have the capacity to carry the traffic, possibly with mixed capacity link types, such as T1, T3, or OC-3. Note that links are logical in the traffic network (IP network in this case). Going back to the air travel example, a flight between two cities (such as Detroit and Copenhagen) defines a logical link while different sizes of aircraft are analogous to different link speeds in this logical network. Now if a flight stops at an airport just for refuelling (no passenger gets on or off) for a flight between two airports, one could argue that this would be somewhat like a physical link level routing.

We now need the aid of a transport network to route these logical links and the associated capacity (see Figure 1.12, bottom). For example, the link capacity unit for the logical link, f, between nodes 1 and 3, in the IP network is connected using the transport network route 1-2-3; similarly, demand unit for the logical link 1-4, between nodes 1 and 4 in the traffic network, is connected via the transport route 1-2-3-4.

Based on mapping between just two layers in the network hierarchy, an important picture emerges. For example, in the IP network, we see three node-diverse and link-wise logically-diverse routes between nodes 1 and 4; they are: 1-4, 1-2-4, and 1-3-4. By diverse we mean, there is no common link (in the logical view) from one route to another. In reality, the actual topology view can be different at a different layer. This is shown in the bottom of Figure 1.12 from which we see that the logical links are actually all routed on the same transport network path, i.e., there is no diversity. Thus, a network that may look logically diverse in one layer but may not be diverse in another layer—this also has implications in protection and restoration design (*network robustness*) due to inter-relation between layers. Thus, multi-layer network design is an important problem to consider; this topic is covered in detail in the latter part of this book.

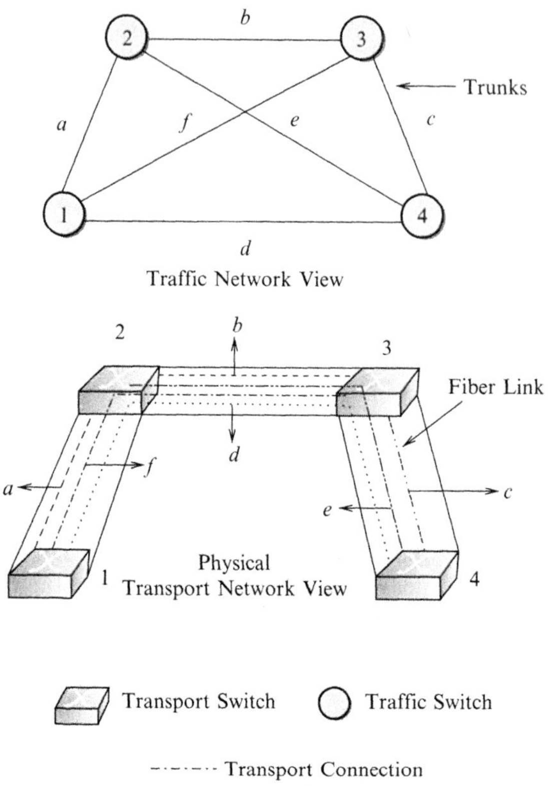

FIGURE 1.12 Traffic (Logical) Network and Transport Network View

As we have pointed out earlier, there are different service networks possible, e.g., voice, data, private-line, and so on. Those may be stacked in a physical network architecture. We show both a functional architecture view (Figure 1.13) and a network architecture view[23] (Figure 1.14). By the functional architecture view, we mean an application services (or traffic) network layer (such as the telephone service or the Internet), which requires logical capacity in units such as T1, T3, or OC-3 in the first transport layer which, in turn, may use an optical network layer and finally the actual media (or duct) layer. For the network architecture view, a simple picture to consider is an IP or telephone network at the top layer; this uses a first layer transport network which in turn uses an optical network.

No doubt that these views are complicated. We do not expect you to comprehend all of it, at least at first reading. Our point here is that a network architecture can be complicated which can impact what we can model, especially in regard to multi-layer design; furthermore, good design methods must be used for designing such networks that capture properties of each

[23] Figure 1.14 is originally from Robert Doverspike [Dov]. It has been somewhat modified in our presentation here.

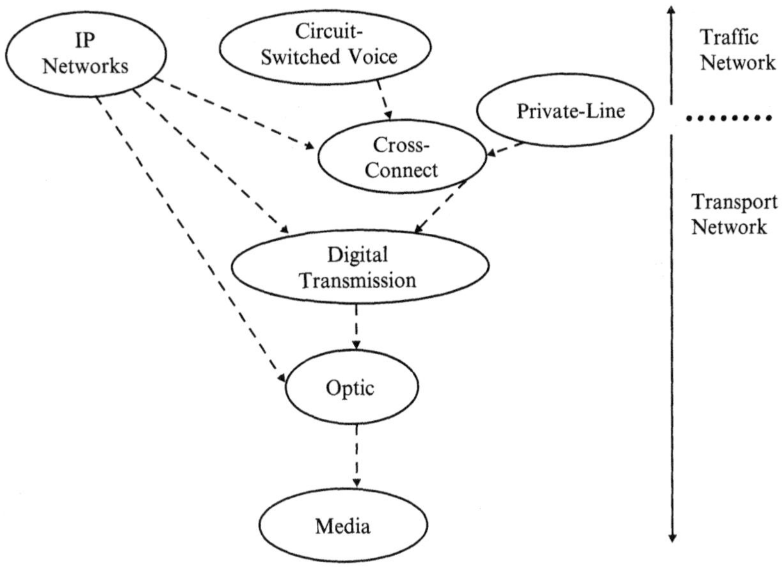

FIGURE 1.13 Functional View

network layer appropriately. This is especially true, for example, if you want to understand the implication of restoration design done at different layers.

1.7 NETWORK MANAGEMENT CYCLE

An important aspect that encompasses all networks is network management. Different networks may have different network management cycles. Certainly, network management was born the day telephone connection was manned by people manually connecting calls. While the term network management sometimes has a different meaning to different people, we use this term here to mean the entire process from planning a network to deploying a network and then to operate the network on a day-to-day basis; in order to do this, various network management *systems* and *protocols* may be necessary. To bring back our air travel analogy, it is probably not hard to see that beneath the actual air travel, there is a huge ongoing management function that ensures that there are enough aircrafts available, maintenance is done on a timely manner, acquisition of aircrafts (new capacity?) is planned, and so on. In essence, a similar functionality is needed for communication and computer networks which is broadly referred to as network management.

In this section, we will attempt to give you an overall view so that it is easier to see where and how network design comes into the picture in regard to the network management cycle. Thus, we start with the broader picture of network management cycles. For any network that is deployed, various issues and decisions need to be addressed. This can be best described using time granularity (Figure 1.15). For example, in a packet-based network, decisions that need to be made in micro-second time windows are, for example, scheduling packets and buffer management. In ms to second time windows, decision can be on reactive feedback

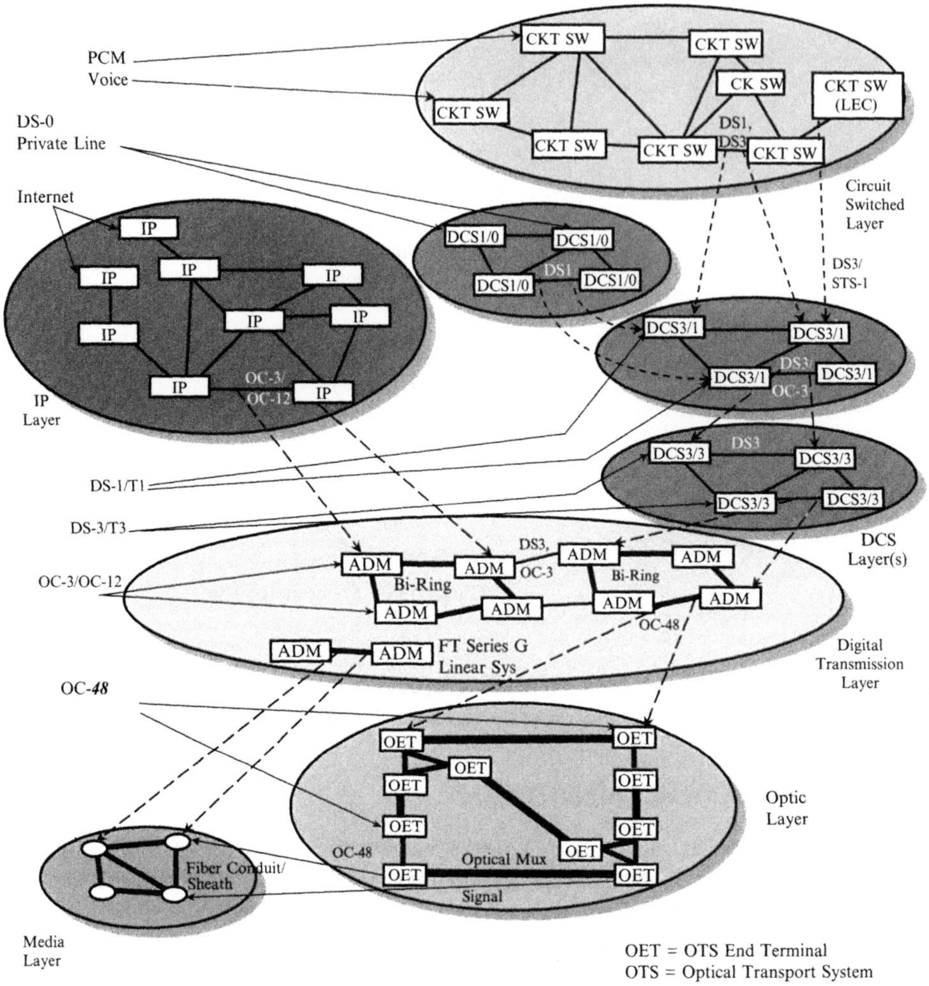

FIGURE 1.14 Network Architecture View (Adapted from [Dov])

controls such as the one that occurs with TCP protocol for rate adjustment. In the seconds to minutes window, typically we face call set up, call admission control, and call routing decisions. All the issues so far can be broadly classified under *real-time traffic management.* From minutes to hours, centralized network management controls can be applicable.

Going beyond that (i.e., from minutes time frame to days/weeks time frame), networks typically face what can be best classified as *capacity management*, or *traffic engineering*. At this point, the capacity is already installed. Based on short-term traffic trend/forecasting, some arrangement or re-arrangement may allow better usage of the network (i.e., network utilization). Thus, this may involve capacity re-allocation (from one service to another, and, within a service, from one demand to another) and re-configurability. This may further result in some re-routing—this re-routing should not be confused with call or packet level

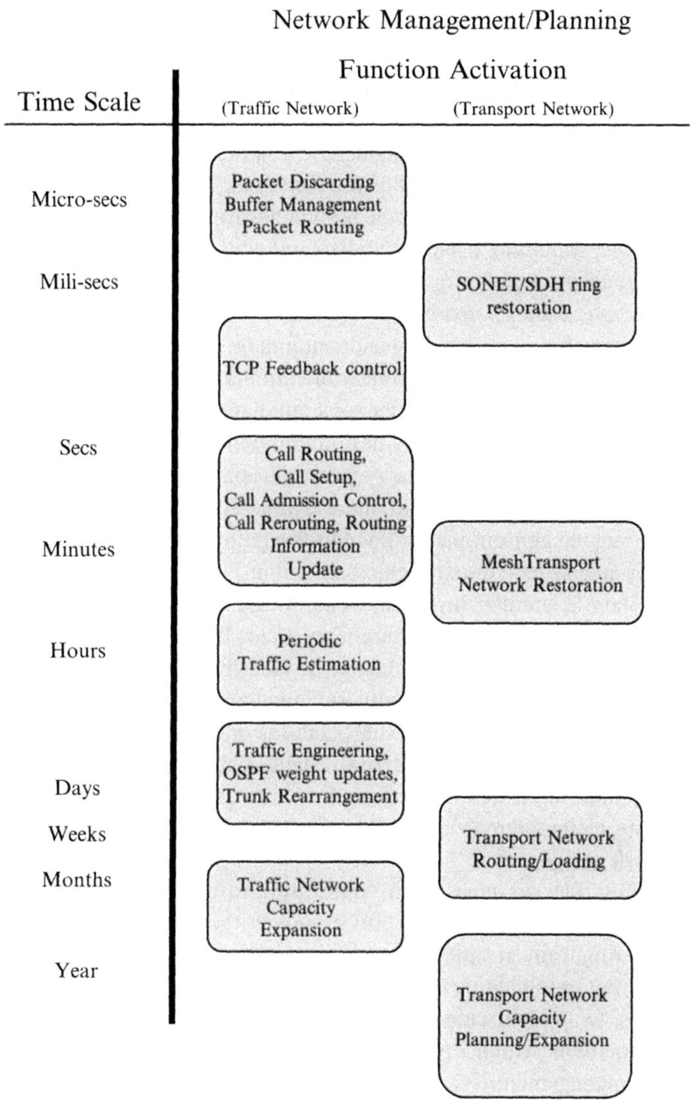

FIGURE 1.15 Time Line of Invocation of Different Functionality

routing. This routing is at the flow allocation level (or flow routing). In some instances, some capacity expansion may be necessary and possible. Finally, going from weeks to months (and sometimes to years), the overall network planning and engineering issues need to be addressed. Capacities and routes can usually be added on a monthly cycle. Large network providers may deploy a semi-optimized network and then do incremental capacity adds as needed until the network is far enough from optimal which then requires mass network capacity re-arrangement to be close to optimal. This mass re-arrangement usually happens every couple of years. In general, it should be noted that the time-window presented in Figure 1.15 between different functions can be reduced with newer technological capabilities. Thus, more than the reference time scale as presented in this figure, functionalities need to be understood in the context of what is possible from a time scale point of view as progress with newer technology and management systems is made.

Based on marketing and traffic forecasts, decisions need to be made for capacity expansion of network links as well as switches/routers. Besides the forecast on demand, there is another important aspect to understand when considering network design and planning. In large network planning and design, networks have two types of cost: 1) capital expenditure (*CapEx*) and 2) operational expenditure (*OpEx*). *CapEx* refers to cost that is primarily due to installation of capacity and equipment in the network (in future) while *OpEx* refers to cost incurred due to day-to-day operational needs of the network. Traditionally, *CapEx* and *OpEx* are considered under separate budgetary authorities and organizations within a network provider. Thus, many design problems are considered under either one or the other category; for example, in many cases, uncapacitated[24] design problems fall under *CapEx* while allocation problems fall under *OpEx*. However, in certain network design scenarios, it can/may be appropriate to develop design models that have cost components from both *CapEx* and *OpEx* (for example, see Section 11.2.1).

There is another important issue to discuss: a network designer might devise a slick solution/design that can decrease *CapEx* cost but on the other hand can increase *OpEx* cost due to implementation complexity. In fact, there have been many cases where solutions that save *CapEx* never made into implementation in actual networks. Thus, a good designer needs to take into account issues, such as operational complexity, to understand various trade-offs—often this consideration changes design rules to engineering rules; furthermore, they should understand issues such as how to coast in a new technology in the midst of existing technologies,[25] and allow for catastrophic scenarios (i.e., reason to do resilient network design).

Now that we have given you a glimpse into what types of decisions are needed at different time scales, it is helpful to look at the time windows of how to relate traffic and forecasting from an entire network management cycle, especially for service networks such as Internet or telephone traffic. This is shown in Figure 1.16.

As we have discussed earlier, we also know that there are networks underneath the traffic network which are transport networks. These do not have the same type of real-time traffic management issues faced by service networks. Restoring a path or a route in case of an actual failure (especially, in the absence of pre-planned stand-by route) would be the type of real-time management problems in transport networks. We provide the network management cycle of transport networks in Figure 1.17.

There is another planning process involved when needed to do a new network design which requires network location design and sometimes topological design. So far, we have primarily talked about designing a network based on traffic or demand, and demand can

[24] Uncapacitated problems and allocations problems are discussed in detail in Chapter 4.

[25] An important issue many of us forget is the need for floor space where equipment such as switches, routers, and cross-connects are physically located. Floor space can be premium. A network design may suggest putting new equipment at a location where there is no floor space left! Thus, constraints such as floor space can be important to understand and incorporate in the models.

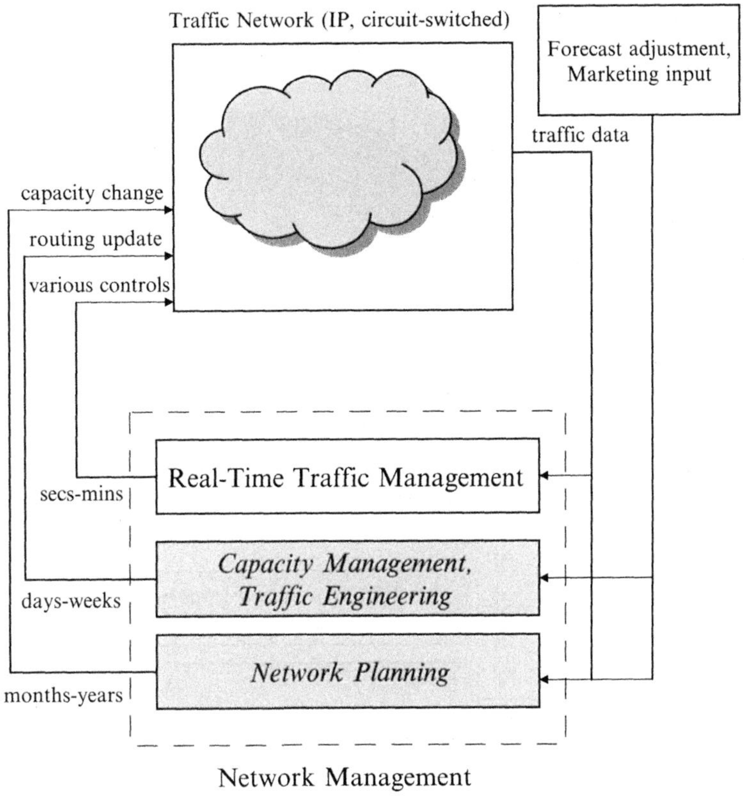

FIGURE 1.16 Network Management Cycle and Feedback Process for Traffic/Service Networks

be construed as what is estimated from traffic measurement or customer demand. In many instances, we should not rule out the fact that we grow a network for the *opportunity* it may provide to offer new service and growth in revenue. Thus, any estimate on demand needs to take into account any opportunity factor along with marketing input on demand.

1.8 SCOPE OF THE BOOK

So far, we have presented you a general picture of traffic, demand, network, routing, and the network management cycle for deploying a network. It is now time to discuss the scope of this book.

Our book primarily addresses *network models, design problems, and optimization algorithms* faced in the *network planning and capacity management* part of the network management cycle for *backbone/core networks*. In doing so, we have made a concerted effort to relate our work to situations in actual networks by incorporating issues that are induced by networking technology, protocols, and operational considerations. For brevity, we will refer to this scope as *network design*.

A critical point to note is that from a time scale point of view, the network design problems considered here are relevant in the time scale of hours to days to months. Thus, the

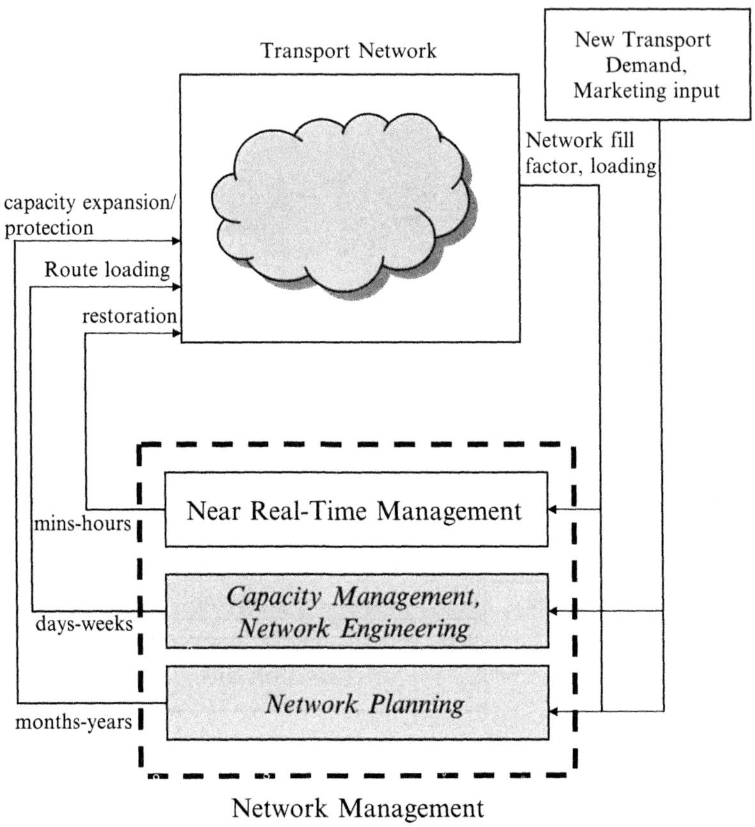

FIGURE 1.17 Network Management Cycle for Transport Networks

large aggregate of traffic and demand is appropriate, rather than the dynamics of individual connections or between connections.[26] With this perspective on time scale, average traffic demand volume for application services or deterministic demand for transport network is a reasonable assumption as input to the models we present in this book. In the context of the network management cycle shown for traffic and transport networks in Figures 1.16 and 1.17, respectively, this book addresses design problems that fall primarily in the shaded boxes (with words in *italics*).

We must point out that understanding the dynamics of connections and packets and their associated statistical properties is extremely important and is of significant interest due to their impact on the real-time management of networks and in understanding protocol behavior. This matter, however, is the subject of the branch of modelling called teletraffic/queueing theory and is outside the scope of our book.

[26]This point has been brought up eloquently in [FGL+00] in the context of deriving traffic demand for IP networks.

In this book, we concentrate on the optimization aspects of network by discussing how problems can be formulated mathematically, how to incorporate different design requirements in the form of constraints and objective functions, how cost can be represented for different problems, how network protocols and technology impact what may be possible in terms of routing and design, and finally how to approach the problems algorithmically. Such problems manifest themselves in many facets of communication and computer networks which are rarely discussed comprehensively in a single book. Thus, an important goal of our book is to provide a place where you can find these aspects considered in a comprehensive manner, especially using a common, uniform terminology.

In many cases, we have found that for lack of the right modelling background by designers, good, realistic and effective models that can be applicable in practical network situations are not actually used. In order to bridge the gap we have started the book by 1) giving simple illustrations of network design problems and how to construct the appropriate equations and conditions (Chapter 2), and 2) providing a set of representative network design problems that arise for different networking technologies such as IP, ATM, digital switching, and digital and optical transmission (Chapter 3).

Many network design problems faced in the real world involve many nodes and links; thus, the mathematical representation leads to what has been commonly called *large-scale* problems. While some such problems can be solved with existing algorithms and available software tools, others may not be easy to solve. Thus, there are often cases where specialized algorithms are required to solve large-scale problems; we have also included material on such specialized (decomposition) algorithms that are applicable for network design problems.

Beyond that, we have tried to cover a variety of different problem domains by taking a three-dimensional approach. These three dimensions can be labeled as follows: 1) different problem variations implied by different technological requirements, 2) network robustness to failures and adaptation to load fluctuations, and 3) multi-layer structure of network resources (the notion you should be able to grasp now from the discussion on network hierarchy). The three dimensions are depicted in Figure 1.18.

Finally, what would we like you, the reader, to get out of this book? There are many ways to summarize this; we will give two views: 1) network view, and 2) approach/algorithm/theory view.

1) Network view:

- Different network design rules are applicable for different types of networks with specific routing, demand flow, and link capacity representation; thus, it is important to understand the subtle differences in the modeling so that proper frameworks can be used.
- Network failure is an important component of network design, and should be taken into account, where applicable.
- Networks are multi-layered (this is a fact).
- Networks tend to be large.

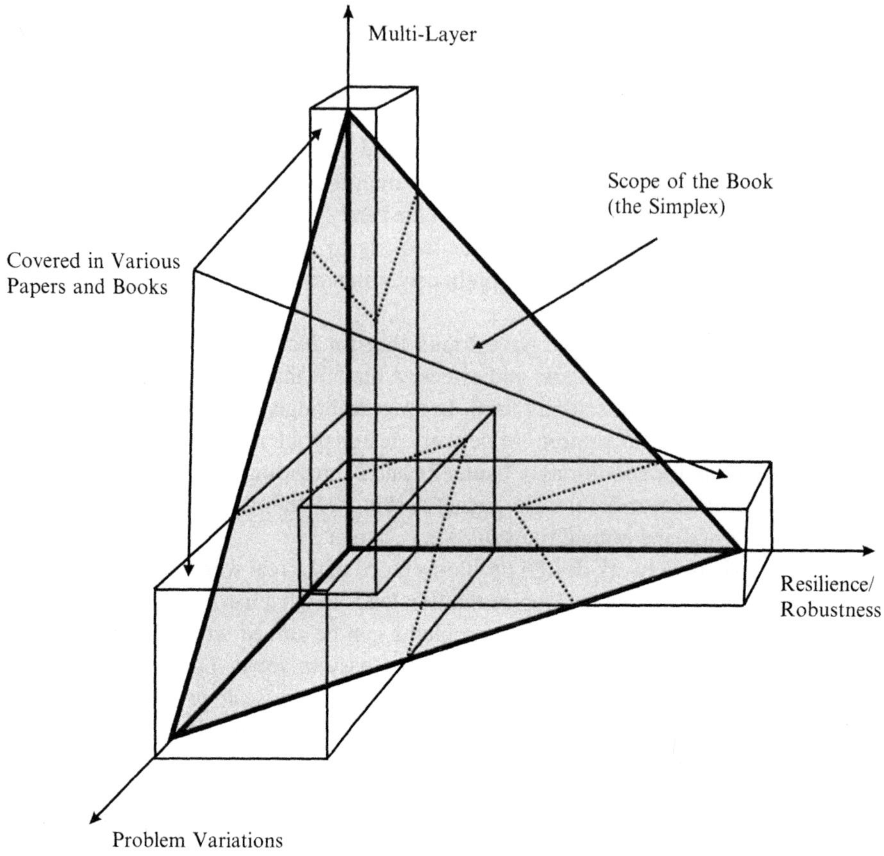

FIGURE 1.18 View on Different Dimensions Covered in this Book

2) Approach/algorithm/theory view:

   - We present different ways to formulate problems so that you can *choose* which ones to use and where to use approximations in the modelling.
   - Even for the same type of network, different network providers may use different rules and constraints in network design. The modeling formulation will help you to see how different rules might be incorporated as constraints.
   - Many practical size problems can be solved with commercial optimization tools. In many cases, this may be enough to solve the problems you might face.
   - As soon as a network gets to be bigger than a few nodes, running a network design problem with a canned approach may sometimes take a considerable amount of time; hence, some idea about developing efficient algorithms is necessary. These are important points to note. However, depending on your interest, you can concentrate primarily on the material on modeling and/or existing algorithms.

- In many cases, the "optimal to the last bit" rule is not necessary; in practice, an approximate or heuristic approach is sufficient.
- Some fundamental principles are important. A simple case in point is linear programming duality. Who would have thought that for IP networks running OSPF protocol, the determination of the link weight is related to solving the dual linear programming problem of a multi-commodity-based network flow allocation problem (see Chapter 7)!

Having read our discussion so far, you will notice that our book does not cover the stochastic topics such as queueing analysis and simulation. While these tools are used for evaluating the network, their role is more to understand dynamics at shorter time granularity which is labelled *real-time traffic management* in Figure 1.16; this is outside the scope of this book.

Finally, throughout the book we present various algorithms. Many of these algorithms have been implemented by one or the other author and their students. Thus, extensive numerical results, including large-scale network design problems of practical size, are included to provide insight. However, to avoid sounding monotonous, we have presented results with different flavors from one chapter to another, especially taking into account the relevance of a model. For example, on location design problems (Chapter 6), we choose to present results with pictorial depictions while comparative performance of one algorithm over another is discussed in Chapter 7.

1.9 NAMING AND NUMBERING CONVENTION

Before we conclude this chapter, we briefly discuss conventions used in the book in regard to naming and numbering. Our equation numbering convention has three parts: chapter number followed by section number followed by the equation number; for example, equation (1.3.1) is the first equation in Chapter 1, Section 3. We believe this will help you especially when we cross-reference because this notes the chapter/section location of the book where the referenced equation was presented/discussed. In regard to numbering of all the other items such as figures, tables, proposition, examples, and so on, our numbering is only chapter-dependent, e.g., Figure 1.3. Each time a proof of a proposition or a theorem is presented, the end of the proof is denoted by ■. Each example described is given a chapter-dependent number and the end of an example is marked using ●. Similarly, each remark is given a chapter dependent number and the end of a remark is marked with ♦.

In this book, we have introduced many terms. The first time a new term is introduced or to emphasize a particular aspect, we use the text/italics mode. Our rule about footnotes can be found in this footnote.[27] In Chapter 2, most of the mathematical notations are defined as they are introduced. We have provided two levels of section headings in each chapter. Difficult sections are marked with asterisks and, sometimes with double asterisks.

In most of the chapters, especially starting in Part II, you will find that we have given a name for a problem formulation when it is first stated. The idea behind this naming is to capture some details about the specific problem considered. To be consistent, we have

[27] Chapter 1 is the only chapter that includes footnotes. In fact, this is the last footnote in this book!

labeled all uncapacitated design problems starting with "D" while all allocation problems are labeled starting with "A." In some cases, the naming identifies certain specific aspects of a problem type, while in other cases, it signifies a problem's variables or the objective. Hopefully, this will become clear as you work through this book.

1.10 SUMMARY

In this introductory chapter, we have provided a general overview of communication and computer networks. By drawing analogy to airline network, we explained the different types of network design problems that arise in design of backbone communication and computer networks.

In network design, an important component is the notion of traffic, or more generally, demand. We explained how this can be represented differently in different networks such as the Internet, the telephone network, and the transport network. We then gave a simple design example to illustrate how routing can play an important role in network design.

Further, we elaborated how networks are structured, specifically making the point that networks are inherently multi-layered from the resource point of view. We also see a relation between capacity and demand since the capacity from an upper layer becomes the demand to the layer below. We then presented a discussion of the network management cycle and show where and how the work on network design presented in this book fits into the network management cycle.

Finally, we provided a brief description on the scope of the book. Our hope is that this will give you, the reader, an idea about the world of network design and how different problems are important to understand and solve. In later chapters, we will go into depth on how to go about modeling different requirements for different networks and what types of algorithms may be applicable. Along the way, we will discuss many different network technological examples to give relevance to the material presented.

Due to our example on air travel and the analogy we have drawn, you might be curious if mathematical modeling and optimization techniques are used for airline network design and routing. Indeed this is the case; for example, see references such as [Jen88], [KG85], and [LN98].

CHAPTER 2

Network Design Problems—Notation and Illustrations

In Chapter 1, we have presented basic ideas about communication and computer network design problems that a network provider is likely to face. In this chapter, we illustrate a representative set of network design problems through simple numerical examples to help understand different aspects of network design. We will consider only a sampling of design problems here; the later chapters will cover many more models, including in-depth variations and extensions of the samples presented in this chapter.

As you will see, network design problems can be formally formulated using mathematical notations. The advantage of a good mathematical notation is that it can represent a specific design problem in a compact and unambiguous way, and moreover, it eventually helps to understand the problem at hand. In the process, we will show how the same problem can be represented in different ways, discussing advantages and disadvantages of notations; this will lead us to the notation used throughout this book. It is important to understand how we use the notation for different problems as it is essential in understanding different design models covered in this book.

Thus, the purpose of this chapter is basically two-fold: 1) to introduce the mathematical notation used throughout this book for network design problems; and 2) to illustrate the network design problem formulations through a sample of simple numerical examples.

The first three sections, 2.1 through 2.3, of this chapter are the basics on how to formulate a problem for a three-node network example, and then discussing merits and demerits of different notations. This is also where terms such as node-link and link-path formulation are introduced. The experienced reader may skip these three sections. In Section 2.4, we consider a four-node problem and illustrate the network dimensioning problem—this is also where we introduce the formal notation to be used in the rest of the book. In Section 2.5, we discuss shortest-path routing and related network design by considering the same four-node example. Shortest-path routing is important since it is used for packet routing in the Internet. Afterwards, we illustrate fair networks in Section 2.6. Another important problem is topological design—this is illustrated in Section 2.7. We then consider network restoration design (Section 2.8) that addresses failure situations such as a fiber cable cut, and show how the basic notation can be extended to consider restoration design as well. As discussed in Section 1.6 of Chapter 1, an important issue is multi-layer network modeling. Thus, we present a detailed illustration of multi-layer networks in Section 2.9 so that you can understand what extensions are required to be introduced when more than one layer of

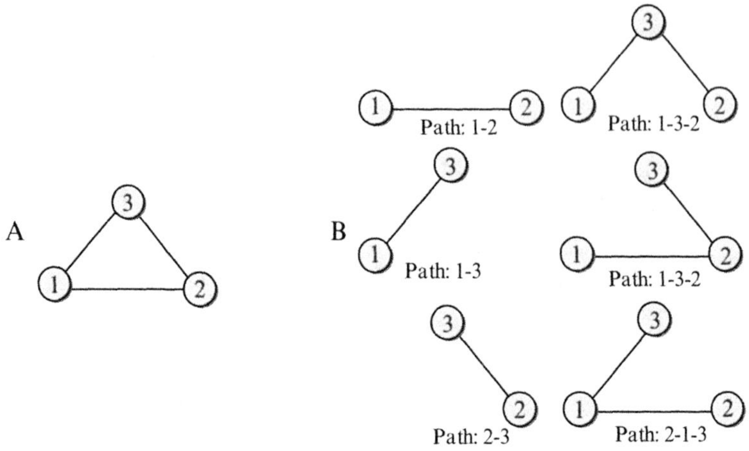

FIGURE 2.1 (A) Three-Node Network Example and (B) All Possible Paths for the Three-Node Example

resources is involved, and how the modeling works. Despite its importance, this section may be skipped in first reading; the reader should come back to it before going into Chapter 12.

2.1 A NETWORK FLOW EXAMPLE IN LINK-PATH FORMULATION

We will start with a simple network that consists of three nodes where each node is connected to the other two nodes, i.e., the network topology looks like a triangle (see Figure 2.1a). In this example, nodes can be routers in the Internet, telephone switches in the telephone network, or digital cross-connects in the SONET network. *Node* is a good generic term to identify different types of routing or switching devices in a network, and we will use this name throughout the book. *Demand volume* represents either the traffic volume (as in the Internet or the telephone network) or the required bandwidth (as in SONET) between a pair of nodes, depending on the considered type of network. Such a pair of nodes is called a *demand pair*, or simply *demand*. Suppose that the demand volume between nodes 1 and 2 is 5, between nodes 1 and 3 is 7, and between nodes 2 and 3 is 8 (units). Note that the demand is assumed to be bi-directional (undirected), given as "between" rather than "from-to". This is to keep this example simple as we assume here that the links are also undirected (in general the demand and/or links can be directed, i.e., uni-directional). We will use $\hat{h}$ to identify the demand volume:

$$\hat{h}_{12} = 5, \quad \hat{h}_{13} = 7, \quad \hat{h}_{23} = 8.$$

As you can see, subscripts with $\hat{h}$ are used for identifying the associated end nodes of demands. While the use of "hat" (^) notation may seem a bit odd, its appropriateness will become clear as we go through this chapter, especially by the end of Section 2.3.

The demand volume for a pair of nodes can possibly be routed over two paths in this three-node network. For example, for the demand pair with end nodes 1 and 2 (to be denoted as $\langle 1,2 \rangle$), its demand volume can be routed over the direct-link route 1-2, and the alternate route 1-3-2 via node 3 (Figure 2.1b). How much of the demand volume will be routed on each path really depends on the network design objective (we will discuss this later in this section). So, if we use $\hat{x}$ with an appropriate subscript identifier to denote the unknown *demand path-flow variables* (flow variables, or flows, in short), then for demand pair $\langle 1,2 \rangle$, we can write:

$$\hat{x}_{12} + \hat{x}_{132} = 5 \quad (= \hat{h}_{12}).$$

Note that we have used subscripts with $\hat{x}$ variables to identify the route or the path; in this case, paths 1-2, and 1-3-2. The summation on the left hand of the above equation holds since the demand flow allocated to different paths for a demand pair adds up to the total demand volume for that pair. Similarly, for demand pairs $\langle 1,3 \rangle$ and $\langle 2,3 \rangle$, respectively, we can write the following equations after identifying the possible paths (Figure 2.1b):

$$\hat{x}_{13} + \hat{x}_{123} = 7 \quad (= \hat{h}_{13})$$

$$\hat{x}_{23} + \hat{x}_{213} = 8 \quad (= \hat{h}_{23}).$$

Note that path-flows are non-negative, i.e., $\hat{x} \geq 0$ for all paths. The next item we need to consider is the *link capacity*, sometimes also referred to as *link bandwidth*. In order to distinguish demands from links, we will denote the links by 1-2, 1-3, and 2-3, and the capacity associated with these links by $\hat{c}_{12}, \hat{c}_{13}$, and $\hat{c}_{23}$, respectively, where the subscripts denote the end nodes of a link.

It is important to recognize here that the demand volume can be between any pair of nodes while the link connects two nodes directly. Another important point is that the unit of the demand volume needs to be consistent with the unit of link capacities. Thus, if we are considering packets per second (pps) as the unit for demand volume, then the link capacity needs to be expressed in units that can be translated to pps as well. This can be accomplished fairly easily for a link for which the capacity is given in terms of raw link speed such as Megabits per second (Mbps). To relate a link capacity to pps, the traffic measurement process also needs to determine the average packet size. If we have the average packet size, we can obtain the maximal possible total flow on a link in pps by dividing the raw link speed by the average packet size expressed in Mbps; this is then the effective link capacity in pps, sometimes referred to as the service rate of the link in pps. Recall that this was discussed earlier in Section 1.3.1. In any case, we will assume that units are consistent (refer to link capacity units [LCU] and demand volume units [DVU] in Section 1.3.5).

We now want to find out which flows might use different links. Since we are using the subscript identifier for a route, link identifiers are implicit in there. Thus, we can see that flow variables $\hat{x}_{12}$ (for demand pair $\langle 1,2 \rangle$), $\hat{x}_{123}$ (for demand pair $\langle 1,3 \rangle$), and $\hat{x}_{213}$ (for demand pair $\langle 2,3 \rangle$) use link 1-2 which has a capacity of $\hat{c}_{12}$, expressed in pps. A common sensible requirement in any communication and computer network is that the link load cannot exceed the capacity of the link. Thus, we have the following inequality for link 1-2:

$$\hat{x}_{12} + \hat{x}_{123} + \hat{x}_{213} \leq \hat{c}_{12}.$$

Similarly, for other two links 1-3 and 2-3 we can write:

$$\hat{x}_{132} + \hat{x}_{13} + \hat{x}_{213} \leq \hat{c}_{13}$$

$$\hat{x}_{132} + \hat{x}_{123} + \hat{x}_{23} \leq \hat{c}_{23}.$$

In this illustration, we will now assume that the capacity of the first two links is 10 and the third is 15 (units); thus:

$$\hat{c}_{12} = \hat{c}_{13} = 10, \quad \hat{c}_{23} = 15.$$

Summarizing what we have discussed so far, we have the following set (system) of linear equations and inequalities (called *constraints*) where $\hat{x}$ are unknowns for all three demands considered (Exercise 2.1):

$$\begin{array}{llllllll} \hat{x}_{12} & +\hat{x}_{132} & & & & & = & 5 \\ & & \hat{x}_{13} & +\hat{x}_{123} & & & = & 7 \\ & & & & \hat{x}_{23} & +\hat{x}_{213} & = & 8 \\ \hat{x}_{12} & & & +\hat{x}_{123} & & +\hat{x}_{213} & \leq & 10 \\ & \hat{x}_{132} & +\hat{x}_{13} & & & +\hat{x}_{213} & \leq & 10 \\ & \hat{x}_{132} & & +\hat{x}_{123} & +\hat{x}_{23} & & \leq & 15 \end{array} \tag{2.1.1a}$$

$$\hat{x}_{12}, \ \hat{x}_{132}, \ \hat{x}_{13}, \ \hat{x}_{123}, \ \hat{x}_{23}, \ \hat{x}_{213} \geq 0.$$

In fact, system (2.1.1a) has, in general, multiple (continuously many) solutions and defines the set of all *feasible solutions*, i.e., feasible flows $\hat{x}$. This raises a question as to which specific feasible solution is of best interest. To address this, we now need to realize what is essential as far as the goal of network design is concerned. There can be different goals: minimize the total routing cost, minimize the congestion of the most congested link in the network, and so on. In the context of the mathematical representation, these types of goals are expressed through what is known as the *objective function* which is either minimized or maximized.

Suppose our goal is to minimize the total routing cost. Assuming that the cost of routing one unit of flow on every link along its path is simply set to 1, the total routing cost for all the flow variables is:

$$\boldsymbol{F} = \hat{x}_{12} + 2\hat{x}_{132} + \hat{x}_{13} + 2\hat{x}_{123} + \hat{x}_{23} + 2\hat{x}_{213} \tag{2.1.1b}$$

and this is our objective function. Note that the unit path cost on path 1-3-2 is 2 since the path is made up of two links where the unit link cost with respect to routing is 1. Another way to look at this is to say that it is twice as expensive to route on a two-link path compared to a one-link direct path. Finally, our goal here is to:

Minimize the objective function (2.1.1b) subject to the requirements or the constraints given by (2.1.1a). This dilemma will be referred to as Problem (2.1.2).

For completeness, we write the entire routing minimization problem discussed so far:

minimize

$$\boldsymbol{F} = \hat{x}_{12} + 2\hat{x}_{132} + \hat{x}_{13} + 2\hat{x}_{123} + \hat{x}_{23} + 2\hat{x}_{213}$$

subject to (constraints)

$$\begin{array}{llllllll} \hat{x}_{12} & + \hat{x}_{132} & & & & & = & 5 \\ & & \hat{x}_{13} & + \hat{x}_{123} & & & = & 7 \\ & & & & \hat{x}_{23} & + \hat{x}_{213} & = & 8 \\ \hat{x}_{12} & & & + \hat{x}_{123} & & + \hat{x}_{213} & \leq & 10 \\ & \hat{x}_{132} & + \hat{x}_{13} & & & + \hat{x}_{213} & \leq & 10 \\ & \hat{x}_{132} & & + \hat{x}_{123} & + \hat{x}_{23} & & \leq & 15 \end{array} \qquad (2.1.2)$$

$$\hat{x}_{12},\ \hat{x}_{132},\ \hat{x}_{13},\ \hat{x}_{123},\ \hat{x}_{23},\ \hat{x}_{213} \geq 0.$$

A dilemma such as Problem (2.1.2) is an example of a *multi-commodity network flow problem*. The term multi-commodity comes from the fact that there are multiple demands (or commodities) that need to be routed in the network simultaneously and they compete for available resources (link capacities, in this case). This is in fact a very common scenario in communication and computer networks (as opposed to a simpler *single-commodity* network flow problem). In the optimization context, this representation is also known as the *linear programming problem* since all the constraints and the objective function are linear. Finally, we refer to the mathematical description of the problem, as shown in (2.1.2), as the *formulation* (instance) of the problem. This formulation is also called the *arc-path* or *link-path* formulation in the literature; we will use the latter name in this book.

For Problem (2.1.2), we now need to find the *optimal solution*, i.e., feasible values of the decision variables ($\hat{x}$) that minimize the objective function (2.1.1b). It turns out that the optimal solution in this case is easy to find and does not require any fancy tools; in fact, some common sense is all you need. Since the cost is higher on multi-link paths, we try to route everything on direct, single-link paths. The resulting optimal solution (to be denoted with * in the superscript) is:

$$\hat{x}^*_{12} = 5, \quad \hat{x}^*_{13} = 7, \quad \hat{x}^*_{23} = 8$$

while all the other $\hat{x}$ are 0, and the total (optimal) cost is $\boldsymbol{F}^* = 20$ (Exercise 2.2). This solution is optimal because it is feasible (satisfies all the constraints), while minimizing the total cost. Furthermore, the optimal solution in this case is unique meaning that the flows $\hat{x}^*$ achieving the minimal cost $\boldsymbol{F}^*$ are unique; in general, however, the optimal solution may not be unique.

Seeing a simple way to obtain the optimal solution, like in this case, can give the illusion that these problems are always easy to solve. Although we did not mention this above, we actually really needed to make sure that all constraints are satisfied by the optimal solution and, in particular, the link capacity constraints are not violated. To illustrate this point, let us consider a simple variation of this problem where the routing cost of a unit of flow is a bit strange; it is twice as expensive to go on the direct path compared to the alternate path. The new objective function can be written as:

$$\boldsymbol{F} = 2\hat{x}_{12} + \hat{x}_{132} + 2\hat{x}_{13} + \hat{x}_{123} + 2\hat{x}_{23} + \hat{x}_{213}. \tag{2.1.3}$$

This certainly seems like an odd cost function compared to the previous cost function (2.1.1b). Observe that in fact the cost function (2.1.1b) is the sum of link costs, where the link cost is the product of the *link load* (link load is the sum of all flows through the link) times the link unit cost (unit link cost are equal to 1 in this case). Actually, in practical world, we do face situations like the new cost function (2.1.3). For example, often an airplane ticket to go from one city to another city, especially in the U.S., is sometimes more expensive to fly directly than to hop through another city! Although you may wonder why anything like this could happen in a communication network, this kind of situation is not unheard of and can be dictated by the routing policy (although, perhaps not as exaggerated as this cost function). Essentially, we need to accept that the routing cost function can be quite arbitrary (Exercise 2.3).

In the revised problem where the specific objective function (2.1.3) is to be minimized with regard to constraints (2.1.1a), an obvious reaction would be to send all the volume for a demand pair on the cheaper of the two paths, i.e., on path 1-3-2 for demand pair $\langle 1,2 \rangle$ instead of path 1-2, and so on. Well, we immediately hit a snag which is the capacity of the links! Does this mean that the problem is not feasible, i.e., are there no values of $\hat{x}$ that satisfy (2.1.1a)? Certainly not; otherwise, we would not have found a solution to Problem (2.1.2) with the original objective function. Note that for the revised problem of Problem (2.1.2), only objective function (2.1.3) has changed, *not* constraints (2.1.1a). This means that the optimal solution to the original Problem (2.1.2) is still a feasible solution to the revised problem. Taking a closer look, it is easy to see that this is not the optimal solution to the revised problem, and neither is the case when all demand volumes are routed on the cheaper of the two paths (since feasibility is violated). This means that the true optimal solution lies somewhere in between.

Without keeping you in suspense and without telling you for now how we can obtain the optimal solution, we are happy to report that the optimal solution to the revised problem, where we are minimizing (2.1.3) with regard to constraints (2.1.1a), is as given below:

$$\hat{x}^*_{12} = 0, \quad \hat{x}^*_{132} = 5, \quad \hat{x}^*_{13} = 1, \quad \hat{x}^*_{123} = 6, \quad \hat{x}^*_{23} = 4, \quad \hat{x}^*_{213} = 4$$

and the total cost at the optimal solution is $\boldsymbol{F}^* = 25$.

There are a couple of important lessons that can be learned from the above example besides becoming familiarized with a multi-commodity network flow problem:

1. Changing the objective function can affect the optimal solution to a problem, and the way of finding it, sometimes, quite dramatically;
2. We need to carefully understand and use the right goal or objective function for a particular network; otherwise, the optimal solution obtained may not be meaningful.

2.2 NODE-LINK FORMULATION

The mathematical formulation presented in (2.1.2) uses the notions of link and path to describe the network optimization problem (this is why the name, link-path formulation, makes sense). In fact this formulation is valid for both undirected and directed links and demands. Still, there is another way to represent the same problem.

Assume that both links and demands are directed, and consider a fixed demand pair and a fixed node. Instead of tracing the *path flows* realizing the demand volume of the considered demand, we consider the total *link flow* for this demand on each link (many of such flows will be in general equal to 0). Now if you look at these link flows from the point of view of the fixed node, which is not an end node of the considered demand, you can see that the flows come into this node on the incoming links and are sent out on its outgoing links. Moreover, the total flow realizing the considered demand incoming to the node (called transit or intermediate node in this context) is equal to the total flow for this demand outgoing from the node. This is called *flow conservation law*. If the considered fixed node is the source of the considered demand, then the total outgoing flow minus the total incoming flow must be equal to the demand volume. Finally, if the fixed node is the sink, then the total incoming flow minus the total outgoing flow must be equal to the demand volume.

Coming back to the three-node network example from Figure 2.1a we substitute each of the three undirected links by two directed links (directed links are frequently referred to as *arcs*). For instance, undirected link 1-2 is substituted by two arcs: $1 \rightarrow 2$ and $2 \rightarrow 1$. Also all the three demands must be made directed—this time, however, it is sufficient to choose only one direction out of the two possible. Considering the first demand $\langle 1,2 \rangle$ between nodes 1 and 2, we may assume that its demand volume, $\hat{h}_{12}$, is originating at node 1 and is destined for node 2 (Figure 2.2), so demand $\langle 1,2 \rangle$ becomes the directed demand $\langle 1{:}2 \rangle$. As it will soon become clear, this can be viewed in the reverse order as well (using demand $\langle 2{:}1 \rangle$, instead of $\langle 1{:}2 \rangle$). This originating demand has two outlets, arc $1 \rightarrow 2$ and arc $1 \rightarrow 3$, to split and realize the demand volume; we will represent the amount of flow to allocate on these arcs by the (unknown) non-negative variables, $\tilde{x}_{12,12}$ and $\tilde{x}_{13,12}$, respectively. Notation "tilde" ($\tilde{\ }$) is used to identify this type of the variable, to distinguish it from the path-flow representation given earlier. Here, the first part in the subscript before the comma refers to the arc, and the second part refers to the (directed) demand pair. As for an example, $\tilde{x}_{13,12}$ refers to the flow on arc $1 \rightarrow 3$ for demand pair $\langle 1{:}2 \rangle$.

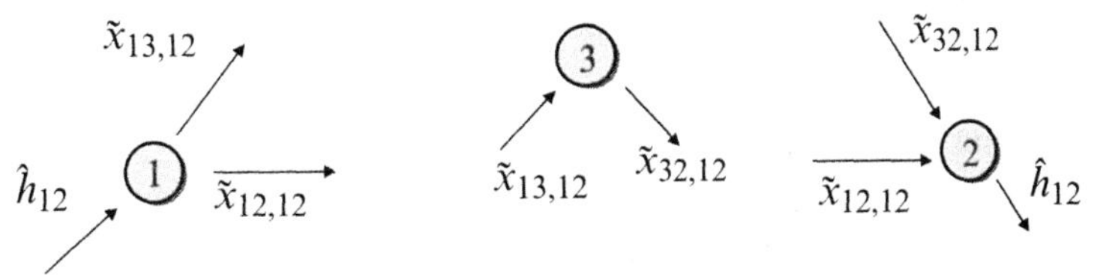

FIGURE 2.2 Flow View for Demand between Nodes 1 and 2

Let us consider demand $\langle 1{:}2\rangle$. Due to the flow conservation law and using the convention that anything going into the node is negative and anything going out is positive, we may write the following equation for node 1:

$$-\hat{h}_{12} - \tilde{x}_{21,12} - \tilde{x}_{31,12} + \tilde{x}_{12,12} + \tilde{x}_{13,12} = 0.$$

Note that node 1 is the source of demand $\langle 1{:}2\rangle$. For node 3, which is a transit node for demand $\langle 1{:}2\rangle$, we have:

$$-\tilde{x}_{13,12} - \tilde{x}_{23,12} + \tilde{x}_{31,12} + \tilde{x}_{32,12} = 0.$$

Finally, at node 2, which is the sink for the considered demand, the flow conservation equation reads:

$$-\tilde{x}_{12,12} - \tilde{x}_{32,12} + \hat{h}_{12} + \tilde{x}_{21,12} + \tilde{x}_{23,12} = 0.$$

It is important to observe that it is sufficient to assume that for each undirected link, at most one out of the two corresponding directed flows is greater than 0 (i.e., one of these two flows is always equal to 0). This is because what really matters is the net flow on a link, e.g., $\tilde{x}_{12,12} - \tilde{x}_{21,12}$. A moment of reflection reveals that in our case we may assume in advance that

$$\tilde{x}_{21,12} = 0, \tilde{x}_{31,12} = 0, \tilde{x}_{23,12} = 0$$

because there is no use to have these flows positive since they are the "backward" flows from the viewpoint of demand $\langle 1{:}2\rangle$. (We need to make a remark here that in general it is not obvious which flows can in advance be assumed to be equal to 0.)

Making use of the above observations we can write the set of *flow conservation equations* for demand $\langle 1{:}2\rangle$ as:

$$\begin{array}{llllll} \tilde{x}_{12,12} & +\tilde{x}_{13,12} & & = & \hat{h}_{12} \\ & -\tilde{x}_{13,12} & +\tilde{x}_{32,12} & = & 0 \\ -\tilde{x}_{12,12} & & -\tilde{x}_{32,12} & = & -\hat{h}_{12}. \end{array} \tag{2.2.1}$$

(An observant reader may notice that the above system of equations is dependent, and one equation can be eliminated—this is a general fact.)

If we now consider the demand $\langle 1{:}3\rangle$ from node 1 to node 3, and assuming $\tilde{x}_{31,13} = 0, \tilde{x}_{32,13} = 0, \tilde{x}_{21,13} = 0$, we can write the analogous equations as follows:

$$\begin{array}{llllll} \tilde{x}_{12,13} & +\tilde{x}_{13,13} & & = & \hat{h}_{13} \\ -\tilde{x}_{12,13} & & +\tilde{x}_{23,13} & = & 0 \\ & -\tilde{x}_{13,13} & -\tilde{x}_{23,13} & = & -\hat{h}_{13}. \end{array} \tag{2.2.2}$$

Finally, assuming $\tilde{x}_{32,23} = 0, \tilde{x}_{31,23} = 0, \tilde{x}_{12,23} = 0$, we have the following equations for the demand $\langle 2{:}3\rangle$ from node 2 to node 3:

$$\begin{array}{lllll} \tilde{x}_{21,23} & +\tilde{x}_{23,23} & = & \hat{h}_{23} \\ -\tilde{x}_{21,23} & +\tilde{x}_{13,23} & = & 0 \\ -\tilde{x}_{13,23} & -\tilde{x}_{23,23} & = & -\hat{h}_{23}. \end{array} \tag{2.2.3}$$

Now, we consider the links. Recall that we have assumed that each undirected link is composed of two arcs, and that for each demand pair, its flow on one of these arcs is equal to zero. The sum of all arc flows realized on a link must not exceed its capacity, which leads to a new set of (capacity) constraints. For example, for link 1→2 the capacity constraint is expressed by the inequality:

$$\tilde{x}_{12,12} + \tilde{x}_{12,13} \le \hat{c}_{12}$$

since we have assumed $\tilde{x}_{21,12} = 0, \tilde{x}_{21,13} = 0, \tilde{x}_{12,23} = 0$. On the other hand, for 1→3, we have the following capacity constraint requirements (due to flow labeling):

$$\tilde{x}_{13,12} + \tilde{x}_{13,13} + \tilde{x}_{13,23} \le \hat{c}_{32}.$$

Similarly, we can write analogous inequalities (capacity constraints) for other links in the network. Putting everything together and eliminating those arc flow variables which are assumed to be equal to 0, we have the following equivalent representation of Problem (2.1.2):

minimize

$$F = \tilde{x}_{12,12} + \tilde{x}_{13,12} + \tilde{x}_{32,12} + \tilde{x}_{12,13} + \tilde{x}_{13,13} + \tilde{x}_{23,13} + \tilde{x}_{21,23} + \tilde{x}_{13,23} + \tilde{x}_{23,23}$$

subject to

$$\begin{array}{ccccccccccc}
\tilde{x}_{12,12} & +\tilde{x}_{13,12} & & & & & & & & = & \hat{h}_{12} \\
 & -\tilde{x}_{13,12} & +\tilde{x}_{32,12} & & & & & & & = & 0 \\
-\tilde{x}_{12,12} & & -\tilde{x}_{32,12} & & & & & & & = & -\hat{h}_{12} \\
 & & & \tilde{x}_{12,13} & +\tilde{x}_{13,13} & & & & & = & \hat{h}_{13} \\
 & & & -\tilde{x}_{12,13} & & +\tilde{x}_{23,13} & & & & = & 0 \\
 & & & & -\tilde{x}_{13,13} & -\tilde{x}_{23,13} & & & & = & -\hat{h}_{13} \\
 & & & & & & \tilde{x}_{21,23} & & +\tilde{x}_{23,23} & = & \hat{h}_{23} \\
 & & & & & & -\tilde{x}_{21,23} & +\tilde{x}_{13,23} & & = & 0 \\
 & & & & & & & -\tilde{x}_{13,23} & -\tilde{x}_{23,23} & = & -\hat{h}_{23} \\
\tilde{x}_{12,12} & & & +\tilde{x}_{12,13} & & & & & & \le & \hat{c}_{12} \\
 & & & & & & \tilde{x}_{21,23} & & & \le & \hat{c}_{21} \\
 & \tilde{x}_{13,12} & & & +\tilde{x}_{13,13} & & & +\tilde{x}_{13,23} & & \le & \hat{c}_{13} \\
 & & & & & \tilde{x}_{23,13} & & & +\tilde{x}_{23,23} & \le & \hat{c}_{23} \\
 & & \tilde{x}_{32,12} & & & & & & & \le & \hat{c}_{32}
\end{array}$$

all $\tilde{x}$ non-negative.

(2.2.4)

This formulation, due to the use of link flows and node flow conservation constraints, is commonly known as the *node-link formulation*.

2.3 NOTIONS AND NOTATIONS

In the specific three-node example studied in Section 2.1, we have used a certain notation to represent nodes, links, demands, and path flows for the link-path representation of a multi-commodity flow problem; this notation can be best referred to as *node-identifier-based notation*. What we mean is that all demands and paths are easy to follow from a node-reference point of view. However, this notation, which works quite well for a three-node network and in some special cases (Exercise 2.4), does not work very well in the general case since: 1) some node pairs may not have any demand and/or not all nodes are directly connected; 2) paths may contain many intermediate nodes; and 3) flow variables have indices of different length. To illustrate this, we will consider the link-path formulation of the instance (2.1.2) described in Section 2.1 for an undirected network with undirected links and bi-directional demands.

Basically, if every node pair has a demand, then for each pair of nodes i and j, we can represent the demand volume by $\hat{h}_{ij}$. Now suppose a pair of nodes in a network has no demand. For example, in a network with 50 nodes, suppose the demand does not exist between node 7 and node 15. Imagine now several pairs of nodes that may not have any demand (this is not unusual in real networks) and hence we somehow need to indicate in the model representation that certain pairs of nodes do not have any demand. With the node-identifier-based notation, this would need to be listed explicitly within the context of the model. That is, we have demand $\hat{h}_{ij}$ between two nodes i and j except, for example, pair $\langle i,j \rangle = \langle 7,15 \rangle$ and so on. At best this takes away from the main flow of understanding a problem formulation and can become a distraction. This distraction concerns also the links. If there is no (direct) link between, for example, nodes 5 and 9, then not only do we have $\hat{c}_{59} = 0$, but we do not need to represent link 5-9 at all in the formulation. In the node-identifier-based notation, you again have the situation of representing such exceptions in the formulation itself.

When the network gets larger, there are many possible paths between two nodes and the paths can be of a variable number of links (hops). Consider a path between nodes i and j of a demand pair going through a third node k; then, the path is represented by i-k-j, and the flow variable is written as $\hat{x}_{ikj}$. On the other hand, if there is another path that goes via two intermediate nodes m and n for the same demand pair, then the path will be i-m-n-j, and the flow variable would be represented as $\hat{x}_{imnj}$, and so on. This notation creates such problems as:

- There is no easy way to represent multiple paths for a specific demand pair when each path may go through a different number of intermediate nodes;
- To complicate this matter, it so happens that even if a network allows for paths having, for example, a maximum two intermediate nodes, not all paths with two intermediate nodes may be acceptable due to the issues such as the distance between nodes; this again forces us to list exceptions for paths which are not used;
- The notation cannot directly handle the situation when there is more than one link between two nodes, i.e., the multi-graph case;
- Also, the situation with multiple demands between the same pair of nodes cannot be explicitly handled; and
- There is virtually no way to write summations over paths, which is necessary for expressing constraints (2.1.1a) in the general form.

To avoid such problems, we will use a different notation (which can be called *link-demand-path-identifier-based notation*) for the majority of the discussion in this book. This notation is compact and allows to list only the necessary objects. While the new notation may seem somewhat non-intuitive or awkward at first reading (at least for the three-node network example), in the long run it is much more handy to capture, formulate, and understand multi-commodity network flow problems, as well as to make algebraical manipulations on the formulated problems.

We now discuss how the link-demand-path-identifier-based notation works. All the demand pairs that have non-zero (i.e., non-negligible) demand volume (and only these pairs) are assigned indices from 1 to the total number of such demand pairs. This way any pair of nodes that does not have any demand is not listed at all. Now consider the three-node example of Section 2.1; we can label and map the demand pairs as follows:

$$\begin{aligned}
&\text{demand pair } \langle 1,2\rangle \longleftrightarrow \text{demand label } 1\\
&\text{demand pair } \langle 1,3\rangle \longleftrightarrow \text{demand label } 2\\
&\text{demand pair } \langle 2,3\rangle \longleftrightarrow \text{demand label } 3.
\end{aligned}$$

In general, we will use the notation D to denote the total number of demand pairs in a network that have positive demand volumes, and index d to label these demands. Thus, in this case $D = 3$ and $d = 1, 2, 3$. Similarly, links that exist in the network are given labels from 1 to the total number of links. As in the case of a demand pair, if there is no link between two specific nodes, we do not need to list it at all in the formulation of the problem. Thus, for the same example, we have

$$\begin{aligned}
&\text{link 1-2} \longleftrightarrow \text{link label } 1\\
&\text{link 1-3} \longleftrightarrow \text{link label } 2\\
&\text{link 2-3} \longleftrightarrow \text{link label } 3.
\end{aligned}$$

Again, in general, we will use the notation E to denote the total number of actual links in the network, and index e to label the links. In this case, we have $E = 3$ and $e = 1, 2, 3$. Note that if there are multiple demands or links between the same pair of nodes, they can be simply included into the list of demands or links, respectively.

With the above background, we can make the following equivalence mapping for demand volumes and link capacities for the three-node problem of Section 2.1:

$$\begin{aligned}
&\hat{h}_{12} \longleftrightarrow h_1, \qquad \hat{h}_{13} \longleftrightarrow h_2, \qquad \hat{h}_{23} \longleftrightarrow h_3\\
&\hat{c}_{12} \longleftrightarrow c_1, \qquad \hat{c}_{13} \longleftrightarrow c_2, \qquad \hat{c}_{23} \longleftrightarrow c_3.
\end{aligned}$$

Having considered the transformation of the demand pairs and the links to the new notation, we are now ready to discuss identifiers for the paths. Since we now have a demand pair identifier, we will use this as the first subscript in a path-flow variable, and then use the second subscript as the label for the path for that particular demand pair. This means that similar to demand pairs and links, the *candidate paths* for a demand pair are numbered from 1 to the total number of candidate paths for this demand pair. The total number of candidate paths for demand d will be denoted by P_d and the paths will be labeled with index p. For example, for demand $\langle 1,2\rangle$ identified by label $d = 1$

we have $P_1 = 2$. The two candidate paths, 1-2 and 1-3-2, are labeled with $p = 1, 2$ (as the second subscript in the path-flow variable), respectively, and identified as (1,1) and (1,2), i.e., as paths number 1 and 2 for demand number 1. In the process, we can re-write the flow variables and their equivalence to the previous markers as listed below:

$$\begin{array}{ll} \hat{x}_{12} \longleftrightarrow x_{11}, & \hat{x}_{132} \longleftrightarrow x_{12}, \\ \hat{x}_{13} \longleftrightarrow x_{21}, & \hat{x}_{123} \longleftrightarrow x_{22}, \\ \hat{x}_{23} \longleftrightarrow x_{31}, & \hat{x}_{213} \longleftrightarrow x_{32}, \end{array}$$

You will notice that we are not using the "hat" with the new set of notations anymore. In fact, you might realize that we used the hat-notation to get to this point, and especially to show equivalence to the new notation (for one-to-one mapping). Since, we have accomplished this, from now on we will not be using the hat- or tilde-notation in the general model formulation. Finally, note also that we can easily map path identifiers and paths from the node-identifier-based notation (with node numbering) to the link-demand-path-identifier-based notation (using link numbering). For example:

node-identifier-based		link-demand-path-identifier-based	
path identifier	path	path identifier	path
132	1-3-2	12	$\{2, 3\}$
213	2-1-3	32	$\{1, 2\}$
23	2-3	31	$\{3\}$

and so on, where for the link-demand-path-identifier notation paths are represented as sets of link labels.

Finally, to complete this exercise, we will now re-write the entire formulation for the three-node example of Section 2.1 for the original instance (2.1.2) where we also include the notations for demand volumes and link capacities, instead of using their values on the right-hand side as was shown in (2.1.2):

minimize

$$\boldsymbol{F} = x_{11} + 2x_{12} + x_{21} + 2x_{22} + x_{31} + 2x_{32}$$

subject to

$$\begin{array}{lllllll} x_{11} & + x_{12} & & & & & = h_1 \\ & & x_{21} & + x_{22} & & & = h_2 \\ & & & & x_{31} & + x_{32} & = h_3 \\ x_{11} & & & + x_{22} & & + x_{32} & \le c_1 \\ & x_{12} & + x_{21} & & & + x_{32} & \le c_2 \\ & x_{12} & & + x_{22} & + x_{31} & & \le c_3 \end{array} \qquad (2.3.1)$$

$$x_{11},\ x_{12},\ x_{21},\ x_{22},\ x_{31},\ x_{32} \ge 0.$$

It should be noted that both formulation (2.3.1) and the previous formulation (2.1.2) represent the same problem and use the link-path representation; the only difference is the notation, whether it is node-identifier based or link-demand-path-identifier based. Additional advantages of link-path formulation, especially with link-demand-path-identifier-based representation, is discussed later in Section 4.6.2.

The link-demand-path-identifier based notation can be used for the node-link representation of the problems discussed in Section 2.2 as well. Then the arc-flow variables are identified by the arc and demand labels, as explained in Section 4.1.1.

Let us now come back to the notation and naming issues. Figure 2.1a depicts a *graph* connecting network's nodes and links. Roughly speaking, the *network* is an object with the structure (often called network *topology*) given by its graph, and with many other attributes, as demand volumes, their candidate path lists, link capacities, etc.

As you already know, a demand pair is a pair of nodes and can be uni-directional (directed) or bi-directional (direction-less, undirected) depending on whether the demand volume is directed or not. Thus, the set-notation such as $\{v, v'\}$ (bi-directional demand) or (v, v') (uni-directional demand) for referring to the demand between nodes v and w makes sense. However, in this book, demand (pair) has a special role; thus, not to confuse with the standard set-notation, we will use $\langle v,v' \rangle$ for referring to demand between nodes v and v' (we have already been doing it!) in the bi-directional case, and use $\langle v{:}v' \rangle$ when referring to the uni-directional demand from node v to node v'. Let us also notice that many books and papers use the name "demand" for the actual volume of demand; in this book we will basically use the term demand to refer to a pair of nodes, and use the expression demand volume to refer to the actual volume (representing traffic or bandwidth) to be realized between the nodes of a particular demand.

We now discuss the case of links. As you know, a link is an object connecting two nodes. In this book, we will use the notation v-v' when referring to the undirected (bi-directional) link between nodes v and v' (if there exists one), and also to distinguish from the notation for a bi-directional demand between the same two nodes. For a directed (uni-directional) link from node v to node v', we will use the notation $v{\to}v'$. Graphs with directed links will be called directed graphs and graphs with undirected links will be called undirected graphs.

Finally, we will discuss the notion of the path. In general, an n-hop path between nodes v and v' is an interlacing sequence of nodes and links of the form

$$(v_1, e_1, v_2, e_2, ..., v_n, e_n, v_{n+1})$$

where $v_1 = v$, $v_{n+1} = v'$, and link e_i connects nodes v_i and v_{i+1} for $i = 1, 2, ..., n$. If the links are directed then the path is directed, and if the links are undirected, so is the path. A path can be represented either by its nodes or links. For instance, taking $n = 2$, the corresponding undirected path is represented by its nodes as v_1-v_2-v_3, and the directed path as $v_1{\to}v_2{\to}v_3$; in the link representation, we write them as $\{e_1, e_2\}$ and (e_1, e_2), respectively.

It is important to note that in most problem formulations studied in this book, nodes, demands, links, and paths will be identified by their generic labels (this is possible due to our link-demand-path-identifier-based notation): v for node (nodes are called vertices in graph theory), d for demand, e for link (links are called edges in graph theory), and p for path. Hence, the somewhat tedious notation needed to distinguish the different cases of the demand and link types will not be much needed. Note that we will use upper-case letters such as D to denote total number of demands, E to denote total number of links, and so on. This is introduced in the next section.

2.4 DIMENSIONING PROBLEMS

In this section, we consider a problem of minimizing the cost of network links with given demand volume between different nodes which can be routed over different paths. We will illustrate this problem through a new four-node example network with three nodes generating demand between each other and one "pure" transit node, not generating any demand. The simple network is shown in Figure 2.3. Our objective function in this case is going to be different than in the previous example.

The structure of this network is represented by the graph depicted in the lower part of Figure 2.3 and consists of $V = 4$ nodes and $E = 5$ undirected links. As shown in the upper part of this figure, there are $D = 3$ bi-directional demands. We have drawn an artificial vertical dotted line between the upper part and the lower part (such as connecting $v = 1$ from the upper part to $v = 1$ in the lower part) to show the corresponding mapping in regard to demand nodes.

We now generalize the labeling a bit more compared to the previous section, and add more formalism as we move forward. Purposefully, we have chosen to repeat certain issues

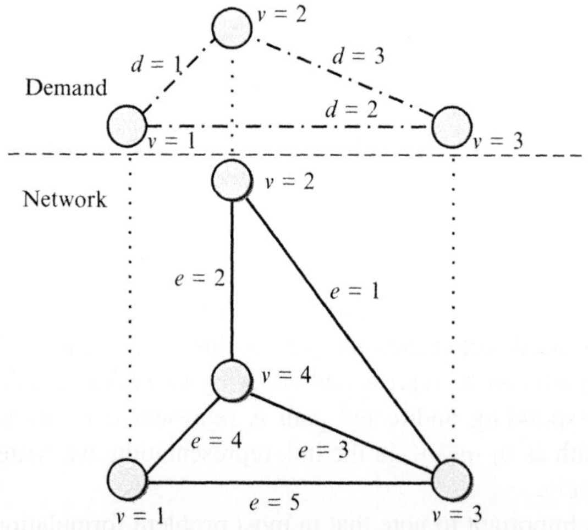

FIGURE 2.3 Four-Node Network Example

discussed in the previous sections for those who skipped reading the first three sections, and to help the beginners better understand mapping, formalism, and formulation. With this, we first introduce generic label for nodes, links, and demands. Nodes (vertices) will be labeled with the generic label v ($v = 1, 2, ..., V$), links (edges) with label e ($e = 1, 2, ..., E$), and demands with label d ($d = 1, 2, ..., D$). Each link connects its end nodes directly, and is identified with the corresponding unordered pair of nodes. For instance, link $e = 1$ is of the form 2-3; here, nodes $v = 2$ and $v = 3$ are the end nodes of link $e = 1$. Similarly, link $e = 5$ connects nod es $v = 1$ and $v = 3$ so is of the form 1-3, and so on. Note that links and demands of the example network are undirected.

Demands correspond to pairs of nodes. In Figure 2.3, demand $d = 1$ corresponds to pair $\langle 1,2 \rangle$, $d = 2$ to pair $\langle 1,3 \rangle$, and $d = 3$ to pair $\langle 2,3 \rangle$. Thus, nodes $v = 1$ and $v = 2$ are the end nodes of demand $d = 1$, and so on. Note that not all pairs of nodes correspond to demands; for instance, there is no demand between nodes $v = 1$ and $v = 4$. In fact, node $v = 4$ is not the end node of any demand in this example and, therefore, is sometimes referred to as a (pure) transit node. Note that end nodes can be transit nodes as well in the sense that they can appear as intermediate nodes for demands with other end nodes. In Figure 2.3 the end nodes are duplicated in the upper part, so the demands between the end nodes are depicted separately.

The capacity of link e ($e = 1, 2, ..., E$) will be denoted by c_e whenever the capacity is given. On the other hand, for certain design problems, the capacity of a link will not be given and will, in fact, be a design variable. For example, consider the design problem where we are to determine demand flows and link capacities required to carry the given demand volumes, sometimes referred to as the *dimensioning problem*. When link capacity is a variable, we will use the notation y_e; the notation c_e will be used when the capacity is given. Generically, we will use link capacity unit—LCU—for expressing capacity of a link. One capacity unit (or, 1 LCU) on link e is assigned the unit (or marginal) cost ξ_e (≥ 0).

Each demand d ($d = 1, 2, ..., D$) is characterized by the demand volume denoted by h_d. Demand volumes are also called commodities in non-telecommunications applications, hence the term multi-commodity when multiple demands are considered, thus leading to the term multi-commodity network problems. Demand volume is expressed in general through demand volume units—DVU. For example, if a DVU is given in Mbps, then for consistency, LCU should be represented in Mbps as well. If however, a DVU is given in pps, LCU need to be mapped to pps even though the actual capacity may be given in link bit-rate (see Section 1.3.1 on how to do proper mapping, and the discussion earlier). In the rest of this section, we shall assume that LCU and DVU are in Mbps, unless stated otherwise.

Figure 2.4 depicts the unit costs and demand volumes assigned to the links and demands, respectively. Each demand d is assigned a list of paths (called also routes) that can carry flows. For demand d the total number of assigned paths is denoted by P_d and they are labeled with p from the first path to the total number of paths, i.e., $p = 1, 2, ..., P_d$; this sequence is called the *list of candidate paths* (or path list, or routing list, in short). To tie it to generic demand d, we write the list of paths as $\mathbb{P}_d = (\mathcal{P}_{d1}, \mathcal{P}_{d2}, ..., \mathcal{P}_{dP_d})$.

It is important to note that each path $\mathcal{P}_{dp}(p = 1, 2, ..., P_d)$ connects the end nodes of demand d. Each path is described as the set of links of which the path is composed of.

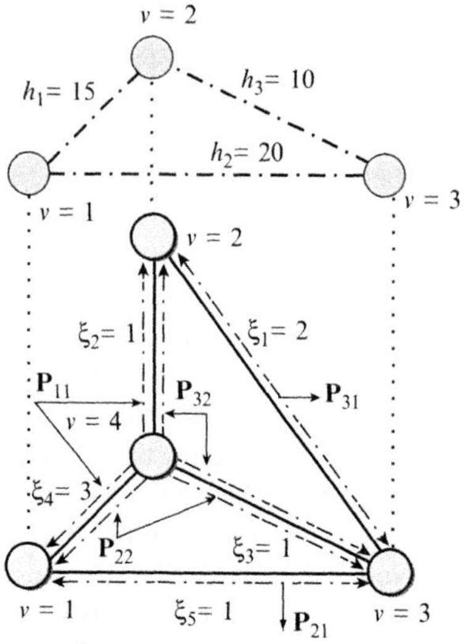

FIGURE 2.4 Four-Node Network Example: Demand Volume and Link Cost

Demand volumes are *realized* by means of flows assigned to paths on their routing lists. The flow realizing demand d on path p is denoted by x_{dp} $(p = 1, 2, ..., P_d)$.

Now, consider the example in Figure 2.4. Here, demand $d = 1$ is allowed to have, for example, just one path: $\mathcal{P}_{11} = \{2, 4\}$ which means that the path consists of link number 2 and link number 4. This then means that $\mathbb{P}_1 = (\mathcal{P}_{11})$. In this case, there is only one flow variable x_{11}. For demand $d = 2$ two paths are allowed: $\mathcal{P}_{21} = \{5\}$, $\mathcal{P}_{22} = \{3, 4\}$ and the associated flow variables are x_{21} and x_{22}, respectively. Note that $\mathbb{P}_2 = (\mathcal{P}_{21}, \mathcal{P}_{22})$. Finally, demand $d = 3$ is also allowed to have two paths: $\mathcal{P}_{31} = \{1\}$, $\mathcal{P}_{32} = \{2, 3\}$ $(\mathbb{P}_3 = (\mathcal{P}_{31}, \mathcal{P}_{32}))$, and associated flow variables, x_{31} and x_{32}. Notice that path $\mathcal{P}_{12} = \{1, 5\}$ could have been a possible path for demand $d = 1$, but is not included into the path list $\mathbb{P}_1$ in the first part of our illustration, and will be considered later.

Since demand volume for each demand d needs to be realized through flows on candidate paths, we can now write the following equations (known as the *demand constraints*):

$$\begin{aligned} x_{11} &= 15 \\ x_{21} + x_{22} &= 20 \\ x_{31} + x_{32} &= 10. \end{aligned} \tag{2.4.1}$$

Note that, in this case, we have $P_1 = 1$, $P_2 = 2$, and $P_3 = 2$. In general, if you notice, the flow variables names and path indices are pretty much the same as in the three-node example from the previous section after we introduced the link-demand-path-identifier-based notation in Section 2.3. This allows you to see the advantage of this notation; although the actual network topology has changed from the previous example, the representation of the problem remains virtually the same.

The demand constraints (2.4.1) can be written in a general form as follows. Suppose we denote the vector of flows assigned to demand d with $\boldsymbol{x}_d = (x_{d1}, x_{d2}, ..., x_{dP_d})$ for path indices $p = 1, 2, ..., P_d$. Then, we arrive at:

$$x_{d1} + x_{d2} + ... + x_{dP_d} = h_d$$

for each demand d. In summation notation, we can write this as:

$$\textstyle\sum_{p=1}^{P_d} x_{dp} = h_d, \quad d = 1, 2, ..., D. \tag{2.4.2}$$

Since, in general, we know that the paths are numbered from 1 to P_d for each demand d, we can write expression (2.4.2) more compactly as:

$$\textstyle\sum_p x_{dp} = h_d, \quad d = 1, 2, ..., D \tag{2.4.3}$$

where, for a fixed demand d, the summation is always carried over all $p = 1, 2, ..., P_d$, unless explicitly stated otherwise. In its general form, equation (2.4.3) is an important one to note and understand as you will see this throughout the book.

In general, the vector of all flows (path-flow variables), will be called *flow allocation vector*, or simply *flow vector*, which can be written as:

$$\begin{aligned} \boldsymbol{x} = (\boldsymbol{x}_1, \boldsymbol{x}_2, ..., \boldsymbol{x}_D) &= (x_{11}, x_{12}, ..., x_{1P_1}, x_{21}, x_{22}, ..., x_{2P_2}, ..., x_{D1}, x_{D2}, ..., x_{DP_D}) \\ &= (x_{dp} : d = 1, 2, ..., D; p = 1, 2, ..., P_d). \end{aligned}$$

By now, you have probably noticed that we are using the bold font to denote a vector, and to distinguish it from a scalar quantity. For example, $\boldsymbol{x}_1$ and x_{11} are both valid notations - the first one (bold), $\boldsymbol{x}_1$, is a vector while the second one, x_{11}, refers to the first scalar entity of vector $\boldsymbol{x}_1$. Since with any rule there is an exception, we also have an exception; throughout this book, we will use the bold font, $\boldsymbol{F}$, for representing the objective function which takes scalar values.

As you may have guessed by now, there is a second set of constraints which assures that for each link e its capacity c_e (or y_e, if the capacity is a variable) is not exceeded by the flows using this link; we call these *capacity constraints*. This requirement leads to the following inequalities for the four-node network:

$$\begin{array}{lllllll} & & & x_{31} & & \le y_1 \\ x_{11} & & & & +x_{32} & \le y_2 \\ & & x_{22} & & +x_{32} & \le y_3 \\ x_{11} & & +x_{22} & & & \le y_4 \\ & x_{21} & & & & \le y_5. \end{array} \tag{2.4.4}$$

The sums on the left-hand sides of the above inequalities are called *link loads*, as they give the total flow through a link, expressed in DVUs. This is very similar to what we did in (2.1.1a) (note the last three inequalities). In general, to write down the link loads, we need to

TABLE 2.1 **Link-Path Incidence Relation δ_{edp}**

$e \setminus \mathcal{P}_{dp}$	$\mathcal{P}_{11} = \{2,4\}$	$\mathcal{P}_{21} = \{5\}$	$\mathcal{P}_{22} = \{3,4\}$	$\mathcal{P}_{31} = \{1\}$	$\mathcal{P}_{32} = \{2,3\}$
1	0	0	0	1	0
2	1	0	0	0	1
3	0	0	1	0	1
4	1	0	1	0	0
5	0	1	0	0	0

know the relationship between links and paths. The relationship can be formally specified by the link-path incidence coefficients. To see this, we refer to Table 2.1.

Observe that Table 2.1 is nothing but an indication of which flow variables appear on the left-hand side of each inequality in (2.4.4). For example, the first path for demand $d = 1$, path $\mathcal{P}_{11}$ does not use link $e = 1$, so this entry is 0. The reason is that $\mathcal{P}_{11}$ consists of links $e = 2$ and $e = 4$; thus, this makes sense. Let us look at another one. The second path for demand $d = 3$ uses link $e = 3$, so this entry is set to 1. If you look at the pattern, you will notice that there are three pieces of information involved, e, d, p; another way to look at it is to determine whether a generic path p for demand d uses link e; if it does for a specific case, we set the entry in the table to be 1, otherwise, it is 0. The good news is that this information can be written in a very nice compact manner by using another notation, δ, which really tells us the link-path relation. Formally, a coefficient δ_{edp} is defined for each triple (e, d, p) where $e = 1, 2, ..., E$, $d = 1, 2, ..., D$, and $p = 1, 2, ..., P_d$, and is defined as:

$$\delta_{edp} = \begin{cases} 1 & \text{if link } e \text{ belongs to path } p \text{ for demand } d \\ 0 & \text{otherwise.} \end{cases} \tag{2.4.5}$$

Note that δ_{edp} is a given quantity since the set of possible paths is already given and the links these paths use are fixed; in other words, it is not a variable. Using the introduced coefficients, the link load on e can be nicely written as the following linear expression:

$$\textstyle\sum_{d=1}^{D}\sum_{p=1}^{P_d}\delta_{edp}x_{dp}.$$

For the 4-node example, this is nothing but the expression on the left-hand side of (2.4.4) for each link. As you can see, the use of the notation δ_{edp} is extremely helpful since it allows us to write the relation between link load and capacity in a nice compact way. This load for link e will be denoted by $\underline{y}_e$, and hence is defined as follows:

$$\underline{y}_e = \underline{y}_e(\boldsymbol{x}) = \textstyle\sum_d\sum_p\delta_{edp}x_{dp} \tag{2.4.6}$$

where we have skipped the bounds for the summation indices as they are known.

The capacity constraints can be generally written as:

$$\textstyle\sum_d\sum_p\delta_{edp}x_{dp} \le y_e, \quad e = 1, 2, ..., E. \tag{2.4.7}$$

The summation on the left-hand side of inequalities (2.4.7) is taken over all paths appearing in the routing lists of all demands, i.e., over all combinations (d, p) such that $d = 1, 2, ..., D$ and $p = 1, 2, ..., P_d$; these are not shown in the above compact form. Now, inequality (2.4.7) is the next important relation to note after equation (2.4.3). For brevity, we will often refer to the capacity variables $y_e, e = 1, 2, ..., E$ through the vector notation $\boldsymbol{y} = (y_1, y_2, ..., y_E)$. It is important to distinguish link capacity variables y_e from the corresponding link loads $\underline{y}_e$; in general, we require that $\underline{y}_e \le y_e$ for each link e.

In this problem, we are interested in minimizing the capacity cost. This objective function can be written as:

$$\begin{aligned} \boldsymbol{F} &= \xi_1 y_1 + \xi_2 y_2 + \xi_3 y_3 + \xi_4 y_4 + \xi_5 y_5 \\ &= 2y_1 + y_2 + y_3 + 3y_4 + y_5. \end{aligned} \tag{2.4.8}$$

In general, this cost function can be denoted as:

$$\boldsymbol{F} = \textstyle\sum_{e=1}^{E} \xi_e y_e = \sum_e \xi_e y_e. \tag{2.4.9}$$

Thus, we can pose the following instance of the *dimensioning problem*, referred to as DP in the sequel, for the four-node network example in its entire form as:

minimize

$$\boldsymbol{F} = 2y_1 + y_2 + y_3 + 3y_4 + y_5$$

subject to

$$\begin{array}{ccccccc} x_{11} & & & & & = & 15 \\ & x_{21} & + x_{22} & & & = & 20 \\ & & & x_{31} & + x_{32} & = & 10 \\ & & & x_{31} & & \le & y_1 \\ x_{11} & & & & + x_{32} & \le & y_2 \\ & & x_{22} & & + x_{32} & \le & y_3 \\ x_{11} & & + x_{22} & & & \le & y_4 \\ & x_{21} & & & & \le & y_5 \end{array} \tag{2.4.10}$$

$$x_{11},\ x_{21},\ x_{22},\ x_{31},\ x_{32} \ge 0, \quad y_1,\ y_2,\ y_3,\ y_4,\ y_5 \ge 0.$$

In the general form, DP (2.4.10) can be written as:

minimize

objective/cost function (2.4.9): $\boldsymbol{F} = \sum_e \xi_e y_e$

subject to

demand constraints (2.4.3):	$\sum_p x_{dp} = h_d,$	$d = 1, 2, ..., D$
capacity constraints (2.4.7):	$\sum_d \sum_p \delta_{edp} x_{dp} \le y_e,$	$e = 1, 2, ..., E$
constraints on variables:	$\boldsymbol{x} \ge \boldsymbol{0}, \boldsymbol{y} \ge \boldsymbol{0}.$	

(2.4.11)

Let us pause now to compare this formulation to what we have discussed in earlier sections in regard to the three-node network example (Exercise 2.5). In the instance of Problem (2.3.1) for the three-node example, we have minimized the total routing cost when capacity was given to carry a given demand using flow variables; for the four-node example here, we are minimizing the total link capacity cost required to carry a given demand also using flow variables, but at the same time capacities are variables as well. A problem such as DP where capacity is to be determined is, as already mentioned, referred to as the dimensioning (or uncapacitated) problem. Note that DP (2.4.11) happens to be a linear programming (LP, refer to Section 5.1.1) problem. It may be noted that a common convention for writing a linear programming problem is to list all variables on the left side of the equation or inequality. We favor keeping the logical (and physical) meaning of a constraint intact in its natural form over this convention. Thus, for (2.4.7), i.e., the capacity constraint in (2.4.11), variable y_e is kept on the right side of the inequality instead of moving it to the left side of the inequality.

Now we are ready to discuss the optimal solution for DP (2.4.11). In this model, when variables take continuous values (as in our case for this example), then for any optimal solution of DP, the capacity feasibility constraints become equalities, i.e., for each link, its load is equal to its capacity because otherwise we would pay for unused capacity on the links (implying the solution is not optimal).

In Figure 2.5, we have shown a set of values for the flow allocation vector $\boldsymbol{x}$. If we calculate the link loads (and hence, link capacities) for this flow allocation vector, then assuming the equalities in constraints (2.4.7) we arrive at the following loads: $\underline{y}_1(\boldsymbol{x}) = y_1 = 5$, $\underline{y}_2(\boldsymbol{x}) = y_2 = 20$, $\underline{y}_3(\boldsymbol{x}) = y_3 = 10$, $\underline{y}_4(\boldsymbol{x}) = y_4 = 20$, and $\underline{y}_5(\boldsymbol{x}) = y_5 = 15$. The so defined feasible solution $(\boldsymbol{x}, \boldsymbol{y})$, where $\boldsymbol{y} = (y_1, y_2, y_3, y_4, y_5) = (5, 20, 10, 20, 15)$, has the total cost $\boldsymbol{F} = 115$.

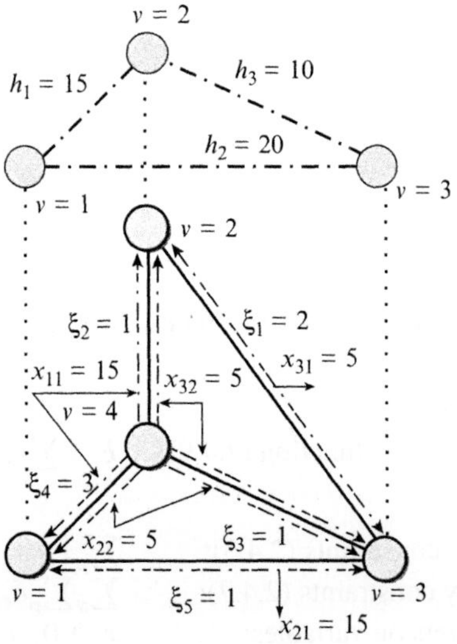

FIGURE 2.5 Four-Node Network Example: Allocation

It is easy to see that the above solution is not optimal, because of the use of the second path of the second demand, $\mathcal{P}_{22}$, carrying flow $x_{22} = 5$. This path is composed of links $e = 3$ and $e = 4$, and has the unit cost equal to the sum of the unit costs of its links, i.e., $\zeta_{22} = \xi_3 + \xi_4 = 1 + 3 = 4$. The other allowable path for demand $d = 2$ is its path number $p = 1$, $\mathcal{P}_{21}$, with $\zeta_{21} = \xi_5 = 1$. In general, the cost of path $\mathcal{P}_{dp}$ for Problem (2.4.11) is given by the formula:

$$\zeta_{dp} = \textstyle\sum_e \delta_{edp}\xi_e, \quad d = 1, 2, ..., D \quad p = 1, 2, ..., P_d. \tag{2.4.12}$$

This also shows another advantage of notation δ_{edp} since it allows us to write the cost of a path in a compact manner if the costs of the links that the path is composed of are available.

In this example, it is profitable then to move all the flow from path $\mathcal{P}_{22}$ to path $\mathcal{P}_{21}$ which gives the saving of $(\zeta_{22} - \zeta_{21}) = 3$ per one unit of flow. In our case, this would give the total saving of 15, since $x_{22}(\zeta_{22} - \zeta_{21}) = 15$. Note that flow x_{11} is trivially optimal since its value is fixed by the demand constraint (2.4.3) for demand $d = 1$; note that there is only one path for demand $d = 1$. Also, the two flows assigned to demand $d = 3$ are optimal since both allowable paths for this demand have the same unit cost $\zeta_{31} = \zeta_{32} = 2$; altogether, we have the optimal cost $\boldsymbol{F}^* = 100$. Note that for this problem, and in the case of demand $d = 3$, any split of its demand volume $h_d = 10$ among the two allowable paths is optimal as well which means that $\boldsymbol{F}^*$ remains the same but there are multiple $\boldsymbol{x}$s with the same optimal cost value. The above observations lead to describing optimal solution $(\boldsymbol{x}^*, \boldsymbol{y}^*)$ in the following way:

$$\begin{aligned}
x^*_{11} &= 15 \\
x^*_{21} &= 20, x^*_{22} = 0 \\
x^*_{31} &= a, x^*_{32} = 10 - a \quad \text{for any } 0 \le a \le 10 \\
y^*_1 &= 10 - a, y^*_2 = 15 + a, y^*_3 = a, y^*_4 = 15, y^*_5 = 20 \\
\boldsymbol{F}^* &= 100.
\end{aligned}$$

Thus, we can make the following statement in regard to obtaining the optimal solution to our specific problem:

***Shortest-Path Allocation Rule for DP*:**

For each demand, allocate its entire demand volume to its shortest path, with respect to links unit costs and candidate path. If there is more than one shortest path for a demand then the demand volume can be split among the shortest paths in an arbitrary way. (2.4.13)

This rule implies that the optimal solution (i.e., optimal flow allocation vector) of DP, in general, may not be unique. This is an important point to note. Moreover, while the above rule works for DP, it is not (at all) a general solution approach for other multi-commodity flow problems.

We can slightly change the four-node design Problem (2.4.10) by putting restrictions on flows. For example, suppose we insist on having an optimal solution with *non-bifurcated* flows (also called *single-path* flows or *unsplittable* flows). This would mean that for $d = 2$

and d = 3, we can choose only one path each although each demand has two possible paths. To obtain the optimal solution, no demand split is allowed. The non-bifurcated solutions are not unique either. For instance in the example here if we impose the requirement for non-bifurcated flows, we can have two such solutions corresponding to $a = 0$ and $a = 10$. We want to emphasize that although in the case considered it is easy to obtain a non-bifurcated optimal solution, in general, the single-path flow requirement makes the problem (much) more difficult to solve.

Now we consider another variation to the original example (2.4.10) while allowing bifurcation. Suppose we add path $\mathcal{P}_{12} = \{1, 5\}$ to the candidate path list of demand $d = 1$. Since this path appears for demand $d = 1$, and for links $e = 1$ and $e = 5$, we need to modify the corresponding equations and inequalities. Specifically, the first equation (2.4.10) corresponding to demand $d = 1$ which is $x_{11} = 5$, the inequality corresponding to link $e = 1$ which is $x_{31} \le y_1$, and the inequality corresponding to link $e = 5$ which is $x_{21} \le y_5$, need to change, respectively, to:

$$\begin{array}{llllcl}
x_{11} & + x_{12} & & & = & 15 \\
 & x_{12} & & + x_{31} & \le & y_1 \\
 & x_{12} & + x_{21} & & \le & y_5.
\end{array}$$

Thus, we have the following modified problem:

minimize

$$\boldsymbol{F} = 2y_1 + y_2 + y_3 + 3y_4 + y_5$$

subject to

$$\begin{array}{lllllllcl}
x_{11} & + x_{12} & & & & & & = & 15 \\
 & & x_{21} & + x_{22} & & & & = & 20 \\
 & & & & x_{31} & + x_{32} & & = & 10 \\
 & x_{12} & & & + x_{31} & & & \le & y_1 \\
x_{11} & & & & & + x_{32} & & \le & y_2 \\
 & & & x_{22} & & + x_{32} & & \le & y_3 \\
x_{11} & & & + x_{22} & & & & \le & y_4 \\
 & x_{12} & + x_{21} & & & & & \le & y_5
\end{array} \qquad (2.4.14)$$

$$x_{11},\ x_{12},\ x_{21},\ x_{22},\ x_{31},\ x_{32} \ge 0, \quad y_1,\ y_2,\ y_3,\ y_4,\ y_5 \ge 0.$$

The optimal solution to the modified Problem (2.4.14) would use the flows $x^*_{11} = 0, x^*_{12} = 15$ and the cost would be further decreased by 15 to $\boldsymbol{F}^* = 85$, since, for demand $d = 1$, the cost for the second path ($\zeta_{12} = 3$) is cheaper than the first path ($\zeta_{11} = 4$). This example shows that, as could be expected, the starting candidate path lists can affect the optimal solution and, hence, the path preprocessing, i.e., initializing or augmenting path lists can be an important part of the network design process.

So far, we have assumed that link capacity can be installed in non-integral, continuous values. Often, in real networks, capacities can be installed only in modular units, e.g., T1, E1, OC-3, and so on. Suppose now we change the original design problem DP (2.4.11) to be addressed in the presence of modular capacity units (i.e., certain modules equal to M DVUs; in this way, one LCU is equal to M DVUs). With such modular links the solution does not, in general, obey the shortest-path allocation rule (2.4.13) (which can be easily anticipated for large values of the module) nor the optimal link load, $\underline{y}_e(\boldsymbol{x})$, being equal to optimal link capacity, y_e (see the example illustrated in Section 1.4). For instance, with $M = 35$ the cheapest solution for this modularized problem is to install one module of capacity on exactly two links: $e = 1$ and $e = 5$ (assuming that $\xi_e = 1$ is the cost of one module of capacity on link e). Also, the optimal flows in the modular link case are, in general, bifurcated, unless additional constraints forcing the single-path solution are imposed. We note that for large networks, the modular design problems, especially when combined with the single-path requirement, are very difficult to solve even with specialized algorithms/heuristics developed for this purpose.

In DP-like problems, link capacities are subject to optimization and, hence, DP is an example of an *uncapacitated* design problem. Another type of problem is *capacitated* design problem where link capacities are given (note we will use c_e as the given capacity of link e when known, instead of y_e). The problem is to find a feasible flow allocation vector that satisfies the demand constraints (2.4.3) and the capacity constraints (2.4.7) with c_e appearing on the right-hand sides. In such a scenario, there may not be any objective function unless, for example, flow routing cost minimization is required as discussed in Sections 2.1 and 2.3. Thus, this shows the connection between the two different cases which are useful for addressing different network design problems. For completeness, we state the capacitated problem in the compact form below:

$$
\begin{array}{lll}
\text{demand constraints:} & \sum_p x_{dp} = h_d, & d = 1, 2, ..., D \\
\text{capacity constraints:} & \sum_d \sum_p \delta_{edp} x_{dp} \le c_e, & e = 1, 2, ..., E \\
\text{constraints on variables:} & \boldsymbol{x} \ge \mathbf{0}. &
\end{array}
\tag{2.4.15}
$$

Note that link costs do not come into the picture in this case; however, the routing cost may appear. Such problems often arise in a network scenario when the network capacity is already built up, but the demand may have changed.

Returning to our original example for this section, suppose that the link capacities are given as follows $\boldsymbol{c} = (c_1, c_2, c_3, c_4, c_5) = (5, 10, 10, 5, 30)$, and that the path lists are extended so that $\mathbb{P}_1 = (\mathcal{P}_{11}, \mathcal{P}_{12}, \mathcal{P}_{13})$, where $\mathcal{P}_{13} = \{4, 3, 1\}$, can also be used for demand $d = 1$ (candidate path lists for the remaining two demands are not altered). It is easy to see that all feasible solutions to the considered capacitated problem are necessarily bifurcated, and an example of one of them is as follows:

$$
\begin{array}{l}
x_{11} = 5, x_{12} = 0, x_{13} = 10 \\
x_{21} = 20, x_{21} = 0 \\
x_{31} = 10, x_{32} = 10.
\end{array}
$$

Note that demand $d = 1$ uses its longest path in terms of the "hop-count".

In general, when non-bifurcated solutions are required, then additional constraints on the flows must be imposed explicitly to force the single-path solution. It may so happen that for given link capacities a bifurcated solution exists but the non-bifurcated does not (think why). You can see this from the above example when you impose the requirement that flows for a demand pair must be non-bifurcated.

Problems along the lines discussed in this section will be covered in detail in Chapter 4. Optimization algorithms related to these problems will be covered in Chapter 5.

2.5 SHORTEST-PATH ROUTING

Now we will consider another design problem. Computer networks use what is often referred to as *shortest-path routing*; for example, OSPF routing in IP networks (see Section 3.1 and Chapter 7 for additional details). It is important not to confuse shortest-path routing with the term shortest-path allocation discussed in the last section. This will hopefully become apparent once you read through this section. Basically, the shortest-path routing means that for each demand d all its volume h_d is realized on its shortest path, with respect to some given link weight system $\boldsymbol{w} = (w_1, w_2, ..., w_E)$ with link weight (cost) w_e for link e, among all possible paths for demand d in the network. Note that the path selection is based on additive calculation of link-weights.

Suppose we are given the link weight system $\boldsymbol{w} = (1,3,1,2,4)$ for the example network of Figure 2.3. Then, the following paths will be used to carry the entire demand volumes for different demands as follows:

$$\begin{array}{llll} d=1 & \mathcal{P}_{13} = \{1,3,4\} & \text{path length } 4 & x_{13} = 15 \\ d=2 & \mathcal{P}_{21} = \{1\} & \text{path length } 1 & x_{21} = 10 \\ d=3 & \mathcal{P}_{32} = \{3,4\} & \text{path length } 3 & x_{32} = 10. \end{array}$$

In this case, the rest of the flow variables are equal to 0. Since in this example of a network scenario, the shortest paths are unique for each demand pair, the resulting flow allocation vector $\boldsymbol{x}(\boldsymbol{w})$, is also unique, and in this case, non-bifurcated. It is important to note the notation in this case: $\boldsymbol{x}(\boldsymbol{w})$ (instead of just $\boldsymbol{x}$), which means that flow allocation $\boldsymbol{x}$ is dictated by the weight system $\boldsymbol{w}$. However, this flow vector is not feasible for the link capacities $\boldsymbol{c} = (5,10,10,5,30)$ used in the previous example! The link loads, which are denoted by $\underline{y}_e$, resulting from the allocation vector $\boldsymbol{x}(\boldsymbol{w})$, are equal to $\underline{\boldsymbol{y}}(\boldsymbol{w}) = (\underline{y}_1, \underline{y}_2, \underline{y}_3, \underline{y}_4, \underline{y}_5) = (25,0,35,35,0)$; they do not satisfy the link capacities in terms of the capacity constraints listed in (2.4.15). Certainly, if we change the link capacity so that $\boldsymbol{c} = \underline{\boldsymbol{y}}(\boldsymbol{w})$, then this shortest-path allocation, with respect to the weight system $\boldsymbol{w}$, will become (trivially) feasible.

In general, the following single shortest-path allocation problem is a complex problem to solve:

> *For given link capacities* $\mathbf{c}$ *and demand volumes* $\boldsymbol{h}$ $(\boldsymbol{h} = (h_1, h_2, ..., h_D))$, *find a link weight system* $\boldsymbol{w}$ *such that the resulting shortest paths are unique and the resulting flow allocation vector* $\boldsymbol{x}(\boldsymbol{w})$ *is feasible, i.e., such that* $\boldsymbol{x}(\boldsymbol{w})$ *satisfies (2.4.15).*

There are three main reasons for this complexity:

- A non-bifurcated (single-path) feasible flow allocation may not exist while bifurcated feasible flow allocations may exist.

- Even if a single-path solution exists, in most cases it can be hard to determine.
- Moreover, even if we find a single-path flow solution, then the weight system to induce it may not exist.

To illustrate the last (least obvious) item more precisely, we note that there can be a feasible non-bifurcated flow allocation vector, $\boldsymbol{x}$, but there may not exist any weight system $\boldsymbol{w}$ such that $\boldsymbol{x} = \boldsymbol{x}(\boldsymbol{w})$ for any such feasible $\boldsymbol{x}$. This issue is illustrated in Figure 2.6. Suppose there are two demands: $d = 1$ between nodes 1 and 7 and $d = 2$ between nodes 2 and 6 with same demand volume $h_1 = h_2 = 1$. Suppose also that all links' capacities are equal to 1 ($c_e \equiv 1$). Here, each demand has two paths; for demand $d = 1$, the first path traverses the nodes 1-3-5-7 (path $\mathcal{P}_{11}$) and the second path traverses the nodes 1-3-4-5-7 (path $\mathcal{P}_{12}$). For demand $d = 2$, paths are 2-3-4-5-6 (path $\mathcal{P}_{21}$) and 2-3-5-6 (path $\mathcal{P}_{22}$). Now, allocating flow $x_{11} = 1$ to path 1-3-5-7 and flow $x_{21} = 1$ to path 2-3-4-5-6 gives the feasible flow allocation vector $\boldsymbol{x} = (x_{11}, x_{21})$ with respect to Problem (2.4.15). Now you may wish to check if any link weight system induces this flow (bad news: it is not possible for single shortest path!).

We now return to our original 4-node example and consider the weight system $\boldsymbol{w} = (1, 1, 1, 1, 1)$. You may recognize this weight system immediately since this is nothing but the system inducing shortest-path routing with respect to hop-count (hop-count rule). Using shortest paths in the sense of the hop count is natural and is a common practice in many actual networks. Consider now demand $d = 1$ for this example; we can immediately find that there are two shortest paths! They are: $\mathcal{P}_{11} = \{2, 4\}$ and $\mathcal{P}_{12} = \{1, 5\}$. In such situations, a common question is which path should be used for routing the traffic. In other words, there must be some additional rule of splitting the demand volume into its different shortest paths.

This problem, for instance, appears in determining link weight in IP-OSPF networks (Section 3.1 and Chapter 7). One such rule used in OSPF routing is the equal-split rule, often referred to as ECMP: "equal-cost multi-path" rule. For a fixed destination, the goal of ECMP is to equally split all the demand outgoing from a node among all its outgoing links

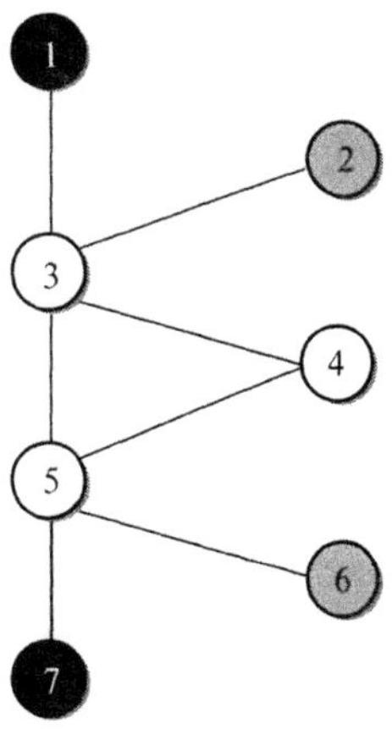

FIGURE 2.6 Infeasible Unique Shortest-Path Case

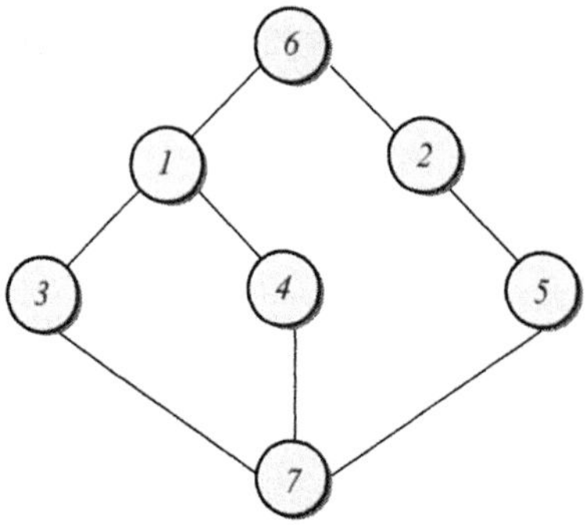

FIGURE 2.7 Equal-Split Rule

that belong to the shortest paths to that destination. This is illustrated through the example network given in Figure 2.7. Assuming link weights to be all equal to 1, there are three shortest paths from node 6 to node 7, i.e., for the directed demand pair ⟨6:7⟩. The shortest paths 6-1-3-7 and 6-1-4-7 carry one-quarter of the total demand volume from node 6 to node 7, while the shortest path 6-2-5-7 carries the remaining one-half of the volume. To complicate matters, in OSPF network routing is directional. This can imply that demand split depends on the direction: if the demand volume were considered from node 7 to node 6, then the shortest paths would remain the same as in the other direction, but the split would change to the uniform one assigning one-third of the volume to each of the three paths.

The process of determining the weight system under the ECMP rule encounters the same difficulties as the single-shortest-path allocation case (Exercise 2.6). Incidently, despite these difficulties, in the example shown in Figure 2.6, the weight system assigning weights equal to 2 on all links except for weight equal to 1 on links 3-4 and 4-5 induces a feasible solution under the ECMP rule.

Shortest-path based routing design will be covered in detail in Chapter 7.

2.6 FAIR NETWORKS

We will now consider another yet different type of design problem. So far, we have assumed that the demand volumes are given and the network is required to route these volumes. Consider a network where the demand is *elastic*. Elasticity means that each demand can consume any bandwidth assigned to its path, perhaps within certain predefined bounds. This assumption corresponds, for instance, to a network with demands generating elastic traffic which can accommodate the changing bandwidth currently assigned to it, such as traffic generated during Internet web sessions.

A general problem with such networks is how and how much of demand volume to assign to each demand so that the capacities of links are not exceeded; to simplify, we will first assume that a fixed path is given for each demand to carry its (elastic) demand volume. In other words, in this problem, we have capacity constraints along the line of those listed in Problem (2.4.15), but no particular value for h_d in the demand constraint is assumed, which means that the demand constraint is needed to be satisfied within some predefined bounds. An obvious initial solution could be to assign demand

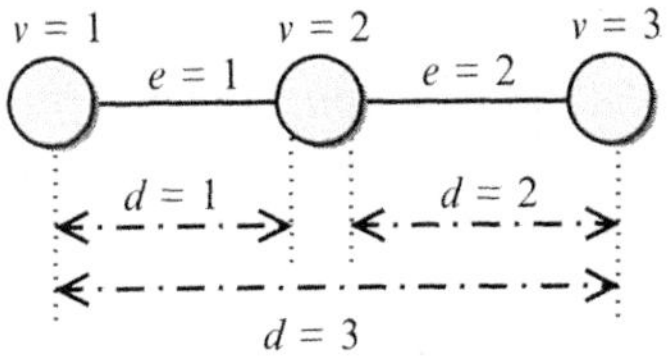

FIGURE 2.8 Two-Link Network

volume on its lower bound if this leads to satisfying the capacity constraints; if not, the problem is not feasible at all. Assuming feasibility, we still want the network to carry more than the lower bound of the demand volume such that some level of fairness among different demands is maintained, raising a question on how to assign volumes to the demands in a fair way. Furthermore, we are interested in understanding the impact on network throughput, which is defined to be the total demand volume carried by the network.

By far, the best known fairness criterion is *Max-Min Fairness* (MMF), also called *equity*. In the pure elastic case with no bounds, the first step of obtaining the MMF solution consists in assigning the same maximal volume to all demands, assuring that minimal assignment is maximized. Consider the network in Figure 2.8. It has $E = 2$ links, $V = 3$ nodes, and $D = 3$ demands. The link capacities are $c_1 = c_2 = 1\frac{1}{2}$. Clearly, all demands have exactly one candidate path. Under the MMF principle, the first step of the solution results in the following flow allocation: $x_{11} = x_{21} = x_{31} = \frac{3}{4}$. In fact, in this case, we are already at the final solution since all capacities are exhausted. Otherwise, if after the first step, some free capacity is still present, the process of increasing demand volumes for those demands (for which it is possible) would be continued. In this way, the second minimal assignment is maximized and so on. To illustrate this point, suppose we increase the capacity of $e = 2$ to 2 units. Then, after the first step, we will have $\frac{1}{2}$ unit of capacity left on link $e = 2$. Thus, demand $d = 2$ (and only this demand) can utilize this unused capacity, thus increasing its assigned demand volume to $1\frac{1}{4}$.

We notice that the MMF solution is fair from the user's viewpoint. On the other hand, if we were to optimize the total throughput in this network, we find that, by returning to the example in Figure 2.8, the maximal throughput is 3 which is achieved with a highly unfair solution $x_{11} = x_{21} = 1.5$ and $x_{31} = 0$. A simple but important observation is that what is good for the network may not necessarily be good for *all* individual users (demand). With the MMF solution, the resulting throughput is equal to $x_{11} + x_{21} + x_{31} = 2\frac{1}{4}$.

Clearly, the throughput degradation observed with the MMF rule is due to the fact that the same volume is assigned to every demand whatever the number of links on its path may be (the demands with long paths use up capacity of many links). Hence, a natural question arises whether there is some compromise solution between MMF and throughput maximization that has better throughput than MMF, yet is not as unfair as pure throughput maximization. The answer is yes, and one such fair allocation principle is called *Proportional Fairness* (PF).

The PF principle uses the *revenue objective* which consists in maximizing the sum of (natural) logarithms of the volumes assigned to demands, i.e., in our case, to maximize $\log x_{11} + \log x_{21} + \log x_{31}$. The rational behind using the logarithmic function is that it does not allow the assignment of zero volumes to demands (this would cause the revenue to be equal $-\infty$), and at the same time it makes it not profitable to assign too much volume to any demand (think why). Note that the objective function is non-linear, in contrast to the examples discussed so far in this chapter. You may check that the solution for the PF principle is $x_{11} = x_{21} = 1$ and $x_{31} = \frac{1}{2}$ (Exercise 2.7).

From the user's point of view, the PF solution is less fair than the MMF solution: the long flow (i.e., the flow using both links) $x_{31} = \frac{1}{2}$ is smaller than the two short flows (i.e., the flows using one link each) $x_{11} = x_{21} = 1$. However, because of favoring shorter flows, the PF allocation is more efficient in terms of throughput, in this case equal to $x_{11} + x_{21} + x_{31} = 2\frac{1}{2}$. This is a general observation: the PF solution does better than the MMF solution in terms of throughput, at the expense of fairness given to the users. Another way to examine this is that addressing fairness can reduce overall throughput. Hence, PF can be viewed as a compromise between throughput maximization and MMF.

From the above example it follows that the capacitated flow allocation problem in the PF case is to find a flow allocation vector $\boldsymbol{x}$ satisfying the capacity constraints (2.4.7) and maximizing the (logarithmic) *revenue function*:

$$\boldsymbol{R}(\boldsymbol{x}) = \textstyle\sum_d r_d \log X_d, \tag{2.6.1}$$

where $X_d = \sum_p x_{dp}$ is the total flow allocated to demand d and r_d is a positive weight (revenue) associated with demand d. This is a tractable mathematical formulation which can be solved, for instance, by introducing a linear approximation of the logarithmic function and solving the resulting linear programming problem.

Solving the MMF capacitated allocation problem is more complicated. In general, it is just not enough to find a flow allocation vector $\boldsymbol{x}$ which maximizes the minimal (over all demands) total flow X_d assigned to all demands; if such a vector $\boldsymbol{x}$ is found, then, in general, some link capacity will still be free and can be used for increasing flow allocations for at least a subset of demands.

To illustrate this point, consider the network depicted in Figure 2.9. Applying solution $\boldsymbol{x}^1$ leaves room for further increase in flow for demand $d = 1$, leading to the final (optimal)

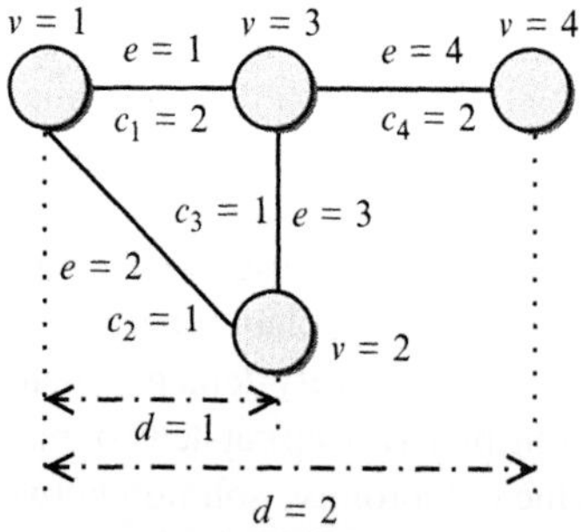

Solution $\boldsymbol{x}^1$: $x^1_{11} = 1$ on path {2}, $x^1_{21} = 1$ on path {1,4}
Solution $\boldsymbol{x}^2$: $x^2_{11} = 1$ on path {1, 3}, $x^2_{21} = 1$ on path {2,3,4}

FIGURE 2.9 Multiple Optimal Allocation Vectors

MMF allocation vector:

$$x_{11} = 1, \quad \mathcal{P}_{11} = \{2\}$$
$$x_{12} = 1, \quad \mathcal{P}_{12} = \{1,3\}$$
$$x_{21} = 1, \quad \mathcal{P}_{21} = \{1,4\}$$

Applying solution $\boldsymbol{x}^2$ does not leave room for any further improvement.

The final total allocation vector $\boldsymbol{X} = (X_1, X_2)$ is equal to (2, 1), and has the crucial property that when sorted, it is *lexicographically maximal* in the set of all feasible sorted total allocation vectors. Recall that a sorted vector $\boldsymbol{X} = (X_1, X_2, ..., X_D)$ is lexicographically greater than another sorted vector $\boldsymbol{Z} = (Z_1, Z_2, ..., Z_D)$ if there exists d, $0 \leq d < D$, such that $X_i = Z_i$ for $i = 1, 2, ..., d$ and $X_{d+1} > Z_{d+1}$. Notice that it is not a straightforward task to find the MMF solution vector, since, as in our example, we do not know in advance which of the possible solutions from the first step leads to the final solution (in general, there can be many steps to perform).

The uncapacitated counterparts of the above presented capacitated allocation problems are also of interest, especially in the PF case. Chapter 8 covers fair network design in depth.

2.7 TOPOLOGICAL DESIGN

Another important class of design problems is *topological design problems*. The basic feature of topological design problems is that in the cost function we take into account not only the capacity-dependent costs of links, ξ_e, but also the link installation ("opening") costs κ_e; thus, the augmented cost function to be minimized is of the form:

$$F = \sum_e \xi_e y_e + \sum_e \kappa_e u_e \qquad (2.7.1)$$

where the binary variable u_e indicates if link e is installed or not (u_e equals 1 or 0, respectively). The resulting uncapacitated design problem consists in minimizing the augmented cost function (2.7.1) subject to the the demand constraints (2.4.3), the capacity constraints (2.4.7), and the additional constraint

$$y_e \leq \Delta u_e, \quad e = 1, 2, ..., E, \qquad (2.7.2)$$

where Δ is an appropriate large constant. Observe that the binary variable $\boldsymbol{u}_e$, through constraint (2.7.2), forces the result $y_e = 0$ whenever $u_e = 0$, i.e., when link e is not installed.

If the installation costs for the network from Figure 2.4 are assumed to be $\boldsymbol{\kappa} = (\kappa_1, \kappa_2, ..., \kappa_5) = (50, 1, 1, 1, 50)$, then the optimal network topology becomes a tree composed of links $e = 2, e = 3$, and $e = 4$ ($u_2^* = u_3^* = u_4^* = 1$ and $u_1^* = u_5^* = 0$) with the installation cost $\sum_e \kappa_e u_e^* = 3$ and the capacity-dependent cost $\sum_e \xi_e y_e = 160$.

The difficulty of the topological design problem is considerable and comparable to that of the uncapacitated design problem with modular links described in Section 2.4. Topological design problems, including not only link but also node location, are discussed in Chapter 6.

2.8 RESTORATION DESIGN

So far in our design problems, we have considered the network to be in normal operational state, i.e., no failure consideration, either for a link or a node, is taken into account. We now add a new dimension to the NDPs by taking failures into account which will be referred to as *restoration design problems*. For example, in restoration design problems the link failures are taken explicitly into account in the formulation of the optimization model. For instance, we may assume a failure scenario in which each link can become totally unavailable, still different links do not fail simultaneously. Hence, each of the resulting *failure states* or *failure situations* consists of the failure of one link at a time, i.e., the rest being fully operative. For the network of Figure 2.3 this results in 5 failure states, $s = 1, 2, ..., 5$ corresponding to each link: in state s link $e = s$ is failed and the remaining links are intact. For convenience, the normal operational state where all components are fully available, is labeled with $s = 0$.

Suppose that we wish to solve the restoration design problem (RDP) for the example network with the link costs and demand volumes given in Figure 2.4. This means that we want to find the cheapest link capacity configuration together with routing and flow allocation in such a way that in all states ($s = 0, 1, ..., 5$) the demand volumes are fully realized (100% demand protection). Recall the design problem presented in (2.4.10) which was modified by augmenting the candidate path list of demand $d = 1$ (refer to (2.4.14)) and consider the RDP for this modified problem. Due to state s, we now need to introduce an identifier for s. Thus, the demand constraint in (2.4.14) for demand $d = 1$, i.e.,

$$x_{11} + x_{12} = 15$$

is extended to reflect the state s by introducing this in the subscript as follows:

$$x_{11s} + x_{12s} = 15, \quad s = 0, 1, ..., 5.$$

Simply put, we now have six equations instead of one for demand $d = 1$ due to the normal state plus all the failure states.

We can now generalize the above demand constraints to capture all the states and demands. That is, we can write the demand constraints for all demands and states as:

$$\textstyle\sum_p x_{dps} = h_d, \quad p = 1, 2, ..., P_d \quad s = 0, 1, ..., S. \tag{2.8.1a}$$

Now, let us consider capacity constraints. If we now incorporate failure state $s = 1 (= e)$, then the capacity feasibility constraints for $e = 1$ are of the following form:

$$\begin{array}{lll} s = 0: & x_{120} + x_{310} & \le y_1 \\ s = 1: & x_{121} + x_{311} & \le 0 \\ s = 2: & x_{122} + x_{312} & \le y_1 \\ \dots & & \end{array}$$

Again, we have six inequalities for each link. Note that since $s = 1$ corresponds to the failure of link $e = 1$, no capacity should be assigned to link $e = 1$ in this state. This is reflected by the right-hand side of the relevant constraint set to zero (see above).

If we use the notation α_{es} to denote 1 if link e is up and 0 if it is down in state s, then we can compactly write the new set of inequalities for capacity constraints in general as:

$$\textstyle\sum_d \sum_p \delta_{edp} x_{dps} \leq \alpha_{es} y_e, \quad s = 0, 1, ..., S \quad e = 1, 2, ..., E. \tag{2.8.1b}$$

This formulation can be referred to as the scenario where we are allowed to freely rearrange the flows in case of a failure. This may not necessarily be the case in all practical networks (refer to Exercise 2.8). The optimal flows for the robust design case (under full re-arrangement) corresponding to Problem (2.4.14) are as follows:

$s = 0$:	$x^*_{110} = 0$	$x^*_{120} = 15$	$x^*_{210} = 20$	$x^*_{220} = 0$	$x^*_{310} = 0$	$x^*_{320} = 10$
$s = 1$:	$x^*_{111} = 15$	$x^*_{121} = 0$	$x^*_{211} = 20$	$x^*_{221} = 0$	$x^*_{311} = 0$	$x^*_{321} = 10$
$s = 2$:	$x^*_{112} = 0$	$x^*_{122} = 15$	$x^*_{212} = 20$	$x^*_{222} = 0$	$x^*_{312} = 10$	$x^*_{322} = 0$
$s = 3$:	$x^*_{113} = 0$	$x^*_{123} = 15$	$x^*_{213} = 20$	$x^*_{223} = 0$	$x^*_{313} = 10$	$x^*_{323} = 0$
$s = 4$:	$x^*_{114} = 0$	$x^*_{124} = 15$	$x^*_{214} = 20$	$x^*_{224} = 0$	$x^*_{314} = 0$	$x^*_{324} = 10$
$s = 5$:	$x^*_{115} = 15$	$x^*_{125} = 0$	$x^*_{214} = 0$	$x^*_{225} = 20$	$x^*_{315} = 0$	$x^*_{325} = 10.$

The optimal capacity y^*_e of link e implied by the above specified flows is computed as the maximum load of the link over all states $s = 0, 1, ..., 5$. Hence:

$$y^*_1 = 25 \quad y^*_2 = 25 \quad y^*_3 = 30 \quad y^*_4 = 35 \quad y^*_5 = 35.$$

This results in the optimal cost of $\boldsymbol{F}^* = 245$, showing that the robust network can be considerably more expensive than the cost of network design for just the normal state; recall from Section 2.4 that the cost of the cheapest network without failure consideration was $F^* = 85$.

In the above example, it so happens that the optimal flow allocations in all situations are non-bifurcated. The following simple example shows that it is not always the case. Consider the network in Figure 2.10 with two nodes (and hence only one demand $d = 1$), three links ($E = 3$), and three failure situations ($S = 3$). The demand volume in all situations is the same, $h_{1s} = 3$, where $s = 0, 1, 2, 3$. The unit cost of all three links is the same and equal to 1. In the failure situations only one link is failed. As shown in the figure, optimal link capacities are all equal to $1\frac{1}{2}$ (figures in parentheses). The optimal flows for all situations are given by the figures without parentheses. The optimal cost is $\boldsymbol{F}^* = 4\frac{1}{2}$.

If we look for non-bifurcated solutions in all situations, then the resulting solution will be more expensive as illustrated in Figure 2.11. The optimal cost $\boldsymbol{F}^* = 6$ is greater than for the previous non-bifurcated solution.

Design problems related to network robustness to failures does not, in general, follow the shortest-path rule (2.4.13) that works for the design of networks for the normal operating state; furthermore, the number of equations, inequalities, and variables grows with the introduction of states to capture different failure situations which can be seen, for example, from (2.8.1). Thus, restoration design problems are often difficult and time consuming to solve; nevertheless, they are an important class of design problems and can help to find network configurations that are resilient and survivable.

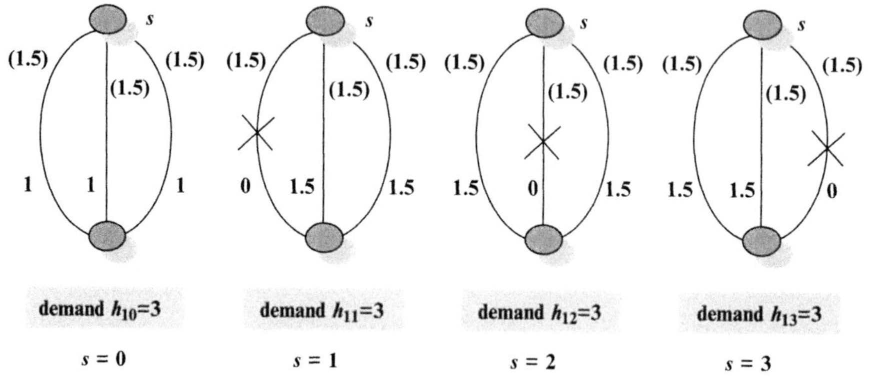

FIGURE 2.10 A Bifurcated Solution

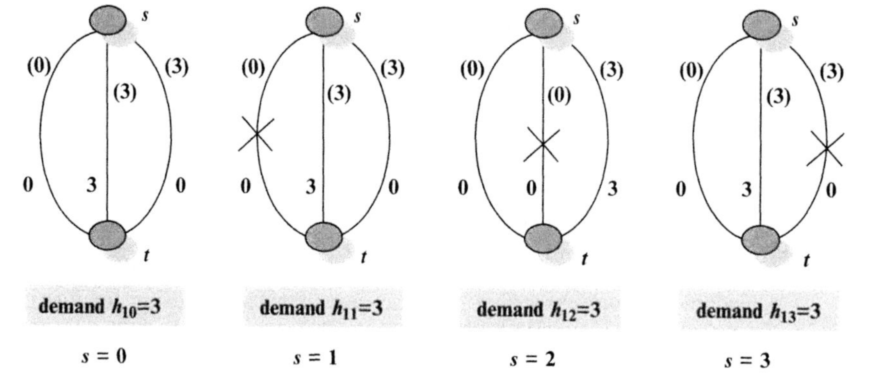

FIGURE 2.11 A Non-Bifurcated Solution

The example restoration design problem considered in this section involves the *path protection mechanism* for flow re-arrangement in failure situations. Note that other mechanisms are possible, for instance *link protection*. It is worth mentioning that these mechanisms make use of a common pool of shared protection capacity. More about restoration design can be found in Chapter 9 and related algorithms are discussed in Chapter 10.

2.9 *MULTI-LAYER NETWORKS MODELING

With respect to design problems presented so far in this chapter, the robustness issue that considers restoration adds a new dimension to NDPs, both in the sense of importance and difficulty. We are now about to introduce yet another important design dimension where the layered structure of the network resources is taken into account in the network modeling. The modeling is going to look complicated when you try to understand the entire relationship for the first time. The best way to think about this is to imagine you have different multi-commodity flow problems for each layer which are combined together in such a way that the upper layer imposes demand on the neighboring lower layer. If you are not ready for it yet, you may skip this section now and come back to it later (especially when you are about to read Chapter 12 in this book). However, we do not want you to ignore its significance since networks are inherently multi-layered (which is still commonly overlooked in the current literature), and it is important to understand how the relationship works between different layers. Recall that we have described the notion of multi-layer earlier in Section 1.6.

In a nutshell, the resources (links and nodes) of communication and computer networks are configured in a multi-layered fashion, forming a hierarchical structure with each layer being a proper network on its own. The links of an upper layer are formed using paths of the lower layer, and this pattern repeats as one goes down the resources hierarchy. For instance, in a public-switched telephone network there is a layer of trunk groups and the trunk groups are realized by means of transmission paths configured in the transmission facility (or simply, facility) layer forming a layer below [Rey83, p. 83]. The digital links in the facility layer are formed by means of the paths in the optical layer, and so on, until eventually the conduit layer is reached. Similarly, IP networks can be provided over ATM, multi-protocol label switching (MPLS), SONET, or WDM. In fact, we can have more than two layers, for example, in the case of IP over ATM over SONET network.

While some network providers may own resources only at one or two neighboring layers, some large network providers own all of the layers. For the latter, it is essential to address the design of multi-layer networks.

Consider the network example depicted in Figure 2.12. The network consists of two layers of resources (Layer 1: equipment layer, Layer 2: virtual capacity layer) and an additional, auxiliary layer (Layer 3: demand layer) used merely to specify the demands. Altogether the network has two resource layers plus an auxiliary layer for the demand—this can be thought of as three layers; taking a similar view, the networks considered in the previous sections can be considered as two-layer networks composed of one resource layer (the lower, resource layer) and one demand layer (the upper, demand layer). In the case considered here, links are formed in the two lower resource layers, which is a natural extension of the one-layer resource network structure considered so far. For each demand d its demand volume h_d is realized by means of flows assigned to paths of Layer 2. The demands can be treated as the links of Layer 3 so we can say that capacity h_d of each link d of Layer 3 is realized by means of flows $\boldsymbol{x}$ in Layer 2. If we sum up the flows through each link e of Layer 2 then the resulting loads determine link capacity vector $\boldsymbol{y}$ of the layer. The next step is analogous. The capacity of each link e in Layer 2 is realized by means of flow in Layer 1, and the resulting Layer 1 flows $\boldsymbol{z}$ determine the load of each link g of Layer 1, and hence it capacity w_g. The cost of the resulting network configuration is eventually determined as the cost of the capacity of the links of Layer 1. In regard to nodes in different layers, we assume that the relationship is as follows: if a node appears in an upper layer, then it automatically appears downwards in the layer hierarchy. The advantage of our assumption is that it simplifies explanation of the model.

Let us assume that node and link numbering are as specified in Figures 2.13a and 2.13b. We will keep the same node number as we traverse down the layers. The following demand volumes (capacities of the Layer 3 links) and the Layer 1 link unit costs are assumed.

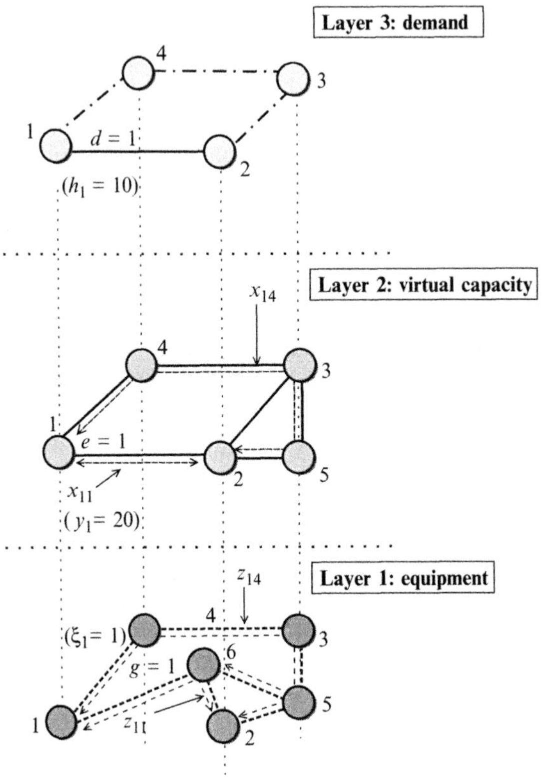

FIGURE 2.12 Three-Layer Network

Layer 3 (demand)

links:	$d = 1$	$d = 2$	$d = 3$	$d = 4$	$d = 5$	$d = 6$
end nodes:	1-2	1-3	1-4	2-3	2-4	3-4
capacities:	20	10	10	10	10	10

Layer 2

links:	$e = 1$	$e = 2$	$e = 3$	$e = 4$	$e = 5$	$e = 6$	$e = 7$
end nodes:	1-2	1-4	2-3	2-4	2-5	3-4	3-5

Layer 1

links:	$g = 1$	$g = 2$	$g = 3$	$g = 4$	$g = 5$	$g = 6$	$g = 7$	$g = 8$
end nodes:	1-4	1-6	2-5	2-6	3-4	3-5	4-6	5-6
unit cost ξ_g:	1	1	1	1	1	1	1	1.

Let us also assume the following candidate path lists where $\mathbb{P}_d = (\mathcal{P}_{d1}, \mathcal{P}_{d2}, ..., \mathcal{P}_{dP_d})$ is used for denoting the Layer 2 candidate path list for demand d while $\mathbb{Q}_e = (\mathcal{Q}_{e1}, \mathcal{Q}_{e2}, ..., \mathcal{Q}_{eQ_e})$ is used for denoting the Layer 1 candidate path list for link e:

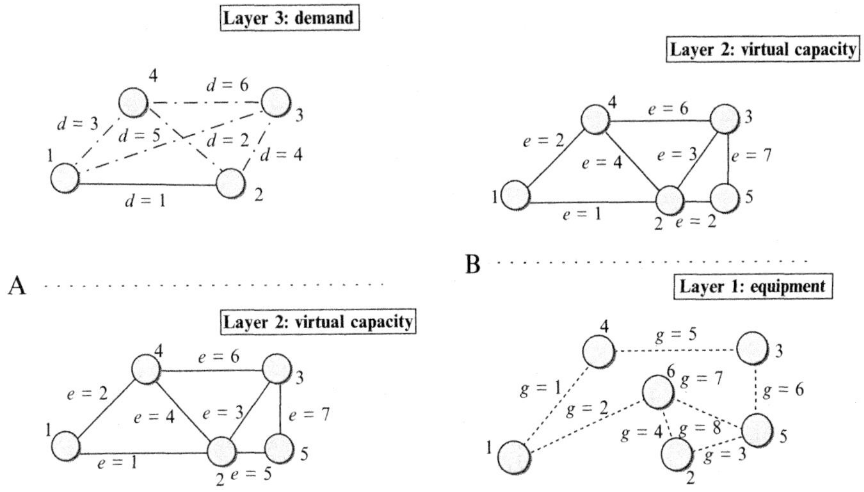

FIGURE 2.13 (A) Node and Link Numbering in Two Upper Layers; (B) Node and Link Numbering in Two Lower Layers

Layer 3/Layer 2

$d = 1$	$\mathcal{P}_{11} = \{1\}$	$\mathcal{P}_{12} = \{2,4\}$	$\mathcal{P}_{13} = \{2,3,6\}$	$\mathcal{P}_{14} = \{2,5,6,7\}$
$d = 2$	$\mathcal{P}_{21} = \{1,3\}$	$\mathcal{P}_{22} = \{2,6\}$	$\mathcal{P}_{23} = \{1,5,7\}$	
$d = 3$	$\mathcal{P}_{31} = \{2\}$	$\mathcal{P}_{32} = \{1,4\}$	$\mathcal{P}_{33} = \{1,3,6\}$	$\mathcal{P}_{24} = \{1,5,6,7\}$
$d = 4$	$\mathcal{P}_{41} = \{3\}$	$\mathcal{P}_{42} = \{4,6\}$	$\mathcal{P}_{43} = \{5,7\}$	$\mathcal{P}_{44} = \{1,2,6\}$
$d = 5$	$\mathcal{P}_{51} = \{4\}$	$\mathcal{P}_{52} = \{1,2\}$	$\mathcal{P}_{53} = \{3,6\}$	$\mathcal{P}_{54} = \{5,6,7\}$
$d = 6$	$\mathcal{P}_{61} = \{6\}$	$\mathcal{P}_{62} = \{3,4\}$	$\mathcal{P}_{13} = \{1,2,3\}$	$\mathcal{P}_{14} = \{1,2,5,7\}$

Layer 2/Layer 1

$e = 1$	$\mathcal{Q}_{11} = \{2,4\}$	$\mathcal{Q}_{12} = \{1,4,7\}$	$\mathcal{Q}_{13} = \{1,3,5,6\}$	
$e = 2$	$\mathcal{Q}_{21} = \{1\}$	$\mathcal{Q}_{22} = \{2,7\}$	$\mathcal{Q}_{23} = \{2,5,6,8\}$	$\mathcal{Q}_{24} = \{2,3,4,5,6\}$
$e = 3$	$\mathcal{Q}_{31} = \{3,6\}$	$\mathcal{Q}_{32} = \{4,5,7\}$	$\mathcal{Q}_{33} = \{4,6,8\}$	$\mathcal{Q}_{34} = \{1,2,4,5\}$
$e = 4$	$\mathcal{Q}_{41} = \{4,7\}$	$\mathcal{Q}_{42} = \{1,2,4\}$	$\mathcal{Q}_{43} = \{3,5,6\}$	
$e = 5$	$\mathcal{Q}_{51} = \{3\}$	$\mathcal{Q}_{52} = \{4,8\}$	$\mathcal{Q}_{43} = \{4,5,6,7\}$	$\mathcal{Q}_{14} = \{1,2,4,5,6\}$
$e = 6$	$\mathcal{Q}_{61} = \{5\}$	$\mathcal{Q}_{62} = \{6,7,8\}$	$\mathcal{Q}_{63} = \{1,2,6,8\}$	$\mathcal{Q}_{14} = \{1,2,3,4,6\}$
$e = 7$	$\mathcal{Q}_{71} = \{6\}$	$\mathcal{Q}_{72} = \{5,7,8\}$	$\mathcal{Q}_{73} = \{3,4,5,7\}$	$\mathcal{Q}_{74} = \{1,2,3,4,5\}$.

Note that the routing lists do not necessarily contain all possible paths. For instance, the middle layer path $\mathcal{P}_{24} = \{2,3,4\}$ is not on the path list of demand $d = 2$, and the lower layer path $\mathcal{Q}_{44} = \{3,7,8\}$ is not on the routing list of link $e = 4$.

Now consider the flow allocation vector $\boldsymbol{x}$ defined by the following individual flows (flows equal to zero are not listed):

$$x_{11} = 10 \quad x_{14} = 10 \qquad (h_1 = x_{11} + x_{14}, \text{ these two flows are depicted in Figure 2.12})$$
$$x_{21} = 10 \quad x_{31} = 10 \quad x_{41} = 10 \quad x_{51} = 10 \quad x_{61} = 10.$$

The above defined flows realize the assumed demand volumes, i.e., fulfill the demand constraints in the middle layer (Layer2):

$$\textstyle\sum_p x_{dp} = h_d, \quad d = 1, 2, ..., D \tag{2.9.1}$$

where the sum is taken over all paths p ($p = 1, 2, ..., P_d$) on the routing list $\mathbb{P}_d$ of demand d. We are already familiar with this and it has been addressed in Section 2.4. The middle layer link capacities, y_e, are equal (in this case) to the link loads, $\underline{y}_e = \underline{y}_e(\boldsymbol{x})$, resulting from the middle layer flow allocation vector $\boldsymbol{x}$ and these are shown below:

$$y_1 = 20 \quad y_2 = 20 \quad y_3 = 20 \quad y_4 = 10 \quad y_5 = 10 \quad y_6 = 20 \quad y_7 = 10.$$

Using the link-path incidence coefficients defined by (2.4.5), the general formula defining the middle layer link loads can be written as:

$$\underline{y}_e = \textstyle\sum_d \sum_p \delta_{edp} x_{dp}, \quad e = 1, 2, ..., E. \tag{2.9.2}$$

The other allocation vector, $\boldsymbol{z}$, is the lower layer flow allocation vector which specifies how the capacity of each middle layer link e is realized by means of flows z_{eq} allocated to its candidate paths from the routing list in Layer 1. Suppose the vector $\boldsymbol{z}$ is as follows (zero flows are not listed):

$$z_{11} = 15 \quad z_{13} = 5 \ (y_1 = z_{11} + z_{13}, \text{ these two flows are depicted in Figure 2.12})$$
$$z_{21} = 20 \quad z_{31} = 20 \quad z_{41} = 10 \quad z_{51} = 10 \quad z_{61} = 20 \quad z_{71} = 10$$

As before, the above defined flows realize the assumed middle layer link capacities, i.e., fulfill the demand constraints in the lower layer:

$$\textstyle\sum_q z_{eq} = y_e, \quad e = 1, 2, ..., E, \tag{2.9.3}$$

where the sum is taken over all paths q ($q = 1, 2, ..., Q_e$) on the routing list $\mathbb{Q}_e$ of link e. The lower link loads resulting from the lower layer flow allocation vector $\boldsymbol{z}$ are equal to the lower layer link capacities w and are as follows:

$$w_1 = 20 \quad w_2 = 15 \quad w_3 = 35 \quad w_4 = 10 \quad w_5 = 25 \quad w_6 = 35 \quad w_7 = 10 \quad w_8 = 0.$$

Introducing the link-path incidence coefficients for Layer 1

$$\gamma_{geq} = \begin{cases} 1 & \text{if Layer 1 link } g \text{ belongs to path } q \text{ realizing Layer 2 link } e \\ 0 & \text{otherwise} \end{cases} \tag{2.9.4}$$

the general formula specifying the lower layer capacity constraint can be stated as:

$$\sum_e \sum_q \gamma_{geq} z_{eq} \leq w_g, \quad g = 1, 2, ..., G, \tag{2.9.5}$$

where G is the total number of links in Layer 1 and the summation for each link g is taken over all flows in the lower layer.

Altogether, we have two demand constraints, (2.9.1) and (2.9.3), and two capacity constraints, (2.9.2) and (2.9.5). The demand vector $\boldsymbol{h} = (h_1, h_2, ..., h_D)$ is defined through the capacities of the uppermost layer links (auxiliary Layer 3), and the cost vector $\boldsymbol{\xi} = (\xi_1, \xi_2, ..., \xi_G)$ specifies the unit costs of the lowermost layer (Layer 1) links. The resulting *two-resource layer dimensioning problem* (TRL-DP), being an extension of DP (2.4.11) from Section 2.4, is as follows:

For given vectors **h** *and* $\boldsymbol{\xi}$, *and the network structure specified by the link-path incidence coefficients* δ_{edp} *and* γ_{gek}, *find flow vectors* $\boldsymbol{x}$ *and* $\boldsymbol{z}$, *and link capacity vectors* $\boldsymbol{y}$ *and* $\boldsymbol{w}$ *in order to:*

minimize $\boldsymbol{F} = \sum_g \xi_g w_g$
subject to *constraints* (2.9.1), (2.9.2), (2.9.3) *and* (2.9.5) (2.9.6)

The example flow vectors $\boldsymbol{x}$ and $\boldsymbol{z}$, and the corresponding link capacity vectors $\boldsymbol{y}$ and $\boldsymbol{w}$ constructed earlier in this section constitute a feasible solution for TRL-DP with $\boldsymbol{F} = 150$ which is not optimal. To see this we observe that the optimal solutions obey the generalized shortest-path allocation rule, that extends the shortest-path allocation rule presented in Section 2.4 for DP (2.4.11):

Shortest-Path Allocation Rule for TRL-DP:

1. For each link e of Layer 2 select one of its shortest paths with respect to the unit costs ξ of the Layer 1 links. Let $q(e)$ be the index of such a shortest path for link e and let λ_e denote its length:

$$\lambda_e = \min \left\{ \sum_g \xi_g \gamma_{geq} : q = 1, 2, ..., Q_e \right\}, \quad e = 1, 2, ..., E. \tag{2.9.7}$$

2. For each demand d (link of Layer 3) select one of its shortest paths with respect to the unit costs $\lambda = (\lambda_1, \lambda_2, ..., \lambda_E)$ of the Layer 2 links defined by (2.9.7). Let $p(d)$ be the index of such a shortest-path for demand d and let μ_d denote its length:

$$\mu_d = \min \{ \sum_e \lambda_e \delta_{edp} : p = 1, 2, ..., P_d \}, \quad d = 1, 2, ..., D. \tag{2.9.8}$$

3. For each demand d allocate its whole demand volume h_d to its shortest path $p(d)$. Compute the resulting capacities (loads) y_e of the Layer 2 links.

4. For each link e allocate its whole capacity y_e to its shortest path $q(e)$. Compute the resulting capacities (loads) w_g of the Layer 1 links.

Any optimal solution $\boldsymbol{x}^*, \boldsymbol{z}^*, \boldsymbol{y}^*, \boldsymbol{w}^*$ resulting from the application of the generalized shortest-path rule is optimal. In any case when there is more than one shortest-path, the demand volume or link capacity can be split arbitrarily among the shortest paths. Notice that the optimal cost is equal to:

$$\boldsymbol{F}^* = \sum_d \mu_d h_d. \tag{2.9.9}$$

For the considered network example one of the optimal solutions resulting from the generalized shortest-path rule is shown below:

$\lambda_1 = 2$	$\lambda_2 = 1$	$\lambda_3 = 2$	$\lambda_4 = 2$	$\lambda_5 = 1$	$\lambda_6 = 1$	$\lambda_7 = 1$	
$q(1) = 1$	$q(2) = 1$	$q(3) = 1$	$q(4) = 1$	$q(5) = 1$	$q(6) = 1$	$q(7) = 1$	
$\mu_1 = 2$	$\mu_2 = 2$	$\mu_3 = 1$	$\mu_4 = 2$	$\mu_5 = 1$	$\mu_6 = 1$		
$p(1) = 1$	$p(2) = 2$	$p(3) = 1$	$p(4) = 2$	$p(5) = 1$	$p(6) = 1$		
$h_1 = 20$	$h_2 = 10$	$h_3 = 10$	$h_4 = 10$	$h_5 = 10$	$h_6 = 10$		
$x_{11} = 20$	$x_{22} = 10$	$x_{31} = 10$	$x_{42} = 10$	$x_{51} = 10$	$x_{61} = 10$		
$y_1 = 20$	$y_2 = 20$	$y_3 = 0$	$y_4 = 10$	$y_5 = 10$	$y_6 = 10$	$y_7 = 10$	
$z_{11} = 20$	$z_{21} = 20$	$z_{31} = 10$	$z_{41} = 10$	$z_{51} = 10$	$z_{61} = 10$	$z_{71} = 10$	
$w_1 = 20$	$w_2 = 20$	$w_3 = 20$	$w_4 = 10$	$w_5 = 10$	$w_6 = 20$	$w_7 = 10$	$w_8 = 20$

$\boldsymbol{F}^* = 110.$

The generalization of the described modeling approach and the resulting TRL-DP to more than two resource layers is straightforward. Also, the shortest-path allocation rule easily generalizes to more layers. This will be discussed later in Chapter 12.

The multi-layer design can also be generalized to take the restoration issue into account. It appears that an acceptable failure model, in most cases, is obtained when the failure situations are restricted only to the failures of the Layer 1 (lower layer) links. Several extensions of TRL-DP are possible, depending on the number of layers in which the flow re-arrangement is admissible. One such generalization is obtained when the flow re-arrangement is allowed in both the "true" resource layers (i.e., in Layer 1 and Layer 2). Two more problems arise when the re-arrangement is permitted only in Layer 1 or only in Layer 2, respectively.

Multi-layer design problems and algorithms will be treated in Chapter 12 and partly in Chapter 13.

2.10 SUMMARY

In this chapter, we have discussed a set of representative NDPs using small network examples. We have started with a simple capacitated allocation problem involving minimization of flow routing. This example served as a means for introducing two basic formulation types: link-path formulation (Section 2.1) and node-link formulation (Section 2.2). In both cases we have used a notation system which we call node-based-identifier representation.

Then, in Section 2.3, we have demonstrated that this seemingly (at first sight) nice notation has certain fundamental drawbacks and that, in fact, another notation, called link-demand-path-identifier notation, is much more convenient for general formulations of NDPs, should they be in the link-path or in the node-link formulation.

Having clarified the notational issues, we have proceeded to discuss an uncapacitated network dimensioning problem (Section 2.4), and then to additional and more complicated problems involving the shortest-path routing (Section 2.5), fair networks (Section 2.6), and topological design (Section 2.7), through restoration design (for network protection against failures, Section 2.8) and to end up with the discussion of multi-layer NDPs.

It should be noted that the design problems we have introduced here are classified as multi-commodity network flow problems. While introducing consecutive design problems we have occasionally mentioned that certain problem formulations are simple and others are difficult or complex. As we are not yet prepared for a more precise discussion of these issues, we will now only make some brief comments. Incidently, multi-commodity network flow problems are frequently linear programming (LP) problems as long as, roughly speaking, the objective function is linear and the bifurcated flows are allowed as independent decision variables. Examples of valid LP design problems can be found in Sections 2.4, 2.8, and 2.9. As you may know, in most cases, LP problems can be effectively solved using the well known simplex algorithm. For some problems (as for DP, refer to Section 2.4), their very special structure permits the creation of even more effective algorithms, such as the shortest-path allocation rule; such problems can be called simple.

Many of the considered problems are not LP problems. These are for example problems involving modular links (Section 2.4), shortest-path routing (Section 2.5), fairness (Section 2.6), and topological design (Section 2.7). These problems are in general difficult; algorithmic approaches to solve such problems will be discussed later in Chapter 5.

Apparently, Kalaba and Juncosa [KJ56] in 1956 were the first to address communication NDPs using a multi-commodity flow approach; incidently, their formulation can be considered as the first node-link-based multi-commodity flow representation where they used the term "message" to generically describe communication demand. The reader may find a comment from this paper rather interesting; to quote "In a system such as the Western Union System, which has some 15 regional switching centers all connected to each other, an optimal problem of this type would have about 450 conditions (constraints) and involve around 3,000 variables". By referencing the Kalaba-Juncosa paper, Ford and Fulkerson [FF58] were perhaps the first ones to introduce link-path representation to formulate the maximal flow multi-commodity problem; incidently, the origin of the "delta" notation (i.e., δ_{edp}) can be attributed to this work.

For solving LP problems, a commonly known method called simplex, originally developed by G.B. Dantzig [Dan63], can be effectively used in most cases, possibly enforced by some kind of decomposition required by large network instances. In effect, the problems enjoying LP formulations can be roughly classified as effectively solvable, as in practice the simplex methods works in the time proportional to the number of optimization variables.

Deviations from linearity in problem formulations can pose problems. This issue will be discussed in more detail in the summary of Chapter 4 (Section 4.7). Here we only mention that whenever binary/integral variables are necessary in the problem formulations, resulting in the so-called mixed-integer programming (MIP) formulations (which are basically LP formulations with additional requirements for some variables to be binary/integral) then we can expect with great likelihood that the problems are $\mathcal{NP}$-complete (refer to Appendix B) and intrinsically cannot be solved in an exact way in a reasonable time for large networks. For such problems approximate or heuristic methods are used.

No further reading is suggested for this particular chapter, as all of its discussion will be extended in the subsequent chapters of this book.

EXERCISES FOR CHAPTER 2

2.1. Consider the formulation (2.1.2). Now suppose there is no demand between node pair 1 and 3, i.e., $\hat{h}_{13} = 0$. Rewrite the complete formulation for this modified problem in link-demand-path-identifier-based notation.

2.2. Find other feasible solutions (other than the one already discussed) that satisfy the set of equations and inequalities (2.1.1a).

2.3. Identify another goal that can be of interest in a network and formulate the corresponding objective function for the three-node example given by constraints (2.1.2). Determine the optimal solution.

2.4. Think of a situation where the node-identifier-based formulation could be advantageous over the link-demand-path-identifier-based formulation. (Hint: consider a situation when a number of hops for a path is fixed at a certain value for all paths and the network nodes are fully connected by links.)

2.5. Apply the general formulation (2.4.11) to specify an instance of problem DP for the three-node network (analogous to Problem (2.3.1)).

2.6. Consider the example depicted in Figure 2.6 with link capacities altered as follows: all link capacities are equal to 1 except for link 3-5 which has capacity $1\frac{1}{2}$ and links 3-4 and 4-5 which have the same capacity $\frac{1}{2}$. Does a weight system exist that induces a feasible solution under the ECMP rule?

2.7. Derive the PF solution for the network in Figure 2.8.

2.8. Variation of (2.8.1): consider the restoration design case where the flow that was originally assigned to the normal state may not be re-arranged in the case of a failure. How would the set of equations and inequalities change corresponding to (2.8.1)?

CHAPTER 3

Technology-Related Modeling Examples

In Chapter 2, we have introduced several types of network design problems (NDPs) and illustrated them with simple examples; in the process, we have shown how to formulate/represent NDPs as multi-commodity flow problems. Reading this book will help make it clear that multi-commodity flow models are of major importance in communication and computer network design. While multi-commodity flow models are now commonly used in many other areas outside telecommunications, it is indeed interesting to note that the first formulation of multi-commodity flow problem was for communication networks [KJ56].

A general belief, totally shared by the authors of this book, is that multi-commodity flow framework provides proper means for unified, generic and strict modeling of flows between different source and destination nodes in a communication/computer network. At the same time, an important issue remains: where and how can we apply the framework to model design problems for a specific network? This chapter provides examples for answering these types of questions. This also leads to a more general question of how to mathematically model a particular NDP if the multi-commodity flow approach is not relevant. Fortunately, according to our experience, the latter cases are very rare, and can be treated individually.

To examine this from another angle, over the years we have continually seen different networking/telecommunication technologies enter the playing field. Certainly, there are differences between technologies; important questions are: what types of design problems are relevant for a specific technology, and why is a given formulation relevant for a considered problem? Also, since we usually need to make certain assumptions and approximations, another question then is: why would such assumptions/approximations be valid and acceptable? Furthermore, along with these questions, we also need to understand the relevance of specific technology-dependent design constraints, objectives, and the like. It should be noted that in many cases it is not easy to figure out what formulations are applicable and how to use them. A potential mistake one can make is to apply a given known formulation to a specific NDP (without fully understanding what the problem is), while such an application is not really valid. Rather, it is important to approach this issue from the reverse angle: understand the actual problem, and then determine what is relevant/possible to model, and whether certain assumptions and approximations leading to multi-commodity formulations make sense. In the end, developing models is more of an art (than science); one hopefully gets better at it over the years through experience.

However, the power of using the multi-commodity flow modeling in network design is hard to overestimate. Once we are able to establish an acceptable multi-commodity formulation then we can apply the entire optimization machinery that has been successfully developed over the years for dealing with such problems.

In this chapter, we will pick a specific set of important and representative technology cases, and describe related design problems and the corresponding multi-commodity flow formulations applicable to these cases. These are only a few samples, and it is impossible to do justice to a wide variety of modeling techniques and approaches related to the multi-commodity flow based framework that researchers have developed over the years. Furthermore, our focus will stay on formulation, i.e., no solution methods will be discussed in this chapter. These will be addressed in subsequent chapters.

Our first example is for traffic engineering in Internet intra-domain routing (Section 3.1). Next we present a tunneling optimization problem for multi-protocol label-switched (MPLS) networks in Section 3.2. In Section 3.3, we present capacity design for virtual path-based asynchronous transfer mode (ATM) networks. This is then followed by a network dimensioning problem for digital circuit-switched telephone networks (Section 3.4) both for single-busy hour and multi-busy hour traffic demand. The rest of the sections include capacity and protection design for synchronous optical networks (SONET) or synchronous digital hierarchy (SDH) based transport networks (Section 3.5), bandwidth design for SONET/SDH rings (Section 3.6), and restoration design with optical cross-connects for wavelength-division multiplexing (WDM) networks (Section 3.7). Finally, in Section 3.8, a design problem for a two-layer IP over SONET network is presented.

The presented examples should provide ample information about the applicability of multi-commodity flow modeling techniques for communication and computer NDPs. In addition, this well help to see a common thread among models related to different technologies in order to realize the need for general solution methods presented in later chapters.

3.1 IP NETWORKS: INTRA-DOMAIN TRAFFIC ENGINEERING

The first example that we consider here is from Internet routing. This issue, referred to as the shortest-path routing problem and initially studied in Section 2.5 of Chapter 2, will be extensively discussed later in Chapter 7. Here, we will give a brief overview of the basic problem and the general modeling approach. Routing in the Internet [Hui00] is divided into two parts: 1) intra-domain, and 2) inter-domain. Typically, an intra-domain network is run by an Internet service provider (ISP) who has in its control the location of routers and links (and their capacity). The provider's job is to establish and operate the network in such a way that packets (IP datagrams) can move efficiently through his/her network, whether the packets are generated by his/her own users, or they are transiting through his/her domain (Figure 3.1).

Before we proceed to examining the specific problem formulations, we need to recall a few things about the IP technology basics in the intra-domain environment. An intra-domain consists of a set of routers connected by IP links. If this domain is for an ISP who serves other providers, then some routers function as edge routers while others function as transit routers (refer to Figure 3.1). For routing in intra-domain, there are two well-established protocols,

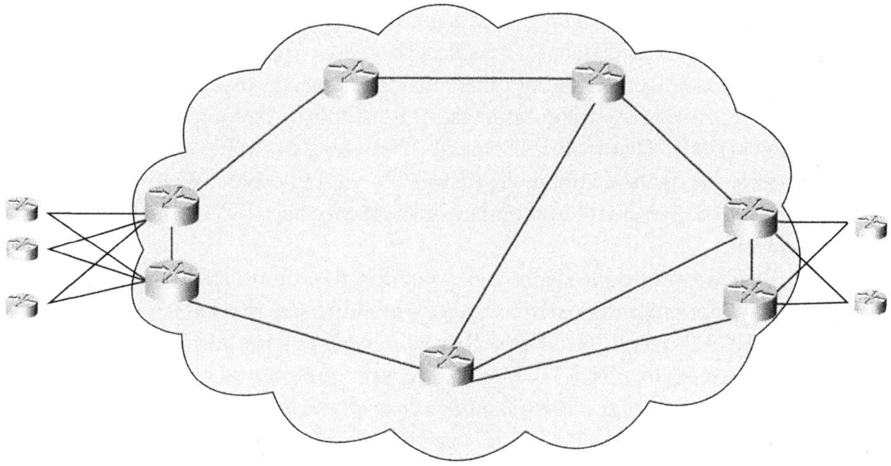

FIGURE 3.1 Intra-Domain IP Network

open shortest-path first (OSPF) and intermediate system—intermediate system (IS-IS) (see Chapter 7 for further discussion, and also [ISO90], [Moy98b], [Moy98a], [Ora90]). Both are link-state protocols with similar functionality. This means that routing systems based on both protocols use some kind of link metric (referred to as link-state) to determine the shortest path between the routers (using some version of Dijkstra's algorithm); such shortest paths are then mapped to the routing tables by keeping track of the next hop (router) on the shortest paths to different destinations. Hence, when an actual data packet arrives at a router, then the router forwards it to the next hop on the shortest path to the packet destination.

Now, what is the particular design (traffic engineering in this case) issue we are interested in solving? The first and foremost question is: *how to minimize the delay for packets traversing through the network?* Note that the focus is not on a particular packet, rather it is on the average delay for the entire stream of packets between sources and destinations (demands), or even on the overall, average packet behavior. Similar to road transportation networks, a link (and in fact, a node as well) in a computer network can get congested causing a delay in packet delivery. Suppose that a link is congested and it happens to be on the shortest path for a particular source-destination pair—certainly this will cause delayed delivery for the packet traffic for this pair (recall the average delay formula (1.3.1) discussed in Chapter 1). In the first place note that, somehow, this link was on the shortest path—this probably happened because the cost of this link (link metric) was too low. Thus, it would be desirable if the shortest path does not use this link. To achieve this, the metric for this link should be increased in order to move some traffic away from it and reduce its congestion. Thus, an important related question is: *how to determine the metrics (costs) of links so that the shortest paths are determined in a way minimizing the delay as an overall network goal?*

To address the two mutually related questions—minimizing delay as a network goal and determining an appropriate link metric system—we need to first understand what the traffic demand volume is for this problem, and where and how multi-commodity flow appears.

Typically, demand volumes in data networks are measured in Megabits per second (Mbps), Gigabits per second (Gbps) or packets per second (pps) (see Chapter 1). Thus, through some measurement system and/or other aids, the demand volume between any two edge routers in a network needs to be estimated, say in Mbps (then one Mbps is the demand volume unit—DVU). That is, for a demand d between two traffic generating routers, we need to specify the demand volume h_d ($d = 1, 2, ..., D$) in Mbps. We also have the capacity of link e, c_e, to be given in the appropriate link capacity unit (LCU) which in this case can be Mbps as well.

Next, we need to define a design objective. In order to minimize the average packet delay, a common approach has been to minimize the maximum link utilization, for example, see [BG92] (recall the relation between average delay and link utilization which we have discussed in Section 1.3.1). Now, the basic question is: *how to formulate the problem of minimizing the maximum link utilization, given that we have demand h_d ($d = 1, 2, ..., D$) and capacity c_e ($e = 1, 2, ..., E$) and the routing is imposed by OSPF/IS-IS?*

As in Section 2.5, let us denote the metric (or weight) of link e by w_e which takes non-negative or positive integer values (depending on the underlying routing protocol) bounded above. Thus, the link metric system $\boldsymbol{w} = (w_1, w_2, ..., w_E)$ will induce the traffic flow for each demand based on the rule of the routing protocol. In the case of OSPF/IS-IS, this is governed by the shortest-path routing. If multiple shortest paths are available for a demand d then flow is equally split among all the shortest paths according to the rule known as the "equal-cost multi-path" (ECMP) rule. Suppose that we can determine a set of possible/allowable paths $p = 1, 2, ..., P_d$ for demand d (instead of assuming which one would be the shortest). Practically, the network designer can determine this set of candidate paths based on his/her knowledge of the network; otherwise, the set of candidate paths can be generated as a set of shortest paths in terms of the number of hops (e.g., using the K-shortest-path algorithm—see Appendix C). Now we denote the flow on path p for demand d induced by the link metric system $\boldsymbol{w}$ by $x_{dp}(\boldsymbol{w})$—this relation is important to point out due to the dependency of the flows on $\boldsymbol{w}$ through the protocol rule. Note that it is acceptable to denote quantity of flow $x_{dp}(\boldsymbol{w})$ on path p for packets flowing on this path, since in practice this would correspond to the portion of the traffic allocated on a path as dictated by the link metric system. Thus, using the convention on summation notation which has been already discussed in Chapter 2 (see for example, the difference between (2.4.2) and (2.4.3)) we have:

$$\textstyle\sum_p x_{dp}(\boldsymbol{w}) = h_d, \quad d = 1, 2, ..., D.$$

Note that this equation is similar to (2.4.2) which has been introduced in Chapter 2. The main difference is that path flow is now dependent on the link-metric system $\boldsymbol{w}$. Let δ_{edp} be the link-path indicator, meaning it takes the value 1 if the route p for demand d uses the link e, otherwise it is 0. Then the link load (also called link flow) $\underline{y}_e$ on link e, induced by the link metric system, is given by the following formula:

$$\underline{y}_e(\boldsymbol{w}) = \textstyle\sum_d \sum_p \delta_{edp} x_{dp}(\boldsymbol{w}), \quad e = 1, 2, ..., E.$$

This is similar to (2.4.7) discussed in Chapter 2. Then, we certainly want the link-flow to be bounded above by the capacity, i.e.,

$$\underline{y}_e(\boldsymbol{w}) \leq c_e, \quad e = 1, 2, ..., E.$$

The link utilization on each link e is denoted by $\underline{y}_e(\boldsymbol{w})/c_e$. Then the maximum utilization over all links is represented by the dependent variable r where:

$$r = \max_{e=1,...,E} \left\{ \underline{y}_e(\boldsymbol{w})/c_e \right\}.$$

The specific link e for which the ratio is the highest is then the link with maximum utilization (i.e., the "most congested" link). The goal of minimizing the maximum link utilization can be formulated as follows:

$$\begin{array}{lll} \textbf{\textit{minimize}}_{\boldsymbol{w}} & \boldsymbol{F} = \max_e \left\{ \underline{y}_e(\boldsymbol{w})/c_e \right\} & \\ \textbf{\textit{subject to}} & \sum_p x_{dp}(\boldsymbol{w}) = h_d & d = 1, 2, ..., D \\ & \sum_d \sum_p \delta_{edp} x_{dp}(\boldsymbol{w}) = \underline{y}_e(\boldsymbol{w}) & e = 1, 2, ..., E \\ & \underline{y}_e(\boldsymbol{w}) \leq c_e & e = 1, 2, ..., E \\ & w_e \text{ non-negative integers.} & \end{array} \quad (3.1.1)$$

In the above formulation, the variables/unknowns (link metrics) are indicated as the subscript with the term 'minimize' to avoid confusion with the known quantities (note that the path-flow vector $\boldsymbol{x}$ and the link load vector $\underline{\boldsymbol{y}}$ are fully determined by $\boldsymbol{w}$). It is fairly easy to see that after introducing an auxiliary variable r and getting rid of the link load equation, the above problem can be re-written in the following format:

$$\begin{array}{lll} \textbf{\textit{minimize}}_{\boldsymbol{w},r} & \boldsymbol{F} = r & \\ \textbf{\textit{subject to}} & \sum_p x_{dp}(\boldsymbol{w}) = h_d & d = 1, 2, ..., D \\ & \sum_d \sum_p \delta_{edp} x_{dp}(\boldsymbol{w}) \leq c_e r & e = 1, 2, ..., E \\ & r \text{ continuous} & \\ & w_e \text{ non-negative integers.} & \end{array} \quad (3.1.2)$$

If at the optimum $r^* < 1$ then no link will be congested. The above formulated problem can help to develop algorithms that determine an appropriate optimal link-metric system $\boldsymbol{w}^*$. In practice, an off-line system (taking into account demand volume and capacity) computes the link-metric system and disseminates this information to all routers.

An important question to ask is whether the "relaxed" routing model (when metric-based shortest-path routing is dropped from the basic model, i.e., when independent decision variables x_{dp} are used instead of $\boldsymbol{w}$ and $x_{dp}(\boldsymbol{w})$) has any significance. In our case, for a given objective, this relaxed routing (which would imply an LP multi-commodity flow model) would in general provide a decrease of the optimal objective r^*. Note that the weight system $\boldsymbol{w}$ has the effect of imposing rather strong constraints on the flows $x_{dp}(\boldsymbol{w})$, and, thus, the weight-dependent optimal network objective value r^* for (3.1.2) would be higher than for the relaxed problem. We will come back to the design problems related to the the shortest-path routing networks in Chapter 7.

3.2 MPLS NETWORKS: TUNNELING OPTIMIZATION

Multi-protocol label switching (MPLS) is a recent technique [DR00] to provide controlled traffic engineering for flow of packets for different service/user (traffic) classes in core IP networks. Roughly speaking, this is done by assigning end-to-end "virtual paths" (called *tunnels*) of predefined capacity to different demand streams corresponding to different service classes associated with certain user groups, with local networks connected by the core IP network, etc., that require differentiated quality of service (QoS) (for example, private data networks for different customers, bank-transaction networks for automated teller machines). In this way a much more flexible packet routing can be achieved as compared to the link-metric dependent shortest-path type of routing described in the previous section, which is identical for all service/user classes.

MPLS achieves control over packet flows (and thus can perform traffic engineering in a flexible way) through a concept called *label switching*. For different classes different tunnels can be established that use the concept of label switching between label-edge routers (LER) where traffic ingresses and egresses (Figure 3.2). The communication between routers to set up such labels can be performed either by using the label distribution protocol (LDP), or the resource reservation protocol (RSVP) [DR00].

The tunnels in the network can have a certain bandwidth (transmission speed) assigned to them, although it should be noted that an MPLS network does not by itself provide QoS. On the other hand, for a traffic class, if the bandwidth needed to meet a certain QoS can be determined, then a tunnel (or multiple tunnels, if this is allowable) that can carry this bandwidth demand can be established. In other words, QoS requirement can be met indirectly if the bandwidth determination process takes into account QoS requirement.

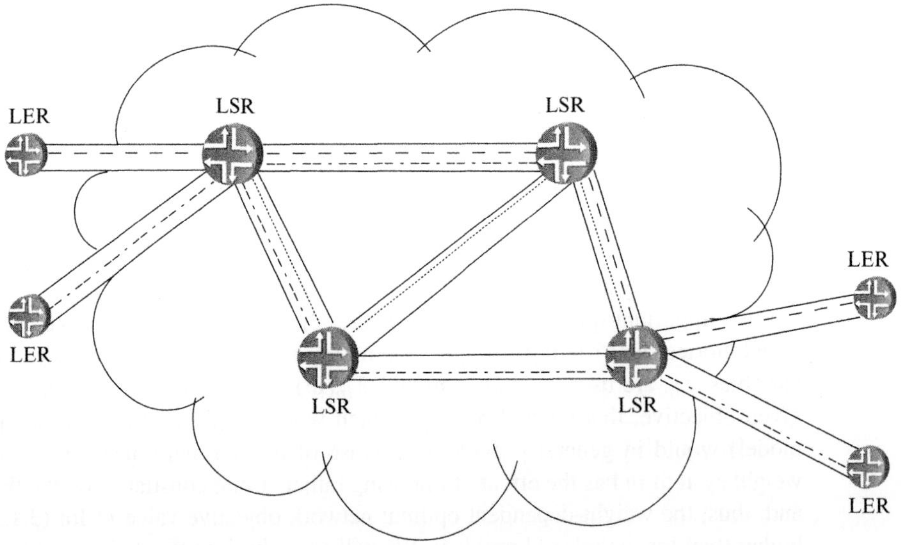

FIGURE 3.2 MPLS Network

While tunneling is a nice concept with great traffic engineering potential and allows separation of diverse traffic of different service/user groups in different tunnels, there is an inherent difficulty since only a limited number of tunnels can be handled by any MPLS router without unduely overloading the router. Furthermore, from a management point of view, it may also be desirable to limit the number of tunnels (e.g., on a router or a link basis). Thus, we can pose the following network engineering question: *how to carry different traffic classes in an MPLS network through the creation of tunnels in such a way that the number of tunnels on each MPLS router/link is minimized and load balanced?*

Again here we will use the identifier d to denote a demand (associated with a node pair and a traffic class) that requires bandwidth h_d (where the bandwidth h_d may be calculated differently for different classes) to be routed in the network. We assume that the demand h_d can be carried over multiple tunnels from ingress to egress MPLS label-edge-router (LER). We denote the different possible tunnels for demand d by P_d and the *fraction* of the demand volume for d to be carried on tunnel p as x_{dp}. We then have the demand constraint:

$$\textstyle\sum_p x_{dp} = 1, \quad d = 1, 2, ..., D.$$

Note the difference in use of the variable x_{dp} here compared to the previous section. Since it is possible to select a flow with a very small fraction, we want to put a lower bound on the fraction of a flow on a path—this is also desirable since we want to minimize the number of tunnels on a link. Thus, if we use a positive quantity ε to be the lower bound on fraction of flow on a tunnel (path) and use the binary variable $u_{dp} = 1$ to denote selection of a tunnel if the lower bound is satisfied (and 0, otherwise), we have the following two relations:

$$\begin{aligned} &\varepsilon u_{dp} \le h_d x_{dp}, \quad d = 1, 2, ..., D \quad p = 1, 2, ..., P_d \\ &x_{dp} \le u_{dp}, \quad d = 1, 2, ..., D \quad p = 1, 2, ..., P_d. \end{aligned}$$

The first one states that if a tunnel is selected, then the tunnel must have at least the fraction of flow which is set to ε; the second one states that if a tunnel is not selected, then the flow fraction associated with this tunnel should be forced to be equal to 0. Hopefully, this provides an idea about the benefit of using the concept of fractional flow variables.

As with earlier models, we have the capacity feasibility constraint:

$$\textstyle\sum_d h_d \sum_p \delta_{edp} x_{dp} \le c_e, \quad e = 1, 2, ..., E.$$

Now, the number of tunnels on link e will be

$$\textstyle\sum_d \sum_p \delta_{edp} u_{dp}.$$

Since our goal is to reduce "tunnel congestion", i.e., total number of tunnels, we want to minimize a number r that represents the maximum number of tunnels over all links. Thus, our entire problem can be formulated as:

$$
\begin{array}{llll}
\textbf{minimize}_{\boldsymbol{x},\boldsymbol{u},r} & \boldsymbol{F} = r & & \\
\textbf{subject to} & \sum_p x_{dp} = 1 & d = 1,2,...,D & \\
 & \sum_d h_d \sum_p \delta_{edp} x_{dp} \le c_e & e = 1,2,...,E & \\
 & \varepsilon u_{dp} \le h_d x_{dp} & d = 1,2,...,D & p = 1,2,...,P_d \\
 & x_{dp} \le u_{dp} & d = 1,2,...,D & p = 1,2,...,P_d \\
 & \sum_d \sum_p \delta_{edp} u_{dp} \le r & e = 1,2,...,E & \\
 & x_{dp} \text{ continuous and non-negative} & & \\
 & u_{dp} \text{ binary} & & \\
 & r \text{ integer.} & &
\end{array}
\qquad (3.2.1)
$$

Note that this problem has both continuous and discrete variables while the constraints and the objective function are linear; thus, this is an example of a mixed-integer linear programming problem (shortly, MIP problem). Certainly, this problem has more related constraints than the problems we have addressed up to now. Variation of the above model where the number of tunnels on each link is limited can also be developed (Exercise 3.1).

3.3 ATM NETWORKS: VIRTUAL PATH DESIGN

The asynchronous transfer mode (ATM) technology [Per01] was proposed more than a decade ago, and has been considered to be one of the early entrants to high-speed networking in the core backbone networks. Among many functionalities, ATM provides the concept of permanent (or semi-permanent) *virtual paths* (VP) along with guaranteed data rate. A VP can conceivably have any demand volume based on the end customer's need or guaranteed data rate requirement, which is to be routed through the ATM network capable of VP switching. Usually, when such a (long-term) VP is set up, it stays that way for a long time (unless the customer does not want it anymore). A simple ATM network is shown in Figure 3.3.

The design question we want to consider is: *how to determine link capacity so that the total link cost is minimized given that the ATM virtual path demand requirement and so that link capacity can be in modular units such as 155 Mbps?* In general, many customers may request for VPs which start at the same origin node network and destined for the same destination; as explained in Section 2.3, we can easily take this requirement into account in the link-demand-path notation by allowing multiple demands d with different demand volumes h_d for the same pair of nodes. Thus, we can say that we have demand volume h_d for demand d ($d = 1,2,...,D$) where D is the total number of demand pairs that have a positive demand volume. While many VP paths may be possible from the source ATM switch to the destination ATM switch of a demand, we assume that only one VP is required to be set up so that the demand volume for that pair is not split. ATM networks originally proposed two link speeds: 1) 155 Mbps, and 2) 622 Mbps. For our illustration, we will assume that only one type of link speed (LCU) is used, 155 Mbps. To be consistent, we assume that the DVU is already given in Mbps.

In many ATM networks, the network designer typically has some idea about possible/acceptable paths between a source and a destination ATM switch. Thus, we number all possible and acceptable candidate paths for a virtual path (VP) for demand d with $p = 1,2,...,P_d$. Since only one of these VP paths is allowed to be accepted in the final

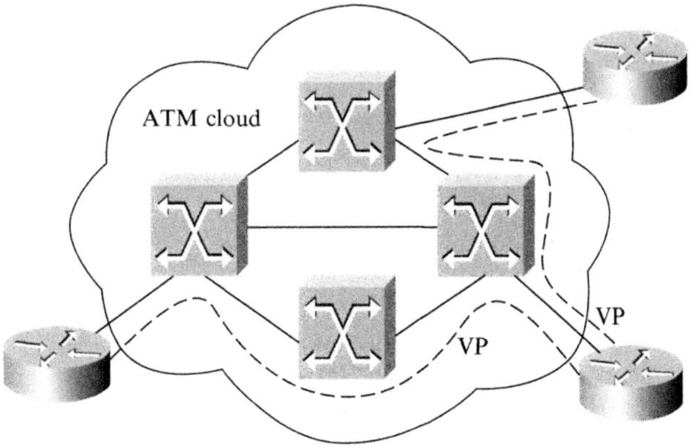

FIGURE 3.3 ATM Network

selection for VP set up for a particular demand d, we need a binary decision variable for this purpose, i.e., either a path p for demand d is chosen or not chosen, but there must be exactly one path chosen. Thus, we introduce the binary decision variable u_{dp} to take the value 1 or 0 depending on whether the path is selected or not. To meet the requirement that only one path for a demand d can be selected we can write:

$$\sum_p u_{dp} = 1, \quad d = 1, 2, ..., D. \tag{3.3.1}$$

As we have done with other formulations so far, we again need the link-path coefficient indicator δ_{edp}. Its meaning essentially remains the same: it is set to 1 if VP path p for demand d uses link e (0, otherwise). Then, the sum

$$\sum_p \delta_{edp} u_{dp}$$

expresses the total number of VPs for demand d that is using link e. Since, the first constraint (3.3.1) ensures that only one VP set up for each demand d is allowable, this summation would mean that at most only one VP for demand d will use link e. Now, if this demand does use link e, we need to carry the entire demand volume h_d on this link, and for all demands the link load on link e is:

$$\sum_d h_d \sum_p \delta_{edp} u_{dp}.$$

Now, if we assume that both demand volume (h_d) and link capacity (y_e) is expressed in the 155 Mbps modules and assume that the variable y_e for link e is an integer, then we have the relation:

$$\sum_d h_d \sum_p \delta_{edp} u_{dp} \le y_e, \quad e = 1, 2, ..., E.$$

Now suppose that the unit cost of a 155 Mbps link (LCU) is given to be ξ_e on link e, then the total cost of all link capacities can be written as:

$$\sum_e \xi_e y_e.$$

Thus, in order to minimize the total capacity cost, the ATM VP network capacity design problem can be written as:

$$
\begin{array}{lll}
\textbf{\textit{minimize}}_{u,y} & \boldsymbol{F} = \sum_e \xi_e y_e & \\
\textbf{\textit{subject to}} & \sum_p u_{dp} = 1, & d = 1, 2, ..., D \\
 & \sum_d h_d \sum_p \delta_{edp} u_{dp} \leq y_e, & e = 1, 2, ..., E \\
 & u_{dp} \text{ binary, } y_e \text{ integers.} &
\end{array}
\tag{3.3.2}
$$

This formulation is an integer programming problem since the variables take only discrete (integer or binary) values. (Observe that in this book the acronym 'IP' is used to abbreviate two different notions: 'Internet protocol' and 'integer programming'; the actual meaning of the acronym should be clear from the context.) You will notice that formulation (3.3.2) is an IP version of the general network design LP formulation (2.4.11) discussed earlier in Chapter 2. This relation is discussed in detail later in Chapter 4. Finally, note that by using the term 'MPLS tunnel' instead of 'virtual path', this model is also applicable in capacity design of MPLS networks.

3.4 DIGITAL CIRCUIT-SWITCHED TELEPHONE NETWORKS: SINGLE-BUSY HOUR AND MULTI-BUSY HOUR NETWORK DIMENSIONING

In digital circuit-switched telephone networks (frequently referred to as IDN—integrated digital networks) the nodes are divided into two categories: 1) end nodes, and 2) transit nodes [Rey83]. End nodes (also called access nodes) represent digital exchanges (switches) generating demand (i.e., telephone traffic) to each other. The demand volume between two end nodes v and w is usually expressed in *Erlangs* (or, *Erl*) (discussed earlier in Section 1.3.2) during the traffic busy hour. Thus, in this case, demand volume and link load is expressed in DVUs equal to *Erl*s (refer to Section 1.3.5). Transit switches do not generate traffic but play a crucial role in establishing connections that join the end nodes in order to carry calls. Calls are established on paths composed of switched 64 Kbps voice circuits traversing a sequence of transit switches. The links between the nodes (end and transit) are called *trunk-groups* or *circuit-groups* and are typically installed in modules of $M = 24$ circuits (T1, U.S. and Japanese standard), or, $M = 30$ circuits (E1, European standard). Hence, the link capacities are modular, with the module value equal to M. The capacity y_e or c_e of link e is expressed as number of modules M. Hence, the LCU (refer to Section 2.4) is equal to one module of M circuits.

An important network dimensioning question is: *how to determine the modular capacity needed in the network so that offered traffic is carried with an acceptable grade-of-service?* We will discuss this problem for both single-busy hour (peak offered traffic estimate over the entire day is used) and multi-busy hour traffic (different offered traffic during the day). First, we start with the single-busy hour design problem.

We must first explain the traffic (call) flow in circuit-switched networks. The paths for calls are established according to a certain fixed routing rule using a set of predefined routes (i.e., paths in the network graph). In Figure 3.4, for instance, we can consider demand d composed of end nodes $v = 1$ and $v = 2$, with $P_d = 3$ routes. The three routes are 1-3-4-2, 1-3-5-4-2, and 1-3-6-2. Note that route 1-3-7-6-2 cannot be applied because it uses end node $v = 7$ as a transit node (which is not allowed).

An example of the routing rule is to split, for each demand d, its demand volume of h_d *Erl* among the set of available routes $p = 1, 2, ..., P_d$. The split results in the set of traffic flows $x_{d1}, x_{d2}, ..., x_{dP_d}$ with the obvious property that the flow conservation is satisfied:

$$\sum_p x_{dp} = h_d, \quad d = 1, 2, ..., D$$

(refer to (2.4.2)). Such a split can be achieved by a technique, often referred to as *load sharing* routing, which consists of routing an incoming call on path number p with probability x_{dp}/h_d. The link loads, as you can guess by now, are:

$$\underline{y}_e = \sum_d \sum_p \delta_{edp} x_{dp}, \quad e = 1, 2, ..., E$$

using the link-path indicator δ_{edp}, where $\delta_{edp} = 1$ if link e belongs to path p of demand d, and $\delta_{edp} = 0$, otherwise. The load of link e is in fact the average *traffic offered* to each link e, expressed in *Erl*. (The value of traffic offered to a link expresses the average number of calls in progress on link e provided there are no losses on the link, i.e., the link has

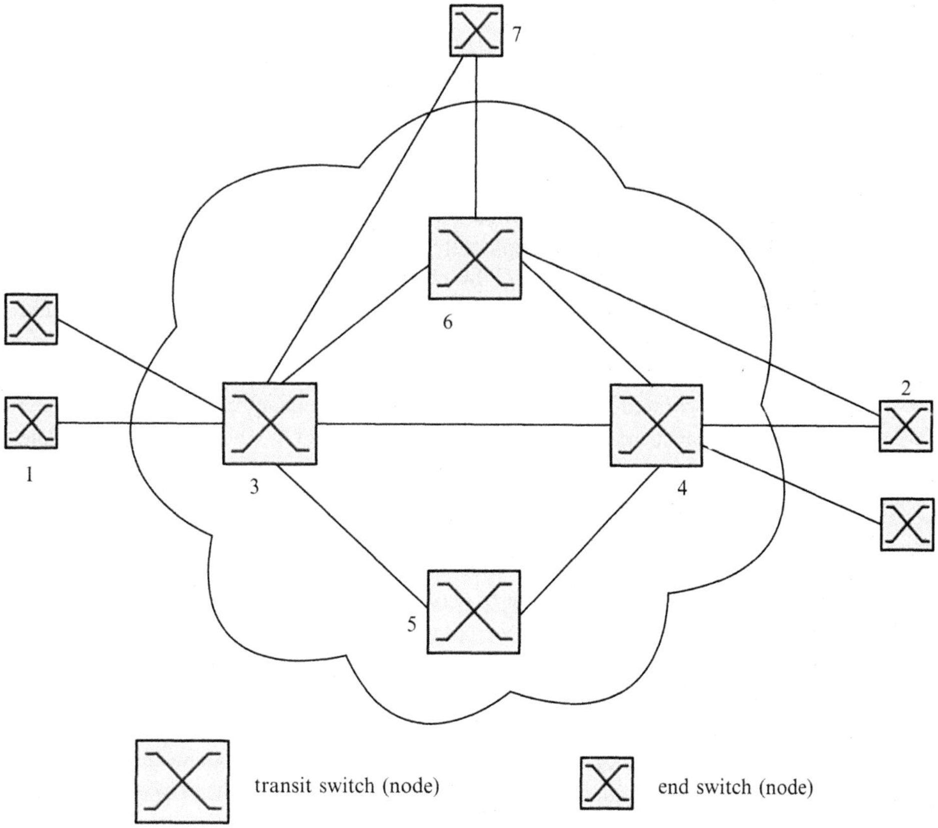

FIGURE 3.4 Circuit-Switched Network

infinite capacity.) Assuming a certain call blocking probability b_e for link e to maintain a certain grade of service (e.g., $b_e = 1\%$) we can dimension the link using the well known Erlang B-loss formula (refer to Section 1.3.2). The formula, denoted by $\mathcal{B}(a, c)$, establishes the relation between link call blocking probability b, offered traffic a, and the number of circuits c as already defined in (1.3.3).

Let $\mathcal{C}(a; b)$ denote the inverse of the Erlang blocking formula (1.3.3) for offered load a and fixed b. When appropriately extended to the real domain, function $\mathcal{C}(a; b)$ is known to be concave (refer to Section 4.3.3) in a for any fixed b $(0 < b < 1)$. In

$$F_e(a) = \mathcal{C}(a; b_e) \tag{3.4.1}$$

we define link-dependent dimensioning functions yielding the (real) number of circuits $F_e(a)$ required to carry the offered load (offered traffic) a with call blocking probability b_e.

Now, we are ready to formally present the dimensioning problem: for offered demand h_d $(d = 1, 2, ..., D)$, acceptable link blocking b_e and unit modular capacity cost of ξ_e, find the modular capacity needed to minimize total cost:

$$\begin{array}{lll} \textbf{\textit{minimize}}_{\boldsymbol{x},\boldsymbol{y}} & \boldsymbol{F} = \sum_e \xi_e y_e & \\ \textbf{\textit{subject to}} & \sum_p x_{dp} = h_d, & d = 1, 2, ..., D \\ & F_e(\sum_d \sum_p \delta_{edp} x_{dp}) \leq M y_e, & e = 1, 2, ..., E \\ & x_{dp} \text{ continuous, non-negative} & \\ & y_e \text{integers.} & \end{array} \tag{3.4.2}$$

The above problem is a combined concave-integer dimensioning problem of the form which will be discussed in Section 4.3.

It may be noted that the implementation of the flow reconfiguration in digital exchanges is achieved in a "software way" by changing the routing tables when required. This is a routine task of the management systems of modern digital exchanges/switches.

So far, demand volumes $\boldsymbol{h} = (h_1, h_2, ..., h_D)$ have been defined as the traffic offered to the demand end nodes in the traffic busy hour, assuming implicitly that the busy hours for all demands coincide (i.e., single-busy hour). This is not necessarily the case, for instance, in a long distance network of a country such as the U.S. where there are multiple time zones. For example, when it is 8:00 AM in the Eastern time zone where cities such as New York, Boston, and Washington, D.C, are located, it is 5:00 AM in the Pacific time zone where cities such as San Francisco, Los Angeles, and Seattle are located. Thus, while there could be a lot of phone traffic among the cities in the Eastern time zone around 8:00 AM, cities in the Pacific time zone are just about to wake up! This time dependent consideration can help in decreasing capacity needed as well as to find capacity in lightly loaded region to route calls.

While originally most digital exchanges had a fixed-order of trying different routes, this aspect changed beginning in early 1980s with the introduction of dynamic or adaptive call routing concepts such as dynamic non-hierarchical routing (DNHR), dynamically controlled routing (DCR), dynamic alternative routing (DAR), and real-time network routing (RTNR) (for example, see [Ash97], [Gir90]). Such dynamic routing techniques have better capability to take advantage of free capacity, especially taking into account non-coincidence of busy hour traffic. Referring back to Figure 3.4, such schemes can be thought of as applied to the network segment consisting of just transit nodes, i.e., for the core backbone network.

Now the design question for us to consider for the multi-busy hour case is: *how to do modular capacity design given that traffic volume is different for different hours of a day, and by taking into account functional characteristics of a routing scheme?*

First, the day can be partitioned into several "traffic hours" $t = 1, 2, ..., T$ such that for each demand its offered traffic is in general different at different times of the day (i.e., hours). Hence, we arrive at a set of demand volume vectors $\boldsymbol{h}_1, \boldsymbol{h}_2, ..., \boldsymbol{h}_T$ with $\boldsymbol{h}_t = (h_{1t}, h_{2t}, ..., h_{Dt})$. Another important item is the determination of candidate paths. In the core network, the path lengths are restricted to a maximum of two links between ingress and egress nodes in most currently implemented dynamic routing schemes. Thus, the set of candidate paths are hop-limited (with a maximum of one intermediate node) and can be easily determined. Due to the dynamic nature of the flow, we need to allow the path-flow estimation to be different for different time periods t; thus, our flow variable for demand d for path p needs to be time dependent, t, as well, i.e., x_{dpt}. While performance impact of different dynamic routing schemes can be different, our interest here is to develop a model that is usable for multi-hour network dimensioning. In fact, from a capacity design modeling point of view, the ability to define time-dependent flow variables along with the notion of load sharing is a good approximation for any reasonable dynamic routing scheme.

Under these circumstances the previously considered uncapacitated design Problem (3.4.2), can be referred to as the *single-hour* design problem which needs to be extended, resulting in the *multi-hour* design problem (sometimes referred to as "multi-hour engineering") with time period-dependent demand traffic flows x_{dpt}. The formulation for the multi-hour problem is as follows:

$$
\begin{array}{llll}
\textbf{\textit{minimize}}_{\boldsymbol{x},\boldsymbol{y}} & \boldsymbol{F} = \sum_e \xi_e y_e & & \\
\textbf{\textit{subject to}} & \sum_p x_{dpt} = h_{dt}, & d = 1, 2, ..., D & t = 1, 2, ..., T \\
 & F_{et}\left(\sum_d \sum_p \delta_{edpt} x_{dpt}\right) \leq M y_e, & e = 1, 2, ..., E & t = 1, 2, ..., T \\
 & x_{dpt} \text{ continuous, non-negative} & & \\
 & y_e \text{ integers.} & &
\end{array}
\tag{3.4.3}
$$

Note that the link dimensioning functions F_{et} can be not only link-dependent but also time-dependent since the link call blocking probabilities b_{et} in the definition (3.4.1) can assume different values in different time periods, allowing for higher blocking during the links' busy hour periods.

Finally, we want to point out that the multi-hour scenario is not necessarily limited to circuit-switched networks. Multi-hour modeling may be the right approach for any network for which considering multiple traffic matrices for different times of the day is appropriate and provides cost savings (refer to Exercises 3.3, 3.4, and 3.5). Thus, we will cover in detail the multi-hour design problem in Chapter 11.

3.5 SONET/SDH TRANSPORT NETWORKS: CAPACITY AND PROTECTION DESIGN

In Section 1.3.3, we have discussed the demand for transport networks and have given a brief idea about the technology used for transport networks. A widely deployed technology for transport networks in North America is SONET; the European counterpart is called SDH (synchronous digital hierarchy). Recall that SONET/SDH fits into the multi-layer network architecture for transport functionality, as discussed in Section 1.6.

We first present a very brief overview of SONET/SDH technology that is pertinent to our discussion. The interested reader is directed to books such as [Muk97, RS02, Wu92] for more details about SONET/SDH. Nodes in SONET or SDH networks are equipped with devices such as terminal multiplexers (TM), digital cross connects (DCS), and add-drop multiplexers (ADM). TMs and DCSs are used in transmission networks with mesh topology, while ADMs are typical nodes of ring networks (Figure 3.5). There are several data rates available for SONET/SDH which are given as synchronous transfer signal (STS) for SONET and synchronous transport module (STM) for SDH (refer to Table 3.1 for these rates). In SONET standard, optical carrier (OC) levels are also defined corresponding to electrical equivalent in STSs. To complicate further, SONET/SDH standard allows subrates

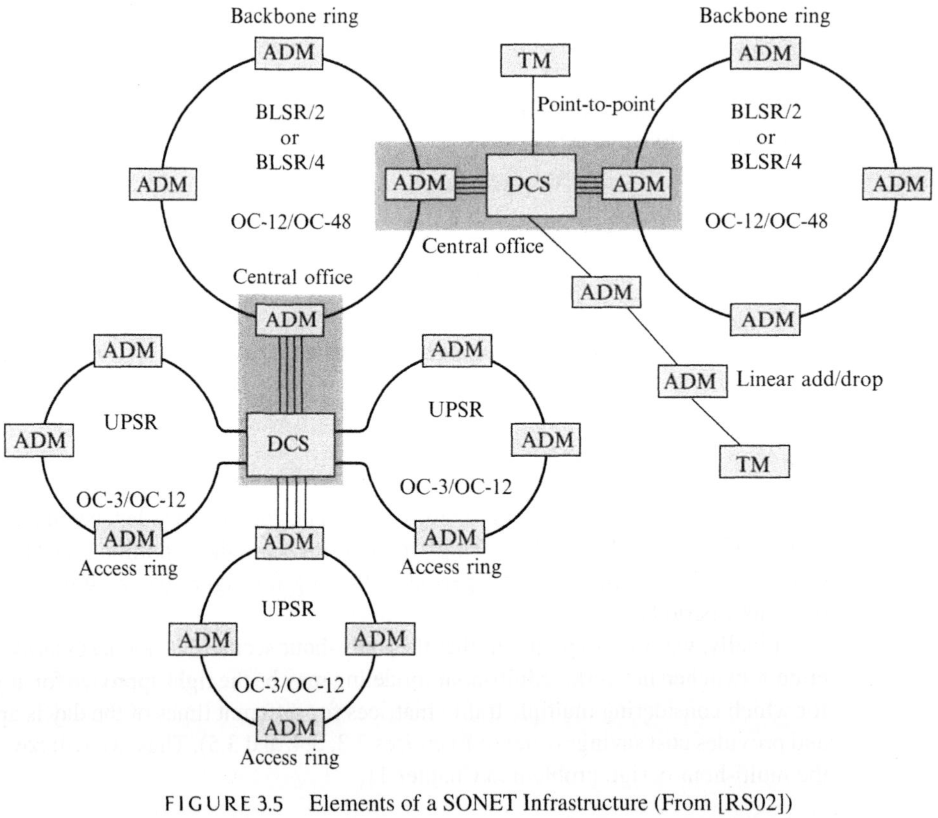

FIGURE 3.5 Elements of a SONET Infrastructure (From [RS02])

TABLE 3.1 **Transmission Rates for SONET/SDH**

SONET Signal	SDH Signal	Bit Rate (Mbps)
STS-1 (OC-1)	–	51.84
STS-3 (OC-3)	STM-1	155.52
STS-12 (OC-12)	STM-4	622.08
STS-48 (OC-48)	STM-16	2,488.32
STS-192 (OC-192)	STM-64	9,953.28

TABLE 3.2 **Rates for VC (Subrates for STM) and VT (Subrates for STS)**

VC Type	Bit Rate (Mbps)
VC-11	1.728
VC-12	2.304
VC-3	48.960
VC-4	150.336

VT Type	Bit Rate (Mbps)
VT-1.5	1.728
VT-2	2.304
VT-3	3.456
VT-6	6.912

for carried demand. These subrates are referred to as virtual tributaries (VT) in SONET and virtual containers (VC) in SDH (see Table 3.2). Furthermore, old-style rates such as T1 and T3 can also be connected to a SONET/SDH nodes through service adapters. See Figure 3.6 for relation among different rates.

Examples of typical services that create demand for the transport provided by SONET/SDH are trunks for digital circuit-switched networks, interface from line-cards for IP networks, and private leased-line services. It may be noted that while SONET/SDH standard did not originally address interfacing with IP network routers, it has been possible to use SONET/SDH as transport for IP network links between two routers through an interfacing mechanism called packet over SONET/SDH (PoS).

The design questions for SONET/SDH transport networks, analogous to the problems discussed earlier in this chapter, are a bit complicated because of the actual data rates and interfaces available for a particular SONET/SDH network. An input demand (sometimes at subrate) could come into one of these interfaces depending on the type of node functionality deployed in a network. For this example, we assume that SONET/SDH nodes are DCS capable, meaning that they can switch signal at any subrate (i.e., VT-1.5, VT-3, VT-6, or VC-12, VC-3, VC-4) level.

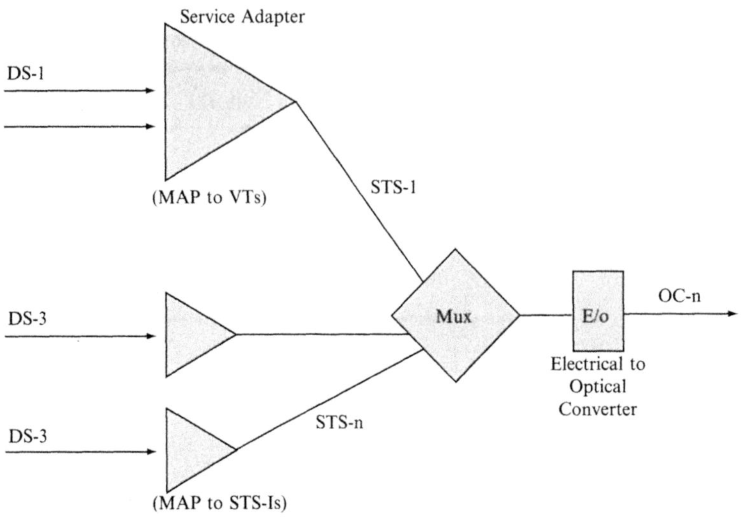

FIGURE 3.6 SONET Multiplexing Interfacing

First, we consider the case where a SONET/SDH network is used as the transport layer for a digital voice circuit-switched network (refer to Section 3.4). Consider this example for a European network where SDH is deployed. The E1 interface from the switch (digital exchange) of the digital circuit-switched network requiring 2.048 Mbps data rate, can be transported on one SDH VC-12. Thus, we count demand between an ingress DCS node (an interface to a digital voice circuit-switched network) to an egress DCS node (another interface to a digital voice circuit-switched network) in terms of VC-12s. In other words, each circuit (or trunk) group d composed of, for example, h_d 30-circuit modules constitutes a (aggregated) demand from the point of view of the SDH network. Here, one DVU is equal to one VC-12.

The links interconnecting the transport nodes are composed of optical transmission systems STM-n, where $n = 1, 4, 16, 64$ (Table 3.1), using optical fibers. Each STM-1 module can carry 63 VC-12 containers. The capacity c_e (or y_e, if the capacity is a variable) of transmission link e is expressed in LCUs being the STM-1 modules (i.e., 1 LCU = 63 DVUs since 1 DVU is a VC-12 unit), and is equal to the total number of STM-1 modules realized by all the transmission systems carried by the link. The links (transmission systems) are terminated at the DCS nodes and the VC-12 containers carried in the STM-1 modules are delivered to the ports of the node's switching matrix.

Hence, for the case considered here, the SDH transport network capacity design problem can be formulated as follows (see also (4.3.1):

$$
\begin{array}{lll}
\textbf{minimize}_{x,y} & F = \sum_e \xi_e y_e & \\
\textbf{subject to} & \sum_p x_{dp} = h_d, & d = 1, 2, ..., D \\
 & \sum_d \sum_p \delta_{edp} x_{dp} \leq M y_e, & e = 1, 2, ..., E \\
 & x_{dp}, y_e \text{ non-negative integers} &
\end{array}
\quad (3.5.1)
$$

where $M = 63$ and ξ_e is the cost of one LCU (STM-1 system) on link e. Observe that Problem (3.5.1) is somewhat simplified because it does not differentiate between the costs of STM-1 modules realized in the transmission systems of different rates. A more accurate formulation assumes that the cost of one transmission system STM-n realized on link e is equal to ξ_{en} and, hence, the above formulated problem is transformed to (refer to Problem D/LMMS presented in (4.3.3) in Section 4.3.1):

$$\begin{aligned} &\textbf{\textit{minimize}}_{x,y} && \boldsymbol{F} = \textstyle\sum_e \sum_n \xi_{en} y_{en} && \\ &\textbf{\textit{subject to}} && \textstyle\sum_p x_{dp} = h_d, && d = 1, 2, ..., D \\ & && \textstyle\sum_d \sum_p \delta_{edp} x_{dp} \le \sum_n M_n y_{en}, && e = 1, 2, ..., E \\ & && x_{dp}, y_{en} \text{ non-negative integers} && \end{aligned} \tag{3.5.2}$$

where y_{en} is the number of STM-n systems realized on link e, and $M_n = 63n$ is the modularity of such a system.

In the example considered, the SDH network forms the transport layer for realizing circuit groups of the digital switched telephone network built on top of it. Hence, a (total) failure of a certain transmission link, say link e, will result in losing all the flows x_{dp} assigned to the paths traversing link e, i.e., to all the paths $\mathcal{P}_{dp}$ with the coincidence coefficient $\delta_{edp} = 1$. In consequence, from the perspective of the upper telephone network layer the failure will be seen as a simultaneous partial failure of several circuit groups d. More precisely, the surviving capacity of the circuit group d in such a *failure situation* s will be equal to

$$h_{ds} = h_d - \textstyle\sum_p \delta_{edp} x_{dp}, \quad d = 1, 2, ..., D. \tag{3.5.3}$$

Hence, from the survivability point of view, the capacities h_d of the circuit groups should be split and realized with as many non-zero flows x_{dp} as economically reasonable, unless some other protection mechanisms are applied. Such a splitting is called *path diversity* (PD) and is commonly used in the case considered here. For instance, we may assume that each circuit group d is realized by means of at least two flows by adding the constraint

$$x_{dp} \le \lceil h_d/2 \rceil, \quad d = 1, 2, ..., D. \tag{3.5.4}$$

In this way, assuming single link failures in the transmission network, the circuit groups *availability coefficients* α_{ds} will be never $< \frac{1}{2}$ for even h_d (and at most only slightly less than $\frac{1}{2}$ for odd h_d). Observe that PD can result in a relatively costly transmission network over-dimensioning because the alternative paths can be longer than the shortest paths (refer to Example 9.1 in Section 9.1).

The cost ineffectiveness of the PD solution is one of the main reasons why modern meshed core SDH networks are often equipped with additional protection/restoration capacity, which combined with the advanced signaling/switching functionality of DCSs provides active protection mechanisms which are capable of restoring failed flows, making the network robust to major failures, e.g., to optical cable cuts.

In the SDH networks, a typical protection mechanism is called *link protection*. This mechanism restores the transmission capacity of the lost links rather than individual flows (the latter mechanism is frequently referred to as path protection). The protection design problem consists in minimizing the cost of the necessary link protection capacity and is as follows (refer to Section 9.5.1):

$$
\begin{array}{lll}
\textbf{\textit{minimize}}_{z,y} & F = \sum_e \xi_e y_e & \\
\textbf{\textit{subject to}} & \sum_q z_{eq} = c_e, & e = 1, 2, ..., E \\
& \sum_e \sum_q \beta_{fek} z_{eq} = y_f, & f = 1, ..., E, \; e = 1, 2, ..., E, \quad f \neq e \\
& z_{eq}, y_e \text{ non-negative integers.} &
\end{array}
\tag{3.5.5}
$$

The above formulation assumes fixed link capacities c_e ($e = 1, 2, ..., E$) assigned for the normal state and minimizes the cost of additional protection link capacities y_e ($e = 1, 2, ..., E$) which are sufficient to restore each failed capacity c_e (single-link failures are assumed). For each link e there is a given list of restoration paths labeled with $q = 1, 2, ..., Q_e$ that can be used for restoring its capacity when the link fails (e.g., the cable on which it is realized is cut). The capacity is restored by means of restoration flows z_{eq} (expressed in LCUs). The link-path incidence coefficients β_{feq} specify whether or not link f belongs to path q restoring link e ($\beta_{feq} = 1$ or $\beta_{feq} = 0$, respectively).

3.6 SONET/SDH RINGS: RING BANDWIDTH DESIGN

An important alternative to mesh SDH networks discussed in the previous section are SDH ring networks (see [Muk97], [RS02], [Wu92]) where the restoration mechanisms are intrinsic to the network functionality. This is contrary to the mesh case where restoration requires inter-DCS signaling. Self-healing rings have been heavily deployed due to its < 50 ms restoration capability from a single-link failure. The nodes of a ring network are called ADMs and are capable of inserting or extracting any VC-12 container out of the set of all containers circulating around the ring. Figure 3.7 depicts a bi-directional line-switched ring (BLSR) with four optical fibers (because of four fibers, they are also referred to as BLSR/4). Now assume that this ring is based on the STM-1 transmission system, i.e., the system with 63 VC-12 containers. The ring is divided into two pairs of fibers, one basic pair and one protection pair. Note that BLSR protection can be classified as link protection (refer to Section 9.1.2). The VC-12 containers destined to a particular node are extracted from the incoming basic fiber (for example, the most outer fiber in Figure 3.7) while the originating containers are inserted into the outgoing (second outer) basic fiber. The design question is: *given the inherent routing nature of a SONET/SDH ring and the demand volume, how do we determine what is the minimal number and type of (parallel) rings needed?*

For example, if demand $d = 1$ between ADMs $v = 1$ and $v = 2$ has volume of $h_1 = 3$ VC-12s, then three selected numbers k, l, and n from the set $\{1, 2, ..., 63\}$ are reserved between nodes $v = 1$ and $v = 2$, and the VCs with these numbers are used for realizing the 90 circuits required between the two considered nodes to form a trunk group d. If the path between two nodes of a demand consists of more *segments* of the ring (a segment is the part of the ring between its two consecutive nodes), then the containers with the same numbers are reserved along all the segments of the path. When one of the ring segments fails, then the protection switches automatically re-switch the STM-1 module to the unaffected part of the inner protection pair of fibers.

The allocation of the demand flows in a BLSR for the given set of demands is not a trivial task, as each demand volume can be split into two parts (in general, not equal), and each part is realized on one of the two complementary parts of the ring. Suppose that nodes are numbered from 1 to V in the clockwise manner starting from some distinguished node $v = 1$. Then it is natural to number the segments from 1 to V (the number of segments E is equal to the number of nodes V as we deal with a ring!) such that segment $e = 1$ connects nodes $v = 1$ and $v = 2$, segment $e = 2$ connects nodes $v = 2$ and $v = 3$, and so on, with segment $e = V$ connecting nodes $v = V$ and $v = 1$ (Figure 3.8). If we assume undirected demands, then demand volume h_{vw} between nodes v and w, with $v < w$ can be realized on two paths: clockwise from v to w and clockwise from w to v. Denote the flow on the first path by u_{vw} and on the second path by z_{vw}. The corresponding design problem is as follows:

$$\begin{array}{lll} \textbf{minimize}_{\boldsymbol{u},\boldsymbol{z},r} & r & \\ \textbf{subject to} & u_{vw} + z_{vw} = h_{vw}, & v, w = 1, 2, ..., V, v < w \\ & \delta_{evw} u_{vw} + (1 - \delta_{evw}) z_{vw} \le Mr, & e = 1, 2, ..., E \\ & u_{vw}, z_{vw}, r \text{ non-negative integers.} & \end{array} \tag{3.6.1}$$

In the formulation, each segment-demand incidence coefficient δ_{evw} reflects the position of the end nodes of demand $d = \langle v,w \rangle$ in the ring, and specifies if segment e belongs to the clockwise path from v to w. Clearly,

$$\delta_{evw} = \begin{cases} 1 & \text{if } v \le e < w \\ 0 & \text{otherwise.} \end{cases}$$

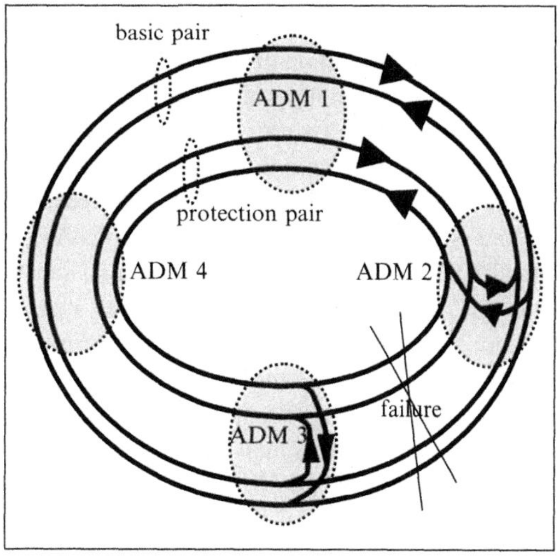

FIGURE 3.7 Bi-Directional Line-Switched Ring (BLSR)

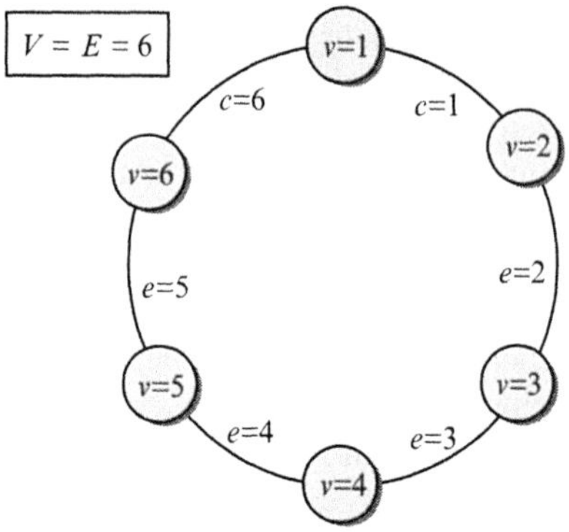

FIGURE 3.8 Node and Segment Labeling of BLSR

In the example considered, $M = 63$, although for other types of SDN/SONET rings this module can be different (e.g., $M = 252$ in an STM-4-based BLSR). The self-healing feature of BLSR means that in the case when one segment of the ring is cut, then the broken basic segment of the ring is restored along the (long) path on the surviving part of the inner protection pair of fibers (Figure 3.7). This is done automatically by means of a functionality called protection switching.

Similar to BLSR, there is another SONET/SDH ring protection mechanism called unidirectional path-switched rings (UPSR) where the protection mechanism can be classified as path protection (refer to Section 9.1.2). The bandwidth design formulation problem is left as an exercise (Exercise 3.6).

3.7 WDM NETWORKS: RESTORATION DESIGN WITH OPTICAL CROSS-CONNECTS

In recent years, wavelength division multiplexing (WDM) has received a lot of attention [Muk97], [RS02] as a technology allowing for a dramatic increase of the rates in optical transmission. In WDM networks, DVUs correspond to *wavelengths* called *lambdas* or *colors*. LCUs correspond to optical fibers. Today, one wavelength (one DVU) is typically capable of carrying 10 Gbps (1 DVU = 10 Gbps which is equivalent to 64 STM-1 modules), while one optical fiber (one LCU) can typically realize up to around 100 different wavelengths (1 LCU = 100 DVUs). The nodes of the WDM network are called Optical Cross-Connects (OXC). There are two basic types of such devices: 1) without wavelength conversion, and 2) with wavelength conversion (Figure 3.9). OXCs without wavelength conversion are technically less complicated than OXC with the conversion. An OXC without conversion is able to switch the same color directly in the optical domain (i.e., without using conversion to electrical signals) between two arbitrary optical fibers connected to its input/output ports. OXCs with the wavelength conversion are more flexible—they can switch (also in the optical domain) different colors between the input/output ports. Hence, if the networks use OXCs without wavelength conversion, then a route (called the light-path) between two end nodes of a demand uses the same color all the way. In the case of the

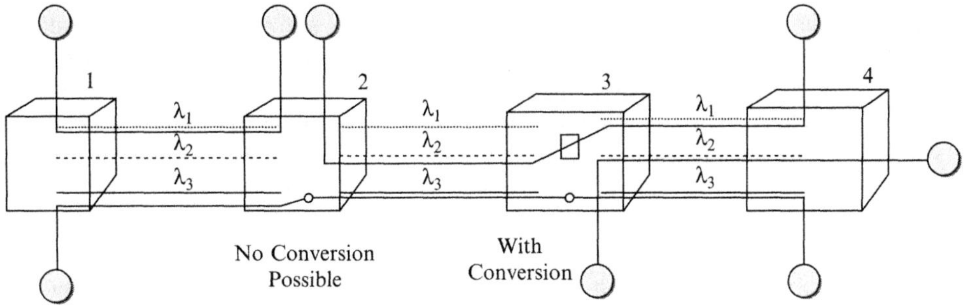

FIGURE 3.9 WDM Network

network using OXCs with the conversion, a light-path can use different colors on different links.

Consider the following design problem which we can refer to as the wavelength assignment problem that is appropriate for a WDM network with path-diversity (refer to Section 3.5 and Subsection 4.2.1) routing and without wavelength conversion.

Demands for capacity to be realized between pairs of nodes are labeled with $d = 1, 2, ..., D$, candidate paths for demand d with $p = 1, 2, ..., P_d$, and links (composed of sets of fibers) with $e = 1, 2, ..., E$. Colors (lambdas, wavelengths) available on the links are labeled with $c = 1, 2, ..., C$. Finally, the failure situations are denoted by $s = 0, 1, ..., S$, where $s = 0$ corresponds to the normal state with no failures, i.e., with all links fully available.

The parameters (constants) of the problem are: (1) h_{ds} ($d = 1, 2, ..., D$) specifying the volume of demand d to be realized in situation s, expressed as the number of light-paths; (2) ξ_e ($e = 1, 2, ..., E$) defining the cost of one LCU (i.e., optical fibre) on link e; and (3) binary link-failure coefficients α_{es} where $\alpha_{es} = 0$ if link e is failed in situation s and $\alpha_{es} = 1$ if the link works (observe that $\alpha_{e0} \equiv 1$). Furthermore, two sets of binary coefficients are assumed to be known: link-path incidence coefficients δ_{edp} with $\delta_{edp} = 1$ if link e belongs to path p realizing demand d (otherwise $\delta_{edp} = 0$), and path-failure coefficients θ_{dps} with $\theta_{dps} = 0$ if path p of demand d is failed in situation s (otherwise $\theta_{dps} = 1$). Observe that $\theta_{dps} = \prod_{\{e:\delta_{edp}=1\}} \alpha_{es}$. Now we wish to find the values of the following variables:

x_{dpc}	flow (number of light-paths) realizing demand d in color c on path p (non-negative integer)
z_{ce}	number of times the color c is used on link e (non-negative integer)
y_e	capacity of link e expressed in the number of fibers (non-negative integer)

to solve the optimization problem for the OXCs without wavelength conversion:

$$\begin{aligned}
&\textbf{\textit{minimize}}_{\boldsymbol{x},\boldsymbol{z},\boldsymbol{y}} && \boldsymbol{F} = \textstyle\sum_e \xi_e y_e \\
&\textbf{\textit{subject to}} && \textstyle\sum_p \theta_{dps} \sum_c x_{dpc} \geq h_{ds}, && d = 1, 2, ..., D \quad s = 0, 1, 2, ..., S \\
& && \textstyle\sum_d \sum_p \delta_{edp} x_{dpc} = z_{ce}, && c = 1, 2, ..., C, \quad e = 1, 2, ..., E \\
& && y_e \geq z_{ce}, && c = 1, 2, ..., C, \quad e = 1, 2, ..., E.
\end{aligned} \tag{3.7.1}$$

The first constraint in (3.7.1) shows that in each failure situation s (including the normal state of the network) the surviving flows (from normal state) realize the assumed number of DVUs for each demand. The second constraint in (3.7.1) sets the number of times the color c is actually used on link e. Finally, the last constraint in (3.7.1) assures that the number of fibers assigned to each link is sufficient to realize the demand for each color on the link.

Problem (3.7.1) is an integer programming problem and as such is difficult to solve, at least for large networks. Nevertheless, its LP relaxation assuming all variables to be continuous can help to find a good approximation of the optimal solution. Notice that if OXCs with wavelength conversion are considered then the appropriate counterpart of Problem (3.7.1) becomes simpler and in fact, identical to the one that would be relevant for the SDH/SONET networks considered in Section 3.5.

Finally, observe that by busing additional (binary) variables we can consider, maintaining the integer programming formulation, the objective function in (3.7.1) extended to take into account the constant "link-opening" costs (implied by e.g., the cost of conduits):

$$\boldsymbol{F} = \sum_e F_e(y_e), \quad F_e(y_e) = \xi_e y_e + \kappa_e \text{ for } y_e > 0, \text{ and } F_e(y_e) = 0 \text{ for } y_e = 0.$$

To achieve this, for each link e we introduce an additional binary variable u_e and add the following (where M is a large number):

$$\begin{array}{llll}
\textbf{minimize}_{\boldsymbol{x},\boldsymbol{z},\boldsymbol{y},\boldsymbol{u}} & \boldsymbol{F} = \sum_e (\xi_e y_e + \kappa_e u_e) & & \\
\textbf{subject to} & \sum_p \theta_{dps} \sum_c x_{dpc} \geq h_{ds}, & d = 1, 2, ..., D & s = 0, 1, 2, ..., S \\
& \sum_d \sum_p \delta_{edp} x_{dpc} = z_{ce}, & c = 1, 2, ..., C, & e = 1, 2, ..., E \\
& y_e \geq z_{ce}, & c = 1, 2, ..., C, & e = 1, 2, ..., E \\
& y_e \leq M u_e, & e = 1, 2, ..., E. &
\end{array} \tag{3.7.2}$$

The last constraint in (3.7.2) simply forces the link capacity y_e to be equal 0 when the link is not installed, i.e., when $u_e = 0$.

3.8 IP OVER SONET: COMBINED TWO-LAYER DESIGN

In Section 1.6 (Chapter 1), we have briefly discussed why communication networks are inherently multi-layered and how different layers of network resources are related, either in a traffic-over-transport or in a transport-over-transport manner. In this section, we will discuss a two-layer design problem for a network consisting of the traffic (IP) and the transport (SONET) layer.

Earlier in Section 3.1, we have discussed an IP traffic engineering problem, and in doing so, we have shown how IP traffic flows depend on the link weight (metric) system with protocols such as OSPF or IS-IS that use shortest paths for routing data packets. In Section 3.5, we have considered another technology, SONET/SDH, for the transport network with cross-connect (DCS) capabilities. Consider now an IP network and suppose that the IP links connecting IP routers need to be physically realized as transmission paths in a SONET network using DCSs. Thus, we have the IP over SONET network with a two-layer resource hierarchy, using the PoS technology. A pictorial view of this hierarchy

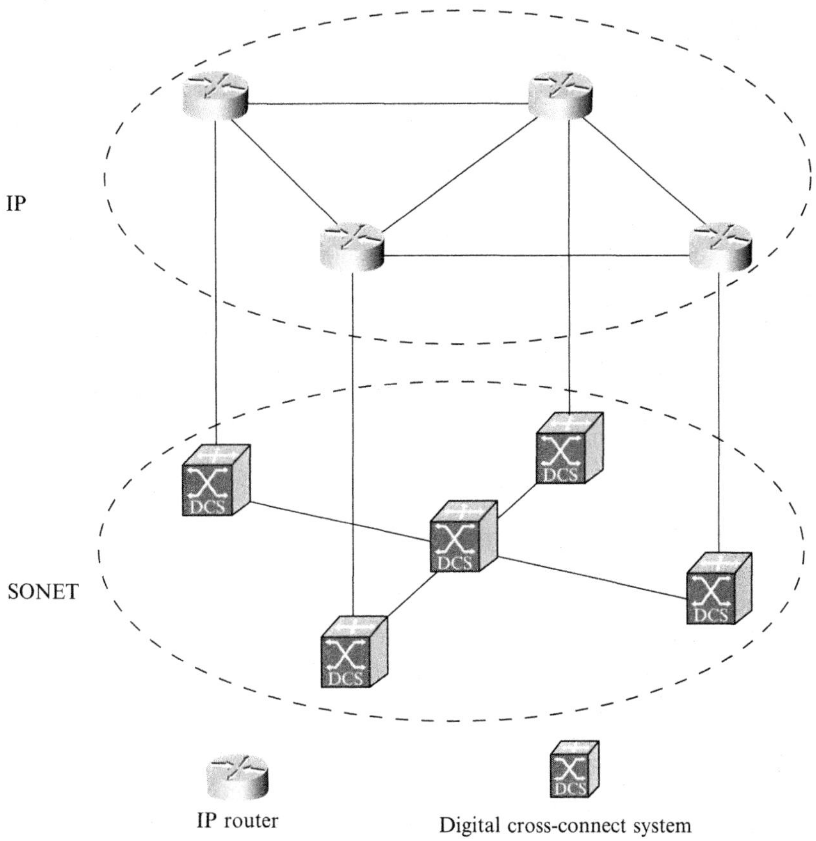

FIGURE 3.10 IP Over SONET: Two-Layer Architecture

is shown in Figure 3.10. Then, the two-layer design question we want to address is: *given an IP intra-domain network and that the IP links are realized as transmission paths over a capacitated SONET network, how do we determine capacity required for the IP links, and the routing of these links in the SONET network in an integrated manner to minimize the IP network cost?*

Such a two-layer integrated design is often possible only for network providers who own both the IP network (upper layer) and the SONET network (lower layer); this will be discussed in detail in Section 12.3.3 of Chapter 12. In any case, we assume that this is the case and that the capacity in the SONET network is given (and hence limited). Now, for the IP network, we need to determine the IP link capacity, given that (packet) flow allocation is driven by the shortest-path routing. Suppose that we are given the demand volume for the IP network in Mbps between different routers. Suppose also that we use OC-3 interface cards to connect the routers; this means that IP links are modular with the speed equal to 155.52 Mbps (refer to Table 3.1), hence the LCU of IP links is then 155.52 Mbps. If one DVU in the IP layer is equal to 1 Mbps, then the IP link module value is given as M = 155.52 Mbps. Now, the capacity of the IP links become demand volumes for the SONET layer, implying that one DVU in the lower layer is equal to one OC-3. This demand is then routed over the lower layer network using high speed SONET transmission links such as OC-48 (or OC-192); this in turn implies that one LCU of the lower layer links is equal to $N = 16M$ because one OC-48 (2,488.32 Mbps, see Table 3.1) system can carry 16 OC-3 modules. Finally, observe that the capacity of an IP link is routed (realized) on a path traversing a series of intermediate DXC nodes between the end DXCs connected to the end IP routers of the considered IP link.

To summarize, the DVU for IP demands is equal to 1 Mbps, and the LCU for IP links is equal to $M = 155.52$ Mbps. The LCU from IP network becomes the DVU for the SONET network in the two-layer architecture, i.e., DVUs for the SONET network can be thought of as OC-3s. We assume that the link capacity in the SONET network is given in multiples of OC-3s, namely in OC-48s. Then the LCU for the SONET network links is equal to OC-48 with modularity $N = 2{,}488.32$ Mbps.

Formally, we denote the IP network traffic demand volume as h_d for demand d, $d = 1, 2, ..., D$. The flow on an allowable path, p, for demand d in the IP layer that is induced by the link weight (metric) system, $\boldsymbol{w} = (w_1, w_2, ..., w_E)$ is given by $x_{dp}(\boldsymbol{w})$. In Section 3.1, we have discussed the IP traffic engineering problem; here we are interested in the IP capacity design, subject to capacity limitations in the SONET transport layer. As before, we will put $\delta_{edp} = 1$ to indicate that path p for demand d if the IP network uses link e ($\delta_{edp} = 0$, otherwise). Then if we write the modular capacity (to be determined) on IP layer link e to be y_e (expressed in modules M), we can see that this new demand volume, y_e, induced in the upper layer would need to be routed on the SONET network using DCSs. It is important to make a distinction between routing in the two considered layers. Routing in the IP layer is at the packet level and generates the aggregated packet flows, while the routing in the SONET network is at the SONET frame level and is set up on a permanent or semi-permanent basis by setting up connection paths of OC-48 modules switched in the DCSs along the path. Note that, analogously to δ_{edp}, we need to use another indicator to map the SONET links onto the SONET paths realizing the IP links. The candidate paths in SONET layer for IP link e would be denoted by $q = 1, 2, ..., Q_e$. Then, γ_{geq} takes value 1 if path q in the transport layer for demand e uses link g; and 0, otherwise. Finally, we denote the capacity of link g in the SONET network by c_g expressed in OC-48 modules denoted by N.

Thus, the design problem, involving variables $\boldsymbol{w}, \boldsymbol{y}$, and $\boldsymbol{z}$, can be written in the link-path formulation as (at this point, the reader may want to read Section 2.9 for an illustration of multi-layer modelling):

$$
\begin{array}{lll}
\textbf{\textit{minimize}}_{\boldsymbol{w},\boldsymbol{y},\boldsymbol{z}} & \sum_e \xi_e y_e + \sum_e \sum_q \zeta_{eq} z_{eq} & \\
\textbf{\textit{subject to}} & \sum_p x_{dp}(\boldsymbol{w}) = h_d, & d = 1, 2, ..., D \\
& \sum_d \sum_p \delta_{edp} x_{dp}(\boldsymbol{w}) \le \rho M y_e, & e = 1, 2, ..., E \\
& \sum_q \sum_c z_{eq} = y_e, & e = 1, 2, ..., E \\
& M \sum_e \sum_q \gamma_{geq} z_{eq} \le N c_g, & g = 1, 2, ..., G \\
& w_e \text{ non-negative integer} & \\
& y_e, z_{eq} \text{ non-negative integer.} &
\end{array}
\qquad (3.8.1)
$$

As you can see, the capacity, y_e, of IP layer link e becomes the demand volume for the lower layer and needs to be routed on the paths in the SONET network. Note that there is a coefficient, ρ, $(0 < \rho < 1)$, called the link utilization coefficient, (refer to Section 7.1.1) used in the upper layer link capacity constraints which can be used for limiting IP link congestion.

There are two cost components. The first is the IP link termination cost, ξ_e, induced by the cost of the OC-3 interfaces at the end routers of link e (ξ_e is in most cases link-independent, i.e., $\xi_e \equiv 2\xi$, where ξ is the cost of one OC-3 interface card). The second cost component is the routing cost in the SONET layer. This component can be used to model various situations. For instance, if we assume $\zeta_{eq} \equiv 1$ then we are in fact maximizing the spare capacity on the SONET links (Exercise 3.7). Another example is when $\zeta_{eq} = \zeta_e, q = 1, 2, ..., Q_e$; then we can interpret ζ_e as the cost rate (e.g., monthly or yearly cost) of one LCU of the IP link e to be paid by the IP provider to the operator of the SONET network for realizing the IP link capacities. More discussion about cost components can be found later in Section 12.1.1 of Chapter 12.

3.9 SUMMARY AND FURTHER READING

In this chapter, we have considered a set of specific network technologies and presented related routing, flow, and capacity design examples. Although it is important to understand what a particular technology may or may not allow, and what design issues are specific to it, we had no space here to describe every technology in detail. Rather, we have given brief yet relevant information about each technology that is required for the purpose of network design. We have also included a few key book references that the reader can refer to for further information on these technologies.

Our examples will hopefully provide a good sense of where and how different types of multi-commodity flow models appear for different design problems. In essence, we have tried to accomplish the following by presenting technology related examples:

- how the multi-commodity flow network approach is applicable to the design of modern communication and computer networks;
- how specific features of particular technologies influence design objectives;
- how specific features of particular technologies lead to certain modelling assumptions that are expressed as relevant technology-dependent sets of constraint (demand and capacity constraints already discussed in Chapter 2);
- how the objectives and constraints are put together in design problem formulations, in a sense to extend the illustration already presented in Chapter 2.

Certainly, the list of technology examples presented here is not exhaustive. We do cover additional design problems in the rest of the book (refer to Section 9.6 in Chapter 9 for protection and restoration design). Similarly, to consider transient failures in IP networks, a model has been presented in Section 7.9. The concept of overlay networks has been recently considered where a virtual network is built for a service or services over an existing network. Location of nodes in such overlay networks depends on the latency cost and other factors. We will discuss location design models in Chapter 6 that can be useful for overlay network location design. Certainly, there are additional models scattered throughout the rest of the book.

The literature on structure, architecture, functionality and general modeling of communication and computer networks is extremely rich as you will notice for instance from the bibliography listed at the end of this book. In fact, the related literature constitutes a very considerable part of the whole literature devoted to telecommunications. This type of knowledge is very widespread and rather easily available in numerous books as well as in specialized journals in telecommunications and networking. Thus, as it is not in the mainstream of this book, we purposely do not list particular bibliographical references here (contrary to the rest of the chapters of this book), not to bias the reader with our favorite selection.

Finally, we wish to note that there are network design models and problems that do not use (or need not to use) the multi-commodity flow framework (e.g., [SWY03, YOY97], and § 8.2.4 in [RS02]); you will find more in open literature.

EXERCISES FOR CHAPTER 3

3.1. Modify formulation (3.2.1) and determine what other objective may be applicable in MPLS networks.

3.2. The example discussed in Section 1.4 can, in fact, be formulated like the model for ATM VP-design considered in Section 3.3. Write the example presented in Section 1.4 explicitly in the form of the multi-commodity flow formulation (3.3.2). Solve it by hand.

3.3. Consider the example presented in (2.4.10). Extend this formulation to consider demand volume at two different time periods (e.g., morning and afternoon) instead of just one time period. Use the existing demand volumes for one time period; the demand volume for the second time period is given as follow: $h_1 = 20, h_2 = 5, h_3 = 15$.

3.4. Generalize formulation (2.4.11) to consider multi-hour demand volumes while minimizing the total network capacity cost (hint: use t notation).

3.5. Generalize formulation (3.3.2) to consider multi-hour demand volumes while minimizing the total network capacity cost.

3.6. Formulate a bandwidth design problem for SONET UPSRs. (Hint: see formulation for BLSR bandwidth design problem discussed in Section 3.6.)

3.7. Formulate Problem (3.8.1) using the actual values of modules M and N for the 2-layer network example considered in Section 2.9.

II

DESIGN MODELING AND METHODS

Part II consists of five chapters that cover basic, normal-state network design: from formulations to algorithms, including numerical illustrations. By basic or normal-state design, we mean the design of the network to carry the normal (usual, everyday) demand volume without taking into consideration failures, demand shifts, complexity of the network architecture, and so on.

In Chapter 4, we begin with an extensive discussion on problem formulations and various types of multi-commodity flow network modelling approaches that may be applicable. Before we continue with discussing selected network design problems in more depth, we survey different optimization approaches, methods, and algorithms that are applicable in multi-commodity flow network design. This is done in Chapter 5.

Location and topological design problems are addressed in Chapter 6; these types of problems are faced at the early stages of network planing in the network management cycle.

In Chapter 7, network design for the shortest-path routing networks, used in modern packet networks, is discussed. Here, we present how to model flow problems where flows are induced by a link metric system. We then present several different formulations and solution approaches to determine optimal link metric system.

This part concludes with Chapter 8 on fair networks. The characteristic feature of fair networks is that the demand volumes between different pairs of nodes are elastic and, hence, the total flows are required to be assigned to demands in a fair way. Thus, we consider different notions of fairness, and discuss how solutions and approaches are affected.

CHAPTER 4

Network Design Problem Modeling

In this chapter we will introduce in a systematic manner a number of basic network design problems (NDPs) associated with the normal design of communication and computer networks. *Normal* (sometimes called "nominal" or regular) network design in our context means that only one state of the network is considered in design problem, namely the normal (or "nominal") operating state, i.e., the one with typical ("average") demand volumes and with all resources fully available.

Simply put, for the given demand volume we want to determine how much resource capacity is needed and how to economically distribute it in the network under a set of routing/flow constraints—this is broadly classified as uncapacitated design. Typically, such problems occur in medium to long term network planning. Once the capacity in a network is known (installed) and the demand volume is given, the problem changes to how to allocate flows on different paths in a manner that optimizes a given network goal (e.g., minimum cost routing or maximum total revenue). Even without any additional goal, we still face the flow allocation problem in the feasibility sense. Usually such allocation (and/or minimum cost routing) problems—called capacitated problems—are faced in short-term or near-time network design when capacity cannot be added to the network. Majority of these problems can be formulated either as link-path or node-link multi-commodity flow problems; we have already seen some examples of these types of problems in Chapters 2 and 3. As we progress through this chapter, we will explain where and how one formulation/model has advantage over the other. Further, we will show where and how routing restrictions, modularity of link capacity, non-linearities in the cost function, and other constraints arise and how to handle them.

As it will soon become clear to the reader, the variety of potentially important NDPs, even for the normal design case, is very large and it is not possible to discuss all of them. Therefore, in this chapter, we aim rather at formulating and discussing a selected set of basic problems and, equally important, at illustrating the basic rules of creating the formulations that will help the reader to devise problems on their own when such a necessity arises.

As we will see in Chapter 9, NDPs become more difficult and complicated when states other than the normal state are taken into account in the design process. Such non-normal states include situations when certain links and/or nodes are totally or partially failed and/or the demand volumes are altered, and lead to the problems of designing networks robust to failures and/or demand variations. In the subsequent chapters, the extensions of the basic design problems formulated below will be used for the purpose of designing resilient (robust) networks (Part III) and for the purpose of other types of normal design problems (Part II).

4.1 BASIC UNCAPACITATED AND CAPACITATED DESIGN PROBLEMS

We start our presentation with relatively simple and well-known formulations. As you will notice, in the formulations, we clearly distinguish between indices, constants, variables, objectives, and constraints. To avoid repetitiveness, sometimes some indices and constants are not explicitly listed when there is no ambiguity with the notation. Besides, unless stated explicitly otherwise, if a type of flow/capacity variable is not specified, then it is assumed to be continuous and non-negative. As you will see, in some formulations we use redundant variables and constraints in order to make the presentation easier to understand. Finally, we note that all formulations in this section define linear programming (LP) problems.

4.1.1 Uncapacitated Problems

Recall the simple uncapacitated NDP in the link-path formulation considered in Section 2.4 for a four-node network (Problem (2.4.11)). Now we give a general formulation of this (very basic) problem.

***LP:* D/SDP** **Link-Path Formulation**

Simple Design Problem

indices

$d = 1, 2, ..., D$ demands

$p = 1, 2, ..., P_d$ candidate paths for flows realizing demand d

$e = 1, 2, ..., E$ links

constants

δ_{edp} = 1, if link e belongs to path p realizing demand d; 0, otherwise

h_d volume of demand d

ξ_e unit (marginal) cost of link e

variables

x_{dp} flow allocated to path p of demand d (continuous non-negative)

y_e capacity of link e (continuous non-negative)

objective

$$\text{minimize } \boldsymbol{F} = \textstyle\sum_e \xi_e y_e \quad \text{(bandwidth cost)} \tag{4.1.1a}$$

constraints

$$\textstyle\sum_p x_{dp} = h_d, \quad d = 1, 2, ..., D \quad \text{(demand constraints)} \tag{4.1.1b}$$

$$\textstyle\sum_d \sum_p \delta_{edp} x_{dp} \le y_e, \quad e = 1, 2, ..., E \quad \text{(capacity constraints).} \tag{4.1.1c}$$

In then sequel vector $\boldsymbol{x} = (\boldsymbol{x}_1, \boldsymbol{x}_2, ..., \boldsymbol{x}_D)$ (where $\boldsymbol{x}_d = (x_{d1}, x_{d2}, ..., x_{dP_d})$ for $d = 1, 2, ..., D$) will be called *flow allocation vector*. Recall that the quantity $\underline{y}_e(\boldsymbol{x}) = \sum_d \sum_p \delta_{edp} x_{dp}$ in the left-hand side of the capacity constraints (4.1.1c) is called the link load, that variables take continuous values, and that (4.1.1) is a linear programming

(LP) problem (Section 5.1). Clearly, in the optimal solution of D/SDP, all constraints (4.1.1c) are binding, i.e., the links loads are equal to the links capacities (otherwise we would pay for the unused capacity). We deliberately use the inequality capacity constraint here because it is consistent with other (non-linear) formulations which soon will be considered. The above link-path formulation of D/SDP requires $\sum_d P_d = \bar{P} \times D$ path-flow variables x_{dp}, where $\bar{P}$ is the average number of the candidate paths per demand, and E link capacity variables. There are $D + E$ constraints (not counting the standard constraints for variables' non-negativity). Note that the link capacity variables are not necessary in the D/SDP formulation, as you will see in the next formulation, still they make it easier to understand the problem.

We would like to drive your attention to the two-line naming convention used for D/SDP as well as for all the problems in this book. In the left-hand side of the first line the type (*LP* - linear program) of the problem is specified, followed by the acronym of the problem (D/SDP), which is used to refer to this problem throughout the book. In this particular acronym, the letter D stands for "dimensioning", followed by the slash and the abbreviated name of this particular problem (SDP) which is given in full in the second line. This type of formulation (link-path in this case) is indicated in the right-hand side of the first line. Similarly, chapter-dependent problem naming conventions will be used throughout this book.

As we already know from Section 2.4, an optimal solution to Problem D/SDP can be obtained by allocating, for each demand d, all its demand volume h_d to one of its shortest candidate paths, with respect to the links unit costs. This property is called the shortest-path allocation rule (2.4.13). To investigate this issue in more detail we substitute the load of link e, i.e., the left-hand side of equation (4.1.1c), for variable y_e in the cost function (4.1.1a). In effect, we eliminate the link capacity variables and arrive at a new cost function:

$$\boldsymbol{F} = \sum_e \xi_e \sum_d \sum_p \delta_{edp} x_{dp} = \sum_d \sum_p x_{dp} \sum_e \xi_e \delta_{edp} = \sum_d \sum_p \zeta_{dp} x_{dp} \quad (4.1.2)$$

where $\zeta_{dp} = \sum_e \xi_e \delta_{edp}$ is the length (cost) of path p of demand d. Hence, Problem D/SDP can be equivalently rewritten as:

_LP:_ D/SDP/DLPF **Link-Path Formulation**

SDP—Decoupled Link-Path Formulation

variables

x_{dp} flow variable allocated to path p of demand d

objective

$$\text{minimize } \boldsymbol{F} = \sum_d \sum_p \zeta_{dp} x_{dp} \quad (4.1.3a)$$

constraints

$$\sum_p x_{dp} = h_d, \quad d = 1, 2, ..., D. \quad (4.1.3b)$$

D/SDP/DLPF is a decoupled version of the original problem D/SDP. In fact, it is a set of D independent minimization problems, each for a fixed demand d, of the form:

$$\textbf{\textit{minimize}} \quad F = \sum_p \zeta_{dp} x_{dp} \quad (4.1.4a)$$

$$\textbf{\textit{subject to}} \ \sum_p x_{dp} = h_d, \quad \text{all } x_{dp} \geq 0. \tag{4.1.4b}$$

This natural decoupling is due to the linear structure of the objective (4.1.3a). It is easy to see from (4.1.4) that the optimal solution allocates flows only to the shortest paths from the sets of candidate paths (route or routing lists), and that in the case of a demand d with more than one shortest path, the split of h_d among its shortest paths can be done arbitrarily.

The link-path formulation (4.1.1) is valid for both undirected and directed graphs. It requires using predetermined sets of candidate paths as an input (recall illustrations from Chapter 2); such a candidate path list can be generated ahead of time, for example, using K-shortest-path algorithms (refer to Appendix C) for an acceptable value K of the number of candidate paths. An alternative formulation, based on the node-link formulation for directed graphs, for Problem (4.1.1) is also possible (refer to Section 2.2). For this formulation, there are link-flow variables (instead of path-flow variables) needed for each demand d and link e and specifying the part of the demand volume h_d traversing link e. For the node-link formulation we need to introduce the link-node incidence relation; in order to do that, we introduce notations a_{ev} and b_{ev} for link-node incidence as explained in the formulation below.

***LP:* D/SDP** **Node-Link Formulation**

Simple Design Problem

indices

- $d = 1, 2, ..., D$ demands
- $e = 1, 2, ..., E$ arcs (directed links)
- $v = 1, 2, ..., V$ nodes

constants

- a_{ev} = 1 if link e originates at node v; 0, otherwise
- b_{ev} = 1 if link e terminates in node v; 0, otherwise
- s_d source node of demand d
- t_d sink node of demand d
- h_d volume of demand d
- ξ_e unit cost of link e

variables

- x_{ed} flow realizing demand d allocated to link e (continuous non-negative)
- y_e capacity of link e (continuous non-negative)

objective

$$\text{minimize } \boldsymbol{F} = \sum_e \xi_e y_e \tag{4.1.5a}$$

constraints

$$\sum_e a_{ev} x_{ed} - \sum_e b_{ev} x_{ed} = \begin{cases} h_d, & \text{if } v = s_d \\ 0, & \text{if } v \neq s_d, t_d, \\ -h_d, & \text{if } v = t_d \end{cases} \quad v = 1, 2, ..., V \quad d = 1, 2, ..., D \tag{4.1.5b}$$

$$\sum_d x_{ed} \leq y_e, \quad e = 1, 2, ..., E. \tag{4.1.5c}$$

The demand constraint (4.1.5b) is commonly referred to as the *flow conservation law*. Note that the left-hand side of (4.1.5c) is nothing but the load, $\underline{y}_e(\boldsymbol{x})$, of link e in Problem (4.1.1). The node-link formulation (4.1.5) of D/SDP requires $D \times E$ flow variables (link capacity variables are auxiliary), and $E + D \times V$ constraints (not counting the standard constraints for variables non-negativity).

Formulation (4.1.5) can be applied to undirected graphs as well, by substituting each (undirected) link by two directed, oppositely oriented links (arcs) with the same unit costs as the original link (refer to Exercise 4.1). Certainly, D/SDP in the node-link formulation can still be solved directly by allocating all demand volumes to their shortest paths, but this time the shortest paths are to be found by some shortest-path algorithm, as all possible paths for each demand are involved in formulation (4.1.5). For a survey of shortest-path algorithms (such as the Dijkstra algorithm or the Breadth-Search-First algorithm) see Appendix C.

Actually, we can introduce another node-link formulation involving less flow variables than formulation (4.1.5).

LP: D/SDP/MNLF **Node-Link Formulation**

SDP—Modified Node-Link Formulation

indices

$d = 1, 2, ..., D$ demands

$e = 1, 2, ..., E$ links

$v, v' = 1, 2, ..., V$ nodes

constants

a_{ev} = 1 if link e originates at node v; 0, otherwise

b_{ev} = 1 if link e terminates in node v; 0, otherwise

$h_{vv'}$ volume of demand d originating at node v and terminating at node v'

H_v $= \sum_{v' \neq v} h_{vv'}$ - total demand volume originating in node v

ξ_e unit cost of link e

variables

x_{ev} flow realizing *all* demands originating at node v on link e

y_e capacity of link e

objective

$$\text{minimize } \boldsymbol{F} = \sum_e \xi_e y_e \tag{4.1.6a}$$

constraints

$$\sum_e a_{ev} x_{ev} = H_v, \quad v = 1, 2, ..., V \tag{4.1.6b}$$

$$\sum_e b_{ev'} x_{ev} - \sum_e a_{ev'} x_{ev} = h_{vv'}, \quad v, v' = 1, 2, ..., V, \ v \neq v' \tag{4.1.6c}$$

$$\sum_v x_{ev} \leq y_e, \quad e = 1, 2, ..., E. \tag{4.1.6d}$$

TABLE 4.1 Model Comparison

	Number of Variables	Number of Constraints
Link-path formulation	$\bar{P} \times V'(V'-1) + \frac{1}{2}\bar{k} \times V = O(V^2)$	$\bar{P} \times V'(V'-1) + \frac{1}{2}\bar{k} \times V = O(V^2)$
Node-link formulation	$\frac{1}{2}\bar{k} \times V \times V'(V'-1) = O(V^3)$	$V \times V'(V'-1) + \frac{1}{2}\bar{k} \times V = O(V^3)$
Modified node-link formulation	$\frac{1}{2}\bar{k} \times V \times (V'+1) = O(V^2)$	$V'(V+1) + \frac{1}{2}\bar{k} \times V = O(V^2)$

The trick here is that constraint (4.1.6c) forces the total demand H_v generated in node v to flow out of node v, and constraint (4.1.6d) forces portion $h_{vv'}$ of the flow originated at node v which is destined for node v' to remain in v'.

The three alternative formulations of D/SDP (formulations (4.1.1), (4.1.5), and (4.1.6)) have certain advantages and disadvantages. As far as the number of variables and the number of constraints are concerned, we observe that for a directed graph the number of links is $E = \frac{1}{2}(\bar{k} \times V)$ assuming $\bar{k}$ to be the average degree of a node, and the number of demands $D = V' \times (V'-1)$ where $V'(\leq V)$ is the number of nodes generating demand to each other. Suppose that the average node degree $\bar{k}$ and the average number $\bar{P}$ of candidate paths per demand do not increase with V and that $V' = V$, i.e., every node has demand to another node. Then, the numbers of variables and constraints for the three formulations of D/SDP are as shown in Table 4.1.

Hence, asymptotically the link-path formulation (4.1.1) and the modified node-link formulation (4.1.6) require one order of magnitude (in terms of the number of nodes V) less variables and constraints than the standard node-link formulation (4.1.5). This observation suggests that the modified node-link formulation (4.1.6) is more efficient than the first node-link formulation (4.1.5). According to [JLFP93], the former one, due to dense coefficient matrix, can be harder to solve than the latter which is sparse in the same sense. In fact, the number of variables and constraints in the D/SDP formulations is not important in practice because the shortest-path allocation rule (2.4.13) applies; this issue becomes significant in the capacitated problems specified in the next section and in all non-trivial extensions of D/SDP.

Comparing the two types of formulations, we should notice that the link-path formulation (4.1.1) requires some preprocessing for computing sets of candidate paths for the demands and, hence, may be sometimes troublesome. On the other hand, predefined sets of paths can be very convenient since they allow for controlling the properties of actually allowable paths in an easy way; for instance, we may require to use only the paths with a limited number of hops which is in general not possible in the node-link formulation. Using the node-link formulations (4.1.5) and (4.1.6) we automatically scan all network paths and have no direct means for eliminating paths of certain undesirable features (e.g., too long) from consideration. Sometimes, however, we may exclude certain types of paths by setting certain link flows to zero. This issue is discussed in Section 6.3.4, after the formulation of Problem (6.3.7), and in the following example.

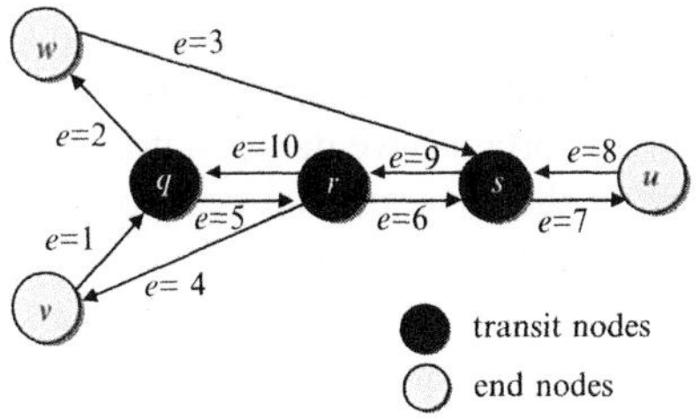

FIGURE 4.1 Network with Separate End and Transit Nodes

Example 4.1 *Eliminating Paths*

Consider the network in Figure 4.1 with separate sets of end and transit nodes, where the end nodes cannot be used as transit nodes in the paths. Suppose all links between end nodes and transit nodes have unit cost equal to 1 and the rest of the links (between transit nodes) have unit costs equal to 2. In such a case the node-link formulation (4.1.5) cannot be directly used because the shortest path for demand $d = 1$ from end node v to end node u traverses nodes q, w, and s. The resulting path composed of links $\{1, 2, 3, 7\}$ of length 5 is forbidden since it goes through the end node w, and the appropriate path for this demand is path $\{1, 5, 6, 7\}$ with length 6. To exclude this path we should assume $x_{21} = 0$ and not use this flow in the problem formulation (in constraints (4.1.5b) to (4.1.5c). In general, for each link e incoming to end node v, flow variables x_{ed} can be non-zero only for demands d with node v as the terminating node; similarly for link e outgoing from end node v the flow variables x_{ed} can be non-zero only for demands d with node v as the originating node. This will force the access links between end nodes and transit nodes to be used only by the demands from/to the considered end node.

In order to avoid the above described situation in the modified node-link formulation (4.1.6), for each link e outgoing from end node v ($a_{ev} = 1$) only the flow variables x_{ev} can be non-zero. All the other variables of the form x_{ew} (for all end nodes w different from v) must be equal to 0; this will forbid the use of links outgoing from node v for other demands than those originating at v. Certainly, similar assumptions must be used for links incoming to end nodes.

And what about the link-path formulation? Clearly, path $\{1, 2, 3, 7\}$ will be excluded from the route list of demand $d = 1$; it is as simple as that! ●

In order to find a solution for the node-link formulation we can either use a shortest-path algorithm or an LP solver (e.g., [CPL99]). In the latter case, however, we encounter a problem of postprocessing the LP solution in order to restore the path flows corresponding to the optimal link flows specified by the LP solution. This is not a difficult task; still, it requires some programming (refer to Exercise 4.2). In this context we emphasize a very important fact—using the link-path formulation we are still able to effectively take into account all the paths we wish to consider by means of the column generation technique for LP (refer to Section 5.4.2). For this to work, we only need an efficient algorithm for generating the paths. This is for instance the case when we wish to use paths that are limited in terms of the number of hops (links).

Recall that for the considered design problem D/SDP with the simple solution based on the shortest-path allocation rule, the question of whether to use the link-path or the node-link notation is not important—we may just use an appropriate path algorithm omitting the explicit use of any of the LP formulations. However, in almost all the problems that will be dealt with further in this book the considered issue can be of significant importance. We should add here that the link-path formulation always works while in some cases the node-link formulation is not applicable (at least in an efficient way—see Section 9.3.2). To this end, in our opinion the link-path formulation is generally more effective for practical NDPs, and we will usually use this formulation in the rest of the book. Advantages of a link-path formulation are further discussed later in Section 4.6.2.

4.1.2 Capacitated Problems

Problem D/SDP considered in Section 4.1.1 involves simultaneous flow allocation and link capacity optimization; the latter feature justifies the name "uncapacitated". Now suppose we want to consider problems where the capacity of the network links is given; this is a common case in a network that is already built. Such capacitated problems will be referred to through letter A (for Allocation). Probably the simplest capacitated problem is as follows:

***LP:* A/PAP** **Link-Path Formulation**

Pure Allocation Problem

constants

δ_{edp} = 1 if link e belongs to path p realizing demand d; 0, otherwise

h_d volume of demand d

c_e capacity of link e

variables

x_{dp} flow allocated to path p of demand d (continuous non-negative)

constraints

$$\textstyle\sum_p x_{dp} = h_d, \quad d = 1, 2, ..., D \tag{4.1.7a}$$

$$\textstyle\sum_d \sum_p \delta_{edp} x_{dp} \le c_e, \quad e = 1, 2, ..., E. \tag{4.1.7b}$$

The set of notations is almost the same as in Problem (4.1.1) except that we have c_e for given capacity instead of variable y_e in (4.1.1). Further, note that A/PAP has *no* objective function, hence solving A/PAP is equivalent just to finding a feasible solution, i.e., finding a flow allocation vector $\boldsymbol{x} = (\boldsymbol{x}_1, \boldsymbol{x}_2, ..., \boldsymbol{x}_D)$ (where $\boldsymbol{x}_d = (x_{d1}, x_{d2}, ..., x_{dP_d})$ for $d = 1, 2, ..., D$) which satisfies constraints (4.1.7). Problem A/PAP is again an LP problem; thus, such a solution can be found by Phase I of the simplex algorithm (see §1.2 in [Las70]). For A/PAP, no simple counterpart of the shortest-path allocation rule of D/SDP is available, since no reasonable notion of the shortest path can be thought of, at least in a straightforward way.

Note that the pure allocation problem A/PAP may be non-feasible. Therefore, it is sometimes convenient to use its modified formulation ensuring feasibility. This is shown below:

***LP:* A/PAP/MLPF** **Link-Path Formulation**

PAP—Modified Link-Path Formulation

variables

x_{dp} flow allocated to path p of demand d

z auxiliary continuous variable (of unrestricted sign)

objective

$$\text{minimize } z \tag{4.1.8a}$$

constraints

$$\textstyle\sum_p x_{dp} = h_d, \quad d = 1, 2, ..., D \tag{4.1.8b}$$

$$\textstyle\sum_d \sum_p \delta_{edp} x_{dp} \leq z + c_e, \quad e = 1, 2, ..., E. \tag{4.1.8c}$$

The modified allocation problem is always feasible and when its optimal objective, z^*, is non-positive then the corresponding optimal flows x^*_{dp} determine a feasible solution for the original allocation problem A/PAP (4.1.7). If not, then z^* determines the minimal necessary extra capacity required on at least one link (and possible on more, even on all, links) to ensure that the original problem is feasible.

Problem A/PAP can be written in the node-link formulation (refer to Exercise 4.3) and all the differences between the two alternative formulations discussed for the case of D/SDP concern A/PAP as well. The fact that A/PAP is an LP problem has a desirable consequence expressed by the following proposition.

PROPOSITION 4.1 *If A/PAP is feasible, then a solution $\boldsymbol{x}$ with at most $D + E$ non-zero flows exists.*

Proof:

Adding non-negative slack variables $\boldsymbol{s} = (s_1, s_2, ..., s_E)$ to constraints (4.1.7b), we arrive at the following equivalent LP problem in the standard form:

$$\textstyle\sum_p x_{dp} = h_d, \quad d = 1, 2, ..., D \tag{4.1.9a}$$

$$\textstyle\sum_d \sum_p \delta_{edp} x_{dp} + s_e = c_e, \quad e = 1, 2, ..., E. \tag{4.1.9b}$$

The number of non-zero (basic) variables in any basic feasible solution is at most equal to the number of equations in (4.1.9a) and (4.1.9b) (see §1.2 in [Las70]), implying the desired result (for details see Example 5.3 in Section 5.1.3). ∎

The above proof reveals even more; for instance, if all slack variables are greater than 0 in the optimal solution (i.e., all links are *unsaturated*) then exactly D non-zero flows suffice, resulting in a single-path flow allocation. Proposition 4.1 is actually a very important result and has far-reaching implications, specifically, how many paths are likely to carry non-zero flows in practical networks. It implies that demand volumes can be realized by means of a relatively small number of non-zero flows since D is, in most practical cases, much greater than E. For instance, in large networks of a grid structure (such as the Manhattan Street Network) and with demands defined for all node pairs, almost all demands are realized by means of only one non-zero flow.

Example 4.2 *Implication of Proposition 4.1*

Consider an undirected network with $V = 100$ nodes and the average node degree equal to 5. Then $E = 250$ and D is almost equal to 5,000. Proposition 4.1 implies that if A/PAP is feasible then we can realize at least 95% of demands on single paths and the remaining 5% (or less if some links are not saturated) on two paths, on the average. ●

Example 4.3 *A Fact*

Another interesting result for A/PAP is as follows:

Assign the entire demand volume of each demand d to one of its shortest paths with respect to the number of links. If in the resulting (non-bifurcated) solution all links are saturated (i.e. $\sum_d \sum_p \delta_{edp} x_{dp} \geq c_e$ *for* $e = 1, 2, ..., E$*) and at least one link is overloaded (i.e.,* $\sum_d \sum_p \delta_{edp} x_{dp} > c_e$ *for some e), then A/PAP is infeasible.*

The above result yields a necessary condition for feasibility of A/PAP. Although the condition is not directly usable in practice, it has an interesting dual interpretation and can be used in the Benders decomposition algorithm (see the proof based on the dual method in the solution of Exercise 5.17, Example 10.1 and Exercise 10.10). Exercise 4.4 asks the reader to prove the result in the straightforward way. ●

In many cases we may wish not only to find a feasible solution of A/PAP but the *best* feasible solution (in some sense). Such a sense can be expressed by introducing an objective function to the problem. For instance, objective (4.1.8a) leads to maximizing the minimal unused capacity (over all links). If we wish to explicitly maximize the total unused capacity left after flow allocation, this can be expressed by the objective:

$$\textbf{\textit{maximize}}\ \boldsymbol{F} = \sum_e r_e \left(c_e - \sum_d \sum_p \delta_{edp} x_{dp} \right) = \sum_e r_e (c_e - \underline{y}_e(\boldsymbol{x})) \tag{4.1.9}$$

where for each link e, $\underline{y}_e(\boldsymbol{x})$, is, as usual, the link load induced by the flow allocation vector $\boldsymbol{x}$, and r_e is the revenue associated with one unit of unused capacity of the link. Certainly, other revenue functions $\boldsymbol{F}$ can be considered, not necessarily linear. Incidently, objective (4.1.9) is equivalent to:

$$\textbf{\textit{minimize}}\ \boldsymbol{F} = \sum_d \sum_p \rho_{dp} x_{dp} \tag{4.1.10}$$

where $\rho_{dp} = \sum_e r_e \delta_{edp}$ is the unit revenue from path $\mathcal{P}_{dp}$ of demand d in terms of link revenue r_e. We will utilize this fact in Section 7.2.2.

Note that Proposition 4.1 applies to the above cases as well as to the problem formulated in the next section.

4.1.3 Mixed Problems

A mixed capacitated/uncapacitated problem (marked as AD) arises when we wish to dimension the link capacities within certain upper bounds, i.e., there are link capacity variables, but upper bounds on link capacities are given. This is a fairly simple extension of what we have discussed so far.

***LP:* AD/BLC** **Link-Path Formulation**

Bounded Link Capacities

constants

δ_{edp} = 1 if link e belongs to path p realizing demand d; 0, otherwise

h_d volume of demand d

c_e upper bound on the capacity of link e

ξ_e unit cost of link e

variables

x_{dp} flow allocated to path p of demand d (continuous non-negative)

y_e capacity of link e (continuous non-negative)

objective

$$\text{minimize } \boldsymbol{F} = \textstyle\sum_e \xi_e y_e \tag{4.1.11a}$$

constraints

$$\textstyle\sum_p x_{dp} = h_d, \quad d = 1, 2, ..., D \tag{4.1.11b}$$

$$\textstyle\sum_d \sum_p \delta_{edp} x_{dp} \le y_e, \quad e = 1, 2, ..., E \tag{4.1.11c}$$

$$y_e \le c_e, \quad e = 1, 2, ..., E. \tag{4.1.11d}$$

Another interpretation of this problem is that we wish to minimize the cost of routing implied by the link unit costs. To see this we may eliminate variables y_e (which are interpreted as link loads in this case: $y_e = \underline{y}_e(\boldsymbol{x}) = \sum_d \sum_p \delta_{edp} x_{dp}$) and transform the cost function into $\boldsymbol{F} = \sum_d \sum_p \zeta_{edp} x_{dp}$ where $\zeta_{dp} = \sum_e \delta_{edp} \xi_e$ is the cost of routing one unit of flow on path $\mathcal{P}_{dp}$ induced by the link unit costs. Note that other routing costs can be used as well (refer to Section 2.1).

4.2 ROUTING RESTRICTIONS

The optimization problems considered in Section 4.1 assume no routing constraints (besides the fact that in the link-path formulations the sets of candidate paths are predefined) and, hence, D/SDP can be solved by means of the shortest-path allocation rule. There are many cases, however, where additional constraints arise naturally in the network and can even be necessary for the technological requirements as well as operational restrictions. Below we will discuss several important problems involving such additional routing constraints. For this purpose we will use extensions of the capacitated problem A/PAP, keeping in mind that the considerations are valid for the uncapacitated tasks of the D/SDP type as well.

4.2.1 Path Diversity

Path diversity (PD) is a common requirement that forces splitting demand volumes into more than one path. Typically, this is considered so that a single link (node) failure cannot affect too much any demand, provided that the paths used for a demand pair are link-disjoint (node-disjoint).

***LP:* A/PD** **Link-Path Formulation**

Path Diversity

constants

- δ_{edp} = 1 if link e belongs to path p realizing demand d; 0, otherwise
- h_d volume of demand d
- n_d diversity factor for demand d
- c_e capacity of link e

variables

- x_{dp} flow allocated to path p of demand d (continuous non-negative)

constraints

$$\textstyle\sum_p x_{dp} = h_d, \quad d = 1, 2, ..., D \tag{4.2.1a}$$

$$\textstyle\sum_d \sum_p \delta_{edp} x_{dp} \leq c_e, \quad e = 1, 2, ..., E \tag{4.2.1b}$$

$$x_{dp} \leq h_d / n_d, \quad d = 1, 2, ..., D \quad p = 1, 2, ..., P_d. \tag{4.2.1c}$$

If *diversity factor*, n_d, appearing in constraint (4.2.1c) is an integer, then it will force the demand volume h_d to be split onto at least n_d different paths and that each individual flow will not exceed $(100/n_d)\%$ of the demand volume. The PD requirement combined with the appropriately specified sets of candidate paths makes it possible to have the flow allocation solution more robust to failures. For instance, if we require that for each demand the candidate paths are link-disjoint, then in the case of a single link failure any demand can loose at most $(100/n_d)\%$ of its volume.

Basically, formulation (4.2.1) makes sense when routing lists contain mutually disjoint paths (more precisely, when any two paths on a demand's list do not fail simultaneously). Assuming only single-link failures, a more general formulation than (4.2.1), not requiring preprocessed lists of link-disjoint paths (for algorithms of generating disjoint paths refer to Appendix C), is as follows.

LP: A/GD **Link-Path Formulation**
Generalized Diversity
variables

x_{dp} flow allocated to path p of demand d

constraints

$$\sum_p x_{dp} = h_d, \quad d = 1, 2, ..., D \tag{4.2.2a}$$

$$\sum_d \sum_p \delta_{edp} x_{dp} \le c_e, \quad e = 1, 2, ..., E \tag{4.2.2b}$$

$$\delta_{edp} x_{dp} \le h_d/n_d, \quad e = 1, 2, ..., E \quad d = 1, 2, ..., D \quad p = 1, 2, \ldots, P_d \tag{4.2.2c}$$

Constraint (4.2.2c) assures that no link carries more than the allowed portion of the demand volume. A drawback of both diversity formulations, A/PD and A/GD, is the large number of diversity constraints, (4.2.1c) and (4.2.2c), respectively. We will return with a way to resolve this issue later in Section 4.6.1.

Now, consider the uncapacitated problem D/SDP where PD is also imposed. An immediate question is: does the simple shortest-path allocation rule apply to D/SDP extended by adding PD requirement? The answer is essentially yes. The optimal rule is to allocate flow equal to h_d/n_d to the shortest path (with respect to link unit costs) of demand d, then the next portion h_d/n_d of demand volume to the next shortest path, and so on (note than less flow than h_d/n_d will in general be allocated to the last shortest path).

Finally, let us consider the diversity requirement for the node-link formulation. The generalized diversity requirement fits well into the node-link formulation since the constraint

$$x_{de} \le h_d/n_d$$

provides the node-link counterpart of (4.2.2c). Also, the node-disjoint paths can be handled, as explained later in Section 4.6.1.

4.2.2 Lower Bounds on Non-Zero Flows

In the PD case, the flows are bounded from above. A natural counterpart of PD is the requirement that non-zero flows are bounded from below, i.e., non-zero flows are not less than a predefined positive number. It appears that this lower-bound assumption adds a lot of difficulty to A/PAP (and D/SDP). The issue is that the statement "non-zero flow is greater than ..." is difficult to express as a mathematical programming constraint. In fact such a statement requires extra variables which are binary (0/1); this results in a mixed-integer linear programming (MIP) problem (see Section 5.2).

In order to formulate this problem, a binary variable is associated with each path-flow variable. If this binary variable takes value 1, then the associated path flow variable should carry at least the lower bounded flow; however, if flow is likely to be below this threshold, then we want the flow to be set to zero. We can accomplish this by introducing two additional sets of constraints as shown below:

MIP: **A/LBF** **Link-Path Formulation**

Lower-Bounded Flows

constants

δ_{edp} = 1 if link e belongs to path p realizing demand d; 0, otherwise

h_d volume of demand d

b_d lower bound on non-zero flows of demand d

c_e capacity of link e

variables

x_{dp} continuous flow variable allocated to path p of demand d

u_{dp} binary variable corresponding to x_{dp}

constraints

$$\sum_p x_{dp} = h_d, \quad d = 1, 2, ..., D \tag{4.2.3a}$$

$$x_{dp} \leq h_d u_{dp}, \quad d = 1, 2, ..., D \quad p = 1, 2, ..., P_d \tag{4.2.3b}$$

$$b_d u_{dp} \leq x_{dp}, \quad d = 1, 2, ..., D \quad p = 1, 2, ..., P_d \tag{4.2.3c}$$

$$\sum_d \sum_p \delta_{edp} x_{dp} \leq c_e, \quad e = 1, 2, ..., E. \tag{4.2.3d}$$

Constraints (4.2.3b) and (4.2.3c) assure that $x_{dp} > 0$ if, and only if, $u_{dp} = 1$, and that the non-zero flows are bounded from below by a positive demand-dependent limit b_d, as required. Note that constraint (4.2.3b) bounds the non-zero flows from above by h_d; this constraint is redundant (and can be removed) as it is implied by (4.2.3a). The presence of binary variables in the formulation of A/LBF makes the problem difficult to solve. In fact, no methods significantly different from the full search in the binary variables space (refer to branch-and-bound and branch-and-cut, Section 5.2) are known for this problem.

Clearly, the lower-bound requirement can be combined with PD in the link-path formulation. You will notice that the node-link formulation cannot be used for A/LBF at all.

4.2.3 Limited Demand Split

We now consider another type of possible requirement, referred to as *limited demand split*. The requirement of limited split of the demand volumes is somewhat contrary to PD - it assures that the demand volumes are realized with (at most) a predetermined number of non-zero path-flows, for instance, with just one non-zero flow. Incidently, the single-flow allocation is also called single-path allocation (routing), unsplittable allocation, or non-bifurcated allocation. In Section 2.4, we did illustrate this case, without presenting a formulation.

We first present a formulation for the non-bifurcated (single-path) flow allocation requirement. This formulation takes a somewhat different approach than using the usual flow allocation variables. Since, the flow is non-bifurcated, you either pick one path or another to carry the entire demand volume for a demand pair. As you can probably sense, this sounds a lot like a binary decision, which happens to be the case here. Also, we need to make sure, using binary variables, that the entire flow is carried on just one path.

***MIP:* A/SPA** **Link-Path Formulation**
Single-Path Allocation
constants
δ_{edp} = 1 if link e belongs to path p realizing demand d; 0, otherwise
h_d volume of demand d
c_e capacity of link e
variables
x_{dp} flow allocated to path p of demand d
u_{dp} binary variable associated with flow x_{dp}
constraints

$$x_{dp} = h_d u_{dp}, \quad d = 1, 2, ..., D \quad p = 1, ..., P_d \tag{4.2.4a}$$

$$\sum_p u_{dp} = 1, \quad d = 1, 2, ..., D \tag{4.2.4b}$$

$$\sum_d \sum_p \delta_{edp} x_{dp} \leq c_e, \quad e = 1, 2, ..., E. \tag{4.2.4c}$$

Constraint (4.2.4b) assures that only one binary variable associated with a given demand d is equal to 1 and, together with constraint (4.2.4a), imply that the path corresponding to the non-zero binary variable carries all the demand volume h_d. Again, the necessity of using the binary variables makes the problem difficult and virtually impossible to solve efficiently for large networks. In fact, there is not much hope for an efficient solution for the case of large networks since the problem is $\mathcal{NP}$-complete (for the importance of $\mathcal{NP}$-completeness the reader is referred to Appendix B), as the following proposition shows.

PROPOSITION 4.2 *The flow allocation problem A/SPA is $\mathcal{NP}$-complete.*

Proof:

The thesis of the proposition is a consequence of the two following facts.
Fact 1: The allocation flow problem A/PAP with only two demands ($D = 2$) and with integral flows (all x_{1p} and x_{2p} are integers) is $\mathcal{NP}$-complete.

This is shown both for directed graphs (Problem D2CIF) and for undirected graphs (Problem U2CIF) in Section 4 of [EIS76] and in Section B.8 of Appendix B.
Fact 2: The integral flow problem A/PAP is $\mathcal{NP}$-complete in the special case of homogeneous unit demands ($h_d \equiv 1$).

This follows from a simple modification of the basic construction for Problem D2CIF. The source node of the second demand (commodity) with demand volume equal to k can be replaced by k sources, each with demand volume equal to 1, and the source nodes of the new demands are connected to the source node of the replaced demand with directed links of capacity 1. Fact 2 directly implies that the problem of finding non-bifurcated flows is $\mathcal{NP}$-complete. ■

Note that A/SPA can be simplified and written in the form of the following integer programming (IP) problem:

***IP:* A/SPA** **Link-Path Formulation**

Single-Path Allocation

variables

u_{dp} binary variable corresponding to the flow allocated to path p of demand d

constraints

$$\sum_p u_{dp} = 1, \quad d = 1, 2, ..., D \tag{4.2.5a}$$

$$\sum_d h_d \sum_p \delta_{edp} u_{dp} \leq c_e, \quad e = 1, 2, ..., E. \tag{4.2.5b}$$

Recall that we have already used the same approach in Section 3.3.

The use of binary variables in the above problem combined with the technique applied in Section 4.2.2 for the lower-bounded flows makes it possible to formulate an entirely new variety of limited demand split problems. Below are two examples.

***IP:* A/ES** **Link-Path Formulation**

Equal Split Among k Paths

additional constants

k_d predetermined number of paths for demand d

variables

u_{dp} binary variable corresponding to flow allocated to path p of demand d

constraints

$$\sum_p u_{dp} = k_d, \quad d = 1, 2, ..., D \tag{4.2.6a}$$

$$\sum_d \left(\sum_p \delta_{edp} u_{dp} \right) h_d / k_d \leq c_e, \quad e = 1, 2, ..., E. \tag{4.2.6b}$$

To see why the above formulation assures the equal split you may consider flow variables x_{dp} and additional equations: $x_{dp} = h_d u_{dp} / k_d$ for $d = 1, 2, ..., D, p = 1, 2, ..., P_d$. Then inequalities (4.2.6b) are equivalent to the usual inequalities on link loads: $\sum_d \sum_p \delta_{edp} x_{dp} \leq c_e$ for $e = 1, 2, ..., E$. Hence, constraint (4.2.6a) assures that exactly k_d binary variables associated with a given demand d are equal to 1, and, together with constraint (4.2.6b), imply that each of the paths corresponding to the non-zero binary variable carries the $\left(\frac{1}{k_d}\right)$-th of the demand volume h_d.

MIP: **A/AS** **Link-Path Formulation**

Arbitrary Split Among k Paths

variables

x_{dp} flow allocated to path p of demand d

u_{dp} binary variable corresponding to the flow variable x_{dp}

constraints

$$\sum_p x_{dp} = h_d, \quad d = 1, 2, ..., D \tag{4.2.7a}$$

$$\sum_p u_{dp} = k_d, \quad d = 1, 2, ..., D \tag{4.2.7b}$$

$$x_{dp} \leq u_{dp} h_d, \quad d = 1, 2, ..., D \quad p = 1, 2, ..., P_d \tag{4.2.7c}$$

$$\sum_d \sum_p \delta_{edp} x_{dp} \leq c_e, \quad e = 1, 2, ..., E. \tag{4.2.7d}$$

Constraints (4.2.7b) and (4.2.7c) jointly force that for each demand d non-zero flows can be assigned to at most k_d paths. Formulation of some other capacitated allocation problems related to limited demand split are left to the reader (Exercises 4.5 to 4.9). An uncapacitated problem of this type (i.e., extension of D/SDP) is considered in Exercise 4.10.

At this point, it is important to notice that the node-link formulation *can* be used for the single-path allocation requirement (Problem A/SPA (4.2.5)):

IP: **A/SPA** **Node-Link Formulation**

Single-Path Allocation

indices

$d = 1, 2, ..., D$ demands

$e = 1, 2, ..., E$ links

$v = 1, 2, ..., V$ nodes

constants

a_{ev} = 1 if node v is the originating node of link e; 0, otherwise

b_{ev} = 1 if node v is the terminating node of link e; 0, otherwise

s_d source node of demand d

t_d sink node of demand d

h_d volume of demand d

c_e capacity of link e

variables

u_{de} binary variable corresponding to flow of demand d allocated to link e

constraints

$$\sum_d h_d u_{de} \leq c_e, \quad e = 1, 2, ..., E \tag{4.2.8a}$$

$$\sum_e a_{ev} u_{de} - \sum_e b_{ev} u_{de} = \begin{cases} 1, & \text{if } v = s_d \\ 0, & \text{if } v \neq s_d, t_d, \quad v = 1, 2, ..., V; d = 1, 2, ..., D \\ -1, & \text{if } v = t_d. \end{cases}$$

(4.2.8b)

Observe that formulation (4.2.8) allows for an extension limiting the number of hops in the paths (the problem of using paths with a limited number of hops in the link-path formulation is easily treated by candidate path pre-processing; refer to Appendix C for an algorithm generating shortest paths with the hop limit). To assure that the path for demand d traverses no more than n_d links the additional set of constraints is added:

$$\sum_e u_{de} \leq n_d, \quad d = 1, 2, ..., D. \tag{4.2.8d}$$

To the best of our knowledge, the node-link formulation does not apply to equal demand split nor to arbitrary split among the predefined number of paths. Still, somewhat unexpectedly, one can apply the node-link formulation to split the demand volumes among a fixed number of *link-disjoint paths* in a way shown below:

***IP:* A/ESLDP** **Node-Link Formulation**

Equal Split Among k Link-Disjoint Paths

additional constants

k_d predetermined number of paths for demand d

variables

u_{de} binary variable corresponding to flow of demand d allocated to link e

constraints

$$\sum_d u_{de} h_d / k_d \leq c_e, \quad e = 1, 2, ..., E \tag{4.2.10a}$$

$$\sum_e a_{ev} u_{de} - \sum_e b_{ev} u_{de} = \begin{cases} k_d, & \text{if } v = s_d \\ 0, & \text{if } v \neq s_d, t_d, \quad v = 1, 2, ..., V; d = 1, 2, ..., D \\ -k_d, & \text{if } v = t_d. \end{cases}$$

(4.2.10b)

As before, to see why the above formulation assures the equal split we consider flow variables x_{de} and additional equations: $x_{de} = h_d u_{de} / k_d$ for $d = 1, 2, ..., D, e = 1, 2, ..., E$. Then inequalities (4.2.10a) become equivalent to the standard inequalities on link loads $\sum_d \sum_p x_{de} \leq c_e$ for $e = 1, 2, ..., E$, and equalities (4.2.10b) (through multiplying all equations (4.2.10b) for each demand d by h_d / k_d) to the standard flow conservation equations:

$$\sum_e a_{ev} x_{de} - \sum_e b_{ev} x_{de} = \begin{cases} h_d, & \text{if } v = s_d \\ 0, & \text{if } v \neq s_d, t_d, \quad v = 1, 2, ..., V; d = 1, 2, ..., D \\ -h_d, & \text{if } v = t_d. \end{cases}$$

Also equal split among *node-disjoint paths* can be covered by the node-link notation. To accomplish this, an additional requirement is added to formulation (4.2.10):

$$\sum_e a_{ev} u_{de} \leq 1, \quad \text{if } v \neq s_d, t_d, \quad v = 1, 2, ..., V; d = 1, 2, ..., D. \tag{4.2.10c}$$

Alternatively, if constraint (4.2.10c) is *not* included, then the required node-disjointness can be achieved through preprocessing the network graph by appropriately splitting each node into two parts joined with an auxiliary link of infinite capacity (refer to Section 4.6.1 and Exercise 4.11). Observe that, in both cases, analogous link-path formulations would require only predefined sets of link-disjoint or node-disjoint paths (refer to Appendix C for the disjoint-path algorithms) so the link-path problem formulation remains the same.

4.2.4 Integral Flows

The requirement of integral flow arises naturally when we wish to allocate demand volumes in certain demand modules. For example, in transport networks, demand volume is usually given in terms of modular units such as the number of optical careers OC-3s needed between two nodes in a synchronous optical network (Section 3.5).

MIP: **A/MFA** **Link-Path Formulation**
Modular Flow Allocation
constants

- δ_{edp} = 1 if link e belongs to path p realizing demand d; 0, otherwise
- L_d demand module for demand d
- H_d volume of demand d expressed as the number of demand modules
- h_d demand volume ($h_d = L_d H_d$)
- c_e capacity of link e

variables

- x_{dp} flow allocated to path p of demand d (continuous non-negative)
- u_{dp} non-negative *integral* variable associated with variable x_{dp}

constraints

$$x_{dp} = L_d u_{dp}, \quad d = 1, 2, ..., D \quad p = 1, 2, ..., P_d \tag{4.2.11a}$$

$$\sum_p x_{dp} = h_d, \quad d = 1, 2, ..., D \tag{4.2.11b}$$

$$\sum_d \sum_p \delta_{edp} x_{dp} \leq c_e, \quad e = 1, 2, ..., E. \tag{4.2.11c}$$

Dropping flow variables x_{dp}, we arrive at a simplified formulation:

IP: **A/MFA** **Link-Path Formulation**
Modular Flow Allocation

variables

u_{dp} non-negative integral variable associated with the flow on path p of demand d

constraints

$$\textstyle\sum_p u_{dp} = H_d, \quad d = 1, 2, ..., D \tag{4.2.12a}$$

$$\textstyle\sum_d L_d \sum_p \delta_{edp} u_{dp} \le c_e, \quad e = 1, 2, ..., E. \tag{4.2.12b}$$

The above formulation can be further simplified when the demand module for the entire network is the same, i.e., $L_d \equiv L$ (e.g., all are OC-3s). In this case, the capacity of link c_e can be given in units equal to L, i.e., we replace c_e by c_e/L and constraint (4.2.12b) by $\sum_d \sum_p \delta_{edp} u_{dp} \le c_e$.

The flow modularity requirement is in some cases equivalent to the limited demand split requirement discussed in Section 4.2.3. In particular, the single-path allocation problem A/SPA (4.2.4) is equivalent to A/MFA (4.2.12) with $H_d = 1$ and $L_d = h_d$ for $d = 1, 2, ..., D$. Thus, it follows from Proposition 4.2 that A/MFA is $\mathcal{NP}$-complete. Note that uncapacitated design problems of type D may also have modular flows as we have shown here for capacitated (allocation) problems of type A.

4.3 NON-LINEAR LINK DIMENSIONING, COST, AND DELAY FUNCTIONS

So far, we have mostly discussed the various types of flow variables (continuous, binary, and integral) assuming that link capacities are equal to link loads for the uncapacitated problems. In this section, we will discuss the influence of the other types of link dimensioning functions (besides the so far assumed case of linear dimensioning functions) on the formulation of uncapacitated NDPs. Typically, the notion of the link cost function is built upon the notion of the link dimensioning function. The link dimensioning function $F_e(\underline{y}_e)$ determines the relationship between the link load, $\underline{y}_e$ (the sum of all flows through the link, expressed in demand volume units, DVUs), and the minimal capacity, y_e, of the link (expressed in link capacity units; LCUs) necessary to carry the load. Then the cost of the link is expressed as the link capacity times an appropriate unit cost coefficient, ξ_e. So far the link cost functions, $\xi_e F_e(\underline{y}_e)$, were simply the linear functions (refer to the cost $\boldsymbol{F}$ given by (4.1.1) in the formulation of D/SDP) of the form $F_e(\underline{y}_e) = \xi_e \underline{y}_e$, where the link load is equal to the link capacity. The main cases considered in this section are: modular links, links with convex cost, and links with concave cost.

4.3.1 Modular Links

Link modularity is a common feature in communications networks. For instance, in the North-American pulse-code modulation (PCM) system, the digital trunk groups (Section 3.4) have modularity of $M = 24$ voice circuits; in European PCM system, the digital telephone trunk groups (i.e., PCM primary groups) have modularity of $M = 30$ trunks (in

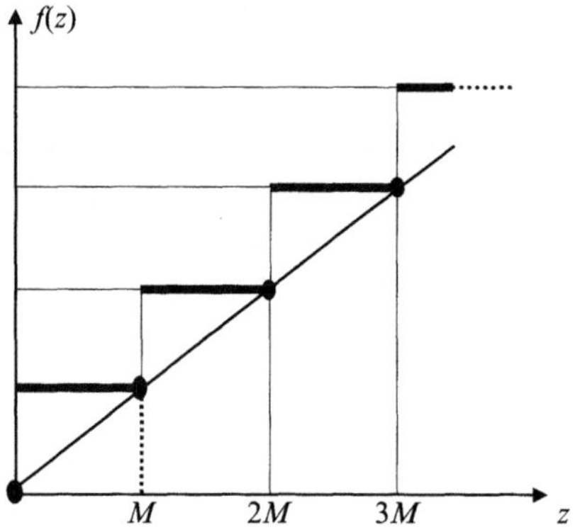

FIGURE 4.2 Cost of a Modular Link Versus Link Load

fact 32, but 2 trunks are used for different purpose than carrying voice); the SDH network at the VC-4 level has links of modularity of 63 PCM primary groups (Section 3.5), and so on. A typical cost function $F(\underline{y})$ of the link load, $\underline{y}$, for modular links is illustrated in Figure 4.2.

Consider again the uncapacitated design problem D/SDP (4.1.1). If we now introduce links with modular capacity, then the role of variable y_e, as given in (4.1.1) where it was a continuous variable, changes to a discrete variable taking into account the modularity aspect. Essentially, this means that Problem (4.1.1) can be modified to obtain the following MIP formulation:

***MIP:* D/ML** **Link Path Formulation**

Modular Links

indices

$d = 1, 2, ..., D$ demands

$p = 1, 2, ..., P_d$ candidate paths for demand d

$e = 1, 2, ..., E$ links

constants

δ_{edp} = 1, if link e belongs to path p realizing demand d; 0, otherwise

h_d volume of demand d

ξ_e cost of one capacity module on link e

M size of the link capacity module

variables

x_{dp} flow allocated to path p of demand d (continuous non-negative)

y_e capacity of link e expressed in the number of modules (non-negative integer)

objective

$$\text{minimize } \boldsymbol{F} = \textstyle\sum_e \xi_e y_e \qquad (4.3.1a)$$

constraints

$$\textstyle\sum_p x_{dp} = h_d, \quad d = 1, 2, ..., D \qquad (4.3.1b)$$

$$\sum_d \sum_p \delta_{edp} x_{dp} \le M y_e, \quad e = 1, 2, ..., E. \tag{4.3.1c}$$

An obvious heuristic rule to solve this problem could consist in assuming a linear approximation of the link dimensioning function (increasing line in Figure 4.2), solving the resulting LP problem and rounding-up the obtained link capacities. In general, this leads to solutions far from optimal and, in fact, it can get worse when the link capacity module, M, is much larger than the flow unit which is a typical case. This is illustrated in Example 4.4.

Example 4.4 *Modular Example*

Consider a fully meshed network with V nodes requesting one unit of flow to be realized between each pair of nodes ($h_d = 1, d = 1, 2, ..., D = V(V-1)/2$). The cost of one capacity module on each link is equal to 1 ($\xi_e \equiv 1$) and the link capacity module M equals to D flow units. Since one link module is able to accommodate all demand volumes, it is clear that every optimal solution of D/ML corresponds to a spanning tree $T \subseteq E$, with $y_e = 1$ if $e \in T$ and $y_e = 0$, otherwise. The minimal cost of every such solution is equal to $V - 1$, since every tree with V nodes has $V - 1$ links. In contrast, the shortest-path allocation rule would lead to a network with all links loaded with one unit of flow. Hence, the rounded-up solution would lead to a full network with $y_e = 1$ for $e = 1, 2, ..., E = V(V - 1)/2$ and with the cost equal to $V(V - 1)/2$, i.e., $V/2$ times greater than the minimal cost! ●

Note that the shortest-path allocation rule does not apply because it may be cheaper to use a longer path to take advantage of the otherwise unused capacity of the installed modules. In fact, D/ML with link modularity is an $\mathcal{NP}$-complete problem which is easy to see using an argument similar to that of Example 4.4, as shown below.

PROPOSITION 4.3 *Problem D/ML (4.3.1) with modular links is $\mathcal{NP}$-complete.*

Proof:

We will show that the considered problem solves the Steiner tree problem (STP) which is known to be $\mathcal{NP}$-complete (see [GJ79]). For our purposes, STP can be stated as follows: given a list of nodes $v = 1, 2, ..., V$, a proper subset of nodes $V' \subseteq V$ and a list of links $e = 1, 2, ..., E$ with given weights ξ_e, find a subgraph $T \subseteq E$ such that T contains a path joining any pair of nodes in V' and minimizes the cost:

$$\xi(T) = \sum_{e \in T} \xi_e. \tag{4.3.2}$$

In other words, STP consists of finding a lightest tree spanning subset V'. The issue is that the Steiner tree can contain some, but not necessarily all, nodes from $V \backslash V'$ and, hence, the problem is not equivalent to just finding the lightest tree spanning the set of all nodes V. In fact, the latter problem is easy to solve by the Kruskal or Prim algorithm (see [Kru56]). Proceeding as in Example 4.4, we assign a demand d with volume h_d equal to 1 to each pair of nodes in V' and put $M = V'(V' - 1)/2$. Then an optimal solution of (4.3.1) solves the introduced version of STP. ■

The following problem is a generalization of D/ML admitting multiple module sizes. Note that this increases the number of variables associated with each link since one set of such variables is needed for each modular unit type ($k = 1, 2, ..., K$).

***MIP:* D/LMMS** **Link-Path Formulation**

Link With Multiple Modular Sizes

additional indices

$k = 1, 2, ..., K$ types of modules

constants

δ_{edp} = 1, if link e belongs to path p realizing demand d; 0, otherwise

h_d volume of demand d

ξ_{ek} cost of one capacity module of type k on link e

M_k size of the link capacity module of type k

variables

x_{dp} flow allocated to path p of demand d

y_{ek} number of modules of type k on link e (non-negative integer)

objective

$$\text{minimize } \boldsymbol{F} = \textstyle\sum_e \sum_k \xi_{ek} y_{ek} \tag{4.3.3a}$$

constraints

$$\textstyle\sum_p x_{dp} = h_d, \quad d = 1, 2, ..., D \tag{4.3.3b}$$

$$\textstyle\sum_d \sum_p \delta_{edp} x_{dp} \le \sum_k M_k y_{ek}, \quad e = 1, 2, ..., E. \tag{4.3.3c}$$

Note that if the link modules are ordered according to the increasing size ($M_1 < M_2 < ... < M_K$) then typically $\xi_{e1} < \xi_{e2} < ... < \xi_{eK}$ for each link e. This property leads to the cost function depicted in Figure 4.3. In this example we have assumed $K = 2$, $M_2 = 2M_1$ and $\xi_{e1} < \xi_{e2} < 2\xi_{e1}$.

Still another way of introducing modular cost functions with different modules is the *incremental characterization* [DS98, Wes00]. Now K denotes the number of steps, and $m_1, m_2, ..., m_K$ are the consecutive incremental values of loads at which the cost function increases (jumps). The cost of each incremental module m_k on link e is equal to ξ_{ek}. The basic assumption of this cost model is that when the module number k is installed on a link, then all incremental modules j with $j < k$ must also be installed. This leads to the following modular formulation:

***MIP:* D/LIM** **Link-Path Formulation**

Links With Incremental Modules

constants

δ_{edp} = 1, if link e belongs to path p realizing demand d; 0, otherwise

h_d volume of demand d

ξ_{ek} incremental cost of one capacity module of type k on link e

m_k incremental size of the link capacity module of type k

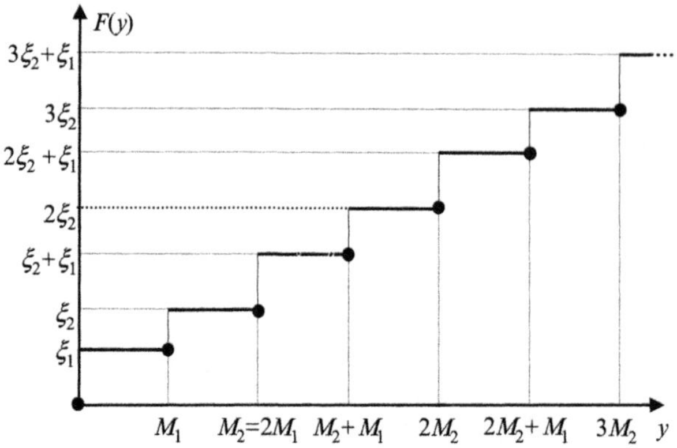

FIGURE 4.3 Cost of a Link with Multiple Modules

variables

x_{dp} flow allocated to path p of demand d

u_{ek} *binary* variable indicating whether incremental module of type k is installed on link e

objective

$$\text{minimize } \boldsymbol{F} = \textstyle\sum_e \sum_k \xi_{ek} u_{ek} \tag{4.3.4a}$$

constraints

$$\textstyle\sum_p x_{dp} = h_d, \quad d = 1, 2, ..., D \tag{4.3.4b}$$

$$\textstyle\sum_d \sum_p \delta_{edp} x_{dp} \leq \sum_k m_k u_{ek}, \quad e = 1, 2, ..., E \tag{4.3.4c}$$

$$u_{e1} \geq u_{e1} \geq ... \geq u_{eK}, \quad e = 1, 2, ..., E. \tag{4.3.4d}$$

This formulation will be mentioned in Section 10.4 discussing methods for solving restoration design problems with modular links. Note that uncapacitated modular design is related to topological design (Section 2.7 and Chapter 6) since the first step of the modular capacity function can represent the cost of introducing a new link.

4.3.2 Convex Cost and Delay Functions

An important type of a non-linear cost function is the convex function (for the notion of convexity refer to Appendix A). We first start with its definition. A function $f : [0, \infty) \to \mathcal{R}$ is *convex* if, and only if, for each two points z_1, z_2 in $[0, \infty)$ and each $\alpha \in [0, 1]$, the following relation holds

$$\alpha f(z_1) + (1 - \alpha) f(z_2) \geq f(\alpha z_1 + (1 - \alpha) z_2).$$

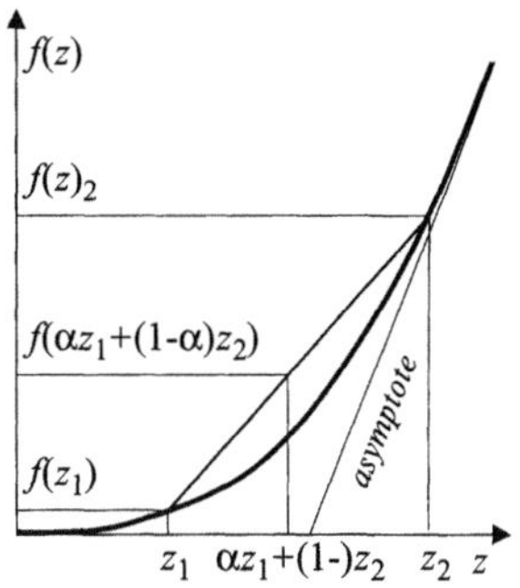

FIGURE 4.4 Convex Function

This is depicted through Figure 4.4. Note that if in the above definition, the strong inequality holds (for $0 < \alpha < 1$), then the function is called *strictly convex.*

Typically, convex cost functions appear in communications network applications to describe delay. For example, link e of a packet network can be modeled as a $M/M/1$ queue (for example, see [BG92] and the discussion in Section 1.3.1), and the average delay experienced by the packets sent along the link is expressed by a convex function of the link load $\underline{y}_e$ given in pps (packets per second), as it goes from 0 to c_e (the given link capacity in pps). The delay function is as follows:

$$F_e(\underline{y}_e) = \frac{1}{c_e - \underline{y}_e}, \qquad 0 \leq \underline{y}_e < c_e. \tag{4.3.5}$$

We now show an extension of A/PAP (4.1.7) by introducing a non-linear (convex) cost function:

***CXP:* A/CCF** **Link-Path Formulation**

Convex Cost Function

indices

$d = 1, 2, ..., D$ demands

$p = 1, 2, ..., P_d$ candidate paths for flows realizing demand d

$e = 1, 2, ..., E$ links

constants

δ_{edp} = 1 if link e belongs to path p realizing demand d; 0, otherwise

h_d volume of demand d

$F_e(\cdot)$ convex cost function of link e

c_e capacity of link e

variables

x_{dp} flow allocated to path p of demand d (continuous non-negative)

$\underline{y}_e$ load of link e (continuous non-negative)

objective

$$\text{minimize } \boldsymbol{F} = \textstyle\sum_e F_e(\underline{y}_e) \tag{4.3.6a}$$

constraints

$$\sum_p x_{dp} = h_d, \quad d = 1, 2, ..., D \tag{4.3.6b}$$

$$\sum_d \sum_p \delta_{edp} x_{dp} = \underline{y}_e, \quad e = 1, 2, ..., E \tag{4.3.6c}$$

$$\underline{y}_e \leq c_e, \quad e = 1, 2, ..., E. \tag{4.3.6d}$$

In the above formulation the acronym CXP stands for convex programming problem (refer to Appendix A for the definition of the convex programming problem). Certainly, we are aware that functions are not constants; we list them among constants not to create another category of problem parameters. Observe that if we use functions

$$F_e(\underline{y}_e) = \frac{\underline{y}_e}{c_e - \underline{y}_e}, \quad e = 1, 2, ..., E \tag{4.3.7}$$

in (4.3.6a) then the resulting objective is proportional to the average network delay experienced by the packets (see Problem (7.1.7) in Section 7.1.1). Note that strictly speaking functions $F_e(\cdot)$ of the form (4.3.5) and (4.3.7) are not meaningful outside interval $[0, c_e]$ and they are infinite for $\underline{y}_e = c_e$.

Convex functions can also be used to convert capacitated flow allocation problems to uncapacitated ones using penalty functions; we need to ensure that the penalty cost chosen is convex and incurs a heavy cost if the link capacity is violated. For example, such a penalty function is obtained by using the following for some large link-dependent positive penalty coefficient ξ_e:

$$F_e(\underline{y}_e) = \begin{cases} 0 & \text{if } \underline{y}_e \leq c_e \\ \xi_e(\underline{y}_e - c_e)^2 & \text{if } \underline{y}_e > c_e. \end{cases}$$

***CXP:* A/CPF** **Link-Path Formulation**

Convex Penalty Function

constants

- δ_{edp} = 1 if link e belongs to path p realizing demand d; 0, otherwise
- h_d volume of demand d
- c_e capacity of link e
- $F_e(\cdot)$ convex penalty function of link e

variables

- x_{dp} flow allocated to path p of demand d
- $\underline{y}_e$ load of link e

objective

$$\text{minimize } \boldsymbol{F} = \sum_e F_e(\underline{y}_e) \tag{4.3.8a}$$

constraints

$$\sum_p x_{dp} = h_d, \quad d = 1, 2, ..., D \tag{4.3.8b}$$

$$\sum_d \sum_p \delta_{edp} x_{dp} = \underline{y}_e, \quad e = 1, 2, ..., E. \tag{4.3.8c}$$

If we additionally assume that the functions $F_e(\cdot)$ are non-decreasing (which is the case in most practical cases), then the optimal flow allocations in the two problems formulated above are, in general, bifurcated. (Observe that $f(0) = 0$ and $f(x) \geq 0$ for $x \geq 0$ is sufficient for a convex function $f(x)$ to be non-decreasing in $[0, \infty)$, refer to Exercise 4.12.) The reason is that for a non-decreasing convex cost function f we have $f(z_1)/z_1 \leq f(z_2)/z_2$ for $z_1 < z_2$ (the strict inequality holds for strictly convex functions) so it is beneficial to split the demand volumes to several paths, at least when the paths are of similar cost (refer to Exercise 4.13).

The considered optimization problems are convex (they address minimization of a convex objective function subject to linear constraints) and as such have no local minima but only one global minimum of the objectives (4.3.8) or (4.3.13), attained possibly in more than one feasible point (the set of optimal points is convex), (refer to [Las70] and Appendix A). That is why in the case when the considered cost functions are differentiable (as in Problem (4.3.6)) some form of constrained gradient minimization techniques can be used (refer to Section 5.5).

In any case, however, the convexity itself is sufficient to convert the considered problems into their close LP approximations. In our case the basic idea is to substitute the cost (or penalty) functions $F_e(\cdot)$ with their *piecewise linear* approximations. We first describe such an approximation before returning to model formulation.

Example 4.5 *Piecewise Linear Approximation of a Convex Function*

Define the function

$$f(z) = \begin{cases} 0 & \text{for } 0 \leq z \leq 1 \\ (z-1)^2 & \text{for } z > 1. \end{cases} \tag{4.3.9}$$

already considered for Problem (4.3.8). A piecewise linear approximation of (4.3.9) consisting of four linear pieces can be as follows (as shown in Figure 4.5):

$$f(z) = \begin{cases} 0 & \text{for } 0 \leq z \leq 1 \\ z-1 & \text{for } 1 \leq z < 2 \\ 3(z-2)+1 = 3z-5 & \text{for } 2 \leq z < 3 \\ 10(z-3)+4 = 10z-26 & \text{for } z \geq 3. \end{cases} \tag{4.3.10}$$

●

In the general case we consider the function $f(z)$ defined as:

$$f(z) = f_k(z) = a_k z + b_k, \quad s_{k-1} \leq z < s_k, \quad k = 1, 2, ..., K \tag{4.3.11}$$

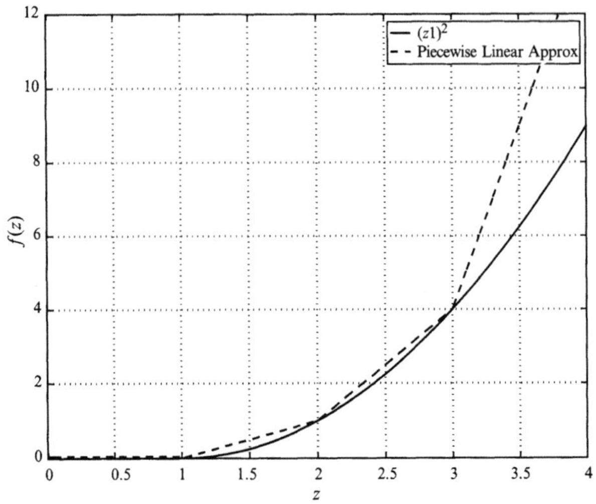

FIGURE 4.5 Piecewise Linear Approximation of a Convex Function

(where $s_1 = 0$ and s_K can be equal to $+\infty$) for a piecewise linear approximation of the convex function $f(z)$, $z \geq 0$ and suppose that we are given a number y where $y \geq 0$. The crucial observation that leads to calculating the value of the value of $f(y)$ within the LP framework is that due to convexity the equality

$$f(z) = \max_{k=1,2,\ldots,K} \{a_k z + b_k\}$$

holds true (Figure 4.5). Hence, the optimal solution of the following LP problem will return the correct value of $f(y)$, i.e. $r = f(y)$ (refer to Exercises 4.14 and 4.15):

$$\begin{aligned} &\textbf{\textit{minimize}} \quad r \\ &\textbf{\textit{subject to}} \quad r \geq a_k y + b_k, \quad k = 1, 2, \ldots, K. \end{aligned} \qquad (4.3.12)$$

The above observation makes it possible to transform convex mathematical programming problems such as (4.3.6) or (4.3.8) to LP problems, as illustrated below for Problem A/CPF (4.3.8) (also see Exercise 4.16).

***LP:* A/CPF/PLA** **Link-Path Formulation**

Convex Penalty Function—Piecewise Linear Approximation

additional indices

$k = 1, 2, \ldots, K_e$ consecutive pieces of the linear approximation of $F_e(\cdot)$

additional constants

a_{ek}, b_{ek} coefficients of the linear pieces of the piecewise linear approximation of $F_e(\cdot)$

variables

x_{dp} flow allocated to path p of demand d

$\underline{y}_e$ load of link e

r_e continuous variable approximating $F_e(\underline{y}_e)$

objective

$$\text{minimize } \boldsymbol{F} = \sum_e r_e \qquad (4.3.13a)$$

constraints

$$\sum_p x_{dp} = h_d, \quad d = 1,2,...,D \qquad (4.3.13b)$$

$$\sum_d \sum_p \delta_{edp} x_{dp} = \underline{y}_e, \quad e = 1,2,...,E \qquad (4.3.13c)$$

$$r_e \geq a_{ek}\underline{y}_e + b_{ek}, \quad e = 1,2,...,E \quad k = 1,2,...,K_e. \qquad (4.3.13d)$$

Assuming that the piecewise linear approximation has the same number K of pieces for every link, the above LP programme contains E additional variables and $E \times K$ additional constraints with respect to the original approximated problem.

In many applications it is not important exactly what the equations (4.3.11) of the linear pieces of the approximation are; only the slopes and where they change really matter. Assuming that the first linear piece starts at the origin (0,0), that the slopes of the consecutive pieces are a_k, $k = 1,2,...,K$, and that the consecutive break points at which the slope changes are $0 = s_0 < s_1 < s_2 < ... < s_K$ (where s_K can be equal to $+\infty$), the approximation analogous to (4.3.12) is as follows:

$$\begin{array}{ll} \textit{minimize} & a_1 z_1 + a_2 z_2 + ... + a_K z_K \\ \textit{subject to} & y = z_1 + z_2 + ... + z_K \\ & 0 \leq z_1 \leq s_1 - s_0 \\ & 0 \leq z_2 \leq s_2 - s_1 \\ & ... \\ & 0 \leq z_K \leq s_K - s_{K-1}. \end{array} \qquad (4.3.14)$$

Due to convexity, we have that $a_1 < a_2 < ... < a_K$; this is why the approximation works. If $s_{k-1} \leq y < s_k$, the minimization in (4.3.14) will set z_1 to s_1, then z_2 to $s_2 - s_1$, ... , z_{k-1} to $s_{k-1} - s_{k-2}$ and z_k to $y - s_{k-1}$; all the remaining s_j will be set to 0. In a more compact form, the problem can be written in the following way:

$$\begin{array}{ll} \textit{minimize} & \sum_k a_k z_k \\ \textit{subject to} & \sum_k z_k = y \\ & 0 \leq z_k \leq m_k, \quad k = 1,...,K. \end{array} \qquad (4.3.15)$$

where $m_k = s_k - s_{k-1}$, so it is also enough to know only the distance m_k between the consecutive break points.

Finally, note that all the problems considered in Section 4.3.2 can be formulated in the node-link notation as well.

We end this section with a classical convex capacity design problem for data networks involving linear objective and convex constraints. The problem is considered under the requirement that the routing is fixed and that the network is required to address a bound for average packet delay ([BG92]). Note that fixed routing implies that the link loads $\underline{y}_e$ are fixed. The delay constraint is convex and is based on the $M/M/1$ delay model (see (7.1.5) in Section 7.1.1 for an explanation on the network-wide delay).

***CXP:* D/CD/FRDC**
Capacity Design With Fixed Routing and Delay Constraint
indices

$e = 1, 2, \ldots, E$ links

constants

$\underline{y}_e$ load on link e induced by fixed routing
ξ_e unit cost of link e
H total traffic volume, $H = \sum_d h_d$, where h_d is the demand volume for demand d
$\hat{\mathcal{D}}$ acceptable delay

variables

y_e capacity of link e (non-negative continuous)

objective

$$\text{minimize } \boldsymbol{F} = \sum_e \xi_e y_e \qquad (4.3.16a)$$

constraints

$$y_e \geq \underline{y}_e, \quad e = 1, 2, ..., E \qquad (4.3.16b)$$

$$\frac{1}{H} \sum_e \frac{\underline{y}_e}{y_e - \underline{y}_e} \leq \hat{\mathcal{D}}. \qquad (4.3.16c)$$

This problem has an analytical solution for capacity y_e which is given as follows:

$$y_e = \underline{y}_e + \frac{1}{\hat{\mathcal{D}}} \sqrt{\frac{\underline{y}_e}{H \xi_e}} \left(\sum_l \sqrt{\frac{\xi_l \underline{y}_l}{H}} \right), \quad e = 1, 2, ..., E. \qquad (4.3.17)$$

The optimal solution can be obtained by observing that for continuous values of capacity variables, the delay constraint (4.3.16c) actually satisfies equality at the optimal solution (otherwise, capacity can be reduced). The above solution can be easily obtained using Karush-Kuhn-Tucker conditions (refer to Section A.2 in Appendix A) or the classical Lagrangian multiplier method (Exercise 4.17). In general, convex constraints can be linearized using the technique described earlier in this section, and the problems with convex constraints can be transformed to their LP approximations as well. This method is applied in Chapter 13.

4.3.3 Concave Link Dimensioning Functions

The flip-side of a convex function is a concave function. We start with the definition (refer to Appendix A). A function $f : [0, \infty) \rightarrow \mathcal{R}$ is *concave* if, and only if, for each two points z_1, z_2 in $[0, \infty)$ and each $\alpha \in [0, 1]$, the following relation holds (Figure 4.6):

$$\alpha f(z_1) + (1 - \alpha) f(z_2) \leq f(\alpha z_1 + (1 - \alpha) z_2).$$

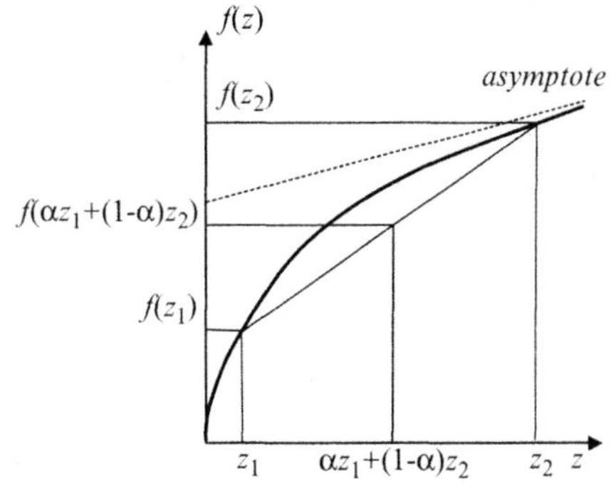

FIGURE 4.6 Concave Function

If for $0 < \alpha < 1$ the strict inequality holds, the function is called *strictly concave*. Typically, link dimensioning functions in communications networks are (strictly) concave rather than convex, since the property $f(z_1)/z_1 \geq f(z_2)/z_2$ for $z_1 < z_2$ of non-decreasing concave functions is more natural than the property $f(z_1)/z_1 \leq f(z_2)/z_2$ for $z_1 < z_2$ of the non-decreasing convex functions (Exercise 4.18).

Example 4.6 *Erlang B-Loss Formula Based Concave Function*

Consider link e (a trunk group) in a telephone network. The link is offered a load of A Erlangs, i.e., $\underline{y}_e = A$. For dimensioning purposes the blocking for the links, b_e, is assumed to be fixed and equal (e.g., $b_e \equiv 0.1\%$) so the corresponding link dimensioning function $y_e = F_e(\underline{y}_e)$ is computed from the inverse of the Erlang Loss formula (see 1.3.3)

$$b_e = \mathcal{B}(A, y_e)$$

extended to the real domain [Sys66]. The value y_e is the (continuous) number of trunks required to carry load A offered to link e on the blocking level b_e. It can be shown that $F_e(0) = 0$ and that $F_e(\cdot)$ is a strictly increasing concave function in $[0, \infty)$ [Sys66]. ●

A concave programming problem (CVP) analogous to D/SDP is as follows:

***CVP:* D/CDF** **Link-Path Formulation**

Concave Dimensioning Functions

indices

$d = 1, 2, ..., D$ demands
$p = 1, 2, ..., P_d$ candidate paths for flows realizing demand d
$e = 1, 2, ..., E$ links

constants

δ_{edp} = 1 if link e belongs to path p realizing demand d; 0, otherwise
h_d volume of demand d
ξ_e unit cost of link e
$F_e(\cdot)$ non-decreasing concave dimensioning function of link e

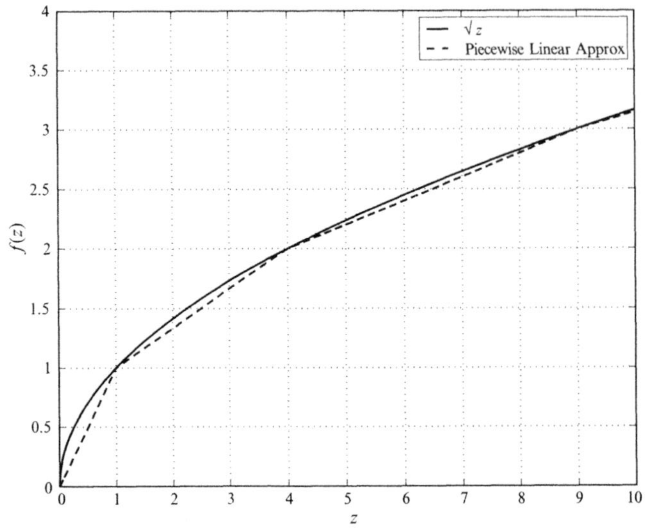

FIGURE 4.7 Piecewise Linear Approximation of a Concave Function

variables

x_{dp} flow allocated to path p of demand d

$\underline{y}_e$ load of link e

objective

$$\text{minimize } \boldsymbol{F} = \textstyle\sum_e \xi_e F_e(\underline{y}_e) \qquad (4.3.18a)$$

constraints

$$\textstyle\sum_p x_{dp} = h_d, \quad d = 1, 2, ..., D \qquad (4.3.18b)$$

$$\textstyle\sum_d \sum_p \delta_{edp} x_{dp} = \underline{y}_e, \quad e = 1, 2, ..., E. \qquad (4.3.18c)$$

Because of the property $f(z_1)/z_1 \geq f(z_2)/z_2$ for $z_1 < z_2$ of the dimensioning functions, the optimal solutions of the above model are non-bifurcated. This is a desirable property that can be utilized for finding flow allocations, as shown in Section 5.6. Unfortunately, since the problem consists of minimizing a concave objective function (4.3.18a) subject to linear constraints, the instances of the considered problem have, in general, numerous local minima attained on the extreme-points ("corners") of the feasible region determined by constraints (4.3.18b) to (4.3.18c), so finding the global minimum can be an extremely difficult task ([Min86] and Section 5.6).

In Subsection 4.3.2 we have shown how problems with convex objective functions and linear constraints can be approximated with LP formulations. For concave objective functions this is not possible; only a MIP approximation can be considered in this case. The basic idea is, as for the convex case, to substitute concave functions $F_e(\cdot)$ with their *piecewise linear* approximations (Figure 4.7).

Example 4.7 *Piecewise Linear Approximation of a Concave Function*
Consider the concave square root function:

$$f(z) = \sqrt{z}, \quad z \geq 0. \tag{4.3.19}$$

A piecewise approximation of the square root consisting of four linear pieces can be as follows (Figure 4.7):

$$f(z) = \begin{cases} z & \text{for } 0 \leq z < 1 \\ (z-1)/3 + 1 = z/3 + 2/3 & \text{for } 1 \leq z < 4 \\ (z-4)/5 + 2 = z/5 + 6/5 & \text{for } 4 \leq z < 9 \\ (z-9)/7 + 3 = z/7 + 12/7 & \text{for } z \geq 9. \end{cases} \tag{4.3.20}$$

●

Let function $f(z)$ defined as

$$f(z) = f_k(z) = a_k z + b_k, \quad s_{k-1} \leq y < s_k, \quad k = 1, 2, ..., K \tag{4.3.21}$$

(s_K can be equal to $+\infty$) be a piecewise linear approximation of the concave function $f(z)$ and suppose that we are given a number y ($y \geq 0$). The optimal solution of the following MIP problem will return the correct value of $f(y)$ (Exercises 4.20 and 4.21):

$$\begin{aligned} \textbf{\textit{minimize}} \quad & \textstyle\sum_k (a_k y_k + b_k u_k) \\ \textbf{\textit{subject to}} \quad & \textstyle\sum_k y_k = y \\ & \textstyle\sum_k u_k = 1 \\ & y_k \leq \Delta u_k, \quad k = 1, 2, ..., K \\ & y_k \text{ non-negative continuous, } u_k \text{ binary.} \end{aligned} \tag{4.3.22}$$

Above, Δ is a number larger than any potential value y. To see why this MIP works, note that formulation (4.3.22) is equivalent to the following problem in binary variables u_k:

$$\begin{aligned} \textbf{\textit{minimize}} \quad & \textstyle\sum_k u_k(a_k y + b_k) \\ \textbf{\textit{subject to}} \quad & \textstyle\sum_k u_k = 1. \end{aligned} \tag{4.3.23}$$

Formulation (4.3.23) works due to concavity of the approximation (4.3.22) (Figure 4.7). However, it is not a MIP formulation because if we treat y as a variable (this will be the case in the next problem) the objective in (4.3.23) contains terms with variables y and u_k multiplied ($\sum_k a_k u_k y + b_k u_k$) which is not allowed. Because of this difficulty, we have introduced auxiliary variables $y_1, y_2, ..., y_K$ and additional constraints listed in (4.3.22) forcing that exactly (and the right) one value of y_k will be non-zero and equal to y in the optimal solution.

The purpose of formulation (4.3.22) is to transform the concave mathematical programming problem (4.3.18) to a MIP problem, as shown below.

***MIP:* D/CDF/PMIA** **Link Path Formulation**

Concave Dimensioning Functions – Piecewise Mixed-Integer Approximation

additional indices

$k = 1, 2, ..., K_e$ consecutive pieces of the linear approximation of $f_e(\cdot)$)

additional constants

a_{ek}, b_{ek} coefficients of the linear pieces of the linear approximation of $f_e(\cdot)$

Δ large number

variables

x_{dp} flow allocated to path p of demand d

$\underline{y}_e$ load of link e

y_{ek} additional continuous variables for link e

u_{ek} additional binary variables for link e

objective

$$\text{minimize } \boldsymbol{F} = \sum_e \sum_k (a_{ek} y_{ek} + b_{ek} u_{ek}) \tag{4.3.24a}$$

constraints

$$\sum_p x_{dp} = h_d, \quad d = 1, 2, ..., D \tag{4.3.24b}$$

$$\sum_d \sum_p \delta_{edp} x_{dp} \leq \underline{y}_e, \quad e = 1, 2, ..., E \tag{4.3.24c}$$

$$\sum_k y_{ek} = \underline{y}_e, \quad e = 1, 2, ..., E \tag{4.3.24d}$$

$$\sum_k u_{ek} = 1, \quad e = 1, 2, ..., E \tag{4.3.24e}$$

$$y_{ek} \leq \Delta u_{ek}, \quad e = 1, 2, ..., E \quad k = 1, 2, ..., K_e. \tag{4.3.24f}$$

Assuming that the piecewise linear approximation involves the same number K of pieces for every link, the above problem contains $E \times K$ additional continuous variables, $E \times K$ additional binary variables, and $E \times (K + 2)$ additional constraints with respect to the original approximated problem. This shows that the problem is difficult to solve—in fact there are no general algorithms for solving Problem (4.3.24) significantly better from the full search in the space of binary variables (e.g., with branch-and-bound, see Section 5.2).

As was the case with convex link cost (dimensioning) functions, in many applications it is not necessary to have the equations (4.3.21) exactly, but rather the slopes of the linear pieces and where they change. Assuming again that the first linear piece starts at the origin, that the slopes of the consecutive pieces are a_k, $k = 1, 2, ..., K$, and that the consecutive break points at which the slope changes are $0 = s_0 < s_1 < s_2 < ... < s_K$ (where s_K can be a large but a finite number Δ), the approximation analogous to (4.3.22) is as follows:

$$
\begin{aligned}
\textbf{\textit{minimize}} \quad & a_1 z_1 + a_2 z_2 + \ldots + a_K z_K \\
\textbf{\textit{subject to}} \quad & y = z_1 + z_2 + \ldots + z_K \\
& u_1 \geq u_2 \geq \ldots \geq u_K \\
& (s_1 - s_0)u_2 \leq z_1 \leq (s_1 - s_0)u_1 \\
& (s_2 - s_1)u_3 \leq z_2 \leq (s_2 - s_1)u_2 \\
& \ldots \\
& (s_{K-1} - s_{K-2})u_K \leq z_{K-1} \leq (s_{K-1} - s_{K-2})u_{K-1} \\
& 0 \leq z_K \leq (s_K - s_{K-1})u_K \\
& z_k \text{ continuous, } u_k \text{ binary.}
\end{aligned}
\tag{4.3.25}
$$

The constraints imply that if $u_k = 1$ and $u_{k+1} = 0$ then $u_1 = u_2 = \ldots = u_k = 1$ and force $z_j = m_j$ for all $j < k$, $0 \leq z_k \leq m_k$ and $z_j = 0$ for all $j > k$ (where $m_k = s_k - s_{k-1}$). In compact form, the problem can be rewritten as:

$$
\begin{aligned}
\textbf{\textit{minimize}} \quad & \textstyle\sum_k a_k z_k \\
\textbf{\textit{subject to}} \quad & \textstyle\sum_k z_k = y \\
& m_k u_{k+1} \leq z_k \leq m_k u_k, \quad k = 1, 2, \ldots, K.
\end{aligned}
\tag{4.3.26}
$$

Note that the constraint $u_1 \geq u_2 \geq \ldots \geq u_K$, as redundant, is omitted.

We end this section with the following capacitated problem (a version of A/PAP) which arises naturally in the context of concave dimensioning functions.

***CVP:* A/CDF** **Link-Path Formulation**

Concave Dimensioning Functions

constants

- δ_{edp} = 1 if link e belongs to path p realizing demand d; 0, otherwise
- h_d volume of demand d
- c_e capacity of link e
- $F_e(\cdot)$ non-decreasing concave dimensioning function of link e

variables

- x_{dp} flow allocated to path p of demand d
- $\underline{y}_e$ load of link e

constraints

$$\textstyle\sum_p x_{dp} = h_d, \quad d = 1, 2, \ldots, D \tag{4.3.27a}$$

$$\textstyle\sum_d \sum_p \delta_{edp} x_{dp} = \underline{y}_e, \quad e = 1, 2, \ldots, E \tag{4.3.27b}$$

$$F_e(\underline{y}_e) \leq c_e, \quad e = 1, 2, \ldots, E. \tag{4.3.27c}$$

This problem has a non-convex feasible solution region defined by the linear constraints (4.3.27a)-(4.3.27b) and concave constraints (4.3.27c), and therefore is difficult to solve.

However, it can be converted into a MIP approximation using formulation (4.3.22) (Exercise 4.22).

Note that all the problems considered in this section can be formulated using the node-link representation.

4.4 BUDGET CONSTRAINT

In many cases the budget constraint can provide better means for the design goal than minimization of the cost function such as in D/SDP. The budget constraint substitutes the explicit minimization of the cost function (4.1.1a) and allows for introducing another objective function, for instance some kind of throughput maximization. To illustrate this issue consider the following uncapacitated problem:

***LP:* D/BC** **Link-Path Formulation**

Budget Constraint

indices

$d = 1, 2, ..., D$ demands

$p = 1, 2, ..., P_d$ candidate paths for demand d

$e = 1, 2, ..., E$ links

constants

δ_{edp} = 1 if link e belongs to path p realizing demand d; 0, otherwise

h_d reference volume of demand d

ξ_e unit cost of link e

B given budget

variables

x_{dp} flow allocated to path p of demand d

y_e capacity of link e

r proportion of the realized demand volumes (continuous non-negative)

objective

$$\text{maximize} \quad r \tag{4.4.1a}$$

constraints

$$\textstyle\sum_p x_{dp} \geq r h_d, \quad d = 1, 2, ..., D \tag{4.4.1b}$$

$$\textstyle\sum_d \sum_p \delta_{edp} x_{dp} \leq y_e, \quad e = 1, 2, ..., E \tag{4.4.1c}$$

$$\textstyle\sum_e \xi_e y_e \leq B. \tag{4.4.1d}$$

The optimal solution of the above LP problem will use entire given budget, B, to allocate all the demand volumes to as great extent as possible, preserving the assumed proportion of demand volumes specified by the given values of h_d ($d = 1, 2, ..., D$). This type of the extension of D/SDP can be combined with other uncapacitated extensions of the problem presented in this chapter (e.g., convex cost functions or concave dimensioning functions). Also, node-link formulation can be used (Exercise 4.23). In the next chapters we will use the extensions of the budget constraint problem D/BC to identify with such problems as topological design (Section 6.3.2), design of fair networks (Section 13.1), and others (Section 9.4.3), since in many cases the budget constraint can provide more appropriate means for the design goal than the the cost minimization itself.

4.5 INCREMENTAL NDPs

The uncapacitated design problems of the D type considered in the previous sections can be modified to take into account an important situation: the network is not designed from scratch (so it is not a "greenfield" network) but rather its existing resources are extended to take note of the increase of demand volumes. Another good reason for extending resources is when the demand volumes are to become protected in an initially unprotected network. These situations are best described as *incremental network design* problems; these will also be referred to as *network extension* problems. Thus, Problem (4.1.1) can be extended as follows:

***LP:* E/SEP** **Link-Path Formulation**

Simple Extension Problem

indices

$d = 1, 2, ..., D$ demands

$p = 1, 2, ..., P_d$ candidate paths for flow realizing demand d

$e = 1, 2, ..., E$ links

constants

δ_{edp} = 1, if link e belongs to path p realizing demand d; 0, otherwise

h_d volume of demand d

ξ_e unit cost of link e

c_e existing capacity of link e

variables

x_{dp} flow variable allocated to path p of demand d (continuous non-negative)

y_e extra capacity of link e on top of c_e (continuous non-negative)

objective

$$\text{minimize } \boldsymbol{F} = \textstyle\sum_e \xi_e y_e \tag{4.5.2a}$$

constraints

$$\textstyle\sum_p x_{dp} = h_d, \quad d = 1, 2, ..., D \tag{4.5.2b}$$

$$\textstyle\sum_d \sum_p \delta_{edp} x_{dp} \le y_e + c_e, \quad e = 1, 2, ..., E. \tag{4.5.2c}$$

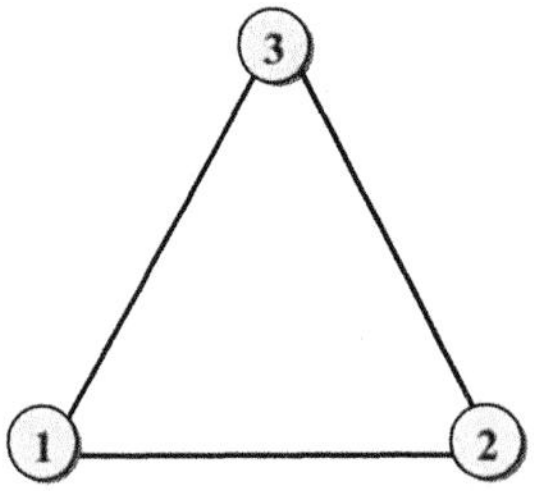

FIGURE 4.8 Extension Example

Problem E/SEP consists of minimizing the cost of the extra link capacity required to realize the (new, increased) demand volumes. The problem corresponds to a major network capacity extension faced during network planning and, hence, it does not usually need to consider maintaining the existing flows.

Note that in general for an optimal solution $\boldsymbol{y}^*$ of E/SEP, the cost $\boldsymbol{F}(\boldsymbol{y}^*)$ given by (4.5.2a) is greater than $\boldsymbol{F}(\hat{\boldsymbol{y}}) - \sum_e \xi_e c_e$ where $\hat{\boldsymbol{y}}$ is an optimal solution of D/SDP (4.1.1) for the same input demand and cost data (in D/SDP the existing link capacities are not taken into account). This property expresses the obvious observation that if we design a network from scratch the already invested budget ($\sum_e \xi_e c_e$) can be better utilized as the original demand volumes for which the existing network has been designed could have been distributed differently than the current (increased) demand.

Example 4.8 *Design From Scratch Example*

Consider the network in Figure 4.8. Suppose that the modularity of links is 24 and that the demand volume between all three node pairs is equal to 13. Assuming module cost equal to 1, the optimal solution results with the cost $\boldsymbol{F} = 3$ and the capacity $c_e = 1$ for each of the three links. Now if demand volumes are increased to 35 for pairs $\langle 1,3 \rangle$ and $\langle 2,3 \rangle$ and remain unchanged for pair $\langle 1,2 \rangle$, then the optimal extension results with two extra modules on links $\langle 1,3 \rangle$ and $\langle 2,3 \rangle$ and the extension cost $\boldsymbol{F}^* = 2$. If we were to design the network for the new demand from scratch, then it would suffice to put two modules of capacity on each of the two links $\langle 1,3 \rangle$ and $\langle 2,3 \rangle$ resulting in cost $\hat{\boldsymbol{F}} = 4$. But $\boldsymbol{F}^* + \boldsymbol{F} = 5$, so the extension is *per saldo* more expensive than the "from scratch" solution. ●

It is important to note that extension problems of the E/SEP type can be adjusted in many ways along essentially the same lines as Problem D/SDP has been extended in earlier sections in this chapter.

4.6 EXTENSIONS OF PROBLEM MODELING

In this section we will explain additional issues that facilitate the use of the modeling framework discussed earlier in this chapter for extended NDPs involving node modeling, multicast connections, etc. We will also come back to advantages of the link-path representation of NDPs.

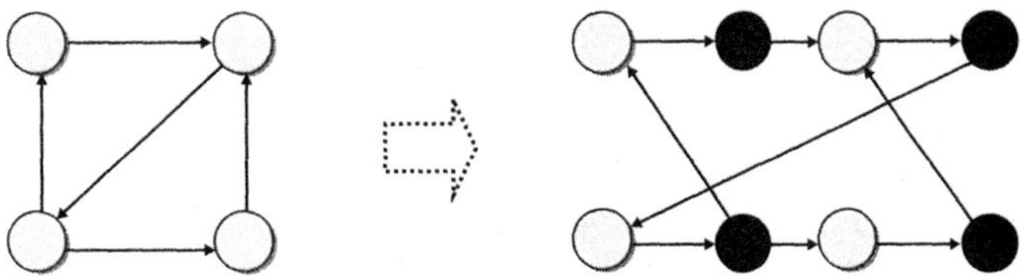

FIGURE 4.9 Directed Graph Adjustment

4.6.1 Representing Nodes

In the problem formulations considered in this chapter the link capacities appear as key network resources and, as you may have noticed (and be annoyed by this), the node capacity is not taken explicitly into account. The node costs associated with the *capacity of the individual links* connected to the nodes (such as the cost of input/output ports and the link terminal equipment) can be taken into account directly in the link costs. Another type of node capacity, resulting from the *total link capacity* connected to the nodes as well as the associated cost (e.g., modular cost of the switching fabric, fixed costs of installing the node, and so on) can be considered in a general way through introducing the following transformation of the original network graph.

For the directed graphs (used, for instance, in the node-link formulations), each node v is substituted with its two copies (nodes v' and v''), and a directed *internal link* $e(v) = (v', v'')$ between the matching copies is added to the set of links of the graph (Figure 4.9). All of the original links incoming to node v are connected to node v' and, similarly, all links outgoing from node v to node v''. For the graphs used in the link-path formulations, which are basically undirected, this is done in an even simpler way. For each node v, an extra (artificial) link $e(v)$ is introduced to the list of links. For the artificial links the coincidence coefficients are defined as follows:

$$\delta_{e(v)dp} = \begin{cases} 1, & \text{if node } v \text{ belongs to path } p \text{ realizing demand } d \\ 0, & \text{otherwise.} \end{cases}$$

The load of the node, $\underline{y}_v = \sum_d \sum_p \delta_{e(v)dp} x_{dp}$, can be used for other purposes, as for instance, to impose an upper bound for the node load:

$$\sum_d \sum_p \delta_{e(v)dp} x_{dp} \le C_v, \quad v = 1, 2, ..., V. \tag{4.6.1}$$

The cost of node v, depending on its load $\underline{y}_v$, can appear in the objective function of the design problem. Observe that the node costs tend to be highly modular due to the structure of the switch/routers fabric.

The concept of the internal link is also very useful to model node failures—to fail a node we simply fail its internal link. Observe that if the diversified link-path formulation (4.2.2) of Section 4.2.1 is to be extended to encompass node failures as well, then the diversity constraints (4.2.2c) become less numerous:

$$\delta_{e(v)dp} x_{dp} \le h_d / n_d, \qquad d = 1, 2, ..., D, \quad v = 1, 2, ..., V, v \ne s_d, v \ne t_d \tag{4.6.2a}$$

$$\delta_{edp} x_{dp} \leq h_d / n_d, \quad d = 1, 2, ..., D,$$
$$e = (s_d, t_d) \text{ (i.e., } e \text{ is the link (direct path) between } s_d \text{ and } t_d), \quad (4.6.2b)$$

where s_d and t_d are the end nodes of demand d.

With node-link formulation, the above two constraints become even simpler.

$$x_{e(v)d} \leq h_d / n_d, \quad d = 1, 2, ..., D, \quad v = 1, 2, ..., V, v \neq s_d, v \neq t_d \quad (4.6.3a)$$

$$x_{ed} \leq h_d / n_d, \quad d = 1, 2, ..., D, \quad e = (s_d, t_d). \quad (4.6.3b)$$

Finally, we turn to the problem of the equal split among node-disjoint paths in the node-link formulation (refer to (4.2.10) with constraint (4.2.10c)). With node splitting, this additional constraint is simply substituted with

$$u_{de(v)} \leq 1, \quad d = 1, 2, ..., D, \quad v = 1, 2, ..., V, v \neq s_d, v \neq t_d. \quad (4.6.4)$$

4.6.2 Capabilities of Link-Path Representation

We have emphasized earlier that the link-path representation is preferable for communication and computer NDP modeling, for example, since pre-processed paths can be an input to link-path-based models. In fact, link-path representation has several additional advantages, especially with our link-demand-path-identifier-based notation; these are highlighted below.

Note that demand identifier d need not to be restricted to mean "exactly one demand for exactly one node pair". For example, if a node pair can have multiple different demands (e.g., due to different services or bandwidth requirements) then labeling with single identifier d is sufficient to capture these variations without needing to change problem formulation. Similarly, link identifier e can be used for representing multiples links between two nodes and this also does not require changes in model formulation.

Interestingly, a demand identifier can be used for identifying other objects than end-to-end demands, e.g., a multi-cast group demand that involves more nodes than just a pair of nodes. Certainly, the demand volume needs to use 'paths' for its flows. The question then is: does the 'path entity' need to change when the meaning of a demand is changed? Not really. For example, when a demand identifier is used for identifying different services, then each service can have a set of candidate paths which can be different from one service to another for the same node pair. When a demand represents a multicast group, then different possible multicast path sets (for example trees spanning the multicast group) can be considered as candidate 'path' sequences. The reason this works is that in the link-capacity constraint of link-path formulation a link needs to check if a path is using it—this can be reflected through the 'delta' indicator, δ_{edp}, without needing to worry if a 'path' is really in the form of a regular path, or other objects such as multi-cast tree.

It may further be noted that even when a demand identifier is associated with a node pair, the path need not be limited to a regular path—in fact, a 'path' can for example be used for representing a pair: primary/back-up path (Section 9.3.4).

Thus, as you can see, there are several very powerful properties of the link-path formulation; such extensions are virtually impossible with the node-link formulation.

In this book, however, while not really necessary, we will still include additional identifiers for different network states, time periods, and services for the same demand pair (refer for example to Chapters 9 and 11). Adding additional identifiers makes it easier to formulate and understand different variations of the considered design models. For example, we have already taken this approach while considering failure states in Section 2.8 of Chapter 2, where we have used h_{ds} to denote demand volume for demand d in state s; other entities such as flow variables x_{dps} are accordingly indexed with s.

4.7 SUMMARY AND FURTHER READING

The purpose of this chapter is two-fold. First, it presents a set of basic design problems that are considered in the further chapters of Part II as well as in numerous papers on network design spread over journals and conference proceedings in telecommunications, data communications, and operations research. The formulations use a general, unified, concise summation notation developed for the purpose of this book. Wherever possible, we have tried to discuss connections between the different problems.

The presented formulations are in the form of optimization problems and are called *mathematical programming problems* (mathematical programmes or mathematical programs, in short) in the field of operations research, which basically means that they are of the form

$$\begin{array}{ll} \textbf{\textit{minimize}} & F(\boldsymbol{x}) \\ \textbf{\textit{subject to}} & \boldsymbol{x} \in S \end{array}$$

with a given objective function $F(\boldsymbol{x})$ and the solution set (optimization space) S which is typically a subset (in most cases either compact or finite) of the n-dimensional Euclidean space (refer to Appendix A). This form of a formulation allows for use of the entire ammunition (i.e., optimization algorithms) developed, for a wide variety of mathematical programs, within optimization theory and operations research.

It should be emphasized, however, that in most cases finding a mathematical formulation (no matter how desirable it can be), which is essentially the last step in problem modeling, does not automatically mean that we have found an effective way to solve the problem at hand. On the contrary, it is in many cases only a beginning of a frequently painful process of: 1) finding, 2) tailoring, and 3) applying (implementing) an efficient algorithm for the instances of the problem we wish to consider. Needless to say, this is especially true for the problem instances corresponding to large networks.

In Chapter 5 we will present and discuss several optimization approaches, methods, and algorithms, including LP, MIP, convex programming, and concave programming. It will then become clear what algorithms can be used for the problems discussed in this chapter. At the same time it will become evident that almost all problems that are not LP problems are difficult to solve, especially when applied to large network examples. First, as a rule, MIP formulations soon become intractable when the number of variables grow, no matter what up-to-date MIP solver we use (and despite a great development of the MIP solving techniques, first of all of branch-and-cut, in the recent years). This is an intrinsic difficulty with MIP formulations as in most cases they are $\mathcal{NP}$-complete. Second, typical large-scale convex network design problems suffer from very slow convergence. Finally, algorithms for concave programming problems usually get stacked in local minima making it virtually impossible to find the true global optimal solution.

It is our conviction that in most cases only the LP formulations allow for successful application of the available (commercial and freeware) solvers and get *exact optimal solutions* in acceptable time, provided the number of variables and constraints is kept at a manageable level. If the number of variables and constraints in the LP formulations gets too large, efficient decomposition methods such as column generation, Lagrangian relaxation, and Benders' decomposition (discussed in later chapters) can be effectively applied allowing for efficient treatment of large network design instances of hundreds of nodes, for example. These decomposition methods, however, may be quite difficult to use for a beginner.

This all leads to a need for using meta-heuristics (such as simulated annealing, simulated allocation, evolutionary algorithms, and tabu search) and the algorithms derived from them for dealing with NDPs involving integral (binary) variables and non-linear cost. With adequate heuristic methods we can at least find approximate solutions in reasonable time (hopefully near-optimal); still, it may sometimes be troublesome to devise and implement an appropriate algorithm. A fair deal of this book discusses the heuristic approach to network design.

The second purpose of this chapter has been to illustrate (and try to teach a beginner) how to build network design models, adding more and more difficulty into the formulations in order to capture the (sometimes quite sophisticated) specific features of the problems imposed by the network structure and the technology used. We have started with the simplest dimensioning and allocation LP formulations (of type D and A, respectively) in Section 4.1 and then we have added various constraints representing different aspects of the problems as we have progressed through the chapter. This methodical treatment will hopefully be useful to you in visualizing the problems and examples discussed earlier in Chapters 2 and 3 in a better and more general perspective and, more importantly, help in understanding design problems arising in subsequent chapters of this book.

In Section 4.2, we have first imposed diversity routing constraints that take failures of links and nodes into account at the design stage. This has been achieved within the LP formulation imposing additional linear constraints on flow variables. Next, we have forbidden the use of too small flows and imposed lower bound on flow allocations; these required binary variables. Then we have imposed limitations on the number of paths with non-zero flows. Here, the most important case is the single-path (unsplittable or non-bifurcated) allocation, calling for binary variables as well. Finally, we have introduced integral (modular) flows, again using binary variables, which is closer to the truth in actual networks.

The next direction in extending the design problems is presented in Section 4.3 where we have discussed the main types of link cost/dimensioning functions, distinct from the simple linear case. Here, the modular functions of different types, convex functions, and concave functions are introduced and used for the most important purposes, such as modular link capacity, convex link cost, convex penalty cost for link overload, delay constraint, and concave dimensioning functions. We have shown that the problems involving convex and concave functions can be approximated by the LP and MIP problems, respectively, sometimes in a nifty way.

Then, in Section 4.4, we have discussed the problems involving the budget constraint on links cost rather than minimizing the links cost iteself - this will become important later in this book. Incremental NDPs, taking into account the existing link capacity, are discussed in Section 4.5. Finally, in Section 4.6.1, we have shown how a simple idea of splitting the nodes can be used to explicitly consider the nodes and all their attributes (as load, capacity, cost, and so on) in the formulations introduced in all the preceding sections, which involve only link attributes. The node splitting can also be used to model node failures, as discussed in Chapter 9.

During the entire presentation in this chapter we have been considering and comparing two basic types of formulations: the link-path notation and the node-link notation. Both notations have their *pros* and *cons*; still, as we have tried to show, the link-path notation is more powerful as it allows for formulation of problems which are not expressible in the node-link notation. This has been demonstrated for the cases of lower bound on the non-zero flows, equal split of demand volume, restriction on number of hops in a path, dealing with generalized path notion (as trees). The advantage of the link-path notation in this aspect will become even more profound in Chapter 9, where the restoration problems are considered. In fact, the only advantage of the node-link notation over link-path is that in the LP formulations the former notation can make effective use of all available network paths to be used by demand flows. This cannot be accomplished so easily by the link-path formulations. In the latter case, some path generation techniques must be used to extend the routing lists if they are not sufficient for achieving optimal solutions, as explained in Section 5.4.2.

Most of the NDPs discussed in this chapter can be found throughout the literature in many different versions and sometimes it is really hard to tell who was the first to consider a particular problem, who first introduced a certain trick, who first noticed that a certain class of the considered multi-commodity optimization problems is relevant for communications and computer network design, and so on. Having said that, apparently, Kalaba and Juncosa [KJ56] were the first to consider NDPs in telecommunications using a multi-commodity flow problem—their formulation can be considered as the first node-link multi-commodity flow representation. In turn, Ford and Fulkerson [FF58] were perhaps the first to formulate the maximal flow multi-commodity problem using link-path representation. Another early work on multi-commodity flows is [GH61].

As for further reading, a discussion on the link-path and node-link notations can be found in the surveys by Assad and Kennington [Ass78], [Ken78], in the paper [JLFP93], and in the book by Ahuja, Magnanti, and Orlin [AMO93]. For the single-commodity flow problems see also the classical book [FF62]). A use of the A type formulation is made in the Minoux paper [Min81]. Use of a convex delay function in a multi-commodity flow formulation for computer network design was first considered by Fratta, Gerla, and Kleinrock [FGK73]. The convex problems of Section 4.3.2 are discussed in detail by Bertsekas and Gallager in [BG92] and by Kershenbaum in [Ker92], although the LP approximations are not discussed there. The concave problems (Section 4.3.3) are treated in [Yag71] and [Min89] by means of certain iterative algorithms. The linear approximation of the convex programming problems is discussed, in a general way, in §4.4 [Las70]. Applications similar to ours are discussed in [Wil93], where MIP approximations of the concave functions are also presented.

The famous Dijkstra shortest-path algorithm is described in [Dij59]. The discussion of shortest-path algorithms required as input to link-path formulations can be found, for example, in Bhandari [Bha99] (the Dijkstra shortest-path algorithm and its variants, algorithms for finding shortest sets of disjoint paths), in [BG92] (Dijkstra, Bellman-Ford, and Floyd-Warshall algorithms), in Lawler [Law76] (k-shortest paths), and in [Wes00] (shortest paths with at most k-hops). All these types of algorithms are discussed in Appendix C.

EXERCISES FOR CHAPTER 4

4.1. Show the following property of the optimal solution of D/SDP in the node-link formulation: if there are two oppositely directed arcs between two nodes then only one of them can have non-zero flow for any fixed demand d.

4.2. *How do we determine path flows corresponding to the link flows obtained by solving D/SDP in the node-link formulation? (Hint: use the Ford-Fulkerson algorithm for single-commodity flow maximization [FF62].)

4.3. Write down the node-link formulation of A/PAP for a directed graph. How does this formulation extend to the undirected graph?

4.4. *Prove (in a straightforward way) the property discussed in Example 4.3.

4.5. *Formulate an allocation (type A) problem in the link-path notation expressing the following requirement: find the largest integer k such that there exists a feasible solution with all demands split equally among k paths. Is this possible to express in the node-link formulation?

4.6. Formulate a type A problem simultaneously assuring path diversity and lower-bounded flows.

4.7. *Specify a link-path formulation for a type A problem assuring that for each demand its volume is split equally among exactly 2 or 3 paths.

4.8. Specify a link-path formulation of a type A problem assuring that each link e carries not more than k_e non-zero flows. Is this possible to express in the node-link formulation?

4.9. *Formulate an LP problem for finding a shortest path (in terms of the number of hops) between two given nodes in a graph. How does the formulation extend to the problem of finding shortest paths for a set of demands? (Hint: use a version of D/SDP in the node-link formulation.)

4.10. Formulate a dimensioning problem (of type D) corresponding to the type A problem from Exercise 4.8.

4.11. *Find a procedure for splitting the nodes and augmenting A/ESLDP in order to assure node-disjointness of the allocated flows. How do we apply this approach to undirected graphs?

4.12. Show that $f(0) = 0$ and $f(x) \geq 0$ for $x \geq 0$ is sufficient for a convex function $f(x)$ to be non-decreasing in $[0, \infty)$.

4.13. Consider a graph composed of just two nodes and two distinct links between the nodes. The demand volume between the nodes is equal to 1, and $f(x) = x^2$ is the cost function of each link. Show that the optimal solution to Problem (4.3.8) consists of splitting the demand equally between the two links (paths). What is the cost difference between this solution and the non-bifurcated solution? Show that for the considered network the property holds for all strictly convex, twice differentiable functions (non-necessarily increasing).

4.14. Solve LP (4.3.12) for $y = 2.5$ using the approximation defined in Example 4.5 and check whether the obtained value is correct.

4.15. Prove that LP (4.3.12) is correct.

4.16. Formulate the linear approximation of the convex problem A/CCF (4.3.6).

4.17. *Solve the capacity design problem (4.3.16) with fixed routing and delay constraint to obtain the optimal solution (4.3.17). Also determine the optimal cost.

4.18. Show that the property $f(z_1)/z_2 \geq f(z_2)/z_2$ for $z_1 < z_2$ holds for non-decreasing concave functions, and that the property $f(z_1)/z_2 \leq f(z_2)/z_2$ for $z_1 < z_2$ holds for non-decreasing convex functions.

4.19. Show that function (4.3.6a) is convex and that function (4.3.18a) is concave.

4.20. Solve MIP (4.3.22) for $y = 5$ for the approximation defined in Example 4.7 and check whether the obtained value is correct.

4.21. Prove that LP (4.3.22) is correct.

4.22. Convert Problem (4.3.27) into an MIP problem.

4.23. Formulate a node-link version of the budget constraint Problem D/BC (4.4.1) for concave dimensioning functions.

CHAPTER 5

General Optimization Methods for Network Design

Chapter 5 is devoted to basic optimization methods and algorithms applicable to the network design problems (NDPs) discussed in Chapter 4 and in all the subsequent chapters. Most of the problems studied in this book are multi-commodity flow NDPs, and as such they often either possess exact linear programming (LP) formulations or can be reasonably approximated with LP formulations. This, and the fact that these are mainly the LP problem formulations that can be effectively solved in the exact way with a fair implementation effort, make the role of LP crucial for network design. For this reason we start the presentation with Section 5.1 on LP, including the discussion of the basics, the famous simplex method, and interior-point algorithms.

On the other hand, as we have already seen in Chapter 4, there are important design problems which are $\mathcal{NP}$-complete and involve such non-linear features as modular links/flows or non-bifurcated routing. Therefore, the LP formulations are in many cases too simplified and require the use of additional integral (binary) variables; this leads to mixed-integer programming (MIP) formulations and, sometimes, to integer programming (IP) formulations, with no continuous variables at all. Practically, the only general exact approach used in professional solvers for MIP and IP problems is the branch-and-bound (BB) technique, presented in Section 5.2 together with its less known enhancement called branch-and-cut (BC).

Integer programming problems are a special case of more general combinatorial (or discrete) optimizations problems, i.e., problems with finite solution space. Although BB can be applicable in this more general case as well, for many problems, especially for large networks, a heuristic approach can be more (even much more) efficient in obtaining close-to-optimal solutions. In recent decades, a number of general heuristic methods (sometimes called meta-heuristics) have been developed, including simulated annealing, evolutionary algorithms, tabu search, and others. All of these methods involve some randomness and, therefore, are called stochastic meta-heuristics. Section 5.3 is devoted to such methods; it also includes a less known method called simulated allocation, well suited for multi-commodity flow problems.

Due to excessive number of variables and constraints in large networks, even the LP approach can fail when applied directly. In such cases, decomposition methods can often solve large-scale problems that may not be solvable by LP solvers in a reasonable time.

Three decomposition methods most relevant for multi-commodity network design are described in Section 5.4. Some of these are quite complicated and can be skipped in the first reading.

Sections 5.5 and 5.6 are devoted to problems involving convex and concave objective functions, respectively. Special methods for the linear constraints, including those not discussed in the general optimization handbooks, are discussed in detail.

Finally, in Section 5.7, we give a summary of applicability of different approaches discussed in this chapter for problems formulated in Chapter 4.

This chapter ends with a summary and a discussion of the relevant literature (Section 5.8). In reading Chapter 5, you are advised to make use of Appendix A which contains an optimization theory refresher with the notation, general notions, and the theoretical results used throughout this book.

Finally, we point out that we do not expect every reader to become an expert in developing algorithms for multi-commodity network design or know all the details of various approaches, especially readers whose primary interest is network modeling. Regardless, this chapter, together with Appendix A, can also serve as a good place to find answers to important, relevant questions that may come to mind regarding optimization algorithms and theory instead of going through many books and papers to search for the answers. All of the methods discussed in this chapter (besides interior-point methods for LP and branch-and-cut for MIP) are presented, in the general context, in an excellent book by Michel Minoux [Min86].

5.1 LINEAR PROGRAMMING

LP is an exact, effective, and easily accessible optimization approach, applicable to NDPs whenever they can be formulated as LP problems. LP solvers are available on both the commercial and freeware basis, and some of them are capable of solving really large linear programs with many thousands of variables and constraints. In Appendix D we show how to use and formulate problems for such tools (almost all numerical examples for the LP problems presented in this book have been solved by means of CPLEX [CPL99], AMPL [FGK02], and MATLAB [MAT]).

5.1.1 Basic Facts About LP

The general form of an LP problem (also called a *linear programme* or *linear program*, refer to Appendix A) is as follows:

LP Problem

indices

$j = 1, 2, ..., n$ variables

$i = 1, 2, ..., m$ constraints

constants

a_{ij} coefficient for variable j in constraint i

b_i right-hand side of constraint i

c_j cost coefficient of variable j

variables

x_j j-th variable

objective

$$\text{minimize } z = \sum_j c_j x_j \tag{5.1.1a}$$

constraints

$$\sum_j a_{ij} x_j \le b_i, \quad i = 1, 2, ..., m. \tag{5.1.1b}$$

We note that an equality constraint of the form $\sum_j a_{ij}x_j = b_i$ is equivalent to two inequalities, $\sum_j a_{ij}x_j \le b_i$ and $-\sum_j a_{ij}x_j \le -b_i$ (refer to Section A.7). Denoting by $\boldsymbol{x} = (x_1, x_2, ..., x_n)$ the vector of variables, by $\boldsymbol{A} = [a_{ij}]$ the $m \times n$ coefficient matrix, by $\boldsymbol{c} = (c_1, c_2, ..., c_n)$ the cost coefficient vector, and by $\boldsymbol{b} = (b_1, b_2, ..., b_m)$ the right-hand side vector, the above problem can be formulated in the matrix form as follows:

$$\begin{aligned} &\textit{minimize} \quad z = \boldsymbol{cx} \\ &\textit{subject to} \quad \boldsymbol{Ax} \le \boldsymbol{b}. \end{aligned} \tag{5.1.2}$$

For ease of writing and when it does not lead to misunderstanding, we do not distinguish between a row and a column vector by putting the transpose sign. For example, in $\boldsymbol{cx}$, vector $\boldsymbol{c}$ is a row vector while $\boldsymbol{x}$ is a column vector. For clarity, we distinguish between matrix-vector and vector-matrix multiplication, i.e., $\boldsymbol{Ax}$ is different from $\boldsymbol{\pi A}$ (where $\boldsymbol{x}$ is a column vector and $\boldsymbol{\pi}$ is a row vector). Another compact notation to represent Problem (5.1.2) is:

$$\min_{\boldsymbol{x}} \{\boldsymbol{cx} : \boldsymbol{Ax} \le \boldsymbol{b}\}, \tag{5.1.3}$$

where the indicator under 'min' ($\boldsymbol{x}$ in this case) is to identify the set of variables for the specific problem in hand.

The convex set $\mathcal{S}$ of the form $\{\boldsymbol{x} : \boldsymbol{Ax} \le \boldsymbol{b}\}$ is called the (convex) *polytope* (a bounded polytope is called (convex) *polyhedron*); hence, feasible points of a linear program form a polytope (or polyhedron). A feasible point $\boldsymbol{x}$ is called an *extreme point* if it cannot be expressed as a convex linear combination $\boldsymbol{x} = \sum_{k=1}^{K} \alpha_k \boldsymbol{x}^k$ ($\alpha_k \ge 0$, $\sum_{k=1}^{K} \alpha_k = 1$) of a (finite) set of other feasible points $\boldsymbol{x}^1, \boldsymbol{x}^2, ..., \boldsymbol{x}^K$. For example, if constraints $x_j \ge 0$, $j = 1, 2, ..., n$ are among inequalities in (5.1.1b) then $\boldsymbol{x} = \boldsymbol{0}$ is an extreme point (Figure 5.1), provided it is a feasible solution. Extreme points of a polytope are called *vertices*. All optimal solutions of a linear program are called the optimal solution set. An important (and intuitively obvious) property of LP problems is as follows.

THEOREM 5.1 *If an LP problem has a bounded global minimum and the solution polytope $\mathcal{S} = \{\boldsymbol{x} : \boldsymbol{Ax} \le \boldsymbol{b}\}$ contains at least one vertex, then the optimal solution set also contains at least one vertex.*

A vertex which is an optimal solution is called *optimal vertex*. Note that the global minimum can be attained at a point which is not a vertex. This follows from the fact that if $\boldsymbol{x}^1, \boldsymbol{x}^2, ..., \boldsymbol{x}^K$ are global minima then all their convex combinations are also global minima, which follows directly from the linearity (in fact from convexity) of the optimal solution set (Section A.1). In general, LP problems can have multiple optimal vertices (Exercise 5.1).

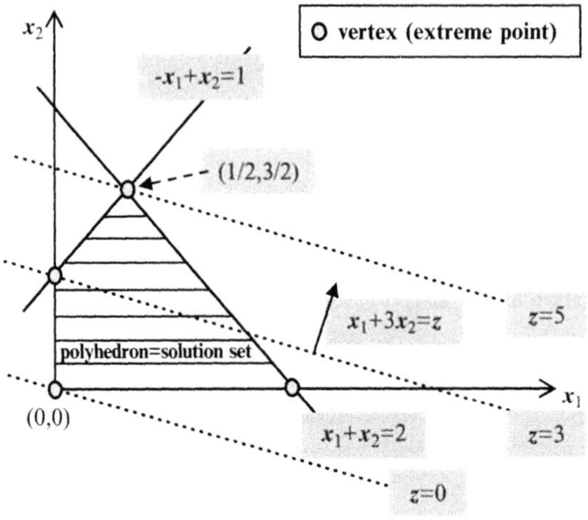

FIGURE 5.1 A Two-Variable LP Problem

Example 5.1 *An LP Problem [Las70]*

Consider the following LP problem:

$$\begin{array}{llcl} \textbf{\textit{maximize}} & z = x_1 + 3x_2 & & \quad (\text{or, } \textbf{\textit{minimize}} \quad z = -(x_1 + 3x_2)) \\ \textbf{\textit{subject to}} & -x_1 + x_2 & \leq & 1 \\ & x_1 + x_2 & \leq & 2 \\ & x_1, x_2 & \geq & 0. \end{array}$$

The solution set is depicted in Figure 5.1; it is the polyhedron bounded by the four straight lines: $x_2 = 0, x_1 + x_2 = 2, -x_1 + x_2 = 1$ and $x_1 = 0$. Using graphical illustration, it is easy to see by moving upwards the objective function contour $z = x_1 + 3x_2$, that the optimal solution z^* is attained at the vertex $\boldsymbol{x}^* = (\frac{1}{2}, 1\frac{1}{2})$. ●

5.1.2 Duality in LP

Duality in optimization theory is a powerful concept. In essence, using duality, an optimization problem given in a particular form, called *primal problem* in this context, can be transformed to a related problem, called its *dual problem*, so that the optimal solutions to both the primal and the dual are closely related. Sometimes this transformed problem can be easier to solve. Furthermore, some efficient algorithms for solving primal problems can be developed using duality. We know it is not possible to do justice to the vast body of wonderful work on this subject in a matter of a few pages. In Appendix A, we have included a brief summary of the duality theory for general optimization problems (Section A.5). Here we will give the basics of duality in LP and discuss its applicability; a more comprehensive presentation of duality in LP can be found, for example, in [Chv83], [Min86], and [Mur83].

We will use a special form of linear programs to discuss duality. Suppose our (original) primal problem is in the following LP form:

Linear Program: Primal Problem
variables
x_j variable j
objective

$$\text{minimize } \sum_j c_j x_j \tag{5.1.4a}$$

constraints

$$\sum_j a_{ij} x_j \geq b_i, \qquad i = 1, 2, ..., m \tag{5.1.4b}$$
$$x_j \geq 0, \qquad j = 1, 2, ..., n. \tag{5.1.4c}$$

Its dual is another LP problem which is of the form:

Linear Program: Dual Problem of (5.1.4)
variables
π_i dual variable i
objective

$$\text{maximize } \sum_i b_i \pi_i \tag{5.1.5a}$$

constraints

$$\sum_i a_{ij} \pi_i \leq c_j, \qquad j = 1, 2, ..., n \tag{5.1.5b}$$
$$\pi_i \geq 0, \qquad i = 1, 2, ..., m. \tag{5.1.5c}$$

The vector of variables in the primal problem is $\boldsymbol{x} = (x_1, x_2, ..., x_n)$ while in the dual problem it is $\boldsymbol{\pi} = (\pi_1, \pi_2, ..., \pi_m)$ so there is a one-to-one correspondence between the dual variables and the constraints (5.1.4b). A compact way to represent the primal/dual problem using matrix notation is shown below:

$$\text{Primal:} \quad \min_{\boldsymbol{x}} \{\boldsymbol{cx} : \boldsymbol{Ax} \geq \boldsymbol{b}, \boldsymbol{x} \geq \boldsymbol{0}\} \tag{5.1.6}$$

$$\text{Dual:} \quad \max_{\boldsymbol{\pi}} \{\boldsymbol{b\pi} : \boldsymbol{\pi A} \leq \boldsymbol{c}, \boldsymbol{\pi} \geq \boldsymbol{0}\}. \tag{5.1.7}$$

There is no rule that says we must have the primal problem in a specific format; in fact, in some books, the dual problem as shown above is called the primal, and the primal problem is called the dual. This can be a bit confusing. We use this particular convention here since many NDPs are minimization problems; what is in fact important is to refer to the specific NDP you are modeling as the primal problem. Furthermore, a primal problem may not be exactly given in the format described above. Then we may transform the primal to the form (5.1.6) or use a general definition of the dual given in Section A.5 of Appendix A—see Exercises 5.2 and 5.3.

While the dual may look like just another problem without any meaning, we want to point out that dual problems do have physical (or economical) interpretation. In multi-commodity flow problems it is often useful to interpret the optimal dual variables corresponding to the capacity constraints as link weights, and the optimal dual variables corresponding to the demand constraints—as lengths of the demands' shortest paths; we will soon see (Section 5.4) that this interpretation leads to useful decomposition algorithms. In general, the optimal dual variables measure (under certain conditions assuring their uniqueness) the sensitivity of the optimal primal objective to the perturbation of the right-hand sides of the constraints (5.1.4b); see Sections A.3 and A.7 in Appendix A. Also, the optimal dual variables can be sometimes used in a quite unexpected way—we will discuss such an application for a shortest-path routing flow allocation problem in Section 7.2.2 of Chapter 7.

Now we will discuss two important theorems concerning duality. The first is called the "strong duality theorem".

THEOREM 5.2 *The primal problem has a bounded optimal solution* $\boldsymbol{x}^* = (x_1^*, x_2^*, ..., x_n^*)$, *if, and only if, the dual also has a bounded optimal solution* $\boldsymbol{\pi}^* = (\pi_1^*, \pi_2^*, ..., \pi_m^*)$, *and then the following holds:*

$$\textstyle\sum_j c_j x_j^* = \sum_i b_i \pi_i^*. \tag{5.1.8}$$

It is important to note that the primal may not always have a bounded optimal solution. This is the case when the problem is infeasible (solution set is empty), or it is unbounded (note that an unbounded solution set does not necessarily imply that there is no bounded optimal solution). In most NDPs, the feasible region (i.e., solution set) is bounded, primarily due to the flow conservation equation. However, a problem can be infeasible; this is similar to stating: carry a demand volume of 15 units when the capacity is only 10 units.

At optimality, the primal and the dual solutions satisfy a set of conditions. For the general optimization problem, these conditions are known as the Karush-Kuhn-Tucker (KKT) conditions (refer to Section A.2 of Appendix A). In the considered case of the LP problems of the form 5.1.4, at optimality, any primal-dual optimal solution pair $(\boldsymbol{x}^*, \boldsymbol{\pi}^*)$ satisfies the following conditions:

$$\textstyle\sum_j a_{ij} x_j^* \geq b_i, \qquad i = 1, 2, \ldots, m \tag{5.1.9a}$$

$$x_j^* \geq 0 \qquad j = 1, 2, \ldots, n \tag{5.1.9b}$$

$$\textstyle\sum_i a_{ij} \pi_i^* \leq c_j, \qquad j = 1, 2, \ldots, n \tag{5.1.9c}$$

$$\pi_i^* \geq 0 \qquad i = 1, 2, \ldots, m \tag{5.1.9d}$$

$$\pi_i^* (\textstyle\sum_j a_{ij} x_j^* - b_i) = 0 \qquad i = 1, 2, \ldots, m \tag{5.1.9e}$$

$$(\textstyle\sum_i a_{ij} \pi_i^* - c_j) x_j^* = 0 \qquad j = 1, 2, \ldots, n. \tag{5.1.9f}$$

The last two conditions are called *complementarity slackness conditions*. As the dual variables are associated with primal constraints they are often referred to as *dual multipliers*.

It is relevant to point out that when we solve an LP problem using the simplex algorithm (see the next section), the information about the primal and dual solutions is readily available (as the algorithm progresses), and, in essence, the optimality condition in the strong duality theorem can be easily checked. Note that if inequality in parenthesis in (5.1.9f) is sharp, then the corresponding optimal x_j^* must be equal to zero (also see Section A.7 in Appendix A).

There is another important result, known as the "weak duality theorem" (see Section A.5 in Appendix A for its version for general optimization problems).

THEOREM 5.3 *For any feasible solutions $\boldsymbol{x}$ for primal and $\boldsymbol{\pi}$ for dual, the following always holds:*

$$\sum_j c_j x_j \geq \sum_i b_i \pi_i.$$

Proof:

The proof is a one liner in this case as shown below:

$$\sum_j c_j x_j \geq \sum_j (\sum_i a_{ij} \pi_i) x_j = \sum_i (\sum_j a_{ij} x_j) \pi_i \geq \sum_i b_i \pi_i.$$

■

The implication of this proposition is that, under no circumstances (including the optimum), the dual cost should be higher than the primal cost.

Example 5.2 *Determining a Dual for a Problem Not in the Assumed Format*

Consider the following (strange looking?) primal problem in matrix notation with vectors of variables $\boldsymbol{x}, \boldsymbol{y}$:

$$\begin{array}{lll} \text{Primal:} & \textbf{\textit{minimize}} & F = \boldsymbol{\xi} \boldsymbol{y} \\ & \textbf{\textit{subject to}} & \boldsymbol{E}\boldsymbol{x} = \boldsymbol{h} \\ & & \boldsymbol{D}\boldsymbol{x} \leq \boldsymbol{y} \\ & & \boldsymbol{x}, \boldsymbol{y} \geq \boldsymbol{0}. \end{array} \tag{5.1.10}$$

First, we need to rewrite this problem in the format given in (5.1.6). To do that we first transform $\boldsymbol{E}\boldsymbol{x} = \boldsymbol{h}$ to be composed of two inequalities:

$$\boldsymbol{E}\boldsymbol{x} \geq \boldsymbol{h}, \quad \boldsymbol{E}\boldsymbol{x} \leq \boldsymbol{h}.$$

and to set in the format we wanted, we can write all the constraints as:

$$\begin{array}{lll} \boldsymbol{E}\boldsymbol{x} & & \geq \boldsymbol{h} \\ -\boldsymbol{E}\boldsymbol{x} & & \geq -\boldsymbol{h} \\ -\boldsymbol{D}\boldsymbol{x} & +\boldsymbol{y} & \geq 0 \end{array}$$

and the primal cost as $\boldsymbol{0} \cdot \boldsymbol{x} + \boldsymbol{\xi} \cdot \boldsymbol{y}$. If we now associate non-negative dual multipliers $\boldsymbol{u}$, $\boldsymbol{v}$, $\boldsymbol{\pi}$ with these three constraints, respectively, we can write the dual constraints as:

$$\begin{array}{rl} \boldsymbol{u}\boldsymbol{E} - \boldsymbol{v}\boldsymbol{E} - \boldsymbol{\pi}\boldsymbol{D} & \leq \boldsymbol{0} \\ \boldsymbol{\pi} & \leq \boldsymbol{\xi} \end{array}$$

and then the dual as

$$\max_{u,v,\pi} \{hu - hv + 0 \cdot \pi : \; uE - vE - \pi D \le 0, \; \pi \le \xi, \; u \ge 0, v \ge 0, \pi \ge 0\}. \tag{5.1.11}$$

It may be noted that the non-negative dual variables u, v can be replaced with unrestricted variables λ where $\lambda = u - v$; then, the dual problem can be rewritten as:

$$\begin{array}{lll} \text{Dual:} & \textit{maximize} & h\lambda \\ & \textit{subject to} & \lambda E - \pi D \le 0 \\ & & \pi \le \xi \\ & & \pi \ge 0, \lambda \text{ unrestricted in sign.} \end{array} \tag{5.1.12}$$

●

5.1.3 Simplex Method

The basic solution method for LP problems, the famous simplex algorithm developed by the American mathematician George B. Dantzig [Dan63] (also see [Las70] and [Min86]), requires (in its simplest form) that the linear program is formulated in the *standard form* involving only non-negative variables and equality constraints.

Linear Program: Standard Form
variables

x_j j-th variable

objective

$$\text{minimize} \quad z = \textstyle\sum_j c_j x_j \tag{5.1.13a}$$

constraints

$$\textstyle\sum_j a_{ij} x_j = b_i \qquad i = 1, 2, ..., m \tag{5.1.13b}$$

$$x_j \ge 0 \qquad j = 1, 2, ..., n. \tag{5.1.13c}$$

Any LP problem can be easily converted to the standard form by introducing an additional non-negative *slack variable* s_i for each inequality in (5.1.1b) and substitute each x_j with an unconstrained sign by $x'_j - x''_j$ where $x'_j \ge 0, x''_j \ge 0$ (Exercise 5.4). We assume that in the resulting linear program there are n variables and m equations (5.1.13b), plus n non-negativity constraints (5.1.13c). Certainly Problem (5.1.13) is non-trivial only if $n > m$. There are potentially $\binom{m}{n}$ *basic solutions* of Problem (5.1.13), each corresponding to one of the non-singular $m \times m$ submatrices of $\boldsymbol{A}$, for instance to matrix $\boldsymbol{B}$, obtained by deleting all the columns from matrix $\boldsymbol{A}$ except m selected columns $j_1, j_2, ..., j_m$. The solution $\boldsymbol{x}^B$ corresponding to submatrix $\boldsymbol{B}$ is defined as:

$$\begin{array}{ll} x_j^B = y_k & \text{if } j = j_k \text{ for some } k = 1, 2, ..., m \\ x_j^B = 0 & \text{otherwise,} \end{array} \tag{5.1.14}$$

where $y = (y_1, y_2, ..., y_m)$ is the unique solution of the system of m linear equations $By = b$. A *basic feasible solution* is a basic solution with non-negative components. The fundamental fact about LP is as follows (refer to [Min86], § 2.2).

THEOREM 5.4 *Basic feasible solutions are identical with the extreme points (vertices) of the solution polytope defined by (5.1.13b) to (5.1.13c). If Problem (5.1.13) is feasible, its minimum is bounded from below, and rank(A) = m, then the minimum of (5.1.13a) is attained at one (or more) of the basic feasible solutions.*

(Recall that a $m \times n$ matrix with $m < n$ is of rank m if it contains at least one square $m \times m$ non-singular submatrix.)

Example 5.3 *Proposition 4.1 Revisited*

We now return to the proof of Proposition 4.1 from Section 4.1.2. LP Problem (4.1.9) is in the standard form, so every extreme point of the solution polyhedron (4.1.9a) to (4.1.9b) has at most $D + E$ non-zero entries, irrespective of the number of candidate paths. Moreover, if a basic feasible solution does not saturate a particular link e then the corresponding slack variable s_e is strictly positive, and this implies that in the simplex solution there are not more than $D + E - U$ non-zero flows where U is the number of unsaturated links. ●

Roughly speaking, the simplex method is a systematic, iterative algorithm of visiting consecutive basic feasible solutions (vertices of the solution polytope), decreasing the objective function during each (or almost each) iteration, and eventually identifying the minimum once it is reached. We point out that in the practical (commercial) simplex implementations, the non-negativity constraint for variables is not necessary; on the contrary, typical simplex implementations (as CPLEX [CPL99], Xpress [XM], and others) make effective use of free variables. For bounded variables the so-called "simple upper bounding" is applied (see [Mar03], [Mur81], [Naz87], and [OH68]). In fact, non-negativity of variables in optimization handbooks is adopted merely to simplify the presentation of the simplex algorithm.

There are also effective ways to assure that the actual problem treated by a simplex solver has linearly independent constraints (5.1.13b), i.e., rank(A) = m. This is important since NDPs often have dependent constraints. The independence of constraints can be assured by using, if necessary, the artificial variables introduced for Phase 1 of the simplex method also in Phase 2 (together with the additional constraints $t_k = 0$, where t_k denotes the artificial variable). Recall that Phase 1 is used to obtain a starting feasible point of (5.1.13) for the main algorithm of Phase 2 used to find the final optimal solution. In general, Phase 1 requires solving of the following linear program:

$$\begin{array}{lll}
\textbf{minimize} & t_1 + t_2 + ... + t_m & \\
\textbf{subject to} & a_{11}x_1 + a_{12}x_2 + ... + a_{1n}x_n + t_1 & = \; b_1 \\
& a_{21}x_1 + a_{22}x_2 + ... + a_{2n}x_n + t_2 & = \; b_2 \\
& \dots & \\
& a_{m1}x_1 + a_{m2}x_2 + ... + a_{mn}x_n + t_m & = \; b_m \\
& x_1, x_2, ..., x_n, t_1, t_2, ..., t_m & \geq \; 0.
\end{array}$$

A crucial property of the simplex method is that although, in general, it is an exponential-time algorithm (Appendix B), in practice it is a very efficient approach, in most cases with the computation time proportional to $n + m$ (in such a case we say that the computational complexity is $O(m + n)$). Although more recent polynomial-time algorithms for LP exist (based on the interior-point approach, see [RTV97] and Section 5.1.4), it still appears that in practice the simplex method is one of the easiest and fastest approaches.

The vertex-based approach gives way to several versions of the simplex algorithm, including primal simplex algorithm, dual simplex algorithm, and primal-dual simplex algorithm. All of these algorithms can be equipped with the commonly known technique—revised simplex algorithm—allowing for the determination of the necessary quantities during the calculation process without explicit use of the whole coefficient matrix $\boldsymbol{A}$. The description of the simplex techniques can be found, e.g., in [Las70], [Min86], [BJS90], [Mur81] and [Pad91]. Also, specialized polynomial-time simplex algorithms (mostly primal-dual) exist for specific classes of LP problems [DT97]; see [KH80] and [BJS90] for such specialized simplex algorithms for single-commodity network flow problems.

Certainly, the simplex method can be used for all the LP formulations presented in Chapter 4. The method produces exact, extreme-point solutions and is applicable even for large networks (for example, of 100 nodes), especially when combined with the column generation technique and Benders' decomposition discussed in Section 5.4.

5.1.4 Interior Point Methods (IPM)

The simplex method, although very efficient in practical applications, exhibits the exponential worst-case behavior, as illustrated by the following example.

Example 5.4 *Exponential-Time Example for the Simplex Method [BJS90]*
Consider the following problem with a fixed parameter $\gamma,\ 0 < \gamma < \frac{1}{2}$:

$$\begin{array}{lll} \textbf{maximize} & x_n & \\ \textbf{subject to} & 0 \le x_1 \le 1 & \\ & \gamma x_{j-1} \le x_j \le 1 - \gamma x_{j-1} & j = 2, 3, ..., n \\ & x_j \ge 0 & j = 2, 3, ..., n. \end{array}$$

It can be shown that starting from $\boldsymbol{x} = \boldsymbol{0}$, the standard simplex algorithm will visit all 2^n vertices of the solution polyhedron until it finds the optimal solution. As pointed out in [BJS90], this particular class of problems can be solved in just one iteration after introducing certain simple enhancements to the basic version of the simplex algorithm. Still, examples are known for which any enhancement of the simplex rules will not help [Jer73]. ●

Since 1947 when G. Dantzig discovered the simplex algorithm, substantial efforts have been spent to find an algorithm that solves *all* LP problems in polynomial time. Such an algorithm was finally found in 1979 by the Soviet mathematician L. Khachian [Kha79]; he applied an *ellipsoidal method*, based on the idea of N.Z. Shor (making use of the old technique of Newton) in the iterative process leading to the optimal solution. This was a remarkable achievement as it showed that all problems that can be formulated as linear programs are polynomial. However, in practical applications the algorithm itself turned out to be far slower than the simplex method. This somewhat strange situation changed in 1984 when the Indian mathematician N. Karmarkar [Kar84] found another polynomial (so-called *projective*) method for LP problems, with the practical efficiency comparable with that of the simplex method.

The general idea of IPM for LP is quite simple, and in fact analogous to general gradient optimization methods for convex programming (Section A.4 in Appendix A and Section 5.5 in this chapter). Instead of considering only vertices of the solution polytope (5.1.1) by moving along its edges (as in the simplex method), IPM algorithms follow a path through the interior of the polytope. There are several (inter-related) methods beyond this general idea, such as ellipsoid, projective, affine scaling, and barrier methods. Developments after 1984 include the method of Gill, Murray, Sanders, Tomlin, and Wright [GMS+86] which shows a close relation between Karmarkar's IPM and the logarithmic barrier approach, the primal-dual method of Monteiro and Adler [MA87], and other methods (see [BJS90], [GT96], and [RTV97]). Today, the so-called *central path-following primal-dual infeasible* IPM algorithms seem to be most efficient in practical applications (see [AGMX96], [GT96] and [Ter01]). They are theoretical bound on the number of iterations to reach an ε-exact solution is $O(\sqrt{n}\log(1/\varepsilon))$. In practice, however, their behavior is much better than the worst case complexity estimate: primal-dual methods with multiple centrality correctors [Gon96] tend to solve very large problems in a number of iterations which is proportional to $\log n$ rather than to $\sqrt{n}$ (although the computational effort for one IPM iteration may significantly exceed that of the simplex method).

Typically, IPM algorithms only approach the optimal solution asymptotically. If the solution is unique (a vertex) then IPMs would identify it. However, this is not often the case; many practical problems (including the ones considered in this book) are degenerate in the sense that they have multiple optimal solutions, either in the primal or dual space. In such a case, IPMs terminate at an approximate *analytical center* of the optimal solution set rather than in an optimal vertex. More precisely, if a linear program has a whole facet of optimal solutions, then the solution $\boldsymbol{x}^*$ generated by the IPM is approximately of the form

$$\boldsymbol{x}^* = \alpha_1\boldsymbol{x}^1 + \alpha_2\boldsymbol{x}^2 + ... + \alpha_K\boldsymbol{x}^K, \tag{5.1.15}$$

where $\boldsymbol{x}^1, \boldsymbol{x}^2, ..., \boldsymbol{x}^K$ are optimal vertices of the optimal facet, $\sum_{k=1}^K \alpha_k = 1$, and $\alpha_k > 0$ for $k = 1, 2, ..., K$ (this means that analytical center 5.1.15 is a strictly convex linear combination of all optimal vertices). This fact can be exploited in some applications, as in Section 8.2.1 Still, if an extreme-point optimal solution is required, appropriate efficient algorithms exist that can convert the optimal point (5.1.15), or its approximation, into a basic feasible solution by producing the corresponding optimal basis (this operation is called *cross-over*). Observe also that the primal-dual IPMs produce the primal solution (5.1.15) along with the corresponding dual solutions, also of the form analogous to (5.1.15).

In recent years, the IPM approach has improved considerably and new algorithms have been devised (see [AG99], [AGMX96], [BJS90], [DT97], [GT96], [Pad91], [RTV97], and [Ter01]). Today, the approach is well understood and efficient IPM algorithms are available in commercial LP solvers, e.g., [AG99], [CPL99], [Gon95], [MAT], and [XM] (for a recent survey of LP/IPM solvers, see [Fou03]). Intuitive (as well as formal) description of

Khanchian's and Karmarkar's algorithms can be found in [BJS90]. A relatively simple IPM of Dikin is described in [BC99]. A survey of today's most efficient IPM algorithms is given in [Fou03] and [GT96] (also see the reference list there); for a recent tutorial on IPMs, see [Ter01].

5.2 MIXED-INTEGER PROGRAMMING

As we already know, not all design problems considered in Chapter 4 (this also concerns many important problems studied in the subsequent chapters) can be formulated in the form of linear programs. This is, for instance, not possible (at least for now) for the $\mathcal{NP}$-complete problems (see Appendix B for the discussion of $\mathcal{NP}$-completeness), e.g., for the single-path allocation problem A/SPA (4.2.4) or for the modular link design problem D/ML (4.3.1) discussed in Chapter 4. For the multi-commodity NDPs studied in this book, however, the general LP form can be often maintained in the problem formulation, and only additional requirement for a certain subset of variables to be integers has to be introduced, leaving the rest of variables continuous. Such problems are called MIP problems. If all variables are to be integral, then the problem is called IP. So far we have seen three reasons for introducing integral variables: 1) routing restrictions (single-path routing and alike, lower bound on non-zero flows, refer to Section 4.2.2); modular links (various types, see Section 4.3.1); and MIP approximations of concave dimensioning functions (Section 4.3.3). In subsequent chapters we will see how MIP formulations can also be applied for other types of problems, not falling into any of these three categories (Section 7.2.1 and Section 8.1.2). In effect, virtually all problems considered in this book are (or can be) formulated as MIP problems.

We wish to point out that it is advantageous to have a MIP formulation of a problem in hand, since MIP problems can be directly treated by means of general purpose MIP solvers (as CPLEX [CPL99], XPRESS-MP [XM], and others). Even though the solvers may not be efficient for the large (or even medium) network problem instances, exact solutions can still be achieved at least for small networks, and used, for example, in verifying approximative heuristic methods. Also, better, problem-specific lower bounds can be obtained in many cases, e.g., through valid inequalities or Lagrangian relaxation, and used to speed up the branch-and-bound (BB) process of solving MIPs.

BB, and especially its important enhancement called branch-and-cut (BC), is virtually the only technique available to solve (exactly) general MIP (and IP) problems. Other approaches, such as the cutting-plane (CP) method and sometimes dynamic programming (DP), in principle can be applied for vast classes of MIPs, but they are not used in practice. In 1979 Land and Powell [LP79] found that all commercial MIP solvers used the BB technique. This finding is still actual if we add the BC extension (see [OZ96], [Sal94], and [Wol89]). In consequence, only the BB method will be described in detail below.

5.2.1 *The Branch-and-Bound (BB) Method*

The application of BB to MIP problems is best illustrated for binary variables. Consider the MIP problem obtained from linear program (5.1.1) by introducing the additional requirement:

$$x_j \in \{0, 1\},\ j=1, 2, ..., k \text{ for some fixed } k, k \leq n, \text{ and } x_j \geq 0,\ j=k+1, k+2, ..., n. \tag{5.2.1}$$

In our description of the recursive BB algorithm (written in a Pascal-like pseudo-code, see Algorithm 5.1), we use the following notation:

$N_U \subseteq \{1, 2, ..., k\}$	set of indices corresponding to unspecified values of binary variables, the binary requirement for these variables is relaxed so that for $j \in N_U$, x_j is a continuous variable from interval [0, 1]
$N_0 \subseteq \{1, 2, ..., k\}$	set of indices corresponding to binary variables equal to 0
$N_1 \subseteq \{1, 2, ..., k\}$	set of indices corresponding to binary variables equal to 1.

Procedure *solution* (N_U, N_0, N_1, x, z) used in the algorithm returns the optimal solution z^* of the LP subproblem being a relaxed (LP) version of the original MIP problem defined by (5.1.1a) to (5.1.1b) and the following additional constraints for variables:

$x_j \geq 0$, x_j continuous	for $j = k + 1, k + 2, ..., n$
$0 \leq x_j \leq 1$, x_j continuous	for $j \in N_U$
$x_j = 0$	for $j \in N_0$
$x_j = 1$	for $j \in N_1$.

If for given N_0 and N_1 such a subproblem is infeasible (which can frequently happen) then, by definition, $z = +\infty$. To initialize the procedure we put $N_0 = N_1 = \emptyset$, $N_U = \{1, 2, ..., k\}$ and assign a large number, greater than the expected optimal objective function of the problem to z^{best}. Note that during the execution of BB, it always holds true that $N_0 \cap N_1 = \emptyset$ (i.e., N_0 and N_1 are disjoint) and that $N_U = \{1, 2, ..., k\} \backslash (N_0 \cup N_1)$. Any such triple (N_0, N_1, N_U) is called a *node of the BB tree*; each such node is associated with the LP problem defined by (5.1.1a), (5.1.1b), and (5.2.1).

In Algorithm 5.1, the lower bounds used for "pruning" the BB tree are usually computed by solving the LP subproblems associated with the nodes of the BB tree procedure *solution* (N_U, N_0, N_1, x, z). Still, for particular problems the lower bounds can be found with other, specific (and more effective) means. Generally, the quality of the lower bounds (the greater the better) and the time required for their computation is decisive for the efficiency of the approach. In particular it may be important to provide the BB procedure with direct means for omitting the combinations of binary variables leading to unfeasible relaxed subproblems. This is important for instance when binary variables are subject to the single-path routing constraint, e.g., see (4.2.5a). Also, the (problem-dependent) criteria assumed for the choice of the particular unspecified variable $i \in N_U$ which enters the sets N_0 and N_1 at each iteration can be important for the effectiveness of BB. It should be noted that although for majority of the problems considered in this book, the BB approach may fail to find the exact optimum for large networks, as its execution time is in general exponential with the number of binary variables, in many cases it is able to find near-optimal solutions.

ALGORITHM 5.1 **Branch-and-Bound Procedure for Binary Variables (BBB)**

```
procedure BBB(N_U, N_0, N_1)
begin
  solution (N_U, N_0, N_1, x, z);
  if N_U = ∅ or for all i ∈ N_U x_i are binary then
    if z < z^best then begin z^best := z; x^best := x end
  else {in the current solution the value of x_i is not binary for some i ∈ N_U}
    if z ≥ z^best then
      return   {bounding}
    else
      begin   {branching}
        choose i ∈ N_U such that x_i is fractional;
        BBB(N_U\{i}, N_0 ∪ {i}, N_1);
        BBB(N_U\{i}, N_0, N_1 ∪ {i})
      end
end { procedure }
```

Now consider the general case when integral variables are not necessarily binary, but can be non-negative integers. Then, first of all, it is possible to transform the integer-valued MIP into its binary counterpart. This can be done by substituting each integral variable x_j by the expression

$$2^0 u_{j0} + 2^1 u_{j1} + 2^2 u_{j2} + \ldots + 2^q u_{jq} \tag{5.2.2}$$

composed of additional binary variables $u_{j0}, u_{j1}, \ldots, u_{jq}$, where q is the smallest integer such that $K \leq 2^{q+1} - 1$ and K is the maximal (integer) value for x_j (refer to [Min86, §7.2]).

In fact, the commercial MIP solvers use BB algorithms dealing directly with integral variables. Below, in Algorithm 5.2, we formulate an example of a BB procedure for a MIP problem with integral variables x_j, $j = 1, 2, \ldots, k$ and continuous variables x_j, $j = k+1, k+2, \ldots, n$. This time a node Ω of the BB tree is identified by a set of inequalities of the form

$$0 \leq d_j(\Omega) \leq x_j \leq g_j(\Omega) \leq M_j \quad j = 1, 2, \ldots, k, \tag{5.2.3}$$

where M_j is the fixed predefined upper bound for variable x_j. The LP problem of the node identified by set Ω, denoted by $\boldsymbol{P}(\Omega)$, is as follows:

$$\begin{array}{lll} \boldsymbol{P}(\Omega): & \textbf{\textit{minimize}} & z = \boldsymbol{cx} \\ & \textbf{\textit{subject to}} & \boldsymbol{Ax} \leq \boldsymbol{b} \\ & & d_j(\Omega) \leq x_j \leq g_j(\Omega) \qquad j = 1, 2, \ldots, k \\ & & x_j \geq 0, x_j \text{ continuous} \quad j = k+1, k+2, \ldots, n. \end{array} \tag{5.2.4}$$

Suppose $(z(\Omega), \boldsymbol{x}'(\Omega), \boldsymbol{x}''(\Omega))$, where

$$\boldsymbol{x}'(\Omega) = (x'_1(\Omega), x'_2(\Omega), ..., x'_k(\Omega)) \text{ and } \boldsymbol{x}''(\Omega) = (x''_{k+1}(\Omega), x''_{k+2}(\Omega), ..., x''_n(\Omega)),$$

denotes an optimal solution of the node problem $\boldsymbol{P}(\Omega)$ and suppose that such a solution is returned by procedure *solution*$(\Omega, z(\Omega), \boldsymbol{x}'(\Omega), \boldsymbol{x}''(\Omega))$. Besides, Boolean function *integer*$(\boldsymbol{x}'(\Omega))$ returns a value of **true** if vector $\boldsymbol{x}'(\Omega)$ is composed entirely of integers, and **false**, otherwise. Initially we put:

$$\Omega = \{0 \le x_j \le M_j : j = 1, 2, ..., k\}, \text{ i.e., } d_j(\Omega) = 0, g_j(\Omega) = M_j \quad j = 1, 2, ..., k. \tag{5.2.5}$$

Most of the remarks made for the binary version of BB apply also for Algorithm 5.2. We must add that non-recursive versions of BB procedures can be easily implemented, using the *waiting list* of the not yet solved nodes of the BB tree (in the recursive procedures *BBB* and *BBI* such a list is handled automatically by the recursion stack). With waiting lists, some other ordering of branching (possibly more effective than the depth-first search used above) and, thus, of solving the BB node problems can be applied.

ALGORITHM 5.2 Branch-and-Bound Procedure for Integer Variables (BBI)

```
procedure BBI(Ω)
begin
  solution(Ω, z(Ω), x'(Ω), x''(Ω));
  if integer(x'(Ω)) then
  if z(Ω) < z^best then
    begin
      z^best := z(Ω); x^best := (x'(Ω), x''(Ω))
    end
  else   {x'(Ω) contains a non-integer component}
    if z(Ω) ≥ z^best then
      return   {bounding}
    else
      begin   {branching}
        choose index i of one of non-integer components of x'(Ω);
        BBI((Ω\{d_i(Ω) ≤ x_j ≤ g_i(Ω)}) ∪ {d_i(Ω) ≤ x_j ≤ ⌊x'_j(Ω)⌋});
        BBI((Ω\{d_i(Ω) ≤ x_j ≤ g_i(Ω)}) ∪ {⌈x'_j(Ω)⌉ ≤ x_j ≤ g_i(Ω)})
      end
end { procedure }
```

The BB process consists of the three consecutive phases: 1) finding an initial yet feasible (integral) solution; 2) finding optimal integral solution; and 3) proving that the solution is optimal. Following [OZ96] we emphasize that computational experiments indicate

([BGG+71]) that for many MIPs the first two phases are completed in a relatively short time (sometimes only several times longer than the time required for the initial, totally relaxed LP solution), whereas the third phase may take an extremely long time. This observation can be used to improve stopping criteria for the BB procedures.

More about BB procedures can be found in optimization handbooks dealing with combinatorial optimization, e.g., [Bea79], [Ber98], [CCPS98], [Min86], [NW88], [OZ96], and [TW93].

5.2.2 The Branch-and-Cut (BC) Method

The efficiency of BB depends heavily on the quality of the lower bounds obtained by solving the BB tree node problems. If these bounds are close to the optimal integer solution then we can expect that the majority of the BB tree nodes will never be visited as most of the BB tree branches will not be entered (this is in fact the basic idea behind BB). Therefore, it may happen that it is advantageous to spend more time in a node and try to find a better lower bound than the one resulting from simple relaxation (i.e., from solving $\boldsymbol{P}(\Omega)$). Application of the lower bound improvement techniques is the heart of the BC enhancement of BB.

The basic way to achieve better lower bounds is to construct *valid inequalities* in the BB tree nodes. Such inequalities are generated and inserted to problems $\boldsymbol{P}(\Omega)$, on top (and sometimes instead) of the standard constraints (5.2.4). The idea is to exploit the integrality of variables in order to produce inequalities that are valid for all integral solutions and at the same time separate parts of the solution polyhedron of $\boldsymbol{P}(\Omega)$ containing the non-integral optimal solutions, leaving the integral optimal solutions within the adjusted polyhedron. It is also desirable that such inequalities define the faces (also called facets) of the *convex hull* of the solution set of the non-relaxed version of $\boldsymbol{P}(\Omega)$ (recall that such a convex hull is the smallest polyhedron containing all feasible solutions of the non-relaxed version of $\boldsymbol{P}(\Omega)$). The following example illustrates this issue.

Example 5.5 *Continuous Versus Integral Solution, Convex Hull for Integral Solutions [Min86]*
Consider the problem:

$$\begin{array}{lll} \textbf{\textit{maximize}} & z = 10x_1 + 11x_2 & \text{(equivalently: } \textbf{\textit{minimize}}\ z = -(10x_1 + 11x_2)) \\ \textbf{\textit{subject to}} & 10x_1 + 12x_2 \le 59 & \\ & x_1, x_2 \ge 0 \text{ and integers.} & \end{array}$$

The reader is kindly asked to draw the polyhedron determined by the three lines: 1) $10x_1 + 12x_2 = 59$; 2) $x_1 = 0$; and 3) $x_2 = 0$ as an exercise (Exercise 5.5). The resulting graphical illustration of the above problem reveals that the continuous optimum (for the relaxed problem with continuous variables x_1, x_2) is $\boldsymbol{x}^* = (5.9, 0)$ ($\boldsymbol{z}^* = 59$), while the integral optimum is $\boldsymbol{x}^* = (1, 4)$ ($\boldsymbol{z}^* = 54$). You may note that these two optima are quite distant from each other, and that rounding-down the continuous optimum yields an integral solution $\boldsymbol{x}^* = (5, 0)$ ($\boldsymbol{z}^* = 50$) which is far from the true integral optimum $\boldsymbol{x}^* = (1, 4)$ both in terms of the distance of the two points and the value of the objective function.

You may note that the convex hull containing all feasible integer solutions is the polyhedron determined by the inequalities: $x_1 + x_2 \leq 5, 0 \leq x_2 \leq 4, x_1 \geq 0$. These are valid inequalities for the above IP problem; if we could generate them in some way, then the continuous problem

$$\begin{array}{ll} \textbf{\textit{maximize}} & z = 10x_1 + 11x_2 \\ \textbf{\textit{subject to}} & x_1 + x_2 \leq 5, 0 \leq x_2 \leq 4, x_1 \geq 0 \end{array}$$

would yield the proper optimal integral solution $\boldsymbol{x}^* = (1, 4)$ (Exercise 5.6). ●

We also note that generation of valid inequalities is important already at the root of the BB tree (i.e. at the initial node, corresponding to the fully relaxed continuous version of the original problem), as they may yield a tighter set of constraints than the standard relaxed formulation, and these additional constraints will be used in the problems defined for all other nodes of the BB tree. It can even happen that solving the root problem will immediately yield a point, which, if an appropriate (feasible) rounding-off of the continuous variables can be found, provides a good near-optimal feasible integral solution.

Improved lower bounds can sometimes be effectively found by the Lagrangian relaxation technique, see, e.g., [Bal89], [CMM03], [GLY02], [JGL99], and [JSMR01] for applications of LR to multi-commodity flow problems. The technique is described in Section 5.4.1. Also, inequalities derived from Benders' decomposition can be used (Section 5.4.3). Finally, we mention that effective problem-specific methods can be sometimes found for this purpose, e.g., for the knapsack-type problems as in Section 6.4.1.

A recent survey of the general BC techniques can be found in [Wol89] (also see the list of references there and [BCC96]). The technique has been extensively used in the multi-commodity flow network design ([BM01], [CMM03], [DS98], [Gef01], [GLY02], [GMS95], [Gün99], [JGL99], [Min01], and [Wes00]). We will return to applications of BC in later chapters of this book.

5.2.3 The Cutting-Plane Method

The basic idea of the cutting-plane (CP) method is to add consecutive constraints to the initial relaxed LP formulation of the considered MIP problem (in the initial relaxed formulation and also in the consecutively constructed problems the integrality requirements for variables are totally skipped) in order to eliminate consecutive non-integral optimal solutions. More precisely, when we solve the initial continuous problem with the simplex algorithm, and the optimal vertex $\boldsymbol{x}^*$ is integral, then we are done; otherwise, we need to look for an additional inequality (defining a hyperplane) that will diminish the initial solution polytope (or polyhedron) (5.1.1) by cutting off vertex $\boldsymbol{x}^*$. Then, we add this inequality (defining a hyperplane called the cutting plane) to the original relaxed problem, and continue the procedure. You may note that for the problem in Example 5.5, the first cutting plane could be defined by inequality $x_1 \leq 5$.

The issue of how the consecutive planes should be selected is difficult, as no systematic way of generating the linear equations or inequalities defining the minimal convex hull of all the integer points contained in a given convex polyhedron is known. In fact such a convex hull can contain an enormous number of facets, even for MIP problems with only few variables and constraints. In this context, the main breakthrough in the CP method was the discovery by R.E. Gomory [Gom60] of a special class of CPs leading to finitely convergent CP algorithms (note that in general the number of generated planes must be exponential with the size of the problem, as the CP method aims at solving $\mathcal{NP}$-complete problems).

Clearly, the CP method can be used within the BC algorithms. For a more detailed development of the CP method the reader is referred to § 7.4 of [Min86] and to [Gol67] (also see [BCC96] and [Kiw97]).

5.2.4 Dynamic Programming

In the context of this book, dynamic programming (DP) can be regarded as a recursive way of solving MIP problems which obey so-called *principle of optimality*. Roughly speaking, the principle says that at any stage of the solution process, the partial optimal solutions obtained so far can be extended (without any change) towards the final optimal solution, and the optimal decision on how to extend the current partial solutions does not depend on the way a particular partial solution has been reached. The approach, established by R. Bellman [Bel57] (also see [BB96], [Had64], [Min86], and [Nem67]), is commonly used in the mathematical theory of optimal control, where the optimal solutions are functions of time, as the dynamic system evolves in time. In the context of MIP, the dynamic feature of the problem is introduced artificially, as we will see for the "knapsack problem" below. In the area of multi-commodity flow network design, the commonly known example of application of DP are the shortest-path algorithms, since the property: any initial part of a shortest path is also a shortest path, is an instance of the principle of optimality.

Below we will illustrate the idea of DP on the algorithm for solving the knapsack problem:

$$\begin{array}{ll} \textbf{\textit{maximize}} & \boldsymbol{F} = r_1x_1 + r_2x_2 + \ldots + r_nx_n \\ \textbf{\textit{subject to}} & w_1x_1 + w_2x_2 + \ldots + w_nx_n \leq W \\ & x_1, x_2, \ldots, x_n \text{ binary.} \end{array} \tag{5.2.6}$$

Constant integer W is the upper bound of the knapsack weight, and index $j = 1, 2, \ldots, n$ labels the objects (of weight $w_j > 0$ and value $r_j > 0$) that can be put into the knapsack. The problem is to maximize the total value of the objects put into the knapsack without exceeding the weight limit. The knapsack problem, although it enjoys a very simple formulation, is $\mathcal{NP}$-complete ([GJ79]) with respect to the problem size $n + W$.

Let $\boldsymbol{F}^*(k, w)$ denote the optimal objective value for Problem (5.2.6) for given parameters k and w (instead of n and W). Then the principle of optimality for the knapsack problem reads:

$$\boldsymbol{F}^*(k, w) = \max \left\{ \boldsymbol{F}^*(k-1, w), \boldsymbol{F}^*(k-1, W - w_i) + r_i \right\}. \tag{5.2.7}$$

TABLE 5.1 **Optimal Objectives in Knapsack Subproblems**

$k \backslash w$		0	1	2	3	4	5	6	7	8	9	10	11
1	$w_1 = 1, r_1 = 1$	0	1	1	1	1	1	1	1	1	1	1	1
2	$w_2 = 2, r_2 = 6$	0	1	6	7	7	7	7	7	7	7	7	7
3	$w_3 = 5, r_3 = 18$	0	1	6	7	7	18	19	24	25	25	25	25
4	$w_4 = 6, r_4 = 22$	0	1	6	7	7	18	22	24	28	29	29	40
5	$w_5 = 7, r_5 = 28$	0	1	6	7	7	18	22	28	29	34	35	40

Assuming initial values $\boldsymbol{F}^*(k, w) = 0$ for all $w \geq 0$ and $\boldsymbol{F}^*(k, w) = -\infty$ for all k when $w < 0$, we may compute consecutive values of $\boldsymbol{F}^*(k, w)$, starting from $\boldsymbol{F}^*(1, 1)$, until we reach $\boldsymbol{F}^*(N, W)$. Exercise 5.7 asks the reader is write down a recursive algorithm based on formula (5.2.7).

Example 5.6 *Knapsack Problem [BB96]*

Table 5.1 illustrates the application of DP to the knapsack problem with parameters $W = 11$, $\boldsymbol{w} = (1, 2, 5, 6, 7)$, and $\boldsymbol{r} = (1, 6, 18, 22, 28)$. Observe that Table 5.1 makes it possible to recover not only the optimal value of the knapsack load, but also its optimal composition (Exercise 5.8).

●

The knapsack-type problems are important as they appear in many operations research applications, including multi-commodity flow NDPs (for example, see Section 6.4.1 and [SKMP03]).

5.3 STOCHASTIC HEURISTIC METHODS

In this section we will discuss basic heuristic methods ([OL96]) applicable for the IP formulations created in Chapter 4 and for the problems considered in subsequent chapters. Except for local search, all the methods are stochastic in the sense that there is a random element guiding the sequence of generated solution points. The methods aim at finding suboptimal solutions to *combinatorial (discrete) optimization problems* of the following form:

$$\textit{\textbf{minimize}}\ \boldsymbol{F}(\boldsymbol{x}) \text{ for } \boldsymbol{x} \in \mathcal{S}, \tag{5.3.1}$$

where $\mathcal{S}$ is a finite set of feasible points (i.e., solution space, optimization space).

5.3.1 Local Search

Probably the simplest and most commonly known heuristic for Problem (5.3.1) is the local search (LS, see [AL97] and [OL96]) approach. LS uses a notion of *neighborhood*. A neighborhood of point $\boldsymbol{x} \in \mathcal{S}$, $\mathcal{N}(\boldsymbol{x})$, is a subset of the solution space S, $\mathcal{N}(\boldsymbol{x}) \subseteq \mathcal{S}$, such that $x \notin \mathcal{N}(x)$. The main requirement imposed on the family of all the neighborhoods $\{\mathcal{N}(x), x \in \mathcal{S}\}$ is that for any two points $x, y \in \mathcal{S}$ there exists a sequence $z_1, z_2, ..., z_p$ of points in $\mathcal{S}$ such that $z_1 \in \mathcal{N}(x), z_2 \in \mathcal{N}(z_1), ..., z_p \in \mathcal{N}(z_{p-1})$ and $y \in \mathcal{N}(z_p)$, i.e., that any point $y \in \mathcal{S}$ can be reached from any other point $x \in \mathcal{S}$ by traversing a sequence of neighborhoods.

ALGORITHM 5.3 **Local Search with Steepest Descent (LS)**

```
procedure SDLS
begin
  choose_initial_point(x);
  repeat
    z := x;
    for y ∈ N(x) do if F(y) < F(z) then z := y;
  until z = x
end { procedure }
```

The version of LS presented as Algorithm 5.3 is called the *steepest descent* LS since in each step it looks for the best improvement. Of course, if we put $\mathcal{N}(x) = \mathcal{S}$ for the initial point x then local search will find the global minimum just by searching through the whole solution space. This, however, is not practical, since to make the algorithm efficient the neighborhoods should be relatively small. Then, in turn, the algorithm can very soon get trapped in a local minimum.

Another version of LS, called *first descent*, is obtained when the **for** instruction terminates immediately after the first point y, thereby improving the objective function (Exercise 5.9).

5.3.2 *Simulated Annealing (SAN)*

We start with the oldest (at least among the commonly known approaches) general stochastic method called simulated annealing ([KGV83], [JAMS89], and [KAK89]), referred to as SAN in the sequel. SAN (see Algorithm 5.4) is a heuristic method for solving problems of type (5.3.1). As local search, SAN also uses the notion of a neighborhood.

After selecting an initial point $x \in \mathcal{S}$ and setting the initial temperature T^0 (initial temperature is a parameter, typically a large number), the algorithm proceeds into the outer **while-end** loop with a fixed temperature. Then the inner **while-end** loop is executed L times (L is another parameter of the algorithm, also typically a large number). Each execution of the inner loop consists in selecting a neighbor y of the current point x ($y \in N(x)$) at random and performing the so called *Metropolis test* in order to accept a move from x to y or not. The move is always accepted if it does not increase the objective function $F(x)$. Moreover, the (uphill) move is accepted with probability $e^{-\Delta F/T}$ even though it results in an increase of $F(x)$. For fixed T, the acceptance probability is an exponentially decreasing function of ΔF so the acceptance probability quickly becomes very small with the increase of ΔF. The use of the Metropolis test allows for leaving the local minima encountered during the process of wandering around the solution space within the inner loop. Once L steps of the inner loop are performed, the temperature is decreased and the inner loop is started again. An example of the temperature reduction is $T := \tau T$, for some parameter τ from interval (0, 1), e.g., $\tau = 0.99$. For fixed $\Delta \boldsymbol{F}$ the acceptance probability decreases with T, so in the consecutive execution of the inner loop the uphill moves are more and more rare. The stopping criterion can be, for instance, the condition $T = 1$ or the lack of significant improvement of the objective function in two consecutive executions of the outer loop. Also, reaching a solution not exceeding a certain predefined cost could be used to stop the procedure.

ALGORITHM 5.4 **Simulated Annealing (SAN)**

```
procedure SAN
begin
choose_initial_point(x); x^best := x; F^best = F(x^best);
T := T^0;
while stopping_criterion not true
  begin
    l := 0;
    while l < L do
      begin
        z := random_neighbor(N(x));
        ΔF := F(z) − F(x);
        if ΔF ≤ 0 then
          begin
            x := z;
            if F(x) < F^best then begin F^best := F(x); x^best := x end;
          end
        else if random(0, 1) < e^(−ΔF/T) then x := z;
        l := l + 1;
      end
    reduce_temetarture(T);
  end
end { procedure }
```

Observe that for each fixed temperature, the random process of visiting consecutive points in the optimization space is a Markov process (Exercise 5.10). Under certain additional assumptions it can be shown that the process is *ergodic* and its statistical equilibrium (or stationary) distribution is given by the Boltzmann distribution:

$$\text{Prob}\,\{\text{ the process is in state } x \text{ at step } n\,\} = e^{-\boldsymbol{F}(\boldsymbol{x})/T} / \textstyle\sum_{x \in \mathcal{S}} e^{-\boldsymbol{F}(\boldsymbol{x})/T}. \qquad (5.3.2)$$

It can be further proved that if parameter L is large enough, then the final solution as T approaches 0 is optimal with probability 1 (refer to [Ber98] §10.4.3). However, the issue is that in order to reach a global minimum, the number of steps L in the inner loop must in general be very large, possibly greater than the number of points in the solution space ($L > |S|$), which makes such an exact approach useless. Hence, SAN should be in fact treated as a heuristic method. In the next chapters we shall occasionally apply it for certain design problems; here, we show how to apply SAN to the concave problem D/CDF (4.3.18) discussed earlier in Chapter 4.

Since D/CDF admits non-bifurcated optimal solutions then the points of the solution space S can be coded as vectors $\boldsymbol{x} = (x_1, x_2, ..., x_D)$ where for $d = 1, 2, ..., D, 1 \leq x_d \leq P_d$ and x_d denotes the number of the path actually used to allocate demand volume h_d. A neighborhood of $\boldsymbol{x} \in S$ can be defined as:

$$\mathcal{N}(\boldsymbol{x}) = \{\boldsymbol{y} \in S : \boldsymbol{x} \text{ and } \boldsymbol{y} \text{ differ exactly at one position } \}. \tag{5.3.3}$$

Having defined the neighborhood structure, the SAN procedure can be run from some starting point $\boldsymbol{x} \in S$ with some fixed parameters T^0, L, and τ.

5.3.3 Evolutionary Algorithm (EA)

EA is another stochastic heuristic method of general purpose ([Gol89], [Mic96]). There are many versions of EAs. In this book, we will discuss a version called $(M + L)$-evolutionary algorithm specified by Algorithm 5.5.

ALGORITHM 5.5 **$(M + L)$-Evolutionary Algorithm (EA)**

---

procedure *MLEA*
begin
  initialize($\boldsymbol{P}$); $k := 0$;
  while *stopping_criterion* **not true**
    begin
      $\Theta := \emptyset$;
      for $i := 1$ **to** L **do** $\Theta := \Theta \cup$ *crossover*($\boldsymbol{P}$);
      for $\boldsymbol{x} \in \Theta$ **do if** *random*(0, 1) $< q$ **then** *mutate*($\boldsymbol{x}$);
      $\boldsymbol{P}$:= *select_best*($\Theta \cup \boldsymbol{P}$)
      $k := k + 1$;
    end
end { *procedure* }

The algorithm aims at maximizing the objective $\boldsymbol{F}(\boldsymbol{x})$, called the fitness function in the context of EA. The algorithm starts with forming an initial *population* $\boldsymbol{P} \subseteq S$ consisting of M *chromosomes*, i.e., solution points (the population size, M, is the basic parameter of EA). A chromosome is a sequence of *genes*, representing the internal structure of chromosome. Then the algorithm enters the main loop which is repeated until the stopping criterion is satisfied. The stopping criterion can be reaching a certain iteration limit or, as in SAN, lack of improvement of the objective function or, reaching a solution exceeding a certain predefined lower bound.

In the main loop, an auxiliary set $\mathbf{\Theta}$ of L chromosomes is first formed (L is the second basic parameter of the algorithm) by applying L times the so-called *crossover operation* to the current population $\boldsymbol{P}$. The crossover operation is applied to a pair of parent chromosomes selected from the current population $\boldsymbol{P}$. The parents $\boldsymbol{x}, \boldsymbol{y} \in \boldsymbol{P}$ are selected with probabilities proportional to the values of their fitness function $F(\boldsymbol{x})$ and $F(\boldsymbol{y})$, respectively, so the points that "better fit" have a larger chance to become parents. As the result of the crossover operation, the pair of selected parents produce an *offspring* by exchanging the genes, and the offspring is added to set $\mathbf{\Theta}$. The crossover rule is problem-dependent. Once the set $\mathbf{\Theta}$ is formed, each of its elements can be subject to the *mutation operation*. The mutation procedure on offspring $\boldsymbol{x}$ is performed with probability q (this is the third basic parameter) and is also problem-dependent. The result of procedure *mutate*($\boldsymbol{x}$) is a chromosome with randomly perturbed genes in chromosome $\boldsymbol{x}$. Each iteration of the main loop ends with selecting the M best fit chromosomes from the joint pool of chromosomes from $\boldsymbol{P}$ and $\mathbf{\Theta}$.

As already mentioned, EA can be modified in many ways, and a great variety of crossover and mutation operations can be thought of. Frequently, as the result of a crossover, two offspring are formed (as in the application described below).

In the next chapters, EAs will be applied to several NDPs. Here, we show how to apply EA to the single-path allocation problem A/SPA (4.2.4) formulated in Section 4.2.3.

The solution of A/SPA consists in finding a non-bifurcated feasible solution; hence, the chromosomes (i.e., the points of the solution space $\mathcal{S}$) can be coded as vectors $\boldsymbol{x} = (x_1, x_2, ..., x_D)$ where $d = 1, 2, ..., D$, $1 \le x_d \le P_d$ and x_d denotes the number of candidate paths actually used to allocate demand volume h_d. Recall that entries of each chromosome are referred to as genes. The fitness function can defined as:

$$\boldsymbol{F}(\boldsymbol{x}) = -\sum_e \left(\max\{\underline{y}_e(\boldsymbol{x}) - c_e, 0\}\right)^2, \tag{5.3.4}$$

where $\underline{y}_e(\boldsymbol{x})$ is the load of link e determined by the flow allocation corresponding to chromosome $\boldsymbol{x}$. Crossover of two chromosomes $\boldsymbol{x}$ and $\boldsymbol{y}$ results in two offspring $\boldsymbol{x}'$ and $\boldsymbol{y}'$ defined as:

$$x'_d = x_d + y_d - \omega y_d - (1-\omega)x_d, \quad y'_d = x_d + y_d - \omega x_d - (1-\omega)y_d, \quad d = 1, 2, ..., D, \tag{5.3.5}$$

where ω is a random binary number. Finally, the mutation operation changes chromosome $\boldsymbol{x}$ by randomly changing the numbers of paths x_d coded by its genes. This means that x_d is changed to some other number chosen randomly from set $\{1, 2, ..., P_d\}$.

5.3.4 Simulated Allocation (SAL)

The two methods from the previous sections, i.e., SAN and EA, are well known and have been applied in many different areas including communication network design. The method presented in this paragraph, called SAL [Pió97b], is less known although it is simpler, often faster, and in many cases more efficient in finding near-optimal solutions for the multi-commodity flow problems than SAN and EA.

Below we shall illustrate the idea of SAL using the modular link dimensioning problem D/ML (4.3.1) with modular demands as in A/MFA (4.2.11).

***LP:* D/ML/MF** **Link-Path Formulation**

Modular Links and Modular Flows

indices

$d = 1, 2, ..., D,$ demands
$p = 1, 2, ..., P_d$ candidate paths for demand d
$e = 1, 2, ..., E$ links

constants

δ_{edp} = 1, if link e belongs to path p realizing demand d; 0, otherwise
L size of the demand flow capacity module
h_d volume of demand d expressed as the number of demand modules
ξ_e cost of one capacity module on link e
M size of the link capacity module

variables

x_{dp} number of demand modules allocated to path p of demand d
y_e capacity of link e expressed in the number of modules

objective

$$\min \boldsymbol{F} = \sum_e \xi_e y_e \tag{5.3.6a}$$

constraints

$$\sum_p x_{dp} = h_d \qquad d = 1, 2, \ldots, D \tag{5.3.6b}$$

$$\sum_d \sum_p \delta_{edp} x_{dp} \leq (M/L) y_e \qquad e = 1, 2, \ldots, E \tag{5.3.6c}$$

$$x_{dp} \text{ and } y_e \text{ non-negative integers} \tag{5.3.6d}$$

Application of SAL to D/ML/MF results in Algorithm 5.6. The constant H denotes the sum of all demanded numbers of flow modules, $H = \sum_d h_d$ and it is assumed that the link module size is divisible by the demand module size and that $M/L = K$. Let $\boldsymbol{x} = (x_{dp} : d = 1, 2, ..., D, p = 1, 2, ..., P_d)$ and $|\boldsymbol{x}| = \sum_d \sum_p x_{dp}$ ($|\boldsymbol{x}|$ is the height of the allocation state $\boldsymbol{x}$).

In general, SAL works with partial allocation states (flow allocations) not necessarily fulfilling constraint (5.3.6b). From time to time, however, the algorithm will reach a full allocation state yielding a feasible solution for the considered problem. The best full allocation state found by the algorithm serves as the final solution.

ALGORITHM 5.6 Simulated Allocation (SAL)

```
procedure SAL
begin
  n := 0; x := 0; F^best := +∞;
  repeat
    if random(0, 1) < q(|x|) then allocate(x) else disconnect(x);
    if |x| = H then
      begin
        n := n + 1;
        if F(x) < F^best then
          begin
            F^best := F(x);
            x^best := x
          end
      end
  until n = N or F^best ≤ cost_lower_bound
end { procedure }
```

The procedure terminates when the number of visited full allocation states reaches the limit N or when the cost of the best full allocation state does not exceed a predefined value *cost_lower_bound*. The best solution is stored in $\boldsymbol{x}^{best}$. Two basic procedures of SAL are *allocate* ($\boldsymbol{x}$) and *disconnect* ($\boldsymbol{x}$). Procedure *allocate* ($\boldsymbol{x}$) is executed with the state-dependent probability $q(|\boldsymbol{x}|)$ and procedure *disconnect* ($\boldsymbol{x}$) with probability $1 - q(|\boldsymbol{x}|)$. Function $q(k)$ is defined for $0 \le k \le H$ and has the properties: $q(0) = 1$ and $q(H) = 0$, $\frac{1}{2} < q(k) \le 1$ for $0 < k < H$.

Procedure *allocate*($\boldsymbol{x}$) picks up one of the currently non-allocate d modules at random and allocates it to one of the allowable paths. This means that the demand d for which a demand module will be allocated is chosen with probability:

$$\left(h_d - \textstyle\sum_p x_{dp}\right) / (H - |\boldsymbol{x}|) \quad d = 1, 2, ..., D. \tag{5.3.7}$$

The path for allocating the considered demand module is chosen to be the shortest path with respect to the state-dependent link weights κ_e ($e = 1, 2, ..., E$) defined as follows:

$$\kappa_e = \begin{cases} \xi_e & \text{if } \sum_d \sum_p \delta_{edp} x_{dp} = K y_e \\ 0 & \text{if } \sum_d \sum_p \delta_{edp} x_{dp} < K y_e. \end{cases} \tag{5.3.8}$$

Then the capacities of the saturated links belonging to the selected shortest path are increased by 1 (this happens when the shortest path has a non-zero length) and the demand module allocated.

Procedure *disconnect* ($\boldsymbol{x}$) is even simpler. An allocated demand module is selected at random and disconnected from the path it uses. If this results in making a capacity module on one or more links on the path empty then the capacities of such links are decreased by 1. More precisely, the demand d for which a demand module will be disconnected is chosen with probability

$$\textstyle\sum_p x_{dp}/|\boldsymbol{x}|, \quad d = 1, 2, ..., D \tag{5.3.9}$$

and then a particular module is chosen at random, i.e., the probability of choosing a particular path $\mathcal{P}_{d,p}$ is proportional to x_{dp}. The capacity of a link on the chosen path is decremented by one module if

$$\textstyle\sum_d \sum_p \delta_{edp} x_{dp} - 1 = K(y_e - 1). \tag{5.3.10}$$

It can be shown using the methods described in [Fel68, Chapter XIV] (Exercise 5.11) that if

$$q(|\boldsymbol{x}|) = q_0 \geq \tfrac{1}{2} \quad \text{for } 0 < |\boldsymbol{x}| < H \tag{5.3.11}$$

then the expected (average) number of steps (allocations and disconnections) required to reach a full allocation state starting from state $\boldsymbol{x}$ is not greater than

$$(H - |\boldsymbol{x}|)/(2q_0 - \tfrac{1}{2}). \tag{5.3.12}$$

For instance, if $q_0 = \frac{2}{3}$ then a full allocation state will be reached from the zero allocation state in only $3H$ steps on the average.

Allocation and disconnection procedures of SAL can be improved in many ways in order to tailor the procedure to other design problems. We will present other applications of SAL in the rest of the book. Here we only state that for the considered problem D/ML/MF a significant time-efficiency improvement is achieved with the so-called "bulk disconnections". Bulk disconnection can be performed every N-th time a full allocation time is reached (for example, every tenth time) and consists in setting the capacities of a set of randomly chosen (with certain probability) links to 0 and disconnecting all flows through these links. For instance each link can be considered for deleting with probability $\frac{1}{4}$; then, on average, the capacities of one-fourth of the links will be set to zero.

5.3.5 *Tabu Search (TS)*

Tabu search is a neighborhood search descent method which avoids the "local minimum traps" by accepting worse (or even infeasible solutions) and constraining the current solution neighborhood by the solutions' "search history." The search history is stored in the form of a *tabu* (forbidden) list. The tabu list does not contain recent solutions to be excluded, but rather particular changes of the solution attributes, called moves, that cannot be applied in the subsequent iteration(s). The attribute-based tabu memory helps to diversify the search by avoiding short-term cycles or sequences of similar solutions. Each such tabu move is put on the tabu list and hence is forbidden for a specified number of iterations (this is called "tabu tenure"). Additionally, aspiration criteria can be introduced to weaken the tabu list restrictions. For example, an aspiration criterion can admit a solution, even if it is forbidden by the tabu list, when it outperforms the best result found so far. Both solution attribute choice and aspiration criterion are problem-specific. Below we present an example of the TS algorithm (Algorithm 5.7).

ALGORITHM 5.7 Tabu Search (TS)

procedure TS
begin
  choose_initial_point(x); $F^{best} := F(x)$; $x^{best} := x$;
  $\mathcal{T} := \emptyset$;
  while *stopping_criterion* **not true do**
    begin
      $\mathcal{N}^* := \mathcal{N}(x)$;
      repeat
          $y :=$ *best_neighbor* ($\mathcal{N}^*$);
          $\mathcal{N}^* := \mathcal{N}^* \backslash \{y\}$
      until $(y, x) \notin \mathcal{T}$;
      update ($\mathcal{T}$);
      $\mathcal{T} := \mathcal{T} \cup \{(y, x)\}$;
      if $F(x) \leq F^{best}$ **then begin** $F^{best} := F(x)$; $x^{best} := x$ **end;**
      $x := y$
    end
end { *procedure* }

To diversify the search, a frequency-based memory can be involved. In such a case we monitor the frequency of moves, but only on particular occasions (for example when no improvement is possible). For a long-term diversification, a penalty for these moves that are performed frequently is added to the objective function. Another complementary strategy, arising from the frequency memory, combines the solution attributes that are most often used in the previously noted local optima, but come from different subsets of past solutions, to generate a new solution.

Extensive literature on TS exists, for example refer to [Glo89], [Glo90], [LG93], [AFPR93], and [GL97].

5.3.6 Other Methods

In fact, there are many variations of the meta-heuristic methods described so far in Section 5.3, as well as other meta-heuristics applicable for multi-commodity network optimization (for example see [CLH99]); almost all of these methods are stochastic in nature. In many cases, it is hard to declare if a particular method (or approach) is an instance of a more general meta-heuristic or if is it a well-established method of its own. However, this does not matter much, as long as a method or algorithm is useful for solving a class of multi-commodity flow problems.

Here we will mention one particular approach, the greedy randomized adaptive search procedure (GRASP) ([FR95]); this procedure provides a more general framework for using the methods considered so far. Roughly speaking, GRASP is an iterative procedure in which each iteration is composed of two phases. In the first ("construction") phase we construct an initial solution, called greedy randomized solution, in some simple yet greedy way. For instance, if the decision variables are binary we choose their values in some random order according to a locally optimal rule. Once a feasible initial solution is constructed, we start the second ("improvement") phase, which consists in improving the greedy randomized solution with some other method, e.g., local search. Then the idea is to perform a large number of the combined iterations and adopt the best resulting solution.

You may easily notice that the GRASP framework can be used, for instance, to combine SAN and SAL approaches. SAL can be used for the construction phase (as it works with partial allocation states), and once the first feasible solution is reached, the improvement phase can be performed using SAN.

5.4 LP DECOMPOSITION METHODS

In this section we discuss three decomposition methods: Lagrangian relaxation (LR), the LP column generation technique useable for candidate path lists augmentation (CPLA), and Benders' decomposition (BD). All of these methods are among the most important approaches applicable to large NDPs of the LP and/or MIP form. As such, they will be used in subsequent chapters.

5.4.1 *Lagrangian Relaxation (LR)*

The way LP duality is discussed in Section 5.1.2 may give the impression that for a given problem there is only one way to write its dual. As you may have already noticed reading Section A.5 of Appendix A, this is actually not the case. In fact, there are many ways to write a dual, and what has been discussed in Section 5.1.2 can be classified as the "classical" (or 'full') dual for LP problems.

Generalized Dual

In the classical dual, we dualize all the constraints in the primal problem (except for non-negativity of variables). In the generalized dual approach it is not necessary to dualize all the constraints of the primal problem; only a suitable subset of actually relaxed constraints is chosen.

We will illustrate the generalized dual using a MIP version of Example 5.2 where the link capacity vector y is allowed to take only integral values and the link capacities are modular with module M. This is in fact Problem D/ML discussed in Section 4.3.1 (also, see Section 3.3). In the matrix form D/ML is as follows:

$$\begin{aligned} \textbf{\textit{minimize}} \quad & F = \xi y \\ \textbf{\textit{subject to}} \quad & Ex = h \\ & Dx \le My \\ & x \ge \mathbf{0};\, , y \text{ non-negative integer.} \end{aligned} \tag{5.4.1}$$

We consider dualizing with respect to a subset of constraints; from (5.4.1), we choose $\boldsymbol{D}\boldsymbol{x} \leq M\boldsymbol{y}$ for dualization (called *relaxation* in the present context). The Lagrangian function (refer to Section A.5) is written using the dual multipliers associated only with this subset of constraints and the original objective function as follows:

$$L(\boldsymbol{x}, \boldsymbol{y}; \boldsymbol{\pi}) = \boldsymbol{\xi}\boldsymbol{y} + \boldsymbol{\pi}(\boldsymbol{D}\boldsymbol{x} - M\boldsymbol{y}).$$

First, notice that the Lagrangian can be rewritten as

$$L(\boldsymbol{x}, \boldsymbol{y}; \boldsymbol{\pi}) = (\boldsymbol{\pi}\boldsymbol{D})\boldsymbol{x} + (\boldsymbol{\xi} - M\boldsymbol{\pi})\boldsymbol{y}.$$

Now, if we try to minimize the Lagrangian with respect to primal variables $\boldsymbol{x}, \boldsymbol{y}$ in regard to the remaining constraints, we arrive at a following new problem in variables $\boldsymbol{x}$ and $\boldsymbol{y}$

$$\begin{array}{ll} \textbf{\textit{minimize}} & L(\boldsymbol{x}, \boldsymbol{y}; \boldsymbol{\pi}) = (\boldsymbol{\pi}\boldsymbol{D})\boldsymbol{x} + (\boldsymbol{\xi} - M\boldsymbol{\pi})\boldsymbol{y} \\ \textbf{\textit{subject to}} & \boldsymbol{E}\boldsymbol{x} = \boldsymbol{h}, \quad \boldsymbol{x} \geq \boldsymbol{0}, \quad \boldsymbol{y} \text{ non-negative integer.} \end{array} \tag{5.4.2}$$

Note that this problem is parameterized by the vector of multipliers $\boldsymbol{\pi}$ ($\boldsymbol{\pi} \geq \boldsymbol{0}$) and that it can be divided into two separate subproblems since dependency between $\boldsymbol{x}$ and $\boldsymbol{y}$ in the constraints no longer exists. This is a highly desired feature (in fact motivating the use of LR in this case) which helps to solve Problem (5.4.2) leading to the following formulation of the Lagrangian minimization problem:

$$\begin{aligned} W(\boldsymbol{\pi}) &= \min_{\boldsymbol{x},\boldsymbol{y}} \{L(\boldsymbol{x}, \boldsymbol{y}; \boldsymbol{\pi}) \; : \boldsymbol{E}\boldsymbol{x} = \boldsymbol{h}, \; \boldsymbol{x} \geq \boldsymbol{0}, \boldsymbol{y} \geq \boldsymbol{0} \text{ and integer}\} \\ &= \min_{\boldsymbol{x}} \{(\boldsymbol{\pi}\boldsymbol{D})\boldsymbol{x} \; : \; \boldsymbol{E}\boldsymbol{x} = \boldsymbol{h}, \; \boldsymbol{x} \geq \boldsymbol{0}\} + \min_{\boldsymbol{y}} \{(\boldsymbol{\xi} - M\boldsymbol{\pi})\boldsymbol{y} : \boldsymbol{y} \geq \boldsymbol{0} \\ &\qquad\qquad\qquad\qquad\qquad\qquad\qquad\qquad \text{and integer}\}. \end{aligned}$$

It is now easier to see the two decoupled problems, one over the variable $\boldsymbol{x}$ and the other over the variable $\boldsymbol{y}$, which are certainly dependent on the assumed values of $\boldsymbol{\pi}$. The advantage of such decoupling is the ability to solve these subproblems efficiently. To illustrate this point, consider the second subproblem:

$$\min_{\boldsymbol{y}} \{(\boldsymbol{\xi} - M\boldsymbol{\pi})\boldsymbol{y} \; : \; \boldsymbol{y} \geq \boldsymbol{0} \text{ and integer}\}.$$

This subproblem can be solved for each component of $\boldsymbol{y}$ independently. If $\boldsymbol{y}$ is a E-dimensional vector, then for component y_e, $e = 1, 2, ..., E$, we have the single variable problem:

$$\min_{y_e} \{(\xi_e - M\pi_e)y_e \; : \; y_e \geq 0 \text{ and integer}\}, \qquad e = 1, 2, ..., E.$$

It is easy to see that the solution is readily available since optimal y_e takes the value 0 if $\xi_e \geq \pi_e$, otherwise ∞. In practical implementation of an algorithm, we cannot allow an infinite value; thus, the feasible region for y_e is typically upper bounded with an artificial high number.

Remark 5.1

On Artificial Bound

Instead of using the artificial upper bounds for $\boldsymbol{y}$ we can specify the proper domain for the dual variables in which minimization of the Lagrangian makes sense, i.e., the set $Dom(W) = \{\boldsymbol{\pi} : 0 \le \pi_e \le \xi_e/M,\ e = 1, 2, ..., E\}$ in the considered case. This set is the domain of the dual objective function W, as explained in Appendix A. ♦

To recap, we have the following parameterized problem:

$$\begin{aligned} W(\boldsymbol{\pi}) &= \min_{\boldsymbol{x},\boldsymbol{y}} \{L(\boldsymbol{x}, \boldsymbol{y}; \boldsymbol{\pi}) \ : \ \boldsymbol{Ex} = \boldsymbol{h},\ \boldsymbol{x} \ge \boldsymbol{0},\ \boldsymbol{y} \ge \boldsymbol{0}\} \\ &= \min_{\boldsymbol{x}} \{(\boldsymbol{\pi D})\boldsymbol{x} \ : \boldsymbol{Ex} = \boldsymbol{h},\ \boldsymbol{x} \ge \boldsymbol{0}\} + \min_{\boldsymbol{y}} \{(\boldsymbol{\xi} - M\boldsymbol{\pi})\boldsymbol{y} \ : \ \boldsymbol{y} \ge \boldsymbol{0}\} \\ &= \min_{\boldsymbol{x}} \ \{L_x(\boldsymbol{\pi}) \ : \ \boldsymbol{Ex} = \boldsymbol{h},\ \boldsymbol{x} \ge \boldsymbol{0}\} + \min_{\boldsymbol{y}} \ \{L_y(\boldsymbol{\pi}) \ : \ \boldsymbol{y} \ge \boldsymbol{0}\}, \end{aligned}$$

where $L_x(\boldsymbol{\pi}) = (\boldsymbol{\pi D})\boldsymbol{x}$ and $L_y(\boldsymbol{\pi}) = (\boldsymbol{\xi} - M\boldsymbol{\pi})\boldsymbol{y}$. Then, the generalized dual problem of Problem (5.1.10) is:

$$\max_{\boldsymbol{\pi}} \ \{W(\boldsymbol{\pi}) \ : \ \boldsymbol{\pi} \ge 0\}. \tag{5.4.3}$$

As stated in Section A.5 of Appendix A, both the classical dual and the generalized dual obey the weak-duality theorem (i.e. the maximum of the generalized dual objective can never be higher than the minimum of the primal objective). Further, note that the function $W(\boldsymbol{\pi})$ is a piecewise linear concave function (Figure 5.2) since it is the minimum of the linear functions arising in the solution of the subproblems. Hence, because we are maximizing the (concave) dual function, any locally optimal solution to $W(\boldsymbol{\pi})$ is also globally optimal. It is also important to note that in the considered non-convex optimization problem (with integral variables), the minimum of the primal objective is in general strictly greater than the maximum of the dual function. This phenomenon is called *duality gap* (see Section A.5).

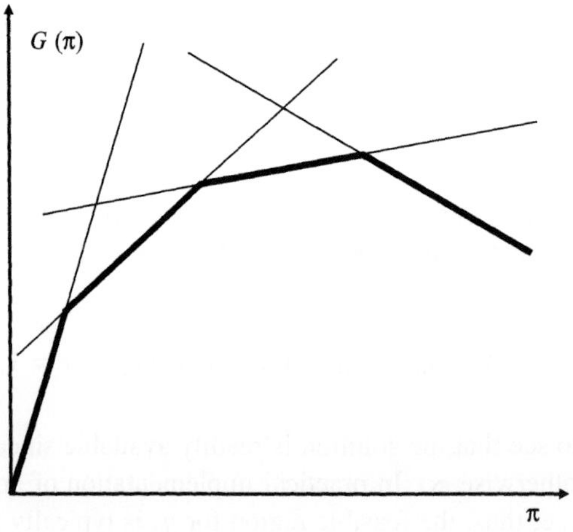

FIGURE 5.2 Piecewise Linear Concave Function

Generalized dual is a powerful concept since you can dualize with respect to *any* subset of constraints. Thus, for a specific design problem, you should examine the structure of the problem and choose the subset that is the best to dualize, which leads to decoupled minimization of the Lagrangian. This can, in many cases, be beneficial since it is possible to develop some efficient algorithms for the parameterized subproblems (e.g., as in (5.4.3)) as well as to use some efficient techniques for the maximization of the dual function.

Note that we have formed the Lagrangian by relaxing a subset of constraints; hence, the process is also called LR, especially in the context of developing algorithms for solving the dual problem. In addition note the difference between the classical dual Problem (5.1.12) and the generalized dual Problem (5.4.3). The classical dual of an LP problem is again an LP problem while the generalized dual of an LP problem for a proper subset of constraints is a concave maximization problem over a piecewise linear concave function in dual variables that requires solving the Lagrangian minimization subproblems. Hence, the dual is a convex problem, involving maximization of a concave function over linear constraints. Finally, let us note that the the generalized dual (involving the Lagrangian) taken with respect to all constraints of an LP problem turns out to be the classical dual discussed in Section 5.1.2.

Solving the Dual Problem

Recall that $W(\pi)$ is a piecewise linear concave function. This means that at the intersection point of adjacent linear pieces (Figure 5.2), $W(\pi)$ is not differentiable, but it is subdifferentiable (see Section A.8 and A.9 of Appendix A). Note that the *subdifferential* of function $W(\pi)$ at point π is a set of all its *subgradients* at this point and is denoted by $\partial W(\pi)$.

The general definition of a subgradient is given in Section A.8 in Appendix A. In the example considered in this section each subgradient, $\nabla W(\pi)$, at a given point π is obtained in the following way (following from the general formula derived in Section A.9 of Appendix A). Given multiplier π, we can solve each of the subproblems given in (5.4.3) which are both LPs (the second of them is further specialized as we have illustrated earlier). Suppose that the π-dependent optimal solutions for these subproblems are denoted by $\boldsymbol{x}^*(\pi)$ and $\boldsymbol{y}^*(\pi)$. Then the corresponding subgradient of the dual function W at π is given by:

$$\nabla W(\pi) = \boldsymbol{D}\boldsymbol{x}^*(\pi) - M\boldsymbol{y}^*(\pi). \tag{5.4.4a}$$

Note that it is possible that there are multiple optimal solutions for subproblems (5.4.3) associated with π; in fact, the above method for determining the subgradient implies that different optimal solutions $\boldsymbol{x}^*(\pi)$ and $\boldsymbol{y}^*(\pi)$ in general determine different subgradients. Thus, there are other subgradients possible depending on the optimal solutions generated by solving the subproblems. For our purpose, however, we just need one optimal solution for the subproblem associated with π and compute the resulting subgradient, $\nabla W(\pi)$. Note that the subgradient is similar to the gradient of the Lagrangian with respect to π.

Now, suppose we are at dual iteration k with dual multiplier π^k and the computed subgradient is denoted by $\nabla W(\pi^k)$. Then, the dual iteration can be updated as follows:

$$\pi^{k+1} = \max\left\{\pi^k + t_k \nabla W(\pi^k), 0\right\}. \tag{5.4.4b}$$

Here max is used to ensure non-negativity of dual multipliers, and the step-size, t_k, can be given by the following:

$$t_k = \rho\left(\overline{W} - W(\pi^k)\right)/||\nabla W(\pi^k)||^2 \quad (5.4.4c)$$

as first described in [HWC74] (see also [Sho85]). Note that ρ is commonly used in the range $0 \le \rho \le 2$. Finally, $\overline{W}$ is an upper bound on the dual objective; this is easy to attain since by the weak duality result, any feasible solution to the primal problem is an upper bound. Note that other step-size calculations are possible as long as convergence can be guaranteed (for example, see § 6.3.2 in [KH80]). The dual iteration is continued until a user-defined stopping rule such as maximum number of iterations or no progress in the dual objective. A schematic view of the LR based dual approach is given in Algorithm 5.8.

ALGORITHM 5.8 **Lagrangian Relaxation (LR) Based Dual Algorithm**

Step 0: Choose an initial π^0, k_{max} and $\rho_{maxiter}$. Set $\rho = 2$, $\rho_{min} = 0.005$, $k = 0$, $\rho_{iter} = 0$, $\boldsymbol{F}^{best} = \infty$.

Step 1: $k := k + 1$, $\rho_{iter} := \rho_{iter} + 1$.
Given π^k, solve (5.4.2) as decoupled subproblems in $\boldsymbol{x}$ and $\boldsymbol{y}$ to obtain solutions $\boldsymbol{x}^k$, and $\bar{\boldsymbol{y}}^k$.

Step 2: Use $\boldsymbol{x}^k$ to compute feasible $\boldsymbol{y}^k$ (integer valued) that satisfies $D\boldsymbol{x}^k \le M\boldsymbol{y}^k$.
Use $\boldsymbol{x}^k$ and $\boldsymbol{y}^k$ to compute primal objective $\boldsymbol{F}$.
If $\boldsymbol{F} < \boldsymbol{F}^{best}$ then $\boldsymbol{F}^{best} := \boldsymbol{F}, \boldsymbol{x}^{best} := \boldsymbol{x}^k, \boldsymbol{y}^{best} := \boldsymbol{y}^k, \overline{W} := \boldsymbol{F}^{best}$.
If ($\rho_{iter} > \rho_{maxiter}$) then begin $\rho = \max\{\rho/2, \rho_{min}\}$; $\rho_{iter} = 0$ end

Step 3: Use decoupled solutions $\boldsymbol{x}^k$ and $\bar{\boldsymbol{y}}^k$ to compute
subgradient: $\nabla W(\pi^k)$ (refer to (5.4.4a))
dual objective: $W(\pi^k) = \xi\bar{\boldsymbol{y}}^k + \pi^k(D\boldsymbol{x}^k - M\bar{\boldsymbol{y}}^k)$
step size: t_k (refer to (5.4.4c))
dual variable: π^{k+1} (refer to (5.4.4b)).

Step 4: If $k > k_{max}$, stop; otherwise go to Step 1.

In essence, we can take the dual subgradient-based approach to solve for the approximate primal optimal objective. However, there is one more major problem (except for the duality gap) associated with the dual approach: in general the optimal primal solution point $(\boldsymbol{x}^*, \boldsymbol{y}^*)$ (or even the primal feasible solution point, although this is not the case in this example) may not be available from the optimal dual solution. As the iteration progresses, a primal feasible solution can be computed based on the optimal $\boldsymbol{x}^k$ at iteration k to obtain a feasible $\boldsymbol{y}$ that satisfies $D\boldsymbol{x} \le M\boldsymbol{y}$ (note $\boldsymbol{y}$ is variable); we need to store this primal feasible solution with the minimal primal cost until the end. Note that this works because $\boldsymbol{y}$ is a variable; if the right-hand side was given as a constant (e.g., capacity), it would not be easy to obtain a primal feasible solution at each dual iteration k.

Finally, we want to comment on the dual function. While, in general, the dual objective function remains subdifferentiable, especially when a LP problem is dualized, there are situations under which it is possible that the generalized dual is differentiable—for sufficient conditions see [Roc70], and [Rob87].

Example 5.7 *Node Location Problem: Illustration*

Consider Problem (6.1.1) discussed later in Chapter 6 for determining node location (where explanation of variables and constants are given):

$$\begin{array}{lll} \textbf{minimize}_{\boldsymbol{u},\boldsymbol{r}} & \boldsymbol{F} = \sum_i \sum_j \xi_{ij} u_{ij} + \sum_j \eta_j r_j & \\ \textbf{subject to} & \sum_j u_{ij} = 1 & i = 1, 2, ..., N \\ & \sum_i u_{ij} \leq K_j r_j & j = 1, 2, ..., M \\ & \boldsymbol{u}, \boldsymbol{r} \text{ binary} & \end{array} \tag{5.4.5}$$

in variables $\boldsymbol{u} = (u_{ij} : i = 1, 2, ..., N, j = 1, 2, ..., M)$ and $\boldsymbol{r} = (r_1, r_2, ..., r_M)$.

In this case, we will consider dualizing with respect to the second constraint in (5.4.5). The Lagrangian can be written as:

$$L(\boldsymbol{u}, \boldsymbol{r}; \boldsymbol{\pi}) = \sum_i \sum_j \xi_{ij} u_{ij} + \sum_j \eta_j r_j + \sum_j \pi_j \left(\sum_i u_{ij} - K_j r_j \right).$$

On simplifying, we get:

$$L(\boldsymbol{u}, \boldsymbol{r}; \boldsymbol{\pi}) = \sum_i \sum_j (\xi_{ij} + \pi_j) u_{ij} + \sum_j (\eta_j - K_j \pi_j) r_j.$$

Here, the dual problem is:

$$\max_{\boldsymbol{\pi}} \{ W(\boldsymbol{\pi}) \ : \boldsymbol{\pi} \geq \boldsymbol{0} \} \tag{5.4.6}$$

where

$$W(\boldsymbol{\pi}) = \min_{\boldsymbol{u},\boldsymbol{r}} L(\boldsymbol{u}, \boldsymbol{r}; \boldsymbol{\pi}) = \min_{\boldsymbol{u}} L_u(\boldsymbol{\pi}) + \min_{\boldsymbol{r}} L_r(\boldsymbol{\pi}), \tag{5.4.7}$$

and

$$\min_{\boldsymbol{u}} L_u(\boldsymbol{\pi}) = \min_{\boldsymbol{u}} \left\{ \sum_i \sum_j (\xi_{ij} + \pi_j) u_{ij} \ : \ \sum_j u_{ij} = 1, i = 1, 2, ..., N, \boldsymbol{u} \text{ binary} \right\} \tag{5.4.8}$$

$$\min_{\boldsymbol{r}} L_r(\boldsymbol{\pi}) = \min_{\boldsymbol{r}} \left\{ \sum_j (\eta_j - K_j \pi_j) r_j \ : \ \boldsymbol{r} \text{ binary} \right\}. \tag{5.4.9}$$

It is easy to see that for given $\boldsymbol{\pi}$, Problem (5.4.8) is further decomposable for each i, and the problem for each i is easily solvable by selecting j and setting $u_{ij} = 1$ corresponding to the lowest cost-coefficient $\xi_{ij} + \pi_j$ among all j. Similarly, for (5.4.9), we set r_j to 0 or 1 depending on whether the quantity $\eta_j - K_j \pi_j$ is positive or negative.

For a given $\boldsymbol{\pi}$, the subgradient corresponding to an optimal solution $\boldsymbol{u}^*$ and $\boldsymbol{r}^*$ of the minimization problem in 5.4.7 is obtained as $\nabla W(\boldsymbol{\pi}) = (\partial W(\boldsymbol{\pi})/\partial \pi_1, \partial W(\boldsymbol{\pi})/\partial \pi_2, \ldots, \partial W(\boldsymbol{\pi})/\partial \pi_M)$ where

$$\partial W(\boldsymbol{\pi})/\partial \pi_j = \sum_i u_{ij}^* - K_j r_j^* \quad j = 1, 2, ..., M. \tag{5.4.10}$$

As explained earlier in this section, this dual subgradient can be used for updating the dual multipliers at iteration k. Then, the subproblems are solved again for the next iteration and so on, until the stopping rule is reached. ●

To end this section, we note that in the applications to multi-commodity networks, the LR technique is basically used to find approximate, close-to-optimal solutions to MIP problems (refer for example to [Dia03], [HY98], [JSMR01], [Med95], and [MT00b]) and in particular to compute lower bounds in the BC algorithms ([HY00]).

5.4.2 Column Generation Technique for Candidate Path List Augmentation (CPLA)

As explained in Section 4.1.1 (and in Chapter 2) there are two basic types of formulations of the multi-commodity flow NDPs: node-link and link-path. The basic difference is in the way the formulation includes the demands' paths. The node-link formulation takes (indirectly) into account all possible paths in the network (the set of all network paths is denoted by $\mathcal{P}_{all}$), while the link-path formulation makes direct use of the predefined lists of candidate paths (the set of all paths actually appearing on the candidate path lists is denoted by $\mathcal{P}_{cand}$). The paths that are allowed to appear on the candidate lists (recall that these lists are also called routing lists) can be restricted by some requirement, for instance, the paths can have a limited number of links (hops). The set of network paths that satisfy such a requirement is called the set of allowable paths and denoted by $\mathcal{P}_{allow}$ (Figure 5.3). It is important that, in general, node-link does not allow for such additional restriction, so for node-link, $\mathcal{P}_{cand} = \mathcal{P}_{allow} = \mathcal{P}_{all}$. On the contrary, for link-path it is typical that $\mathcal{P}_{cand} \subsetneq \mathcal{P}_{allow} \subsetneq \mathcal{P}_{all}$.

The size (number of flow variables) of the LP problems in the link-path formulations depends on the total size $|\mathcal{P}_{cand}|$ of the candidate path lists. Since the total number of network paths $|\mathcal{P}_{all}|$ grows exponentially with the number of nodes, the total number of potential flow variables also grows exponentially. Thus, we can arrive at a situation where we have a reasonable number of constraints but a very large number of variables. It is not always easy to effectively use the simplex method in such cases to obtain an optimal solution in a reasonable amount of time; in fact, sometimes it is not even possible to obtain a solution and, for that matter, just generating a reasonable initial set of candidate paths for a large network can pose a problem. At the same time, as shown in Example 5.3 (and in Example 4.1 in Section 4.1),

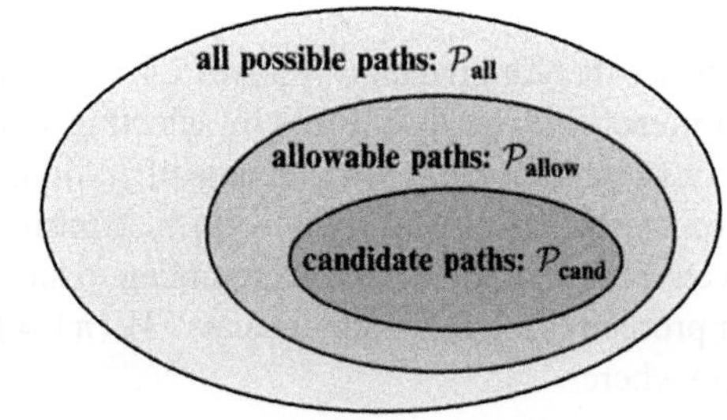

FIGURE 5.3 Relation between Sets of Paths

the total number of non-zero flows in the optimal solution for a multi-commodity flow network problem can be very small as compared to the total number of paths that are potentially allowed to carry the flows. Hence, if we consider the routing lists containing only the paths with non-zero optimal flows, then for large networks we typically have $|\mathcal{P}_{cand}| \approx D \ll |\mathcal{P}_{allow}|$.

Thus, one may wonder if there is a way to reduce the number of variables so that the problem is manageable. A possible way is to generate small routing lists to start with, so the total number of variables is still manageable for the simplex method to solve. The issue then is how many and, for that matter, which paths outside of the initial routing lists to include in the initial set so that we can arrive at the optimal solution for the entire problem. While generating a small set of candidate paths as a feeder to the design problem can still generate close to optimal (and sometimes the optimal) solutions to the entire problem, a nice technique is available which can be used to select the set of paths iteratively so that the problem remains reasonable and, at the same time, we can arrive at the optimal solution. This technique, called *path generation* for candidate path lists augmentation, and referred to as PG or CPLA in the rest of this book, is an application of the *generalized* LP (see § 8.1.3 in [Min86]) or *column generation* (see [Raw69] and Section 17.5 in [AMO93]); for applications relevant to this book also see [DS98], [KPNG02], [Nac02], and [Wes00].

Below, we apply CPLA to solve the flow allocation problem A/PAP (4.1.7) from Section 4.1 to illustrate benefits of the technique; further applications are discussed in Section 8.2.1, Section 10.1, and Section 12.4.3. Recall that A/PAP is a pure allocation problem and consists in finding any of the feasible flow allocation vectors in a capacitated network. Thus, even if the problem is feasible within set $\mathcal{P}_{allow}$, there is no guarantee that a given instance of the problem with routing lists limited to $\mathcal{P}_{cand}$ is feasible. We start with augmenting the problem with artificial variables $\boldsymbol{z}$, expressing the overload of links, to make the problem feasible for any fixed set of non-empty routing lists $\mathcal{P}_{cand}$.

***LP:* A/ALC** **Link-Path Formulation**

Augmented Link Capacities

indices

$d = 1, 2, ..., D$ demands
$p = 1, 2, ..., P_d$ candidate paths for demand d
$e = 1, 2, ..., E$ links

constants

δ_{edp} = 1 if link e belongs to path p realizing demand d; 0, otherwise
h_d volume of demand d
c_e capacity of link e

variables

x_{dp} flow allocated to path p of demand d, $\boldsymbol{x} = (x_{dp} : d = 1, 2, ..., D, p = 1, 2, ..., P_d)$
z_e variable measuring overload of link e, $\boldsymbol{z} = (z_e : e = 1, 2, ..., E)$

objective

$$\text{minimize } \boldsymbol{F}(\boldsymbol{z}) = \textstyle\sum_e z_e \qquad (5.4.11a)$$

constraints

$$\sum_p x_{dp} = h_d, \qquad d = 1, 2, \ldots, D \tag{5.4.11b}$$
$$\sum_d \sum_p \delta_{edp} x_{dp} \leq c_e + z_e, \qquad e = 1, 2, \ldots, E \tag{5.4.11c}$$
$$\boldsymbol{x} \geq \mathbf{0}, \boldsymbol{z} \geq \mathbf{0}. \tag{5.4.11d}$$

If an optimal solution $(\boldsymbol{x}^*, \boldsymbol{z}^*)$ of A/ALC exists and if $\boldsymbol{F}(\boldsymbol{z}^*) = 0$, then $(\boldsymbol{x}^*, \boldsymbol{z}^*)$ is a feasible solution of A/PAP we are looking for and, therefore, such a solution $(\boldsymbol{x}^*, \boldsymbol{z}^*)$ is called *optimal in the wider sense*. Simply put, set $\mathcal{P}_{cand}$ (i.e., the assumed lists of candidate paths) contains enough "necessary" paths, so the solution $(\boldsymbol{x}^*, \boldsymbol{z}^*)$ is optimal also when all allowable paths are included to the routing lists ($\mathcal{P}_{cand} = \mathcal{P}_{allow}$).

CPLA works with dual variables, so we first need to look at the Lagrangian for Problem (5.4.11), the associated dual variables, and the optimality conditions. Let $\boldsymbol{\lambda} = (\lambda_1, \lambda_2, \ldots, \lambda_D)$ be the vector of the dual variables (with unconstrained signs) corresponding to constraints (5.4.11b) and $\boldsymbol{\pi} = (\pi_1, \pi_2, \ldots, \pi_E)$, $\boldsymbol{\pi} \geq 0$ be the vector of dual variables corresponding to constraints (5.4.11c). The Lagrangian function (refer to Section A.5 of Appendix A) for A/ALC is as follows:

$$\begin{aligned} L(\boldsymbol{x}, \boldsymbol{z}; \boldsymbol{\lambda}, \boldsymbol{\pi}) &= \sum_e z_e + \sum_d \lambda_d \left(h_d - \sum_p x_{dp}\right) + \\ &\quad + \sum_e \pi_e \left(\sum_d \sum_p \delta_{edp} x_{dp} - c_e - z_e\right) \\ &= \sum_d \lambda_d h_d - \sum_e \pi_e c_e + \sum_e (1 - \pi_e) z_e + \\ &\quad + \sum_d \sum_p \left(\sum_e \delta_{edp} \pi_e - \lambda_d\right) x_{dp}. \end{aligned} \tag{5.4.12}$$

The following optimality conditions hold for any saddle point $(\boldsymbol{x}^*, \boldsymbol{z}^*, \boldsymbol{\lambda}^*, \boldsymbol{\pi}^*)$ of (5.4.12):

$$0 \leq \pi_e^* \leq 1, \qquad e = 1, 2, \ldots, E \tag{5.4.13a}$$
$$\sum_d \sum_p \delta_{edp} x_{dp}^* < c_e \text{ implies } \pi_e^* = 0, \qquad e = 1, 2, \ldots, E \tag{5.4.13b}$$
$$z_e > 0 \text{ implies } \pi_e^* = 1, \qquad e = 1, 2, \ldots, E \tag{5.4.13c}$$
$$\lambda_d^* = \min\left\{\sum_e \delta_{edp} \pi_e^* : p = 1, 2, ..., P_d\right\}, \qquad d = 1, 2, ..., D \tag{5.4.13d}$$
$$\sum_e \delta_{edp} \pi_e^* < \lambda_d^* \text{ implies } x_{dp}^* = 0, \qquad d = 1, 2, ..., D \quad p = 1, 2, ..., P_d \tag{5.4.13e}$$

and are implied by the complementary slackness property of saddle point (their proof is left to the reader as Exercise 5.12). If the optimal dual variable (multiplier) π_e^* is treated as the weight (metric, dual cost) of link e, then properties (5.4.13) have the following interpretation:

- the weights are real numbers from interval [0,1] (by property (5.4.13a))
- the quantity $\sum_e \delta_{edp} \pi_e^*$ is the length of path number p of demand d with respect to the weight system π^* (by the definition of link-path coincidence coefficients δ_{edp})

– if link e is not saturated (i.e. $\sum_d \sum_p \delta_{edp} x^*_{dp} < c_e$) then $\pi^*_e = 0$ (by property (5.4.13b))

– $0 < \pi^*_e < 1$ implies, i.e. that link e is saturated ($\sum_d \sum_p \delta_{edp} x^*_{dp} = c_e$) but not overloaded (by properties (5.4.13b) to (5.4.13c))

– $z^*_e > 0$ means that link e is overloaded (i.e. $\sum_d \sum_p \delta_{edp} x^*_{dp} > c_e$) and implies that $\pi^*_e = 1$ (by property (5.4.13c))

– for each d, λ^*_d is equal to the length of the shortest path from the list of allowable paths for demand d (there may be more than one shortest allowable paths on the list) (by property (5.4.13d))

– for the current list of allowable paths the non-zero primal optimal flows can be assigned only to the shortest paths from the list: $x^*_{dp} > 0$ implies $\sum_e \delta_{edp} \pi^*_e = \lambda^*_d$ (by property (5.4.13e)).

Problem A/ALC with routing lists restricted to set $\mathcal{P}_{cand}$ will be called *restricted problem*, while A/ALC with full routing lists $\mathcal{P}_{allow}$ will be called *maximal problem*. Now comes the key observation.

PROPOSITION 5.1 *Let $(\boldsymbol{x}^*, \boldsymbol{z}^*, \boldsymbol{\lambda}^*, \boldsymbol{\pi}^*)$ be a saddle point of restricted problem. Let $\mathcal{P}_d \in \mathcal{P}_{allow}$ be the shortest path for demand d (among all allowable paths) with respect to optimal multipliers $\boldsymbol{\pi}^*$, and let $\zeta_d(\boldsymbol{\pi}^*) = |\mathcal{P}_d|$ denote the corresponding length of $\mathcal{P}_d$. If for all d, $\zeta_d(\boldsymbol{\pi}^*) = \lambda^*_d$ (i.e., set $\mathcal{P}_{cand}$ already contains paths with the shortest possible lengths) then the primal solution $(\boldsymbol{x}^*, \boldsymbol{z}^*)$ is optimal in the wider sense. Otherwise, if for some demand d a path $\mathcal{P}_d$ with $\zeta_d(\boldsymbol{\pi}^*) < \lambda^*_d$ does exist, then the primal solution $(\boldsymbol{x}^*, \boldsymbol{z}^*)$ can be possibly (but not necessarily) improved by adding path $\mathcal{P}_d$ to the current routing list of the paths allowable for d ($\mathcal{P}_{cand} := \mathcal{P}_{cand} \cup \{\mathcal{P}_d\}$).*

Proof:

Let $V(\boldsymbol{\pi}, \boldsymbol{\lambda})$ be the dual function of the maximal problem. It follows from (5.4.12) that $(\boldsymbol{\pi}, \boldsymbol{\lambda}) \in Dom(V)$ (i.e., $V(\boldsymbol{\pi}, \boldsymbol{\lambda}) > -\infty$) if and only if:

$$0 \le \pi_e \le 1, \qquad e = 1, 2, \dots, E \qquad (5.4.14a)$$

$$\lambda_d \le \sum_d \delta_{edp} \pi_e, \qquad d = 1, 2, ..., D \quad p = 1, 2, ..., \bar{P}_d \qquad (5.4.14b)$$

where $\bar{P}_d$ is the length of the maximal routing list (containing all allowable paths). In its domain (5.4.14a to 5.4.14b) the dual function is given by the formula:

$$V(\boldsymbol{\pi}, \boldsymbol{\lambda}) = \sum_d \lambda_d h_d - \sum_e \pi_e c_e. \qquad (5.4.14c)$$

The dual function of the restricted problem, $W(\boldsymbol{\pi}, \boldsymbol{\lambda})$, is also given by the right-hand side of (5.4.14c), and its domain, $Dom(W)$, is defined by (5.4.14a) and (5.4.14b) with $\bar{P}_d$ substituted with P_d. Hence, dual functions $V(\boldsymbol{\pi}, \boldsymbol{\lambda})$ and $W(\boldsymbol{\pi}, \boldsymbol{\lambda})$ differ only by the domains, and

$Dom(V)$ is a subset of $Dom(W)$, because $\mathcal{P}_{cand} \subsetneq \mathcal{P}_{allow}$. Further, $Dom(V) \subseteq Dom(W)$ implies that the maximum of $V(\boldsymbol{\pi}, \boldsymbol{\lambda})$ cannot be greater than the maximum of $W(\boldsymbol{\pi}, \boldsymbol{\lambda})$.

Consider dual vectors $\boldsymbol{\pi}^*$ and $\boldsymbol{\lambda}^*$ of the saddle point of the restricted problem, $(\boldsymbol{\pi}^*, \boldsymbol{\lambda}^*) \in Dom(W)$. If $\lambda_d^* = \zeta_d(\boldsymbol{\pi}^*)$ for $d = 1, 2, \ldots, D$, and $(\boldsymbol{\pi}^*, \boldsymbol{\lambda}^*) \in Dom(V)$, this implies that the optimal multipliers $(\boldsymbol{\pi}^*, \boldsymbol{\lambda}^*)$ of the restricted problem also maximize the dual function of the maximal problem. Hence, the primal solution $(\boldsymbol{x}^*, \boldsymbol{z}^*)$ is optimal in the wider sense, proving the first part of the proposition.

Now suppose that for some demand d' the length $\zeta_{d'}(\boldsymbol{\pi}^*)$ of path $\mathcal{P}_{d'} \in \mathcal{P}_{allow}$ is strictly smaller than $\lambda_{d'}^*$, and consider a new problem, A/ALC*, obtained for some fixed $\varepsilon > 0$ from the original restricted problem A/ALC by the following two modifications:

$$\textstyle\sum_p x_{d'p} = h_{d'} - \varepsilon \tag{5.4.15a}$$

$$c_e := c_e - \psi_e \varepsilon, \qquad e = 1, 2, \ldots, E \tag{5.4.15b}$$

where for each $e, \psi_e = 1$ if link e belongs to path $\mathcal{P}_{d'}$, and $\psi_e = 0$, otherwise. In other words, problem A/ALC* is obtained from A/ALC by assigning fixed flow $x = \varepsilon$ realizing demand d' to path $\mathcal{P}_{d'}$. It is easy to show that the relation between the dual function $W(\boldsymbol{\lambda}, \boldsymbol{\pi})$ of A/ALC and the dual function $W^*(\boldsymbol{\lambda}, \boldsymbol{\pi})$ of A/ALC* is as follows (Exercise 5.13):

$$Dom(W^*) = Dom(W) \tag{5.4.16a}$$

$$W^*(\boldsymbol{\lambda}, \boldsymbol{\pi}) = W(\boldsymbol{\lambda}, \boldsymbol{\pi}) - \sigma\varepsilon \tag{5.4.16b}$$

where

$$\sigma = \lambda_{d'} - \zeta_{d'}(\boldsymbol{\pi}). \tag{5.4.16c}$$

This means that if for some $\varepsilon > 0$ dual variables $(\boldsymbol{\pi}^*, \boldsymbol{\lambda}^*)$ are optimal for both A/ALC and A/ALC*, then introducing path $\mathcal{P}_{d'}$ to the routing list of demand d' and assigning flow $x = \varepsilon$ to it, will decrease the primal objective function by $\sigma^*\varepsilon$, where $\sigma^* = {\lambda^*}_{d'} - \zeta_{d'}(\boldsymbol{\pi}^*)$. For instance this is the case when $(\boldsymbol{x}^*, \boldsymbol{z}^*)$ is an optimal basic simplex solution of A/ALC, $(\boldsymbol{\pi}^*, \boldsymbol{\lambda}^*)$ are the corresponding optimal simplex multipliers, and A/ALC* has the same optimal simplex basis as A/ALC. It can happen, however, that the optimal basis corresponding to $(\boldsymbol{x}^*, \boldsymbol{z}^*)$ is not optimal for A/ALC* for all $\varepsilon > 0$ in some neighborhood of $\varepsilon = 0$; then using path $\mathcal{P}_{d'}$ may not decrease the objective function (5.4.11) (in fact in can sometimes increase it). ■

It should be emphasized that quantity $-\sigma^*$ is exactly the reduced cost of the variable corresponding to the flow on path $\mathcal{P}_{d'}$ c omputed according to the rules of the revised simplex algorithm. Also, the possibility that the objective function (5.4.11) cannot be decreased even though $\sigma^* > 0$ follows from the possible degeneracy of the current basic solution.

Proposition 5.1 implies that a solution of A/PAP (with full routing lists of admitting all allowable paths) can be found by finding a solution of A/ALC optimal in the wider sense using the following procedure.

ALGORITHM 5.9 Solving A/ALC by CPLA

Step 0: Form the initial instance of A/ALC with short lists of candidate paths.
Step 1: Solve A/ALC (using the solution of the previously solved task as the starting point, when Step 1 is entered from Step 2). Let $(\boldsymbol{x}^*, \boldsymbol{z}^*)$ be the solution of the current problem. If $\boldsymbol{F}(\boldsymbol{z}^*) = 0$ (then $\boldsymbol{z}^* = \boldsymbol{0}$) and trivially the solution is optimal in wider sense) the algorithm terminates
Step 2: Let $(\boldsymbol{x}^*, \boldsymbol{z}^*, \boldsymbol{\lambda}^*, \boldsymbol{\pi}^*)$ be a saddle point of the problem. Using the optimal multipliers $\boldsymbol{\pi}^*$ as links' weights run a shortest path algorithm to determine a shortest path $\mathcal{P}_d$ for each demand d. If for every demand d there is no path shorter than λ_d^*, then the solution of A/ALC is optimal in the wider sense and the algorithm terminates. If such paths exist, then form a new instance of A/ALC by adding shortest path $\mathcal{P}_d$ to the current routing list for each demand d with $\zeta_d(\boldsymbol{\pi}^*) < \lambda^*$. Go to Step 1.

In the considered case, we know that $\boldsymbol{F} = 0$ is the lower bound of the optimal objective solution (such information is not always available). We exploit this fact in Step 1: if $\boldsymbol{F}(\boldsymbol{z}^*) = 0$ ($\boldsymbol{z}^* = 0$) then the solution obtained in Step 1 solves A/ALC. However, if the feasible solution of the original problem A/PAP (4.1.7) does not exist, then solutions optimal in the wider sense have the objective function > 0 and the criterion of Step 1 will never terminate the algorithm. Nevertheless, in some cases stopping criteria based on the value of the dual function can be applied. In our case to introduce such a criterion, the value of the dual function calculated for the current optimal values of $\boldsymbol{\pi}^*$ (calculated in Step 1) is used:

$$W(\boldsymbol{\pi}^*, \zeta_d(\boldsymbol{\pi}^*)) = \sum_d \zeta_d(\boldsymbol{\pi}^*) h_d - \sum_e \pi_e^* c_e. \tag{5.4.17}$$

Of course, $W(\boldsymbol{\pi}^0, \zeta_d(\boldsymbol{\pi}^0))$ is the lower bound for the primal solution of A/ALC optimal in the wider sense. Hence, Step 2 can be adjusted in the following way:

Step 2: Let $(\boldsymbol{x}^*, \boldsymbol{z}^*, \boldsymbol{\lambda}^*, \boldsymbol{\pi}^*)$ be a saddle point of (5.4.12). Run the shortest path algorithm to find the shortest path $\mathcal{P}_d$ for each demand d. If for every d there is no path shorter than λ_d^*, then the solution of A/ALC is optimal in the wider sense, and the algorithm terminates. If such paths exist, then form a new instance of A/ALC by adding shortest path $\mathcal{P}_d$ to the routing list of each demand d with $\zeta_d(\boldsymbol{\pi}^*) < \lambda_d^*$. Compute the difference $\Delta = \boldsymbol{F}(\boldsymbol{x}^*, \boldsymbol{z}^*) - W(\boldsymbol{\pi}^*, \zeta_d(\boldsymbol{\pi}^*))$. If $\Delta \leq \eta$ (for some given small threshold $\eta > 0$) then solve the new instance of A/ALC and stop. Otherwise go to Step 1.

Observe that the consecutive values of (5.4.17) do not need to be non-decreasing so the largest value $W(\boldsymbol{\pi}^*, \zeta_d(\boldsymbol{\pi}^*))$ found so far in the iterative process should be used for the test (Exercise 5.14).

There are many possible heuristic policies to adjust the routing lists in Step 2. For instance, we can add only one path in each iteration, namely the first path with $\zeta_d(\boldsymbol{\pi}^*) < \lambda_d^*$

found during the shortest path computation. This will considerably decrease the time spent in the shortest path algorithm during one iteration, but, certainly, increase the number of iterations. We could also modify the lists of allowable paths by deleting all the paths that are longer than λ_d^* (i.e., all the paths (d, p) with $\sum_e \delta_{edp} \pi_e^* > \lambda_d^*$)) from the routing lists. The latter option leads to intermediate instances of A/ALC with less flow variables; at the same time this policy may require more iterations of the procedure, and can even introduce cycling (i.e., a set of paths may cyclically leave and re-enter the routing lists) preventing the algorithm from converging. We shall return to these issues in Example 5.8 below and in Section 10.1.4.

Algorithm 5.9 can be based on any standard LP solver, as both primal solution $(\boldsymbol{x}^*, \boldsymbol{z}^*)$ and the corresponding dual solution $(\boldsymbol{\pi}^*, \boldsymbol{\lambda}^*)$ are returned in the solver output, so the entire saddle point $(\boldsymbol{x}^*, \boldsymbol{z}^*, \boldsymbol{\lambda}^*, \boldsymbol{\pi}^*)$ of Lagrangian (5.4.12) is available. As mentioned in Step 1, when solving the current problem with adjusted routing lists, the recent optimal solution from the previous iteration should be used as the starting point, as this will considerably accelerate the computations.

CPLA is one of the most important techniques for multi-commodity networks because it leads to the possibility of effectively using the sets of allowable paths while solving flow allocation/routing problems. Below we will illustrate its effectiveness for A/ALC. More results of the CPLA applications will be given in Section 10.1.4.

Example 5.8 *Illustrative Example of Path Generation*

Consider the network in Figure 5.4. The link capacities have been computed by assuming an equal split of the demands into their shortest (in the number of hops) paths and by assuming the resulting loads as the link capacities. In this way, the network becomes saturated, i.e., all available link capacity must be used for any feasible solution of A/PAP. The demand volumes are given in Table 5.2.

We start with one-path routing lists (composed of randomly selected shortest paths) and augment them with the CPLA algorithm, considering the following three routing list updating principles in Step 2:

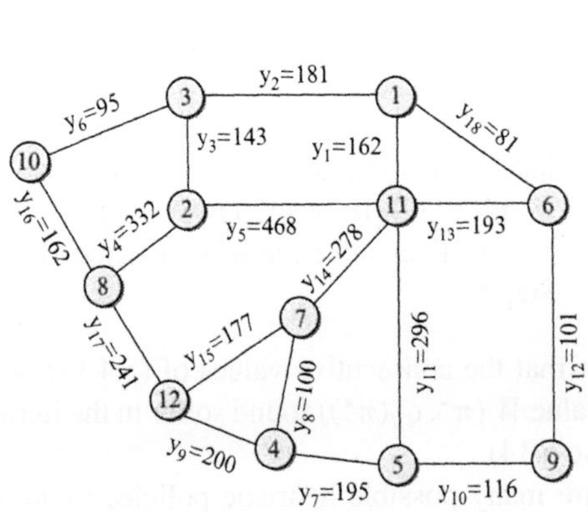

FIGURE 5.4 12-Node, 18-Link Network

TABLE 5.2 **Demand Volumes**

	2	3	4	5	6	7	8	9	10	11	12
1	10	11	13	13	16	7	19	10	6	13	14
2	0	3	21	19	21	14	32	14	5	68	32
3	0	0	27	21	25	17	35	14	3	107	24
4	0	0	0	11	21	15	51	21	19	84	40
5	0	0	0	0	13	20	35	5	18	74	28
6	0	0	0	0	0	16	34	4	9	30	18
7	0	0	0	0	0	0	21	14	12	4	15
8	0	0	0	0	0	0	0	28	47	129	14
9	0	0	0	0	0	0	0	0	7	61	13
10	0	0	0	0	0	0	0	0	0	24	19
11	0	0	0	0	0	0	0	0	0	0	97

AA (add-all): for each demand d compute a shortest path with respect to the current optimal multipliers π^*, and if the path is shorter than λ_d^* then add it to the list;

AB (add-best): add only one path, the path with the largest difference $\lambda_d^* - \zeta_d(\pi^*)$;

AF (add-first): add only one path, the first path with positive difference $\lambda_d^* - \zeta_d(\pi^*)$.

Figure 5.5 shows that the AA policy by far performs the best, as it requires only 5 iterations (CPU time 0.02 seconds), as compared to 29 iterations for AB (CPU time 0.05 seconds), and 44 for AF (CPU time 0.05 seconds). However, there is an expense introduced by using AA. In the final (optimal in the wider sense) solution, the AA policy uses a total of 128 candidate paths, while AB uses 94 paths and AF uses 109 paths. All of the policies use 76 non-zero flows in the final solution. Also note that AA and AB require the computation of the shortest paths for all demands. This makes AB not too practical since AA is, in general, much faster than AB (jointly considering the time spent for the shortest paths computation and the time spent by the LP solver). Finally, note that the plots for AF and AB show that sometimes new generated paths do not decrease the objective function. ●

In Exercise 5.15 we show a (somewhat degenerated) situation when introducing a shorter path doesn't lead to the decrease of the objective function. This, also, illustrates the last statement in the proof of Proposition 5.1. After examining this tedious (but instructive) example, we ask the reader to solve Exercise 5.16 for an alternative formulation of A/ALC.

We end this section by noting out that the dual properties and the reasoning behind the column generation approach can be used to prove the fact stated in Example 4.3 from Section 4.1 (Exercise 5.17).

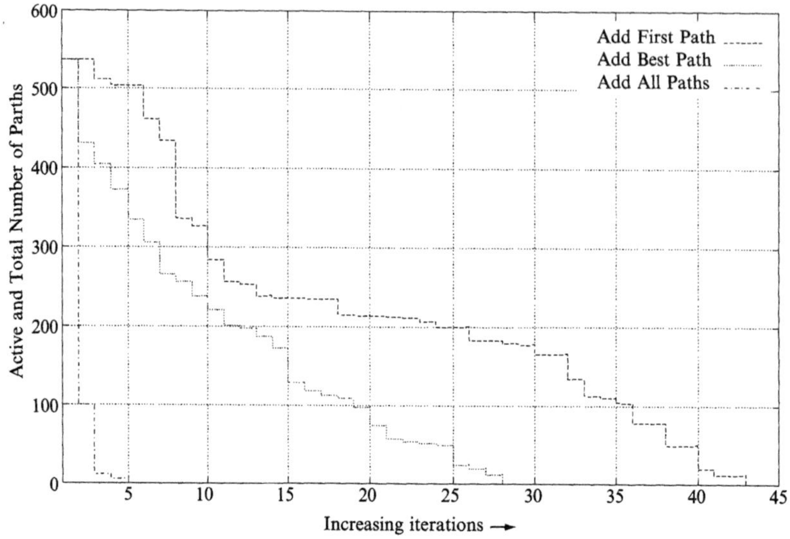

FIGURE 5.5 Objective Value for Three Augmenting Rules

5.4.3 Benders' Decomposition

Benders decomposition (BD) is a general method applicable to LP and MIP problems that can be partitioned with respect to variables ([Ben62], [Las70], and [Min86]). In the multi-commodity network design, BD has been used for restoration and/or modular design in [BL99], [DS98], [KPNG02], [Min81], [MS81b], and [Wes00]. Applications of BD will be presented in Chapters 10 and 13, and the reader is referred to Section 10.3 for a detailed discussion of the approach.

Roughly speaking, BD is applicable when we can distinguish a subset of *master variables* (e.g., link capacities) and decompose the original problem into a *master* problem involving minimization of the original objective function using only the distinguished variables, and a set of auxiliary problems (called *feasibility tests*) which generate inequalities for the master problem. The BD algorithm is iterative: the master problem minimizes the objective function, and then the resulting optimal master variables are tested for feasibility in the sense of the original problem. When a feasibility test fails, a new (linear) inequality is added to the master problem.

To see how BD works, consider the modular design MIP problem D/ML (4.3.1)

minimize $\quad F = \sum_e \xi_e y_e \qquad$ (5.4.18a)

subject to $\quad \sum_p x_{dp} = h_d, \qquad d = 1, 2, \ldots, D \qquad$ (5.4.18b)

$\sum_d \sum_p \delta_{edp} x_{dp} \le M y_e, \qquad e = 1, 2, \ldots, E \qquad$ (5.4.18c)

x_{dp} non-negative continuous, y_e non-negative integer. $\qquad$ (5.4.18d)

As we already know from Section 4.2.3, the problem is $\mathcal{NP}$-complete and the BB technique may be considered to find the exact optimal solution. To make BB more effective, we can use BD and apply BB only to the master problem which has less variables than the original MIP formulation.

We choose the master variables to be the link capacities $\boldsymbol{y} = (y_1, y_2, ..., y_E)$ and define the master problem:

$$\textbf{(MP)}\ \textbf{\textit{minimize}} \quad F = \textstyle\sum_e \xi_e y_e \tag{5.4.19a}$$

$$\textbf{\textit{subject to}} \quad \boldsymbol{y} \in \Omega, \boldsymbol{y} \text{ integer}, \ \boldsymbol{y} \geq 0, \tag{5.4.19b}$$

where the set of inequalities Ω is initially empty. Now, we solve MP (the first optimal solution is trivial: $\boldsymbol{y}^* = 0$) and check, by means of the feasibility test, whether $\boldsymbol{y}^*$ is feasible with respect to the original constraints in formulation (5.4.18). The feasibility test is nothing else but a test of problem A/PAP (4.1.7), with link capacities fixed to $\boldsymbol{c} = M\boldsymbol{y}^*$, for feasibility. If the check is positive we conclude that $\boldsymbol{y}^*$ is the optimal solution of (5.4.18). If not (this is the case for instance for $\boldsymbol{y}^* = \mathbf{0}$) we generate a new inequality for set Ω and return to the master problem. The check and the generation of the inequality can be done simultaneously by considering the dual to problem A/PAP augmented in the following way:

$$\textbf{\textit{minimize}} \quad F = z \tag{5.4.20a}$$

$$\textbf{\textit{subject to}} \quad \textstyle\sum_p x_{dp} = h_d, \qquad d = 1, 2, \ldots, D \tag{5.4.20b}$$

$$\textstyle\sum_d \sum_p \delta_{edp} x_{dp} \leq M y_e^* + z, \qquad e = 1, 2, ..., E \tag{5.4.20c}$$

$$\textstyle\sum_d \sum_p \delta_{edp} x_{dp} \leq c_e, \qquad e = 1, 2, \ldots, E \tag{5.4.20d}$$

$$x_{dp} \text{ continuous and non-negative, } z \text{ continuous.} \tag{5.4.20e}$$

Note the difference between (5.4.20a) and A/ALC (5.4.11a) from the previous section. The problem dual to (5.4.20) (the feasibility test) is as follows (Exercise 5.16):

$$\textbf{(FT)}\ \textbf{\textit{maximize}} \quad W(\boldsymbol{\pi}, \boldsymbol{\lambda}) = \textstyle\sum_d \lambda_d h_d - \sum_e \pi_e M y_e{}^* \tag{5.4.21a}$$

$$\textbf{\textit{subject to}} \quad \textstyle\sum_e \pi_e = 1 \tag{5.4.21b}$$

$$\lambda_d \leq \textstyle\sum_e \delta_{edp} \pi_e, \qquad d = 1, 2, ..., D \quad p = 1, 2, ..., P_d \tag{5.4.21c}$$

$$\pi_e \geq 0, \qquad e = 1, 2, \ldots, E. \tag{5.4.21d}$$

Let $(\boldsymbol{\pi}^*, \boldsymbol{\lambda}^*)$ be the optimal solution of FT. Then $W(\boldsymbol{\pi}^*, \boldsymbol{\lambda}^*)$ is equal to the primally optimal z^*, so if $W^* \leq 0$ the test is positive. Otherwise, the current vector is not feasible in the sense of the constraints in Problem (5.4.18) and the following inequality, for given values of π_e^* and λ_d^*, is added to set Ω (this is the crucial step of BD):

$$\textstyle\sum_d \lambda_d^* h_d - \sum_e \pi_e^* M y_e \leq 0. \tag{5.4.22}$$

It can be proved ([Las70] and [Min86]) that the procedure will terminate after a finite number of steps (one step = MP + FT). The rationale behind applying BD is that the MIP problem that is actually solved (Problem (5.4.19)) has much less variables than the original Problem (5.4.18), and that the inequalities in Ω may eventually become more tight than the flow and capacity constraints in (5.4.18). Also note that at the initial steps of BD, problem MP can be relaxed, and its proper IP version treated only in the final iteration(s).

It is worth noticing that BD can be well applied for the node-link formulation of Problem (5.4.18), as illustrated in Exercise 5.18. Finally, we observe that although in the original work of Benders [Ben62] his decomposition method was developed for MIP problems and as such can be used in the BC techniques for solving, e.g., modular restoration design problems, BD can also be used to decompose and then effectively solve large linear programs (Section 10.3).

5.5 GRADIENT MINIMIZATION AND OTHER APPROACHES FOR CONVEX PROGRAMMING PROBLEMS

Note that Problem A/CPF (4.3.8) from Chapter 4 is a non-linear optimization problem; specifically, it is a convex multi-variable function minimization problem with linear constraints. In Section 4.3.2, we have shown how a convex programming problem can be approximated with a LP problem using piecewise linear approximation. The two most commonly known general methods for such problems are the gradient projection method (GP) of Rosen [Ros60] and the reduced gradient method of Wolfe [Wol62]. Due to the simple structure of the constraints (4.3.8b), a substantially simplified version of the projection method can be applied, and the Frank-Wolfe method [FW56] can be used instead of the reduced gradient approach. Often in the context of computer NDPs, the Frank-Wolfe method has been referred to as the flow deviation (FD) method, based on the work [FGK73].

Before discussing the two solution methods we shall transform Problem (4.3.8) into an equivalent form by substituting the link load variables $\underline{y}_e$ in the objective function (4.3.8a) with the left-hand sides of equations (4.3.8c).

***LP:* A/CPF** **Link-Path Formulation**

Convex Penalty Functions

constants

δ_{edp} = 1 if link e belongs to path p realizing demand d; 0, otherwise
h_d volume of demand d
$F_e(\cdot)$ convex cost function of link e

variables

x_{dp} flow allocated to path p of demand d

objective

$$\min \boldsymbol{F} = \textstyle\sum_e F_e(\sum_d \sum_p \delta_{edp} x_{dp}) \quad (5.5.1a)$$

constraints

$$\textstyle\sum_p x_{dp} = h_d \qquad d = 1, 2, \dots, D \quad (5.5.1b)$$

x_{dp} non-negative. (5.5.1c)

As a convex problem (convex objective function plus linear constraints) A/CPF has only one global minimum $\boldsymbol{F}^{min}$, and this minimum is attained either at one single point or at a convex set of feasible points (Exercise 5.19). Also, optimal solutions are in general bifurcated (refer to the discussion in Section 4.3.2).

5.5.1 The Flow Deviation (FD) Method

The following Algorithm 5.10 implements the well-known FD method, based on a general approach for solving minimization problems with convex objective function and linear constraints.

ALGORITHM 5.10 **Algorithm for Solving A/CPF (FD)**

Step 1: Assume initial flow allocation vector $\boldsymbol{x}^0 = (x^0_{dp} : d=1,2,...,D, p=1,2,...,P_d)$. Set iteration counter k to 0.

Step 2: Compute link loads $\underline{y}^k_e = \sum_d \sum_p \delta_{edp} x^k_{dp}$ and the derivatives (link unit costs)

$$\xi^k_e = dF_e(y)/dy \text{ at point } y = \underline{y}^k_e,\ e = 1,2,...,E. \tag{5.5.2}$$

For each demand d find the *minimum first derivative length* path $\bar{p}(d)$ ($1 \leq \bar{p}(d) \leq P_d$), i.e., any of the shortest paths with respect to the link costs (5.5.2). Define the flow allocation vector $\bar{\boldsymbol{x}} = (\bar{x}_{dp} : d = 1,2,...,D, p = 1,2,...,P_d)$:

$$\bar{x}_{dp} = \begin{cases} h_d & \text{for } p = \bar{p}(d) \\ 0 & \text{otherwise.} \end{cases} \tag{5.5.3}$$

Step 3: Perform one-dimensional search and find the scalar step-size $\bar{t}$ such that:

$$\boldsymbol{F}(\boldsymbol{x}^k + \bar{t}(\bar{\boldsymbol{x}} - \boldsymbol{x}^k)) = \min_{0 \leq t \leq 1} \boldsymbol{F}(\boldsymbol{x}^k + t(\bar{\boldsymbol{x}} - \boldsymbol{x}^k)). \tag{5.5.4}$$

Set:

$$\boldsymbol{x}^{k+1} := \boldsymbol{x}^k + \bar{t}(\bar{\boldsymbol{x}} - \boldsymbol{x}^k).$$

Step 4: Set $k := k + 1$. If

$$|\boldsymbol{F}(\boldsymbol{x}^k) - \boldsymbol{F}(\boldsymbol{x}^{k-1})| \leq \varepsilon \boldsymbol{F}(\boldsymbol{x}^k) \tag{5.5.5}$$

then stop ($\boldsymbol{x}^k$ is close to optimal); otherwise go to Step 2.

The FD method is an application of the Frank-Wolfe method [FW56]. As shown in [Min86, §5.3.6.1], the method is convergent for any positive ε in a finite number of steps. An issue is the slow convergence of the procedure near optimum because of the zig-zagging effect ([BG92, §5.6.1]). To overcome the zig-zagging effect of the FD method, some other flow-shifting algorithms can be applied as discussed in [Ker92, §6.3].

5.5.2 The Gradient Projection (GP) Method

An alternative method to FD is the GP method, being a special case of Rosen's GP method for linear constraints ([Min86, §5.3.3]). The basic idea behind the application of Rosen's method to A/CPF is that if a point $\boldsymbol{x}$ satisfies constraints (5.5.1b) and (5.5.1c) then the steepest descent feasible direction emanating from $\boldsymbol{x}$ is the projection $W = \left(w_{dp} : d = 1, 2, ..., D, p = 1, 2, ..., P_d\right)$ of the minus gradient of the cost function $\boldsymbol{F}$ at $\boldsymbol{x}$ $(-\nabla \boldsymbol{F}(\boldsymbol{x}))$ onto the set of points satisfying the constraints:

$$\textstyle\sum_p w_{dp} = 0 \qquad d = 1, 2, \ldots, D \tag{5.5.6a}$$

$$w_{dp} \geq 0 \qquad \text{for } d = 1, 2, \ldots, D,\ p = 1, 2, \ldots, P_d \text{ such that } x_{dp} = 0. \tag{5.5.6b}$$

The GP algorithm can be found later, labeled as Algorithm 5.11.

ALGORITHM 5.11 **Algorithm for Solving A/CPF (GP)**

Step 0: Assume an initial flow allocation vector $\boldsymbol{x}^0 = (x^0_{dp} : d = 1, 2, ..., D, p = 1, 2, ..., P_d)$. Set iteration counter k to 0.

Step 1: Compute link loads $\underline{y}^k_e = \sum_d \sum_p \delta_{edp} x^k_{dp}$, the derivatives (link unit costs)

$$\xi^k_e = dF_e(y)/dy \text{ at point } y = \underline{y}^k_e,\ e = 1, 2, ..., E \tag{5.5.7}$$

and the gradient

$$\nabla \boldsymbol{F}(\boldsymbol{x}^k) = \left(\textstyle\sum_e \xi^k_e \delta_{edp} : d = 1, 2, ..., D, p = 1, 2, ..., P_d\right). \tag{5.5.8}$$

Project vector $\boldsymbol{x}^k - \nabla \boldsymbol{F}(\boldsymbol{x}^k)$ onto set (5.5.1b), (5.5.1c) and let $\boldsymbol{w}^k$ be the resulting projection vector.

Step 2: Perform one-dimensional search and find the scalar step-size $\bar{t}$ such that

$$\boldsymbol{F}(\boldsymbol{x}^k + \bar{t}\boldsymbol{w}^k) = \min_{0 \leq t \leq T} \boldsymbol{F}(\boldsymbol{x}^k + t\boldsymbol{w}^k), \tag{5.5.9}$$

where $T = \max\left\{t : \boldsymbol{x}^k + t\boldsymbol{w}^k \geq 0, t \geq 0\right\}$. $\boldsymbol{x}^{k+1} := \boldsymbol{x}^k + \bar{t}\boldsymbol{w}^k$.

Step 3: Set $k := k + 1$. If

$$|\boldsymbol{F}(\boldsymbol{x}^k) - \boldsymbol{F}(\boldsymbol{x}^{k-1})| \leq \varepsilon \boldsymbol{F}(\boldsymbol{x}^k) \tag{5.5.10}$$

then stop ($\boldsymbol{x}^k$ is close to optimal); otherwise go to Step 1.

Note that the quantity $\sum_e \xi^k_e \delta_{edp}$ in (5.5.8), being the partial derivative of the cost function $\boldsymbol{F}$ with respect to x_{dp}, is the current cost of flow x_{dp}, i.e., the length of path (d, p) for the current link weights (5.5.7). As discussed in [Min86, § 5.3.3], the GP procedure, as a special case of the Rosen's GP method, in practice will converge for a positive ε in a finite number of steps. Again, an issue is the slow convergence of the procedure near the optimum.

The difference between the two methods is that in GP the linear search is performed along the vector being the projection of the direction of the steepest descent, while in FD along a feasible direction that shifts, for each path (d, p) such that $p \neq \bar{p}(d)$, a proportion $\bar{t}$ of flow x^k_{dp} to the currently shortest path $\bar{p}(d)$.

It should be noted that in the general case GP can be computationally difficult. Fortunately, in the case of A/CPF the projection is easy due to the special form of linear constraints (5.5.6). In order to compute the projection $\boldsymbol{w}^k$ consider a vector $\boldsymbol{y} = (y_1, y_2, ..., y_n)$ and its projection $\boldsymbol{x} = (x_1, x_2, ..., x_n)$ onto the set

$$x_1 + x_2 + ... + x_n = 0 \tag{5.5.11a}$$

$$x_i \geq 0, \quad i \in \boldsymbol{I}^0 \subseteq \{1, 2, ..., n\}. \tag{5.5.11b}$$

For a given vector $\boldsymbol{y}$, the projection vector $\boldsymbol{x}$ is the unique solution of the optimization problem:

$$\textbf{\textit{minimize}} \sum_{i=1}^{n}(x_i - y_i)^2 \textbf{\textit{ subject to }} (5.5.11). \tag{5.5.12}$$

In order to find the solution (projection vector) $\boldsymbol{x}$ of (5.5.12) the following modification of a method based on the Kuhn-Tucker conditions derived in [HWC74] can be used. Let us order the coordinates of $\boldsymbol{y}$ such that $\boldsymbol{I}^0 = \{1, 2, ..., m\}$ and $y_1 \leq y_2 \leq ... \leq y_m$ and put

$$j = \max\{i : 1 \leq i \leq m, (y_{i+1} + y_{i+2} + ... + y_n)/(n - i) > y_i\} \tag{5.5.13a}$$

$$\lambda = (y_{j+1} + y_{j+2} + ... + y_n)/(n - j) \tag{5.5.13b}$$

(by definition $j = 0$ if $\boldsymbol{I}^0 = \emptyset$ or $(y_{i+1} + y_{i+2} + ... + y_n)/(n - i) \leq y_i$ for $i = 1, 2, ..., m$). Then the projection vector $\boldsymbol{x}$ is defined by the following formula:

$$x_i = \begin{cases} \max\{y_i - \lambda, 0\} & \text{for } i = 1, 2, ..., m \\ y_i - \lambda & \text{for } i = m + 1, m + 2, ..., n. \end{cases} \tag{5.5.14}$$

The required projection $\boldsymbol{w}^k$ is found by applying formulae (5.5.13) to (5.5.14) separately to each part of vector $-\nabla \boldsymbol{F}(x^k)$ corresponding to the flows of each demand d, i.e., to the each subvector $(-\sum_e \xi_e^k \delta_{ed1}, -\sum_e \xi_e^k \delta_{ed2}, ..., -\sum_e \xi_e^k \delta_{edP_d})$ (Exercises 5.20 and 5.21).

The Rosen's GP technique can also be used to solve problem A/CCF (4.3.6). An initial solution $\boldsymbol{x}^0$ can be found by solving the LP problem without objective function (4.3.6a) and then the iterative procedure described above can be applied. In the considered case, however, the projection is not straightforward and requires either a projection method discussed in [Min86, § 5.3.3] or quadratic programming (available, e.g., within CPLEX) to find the projection $\boldsymbol{z} = (z_{dp} : d = 1,2,...,D, p = 1,2,...,P_d)$ of the negative gradient of the cost function (4.3.6a) for given flows $\boldsymbol{x} = (x_{dp} : d = 1,2,...,D, p = 1,2,...,P_d)$:

$$\textbf{\textit{minimize}} \quad \sum_d \sum_p (z_{dp} - x_{dp} + \sum_e \xi_e^k \delta_{edp})^2 \tag{5.5.15a}$$

$$\textbf{\textit{subject to}} \quad \sum_p z_{dp} = h_d, \qquad d = 1,2,\dots,D \tag{5.5.15b}$$

$$\sum_d \sum_p \delta_{edp} z_{dp} \le c_e, \quad e = 1,2,\dots,E \text{ and } \sum_d \sum_p \delta_{edp} x_{dp} = c_e. \tag{5.5.15c}$$

5.5.3 Dual Method

As explained in Section 4.3.2, both A/CPF and A/CCF can be approximated by LP problems and solved by Simplex. For A/CPF still another possibility, not commonly known, is to use the dual approach to find the optimal link capacities, and then to solve the resulting capacitated LP problem A/PAP in order to find the corresponding flows. The method is as follows.

Consider the Lagrangian function for problem A/CPF (4.3.8) constructed by dualizing only constraints (4.3.8c):

$$\begin{aligned} L(\boldsymbol{x}, \boldsymbol{y}; \boldsymbol{\pi}) &= \sum_e F_e(\underline{y}_e) + \sum_e \pi_e \left(\sum_d \sum_p \delta_{edp} x_{dp} - \underline{y}_e \right) \\ &= \sum_e \left(F_e(\underline{y}_e) - \pi_e y_e \right) + \sum_d \sum_p \left(\sum_e \delta_{edp} \pi_e \right) x_{dp} \end{aligned} \tag{5.5.16}$$

where $\boldsymbol{\pi} = (\pi_1, \pi_2, ..., \pi_E)$ are the dual variables associated with constraints (4.3.8c), and the corresponding dual function

$$W(\boldsymbol{\pi}) = \min_{\boldsymbol{x} \in \boldsymbol{X}, \boldsymbol{y} \ge \boldsymbol{0}} L(\boldsymbol{x}, \boldsymbol{y}; \boldsymbol{\pi}), \quad \pi \ge 0, \tag{5.5.17}$$

where $\boldsymbol{X}$ is the set of constraints determined by (4.3.8b) and the non-negativity constraint. For further considerations, we shall assume that for each e the penalty function F_e is strictly convex, increasing and $F_e(0) = 0$. Let $f_e = \sup_{y \ge 0} F_e'(y)$ (possibly $f_e = +\infty$). Then it is not difficult to see (Exercise 5.22) that this implies that the optimal multipliers satisfy the inequalities

$$\pi_e^* \le f_e, \quad e = 1,2,...,E \tag{5.5.18}$$

and that at the saddle point $(\boldsymbol{x}^*, \boldsymbol{y}^*, \boldsymbol{\pi}^*)$ of Lagrangian (5.5.16) the values $\underline{y}_e^*$ are unique and can be computed from the equalities:

$$F_e'(\underline{y}_e^*) = \pi_e^* \quad \text{if } F_e'(0) \le \pi_e^* < f_e \tag{5.5.19a}$$

$$\underline{y}_e^* = +\infty \quad \text{if } \pi_e^* = f_e \tag{5.5.19b}$$

$$\underline{y}_e^* = 0 \quad \text{if } \pi_e^* < F_e'(0). \tag{5.5.19c}$$

Because of constraints (5.5.18), the domain of the dual function (5.5.17) can be restricted to:

$$\boldsymbol{\Pi} = \{\boldsymbol{\pi} : 0 \le \pi_e \le f_e, e = 1,2,...,E\}. \tag{5.5.20}$$

Furthermore, if the multipliers π_e are interpreted as links' weights, then the quantity $\zeta_{dp}(\boldsymbol{\pi}) = \sum_e \delta_{edp}\pi_e$ is the length of path (d, p), and then any subgradient of $W(\boldsymbol{\pi})$ is of the form

$$\partial W(\boldsymbol{\pi})/\partial\pi_e = -\underline{y}_e + \underline{Y}_e, \quad e = 1, 2, ..., E, \tag{5.5.21}$$

where for a given $\boldsymbol{\pi}$, the unique values of $\underline{y}_e$ are computed according to (5.5.19) (where superscript * is skipped), and $\underline{Y}_e$ is the load of link e resulting from any flow $\boldsymbol{x} \in \boldsymbol{X}$ resulting from allocating each demand volume h_d to its shortest paths with respect to the lengths $\zeta_{dp}(\boldsymbol{\pi})$ (Exercise 5.23).

Solving the dual problem:

$$\max \; \{W(\boldsymbol{\pi}) : \quad \boldsymbol{\pi} \in \boldsymbol{\Pi}\} \tag{5.5.22}$$

by means of a subgradient maximization algorithm (refer to Algorithm 5.8, Section 5.4.1) we arrive at the optimal dual multipliers π_e^*, and optimal link loads $\underline{y}_e^*$ uniquely determined by formula (5.5.19). Note that this is not the case for the flows. Using the dual approach in general we do not find optimal flows, since the flows used to minimize the Lagrangian (and, hence, compute the dual function) for optimal π_e^* are not unique.

Finally, having computed the optimal link loads $\underline{y}_e^*$ we may use A/PAP (4.1.7) with $c_e = \underline{y}_e^*$ to find the correct optimal flows $\boldsymbol{x}^*$ for the primal problem.

Example 5.9 *Dual Problem*

Let $F_e(\underline{y}_e) = \underline{y}_e^2$ for $\underline{y}_e \geq 0$. Then $f_e = +\infty$, $F_e'(0) \equiv 0$ and for each link e formula (5.5.19) yields $\underline{y}_e = -\pi_e^2/4$. Hence, the dual Problem (5.5.22) becomes:

$$\begin{array}{ll} \textbf{\textit{maximize}} & W(\boldsymbol{\pi}) = -\sum_e \pi_e^2/4 + \min_{x\in X} \sum_e (\sum_d \sum_p \delta_{edp} x_{dp})\pi_e \\ \textbf{\textit{subject to}} & \boldsymbol{\pi} \geq \mathbf{0}. \end{array} \tag{5.5.23}$$

The subgradient of $W(\pi)$ is defined through:

$$\partial W(\boldsymbol{\pi})/\partial\pi_e = -\pi_e/2 + \sum_d \delta_{ed\,p(d)} h_d \quad e = 1, 2, ..., E, \tag{5.5.24}$$

where $p(d)$ is one of the allowable shortest paths of demand d. The optimization Problem (5.5.23) can be formulated directly as the following quadratic programming problem.

$$\begin{array}{ll} \textbf{\textit{maximize}} & W(\boldsymbol{\pi}) = -\sum_e \pi_e^2/4 + \sum_d \lambda_d h_d \\ \textbf{\textit{subject to}} & \boldsymbol{\pi} \geq 0 \\ & \lambda_d \leq \sum_e \delta_{edp}\pi_e, \qquad d = 1, 2, ..., D \quad p = 1, 2, ..., P_d. \end{array} \tag{5.5.25}$$

It is possible that solving (5.5.25) may not be much easier than solving the original primal problem. ●

5.6 SPECIAL HEURISTICS FOR CONCAVE PROGRAMMING PROBLEMS

The strictly concave increasing dimensioning functions relating the link load to the link capacity express the so-called economy of scale phenomenon observed in communication networks. Such functions $F(y)$ are characterized by decreasing incremental cost (first derivative) $F'(y)$ and decreasing cost per unit carried load $F(y)/y$, and by $F(0) = 0$ (Figure 5.6).

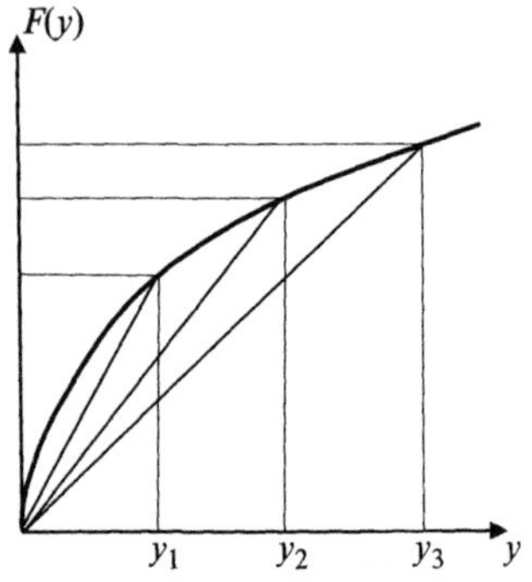

FIGURE 5.6 A Concave Function and its Approximations

As discussed in Section 4.3.3, the concave dimensioning problem D/CDF (4.3.18) is difficult to solve as it is characterized by numerous local minima which can be far from the global one. As also shown in Section 4.3.3, the considered concave problems can be approximated by mixed-integer LP problems involving binary variables. Of course, using MIP solvers would be excessively time-consuming for large networks; hence, methods for finding a local minimum can be of some value since one may use many starting points and apply a procedure for finding a local minimum for each of them. Below, we shall describe two such algorithms for finding local minima of Problem (4.3.18). Both methods take advantage of the fact that the optimal flow allocation is non-bifurcated.

5.6.1 Minimum First Derivative Length Path (MFDLP) Method

The MFDLP method, due to [Yag71], is shown in Algorithm 5.12.

ALGORITHM 5.12 **Algorithm for Solving D/CDF (MFDLP)**

Step 0: Assume an initial non-bifurcated flow allocation vector $\boldsymbol{x}^0 = (x^0_{1\,p(1)}, x^0_{2\,p(2)}, ..., x^0_{D\,p(D)})$ where $p(d) \in \{1, 2, ..., P_d\}$ and $x^0_{d\,p(d)} = h_d$ for $d = 1, 2, ..., D$. Set iteration counter k to 0.

Step 1: Compute link loads $\underline{y}^k_e = \sum_d \delta_{ed\,p(d)} x^k_{d\,p(d)}$ and the derivatives (link unit costs)

$$\kappa_e = \xi_e dF_e(y)/dy \text{ at point } y = \underline{y}^k_e,\ e = 1, 2, ..., E. \tag{5.6.1}$$

For each demand d compute the shortest path $p(d) \in \{1, 2, ..., P_d\}$ with respect to costs (5.6.1).

Step 2: Set $k := k + 1$ and $x^k_{d\,p(d)} = h_d$ for $d = 1, 2, ..., D$. If $\boldsymbol{F}(\boldsymbol{x}^k) = \boldsymbol{F}(\boldsymbol{x}^{k-1})$ then stop ($\boldsymbol{x}^k$ is a local minimum); otherwise, go to Step 1.

It can be shown (§ 2.1.2 of [Min89] and [Yag71]) that Algorithm 5.12 converges to a local minimum in a finite number of steps (Exercise 5.24). In practice, the convergence is very fast and the main problem is that, in most cases, the value of the cost function $\boldsymbol{F}$ at the minimum that has been found is not much smaller than the initial cost. This is caused mainly by the fact that when a link is not used in some iteration, then it will be dropped for good since when its load becomes 0 then it is assigned a relatively high unit cost κ_e (5.6.1), as the derivative of the convex dimensioning function F_e is maximal at 0.

To overcome this difficulty some modification of the path cost computation were already proposed in the original Yaged's paper [Yag71]. Another modification is described in [KKP99]. The idea of the latter modification is to use the MFDLP algorithm for certain consecutive approximations of the dimensioning functions F_e, starting from a linear approximation and then gradually increasing the slope of the function at the origin. To illustrate this idea suppose that the dimensioning function for each link is the same and is of the shape depicted in Figure 5.6. Let $y_0 = 0$ and $y_0, y_1, ..., y_N$ (in the depicted case $N = 3$) be some given equidistant points, where y_N is large enough to be greater than any feasible link load. The original MFDLP algorithm is run $N + 1$ times using the following dimensioning function F^n in the nth run:

$$F^{N-n+1}(y) = \begin{cases} (F(y_{N-n+1})/y_{N-n+1}) \cdot y & \text{for } 0 \le y \le y_{N-n+1} \\ F(y) & \text{for } y > y_{N-n+1}. \end{cases} \tag{5.6.2}$$

Note that the modified algorithm does not depend on the starting point. The modification is quite effective as illustrated in Section 5.6.3.

5.6.2 Greedy Descent (GD) Method

An alternative to the MFDLP algorithm, called *the greedy algorithm for minimum concave cost network problem*, is presented in § 2.1.2 of [Min89]. This approach is based on a simple observation that a minimum solution $\boldsymbol{x}^* = (x^*_{1\,p(1)}, x^*_{2\,p(2)}, ..., x^*_{D\,p(D)})$ of problem D/CDF (4.3.18) must have a property that deleting any link e with positive load $\underline{y}_e(\boldsymbol{x}^*)$ ($\underline{y}_e(\boldsymbol{x}^*) = \sum_d \delta_{ed\,p(d)} x^*_{d\,p(d)} > 0$) and restoring load $\underline{y}_e(\boldsymbol{x}^*)$ on any path around link e will not lead to a decrease in the links' cost $\boldsymbol{F}(\boldsymbol{x}^*)$. In each iteration of the GD algorithm a link with the maximum cost decrease is found and deleted from the network.

ALGORITHM 5.13 **Algorithm for Solving D/CDF (GD)**

Step 0: Assume an initial non-bifurcated flow allocation vector $\boldsymbol{x}^0 = (x^0_{1\,p(1)}, x^0_{2\,p(2)}, ..., x^0_{D\,p(D)})$ where $p(d) \in \{1, 2, ..., P_d\}$ and $x^0_{d\,p(d)} = h_d$ for $d = 1, 2, ..., D$. Set iteration counter k to 0. Compute link loads $\underline{y}^0_e = \sum_d \delta_{ed\,p(d)} x^0_{d\,p(d)}$.

Step 1: For each link ℓ find the shortest path P_ℓ between the end nodes of link ℓ and its length L_ℓ using the following link weights:

$$w_e = \begin{cases} +\infty & \text{if } e = \ell \\ F_e(\underline{y}_e^k + \underline{y}_\ell^k) - F_e(\underline{y}_e^k) & \text{if } e \neq \ell. \end{cases} \quad (5.6.3)$$

Find link ℓ with positive load $\underline{y}_e(\bar{x}^k)$ maximizing the cost gain

$$\Delta_\ell = F_\ell(\underline{y}_\ell^k) - L_\ell. \quad (5.6.4)$$

Step 2: If $\Delta_\ell \leq 0$ then stop ($\boldsymbol{x}^k$ is a local minimum); otherwise set $k := k + 1$, modify the link loads

$$\underline{y}_e^k = \begin{cases} 0 & \text{if } e = \ell \\ \underline{y}_e^{k-1} + \underline{y}_\ell^k & \text{if } e \in P_\ell \\ \underline{y}_e^{k-1} & \text{if } e \notin P_\ell \end{cases} \quad (5.6.5)$$

and go to Step 1.

As shown in [Min89], the GD algorithm can be, in some cases, substantially accelerated; still it has the same drawback as the MFDLP approach discussed in the previous section: once link ℓ is eliminated (5.6.5) it will not be used in consecutive iterations.

5.6.3 Numerical Example

Since algorithms for concave multi-commodity problems are less commonly known than algorithms for their convex counterparts discussed in Section 5.5, we will illustrate their performance on a network example. The network is the upper layer of the three-layer structure described in Figure 5.4 in [KKP99]. It consists of $V = 19$ nodes, $E = 75$ links, and $D = 171$ demands. The concave dimensioning function used in the calculations is as follows:

$$F_e(y) = (0.03y + 50)(1 - e^{-0.01y}) \quad e = 1, 2, ..., E. \quad (5.6.6)$$

Table 5.3 shows the results for the original Yaged's method (MFDLP), Yaged's method with modifications of dimensioning functions (5.6.2) (MFDLP/MOD with $N = 50$ and $y_N = 10,000$), Minoux's method (GD), and the combination consisting of GD followed by MFDLP (GD+MFDLP). We also give results for a modification of the GD algorithm, called GD/BFS (GD with bulk flow shifting, see later). Additionally, we give results for two more algorithms: application of EA (Section 5.3.3) and of SAL (Section 5.3.4).

Columns 2, 3, 4 and 8 of Table 5.3 show the averages over 10 runs for each algorithm (except for MFDLP/MOD which is completely deterministic) starting from 10 different randomly generated initial solutions. In column 5, the best solution out of ten is displayed; the standard deviation of the ten results from the average is shown in column 6. In column 7,

TABLE 5.3 **Results for Concave Dimensioning (Averaged Over 10 Runs)**

Algorithm	Initial Objective	Average No. of Iterations	Average Final Objective	Best Objective	Standard Deviation	% From Lowest Average Final Objective	Average Time (s)
MFDLP	7,115	7.2	4,908	4,635	133	27.5%	0.1
MFDLP/MOD	6,352	50×2.2	4,215	4,215	0	9.5%	0.3
GD	7,115	19.6	5,907	5,265	347	53.5%	0.1
GD+MFDLP	7,115	19.6+1.8	4,430	4,217	156	15.1%	0.1
GD/BFS	7,115	12.2	3,889	**3,815**	83	1.0%	1.3
EA	–	–	3,849	3,827	14	–	35.2
SAL	–	–	3,959	3,865	67	2.9%	8.0

we list how far the average final objective is for each method compared to the lowest average final objective (EA, in this case) in terms of percentage. Note that the best result (in bold) has been achieved with a modification of GD consisting of restoration of the individual flows using the link that is currently deleted, with each flow restored on its individual, shortest path; recall that in original GD the entire load of the deleted link is restored entirely onto one of the shortest paths (5.6.3). In fact, GD/BFS is similar to algorithm H3 (with BFS) described for topological design in Section 6.3.5.

It is clear from this example that GD gives results furthest away from the best known (local) optimum, and MFDLP is also not very effective in terms of providing good near-optimal solutions; note that MFLDP/MOD helps quite a bit, especially as it consists of one run (although this run is longer than the pure MFLDP run). Combination GD+MFDLP is better than any of its combined components, still it is inferior to MFDLP/MOD. Applications of EA and SAL perform much better that the previous methods (except for GD/BFS) but take comparatively more time (especially EA). However, each run of EA took only about 35 seconds (on today's computer); thus, any of the bottom three algorithms (GD/BFS, EA, SAL) provides good results and can be usable in practice. Still, considering implementation simplicity, MFDLP/MOD seems to be the most attractive option for fast approximate calculations.

5.7 SOLVING MULTI-COMMODITY FLOW PROBLEMS

The main purpose of Chapter 5 has been to discuss optimization methods for NDPs arising from modeling and design of communication and computer networks. Many important types of such problems will be discussed in the next chapters of this book, and in particular it will be shown how the methods of Chapter 5 can be applied in different situations. Still, as we are not able to deal in a detailed way with all of the potentially important cases, in this section we will summarize what optimization methods are appropriate for different classes of basic problem formulations discussed in Chapter 4. This should help the reader to be able to address these problems even though not all of them are directly considered in the rest of the book.

5.7.1 LP Formulations

First of all, we notice that essentially all of the problems in Chapter 4 that are formulated as LP problems can be effectively solved by a direct application of any commercial LP solver available on the market. Within such solvers, either a version of the simplex method (Section 5.1.3) or of the interior point method (Section 5.1.4) can be used. It should be noted that many problems are formulated using link-path formulation since this formulation usually fits better with many practical design problems. This also means that for these formulations, we need to enter a set of pre-processing paths. In many instances, a set of pre-processed paths either generated using the K-shortest path algorithm (Appendix C) or determined based on a network designer's prior knowledge of the network can be used. However, it is not always clear how many pre-processed paths to use for a given problem. In such cases, the column generation technique (Section 5.4.2) can be additionally applied, if necessary, to avoid computation (in the pre-processing phase) of large candidate path lists which may lead to excessive number of variables. Hence, roughly speaking, all the design problems discussed in Section 4.1 can be effectively covered by the LP optimization framework.

5.7.2 Non-Bifurcated Flows

Section 4.2 introduces routing restrictions to the LP problem formulations of Section 4.1 which as a rule assume bifurcated routing with unrestricted split of demand volumes into flows assigned to the candidate paths. We note that (simple) restrictions associated with the path-flow diversity requirements introduced in Section 4.2.1 still keeps the overall formulations as LP problems; thus, the remarks from Section 5.7.1 remain valid. However, all other formulations (Sections 4.2.2 to 4.2.4) lead in general to computationally difficult problems expressed in the form of MIPs, using in most cases binary variables to express the single-path flow requirement; recall that single-path routing is also called non-bifurcated routing or unsplittable routing. The most representative formulation here is the allocation problem A/SPA (4.2.4) which is shown to be $\mathcal{NP}$-complete (refer to Proposition 4.2 in Section 4.2.3). Problem A/SPA (and its mixed versions with objective functions, refer to Section 4.1.3) can be directly approached using the standard BB algorithm (Section 5.2.1); however, this approach is in general ineffective because of the low quality of the lower bounds. Therefore, more effective ways for computing lower bounds must be applied, using the decomposition techniques such as LR (Section 5.4.1), as explained in [AV03] where the node-link formulation of the problem is considered. When LR is applied to the capacity constraints (4.2.5b), then the resulting subproblems are based on the shortest path computations, separately for each demand. This leads to the calculation of the lower bounds in the nodes of the BB tree using column generation (Section 5.4.2), and results in the branch-and-price algorithm (surveys on the branch-and-price approach, combining linear relaxation with column (path) generation can be found in [BJN⁺98], [LD02], and [Wil01]). Another possibility is to dualize the demand constraints (4.2.5a); this leads to the lower-bound computation subproblems of the knapsack type (Section 5.2.4) and in fact to better lower bounds than the first relaxation (of capacity constraints). In any case, according to [AV03], in most of the considered cases (only small network examples were considered) CPLEX gives better results than the specialized methods initially developed in [AV03].

Other works dealing with exact methods for solving the single-path routing problems of the A/SPA type are [BB03], [BHV00], [Gef01], [GNS98], [GNS99], [PK96], and [PKL03]. These works add valid inequalities (Section 5.2.2) to the linear relaxation problems solved at the BB tree nodes to strengthen the lower bounds computation, and lead to some kinds of the branch-and-cut (BC) algorithms.

We wish to emphasize that the application of exact (BB type) methods to the single-path flow allocation (or mixed) problems is limited to at most medium-size networks (of 20 nodes, for example) and, thus, the approximate and heuristic methods are of interest. Such approximate methods are discussed in [KS99]. As far as heuristic methods are concerned, we have already illustrated (Section 5.3.3) an application of an EA to A/SPA. Applications of tabu search (Section 5.3.5) are presented in [AFPR93] and [LG93]. Additional information about approximate and heuristic methods for the single-path routing allocation problems will be presented in Chapter 7. It should be noted that the LR method, where applicable, can also be used as a heuristic since the user has a control on the number of dual iterations to run the algorithm.

5.7.3 Modular Links

As the third group of problems, we consider the formulations using modular link cost functions discussed in Section 4.3.1 (the convex and concave cost functions discussed in Sections 4.3.2 and 4.3.3 are dealt with in Sections 5.5 and 5.6, respectively). Such problems are $\mathcal{NP}$-complete (see Proposition 4.3.4 and [Min01]) and can be formulated as MIP problems of the form depending on the kind of the involved modular cost function (see formulations (4.3.1) to (4.3.4)). In fact, such "modular dimensioning problems" (referred to as MDP henceforth in this section) with integral (or binary in the case of formulation (4.3.3)) link capacity variables and bifurcated continuous flows are central to the optimization theory of multi-commodity flow networks.

In Section 5.4.3 we have already shown how the BD method works for Problem (4.3.1) and discussed why BD can help in solving the considered MIP problem. In fact, the classical BD approach can be enriched by generating the sets of valid inequalities, leading to different BC algorithms. The form of valid inequalities depend on the type of the modular cost function used in a problem. Most of these inequalities are of the cut type, i.e., they make use of the property that the total (modular) capacity of the links in a cut (be it a single cut between two sets of vertices, or a collection of cuts between a family of subsets of nodes partitioning the set of all nodes) must be greater or equal to the sum of all demand volumes between the vertices belonging to different node subsets. In any case, valid inequalities aim at defining facets of the smallest convex hull spanned over all integral solutions of the considered MDP. It is worth mentioning that the step function used in formulation (4.3.4) is particularly well suited for the BC approach as the monotonic constraints (4.3.4d) help to derive good lower bounds for the BC process ([DS98], [GKM99], [Wes00]).

The MDP problems are classified with respect to the form of the cost function ([GKM99], [Min01]). In particular, model (4.3.1) is referred to as single-facility problem, Problem (4.3.3) as a multiple-facility problem, and Problem (4.3.4) as a general step cost function. It should be noted that a special case with exactly two different capacity modules ($K = 2$ in Problem (4.3.3)) is referred to as two-facility problem [MM95]. Exact methods and approaches related to BC can be found in such papers as [GKM99], [MM95], [Gün99]; for a recent survey, see [Min01]. We also note that problems similar to MDP are considered and addressed later in Chapters 9, 10, and 11. Such problems (referred to as restoration modular dimensioning and multi-hour dimensioning problems) are in general treated with similar means, so we will return to the MDP-related issues in Section 10.4 and 11.1.4 (and, in fact, in Sections 12.1.5 and 12.2.5, in the context of multi-layer networks).

It should be noted that even the best exact BC methods for MDP are of limited capability in terms of time efficiency. As stated in a recent paper [GKM03], the best currently available methods are capable of solving network instances with the number of nodes and links limited by 30 and 40, respectively. Therefore, approximate solution algorithms for MDP are of great interest. Such methods based on cut inequalities are discussed in [GKM03] (see also the PhD dissertation [Kni01]). Certainly, also stochastic heuristics can be used for this purpose, as illustrated in Section 5.3.4 (also, see [AK01], [CL99], [FCR+98], and [PG97]).

Finally, we mention that the combination of the single-path routing and modular cost leads to a class of difficult dimensioning problems; later in Sections 11.1.4 and 11.1.5 we will explain that a LR-based dual approach can be used to solve such problems effectively even for a network with large number of nodes in presence of multi-hour traffic demand (also see [Med95] and [MT00b]). Note that the application of the simulated allocation heuristic described in Section 5.3.4 is valid for this class of problems as well; also other meta-heuristics described in Section 5.3 are applicable.

5.8 SUMMARY AND FURTHER READING

In this chapter we have presented basic optimization techniques that can be used for solving problems studied in this book. Many of the problems discussed in Chapter 4 have linear constraints and linear objectives. Such problems can be solved using LP methods, possibly enriched with some decomposition, as long as all variables are continuous. However, for many problems, all variables take only discrete integral values (often taking only binary values 0 or 1); these problems are typically referred to as IP problems, or combinatorial optimization problems. Some models fall into the category of MIP problems if some variables take continuous values while others take discrete values. For MIP and IP problems, the well-known BB technique (and its enhancement, BC) is the most effective. Another commonly known but less efficient technique is the CP method; sometimes also LR with subgradient maximization is used. There are also new approaches (based on meta-heuristics) to solving IP problems, especially for the type of problems we will discuss in Chapter 7. Notably, among them are stochastic heuristics such as SAN, EA, SAL, and tabu search. Yet, there are some not so well-known methods for convex and concave problems that are applicable in solving various NDPs.

The basic optimization techniques discussed in this chapter (especially in Sections 5.1 to 5.4) are described in numerous handbooks, monographs, and research papers in the optimization theory and operations research, including the works specialized in communication and computer networks. Below we shall try to suggest further reading, realizing that no complete literature survey is feasible in a book like this, due to the enormous number of books and papers that are available in the field.

LP, perhaps the single most important real-life mathematical problem (to use the wording of [Dev99]), is discussed in virtually every optimization and operations research handbook. Since 1947, i.e., the pioneering work of the American mathematician George Dantzig [Dan63], the simplex method has become a standard and extremely successful approach, commonly available in commercial and freeware software tools. Our presentation in Section 5.1 is based on the books [Min86] and [Las70]. More advanced problems of LP, duality and the implementation issues of the advanced simplex algorithms can be found in [BJS90], [Mur81], [Naz87], [OH68], and [Pad91].

For an elementary, easy-to-understand description of LP and the simplex method, there are many good books such as [Chv83], [Gas90], [Mur83], and [Van98]. Interior-point methods of LP are described in [BJS90] (short treatment) and in [DT97], [Fou03], [GT96], [Pad91], and [RTV97]. The Karmarkar method is discussed in his paper [Kar84], as well as in the above cited books while a relatively simple interior-point method due to I.I. Dikin can be found in [BC99]. A recent tutorial on interior-point methods can be found in [Ter01].

The BB method is a commonly known method for combinatorial problems (including IP problems), at least in its naive version with branching but without using lower bounds. More on BB can be found in such books as [BGG+71], [Ber98], [LP79], [Min86], [OZ96], [Tom70], and [TW93] and many others. The more recent BC approach, which has in fact almost definitely replaced BB in the MIP applications and MIP solvers ([Wol03]), is discussed in [ZO81]; also see [BCC93], [NW88], [Wol89], and [Wol98]. The CP method, underlying the BC approach, is described in [Min86] and [Ber98] (also see [Gol67], [Gom60], and [Gom63]). For DP, see [BB96], [Had64], [Min86], and [Nem67].

The use of stochastic meta-heuristics for combinatorial problems has gained a great deal of popularity in recent decades, due to their implementation simplicity of not requiring basically any theoretical background (as in the case of BC for instance). A popular description of SAN can be found in [KGV83]. More advanced presentation is given in [DA91], [JAMS89], and [Ber98]; for a multi-commodity network design application see [LP95]. Genetic EAs are treated in detail in the monographs [Ber98], [Gol89], [Mic96], [Muh92] and the classical paper [RTB67]. Telecommunication applications of EAs are listed in [Sin99]. SAL, a less known stochastic meta-heuristic devised especially for the multi-commodity flow applications, is presented in [Pió97b] and [PG97]. Tabu search was introduced in the works of [Glo86] and [Han86]; also see monograph in [GL97], surveys in [Glo89] and [Glo90], discussion in [Ber98], and papers [CS99] and [GM84].

General description of decomposition methods in LP presented in Section 5.4 (LR, column generation, and BD) can be found in [Las70], [Min86] and other optimization handbooks. LR is also discussed in [AMO93], [Ber98], [Min86], and [Sha79]; subgradient maximization methods are also presented in [HWC74], [Sho85], and [Min84]. Column generation is treated in [Wol03], and for multi-commodity network design applications in [AMO93], [DS98], [KSPM03], and [Wes00]. Benders Decomposition, introduced in [Ben62], is also discussed in [Min89], [Min81], [Min84], and [PS01] for multicommodity network design applications.

Theoretical background for general convex optimization problems is given in [Ber98], [Min86], [Rob87], and [Roc70], and for convex problems with linear constraints (i.e., for the problems treated in Section 5.5) in [Ber95]. General GP methods and reduced gradient methods for such problems are presented in [Rosen] and [Min86]. GP and reduced gradient methods for multi-commodity network design are described in [BH75], [BG92], [Ber98], [Har76], and [Ker92].

The algorithms for the concave optimization discussed in Section 5.6 are presented in [Yag71], [Min89], and [KKP99].

EXERCISES FOR CHAPTER 5

5.1. Consider the LP problem from Example 5.1 and change its objective to: maximize $z = x_1 + x_2$. Characterize the set of all optimal solutions.

5.2. Obtain the LP dual of the following problem where variables are also bounded from above:

$$\textbf{\textit{minimize}} \quad cx \quad \textbf{\textit{subject to}} \quad \boldsymbol{A}x = \boldsymbol{b}, \quad \boldsymbol{0} \leq x \leq \boldsymbol{M}.$$

5.3. ([Min93]) Suppose we need to put two transmission media of different characteristics in an existing conduit. The first medium requires 8 mm^2 section area per cable while the second medium requires 4 mm^2. The first medium holds 3 T1s while the second medium holds 5 T1s. The distance-based unit cost for the first medium is \$10 and for second medium is \$70. We are given that the total available area in the conduits is 4,800 mm^2, and the total budget available is \$38,500. There is an additional requirement: the maximum number of pairs of the first medium that can be put in a conduit before electrical interference arises is 500. The objective is to maximize T1-bandwidth in the conduit. Formulate this as a linear programming problem and determine the optimal solution. Write the dual counterpart of this problem and solve it. Is there a physical interpretation of the optimal dual variables and the dual problem? (Hint: note that the electrical interference requirement and the conduit's capacity requirement are not binding at the optimal solution of the primal problem.)

5.4. Drop the constraint $x_1 \geq 0$ from the problem of Example 5.1 and formulate the resulting LP in the standard form.

5.5. Draw the solution polyhedron for the relaxed problem of Example 5.5 and confirm that the given solution is correct.

5.6. Solve the modified continuous problem of Example 5.5.

5.7. *Derive formula (5.2.7) and write down a Pascal-like pseudo-code for the recursive algorithm for solving Problem (5.2.6) using formula (5.2.7).

5.8. Tracing back Table 5.1 from the value $\boldsymbol{F}^*(5, 11) = 40$ find the composition of the optimal knapsack.

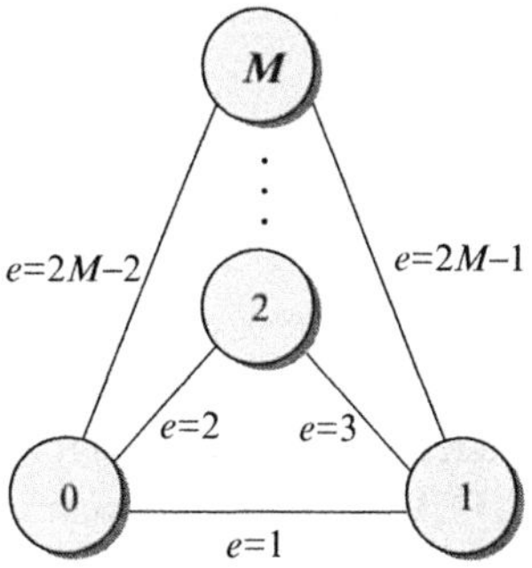

FIGURE 5.7 A "Nasty" Example

5.9. Formulate the first descent LS version of local search.

5.10. Find the transition probability matrix $\boldsymbol{P} = [p_{xy}]_{x,y \in X}$ for the Markov chain of the inner loop of the SAN algorithm.

5.11. *Derive formula (5.3.12).

5.12. Using the properties of the saddle point of the Lagrangian function given in Appendix A prove properties (5.4.13).

5.13. Derive formula (5.4.16).

5.14. *Formulate and proof a proposition analogous to Proposition 5.1 for problem A/PAP (4.1.7) with objective function (4.1.10) Show that the stopping criterion analogous to that based on the dual function (5.4.17) is valid. (Hint: the problem is solved in [AMO93].)

5.15. ** Consider the network of Figure 5.7. Suppose that the demands correspond to links (links and the corresponding demands have the same end nodes), and the numbering of links and demands coincide. Let demand volume h_1 of demand $d = 1$ between nodes $v = 0$ and $v = 1$ be equal to 12, and the rest of the demand volumes be $h_d = 10$. Assume that all link capacities are equal to 10. Finally, assume that each demand $d > 1$ has only one allowable path - the direct path composed of link $e = d$ and that, exceptionally, demand $d = 1$ has the set of allowable paths composed of the direct path $\mathcal{P}_1 = \{1\}$ (i.e., $\mathcal{P}_1$ consists of link $e = 1$), and all two-link paths $\mathcal{P}_v = \{2v-2, 2v-1\}$, for $v = 2, 3, ..., M$.

Show that the optimal solution of A/ALC consists in assigning all demand volumes to their direct one-link paths, leading to the optimal primal objective $\boldsymbol{F}^* = 2$.

Note that if you start Algorithm 5.9 with the routing list for demand $d = 1$ consisting of only one (direct) path $\mathcal{P}_1$, then you will immediately get the optimal solution. However, if you do not know this and continue to apply the algorithm, then show that you will be forced to check all the allowable two-link paths for demand $d = 1$ before the algorithm terminates. Show a way to avoid this situation. (Hint: note that some sets of optimal dual variables can be better than others in generating new paths.)

5.16. *Consider the modified problem A/ALC (5.4.11):

$$\begin{array}{lll} \textbf{\textit{minimize}} & F(z) = z & \\ \textbf{\textit{subject to}} & \sum_p x_{dp} = h_d & d = 1, 2, \dots, D \\ & \sum_d \sum_p \delta_{edp} x_{dp} \leq c_e + z & e = 1, 2, \dots, E \\ & \boldsymbol{x} \geq 0, z \geq 0. & \end{array} \tag{5.8.1}$$

Formulate the corresponding dual problem, and apply the CPLA technique to the network from Exercise 5.15. Show that for this formulation of the augmented problem, before stopping, CPLA will always have to examine the last allowable two-link path, no matter what optimal dual solutions are used.

5.17. *Prove the fact from Example 4.3 using arguments of the dual theory.

5.18. *Write down Problem (5.4.20) in the node-link formulation and derive the corresponding feasibility test for generating inequalities for $\boldsymbol{y}$ for the master problem.

5.19. Show that the set of optimal solutions of Problem (5.5.1) is convex. Give an intuitive explanation of the bifurcated nature of the optimal flows.

5.20. Check formula (5.5.14) for the vector $y = (1, 2)$ and the constraints $x_1 + x_2 = 1$, $x \geq 0$. Write down formula (5.5.14) for a fixed demand d assuming that the part of $-\nabla F(x^k)$ corresponding to demand d is equal to $\boldsymbol{f} = (f_{d1}, f_{d2}, \dots, f_{dP_d})$.

5.21. Derive formulae (5.5.13-5.5.14). (Hint: use Karush-Kuhn-Tucker conditions, Section A.2, Appendix A.)

5.22. *Prove formulae (5.5.18) and (5.5.19).

5.23. *Prove formula (5.5.21) for the subgradient of the dual function (5.5.17).

5.24. **Assume that $\boldsymbol{x}^*$ is the flow vector obtained as a result of the Algorithm 5.12. Show that $\boldsymbol{x}^*$ is the local minimum of the considered problem. (Hint: use Karush-Kuhn-Tucker conditions.)

CHAPTER 6

Location and Topological Design

In this chapter, we introduce a new element which has a significant impact on the nature of the network design problems (NDPs): the installation, "opening" cost of links (and nodes). An implicit assumption underlying the uncapacitated design problems considered so far (for example, see Chapter 4) was that links (and nodes) are already located and installed in the network and that the cost of the network depends only on the capacity assigned to links (and nodes). Although such "dimensioning" problems are of major importance, in many cases, especially at the early stages of the long-term network planning process, the decision where to install network nodes and links interconnecting the located nodes must be made on an economical basis, i.e., also taking into account the capacity-independent, "fixed" costs associated with installation of nodes and links. Since the particular location of nodes and links determines the topology (structure) of the resulting network graph, these types of problems are called *topological design* problems.

There are two main types of topological design problems. In the first type, which are frequently referred to as *location problems* (and can be labeled as "pure" topological design), demand volumes generated between the nodes are not considered, since for instance they may not be known at the early stages of network planning. Thus, only the fixed capacity-independent installation cost of nodes and links is taken into account, and the nodes and links are located in order to achieve a network topology that assures a certain degree of connectivity between origin-destination demand pairs at the lowest total installation cost. The second type of problems adds demand volume into the picture together with the capacity-dependent costs, and both cost factors are considered in the total network cost in network design. As a result, link/node locations are determined simultaneously with flow and capacity allocation.

In planning of any network, we can envision scenarios such as the following: 1) Given possible access node locations, where do I want to locate transit nodes (or access nodes in the backbone network)? 2) Where and how do I want to interconnect the core nodes taking into account possible locations for access networks? 3) Once I know the location of core nodes and the graph of the network, how do I determine where to have links expanded so that traffic demand can be met? This chapter, therefore, attempts to answer such questions through presentation of relevant optimization models.

The technology area where these scenarios can be applicable is numerous. The basic node location problem can be used in access network design, as it has been traditionally used in hub location problems for network design and other areas as well (e.g., warehouse location, factory location, and so on). Here, we will consider a scenario of access/transit node location, which can be applied, for example, to multi-protocol label switching (MPLS)-capable IP networks, with the access nodes representing ingress/egress label edge routers (LER), and the transit nodes being label switching routers (LSR). Since evolving IP/MPLS networks can be a collection of large numbers of LERs and LSRs to be placed in many possible sites, the problem of optimal node and link location becomes important, especially for economical network extension. Similarly, many other applications of these problems, also for other networking technologies, can be thought of, not just in the core network design but also to locate critical services in overlay networks, for example, actual web server locations for a major website, service node locations in SS7 signalling networks [Rus02], and so on.

We consider two location design problems. In Section 6.1, we study a classical location design problem to determine how to connect areas to a particular location for a generic cost structure. We then describe a well-known add heuristic to solve this problem. It may be noted that Lagrangian-based dual approach is a successful approach for this problem—how this approach can be used has been described earlier in Chapter 5 (Example 5.4.1). In Section 6.2, we extend the considerations to include network connectivity issues.

Topological design problems combining both the installation and capacity-dependent cost factors are considered in Section 6.3, together with appropriate exact and heuristic optimization methods. We start with discussing the classical topological design problems explicitly considering only link locations. First, the case with the budget constraint for the installation cost and the capacity-dependent cost minimization as the optimization objective is formulated (Section 6.3.2). Then, in Section 6.3.3, the models with the installation cost moved to the objective function are considered. Although the nodes can be represented using auxiliary, artificial links and, hence, there is no necessity of dealing with nodes explicitly (this technique is explained in Section 4.6.1), it may be computationally more efficient to use problem formulations where nodes are explicitly represented by optimization variables. Such formulations are presented in Section 6.3.4. Optimization methods for topological design are presented in Section 6.3.5, and the corresponding numerical examples are given in Section 6.3.6.

Section 6.4 is devoted to discussing methods for the computation of the lower bounds useful in solving the topological design problems by means of the branch-and-bound (BB) technique. The problems and optimization methods presented in this chapter are illustrated with numerical results. The summary and suggested reading is given in Section 6.5.

6.1 NODE LOCATION PROBLEM

In the long-term planning phase of a network designed for initial configuration, an important problem is determination of location of nodes. The use of the term 'node' can be applicable for problems related to a variety of different networks such as consisting of switches, routers, hubs, or even a location for point-of-presence (PoP). Thus, we will use the generic name 'node' to describe this problem.

The problem can be stated as follows: we are to connect N areas ("access" regions) through a list of possible node locations M so that the total cost is minimized. We are given the possible cost information for connecting each area to each possible node location. Secondly, we know that any sites for a node, if opened, can handle only up to a certain number of termination (e.g., to address the requirement of the maximum number of ports in a router) and that each area needs to be connected to only one node; this means there is only a single access link for an area to the core network. This is a classical node location problem. We first present the formulation before describing the constraints involved.

***IP:* D/NLD**
Node Location Design
indices

$i = 1, 2, ..., N$ areas (sources) to be connected
$j = 1, 2, ..., M$ possible locations for nodes

constants

ξ_{ij} cost of connecting area i to possible location j
η_j cost of location j, if opened
K_j maximum number of areas that can be handled at possible location j

variables

u_{ij} = 1, if area i is connected to location j; 0, otherwise
r_j = 1, if a node is decided to be located at site j; 0, otherwise

objective

$$\text{mininimize } \boldsymbol{F} = \textstyle\sum_i \sum_j \xi_{ij} u_{ij} + \sum_j \eta_j r_j \tag{6.1.1a}$$

constraints

$$\textstyle\sum_j u_{ij} = 1, \qquad i = 1, 2, ..., N \tag{6.1.1b}$$

$$\textstyle\sum_i u_{ij} \leq K_j r_j, \qquad j = 1, 2, ..., M. \tag{6.1.1c}$$

In this problem, we want to select a subset of node locations, $j = 1, 2, ..., M$ for optimal design to minimize the total location cost and access cost. We are given that the cost of opening a node at site j to be $\eta_j, j = 1, ..., M$ and the cost of connecting area i to site j to be ξ_{ij} (only if connected), and that each switch location j can handle a maximum of K_j areas. The entire formulation is developed using binary decision variables.

The first condition to be met is that each area is to be connected to only one site. This is reflected through equation (6.1.1b). Since u_{ij}'s are binary decision variables and the summation over $j = 1, 2, ..., M$ is 1, we can have only a particular j that takes the value 1 (when i is fixed); this needs to be considered for each $i = 1, 2, ..., N$.

Secondly, each switch location can handle up to K_j areas if a switch is located at site j. Note that this is a *conditional* request and that inequality (6.1.1c) shows how to handle such conditional statements by using site binary decision variables r_j. If a location j is not selected, then the associated r_j will take the value 0; this will then force each u_{ij} for this j to take the value 0—this means that no area is connected to this location. On the other hand, if the location j is open, the associated decision variable r_j will take the value 1; in this case, this site is limited by its capacity K_j for how many areas it can handle.

The total cost is the connection (access) cost due to ξ_{ij} and the location cost due to η_j; this is reflected in objective (6.1.1a). An important variation of this problem is faced in the location design of SS7 networks [Rus02] where every access node is required to be connected to two transit (or core) nodes for network reliability; this is left as an exercise (Exercise 6.1).

The above problem is a 0-1 integer programming problem since decision variable vectors $\boldsymbol{u} = (u_{11}, u_{12}, ..., u_{NM})$ and $\boldsymbol{r} = (r_1, r_2, ..., r_M)$ can only take the values 0 or 1; this is also known as a combinatorial optimization problem. You can use integer programming solvers to solve this problem as long as the problem is not too large. Exhaustive search can be very expensive when the problem size grows; thus, we need to resort to heuristic algorithms for large problems. There are several methods. As we have discussed for many problems, Lagrangian relaxation (LR)-based subgradient dual approach (Section 5.4.1) can be used for solving this problem by relaxing constraint (6.1.1c); this has already been illustrated in Section 5.4.1. We will cover here a special heuristic called *add heuristic*.

6.1.1 Add Heuristic

This is a local search procedure, similar to what we have described in Section 5.3.1. In this procedure, we start with any location and all the sources connected to this location. In actuality, the problem may not be feasible since it may go over the limit imposed by K_j—this is acceptable as the starting point. In the next iteration, all the rest of the possible locations are checked one at a time to determine reduction in cost while trying to address the termination constraint (6.1.1c). Once all of them are considered one at a time, the location with the best savings is considered for opening as an acceptable site. Then in the next iteration, all the potential locations are compared to the locations already opened thus far, and the process goes on until all of the locations are considered for opening. The add heuristic is formally described in Algorithm 6.1. How about complexity of the add heuristic? The effort to select the next location is $O(NM)$ where N is the number of sources (areas) and M is the number of potential locations. The overall complexity of the algorithm is $O(NM^2)$, since we can select at most $O(M)$ locations. We illustrate add heuristic through the following example from [Sch77].

ALGORITHM 6.1 Add Heuristic for Node Location Design Problem (6.1.1)

Step 0: Select an initial location $\hat{\jmath}$ and assume that all areas are connected to this location. Set $\mathcal{S}_0 = \{\hat{\jmath}\}$. and iteration count to $k = 0$. Compute cost $\boldsymbol{F}^0$ with this configuration. Set $\xi'_i = \xi_{i\hat{\jmath}}, i = 1, 2, ..., N$. Let $\mathcal{M}$ denote the set of locations.

Step 1: For $j \in \mathcal{M} \setminus \mathcal{S}_k$, do

$$\boldsymbol{F}_j^{k+1} = \boldsymbol{F}^k + \sum_{i \in I_j} (\xi_{ij} - \xi'_i) + \eta_j \quad \text{where } I_j = \{i \,|\, \xi_{ij} - \xi'_i < 0\}.$$

Step 2: Determine a new $\hat{\jmath}$ such that

$$\boldsymbol{F}_{\hat{\jmath}}^{k+1} = \min_{j \in \mathcal{M} \setminus \mathcal{S}_k} \{\boldsymbol{F}_j^{k+1}\} < \boldsymbol{F}^k.$$

If there is no such $\hat{\jmath}$, go to Step 4.

Step 3: Update

$$\mathcal{S}_{k+1} = \mathcal{S}_k \cup \{\hat{\jmath}\}$$

and

$$\xi'_i = \xi_{i\hat{\jmath}} \qquad \text{for } i \in I_{\hat{\jmath}}.$$

Set $\boldsymbol{F}^{k+1} = \boldsymbol{F}_{\hat{\jmath}}^{k+1}$ and $k := k + 1$ and go to Step 1.

Step 4: No more improvement possible; stop.

***Example 6.1** Illustration of Add Heuristic*

Table 6.1 shows the cost ξ_{ij} of connecting source i to switch location j. For this example, we are given that $K_j = 3, \quad j = 1, 2, 3, 4, \quad$ and $\quad \eta_1 = 0, \eta_2 = \eta_3 = \eta_4 = 2$. We will denote ξ'_i to be the cost of connecting to a location (when it has already been decided) during the iterative procedure.

Iteration 0: First, we connect all the the sources to the location S1 (a "must" location for this example since $\eta_1 = 0$). The total cost is

$$\boldsymbol{F}^0 = \sum_{i=1}^{6} \xi_{i1} = 2 + 1 + 4 + 1 + 2 + 4 = 14.$$

In this instance, $\xi'_i := \xi_{i1}$ since all are connected to location S1.

Iteration 1: Now, we check one location at a time to determine which one provides the best savings. Suppose we open S2. Consider the set of sources for which the cost is reduced compared to being connected to S1. To see this, observe the following:

TABLE 6.1 **Cost ξ_{ij} Information for Example 6.1**

	S1	S2	S3	S4
1	2	1	2	4
2	1	0	1	2
3	4	1	2	2
4	1	2	1	2
5	2	3	2	0
6	4	4	3	2

$\xi_{12}-\xi_{11}$	$\xi_{22}-\xi_{21}$	$\xi_{32}-\xi_{31}$	$\xi_{42}-\xi_{41}$	$\xi_{52}-\xi_{51}$	$\xi_{62}-\xi_{61}$
$=1-2$	$=0-1$	$=1-4$	$=2-1$	$=3-2$	$=4-4$
$=-1$	$=-1$	$=-3$	$=1$	$=1$	$=0.$

From the above, we can see that there is good reason to connect the first three sources to the new location since it will reduce cost; otherwise, for sources 4 and 5 it will cost more and should not be added, while for source 6 since the cost difference is 0, it can be connected to either location. Thus, the new cost is

$$\boldsymbol{F}_2^1 = \boldsymbol{F}^0 + \textstyle\sum_{i\in I_2}(\xi_{i2}-\xi_{i1}) + \eta_2 = 14 + [-1-1-3] + 2 = 11.$$

Note that I_2 here refers to the set of sources for which there is cost savings if connected to location 1; in this instance, $I_2 = \{1,2,3\}$ and we incur an additional cost η_2 for opening site S2.

Now we do the same assessment for location 3, i.e., open S3 (independent of what we just did for location S2). In this case, we can see that the savings are for sources 3 and 6. Thus, here $I_3 = \{3,6\}$, and the overall cost assessment is:

$$\boldsymbol{F}_3^1 = \boldsymbol{F}^0 + \textstyle\sum_{i\in I_3}(\xi_{i3}-\xi_{i1}) + \eta_3 = 14 + [-2-1] + 2 = 13. \tag{6.1.2}$$

Finally, we open location S4 to do the same exercise. In this case, we see that the savings can be obtained for connecting to location 3 are sources 3, 5, and 6, i.e., $I_4 = \{3,5,6\}$,

$$\boldsymbol{F}_4^1 = \boldsymbol{F}^0 + \textstyle\sum_{i\in I_4}(\xi_{i4}-\xi_{i1}) + \eta_4 = 14 + [-2-2-2] + 2 = 10. \tag{6.1.3}$$

Now, comparing all the possible locations for opening, we see that it would be the cheapest to open S4 since with S4, we reduce total cost the most to 10. If we do so, then sources 3, 5, and 6 should now be connected to S4 while 1, 2, and 4 remain connected to S1. Thus, we have the new configuration and each updated ξ' is as follows:

$$\xi'_1 = \xi_{11},\ \xi'_2 = \xi_{21},\ \xi'_3 = \xi_{34},\ \xi'_4 = \xi_{41},\ \xi'_5 = \xi_{54},\ \xi'_6 = \xi_{64}.$$

Hence, we have now completed iteration 1 with new reduced cost

$$\boldsymbol{F}^1 = \min\{\boldsymbol{F}_2^1, \boldsymbol{F}_3^1, \boldsymbol{F}_4^1\} = 10.$$

Iteration 2: Now that we have locations S1 and S4 open (with each of them "homing" certain areas), we can consider opening S2 and S3 one at a time compared to the present assignment and relative reduction in cost. Thus, if we check, the cost differential for S1 relative to the currently assigned allocation, we see that

$\xi_{12} - \xi_1'$	$\xi_{22} - \xi_2'$	$\xi_{32} - \xi_3'$	$\xi_{42} - \xi_4'$	$\xi_{52} - \xi_5'$	$\xi_{62} - \xi_6'$
$= \xi_{12} - \xi_{11}$	$= \xi_{22} - \xi_{21}$	$= \xi_{32} - \xi_{34}$	$= \xi_{42} - \xi_{41}$	$= \xi_{52} - \xi_{54}$	$= \xi_{62} - \xi_{64}$
$= 1 - 2$	$= 0 - 1$	$= 1 - 2$	$= 2 - 1$	$= 3 - 0$	$= 4 - 2$
$= -1$	$= -1$	$= -1$	$= 1$	$= 3$	$= 2.$

This indicates that sources 1, 2, and 3 are up for consideration, i.e., $I_2 = \{1, 2, 3\}$. Thus, we have the following cost

$$\boldsymbol{F}_2^2 = \boldsymbol{F}^1 + \sum_{i \in I_2} (\xi_{i2} - \xi_i') + \eta_2 = 10 + [-1 - 1 - 1] + 2 = 9. \quad (6.1.4)$$

Now we check S3 independently for any improvement; no allocation reduces cost, i.e., $I_3 = \emptyset$! Thus, opening S2 with the new allocation, i.e., sources 1, 2, 3 to location S2, source 4 to location S1, and sources 5 and 6 to location S4, will result in the new cost of $\boldsymbol{F}^2 = 9$.
Iteration 3: Given the allocation as in iteration 2, the only location left to check is S3—it can be easily seen that there is no additional gain. Thus, the algorithmic steps have been completed and the solution is the one obtained at the end of Iteration 2. ●

Remark 6.1

1) From the solution to the above example, it may seem that we could have picked the location for each source for which the cost is the smallest (Table 6.1) and that this assignment would determine optimality immediately; this would actually work if each η_i is set to *zero*! If some of the η_is are positive, then this simple rule would not work. 2) The add heuristic can be modified for the SS7 network location design problem (Exercise 6.3). ♦

To get a better sense of what a network may look like after solving the node location design problem D/NLD, we consider an example with 30-access areas (denoted by circles) and 10 possible locations (denoted by triangles) as shown in Figure 6.1a. We have set $K_j = 6$; the resulting optimal solution is then shown pictorially in Figure 6.1b where five sites are selected for optimal location of nodes.

6.2 JOINT NODE LOCATION AND LINK CONNECTIVITY PROBLEM

Beyond locating nodes to connect access areas, the nodes themselves need to be connected as well in the core to form a network. Certainly, there is a link cost associated with connecting core nodes. We are interested in the optimal location of the core network nodes which minimizes the access connectivity cost (the cost of the access network to the core network connectivity) and the node placement cost *as well as* the cost of *connecting* core network

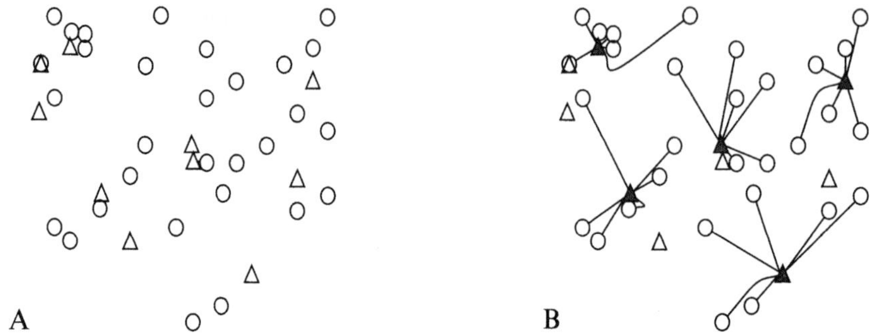

FIGURE 6.1 Illustration of Node Location Design

nodes. This combined problem is called the optimal node location and link connectivity (ONLLC) problem.

This scenario appears to be similar to the classical node location problem (Section 6.1). However, problem ONLLC addresses both location as well as connectivity of the network. Due to changing cost structure and domain of operations of networks (and network providers), the ONLLC problem is sometimes more applicable than just the node location problem for some network providers.

We will present two different models. In the first model, all of the nodes are considered to be of the same type (e.g., all IP routers), but not necessarily of the same capacity. In the second model, we consider two types of nodes that are applicable in the overlay-underlay network design. Two good cxamples would be IP over MPLS networks or IP over WDM networks. Let us elaborate this second case a bit more. A group of IP routers may be clustered to connect to another cluster of IP networks through an MPLS-based network (or WDM network) where a set of possible sites for MPLS nodes are available; in this case, the problem is which IP router should be homed to a specific MPLS switch so that access/location as well as interconnection cost between the switches is minimized. In this case, the IP routers in a cluster can be thought of as in an access network environment or edge devices, and MPLS switch network as the core network. To avoid confusion between routers and switches, which is immaterial in the formulation of the models to be presented, we will use the generic term *node device* in the rest of the discussion.

6.2.1 Design Formulation: One-Level

In the first case, we consider the scenario that every site can possibly be a candidate site for node device location. Thus, any site can either be an access site or a node location site.

Note that the optimal node location design for $N = 30$ and $M = 10$ was already shown in Figure 6.1b; if we were to also consider the core network interconnection cost for this example, we obtain a solution as shown in Figure 6.2—note that we can get a different set of core nodes than for "pure" node location design due to the additional consideration of core network connectivity cost. If a node device is located at a site, it is assumed to have a

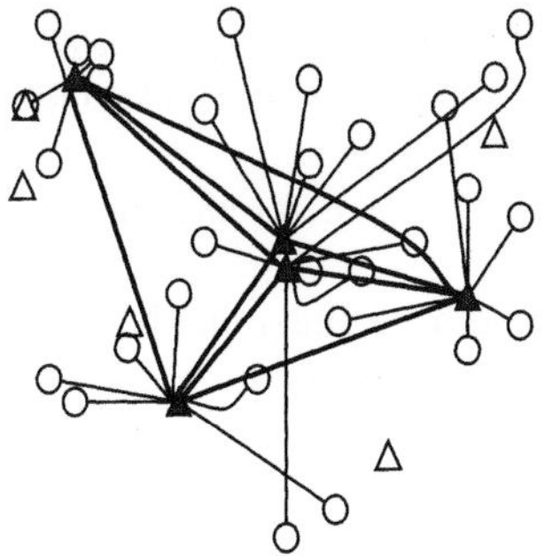

FIGURE 6.2 Combined Node Location and Core Network Interconnection Design for $N = 30$ and $M = 10$

finite 'source' termination capacity (e.g., interfaces or ports) and can connect to other node devices. We specifically consider the case where the selected sites in the core are needed to be fully-interconnected (fully-mesh).

We now need to construct the constraints imposed by this problem. This requires a bit of elaboration. To start with, consider that we have N sites to be connected of which P are node locations to be selected. We are given that the cost of connecting site i to site j is ξ_{ij} and cost of location j, if opened, is η_j. Let K_j be the maximum number of terminations that can be handled at location j. We introduce two sets of variables: u_{ij} denotes the decision variable that takes the value 1 if site i is to be connected to site j (0, otherwise), and r_j is the decision variable that indicates the opening of site j. We assume here symmetry on the connectivity cost, i.e., $\xi_{ij} = \xi_{ji}$; this implies that u_{ij} is indifferent from u_{ji}. Hence, the problem can be restricted to the i and j which are diagonal or upper diagonal, i.e., $i \leq j$ with $i, j = 1, 2, ..., N$.

Since we have all locations of the same type to start with, of which some will become access location while others will become core locations, we need to consider each site's possibility separately. If site i turns out to be an access site, then it is required that it be connected to exactly one node device site; this can be related as follows:

$$\sum_{j=1}^{N} u_{ij} = 1, \text{ for any access site } i.$$

This is equivalent to

$$\sum_{j=1}^{N} u_{ij} \geq 1, \text{ for any access site } i \tag{6.2.1}$$

$$\sum_{j=1}^{N} u_{ij} \leq 1, \text{ for any access site } i. \tag{6.2.2}$$

Note that if site j is chosen to be a core site, then it needs to support at least one access site (which could be itself). If the overall goal is to create a fully interconnected backbone/core network, then each core site j is required to be connected to $(P - 1)$ other core sites; thus, we have the following relation:

$$\sum_{i=1}^{N} u_{ij} \geq P, \text{ for each core site } j. \tag{6.2.3}$$

Taking advantage of the symmetry ($u_{ij} = u_{ji}$), we can combine relation (6.2.3) with relation (6.2.1) by introducing the node selection variable r_j to obtain the following:

$$\sum_{i=1}^{N} u_{ij} \geq P r_j + (1 - r_j), \text{ for any site } j. \tag{6.2.4}$$

Similarly, a node device site j can be connected to $P - 1$ other core nodes (due to requirement for being fully-interconnected in the core) and can handle up to a maximum of K_j access sites; thus, we have:

$$\sum_{i=1}^{N} u_{ij} \leq K_j + P - 1, \text{ for any core site } j. \tag{6.2.5}$$

In this case, combining relation (6.2.5) with (6.2.2) and taking advantage again of symmetry, we can write:

$$\sum_{i=1}^{N} u_{ij} \leq (K_j + P - 1) r_j + (1 - r_j), \text{ for any site } j. \tag{6.2.6}$$

To recap, every site satisfies both (6.2.4) and (6.2.6).

We now need to determine the total number of links that should exist in the network. Each access site should be connected to one core node for the access network connectivity, and in the core network, all the P nodes are to be fully interconnected. Again, due to symmetry, this requirement can be reflected by considering the diagonal and upper diagonal $\boldsymbol{u}$ as follows:

$$\sum_{i=1}^{N} \sum_{j=i}^{N} u_{ij} = N + P(P - 1)/2. \tag{6.2.7}$$

Note the range of the second summation to accomplish this requirement. Finally, we address the total number of sites that should be core node sites, and the fact that the access site at i is connected to itself as the core site. Thus, we have:

$$\sum_{j=1}^{N} r_j = P \tag{6.2.8}$$

$$\sum_{i=1}^{N} u_{ii} = P. \tag{6.2.9}$$

The goal is to minimize the total cost due to access as well as core network links for full-interconnection, and due to the selection of the core node location sites. The objective function, then, is:

$$\boldsymbol{F} = \sum_{i=1}^{N} \sum_{j=i}^{N} \xi_{ij} u_{ij} + \sum_{j=1}^{N} \eta_j r_j. \tag{6.2.10}$$

In this representation, ξ_{ij} corresponds to either access links or interconnection links depending on the selected u_{ij} along with the sites selected (r_j). The NDP is to minimize (6.2.10) under the requirements given in (6.2.4), (6.2.6), (6.2.7), (6.2.8), and (6.2.9), and that the variables take only the values 0 or 1. Rearranging (6.2.4) and (6.2.6), we can now summarize the formulation.

***IP:* D/ONLLC/A** **Fully-Connected Core**

Node Location and Link-Connectivity

indices

$i, j = 1, 2, ..., N$ sites to be connected

constants

P number of switch locations ($P < N$)

ξ_{ij} cost of connecting site i to site j (assume symmetry, i.e., $\xi_{ij} = \xi_{ji}$)

η_j cost of location j, if opened

K_j maximum number of sites that can be handled at location j (if j is selected)

variables

u_{ij} =1, if site i is connected to site j; 0, otherwise

r_j =1, if site j is chosen for location of a switch; 0, otherwise

objective

$$\text{minimize } \boldsymbol{F} = \sum_{i=1}^{N} \sum_{j=i}^{N} \xi_{ij} u_{ij} + \sum_{j=1}^{N} \eta_j r_j \tag{6.2.11a}$$

constraints

$$\sum_{i=1}^{N} u_{ij} - (P-1) r_j \geq 1, \quad j = 1, 2, ..., N \tag{6.2.11b}$$

$$\sum_{i=1}^{N} u_{ij} - (K_j + P - 2) r_j \leq 1, \quad j = 1, 2, ..., N \tag{6.2.11c}$$

$$\sum_{i=1}^{N} \sum_{j=i}^{N} u_{ij} = N + P(P-1)/2 \tag{6.2.11d}$$

$$\sum_{j=1}^{N} r_j = P \tag{6.2.11e}$$

$$\sum_{i=1}^{N} u_{ii} = P. \tag{6.2.11f}$$

Thus, we have formulated the first case of problem D/ONLLC/A as a 0/1 integer linear programming problem. It may be noted that since the cost between two sites is given using ξ_{ij} which need *not* be based on Euclidean distance, the model is quite general. Typically, we assume that $\xi_{ii} > 0$ is different for each i (i.e., $\xi_{ii} \neq \xi_{kk}$ if $i \neq k$). It may also be noted that P, the minimum number of node locations to be chosen, should be in the order of $N^2/(\sum_{j=1}^{N} K_j)$ for the optimization problem to be feasible. For instance, if $K_j = K$ for all j, then for the feasibility of the problem, we must have $P \geq \lceil N/K \rceil$.

Optimal Number of Node Locations (Special Case)

A natural extension would be to consider P, the number of locations to be selected, also as a variable to determine optimal P instead of providing a specific value P as an input parameter; however, this should not be confused with optimal location of nodes.

The primary disadvantage of developing a formulation for this extension is that the entire problem becomes a *non-linear* integer programming problem. In general, non-linear integer programming problems are very hard to solve and, in fact, no general solution approach is known. Fortunately, for problem D/ONLLC/A, it appears that the optimal P in the optimal ONLLC design is likely the one with the smallest P for which the formulation is feasible. That is, consider problem D/ONLLC/A for $N = 25$, and $K_j = 5$ for all sites j; in this case, the optimal cost is obtained by solving D/ONLLC/A with $P = 5$—this cost is smaller than the optimal cost obtained with any other $P > 5$.

To illustrate this in another way, consider the hypothetical case where we set $\xi_{ij} = \xi$ and $\eta_j = \eta$. Let us denote the optimal cost by $\boldsymbol{F}_P$ for D/ONLLC/A when P sites are to be selected. From formulation (6.2.11), using (6.2.11a) along with (6.2.11d), and (6.2.11e) for fixed values ξ and η, the optimal cost for fixed P becomes

$$\boldsymbol{F}_P = \xi N + \xi P(P-1)/2 + \eta P.$$

If we now solve formulation (6.2.11) for selection of $P+1$ number of locations, the optimal cost changes to

$$\boldsymbol{F}_{P+1} = \xi N + \xi(P+1)P/2 + \eta(P+1).$$

Clearly, $\boldsymbol{F}_P < \boldsymbol{F}_{P+1}$ for positive cost components ξ and η showing that the optimal P is the smallest P for which formulation (6.2.11) is feasible. Another way to illustrate this is that when we go from P to $P+1$, we need to add additional P links in the core network for the interconnection cost besides the cost for the additional switch site. Yet, it is hard to generalize this result.

Next, we introduce two special instances of problem D/ONLLC/A.

Variation: A1

If in addition to the requirements described above for formulation (6.2.11), we are also given that $K_j = K$ and $\eta_j = \eta$ for all sites, then the following simplification takes place for the second part of the objective function (6.2.11a) when coupled with (6.2.11e):

$$\sum_{j=1}^{N} \eta r_j = \eta \sum_{j=1}^{N} r_j = bP.$$

Since this is a constant, the second part of the objective function does not need to be explicitly listed in the objective function, i.e., we need to minimize the following cost:

$$\boldsymbol{F} = \sum_{i=1}^{N} \sum_{j=i}^{N} \xi_{ij} u_{ij}.$$

Variation: A2

If a node device site is required to be connected to an access site besides itself, as well as all the other core networks, then (6.2.3) will change to:

$$\sum_{i=1}^{N} u_{ij} \geq P+1, \quad \text{for core node site } j. \tag{6.2.12}$$

Consequently, (6.2.4) will change to:

$$\sum_{i=1}^{N} u_{ij} \geq (P+1) r_j + (1 - r_j), \quad \text{for all site } j. \tag{6.2.13}$$

Note that with this condition, the number of node locations P cannot be less than $N/2$ to maintain feasibility of the problem.

6.2.2 Design Formulation: Two-Level

This model is applicable to scenarios such as the IP/MPLS environment describe earlier. In this case, the list of access sites and the list of possible core node location sites are different to indicate the different types of nodes. As before, we are operating under the requirement that the backbone network is to be fully interconnected. In figures, we will use a circle to denote an access site and a plain triangle to denote a possible core node location site as we did in Section 6.1. Figure 6.1a shown earlier in Section 6.1 is an example of the initial scenario of access sites and possible core node location sites.

We first start with the notations for the given information. Let N be the total number of access sites. Let M be the possible location of core nodes for the second level of the network architecture of which P locations are to be chosen. Let K_j denote the maximum number of access sites that can be connected to a core node located at $j = 1, 2, ..., M$. Let ξ_{ij} denote the cost of connecting access site i to possible core node site j. Another cost is: η_j, the cost of node device with maximum access link termination condition of K_j if located at j with interfaces to other selected router sites. Finally, ζ_{jk} denotes the cost of connecting possible core node site j to possible core node site k; in this case, the cost is assumed to be symmetrical, i.e., $\zeta_{jk} = \zeta_{kj}$.

Here, we introduce three sets of 0/1 variables: one set for the decision of connected access site to a possible router site, the second set for the decision to select a core node site, and the third set for the decision of interconnection in the core network. Specifically, we have

u_{ij} = 1, if access site i is connected to possible router site j if a router is located at site j; 0, otherwise (binary variable)
r_j = 1, if possible router site j is chosen for locating a switch; 0, otherwise
s_{jk} = 1, if possible switch site j is connected to possible switch site k (if switches are located at both sites); 0, otherwise (binary variable).

Here, decision vectors for access and locations are $\boldsymbol{u}$ and $\boldsymbol{r}$. We also have interconnecting decision vector $\boldsymbol{s}$ in the core between any two possible core sites with component $s_{jk}, j = 1, 2, ..., M, k = 1, 2, ..., M$. Due to symmetry of cost in the core, we need to only consider the strict upper diagonals ones, i.e., $j < k$, $((k = j+1, j+2, ..., M); j = 1, 2, ..., M-1)$. For notational purpose, any u_{j_1,j_2}, where j_1 appears to be greater than j_2, actually refers to u_{j_2,j_1}.

We first start with the requirement that every access site i needs to be connected to exactly one core network node site:

$$\sum_{j=1}^{M} u_{ij} = 1, \text{ for all } i. \tag{6.2.14}$$

A core network node site j, if chosen, can accommodate only up to K_j access sites whereas a possible core network node site, not selected to be in the core network, should not "home" any access site. This can be given as follows by incorporating the site selection variables r_j:

$$\sum_{i=1}^{N} u_{ij} \leq K_j r_j, \text{ for all } j. \tag{6.2.15}$$

In the case of interconnecting the core, a core network site j, if chosen, is required to have exactly $(P - 1)$ links to other chosen core network sites. This is only true for the selected core node sites which can be reflected through the following equation:

$$\sum_{k=1,k\neq j}^{M} s_{jk} = (P-1)r_j, \text{ for every possible core site } j. \tag{6.2.16}$$

Since the core network is fully-interconnected, only $P(P-1)/2$ interconnection decision variables should be active. Thus, we have:

$$\sum_{j=1}^{M-1}\sum_{k=j+1}^{M} s_{jk} = P(P-1)/2. \tag{6.2.17}$$

Finally, only P core sites should be selected:

$$\sum_{j=1}^{M} r_j = P. \tag{6.2.18}$$

To complete this discussion, there are three cost components for this problem: 1) the cost of connecting access sites to core node sites, 2) the cost of locating node devices at each core site (if selected), and 3) the cost of interconnecting links in the core network. Thus, the objective function can be written as follows:

$$\sum_{i=1}^{N}\sum_{j=1}^{M}\xi_{ij}u_{ij} + \sum_{j=1}^{M}\eta_j r_j + \sum_{j=1}^{M-1}\sum_{k=j+1}^{M}\zeta_{jk}s_{jk}. \tag{6.2.19}$$

Thus, problem D/ONLLC/B is to minimize the total cost given the constraints described above as well as the requirement that the variables only take the values 0 or 1. The complete formulation is summarized below.

***IP:* D/ONLLC/B** **Fully-Connected Core**

Node Location and Link-Connectivity: Two-Level nodes/sites

indices

$i = 1, 2, ..., N,$ access sites to be connected

$j, k = 1, 2, ..., M,$ possible location of core nodes

constants

P number of node locations to be chosen ($P < M$)

ξ_{ij} cost of connecting access site i to core site j

η_j cost of core location j, if opened

ζ_{jk} cost of connecting possible core site j to possible core site k

K_j maximum number of sites that can be handled at core location j (if j is selected)

variables

u_{ij} = 1, if access site i is connected to core node site j; 0, otherwise

r_j = 1 if core node site j is chosen for location of a node device; 0, otherwise

s_{jk} = 1, if core site site j is connected to core site k; 0, otherwise

objective

$$\text{minimize } \boldsymbol{F} = \sum_{i=1}^{N}\sum_{j=1}^{M}\xi_{ij}u_{ij} + \sum_{j=1}^{M}\eta_j r_j + \sum_{j=1}^{M-1}\sum_{k=j+1}^{M}\zeta_{jk}s_{jk} \tag{6.2.20a}$$

constraints

$$\sum_{j=1}^{M} u_{ij} = 1, \quad i = 1, 2, ..., N \tag{6.2.20b}$$

$$\sum_{i=1}^{N} u_{ij} \leq K_j r_j, \quad j = 1, 2, ..., M \tag{6.2.20c}$$

$$\sum_{k=1, k \neq j}^{M} s_{jk} = (P - 1) r_j, \quad j = 1, 2, ..., M \tag{6.2.20d}$$

$$\sum_{j=1}^{M-1} \sum_{k=j+1}^{M} s_{jk} = P(P - 1)/2 \tag{6.2.20e}$$

$$\sum_{k=1}^{M} r_j = P. \tag{6.2.20f}$$

This formulation is also a 0/1 integer linear programming formulation and will be referred to as problem D/ONLLC/B. It is important to note that this model reduces to the node location design problem D/NLD if we do *not* consider the cost of interconnecting the core network nodes, drop the terms or equations associated with s_{jk} from formulation (6.2.20) and drop (6.2.20f).

Optimal Number of Core Node Locations (Special Case)

We consider the special case where we assume $\xi_{ij} = \xi$, $\eta_j = \eta$, and $\zeta_{jk} = \zeta$. If now, for a given P, we denote the optimal cost by $\boldsymbol{F}_P$ for D/ONLLC/B, then using (6.2.20a), (6.2.20b), (6.2.20e), and 6.2.20f), we get:

$$\boldsymbol{F}_P = \xi N + \eta P + \zeta P(P - 1)/2.$$

If we now change the number of locations to be selected to $P + 1$, we then have:

$$\boldsymbol{F}_{P+1} = \xi N + \eta(P + 1) + \zeta(P + 1)P/2.$$

Thus, we have $\boldsymbol{F}_P < \boldsymbol{F}_{P+1}$.

Non–Fully-Interconnected Core Network

In both D/ONLLC/A and D/ONLLC/B, we have assumed the interconnected core network to be fully mesh. Although this assumption is valid in practice for many real networks, it is desirable to generate a core network topology that will work for a less than fully interconnected core case as well. However, this is not so easy to model since the connectivity (not full-connectivity) of the core network is somehow needed to be addressed to avoid networks being isolated into two or more sub-networks. On the other hand, it is easy to develop a heuristic based on the formulations we have already presented. Note that both formulations guarantee the connectivity (albeit, full-connectivity) of the core network. Thus, a simple heuristic can be developed if the goal is to connect the core network with, say, L links (where $P-1 \leq L \leq P(P-1)/2$). This heuristic is referred to as the delete heuristic and is shown as Algorithm 6.2 for D/ONLLC/B; the one for D/ONLLC/A can be done following similar steps. As you can see, the delete heuristic provides a way to obtain the network topological architecture where the core network need not be fully-interconnected.

ALGORITHM 6.2 **Delete Heuristic to Generate a Less-Than Fully-Connected Topology**

Step 1: Solve D/ONLLC/B (6.2.20)

Step 2: If the minimum number of core network links, L, is specified to be $P(P-1)/2$, then stop; otherwise go to Step 3.

Step 3: Sort all core network links in descending order of their cost values, i.e., appropriate ζ_{jk} corresponding to optimal solution for (6.2.20)

Step 4: While (the number of remaining core-network links $\geq L$) do

(a) Select the core network link with the highest cost from the current list of links not yet tested

(b) Delete it if the overall core network connectivity is not violated; otherwise, mark it and ignore if the connectivity is violated

endwhile

6.2.3 *Design Results*

General Remark

First, we remark about using the CPLEX 8.0 solver to solve (6.2.11) and (6.2.20). We found that for 15-site examples for D/ONLLC/A, the solver obtains the optimal solution in < 1 second. However, for 25-site examples, in some (not all) cases, the solver took about a minute to solve the problem, while taking several minutes for others. On inspecting the CPLEX output log for the specific cases where it took a longer time to solve, we found that the actual optimal solution was obtained within a minute or so, but since the mixed-integer programming (MIP) solver in CPLEX uses the branch and cut technique (see Section 5.2.2), the solver needs to prune all the other branches before reporting the optimality. Fortunately, CPLEX provides a parameter that can be set up before starting a run which allows a user to limit the number of nodes to be visited in the BC tree; in our case, we have used 30,000 (by declaring `set mip limits nodes 30000` in CPLEX). We have found that the best cost (with 30,000 node limits) is less than a fraction of 1% cheaper than the cost found when the limit was set to 10,000 nodes (visited in the BC implementation of the CPLEX solver); this is achieved without consuming more than one minute of computing time. Thus, for many practical problems, close-to-optimal solutions may be obtainable in a reasonable computing time by limiting number of nodes visited in solvers such as CPLEX.

Another interesting phenomenon we observed is that it can take more computing time to solve tighter problems for D/ONLLC/B; for example, with $N = 30$, $M = 10$, and for $K_j = 6$, we need a minimum value of P to be 5 for the problem to be feasible—this is the 'tightness' of the problem. This example (i.e., with $P = 5$) took relatively more computing time to solve than the corresponding case with $P = 7$. On the other hand, note that both the problems have the same number of binary variables, 410, and the same number of constraints, 52 (refer to Exercise 6.5). Finally, solving larger problems (where N is high) can be computationally intensive and time consuming in an MIP solver. Networks of large size may have a natural decomposition. For example, a large nationwide network may have 120 sites. This network may be divided into four regional areas of approximately 30 sites; thus, the model discussed here can be solved for each region separately using CPLEX.

Results for D/ONLLC/A

We will now present results for both D/ONLLC/A considering a 15-site example and a 25-site example. These examples are randomly generated on an x-y grid. For cost ξ_{ij}, we use the following relation $\xi_{ij} = \alpha + \beta * dist(i, j)$ where $dist(i, j)$ is the Euclidean distance between site i and site j. We have set $K_j = 5$ for each j. The cost η_j is randomly generated. Since $K_j = 5$, for the feasibility of the problem we need $P \geq 3$ when $N = 15$ (or $P \geq 5$ when $N = 25$). Note that when we set $\alpha = 0$, and $\beta = 1$, the cost $\xi_{ij} = dist(i, j)$ is based purely on distance. We will refer to the case of $\alpha = 0, \beta = 1$ as the distance-based example.

The first set of figures is for the distance-based case when $N = 15$; specifically, refer to Figures 6.3a, 6.3b and 6.3c for $P = 3, 4, 5$, respectively. Note that in the figures, selected switch sites are marked as diamond-shaped. From these figures, we see that the same set of three core nodes selected when $P = 3$ are also selected when $P = 4$ and $P = 5$. This may give the impression that the same core nodes are always selected when P is increased. This is only an artifact and, in general, the same set of core nodes may not be included in the optimal design whenever P is increased. To see this, consider the case of $N = 25$. For the distance-based case, the optimal designs are shown in Figure 6.4a, Figure 6.4b, and Figure 6.4c for $P = 5, 6, 7$, respectively, where we see that the same core nodes are not always selected when P is increased.

For the scenarios discussed above (for the distance-based case), the optimal design layout appears to be somewhat intuitive (at least in some of them) as far as the selection of the core nodes is concerned. This may give the impression that by looking at the locations of the sites, it is reasonably predictable where the likely sites of the core nodes are going to be located. This is not obvious at all when cost ξ_{ij} is not based purely on Euclidean distance. To see this, we consider the same 15-site and 25-site examples, but this time with $\alpha = 10$ and $\beta = 0.1$—these cases will be referred to as the *skewed-distance* cases. The optimal

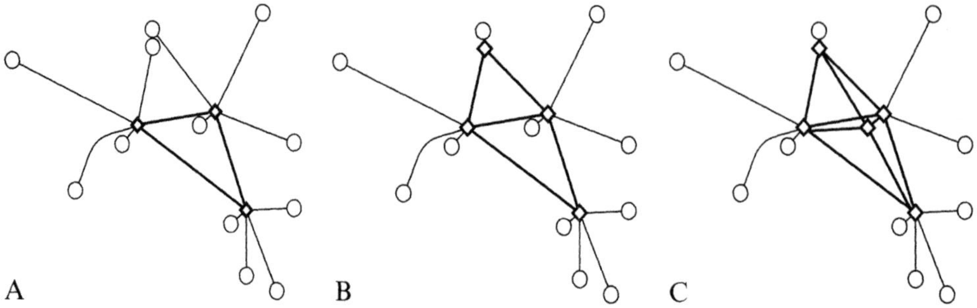

FIGURE 6.3 Design (Distance-Based Cost)—(A) D/ONLLC/A: $N = 15, P = 3$; (B) D/ONLLC/A: $N = 15, P = 4$; (C) D/ONLLC/A: $N = 15, P = 5$

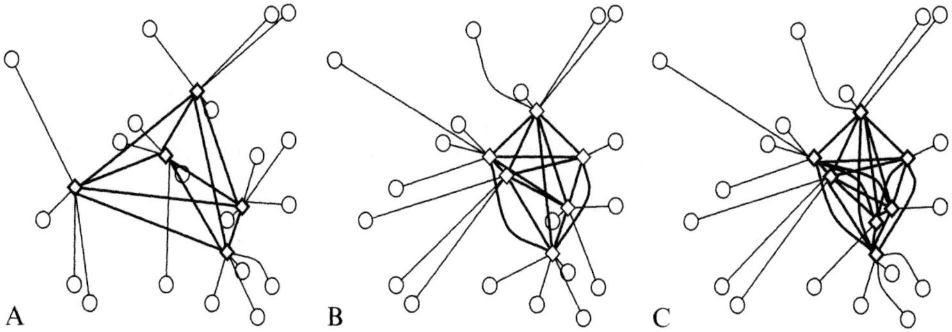

FIGURE 6.4 Design (Distance-Based Cost)—(A) D/ONLLC/A: $N = 25, P = 5$; (B) D/ONLLC/A: $N = 25, P = 6$; (C) D/ONLLC/A: $N = 25, P = 7$

designs for $N = 15$ are shown in Figure 6.5a, Figure 6.5b, and Figure 6.5c, for $P = 3, 4, 5$, respectively, and for $N = 25$ with $P = 5, 6, 7$ in Figure 6.6a, Figure 6.6b, and Figure 6.6c, respectively. From these skewed-distance examples, we can see that the optimal ONLLC design is often non-intuitive. This also shows the advantage of the model formulation since the cost between two sites are generic and is not required to be based purely on the Euclidean distance. We do want to point out that in one case ($N = 25$ with $P = 5$) whether we used distance-based or skewed-distance costs, the optimal design layout turned out to be the same (compare Figure 6.4a and Figure 6.6a), although the actual optimal cost was different (since ξ_{ij} were different).

Results for D/ONLLC/B

We will now present results for D/ONLLC/B using a 30-site example (Figure 6.1a). In the results shown here, we have set $K_j = 6$. Recall that in this case, a set of possible core node sites is given—see Figure 6.1a which is actually the input set of sites and potential core nodes for this set of results. We have considered scenarios with both distance-based and skewed-distance for ξ_{ij} and ζ_{jk}. The optimal design layouts for $N = 30$ sites with $M = 10$ possible core node sites when P was set to 5, 6, and 7 are shown in Figure 6.7a,

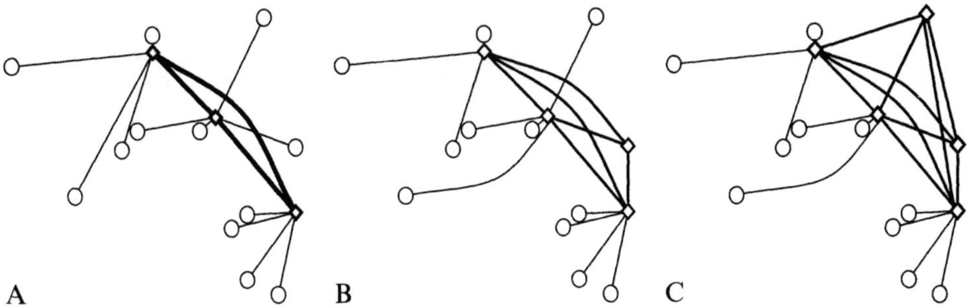

FIGURE 6.5 Design Using Skewed Distance—(A) D/ONLLC/A: $N = 15, P = 3$; (B) D/ONLLC/A: $N = 15, P = 4$; (C) D/ONLLC/A: $N = 15, P = 5$

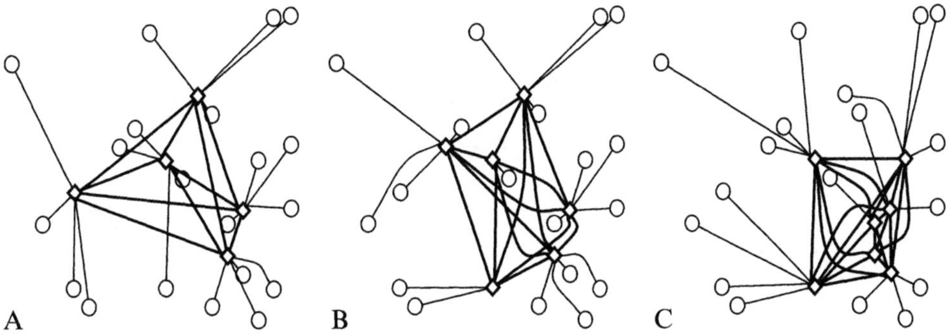

FIGURE 6.6 Design Using Skewed-Distance—(A) D/ONLLC/A: $N = 25, P = 5$; (B) D/ONLLC/A: $N = 25, P = 6$; (c) D/ONLLC/A: $N = 25, P = 7$

Figure 6.7b, and Figure 6.7c, respectively, when costs (ξ_{ij} and ζ_{jk}) are based only on distance; the corresponding figures for the skewed-distance cases are shown in Figure 6.8a, Figure 6.8b, and Figure 6.8c. Observe the difference in the optimal network design between the distance-based and skewed-distance cases.

An important observation is that the same set of selected core node sites may not always be selected when P is increased, from $P = 5$ to $P = 6$. Since we did both the design runs (from scratch) this is not surprising. On the other hand, in a real network environment, a core network optimal location is obtained initially (say for $P = 5$) and then incrementally additional core nodes are added as the network grows—this means that the initial optimal core node locations do not change over time. In such a case, we do not want to run the same model from scratch to get the optimal results for $P = 6$; instead a different scenario run is appropriate where the currently optimal core node locations are kept fixed, and the design problem is to determine *additional* core node locations optimally (Exercise 6.4).

Finally, an obvious question is what advantage does formulation D/ONLLC/B provide over the classical node location formulation D/NLD presented in Section 6.1. The optimal

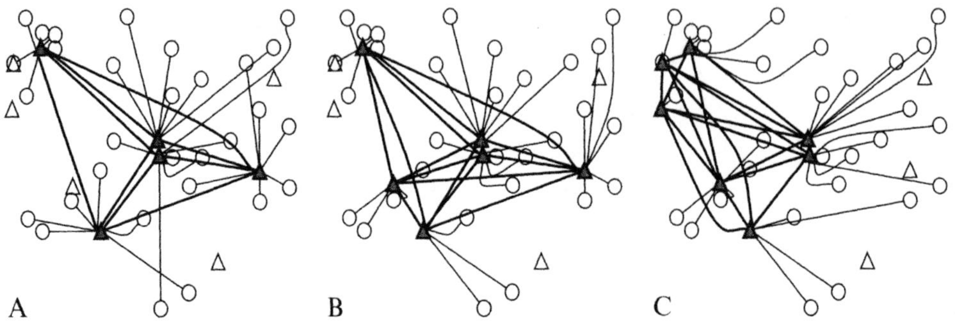

FIGURE 6.7 Design with Distance-Based—(A) D/ONLLC/B: $N = 30, P = 5$; (B) D/ONLLC/B: $N = 30, P = 6$; (C) D/ONLLC/B: $N = 30, P = 7$

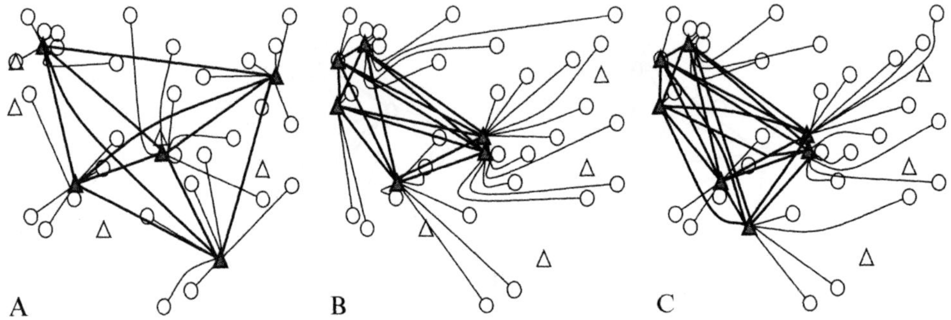

FIGURE 6.8 Design with Skewed-Distance—(A) D/ONLLC/B: $N = 30, P = 5$; (B) D/ONLLC/B: $N = 30, P = 6$; (C) D/ONLLC/B: $N = 30, P = 7$

node location design for $N = 30$, $M = 10$ with $P = 5$ was already shown in Figure 6.1b; compare this to Figure 6.7a. As can be seen, the classical formulation favors core node sites that are closer to a cluster of sites which are in general not good for ONLLC-based network design since the *interconnection* cost of the core network is not taken into account in the node location design model.

6.3 TOPOLOGICAL DESIGN

In the problems of node and link location addressed in the two previous sections of this chapter the demand volumes have (purposely) not been considered, as traditionally in the network planning process the traffic demand is taken into account at a stage which comes after the node location and/or the core network connectivity (link location) design. An integrated formulation for node location, connectivity and demand/capacity allocation (all together in one model) is nevertheless important, at least for the core network, as the demand volume can have a significant impact on the cost of a particular node/link location selection.

Hence, in this section we move to the next set of topological design problems where traffic demand is taken into account.

In the rest of this section we will adopt an assumption that access networks are represented by their corresponding access nodes which are already located (installed). Hence, we consider two basic cases:

1) Core nodes are also already installed (e.g., obtained using D/NLD), so the issue is to find core link locations and the corresponding flow and link capacity allocation; this problem will be discussed in Sections 6.3.2 and 6.3.3.
2) Only access nodes are located and, hence, the core node and link locations, together with appropriate flow and link capacity allocation must be found simultaneously; this problem will be dealt with in Section 6.3.4.

In the first case, we need to determine where to install core network links, given traffic demand between access sites. In the second case, we have to also find the core network node locations in the presence of demand between access sites. Thus, in general, the topological design problem is to consider traffic demand (generated by access nodes/networks) along with determination of core network link connectivity (and possibly determination of node locations).

6.3.1 Discussion

To illustrate the relevance of the above problems let us consider the network in Figure 6.9. There are two types of nodes: 1) access and 2) transit. We assume that the access nodes are fixed and installed, and that demand volume exists only between the access nodes. The transit nodes are necessary to transit flows realizing demand volumes between pairs of access nodes, in the case when the access nodes cannot play this role. The transit nodes may be, or may not be, installed; in the latter case, only the potential transit node locations are given in advance. In both cases, links are not installed, only their potential locations. Each potential site, either for a link or a transit node, has a fixed installation (opening)

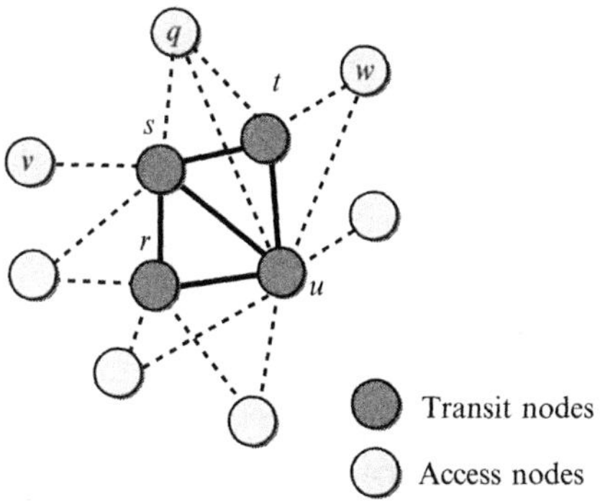

FIGURE 6.9 Access/Transit Node Network

cost associated with placing a link or node there, independent of its eventually assigned capacity. The main objective is to find the cheapest configuration of links (or links and nodes) with capacity sufficient to route the assumed demand volumes between the access nodes. Certainly, any admissible configuration of transit nodes and links must result in a network which is connected from the access nodes' perspective, which means that there must be at least one available path for each pair of access nodes with non-zero demand volume.

In regard to the above remarks, it is important to point out that there are basically three categories of nodes in a core network: 1) pure access nodes, 2) pure transit nodes, and 3) nodes with mixed functionality. Pure access nodes cannot transit traffic and, hence, they appear only as the end nodes in allowable paths. Pure transit nodes, in turn, do not generate traffic demand and only transit the traffic between pairs of access nodes. Hence, (pure) transit nodes appear only as intermediate nodes of allowable paths. These restrictions do not concern mixed nodes. However, if for some reason we wish to deal only with either access or transit nodes, and do not want to treat the mixed nodes explicitly, then each such node can be split into the pure access part and the pure transit part, connected with an internal link of infinite capacity and zero cost.

An example of the application of the considered model is a core MPLS-capable IP network where access nodes can represent LERs and the transit nodes can be LSRs. Note that in this case we have pure access nodes and pure transit nodes.

6.3.2 Design with Budget Constraint

We start the discussion of topological design problems with probably the oldest problem of this type, referred to in the literature as the "optimal network problem" ([BFW73], [DF79], [Sco69]). This problem belongs to the first type of topological problems discussed in the introduction to Section 6.3, and assumes that access nodes and transit nodes are already located and that we are interested in the optimal link (and their capacity) allocation. The problem takes into account an upper bound B for the total fixed cost of links (installation cost cannot exceed the assumed budget), and that the capacity-dependent cost of links is subject to minimization. In this way, budgeting for network design can be separated into two parts: 1) capital (installation) cost, and 2) maintenance/operational capacity-dependent cost (refer to Sections 1.7 and 2.7).

***MIP:* Problem D/TDBC:** **Link-Path Formulation**
Topological Design with Budget Constraint

indices

$d = 1, 2, ..., D$ demands
$p = 1, 2, ..., P_d$ candidate paths for demand d
$e = 1, 2, ..., E$ links

constants

B	upper bound for capital budget
h_d	volume of demand d
δ_{edp}	= 1 if link e belongs to path p realizing demand d; 0, otherwise
ξ_e	unit maintenance cost on link e
κ_e	cost of installing link e (for capital budget)
M_e	upper bound for the capacity of link e

variables

x_{dp}	non-negative flow realizing demand d allocated to path p (non-negative continuous)
y_e	capacity of link e (non-negative continuous)
u_e	= 1 if link e is provided; 0, otherwise (binary)

objective

$$\text{minimize } \boldsymbol{F} = \sum_e \xi_e y_e \qquad (6.3.1a)$$

constraints

$$\sum_e \kappa_e u_e \leq B \qquad (6.3.1b)$$

$$\sum_p x_{dp} = h_d, \quad d = 1, 2, ..., D \qquad (6.3.1c)$$

$$\sum_d \sum_p \delta_{edp} x_{dp} \leq y_e, \quad e = 1, 2, ..., E \qquad (6.3.1d)$$

$$y_e \leq M_e u_e, \quad e = 1, 2, ..., E. \qquad (6.3.1e)$$

Capital budget constraint (6.3.1b) keeps the total fixed cost of actually-provided links below the given bound. As usual, demand constraint (6.3.1c) assures that the demand volumes are realized, while capacity constraint (6.3.1d) indicates that the actually-provided capacity of a link is not less than its link load. Finally, constraint (6.3.1e) assures that the capacity of a non-provided link is equal to 0. The objective is to minimize the (linear) link maintenance cost (with respect to the capital budget constraint). Again, an important point to note about this formulation is that there are two cost components associated with a link: 1) cost of creating a new link (associated with capital cost), and 2) cost of capacity on the link (associated with maintenance cost).

We need to make an important point: the access node may need to be obligatory connected to more than one different transit node for diversity (and hence survivability) purposes. However, this does not change the basic nature of the topological design problems because such kind of requirements can be forced by introducing additional diversity constraints, as demonstrated earlier in Section 4.2.1.

Finally, we note that it has been shown in [JLK78] that problem D/TDBC is $\mathcal{NP}$-complete. As (6.3.1) is a MIP formulation, the BB (or BC) approach can be directly applied. For large networks, however, heuristic methods are of interest since BB may become time inefficient. This will be further discussed in Sections 6.3.5 and 6.4.1.

6.3.3 Design with Extended Objective

Another version of topological design problem D/TDBC is obtained when the capital budget constraint is moved to the objective function. This can be interpreted as minimizing the total capital budget and maintenance cost together. This is shown below.

MIP: **D/TDEO** **Link-Path Formulation**

Topological Design with Extended Objective

variables

x_{dp} flow realizing demand d allocated to path p (non-negative continuous)

y_e capacity of link e (non-negative continuous)

u_e = 1 if link e is provided; 0, otherwise (binary)

objective

$$\text{minimize } \boldsymbol{F} = \sum_e \xi_e y_e + \sum_e \kappa_e u_e \tag{6.3.2a}$$

constraints

$$\sum_p x_{dp} = h_d, \quad d = 1, 2, ..., D \tag{6.3.2b}$$

$$\sum_d \sum_p \delta_{edp} x_{dp} \leq y_e, \quad e = 1, 2, ..., E \tag{6.3.2c}$$

$$y_e \leq M_e u_e, \quad e = 1, 2, ..., E. \tag{6.3.2d}$$

Problem D/TDEO is as difficult to solve as problem D/TDBC from the previous section.

PROPOSITION 6.1 *Problem D/TDEO is $\mathcal{NP}$-complete.*

Proof:

Recall the proof of Proposition 4.3 from Section 4.3.1 where we stated that the modular link dimensioning problem D/ML is $\mathcal{NP}$-complete. The argument used there can be adapted to prove the $\mathcal{NP}$-completeness of D/TDEO. It is enough to assume that the unit capacity costs ξ_e are negligible with respect to the fixed costs κ_e. Then, clearly, D/TDEO solves the Steiner tree problem for the link costs κ_e. As the latter problem is $\mathcal{NP}$-complete ([Kar72], [GJ79]), this ends the proof. ■

As a MIP, D/TDEO can be directly solved by the BB (BC) method. To improve computation of the lower bounds, the Lagrangian relaxation (LR) approach can be applied by relaxing constraint (6.3.2c), as proposed in [Bal89], [BBP00] and [HH98].

In Section 5.6.2, we described a heuristic method (called greedy descent) of Minoux [Min89] for uncapacitated network design with concave dimensioning functions. In Section

2.2 of the same paper, Minoux shows how this method can be adapted for the considered topological design problem.

Let $\boldsymbol{u} = (u_e : e = 1, 2, ..., E)$ be a fixed binary *link-status vector* and let $S(\boldsymbol{u})$ denote the corresponding *sub-network* composed of all links with $u_e = 1$ but not of links with $u_e = 0$. Suppose that $\boldsymbol{y} = (y_e : e = 1, 2, ..., E)$ is the vector of link capacities resulting from the shortest path allocation rule (Section 4.1.1) applied to sub-network $S(\boldsymbol{u})$ corresponding to vector $\boldsymbol{u}$. Further, let $f_e(\boldsymbol{u})$ be the length of the shortest path (with respect to link unit costs ξ_e) in sub-network $S(\boldsymbol{u})$ between the end nodes of link e. Define

$$\Delta_e(\boldsymbol{u}) = y_e \cdot f_e(\boldsymbol{u} - \boldsymbol{u}(e)) - (\xi_e y_e + \kappa_e) \tag{6.3.3}$$

for all links e with $u_e = 1$, where $\boldsymbol{u}(e)$ denotes the E-vector with all components equal to 0 except for the e-th component which is equal to 1. The quantity $\Delta_e(\boldsymbol{u})$ measures the effect of deleting link e from sub-network $S(\boldsymbol{u})$, assuming that the current load of link e is shifted to one of the shortest paths "around" link e.

Note that $\Delta_e(\boldsymbol{u})$ is greater or equal to the quantity

$$\Theta_e(\boldsymbol{u}) = \boldsymbol{F}(\boldsymbol{u} - \boldsymbol{u}(e)) - \boldsymbol{F}(\boldsymbol{u}) \tag{6.3.4}$$

(where function $\boldsymbol{F}(\boldsymbol{u})$ is the extended network cost given by (6.3.2a)) because in the case of $\Theta_e(\boldsymbol{u})$ the flows realized on the deleted link are restored individually without any constraints, contrary to $\Delta_e(\boldsymbol{u}^k)$.

In this heuristic, we start with the link status vector $\boldsymbol{u}^0$ with all components equal to 1 (i.e., with full network). In each iteration k we look for link e' maximizing $\Delta_e(\boldsymbol{u}^k)$ over all links with $u_e^k = 1$. If gain $\Delta_{e'}(\boldsymbol{u}^k)$ is non-positive, the algorithm terminates; otherwise, the capacity of link e' is rerouted to one of its shortest paths, the capacities on all the links along this shortest path are increased by $y_{e'}^k$, link e' is removed ($u_{e'}^{k+1} = 0$), and the main step repeated. This greedy algorithm can be substantially accelerated using the so-called 'monotonicity property'

$$\Delta_e(\boldsymbol{u}^k) \geq \Delta_e(\boldsymbol{u}^{k+1}) \quad e = 1, 2, ..., E \tag{6.3.5}$$

which holds for the considered problem due to the linear capacity-dependent cost function. The accelerated algorithm is very fast, and according to [Min89], quite effective in finding good suboptimal solutions to D/TDEO.

Finally, following Section 2.3.1 of [Min89], we note that there is a nice connection between the two topological design problems D/TDBC and D/TDEO. Namely if we dualize the budget constraint (6.3.1b) in D/TDBC, then it turns out that the computation of the resulting dual function is equivalent to solving a problem of the D/TDEO type (Exercise 6.6).

6.3.4 Transit Nodes and Links Localization Problem

The next two problems we consider belong to the second type of topological problems discussed at the beginning of Section 6.3 and will be referred to as transit nodes and links localization problems (TNLLPs). TNLLPs are extensions of problem D/TDEO accounting for the fixed installation costs of the transit nodes.

In D/TNLLP1 (the first of the two problems), the set of network nodes is divided into two disjoint subsets: 1) the subset of access/mixed nodes, and 2) the subset of transit nodes. Access/mixed nodes are assumed to be installed, while transit nodes are not. As D/TNLLP1 uses the link-path formulation, the distinction between access and mixed nodes is made in the candidate path lists generation pre-computation. The installation cost is assigned only to transit nodes, as access nodes are known ahead of time.

Problem D/TNLLP1 **Link-Path Formulation**

indices

$d = 1, 2, ..., D$ demands
$p = 1, 2, ..., P_d$ candidate paths for demand d
$e = 1, 2, ..., E$ links
$v = 1, 2, ..., V$ transit nodes

constants

h_d volume of demand d
δ_{edp} = 1 if link e belongs to path p realizing demand d; 0, otherwise
β_{ev} = 1 if link e is incident with node v; 0, otherwise
ξ_e marginal cost of link e
κ_e cost of installing link e
M_e upper bound for the capacity of link e
φ_v cost of installing transit node v
G_v upper bound for the degree of transit node v

variables

x_{dp} flow realizing demand d allocated to path p (non-negative continuous)
y_e capacity of link e (non-negative continuous)
u_e = 1 if link e is installed; 0, otherwise (binary)
s_v = 1 if node v is installed; 0, otherwise (binary)

objective

$$\text{minimize } \boldsymbol{F} = \sum_e(\xi_e y_e + \kappa_e u_e) + \sum_v \varphi_v s_v \qquad (6.3.6a)$$

constraints

$$\sum_p x_{dp} = h_d, \quad d = 1, 2, ..., D \qquad (6.3.6b)$$

$$\sum_d \sum_p \delta_{edp} x_{dp} \le y_e, \quad e = 1, 2, ..., E \qquad (6.3.6c)$$

$$y_e \le M_e u_e, \quad e = 1, 2, ..., E \qquad (6.3.6d)$$

$$\sum_e \beta_{ev} u_e \le G_v s_v, \quad v = 1, 2, ..., V. \qquad (6.3.6e)$$

An important requirement in this formulation is that a link can be created only if the end nodes associated with this link are selected. In D/TNLLP1 constraint (6.3.6e) considers all the links incident to a node and assures that the node degree does not exceed a predefined bound. This also assures that the provision of links and nodes is consistent, i.e., if a particular s_v is 0 which means that node v is not selected, then the associated link variable u_e for the link incident to v is forced to be 0, i.e., the link is also not selected. Note that if the binary vector $\boldsymbol{s} = (s_1, s_2, ..., s_V)$ is fixed then deleting all (transit) nodes with $s_v = 0$ and all links incident with the deleted nodes reduces D/TNLLP1 to D/TDEO.

As the sets of predefined paths used in the link-path formulation D/TNLLP1 can lead to an excessive number of flow variables and constraints, the node-link formulation, denoted with D/TNLLP2 and described below, can in many cases be used more efficiently in the MIP solvers, provided there are no limitations on the allowable paths between transit nodes.

With respect to D/TNLLP1, in D/TLLNP2 it is additionally assumed that there are no mixed nodes, and, moreover, that there are no links between access nodes.

In D/TNLLP2 the demands and the link flows are directed, but the links are not. The resulting (somewhat complicated) formulation aims at using a minimal number of flow variables and follows the formulation of D/SDP/MNLF (4.1.6).

***MIP:* D/TNLLP2** **Node-Link Formulation**

indices

$w = 1, 2, ..., W$ access nodes
$v = 1, 2, ..., V$ transit nodes
$e = 1, 2, ..., E$ links
$f = 1, 2, ..., F$ directed access arcs (between access and transit nodes)
$t = 1, 2, ..., T$ directed transit arcs (between transit nodes)

constants

$h_{ww'}$ volume of demand from access node w to access node w'
H_w $= \sum_{w'} h_{ww'}$ - total demand outgoing from access node w
β_{ev} = 1 if link e is incident with transit node v; 0, otherwise
β_{fv} = −1 if access arc f is incoming to transit node v
= 1 if access arc f is outgoing from transit node v
= 0 otherwise
β_{fw} = −1 if access arc f is incoming to access node w
= 1 if access arc f is outgoing from transit node w
= 0 otherwise
β_{tv} = −1 if transit arc t is incoming to transit node v
= 1 if transit arc t is outgoing from transit node v
= 0 otherwise
ω_{ef} = 1 if access arc f is realized on link e; 0, otherwise
ω_{et} = 1 if transit arc t is realized on link e; 0, otherwise
ξ_e marginal cost of link e
κ_e cost of installing link e

M_e upper bound for the capacity of link e
φ_v cost of installing transit node v
G_v upper bound for the degree of transit node v

variables

x_{fw} flow realizing all demands originating at access node w on access arc f
x_{tw} flow realizing all demands originating at access node w on transit arc t
y_e capacity of link e
u_e = 1 if link e is provided; 0, otherwise
s_v = 1 if transit node v is installed; 0, otherwise

objective

$$\text{minimize } \boldsymbol{F} = \sum_e(\xi_e y_e + \kappa_e u_e) + \sum_v \varphi_v s_v \tag{6.3.7a}$$

constraints

$$\sum_t \omega_{et} \sum_w x_{tw} + \sum_f \omega_{ef} \sum_w x_{fw} \le y_e, \quad e = 1,2,...,E \tag{6.3.7b}$$

$$\sum_f \beta_{fw} x_{fw} = H_w, \quad w = 1,2,...,W \tag{6.3.7c}$$

$$\sum_f \beta_{fw'} x_{fw} = -h_{ww'}, \quad w = 1,2,...,W, \; w' = 1,2,...,W, w \ne w' \tag{6.3.7d}$$

$$\sum_t \beta_{tv} x_{tw} + \sum_f \beta_{fv} x_{fw} = 0, \quad v = 1,2,...,V, \; w = 1,2,...,W \tag{6.3.7e}$$

$$y_e \le M_e u_e, \quad e = 1,2,...,E \tag{6.3.7f}$$

$$\sum_e \beta_{ev} u_e \le G_v s_v, \quad v = 1,2,...,V. \tag{6.3.7g}$$

In the above formulation it is important that, by definition, only the following link flow variables are used (which means that only these variables can be > 0):

- x_{fw}: flow realizing all demands originating at access node w on access link f for all pairs (f, w) such that $f = 1,2,...,F$, $w = 1,2,...,W$ and either access link f is outgoing from access node w (i.e., $\beta_{fw} = 1$) or link f is incoming to some other access node w' with $h_{ww'} > 0$ ($\beta_{fw'} = -1$ and $h_{ww'}$ is the demand between access nodes w and w');

TABLE 6.2 **Model Comparison: D/TNLLP1 and D/TNLLP2**

	Number of Variables	Number of Constraints
D/TNLLP1	$K = W(W-1)P$	$M = W(W-1)$
D/TNLLP2	$K = WV + W(W-1)V$ $+ WV(V-1)$	$M = W + W(W-1) + WV$ $= W(W+V)$

- x_{tw}: flow realizing all demands originating at access node w on transit link t for all pairs (t, w) such that $t = 1, 2, ..., T$, $w = 1, 2, ..., W$.

In D/TNLLP2, each link e supports exactly two directed arcs (either both access or both transit) whose numbers f or t are specified by these coefficients ω_{ef} and ω_{et} (respectively) which are equal to 1. Constraint (6.3.7c) forces the total demand H_w generated in access node w to flow out, constraint (6.3.7d) assures that the portion $h_{ww'}$ of the flow originated at node w and destined for node w' stays in w', and constraint (6.3.7e) shows that no flow stays in a transit node.

In order to illustrate the savings in the number of variables and constraints while using D/TNLLP2 instead of D/TNLLP1 consider a network with full demand matrix with $W(W-1)$ entries. Then the number of flow variables K and the number of constraints M are as shown in Table 6.2. For example, assuming $W = 100$, $V = 10$, $P = 10$ (where P is the number of paths for each demand in D/TNLLP1) we get $K \approx 10^6$ and $M \approx 10^4$ for D/TNLLP1, and $K \approx 10^5$ and $M \approx 10^4$ for D/TNLLP2, which means one order of magnitude gain in the number of flow variables for the latter formulation.

6.3.5 *Heuristic Algorithms*

We briefly present several heuristic algorithms that can be applied to both D/TDEO and D/TNLLP1. The first four heuristics—H1, H2, H3, and H4—are described for D/TDEO; and the last two, simulated allocation (SAL) and simulated annealing (SAN), for D/TNLLP1. Note that H1 through H4 can also be applied to D/TNLLP1, as explained after describing heuristic H4.

H1: Individual Flow Shifting

First an initial flow allocation is found using any greedy algorithm. This means that when allocating a new demand d the cost of link e is equal to $\xi_e h_d$ if link e has already been installed while allocating a previous demand, and to $\xi_e h_d + \kappa_e$ otherwise. In the main loop of the algorithm, demands are checked in a random order, and the first one whose best reallocation gives a decrease in the total cost (6.3.2a) is reallocated. This procedure is repeated until no improvement can be achieved.

H2: Individual Flow Shifting with Cost Smoothing
An outer loop is introduced to H1, which controls the shape of the links cost functions. The cost function $F_e(y)$ of link e depends on parameter χ as follows:

$$F_e(y) = \begin{cases} \xi_e y + \kappa_e(1 - (1 - \chi)/[(y-1)\chi + 1]), & \text{if } y > 0 \\ 0, & \text{otherwise.} \end{cases} \tag{6.3.8}$$

The algorithm starts with $\chi = 0$ (then $F_e(y) = \xi_e y$) and successively (exponentially) increases the parameter, terminating with $\chi = 1$ (then $F_e(y) = \xi_e y + \kappa_e$). For each fixed value of χ, the algorithm finds a local minimum using H1; this solution serves as the starting point for the next run with increased χ. H2 usually performs better than H1 because when a flow is considered for deallocation, a part of the fixed cost is taken into account in the gain calculation; note that in H1, the allocated flow must be the only one on a link in order to remove the link after the flow reallocation. A similar idea of cost smoothing can be found in [BL94].

H3: Bulk Flow Shifting
H3 is a modification of the greedy algorithm from [Min89] described at the end of Section 6.3.3. We identify link e' to be removed from the network using the quantity $\Delta_e(\boldsymbol{u})$ defined by formula (6.3.3) but we actually reroute the flows that are using the removed link not by shifting them together while restoring the load of link e', but by restoring these flows individually on their shortest (cheapest) paths. Hence, the actual gain after performing the flow shift is equal to the maximal improvement achievable by deleting link e', i.e., to the quatity $\Theta_{e'}(\boldsymbol{u})$ given by formula (6.3.4). In the numerical study presented in the next section, we have considered two variations of H3. In the first, referred to as H3F, the links are scanned in a random order and the first link e' with positive gain $\Delta_{e'}(\boldsymbol{u})$ is removed. A modification of H3F, referred to as H3B, is obtained when all links are checked (using $\Delta_e(\boldsymbol{u})$) and the one with the largest (best) $\Delta_{e'}(\boldsymbol{u})$ is removed. Note that we do not consider testing the links for deleting using $\Theta_{e'}(\boldsymbol{u})$ as this would be very time consuming for large networks.

H4: Bulk Flow Shifting with Cost Smoothing
H4 is a modification of H3 with cost smoothing described for H2. As for H3, two versions of H4 are considered: H4F and H4B.

Remark 6.2

Heuristics H1 through H4 are applicable to problem D/TNLLP1. This is achieved by modifying the calculation of the gains from deleting a link. If deleting link e' results in deleting one or both of its end nodes (this happens when the end node(s) of the deleted link is (are) not incident to any of the remaining links), then the node(s) installation cost φ_v is added to the fixed cost $\kappa_{e'}$. ♦

SAL: Simulated Allocation

Recall that SAL algorithm (refer to Algorithm 5.6 in Section 5.3.4) works with partial flow allocations $\boldsymbol{x} = (x_{dp} : d = 1, 2, ..., D, p = 1, 2, ..., P_d)$. Let $|\boldsymbol{x}| = \sum_d \sum_p x_{dp}$ ($|\boldsymbol{x}|$ is the height of the allocation state $\boldsymbol{x}$) and $H = \sum_d h_d$. The algorithm starts with the zero state ($x_{dp} \equiv 0$) and in each step chooses, with probability $q(|\boldsymbol{x}|)$, between *allocate*($\boldsymbol{x}$), i.e., adding one demand flow to the current state $\boldsymbol{x}$, and *disconnect*($\boldsymbol{x}$), i.e., removing one or more demand flows from current $\boldsymbol{x}$. Whenever a complete allocation state is reached, a check is made whether the cost of the best solution reached so far is improved.

Allocation of a demand consists in finding a shortest path in the current sub-network in which links with zero load are not provided and the nodes with no coincident links are not provided either, and adding the flow on the selected path to the current state $\boldsymbol{x}$. Hence, the link metrics according to which the shortest path for demand d is selected are state-dependent and are of the form:

$\xi_e h_d + \chi(\kappa_e + \varphi_{v'} + \varphi_{v''})$	if link e is not provided, link e connects two transit nodes v' and v'', and the transit nodes v' and v'' are not provided
$\xi_e h_d + \chi(\kappa_e + \varphi_v)$	if link e is not provided and only one of its end nodes, say (transit) node v, is not provided
$\xi_e h_d + \chi\kappa_e$	if link e is not provided and both its end nodes are provided
$\xi_e h_d$	if link e is provided.

The value of parameter $\chi \in [0, 1]$ is equal to the ratio of the sum of the currently allocated demands to the total demand.

Disconnection of a demand means that the flow realizing the demand is removed from $\boldsymbol{x}$. Of course, if this makes certain links (and nodes) not used in the resulting solution, such links (and nodes) are also removed. It is important that whenever a maximal allocation state $\boldsymbol{x}$ is reached, a bulk disconnection takes place with a certain probability (of the order of 10^{-2}). For such a bulk disconnection a set of links provided in state $\boldsymbol{x}$ is selected at random, and these links (and their end nodes if possible), together with all the flows using them are removed from the current solution.

SAN: Simulated Annealing

The SAN heuristic has been described in Algorithm 5.4 in Section 5.3.2 for general optimization problems. Applied to D/TNLLP1, SAN starts with solution $\boldsymbol{x}$ generated by procedure *initialize* ($\boldsymbol{x}$). Then, at each step, the algorithm selects a neighbor of $\boldsymbol{x}$, using function *neighbor* ($\boldsymbol{x}$). The particular way of selecting a neighbor is chosen with a given probability distribution (this distribution is a basic parameter of the SAN algorithm). The neighboring state is obtained in one of the following ways (all selections are made at random):

- switch on one of currently not provided access links
- switch off one of currently provided access links
- switch on one of currently not provided transit links

- switch off one of currently provided transit links
- switch on one of currently not provided transit nodes
- switch off one of currently provided transit nodes.

We finally note that besides SAL and SAN, other stochastic meta-heuristics, as evolutionary algorithm (EA) (Section 5.3.3, see Exercise 6.7), tabu search (see Section 5.3.5 and [CS99]) or GRASP (Section 5.3.6 can be applied to D/TLLNP1.

6.3.6 Numerical Results

For our study, we have considered three artificially generated network structures (N7, N14, and N28) determined by the geographical locations of nodes. The basic parameters of the networks are given in Table 6.3. All links are potentially available. The unit cost ξ_e of link e is in all cases proportional to its geographical length. The fixed installation cost is given by $\kappa_e = \xi_e 10^n$ (where n is a parameter in computations). The fixed installation cost of a transit node is the same for all nodes and is given by $\psi_v = 10^k$ (where k is another parameter in computations).

TABLE 6.3 **Test Networks Parameters**

	W	V	F	T	D	**min** h_d	**max** h_d	$\sum_d h_d$
N7	7	5	70	20	42	240	1,920	34,320
N14	14	11	308	110	182	120	7,560	172,320
N28	28	15	840	210	756	120	30,240	892,492

For algorithms discussed so far, we present the results for D/TNLLP1 in Tables 6.4 for N7, 6.5 for N14, and 6.6 for N28. Our goal here is to understand the relative merits of different approaches; hence, all network cost obtained are shown, normalized to the lowest cost. To understand the implication of different cost parameters, results are reported by varying the parameter values, n and k.

A common theme is that heuristics such as H1, H2, and H3 give poor performance, especially if k increases. For example, for $N7$ with $n = 4$ and $k = 6$, the result from H1 is about 10% more than the lowest cost. On the other hand, if k is increased to 8, then the cost generated by H1 is 325% more than the lowest cost. We can also see that when n and k are "close" to each other in parameter values, for example $n = 5$ and $k = 6$, heuristics such as H2 can give reasonable results (for example, see N7).

Now we will examine the case when the network size changes. Going from N7, N14, to N28, we see that for $(n, k) = (5, 8)$, the relative cost drops from 136% more than the lowest cost to 69% more than the lowest cost; nevertheless, this cost is relatively high by any measure.

When we consider methods such as SAL and BB, we see that the performance is quite comparable, and they invariably give the best results. In regard to SAN, the performance is not consistent; while it works well in some cases, it does not work well in other cases.

TABLE 6.4 **TNLLP1 (N7)**

net	n	k	H1	H2	H3F	H3B	H4F	H4B	SAN	SAL	BB
N7	3	6	1.382	1.496	1.382	1.382	1.386	1.382	1.000	1.000	1.000
N7	3	7	3.289	3.343	3.289	3.289	3.291	3.289	1.000	1.000	1.000
N7	3	8	4.727	4.736	4.727	4.727	4.728	4.727	1.019	1.000	1.000
N7	4	6	1.107	1.116	1.023	1.023	1.044	1.044	1.077	1.000	1.000
N7	4	7	2.138	2.188	2.084	2.084	2.106	2.084	1.000	1.000	1.000
N7	4	8	4.254	4.256	4.240	4.240	4.243	4.243	1.000	1.000	1.000
N7	5	6	1.210	1.000	1.000	1.000	1.000	1.000	1.104	1.000	1.000
N7	5	7	1.186	1.150	1.031	1.031	1.039	1.039	1.092	1.000	1.000
N7	5	8	2.363	2.342	2.273	2.273	2.278	2.278	1.308	1.000	1.000

TABLE 6.5 **TNLLP1 (N14)**

N14	3	6	1.144	1.151	1.144	1.144	1.102	1.102	1.005	1.002	1.000
N14	3	7	2.571	2.562	2.571	2.571	2.541	2.541	1.352	1.000	1.000
N14	3	8	7.761	7.757	7.761	7.761	7.749	7.749	1.637	1.000	1.000
N14	4	6	1.227	1.120	1.227	1.227	1.050	1.040	1.252	1.000	1.000
N14	4	7	1.894	1.819	1.894	1.894	1.770	1.763	1.116	1.000	1.000
N14	4	8	6.105	6.067	6.105	6.105	6.042	6.039	1.437	1.000	1.000
N14	5	6	1.246	1.179	1.151	1.151	1.003	1.003	1.560	1.000	1.000
N14	5	7	1.225	1.174	1.153	1.153	1.040	1.040	1.291	1.031	1.000
N14	5	8	2.267	2.207	2.226	2.226	2.161	2.161	1.252	1.000	1.000

Finally, we report the average computing time with each of the algorithms for different networks in Table 6.7. As we can see H1 is the least time-consuming; however, it comes at the price of getting poor solutions. The time for BB increases drastically going from N7 to N14. Regarding SAN and SAL, we find that SAL takes considerably less time. In general, we can conclude that SAL is a very good approach to take since it can solve large problems with good solutions at a reasonable computing time.

6.4 LOWER BOUNDS FOR BRANCH-AND-BOUND

The topological design problems considered in Section 6.3 are $\mathcal{NP}$-complete, and hence, as discussed in Section 5.2.1, the BB approach (or its extended version, BC) is virtually the only way to obtain exact solutions (although even this approach may fail for large networks). Thus, before we end Chapter 6, we will show how to calculate the lower bounds

TABLE 6.6 **TNLLP1 (N28)**

net	n	k	H1	H2	H3F	H3B	H4F	H4B	SAN	SAL
N28	3	6	1.045	1.028	1.045	1.045	1.000	1.001	1.021	1.005
N28	3	7	1.349	1.336	1.349	1.349	1.315	1.315	1.097	1.000
N28	3	8	4.114	4.106	4.114	4.114	4.094	4.094	2.667	1.000
N28	4	6	1.114	1.107	1.102	1.102	1.001	1.000	1.058	1.035
N28	4	7	1.259	1.254	1.250	1.250	1.171	1.170	1.000	1.002
N28	4	8	3.286	3.282	3.280	3.280	3.230	3.230	1.792	1.000
N28	5	6	1.160	1.135	1.123	1.123	1.011	1.000	1.811	1.003
N28	5	7	1.136	1.115	1.105	1.105	1.009	1.000	1.621	1.042
N28	5	8	1.689	1.675	1.669	1.669	1.608	1.602	1.435	1.000

TABLE 6.7 **Average Computing Time for D/TNLLP1 (for N7, N14, and N28)**

net	H1	H2	H3F	H3B	H4F	H4B	SAN	SAL	BB
N7	0.01	0.27	0.01	0.01	0.26	0.27	39.37	0.54	3.18
N14	0.12	3.39	0.15	0.15	3.37	3.44	318.32	16.87	35,073.02
N28	1.05	28.84	1.13	1.23	28.72	29.68	1,117.97	49.56	NA

for the BB algorithms in topological design. The presented derivations can be combined with the BB algorithm given in Section 5.2.1 (Algorithm 5.1), and used to write a complete BB procedure for solving the considered problems. In the calculations we will exploit the special structure of problems D/TDBC, D/TDEO and D/TNLLP1.

6.4.1 Case: Topological Design with Budget Constraint

As you already know, due to linearity of function $\boldsymbol{F}$ defined by (6.3.1a) for any fixed link status vector $\boldsymbol{u} = (u_1, u_2, ..., u_E)$, the cost $\boldsymbol{F}$ of link capacities is minimized by applying the shortest path allocation rule (with respect to unit costs ξ_e) in sub-network $S(\boldsymbol{u})$, i.e., in the network obtained by removing all links e with $u_e = 0$. This observation can be exploited in calculating lower bounds for the BB algorithm for D/TDBC ([BFW73], [DF79], [Hoa73]) (a summary of the approach of [DF79] can be found in [Min89, § 2.3.2]. Below we shall briefly describe how these bounds can be calculated.

Let $f_e(\boldsymbol{u})$ denote the cost of the shortest path (for unit costs ξ_e) between the end nodes of link e in the sub-network $S(\boldsymbol{u})$ and calculate the quantity

$$\eta_e(\boldsymbol{u}) = h_{d(e)} \cdot (f_e(\boldsymbol{u} - \boldsymbol{u}(e)) - f_e(\boldsymbol{u})) \tag{6.4.1}$$

where $h_{d(e)}$ denotes the demand volume between the end nodes of link e (in general this volume can be equal to 0). Hence, $\eta_e(\boldsymbol{u})$ is a local measure which accounts for the local effect of deleting link e from sub-network $S(\boldsymbol{u})$.

Suppose that the set of the link indices $N = \{1, 2, ..., E\}$ is partitioned into three disjoint subsets N_U, N_0 and N_1, and let $\Phi(N_U, N_0, N_1)$ denote the set of all binary E-vectors $\boldsymbol{u}$ such that $e \in N_0$ implies $u_e = 0$, $e \in N_1$ implies $u_e = 1$, and for $e \in N_U$ the value of u_e is either 0 or 1. Let $\boldsymbol{u}^0$ denote the E-vector with $u_e = 0$ only if $e \in N_0$. The following property holds (note that function $\boldsymbol{F}(\boldsymbol{u})$ is defined implicitly by (6.3.1a)).

PROPOSITION 6.2 *For each $\boldsymbol{u} \in \Phi(N_U, N_0, N_1)$*

$$\boldsymbol{F}(\boldsymbol{u}) \geq \boldsymbol{F}(\boldsymbol{u}^0) + \textstyle\sum_{e \in N_U}(1 - u_e)\eta_e(\boldsymbol{u}^0). \tag{6.4.2}$$

A simple proof of Proposition 6.2 is given in [Min89, § 2.3.1] (Exercise 6.8). It can be used to calculate a lower bound for $F(\boldsymbol{u})$, $\boldsymbol{u} \in \Phi(N_U, N_0, N_1)$, with respect to the budget constraint (6.3.1b). The considered lower bound $L(N_0, N_1)$ is equal to the minimum of the following integer programming problem:

$$\begin{aligned} \textbf{\textit{minimize}} \quad & \boldsymbol{F}(\boldsymbol{u}^0) + \textstyle\sum_{e \in N_U}(1 - u_e)\eta_e(\boldsymbol{u}^0) \\ \textbf{\textit{subject to}} \quad & \textstyle\sum_e \kappa_e u_e \leq B \\ & \boldsymbol{u} \in \Phi(N_U, N_0, N_1). \end{aligned} \tag{6.4.3}$$

Problem (6.4.3) is an instance of the 0-1 knapsack problem. As the 0-1 knapsack problem is $\mathcal{NP}$-complete itself [GJ79], its relaxation can be used as proposed in [DF79]:

$$\begin{aligned} \textbf{\textit{minimize}} \quad & U = \textstyle\sum_{e \in N_U} u_e \eta_e(\boldsymbol{u}^0) \\ \textbf{\textit{subject to}} \quad & \textstyle\sum_e \kappa_e u_e \leq B \\ & 0 \leq u_e \leq 1 \text{ if } u_e \in N_U;\ u_e = 0 \text{ if } u_e \in N_0;\ u_e = 1 \text{ if } u_e \in N_1. \end{aligned} \tag{6.4.4}$$

Finally, the lower bound is given as

$$L(N_0, N_1) = \boldsymbol{F}(\boldsymbol{u}^0) + \textstyle\sum_{e \in N_U} \eta_e(\boldsymbol{u}^0) - U^* \tag{6.4.5}$$

where U^* is the optimal solution of (6.4.4). The relaxed knapsack problem is solved efficiently by sorting the variables according to the ratio $\eta_e(\boldsymbol{u}^0)/\kappa_e$ and by assigning value 1 to the consecutive variables with the highest ratio (the last non-zero variable will in general be assigned a fractional value). Using the lower bound (6.4.5), a BB procedure for solving D/TDBC can be constructed, as described in [DF79].

We may suspect that the local measure $\eta_e(\boldsymbol{u})$ given by 6.4.1 used in the lower bound calculations is too pessimistic and the global measure for function (6.3.1a))

$$\Gamma_e(\boldsymbol{u}) = \boldsymbol{F}(\boldsymbol{u} - \boldsymbol{u}(e)) - \boldsymbol{F}(\boldsymbol{u}) \tag{6.4.6}$$

should be used instead. This is not the case, however, since it is not generally true that

$$F(u) \geq F(u^0) + \sum_{e \in N_U} (1 - u_e)\Gamma_e(u^0), \quad u \in \Phi(N_U, N_0, N_1) \tag{6.4.7}$$

as demonstrated in [DF79]. Nevertheless, the measure (6.4.6) can be used to speed up the BB process at the expense of possibly overlooking optimal solutions.

6.4.2 Case: Transit Node and Link Localization Problem

Consider for a while the case when D/TNLLP1 (6.3.6) is reduced to D/TDEO (6.3.2). Then, using the notation from the previous section, for any given triple (N_U, N_0, N_1) the lower bound (analogous to $L(N_0, N_1)$ shown in (6.4.5)) is the solution of the following integer programming problem:

$$\begin{array}{ll} \textbf{\textit{minimize}} & F(u^0) + \sum_{e \in N_1} \kappa_e + \sum_{e \in N_U} (1 - u_e)\eta_e(u^0) + \sum_{e \in N_U} \kappa_e u_e \\ \textbf{\textit{subject to}} & u \in \Phi(N_U, N_0, N_1) \end{array} \tag{6.4.8}$$

where $F(u^0)$ denotes the capacity-dependent part of the network cost. Then, formally, the lower bound is calculated using the solution of the problem:

$$\begin{array}{ll} \textbf{\textit{minimize}} & \sum_{e \in N_U} (\kappa_e - \eta_e(u^0))u_e \\ \textbf{\textit{subject to}} & u \in \Phi(N_U, N_0, N_1). \end{array} \tag{6.4.9}$$

The solution of (6.4.9) is straightforward: $u_e = 0$ if $\kappa_e \geq \eta_e(u^0)$; and $u_e = 1$, otherwise. Hence, we note that the lower bound resulting from (6.4.9) is of limited value since $\eta_e(u) = 0$ for all transit links e (because $h_{d(e)} = 0$ for all transit links e).

Thus, some other lower bound should be used in the BB algorithms for D/TNLLP1. One possibility is to use the global measure $\Gamma_e(u)$ (6.4.6) instead of $\eta_e(u)$ (6.4.1), as suggested in [DF79]. However, since the value of $\Gamma_e(u)$ is not always the lower bound, we will consider still another lower bound, based on the relaxation of the binary variables u and s.

Suppose that besides N, also the set of transit node indices $K = \{1, 2, ..., V\}$ is partitioned into three disjoint subsets K_U, K_0 and K_1, and let $\Psi(K_U, K_0, K_1)$ denote the set of all V-vectors s such that $v \in K_0$ implies $s_v = 0$, $v \in K_1$ implies $s_v = 1$, and for $v \in K_U$ the s_v can assume any continuous value from the unit interval $[0, 1]$. The same assumption concerns the set $\Phi\ (N_U, N_0, N_1)$ of vectors u. We also assume that K_0 and N_0 are consistent in the sense that $v \in K_0$ and $\beta_{ev} = 1$ imply $e \in N_0$. Below we consider the relaxation of D/TNLLP1 (6.4.10) where the unspecified components of vectors u and s are continuous in the interval [0,1]. The relaxed problem is as follows.

***MIP:* D/TNLLP1/AR** **Node-Link Formulation**
Adjusted Relaxation
variables

- x_{dp} flow realizing demand d allocated to path p (non-negative continuous)
- y_e capacity of link e (non-negative continuous)
- u_e link status variable, $u = (u_1, u_2, ..., u_E)$ (binary)
- s_v node status variable $s = (s_1, s_2, ..., s_V)$ (binary)

objective

$$\text{minimize } \boldsymbol{F} = \sum_e(\xi_e y_e + \kappa_e u_e) + \sum_v \varphi_v s_v \tag{6.4.10a}$$

constraints

$$\sum_p x_{dp} = h_d, \quad d = 1, 2, ..., D \tag{6.4.10b}$$

$$\sum_d \sum_p \delta_{edp} x_{dp} = y_e, \quad e = 1, 2, ..., E \tag{6.4.10c}$$

$$y_e \le M_e u_e, \quad e = 1, 2, ..., E \tag{6.4.10d}$$

$$\sum_{e \in N_U} \beta_{ev} u_e \le g_v s_v, \quad v \in K_U \tag{6.4.10e}$$

$$0 \le u_e \le 1, \quad e \in N_U; \quad u_e = 1, \quad e \in N_1; \quad u_e = 0, \quad e \in N_0 \tag{6.4.10f}$$

$$0 \le s_v \le 1, \quad v \in K_U; \quad s_v = 1, \quad v \in K_1; \quad s_v = 0, \quad v \in K_0. \tag{6.4.10g}$$

The constant in constraint (6.4.10e) is defined as:

$$g_v = G_v - \sum_{e \in N_1} \beta_{ev} \tag{6.4.11}$$

where G_v is the maximal degree of node v, $G_v \le \sum_e \beta_{ev}$.

In the optimal solution of the above problem constraints (6.4.10d) and (6.4.10e) are binding for $e \in N_U$ and $v \in K_U$, respectively, so the problem becomes the simple uncapacitated problem:

$$\begin{aligned} &\textbf{\textit{minimize}} && \boldsymbol{F} = \sum_e \zeta_e y_e + \sum_{e \in N_1} \kappa_e + \sum_{v \in K_1} \varphi_v \\ &\textbf{\textit{subject to}} && \text{(6.4.10b) to (6.4.10c) and} \\ & && \boldsymbol{u} \in \Phi(N_U, N_0, N_1), \ \boldsymbol{s} \in \Psi(K_U, K_0, K_1) \end{aligned} \tag{6.4.12}$$

where

$$\begin{aligned} &\zeta_e = \xi_e + (\kappa_e + \sum_{v \in K_U} \beta_{ev} \varphi_v / g_v)/M_e, \ \text{for } e \in N_U \\ &\zeta_e = \xi_e \text{ for } e \in N_1, \zeta_e = +\infty, \ \text{for } e \in N_0. \end{aligned} \tag{6.4.13}$$

Problem (6.4.13) is efficiently solved by allocating all demands to their shortest paths according to link metrics ζ_e.

Observe that the quality of the lower bound calculated as the solution of the above problem is strictly related to the values of the constants M_e and G_v: the lower the values the better the lower bound. The constants (which are the upper limits for the capacities of links and the degrees of nodes, respectively) should not be decreased too much since this can lead to false (too high) lower bounds, excluding optimal solutions of the original problem in the bounding process of BB. The issue is that if these bounds are too low, then the bounding is more effective (resulting in shorter computation times) but this can be achieved at the expense of overlooking the true optimal solutions. For example, we could assume the following values of the quantities in (6.4.10d) and (6.4.10e):

$$\text{for access link } e\text{: } M_e = \text{total demand generated and terminated at its access end node} \tag{6.4.14a}$$

$$\text{for transit link } e\text{: } M_e = \text{total demand generated by all access nodes divided by 2} \tag{6.4.14b}$$

$$\text{for transit node } v\text{: } G_v = V(v) + W(v). \tag{6.4.14c}$$

The first bound is obvious and follows from the assumption that access nodes do not transit traffic. The second bound (in general not very tight) is based on the reasonable assumption that at most one half of the total demand volume can go through any of the transit links (note that a factor much higher than 2 could be used, especially in large networks). Finally, the bound on the degree of transit node v is simply determined by the maximal assumed number, $V(v)$, of the neighboring transit nodes and the maximal number, $W(v)$ of access nodes that can be connected to v, with the obvious additional (and already used) condition $G_v \leq \sum_e \beta_{ev}$. For instance, in a grid network a typical value would be $V(v) = 5$.

A natural way for improving the lower bounds M_e on link capacities is achieved through limiting the number of paths using a link, as in the following form of D/TNLLP1 using binary variables u_{dp}.

$$\begin{aligned}
&\textbf{\textit{minimize}} && F = \textstyle\sum_e \sum_d \sum_p \xi_e \delta_{edp} u_{dp} h_d + \sum_e \kappa_e u_e + \sum_v \varphi_v s_v \\
&\textbf{\textit{subject to}} && \text{(6.4.10b), (6.4.10d-e) and} \\
& && \textstyle\sum_d u_{dp} = 1, \quad d = 1, 2, ..., D \\
& && \textstyle\sum_d \sum_p \delta_{edp} u_{dp} h_d \leq M_e u_e, \quad e = 1, 2, ..., E.
\end{aligned} \tag{6.4.15}$$

Now M_e is interpreted as the maximal number of flows using link e and the computation of the lower bound resulting from the relaxation of the binary variables leads to the simple design problem:

$$\begin{aligned}
&\textbf{\textit{minimize}} && F = \textstyle\sum_d \sum_p (\sum_e \zeta_{ed} \delta_{edp}) u_{dp} h_d \\
&\textbf{\textit{subject to}} && \textstyle\sum_d u_{dp} = 1, \quad d = 1, 2, ..., D \\
& && \textstyle\sum_d \sum_p \delta_{edp} u_{dp} h_d \leq M_e u_e, \quad e = 1, 2, ..., E.
\end{aligned} \tag{6.4.16}$$

where

$$\zeta_{ed} = \xi_e h_d + (\kappa_e + \textstyle\sum_v \beta_{ev} \varphi_v / G_v)/M_e, \quad e = 1, 2, ..., E, \; d = 1, 2, ..., D. \tag{6.4.17}$$

TABLE 6.8 **Running Time for Two BB Implementations for D/TNLLP2 [s] (Sun Sparc Ultra-4)**

net	n	k	BBO	CPLEX
N07	3	3	23.01	0.92
N07	3	6	1.66	0.58
N07	4	4	3.29	6.02
N07	5	6	1.53	11.73
N07	5	7	1.3	9.98
N07	5	8	0.03	0.12

The above problem is solved by assigning demand flows to their cheapest paths (the cost of path (d, p) is equal to $\sum_e \zeta_{ed}\delta_{edp}$). A disadvantage of this approach is that it uses demand-dependent link metrics (see factor h_d in the above formula) for the computation of the shortest paths. When using Dijkstra's algorithm, this implies the necessity of computing the shortest path separately for each demand, instead of the simultaneous computing of the whole tree of shortest paths from each access node to all other access nodes (refer to Section C.2 in Appendix C).

The above described ways of computing lower bounds $L(N_0, N_1)$ can be used by general MIP solvers in the BB process. However, general solvers cannot exploit the fact that the lower bound $L(N_0, N_1)$ is most effectively computed applying the shortest path algorithm for the link metrics defined by (6.4.17).

In Table 6.8 we compare the computation times for D/TNLLP2 of CPLEX and a BB procedure, referred to as BBO (BB own) written especially for D/TNLLP2. The results are given for network N7 (see Section 6.3.6, where also the meaning of parameters n and k is explained). It is interesting to note that in some cases CPLEX is faster while in others BBO is faster. This shows that it is not that easy to beat commercial solvers, and that it is probably not worthwhile to spend too much time on implementing personal branch-and-bound procedures when good commercial solvers are available.

6.5 SUMMARY AND FURTHER READING

In this chapter, we have covered location and topological design problems for communication and computer networks. Typically, these types of problems are faced in the network planning phase where the decision to determine the location of nodes and links are addressed.

Node location problems are generally known as facility location problems with a rich history in literature outside communication and computer networks. We have presented a formulation for node location problems, along with a presentation of add heuristics to solve these problems; as noted, LR-based dual approach is another popular approach for this purpose. Such node location problems are typically faced in designing tributary networks, or access networks where access nodes are needed to be connected to a core or backbone network node. Thus, the name 'node', depending on the networking environment and technology, can mean to reflect concentrators, switches, routers, access points, and so on. While we presented node location problems where an access area is to be connected only to a location, other variations such as dual-homing for access areas are also related problems.

We then consider integrated node location and inter-connectivity design problem and presented two different formulations depending on classification of nodes and sites. It may be noted that this type of design can be considered as integrated access and backbone network design with location of nodes and link connectivity, and we have presented a new formulation based on [LGM98], not found in existing literature.

The next set of problems we have considered is topological design problems. Topological design problems consider determination of links in a network (when node sites are given) in the presence of demand volumes. (Note that the first two classes of problems, location, and interconnectivity, do not consider traffic demand.) We have considered topological design with budgeting requirements (either as constraints or in the objective), and transit node and link location problems in the presence of demand volume. We then presented a set of heuristics and discussed their advantages and disadvantages through computational studies.

The add heuristic discussed in this chapter for the concentrator location problem dates back to Kuehn and Hamburger [KH63]. In general, it is well known that the concentrator location problem is equivalent to the capacitated facility location problem with single-source constraints (for example, see [Bof89], [Min89]). The LR-based dual approach has been proposed by several researchers, [KL86], [Pir87], [Sri93], and has been found to be an excellent computational approach. Variations of formulation (6.1.1) for different types of nodes have been proposed in [Lee93] that employs a solution method that involves Benders subproblem and a Lagrangian subproblem. An extension to hierarchical concentrator location problem can be found in [NP92]. An algorithmic approach can be found in [Ros01].

The joint problem of location and core network interconnection has been an important design problem for computer networks. This problem is related in the literature as the hub location problem outside of computer networks. We refer the reader to survey articles such as [Cam94] and [OM94] for additional work on hub location problems. For an excellent survey on different variations of models and algorithms proposed, for both node location and hub location-related problems, we refer the reader to [GLY02] and [Kli98].

Topological design problems discussed in Section 6.3 have been studied for quite a long time now. The link localization problem with the budget constraint (D/TDBC—(6.3.1)) is called "network design problem" in the older literature, e.g., see [BFW73], [DF79], [FC72], and [Hoa73] (certain generalizations are discussed in [Sco69]), as well as a more recent survey in [Min89]. $\mathcal{NP}$-completeness of D/TDBC was demonstrated in [JLK78]. The similar problem, D/TDEO (6.3.2), has been studied in [Min89]. A LR-based dual method for D/TDEO is presented, e.g., in [Bal89], [HY98], [HH98], and [HY00], while a simple SAN approach can be found in [LP95]; some heuristics are discussed in [Ker92]. As mentioned in Section 6.3.3, the latter problem is closely related to the famous Steiner tree problem (refer to [BBP00] and the literature survey there, and an older paper [Hu74]) which is $\mathcal{NP}$-complete (refer to [GJ79], and [Kar72]). The two extended problems of Section 6.3.4, also directly taking into account node localization, are discussed in more detail in Section 6.3.5 where the heuristic methods are introduced. The lower bounds for the BB computations are discussed in [DF79], [Hoa73], [Min89], [PJH+01], and [PMJ+01].

There have been many other works for a wide variety of topological design problems; see, for example, [Alt94], [AY92], [BF77], [CG93], [CMS96], [DD76], [Gav82], [Gav91], [GK77], and [LN94].

EXERCISES FOR CHAPTER 6

6.1. In SS7 network, an access node needs to be connected to two switches. Formulate the problem when a site needs to be connected to exactly two areas in the presence of both access link cost and node location cost.

6.2. Develop the Lagrangian relaxation-based dual approach to solve the model D/NLD (6.1.1).

6.3. For the SS7 network location design problem (Exercise 6.1), develop a variation of the add heuristic.

6.4. Develop a formulation for incremental ONLLC design given that a set of core sites and inter-connectivity is given for: 1) when access to core can be rearranged, and 2) where current access to core cannot be rearranged but additional access sites need to be considered for connectivity.

6.5. Determine the general formulation for the number of constraints and the number of variables in terms of N and M for the design problem D/ONLLC/B (6.2.20).

6.6. Write down the problem dual to D/TDBC (6.3.1) by dualizing the budget constraint (6.3.1b) and show that the computation of the corresponding dual function involves a problem of the D/TDEO type (i.e., Problem (6.3.2)).

6.7. Formulate an evolutionary algorithm for D/TDEO (6.3.2).

6.8. *Prove Proposition 6.2.

CHAPTER 7

Networks With Shortest-Path Routing

Shortest-path routing algorithms have existed since two independent seminal works by Bellman [Bel58] and Ford [FF62], and Dijkstra [Dij59] in 1950's. The difference between these two algorithms is the way information needed for computing the shortest-path is used. In the context of packet-switched networks and Internet routing, in particular, Bellman-Ford's algorithm has enabled the development of distance-vector routing protocols while Dijkstra's algorithm has paved the way to the introduction of link-state routing protocols [Hui00]. In this chapter, we focus on network design problems (NDPs) related to the latter type of routing protocols since they have gained popularity due to deployment of open shortest-path first (OSPF) [Moy98b]) and intermediate system to intermediate system (IS-IS) [Cal90], [ISO90], [Ora90])—the most common Internet intra-domain routing protocols.

The shortest-path routing principle in packet networks is attractive because it solves the immanent trade-off between routing implementation complexity and traffic effectiveness. The main advantage of shortest-path routing is that it can be implemented in a distributed way, not losing too much out of the traffic effectiveness achievable with more complicated routing strategies. The idea is to assign a cost metric (weight) to each link in the network, and to route packets incoming to a node using the shortest-path to the packet destination where the path cost (length) is computed using this cost metric. Nodes are aware of the current metrics used for the links, and compute shortest-paths to other destinations, storing in their routing tables the next hop for each destination. When for some reason the metrics in the system are changed (for instance, when a link fails, then it is assigned an infinite weight), nodes are informed about the changes in a distributed manner through a protocol mechanism where the originator (e.g., the node to which a failed link is connected) generates the link metric (and other information about the link), called *link-state* in the OSPF context, and floods it throughout the network—this process is commonly referred to as the link-state advertisement in a link-state routing protocol. Once a node receives the updated state of a particular link, it can locally re-compute and update the shortest-paths.

Both OSPF and IS-IS protocols use some versions of Dijkstra's shortest-path routing algorithm for the local computations of the shortest-path at the nodes, based on the known metric for each link in the network. Collectively, the set of link-cost metrics for all links is referred to as *link metric system* or *link weight system*. A common practice is to use the fixed hop-count (all link weights equal to 1), or the inverse of the link rate as the link metrics.

Thus, traffic between end nodes of a demand is routed on the shortest-paths with respect to the given link metric system, with the shortest-path to destinations computed locally at the network nodes. If there are multiple shortest-paths to a particular destination, the node routing table contains the next hop for each of the shortest-paths to this destination, and the corresponding traffic is equally split over the outgoing links belonging to these shortest-paths; this is called equal-cost multi-path (ECMP) split rule and is used in OSPF networks whenever there are multiple shortest paths for a pair of origin-destination nodes (routers). One may wonder how multiple shortest paths are calculated for recording in the routing table given that Dijkstra's algorithm is used for shortest-path computation in OSPF. Recall that Dijkstra's algorithm (see Algorithm C.1) as originally proposed results in determination of a single shortest-path to a destination, even if there are more than one. In the case of OSPF and IS/IS implementation, Dijkstra's algorithm is often used with a minor variation; instead of strict inequality in the minimum cost test of Dijkstra's algorithm (refer to line-9, i.e., **if** condition, of Algorithm C.1), a less than or equal ($\leq$) condition is used which allows the ability to capture additional shortest paths; this is, in turn, finally reflected through the routing table.

It may be noted that, in practice, the split may not exactly follow ECMP in its true sense; that is, the split decision is not done on a packet-by-packet basis in a round robin manner among the multiple outgoing links that fall on the (multiple) shortest paths; in other words, the total traffic for the same origin-destination node pair may not be exactly equally split among its multiple shortest paths. Note that, as of now, IP networks primarily carry TCP traffic for end computers; it is, thus, important to ensure that a particular TCP session is not drastically affected if packets for this session take two different paths through an OSPF network; note that these paths can conceivably have different latency even if both paths are marked as ECMP paths in the routing table. This is possible since the link-weight system may be determined based on other factors than just latency. The consequence of the path latency problem is that TCP throughput can be significantly affected due to likely impact on reassembly of packets in a timely manner at the receiving end (for example, see [RM01]). Thus, in most router implementations, packets that belong to a particular TCP session (i.e., going to a specific destination in terms of IP address of the end computer) are routed on a specific shortest-path (even if multiple shortest paths are available). Packets for another TCP session, which may have the same pair of origin-destination routers as the first TCP session, can take a different shortest path than the first one (when multiple shortest paths are available). Thus the ECMP split may be decided based on per (TCP) session, rather than on a packet-by-packet basis. Similarly, other ECMP split rules (such as on an entire IP address block) may be possible and conceivable. However, in the rest of the discussion in this chapter, we will assume ECMP to mean split equally in terms of traffic volume since our interest here is on network level impact rather than the impact on a specific TCP session.

Observe that if the link metric is, for example, based on hop-count, then traffic is routed on the minimum hop paths which can lead to high utilization in parts of the network since this metric does not take into account the load of links. Thus, it has been recognized that the metric system should be optimized, i.e., determined in a way to control the flow of traffic and, in turn, to accomplish such traffic engineering goals as minimizing the average network delay or minimizing the maximum link congestion.

If the traffic load is to be counted for in the determination of an optimal weight system, then optimization of the weights is typically done at a central processor and then communicated to each node in the network. After that, each node can use the metric to locally invoke Dijkstra's algorithm and update its routing table by determining the next hop of the shortest-paths to each destination.

In this regard, it is important to note that neither OSPF nor IS-IS says what actual link metric values are to be used in the link metric system to fulfill the network performance objectives—this is where the design problems come into the picture in the shortest-path routing networks. Finding the optimal weight system (under certain performance criterion) for given link capacities is nothing else but the shortest-path routing counterpart of the classical capacitated flow allocation problems studied in Chapter 4. The shortest-path routing counterpart of the classical uncapacitated multi-commodity flow problems consist in adding bandwidth to the network links with simultaneous re-optimization of the link weight system. Both types of problems differ from the classical counterparts in that in the shortest-path routing case these are the link weights (determining the demand flows) which are the decision variables, rather than the demand flows. This problem has received considerable attention for Internet routing in the recent years (for example, see [BGL00], [GPS+00], [FT00], [PSH+02], [RR01]).

There are a broad class of questions one needs to understand in regard to network design of OSPF/IS-IS networks: 1) Given my network, how can I best utilize my network without overly congesting parts of the network and what are the implications of one set of link weights over another? 2) What is the "best" link weight system that can be used for the best usage of my network? 3) Is it possible to have a feasible link weight system that achieves optimal routing? and 4) Is there a good algorithm that can be used off-line to generate the "best" link weight system, and given a number of approaches to finding the link weight systems, what are the trade-offs? From a planning point of view, an important additional question to address is: where do I need to add more bandwidth in the network and how is this related to the link weight system? While some of these questions are not necessarily new compared to what we have discussed so far in this book, they do take a new meaning when shortest-path routing is employed.

This chapter is organized as follows. Chapter 7 deals mostly, although not entirely, with formulating and solving design problems (involving weight system optimization) for the shortest-path routing networks of the OSPF/IS-IS type. In Section 7.1 we introduce the basic shortest-path routing flow allocation problems, considering different optimization objectives and present an illustrative example. Section 7.2 introduces direct mixed integer programming (MIP) formulations of the problems introduced in Section 7.1, and discusses the relevance of the dual formulations for the weight systems optimization. In Section 7.4, we discuss possible methods for direct optimization of the link weights treated as decision variables (including a local search method, simulated annealing (SAN) algorithm and a dual-based approach) for the problems introduced in Section 7.1. Section 7.5 presents a two-phase approach to the weights optimization in which, first, an optimal non-bifurcated flow allocation pattern is established, and then a weight system that generates this pattern is found (if possible). Numerical examples illustrating the methods of Sections 7.4 and 7.5 are shown in Section 7.8, followed by an important discussion (Section 7.6) on the impact of different classes of weight systems for efficient traffic routing. In Section 7.8, we formulate basic uncapacitated counterparts of the previously studied capacitated problems. In Section 7.9, we discuss the selection of optimal weights in under transient failures. Then, in Section 7.10, we provide a proof of an important result stating that the basic shortest-path routing allocation problem is $\mathcal{NP}$-complete and, thus, hard to solve effectively for large networks; this section is rather technical and can be skipped during first reading. Section 7.11 discusses selfish routing which assumes traffic-dependent link weights of a special form (reflecting link congestion). The issue is what happens with the overall traffic efficiency when each individual demand pair routes its demand volume trying to minimize (selfishly, but not deliberately trying to disturb other users) some delay measure; we discuss this work in relation to optimal routing. The chapter is summarized in Section 7.12 where further reading is suggested.

7.1 SHORTEST-PATH ROUTING ALLOCATION PROBLEM

In this section, we will consider formulations for the shortest-path routing allocation problem, i.e., given the requirement that the link weight system is to be considered; our discussion will center around different possible objectives for packet networks.

7.1.1 Basic Problem Formulation

We start with the general problem formulation related to the determination of the link metric system for a shortest-path routing network where traffic demand volumes and link capacities are given. The problem can be labeled as an allocation problem as we aim at finding the link metrics which determine the demand flow pattern that fits into the link capacities and, at the same time, takes into account some network objective (e.g., related to packet delay). Unlike multi-commodity flow formulations presented in Chapter 4, flows in this problem are induced by the link metric system $\boldsymbol{w}$. Suppose $\boldsymbol{w} = (w_1, w_2, ..., w_E)$ is the link metric vector (which is unknown in our case); this will induce a $\boldsymbol{w}$-dependent flow allocation vector $\boldsymbol{x}(\boldsymbol{w}) = (x_{dp}(\boldsymbol{w}) : d = 1, 2, ..., D, p = 1, 2, ..., P_d)$ for routing the demand volumes in the network. Note that here demand volume is considered between two ingress and egress nodes in a network, usually given in Mbps (see also Section 3.1). In practice, many networks are deployed with two routers together at each point-of-presence (PoP) for resiliency; for the purpose of our discussion, such "dual" routers at a PoP can be considered as one node for demand volume to ingress or egress a core network.

By assumption, the metric system $\boldsymbol{w}$ induces the flows according to the ECMP rule. We have briefly discussed the ECMP rule in the introduction to this chapter and through an example in Section 2.5. We now re-visit this example.

Example 7.1 *Illustration of equal split rule*

Consider Figure 7.1. Assuming link weights to be all equal to 1 (i.e., hop-count metrics), there are three shortest-paths from node 6 to node 7. Each of the shortest-paths 6-1-3-7 and 6-1-4-7 carries $\frac{1}{4}$ of the total demand volume from node 6 to node 7, and the shortest-path 6-2-5-7 carries the remaining $\frac{1}{2}$ of the volume. This is because traffic

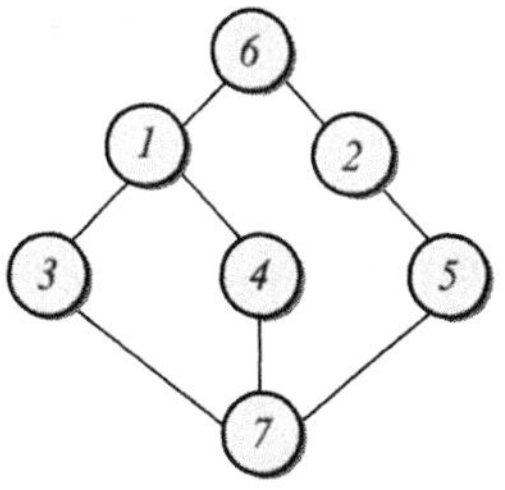

FIGURE 7.1 Illustration of ECMP Flow Splitting Rule

is equally split at the originating node 6 due to two outgoing links; traffic taking the link 6–1 is further split at node 1 to take its two outgoing links. In the OSPF network, routing is directional. This means that the demand split depends on the direction: if the demand volume were considered from node 7 to node 6 with the same weight system, then the length of the shortest-paths would remain the same as in the other direction, but the split would change to the uniform one assigning $\frac{1}{3}$ of the volume to each of the three paths. ●

In order to make the ECMP flow splitting procedure consistent (unambiguous), it is assumed that the link weights are positive, which assures that there are no loops in the shortest-paths. In general, some extra limitations can be imposed on values of the weights, and the space of all allowable weight systems $\boldsymbol{w}$ will be denoted with $\boldsymbol{W}$. A typical example of a weight system space assuring the consistency of the weight systems is:

$$1 \leq w_e \leq K \text{ and } w_e\text{— integer}, \quad e = 1, 2, ..., E. \tag{7.1.1}$$

Note that the requirement that weights take positive integral values corresponds to the fact that OSPF can handle only integer weights from 1 to $2^{16} - 1$ (= K) for shortest-path computation. In the original specification of IS-IS, the lowest value allowed was 0 while upper bound was $K = 63$ [Ora90]; the upper bound has been then modified to $K = 2^{24} - 1$ [NSB⁺02].

Observe that there is no simple function $x_{dp} = x_{dp}(\boldsymbol{w})$ for determining the flow of demand d on path p induced by system $\boldsymbol{w}$. This is the fundamental reason why the design problems considered in this chapter are substantially different from the classical problems considered in Chapter 4; in fact, the considered shortest-path routing design problems are $\mathcal{NP}$-complete, as demonstrated later in Section 7.10.

Now assume that both demand volume units (DVU) and link capacity units (LCU) are in packets per second (pps). The simplest way of taking into account the objective of the packet delay minimization is to assure that no link introduces too much delay. As you already know from Section 1.3.1, when a link of capacity c_e is offered a Poissonian packet arrival rate of $\underline{y}_e$ pps (recall that this means that packets arrive according to the Poissonian process, and that the packet length is exponentially distributed), it then introduces the average packet delay (assuming normalized unit average packet length) of

$$1/(c_e - \underline{y}_e) \tag{7.1.2}$$

seconds, according to the *M/M/*1 queueing model. This is then called the *latency function* of link e. Of course, this function may not be applicable if the Poissonian assumption is not satisfied (in fact this is usually the case) and the link does not "behave" as the *M/M/*1 system (for example, see [GSS96] for routing optimization when delay is based on non-Poissonian traffic). Still this is a good function to understand the essence of delay. If we for instance assume that for each link the delay has to be limited to T seconds (in fact mili-second, ms, is a better unit in this context), then this assumption results in the following link capacity-dependent bound on the link load:

$$\underline{y}_e \leq c_e - 1/T \tag{7.1.3a}$$

or

$$\underline{y}_e \leq \gamma_e c_e \quad \text{(equivalently: } \underline{y}_e/c_e \leq \gamma_e) \tag{7.1.3b}$$

where $\gamma_e = 1 - 1/(c_e T)$ (under obvious assumption that $T > 1/c_e$.). Note that $\gamma_e < 1$ and, hence, the introduced capacity- and delay-dependent coefficient γ_e can be interpreted as the link utilization-level adjustment factor. Finally, the basic weight system optimization problem can be stated as follows.

A/ECMP/BLD **Link-Path Formulation**

ECMP Shortest-Path Routing: Bounded Link Delay

indices

- $d = 1, 2, ..., D$ demands
- $p = 1, 2, ..., P_d$ paths for demand d (all simple paths in the network graph)
- $e = 1, 2, ..., E$ links

constants

- h_d volume of demand d
- δ_{edp} = 1 if link e belongs to path p realizing demand d; 0, otherwise
- c_e capacity of link e
- γ_e link utilization factor for link e ($\gamma_e = 1 - 1/(c_e T)$)

variables

- w_e metric of link e, $\boldsymbol{w} = (w_1, w_2, ..., w_E)$
- $x_{dp}(\boldsymbol{w})$ (non-negative) flow induced by link metric system $\boldsymbol{w}$ for demand d on path p

constraints

$$\textstyle\sum_p x_{dp}(\boldsymbol{w}) = h_d, \quad d = 1, 2, ..., D \tag{7.1.4a}$$

$$\textstyle\sum_d \sum_p \delta_{edp}\, x_{dp}(\boldsymbol{w}) \leq \gamma_e c_e, \quad e = 1, 2, ..., E \tag{7.1.4b}$$

$$\boldsymbol{w} \in \boldsymbol{W}. \tag{7.1.4c}$$

Simply put, Problem A/ECMP/BLD consists in finding an ECMP metric system $\boldsymbol{w}$ that induces the flow allocation vector which satisfies demand constraints (7.1.4a) and link capacity (link delay) constraints (7.1.4b). It is important to emphasize that the above problem is *not* a mathematical programming problem in the common sense (Appendix A) because of the implicit relation $\boldsymbol{x} = \boldsymbol{x}(\boldsymbol{w})$. In Section 7.2.1, we will introduce a MIP formulation of A/ECMP/BLD, and in Section 7.1.2 we will show how to compute the ECMP flows $\boldsymbol{x}(\boldsymbol{w})$ algorithmically. Since the problem is $\mathcal{NP}$-complete (see Section 7.10), it is not possible to formulate any linear program with a polynomial number of constraints equivalent to Problem (7.1.4).

Observe that Problem (7.1.4) will yield a good solution if non-zero flows are assigned to paths that are short in terms of the number of hops. Additionally, the problem can be equipped with an objective consisting not only in limiting the maximal link delay through constraints (7.1.4c) but also in minimizing the average packet delay. Putting $H = \sum_d h_d$ and using the link delay function (7.1.2) showing its dependency on $\boldsymbol{w}$, the average packet delay can be expressed as:

$$\boldsymbol{F}(\boldsymbol{w}) = \frac{1}{H}\sum_d \sum_p x_{dp}(\boldsymbol{w}) \sum_e \delta_{edp} \frac{1}{c_e - \underline{y}_e} = \frac{1}{H}\sum_e \frac{\underline{y}_e}{c_e - \underline{y}_e}. \qquad (7.1.5)$$

where link load $\underline{y}_e$ on link e is defined, as usual, as

$$\underline{y}_e = \sum_d \sum_p \delta_{edp}\, x_{dp}(\boldsymbol{w}), \quad e = 1, 2, ..., E. \qquad (7.1.6)$$

Note that we have assumed the arrivals to each link to be independent, often known as the Kleinrock's independence assumption [BG92], which then allows the use of the average delay formula (7.1.2) on a link-by-link basis. The term $\underline{y}_e/(c_e - \underline{y}_e)$ for link e in (7.1.5) is referred to as the link cost function and corresponds to the average number of packets in the *M/M/*1 system. Adding objective function (7.1.5) (note that the constant factor $1/H$ can be skipped) and equation (7.1.6) to the formulation of A/ECMP/BLD, we arrive at the following modified formulation.

A/ECMP/MAD **Link-Path Formulation**

ECMP shortest-path routing: Minimum Average Delay

variables

w_e metric of link e, $\boldsymbol{w} = (w_1, w_2, ..., w_E)$

$x_{dp}(\boldsymbol{w})$ flow induced by link metric system $\boldsymbol{w}$ for demand d on path p

$\underline{y}_e$ load of link e

minimize

$$\boldsymbol{F} = \sum_e \frac{\underline{y}_e}{c_e - \underline{y}_e} \qquad (7.1.7a)$$

constraints

$$\sum_p x_{dp}(\boldsymbol{w}) = h_d, \quad d = 1, 2, ..., D \qquad (7.1.7b)$$

$$\underline{y}_e = \sum_d \sum_p \delta_{edp}\, x_{dp}(\boldsymbol{w}), \quad e = 1, 2, ..., E \qquad (7.1.7c)$$

$$\underline{y}_e \leq \gamma_e c_e, \quad e = 1, 2, ..., E \tag{7.1.7d}$$

$$w \in W. \tag{7.1.7e}$$

Note that although objective function (7.1.7a) is convex in its domain, the above problem is not a (convex) mathematical programming problem, for the same reasons as for Problem (7.1.4).

An important special case of either (7.1.4) or (7.1.7) in regard to the link weight system arises when we are interested in determining the unique shortest-path for every demand. This problem, discussed earlier in Section 2.5, is clearly a complex problem to solve. There are three main reasons for this complexity:

- A non-bifurcated (unique-path) feasible flow allocation may not exist while bifurcated feasible flow allocations may exist.
- Even if a unique-path solution exists, in most cases it can be hard to determine.
- Moreover, even if we find a unique-path solution, a weight system may not exist to induce it.

7.1.2 Adjustments of the Basic Problem

Model A/ECMP/BLD (7.1.4) can be adjusted by introducing link penalty functions instead of the link capacity constraints (7.1.4b). The resulting uncapacitated problem uses the objective function that incurs cost whenever the condition (7.1.4b) is violated, e.g.,

$$f_e(\underline{y}_e) = \begin{cases} B_e(\gamma_e c_e - \underline{y}_e)^2, & \text{if } \underline{y}_e > \gamma_e c_e \\ 0, & \text{otherwise} \end{cases} \tag{7.1.8}$$

where constant, B_e, is a fixed link-dependent cost coefficient.

A/ECMP/BLD/PF **Link-Path Formulation**

ECMP shortest-path routing: Penalty Function

variables

w_e metric of link e, $w = (w_1, w_2, ..., w_E)$

$x_{dp}(w)$ flow induced by link metric system w for demand d on path p

$\underline{y}_e$ load of link e

objective

$$F = \sum_e f_e(\underline{y}_e) \tag{7.1.9a}$$

constraints

$$\sum_p x_{dp}(w) = h_d, \quad d = 1, 2, ..., D \tag{7.1.9b}$$

$$\sum_d \sum_p \delta_{edp} x_{dp}(\boldsymbol{w}) = \underline{y}_e, \quad e = 1, 2, ..., E \tag{7.1.9c}$$

$$\boldsymbol{w} \in \boldsymbol{W}. \tag{7.1.9d}$$

Instead of using the link-cost function $\underline{y}_e/(c_e - \underline{y}_e)$ as given in (7.1.7a), the following convex piecewise linear approximation can be used as proposed by Fortz and Thorup [FT00], [FT02] for each link e:

$$f_e(\underline{y}_e) = \begin{cases} \underline{y}_e & \text{for} \quad 0 \leq \underline{y}_e/c_e < 1/3 \\ 3\,\underline{y}_e - \frac{2}{3}\,c_e & \text{for} \quad 1/3 \leq \underline{y}_e/c_e < 2/3 \\ 10\,\underline{y}_e - \frac{16}{3}\,c_e & \text{for} \quad 2/3 \leq \underline{y}_e/c_e < 910 \\ 70\,\underline{y}_e - \frac{178}{3}\,c_e & \text{for} \quad 9/10 \leq \underline{y}_e/c_e < 1 \\ 500\,\underline{y}_e - \frac{1,468}{3}\,c_e & \text{for} \quad 1 \leq \underline{y}_e/c_e < 11/10 \\ 5,000\,\underline{y}_e - \frac{16,318}{3}\,c_e & \text{for} \quad 11/10 \leq \underline{y}_e/c_e < \infty. \end{cases} \tag{7.1.10}$$

There are some advantages of this approximation. This function is defined beyond c_e as opposed to the link cost function $\underline{y}_e/(c_e - \underline{y}_e)$; note that the derivative of this function increases from 1 to 5,000 as the utilization, z/c_e, increases. The basic idea behind using this function is that it costs little (in terms of link cost) to send flow over a link with low utilization while it is expensive when the utilization approaches 100%, and to penalize heavily once it crosses over 100% of the assumed utilization. That is, the function can handle an overloaded link as opposed to $\underline{y}_e/(c_e - \underline{y}_e)$ (see Figure 7.2 for a comparison). Since, in practice, an overloaded link does not bring down the entire network [FT02], the link capacity constraint can be ignored, especially in the presence of this function in the objective. Recall from Section 4.3.2 that a convex piecewise linear function can be replaced by an equivalent linear programming (LP) problem by introducing additional variables r_e (refer to Section (4.3.2)).

The entire problem formulation can be stated as follows.

***IP:* A/ECMP/MDA** **Link-Path Formulation**

Piecewise Linear Penalty Functions

variables

- w_e metric of link e, $\boldsymbol{w} = (w_1, w_2, ..., w_E)$
- $x_{dp}(\boldsymbol{w})$ flow induced by link metric system $\boldsymbol{w}$ for demand d on path p
- $\underline{y}_e$ load of link e
- r_e penalty cost of link e

objective

$$\text{minimize } \boldsymbol{F} = \sum_e r_e \tag{7.1.11a}$$

constraints

$$\sum_p x_{dp}(\boldsymbol{w}) = h_d \quad d = 1, 2, ..., D \tag{7.1.11b}$$

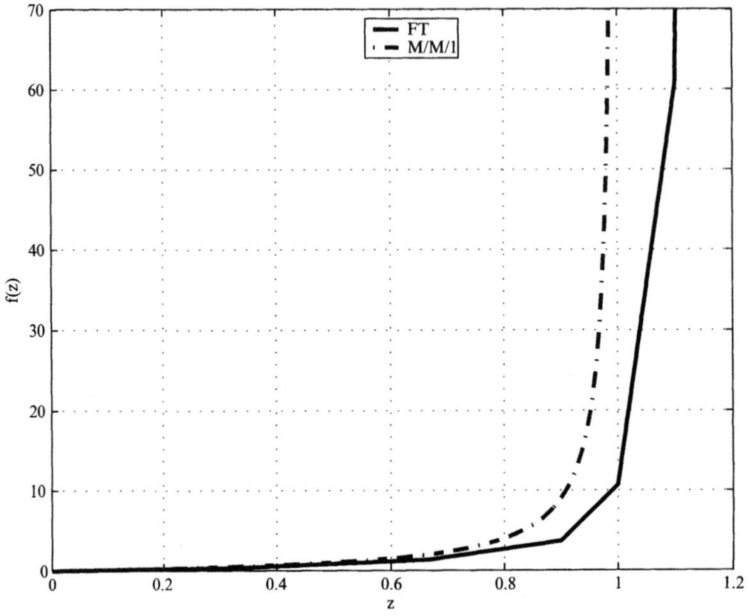

FIGURE 7.2 Comparison of Fortz-Thorup Function and *M/M/*1 Link Cost Function (shown for $c_e = 1$)

$$\textstyle\sum_d \sum_p \delta_{edp} x_{dp}(\boldsymbol{w}) = \underline{y}_e, \quad e = 1, 2, ..., E \tag{7.1.11c}$$

$$r_e \geq \underline{y}_e, \quad e = 1, 2, ..., E \tag{7.1.11d}$$

$$r_e \geq 3\,\underline{y}_e - \tfrac{2}{3}\,c_e, \quad e = 1, 2, ..., E \tag{7.1.11e}$$

$$r_e \geq 10\,\underline{y}_e - \tfrac{16}{3}\,c_e, \quad e = 1, 2, ..., E \tag{7.1.11f}$$

$$r_e \geq 70\,\underline{y}_e - \tfrac{178}{3}\,c_e, \quad e = 1, 2, ..., E \tag{7.1.11g}$$

$$r_e \geq 500\,\underline{y}_e - \tfrac{1{,}468}{3}\,c_e, \quad e = 1, 2, ..., E \tag{7.1.11h}$$

$$r_e \geq 5{,}000\,\underline{y}_e - \tfrac{16{,}318}{3}\,c_e, \quad e = 1, 2, ..., E \tag{7.1.11i}$$

$$\boldsymbol{w} \in \boldsymbol{W}. \tag{7.1.11j}$$

Another relevant objective for packet networks is the minimization of maximum link utilization, i.e., minimization of the utilization of the link with the highest delay. We have discussed this objective already in Section 3.1 (refer to formulation (3.1.2)) without the link metric $\boldsymbol{w}$. Thus, incorporating $\boldsymbol{w}$, Problem (3.1.2) takes the following form:

A/ECMP/MMLU **Link-Path Formulation**
Minimization of Maximum Link Utilization
constants

γ_e link-based adjustment for acceptable link utilization

variables

w_e metric of link e, $\boldsymbol{w} = (w_1, w_2, ..., w_E)$
$x_{dp}(\boldsymbol{w})$ flow induced by link metric system $\boldsymbol{w}$ for demand d on path p
r maximum link utilization variable

objective

$$\text{minimize } \boldsymbol{F} = r \tag{7.1.12a}$$

constraints

$$\textstyle\sum_p x_{dp}(\boldsymbol{w}) = h_d, \quad d = 1, 2, ..., D \tag{7.1.12b}$$

$$\textstyle\sum_d \sum_p \delta_{edp} x_{dp}(\boldsymbol{w}) \le \gamma_e c_e\, r, \quad e = 1, 2, ..., E \tag{7.1.12c}$$

$$\boldsymbol{w} \in \boldsymbol{W}. \tag{7.1.12d}$$

Remark 7.1

Note that in all of the above problems we have deliberately kept link metric system $\boldsymbol{w}$ in the problem formulations to ensure that this is indeed important to account for if the flow were to be determined based on $\boldsymbol{w}$, and especially when a particular rule such as the equal split rule were to be used. Then, what is the meaning of the shortest-path routing allocation problem when $\boldsymbol{w}$ is *ignored*? If we ignore the fact that there is a metric system involved, then $\boldsymbol{w}$ can be dropped from the formulation and we can simply consider flows x_{dp} not constrained by the additional requirement that the flows be determined based on $\boldsymbol{w}$.

From the viewpoint of the optimal value (cost) of the objective function, the model *without* $\boldsymbol{w}$ (as less constrained) results in lower cost than the corresponding model where $\boldsymbol{w}$ is taken into account, meaning that we can obtain a lower bound to the actual problem. For example, the optimal cost $\boldsymbol{F}$ obtained for formulation (7.1.11) when $\boldsymbol{w}$ is ignored serves as the lower bound compared to the optimal cost $\boldsymbol{F}$ obtained for (7.1.11) when the link weight system $\boldsymbol{w}$ is explicitly taken into account since $\boldsymbol{w}$ imposes additional constraints on the problem. As you may have already noticed, dropping the requirement of $\boldsymbol{w}$ makes the considered problem take the classical form considered in Chapter 4 and is, thus, easier to solve. For several models where only linear relations are involved, i.e., for (7.1.11) and (7.1.12), corresponding problems without $\boldsymbol{w}$ are simply LP problems. Hence, these models can be solved by LP solvers to obtain lower bounds or to be utilized in a different way (as shown in Section 7.4). ♦

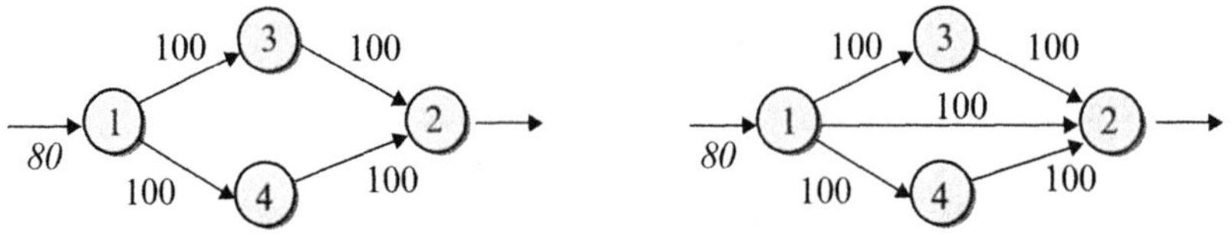

A Original network B Upgraded network

FIGURE 7.3 Four-Node "Diamond" Network Example to Illustrate "Paradoxical" Behavior in Packet Networks

7.1.3 Minimum-Hop Routing versus Network Delay: An Illustration

As discussed before, an important traffic engineering objective is to determine a link metric system so that the average delay is reduced. Below, we show that the commonly used system of unit link metrics leading to the use of the shortest-hop paths may be in general not good for this purpose, and discuss the related issues.

Consider the simple diamond-shaped four-node OSPF network (E = 4) with directed links as shown in Figure 7.3a. We start by assigning link metric system, $\boldsymbol{w}$, with weight equal to 1 for all links (i.e., the hop-count weight system), $w_e \equiv 1$. Suppose that all links in the network are 100 kilobits per second (Kbps) links, and there is only one traffic stream from node 1 to node 2 which is assumed to be on average 80 Kbps, i.e., the packet arrival intensity times the average packet length is 80 Kbps. Thus, here D = 1 and $h_1(= h)$ = 80. Furthermore, note that 1 DVU = 1 LCU = 1 Kbps. Then in this network, due to the ECMP rule, we have two equal cost paths from node 1 to node 2 where 50% of the traffic will take path 1-3-2 (path p = 1) while the other 50% will take path 1-4-2 (path p = 2), i.e., $x_{11}(\boldsymbol{w})$ = 40 = $x_{12}(\boldsymbol{w})$ for link metric vector $\boldsymbol{w}$ = **1**. Using the *M/M/*1 delay formula, we see that the average delay on each link is $1/(100 - 40)$ seconds, or $16\frac{2}{3}$ ms (assuming average packet size of 1 Kbits). Thus, the path delay on either path (due to the hop-by-hop nature of routing, and here with one intermediate hop) is $16\frac{2}{3} + 16\frac{2}{3} = 33\frac{1}{3}$ ms.

Now, suppose we increase the capacity in this network by directly connecting a link from node 1 to node 2 at a link capacity of 100 Kbps (Figure 7.3b). Suppose that the link metric for this (like for the rest of the links) is set to 1 as well in order to maintain the hop-count weight system. Then, in such an upgraded network, the shortest-path from node 1 to node 2 is the direct link 1-2, instead of the other two paths which were used prior to the network upgrade; now, due to the shortest-path routing principle, all of 80 Kbps of traffic will be exerted to the direct path. Using the delay formula, the average delay on this direct link path is $1/(100 - 80)$ second, or 50 ms. That is, we have added a new link and capacity in the network, and the average delay has increased from $33\frac{1}{3}$ ms to 50 ms! Thus, for this example, the hop-count based link weight system induces an increase in delay. This leads to the conclusion: for delay minimization the values assumed by the link metrics should reflect the link delay and not be set having some other performance measure in mind (hop minimization in this case).

We ask the reader to solve (Exercise 7.1) to show that such unwanted behavior occurs for the hop-count link metric system only when $h > 66\frac{2}{3}$, where h is the demand volume (above we have assumed $h = 80$). This suggests that disadvantageous behavior is more likely to occur when the load in the network is above a certain threshold.

Clearly, this disadvantageous behavior in the above example can be easily avoided if in the upgraded network we set the link metric of link 1-2 to 2, and keep the weights of the remaining four links equal to 1. Now all three paths are of equal cost, and due to the ECMP rule, the traffic will be equally split resulting in the average delay of $22\frac{8}{11}$ ms, which is lower than $33\frac{1}{3}$ ms (Exercise 7.1). This average network delay (dictated by the best ECMP link metric system) is still slightly higher than the metric-independent minimum $\frac{125}{11}\frac{(-44+25\sqrt{2})}{(-4+\sqrt{2})(-1+2\sqrt{2})} \approx 20.777$ ms. At the global optimal solution, $-\frac{180}{7}+\frac{220\sqrt{2}}{7} = 18.7325$ units of flow is offered to the direct-link path and 42.535 units to each of the long paths (Exercise 7.1; see also Exercise 7.2).

As a by-product, the above illustration also points out that trying to achieve a unique shortest-path in a network could lead to higher delay (equal to 50 ms no matter which of the three paths is chosen). While this is certainly true in this small single-commodity example, in most practical cases of large networks, using unique shortest-path can result in near-optimal delay-wise solutions. This statement is justified by the property expressed by Proposition 4.1 of Section 4.1.2, which can be applied to linear programming relaxation of Problem (7.1.4) when flows are assumed to be weight-independent. This property implies that a solution exists with at most $D + E$ non-zero flows; thus, in a large network (with $D \gg E$) almost all demands are routed on unique paths. If the resulting flows (paths) could be induced by a certain weight system then we would approximately achieve the desired solution. Identifying such paths is an important problem—this is discussed further in Section 7.4.

Interestingly, for the upgraded four-node diamond network, the same average network delay as for the optimized ECMP weight system is obtained by means of a very special flow split requiring that all paths have the same latency (delay). Denoting x as the flow assigned to the direct link, this requirement leads to the condition $1/(100-x) = 2/(100-(80-x)/2)$, and results in the Nash equilibrium solution which is defined formally in Section 7.11. In fact, the resulting flow on each path under the Nash equilibrium (assuming the sum of average link delays to constitute the path latency) would lead to the same latency on each of the three paths equal to $22\frac{8}{11}$ ms, i.e., equal to the average ECMP optimized network delay (note that in the ECMP case, the latency on the long paths is different from the latency of the direct path).

In fact, the above result can be generalized for a network with n multi-link paths, each of m links between two end nodes, and one single direct-link path between the same two end nodes; in such a network the Nash equilibrium solution indicates the same average delay as the average delay in the ECMP-optimized flows (see Exercise 7.3).

Although equivalent in terms of the average delay, the Nash equilibrium solution is superior to the ECMP one, as in the former all flows experience the same delay. Nash equilibrium flows are achieved when each packet is routed on the path with the currently minimal latency calculated as the sum of the current delays of its links resulting from the current link loads. Hence, Nash equilibrium flows are hard to achieve in practice, since they require on-line knowledge of time-dependent link loads on a packet-by-packet basis. Note that even if the Nash equilibrium link delays were used as link metrics in an OSPF network, the ECMP solution would be different from the Nash equilibrium solution due to the equal demand volume split induced by the ECMP rule.

To summarize: in order to obtain near optimal behavior in the case of the simple network, the ECMP metric system must be optimized for the average delay objective. One way to achieve this, discussed extensively in later sections of this chapter, is to solve the allocation Problem (7.1.4) and use the resulting link metrics. Another, rather theoretic, possibility, discussed in Section 7.11, is to let the users (e.g., packets of the demands) use the load-dependent delay link metrics leading to the Nash equilibrium flows.

7.2 MIP FORMULATION OF THE SHORTEST-PATH ROUTING ALLOCATION PROBLEM AND DUAL PROBLEMS

In this section, we discuss an MIP formulation of the shortest-path routing allocation Problem (7.1.4). We also present the linear programming dual of (7.1.4) where the ECMP requirement is relaxed, and show the relation of the dual solution to the link metric system.

7.2.1 MIP Formulation of the Shortest-Path Routing Allocation Problem

In [Tom00] shortest-path routing Problem (7.1.4) is presented in the form of a MIP problem, explicitly using the link metric variables in the formulation (for a different formulation, that is for the capacity design problem, see [HY]). This formulation uses the node-link representation of the multi-commodity problems and, hence, requires directed links and demands. As you already know from the discussion of Section 4.6 this is not a limitation since any undirected network can be easily transformed to a directed one.

In this formulation, the demand volume to be allocated from node v to node t is given by h_{vt}. Additionally, notations $i(e)$ and $j(e)$ denote starting and end nodes of link e, respectively.

***MIP:* A/ECMP-NL** **Node-Link Formulation**

ECMP Shortest-Path Routing

indices

$t, v, s = 1, 2, ..., V$ nodes

$e = 1, 2, ..., E$ links

constants

h_{vt} demand volume from node v to node t

$i(e)$ starting (originating) node of link e

$j(e)$ terminating node of link e

M large number

c_e capacity of link e

variables

w_e metric of link e (non-negative integer or continuous)

r_{vt} length of the shortest-path from v to t ($v \neq t$) (non-negative integer or continuous)

x_{et} flow to node t on link e (non-negative continuous)

y_{vt} common value of non-zero flow from node v to node t assigned to links outgoing from v and belonging to the shortest-paths from v to t (non-negative continuous)

u_{et} binary variable equal to 1 if and only if link e is on a shortest-path to node t

constraints

$$\textstyle\sum_{\{e:j(e)=t\}} x_{et} = \sum_{s \neq t} h_{st}, \qquad t = 1, 2, ..., V \tag{7.2.1a}$$

$$\textstyle\sum_{\{e:i(e)=v\}} x_{et} - \sum_{\{e:j(e)=v\}} x_{et} = h_{vt}, \qquad t = 1, 2, ..., V \quad v = 1, 2, ..., V, \; v \neq t \tag{7.2.1b}$$

$$\textstyle\sum_t x_{et} \leq c_e, \qquad e = 1, 2, ..., E \tag{7.2.1c}$$

$$\textstyle 0 \leq y_{i(e)t} - x_{et} \leq (1 - u_{et}) \sum_v h_{vt}, \qquad t = 1, 2, ..., V \quad e = 1, 2, ..., E \tag{7.2.1d}$$

$$\textstyle x_{et} \leq u_{et} \sum_v h_{vt}, \qquad t = 1, 2, ..., V \quad e = 1, 2, ..., E \tag{7.2.1e}$$

$$0 \leq r_{j(e)t} + w_e - r_{i(e)t} \leq (1 - u_{et})M, \qquad t = 1, 2, ..., V \quad e = 1, 2, ..., E \tag{7.2.1f}$$

$$1 - u_{et} \leq r_{j(e)t} + w_e - r_{i(e)t}, \qquad t = 1, 2, ..., V \quad e = 1, 2, ..., E \tag{7.2.1g}$$

$$w_e \geq 1, \qquad e = 1, 2, ..., E. \tag{7.2.1h}$$

Constraint (7.2.1a) assures that the total flow incoming and, at the same time, destined to node t is equal to the demand destined to node t generated in all remaining nodes $s \neq t$. Constraint (7.2.1b) forces that demand volume h_{vt} from node v to node t is actually generated in node v. Constraint (7.2.1c) is the link capacity constraint. Constraint (7.2.1d) assures that if link e belongs to one of the shortest-paths from node $i(e)$ to node t then its flow to node t is equal to $y_{i(e)t}$—a value common to all links outgoing from node $i(e)$ and belonging to the shortest-paths to destination t. Constraint (7.2.1e) forces the zero flow to t ($x_{et} = 0$) in the case when link e is not on the shortest-path to t. Finally, constraint (7.2.1f) assures that if $u_{et} = 1$, then link e is on the shortest-path to t; constraint (7.2.1g) assumes that if $u_{et} = 0$, then link e is not on the shortest-path to t. In this case, the link weights need to be ≥ 1, see constraint (7.2.1h).

Note that by adding the constraint

$$\textstyle\sum_{\{e:i(e)=v\}} u_{et} = 1, \quad t = 1, 2, ..., V \quad v = 1, 2, ..., V, v \neq t \tag{7.2.1i}$$

we force the shortest-paths to be unique provided such a solution is feasible.

The value of formulation (7.2.1) follows from the fact that it is a valid mathematical programming (MIP) formulation for the basic shortest-path routing allocation problem discussed in Section 7.1, contrary to formulation (7.1.4) which, as already mentioned, is not a straightforward mathematical programming formulation because of the implicit relationships $x_{dp} = x_{dp}(\boldsymbol{w})$.

Although the above MIP formulation may be difficult to solve even for moderate-size networks, this allows up to obtain exact solutions. In general, Problem (7.2.1) can be treated by MIP solvers, such as CPLEX [CPL99] and XPRESS-MP [XM], with their built-in branch-and-cut (BC) procedures (Section 5.2.2) Also, valid inequalities specific for Problem (7.2.1) can be devised and used in the BC process.

Finally, we note that the average delay minimization objective can be added to formulation (7.2.1) using the piecewise linear approximation (7.1.11a) and (7.1.11d) to (7.1.11i) (refer to Exercise 7.4).

7.2.2 Duality and Shortest-Path Routing

In Section 5.1.2, we have shown how to use the dual of an LP problem. Furthermore, as we have discussed in Remark 7.1, when we ignore the dependency of the flows on the weight system $\boldsymbol{w}$ and use a linear objective function we arrive at an LP problem. Below we will show that there is an important relation between the optimal dual variables (multipliers) of the classical capacitated flow allocation problems and the link weights for the shortest-path routing (weight system-dependent) allocation problem. Roughly speaking, a subset of the optimal multipliers can be used as a link weight system to solve approximately the basic shortest-path routing problem. To illustrate this, we will consider the allocation problem for yet another (linear) objective, maximization of the residual capacity, where we consider the flow allocation vector without any dependency on link metric system, $\boldsymbol{w}$. This relation, discussed in [PSH+02] (also see [AMO93] and [WWZ01]), will be exploited in Section 7.3.3.

***LP:* A/ECMP/RCM** **Link-Path Formulation**
Residual Capacity Maximization
constants (additional)

c_e capacity of link e
γ_e link adjustment factor of link e
b_e value of one unit of idle capacity on link e

variables

x_{dp} non-negative flow on path p for demand d

objective

$$\text{maximize } \boldsymbol{F} = \textstyle\sum_e b_e(\gamma_e c_e - \sum_d \sum_p \delta_{edp} x_{dp}) \tag{7.2.2a}$$

constraints

$$\textstyle\sum_p x_{dp} = h_d, \quad d = 1, 2, ...D \tag{7.2.2b}$$

$$\textstyle\sum_d \sum_p \delta_{edp} x_{dp} \le \gamma_e c_e, \quad e = 1, 2, ..., E. \tag{7.2.2c}$$

First, we rewrite the objective in terms of minimization. Since the term $\sum_e b_e \gamma_e c_e$ is fixed, we can ignore it; thus, we have

$$\textbf{\textit{minimize}} \textstyle\sum_e \sum_d \sum_p b_e \delta_{edp} x_{dp}. \tag{7.2.3}$$

The dual of the above problem (Exercise 7.5) can be written as:

***LP:* Dual of (7.2.2)**
variables
- λ_d (unrestricted) dual multiplier associated with constraints (7.2.2b)
- π_e non-negative dual multiplier associated with constraints (7.2.2c)

objective

$$\text{maximize } G(\boldsymbol{\pi}, \boldsymbol{\lambda}) = \sum_d \lambda_d h_d - \sum_e (b_e + \pi_e)\gamma_e c_e \tag{7.2.4a}$$

constraints

$$\lambda_d \le \sum_e \delta_{edp}(b_e + \pi_e), \quad p = 1, 2, ..., P_d, \quad d = 1, 2, ..., D. \tag{7.2.4b}$$

Note that the dual formulation says that λ_d is unrestricted; however, in reality, it is non-negative since this corresponding constraint in the primal problem can be written with a greater than equal to condition instead of equality without changing the intent of the primal problem.

Suppose that optimal dual multipliers are denoted by $\boldsymbol{\pi}^* = (\pi_1^*, \pi_2^*, ..., \pi_E^*)$ and $\boldsymbol{\lambda}^* = (\lambda_1^*, \lambda_2^*, ..., \lambda_D^*)$. Due to constraints of the dual problem, at optimality we have

$$\lambda_d^* = \min_{p=1,2,\dots,P_d} \left\{\sum_e \delta_{edp}(b_e + \pi_e^*)\right\}, \quad d = 1, 2, ..., D \tag{7.2.5}$$

and $\pi_e^* \ge 0$. Now if we define the optimal link weights as

$$w_e^* = b_e + \pi_e^*, \quad e = 1, 2, ..., E, \tag{7.2.6}$$

then the link metric system, $\boldsymbol{w}^* = (w_1^*, w_2^*, ..., w_E^*)$, has the property that all the non-zero primal optimal flows can be realized only on the paths that are the shortest with respect to weights $\boldsymbol{w}^*$. This property follows from the general complementary slackness property discussed in Section A.7 of Appendix A.

It is important to note that the link metric system obtained from the dual problem depends on the objective function of the primal problem. To illustrate this difference, consider the primal problem based on minimizing the maximum link utilization A/ECMP/MMLU (7.1.12), neglecting the dependence on the weight system $\boldsymbol{w}$:

***LP:* A/SPR/MMLU** **Link-Path Formulation**
Minimization of Maximum Link Utilization
variables
- x_{dp} non-negative flow on path p for demand d
- r link utilization variable

objective

$$\text{minimize } \boldsymbol{F} = r \tag{7.2.7a}$$

constraints

$$\sum_p x_{dp} = h_d \quad d = 1, 2, ..., D \tag{7.2.7b}$$

$$\sum_d \sum_p \delta_{edp} x_{dp}(\boldsymbol{w}) \leq \gamma_e c_e \, r \quad e = 1, 2, ..., E. \tag{7.2.7c}$$

Derivation and formulation of the dual of Problem (7.2.7) is left as an exercise (Exercise 7.6; see also Exercise 7.7). In this case, if $\boldsymbol{\pi}^*$ are optimal multipliers associated with constraints (7.2.7c), then the appropriate optimal weight system $\boldsymbol{w}^* = (w_1^*, w_2^*, ..., w_E^*)$ would be

$$w_e^* = \pi_e^*, \quad e = 1, 2, ..., E, \tag{7.2.8}$$

where $\pi_e^* \geq 0$ and $\sum_e \gamma_e c_e \pi_e^* = 1$. Compared to (7.2.6), we need to be aware of a critical issue. Since at optimality, some π_e^* can be equal to 0, this means that link metric system w_e^* as given in (7.2.8) can produce zero weights. This will not be acceptable for the OSPF protocol since it requires the link weight values to be at least 1; on the other hand, this will work in the IS-IS protocol where a link metric of value 0 is allowed. Thus, the use of a specific primal objective function for obtaining the dual-based weights can matter depending on the link-state routing protocol.

Suppose, we associate artificial weights to both the residual capacity (refer to (7.2.3)) and the maximum link utilization. We can then consider minimizing the following composite function:

$$\boldsymbol{F} = \alpha \sum_e b_e \sum_d \sum_p \delta_{edp} x_{dp} + \beta r. \tag{7.2.9}$$

subject to constraints (7.2.7b) and (7.2.7c). Note that weights $\alpha \geq 0$ and $\beta \geq 0$ used in the above (composite) objective function has no relation to link weights, w_e. In this case, the appropriate optimal weight system $\boldsymbol{w}^* = (w_1^*, w_2^*, ..., w_E^*)$ would be (Exercise 7.8)

$$w_e^* = \alpha b_e + \pi_e^*, \quad e = 1, 2, ..., E. \tag{7.2.10}$$

Thus, as you can see, depending on the objective, different weight systems can be determined (Exercise 7.9). We finally add that both OSPF and IS-IS additionally require integral, upper-bounded weights. This requirement can be fulfilled by multiplying the largest weight by an appropriate factor W to make it equal to the upper bound, multiply the rest of the weights by the same factor W, and round them up.

In the above cases, if for each demand d only one shortest-path exists, the basic ECMP shortest-path routing allocation problem A/ECMP/BLD is automatically solved. However, in general, the uniqueness of the shortest-paths cannot be guaranteed. If the uniqueness is not possible for a particular problem, we can still try to use link metric system $\boldsymbol{w}^*$ according to the ECMP rule. In general, this can lead to a non-feasible solution to A/ECMP/BLD, since flows that solve primal Problem (7.2.2) are in general different than those generated with the ECMP rule (Exercise 7.10). However, since in many practical networks, the network capacity is designed to be maintained at a utilization of, for example, 60% or less, we can use the optimal link metric system $\boldsymbol{w}^*$ to re-compute the ECMP based flow allocation $x_{dp}(\boldsymbol{w}^*)$ and check if the feasibility of A/ECMP/BLD is maintained (see Algorithm 7.1 for how to compute ECMP flow allocation). Nevertheless, if the number of demands with multiple shortest-paths is not large and when the number of the shortest-paths for such demands is low (2 to 3 shortest-paths) then we may expect that ECMP flows will generate link loads about the same as the non-ECMP based optimal solution.

The connection between link metric and the dual multipliers is important. It gives us ways to develop good algorithms for determining link metrics as shown in Section 7.3.3.

7.3 HEURISTIC DIRECT METHODS FOR DETERMINING THE LINK METRIC SYSTEM

As shown in Section 7.10, the shortest-path routing allocation Problem (7.1.4) is $\mathcal{NP}$-complete and, hence, it is difficult to solve as the problem size grows. Also, the branch-and-bound (BB) and branch-and-cut (BC) methods may not always be effective for the MIP formulations introduced in Section 7.2.1. Hence, heuristic methods are needed. In this section, we present three heuristic algorithms, based on local search, SAN and Lagrangian relaxation (LR). We refer to them as direct methods since these approaches work directly with the link weight systems as decision variables. Numerical results illustrating the introduced methods will be discussed later in Section 7.5.

7.3.1 *Weight Adjustment (WA)*

The method presented below is an intuitive, local search procedure (Section 5.3.1) that tries to directly compute a feasible link weight system for A/ECMP/BLD. The method is based on an iterative adjustment of the link weights on the basis of the current link loads with respect to their (fixed) capacities. The algorithm increases the weights of overloaded links and reduces the weights of under-loaded links and handles the integral weight systems of the form (7.1.1):

$$1 \le w_e \le K, \text{ and } w_e\text{—integer}, \quad e = 1, 2, ..., E. \tag{7.3.1}$$

The method is described in detail in [GPS⁺00], [PSH⁺02] and is briefly summarized later, as a reference point method used for comparisons with more sophisticated algorithms (Section 7.5).

WA algorithm starts from some initial weight system $\boldsymbol{w}$, e.g., from randomly generated link weights according to (7.3.1), independently for each link. This heuristic works iteratively and is based on two local search procedures:

weight adjustment: when the network is overloaded (i.e., when there is at least one link e with the load $\underline{y}_e$ exceeding its "effective" capacity $\gamma_e c_e$) the procedure decrements by weights of overloaded links, and decreases weights for under-loaded links.

load optimization: when the network is under-loaded, exactly two links are selected—the most and the least loaded ones—and their weights are adjusted to achieve the highest network utilization.

The idea is as follows. In each iteration, first all of the demands are routed using the ECMP rule according to the current weight system, and then the current cost of each link (ξ_e) is calculated as follows. If link e is overloaded, its cost is made equal to the sum of its effective capacity and the square of its load minus its effective capacity, i.e., $\xi_e = \gamma_e c_e + (\underline{y}_e - \gamma_e c_e)^2$. If link e is under-loaded, its cost is made equal to its current load $\underline{y}_e$, i.e., $\xi_e = \underline{y}_e$.

If a link is overloaded, its weight is increased in order to attempt to remove some flows from it. The magnitude of the increase depends on the value of ξ_e and the absolute value of the difference between the previous cost ξ_e and the current cost ξ_e.

The metric of an under-loaded link is adjusted only at every several iterations. It was discussed in [PSH+02] that if the weights of under-loaded links are updated too frequently (e.g., at each iteration), undesirable cycles can occur, disturbing the convergence of the algorithm. To positively overcome this difficulty, we use the following procedure. Each link e is assigned a randomly initialized integral attribute — counter(e). If link e is under-loaded, the value of counter(e) is decremented at each iteration, and the link weight is updated only if it becomes overloaded or if counter(e) becomes negative. When the link weight is adjusted due to the under-load condition, counter(e) is reset randomly. The random setting is another factor helping to avoid cycles in the optimization process. At each iteration the algorithm evaluates the current weight system with respect to: 1) minimization of the number of overloaded links, and 2) minimization of the magnitude of the average link overload.

If the algorithm finds a weight system at which the network is under-loaded, the goal of the optimization is changed. One of the three following alternative objectives can be selected: 1) maximizing the average residual capacity in the network, 2) maximizing the total residual capacity in the network, or 3) minimizing the variance of the residual capacity volumes on the links. The most loaded and least loaded links are found and their weights are increased and decreased by 1, respectively. Then all the demands are routed according to the new weight system, and the utilization of the network and other performance parameters are calculated. If the utilization of the network has decreased (i.e., the algorithm has moved towards the dedicated goal) the optimization is continued. If the utilization has increased, the algorithm uses randomly an acceptability criterion to decide whether the new weight system is acceptable or not. This criterion is similar to the one used in the SAN process (Section 7.3.2).

7.3.2 Simulated Annealing (SAN)

The SAN approach for integer programming problems has been discussed earlier in Section 5.3.2. Now, we will discuss its application to the ECMP shortest-path routing allocation Problem (7.1.4). Here, we will assume that we are interested in maintaining integral weight systems (7.3.1). Depending on the particular interest/goal of a network, an appropriate objective function can be used. Since we have already described several different objective functions, we will consider a generic objective $\boldsymbol{F}(\boldsymbol{w})$ which is to be minimized. In the description of SAN, described earlier in Algorithm 5.4, the function to be optimized was

was given in terms of $\boldsymbol{x}$. Therefore, for the ECMP problem, based on weight system $\boldsymbol{w}$, we can determine the induced flow $\boldsymbol{x}(\boldsymbol{w})$, which, in turn, is used to determine the objective function value, $\boldsymbol{F}(\boldsymbol{w})$.

Steps given in Algorithm 5.4 for the SAN approach are the same here except that now: 1) we need to assign a starting link weight system $\boldsymbol{w}$ at the start of the algorithm (analogous to initial $\boldsymbol{x}$ in Algorithm 5.4), 2) store the best weight system $\boldsymbol{w}^{best}$ (along with the best objective value $\boldsymbol{F}^{best}$) as the iteration progresses, and 3) we need to define the neighborhood movement given that we are at inner iteration k of the SAN algorithm (Algorithm 5.4).

In our case here, the starting metric system $\boldsymbol{w}$ can be randomly chosen or all weights can be set to 1 (i.e., the hop-count metric). Given a link metric system $\boldsymbol{w}$ at inner iteration k, a neighboring state (rather, a new link metric system in our case), $\boldsymbol{z}$, can be obtained by selecting a random link e' and incrementing or decrementing its weight by 1 randomly, i.e.,

$$\begin{aligned} e' &:= random\{1, 2, ..., E\} \\ z_{e'} &:= w_{e'} + random\{-1, 1\} \\ z_e &:= w_e \quad \text{if } e \neq e'. \end{aligned} \tag{7.3.2}$$

Certainly, we need to ensure in the above calculation that the new weight is in the acceptable range.

An important point to note in regard to using SAN in the case of the ECMP problems is that a neighboring state (which is another link metric system) may result in the same shortest-path system as before, and the objective function value would remain the same, unnecessarily increasing the overall computation time. Thus, other neighborhood selection processes can be thought of. For example, in [BGLM00a], a new weight system is defined with probability q in the way described above; with probability $1-q$ the weights are altered more drastically: a node is chosen randomly, and the weights of all its coincident links are set (randomly) to either the maximum or minimum value from the given predefined set of weight values.

7.3.3 Lagrangian Relaxation (LR)-Based Dual Approach

The LR-based dual approach (Section 5.4.1) is typically used for exploiting specially structured problems to develop decomposition algorithms, and to obtain a lower bound on the primal problem. In this section, we will show how the LR approach can be useful for determining the link metric system.

We start with Problem (7.2.2) where our objective was to maximize the residual capacity. Consider the generalized dual with respect to constraints (7.2.2c) which allows us to write the following Lagrangian:

$$\begin{aligned} L(\boldsymbol{x};\boldsymbol{\pi}) &= -\sum_e b_e(c_e - \sum_d\sum_p \delta_{edp}x_{dp}) + \sum_e \pi_e(\sum_d\sum_p \delta_{edp}x_{dp} - \gamma_e c_e) \\ &= \sum_e (b_e + \pi_e)\sum_d\sum_p \delta_{edp}x_{dp} - \sum_e b_e c_e - \sum_e \gamma_e c_e \pi_e \\ &= \sum_d\sum_p(\sum_e (b_e + \pi_e)\delta_{edp})x_{dp} - \sum_e b_e c_e - \sum_e \gamma_e c_e \pi_e \\ &= L_1(\boldsymbol{x};\boldsymbol{\pi}) - \sum_e b_e c_e - \sum_e \gamma_e c_e \pi_e, \end{aligned} \tag{7.3.3}$$

where $L_1(\boldsymbol{x};\boldsymbol{\pi}) = \sum_d\sum_p(\sum_e(b_e+\pi_e)\delta_{edp})x_{dp}$. The dual function is

$$W(\boldsymbol{\pi}) = \min_{\boldsymbol{x}\geq\boldsymbol{0}} L(\boldsymbol{x};\boldsymbol{\pi}) = -\sum_e b_e c_e - \sum_e \gamma_e c_e + \min_{\boldsymbol{x}\geq\boldsymbol{0}} L_1(\boldsymbol{x};\boldsymbol{\pi}) \quad \boldsymbol{\pi}\geq\boldsymbol{0}. \tag{7.3.4}$$

The subgradient maximization approach for finding optimal dual variables $\boldsymbol{\pi}$ is to start with some initial $\boldsymbol{\pi}^0$ (at iteration $k = 0$), and then iteratively update these multipliers in the dual optimization space in order to maximize the dual function. Suppose we are at iteration k with dual multipliers $\boldsymbol{\pi}^k$. Since the last two terms of the Lagrangian are not dependent on $\boldsymbol{x}$, we need to solve the following subproblem associated with $L_1(\boldsymbol{x};\boldsymbol{\pi})$ at iteration k:

$$\begin{aligned} \textit{minimize} \quad & \textstyle\sum_d\sum_p(\sum_e(b_e+\pi_e^k)\delta_{edp})x_{dp} \\ \textit{subject to} \quad & \textstyle\sum_p x_{dp} = h_d, \quad d = 1,2,\dots,D \\ & \boldsymbol{x}\geq\boldsymbol{0}. \end{aligned} \tag{7.3.5}$$

Note that the subproblem in $\boldsymbol{x}$ (when dual multipliers $\boldsymbol{\pi}^k$ are given) is separable for each demand d and is a simple linear programming problem that can be solved using the shortest-path allocation rule (refer to (4.1.4) in Section 4.1.1) with respect to link costs $b_e+\pi_e^k$. We'll denote such a dual multiplier dependent solution (dependent on the particular selection of the shortest-path flow allocation) by $\boldsymbol{x}^k(\boldsymbol{\pi}^k) = (x_{dp}^k : d = 1,2,\dots,D,\ p = 1,2,\dots,P_d)$.

We also need to determine a subgradient of dual function $W(\boldsymbol{\pi})$ at iteration k for updating the dual multipliers. Such a subgradient depends on the link loads resulting from the particular shortest-path allocation chosen and is given by:

$$\left.\frac{\partial W(\boldsymbol{\pi})}{\partial \pi_e}\right|_{\boldsymbol{\pi}=\boldsymbol{\pi}^k} = \sum_d\sum_p\delta_{edp}x_{dp}^k - \gamma_e c_e. \tag{7.3.6}$$

The above expression shows that a subgradient is equal to the link load minus the effective capacity. Now recall that the dual multipliers update computation as given by (5.4.4) in Section 5.4.1 implies that if the subgradient entry corresponding to a particular link is positive, i.e., when the link is overloaded, then the corresponding dual multiplier is increased (hence, the corresponding link will tend to appear in less shortest-paths); if this is negative, i.e., when the link is underloaded, then the multiplier is decreased (with lower bound 0; hence, the corresponding link will tend to appear in more shortest-paths).

We can consider a different objective function and go through the same exercise. For example, if we consider the composite function given in (7.2.9) as the primal objective to be minimized with constraints (7.2.7b) and (7.2.7c), we can again consider the Lagrangian dual as described above (see Exercise 7.11 for a detailed treatment). In this case, at dual iteration k, the subproblem analogous to (7.3.5) can be written as:

$$\begin{aligned} \textit{minimize} \quad & \textstyle\sum_d\sum_p(\sum_e(\alpha b_e+\pi_e^k)\delta_{edp})x_{dp} \\ \textit{subject to} \quad & \textstyle\sum_p x_{dp} = h_d, \quad d = 1,2,\dots,D \\ & \boldsymbol{x}\geq\boldsymbol{0}. \end{aligned} \tag{7.3.7}$$

ALGORITHM 7.1 ECMP Flow Allocation Algorithm (Given Demand d with Start Node i and End Node j and the Set of ECMP paths $\hat{\mathbb{P}}_{ij}$)

```
procedure ECMP_Allocation(i, j, h_d, P̂_ij)
begin
  S_ij = {e : e is first link of path P ∈ P̂_ij};
  n_ij := |S_ij|;        // number of elements in S_ij
  h' := h_d / n_ij;
  for e ∈ S_ij do
    begin
      i' := otherendoflink(e, i);
      y_e := y_e + h';
      if i' ≠ j then
        begin
          P̂_i'j = {P\{e} : e is first link of path P ∈ P̂_ij};
              // set of ECMP paths but exclude link e
          ECMP_Allocation(i', j, h', P̂_i'j)
        end
      return
    end
end { procedure }
```

Note that in this case, the link cost at iteration k is $\alpha b_e + \pi_e^k$. Regardless of the original objective, it is important to note that at iteration k the subproblem solution flow x_{dp}^k may not be feasible for the original problem since the capacity constraint may not be satisfied. Secondly, we are primarily interested in a weight system that is workable with the ECMP rule. Since link weight, $\alpha b_e + \pi_e^k$, at iteration k can lead to minimizing subproblem (7.3.7) where multiple shortest-paths for a particular demand d are found, we can apply the ECMP rule for flow allocation when solving problem (7.3.7) at iteration k. That is, we spread flow allocation x_{dp}^k of demand volume h_d on all the shortest-paths so that the allocation is ECMP compliant (see Algorithm 7.1 for details on how the ECMP flow allocation works; see also [ERP02]). Note that when link metric, $\alpha b_e + \pi_e^k$, induces multiple shortest-paths for a particular demand d, it is indeed possible to allocate all demand volume for this d to just one of the shortest-paths, instead of doing ECMP flow. The difference now is that the ECMP-based flow allocation at each iteration k would drive towards computing a subgradient which is different than the one corresponding to allocating flow on just one of the shortest-paths at the same iteration k for a specific demand d—this, in turn, impacts the updating of π and as a result could conceivably lead us to an eventual weight system that is primal feasible under the ECMP rule. Computational results are presented later in Section 7.7.

7.4 TWO-PHASE SOLUTION APPROACH

Below we discuss a two-phase approach for Problem (7.1.4), presented in [GPS+00]. Both phases are based on mathematical programming problems: Phase 1 on a mixed integer programming problem, and Phase 2 on a linear programming problem. The idea is to allocate all demands to single paths (Phase 1) and then try to find a weight system for which the paths realizing demands are the unique shortest-paths (Phase 2).

An additional motivation behind the two-phase approach is that it leads to weight system w with the property that for each demand there is only one unique shortest-path with respect to w (Exercise 7.12). The reader may wonder why we are interested in obtaining unique shortest-paths when the diamond network example discussed in Section 7.1.3 has demonstrated that unique shortest-paths are not necessarily good. This is where we need to understand the difference between a specific example and a general typical case. It is often possible to devise examples where a certain principle (such as a unique shortest-path requirement) may not be a good choice. On the other hand, as already mentioned, we need to remember an important property (refer to Proposition 4.1 and its illustration through Example 4.2) which says that for the considered weight-independent flow allocation problems there are at most $D+E$ non-zero flows. This means that for a large network (a typical case) we have mostly unique shortest-paths and only a small percentage of demand pairs that have multiple shortest-paths. In a nutshell, this means that a procedure to determine the unique shortest-path is scalable in the sense of the quality of results and, hence, is of great importance.

Having the situation of unique shortest-paths allows us to apply the simplest version of the Dijkstra's shortest-path algorithm at the nodes in order to determine routing tables. Unfortunately, no effective necessary and sufficient condition for a system of unique paths to be generated by a certain weight system from $\boldsymbol{W}$ is available (for discussion of this problem, for example, see [BGL00], [FSS98]). Hence, the two-phase approach, although simpler than the direct one, does not always lead to a feasible solution because of possible non-feasibility of the Phase 2 problem.

7.4.1 Formulation of the Two-Phase Optimization Problem

We first present Phase 1 using the maximum residual capacity as the objective (certainly, other objectives can be used).

Phase 1: **Link-Path Formulation**

Single-Path Flow allocation Problem

indices

- $d = 1, 2, ..., D$ demands
- $p = 1, 2, ..., P_d$ candidate paths for demand d
- $e = 1, 2, ..., E$ links

constants

- h_d volume of demand d
- b_e value of one capacity unit of link e
- δ_{edp} = 1 if e belongs to path p realizing demand d; 0, otherwise

c_e capacity of link e

γ_e capacity utilization coefficient for link e

variables

u_{dp} binary variables forcing the single-path flow of demand d on path p

objective

$$\text{maximize } \boldsymbol{F} = \textstyle\sum_e b_e(c_e - \sum_d(\sum_p \delta_{edp} u_{dp}) h_d) \qquad (7.4.1a)$$

constraints

$$\textstyle\sum_p u_{dp} = 1, \quad d = 1, 2, ..., D \qquad (7.4.1b)$$

$$\textstyle\sum_d(\sum_p \delta_{edp} u_{dp}) h_d \leq \gamma_e c_e, \quad e = 1, 2, ..., E. \qquad (7.4.1c)$$

For the purpose of Phase 2 the paths obtained from Phase 1 are renumbered so that the paths with $p = 0$ are the ones that carry the entire demand volume (i.e., $u_{d0} = 1$ for each demand d). The following LP problem [BGL00] gives the necessary and sufficient condition for existence of a weight system $\boldsymbol{w}$ yielding the paths identified by $(d, 0)$ as the unique shortest-paths. This LP problem is feasible if and only if the required weight system uniquely generating the shortest-paths $(d, 0)$ exists.

Phase 2: Shortest-Path Uniqueness Test

variables

w_e metric of link e (continuous variable)

constraints

$$\textstyle\sum_e \delta_{ed0} w_e + 1 \leq \sum_e \delta_{edp} w_e, \quad d = 1, 2, ..., D \quad p = 1, 2, ..., P_d \qquad (7.4.2a)$$

$$w_e \geq 1, \quad e = 1, 2, ..., E. \qquad (7.4.2b)$$

Although, formally, the list $p = 0, 1, ..., P_d$ should contain all the network simple paths for each demand d, the above LP can be easily solved without generating all constraints (7.4.2a). This is simply because if the above LP is not feasible for a certain set of routing lists then it is not feasible. However, if the LP is feasible for a certain set of candidate path lists, then it can be infeasible for larger lists. To examine this possibility we generate, for the solution $\boldsymbol{w}$ for the current lists, two shortest-paths for each demand (see Appendix C for how to compute k-shortest-path algorithm) and if paths which are not on the current lists appear, they are added to the candidate path lists and the LP (7.4.2) is solved again.

This iterative path-generation process is repeated until either the problem is infeasible or no new shortest-paths can be found, implying that the required weight system $\boldsymbol{w}$ exists.

An important variation of Problem (7.4.2) is to consider determination of the positive integer weight system; in this case, constraints (7.4.2b) can be replaced by $1 \le w_e \le K, e = 1, 2, ..., E$ where w_e take integer values (for example, see [BMLG01]).

7.4.2 Solving Phase 1

Phase 1 includes solving integer programming problems which can be effectively solved for small networks by means of MIP solvers, such as CPLEX [CPL99] and XPRESS-MP [XM]. However, available exact methods for MIPs (for example, BB methods, see Chapter 5 and [Gef01]) can fail for large networks because of excessive time and memory requirements. Fortunately, in the considered single-path allocation case, the approximate heuristic methods can be effective in terms of solution quality (suboptimality) and of acceptable computation times. Below we describe two such approaches for solving Phase 1: evolutionary algorithm (EA) and simulated allocation (SAL).

Evolutionary Algorithm (EA)

Application of the EA approach to the single-path allocation problem A/SPA presented in Section 4.2.3 has been discussed earlier in Section 5.3.3. Here, we briefly recall this application to show its relevance to problem A/ECMP/BLD. EA works with full allocation states $\boldsymbol{u} = (u_{dp} : d = 1, 2, ..., D, p = 1, 2, ..., P_d)$, called chromosomes, satisfying constraints (7.4.1b). Within a chromosome, each subsequence $\boldsymbol{u}_d = (u_{dp} : p = 1, 2, ..., P_d)$ is called a gene (corresponding to demand d). Constraints (7.4.1c) are taken into account via a penalty function, as will be shown below.

The algorithm starts with forming an initial population $\boldsymbol{P}$ of M chromosomes, each generated randomly, with all genes satisfying constraints (7.4.1b). At each step k, a set Θ of L chromosomes is formed. Each element of this set is obtained as an outcome of the crossover operations on two (parent) chromosomes of population $\boldsymbol{P}$ (parents). Each parent is selected from the population with the probability proportional to its fitness function

$$\boldsymbol{F}(\boldsymbol{u}) = \sum_e \left(\max \left\{\sum_d (\sum_p \delta_{edp} u_{dp}) h_d - \gamma_e c_e, 0\right\}\right)^2. \tag{7.4.3}$$

Having fixed the parents, their offspring is formed by randomly taking gene by gene from the parents (gene $\boldsymbol{u}_d$, $d = 1, 2, ..., D$, is taken from a parent with probability $\frac{1}{2}$).

Next, each chromosome from the so-formed set Θ is mutated. The mutation consists in randomly changing the current allocation path in each gene of the mutated chromosome with a low probability q (e.g., $q = 1/D$).

Finally, the next population is formed by taking the best, according to the fitness function, elements out of the previous population $\boldsymbol{P}$ and the set Θ. The main step is repeated until the fitness function of the best chromosome in the current population is equal to 0, or there is no improvement in the consecutive k steps (i.e., the best chromosome has the same positive value of the fitness function in k consecutive steps).

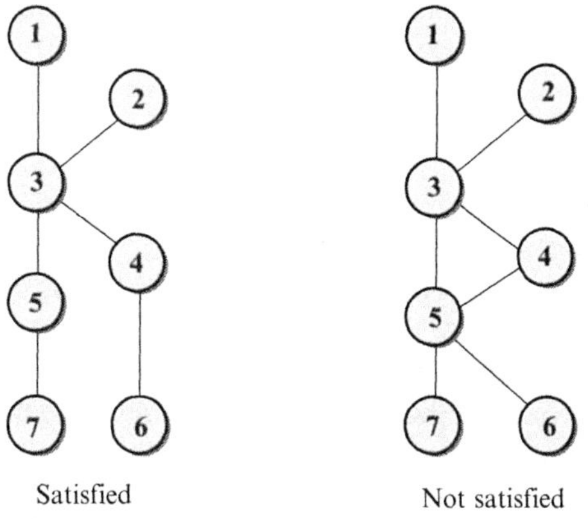

FIGURE 7.4 A Necessary Condition

Simulated Allocation (SAL)
Below we describe an application of SAL (refer to Section 5.3.4) described in [GPS⁺00]. This approach is particularly well suited for Phase 1 because of the assumed single-path allocation and because the generated paths can be forced to fulfill a necessary shortest-path uniqueness condition. In the proposed application any set of currently used paths fulfills a simple necessary uniqueness condition illustrated in Figure 7.4. This condition ([BGL00], [FSS98]) requires that if two paths meet at a certain node, they must continue their way along a common sequence of links until they split for good; for example, in Figure 7.4 the paths 1-3-5-7 and 2-3-4-6 on the left side satisfy this condition; on the other hand, the paths 1-3-5-7 and 2-3-4-5-6 to the right do not (also, see Section 2.5). The condition is known to be rather powerful [BGL00], [FSS98]. Note that for undirected graphs it is easy to check the condition for a given pair of paths: if the paths are not disjoint, the number of common nodes must be exactly equal to the number of common links plus 1.

The SAL algorithm works with partial allocation flow vectors (states) $\boldsymbol{u} = (u_{dp} : d = 1, 2, ..., D, p = 1, 2, ..., P_d)$ of variable "length": $|\boldsymbol{u}| = \sum_d \sum_p u_{dp}$. The algorithm starts with the all zero-flow solution ($u_{dp} \equiv 0$) and in each step chooses, with probability $q(|\boldsymbol{u}|)$, between *allocate*($\boldsymbol{u}$), i.e., adding one demand allocation to the current flow vector $\boldsymbol{u}$, and disconnect($\boldsymbol{u}$), i.e., removing one or more demand allocations from the current solution $\boldsymbol{u}$. We require that $q(|\boldsymbol{u}|) > \frac{1}{2}$, except for maximal allocation states $\boldsymbol{u}$ for which $q(|\boldsymbol{u}|) = 0$; we say that $\boldsymbol{u}$ is a maximal allocation state if all demands are allocated: i.e., $|\boldsymbol{u}| = D$). Whenever a complete allocation state is reached, a check is made whether the best cost reached so far, $\boldsymbol{F}^{best}$, is improved. Procedure disconnect($\boldsymbol{u}$) can be used in two different ways:

disconnect_1($\boldsymbol{u}$):	remove from $\boldsymbol{u}$ one previously allocated demand flow (at random)
disconnect_2($\boldsymbol{u}$):	remove from $\boldsymbol{u}$ all the demand flows which use all the overloaded links and, additionally, from a set of randomly, independently chosen links (with a certain probability).

The second variation is applicable if (and only if) the maximal allocation state is reached or if the current auxiliary cost

$$F(u) = \sum_e \max\{\sum_d(\sum_p \delta_{edp} u_{dp}) h_d - \gamma_e c_e), 0\} \qquad (7.4.4)$$

(expressing the total exceeded link capacity in the current allocation state) becomes greater than the current value of F^{best}.

Procedure *allocate*(u) assigns demand flow h_d to a selected path and increments the corresponding entry u_{dp} by 1. The demand d to be allocated is chosen at random from the set of the not yet allocated demands; for a given d, the allocation path p is selected using a shortest-path algorithm (see below). It is of crucial importance that a new demand be allocated only to a path that satisfies, together with the allocation paths used in the current solution u, the necessary single-path feasibility condition described at the beginning of this section.

The allocation probability q depends on the state through the number of allocated demands, i.e., $q = q(|u|)$ (note that $q(0) = 1$ and $q(D) = 0$). One way to settle the allocation probabilities is to choose a threshold $\underline{D}$ ($0 \leq \underline{D} \leq D$, e.g., $\underline{D} = 0.8D$), and to set $q(k) = 1$ for $k \leq \underline{D}$ and $q(k) = \underline{q}$ for $\underline{D} < \underline{k} < D$, for some fixed $\underline{q} > \frac{1}{2}$.

The algorithm is terminated either when a feasible solution to the Phase 1 allocation problem is found or when the assumed limit on the number of steps (execution of the main loop) is reached.

To find an allocation path for the currently selected demand, any standard shortest-path labeling algorithm can be used (e.g., Dijkstra's algorithm) with a modified way of labeling the nodes. The modification affects the way new nodes are labeled from the already labeled ones. Consider a graph with undirected links. For each node pair $\langle a,b \rangle$ there is a specified attribute $n(a,b)$ equal to the number of times the two nodes belong to the same path in the set of the currently allocated paths. When a demand is removed, the attribute $n(a,b)$ is decremented by 1 for all node pairs $\{a,b\}$ belonging to the path being just disconnected.

When a demand between nodes s and t is to be allocated, the shortest-path tree starting from node s is built according to the standard labeling rule with the following, important adjustments.

Suppose we are at a labeled node a and node a is on the path s-c-...-d-f-...-a from node s in the tree under construction, and we consider labeling node b from node a. Then, we can label node b only when (Figure 7.5) the following cases hold.

Case 1.
Nodes a and b do not belong to a common path ($n(a,b) = 0$): the path s-c-...-d-f-...-a in the currently constructed tree cannot contain any node v belonging to a common allocation path with node b ($n(v,b) = 0$ for $v = s, c, ..., d, f, ..., a$).

Case 2.
Nodes a and b belong to at least one common allocation path ($n(a,b) > 0$): the path s-c-...-d-f-...-a in the currently constructed tree has the following property: nodes from s to d do not belong to a common allocation path with node b, and f-...-a-b is a sub-path of one of the currently allocated paths. The latter condition is equivalent to: edge a-b belongs to at least one path, and nodes f, a and b belong to at least one common path.

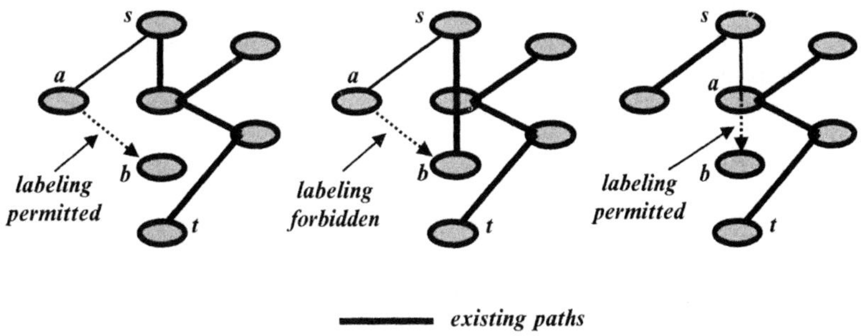

FIGURE 7.5 Node's Labeling

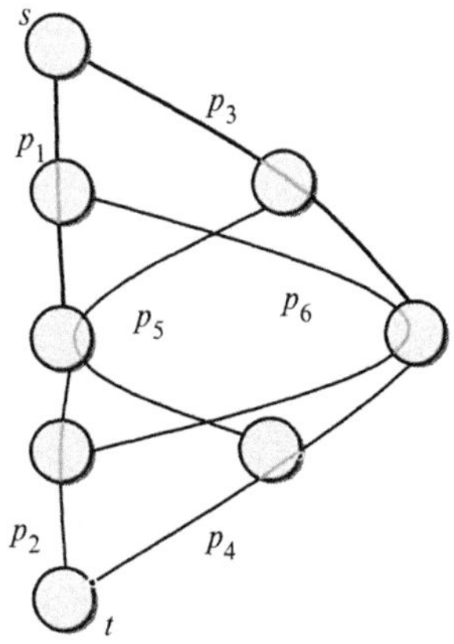

FIGURE 7.6 A Blocking Situation in SAL

If node t is reached, an allocation path is found and the demand volume between nodes s and t is allocated to this path. Then the attribute $n(a, b)$ is incremented by 1 for all node pairs $\langle a,b \rangle$ belonging to the selected path.

When demand d is being allocated in state $\boldsymbol{u}$, the metric of link e used in the labeling decisions is equal to $1 + K \cdot (\max\{0, \underline{y}_e(\boldsymbol{u}) + h_d - \gamma_e c_e\})^2 + b_e$. In the preceding definition $\underline{y}_e(\boldsymbol{u})$ is the load of link e in state $\boldsymbol{u}$ (i.e., $\underline{y}_e(\boldsymbol{u}) = \sum_d(\sum_p \delta_{edp} u_{dp})h_d)$) and K is a fixed positive number. The definition of b_e, which takes the history of the process into account, is somewhat more complicated: b_e is incremented each time the capacity of link e is exceeded during optimization. Still, b_e is bounded—its value cannot exceed a certain fixed upper bound B (if b_e reaches bound B then it stays with this value).

The above described labeling procedure works as well for directed graphs. Note, however, that in both cases there may be situations when a new path cannot be allocated because the existing consistent set of paths blocks all the paths from s to t. An example shown in Figure 7.6 [Tom00] depicts such a situation: all paths from s to t are inconsistent with the consistent set of paths $\{p_1, p_2, ..., p_6\}$. Such situations are more frequent the higher the ratio D/E is. Fortunately, due to the stochastic character of SAL, when a blocking situation is encountered for some current set $\mathbb{P}$ of allocated paths and for some demand d, sooner or later demand d will be allocated because the current set $\mathbb{P}$ is constantly changing in a stochastic manner.

7.4.3 Solving Phase 2

Problem (7.4.2) for Phase 2 can be effectively solved by considering only the meaningful constraints through consecutive generating of two shortest-paths for each demand [BGL00]. An alternative formulation is discussed in [FSS98]. Below we give another necessary and sufficient condition based on the duality theory, especially useful for testing a system of paths for not being realizable. The following property holds.

Property 7.1

A system of weights $\boldsymbol{w} = (w_1, w_2, ..., w_E)$ exists with $w_e \geq 0$ and $\sum_e w_e = 1$, such that for each demand $d = 1, 2, ..., D$ the path $(d, 0)$ is the unique shortest-path if and only if the following LP problem is feasible.

Dual of Shortest Path Uniqueness Test

constants

r_{edp} $= 0$ if both path number 0 and path number p ($p = 1, 2, ..., P_d$) realizing demand d contain link e, or both paths do not contain link e

$= 1$ if path p ($p = 1, 2, ..., P_d$) realizing demand d contains link e, and path number 0 does not

$= -1$ if path p ($p = 1, 2, ..., P_d$) realizing demand d does not contain link e, and path number 0 does

variables

σ_{dp} non-negative continuous variable

constraints

$$\sum_d \sum_{p>0} r_{edp} \sigma_{dp} \leq 0, \quad e = 1, 2, ..., E \tag{7.4.5a}$$

$$\sum_d \sum_{p>0} \sigma_{dp} = 1 \tag{7.4.5b}$$

The proof is based on considering the dual to the following LP:

LP for Uniqueness Test

variables

w_e non-negative metric of link e (continuous variable)

z auxiliary continuous variable

objective

$$\text{maximize } \boldsymbol{F} = z \tag{7.4.6a}$$

TABLE 7.1 **Example Networks**

	No. of Links	Links Capacity	Total Capacity (Medium Overdim.)	Total Capacity (High Overdim.)	No. of Demands	Total Demand	Nodes/ Links Ratio
7 nodes	22	48,000	52,164	55,968	42	34,320	0.32
14 nodes	42	329,280	342,342	352,308	182	172,320	0.33
28 nodes	84	2,192,744	2,283,988	2,347,868	756	892,492	0.33
56 nodes	224	9,784,716	9,863,190	11,040,272	3,080	3,340,320	0.25

constraints

$$\sum_e \delta_{ed0} w_e + z \leq \sum_e \delta_{edp} w_e, \quad d = 1, 2, ..., D \quad p = 1, 2, ..., P_d \tag{7.4.6b}$$

and showing that Problem (7.4.5) is infeasible if and only if Problem (7.4.6) is feasible and unbounded; the proof is left to the reader as Exercise 7.13.

7.5 IMPACT DUE TO STOCHASTIC APPROACHES

In this study, we consider four examples consisting of 7, 14, 28 and 56-node directed networks. The results are given for the basic shortest-path routing Problem (7.1.4) when γ_e is equal to 1. Each network was first dimensioned using a design (dimensioning) version of WA to generate three situations: saturated, with medium, and with high over-dimensioning of the links. Saturation means that the realization of demands consumes all available link capacity.

The example networks are characterized in Table 7.1. The results are reported for WA, SAN and SAL (in two-phase method). Note that an intrinsic feature of the SAL approach is the uniqueness of shortest paths. For all of the methods, the time values are averages over several runs, and they give the values for reaching the reported solutions for the first time during a single run. The following notation is used in the tables for this section:

AVRT = the average running time (in seconds)
POPT = the percent of feasible solutions found in all the runs
AVOL = the average number of overloaded links

Table 7.2 summarizes the performance of the methods for all four examples for the saturated case. Results for the remaining two cases, medium over-dimensioned and highly over-dimensioned, are given in Tables 7.3 and 7.4, respectively.

It may be noted that for small networks (7-node and 14-node networks) all the stochastic algorithms are comparable in terms of quality of results and computation time. For larger

TABLE 7.2 **Results for Saturated Case**

	7-Node Network			14-Node Network		
	WA	SAN	SAL	WA	SAN	SAL
AVRT	0.03	–	0.06	0.2	–	1.31
POPT	100	100	100	100	100	100
AVOL	0	0	0	0	0	0
	28-Node Network			**56-Node Network**		
	WA	SAN	SAL	WA	SAN	SAL
AVRT	13.7	–	198.96	155.8	–	1352
POPT	48	100	0	0	0	0
AVOL	4.3	0	7.4	61	18	85

TABLE 7.3 **Results for Medium Over-Dimensioned Case**

	7-Node Network			14-Node Network		
	WA	SAN	SAL	WA	SAN	SAL
AVRT	0.76	–	0.09	3.31	–	1.43
POPT	100	100	100	100	100	100
AVOL	0	0	0	0	0	0
	28-Node Network			**56-Node Network**		
	WA	SAN	SAL	WA	SAN	SAL
AVRT	19.26	–	47.38	155.77	–	3,211.2
POPT	100	100	100	0	0	0
AVOL	0	0	0	12	4	33.3

and tightly dimensioned networks the best results were obtained with SAN (at the expense of higher computational time). The SAN algorithm, when appropriately tuned, gives almost deterministic results. This is true, for example, for the 56-node networks when the algorithm run time is set to $\frac{1}{2}$ hour. With longer execution time (of about $2\frac{1}{2}$ hours), the algorithm is also almost deterministic and sometimes it finds better results in terms of the unused network capacity in the cases of over-dimensioned networks. WA also produces results of

TABLE 7.4 **Results for Highly Over-Dimensioned Case**

	7-Node Network			**14-Node Network**		
	WA	SAN	SAL	WA	SAN	SAL
AVRT	0.79	–	0.06	3.19	–	1.22
POPT	100	100	100	100	100	100
AVOL	0	0	0	0	0	0
	28-Node Network			**56-Node Network**		
	WA	SAN	SAL	WA	SAN	SAL
AVRT	201.21	–	16.95	156.54	–	2916.5
POPT	100	100	100	10	100	30
AVOL	0	0	0	3	0	9.9

good quality for the saturated and over-dimensioned networks; it is very fast and performs slightly better than SAL. For the 28-node network, SAL was not able to find any feasible solution; WA found feasible solutions in almost 50% of runs. Note, however, that for the 56-node saturated network no algorithm was able to find any feasible solution. For more realistic cases of medium over-dimensioned networks, WA and SAL produce results comparable with SAN, even for the 28-node network, but for 56 nodes the SAN is still the better approach (but, again, at the expense of very long computation times). It may be noted that SAL, while resulting in unique shortest paths, achieves this at the expense of feasibility.

In terms of the computational time, WA is clearly less time consuming than all the other stochastic methods. This method also gives good, consistent results for large networks and is very simple. SAL cannot currently compete with WA in terms of the execution times and the capability of computing near optimal solutions. Note, however, that in case of the medium over-dimensioned networks SAL gives results comparable to the other methods, even for the 56-node network; SAL was able to find a feasible solution in 30% of runs, comparing to 10% for WA (this is also the case for the highly over-dimensioned cases). The slow performance of SAL for large networks is caused by the phenomenon of blocking states, for which the algorithm is not able to find a new path consistent, in the sense of the necessary condition for the existence of a weight system, with the already allocated paths. In large networks with long paths this phenomena can be observed more often, making the method less effective.

7.6 IMPACT OF DIFFERENT LINK WEIGHT SYSTEM

Extensive results have been presented in [FT00] when different link weight systems were considered along with varying demand volumes. Here, we will highlight a subset of results from [FT00].

Two commonly used link weights in operational IP-OSPF networks are: 1) hop-count, and 2) a metric proportional to inverse of the link speed (bandwidth). We have already shown in Section 7.1.3 that the hop-count metric can lead to skewed flow distribution and, in turn, to excessive link congestion. In fact, it has been found in many operational networks that the network utilization is skewed, i.e., some links are highly utilized while others are not. Since we know that high-utilization leads to an increase in delay, this is not necessarily desirable if a highly utilized link is on the shortest-path to destination if hop metric is used. In recent years, another popular link weight has been to consider the inverse of the link speed. Although this does not take into account the traffic, this system has some merit since, in common sense, a high speed link can move packets faster and, thus, the delay is minimized. In fact, a connection between the *M/M/*1 delay function and the inverse of the link speed can be shown by considering the average delay on a link. Recall that for link e, if the capacity (in terms of data rate) is c_e and link load is $\underline{y}_e$ (assuming normalized average packet length), the average delay due to the *M/M/*1 is: $1/(c_e - \underline{y}_e)$. Now, if the link load is much smaller than the capacity, i.e., $\underline{y}_e \ll c_e$, then the link load factor can be essentially ignored. Thus, we can approximate the delay as:

$$\frac{1}{c_e - \underline{y}_e} \approx \frac{1}{c_e} \qquad \text{if } \underline{y}_e \ll c_e. \tag{7.6.1}$$

That is, the inverse of the link speed approximates the average delay quite well *if* the link load is substantially smaller than the capacity of the link. Since in many operational networks, the goal is to keep link utilization down (sometimes as low as 40%!), the use of the inverse of the link speed as the link weight metric can work. On the other hand, this metric still does not account for traffic. Thus, if the traffic in a network is highly asymmetric, the likelihood of the inverse of the link speed as the link metric causing skewed network utilization cannot be completely ruled out. Thus, to keep the utilization at an acceptable level in such an environment (if we still stay with the same rule for link weight: inverse of the link speed), the only option is to increase the capacity of the highly utilized links. On the other hand, using an optimal link weight system, it might be possible to keep the link utilization down (and meet the overall objective) *without* having to add more capacity immediately and prolong the capacity expansion as long as possible.

Now, we are ready to present the results. Besides considering link weights of hop count (labeled UnitOSPF) and the inverse of the link speed (labeled InvCapOSPF), the work presented in [FT00] have also considered Euclidean distance (labeled: L2OSPF), and a random weight (labeled RandomOSPF) along with their local search heuristic (labeled HeurOSPF). They compared them with the general optimal solution minimizing (7.1.11a), described as lower bound earlier in Remark 7.1 (labeled OPTOSPF). We present two types of plots: normalized cost and max-utilization. The normalized cost is the value of the objective ($\sum_e r_e$) (refer to model (7.1.11)) at optimality divided by the value of the same objective at optimality if the network had infinite capacity on each link (which would mean shortest hop-count for shortest path routing). Results for the 90-node AT&T WorldNet IP backbone network are shown in Figure 7.7 while results for a network with 100 nodes generated using a graph modeling tool described in [CDZ97] and [ZCB96] are shown in Figure 7.8.

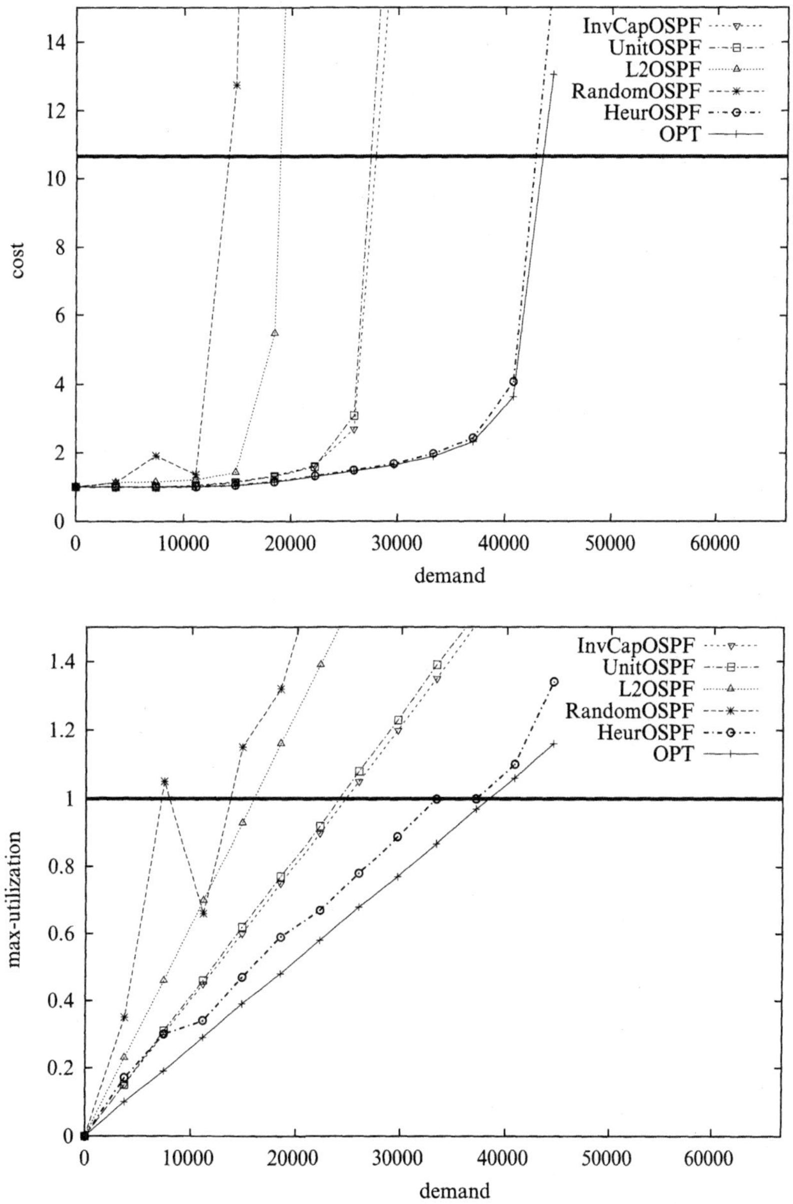

FIGURE 7.7 90-Node AT&T WorldNet Network—Cost and Utilization with Different Weight Systems for Varying Demand Volumes (From [FT00])

As expected, OPTOSPF shows the best results as demand volume increases. Also, as expected, at the low demand volume, all of the different link weight schemes perform about the same. The hop-count-based metric and the inverse of the link speed were found to be

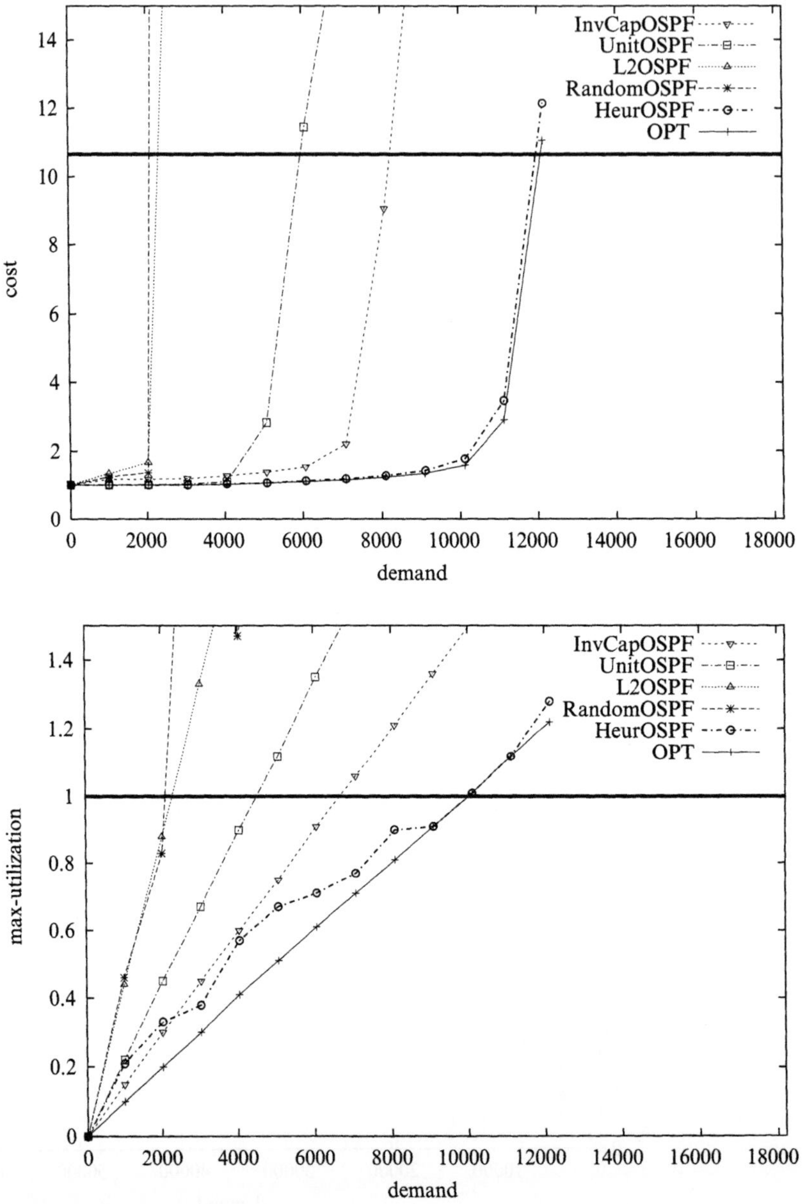

FIGURE 7.8 Two-Level 100-Node Model Network—Cost and Utilization with Different Weight Systems for Varying Demand Volumes (From [FT00])

about the same (in terms of the normalized cost as well as the maximum utilization) for the AT&T WorldNet backbone, while the inverse of the link speed-based metric does better than the hop-count-based metric for the 100-node network. For either network, the local search heuristic was found to be very close to the lower bound.

7.7 IMPACT ON DIFFERENT PERFORMANCE MEASURES

Earlier, we have mentioned several different objectives such as minimize maximum link utilization, maximize residual capacity, minimize a composite function, and minimize the Fortz-Thorup link cost function. In addition, we can also consider percentage of demand pair with unique shortest-path as another performance measure since this allows us to see what percentage of demands would have multiple shortest-paths, thus following the ECMP rule. In order to understand this, we have considered four example networks (Figure 7.9), and the capacity was determined based on a heuristic described later in Section 7.8.

In Table 7.5, we present values of various measures when different objectives were optimized with linear flow and capacity constraints and solved using an LP solver i.e., ignoring constraint due to weight system. The first column shows when the Fortz-Thorup function is optimized, the second column maximizes the residual capacity, and the third column is for minimization of maximum link utilization. For each of them, we have listed four measures when optimality was reached for the objective it was designed for: the value of the normalized Fortz-Thorup function (FT), the fraction of demand with multiple

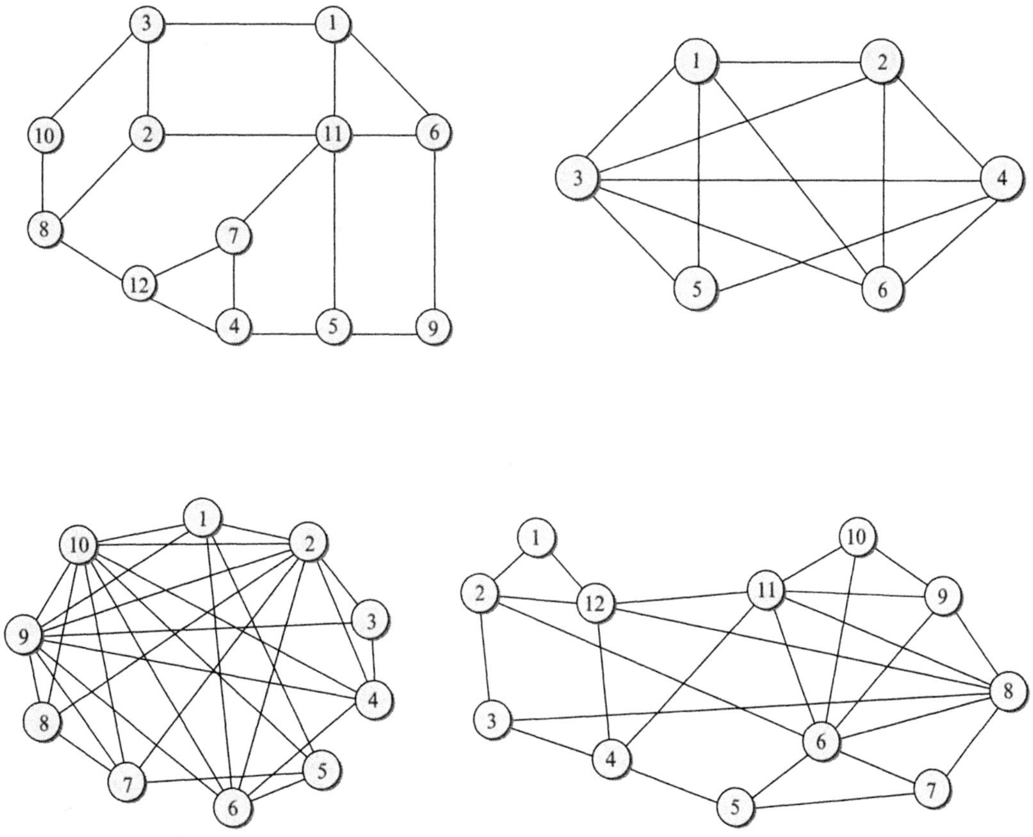

FIGURE 7.9 Example Networks (EN-I, EN-II, EN-III, EN-IV)

TABLE 7.5 **Comparative Performance Measures for Different Objectives**

ENs	(FT-min) FT, FD, FR, ML	(7.2.2a) (RCM) FT, FD, FR, ML	(MinMLU) FT, FT, FR,ML
I	2.00, 1.00, 0.33, 0.67	3.62, 0.20, 0.33, 1.00	2.00, 1.00, 0.33, 0.67
II	2.00, 0.40, 0.34, 0.67	4.51, 0.37, 0.34, 1.00	2.01, 1.00, 0.34, 0.67
III	2.06, 0.24, 0.33, 0.67	4.51, 0.33, 0.35, 1.00	2.07, 1.00, 0.33, 0.67
IV	2.00, 0.71, 0.34, 0.67	3.84, 0.33, 0.34, 1.00	2.02, 0.96, 0.33, 0.66

TABLE 7.6 **Composite Function LP Relaxed Case and LR-Based Dual Approach**

ENs	(α, β)	(Composite-LPmin)	(Composite-LR-ECMP)
ENs		f, FT, FD, FR, ML	f, FT, FD, FR, ML
EN I	$(0.4, 2^{10})$	1409, 2.00, 0.40, 0.33, 0.67	1409, 2.00, 0.00, 0.33, 0.67
EN II	$(0.8, 2^{10})$	5799, 2.00, 0.51, 0.33, 0.67	5958, 2.65, 0.04, 0.34, 0.90
EN III	$(1.1, 2^{10})$	13327, 2.55, 0.29, 0.35, 0.90	13910, 2.74, 0.00, 0.32, 0.91
EN IV	$(0.6, 2^{10})$	9179, 2.00, 0.52, 0.34, 0.67	9353, 2.32, 0.18, 0.34, 0.84

shortest-paths (FD), the fraction of residual capacity (FR), the maximum link utilization (ML). Note that FD was determined from a link metric obtained from the dual optimal solution. As in the last section, the normalized Fortz-Thorup (FT) is the value of the objective $(\sum_e r_e)$ (refer to model (7.1.11)) at optimality, divided by the value of the same objective at optimality if the network had infinite capacity.

In Table 7.6, we present results when the composite function was minimized with linear flow and capacity constraints using an LP solver in the column group "Composite-LPmin". For the results presented in the second column group "Composite-LR-ECMP", we use the Lagrangian-based dual approach with composite objective function (7.2.9); furthermore, in every dual iteration k, if any demand results in multiple shortest-paths, the flow allocation was based on ECMP. In both column groups, the entry f represents the value of the composite objective function at the end. Finally, the link metric obtained via the dual approach was scaled by multiplying by 1,000 and then rounding off to obtain the integer weight systems—the resulting values for different measures are for this integer weight system. As we can see, it appears that it is possible to find a good combination of (α, β) for the composite function (7.2.9), which can result in good maximum link utilization, and yet generate a link metric system that induces the lowest number of demands to have multiple

TABLE 7.7 **50% Additional Capacity: Minimum Maximum Utilization and Composite LR-based Dual Approach**

ENs n_ℓ	(MinMLU) fFT, FD, FR, ML	(Composite-LR-ECMP) FT, FD, FR, ML (α, β)
I	1.49, 0.93, 0.56, 0.44	1.49, 0.00, 0.56, 0.45 $(0.4, 2^{10})$
II	1.51, 1.00, 0.56, 0.45	1.53, 0.04, 0.56, 0.60 $(0.8, 2^{10})$
III	1.56, 1.00, 0.55, 0.45	1.65, 0.00, 0.55, 0.61 $(1.1, 2^{14})$
IV	1.50, 0.99, 0.56, 0.45	1.48, 0.18, 0.56, 0.56 $(0.6, 2^{10})$

shortest-paths. In Table 7.7, we present results for minimizing maximum link utilization and composite function based Lagrangian dual approach when capacity is increased by 50%. Note that even in this case, minimizing maximum utilization objective can make all the demands have multiple shortest-paths.

From the results, we can infer that maximum residual capacity objective tends to force (some) links to have 100% utilization, while minimization of maximum link utilization corrects this at the expense of generating multiple shortest-paths. The composite function can be used to get a happy medium between these two goals: 1) low maximum link minimization and 2) greatly reduced number of pairs with multiple shortest-paths. More details on results can be found in [SAPM03].

7.8 UNCAPACITATED SHORTEST-PATH ROUTING PROBLEM

The capacitated shortest-path routing problems such as A/ECMP/BLD have their uncapacitated counterparts. Thus, we present the network dimensioning problem below.

D/ECMP **Link-Path Formulation**

Design of ECMP Shortest-Path Routing Networks

constants

h_d volume of demand d

δ_{edp} = 1 if link e belongs to path p realizing demand d; 0, otherwise

ξ_e unit cost of modular capacity on link e

M modular capacity unit

variables

w_e non-negative metric of link e, $\boldsymbol{w} = (w_1, w_2, ..., w_E)$

y_e non-negative integral capacity of link e

objective

$$\textbf{minimize } \boldsymbol{F} = \textstyle\sum_e \xi_e y_e \qquad (7.8.1a)$$

constraints

$$\sum_p x_{dp}(\boldsymbol{w}) = h_d, \quad d = 1, 2, ..., D \tag{7.8.1b}$$

$$\sum_d \sum_p \delta_{edp} x_{dp}(\boldsymbol{w}) \leq M y_e, \quad e = 1, 2, ..., E. \tag{7.8.1c}$$

As for D/ECMP, $x_{dp}(\boldsymbol{w})$ denotes the flow realizing demand d on path p, implied by the link weight system $\boldsymbol{w}$. For a given weight system $\boldsymbol{w}$, the flows $x_{dp}(\boldsymbol{w})$ are computed according to the ECMP rule. D/ECMP is not a mathematical programming problem. For solving D/ECMPSPR direct methods of Section 7.4 and two-phase methods of Section 7.5 can be applied, after certain straightforward adjustments. It may be noted that in [HY], a network capacity design formulation is presented where the link metric system is directly considered.

For determining where to add capacity (i.e., the network extension problem), another approach could be to first solve (7.1.11). While this does not generate optimal weights, not necessarily a requirement during the capacity planning phase in OSPF networks, at optimal solution we do know how different links in the network would be utilized. In many cases, due to delay requirement, it is desirable that a network link is not overutilized. For example, a heuristic [SAPM03] would be to start with an initial capacity and solve the LP relaxed version of (7.1.11). Now identify the links that have utilization above an acceptable threshold (e.g., 66%) and increase the capacity of the links to maintain this threshold; the process of solving (7.1.11) is done again with the new capacity. This process continues until all links have utilization less than a certain threshold.

7.9 OPTIMIZATION OF THE LINK METRIC SYSTEM UNDER TRANSIENT FAILURES

In our discussion so far, we have assumed that we are given a demand volume matrix and that we want to find a link metric system that is optimal in terms of a given objective for a network. In doing so, we have also assumed that the network topology has not changed. It is easy to see that the flows in the network could change when a link in the network goes down—this would mean that different link metric systems may be appropriate for each specific link failure for optimal flow of traffic. Thus, a possibility is to enumerate all the failure states of interest, and compute an optimal link metric system for each of these states. While theoretically this can be done, we need to consider the practical aspect about this problem. Based on observation from an actual IP network, it has been pointed out [NSB+03] that 50% of failures last for < 1 minute, and 80% of failures last for < 10 minutes—these short-lived failures are called transient failures. Given the time window of a transient failure, there is usually not enough time to compute a new link-metric system off-line on a central processor and send back this information to all routers so the routers can use the new link metric system and invoke shortest-path computation for updating routing tables. Thus, it is desirable to determine one "good" link weight system in such a way that it works under the normal operating condition *as well as* under transient failures. That is the weight system is computed off-line only once taking into account failure states. This is then loaded to the routers. In case of an actual failure, link-state advertisement can still disseminate the state of the failed link. A router can now recompute (or sometimes partially compute) the routing table considering the same weight except for setting link metric of the failed link to infinity.

However, to be able to work under both conditions, we need to use an objective that captures both normal and transient failure states. It has been suggested that a weighted combination of the maximum link utilization under the normal state and the *worst* maximum link utilization over all failure states is a good objective in this regard as stated in [NSB+03]. Following this approach, we present here a comprehensive formulation of the link metric design problem that addresses both the normal state and all the failures states (also refer to Chapter 9 for related work on protection and restoration design of resilient networks).

In Section 2.8, we have first introduced and illustrated the idea of considering failure states by adding another subscript, s, to account for normal and failure states. Suppose we now have states $s = 0, 1, ..., S$ where $s = 0$ refers to the non-failure state, and failure states refer only to single link failures that do not completely isolate a node or a router. First, this means that we need the network topology to be two-connected. Second, we do not consider node failure; although node failure can be represented by considering failure of all links connected to it, the network also has reduced demand volume to carry/satisfy since no traffic out of the failed node can be routed anymore. Thus, we limit ourselves to link failure states, and primarily to single-link failure states.

Note that here we need to determine the same link metric system $\boldsymbol{w}$ that works for both non-failure and failure states. For clarity, for state $s = 0$, we will refer to this as $\boldsymbol{w}$; however, for failed state $s = e$, weights are the same as in $\boldsymbol{w}$ for all links except for link s, for which $w_s = \infty$; we refer to this weight system as $\bar{\boldsymbol{w}}_s$. For example, in state $s = 0$, the link metric system-induced flow, $x_{dp0}(\boldsymbol{w})$, on path p for demand d must be such that the demand constraint is satisfied. For a failure state s, induced flow $x_{dps}(\bar{w}_s)$ due to $\bar{\boldsymbol{w}}_s$ must satisfy the demand constraint. For state $s = 0$, we are interested in minimizing the maximum link utilization; similarly, for all failure states, we are interested in minimizing, the worst link utilization—this time over all failure states. We introduce a constant α_{es} which takes the value 1 if link e is operational in state s, and 0, if link e is down. For determining how much weight to give to the worst link utilization factor over all failure states, we introduce an artificial constant, ϖ, to allow us to weigh between normal and failure states. The problem formulation can be stated as follows.

Problem A/ECMP/TF **Link-Path Formulation**

ECMP Shortest-Path Routing: Transient Failure

indices

$d = 1, 2, ..., D$	demands
$p = 1, 2, ..., P_d$	allowable paths for flows realizing demand d
$e = 1, 2, ..., E$	links
$s = 0, 1, ..., S$	all possible states ($s = 0$, non-failure state)

constants

h_d	volume of demand d
δ_{edp}	= 1 if link e belongs to path p realizing demand d; 0 otherwise
c_e	capacity of link e
α_{es}	availability co-efficient of link e in state s. That is, if $\alpha_{es} = 1$ link e is available in state s; if $\alpha_{es} = 0$, link e is failed
γ_e	link capacity adjustment factor
ϖ	artificial parameter to weigh between two goals in the objective function ($0 \le \varpi \le 1$)

variables

w_e	metric of link e in normal state, $\boldsymbol{w} = (w_1, w_2, ..., w_E)$
$\bar{w}_{se}$	$\bar{w}_{se} = w_e$ if $e \neq s$; $\bar{w}_{se} = \infty$ if $e = s$.
$x_{dp0}(\boldsymbol{w})$	non-negative flow variable for demand d on path p in normal state $s = 0$, determined by the weight system $\boldsymbol{w}$
$x_{dps}(\bar{\boldsymbol{w}}_s)$	non-negative flow variable for demand d on path p in state s, determined by the weight system $\bar{\boldsymbol{w}}_s$
r	link utilization variable in state $s = 0$
$\bar{r}$	link overload variable over all failure states $s = 1, 2, ..., S$

objective

$$\text{minimize } \boldsymbol{F} = (1 - \varpi)r + \varpi\bar{r} \tag{7.9.1a}$$

constraints

$$\textstyle\sum_p x_{dp0}(\boldsymbol{w}) = h_d, \quad d = 1, 2, ..., D \tag{7.9.1b}$$

$$\textstyle\sum_d\sum_p \delta_{edp}\, x_{dp0}(\boldsymbol{w}) \le \gamma_e c_e r, \quad e = 1, 2, ..., E \tag{7.9.1c}$$

$$\textstyle\sum_p x_{dps}(\bar{\boldsymbol{w}}_s) = h_d, \quad d = 1, 2, ..., D \quad s = 1, 2, ..., S \tag{7.9.1d}$$

$$\textstyle\sum_d\sum_p \delta_{edp}\, x_{dps}(\bar{\boldsymbol{w}}_s) \le \alpha_{es}\gamma_e c_e \bar{r}, \quad e = 1, 2, ..., E \quad s = 1, 2, ..., S \tag{7.9.1e}$$

$$\boldsymbol{w} \in \boldsymbol{W}. \tag{7.9.1f}$$

There are a couple of important points to note here. As we have noted earlier in Section 7.1, 7.9.1 is not strictly a mathematical programming problem due to implicit dependency on the ECMP flow induced by the link metric system. Regardless, it is possible to consider the exact same set of candidate path lists for both normal and failures states. The constraints (7.9.1e) force flow $x_{dps}(\boldsymbol{w})$ (on path p for demand d) to be zero if path p contains the failed link; this is because α_{es}, which is on the right-hand side of these constraints, takes the value 0 in this case and there it forces the zero flow requirement on non-available paths.

Here, we only need one utilization variable, $\bar{r}$, for all failure states to capture the worst maximum utilization over all failure states due to the way constraint (7.9.1e) is structured.

The actual determination of the link metric system can be based on approaches we have already discussed in Sections 7.3 and 7.4, or the tabu search approach (Section 5.3.5) presented in [NSB$^+$03]. The LR-based dual approach (refer to Section 7.3.3) is also applicable here, and is left as an exercise (Exercise 7.14). In regard to the artificial weight ϖ, a general rule that works for all topologies and demand volume matrices is hard to determine; nevertheless, it has been suggested that $\varpi = 0.8$ meaning giving 80% weight to the maximum link utilization over all failure states is a reasonable value [NSB$^+$03].

Note that the objective can be generalized further since it is not clear ahead of time which objective should get higher weight. Thus, a multi-criteria objective (rather bi-criteria in our case) of minimizing the vector valued function $[r, \bar{r}]$ can be considered. As noted in Section A.1 of Appendix A, this results in a Pareto optimal situation. In fact, in a separate work, Yuan [Yua03] has considered a bi-criteria approach to incorporate transient failures. The Fortz-Thorup function was used to determine maximum congestion over both non-failure and failure states which is then minimized; this is left as an exercise (Exercise 7.15).

7.10 * $\mathcal{NP}$-COMPLETENESS OF THE SHORTEST-PATH ROUTING ALLOCATION PROBLEM

In this section, we present the main theoretical result for the shortest-path routing allocation problem showing that this is $\mathcal{NP}$-complete.

To do this we shall show that the so-called X3C Problem (Exact Cover by 3-Sets) ([SP2], [GJ79, p. 221]) can be transformed to (a simplified version of) A/ECMP/BLD (assume $\gamma_e = 1$ in (7.1.4) for this section). X3C is known to be $\mathcal{NP}$-complete and is as follows:

instance
Set $X = \{x_1, x_2, ..., x_p\}$ of $p = 3q$ elements ($|X| = p$) and a family C of n 3-subsets of X, $C = \{C_1, C_2, ..., C_n\}, C_i \subseteq X, |C_i| = 3$ for $i = 1, 2, ..., n$, $n \geq q$.

question
Does C contain a subfamily $C' \subseteq C$, of q ($|C'| = q$) pair-wise disjoint subsets of X?

PROPOSITION 7.1 *Problem A/ECMP/BLD is $\mathcal{NP}$-complete.*

Proof:

Consider the directed single-commodity flow graph depicted in Figure 7.10. Vertex s is the source, and vertex t is the sink. The vertices in the upper row correspond to the 3-sets of family C; on the other hand, the vertices in the lower row correspond to the elements of set X. The edges between the two rows reflect the incidence relation between family C and set X: vertex C_i is connected to vertex x_k if and only if $x_k \in C_i$ (in the considered example $C_1 = \{x_1, x_2, x_3\}$, $C_2 = \{x_2, x_4, x_k\}$ and $C_n = \{x_{k-1}, x_{k+1}, x_p\}$). Henceforth, we will assume that $X \subseteq \cup C$, i.e., that family C covers set X (otherwise X3C is trivial).

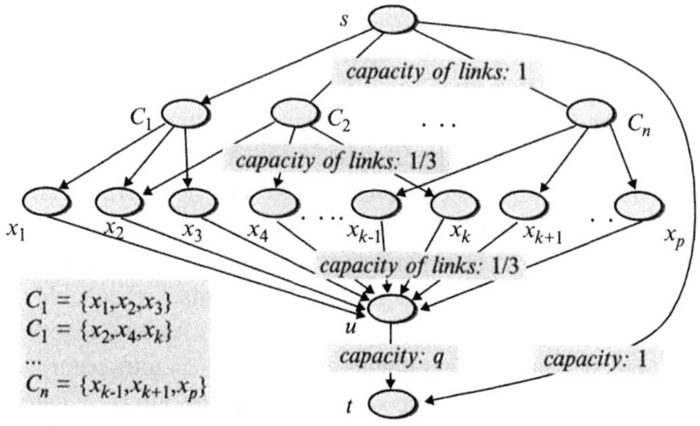

FIGURE 7.10 The Single-Commodity Flow Graph

It is easy to see that for the particular edge capacity values assumed in the considered graph, the value of the maximal flow from s to t is equal to $q + 1$. To see this we first note that the flow cannot be greater than $q + 1$, since no more flow than $q + 1$ can be received by the sink. On the other hand, we can saturate all of the edges incoming to vertex u and, hence, achieve the maximal flow. To do this, for each element of X we select one 3-subset from C that contains the considered element and assign flow $\frac{1}{3}$ to the corresponding edge. This operation determines how much flow must be assigned to each edge from the source to the first row of vertices. The maximal flow from s to t can be easily found in the described way in polynomial time.

Now let us constrain the admissible flows in the considered graph to ECMP flows. Recall that a flow f is an ECMP flow if for each vertex v the flows assigned to the edges outgoing from v are either equal to 0 or to some fixed vertex-dependent positive value. In other words, for any fixed vertex v and each edge of the form (v, w), a number $z(v)$ exists such that either the link flow equals to 0 or to $z(v)$ (i.e., $f(v, w) = 0$ or $f(v, w) = z(v)$). The basic observation leading to the $\mathcal{NP}$-completeness result is that the answer to the question in X3C is positive if and only if the maximal ECMP flow in the considered graph is equal to $q + 1$.

Suppose that the subfamily $C' = \{C_{i(1)}, C_{i(2)}, ..., C_{i(q)}\}$ exactly covers set X. We assign flow equal to 1 to all edges $(s, C_{i(j)})$ for $j = 1, 2, ..., q$ (i.e., $f(s, C_{i(j)}) = 1, j = 1, 2, ..., q$), and flow equal to 0 to the rest of the edges of the form (s, C_l). This assignment will force $f(x_k, u) = \frac{1}{3}$ for $k = 1, 2, ..., p$. Finally, assigning $f(s, t) = 1$ we arrive at an ECMP flow with a value of $q + 1$. Conversely, if the maximal ECMP flow is equal to $q + 1$, then, due to the ECMP assumption, this can be achieved only in one way: flow equal to 1 is assigned to edge (s, t) and to exactly q out of p edges of the form (s, C_l) (with $f(s, t) < 1$ the flow value $q + 1$ could not be achieved because of the capacity q assigned to link (u, t)). Note that this is the reason why edge (s, t) is necessary: without it, it would be possible, as illustrated in Figure 7.11, to find an ECMP flow with value q even if there would be no exact 3-cover. The only possible way to maintain flow of value q down in the main part of the graph (i.e., the left part, without edge (s, t)) is to saturate all edges incoming to vertex u.

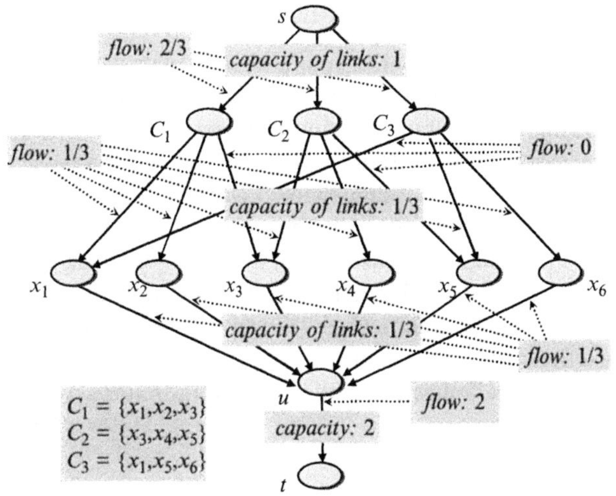

FIGURE 7.11 An Instance of the Single-Commodity Flow Graph

This implies that the vertices C_l with $f(s, C_l) = 1$ define the family C exactly covering set X.

Thus, we have proved our observation: the answer to the X3C question is positive if, and only if, the maximal ECMP flow is equal to $q + 1$. Hence, if we were able to find an ECMP flow equal to $q + 1$, or show that such a flow does not exist, in polynomial time, then we would give an answer to the X3C question in polynomial time. This proves $\mathcal{NP}$-completeness of the following ECMP flow problem:

instance
Integers p, q, n such that $p = 3q$ and $n \geq q$, and a graph of the structure depicted in Figure 7.10.

question
Does there exist an ECMP flow of value $q + 1$?

Note that any instance of the above can be solved by solving a corresponding instance of A/ECMP/BLD. Such instances of A/ECMP/BLD have only one demand $d = D = 1$ (between s and t) with volume h_1 equal to $q + 1$, and the path structure and link capacity specified by the graph in Figure 7.10. The task is to find a link weight system that combined with the ECMP rule defines an ECMP flow answering the question in the above ECMP flow problem. Note that every ECMP flow in the considered graph can be generated by the weight system defined by assigning weights $w = 1$ to all edges with positive flows in the main part of the graph (these flows are either 1, $\frac{1}{3}$, or q), weight $w = 4$ to edge (s, t), and weights $w = +\infty$ to all other edges. Thus, any algorithm solving A/ECMP/BLD solves also the above ECMP problem and, hence, X3C. This proves that A/ECMP/BLD is $\mathcal{NP}$-complete. ■

7.11 * SELFISH ROUTING AND ITS RELATION TO OPTIMAL ROUTING

In many distributed networks (not necessarily data networks), users can decide on a route from origin to destination that is beneficial to themselves rather than the overall benefit of the network. A road transportation network is such an example where the users want to take the least delay path from the origin to destination (as they perceive it); such behavior can be called "selfish", leading to the notion of "selfish routing." In Section 7.1.3, we have already illustrated how selfish routing works and compared its performance to the optimized OSPF/ECMP routing. In this section, following the work presented in [RT02], we discuss the notion of selfish routing in more detail and show a general connection between selfish routing and optimal routing, i.e., the routing with no specific constraints on the way the demand flows are constructed.

Consider the following routing flow optimization problem where $\underline{y}_e \le c_e$ is ignored.

A/FOL **Link-Path Formulation**
Flow Optimization with Latency Function
variables

x_{dp} non-negative flow on path p for demand d
$\underline{y}_e$ link load on link e, determined based on path flow x_{dp}

objective

$$\text{minimize } \boldsymbol{F} = \textstyle\sum_e \ell_e(\underline{y}_e)\underline{y}_e \tag{7.11.1a}$$

subject to

$$\textstyle\sum_p x_{dp} = h_d, \quad d = 1, 2, ..., D \tag{7.11.1b}$$

$$\textstyle\sum_d \sum_p \delta_{edp} x_{dp} = \underline{y}_e, \quad e = 1, 2, ..., E. \tag{7.11.1c}$$

Function $\ell_e(\underline{y}_e)$ is a generic *link-latency function* of the link load $\underline{y}_e$, which is, in turn, dependent on the flow allocation vector $\boldsymbol{x}$, i.e., $\ell_e(\underline{y}_e) = \ell_e(\underline{y}_e(\boldsymbol{x}))$. We assume $\ell_e(\cdot)$ to be non-negative, differentiable, and non-decreasing in its domain, and that $\ell_e(\underline{y}_e)\underline{y}_e$ is a convex function in $\underline{y}_e$. For brevity, we will refer to the product $\ell_e(\underline{y}_e)\underline{y}_e$ as *load-latency product*. You may have noticed that using a derivation similar to (7.1.5) we see that objective function (7.11.1a) is nothing else but the overall latency (with respect to the link-latency functions $\ell_e(\cdot)$) experienced by the network flows.

There are three important examples of the latency function $\ell_e(\cdot)$, especially for packet networks, as shown below:

$\ell_e(\underline{y}_e) = 1/\left(c_e - \underline{y}_e\right)$ – corresponds to average delay minimization (refer to (7.1.2))
$\ell_e(\underline{y}_e) = 1$ – minimum hop-routing
$\ell_e(\underline{y}_e) = 1/c_e$ – inverse of the link capacity.

Note that the first function is differentiable in its domain, $0 \le \underline{y}_e < c_e$. Since the objective function is dependent on the generic link-latency function, we will sometimes write the objective as a function of $\boldsymbol{x}$, and also with the dependency on $\ell_e(\cdot)$, where appropriate:

$$\boldsymbol{F}(\boldsymbol{x}) = \boldsymbol{F}(\boldsymbol{x} \mid \ell_e(\cdot)) = \textstyle\sum_e \ell_e(\underline{y}_e)\underline{y}_e.$$

In general, we will denote the globally optimal solution of the convex optimization Problem (7.11.1) by $\boldsymbol{x}^*$ and, thus, the optimal cost by $\boldsymbol{F}(\boldsymbol{x}^*) = \boldsymbol{F}(\boldsymbol{x}^* \mid \ell_e(\cdot))$ (Exercises 7.16).

In a selfish routing environment, the traffic for demand d tries to optimize its own gain by taking the minimum latency route from origin to destination end points of demand d. Given the link-latency function, we can write the latency "cost" of path p (*path-latency*) for demand d (refer to (2.4.12)) as:

$$\zeta_{dp}(\boldsymbol{x}) = \textstyle\sum_e \delta_{edp} \ell_e(\underline{y}_e) \tag{7.11.2}$$

A crucial property of selfish routing is that under the selfish behavior it is possible to reach traffic equilibrium which is known as *Nash equilibrium* ([Nas50a], [Nas50b]), or *Wardrop's first principle* [War52]. That is, traffic equilibrium is reached in such a way that all routes that are used between an origin-destination node pair have equal costs while all unused routes have a higher cost. Interestingly, the notion of traffic equilibrium goes back to the work of Knight [Kni24] in economics. For clarity, a flow allocation vector that satisfies (7.11.1b) at Nash equilibrium will be denoted by $\boldsymbol{x}^{\mathcal{N}}$ and referred to as the Nash flow vector. Formally, at Nash equilibrium, the Nash flow vector satisfies the following property:

DEFINITION 7.1 *A flow allocation vector $\boldsymbol{x}^{\mathcal{N}}$ satisfying (7.11.1b) is at Nash equilibrium if, and only if, for all demands d ($d = 1, 2, ..., D$) and path $p_{\mathcal{N}}$ where Nash flow is positive, $x_{dp_{\mathcal{N}}} > 0$, the following condition holds:*

$$\zeta_{dp_{\mathcal{N}}}(\boldsymbol{x}^{\mathcal{N}}) \le \zeta_{dp}(\boldsymbol{x}^{\mathcal{N}}) \quad \textit{for all other paths p of demand d.}$$

In other words, for any demand d, all paths that have positive flow at Nash equilibrium will have the same path-latency. Hence, if we denote the path-latency for positive flows of demand d at Nash equilibrium by $\mathcal{D}_d(\boldsymbol{x}^{\mathcal{N}})$, then we have:

$$\boldsymbol{F}(\boldsymbol{x}^{\mathcal{N}}) = \textstyle\sum_d \mathcal{D}_d(\boldsymbol{x}^{\mathcal{N}}) h_d. \tag{7.11.3}$$

Thus, by definition, flows at Nash equilibrium have a nice property that all users "within" one demand experience the same delay for a given network defined latency function.

Now, a natural question arises: what is the relation between optimal flow allocation vector $\boldsymbol{x}^*$ and the Nash flow vector $x^{\mathcal{N}}$? In order to discuss this, we first need to calculate the partial derivative of $\boldsymbol{F}$ with respect to x_{dp} which is given by:

$$\frac{\partial \boldsymbol{F}(\boldsymbol{x})}{\partial x_{dp}} = \textstyle\sum_e \delta_{edp} \dfrac{d(\ell_e(\underline{y}_e)\underline{y}_e)}{d\underline{y}_e} = \zeta_{dp}(\boldsymbol{x}) + \textstyle\sum_e \delta_{edp} \dfrac{\underline{y}_e d(\ell_e(\underline{y}_e))}{d\underline{y}_e} \tag{7.11.4}$$

For the optimal flow allocation vector $\boldsymbol{x}^*$ for Problem (7.11.1), the following optimality condition holds.

Proposition 7.2 *A flow allocation vector $\boldsymbol{x}^*$ is optimal for Problem (7.11.1) if and only if for all demands d ($d = 1, 2, ..., D$) and path p^* where optimal flow is positive, $x_{dp^*} > 0$, the following condition holds:*

$$\frac{\partial \boldsymbol{F}(\boldsymbol{x}^*)}{\partial x_{dp^*}} \leq \frac{\partial \boldsymbol{F}(\boldsymbol{x}^*)}{\partial x_{dp}} \quad \textit{for all other paths p for demand d.}$$

While the above proposition follows from the Karush-Kuhn-Tucker conditions (see Section A.2 in Appendix A), it is also easy to see from another angle [BG92]. Suppose we move a small amount of flow $\varepsilon > 0$ from optimal path p^* (with positive flow) to another path p for the same demand d. This would not improve the overall cost $\boldsymbol{F}$ and, in fact, the first order change in the cost incurred

$$\varepsilon \frac{\partial \boldsymbol{F}(\boldsymbol{x}^*)}{\partial x_{dp}} - \varepsilon \frac{\partial \boldsymbol{F}(\boldsymbol{x}^*)}{\partial x_{dp^*}}$$

must remain non-negative. This then leads to the result given in Proposition 7.2. Interestingly, as [BG92] puts it: *optimal path flow is positive only on paths with minimum first derivative length.* If multiple paths have positive flows in the optimal solution for the same demand d, then they all have the same minimum first derivative length.

Now, we will compare the similarities and differences between Nash flow (Definition 7.1) and optimal-flow (Proposition 7.2). Both refer to minimum path-latency; however, the difference is that the link cost associated with Nash equilibrium is based on the link-latency function, $\ell_e(\underline{y}_e)$, while for optimal flow, the link-latency is based on the *derivative* of $\ell_e(\underline{y}_e)\underline{y}_e$; in other words, they use different link metrics at the equilibrium. This observation was first made by Beckmann, McGuire and Winstem [BMW56] and has lead Roughgarden and Tardos [RT02] to state the following important corollary.

Corollary 7.3 *A flow allocation vector $\boldsymbol{x}^*$ is optimal for Problem (7.11.1) if and only if it is at Nash equilibrium in regard to the derivative link-latency function, $\frac{d(\ell_e(\underline{y}_e)\underline{y}_e)}{d\underline{y}_e}$.*

The above corollary has an important consequence in regard to understanding how far the flow at Nash equilibrium, $\boldsymbol{x}^{\mathcal{N}}$, is from the optimal flow, $\boldsymbol{x}^*$ in terms of the network objective. Specifically, this distance depends on the link-latency function growth rate; [RT02] presents the following important bound that shows the relation between the flow at Nash equilibrium and the optimal flow and, in turn, between selfish routing and optimal routing.

Corollary 7.4 *Consider the latency function $\ell_e(\cdot)$ and the constant $\Upsilon \geq 1$ that satisfy*

$$\ell_e(\underline{y}_e)\underline{y}_e \leq \Upsilon \cdot \int_0^{\underline{y}_e} \ell_e(s)ds \tag{7.11.5}$$

for all links e with $\underline{y}_e > 0$. Then

$$\boldsymbol{F}\left(\boldsymbol{x}^{\mathcal{N}} \mid \ell_e(\cdot)\right) \leq \Upsilon \cdot \boldsymbol{F}\left(\boldsymbol{x}^* \mid \ell_e(\cdot)\right).$$

An important question for us is: can we use this relation for a OSPF network environment? Indeed, this is possible if we consider special cases of the latency function stated at the beginning of this section which are relevant to packet networks. First consider the link-latency function, $\ell_e(\underline{y}_e) = 1$. This refers to the hop-count metric and the optimization Problem (7.11.1) which corresponds to minimizing total link occupancy due to minimum hop routing. In this case, we note that in fact $\Upsilon = 1$ and the following equality holds:

$$\ell_e(\underline{y}_e)\underline{y}_e = 1 \cdot \underline{y}_e = 1 \cdot \int_0^{\underline{y}_e} ds.$$

Thus, from Corollary 7.4, we have the (trivial) observation that the optimal flow and the Nash flow are the same from the objective function point of view for the link-latency function based on the hop-count metric, i.e., $\boldsymbol{F}\left(\boldsymbol{x}^{\mathcal{N}} \mid \ell_e(\cdot) = 1\right) = \boldsymbol{F}\left(\boldsymbol{x}^* \mid \ell_e(\cdot) = 1\right)$.

Recall now the objective of maximization of weighted residual capacity, A/ECMP/RCM (7.2.2), i.e., $\boldsymbol{F} = \sum_e b_e(c_e - \underline{y}_e)$, but this time constraint $\underline{y}_e \leq c_e$ ignored. By re-arranging, we have the equivalent problem of minimizing the weighted link load $\sum_e b_e \underline{y}_e$. If we consider the latency function $\ell_e(\underline{y}_e) = b_e = 1/c_e$, then the objective corresponds to considering the inverse of the link capacity as the latency function, and the overall objective (7.11.1a) becomes the minimization of the sum of the link utilization ratios $\boldsymbol{F} = \sum_e \underline{y}_e/c_e$. Since $1/c_e$ is a constant (similar to $\ell_e(\cdot) = 1$), the flow at the Nash equilibrium is also the optimal flow in regard to this objective function, i.e., $\boldsymbol{F}\left(\boldsymbol{x}^{\mathcal{N}} \mid \ell_e(\cdot) = 1/c_e\right) = \boldsymbol{F}\left(\boldsymbol{x}^* \mid \ell_e(\cdot) = 1/c_e\right)$.

Finally, the latency function of most interest to us is based on the *M/M/*1 delay function, $\ell_e(\underline{y}_e) = 1/(c_e - \underline{y}_e)$. However, in this case, we face the issue of the function growing quickly as the link load approaches the capacity. Note that to be able to apply Corollary 7.4, (7.11.5) must be satisfied. For the *M/M/*1 delay function, the left-hand side of (7.11.5) can be written as $\frac{\rho_e}{1-\rho_e}$, where $\rho_e = \underline{y}_e/c_e$ is link utilization (ratio) for link e. Recall that $\int 1/(c-s)ds = -\ln(c-s)$. Thus, after simplification, we find that condition (7.11.5) translates to:

$$\frac{\rho_e}{1-\rho_e} \leq -\Upsilon \ln(1-\rho_e). \tag{7.11.6}$$

In Figure 7.12, we plot the left side of relation (7.11.6) to the right side for three different values of $\Upsilon (= 1, 1.5, 2)$. From this figure, we find that condition (7.11.6) holds for $\Upsilon = 1.5$ if utilization, ρ_e, is $< 50\%$. If Υ is increased to 2, the condition holds at a higher utilization of 70%. In other words, if the demand volume is such that the link utilization is maintained below 50% for all links, the Nash equilibrium solution can be off by as much as 50% from the optimal flow solution. On the other hand, if the demand volume is such that the link utilization is maintained below 70%, then the Nash equilibrium solution can be twice as far off from the optimal-flow solution. We can write them as follows:

If $\rho_e \leq 0.5$ for all e, then

$$\boldsymbol{F}\left(\boldsymbol{x}^{\mathcal{N}} \mid \ell_e(\underline{y}_e) = 1/(c_e - \underline{y}_e)\right) \leq 1.5 \cdot \boldsymbol{F}\left(\boldsymbol{x}^* \mid \ell_e(\underline{y}_e) = 1/(c_e - \underline{y}_e)\right). \tag{7.11.7a}$$

If $\rho_e \leq 0.7$ for all e, then

$$\boldsymbol{F}\left(\boldsymbol{x}^{\mathcal{N}} \mid \ell_e(\underline{y}_e) = 1/(c_e - \underline{y}_e)\right) \leq 2 \cdot \boldsymbol{F}\left(\boldsymbol{x}^* \mid \ell_e(\underline{y}_e) = 1/(c_e - \underline{y}_e)\right). \tag{7.11.7b}$$

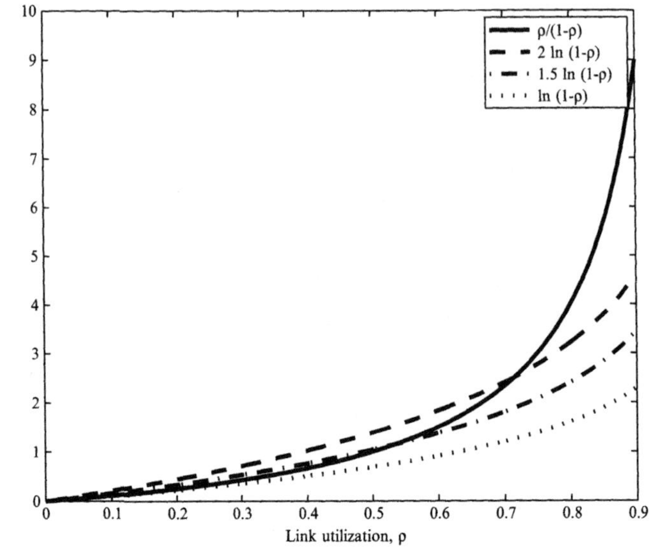

FIGURE 7.12 Bound Comparison

In other words, if a packet network were to use the *M/M/*1 delay based load-sensitive link cost, the network may reach equilibrium; however, it can be quite far off from the optimal flow in the network depending on the network load. Incidently, such a routing metric was proposed for routing in old ARPAnet [KZ89]).

Let us return to the discussion of Section 7.1.3. The inferior behavior of the minimum-hop routing discussed in Section 7.1.3 has a similarity to what is referred to as *Braess' paradox*. In [Bra68] Braess provided, in the context of road transportation, an example of a single-commodity network with a certain (somewhat artificial) set of link-load–dependent link-latency functions, in which the travel delay under selfish routing increases when a link is added to the network, despite that the drivers are choosing the path with currently least delay. (For additional discussion about Braess' paradox, see [Hag] and [Mar70].) In our example discussed in Section 7.1.3, we have illustrated that in packet networks with shortest-path routing such as OSPF networks, such a behavior, somewhat similar to that of Braess' paradox, can be induced as well when the assumption that the link metrics and the objective are correlated is relaxed.

In general, selfish flows at Nash equilibrium and optimal flows do not correspond to the flows induced by some link weight system, since they are not generated according to the ECMP rule.

Recall that selfish routing has a desirable property in that all users of one demand experience the same delay for a given network-defined latency function; this property does not hold in general for optimal flows, as demonstrated, e.g., in Section 7.1.3. As already stated in Section 7.1.3, Nash flows could be achieved in a data network if we let each packet be routed on the path with the currently minimal latency. Hence, Nash equilibrium would be rather hard to achieve in practice, since it requires online knowledge of time-dependent link loads on the packet-by-packet basis. Still, the above discussion suggests that link delay could be considered for the link metric in the OSPF/ECMP environment. Although these metrics (even if frequently updated) will not produce Nash equilibrium, they could induce flows close to Nash flows, which are in general superior, with respect to the delay objective, than simple metrics.

Finally, we can draw an important connection between selfish routing and optimal routing. We can say that optimal flow also leads to an equilibrium; however, the difference between optimal flow and Nash flow is that for calculation of the path lengths we use the link metric equal to the derivative of the load-latency product in the former case, as opposed to the straight link-latency used as the link metric in the latter case. Because of the connection between the derivative of the load-latency product and the link-latency function, eventually we could say that there is nothing called selfish routing, at least for computer networks—it is only a question of what is the link-latency function to be used or defined in the objective for a particular network. For example, for OSPF networks we can decide on an appropriate link-latency function we want to use by programming the routers; then, in the metric calculation of a link, use the derivative of the load-latency product. This is, however, not the case in road transportation networks since in such networks users (not routing nodes) decide routing based on actual latency perceived.

7.12 SUMMARY AND FURTHER READING

In this chapter, we have focused on determining optimal link weight systems for designing and traffic engineering of shortest-path routing networks which is faced in Internet intra-domain routing environment running OSPF and IS-IS. Note that private network-to-network interface (PNNI) routing [For96] in ATM networks also have an extended link-state protocol, thus any shortest-path routing algorithm can be used in PNNI; due to quality-of-service requirement for different traffic classes, approaches other than standard shortest-path routing may be more applicable for PNNI (for example, see [FSS98] and [MSS00]).

Shortest-path routing (SPR) induces new design problems that are intrinsically hard, and substantially different from the classical problems presented in Chapter 4. As you may have noticed already, the basic capacitated problem with continuous flows formulated in Section 7.1.1 is $\mathcal{NP}$-complete, as shown is Section 7.10. This implies that for the shortest-path routing routing with the ECMP rule it is not possible to formulate design problems in the form of LPs, even for the capacitated cases with continuous flows. This makes the shortest-path routing-related design problems different in nature from the classical multi-commodity flow problems, even from those which are also $\mathcal{NP}$-hard, as the non-bifurcated routing Problem (4.2.4). For the latter problems, the linear relaxation leads to natural bifurcated approximate solutions. In Section 7.2.1 we have demonstrated a MIP formulation of the basic shortest-path routing allocation problem; the LP relaxation of this MIP formulation, however, does not yield any reasonable LP approximation of the original problem.

In practice, large shortest-path routing networks can be treated virtually only by heuristic methods. In Section 7.2, we have presented several direct heuristics for solving capacitated shortest-path routing allocation problems, based on the local search (WA), SAN and LR-based dual approaches. The direct methods use the link metrics as optimization variables (either discrete of continuous) and try to find a feasible (or optimal in the case when an objective function is added to the problem formulation) solution. In the case of WA and SAN, the solution space is searched according to the general rules of local search and SAN (for an original SAN-based approach see [LP95]; another interesting approach can be found in [BGLM00a]). As illustrated by the results of Section 7.5, the WA and SAN approaches described in Section 7.2 are not very reliable in the sense that in some cases they work fairly well, but sometimes they may not provide satisfactory solutions at all (in reasonable time). Relation of optimal dual multipliers to link metrics is presented in [PSH+02], [WWZ01], also see [AMO03]. The LR-based dual approach with ECMP computation at each iteration is presented in [SAPM03]. Although the LR solutions can be obtained in a computationally effective way, they are not always feasible in the sense that the resulting ECMP routing yields only an approximate solution to the considered problem. Also an EA-based direct method can be found in [MK00]; the method seems to neglect the ECMP rule, but this important feature of the OSPF routing could be easily added to the algorithm, using for example the recursive ECMP flow calculation algorithm described in Section 7.3.

The two-phase approach to the weights optimization considered in Section 7.4 consists first, in establishing an optimal non-bifurcated flow allocation pattern, and then finding a weight system that generates this pattern (if possible). The idea of such an approach has been suggested in [FSS98] and developed in [GPS+00], [KP00], and [PSH+02], and in a series of papers [BGL00], [BGLM00b]. It seems (refer to Section 7.5) that in many cases it can be superior to the direct, link-metric based approach, although implementing the SAL algorithm for Phase 1 may require some programming effort. Alternatively, an EA algorithm can be used in the first phase but then the produced paths are much more frequently unrealizable with any weight system. Necessary conditions for a set of paths to be realizable as the set of unique shortest-paths (for some weight system) are discussed in [BGL00], [BT92], and [FSS98], where relevant LP formulations for finding such weight systems (provided they exist) are also discussed.

In practice, IP routers (Internet network nodes) have frequently used very simple weight systems such as unit metric systems or inverse proportional systems until recently. In Sections 7.5 and 7.6, we compare the traffic efficiency of the simple systems with the optimized ones, and show that the former can perform much worse under certain traffic conditions; this shows that the weight optimization is really an issue. These issues are treated also in [ERP02], [FT00], [LORS01], and [RR01].

Extensions of the capacitated problems involving link metric optimization for different nominal/failure scenarios and uncapacitated dimensioning problems for shortest-path routing networks have been treated in the literature to a much less extent than the basic capacitated problems of Section 7.1. Extensions of the first kind are discussed in [BGLM00a], [NSB+03], and [Yua03] and are summarized along with uncapacitated problems, in Sections 7.9 and 7.8, respectively.

The $\mathcal{NP}$-completeness of the equal-split shortest-path routing capacitated design problem is proved in Section 7.10. The proof was first published in [JSHP00]. Certain consideration associated with this issue can be found also in [LORS01]. Finally, in Section 7.11, which is based on [RT02], we consider the issue of how far from optimum can the selfish routing be so that each individual demand pair routes its demand volume trying to minimize end-to-end delay measure.

EXERCISES FOR CHAPTER 7

7.1. For the 4-node diamond network example, derive the condition that under $h < 66\frac{2}{3}$ and with hop-count link metric, the upgraded network has less average delay than the original network. For the same example, show that under the hop-count metric, the average delay is $22\frac{8}{11}$ ms in the upgraded network.

7.2. For the 4-node diamond network example discussed in Section 7.1.3, consider the objective function of minimizing maximum utilization. Determine a link weight system for which this objective is minimized and compare this result to the other objectives already discussed in Section 7.1.3.

7.3. Consider a network with n multi-link paths each of m links between two end nodes and a single direct-link path between the same two end nodes (Figure 7.13). 1) Determine an optimal weight system, the ECMP flow on each path and compute the average network delay. 2) Determine the flow at Nash equilibrium based on the average link delay as the link-latency function, compute the path delay, and the average network delay. 3) Determine the optimal flow allocation in the network along with the average network delay.

7.4. Define a convex piecewise linear penalty function and modify the MIP formulation of Section 7.2.1.

7.5. Derive the dual (7.2.2) of A/ECMP/RCM (7.2.2).

7.6. Write the LP dual of (7.2.7).

7.7. Formulate the dual problem for the following "overload minimization" problem and determine the link metric system induced by the dual solution

minimize $\boldsymbol{F} = r$
subject to

$$
\begin{aligned}
&\textstyle\sum_p x_{dp} = h_d && d = 1, 2, ..., D \\
&\textstyle\sum_d \sum_p \delta_{edp} x_{dp} - c_e \le r && e = 1, 2, ..., E \\
&x_{dp},\ r \ge 0.
\end{aligned}
$$

7.8. Write the primal problem associated with the objective (7.2.9). Then, derive its dual and finally, verify the optimal link metric system given in (7.2.10).

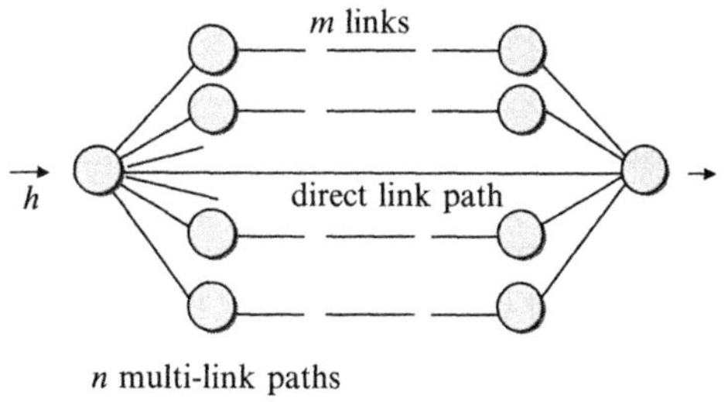

FIGURE 7.13 Network with n Paths Each with m Links Plus a Direct Link

Demand Pair	Volume
⟨1,9⟩	3
⟨4,6⟩	9
⟨3,7⟩	4

FIGURE 7.14 9-Node Manhattan-Street Network

7.9. Derive an example with unique optimal flow with non-ECMP split.

7.10. ([Gou01]) Consider the 9-node Manhattan-street network (Figure 7.14) with three demand pairs as shown below (the numbers next to a link indicates the capacity of the link). Determine optimal weight systems under different objectives considered in this chapter.

7.11. Consider problem P: minimize (7.2.9) subject to constraints (7.2.7b) and (7.2.7c). Formulate the generalized dual of P by introducing multipliers $\boldsymbol{\pi}$ only for constraint (7.2.7c). Show that 1) assuming $0 \leq r \leq 1$, $Dom(W) = \{\boldsymbol{\pi} : \boldsymbol{\pi} \geq 0\}$; and 2) assuming only $r \geq 0$, $Dom(W) = \{\boldsymbol{\pi} : \boldsymbol{\pi} \geq \mathbf{0}, \sum_e \gamma_e c_e \pi_e \leq \beta\}$, and any optimal $\boldsymbol{\pi}^*$ satisfies $\sum_e \gamma_e c_e \pi_e^* = \beta$ (here, P is always feasible). In either case, discuss how to compute $W(\boldsymbol{\pi})$ and its subgradients $\nabla W(\boldsymbol{\pi})$. For case 2), observe that subgradient maximization for solving the dual requires either projection onto $Dom(W)$ or an artificial upper bound or r (see Section 5.4.1 and 10.2.1).

7.12. Adjust the weight system $\boldsymbol{w} = (1, 1, ..., 1)$ ($w_e \equiv 1$) to obtain a weight system that generates the unique shortest-paths with respect to the number of hops. (Hint: add term 2^{-e} to weight w_e [FSS98].)

7.13. *Prove Property 7.1.

7.14. Consider formulation (7.9.1) for determination of an optimal link metric system for transient failures. 1) For the relaxed LP problem that is without the dependency on the link metric system, write the LP dual. 2) Develop and implement a Lagrangian-based dual approach and determine a feasible link metric system.

7.15. Write the formulation (analogous to (7.9.1)) that incorporates normal and failure states when the Fortz-Thorup (congestion) function is used in the objective under the requirement that worst congestion over normal and failures states are to be minimized in this combined formulation. Study and implement Yuan's local search algorithm [Yua03].

7.16. Refer to flow deviation algorithm, Algorithm 5.10, described in Section 5.5.1. Adapt and implement this algorithm for Problem (7.11.1) with $\ell_e(\underline{y}_e) = 1/(c_e - \underline{y}_e)$ to determine the optimal flow. Test your implementation on the example given in Exercise 7.10. (Hint: it is not that easy to implement FD algorithm due to discontinuity at $\underline{y}_e = c_e$, see [BG92] for a clue.)

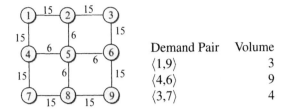

CHAPTER 8

Fair Networks

So far, in Chapters 4 and 7, we have assumed that the volume for each demand is a given, fixed quantity. Now we drop this assumption and assume that the demands between node pairs can utilize any total bandwidth assigned to them by means of their path flows, perhaps within certain bounds (in the limiting case when the lower bounds on demand volumes are equal to the upper bounds, we arrive back at the classical problems with fixed demand volumes). With such elastic demands a natural question arises: what should be the principle governing the distribution of demand volumes within given network resources (link capacities) leading to assignments fulfilling some kind of a fairness criterion? An intuitive way to solve this is to assign as much volume as possible to each demand, at the same time keeping the assigned volumes as equal as possible. This intuitive requirement leads to the assignment principle called Max-Min Fairness (MMF), known also as equity or justice in other applications. In fact, MMF is a very strict principle, implying lexicographically maximal vectors of volumes assigned to demands.

It appears that MMF is a special case of a more general fairness principle based on maximization of a utility function (called the Schur-concave function [MO79]) of the commodities (demand volumes), with respect to the resource (link capacity) constraints. A well-known utility function is the sum of the logarithms of the volumes assigned to demands. Maximization of this sum leads to the principle called Proportional Fairness (PF). As we will soon see, the main difference between MMF and PF is that the latter is in a sense less fair in terms of the demand volume assignment, but more effective in terms of the total throughput achieved by the network.

The notion of fairness arises in the context of packet-switched networks carrying elastic traffic between the node pairs, i.e., the traffic streams that can exhaust, perhaps within certain bounds, any bandwidth that is assigned to them. The most important example of such traffic is the best effort traffic carried under the transmission control protocol (TCP) in Internet; another example is the available bit rate traffic in asynchronous transfer mode (ATM). Fair demand volume allocation can also be used in the situation when the demand matrix for network design is not known, and only the bounds for the demand volumes are given; then, a reasonable design approach is to dimension the network within the assumed budget under the MMF principle with the assumed bounds on demand volumes.

In this chapter, we will study design problems and optimization methods associated with fair demand volume allocation. As for the shortest-path routing network studied in Chapter 7, the design problems and optimization algorithms related to fair networks are quite different in nature from the classical cases studied in Chapters 4 and 6.

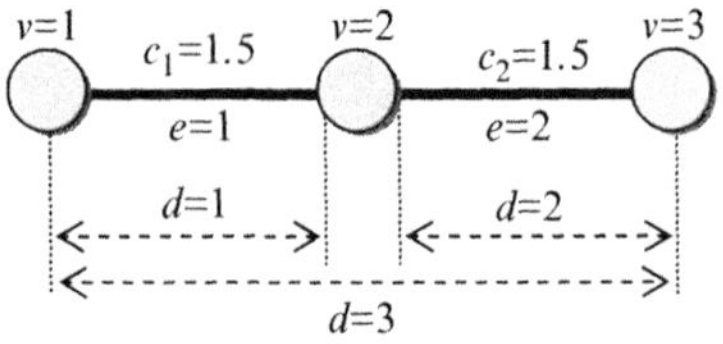

FIGURE 8.1 Two-Link Network

In Section 8.1, we will discuss the notions of MMF, PF and simple capacitated design problems with predefined single-path routing. Section 8.2 extends the considerations for the routing optimization in the capacitated and uncapacitated MMF networks. Analogous problems for PF networks are discussed in Section 8.3. Summary and suggested reading are provided in Section 8.4.

8.1 NOTIONS OF FAIRNESS

Consider a network with *elastic* demands. The elasticity means that each demand can consume any aggregated bandwidth assigned to its individual path(s), perhaps within certain predefined limits. This assumption corresponds, for instance, to a network with demands generating elastic traffic which accommodates to the changing bandwidth currently assigned to them. A general problem with this type of network is how to assign flows (bandwidth) to the demand paths so that the capacities of links are not exceeded and that the actual aggregated bandwidth volumes assigned to demands are distributed in a fair way. One way to do this is to apply the well-known *Max-Min Fairness* (MMF) principle (see [BG92]) for allocating aggregated demand volumes; an alternative to MMF is the concept of *Proportional Fairness* (PF) (see [MMD91] and [Kel97]). As already mentioned in the introduction, there are also other notions of fairness. A class of such notions, including MMF, PF, and other notions considered for communication networks, is referred to as α-fairness and described in [MW00]; more general approaches to the fairness characterization can be found in the optimization literature, e.g., [Raw71] and [Sen73].

8.1.1 An Example

Consider the simple "linear" network depicted in Figure 8.1, with $E = 2$ links, $V = 3$ nodes, and $D = 3$ demands. The link capacities are $c_1 = c_2 = 1\frac{1}{2}$. Each demand has exactly one allowable path ($P_d = 1$ for $d = 1, 2, 3$; $\mathcal{P}_{11} = \{1\}$, $\mathcal{P}_{21} = \{2\}$, $\mathcal{P}_{31} = \{1, 2\}$). Assuming elastic demands, a question arises: how to assign the volumes to the demands in a fair way? This example has already been discussed in Section 2.6, so we only recall that the MMF solution consists in assigning the maximal volume to the demands with the minimal assignment. This results in the following flow allocation: $x_{11} = x_{21} = x_{31} = \frac{3}{4}$. The PF solution requires that the sum of logarithms of the flows is maximized, i.e., in our case we seek to maximize $\log x_{11} + \log x_{21} + \log x_{31}$. The solution is $x_{11} = x_{21} = 1$ and $x_{31} = \frac{1}{2}$.

We notice that the MMF solution is entirely fair as far as the equity of demands (users) is concerned, with the resulting throughput $x_{11} + x_{21} + x_{31}$ equal to $2\frac{1}{4}$. The PF solution is less fair: the "long" flow (i.e., the flow using both links) $x_{31} = \frac{1}{2}$ is smaller than the two "short" flows (i.e., the flows using one link each) $x_{11} = x_{21} = 1$. Still, because optimal flows do not have to be equal in the optimal solution for PF (this, in fact, favors short flows), its flow allocation is more efficient in terms of the throughput, which is equal to $x_{11} + x_{21} + x_{31} = 2\frac{1}{2}$ in this case. This is a general observation: the PF solutions outperform the MMF solutions in terms of throughput, at the expense of fairness. Hence, PF can be viewed as a compromise between throughput maximization (in the considered example the maximal throughput is 3, achieved with a highly unfair solution $x_{11} = x_{21} = 1\frac{1}{2}$ and $x_{31} = 0$) and MMF.

8.1.2 Max-Min Fairness (MMF) Allocation Problem for Fixed Paths

To gain a more general insight into the issue of MMF consider a capacitated network with fixed capacities of links and predefined fixed single paths ($P_d \equiv 1$) assigned to carry the demand flows. First we need the following definition.

DEFINITION 8.1

A n-vector $\boldsymbol{x} = (x_1, x_2, \ldots, x_n)$ sorted in non-decreasing order ($x_1 \le x_2 \le \ldots \le x_n$) is *lexicographically greater* than another n-vector $\boldsymbol{y} = (y_1, y_2, \ldots, y_n)$ sorted in non-decreasing order ($y_1 \le y_2 \le \ldots \le y_n$) if an index k, $0 \le k \le n$ exists, such that $x_i = y_i$ for $i = 1, 2, \ldots, k$ and $x_k > y_k$.

For example, a sorted 3-vector $\boldsymbol{x} = (2, 2, 2)$ is lexicographically greater than $\boldsymbol{y} = (1, 10, 100)$. The following problem formulation expresses the MMF requirement by means of the notion of lexicographical ordering of sorted vectors. Below, the abbreviation 'LXM' stands for *lex-maximization.*

***LXM:* A/MMF/FIXSP** **Link-Path Formulation**

MMF With Fixed Single Paths

indices

$d = 1, 2, ..., D$ demands

$e = 1, 2, ..., E$ links

constants

δ_{ed} = 1 if link e belongs to the fixed path of demand d; 0, otherwise

c_e capacity of link e

variables

x_d flow assigned to demand d, $\boldsymbol{x} = (x_1, x_2, \ldots, x_D)$

objective

find allocation vector $\boldsymbol{x}$ which, when sorted in non-decreasing order, is lexicographically maximal among all allocation vectors sorted in non-decreasing order

constraints

$$\textstyle\sum_d \delta_{ed} x_d \le c_e, \qquad e = 1, 2, \ldots, E. \tag{8.1.1a}$$

$$\boldsymbol{x} \ge \mathbf{0}. \tag{8.1.1b}$$

By Definition 8.1, the solution $\boldsymbol{x}^*$ of A/MMF/FIXSP has the property that for any other feasible vector $\boldsymbol{x} = (x_1, x_2, \ldots, x_D)$, when both vectors are sorted ($x^*_{i(1)} \leq x^*_{i(2)} \leq \ldots \leq x^*_{i(D)}$ and $x_{j(1)} \leq x_{j(2)} \leq \ldots \leq x_{j(D)}$) then an index d, $0 \leq d \leq D$ exists, such that $x^*_{i(l)} = x_{j(l)}$ for $l = 1, 2, \ldots, d$ and $x^*_{i(d+1)} > x_{j(d+1)}$.

The following definition and proposition establish equivalence of the lexicographical characterization of the optimal solution of A/MMF/FIXSP and a more commonly known max-min fairness characterization for the considered fixed single-path case (refer to Section 6.5.2 in [BG92] and [MR99]).

DEFINITION 8.2

A feasible flow allocation vector $\boldsymbol{x}$ satisfying (8.1.1a - 8.1.1b) is *max-min fair* if for each demand d a saturated link e ($\sum_d \delta_{ed} x_d = c_e$) exists, belonging to the path realizing demand d ($\delta_{ed} = 1$) such that flow x_d is maximal on e ($x_d = \max\{x_{d'} : d' = 1, 2, \ldots, D, \delta_{ed'} = 1\}$).

PROPOSITION 8.1 *An allocation vector $\boldsymbol{x}^*$ solves A/MMF/FIXSP if and only if it is max-min fair in the sense of Definition 8.2. The solution $\boldsymbol{x}^*$ of A/MMF/FIXSP is unique.*

Proof:

Suppose that $\boldsymbol{x}^* = (x^*_1, x^*_2, \ldots, x^*_D)$ is not max-min fair, i.e., there is a demand d with the property that flow x^*_d is not maximal on all saturated links on the path assigned to d. Then x^*_d can be increased by some $\varepsilon > 0$ at the expense of decreasing the flows that are greater than x^*_d on the saturated links, and still keep these flows not less than x^*_d. But this means that $\boldsymbol{x}^*$ is not lexicographically maximal. Hence, if $\boldsymbol{x}^*$ is lexicographical maximal then it is max-min fair.

Now assume that $\boldsymbol{x}^*$ is max-min fair and there is a vector $\boldsymbol{x} = (x_1, x_2, \ldots, x_D)$ lexicographically greater than $\boldsymbol{x}^*$. Consider convex combinations $\boldsymbol{x}^\alpha = (1-\alpha)\boldsymbol{x}^* + \alpha\boldsymbol{x}$ ($0 \leq \alpha \leq 1$) of $\boldsymbol{x}^*$ and $\boldsymbol{x}$. Clearly, each $\boldsymbol{x}^\alpha$ is a feasible solution of problem A/MMF/FIXSP (8.1.1). There is at least one demand d for which $x^*_d < x_d$ since otherwise $\boldsymbol{x}$ would not be lexicographically greater than $\boldsymbol{x}^*$. Hence, let d be such a demand with the smallest value of x^*_d and define set $S = \{d' : x^*_{d'} \leq x^*_d\}$. Now note that for all demands $d' \in S$, if $x^*_{d'} \leq x^*_d$ then $x^*_{d'} \leq x_{d'}$ (in the opposite case $\boldsymbol{x}$ would be lexicographically less then $\boldsymbol{x}^*$). This implies that if $\boldsymbol{x}^*$ is transformed into $\boldsymbol{x}$ by increasing α from 0 to 1 in $\boldsymbol{x}^\alpha$, then x^*_d is increased without decreasing the flow for any demand in set S (i.e., for any demand with flow less or equal to x^*_d). This is again a contradiction because Definition 8.2 does not allow for such a transformation, as any increase of the flow x^*_d on the saturated link on which x^*_d is the maximal flow must result in a decrease of one of other flows which are not greater than x^*_d.

To prove the uniqueness suppose we have two different lexicographically maximal vectors $\boldsymbol{x}'$ and $\boldsymbol{x}''$ solving problem A/MMF/FIXSP ($\boldsymbol{x}'$ and $\boldsymbol{x}''$ are equal when sorted). Then any convex combination $\boldsymbol{x}^\alpha = (1-\alpha)\boldsymbol{x}' + \alpha\boldsymbol{x}''$ is feasible and lexicographically not less than both $\boldsymbol{x}'$ and $\boldsymbol{x}''$. If $x'_d < x''_d$ and $0 < \alpha < 1$, then $x'_d < x^\alpha_d < x''_d$ and an appropriate choice of α can make x^α_d different from all other elements of $\boldsymbol{x}'$ and $\boldsymbol{x}''$, which is a contradiction. ■

Note that the formulation (8.1.1) of problem A/MMF/FIXSP is not a mathematical program since it is not of the form: ***maximize*** or ***minimize*** $\boldsymbol{F}(\boldsymbol{x})$ ***subject*** *to* $\boldsymbol{x} \in X$. Still, mathematical programming formulations are possible. A tricky (and somewhat challenging) mixed integer programming (MIP) formulation of A/MMF/FIXSP based on Definition 8.2 is due to [Tom00].

***MIP:* A/MMF/FIXSP** **Link-Path Formulation**
MMF With Fixed Single Paths
variables

x_d flow assigned to demand d

u_{ed} auxiliary binary variable, $u_{ed} = 0$ if link e belongs to the path of demand d, e is saturated and x_d is maximal on e; otherwise $u_{ed} = 1$

z_e auxiliary flow variable for link e

constraints

$$\sum_d \delta_{ed} x_d \leq c_e, \quad e = 1, 2, \dots, E \tag{8.1.2a}$$

$$\sum_e \delta_{ed}(1 - u_{ed}) \geq 1, \quad d = 1, 2, \dots, D \tag{8.1.2b}$$

$$u_{ed} c_e \geq c_e - \sum_{d'} \delta_{ed'} x_{d'}, \quad e = 1, 2, \dots, E, \quad d = 1, 2, \dots, D \tag{8.1.2c}$$

$$u_{ed} c_e \geq z_e - x_d, \quad e = 1, 2, \dots, E, \quad d = 1, 2, \dots, D \text{ and } \delta_{ed} = 1 \tag{8.1.2d}$$

$$x_d \geq z_e, \quad e = 1, 2, \dots, E, \quad d = 1, 2, \dots, D \text{ and } \delta_{ed} = 1 \tag{8.1.2e}$$

all x_d and z_e non-negative continuous and all u_{ed} binary. (8.1.2f)

Note that the above formulation does not have an objective function. Constraint (8.1.2a) assures that link loads do not exceed the link capacities. Constraint (8.1.2b) guarantees that $u_{ed} = 0$ for at least one link e on the path of demand d. Further, (8.1.2c) implies that if $u_{ed} = 0$ then link e is saturated. Finally, using auxiliary link flow variables z_e, constraints (8.1.2d) and (8.1.2e) assure that if $u_{ed} = 0$ then x_d is the maximal flow on link e. Hence, by Proposition 8.1, Problem (8.1.2) has a unique solution $\boldsymbol{x}^* = (x_1^*, x_2^*, \dots, x_D^*)$, identical to the solution of the initial Problem (8.1.1).

Despite the complicated form of the MIP formulation (8.1.2), the considered problem can be easily solved due to the uniqueness property of the solutions of A/MMF/FIXSP. The unique max-min fair vector (lexicographically maximal allocation vector) $\boldsymbol{x}^* = (x_1^*, x_2^*, \dots, x_D^*)$ can be found using Algorithm 8.1.

ALGORITHM 8.1 Algorithm for Solving A/MMF/EFIXSP

Step 0: Put $\boldsymbol{x}^* = \boldsymbol{0}$.

Step 1: $t := \min\{c_e / \sum_d \delta_{ed} : e = 1, 2, \dots, E\}$.

Step 2: $c_e := c_e - t(\sum_d \delta_{ed})$ for $e = 1, 2, \dots, E$; $x_d^* := x_d^* + t$ for $d = 1, 2, \dots, D$. Remove all saturated links (all e with $c_e = 0$). For each removed link e remove all paths and corresponding demands that use the removed link (all d with $\delta_{ed} = 1$).

Step 3: If there are no demands left then stop, otherwise go to Step 1.

Observe that the quantity, t, calculated in Step 1 is the solution of the following linear programming (LP) problem:

$$\textit{maximize} \quad t \tag{8.1.3a}$$

$$\textit{subject to} \quad t(\textstyle\sum_d \delta_{ed}) \le c_e, \quad e = 1, 2, \ldots, E. \tag{8.1.3b}$$

This simple observation will allow us to extend the notion and solution algorithms for more general MMF problems considered below and in Section 8.2.

A more general problem is obtained when demand weights and lower and upper bounds imposed on the flows allocated to demands are added to A/MMF/FIXSP.

A/MMF/EFSP **Link-Path Formulation**

Extended MMF/EFIXSP

indices

$d = 1, 2, ..., D$ demands

$e = 1, 2, ..., E$ links

constants

δ_{ed} = 1 if link e belongs to the fixed path of demand d; 0, otherwise

c_e capacity of link e

w_d weight of demand d

h_d lower bound for the flow of demand d

H_d upper bound for the flow of demand d

variables

x_d flow assigned to demand d, $\boldsymbol{x} = (x_1, x_2, \ldots, x_D)$

objective

find allocation vector $\boldsymbol{x}$ which, when sorted in non-decreasing order, is lexicographically maximal among all allocation vectors sorted in non-decreasing order

constraints

$$h_d \le x_d \le H_d, \quad d = 1, 2, \ldots, D \tag{8.1.4a}$$

$$\textstyle\sum_d \delta_{ed} w_d x_d \le c_e, \quad e = 1, 2, \ldots, E \tag{8.1.4b}$$

$$\boldsymbol{x} \ge \mathbf{0}. \tag{8.1.4c}$$

Notice that in constraint (8.1.4b) the load of link e induced by flow x_d is equal to $\delta_{ed} w_d x_d$, implying that the actual flow assigned to demand d is equal to $w_d x_d$. Also observe that due to the presence of lower bounds, the problem can become infeasible. As will soon become clear, problem A/MMF/EFIXSP also enjoys the uniqueness property and, hence, its unique solution $\boldsymbol{x}^* = (x_1^*, x_2^*, \ldots, x_D^*)$ can be found using Algorithm 8.2 which is similar to Algorithm 8.1. The algorithm makes use of the following LP problem:

$$\textit{maximize} \quad t \tag{8.1.5a}$$

$$\textit{subject to} \quad t(\textstyle\sum_d w_d \delta_{ed}) \le c_e, \quad e = 1, 2, \ldots, E. \tag{8.1.5b}$$

ALGORITHM 8.2 Algorithm for Solving A/MMF/EFIXSP

Step 0:	Put $x_d^* = h_d$ for $d = 1, 2, \ldots, D$ and $c_e := c_e - \sum_d \delta_{ed} w_d h_d$ for $e = 1, 2, \ldots, E$. Remove all saturated links (all e with $c_e = 0$). For each removed link e remove all paths and corresponding demands that use the removed link (all d with $\delta_{ed} = 1$).
Step 1:	Solve the LP Problem (8.1.5) to obtain t.
Step 2:	$c_e := c_e - t(\sum_d w_d \delta_{ed})$ for $e = 1, 2, \ldots, E$; $x_d^* := x_d^* + t$ for $d = 1, 2, \ldots, D$. Remove all saturated links (all e with $c_e = 0$). For each removed link e remove all paths and corresponding demands that use the removed link (all d with $\delta_{ed} = 1$).
Step 3:	If there are no demands left then stop, otherwise go to Step 1.

Remark 8.1

The upper bounds H_d are taken into account by adjusting the network graph before applying Algorithm 8.2. For each demand d an auxiliary leaf node and an extra link of capacity $w_d H_d$ connecting the leaf to one of the demand end nodes are added; the link is added also to the path realizing demand d. ♦

Example 8.1

Consider the network depicted in Figure 8.2. Initially the network has $V = 5$ nodes, $E = 6$ links, and $D = 3$ demands. In order to take into account upper bounds H_d $(d = 1, 2, 3)$, three new nodes $(v = 6, 7, 8)$ and the corresponding links with appropriate capacities are added $(e = 7, 8, 9)$, resulting in the augmented network. ●

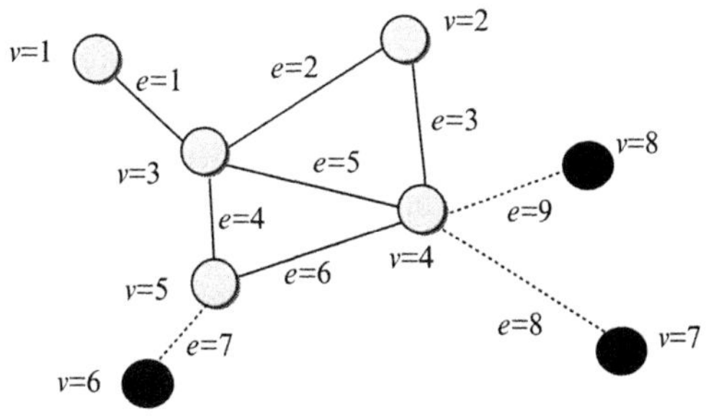

$c_7 = w_1 H_1$, $c_8 = w_2 H_2$, $c_9 = w_3 H_3$
d=1 between v=1 and v=5, path {1,5,6}: leaf node v=6, new path {1,5,6,7}
d=2 between v=1 and v=4, path {1,4,6}: leaf node v=7, new path {1,4,6,8}
d=3 between v=2 and v=4, path {3}: leaf node v=8, new path {3,9}

FIGURE 8.2 Augmented Network

8.1.3 Proportional Fairness (PF) Allocation Problem for Fixed Paths

The counterpart of problem A/MMF/FIXSP for PF is as follows.

***CXP:* A/PF/FIXSP** **Link-Path Formulation**
PF with Fixed Single Paths
variables

x_d flow assigned to demand d, $\boldsymbol{x} = (x_1, x_2, \dots, x_D)$

objective

$$\text{maximize } \boldsymbol{F}(\boldsymbol{x}) = \textstyle\sum_d \log x_d \tag{8.1.6a}$$

constraints

$$\textstyle\sum_d \delta_{ed} x_d \le c_e, \qquad e = 1, 2, \dots, E \tag{8.1.6b}$$

$$\boldsymbol{x} \ge \mathbf{0}. \tag{8.1.6c}$$

Note that formally $x_d = 0$ is outside the domain of the objective function; in fact, constraint (8.1.6c) should be substituted with

$$x_d \ge \varepsilon, \quad d = 1, 2, \dots, D \tag{8.1.6c'}$$

for some small positive constant ε. This remark concerns all the problems involving PF considered in the balance of this chapter.

In the considered context, the logarithmic function $U(x_d) = \log x_d$ is called *utility function*; in general, other convex utility functions $U(x_d)$ can be used for expressing fairness (see Section 8.3.5). The idea behind using the logarithmic utility function is to eliminate zero demand volume allocations (since $\log 0 = -\infty$), and not to promote allocations that are too large (the derivative of $\log x$, equal to $1/x$, is rapidly decreasing with increasing x, so the marginal gain in increasing x reflected by the increase of the objective function is also substantially decreasing).

A/PF/FIXSP is a convex optimization problem (CXP) with linear constraints, and as such can be solved by means of the Rosen projection method discussed in Section 5.5.2. Since no flows can be equal to zero, a good initial point for starting the Rosen procedure is the MMF solution. The gradient projection required in the Rosen method becomes quite easy if we assume that each link e serves as a predefined path for one of the demands. Then the inequality constraint (8.1.6b) become equality:

$$\textstyle\sum_d \delta_{ed} x_d = c_e, \quad e = 1, 2, ..., E \tag{8.1.6d}$$

Also the inequality constraint (8.1.6c) can be skipped since during the maximization process no variable x_d will be set to 0 (this would lead to $\boldsymbol{F}(\boldsymbol{x}) = -\infty$). With constraint

(8.1.6d) the projection is simple. At each stage the steepest ascent direction $\boldsymbol{g}$ is given by the formula

$$\boldsymbol{g} = \boldsymbol{P} \cdot \nabla \boldsymbol{F}(\boldsymbol{x}^k) \tag{8.1.7a}$$

where $\boldsymbol{x}^k$ is the current solution point and the (constant) projection matrix $\boldsymbol{P}$ is a $D \times D$ matrix given by

$$\boldsymbol{P} = \boldsymbol{I} - \boldsymbol{A}^T \cdot [\boldsymbol{A} \cdot \boldsymbol{A}^T]^{-1} \cdot \boldsymbol{A} \tag{8.1.7b}$$

In formula (8.1.7b), $\boldsymbol{I}$ is the unit $D \times D$ matrix and $\boldsymbol{A}$ is a $E \times D$ matrix of the link-path incidence coefficients: $\boldsymbol{A} = [\delta_{ed}]$.

An alternative method is to solve the problem dual to A/PF/FIXSP by means of subgradient maximization, as suggested in [Kel97]. It seems that the best approach, however, is to introduce a piecewise linear approximation of the logarithmic function and transform A/PF/FIXSP to a LP problem (refer to Section 4.3.2).

***LP:* A/PF/LAFIXSP** **Link-Path Formulation**

Linear Approximation of A/PF/FIXSP

indices

$d = 1, 2, \ldots, D$ demands

$e = 1, 2, \ldots, E$ links

$k = 1, 2, \ldots, K$ consecutive pieces of the approximation of $\log x$

constants

δ_{ed} = 1 if link e belongs to the fixed path of demand d; 0, otherwise

c_e capacity of link e

a_k, b_k coefficients of the linear pieces of the linear approximation of $\log x$

variables

x_d flow assigned to demand d, $\boldsymbol{x} = (x_1, x_2, \ldots, x_D)$

f_d approximation of $\log x_d$

objective

$$\text{maximize } \boldsymbol{F} = \textstyle\sum_d f_d \tag{8.1.8a}$$

constraints

$$f_d \le a_k x_d + b_k, \quad d = 1, 2, \ldots, D \quad k = 1, 2, \ldots, K \tag{8.1.8b}$$

$$\textstyle\sum_d \delta_{ed} x_d \le c_e, \quad e = 1, 2, \ldots, E \tag{8.1.8c}$$

$$\boldsymbol{x} \ge \boldsymbol{0}. \tag{8.1.8d}$$

Problem A/PF/FIXSP can be easily extended to take the demand weights and the lower and upper allocation bounds as shown below.

***CXP:* A/PF/EFIXSP** **Link-Path Formulation**
Extended A/PF/FIXSP
variables
x_d flow assigned to demand d, $\boldsymbol{x} = (x_1, x_2, \ldots, x_D)$
objective

$$\text{maximize } \boldsymbol{F}(\boldsymbol{x}) = \sum_d w_d \log x_d \tag{8.1.9a}$$

constraints

$$h_d \leq x_d \leq H_d, \quad d = 1, 2, \ldots, D \tag{8.1.9b}$$
$$\sum_d \delta_{ed} x_d \leq c_e, \quad e = 1, 2, \ldots, E \tag{8.1.9c}$$
$$\boldsymbol{x} \geq \mathbf{0}. \tag{8.1.9d}$$

Note that for PF, demand weights would have quite a different meaning than for MMF. A/PF/EFIXSP can be effectively solved using the LP approximation as well.

8.2 DESIGN PROBLEMS FOR MAX-MIN FAIRNESS (MMF)

In this section, we will consider more general capacitated and uncapacitated problems for MMF, involving simultaneous optimization of paths and flows. We refer to these types of problems as flexible path problems, in contrast to the fixed path problems presented earlier in Section 8.1.

8.2.1 Capacitated Problems for Flexible Paths

We will now give a detailed description of an efficient approach for solving a capacitated problem for MMF involving routing and (bifurcated) flow optimization. We will consider the case with several candidate paths on the routing list assigned to each demand, rather than with single paths as has been assumed in the previous section. Then, in general, the flows realizing each demand volume are split among the allowable paths which will result, in general, in a volume allocation vector lexicographically greater than the one solving the fixed paths case. We consider the following problem.

***LMX:* A/MMF/FLMP** **Link-Path Formulation**
MMF With Flexible Multiple Paths
indices
$d = 1, 2, \ldots, D$ demands (pairs of nodes)
$p = 1, 2, \ldots, P_d$ candidate paths for demand d
$e = 1, 2, \ldots, E$ links

constants

δ_{edp} = 1 if link e belongs to path p of demand d; 0, otherwise

c_e capacity of link e

variables

x_{dp} flow (bandwidth) allocated to path p of demand d

X_d total flow (bandwidth) allocated to demand d, $\boldsymbol{X} = (X_1, X_2, \dots, X_D)$

objective

find total flow allocation vector $\boldsymbol{X}$ which, when sorted in non-decreasing order, is lexicographically maximal among all total allocation vectors sorted in non-decreasing order.

constraints

$$\textstyle\sum_p x_{dp} = X_d \qquad d = 1, 2, \dots, D \qquad (8.2.1a)$$

$$\textstyle\sum_d \sum_p \delta_{edp} x_{dp} \le c_e \qquad e = 1, 2, \dots, E \qquad (8.2.1b)$$

$$\text{all } x_{dp} \ge 0. \qquad (8.2.1c)$$

Problem A/MMF/FLMP is more difficult to solve than its fixed single-path counterpart A/MMF/FIXSP because the solutions of the appropriate extension of the LP Problem (8.1.3) are, in general, not unique. The extension is as follows.

$$\textbf{\textit{maximize}} \quad t \qquad (8.2.2a)$$

$$\textbf{\textit{subject to}} \quad X_d = \textstyle\sum_p x_{dp} \qquad d = 1, 2, \dots, D \qquad (8.2.2b)$$

$$t - X_d \le 0 \qquad d = 1, 2, \dots, D \qquad (8.2.2c)$$

$$\textstyle\sum_d \sum_p \delta_{edp} x_{dp} \le c_e \qquad e = 1, 2, \dots, E \qquad (8.2.2d)$$

$$\text{all } x_{dp} \ge 0. \qquad (8.2.2e)$$

Observe that objective function (8.2.2a) together with constraint (8.2.2c) are equivalent to the objective that we are in fact interested in:

$$\textbf{\textit{maximize}} \quad \min\{X_d : d = 1, 2, \dots, D\}.$$

As shown below, Problem (8.2.2) (and Problem (8.2.4) specified below) can have multiple solutions.

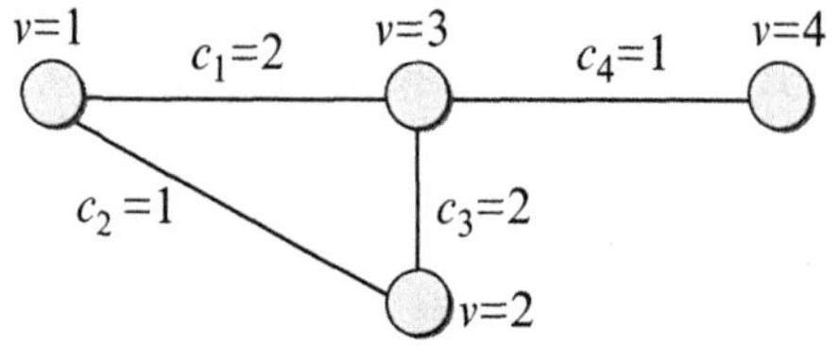

$d = 1$ between $v = 1$ and $v = 2$

$d = 2$ between $v = 1$ and $v = 4$

solution 1: $x1_2^1 = 1$ on path{2} and $x_2{}^1 = 1$ on path {1,4}

solution 2: $x_1{}^2 = 1$ on path{1,3} and $x_2{}^2 = 1$ on path {2,3,4}

FIGURE 8.3 Multiple Optimal Solutions

Example 8.2

Consider the network depicted in Figure 8.3. Optimal solution $\boldsymbol{x}^1$ of Problem (8.2.2) allows for further improvement, leading to the final (optimal for Problem A/MMF/FLMP (8.2.1)) allocation vector $\boldsymbol{x}^*$: $x^*_{11} = 1$ (on path $\mathcal{P}_{11} = \{1, 3\}$), $x^*_{12} = 1$ (on path $\mathcal{P}_{12} = \{2\}$) and $x^*_{21} = 0$ (on path $\mathcal{P}_{21} = \{2, 3, 4\}$), $x^*_{22} = 1$ (on path $\mathcal{P}_{22} = \{1, 4\}$). The final optimal total allocation vector $\boldsymbol{X}^* = (X^*_1, X^*_2)$ is equal to (2, 1). However, the second optimal solution, $\boldsymbol{x}^2$, does not allow for further increase of demand volume for demand $d = 1$. ●

Hence, Algorithm 8.1 for solving A/MMF/FIXSP (fixed single paths) cannot be straightforwardly generalized for the flexible multiple paths case A/MMF/FLMP. The solution of problem A/MMF/FLMP, such as Algorithm 8.3, although still effective, is substantially more complicated. It also consists in an iterative application of an extension of LP (8.2.2), but the use of the extension is interlaced with a step that checks which total demand allocations X_d can be further increased.

The practical efficiency of Algorithm 8.3 depends heavily on the efficiency of the non-blocking test (NBT) used in Step 1. One such straightforward test, referred to as NBT1, involves solving the following LP problem for each fixed demand $d \in Z_1$:

maximize	X_d		(8.2.3a)
subject to	$X_{d'} = \sum_p x_{d'p},$	$d' = 1, 2, \dots, D$	(8.2.3b)
	$t_{d'} - X_{d'} \le 0,$	$d' = 1, 2, \dots, D$ ($t_{d'}$ – constants)	(8.2.3c)
	$\sum_{d'} \sum_p \delta_{ed'p} x_{d'p} \le c_e,$	$e = 1, 2, \dots, E$	(8.2.3d)
	all $x_{d'p} \ge 0.$		(8.2.3e)

ALGORITHM 8.3 Algorithm for Solving A/MMF/FLMP (With NBT1)

Step 0: Solve LP (8.2.2) and let $(t^*, \boldsymbol{x}^*, \boldsymbol{X}^*)$ be the optimal solution of LP (8.2.2). Put $n := 0$, $Z_0 := \emptyset$, $Z_1 := \{1, 2, \ldots, D\}$, and $t_d := t^*$ for each $d \in Z_1$.

Step 1: Put $n := n + 1$. Start considering demands $d \in Z_1$ one by one to check whether the total allocated volume X_d^* can be made greater than t^*, without decreasing the already found maximal allocations $t_{d'}$ for all other demands d'. The check is performed by an appropriate *non-blocking test* (see (8.2.3) below). If there are no blocking demands in Z_1 (demand $d \in Z_1$ is *blocking* if X_d cannot be further increased) then go to Step 2. Otherwise, when the first *blocking* demand, say demand d, is detected, then add d to set Z_0 and delete it from set Z_1 ($Z_0 := Z_0 \cup \{d\}$, $Z_1 := Z_1 \backslash \{d\}$). If $Z_1 = \emptyset$ then stop (vector $\boldsymbol{X}^* = (X_1^*, X_2^*, \ldots, X_D^*) = (t_1, t_2, \ldots, t_D)$ is the solution of Problem (8.2.1)); else proceed to Step 2.
{Set Z_0 is the current set of blocking demands. Note that all demands $d \in Z_1$, for which $X_d^* > t^*$ (the volume resulting from the optimal solution of Step 0 or Step 2 is greater than t^*) are not tested, as this means that they are non-blocking.}

Step 2: Solve the following LP (a modification of (8.2.2)) to improve the currently best total allocations:

$$\begin{aligned}
&\textbf{\textit{maximize}} \quad && t && && \text{(8.2.4a)}\\
&\textbf{\textit{subject to}} \quad && X_d = \textstyle\sum_p x_{dp}, && d = 1, 2, \ldots, D && \text{(8.2.4b)}\\
& && t - X_d \le 0, && d \in Z_1 && \text{(8.2.4c)}\\
& && t_d - X_d \le 0, && d \in Z_0 \ (t_d - \text{constants}) && \text{(8.2.4d)}\\
& && \textstyle\sum_d \sum_p \delta_{edp} && e = 1, 2, \ldots, E && \\
& && x_{dp} \le c_e, && && \text{(8.2.4e)}\\
& && \text{all } x_{dp} \ge 0. && && \text{(8.2.4f)}
\end{aligned}$$

Let $(t^*, \boldsymbol{x}^*, \boldsymbol{X}^*)$ be the solution of (8.2.4). Put $t_d := t^*$ for each $d \in Z_1$ and go to Step 1.
{Note that it may happen that the optimal solution of (8.2.4) will not increase current t^* because there may be more blocking demands besides the one detected in Step 1.}

The outcome of NBT1 (8.2.3) is positive, meaning that demand d is *non-blocking*, if optimal X_d is strictly greater than t^*. Otherwise, the considered demand turns out to be blocking. Notice that a solution of NBT1 for some $d \in Z_1$ can reveal that for some other $d' \in Z_1$ the resulting volume $X_{d'}$ is greater than t^*. Such demands d' are non-blocking and do not need separate tests. Obviously, the calculations should be performed using the solution resulting from Step 0 (or Step 2) as the initial solution of NBT1 for each $d \in Z_1$.

Observe that due to convexity of Problem (8.2.4), it is sufficient to perform NBT1 separately for each $d \in Z_1$ because a solution that increases the volumes X_d simultaneously for all $d \in Z_1$ for which this is possible can be easily established afterwards. Such a solution can be defined as a convex combination ($\sum_{d \in Z_1} \alpha_d \boldsymbol{X}(d)$, $\sum_{d \in Z_1} \alpha_d = 1$, and $\alpha_d > 0$) of the solutions $\boldsymbol{X}(d)$, $d \in Z_1$ of NBT1s. This implies that after each completion of Step 1, the resulting set Z_1 of non-blocking demands and the set Z_0 of blocking demands are unique, resulting in the property (Exercise 8.1) expressed by the following proposition.

PROPOSITION 8.2 *The final total volume allocation vector $\boldsymbol{X}^* = (X_1^*, X_2^*, \ldots, X_D^*)$ (resulting from the solution of Problem (8.2.4) obtained in the last iteration of Algorithm 8.3) is unique. (Certainly, in general, the unique vector $\boldsymbol{X}^*$ can be achieved by more than one optimal configuration of the individual flows $\boldsymbol{x}^* = (x_{dp}^* :\ d = 1, 2, \ldots, D,\ p = 1, 2, \ldots, P_d)$.)*

Remark 8.2

Test NBT1 (consisting in solving (8.2.3)) can be used in a different way. In Step 1 we test *all* demands $d \in Z_1$ (without terminating Step 1 after finding the first blocking demand) and form the resulting set Z containing all non-blocking demands d from set Z_1. Then we modify sets Z_0 and Z_1 by putting $Z_0 := Z_0 \cup (Z_1 \backslash Z)$ and $Z_1 := Z$, check whether $Z_1 = \emptyset$, and if not proceed to Step 2. The modification is the subject of Exercise 8.2. It is also important to observe that the NBTs are not needed at all if a proper interior point method (IPM) of LP is applied (see Section 5.1.4). The optimal solution $\boldsymbol{x}^*$ yielded by some IPM algorithms has an advantageous property of being the analytical center of the optimal solution set, i.e., an appropriate convex combination of all optimal simplex vertices. This simply means that the corresponding vector $\boldsymbol{X}^*$ has the property that for each demand $d \in Z_1$, $X_d^* > t^*$ if and only if d is non-blocking (note that "and only if" is of crucial importance here). ♦

In Section 8.1 problem A/MMF/FIXSP (8.1.1) has been extended to Problem (8.1.4) by adding demand weights and lower and upper bounds for demand volumes. Such weights and lower and upper bounds can be easily added to the formulation of A/MMF/FLMP (Exercise 8.3); Algorithm 8.3 can be used for the modified formulation after some minor changes (Exercise 8.4).

Algorithm 8.3 is clearly of polynomial complexity (recall that any LP problem can be solved in polynomial time, refer to Section 5.1.4). However, due to the necessity of solving a large number of NBT1s, it can become very time-consuming for large networks with thousands of demands. Hence, more efficient NBTs are required. A more efficient test, referred to as NBT2, can be derived from properties of the simplex tableau and is the subject of Exercise 8.5. However, the most efficient test known to us, called NBT3, is based on the dual variables and is described below.

Tests NBT3 based on Dual Variables and Improved Algorithm

The vector $\boldsymbol{\lambda}^* = (\lambda_1^*, \lambda_2^*, \ldots, \lambda_D^*)$ of the optimal dual variables corresponding to constraint (8.2.2c) or the vector $\boldsymbol{\lambda}^* = (\lambda_d^* : d \in Z_n)$ corresponding to constraint(8.2.4c)) can be used in very efficient NBTs for Step 1 of Algorithm 8.3, referred to as Algorithm 8.4.

Consider the solution of the dual to Problem (8.2.2). It follows from the dual theory that if $\lambda_d^* > 0$ then demand d is blocking and its volume X_d cannot be made greater than t^* (maximum of (8.2.2a)) in any optimal solution of Problem (8.2.2). We will not prove this result here; the reader is referred to the derivation of an analogous fact stated in Proposition 13.1 in Section 13.1.2 and Exercise 13.3. Hence, $\lambda_d^* > 0$ indicates that demand d is blocking, i.e., $d \in Z_0$ after the first execution of Step 1. Unfortunately, the fact that $\lambda_d^* = 0$ does not, in general, imply that d is non-blocking, as shown in Example 8.3.

The modification of Algorithm 8.3 based on NBT3 is described in Algorithm 8.4.

ALGORITHM 8.4 Algorithm for Solving A/MMF/FLMP (With NBT3)

Step 0: Put $n := 0$, $Z_0 := \emptyset$, $Z_1 := \{1, 2, \ldots, D\}$ and $t_d := 0$ for all demands d.

Step 1: Solve the problem

$$\begin{aligned}
&\textbf{\textit{maximize}} && t && \text{(or } \textbf{\textit{minimize}} - t) && (8.2.5a)\\
&\textbf{\textit{subject to}} && X_d = \textstyle\sum_p x_{dp}, && d = 1, 2, \ldots, D && (8.2.5b)\\
& && t - X_d \le 0, && d \in Z_1 && (8.2.5c)\\
& && t_d - X_d \le 0, && d \in Z_0 \ \ (t_d - \text{constants}) && (8.2.5d)\\
& && \textstyle\sum_d \sum_p \delta_{edp} x_{dp} \le c_e, && e = 1, 2, \ldots, E && (8.2.5e)\\
& && \text{all } x_{dp} \ge 0. && && (8.2.5f)
\end{aligned}$$

Let t^* be the optimal value of (8.2.5a) and λ_d^*, $d \in Z_1$ be the optimal dual variables corresponding to constraints (8.2.5c).

Step 2: Put $n := n + 1$ and $t_d = t^*$ for each $d \in Z_1$. Put $Z_0 := Z_0 \cup \{d \in Z_1 : \lambda_d^* > 0\}$ and $Z_1 = \{d \in Z_1 : \lambda_d^* = 0\}$. If $Z_1 = \emptyset$ then stop (vector $\boldsymbol{X} = (X_1, X_2, \ldots, X_D) = (t_1, t_2, \ldots, t_D)$ is the solution of Problem (8.2.1)); else go to Step 1.

In Algorithm 8.4, if the optimal t^* in Step 1 happens to be strictly greater than the optimal solution of Problem (8.2.5) obtained in the previous iteration, then all demands d in set Z_1 are non-blocking. If not, then one or more demands in set Z_1 are blocking (they are "false" non-blocking demands) and t^* cannot be increased. Still, and this is the crucial observation, among the newly obtained optimal dual variables λ_d^* for $d \in Z_1$, there will appear at least one with $\lambda_d^* > 0$. Hence, at least one blocking demand will be detected. This is implied by the fact that in the optimal dual solution of (8.2.5) dual variables corresponding to (8.2.5c), λ_d^*, have the property:

$$\textstyle\sum_{d \in Z_1} \lambda_d^* = 1 \text{ and } \lambda_d^* \ge 0 \text{ for } d \in Z_1. \qquad (8.2.6)$$

Example 8.3

Consider the network from Figure 8.4. In this case, problem A/MMF/FLMP (8.2.1) will be solved in the first iteration of Algorithm 8.4, yielding $X_1^* = x_{11}^* = X_2^* = x_{21}^* = X_3^* = x_{31}^* = 1$

(there is only one path for each demand). However, although all of the three demands are blocking, the removal of any one of the two first demands ($d = 1$ or $d = 2$) will not result in any increase of t^* (in the considered case $t^* = 1$). Because of this, assuming that $\lambda_d^* = 0$ implies that demand d is non-blocking, can lead to a false non-blocking demand ($d = 1$ or $d = 2$) in set Z_1, causing no increase of t^* in the next iteration. In fact, it can be checked (Exercise 8.6) that in the considered case the simplex algorithm will always set one of the two first values in the optimal multiplier vector $\boldsymbol{\lambda}^* = (\lambda_1^*, \lambda_2^*, \lambda_3^*)$ ($\boldsymbol{\lambda}^*$ corresponds to constraint (8.2.2c)) to 0, yielding one of the two optimal dual solutions: $\lambda^* = (0, \frac{1}{2}, \frac{1}{2})$ or $\lambda^* = (\frac{1}{2}, 0, \frac{1}{2})$. ●

Consider set Z_0 of blocking demands and the complementary set Z_1, obtained as the result of Step 1 of Algorithm 8.4. To assure that $d \in Z_1$ (i.e., $\lambda_d^* = 0$) implies that d is non-blocking, an additional condition must be fulfilled. For that, we need the following definition.

DEFINITION 8.3

Set Z_0 of blocking demands is called *regular* if it has the following property: when any proper subset Z of the set Z_0 is removed from the formulation of Problem (8.2.5), then in the resulting reduced optimization problem (with smaller number of demands) at least one demand $d \in Z_0 \backslash Z$ becomes non-blocking (i.e., its volume X_d can be increased above t^*).

The condition can now be stated as the following proposition.

PROPOSITION 8.3 *Set Z_0 is regular if and only if for each d, $\lambda_d^0 = 0$ ($d \in Z_1$) implies that d is non-blocking.*

Proposition 8.3 can be proved similar to Proposition 13.2 in Section 13.3 (see Exercise 13.3). Note that if Proposition 8.3 holds, then after solving Step 1 in Algorithm 8.4, d is non-blocking if and only if $\lambda_d^* = 0$. Hence, Proposition 8.3 assures that, in Step 1 of Algorithm 8.4, optimal t^* will be always increased.

Column Generation

The instances of the LP Problem (8.2.5) solved by consecutive iterations of Algorithm 8.4 use the link-path formulation and as such are limited to the pre-processed routing lists of allowable paths. However, this should not be considered a major difficulty since the path generation technique presented in Section 5.4.2 can be applied here as well. The potential efficiency of column generation for problem A/MMF/FLMP is implied by the following

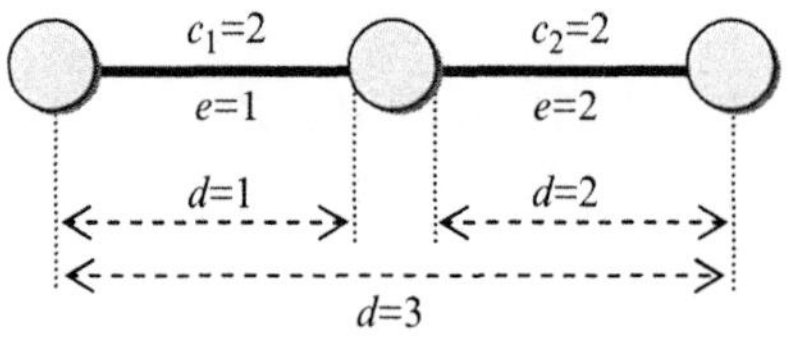

FIGURE 8.4 Two-Link Network

property, analogous to that given by Proposition 4.1 (also see Example 4.2), and implied by the number of basic variables in (8.2.5).

PROPOSITION 8.4 *An optimal solution $\boldsymbol{x}^*$ of problem A/MMF/FLMP exists with at most $D+E$ non-zero flows x^*_{dp}.*

The application of the column generation technique for the LP Problem (8.2.5), called frequently problem AMMF in the rest of the discussion, can be developed as follows. We use (8.2.5b) to substitute $\sum_p x_{dp}$ for X_d in the left-hand side of (8.2.5c), and let λ_d be the Lagrange multipliers (dual variables) corresponding to constraints (8.2.5c) and (8.2.5d). Finally, let π_e be the multipliers corresponding to constraint (8.2.5e). Now, we construct the Lagrangian function

$$\begin{aligned} L(t, \boldsymbol{x}; \boldsymbol{\lambda}, \boldsymbol{\pi}) &= -t + \textstyle\sum_{d\in Z_1} \lambda_d (t - \sum_p x_{dp}) + \sum_{d\in Z_0} \lambda_d (t_d - \sum_p x_{dp}) + \\ &+ \textstyle\sum_e \pi_e (\sum_d \sum_p \delta_{edp} x_{dp} - c_e) \\ &= (\textstyle\sum_{d\in Z_1} \lambda_d - 1)t + \sum_d \sum_p (\sum_e \delta_{edp}\pi_e - \lambda_d) x_{dp} + \\ &+ \textstyle\sum_{d\in Z_0} t_d \lambda_d - \sum_e c_e \pi_e \end{aligned} \tag{8.2.7}$$

where $\boldsymbol{x} = (x_{dp} : d = 1, 2, \ldots, D,\ p = 1, 2, \ldots, P_d)$, $\boldsymbol{\lambda} = (\lambda_1, \lambda_2, \ldots, \lambda_D)$, and $\boldsymbol{\pi} = (\pi_1, \pi_2, \ldots, \pi_E)$.

The dual function, defined as

$$W(\boldsymbol{\lambda}, \boldsymbol{\pi}) = \min\{L(t, \boldsymbol{x}; \boldsymbol{\lambda}, \boldsymbol{\pi}) : \boldsymbol{x} \geq \boldsymbol{0}, t \text{ unrestricted in sign}\} \tag{8.2.8}$$

leads to the following dual problem in variables $\boldsymbol{\lambda}$ and $\boldsymbol{\pi}$:

maximize	$W(\boldsymbol{\lambda}, \boldsymbol{\pi}) = \sum_{d\in Z_0} t_d \lambda_d - \sum_e c_e \pi_e$	(8.2.9a)
subject to	$\sum_{d\in Z_1} \lambda_d = 1$	(8.2.9b)
	$\lambda_d \leq \sum_e \delta_{edp} \pi_e, \quad d = 1, 2, \ldots, D, \quad p = 1, 2, \ldots, P_d$	(8.2.9c)
	$\boldsymbol{\lambda} \geq \boldsymbol{0}$ and $\boldsymbol{\pi} \geq \boldsymbol{0}$.	(8.2.9d)

Notice that constraints (8.2.9b) to (8.2.9c) assure that $W(\boldsymbol{\lambda}, \boldsymbol{\pi}) > -\infty$, and that $W(\boldsymbol{\lambda}, \boldsymbol{\pi}) = -\infty$ when constraints (8.2.9b) to (8.2.9c) are not satisfied. Observe that the solution of (8.2.9) yields optimal multipliers $\boldsymbol{\lambda}^*, \boldsymbol{\pi}^*$ with the following properties:

$$\textstyle\sum_{d\in Z_1} \lambda^*_d = 1 \tag{8.2.10a}$$

$$\lambda^*_d = \min\{\textstyle\sum_e \delta_{edp} \pi^*_e : p = 1, 2, \ldots, P_d\}, \quad d = 1, 2, \ldots, D \tag{8.2.10b}$$

$$\boldsymbol{\lambda}^* \geq \boldsymbol{0}, \ \boldsymbol{\pi}^* \geq \boldsymbol{0}. \tag{8.2.10c}$$

As in Section 5.4.2, the optimal multipliers π^*_e can be treated as link weights. Then the quantity $\sum_e \delta_{edp} \pi^*_e$ is the length of path p of demand d, and equality (8.2.10b) implies that λ^*_d is the length of the shortest allowable path for demand d. The equalities in (8.2.10b) follow from the complementary slackness property (refer to Section A.7 in Appendix A): a strictly positive flow x^*_{dp} in the optimal primal solution $\boldsymbol{x}^*$ can be assigned only to a path

p of demand d for which the equality (8.2.10b) holds; such a path is the shortest path with respect to $\boldsymbol{\pi}^*$. For other, longer paths p, x^*_{dp} must be equal to 0, because for paths with $\sum_e \delta_{edp}\pi^*_e > \lambda^*_d$ the value $x^*_{dp} = 0$ minimizes the Lagrangian (8.2.7) for given $\boldsymbol{\lambda}^*$ and $\boldsymbol{\pi}^*$.

The following proposition, analogous to Proposition 5.4, also holds for AMMF (the reader is asked to prove Proposition 8.5 in Exercise 8.7).

PROPOSITION 8.5 *Let $(t^*, \boldsymbol{x}^*; \boldsymbol{\lambda}^*, \boldsymbol{\pi}^*)$ be a saddle point of problem AMMF with a given fixed set of routing (candidate path) lists. Let $\mathcal{P}_d$ be the shortest path for demand d (among all allowable paths, not necessarily on the routing list of demand d) with respect to optimal multipliers $\boldsymbol{\pi}^*$, and let $\zeta_d(\boldsymbol{\pi}^*)$ denote the length of $\mathcal{P}_d$. If for all d, $\zeta_d(\boldsymbol{\pi}^*) = \lambda^*_d$ (i.e., for each demand, its candidate path list already contains a path with the shortest possible length) then the primal solution $(t^*, \boldsymbol{x}^*)$ of AMMF is optimal in the wider sense (i.e., when all allowable paths are on the routing lists). Otherwise, if for some demand d a path $\mathcal{P}_d$ with $\zeta_d(\boldsymbol{\pi}^*) < \lambda^*_d$ does exist, then the primal solution t^* can be possibly (but not necessarily) improved by introducing path $\mathcal{P}_d$ to the current routing list of candidate paths for demand d. If the improvement is possible, then its rate is equal to $\lambda^*_d - \zeta_d(\boldsymbol{\pi}^*)$.*

Proposition 8.5 leads to a column generation algorithm for Problem (8.2.5), analogous to Algorithm 5.9 in Section 5.4.2 (see Exercise 8.8). Observe, however, that the stopping criterion based on the value of the dual function $W(\boldsymbol{\lambda}, \boldsymbol{\pi})$, analogous to that of Section 5.4.2, cannot be applied in this case. The reason is that the values $\zeta_d(\boldsymbol{\pi}^*)$, $d \in Z_1$ do not in general fulfill constraint (8.2.10a), since it can happen that $\sum_{d \in Z_1} \zeta_d(\boldsymbol{\pi}^*) < 1$, and hence the dual point $(\boldsymbol{\lambda}', \boldsymbol{\pi}^*)$, where $\lambda'_d = \zeta_d(\boldsymbol{\pi}^*), d = 1, 2, \ldots, D$, is in general not in the domain, $Dom(W)$, of $W(\boldsymbol{\lambda}, \boldsymbol{\pi})$.

Remark 8.3

Dual tests NBT3 can be effectively combined with path generation. Even if we reach optimal solution t^* at a certain stage of Algorithm 8.4, we should keep on adding shortest paths according to optimal multipliers π^*_e (using the PG technique) to candidate path lists, and continue solving the currently considered problem with extended lists of candidate paths. Although the maximum t^* will certainly not improve, adding new paths will prepare ground for improvement in further iterations. If we did not do this then we could arrive at an intermediate solution not allowing for reaching optimal final solution.

This can happen because after solving Problem (8.2.5) we may get $\lambda^*_d > 0$ for a ceratin demand d and hence classify this demand as blocking, still in fact λ^*_d is greater than 0 only due to limited current candidate path lists, while adding new paths to the routing list of demand d can make λ^*_d equal to 0 (whether or not the demand is actually non-blocking).

For instance, for the network depicted in Figure 8.3 of Example 8.2 assume the routing lists consisting of paths $\mathcal{P}_{11} = \{1, 3\}$ and $\mathcal{P}_{21} = \{2, 3, 4\}$ for demands $d = 1$ and $d = 2$, respectively. These lists are sufficient to solve Problem (8.2.5) considered in the first iteration of Algorithm 8.4, setting both flows to 1 ($t^* = 1$). Now if we take the following optimal dual variables: $\pi^*_3 = \frac{1}{2}$ and the rest of optimal π^*_e equal to 0, then the corresponding λ^*_d are $\lambda^*_1 = \lambda^*_2 = \frac{1}{2}$. This will stop Algorithm 8.4 with the false optimal solution $X^*_1 = X^*_2 = 1$, although it is obvious that if we add the two remaining paths, $\mathcal{P}_{12}$ and $\mathcal{P}_{22}$, to the respective routing lists, the volume X_1 assigned to demand $d = 1$ can be further increased to 2 (from the initial allocation equal to 1). Observe that for the assumed π_e^* the length of $\mathcal{P}_{12}$ and $\mathcal{P}_{22}$ is 0 so they are shorter than the actually used paths $\mathcal{P}_{11}$ and $\mathcal{P}_{21}$, whose length is equal to $\frac{1}{2}$. Using PG, paths $\mathcal{P}_{12}$ and $\mathcal{P}_{22}$ will be detected and added to the routing lists. Then after solving the considered LP with extended routing lists we will obtain $\lambda_1^* = 0$ and $\lambda_2^* = 1$ (as the reader can check using an LP solver). ♦

It is clear that when solving Problem (8.2.5) by Algorithm 8.3, path generation can be used as well.

Node-Link Formulation

As we already know from Section 4.1, a way of assuring the potential use of all the paths in the optimal solution is to apply the node-link formulation for the problems underlying Algorithm 8.4. Below we give such a formulation for Problem (8.2.2) assuming, for simplicity, non-zero demand between each ordered pair of nodes (Exercise 8.9 asks the reader for a more general formulation). Recall that node-link formulations use directed links, referred to as arcs.

***LP:* A/MMF/FLMP** **Node-Link Formulation**

MMF with Flexible Multiple Paths - First Step

indices

$d = 1, 2, \dots, D$	demands
$e = 1, 2, \dots, E$	directed links (arcs)
$v, v' = 1, 2, \dots, V$	nodes

constants

a_{ev}	= 1 if arc e originates at node v; 0, otherwise
b_{ev}	= 1 if arc e terminates in node v; 0, otherwise
c_e	capacity of link e

variables

$X_{vv'}$	total volume assigned to demand originating at node v and terminating in node v'
S_v	$(= \sum_{v'} X_{vv'})$ total demand volume originating at node v
x_{ev}	continuous non-negative flow realizing all demands originating at node v on arc e

objective

$$\text{maximize } t \tag{8.2.11a}$$

constraints

$$\sum_e b_{ev'} x_{ev} - \sum_e a_{ev'} x_{ev} = X_{vv'}, \quad v, v' = 1, 2, \dots, V \quad v \neq v' \tag{8.2.11b}$$

$$S_v = \sum_{v'} X_{vv'}, \quad v = 1, 2, \dots, V \tag{8.2.11c}$$

$$\sum_e a_{ev} x_{ev} = S_v, \quad v = 1, 2, \dots, V \tag{8.2.11d}$$

$$t - X_{vv'} \leq 0, \quad v, v' = 1, 2, \dots, V \quad v \neq v' \tag{8.2.11e}$$

$$\sum_v x_{ev} \leq c_e, \quad e = 1, 2, \dots, E. \tag{8.2.11f}$$

In this formulation, constraint (8.2.11d) forces the total demand volume S_v generated in node v to flow out of node v, and constraint (8.2.11b) - that the portion $X_{vv'}$ of the flow originated at node v and destined for node v' stays in v'. Note that $X_{vv'}$ is equivalent to X_d used in the formulation (8.2.2). The node-link formulation requires directed graphs with directed links (or at least directed link flows). Hence, if in the original network the links are undirected, then with each link e we associate two oppositely directed arcs e' and e'' between the end nodes of link e and substitute constraint (8.2.11f) with

$$\sum_v (x_{e'v} + x_{e''v}) \leq c_e \quad e = 1, 2, \ldots, E. \tag{8.2.11g}$$

Observe the similarity of the above formulation to problem D/SDP/MF (4.1.6). Also recall that with the node-link formulation it is not possible to impose constraints on the allowable paths (as the limited number of hops; see a remark in Section 5.4.2). Algorithm 8.4 can be easily adjusted for the node-link formulation; in such an extension, the dual variables used in dual NBT3 are λ^*_{vw} corresponding to constraint (8.2.11e) (see Exercise 8.10).

Efficiency Issues and Other Approaches

Algorithm 8.4, combined with the column generation technique, provides a time-efficient and relatively easy to implement model for solving Problem (8.2.1). Certainly, the number of iterations required by Algorithm 8.4 (or Algorithm 8.3) to reach the final solution is not greater than D. Moreover, as shown by Proposition 8.6 below, the optimal vector $\boldsymbol{X}^*$ solving Problem A/MMF/FLMP (8.2.1) has at most E different elements. This in practice means that the number of iterations is bounded by the number E of network links (strictly speaking, for this we need to assume regularity, refer to Definition 8.3, which is a common property in practice). Hence, the algorithm is scalable, since in practical networks the number E grows linearly with the number of nodes N (assuming a fixed average node degree), while the number D of demands grows with N^2.

PROPOSITION 8.6 *The optimal vector $\boldsymbol{X}^*$ solving Problem A/MMF/FLMP (8.2.1) has at most E different elements. (Observe that this approximately implies that the number of iterations performed by Algorithm 8.4 is not greater than the number E of links in the network graph.)*

Proof:

The proposition follows from the fact, which we shall prove below, that after each iteration of Algorithm 8.3 at least one new link becomes saturated and remains saturated in all the future iterations.

Consider the LP Problem (8.2.2) of Step 0. Suppose that t^0 is the maximum of (8.2.2a) and Y_0 is the set of all optimal solutions $\boldsymbol{x} = (x_{dp} : d = 1, 2, \ldots, D,\ p = 1, 2, \ldots, P_d)$ of Problem (8.2.2). Let S_0 denote the set of all links saturated for every optimal solution of (8.2.2):

$$(e \in S_0) \Leftrightarrow (\forall \boldsymbol{x} \in Y_0,\ y_e(\boldsymbol{x}) = c_e), \tag{8.2.12}$$

where $y_e(\boldsymbol{x}) = \sum_d \sum_p \delta_{edp} x_{dp}$ is the load of link e. The set S_0 is not empty. To see this let us assume that for each link e a solution $\boldsymbol{x}^e \in Y_0$ exists such that $y_e(\boldsymbol{x}^e) < c_e$.

Then, because the considered optimization problem is convex, any convex combination $\boldsymbol{x}^{\alpha} = \sum_e \alpha_e \boldsymbol{x}^e$ (with $\sum_e \alpha_e = 1$ and $\alpha_e \geq 0$) is also an optimal solution of (8.2.2), i.e., $\boldsymbol{x}^{\alpha} \in Y_0$. Taking such a combination with all coefficients α_e strictly positive we arrive, for each link $e = 1, 2, \ldots, E$, at the inequality

$$\begin{aligned} y_e(\boldsymbol{x}^{\alpha}) &= \textstyle\sum_{e'} \alpha_{e'} y_{e'}(\boldsymbol{x}^{e'}) = \alpha_e y_e(\boldsymbol{x}^e) + \sum_{e' \neq e} \alpha_{e'} y_{e'}(\boldsymbol{x}^{e'}) < \\ &< \alpha_e c_e + \textstyle\sum_{e' \neq e} \alpha_{e'} y_{e'}(\boldsymbol{x}^{e'}) \leq c_e. \end{aligned} \tag{8.2.13}$$

This is a contradiction, because if all links are not saturated then all demand volumes X_d can be increased above t^0, so $\boldsymbol{x}^{\alpha}$ cannot be an optimal solution of Problem (8.2.2).

Now let us proceed to Step 2 and consider Problem (8.2.4) for $n = 1$ (n is the iteration counter). Let Y_1 denote the set of all optimal solutions of Problem (8.2.4) and let S_1 be the set of links that are saturated for every optimal solution of (8.2.4) for $n = 1$. Clearly $S_0 \subseteq S_1$, since any optimal solution $\boldsymbol{x}$ of (8.2.4) is at the same time an optimal solution of (8.2.2), i.e., $Y_1 \subseteq Y_0$. Moreover, if the maximum t^1 (8.2.4a) is greater than the maximum t^0 (8.2.2a), then S_0 is a proper subset of S_1. Otherwise, for each link $e \notin S_0$ a solution $\boldsymbol{x}^e \in Y_1$ would exist such that $y_e(\boldsymbol{x}^e) < c_e$ and, hence, as shown in the case of Problem (8.2.2), there would be an solution $\boldsymbol{x}^{\alpha} \in Y_1$ for which all links outside S_0 would be non-saturated. But since for all demands $d \in Z_1$ (i.e., for all demands for which the volumes X_d have been increased in Step 2) the increase of their volumes X_d (at least) up to t^1 has been achieved by means of flows using paths disjoint with the set S_0, then again if all links outside the set S_0 are not saturated then $\boldsymbol{x}^{\alpha}$ cannot be the optimal solution of (8.2.4) (and t^1 cannot be the maximum of (8.2.4a)).

Proceeding in the above-described way, we shall finally encounter a situation when all links in all the optimal solutions of Problem (8.2.4) of Step 2 will be saturated, i.e., when $S_n = \{1, 2, \ldots, E\}$ for some iteration n, which will simply mean that $Z_1 = \emptyset$ (no further improvement is possible) and the algorithm terminates after n iterations (more precisely, after n runs of Step 2).

This also means that in the optimal volume allocation vector $\boldsymbol{X}^*$ all elements belong to the set $\{t^0, t^1, \ldots, t^n\}$ with $t^0 < t^1 < \ldots < t^n$ and $n \leq E - 1$. ■

Adding weights w_d to formulation (8.2.1) of A/MMF/FLMP, i.e., substituting constraint (8.2.1b) with

$$\textstyle\sum_d w_d (\sum_p \delta_{edp} x_{dp}) \leq c_e \quad e = 1, 2, \ldots, E \tag{8.2.1d}$$

we arrive exactly at the problem studied in [Nac02] where the weights w_d correspond to the quantities called "input traffic" and are denoted with T_d. However, we note that Algorithm 8.4 offers a more straightforward and efficient solution to the studied problem A/MMF/FLMP (8.2.1) than the algorithm proposed in Section 7.2 of [Nac02]. The latter algorithm is based on a different characterization of the MMF solution, using a lexicographically maximal vector related to the saturated links in the optimal solution of A/MMF/FLMP.

Let us finally note that the lexicographical characterization of the MMF problems has been widely used outside telecommunications, e.g., in [KLS92], [Ogr97] and [Lus99]; for the multi-commodity flow network applications see [KRT99], [Nac02] and [NPD03], and for other telecommunications applications see [LV01] and [GGFS01]. Our approach makes effective use of the general ideas presented in [Ogr97], [KLS92], [MO92], and [Tom02] (see [OS03] for an alternative approach). The original tests NBT3 have their source in [KLS92].

Example 8.4

To illustrate the performance of Algorithm 7.4, consider a network with $V = 12$ nodes, $E = 18$ links, and $D = 66$ demands (demands are all undirected S-D pairs, numbered in the natural order: $\{1,2\}, \{1,3\}, \ldots, \{11,12\}$). Figure 8.5 shows the network topology, node numbers, and link capacities. Each demand is assigned the routing sequence of all simple paths, resulting in the P_d values varying from 6 to 13.

In the numerical study, we have used two LP solvers: the CPLEX simplex solver version 7.1 and the LP solver using an IPM provided by the MATLAB optimization toolbox. We have implemented Algorithm 8.1 (single predefined path case) and Algorithm 8.4 (flexible-path case) with NBT3. Figure 8.6 shows the successive demand volume allocations X_d of Algorithm 8.4 obtained with: 1) a simplex solver, and 2) an interior point solver. The experiment required 8 iterations (in both cases) and took several seconds of the CPU time on a SUNW Ultra-4 WS for case 1), and a comparable time on a Dell WS for case 2). In both cases, the sets of non-blocking demands were regular (Definition 8.3) in all iterations. It is important to note that from the NBTs viewpoint, IPMs have an advantageous property of returning solutions which are close to analytical centers of the optimal solution set (Section 5.1.4), and are not optimal vertices, as is the case with the simplex method. This is adequately visible in Figure 8.6(b). For instance, the solution of Step 0 assigns total demand X^*_d greater than t^* (although not much greater) to many demands d, so no NBTs are required for these demands. In contrast, the simplex solution in Figure 8.6(a) assigns total demand volume equal to t^* for all the demands, calling for a NBT (fortunately, very fast) for each demand.

The benefit from using flexible paths for this network is illustrated in Figure 8.7. The left diagram illustrates the final demand volume allocation after applying Algorithm 8.1 (the predefined paths are the shortest paths in terms of the number of hops). This should be compared to the right diagram, which is the final allocation pattern of Algorithm 8.4 (equal to the last row in Figure 8.6). The total throughput of the flexible solution is greater than the throughput of the fixed-path solution by 16%. ●

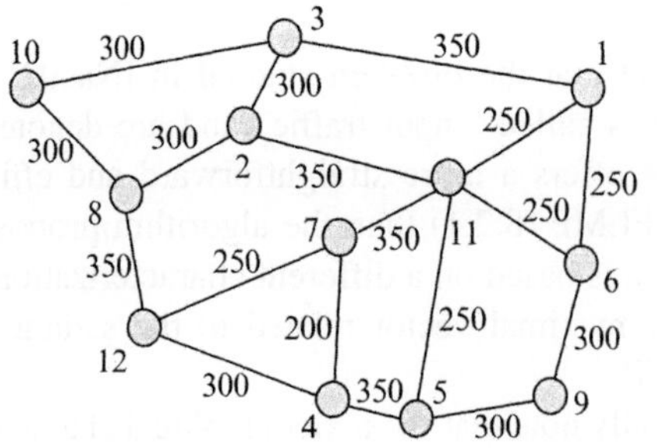

FIGURE 8.5 12-Node, 18-Link Network

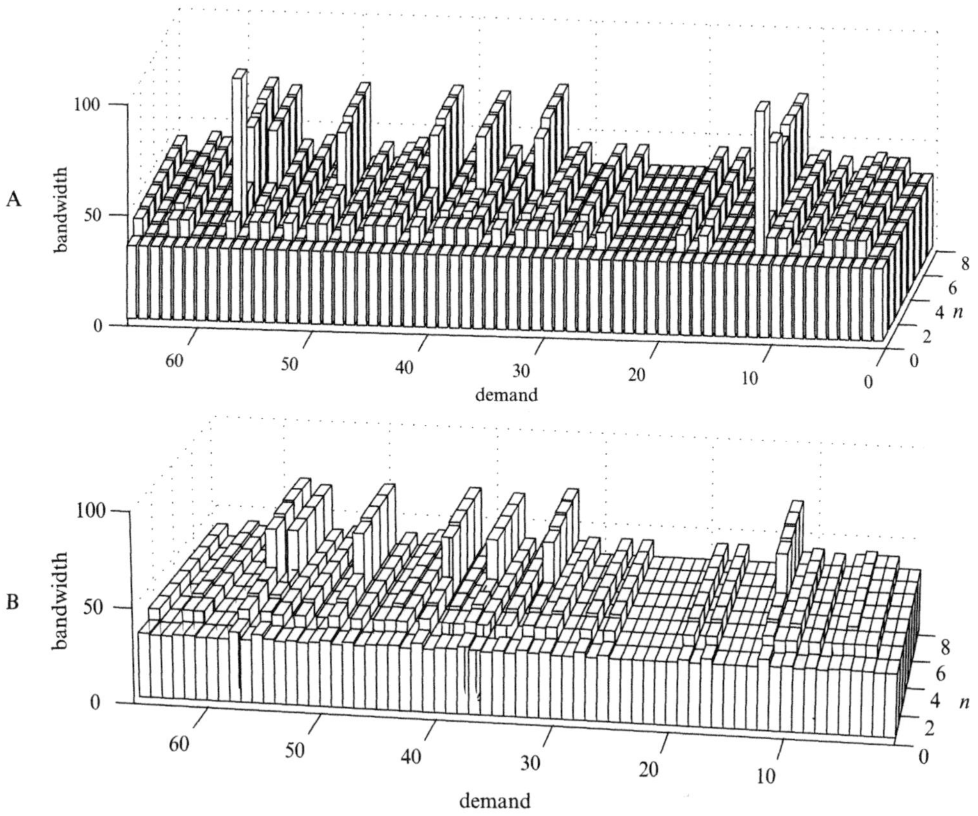

FIGURE 8.6 Evolution of Allocated Demand Volumes

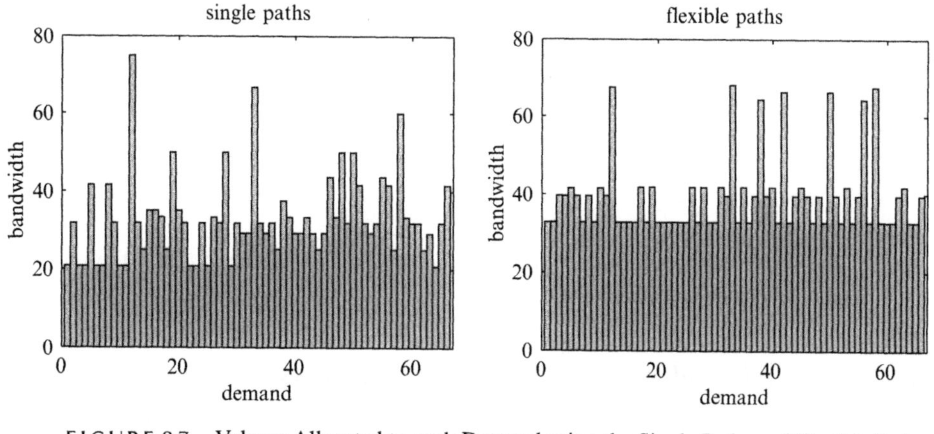

FIGURE 8.7 Volume Allocated to each Demand using the Single Paths and Flexible Paths

8.2.2 Uncapacitated Problems for Flexible Paths

The uncapacitated counterpart of A/MMF/FLMP involving simultaneous flow optimization and optimal link dimensioning under a given budget is as follows.

***LP:* D/MMF/FLMP** **Link-Path Formulation**
MMF With Flexible Multiple Paths

indices
$d = 1, 2, ..., D$ demands
$p = 1, 2, \ldots, P_d$ candidate paths for demand d
$e = 1, 2, ..., E$ links

constants
δ_{edp} = 1 if link e belongs to path p of demand d; 0, otherwise
ξ_e unit cost of link e
ζ_d $= \sum_e \xi_e \delta_{edp(d)}$ - cost (length) of the shortest candidate path, denoted by $p(d)$, realizing demand d
B assumed budget

variables
x_{dp} flow (bandwidth) allocated to path p of demand d
X total flow allocated to demand d (the same for all demands)
y_e capacity of link e

objective

$$\text{maximize } X \tag{8.2.14a}$$

constraints

$$\sum_e \xi_e y_e \le B \tag{8.2.14b}$$

$$\sum_p x_{dp} = X, \quad d = 1, 2, \ldots, D \tag{8.2.14c}$$

$$\sum_d \sum_p \delta_{edp} x_{dp} \le y_e, \quad e = 1, 2, \ldots, E \tag{8.2.14d}$$

$$\text{all } x_{dp} \ge 0. \tag{8.2.14e}$$

Obviously, the lexicographically maximal total allocation vector in the uncapacitated case has all the elements equal to each other, which is reflected in the form of the objective function. Also, the shortest path allocation rule (Section 4.1.1) applies, so to solve D/MMF/FLMP the flow equal to

$$x_{dp(d)} = \frac{B}{\sum_d \zeta_d} \tag{8.2.15}$$

should be allocated to the shortest path $p(d)$ for each demand d and the rest of the flows should be set to 0 (Exercise 8.11).

8.2.3 Capacitated Problems With Non-Bifurcated Flows

The non-bifurcated counterpart of the capacitated problem A/MMF/FLMP (8.2.1) is as follows.

LXM: **A/MMF/SPA** **Link-Path Formulation**
MMF/FLMP with Single-Path Allocation
variables

s_{dp} binary variable corresponding to the flow allocated to path p of demand d
X_d total flow (bandwidth) allocated to demand d, $\boldsymbol{X}= (X_1, X_2, \ldots, X_D)$

objective

find allocation vector $\boldsymbol{X}$ which, when sorted in non-decreasing order, is lexicographically maximal among all total allocation vectors sorted in non-decreasing order

constraints

$$\textstyle\sum_p x_{dp} = X_d, \qquad d = 1, 2, \ldots, D \tag{8.2.16a}$$
$$\textstyle\sum_p s_{dp} = 1, \qquad d = 1, 2, \ldots, D \tag{8.2.16b}$$
$$x_{dp} \le s_{dp} M_d, \qquad d = 1, 2, \ldots, D, \quad p = 1, 2, \ldots, P_d \tag{8.2.16c}$$
$$\textstyle\sum_d \sum_p \delta_{edp} x_{dp} \le c_e, \qquad e = 1, 2, \ldots, E \tag{8.2.16d}$$

all x_{dp} non-negative continuous and all s_{dp} binary. (8.2.16e)

The value of the demand-dependent constant M_d in constraint (8.2.16c) can be taken for example as

$$M_d = \textstyle\sum_p \min\{c_e : e = 1, 2, \ldots, E, \delta_{edp} = 1\} \quad d = 1, 2, \ldots, D, \tag{8.2.17}$$

that is equal to the sum of maximal flows on the allowable paths assigned to a demand. The requirement of the unsplittable flow allocation makes problem A/MMF/FLMP $\mathcal{NP}$-complete. In fact, as demonstrated in [KRT99], already a simpler MMF single-source unsplittable allocation problem (all demands originate from one node) is $\mathcal{N}P$-complete. In [KRT99] approximate algorithms for the single-source problem are also discussed. An approximate formulation of (8.2.16) and related heuristic approaches are presented in [CL02].

8.3 DESIGN PROBLEMS FOR PROPORTIONAL FAIRNESS (PF)

The essence of PF is to assign flows to demand paths so that the (weighted) sum of the logarithms of these flows is maximized. The use of the logarithmic function, instead of, for instance, a linear function (which would lead to throughput maximization), makes it impossible to assign zero flow to any demand, and at the same time, makes it not profitable to assign too much flow to any individual demand. Below we shall discuss the PF design problems with flexible paths.

8.3.1 Capacitated Problems for Flexible Paths

***CXP:* A/PF/FLMP** **Link-Path Formulation**
PF With Flexible Multiple Paths

indices

$d = 1, 2, ..., D$ demands (pairs of nodes)
$p = 1, 2, \ldots, P_d$ allowable paths for demand d
$e = 1, 2, ..., E$ links

constants

δ_{edp} = 1 if link e belongs to path p of demand d; 0, otherwise
w_d weight of demand d
c_e capacity of link e

variables

x_{dp} flow (bandwidth) allocated to path p of demand d
X_d total flow (bandwidth) allocated to demand d

objective

$$\text{maximize } \boldsymbol{F} = \textstyle\sum_d w_d \log X_d \tag{8.3.1a}$$

constraints

$$\textstyle\sum_p x_{dp} = X_d, \quad d = 1, 2, \ldots, D \tag{8.3.1b}$$
$$\textstyle\sum_d \sum_p \delta_{edp} x_{dp} \le c_e, \quad e = 1, 2, \ldots, E \tag{8.3.1c}$$
all x_{dp} continuous and non-negative. (8.3.1d)

Comparing A/MMF/FLMP with its fixed single-path counterpart A/MMF/FIXSP, note that the Rosen projection technique is now more complicated since the zero values of individual flows x_{dp} are now feasible - only the total flows X_d are > 0. Hence, the projection matrix can vary during the minimization process, which makes the implementation more time consuming. In any case, the linear approximation of the logarithmic function can be used to transform the problem into an approximate LP formulation (Exercise 8.12). To summarize, contrary to MMF, the flexible case for PF is comparable in numerical complexity with the fixed single-path case. Adding the lower and upper bounds can also be easily done.

8.3.2 Uncapacitated Problems With a Budget Constraint

In this section we address uncapacitated network design problems where link capacities are also subject to optimization under an overall budget constraint. In the balance of this section, we shall consider two optimal design problems constrained by the assumed budget: one for the unbounded flow case and one for the bounded flow case. We start with the unbounded case and, for reasons that will soon become clear, assume that, for each demand d, its single flow-path $p(d)$ is fixed and given.

CXP: **D/PF/BCUF** **Link-Path Formulation**

Budget Constraint, Unbounded Flows

indices

$d = 1, 2, ..., D$ demands

$e = 1, 2, ..., E$ links

constants

B assumed budget

δ_{ed} = 1 if link e belongs to path p of demand d; 0, otherwise

w_d weight of demand d

ξ_e unit cost of link e

ζ_d = $\sum_e \xi_e \delta_{ed}$ - cost (length) of the path realizing demand d

variables

x_d flow (bandwidth) allocated to the path of demand d

y_e capacity of link e

objective

$$\text{maximize } \boldsymbol{F}(\boldsymbol{x}) = \sum_d w_d \log x_d \tag{8.3.2a}$$

constraints

$$\sum_e \xi_e y_e \leq B \tag{8.3.2b}$$

$$\sum_d \delta_{ed} x_d \leq y_e, \qquad e = 1, 2, \ldots, E \tag{8.3.2c}$$

all x_d and y_e continuous and non-negative. (8.3.2d)

PROPOSITION 8.7 *Let* $\boldsymbol{x}^* = (x_1^*, x_2^*, \ldots, x_D^*)$ *and* $\boldsymbol{y}^* = (y_1^*, y_2^*, \ldots, y_D^*)$ *be the solution to D/PF/BCUF (8.3.2). Then, the following equalities hold:*

$$\boldsymbol{F}(\boldsymbol{x}^*) = (\log B)\sum_d w_d - \sum_d w_d \log \zeta_d + \sum_d w_d \log w_d - (\log \sum_d w_d)\sum_d w_d \tag{8.3.3a}$$

$$x_d^* = \frac{B w_d}{(\sum_d w_d)\zeta_d} \tag{8.3.3b}$$

$$y_e^* = \sum_d \delta_{ed} x_d^*. \tag{8.3.3c}$$

Proof:

The above formulae follow from the explicit solution of the problem dual to (8.3.2). To obtain the dual solution we first note that in the optimal solution of the primal problem D/PF/BCUF, both inequalities become equalities, and then we insert equation (8.3.2c) to equation (8.3.2b)

$$\sum_e \xi_e \sum_d \delta_{ed} x_d = B. \tag{8.3.4}$$

Now, we dualize constraint (8.3.4), form the Lagrangian function (σ is the Lagrangian multiplier with unconstrained sign),

$$L(\boldsymbol{x};\sigma) = -\sum_d w_d \log x_d + \sigma(\sum_e \xi_e \sum_d \delta_{ed} x_d - B) \tag{8.3.5}$$

and transform it into the following form:

$$L(\boldsymbol{x};\sigma) = \sum_d((\sigma \sum_e \xi_e \delta_{ed}) x_d - w_d \log x_d) - \sigma B. \tag{8.3.6}$$

Next, we form the dual function

$$W(\sigma) = \min_{\boldsymbol{x} \geq \mathbf{0}} L(\boldsymbol{x};\sigma) \tag{8.3.7}$$

and begin to solve the dual problem, i.e., to find a multiplier σ^* maximizing the dual function:

$$W(\sigma^*) = \max_\sigma W(\sigma). \tag{8.3.8}$$

where

$$W(\sigma) = \min_{\boldsymbol{x} \geq \mathbf{0}} \sum_d(\sigma \zeta_d x_d - w_d \log x_d) - \sigma B. \tag{8.3.9}$$

The flows $x_d(\sigma)$ minimizing the Lagrangian for a fixed σ are obtained from the stationary point of the sum in (8.3.9) and, hence, the individual flows are obtained by differentiating the terms of this sum and setting the consecutive derivatives equal to zero:

$$\frac{w_d}{x_d(\sigma)} - \sigma \zeta_d = 0, \tag{8.3.10}$$

resulting in

$$x_d(\sigma) = \frac{w_d}{\sigma \zeta_d}. \tag{8.3.11}$$

Inserting (8.3.11) into (8.3.9) we finally arrive at

$$W(\sigma) = \sum_d(w_d - w_d \log \frac{w_d}{\sigma \zeta_d}) - \sigma B. \tag{8.3.12}$$

The maximum of the dual function is attained at the stationary point of (8.3.12) with respect to the multiplier σ obtained from the equality

$$\sum_d \frac{w_d}{\sigma} - B = 0. \tag{8.3.13}$$

Hence, the optimal multiplier σ^* is given by

$$\sigma^* = \sum_d \frac{w_d}{B} \tag{8.3.14}$$

which immediately implies (8.3.3a) and (8.3.3b). ■

Note that the maximum of the objective function (8.3.3a) depends only on B (provided that the rest of the constants are fixed); (8.3.3a) implies that this maximum is of the form:

$$F(B) = a \log B + b. \qquad (8.3.15)$$

Furthermore, from formula (8.3.3a) it is deduced that when the paths for the flows realizing the demands are also subject to optimization, then the optimal solution will assign each demand flow x_d to its shortest path. This is because only the second term on the right-hand side of (8.3.3a) depends on the path selection and it is minimized when the shortest paths are used.

Now consider problem D/PF/BCUF with additional constraints on flows:

$$h_d \le x_d \le H_d, \quad d = 1, 2, \dots, D. \qquad (8.3.2e)$$

The resulting optimization problem is referred to as D/PF/BCBF (budget constraint and bounded flows). We allow lower bounds to be 0 and the upper bounds to be $+\infty$. Without loss of generality, we assume that the sharp inequalities $h_d < H_d$ hold, and that the lower bound, the upper bounds, and the budget fulfill the inequality $\sum_d h_d \zeta_d < B < \sum_d H_d \zeta_d$. Problem D/PF/BCBF can be effectively treated by the dual approach as well. The additional constraint (8.3.2e) is not dualized and is taken into account explicitly in the minimization of the Lagrangian (8.3.6) for a fixed multiplier σ. This implies that formula (8.3.11) takes the form:

$$x_d(\sigma) = \begin{cases} h_d & \text{if } \frac{w_d}{\sigma\zeta_d} < h_d \\ \frac{w_d}{\sigma\zeta_d} & \text{if } h_d \le \frac{w_d}{\sigma\zeta_d} \le H_d \\ H_d & \text{if } H_d < \frac{w_d}{\sigma\zeta_d}. \end{cases} \qquad (8.3.16)$$

In this case the dual function can be maximized in an exact way, but explicit formulae like (8.3.3a) to (8.3.3b) are not available. To maximize the dual function we first calculate the threshold values for σ following (8.3.16):

$$\sigma_d^1 = \frac{w_d}{H_d \zeta_d} \qquad (8.3.17a)$$

$$\sigma_d^2 = \frac{w_d}{h_d \zeta_d}. \qquad (8.3.17b)$$

Note that, for a given d, $\sigma_d^1 < \sigma_d^2$ because $h_d < H_d$, and also that $\sigma_d^1 = 0$ if $H_d = +\infty$, and $\sigma_d^2 = +\infty$ if $h_d = 0$. Now the relation (8.3.16) can be rewritten as:

$$x_d(\sigma) = \begin{cases} h_d & \text{if } 0 \le \sigma < \sigma_d^1 \\ \frac{w_d}{\sigma\zeta_d} & \text{if } \sigma_d^1 \le \sigma \le \sigma_d^2 \\ H_d & \text{if } \sigma > \sigma_d^2. \end{cases} \qquad (8.3.18)$$

The next step is to sort all σ_d^1 and σ_d^2 in non-decreasing order (note that in the sorted sequence some of the elements can be equal). Then, from each subsequence of equal elements all but one element is deleted yielding a shorter sequence $(s_1, s_2, \dots, s_n)$ with the property

$$s_1 < s_2 < \dots < s_n, \qquad (8.3.19)$$

where s_1 may be equal to 0 and s_n may be equal to $+\infty$. Now we form the following $n-1$ intervals:

$$[s_1, s_2],\ [s_2, s_3],\ \dots, [s_{n-1}, s_n] \tag{8.3.20}$$

and for each of them ($[s_j, s_{j+1}]$, $j = 1, 2, \dots, n-1$) we introduce three sets of indices (demands):

$$\begin{aligned} L_j &= \{d:\ x_d(\sigma) = h_d \text{ for } [s_j, s_{j+1}]\} \\ F_j &= \{d:\ x_d(\sigma) = \tfrac{w_d}{\sigma\zeta_d} \text{ for } [s_j, s_{j+1}]\} \\ U_j &= \{d:\ x_d(\sigma) = H_d \text{ for } [s_j, s_{j+1}]\}. \end{aligned} \tag{8.3.21}$$

Note that $L_j \cup F_j \cup U_j = \{1, 2, \dots, D\}$ for $j = 1, 2, \dots, n-1$, which merely states that for each p the demands are partitioned into three disjoint sets. Also, $F_i \neq F_j$ for $i \neq j$, $i, j = 2, 3, \dots, n-2$ (provided F_i and $F_j \neq \emptyset$). For each interval $[s_j, s_{j+1}]$ the dual function takes the form

$$\begin{aligned} W(\sigma) = \ & \min_{\boldsymbol{x}\geq\mathbf{0}}\{\textstyle\sum_{d\in F_j}(\sigma\zeta_d x_d - w_d \log x_d) - \\ & -\sigma(B - \textstyle\sum_{d\in L_j}\zeta_d h_d - \sum_{d\in U_j}\zeta_d H_d) - \\ & -\textstyle\sum_{d\in L_j} w_d \log h_d - \sum_{d\in U_j} w_d \log H_d\} \end{aligned} \tag{8.3.22}$$

or equivalently

$$\begin{aligned} W(\sigma) = \ & \textstyle\sum_{d\in F_j}(w_d - w_d \log(\frac{w_d}{\sigma\zeta_d})) - \\ & -\sigma(B - \textstyle\sum_{d\in L_j}\zeta_d h_d - \sum_{d\in U_j}\zeta_d H_d) - \\ & -\textstyle\sum_{d\in L_j} w_d \log h_d - \sum_{d\in U_j} w_d \log H_d. \end{aligned} \tag{8.3.23}$$

Example 8.5

Consider the dual function of problem D/PF/BCBF for a simple network with $D = 3$ demands and with path costs $\zeta_1 = \zeta_2 = \zeta_3 = 1$, reward coefficients $w_1 = 1$, $w_2 = 2, w_3 = 10$, and the budget $B = 13$. The bounds are as follows: $h_1 = 3, h_2 = 2, h_3 = 0, H_1 = +\infty, H_2 = +\infty, H_3 = 5$. The parameters imply that the intervals (8.3.20) are: $[0, \frac{1}{3}], [\frac{1}{3}, 1], [1, 2], [2, +\infty)$. Figure 8.8 illustrates the dual function for the considered network. ●

Function (8.3.23), as the dual function of the convex Problem (8.3.2a) to (8.3.2e), is concave and, thus, continuous (refer to Section A.6 of Appendix A). Figure 8.8 suggests that it is also differentiable, which indeed is the case. Note that according to (8.3.23), the first derivative of the dual function in interval $[s_j, s_{j+1}]$ is equal to

$$W(\sigma) = B - \textstyle\sum_{d\in L_j}\zeta_d h_d - \sum_{d\in U_j}\zeta_d H_d + \sum_{d\in F_j}\dfrac{w_d}{\sigma} \tag{8.3.24}$$

and consider a point s_j ($j \geq 2$). Because of (8.3.18), for all demands d that change category from U_j to F_j at this point, the equalities

$$H_d = \frac{w_d}{s_j\zeta_d} \tag{8.3.25}$$

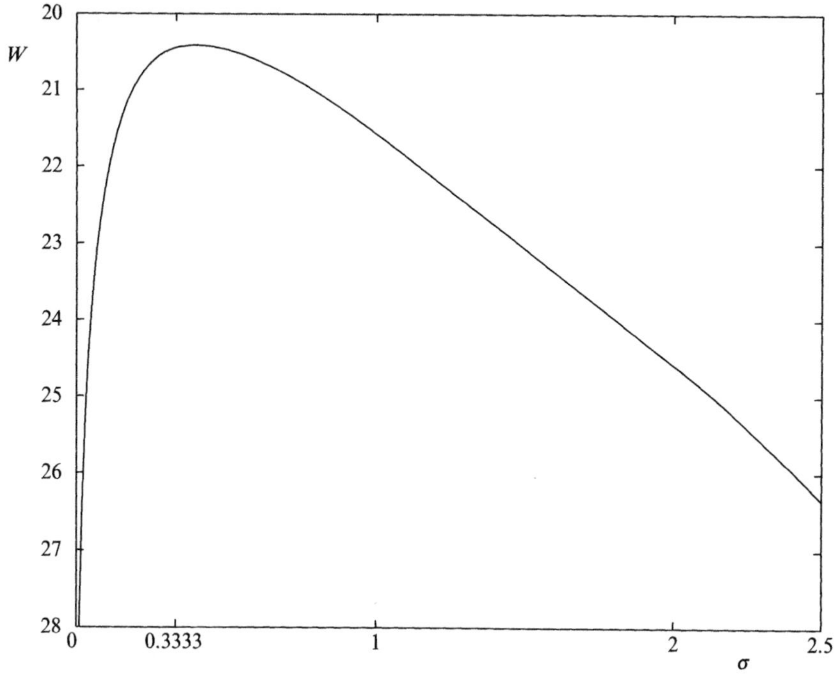

FIGURE 8.8 A Dual Function

hold, so the terms $\zeta_d H_d$ and $\frac{w_d}{s_j}$ cancel each other in (8.3.24). The same holds for F_j and L_j, and for the lower bound h_d at point s_j. Hence, the left and right derivatives of the dual function are equal at each point $s_j, j = 2, 3, \ldots, n-1$.

Observe that the dual function (8.3.23) is not differentiable twice. According to (8.3.24), in interval $[s_j, s_{j+1}]$ its second derivative is equal to

$$W''(\sigma) = -\sum_{d \in F_j} \frac{w_d}{\sigma^2}, \tag{8.3.26}$$

so in general it is discontinuous at the ends of the intervals (8.3.20) where sets F_j change. Also note that in the case when the set F_j is empty the dual function $W(\sigma)$ is linear in $[s_j, s_{j+1}]$ implying that

$$W'(\sigma) = const \;\text{ and }\; W''(\sigma) = 0 \;\text{ for }\; [s_j, s_{j+1}] \quad \text{(refer to (8.3.24) and (8.3.26))}.$$

The dual function is convex and differentiable, so its maximum is attained at a stationary point σ^0 resulting from the equation:

$$W'(\sigma) = 0, \quad \sigma \in [0, +\infty). \tag{8.3.27}$$

A stationary point σ^0 can only belong to one of the intervals (8.3.20). Let j be the index of interval $[s_j, s_{j+1}]$ such that $\sigma^0 \in [s_j, s_{j+1}]$. This interval has the unique property that when we use the dual function given by formula (8.3.23) for the considered j in equation (8.3.27) then the resulting stationary point(s) actually belongs to $[s_j, s_{j+1}]$. Hence, the considered stationary point is given by the formula

$$\sigma^* = \begin{cases} \sum_{d \in F_j} \frac{w_d}{B - \sum_{d \in L_j} \zeta_d h_d - \sum_{d \in U_j} \zeta_d H_d} & \text{if } F_j \neq \emptyset \\ \text{any } \sigma \in [0, +\infty) & \text{if } F_j = \emptyset \text{ and } B = \sum_{d \in L_j} \zeta_d h_d + \sum_{d \in U_j} \zeta_d H_d \\ \text{does not exist} & \text{if } F_j = \emptyset \text{ and } B \neq \sum_{d \in L_j} \zeta_d h_d + \sum_{d \in U_j} \zeta_d H_d. \end{cases} \tag{8.3.28}$$

Note that the unique interval j with the property $\sigma^0 \in [s_j, s_{j+1}]$ can be identified by the property

$$W'(s_j) \geq 0 \text{ and } W'(s_{j+1}) \leq 0 \tag{8.3.29}$$

and that it may happen that the dual function is constant in this interval. The optimal multiplier defines the optimal demand flows via formula (8.3.18).

***Example 8.5** (Continued)*

It can be easily verified that for the consecutive intervals $[0, \frac{1}{3}], [\frac{1}{3}, 1], [1, 2], [2, +\infty)$, the respective stationary points given by (8.3.28) are: $\frac{3}{8}, \frac{2}{5}$, no stationary point, $\frac{5}{4}$. Thus, as expected from Figure 8.8, the stationary point of the dual function belongs only to the second interval: $\frac{2}{5} \in [\frac{1}{3}, 1]$. The corresponding optimal flows are $x_1^* = 3, x_2^* = 5$, and $x_3^* = 5$. Note that the dual function is linear in interval $[1, 2]$ and it has no stationary point there. ●

8.3.3 Uncapacitated Problems With an Extended Objective Function

The budget constraint (8.3.2b) can be moved to the objective function, resulting in the following optimization problem with an extended objective function for unbounded flows.

***XX:* D/PF/EOUF** **Link-Path Formulation**

Extended Objective and Unbounded Flows

additional constant

B_0 upper bound for the cost of links (in general different than budget B in D/PF/BCUF)

variables

x_d flow (bandwidth) allocated to the path of demand d, $\boldsymbol{x} = (x_1, x_2, \dots, x_D)$

y_e capacity of link e, $\boldsymbol{y} = (y_1, y_2, \dots, y_E)$

objective

$$\text{maximize } \boldsymbol{F}(\boldsymbol{x}, \boldsymbol{y}) = \sum_d w_e \log x_d - \sum_e \xi_e y_e \tag{8.3.30a}$$

constraints

$$\sum_e \xi_e y_e \le B_0 \qquad (8.3.30b)$$

$$\sum_d \delta_{ed} x_d \le y_e, \qquad e = 1, 2, \ldots, E \qquad (8.3.30c)$$

$$\boldsymbol{x}, \boldsymbol{y} \ge \boldsymbol{0}. \qquad (8.3.30d)$$

The interpretation of the objective function (8.3.30a) is as follows. The client associated with demand d does not pay for x_d (assigned bandwidth) but for the logarithm of x_d. The value of w_d is interpreted as the unit revenue from demand d in a certain (long) time interval. Hence, the whole objective function determines the revenue from the network minus the investment cost.

Remark 8.4

The revenue from a demand (network user) can be negative if it is not assigned enough bandwidth. With function (8.3.30a) this happens if the flow assigned to the user is $<$ 1. Certainly, the threshold equal to 1 can be easily modified and even made demand dependent. ♦

Due to (8.3.15) and (8.3.3a), the maximal value of the objective function (8.3.30a) is attained at the maximum, with respect to variable B, of the one-variable function (constant b in (8.3.15) is skipped)

$$\boldsymbol{G}(B) = (\log B)\sum_d w_d - B \qquad (8.3.31a)$$

$$\text{over } 0 \le B \le B_0. \qquad (8.3.31b)$$

The optimum of (8.3.31a) is attained either at $B = \sum_d w_d$ (if $\sum_d w_d \le B_0$) or at B_0 (if $\sum_d w_d > B_0$). Clearly, the optimal B is the optimal total cost of links $\sum_e \xi_e y_e$. Furthermore, from (8.3.3a) it follows that if $\sum_d w_d \le B_0$ then the optimal value of (8.3.30a) is equal to

$$\boldsymbol{F}^* = \sum_d w_d \log(\frac{w_d}{\zeta_d}) - \sum_d w_d \qquad (8.3.32)$$

and the optimal flows are given by

$$x_d^* = \frac{w_d}{\zeta_d}, \quad d = 1, 2, \ldots, D. \qquad (8.3.33)$$

Note that D/PF/EOUF can be formulated equivalently as follows.

$$\textbf{maximize} \quad \boldsymbol{F}(\boldsymbol{x}) = \sum_d (w_d \log x_d - \zeta_d x_d) \qquad (8.3.34a)$$

$$\textbf{subject to} \quad \sum_d \zeta_d x_d \le B_0. \qquad (8.3.34b)$$

The objective function (8.3.34a) is strictly convex and its unique solution, not taking the budget constraint (8.3.34b) into account, is obviously given by (8.3.33). A problem arises, however, when the budget constraint is not satisfied at such a solution, i.e., when

$\sum_d \zeta_d x_d^* > B_0$. If this is the case then in order to find the optimal solution we have to solve problem D/PF/BCUF (8.3.2) from Section 8.3.2 for the fixed budget $B = B_0$.

For the bounded flows case, constraint (8.3.2e) is added to the formulation (8.3.30) of D/PF/EOUF. The resulting problem will be referred to as D/PF/EOBF (extended objective and bounded flows). The unique solution of D/PF/EOBF, again not taking the budget constraint (8.3.34b) into account, is given by

$$x_d^* = \begin{cases} h_d & \text{if } \frac{w_d}{\zeta_d} \le h_d \\ \frac{w_d}{\zeta_d} & \text{if } h_d \le \frac{w_d}{\zeta_d} \le H_d \\ H_d & \text{if } \frac{w_d}{\zeta_d} \ge H_d. \end{cases} \qquad d = 1, 2, \dots, D \tag{8.3.35}$$

Again, a problem arises when the budget constraint is not satisfied at this solution. Then the optimal solution is found by solving problem D/PF/BCUF (8.3.2) from Section 8.3.2 for the fixed budget $B = B_0$. Here, it is assumed that $\sum_d h_d \zeta_d < B < \sum_d H_d \zeta_d$ in order to make the considered problem feasible and non-trivial.

8.3.4 Numerical Examples

In this section we provide several numerical examples illustrating the effectiveness of the introduced solutions. We start, however, with a general example showing the essence of the difference between the concepts of PF and MMF.

Example 8.5 *A General Example*

Consider problem D/PF/EOUF (8.3.30) from Section 8.3.3 for the special case with all instances of w_d and ξ_e equal to 1. Then at the optimal solution (we skip constraint (8.3.30b)) the following equalities hold:

$$B = \sum_e y_e = D \tag{8.3.36a}$$

$$x_d^* = \frac{1}{n_d}, \qquad d = 1, 2, \dots, D, \tag{8.3.36b}$$

where n_d is the length of the shortest path of demand d (i.e., number of links in the path). Hence, the flow of demand d is equal to the reciprocal of the length of its shortest path. This property justifies the name "proportionally fair" used for the solution of D/PF/EOUF.

Now consider the MMF counterpart of problem D/PF/BCUF (8.3.2) with $B = D$. This problem consists essentially in finding the link capacity allocation that maximizes the minimal demand flow for a fixed total cost of links (constraint (8.3.2b)). This is in fact equivalent to assuming that all demand flows are equal to each other ($x_d \equiv \underline{x}$, for some $\underline{x}$). The optimal solution of such a problem is to allocate, for each demand d, the flow $\underline{x}$ to one of its shortest paths. Assuming (8.3.36a) we get

$$\underline{x} = x_d^* = \frac{D}{\sum_d n_d}, \qquad d = 1, 2, \dots, D. \tag{8.3.37}$$

It is intuitively obvious that the throughput from a PF network equal to

$$\sum_d \frac{1}{n_d} \tag{8.3.38}$$

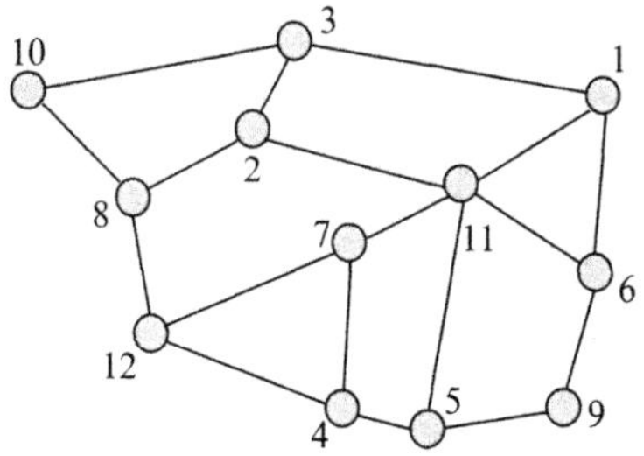

FIGURE 8.9 A Backbone Network

is not less than the throughput from a MMF network equal to

$$\frac{D^2}{\sum_d n_d}. \tag{8.3.39}$$

Formally, this fact follows from a known inequality

$$(\sum_d \frac{1}{n_d})(\sum_d n_d) \geq D^2, \tag{8.3.40}$$

that can be easily proven by mathematical induction. In fact the equality in (8.3.40), implying that the two throughputs (8.3.38) and (8.3.39) are equal, holds if (and only if) the shortest paths for all the demands are of equal lengths. ●

Example 8.6 *A Backbone Network*

Consider the 12-node backbone network (Figure 8.9) with $E = 18$ links and $D = 66$ demands. Consider, as before, the case with all instances of w_d and ξ_e equal to 1. The objective function (8.3.30a) of problem D/PF/EOUF is shown in Figure 8.10; this figure reveals that the maximum is attained, as stated in Example 8.5, at $B = D = 66$, with the optimal multiplier $\sigma = 1$. Optimal flows are equal to reciprocals of the lengths of the shortest paths measured as the number of links in a path. The dual function for the optimal budget $B = 66$ is depicted in Figure 8.11. Note that $F(66) = -W(1) - D$.

In the next case, described in Table 8.1, we consider the backbone network with link unit costs proportional to their length (column 4 in Table 8.1), resulting in the shortest paths of lengths given in column 8. Three trials have been carried out for this case. The first trial corresponds to D/PF/EOUF - the unbounded flow case with the extended objective function and the budget constraint (8.3.30b) skipped. The optimal flows are given in column 3 (the optimal budget $B = 66$).

In the next two trials bounds (8.3.2e) have been imposed on the flows and applied to Problem D/PF/EOBF. The bounds have been generated randomly and are given in columns 5 and 6 (in effect, $\sum_d h_d \zeta_d = 245.64$). In the second trial we have again assumed $B_0 = 250$. In this case the solution of D/PF/BCBF applies (for $B = 250$). The optimal multiplier for budget $B = 250$ is $\sigma = 2.12$ (Figure 8.12) and the maximum of the primal function (2a) is

TABLE 8.1 **Results for the Backbone Network Diverse Unit Cost Link**

Node	Node	x (No Bounds)	Direct Link Unit cost	h	H	w	ζ	x $B_0=250$	x $B_0=300$
1	2	0.241	∞	0.5568	10.0000	1.0000	4.1500	h	h
1	3	0.2941	3.4	1.4273	2.0593	1.0000	3.4000	h	h
1	4	0.2128	∞	0.0500	0.5785	1.0000	4.7000	0.1005	0.2128
1	5	0.241	∞	1.0318	100.0000	1.0000	4.1500	h	h
1	6	0.5882	1.7	0.9636	1.8253	1.0000	1.7000	h	h
1	7	0.3226	∞	0.7455	100.0000	1.0000	3.1000	h	h
1	8	0.1786	∞	1.4273	100.0000	1.0000	5.6000	h	h
1	9	0.3226	∞	0.7455	100.0000	1.0000	3.1000	h	h
1	10	0.5405	∞	1.6182	100.0000	1.0000	6.3000	h	h
1	11	0.5045	1.85	0.4045	100.0000	1.0000	1.8500	h	0.5405
1	12	0.1852	∞	1.9727	3.3252	1.0000	5.4000	h	h
2	3	1	1	0.7727	2.2299	1.0000	1.0000	h	h
2	4	0.2	∞	1.8636	3.7531	1.0000	5.0000	h	h
2	5	0.2174	∞	1.1545	100.0000	1.0000	4.6000	h	h
2	6	0.2532	∞	0.9773	100.0000	1.0000	3.9500	h	h
2	7	0.2817	∞	1.4682	2.7909	1.0000	3.5500	h	h
2	8	0.6897	1.45	0.2955	100.0000	1.0000	1.4500	0.3256	0.6897
2	9	0.1869	∞	0.6701	10.0000	1.0000	5.3500	h	h
2	10	0.3333	∞	0.7182	100.0000	1.0000	3.0000	h	h
2	11	0.4348	2.3	1.1273	2.7858	1.0000	2.3000	h	h
2	12	0.3571	∞	0.0500	0.3242	1.0000	2.8000	0.1686	h
3	4	0.1667	∞	2.1364	3.2286	1.0000	6.0000	h	h
3	5	0.1786	∞	0.9701	10.0000	1.0000	5.6000	h	h
3	6	0.202	∞	0.0500	0.8940	1.0000	4.9500	0.0954	0.2020
3	7	0.2198	∞	1.7409	2.6524	1.0000	4.5500	h	h
3	8	0.4082	∞	0.1607	10.0000	1.0000	2.4500	0.1927	0.4082
3	9	0.1575	∞	2.2318	3.6475	1.0000	6.3500	h	h
3	10	0.3448	2.9	0.6909	100.0000	1.0000	2.9000	h	h
3	11	0.303	∞	0.6957	10.0000	1.0000	3.3000	h	h
3	12	0.2632	∞	0.9364	100.0000	1.0000	3.8000	h	h
4	5	1	1	0.0500	0.0543	1.0000	1.0000	h	h

continues

TABLE 8.1 **Results for the Backbone Network Diverse Unit Cost Link** ***continued***

4	6	0.2564	∞	0.9636	100.0000	1.0000	3.9000	*h*	*h*
4	7	0.625	1.6	0.0500	0.9533	1.0000	1.6000	0.2951	0.6250
4	8	0.2817	∞	0.4364	10.0000	1.0000	3.5500	*h*	*h*
4	9	0.4	∞	0.0500	0.6348	1.0000	2.5000	0.1889	0.4000
4	10	0.1961	∞	1.8909	2.0246	1.0000	5.1000	*h*	*h*
4	11	0.3509	∞	1.2773	2.0567	1.0000	2.8500	*h*	*h*
4	12	0.4545	2.2	0.0500	0.4358	1.0000	2.2000	0.2146	*h*
5	6	0.3448	∞	1.2909	2.6090	1.0000	2.9000	*h*	*h*
5	7	0.3846	∞	1.2091	2.2864	1.0000	2.6000	*h*	*h*
5	8	0.2198	∞	1.1409	100.0000	1.0000	4.5500	*h*	*h*
5	9	0.6667	1.5	0.3091	100.0000	1.0000	1.5000	0.3148	0.6667
5	10	0.1639	∞	1.5636	100.0000	1.0000	6.1000	*h*	*h*
5	11	0.4348	2.3	0.0500	0.5710	1.0000	2.3000	0.2053	0.4348
5	12	0.3125	∞	0.0553	10.0000	1.0000	3.2000	0.1476	0.3125
6	7	0.3448	∞	0.0500	0.2103	1.0000	2.9000	0.1628	*h*
6	8	0.1852	∞	1.9727	2.5668	1.0000	5.4000	*h*	*h*
6	9	0.7143	1.4	0.0500	0.5278	1.0000	1.4000	0.3373	*h*
6	10	0.1439	∞	1.7955	100.0000	1.0000	6.9500	*h*	*h*
6	11	0.6061	1.65	0.3500	100.0000	1.0000	1.6500	*h*	0.6061
6	12	0.1923	∞	1.3182	100.0000	1.0000	5.2000	*h*	*h*
7	8	0.274	∞	1.4955	2.6510	1.0000	3.6500	*h*	*h*
7	9	0.2439	∞	1.6182	2.2805	1.0000	4.1000	*h*	*h*
7	10	0.1923	∞	0.0500	1.0369	1.0000	5.2000	0.0908	0.1923
7	11	0.8	1.25	0.8409	0.8442	1.0000	1.2500	*h*	*h*
7	12	0.4348	2.3	0.3776	10.0000	1.0000	2.3000	*h*	0.4348
8	9	0.1653	∞	1.5500	100.0000	1.0000	6.0500	*h*	*h*
8	10	0.6452	1.55	0.9227	2.2814	1.0000	1.5500	*h*	*h*
8	11	0.2667	∞	1.5227	1.5939	1.0000	3.7500	*h*	*h*
8	12	0.7407	1.35	0.0500	1.0234	1.0000	1.3500	0.3498	0.7407
9	10	0.1316	∞	0.0500	0.4013	1.0000	7.6000	0.0621	0.1316
9	11	0.3279	∞	1.3318	2.5470	1.0000	3.0500	*h*	*h*
9	12	0.2128	∞	0.0500	0.6029	1.0000	4.7000	0.1005	0.2128
10	11	0.1887	∞	0.8381	10.0000	1.0000	5.3000	*h*	*h*
10	12	0.3448	∞	0.2515	10.0000	1.0000	2.9000	*h*	0.3448
11	12	0.2817	∞	0.8682	100.0000	1.0000	3.5500	*h*	*h*

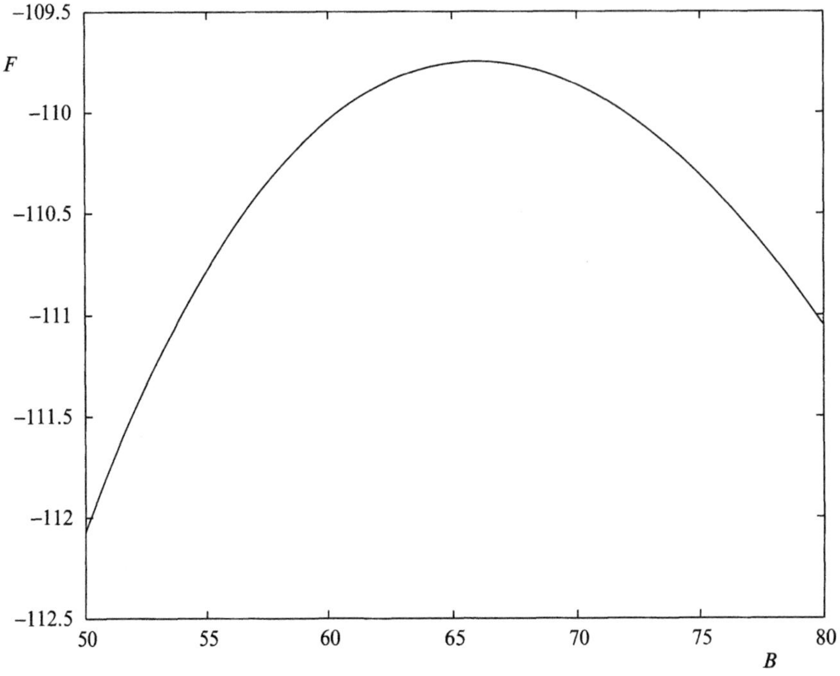

FIGURE 8.10 The Primal Function of D/PF/EOUF

$\boldsymbol{F}(\boldsymbol{x}) = -30.65$ (the optimal flows are given in column 9). Note that assuming $x_d = h_d$ for $d = 1, 2, \ldots, 66$, we would get $\boldsymbol{F}(\boldsymbol{x}) = -47.09$.

Finally, in the third trial we have assumed that the budget constraint is large enough ($B_0 = 300$) and, in the resulting trivial solution of problem (column 10), the optimal budget $\sum_d \zeta_d x_d$ equals 259.49 and the optimal primal solution is $\boldsymbol{F}(\boldsymbol{x}) = -17.27$.

The following conclusions can be derived from the results of Table 8.1.

- It can be verified that the flows with small lower bound are likely to exceed the lower bound so that $x_d > h_d$.
- In trials 2 and 3, the number of flows x_d different from h_d and H_d in the optimal solution is approximately 30%. This relatively small percentage should be compared to the objective function gain, using optimal flows instead of the lower bounds.
- An obvious way to proceed for a network operator who wishes to apply the solution of problem D/PF/EOBF, is to first assign all flows according to (8.3.35) and then compute $\sum_d \zeta_d x_d$ and $\sum_d \zeta_d h_d$. If the resulting budget $B^{opt} = \sum_d \zeta_d x_d$ is acceptable, the corresponding solution can be applied. Otherwise some $B_0 > \sum_d \zeta_d h_d$ should be chosen and D/PF/BCBF applied. Then it can be checked what is the actual loss with respect to the objective function choosing this B_0 instead of B^{opt}.

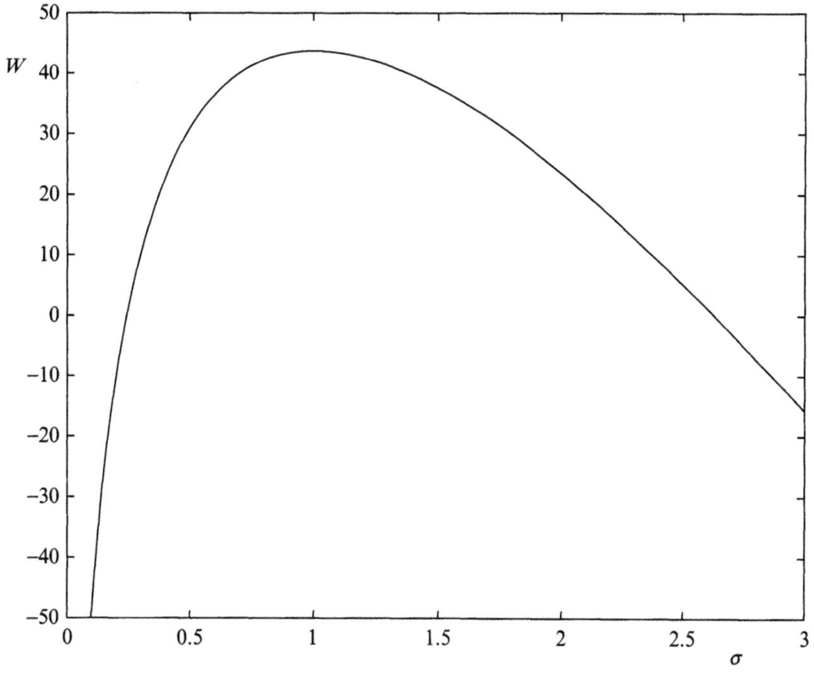

FIGURE 8.11 The Dual Function of D/PF/BSUF

8.3.5 Minimum Delay

It should be emphasized that other utility functions (besides the logarithmic one) can be used for specifying the optimization objective. For instance, instead of the logarithmic revenue (8.3.2a) in problem D/PF/BCUF, the so-called *minimum delay* [MR99] objective can be used:

$$\textit{maximize} \quad \boldsymbol{F}(\boldsymbol{x}) = -\textstyle\sum_d w_d(\frac{1}{x_d}) \qquad (\textit{minimize} \quad \boldsymbol{F}(\boldsymbol{x}) = \textstyle\sum_d \frac{w_d}{x_d}) \tag{8.3.41}$$

With the reciprocal of the demand volume used as the utility function, objective (8.3.41) may be interpreted as minimizing the overall potential delay of the transfers in progress. For objective (8.3.41) the formula (8.3.3) from Proposition 8.7 become as follows (Exercise 8.13):

$$F(\boldsymbol{x}^*) = \frac{(\sum_d \sqrt{\sum_d w_d \zeta_d})^2}{B} \tag{8.3.42a}$$

$$x_d^* = \frac{B\sqrt{\frac{w_d}{\zeta_d}}}{\sum_d \sqrt{\sum_d w_d \zeta_d}} \tag{8.3.42b}$$

$$y_e^* = \textstyle\sum_d \delta_{ed} x_d^*. \tag{8.3.42c}$$

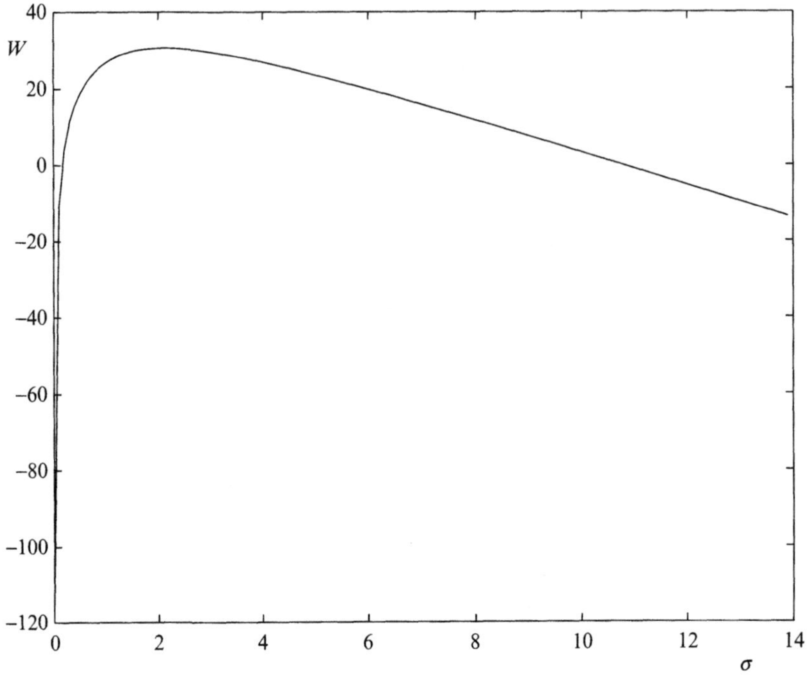

FIGURE 8.12 The Dual Function for Trial 2

8.3.6 Non-Bifurcated Flows

The design problems for PF assuming unsplittable flows are probably as difficult (i.e., $\mathcal{NP}$-complete) as those for MMF. It is possible to approach them with the BB method applied to the MIP formulation for the linear approximation of the logarithmic function (Exercise 8.14). Also, the stochastic heuristic methods of Section 5.3 are applicable.

8.4 SUMMARY AND FURTHER READING

In this chapter we have discussed design problems implied by the application of the principles of MMF and PF for the demand volume assignment. In Section 8.1, we have presented the two principles as well as summarized algorithms for solving simple capacitated problems associated with MMF and PF assuming fixed single paths. The algorithms for MMF are commonly known; however, we have formulated them in a general and concise form (Algorithms 8.1 and 8.2) allowing for further extensions required in Section 8.2. Besides, we have given basic theoretical facts underlying the MMF approach.

In Section 8.2, we discussed capacitated and uncapacitated problems involving routing optimization. Its most important part (Section 8.2.1) discusses in detail an efficient algorithmic approach (Algorithms 8.3 and 8.4) for solving the capacitated bifurcated routing problem, together with the theoretical results underlying the approach. The column generation technique is also described and the numerical results are provided. We also briefly discuss the related uncapacitated problems (Section 8.2.2) and capacitated non-bifurcated problems (Section 8.2.3).

Section 8.3 is devoted to a less known material on PF networks optimization. The focus is on the uncapacitated design problem with bifurcated routing under the budget constraint. The dual optimization approach is used to derive the main results leading to efficient solution methods, illustrated with the results of a numerical study.

The issues of fairness have been extensively studied in the field of economics since 1912 [Pig12] and 1920 [Dal20], resulting in a general axiom (called the Pigou-Dalton principle of equitable transfers) used as the starting point for the formal introduction of the notion of fairness ([Sen73] and [You94]), and leading to the majorization theory of fairness ([MO79]), based on the work of [HLP29] and [HLP52]. Applications of fairness in operations research and management sciences can be found in [KO99] and [MS94]. An equivalent mathematical methodology was developed for decisions under risk (more equal distribution can be interpreted as less risky) ([BRT88] and [Lev93]).

Generally, many approaches to general fair (equitable) optimization (the names of fairness, equity and justice are also used in this context) exist. One may use L_p norms for this purpose (e.g., to cover the PF case), with the limiting case $p \to \infty$ representing the lexicographical max-min [MO79]. The notion of MMF (called "state of justice" in [Raw71]; also see [Beh86], [BR91], [Ehr98] and [Ogr97]) is quite intuitive (although complicated mathematically) and can be formally introduced through the axiom of equitable transfer; MMF is known as the nucleolar approach in game theory [PT92].

In practice, in order to achieve different fair solutions (including MMF, PF, and minimum delay) a suitable Schur-concave function aggregating the results (as demand volumes) is maximized [MO79]. The logarithmic function (leading to PF) is a commonly used utility function in economics for decisions under risk [Lev93].

In the telecommunication network context the notion of MMF has been traditionally introduced through the "bottleneck" characterization (see Definition 8.1), and used for modeling data networks ([BG92], [Jaf81], [MR99], [Meg74] and [MW00]). More recent works of [KRT99], [Nac02], [NP02], and [PMF02] use a (more intuitive) lexicographical characterization, extensively used throughout this chapter.

The simple MMF capacitated problems with single predefined paths discussed in Section 8.1 have gained a lot of attention in modeling data networks. Different procedures equivalent to Algorithms 8.1 and 8.2 can be found in [BG92], [FPS+00], [HTP97], and [HTP98]. Approximative distributed algorithms for achieving suboptimal MMF flows (an important practical issue) are presented in [AC96], [HBCN97], and [MOY96].

Capacitated problems involving path (routing) optimization with bifurcated flows, studied in detail in Section 8.2.1, have been considered in [Nac02], [NDGL03], and [PMF02] (also refer to [FMP02] and [PNKF03]). Procedures similar to Algorithm 8.3 have been described in [Nac02] and [Tom02] (they are based on the general idea presented in [Ogr97]; also see [MO92]). Algorithm 8.4, a remarkably effective procedure, is based on the idea presented for another setting in [KLS92]. An analogous problem for a special case of the set of demands with one common source node is considered in [Meg74], where an algorithm for optimal bifurcated MMF allocation is given, and the intuitive result stating that in this particular case the MMF solution maximizes the total throughput is proved. The path generation technique is considered in [Nac02] and [PMF02]. The non-bifurcated (unsplittable) flow optimization problem in capacitated MMF networks (formulated in Section 8.2.3) is considered in [KRT99], where its $\mathcal{NP}$-completeness is demonstrated, and some heuristic solution methods are for the single-source case are discussed (also see [DGG98], [Kle96], and [KS97]). An approximative formulation of the unsplittable capacitated MMF problem and related heuristic methods are presented in [CL02].

The idea underlying the use of convex utility functions for distribution commodities (implying PF) was introduced as early as 1854 by the German economist H.H. Gossen in his book *"The Development of the Laws of Exchange among Men and of the Consequent Rules of Human Action"*. Gossen's first law states that "the pleasure obtained from each additional amount consumed of the same commodity diminishes until satiety is reached" [BBD98]. (A symmetric law could be a statement that the pleasure approaches $-\infty$ as the amount of the consumed commodity tends to 0.) For data/broadband network applications, PF was proposed in [Kel97], with its origin going back to [MMD91] where a product form was presented for such fairness. In [KMT97], the capacitated PF allocation problem with fixed single paths (Section 8.1.3) is studied, and a solution based on the dual approach is proposed. Uncapacitated design problems for PF networks (considered in Section 8.3) have been previously treated in papers [PMF02] and [NP02]. A distributed algorithm for approximative computation of PF flows in a given network is described in [KMT97], [KST01b], and [KST01a].

Let us recall that in the context of data networks, a class of fairness principles referred two as α-fairness, using the utility function of the form $U(X_d) = \frac{w_d X_d^{1-\alpha}}{1-\alpha}$ in the maximized objective is described in [MW00] (also see [Kel03] and [Bou00]). This general utility function covers throughput maximization ($U(X_d) = w_d \log X_d,\ \alpha = 0$), MMF ($\alpha \to \infty$), PF ($U(X_d) = w_d \log X_d,\ \alpha \to 1$), and minimum delay ($U(X_d) = w_d/X_d,\ \alpha = 2$). As already mentioned, more general approaches for characterizing fairness can be found in the optimization literature on fairness (see [MO79], [Sen73], and [You94]).

We also note that a substantial literature exists on the performance of the flow rate control algorithms (protocols) in data/broadband networks from the fairness point of view (see [Jac88], [CJ89], and [KMT97], and a review in [HBCN97]). Certain protocols in data networks tend to approximately realize MMF flows [CCJ95], while some (as TCP) tend to be proportionally fair ([Jac88] and [KMT97]). The issue of how the minimum delay flows can be achieved is discussed in [MR99].

Finally, we mention that there is a substantial number of papers discussing other applications of fairness in computer networks, different from those discussed in this chapter (see [ZS03] and other papers in the same issue of LNCS).

EXERCISES FOR CHAPTER 8

8.1. *Prove Proposition 8.2.

8.2. Formulate the modification of Algorithm 8.3 discussed in Remark 8.2. Compare the computational efficiency of the original algorithm and the modification.

8.3. Formulate a counterpart of A/MMF/FLMP (8.2.1) with demand weights, and upper and lower bounds for demand volumes.

8.4. *Adjust Algorithm 8.3 for the problem specified in Exercise 8.3.

8.5. **Formulate test NBT2 based on the simplex tableau and accounting for the fact that in NBT1 we do not have to find maximal X_d but only to check whether X_d can be increased above t^*.

8.6. *Consider Example 8.3. Let $\boldsymbol{\lambda}^* = (\lambda_1^*, \lambda_2^*, \lambda_3^*)$ be a vector of optimal dual variables corresponding to constraint (8.2.2c) in Problem (8.2.2). Show that the values of $\boldsymbol{\lambda}^*$ computed according to the simplex method have the property: $\boldsymbol{\lambda}^* = (0, \frac{1}{2}, \frac{1}{2})$ or $\boldsymbol{\lambda}^* = (\frac{1}{2}, 0, \frac{1}{2})$.

8.7. *Prove Proposition 8.5.

8.8. Formulate the column generation algorithm for Problem (8.2.5).

8.9. Write down Problem (8.2.5) with arbitrary demand pairs in the node-link formulation.

8.10. Formulate Algorithm 8.4 with Problem (8.2.5) in the node-link formulation.

8.11. Prove that allocation (8.2.15) solves D/MMF/FLMP.

8.12. Formulate the LP approximation of A/PF/FLMP (8.3.1).

8.13. *Derive formulae (8.3.42).

8.14. Formulate the LP approximation of A/PF/FLMP assuming non-bifurcated flows.

III

ADVANCED MODELS

In Part III we deal with more advanced network design models and algorithms building on the background covered thus far.

We start with the protection and restoration design modeling of resilient networks in Chapter 9. These models typically need to take into consideration failure states (for different failure situations) as well as assume some particular type of reconfigurablity (or lack thereof) that may be possible in a specific networking environment. We present different models to capture different flow/capacity reconfiguration/protection options. We then discuss applicability of various models to networks such as digital voice, IP/MPLS, optical, and so on.

The models presented in Chapter 9 usually result in large problem sizes, for example, due to consideration of failure states on top of the normal state. Therefore, we give an extensive discussion on applicability of various decomposition methods and resulting numerical algorithms for such large problems in Chapter 10. We also present numerical results to illustrate the performance of the algorithms. In particular we present a numerical study of a WDM network design.

We then present multi-hour and multi-period network design in Chapter 11. Multi-hour problems typically arise in dynamic traffic networks. The idea here is to capture the traffic dynamics through a discrete set of time-dependent traffic matrices, especially to take advantage of non-coincidence of busy hours, in order to do efficient network design. Multi-time period models are typically faced in transport network planning and deployment where incremental demand over time and possibility of capacity augmentation can affect transport layout design decisions.

Chapter 12 covers all important multi-layer network design. As we have briefly explained in Chapter 1 and illustrated through examples in Chapters 2 and 3, networks are inherently multi-layered. Furthermore, it is important to note that capacity of an upper layer becomes demand for the layer below it; e.g., capacity of links in a traffic network becomes demand volume for the transport network over which this traffic network is provided. This observation leads to a number of important models. Furthermore, the issue of protection/restoration and multi-hour traffic needs also be considered for multi-layer design. Thus, in this chapter, we have extended concepts and models discussed in Chapters 9 and 11 to the multi-layer framework.

Part III culminates with Chapter 13 which presents less known (and quite peculiar) extensions of previously discussed “classical" restoration/multi-layer design models to fair networks which carry elastic traffic. The models discussed in this chapter can be used for restoration design of IP networks, IP over SONET networks, and so on. Chapter 13 builds on the knowledge developed in Chapter 8.

CHAPTER 9

Restoration and Protection Design of Resilient Networks

In this chapter, we generalize material presented in Chapter 4 by adding a new (resilience) dimension to the considered design problems. Now we will discuss network optimization problems not only for the normal network operating state, but also for a set of states corresponding to a selected set of failure situations. The different failure situations are specified by the availability status of the links and nodes and, additionally, by (possibly decreased) demand volumes requested for a particular situation. The resulting optimization problems will be referred to as *restoration design problems*. The issue is that designed networks are resilient (robust) to failures, i.e., the networks are able to carry (possible decreased) demands also when a part of network resources are temporarily failed. In this chapter we will formulate a set of selected representative design problems for resilient networks, corresponding to basic resource protection/restoration mechanisms, illustrating them with appropriate examples. The methods for solving the introduced problems will be discussed in Chapter 10. We will return to multi-state network design in Chapter 11, and discuss multi-hour and multi-period design problems which are closely related to the restoration design considered in this chapter and in Chapter 10.

In Section 9.1, we discuss basic notions associated with network resource failures and protection/restoration mechanisms (jointly called re-establishment mechanisms). Also, simple protection by diverse allocation of demands is illustrated. Section 9.2 deals with design problems related to the link capacity re-establishment mechanisms, including link restoration with shared capacity and hot-standby link protection with dedicated capacity. In Section 9.3, we continue to deal with restoration problems, detailing their relation to path (flow) restoration mechanisms with shared capacity and to hot-standby path protection with dedicated capacity. Section 9.4 discusses various extensions of the problems introduced in the two previous sections, including modular links, unsplittable flows, and so on. In Section 9.5 we briefly present network protection problems, assuming that the normal network capacities and flows are known and given, and the issue is to optimize the allocation of protection capacity for re-establishment of normal demand volumes. We end the chapter with a discussion of the practical applications of the introduced problems (Section 9.6), and provide a summary and further reading (Section 9.7).

In the previous chapters we have used (chapter-dependent) abbreviation conventions for denoting problem formulations. We will continue to use such conventions also in this and subsequent chapters. Since the convention for Chapter 9 becomes quite complex we will now explain its basic elements. For example consider the following abbreviation: DR/CF/BR/CC/LIN/GD. Here DR stands for restoration design, CF for continuous flows, BR for bifurcated routing, CC for continuous link capacity, LIN for linear cost function, and, finally, GD denotes the generalized diversity, i.e., the type of assumed protection/restoration mechanism. We will use such a six-position convention for all problems considered in this chapter. The options for the the first five positions are as follows:

1. DR (restoration design), D (dimensioning for the normal state), P (protection design), D+P (normal design plus protection design)
2. CF (continuous flows), MF (modular flows)
3. BR (bifurcated routing), NBR (non-bifurcated, i.e., single-path routing)
4. CC (continuous link capacity), MC (modular link capacity)
5. LIN (linear cost), MOD (modular cost), CX (convex cost), CV (concave cost), BC (budget constraint); we will use mostly the LIN option.

We will not list options for the sixth position (denoting the re-establishment mechanism type) here because there are too many possibilities, some of them quite complicated. The options will be introduced gradually in the subsequent sections. Some examples of the last position are: LR+BR (bifurcated link restoration), PR+FSBP (path restoration with fixed single back-up path), PR+UR+LBF (path restoration with unrestricted flow reallocation and lower-bounded flows).

Finally, let us recall that if we do not assume the type of a variable then it is continuous and non-negative.

9.1 FAILURE STATES, PROTECTION/RESTORATION MECHANISMS, AND DIVERSITY

Below we will discuss the basic mechanisms for protecting/restoring demand volumes against failures. The capacity/demand protection/restoration mechanisms are activated when a failure situation occurs during the network operation. Roughly speaking, the protection/restoration mechanisms take care of the affected capacities or demand flows by re-establishing them on paths composed of links and nodes that survive the considered failure situation. At the end of this section we will present the two simplest restoration design problems related to diversity in the flow assignment.

9.1.1 *Characterization of Failure States*

Recall that in Section 2.8 in Chapter 2, we first illustrated a protection and restoration model. We will continue our discussion using the same notation, and it may be useful to revisit that section before proceeding further.

Each *failure state* (situation) s is characterized by a vector of link *availability coefficients* $\boldsymbol{\alpha}_s = (\alpha_{1s}, \alpha_{2s}, ..., \alpha_{Es})$ with $0 \le \alpha_{es} \le 1$. Each coefficient α_{es} determines a proportion of the normal capacity y_e of link e, $\alpha_{es} y_e$, that is available on link e in situation

s, where $s = 1, 2, ..., S$ is the predefined list of failure situations. Frequently we will assume that the availability coefficients are binary, i.e., $\alpha_{es} \in \{0, 1\}$. In any case, we do not assume that only one link can fail at a time, although this is a common practice in the literature.

Failure situations are also characterized by vectors of demand coefficients $\boldsymbol{\chi}_s = (\chi_{1s}, \chi_{2s}, ..., \chi_{Ds})$. Each coefficient χ_{ds} determines the proportion of the *reference demand volume* h_d of demand d, $h_{ds} = \chi_{ds} h_d$, that must be realized in situation s. The demand coefficients are used to account for a possible decrease in the volume of demand d realized in failure situation s ($\chi_{ds} < 1$), i.e., to allow for $< 100\%$ demand protection/restoration (the case of $\boldsymbol{\chi}_s = \mathbf{1}$). For example, this factor can be used as a traffic restoration objective is state s.

In many restoration design problems a necessity of distinguishing the normal state arises. This particular situation (state) will be denoted by $s = 0$ and characterized with $\alpha_{e0} \equiv 1$ and $\chi_{d0} \equiv 1$. The demand volume at the normal network operating state becomes the reference demand volume.

Link availability coefficients can be used to model other failure situations, e.g., to model node failures. If a node v fails, we simply set $\alpha_{es} = 0$ for all links incident to the failed node v, and, more importantly, $\chi_{ds} = 0$ for all demands d incident with the failed node (node v is one of the end nodes of demand d). In other words, a side impact of a node failure is that the network is to carry *less* load then before.

Note that if we skip the assumption that demand coefficients are less or equal to 1, and assume no failures ($\boldsymbol{\alpha}_s = \mathbf{1}$ for all situations s), then we can model the multi-hour problems studied in Section 11.1. In this case, the situation-dependent demand coefficient vectors $\boldsymbol{\chi}_s$ allow for specifying different demand volumes ($h_{ds} = \chi_{ds} h_d, d = 1, 2, ..., D$) for different times of the day. On the other hand, the demand volume at various times during the day is not necessarily a scale factor of demand volume at a particular time of the day; thus, in the multi-hour case, it makes more sense to use the term h_{ds} directly to depict the demand volume of demand d at time s, rather than use the product $\chi_{ds} h_d$.

9.1.2 Re-Establishment Mechanisms

An important feature of the mechanisms assuring network robustness (resilience) is the way resources are re-established in case of failures, i.e., protection versus restoration. In standard bodies the term *protection* is used to describe mechanisms that take action to restore connections *before* the failure happens, while restoration refers to mechanisms with such actions taken *after* the failure. In fact, with protection no actions at all may be taken and still the network can be resilient; this is the case, e.g., for networks designed under the path diversity requirement (refer to Section 4.2.1). The term re-establishment will be used jointly for protection or restoration.

We must clearly understand the relevance in terms of the layers or networks where our interest lies as far as protection/restoration is concerned—the role of layers have been discussed in Chapter 1. Protection/restoration capacity is needed for both traffic networks and transport networks. In case of a substantial link failure in a traffic layer, such as circuit-switched voice network, calls that are active on the link would be dropped and the user may re-try—thus, restoration capacity is needed so that retried calls can find capacity; note that for traffic layer, no distinction can be made between normal capacity and capacity needed for restoration. Similar for packet routing on the Internet, packets will be re-routed around the failure. On the other hand for transport network, the protection is provided for automated switch over, i.e., protected capacity cannot be used for normal purpose. Thus, in the rest of the discussion, our restoration mechanism does not refer to how a call or a packet may be re-routed, rather how much restoration capacity is needed so the network has the ability to handle rerouted/reattempted calls or packets.

A second important feature is link versus path re-establishment. *Link re-establishment* means that the capacity of a link is re-established in case of its failure. With *path re-establishment* the end-to-end flows that use failed links are re-established (individually). In Figure 9.1, we illustrate the difference between the link-based mechanism and the path based mechanism. Consider a flow established on path 1-3-4-2 for demand pair $\langle 1,2 \rangle$. If link 3-4 now fails, then with a link-based mechanism a new path will be established around the failed link 3-4, e.g., the path 3-5-6-4. On the other hand, with the path based mechanism, a new end-to-end path for demand pair $\langle 1,2 \rangle$ can be established along the path 1-5-6-2.

Now we will discuss the difference between protection and restoration. *Path protection* (PP) is understood as reservation of resources at the time the flow on the path is set up, so when the failure occurs the restoration is guaranteed. Therefore, path protection mechanism refers to the case where protection (back-up) paths are pre-calculated in advance and the necessary protection (spare) capacity is reserved. When a particular path is broken (in most cases several paths break simultaneously because of link or node failures), then it re-establishes the flow on the predefined back-up path. In *path restoration* (PR) schemes, when a path is broken the network control starts the restoration process by first calculating the back-up path using the available restoration (spare and released) capacity and then by re-establishing the flow. From a capacity design point of view, there is no difference. However, it makes a difference in terms of how a network management system may or may not need to be invoked when an actual failure occurs, similar to link protection or link restoration. We note that typically protection re-establishment mechanisms are used only against single link failures. We will use the term path re-establishment and flow re-establishment interchangeably.

Finally, the re-establishment mechanisms can use either dedicated (reserved) or shared capacity. *Dedicated capacity* is used as the term for the spare capacity required to re-establish a link (or path) that is reserved exclusively for re-establishing this link (or path), and that cannot be used for re-establishing other links (or paths). Mechanisms with dedicated

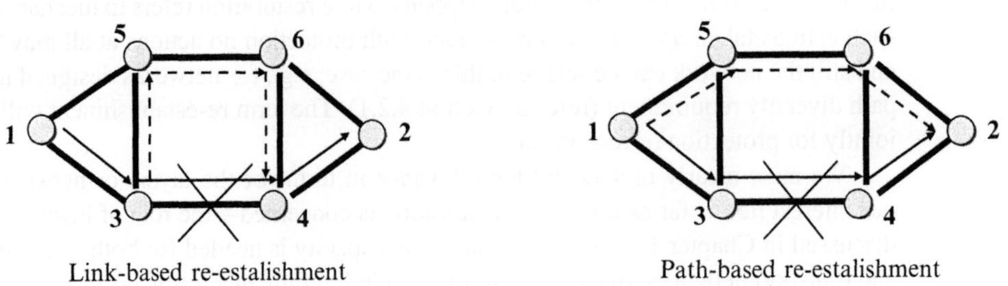

FIGURE 9.1 Link Re-Establishment Versus Path Re-Establishment

capacity are expensive resource-wise, yet relatively simple to operate. Dedicated capacity is typically used in protection schemes, for instance, in the hot-standby protection (also called automated protection switching, or APS for short). Shared capacity means that a common pool of spare resources is used for re-establishing, typically for restoration, broken links or paths, and that the same capacity unit may be used for protecting different resources in different situations. Mechanisms with shared capacity require less spare capacity as compared with those with dedicated capacity but may be much more complicated to control. Protection mechanisms typically use spare capacity, dedicated for this purpose and not used in the normal network operating state. Restoration schemes, however, can also utilize the normal capacity released along the broken paths (e.g., because only one link on a path is broken) for restoring other affected paths.

Perhaps it is time to emphasize that the ultimate goal of any re-establishment mechanism is to protect demand volumes, at least a certain proportion of them, when a failure occurs. This goal can be achieved directly, by the schemes that re-establish the volumes through reconstructing their broken flows (*path re-establishment* (PR)), or in an indirect way through restoring the affected flows by reconstructing the link capacities of failed links (*link re-establishment* (LR)). In the latter scheme, all the flows that use the failed link are reconstructed together which may in fact lead to an ineffective use of the spare capacity (Example 9.2). It is important to note that in fact the link capacity re-establishment scheme works at the neighboring lower layer of network resources than the considered one, in which the PR is realized. To reconstruct the capacity of a link we have to establish a path (or several paths) between the end nodes, for example, nodes v and w, of the failed link and switch the modules reconstructing the failed link capacity units (LCUs) of the capacity of the failed link in the nodes along the back-up path. Note that in the path re-establishment scheme, we reconstruct the failed demand capacity unit (DCU) using the switching mechanism of the considered layer. Also note that the link capacities and LCUs in the considered layer become demand volumes and DCUs, respectively, in the layer below so LR is actually PR in the neighboring lower layer. We will return to this issue in Chapter 12, as we need to know more about the layered architecture of network resources in order to explain it precisely. Henceforth, when considering link re-establishment we will simply assume that the network topology is the same for the two layers in question which makes the use of the single-layer modeling approach correct.

Note that the classical hot-standby path protection mechanism is called the 1+1 *protection* when the signal between its end nodes is transmitted simultaneously on the protected (normal) path and on the protecting back-up path (with dedicated capacity). Then, in case of the failure of the normal path, the receiving nodes switch automatically to the back-up path, making the mechanism simple and fast. Otherwise, when the signal is transmitted only on the normal path, the mechanism is called 1:1 *protection*. Then, both transmitting and receiving nodes have to switch to the back-up path when the failure occurs. A generalization of the 1:1 scheme is the 1:N *protection*, when one back-up path protects N regular paths (then it is assumed that only one of N paths can fail at a time).

Re-establishment of a link or path can be entire or partial. For instance, if links are modular then only a part of its modules may be re-established (partial re-establishment). Also, re-establishment may be splittable (bifurcated) or unsplittable (non-bifurcated). This means that the link or path is re-established on several back-up paths or on exactly one back-up path, respectively. We also mention that there are many variants of the general mechanisms described above. Examples are such mechanisms as the sub-path protection, shared risk link group, ring protection, and so on.

Finally, let us note that from the design problem formulation point of view it is not important whether the re-establishment scheme is of the protection or restoration type. What is really important is, as will soon become clear, whether they use dedicated or shared capacity, and, in the latter case, if they further can use or cannot use the *released* capacity. Therefore, in the sequel we will sometimes use, when it does not lead to misunderstanding, the terms protection and restoration interchangeably.

9.1.3 Protection by Diversity

We end this introductory section with discussing design problems related to the simplest re-establishment (protection) mechanism related to the diversity in the demand flow assignment. In case of failures this mechanism does not take any action at all; due to the diverse flow assignment an assumed portion of demand volumes will simply survive the failure. Consider design problem D/PD, the uncapacitated counterpart of the allocation problem A/PD (4.2.1), assuming path diversity (PD) in allocating demand volumes. Recall that PD is a requirement to split demand volumes into several (link or node disjoint) paths.

***LP:* D/CF/BR+PD/CC/LIN** **Link-Path Formulation**

Normal Design With PD

indices

$d = 1, 2, ..., D$ demands

$p = 1, 2, ..., P_d$ link or node disjoint candidate paths for demand d

$e = 1, 2, ..., E$ links

constants

δ_{edp} = 1 if link e belongs to path p realizing demand d; 0, otherwise

h_d volume of demand d

n_d diversity factor for demand d

ξ_e marginal (unit) cost of link e

variables

x_{dp} (non-negative) flow allocated to path p of demand d

y_e (non-negative) capacity of link e

objective

$$\text{minimize } \boldsymbol{F} = \textstyle\sum_e \xi_e y_e \qquad (9.1.1a)$$

constraints

$$\textstyle\sum_p x_{dp} = h_d, \quad d = 1, 2, ..., D \qquad (9.1.1b)$$

$$x_{dp} \le h_d / n_d, \quad d = 1, 2, ..., D \quad p = 1, 2, ..., P_d \qquad (9.1.1c)$$

$$\textstyle\sum_d \sum_p \delta_{edp} x_{dp} \le y_e, \quad e = 1, 2, ..., E. \qquad (9.1.1d)$$

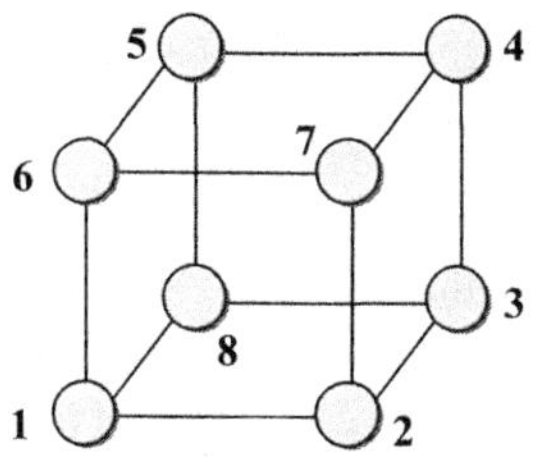

FIGURE 9.2 Cube Network

As already mentioned in Section 4.2.1, the shortest-path allocation rule applies to the LP problem D/CF/BR+PD/CC/LIN with the PD requirement. The optimal rule is to allocate flow equal to h_d/n_d to the shortest path (with respect to link unit costs) of demand d, then the next portion h_d/n_d of flow to the next shortest path, and so on. Note that when the candidate paths are link (node) disjoint then in the case of a single link (node) failure at most $100/n_d$ % of the demand volume is lost and the rest survives.

From the network robustness viewpoint, the PD solution is advantageous because in case of a failure it is likely that only parts of realized demand volumes will be lost, especially when the paths carrying non-zero flows of a demand are link-disjoint (or node-disjoint).

Example 9.1 *Cube Network*

Consider a cube network (Figure 9.2) with E = 12 (undirected) links and D = 12 (undirected) demands (the demands coincide with the links). All link unit costs are equal to 1 ($\xi_e \equiv 1$) and all demand volumes are equal to 3 ($h_d \equiv 3$). The solution of the simple design problem D/SDP (4.1.1) is of course flow allocation $\boldsymbol{x}'$ with all demand volumes allocated to their direct paths, with the cost $\boldsymbol{F}(\boldsymbol{x}') = 36$.

Now let us consider a failure situation scenario with $S = E$ and each situation $s > 0$ corresponding to the total failure of link $e = s$, i.e., $\alpha_{ss} = 0$ and $\alpha_{es} = 1$ for $e \neq s$. If we assume PD with $n_d \equiv 3$ and split each demand volume $h_d \equiv 3$ into three equal flows $x''_{d1} = x''_{d2} = x''_{d3} = 1$ allocated to the shortest set of three node disjoint paths (one short one-link path and two three-link paths) then we get an optimal solution $\boldsymbol{x}''$ of D/CF/BR+PD/CC/LIN with the cost $\boldsymbol{F}(\boldsymbol{x}'') = 12 \cdot (1 + 2 \cdot 3) = 84$. At the same time solution $\boldsymbol{x}''$ realizes at least $\frac{2}{3}$ of each demand volume in any failure situation $s = 1, 2, ..., S$. To summarize, we have achieved a 66% protected network at the expense of a significant cost increase of 48 (from 36 to 84). ●

The general formulation of the protection problem illustrated in Example 9.1 is as follows.

***LP:* DR/CF/BR/CC/LIN/GD** **Link-Path Formulation**

Restoration Design With Generalized Diversity

indices

$d = 1, 2, ..., D$	demands
$p = 1, 2, ..., P_d$	candidate paths for demand d
$e = 1, 2, ..., E$	links
$s = 0, 1, ..., S$	situations or states ($s = 0$ denotes the normal state)

constants

δ_{edp} = 1 if link e belongs to path p realizing demand d; 0, otherwise
h_d volume of demand d
χ_{ds} demand coefficient of demand d in state s, $h_{ds} = \chi_{ds} h_d$
ξ_e unit cost of link e
α_{es} binary availability coefficient of link e in situation s ($\alpha_{es} \in \{0, 1\}$)
θ_{dps} binary availability coefficient of path (d, p) in situation s, $\theta_{dps} = \prod_{\{e:\delta_{edp}=1\}} \alpha_{es}$

variables

x_{dp0} flow allocated to path p of demand d in normal state
y_e capacity of link e

objective

$$\text{minimize } \boldsymbol{F} = \sum\nolimits_e \xi_e y_e \tag{9.1.2a}$$

constraints

$$\sum\nolimits_p \theta_{dps} x_{dp0} \geq h_{ds}, \quad d = 1, 2, ..., D \quad s = 0, 1, ..., S \tag{9.1.2b}$$

$$\sum\nolimits_d \sum\nolimits_p \delta_{edp} x_{dp0} \leq y_e, \quad e = 1, 2, ..., E. \tag{9.1.2c}$$

In the above problem it is important that link availability coefficients α_{es} are binary, and that availability coefficient θ_{dps} of path $\mathcal{P}_{dp}$ in state s is equal to the product of the availability coefficients of all the links belonging to the path, so that $\theta_{dps} = 1$ if (and only if) all links $e \in \mathcal{P}_{dp}$ are available. The assumption of binary availability coefficients is necessary because in general in the case of a partial failure (represented by a fractional coefficient, $0 < \alpha_{es} < 1$) it is not known which particular flows going through the link are broken and lost. In fact, the only reasonable way of modeling partial link failures is to use multi-links between pairs of nodes. If an original multi-link is split into several links and its capacity is appropriately divided among them, then a partial failure of the multi-link is equivalent to a total failure of a subset of these links. This is illustrated in Figure 9.3 where capacity of the multi-link is split equally into its four links.

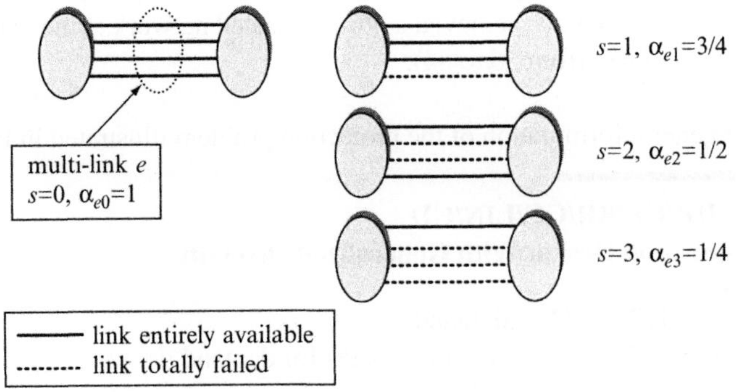

FIGURE 9.3 Representation of Partial Link Failures

If modular links are to be considered then constraint (9.1.2c) should be substituted with

$$\textstyle\sum_d \sum_p \delta_{edp} x_{dp0} \le M y_e \quad e = 1, 2, ..., E \tag{9.1.2d}$$

with the additional requirement that y_e are non-negative integers, and where M denotes the link capacity module (LCU). The resulting mixed integer programming (MIP) problem becomes $\mathcal{NP}$-complete (refer to Proposition 4.3 in Section 4.3.1) and, of course, the shortest-path allocation rule can no longer be applied.

9.2 LINK CAPACITY PROTECTION/RESTORATION

In the next two sections we will survey restoration design problems related to the two basic types of re-establishment mechanisms, for link capacity and demand flows. In this section, we will consider re-establishment of link capacity.

9.2.1 *Link Restoration*

The PD demand volume protection mechanism is costly and *par excellence* passive. In this and the next section we will deal with active protection mechanisms, capable of more efficient demand re-establishment in the case of failures. We start with the link re-establishment mechanism, i.e., link protection or link restoration. Link re-establishment assumes single, total failures of individual links, and restores the entire (or part of) capacity of the failed link on one or several paths between the two end nodes of the link in question (in this way individual flows are re-established indirectly). In link re-establishment the spare capacity is shared.

***LP:* DR/CF/BR/CC/LIN/LR+BR** **Link-Path Formulation**
Design with Link Restoration

indices

- $d = 1, 2, ..., D$ demands
- $p = 1, 2, ..., P_d$ candidate paths for demand d
- $e, \ell = 1, 2, ..., E$ links
- $q = 1, 2, ..., Q_e$ candidate restoration paths for link e

constants

- δ_{edp} = 1 if link e belongs to path p realizing demand d; 0, otherwise
- h_d volume of demand d
- ξ_e unit cost of link e
- $\beta_{\ell eq}$ = 1 if link ℓ belongs to path q restoring link e; 0, otherwise

variables

- x_{dp0} (non-negative) normal flow allocated to path p of demand d
- y_e (non-negative) normal capacity of link e
- z_{eq} (non-negative) flow restoring normal capacity of link e on restoration path q
- y'_e (non-negative) spare, protection capacity of link e (not used in the normal network operating state)

objective

$$\text{minimize } \boldsymbol{F} = \textstyle\sum_e \xi_e (y_e + y'_e) \tag{9.2.1a}$$

constraints

$$\sum_p x_{dp0} = h_d \quad d = 1, 2, ..., D \tag{9.2.1b}$$

$$\sum_d \sum_p \delta_{edp}\, x_{dp0} \leq y_e, \quad e = 1, 2, ..., E \tag{9.2.1c}$$

$$\sum_q z_{eq} = y_e, \quad e = 1, 2, ..., E \tag{9.2.1d}$$

$$\sum_q \beta_{\ell eq} z_{eq} \leq y'_\ell, \quad \ell = 1, 2, ..., E \quad e = 1, 2, ..., E \quad \ell \neq e. \tag{9.2.1e}$$

Constraints (9.2.1b) to (9.2.1c) assure that the normal demand volumes are carried using only the normal link capacities, while constraints (9.2.1d) to (9.2.1e) assure that normal capacity of each link e can be restored using only the protection capacity of the remaining links ℓ ($\ell \neq e$). In this way the normal demand volumes are realized in all single (but total) link failure situations.

Note that spare capacity y'_e of the links is not used in the normal network operating state, and serves only the link capacity restoration purpose. Hence, to obtain the version of Problem (9.2.1) with modular links, we have to assume that

all z_{eq}, y_e and y'_e are non-negative integers. (9.2.2)

Note that the integrality of z_{eq} is essential, since these flows are expressed in LCUs (refer to the discussion in Section 9.1.2).

Example 9.2 *DR/CF/BR/CC/LIN/LR+BR Illustration*

The solution of DR/CF/BR/CC/LIN/LR+BR for the network of Figure 9.2 is first to allocate the normal flows to the shortest single-link paths. This results in $y_e = 3$ for all links. Then we put extra protection capacity on each link equal to $y'_e = 1\frac{1}{2}$. It is easy to check that each link can be restored using two three-link paths. The extra protection cost is 18 and the final cost $\boldsymbol{F} = 36 + 18 = 54$. This is a substantial gain compared to the PD solution of Example 9.1 (where the extra cost was 48).

Moreover, if we admit restoration of only 66% of link capacity, then the extra cost will only be equal to 12 (compared to as much as 48 needed for the PD solution in Example 9.1).

Assume for a moment that on top of the 12 demands corresponding to links we have one more demand, $d = 13$, between nodes $v = 1$ and $v = 4$ with a certain demand volume h_{13} realized on path 1-2-7-4. Suppose that link 2-7 fails and its capacity is restored on path 2-3-4-7. We then see that the affected flow 1-2-7-4 is effectively restored on path 1-2-3-4-7-4, which is not a simple path, and traverses link 7-4 twice! This example illustrates the intrinsic inefficiency of the link re-establishment scheme. ●

Similar to the case of partial links failures discussed in Section 9.1.3, when we admit partial restoration of the link capacity, we must use the notion of the multi-link and its associated links, even though the entire multi-link fails (i.e., all its links fail totally and simultaneously). This is necessary because we must know exactly how the flows using the multi-link are realized, and which part of the multi-link is and is not protected. For instance, if we consider multi-link e in Figure 9.3 then we may assume that only its two upper links are reconstructed in the case of its failure, so in effect we reconstruct only 50% of the capacity, with one-half of the capacity protected and the other one-half not protected.

In practice, link re-establishment requires that the failed link capacity is restored on a single path. This leads to the following MIP modification of DR/CF/BR/CC/LIN/LR+BR, involving (as usual) binary flow variables.

MIP: DR/CF/BR/CC/LIN/LR+SBP **Link-Path Formulation**

Design With Link Restoration on Single Path

indices

$d = 1, 2, ..., D$ demands
$p = 1, 2, ..., P_d$ candidate paths for demand d
$e, \ell = 1, 2, ..., E$ links
$q = 1, 2, ..., Q_e$ candidate restoration paths for link e

constants

δ_{edp} = 1 if link e belongs to path p realizing demand d; 0, otherwise
h_d volume of demand d
ξ_e unit cost of link e
$\beta_{\ell eq}$ = 1 if link ℓ belongs to path q restoring link e; 0, otherwise
K_e upper bound on the normal capacity y_e of link e

variables (all non-negative)

x_{dp0} normal flow allocated to path p of demand d
y_e normal capacity of link e
z_{eq} flow restoring normal capacity of link e on restoration path q
u_{eq} binary flow variable associated with z_{eq}
y'_e protection capacity of link e

objective

$$\text{minimize } \boldsymbol{F} = \textstyle\sum_e \xi_e (y_e + y'_e) \tag{9.2.3a}$$

constraints

$$\textstyle\sum_p x_{dp0} = h_d, \quad d = 1, 2, ..., D \tag{9.2.3b}$$

$$\textstyle\sum_d \sum_p \delta_{edp}\, x_{dp0} \le y_e, \quad e = 1, 2, ..., E \tag{9.2.3c}$$

$$\textstyle\sum_q z_{eq} = y_e, \quad e = 1, 2, ..., E \tag{9.2.3d}$$

$$\textstyle\sum_q u_{eq} = 1, \quad e = 1, 2, ..., E \tag{9.2.3e}$$

$$z_{eq} \le K_e u_{eq}, \quad e = 1, 2, ..., E \quad q = 1, 2, ..., Q_e \tag{9.2.3f}$$

$$\sum_q \beta_{\ell eq} z_{eq} \leq y'_\ell, \quad \ell = 1,2,...,E \quad e = 1,2,...,E \quad \ell \neq e. \tag{9.2.3g}$$

Note that new constraints (9.2.3e) to (9.2.3f) force that $z_{eq} = u_{eq} y_e$, but the right-hand side cannot be used directly in the formulation because it is a term containing a multiplication of two variables which is forbidden in MIP formulations.

Example 9.3 *DR/CF/BR/CC/LIN/LR+SBP Illustration*

The non-bifurcated solution of DR/CF/BR/CC/LIN/LR+SBP for the cube network of Figure 9.2 is different than that of bifurcated LR from Example 9.2. Proceeding as in Example 9.2 we would assign $y'_e = 3$ to each link and, hence, double the normal capacity. For the considered network a cheaper, and in fact in this case optimal, solution is obtained when we form a Hamiltonian cycle (e.g., 1-2-3-4-7-6-5-8-1) and allocate spare capacity $y'_e = 3$ to every link on the cycle. As there are 8 links in the cycle the extra protection cost is 24 and the final cost $\boldsymbol{F} = 36 + 24 = 60$. This is more than for bifurcated LR (36 + 18) but still much less than for PD (36 + 48). If we admit only 66% restoration then the extra cost is equal to 16 (12 for bifurcated LR). ●

9.2.2 *Hot-Standby Link Protection*

Link protection can be achieved also with the hot-standby protection (HS) mechanism. In HS the links are protected by means of dedicated protection paths, so the protection (spare) capacity for one link is not shared with the protection capacity used for other links that fail in other failure situations, as was the case for the previously considered link restoration mechanism. The failed link is restored (entirely in the case of 100% protection) on one single path. In the considered case of link protection, HS assumes single link failures.

MIP: **DR/CF/BR/CC/LIN/LP+HS** **Link-Path Formulation**
Link Protection With Hot-Standby

indices

as in DR/CF/BR/CC/LIN/LR+SBP (9.2.3)

variables

x_{dp0} (non-negative) normal flow allocated to path p of demand d
y_e (non-negative) normal capacity of link e
z_{eq} (non-negative) flow restoring normal capacity of link e on restoration path q
u_{eq} binary flow variable associated with z_{eq}
y'_e (non-negative) protection capacity of link e

objective

$$\text{minimize } \boldsymbol{F} = \sum_e \xi_e (y_e + y'_e) \tag{9.2.4a}$$

constraints

$$\sum_p x_{dp0} = h_d, \quad d = 1,2,...,D \tag{9.2.4b}$$

$$\sum_d \sum_p \delta_{edp} x_{dp0} \leq y_e, \quad e = 1, 2, ..., E \tag{9.2.4c}$$

$$\sum_q z_{eq} = y_e, \quad e = 1, 2, ..., E \tag{9.2.4d}$$

$$\sum_q u_{eq} = 1, \quad e = 1, 2, ..., E \tag{9.2.4e}$$

$$z_{eq} \leq K_e u_{eq}, \quad e = 1, 2, ..., E \quad q = 1, 2, ..., Q_e \tag{9.2.4f}$$

$$\sum_{e \neq \ell} \sum_q \beta_{\ell eq} z_{eq} \leq y'_\ell, \quad \ell = 1, 2, ..., E. \tag{9.2.4g}$$

Observe the difference between constraints(9.2.3g) in DR/CF/BR/CC/LIN/LR+SBP, and (9.2.4g) which reflects the fact that Problem (9.2.3) assumes shared protection capacity and Problem (9.2.4) does not. Now, the spare capacity on link ℓ, y'_ℓ, must be sufficient for restoring all other links as if they fail simultaneously. An analogous problem for PR will be formulated in Section 9.3.5 (Problem (9.3.8)), and problems DR/CF/BR/CC/LIN/LP+HS and (9.3.8) will be compared in Example 9.8.

9.3 DEMAND FLOW RE-ESTABLISHMENT

The PR mechanisms (path protection and path restoration) deal directly with demand flows. Contrary to link re-establishment, the PR mechanisms restore individual flows rather than link capacities, and are not restricted to single-link failures. Also, the PR schemes use not only shared spare capacity, but are also able to reuse the capacity released by the failed flows on those links of the broken paths which survive the failure. The PR design problems are extensions of the simultaneous multi-commodity flow problem in [Min81] and [Min89].

9.3.1 *Unrestricted Reconfiguration*

We start considering PR mechanisms with unrestricted flow reconfiguration.

***LP:* DR/CF/BR/CC/LIN/PR+UR {DR-U}** **Link-Path Formulation**

PR With Unrestricted Reconfiguration

indices

$d = 1, 2, ..., D$	demands
$p = 1, 2, ..., P_d$	candidate paths for demand d
$e = 1, 2, ..., E$	links
$s = 0, 1, ..., S$	situations

constants

δ_{edp}	= 1 if link e belongs to path p realizing demand d; 0, otherwise
h_d	volume of demand d
χ_{ds}	demand coefficient of demand d in state s, $h_{ds} = \chi_{ds} h_d$
ξ_e	unit cost of link e
α_{es}	fractional availability coefficient of link e in state s ($0 \leq \alpha_{es} \leq 1$)

variables

x_{dps} flow allocated to path p of demand d in state s

y_e capacity of link e

objective

$$\text{minimize } \boldsymbol{F} = \sum_e \xi_e y_e \tag{9.3.1a}$$

constraints

$$\sum_p x_{dps} = h_{ds}, \quad d = 1, 2, ..., D \quad s = 0, 1, ..., S \tag{9.3.1b}$$

$$\sum_d \sum_p \delta_{edp} x_{dps} \le \alpha_{es} y_e, \quad e = 1, 2, ..., E \quad s = 0, 1, ..., S. \tag{9.3.1c}$$

Problem DR/CF/BR/CC/LIN/PR+UR (DR-U for short) admits unconstrained reconfiguration of flows in case of a failure. This means that in state s all the normal flows can be first disconnected and then a new flow pattern can be established in the surviving link capacities $\alpha_{es} y_e$, $e = 1, 2, ..., E$. Note that in this case the normal network operating state $s = 0$ does not play any particular role and the situations could be labeled with $s = 1, 2, ..., S$ as well.

It is important to note that the optimal solution of DR-U (9.3.1) and all the other restoration design problems considered in this chapter are in general bifurcated, and that the simple flow allocation rule valid for D/SDP (4.1.1) and similar normal design problems does not apply anymore, as demonstrated in the next example. However, bifurcation is acceptable from a modeling point of view for problems of traffic networks/layers since this represents the bifurcated traffic.

Example 9.4 *Illustration for Different Demand Situations*

Consider the network in Figure 2.10 with two nodes and only one demand $d = 1$, and with 4 situations (three of them failure situations, $S = 3$). The demand volume in all of the situations is the same, $h_{10} = h_{11} = h_{12} = h_{13} = h_{14} = 3$. The unit cost of all three links is the same and equal to 1. In the failure situations only one link is failed as illustrated in the figure. As also shown in the figure, optimal link capacities are all equal to 1.5. The optimal (bifurcated) flows for all situations are given by the figures without brackets. The optimal cost is $\boldsymbol{F} = 4.5$. Note that if we insisted on non-bifurcated flows, the optimal cost would increase to 6, as illustrated in Figure 2.11.

Figure 9.4 illustrates the case with two different situations that differ only in the demanded volume of the two demands (no failures). Assume all unit link costs equal to 1. It easy to see that the optimal solution with the bifurcated flows is $\boldsymbol{F} = 4$, while with the non-bifurcated flows is $\boldsymbol{F} = 5$ (Exercise 9.1). ●

Observe that for the network from Figure 9.2 the optimal solutions for DR-U (9.3.1) and DR/CF/BR/CC/LIN/LR+BR are equivalent. This is not always the case as illustrated by Example 9.5. In fact, assuming single-link failures and 100% restoration, the solution of DR-U (9.3.1) is never more expensive than the solution of DR/CF/BR/CC/LIN/LR+BR,

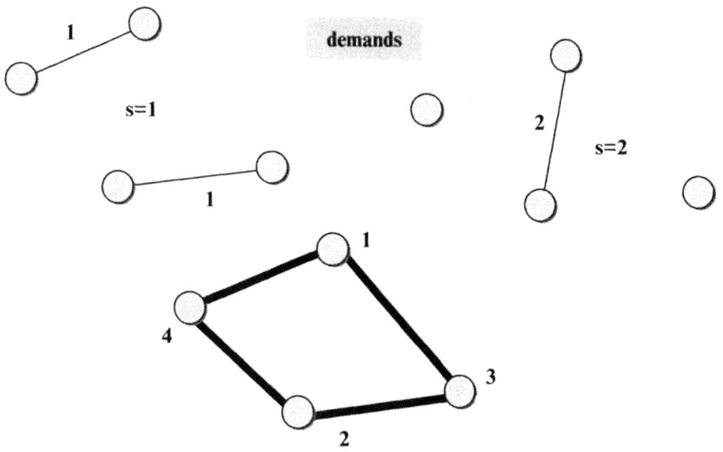

FIGURE 9.4 Two Different Demand Situations

as the optimal solution of the latter can be converted to a feasible solution of the former (Exercise 9.2).

Example 9.5 *Backhaul Due to Restoration*

Consider the network depicted in Figure 9.5. Suppose that there is only one demand $d = 1$ between nodes 1 and 2 with $h_1 = 1$. In the normal network operating state the demand is realized on path 1-3-4-2. Consider only one failure state $s = 1$ with the link between nodes 3 and 4 totally failed. Using link re-establishment we restore the lost link capacity along the path 3-1-5-6-2-4 so the protection cost is 5 (cost of the protection capacity on the five paths used to restore the failed link). The use of PR is more economical. We restore the broken flow on path 1-5-6-2 which gives the extra protection cost equal to 3. The main reason of the ineffectiveness of link re-establishment is that the restored flow traverses links 1-3 and 4-2 twice (Example 9.2)—a situation sometimes referred to as *backhauling*. ●

Note that if modular links are considered then y_e must be non-negative integers and constraint (9.3.1c) substituted with

$$\sum_d \sum_p \delta_{edp} x_{dps} \le \alpha_{es} M y_e \quad e = 1, 2, ..., E \quad s = 0, 1, ..., S. \tag{9.3.1d}$$

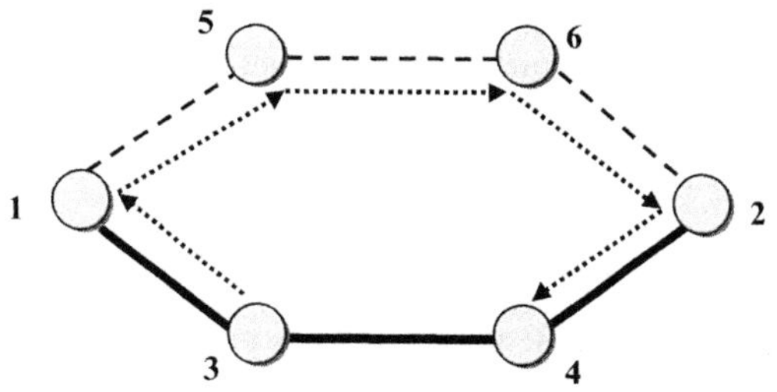

FIGURE 9.5 LR Versus FR

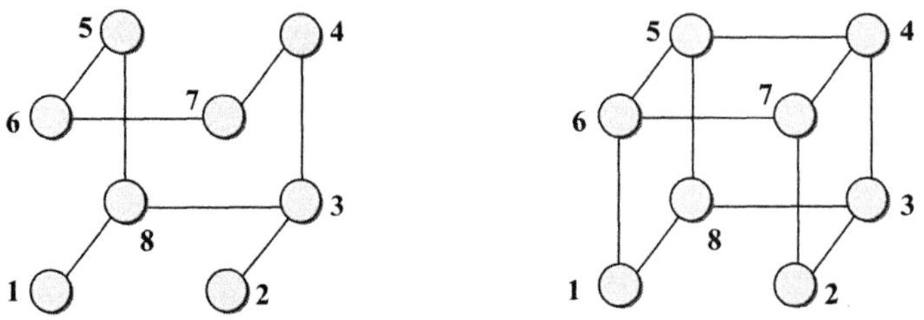

A Normal State Optimal Design B Restoration Design

FIGURE 9.6 Cube Network: Modular Capacity Case

Example 9.6 *Modular Capacity: Cube Network Example Revisited*

Consider the cube network discussed in Example 9.1. Suppose we have the same demand volume set up, i.e., 3 units between adjacent vertices, i.e., $D = 12$, $h_d = 3$, and $d = 1, 2, \ldots, D$. Now we assume that bifurcated flow is allowed, however, capacity needs are modular and in packs of 10 units. The unit modular link cost of a 10-unit pack is assumed to be 1. Then, an optimal design for the normal network case will result in the reduced topology as shown in Figure 9.6a that has 8 links each with one 10-unit pack, thus, the optimal cost is $\boldsymbol{F} = 8$. That is although all the 12 links in the cube network are given as candidate links, only 8 are picked.

Now consider the case where we need to design for any possible link failure (in the original candidate cube network). With modular capacity of 10-unit packs, consider all 13 states (normal state plus 12 single-link failure cases), the optimal design will result in requiring only 11 links each with a single 10-unit pack (Figure 9.6b) and the optimal cost is $\boldsymbol{F} = 11$. Thus, going from base network design to design for restoration, the cost increases by 37.5%.

It is interesting to note that if the modular capacity requirement is relaxed, then the optimal design for the normal state will have all 12 links, with total capacity required as 36 units. If failure of each link is considered (encompassing all links), then the optimal design will still be the cube network, however, with the total capacity of 54 units. Thus, for the case with continuous capacity variable, the increase in network cost is 50% which is more than the modular case. ●

Problem DR-U (9.3.1) with modular links of the form in (4.3.3) and binary link availability coefficients was considered in [GTD+89]. A variant of DR-U (9.3.1) with modular links of the form in (4.3.4), binary availability coefficients, and general diversity assumed for the normal network operating state (i.e., uncapacitated version of problem A/GD (4.2.2); also see formulae (4.6.2) and (4.6.3) in Section 4.6.1 and Exercise 9.3) is studied in [DS98] (also see [Wes00] and references therein).

9.3.2 *Restricted Reconfiguration*

In the case of transport networks, full reconfiguration permitted in problem DR-U (9.3.1) is not too practical. Hence, more restricted flow reconfiguration mechanisms are to be considered. The first natural restriction in flow reallocation is the rule "unbroken flows are not moved," leading to the following problem.

***LP:* DR/CF/BR/CC/LIN/PR+RR {DR-R}** **Link-Path Formulation**
Path Restoration With Restricted Reconfiguration

indices

$d = 1, 2, ..., D$ demands
$p = 1, 2, ..., P_d$ candidate paths for demand d
$e = 1, 2, ..., E$ links
$s = 0, 1, ..., S$ situations

constants

δ_{edp} = 1 if link e belongs to path p realizing demand d; 0, otherwise
h_d volume of demand d
χ_{ds} demand coefficient of demand d in state s, $h_{ds} = \chi_{ds} h_d$
ξ_e unit cost of link e
α_{es} binary availability coefficient of link e in state s ($\alpha_{es} \in \{0, 1\}$)
θ_{dps} binary availability coefficient of path (d, p) in state s, $\theta_{dps} = \prod_{\{e:\delta_{edp}=1\}} \alpha_{es}$

variables

x_{dps} flow allocated to path p of demand d in state s
y_e capacity of link e

objective

$$\text{minimize } \boldsymbol{F} = \textstyle\sum_e \xi_e y_e \tag{9.3.2a}$$

constraints

$$\textstyle\sum_p x_{dps} \geq h_{ds}, \quad d = 1, 2, ..., D \quad s = 0, 1, ..., S \tag{9.3.2b}$$

$$\textstyle\sum_d \sum_p \delta_{edp} x_{dps} \leq \alpha_{es} y_e, \quad e = 1, 2, ..., E \quad s = 0, 1, ..., S \tag{9.3.2c}$$

$$x_{dps} \geq \theta_{dps} x_{dp0}, \quad d = 1, 2, ..., D \quad p = 1, 2, ..., P_d \quad s = 1, 2, ..., S. \tag{9.3.2d}$$

Note that now binary link availability coefficients are required (for the similar reason as for Problem (9.1.2)), contrary to the previous formulation, admitting also fractional coefficients. Although constraint (9.3.2d) assures that the normal flows unaffected by a failure are not moved, it is still possible to use unaffected paths for restoring flows from failed paths. A disadvantage of formulation (9.3.2) is a large number of constraints (9.3.2d). The following formulation has much less constraints than (9.3.2).

***LP:* DR/CF/BR/CC/LIN/PR+RR {MODIFIED}** **Link-Path Formulation**

Path Restoration With Restricted Reconfiguration—Modified Formulation

variables

- x_{dp0} normal flow allocated to path p of demand d
- x_{dps} flow allocated to path p of demand d in state s (these flows are provided on top on the surviving normal flows)
- y_e capacity of link e
- z_{ds} volume of demand d surviving in failure state s
- y'_{es} capacity of link e not occupied by surviving normal flows in state s (provided e is not failed in state s)

objective

$$\text{minimize } \boldsymbol{F} = \sum_e \xi_e y_e \tag{9.3.3a}$$

constraints

$$\sum_p x_{dp0} = h_{d0}, \quad d = 1, 2, ..., D \tag{9.3.3b}$$

$$\sum_d \sum_p \delta_{edp} x_{dp0} \leq y_e, \quad e = 1, 2, ..., E \tag{9.3.3c}$$

$$z_{ds} = \sum_p \theta_{dps} x_{dp0}, \quad d = 1, 2, ..., D \quad s = 1, 2, ..., S \tag{9.3.3d}$$

$$\sum_p x_{dps} \geq h_{ds} - z_{ds}, \quad d = 1, 2, ..., D \quad s = 1, 2, ..., S \tag{9.3.3e}$$

$$y'_{es} = y_e - \sum_d \sum_p \delta_{edp} \theta_{dps} x_{dp0}, \quad e = 1, 2, ..., E \quad s = 1, 2, ..., S \tag{9.3.3f}$$

$$\sum_d \sum_p \delta_{edp} x_{dps} \leq \alpha_{es} y'_{es}, \quad e = 1, 2, ..., E \quad s = 1, 2, ..., S. \tag{9.3.3g}$$

Note that variables z_{ds} and y'_{es}, and constraints (9.3.3d) and (9.3.3f) are auxiliary and are used in the above formulation merely to increase its clarity. Variable z_{ds} is equal to the volume of demand d surviving in failure state s while $\alpha_{es} y'_{es}$ is the capacity of link e not occupied by surviving normal flows in state s, i.e., y'_{es} is the sum of spare and released capacity on link e in state s. Note that spare capacity on link e is equal to $y_e - \sum_d \sum_p \delta_{edp} x_{dp0}$ and the released capacity (when link survives) is equal to $y''_e = \sum_d \sum_p \delta_{edp} x_{dp0} - \sum_d \sum_p \delta_{edp} \theta_{dps} x_{dp0}$ (see Exercise 9.4).

The first formulation, (9.3.2), of DR/CF/BR/CC/LIN/PR+RR (DR-R in short) has a rare LP coefficient matrix (i.e., its coefficient matrix in the LP formulation has majority of 0s). The second formulation, although it has much less constraints, is dense, so in general it is not known in advance which formulation is more efficiently solvable by an LP solver.

DR-R assumes binary link availability coefficients instead of the arbitrary fractional ones used in DR-U (9.3.1). As illustrated for problem DR/CF/BR/CC/LIN/GD in Section 9.1.3, this limitation can be overcome by introducing multi-links between nodes. Each link that can partially fail is substituted with a set of links which fail completely but in general not at the same time. For instance, if for some link e all possible availability coefficients α_{es} are in the set $\{0, \frac{1}{3}, \frac{2}{3}, 1\}$, then link e can be substituted with three parallel links of the same capacity ($\frac{1}{3}$ of the total link capacity y_e), each with appropriately chosen binary availability coefficients. This in fact leads to a more detailed failure characterization. We will return to this issue while discussing the failure propagation in multi-layer networks in Chapter 12.

Clearly, the solutions of problems of the DR-R type (restricted reconfiguration) are never cheaper than the corresponding solution of problem DR-U (9.3.1) (unrestricted reconfiguration) as the solution space for DR-R is (in general, a proper) subset of the solution space for DR-U (9.3.1). The feasible solution $(\boldsymbol{x}', \boldsymbol{y})$ of DR-U (9.3.1) resulting from an optimal solution $(\boldsymbol{x}, \boldsymbol{y})$ of DR-R is defined as follows:

$$
\begin{aligned}
&x'_{dp0} = x_{dp0} && d = 1,2,...,D \quad p = 1,2,...,P_d \\
&x'_{dps} = x_{dps} + \theta_{dps} x_{dp0} && d = 1,2,...,D \quad p = 1,2,...,P_d \quad s = 1,2,...,S.
\end{aligned}
\tag{9.3.4}
$$

As the following example shows, in general $(\boldsymbol{x}', \boldsymbol{y})$ is not an optimal solution of DR-U (9.3.1).

Example 9.7 *Comparison of DR-U (9.3.1) and DR-R (9.3.2)*

Consider the network from Figure 9.7. There are $D = 3$ demands: between nodes 1 and 2, 3 and 4, and 5 and 6. All demand volumes are equal to 1 in all situations, and all link unit costs are equal to 1. There are $S = 4$ failure states and the normal network operating state ($s = 0$). Failure state $s = 1$ consists in the total failure of link 3-4, $s = 2$ in the total failure of link 5-6, $s = 3$ in the total failure of link 7-8, and $s = 4$ in the total failure of link 9-10. The optimal solution of DR-U (9.3.1) is to assign capacity $y_e = 1$ to all links (resulting in the optimal cost $\boldsymbol{F} = 12$) and realize the demand volumes in the following way: demand $\langle 1,2 \rangle$ on path 1-7-8-2, demand $\langle 3,4 \rangle$ on path 3-4, and demand $\langle 5,6 \rangle$ on path 5-6 (Figure 9.7). In state $s = 1$ the normal flow 1-7-8-2 is moved to path 1-9-10-2 and flow on 3-4 to path 3-7-8-4. In state $s = 2$ flow 5-6 is moved to path 5-9-10-6, and in state $s = 3$ flow 1-7-8-2 to path 1-9-10-2 (in state $s = 4$ no flow is affected and moved). Note that this solution requires moving the unaffected normal flow on 1-7-8-2 in state $s = 1$.

The optimal solution of DR-R, for which such a rearrangement is not possible, is more expensive. An optimal solution of DR-R can be readily obtained from the above solution of DR-U (9.3.1) by adding one capacity unit to link 7-8, resulting in the cost $\boldsymbol{F} = 13$. For DR-R, the normal flows and the flows in situations $s = 2, 3$ are the same as for DR-U (9.3.1), but in state $s = 1$ we do not move flow on 1-7-8-2 but only shift flow on 3-4 to path 3-7-8-4.

●

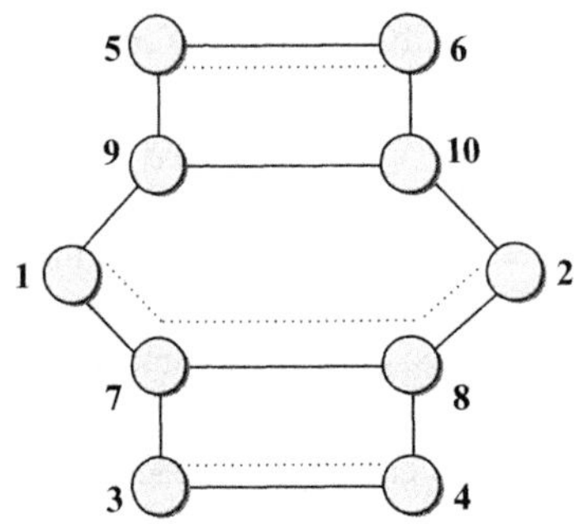

FIGURE 9.7 DR-U (9.3.1) Versus DR-R (9.3.2)

Problem DR-R with modular links is studied in detail in [Wes00] (also see references there in).

9.3.3 *Path Restoration With Situation-Dependent Back-up Paths

The next restriction that can be imposed on the path restoration mechanism is to assume not only that the surviving normal flows are not touched, but also that each affected normal flow is moved entirely to one situation-dependent back-up path (hence, 100% restoration is assumed). In the following formulation, index p (so far labeling candidate paths) is used in a somewhat different way. Now, it labels not a single path but a whole sequence of paths $\mathbb{P}_{dp} = (\mathcal{P}_{dps}, s = 0, 1, ..., S)$ pre-assigned to demand d. Each such sequence of paths for fixed d and p is composed of normal path $\mathcal{P}_{dp0}$, back-up path $\mathcal{P}_{dp1}$ used to protect the normal path in state $s = 1$, back-up path $\mathcal{P}_{dp2}$ used in for the same purpose in state $s = 2$, and so on until $\mathcal{P}_{dpS}$, where back-up path $\mathcal{P}_{dpS}$ is used to protect $\mathcal{P}_{dp0}$ in state $s = S$. Note that if the normal path is not broken in state s then the choice of the path for this situation is arbitrary, since the normal path will be used anyway. Otherwise, it is assumed that each back-up path works in the situation it is used, i.e., if normal path $\mathcal{P}_{dp0}$ is not available in state s, then its back-up path in this situation, $\mathcal{P}_{dps}$, must be available.

***LP:* DR/CF/BR/CC/LIN/PR+SDBP {DR-SD}** **Link-Path Formulation**

Path Restoration With Situation-Dependent Back-up Paths

indices

$d = 1, 2, ..., D$ demands
$p = 1, 2, ..., P_d$ candidate path-sequences for demand d
$e = 1, 2, ..., E$ links
$s = 0, 1, ..., S$ situations

constants

β_{edps} = 1 if link e belongs to path no. s in path-sequence $\mathbb{P}_{dp}$
h_d volume of demand d
ξ_e unit cost of link e
α_{es} binary availability coefficient of link e in state s ($\alpha_{es} \in \{0, 1\}$)
θ_{dps} binary availability coefficient of normal path p realizing demand d in state s, $\theta_{dps} = \prod_{\{e:\beta_{edp0}=1\}} \alpha_{es}$

variables

x_{dp0} flow allocated to the normal path of path-sequence p of demand d in state $s = 0$
y_e capacity of link e

objective

$$\text{minimize } \boldsymbol{F} = \textstyle\sum_e \xi_e y_e \tag{9.3.5a}$$

constraints

$$\textstyle\sum_p x_{dp0} = h_d, \quad d = 1, 2, ..., D \tag{9.3.5b}$$

$$\textstyle\sum_d \sum_p (\beta_{edp0}\theta_{dps} + \beta_{edps}(1 - \theta_{dps}))x_{dp0} \leq \alpha_{es} y_e, \qquad e = 1, 2, ..., E \quad s = 0, 1, ..., S. \tag{9.3.5c}$$

The assumption that for each (d, p) if the normal path $\mathcal{P}_{dp0}$ is not available in state s, then its back-up path in this situation, $\mathcal{P}_{dps}$, must be available can be expressed formally as: $\theta_{dps} = 0$ implies $\omega_{dps} = 1$ for all situations $s = 1, 2, ..., S$, where ω_{dps} is the binary availability coefficient of the back-up path used to protect normal path $\mathcal{P}_{dp0}$ in state s, $\omega_{dps} = \prod_{\{e:\beta_{edps}=1\}} \alpha_{es}$.

The (somewhat complicated) left-hand side of constraint (9.3.5c) is equal the load of link e in state s, since the expression in brackets is equal to part of the load of link e induced by the normal flow x_{dp0} in state s, either directly (because the flow survives in state s, including the normal network operating state $s = 0$ for which $1 - \theta_{dp0} = 0$) or indirectly, because link e belongs to the back-up path for $\mathcal{P}_{dp0}$.

Observe that a path, for example, path P_d for demand d, can appear more than once in the candidate path sequences $p = 1, 2, ..., P_d$. Then path $\mathcal{P}_d$ can be assigned a non-zero flow in more than one path sequence. In effect, the total flow assigned to path P_d, in general, can be restored on several paths. This, in fact, makes LP formulations of DR-R and DR/CF/BR/CC/LIN/PR+SDBP (DR-SD for short) equivalent in the case with $\chi_{es} = 1$ (100% restoration) required for DR-SD. The advantage of formulation DR-SD lies in the fact that formulations DR-R and DR-SD become significantly different when the single-path - type restrictions are applied. Then formulation (9.3.5), contrary to formulations (9.3.2) or (9.3.3), allows for a simple and precise expression of the requirement underlying the formulation of DR-SD: normal flows of a demand can be bifurcated but the restoration flows cannot (see Section 9.4.4). This issue, also discussed in the next section for a similar problem, is the subject of Exercise 9.5.

9.3.4 *Path Restoration With Single Back-up Paths

To end the series of design problems with path restoration we finally assume not only that each affected normal flow is moved entirely to a back-up path, but also that this back-up path is the same for all the failure situations affecting the normal flow. This of course requires that the normal path $\mathcal{P}_{dp}$ and its (single) back-up path $\mathcal{Q}_{dp}$ are *situation-disjoint*, which means that in all situations when path $\mathcal{P}_{dp}$ is not available, its back-up path $\mathcal{Q}_{dp}$ must be available. In the particular case when the two paths in the pair normal–back-up path are node disjoint, then they are sometimes referred to as cycles [Med91a].

***LP:* DR/CF/BR/CC/LIN/PR+FBP {DR-F}** **Link-Path Formulation**

Path Restoration With Fixed Back-up Paths

indices

$d = 1, 2, ..., D$ demands

$p = 1, 2, ..., P_d$ candidate pairs $(\mathcal{P}_{dp}, \mathcal{Q}_{dp})$ of situation disjoint paths for demand d; normal path $\mathcal{P}_{dp}$, and back-up path $\mathcal{Q}_{dp}$

$e = 1, 2, ..., E$ links

$s = 0, 1, ..., S$ situations

constants

δ_{edp} = 1 if link e belongs to normal path $\mathcal{P}_{dp}$; 0, otherwise

β_{edp} = 1 if link e belongs to back-up path $\mathcal{Q}_{dp}$; 0, otherwise

h_d volume of demand d

ξ_e unit cost of link e

α_{es} binary availability coefficient of link e in state s ($\alpha_{es} \in \{0, 1\}$)

θ_{dps} binary availability coefficient of path $\mathcal{P}_{dp}$ in state s, $\theta_{dps} = \prod_{\{e:\delta_{edp}=1\}} \alpha_{es}$

variables

x_{dp0} flow allocated to basic path p of demand d in the normal state

y_e capacity of link e

objective

$$\text{minimize } \boldsymbol{F} = \textstyle\sum_e \xi_e y_e \tag{9.3.6a}$$

constraints

$$\textstyle\sum_p x_{dp0} = h_d, \quad d = 1, 2, ..., D \tag{9.3.6b}$$

$$\textstyle\sum_d \sum_p \left(\delta_{edp}\theta_{dps} + \beta_{edp}(1 - \theta_{dps})\right) x_{dp0} \le \alpha_{es} y_e, \qquad e = 1, 2, ..., E \quad s = 0, 1, ..., S. \tag{9.3.6c}$$

As previously mentioned, it is assumed that when normal path $\mathcal{P}_{dp}$ is not available, then its back-up path must be available, i.e., $\theta_{dps} = 0$ implies $\omega_{dps} = 1$ for all situations $s = 1, 2, ..., S$, where ω_{dps} is the binary availability coefficient of the back-up path p of demand d in state s, $\omega_{dps} = \prod_{\{e:\beta_{edp}=1\}} \alpha_{es}$ (this precisely expresses the fact that the normal and back-up paths are situation-disjoint).

Formulation (9.3.6) is similar to (9.3.5) and the interpretation of constraint (9.3.6c) is analogous to the interpretation of (9.3.5c). In (9.3.6c) we use two types of coincidence coefficients, δ_{edp} and β_{edp}, since this seems to be more natural in the single back-up path case.

As in problem DR-SD, a normal path, for example, path $\mathcal{P}_{dp}$ for demand d, can appear more than once in pairs $p = 1, 2, ..., P_d$, which can lead to a solution with the total flow on path $\mathcal{P}_{dp}$ restored on several paths. In order to assure that the entire path flow is moved to another path in case of a failure, binary variables have to be added to transform DR/CF/BR/CC/LIN/PR+FBP (DR-F for short) into an appropriate MIP problem. For instance, this can be done in the following way. We change the numbering of the candidate pairs for each demand d introducing a double indexing (p, q) instead of the single indexing p used so far. For each fixed d, index p labels all candidate normal paths for demand $d, p = 1, 2, ..., P_d$, where P_d is the total number of such paths. Then, for each normal path $\mathcal{P}_{dp}$, index q labels all candidate back-up paths $\mathcal{Q}_{dpq}$, situation-disjoint with path $\mathcal{P}_{dp}, q = 1, 2, ..., Q_{dp}$, where Q_{dp} is the total number of such back-up paths. Hence, for each d, a pair of indices (p, q) $(1 \le p \le P_d, 1 \le q \le Q_{dp})$ identifies a pair of situation-disjoint paths $(\mathcal{P}_{dp}, \mathcal{Q}_{dpq})$, where for fixed d and different p normal paths $\mathcal{P}_{dp}$ are different.

***MIP:* DR/CF/BR/CC/LIN/PR+FSBP** **Link-Path Formulation**
Path Restoration With Fixed Single Back-up Paths

indices

$d = 1, 2, ..., D$ demands
$p = 1, 2, ..., P_d$ candidate normal paths for demand d
$q = 1, 2, ..., Q_{dp}$ candidate back-up paths for normal path $\mathcal{P}_{dp}$ (each path $\mathcal{Q}_{dpq}$ is situation-disjoint with path $\mathcal{P}_{dp}$)
$e = 1, 2, ..., E$ links
$s = 0, 1, ..., S$ situations

constants

δ_{edp} = 1 if link e belongs to normal path $\mathcal{P}_{dp}$; 0, otherwise
β_{edpq} = 1 if link e belongs to back-up path $\mathcal{Q}_{dpq}$ protecting normal path $\mathcal{P}_{dp}$; 0, otherwise
h_d volume of demand d
ξ_e unit cost of link e
α_{es} binary availability coefficient of link e in state s ($\alpha_{es} \in \{0, 1\}$)
θ_{dps} binary path availability coefficient indicating whether normal path $\mathcal{P}_{dp}$ is available in state s, $\theta_{dps} = \prod_{\{e:\delta_{edp}=1\}} \alpha_{es}$

variables

x_{dpq0} normal flow of demand d allocated to pair $(\mathcal{P}_{dp}, \mathcal{Q}_{dpq})$
u_{dpq} binary variable corresponding to flow x_{dpq0}
y_e capacity of link e

objective

$$\text{minimize } \boldsymbol{F} = \textstyle\sum_e \xi_e y_e \tag{9.3.7a}$$

constraints

$$\textstyle\sum_p \sum_q x_{dpq0} = h_d, \quad d = 1, 2, ..., D \tag{9.3.7b}$$

$$\textstyle\sum_q u_{dpq} \le 1, \quad d = 1, 2, ..., D \quad p = 1, 2, ..., P_d \tag{9.3.7c}$$

$$x_{dpq0} \le h_d u_{dpq}, \quad d = 1, 2, ..., D \quad p = 1, 2, ..., P_d \quad q = 1, 2, ..., Q_{dp} \tag{9.3.7d}$$

$$\sum_d \sum_p \sum_q (\delta_{edp}\theta_{dps} + \beta_{edpq}(1-\theta_{dps}))x_{dpq0} \le \alpha_{es} y_e, \quad e = 1,2,...,E \quad s = 0,1,...,S. \tag{9.3.7e}$$

Constraint (9.3.7c) imposed on each vector of binary variables ($u_{dpq}, q = 1,2,...,Q_{dp}$), together with constraint (9.3.7d), assure that there is at most one non-zero flow assigned to the set of all routing pairs with the same normal path, and that the flow assigned to back-up path $\mathcal{Q}_{dpq}$ of normal path $\mathcal{P}_{dp}$ is equal to $u_{dpq}x_{dpq0}$. An analogous transformation can be applied to DR-SD (9.3.5) leading to a modified problem DR-SD with forced non-bifurcated restoration (see already referenced Exercise 9.5).

9.3.5 Hot-Standby Path Protection

As for the links (see Section 9.2.2), PP can also be achieved with the HS mechanism. Now the paths (flows) are protected by means of dedicated protection paths, so the protection (spare) capacity for one path is not shared with the protection capacity used for other paths that fail in other failure situations. Each failed flow is restored (entirely in the case of 100% protection) on one single path. PP/HS assumes that the normal protected path and its standby path are situation-disjoint.

***MIP:* DR/CF/BR/CC/LIN/PP+HS** **Link-Path Formulation**
PP With Hot-Standby
indices
as in DR/CF/BR/CC/LIN/PR+FSBP (9.3.7)
variables
x_{dpq0} flow of demand d allocated to pair ($\mathcal{P}_{dp}$, $\mathcal{Q}_{dpq}$) in state $s = 0$
u_{dpq} binary variable corresponding to flow x_{dpq0}
y_e capacity of link e
objective

$$\text{minimize } \boldsymbol{F} = \sum_e \xi_e y_e \tag{9.3.8a}$$

constraints

$$\sum_p \sum_q x_{dpq0} = h_d \quad d = 1,2,...,D \tag{9.3.8b}$$

$$\sum_q u_{dpq} \le 1, \quad d = 1,2,...,D \quad p = 1,2,...,P_d \tag{9.3.8c}$$

$$x_{dpq0} \le h_d u_{dpq}, \quad d = 1,2,...,D \quad p = 1,2,...,P_d \quad q = 1,2,...,Q_{dp} \tag{9.3.8d}$$

$$\sum_d \sum_p \sum_q (\delta_{edp} + \beta_{edpq})x_{dpq0} \le \alpha_{es} y_e, \quad e = 1,2,...,E \quad s = 0,1,...,S. \tag{9.3.8e}$$

Again, observe the difference between constraints (9.3.7e) in DR/CF/BR/CC/LIN/PR+FSBP and (9.3.8e).

Example 9.8 *Illustration of PP With Hot-Standby*
The optimal solution of DR/CF/BR/CC/LIN/LP+HS (9.2.4) for the network of Figure 9.2 costs $\boldsymbol{F} = 36+12\times 9 = 36+108 = 144$. In this case, the optimal solution of DR/CF/BR/CC/LIN/PP+HS is equivalent to the solution of DR/CF/BR/CC/LIN/LP+HS. ●

9.4 EXTENSIONS

As you can imagine, restoration design problems formulated in the previous sections can be extended in many ways. In the rest of this section we will consider the following extensions: (1) non-linear cost/dimensioning functions, (2) modular link capacities and/or integer flows, (3) budget constraint, (4) routing restrictions, (5) separated normal and for protection capacity, and (6) separated normal and protection design. Although each of these extensions can be applied separately, many of them can be combined. Which combinations are valid should be clear for the reader after reading this section.

9.4.1 *Non-Linear Cost/Dimensioning Functions*

Introducing non-linear link-dependent cost functions $F_e(\underline{y}_e)$ or dimensioning functions $F_e(\underline{y}_e)$ (convex or concave; refer to Section 4.3) into the problem formulations is achieved with modifying the objective function or the capacity constraint, respectively:

$$\boldsymbol{F} = \textstyle\sum_e \xi_e F_e(\underline{y}_e) \tag{9.4.1a}$$

$$F_e(\textstyle\sum_d \sum_p \delta_{edp} x_{dp}) \le y_e \quad e = 1, 2, ..., E. \tag{9.4.1b}$$

Recall that the dimensioning function (and link load $\underline{y}_e = \sum_d \sum_p \delta_{edp} x_{dp}$) can be also made situation-dependent.

9.4.2 *Modular Link Capacities and/or Integral Flows*

In this chapter we have already presented a considerable set of restoration design problems, assuming continuous flows and continuous or integer (modular) link capacities. The assumption of continuous variables usually leads to desirable LP formulations, which can be solved effectively even for large networks, using appropriate LP decomposition approaches (see Chapter 10). We should note, however, that in many practical cases not only link capacities but also flows are integral (modular). In such a case the value of the LP formulations lies in the fact that rounding-off the continuous solutions is in most cases a reasonable, near-optimal, and practical solution to network dimensioning with modular flows and/or links. As we already know from Chapters 4 and 5, the modularity of variables leads to difficult, usually $\mathcal{NP}$-complete, integer programming (IP) problems. Fortunately, in most cases the integrality of flows can be relaxed, as the size of the flow modules is usually negligible with respect to the size of link modules. For such cases the considered problems become MIP problems. This can be important for the efficiency of the applied solution methods as the number of flow variables is typically much greater than the number of capacity variables.

In the simplest case modular links are taken into account in an analogous way as in D/ML (4.3.1) leading, for example, to the formulation of DR-U (9.3.1) with capacity constraints (9.3.1d). If flows are also assumed to be integral, then DR-U (9.3.1) becomes an IP problem. If $M = 1$ (M is equal to LCU) then link capacities can be assumed continuous since in the optimal solution they will be integers anyway. On the other hand, if $M \gg 1$ then, for practical applications, the flows can be assumed continuous (leading, as already mentioned, to a MIP problem with much less number of integral variables) and rounded-off to integers in the final solution.

For the more precise modular link model (4.3.4) from Section 4.3.1 assuming binary link availability coefficients, capacity constraint (9.3.1c) in DR-U is substituted with

$$\begin{array}{lll} \sum_d \sum_p \delta_{edp} x_{dps} \le \alpha_{es} y_e & e = 1, 2, ..., E & s = 0, 1, ..., S \\ y_e = \sum_k m_k u_{ek} & e = 1, 2, ..., E & \\ u_{e1} \ge u_{e2} \ge ... \ge u_{eK} & e = 1, 2, ..., E & \end{array} \qquad (9.4.2)$$

where u_{ek} are binary variables corresponding the incremental module sizes, and flows x_{dps} are non-negative integers (refer to (4.3.4c) to (4.3.4d)).

Example 9.9 *Illustration of DR-U (9.3.1) with Integral Flows*

Consider the network from Example 9.4 shown in Figure 2.10. The optimal solution for integral flows is depicted in Figure 9.8. For $M = 1$ the optimal cost $\boldsymbol{F} = 5$ is greater than for the optimal solution of Example 9.4 (without the integer requirement $\boldsymbol{F} = 4.5$). If $M = 2$ the optimal value $\boldsymbol{F} = 6$ is the same for both continuous and integral flows. ●

When links and/or flows are assumed to be integers, the branch-and-bound (BB) method (Sections 5.2.1 and 5.2.2) can be used. However, as already discussed on many occasions, in general the approach is ineffective for networks of practical size. In many cases, LR-based

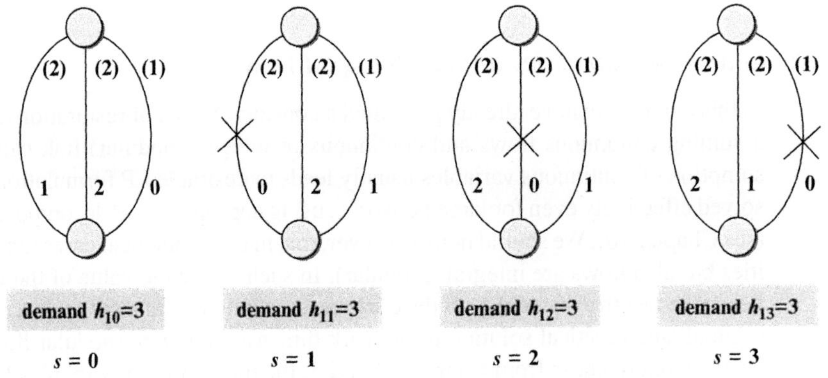

FIGURE 9.8 Solution for DR-U (9.3.1) with Integral Flows

approach can be applicable as shown in the case of multi-service with modular capacity and non-bifurcated flows; see Section 11.1.4. When the integer flow constraint is relaxed and only link capacities are integral (modular), the Benders' decomposition (BD) method can be applied, as discussed in Section 10.3, extending the range of effectively tractable network sizes. Note that restoration design problems with modular links/flows can also be solved in an approximative way using stochastic meta-heuristics described in Section 5.3 (see Section 10.5).

9.4.3 *Budget Constraint*

The minimization of the link cost function can be substituted with a budget constraint (for normal design this is done in problem D/BC (4.4.1)). You may notice that if the assumed budget B is greater than the minimum of the cost function then the budget constraint is not active and, if we consider problem DR-U, formulation (9.3.1) with the cost function minimization is sufficient. However, when this is not the case the solution with the budget constraint can be substantially different which can be easily assessed from the following formulation.

***LP:* DR/CF/BR/CC/BC/PR+UR** **Link-Path Formulation**
Path Restoration Problem DR/CF/BR/CC/LIN/PR+UR With Budget Constraint

indices

$d = 1, 2, ..., D$ demands
$p = 1, 2, ..., P_d$ candidate paths for demand d
$e = 1, 2, ..., E$ links
$s = 0, 1, ..., S$ states

constants

δ_{edp} = 1 if link e belongs to path p realizing demand d; 0, otherwise
h_d volume of demand d
χ_{ds} demand coefficient of demand d in state s, $h_{ds} = \chi_{ds} h_d$
ξ_e unit cost of link e
α_{es} fractional availability coefficient of link e in state s ($0 \leq \alpha_{es} \leq 1$)
B assumed maximal budget

variables

x_{dps} flow allocated to path p of demand d in state s
y_e capacity of link e
r minimal proportion of the realized demand volumes

objective

$$\text{maximize } r \tag{9.4.3a}$$

constraints

$$\textstyle\sum_p x_{dps} \geq h_{ds} r, \quad d = 1, 2, ..., D \quad s = 0, 1, ..., S \tag{9.4.3b}$$

$$\textstyle\sum_d \sum_p \delta_{edp} x_{dps} \leq \alpha_{es} y_e, \quad e = 1, 2, ..., E \quad s = 0, 1, ..., S \tag{9.4.3c}$$

$$\sum_e \xi_e y_e \leq B. \tag{9.4.3d}$$

We note that once the maximal r^* is found, there may be room to further increase a subset of the demand volumes for some demands in some situations (within the assumed budget). Then the next step of r can be considered as leading to a MMF type of a solution. We will discuss this issue for a different problem in Section 9.5.1.

9.4.4 *Routing Restrictions

Routing restrictions similar to those discussed in Section 4.2 for normal design can also be imposed on restoration design problems. For instance, we could state, as in problem A/LBF (4.2.3), that non-zero flows cannot be too small. In the case of DR-U (9.3.1) this would lead to the following MIP problem (with a large number of binary variables).

***MIP:* DR/CF/BR/CC/LIN/PR+UR+LBF** **Link-Path Formulation**

Path Restoration Problem DR/CF/BR/CC/LIN/PR+UR With Lower-Bounded Flows

additional constants

b_{ds} lower bound on non-zero flows of demand d in state s

variables

x_{dps} (non-negative) flow allocated to path p of demand d in state s

y_e capacity of link e

u_{dps} binary variable corresponding to flow allocated to path p of demand d in state s

objective

$$\text{minimize } \boldsymbol{F} = \sum_e \xi_e y_e \tag{9.4.4a}$$

constraints

$$\sum_p x_{dps} = h_{ds}, \quad d = 1, 2, ..., D \quad s = 0, 1, ..., S \tag{9.4.4b}$$

$$u_{dps} b_{ds} \leq x_{dps} \leq u_{dps} h_{ds}, \quad d = 1, 2, ..., D \quad p = 1, 2, ..., P_d \quad s = 0, 1, ..., S \tag{9.4.4c}$$

$$\sum_d \sum_p \delta_{edp} x_{dps} \leq \alpha_{es} y_e, \quad e = 1, 2, ..., E \quad s = 0, 1, ..., S. \tag{9.4.4d}$$

Constraint (9.4.4c) ensures that the flows corresponding to non-zero u_{dps} are between b_{ds} and h_{ds}, and that the flows corresponding to $u_{dps} = 0$ are also equal to 0. Also the single-path–type requirements can be imposed on the problems considered in the previous paragraphs of this section. Such a requirement has already been considered in the single-path link restoration problem DR/CF/BR/CC/LIN/LR+SBP (9.2.3). Binary variables can be introduced to the flow restoration problems as well, forcing non-bifurcated flows in all situations. The resulting formulations are MIP problems. The modification for DR-U (9.3.1) is as follows.

***MIP:* DR/CF/NBR/CC/LIN/PR+UR+NBR** **Link-Path Formulation**
Path Restoration Problem DR/CF/BR/CC/LIN/PR+UR With Single-Path Allocation
variables

u_{dps} binary variable associated with flow on path p of demand d in state s
y_e capacity of link e

objective

$$\text{minimize } \boldsymbol{F} = \textstyle\sum_e \xi_e y_e \tag{9.4.5a}$$

constraints

$$\textstyle\sum_p u_{dps} = 1, \quad d = 1, 2, ..., D \quad s = 0, 1, ..., S \tag{9.4.5b}$$

$$\textstyle\sum_d h_{ds} \sum_p \delta_{edp} u_{dps} \leq \alpha_{es} y_e, \quad e = 1, 2, ..., E \quad s = 0, 1, ..., S. \tag{9.4.5c}$$

Note that constraints (9.4.5b) to (9.4.5c) can be formulated in a more explicit way as

$$\begin{aligned}
&\textstyle\sum_p x_{dps} = h_{ds}, && d = 1, 2, ..., D \quad s = 0, 1, ..., S \\
&\textstyle\sum_p u_{dps} = 1, && d = 1, 2, ..., D \quad s = 0, 1, ..., S \\
&x_{dps} = u_{dps} h_{ds}, && d = 1, 2, ..., D \quad p = 1, 2, ..., P_d \\
& && s = 0, 1, ..., S \\
&\textstyle\sum_d \sum_p \delta_{edp} x_{dps} \leq \alpha_{es} y_e, && e = 1, 2, ..., E \quad s = 0, 1, ..., S.
\end{aligned} \tag{9.4.6}$$

It should be noted that Proposition 4.1 can be applied for problem DR-U (with bifurcated flows), showing the existence of the optimal solution with a limited number of non-zero flows. Once the problem is solved, the resulting optimal link capacities can be fixed for each situation ($c_{es} = \alpha_{es} y_e^*$ for $e = 1, 2, ..., E$ and $s = 0, 1, ..., S$) and the basic allocation problem A/PAP (4.1.7) solved by the simplex method for each state separately. The resulting flows $\boldsymbol{x}_s$ will have the property (see Proposition 4.1) that in each situation there are at most $D + E$ non-zero flows in the vector $\boldsymbol{x}_s$. This suggests the following heuristic procedure for solving (9.4.5): for each state s consider the demands with bifurcated flows one by one, and for each such demand d assign all the demand volume to the path with maximal flow x_{dps}. After this, re-dimension the network to retrieve a feasible solution. The final solution will be sub-optimal, still there is a chance for a good solution because of the small number of bifurcated demands.

For DR-R the single-path formulation is somewhat more complicated.

***MIP:* DR/CF/NBR/CC/LIN/PR+RR+NBR** **Link-Path Formulation**
Path Restoration Problem DR/CF/BR/CC/LIN/PR+RR With Single-Path Allocation
variables

u_{dp0} binary variable for normal flow allocated to path p of demand d
x_{dps} flow allocated to path p of demand d in state s
u_{dps} binary variable for flow allocated to path p of demand d in state s
y_e capacity of link e

objective

$$\text{minimize } \boldsymbol{F} = \sum_e \xi_e y_e \tag{9.4.7a}$$

constraints

$$\sum_p u_{dp0} = 1, \quad d = 1, 2, ..., D \tag{9.4.7b}$$

$$\sum_d h_{d0} \sum_p \delta_{edp} u_{dp0} \leq y_e, \quad e = 1, 2, ..., E \tag{9.4.7c}$$

$$\sum_p u_{dps} \leq 1, \quad d = 1, 2, ..., D \quad s = 1, 2, \ldots, S \tag{9.4.7d}$$

$$x_{dps} \leq u_{dps} h_{ds}, \quad d = 1, 2, ..., D \quad p = 1, 2, ..., P_d \quad s = 1, 2, ..., S \tag{9.4.7e}$$

$$\sum_p x_{dps} \geq h_{ds} - \sum_p \theta_{dps} x_{dp0}, \quad d = 1, 2, ..., D \quad s = 1, 2, ..., S \tag{9.4.7f}$$

$$\sum_d \sum_p \delta_{edp} x_{dps} \leq \alpha_{es}(y_e - \sum_d h_{d0} \sum_p \delta_{edp} \theta_{dps} u_{dp0}),$$
$$e = 1, 2, ..., E \quad s = 1, 2, ..., S. \tag{9.4.7g}$$

Constraint (9.4.7b) ensures non-bifurcated normal flows, while constraint (9.4.7d) allows for one additional restoration flow for demand d in state s. Such an additional flow is required when the surviving normal flow is not sufficient to realize the demand volume h_{ds}. Since the amount of the restoration flow, x_{dps}, is a variable not known in advance, we have to use two constraints (9.4.7d) and (9.4.7e) to force the single restoration flow.

The single-path normal flow allocation requirement in the situation-dependent back-up path restoration problem DR-SD is taken into account as follows.

***MIP:* DR/CF/NBR/CC/LIN/PR+SDBP** **Link-Path Formulation**
Path Restoration Problem DR/CF/BR/CC/LIN/PR+SDBP With Single-Path Allocation

variables

u_{dp} binary flow variable associated with candidate path-sequence p of demand d

y_e capacity of link e

objective

$$\text{minimize } \boldsymbol{F} = \sum_e \xi_e y_e \tag{9.4.8a}$$

constraints

$$\sum_p u_{dp} = 1, \quad d = 1, 2, ..., D \tag{9.4.8b}$$

$$\sum_d h_d \sum_p (\delta_{edp}\theta_{dps} + \beta_{edps}(1-\theta_{dps}))u_{dp} \le \alpha_{es} y_e, \quad e = 1,2,\dots,E \quad s = 0,1,\dots,S. \tag{9.4.8c}$$

Again, the following, more straightforward constraints could be used:

$$\begin{aligned}
&\sum_p x_{dp} = h_d, && d = 1,2,\dots,D \\
&\sum_p u_{dps} = 1, && d = 1,2,\dots,D \\
&x_{dp} = u_{dp} h_d, && d = 1,2,\dots,D \quad p = 1,2,\dots,P_d \\
&\sum_d \sum_p (\delta_{edp}\theta_{dps} + \beta_{edps}(1-\theta_{dps}))x_{dp} \le \alpha_{es} y_e, && e = 1,2,\dots,E \quad s = 0,1,\dots,S.
\end{aligned} \tag{9.4.9}$$

In the case of 100% restoration ($\chi_{ds} \equiv 1$), formulations DR/CF/NBR/CC/LIN/PR+RR+NBR and DR/CF/NBR/CC/LIN/PR+SDBP are formally equivalent. The second formulation, however, requires much less binary variables and, thus, potentially, can be more efficiently solved by MIP solvers.

The single back-up path restoration problem DR-F (9.3.7), with the additional requirement for unsplittable normal flow, takes the following form.

***MIP:* DR/CF/NBR/CC/LIN/PR+FSBP** **Link-Path Formulation**

Path Restoration Problem DR/CF/BR/CC/LIN/PR+FSBP With Single-Path Allocation

variables

u_{dp} binary flow variable associated with pair no. p of demand d

y_e capacity of link e

objective

$$\text{minimize } \boldsymbol{F} = \sum_e \xi_e y_e \tag{9.4.10a}$$

constraints

$$\sum_p u_{dp} = 1, \quad d = 1,2,\dots,D \tag{9.4.10b}$$

$$\sum_d h_d \sum_p (\delta_{edp}\theta_{dps} + \beta_{edp}(1-\theta_{dps}))u_{dp} \le \alpha_{es} y_e, \quad e = 1,2,\dots,E \quad s = 0,1,\dots,S. \tag{9.4.10c}$$

Note that formulation (9.4.10) is simpler than for Problem (9.3.7) without the requirement for unsplittable normal flows.

It is important to realize that the lists of candidate paths (DR-U (9.3.1) and DR-R (9.3.2)), lists of candidate path-sequences (DR-SD (9.3.5)), and lists of candidate path pairs (DR-F (9.3.6)) can be made very short, containing, for example one to three elements. Such lists can be found by solving the relaxed problems (without the SPA requirement) and then finding (and effectively using) the shortest paths for all situations (DR-U and DR-R),

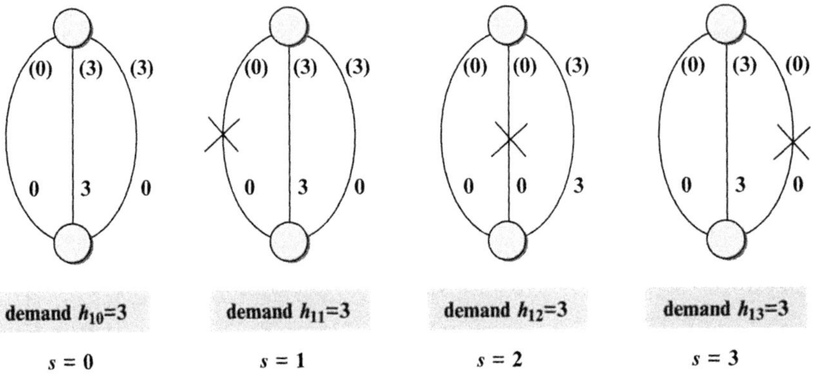

FIGURE 9.9 Solution for DR-U (9.3.1) with Non-Bifurcated Flows

shortest sequences (DR-SD), and shortest pairs (DR-F) using the optimal dual variables as link metrics. This can be done with candidate path list augmentation (column generation) technique introduced in Section 5.4.2, and applied for DR-U to DR-F in Section 10.1.

Example 9.10 *Illustration of DR-U (9.3.1) With Non-Bifurcated Flows*

Consider the network from Example 9.9 and the non-bifurcated optimal solution of DR/CF/NBR/CC/LIN/PR+UR+NBR depicted in Figure 9.9. The optimal cost $\boldsymbol{F} = 6$ is greater than for the solution with the integer flow requirement of Example 9.9, $\boldsymbol{F} = 5$. The presented non-bifurcated solutions also solves the rest of the PR problems DR/CF/NBR/CC/LIN/PR+RR+NBR, DR/CF/NBR/CC/LIN/PR+SDBP, and DR/CF/NBR/CC/LIN/PR+FSBP. ●

9.4.5 *Separating Normal and Protection Capacity*

Consider the case when the "released" normal capacity cannot be reused for protection purposes. This means that the normal capacity and protection capacity are disjoint pools or resources, as has been the case for the link protection mechanism assumed in problems DR/CF/BR/CC/LIN/LR+BR (9.2.1) and DR/CF/BR/CC/LIN/LR+SBP (9.2.3), and for the HS mechanism assumed in problems DR/CF/BR/CC/LIN/LP+HS (9.2.4) and DR/CF/BR/CC/LIN/PP+HS (9.3.8). The considered assumption leads to the following version of DR/CF/BR/CC/LIN/PR+FSBP (9.3.7).

***LP:* DR/CF/BR/CC/LIN/PR+FSBP {CS}** **Link-Path Formulation**

Path Restoration Problem With Capacity Separation

variables

x_{dp0} (non-negative) flow allocated to path p of demand d in the normal state

y_e normal capacity of link e

y'_e protection capacity of link e

objective

$$\text{minimize } \boldsymbol{F} = \sum_e \xi_e (y_e + y'_e) \qquad (9.4.11a)$$

constraints

$$\sum_p x_{dp0} = h_d, \quad d = 1, 2, ..., D \qquad (9.4.11b)$$

$$\sum_d \sum_p \delta_{edp} x_{dp0} \le y_e, \quad e = 1, 2, ..., E \qquad (9.4.11c)$$

$$\sum_d \sum_p \beta_{edp} (1 - \theta_{dps}) x_{dp0} \le \alpha_{es} y'_e, \quad e = 1, 2, ..., E \quad s = 0, 1, ..., S. \qquad (9.4.11d)$$

Note that now the normal load of link e (left-hand side of (9.4.11c)) is realized within the normal link capacity, and the restoration load (left-hand side of (9.4.11d)) is realized within its protection capacity. Analogously, other problems can also be reformulated for the case of the separation of the normal and protection capacity (Exercise 9.6).

9.4.6 *Separated Normal and Protection Design*

In all restoration design problems considered earlier in this section we have assumed that the normal and protection capacity and flow are designed simultaneously in a coordinated way, leading to the cheapest possible solution. In practice, however, the normal and protection design can be made separately: first the normal network is designed, and then the resulting normal link capacity (and normal flows in the PR case) are used while designing the protection capacity and flows. Such an approach leads, in general, to more expensive solutions, because a solution of the separated design problem is of course a solution for the coordinated design problem. Below, we shall formulate the separated design problems for the LR case.

***LP:* D+P/CF/BR/CC/LIN/LR+BR** **Link-Path Formulation**
Design for Normal State + Protection with Link Restoration
Phase 1

indices

$d = 1, 2, ..., D$	demands
$p = 1, 2, ..., P_d$	candidate normal paths for demand d
$e, \ell = 1, 2, ..., E$	links
$q = 1, 2, ..., Q_e$	candidate restoration paths for link e

constants

δ_{edp}	= 1 if link e belongs to path p realizing demand d; 0, otherwise
h_d	volume of demand d
ξ_e	unit cost of link e

variables

x_{dp0}	normal flow allocated to path p of demand d
y_e	normal capacity of link e

objective

$$\text{minimize } \boldsymbol{F} = \sum_e \xi_e y_e \quad (9.4.12a)$$

constraints

$$\sum_p x_{dp0} = h_d \quad d = 1, 2, ..., D \quad (9.4.12b)$$

$$\sum_d \sum_p \delta_{edp} x_{dp0} \le y_e \quad e = 1, 2, ..., E \quad (9.4.12c)$$

Phase 2
additional constants

$\beta_{\ell eq}$ = 1 if link ℓ belongs to path q restoring link e; 0, otherwise
c_e normal capacity of link e, i.e., $c_e = y_e$ from Phase 1 for use in Phase 2

variables

z_{eq} flow restoring normal capacity of link e on restoration path q
y'_e protection capacity of link e

objective

$$\text{minimize } \boldsymbol{F} = \sum_e \xi_e y'_e \quad (9.4.12d)$$

constraints

$$\sum_q z_{eq} = c_e, \quad e = 1, 2, ..., E \quad (9.4.12e)$$

$$\sum_q \beta_{\ell eq} z_{eq} \le y'_\ell, \quad \ell = 1, 2, ..., E \quad e = 1, 2, ..., E \quad \ell \ne e. \quad (9.4.12f)$$

The resulting final link capacities are equal to $y_e = c_e + y'_e$, $e = 1, 2, ..., E$ (Exercise 9.7).

9.5 PROTECTION PROBLEMS

Protection problems arise when the normal network is given, i.e., feasible normal link capacities and flows realizing the demands are given and fixed. Then, basically, the design problem is to find an optimal configuration of protection capacity on top of the normal one so the total resulting link capacity is feasible to fulfill the demands in the assumed failure situations.

9.5.1 *Link Capacity Restoration*

Consider Phase 2 in problem D+P/CF/BR/CC/LIN/LR+BR (9.4.12). Adding the requirement for the single-path link restoration results in the following MIP problem.

***MIP:* P/CF/BR/CC/LIN/LR+SBP** **Link-Path Formulation**
Protection With Link Restoration on Single Path
variables
u_{eq} binary variable determining the flow on path q restoring link e ($z_{eq} = u_{eq}c_e$)
y_e protection capacity of link e
objective

$$\text{minimize } \boldsymbol{F} = \textstyle\sum_e \xi_e y_e \tag{9.5.1a}$$

constraints

$$\textstyle\sum_q u_{eq} = 1, \quad e = 1, 2, ..., E \tag{9.5.1b}$$

$$\textstyle\sum_q j\beta_{\ell eq} u_{eq} c_e \le y_\ell, \quad \ell = 1, 2, ..., E \quad e = 1, 2, ..., E \quad \ell \ne e. \tag{9.5.1c}$$

Example 9.11 *Link Capacity Restoration and Hamiltonian cycle*
As already mentioned in Example 9.3, a simple solution of the above problem is to find a shortest Hamiltonian cycle (the shortest Hamiltonian cycle, the subject of the well-known traveling salesman problem, is a simple closed path going through all the nodes and visiting each node exactly once) with respect to the link unit costs and assign protection capacity equal to $C = \max\{c_e : e = 1, 2, ..., E\}$ to each link along the cycle. This solution can be sometimes improved taking into account that the normal capacity of the links not on the Hamiltonian cycle can be restored on the shortest part of the cycle. To illustrate this point consider the cube network from Figure 9.2. As all link unit costs are equal to 1, each Hamiltonian cycle has a length of 8. Assuming all normal link capacities equal to 3, using for instance the cycle 1-2-3-4-7-6-5-8-1 the resulting protection cost will be equal to 24, as explained in Example 9.3. Now suppose that the normal capacity of link 1-2 is increased to 6 and the normal capacity of all the remaining links is not changed. Then, using the same cycle will result in the protection cost 48 because $C = 6$. If the cycle 1-6-7-2-3-4-5-8-1 were used with the protection capacity 6 assigned to links 1-6, 6-7 and 7-2 and protection capacity 3 assigned to the remaining links on the cycle, the protection cost would be reduced to 33. ●

A new type of problem is obtained when the normal capacities are given and we decide to start using some proportion of the normal capacity on each link as the protection capacity [NPD03]. In this way the demand volumes realized in the network would have to be decreased, still the network will become 100% protected against total single-link failures.

LP: **P/CF/BR/CC/LIN/LR+BR {PAC}** **Link-Path Formulation**

Protection Within Available Capacity Using Link Restoration

indices

$d = 1, 2, ..., D$ demands
$p = 1, 2, ..., P_d$ candidate path p for demand d
$e, \ell = 1, 2, ..., E$ links
$q = 1, 2, ..., Q_e$ candidate restoration paths for link e

constants

h_d "reference" volume of demand d
δ_{edp} = 1 if link e belongs to path p realizing demand d; 0, otherwise
c_e total capacity of link e
$\beta_{\ell eq}$ = 1 if link ℓ belongs to path q restoring link e; 0, otherwise

variables

y_e resulting normal capacity of link e
x_{dp} normal flow realizing demand d on path p
w_e protection capacity of link e
z_{eq} flow restoring capacity of link e on path q
r proportion of the realized demand volumes

objective

$$\text{maximize } r \tag{9.5.2a}$$

constraints

$$r \leq \textstyle\sum_p x_{dp}/h_d, \quad d = 1, 2, ..., D \tag{9.5.2b}$$

$$w_e + y_e \leq c_e, \quad e = 1, 2, ..., E \tag{9.5.2c}$$

$$\textstyle\sum_d \sum_p \delta_{edp} x_{dp} \leq y_e, \quad e = 1, 2, ..., E \tag{9.5.2d}$$

$$y_e \leq \textstyle\sum_q z_{eq}, \quad e = 1, 2, ..., E \tag{9.5.2e}$$

$$\textstyle\sum_q \beta_{\ell eq} z_{eq} \leq w_\ell, \quad \ell = 1, 2, ..., E \quad e = 1, 2, ..., E \quad \ell \neq e. \tag{9.5.2f}$$

Note that constraint (9.5.2b) assures that all demand volumes will be in the worst case decreased by the same optimal proportion r^* since in the optimal solution

$$\textstyle\sum_p x^*_{dp} \geq r^* h_d \quad d = 1, 2, ..., D \tag{9.5.3}$$

(see Exercise 9.8).

Solving P/CF/BR/CC/LIN/LR+BR {PAC} would be in fact only the first step in a procedure leading to a MMF solution for demand volume allocation. Such a procedure, similar to Algorithm 8.4 of Section 8.2.1 for the MMF routing problem A/MMF/FLMP (8.2.1), will assure that the optimal split of the normal capacity between the reduced normal capacity and the (shared) protection capacity leads to the MMF vector of the actually realized demand volumes (refer to [NPD03]).

9.5.2 *Path Restoration

In the case of unrestricted flow reconfiguration, protection of a given normal network using path restoration leads to the following straightforward formulation.

***LP:* P/CF/BR/CC/LIN/PR+UR** **Link-Path Formulation**

Protection With PR+UR

indices

$d = 1, 2, ..., D$ demands

$p = 1, 2, ..., P_d$ candidate paths for demand d

$e = 1, 2, ..., E$ links

$s = 0, 1, ..., S$ situations

constants

δ_{edp} = 1 if link e belongs to path p realizing demand d; 0, otherwise

h_d volume of demand d

χ_{ds} demand coefficient of demand d in state s, $h_{ds} = \chi_{ds} h_d$

ξ_e unit cost of link e

α_{es} fractional availability coefficient of link e in state s ($0 \leq \alpha_{es} \leq 1$)

c_e normal capacity of link e

variables

x_{dps} flow allocated to path p of demand d in state s ($s > 0$)

y_e protection capacity of link e

objective

$$\text{minimize } \boldsymbol{F} = \sum_e \xi_e y_e \tag{9.5.4a}$$

constraints

$$\sum_p x_{dps} = h_{ds}, \quad d = 1, 2, ..., D \quad s = 1, 2, ..., S \tag{9.5.4b}$$

$$\sum_d \sum_p \delta_{edp} x_{dps} \leq \alpha_{es}(c_e + y_e), \quad e = 1, 2, ..., E \quad s = 1, 2, ..., S. \tag{9.5.4c}$$

For the restricted flow reconfiguration case the formulation is as follows.

***LP:* P/CF/BR/CC/LIN/PR+RR** **Link-Path Formulation**

Protection With PR+RR

additional constants

x_{dp0} normal flow allocated to path p of demand d

c_e normal capacity of link e

variables

x_{dps} flow allocated to path p of demand d in state s ($s > 0$)

y_e protection capacity of link e

objective

$$\text{minimize } \boldsymbol{F} = \sum_e \xi_e y_e \tag{9.5.5a}$$

constraints

$$\sum_p x_{dps} \geq h_{ds} - \sum_p \theta_{dps} x_{dp0}, \quad d = 1, 2, ..., D \quad s = 1, 2, ..., S \tag{9.5.5b}$$

$$\sum_d \sum_p \delta_{edp} x_{dps} \leq \alpha_{es}(y_e + c_e - \sum_d \sum_p \delta_{edp} \theta_{dps} x_{dp0}), \quad e = 1, 2, ..., E \quad s = 1, 2, ..., S. \tag{9.5.5c}$$

We note that the BD method can be equally effectively applied for both P/CF/BR/CC/LIN/PR+UR and P/CF/BR/CC/LIN/PR+RR. In fact, for P/CF/BR/CC/LIN/PR+RR the BD method works as efficiently as for P/CF/BR/CC/LIN/PR+UR. As we will see in Section 10.3, this is not the case for the full design counterparts of the two problems, i.e., for DR-U (9.3.1) and DR-R (9.3.2) considered in Section 9.3; application of BD is more effective for the former problem than for the latter.

We skip the counterpart of DR/CF/BR/CC/LIN/PR+SDBP with situation-dependent back-up paths (Exercise 9.9) and proceed to the protection problem for DR/CF/BR/CC/LIN/PR+FSBP, which is the following MIP problem.

***MIP:* P/CF/BR/CC/LIN/PR+FSBP** **Link-Path Formulation**

Protection With PR+FSBP

indices

- $d = 1, 2, ..., D$ demands
- $p = 1, 2, ..., P_d$ given normal paths for demand d (with non-zero flow)
- $q = 1, 2, ..., Q_{dp}$ list of candidate back-up paths $\mathcal{Q}_{dpq}$ for normal path $\mathcal{P}_{dp}$ (each $\mathcal{Q}_{dpq}$ is situation-disjoint with $\mathcal{P}_{dp}$)
- $e = 1, 2, ..., E$ links
- $s = 0, 1, ..., S$ situations

constants

- δ_{edp} = 1 if link e belongs to normal path $\mathcal{P}_{dp}$; 0, otherwise
- β_{edpq} = 1 if link e belongs to back-up path $\mathcal{Q}_{dpq}$ protecting normal path $\mathcal{P}_{dp}$; 0, otherwise
- h_d volume of demand d
- ξ_e unit cost of link e
- α_{es} binary availability coefficient of link e in state s ($\alpha_{es} \in \{0, 1\}$)
- θ_{dps} binary availability coefficient of normal path p realizing demand d in state s, $\theta_{dps} = \prod_{\{e:\delta_{edp}=1\}} \alpha_{es}$
- x_{dp0} normal flow allocated to path $\mathcal{P}_{dp}$, $x_{dp0} > 0$
- c_e normal capacity of link e

variables

- u_{dpq} binary flow variable associated with path $\mathcal{Q}_{dpq}$
- y_e continuous capacity of link e

objective

$$\text{minimize } \boldsymbol{F} = \sum_e \xi_e y_e \tag{9.5.6a}$$

constraints

$$\sum_q u_{dpq} = 1, \quad d = 1,2,...,D \quad p = 1,2,...,P_d \tag{9.5.6b}$$

$$\sum_d \sum_p \sum_q (\delta_{edp}\theta_{dps} + \beta_{edpq}(1 - \theta_{dps}))x_{dp0}u_{dpq} \le \alpha_{es}(c_e + y_e), \quad e = 1,2,...,E \quad s = 1,2,...,S. \tag{9.5.6c}$$

Note that now, contrary to formulation (9.3.7), we can write $x_{dp0}u_{dpj}$ because x_{dp0} is a constant.

All the above formulated protection tasks can be used in Step 2 of the corresponding D+P problems (analogous to D+P/CF/BR/CC/LIN/LR+BR problems discussed in Section 9.4.6), i.e., the problems with separate normal and protection design.

As with link re-establishment (problem P/CF/BR/CC/LIN/LR+BR {PAC} (9.5.2)), a part of normal network capacity can be used to protect the normal flows at the expense of decreasing the normal demand volumes carried in the network. For unrestricted reconfiguration, an appropriate problem is as follows.

***LP:* P/CF/BR/CC/LIN/PR+UR {PAC}** **Link-Path Formulation**

Protection Within Normal Capacity Using PR+UR

indices

- $d = 1,2,...,D$ demands
- $p = 1,2,...,P_d$ candidate paths for demand d
- $e = 1,2,...,E$ links

constants

- h_d volume of demand d
- δ_{edp} = 1 if link e belongs to path p realizing demand d; 0, otherwise
- c_e total capacity of link e

variables

- x_{dps} flow realizing demand d on path p in state s
- r proportion of the realized demand volumes

objective

$$\text{for each state } s = 1,2,...,S \text{ separately maximize } r \tag{9.5.7a}$$

constraints

$$r \le \sum_p x_{dps}/h_d, \quad d = 1,2,...,D \tag{9.5.7b}$$

$$\sum_d \sum_p \delta_{edp} x_{dps} \le \alpha_{es} c_e, \quad e = 1,2,...,E. \tag{9.5.7c}$$

It is implicitly assumed that normal flows are realized in the normal capacity c_e; however, in the failure situations the normal capacities can be insufficient to carry all the normal demand, so a compromise ensured by constraint (9.5.7b) is introduced. Again, as in

P/CF/BR/CC/LIN/LR+BR {PAC} (9.5.2), the optimization process can be continued for each state s separately in order to find the MMF allocation of demands.

For other P problems this type of protection within the normal capacity leads to somewhat different optimization problems (Exercise 9.10).

9.6 APPLICABILITY OF THE PROTECTION/RESTORATION DESIGN MODELS

Most of the protection/restoration mechanisms and design models described in this chapter are actually applicable in real networks. In this section, we consider network technologies applicable in different layers of core networks, and describe which protection/restoration mechanisms they can use and which optimization models are appropriate.

A general comment is that in almost all considered cases modular link capacity is a necessity in the final solution. This may not be explicitly mentioned when discussing a technology, but should be understood. For example, when we say a model (9.3.1) is applicable, we really mean the corresponding version where link capacity takes modular values. Although this statement is true for today's networks, it should be mentioned that with the next generation synchronous network technology (SONET/SDH) it will be possible to form links of arbitrary (continuous) capacity and use them for example as IP links or ATM links, which will allow for dropping the link modularity requirement.

We would also like to point out the particular role of the optimization model DR-U (9.3.1) in protection/restoration studies of communication and computer networks. Unrestricted path (flow) reconfiguration is the most economical solution in terms of spare (protection) capacity since, due to the least constrained way of utilizing resources which are available in failure states, it requires the least amount of protection capacity compared to all other possible re-establishment mechanisms. Thus, the cost of the protection capacity required for a certain re-establishment mechanism can be divided by the cost of the DR-U solution and (expressed in %) used as the efficiency measure for the considered mechanism.

9.6.1 Dynamic Routing Circuit-Switched Networks

Dynamic routing voice digital circuit-switched networks have been around since the mid 1980s [ACM81], [Ash97], [Gir90]. Dynamic routing schemes such as dynamic non-hierarchical routing (DNHR), real-time network routing (RTNR), and dynamically controlled routing (DCR) have been deployed in core backbone wide-area voice networks. An important point to note about all these schemes is that they allow at most two links (i.e., at most one intermediate node) to complete a call within their networks. In this case the candidate path lists are very easy to generate since there is only at most one intermediate node for each path for a demand, and a direct path if the direct link exists. Note that for a V-node network, a maximum of $V - 2$ two-link paths are possible (in case of fully-interconnected networks).

In circuit-switched voice digital networks, the demand imposed on the network is the traffic load between nodes (digital switches) measured in *Erlangs*, i.e., 1 DCU = 1 *Erl*. Hence, h_d is expressed in *Erl* and assumes continuous non-negative values. Thus, link load, $\underline{y}_e$, is also calculated in *Erl*, using, for example, the load sharing model described in Section 3.4. Links between two switches are referred to as trunk groups. Trunk groups are modular; a typical module is equivalent to T1 (1 LCU = 24 circuits) or E1 (1 LCU = 30 or 31 circuits). Then, using, *Erlang-B* inverse formula (3.4.1), the link load can be translated to the number of circuits, and hence, to the number of modules required to carry the link load at a given blocking level.

Trunk groups can be realized in the transport layer using path diversity (PD); thus, once a trunk group between two switches is affected due to a failure, only a part of capacity (or entire capacity if PD is not used) for that group is lost, depending on how many physically diverse transmission paths the circuits of the trunk group are routed in the transport network [MS93]. Thus, in this case, link availability coefficient for trunk group e, α_{es}, is fractional, i.e., $0 \leq \alpha_{es} \leq 1$, since, due to PD, partial failures are common in the trunk group layer. Common values for α_{es} are $0, \frac{1}{3}, \frac{1}{2}, \frac{2}{3}$, and so on. Another characteristic feature is that multiple trunk groups can fail simultaneously because a failure such as a fiber cut can affect many trunk groups (refer to Figure 1.12; see also Section 12.3.4). This is an important issue to understand, leading to multi-layer modeling for failure propagation (see [GS98], [Med94b], [Pió99]), which will be discussed later in Chapter 12.

A digital circuit-switched voice network is an example of a traffic network (traffic layer in a multi-layer telecommunication network, refer to Section 1.6) and as such its typical protection/restoration mechanism is unrestricted path (flow) reconfiguration (restoration). Reconfiguration of call flows is performed automatically by the dynamic routing system controlling call routing tables in some kind of adaptive way. In the context of restoration capacity design for such networks, we do not need to distinguish between normal capacity and restoration capacity since circuits on a trunk group, once provisioned, are made indistinguishable and are freely used for unconstrained flow reconfiguration (note that this feature eliminates the necessity of using more capacity-consuming protection mechanisms, as for example hot-standby). An important benefit of this capability is that a network can use such capacity to complete additional call volumes during a sudden traffic surge (and thereby increase revenue).

In dynamic routing circuit-switched networks, from the capacity design point of view, we can assume unrestricted flow restoration. That is, although there is a transient phase of flow restoration after a failure, the network can be assumed to be in a state with a less capacity of trunk groups available to account for a failed situation. The network in a failure state may be required to have enough surviving capacity to carry offered traffic at an acceptable grade-of-service (blocking). The grade-of-service for a normal state is typically below 1% call-blocking; however, under a failure state, it may be acceptable to have blocking as high as 5% to 10% (note that this influences link dimensioning functions, refer to Example 4.6 in Section 4.3.3). Moreover, we can use the parameter χ_{ds} described in Section 9.1 to account for any adjustment of traffic due to a failure state. For example, we may control (and thus define) the demand coefficients χ_{ds} using a suitable congestion control mechanism (for example, call gapping [Tow88]) to throttle the traffic h_d allowed to enter the network in failure situation s.

It so happens that the dynamic routing networks can be modeled in an approximate way using the load-sharing traffic model (refer to Section 3.4). If we then assume (as in

Section 11.1.2) that the relationship between the link load and the number of required circuits is linear (which is approximately the case for large trunk groups), then the unrestricted path restoration model DR-U (9.3.1) with modular dimensioning (that uses (9.3.1d)) is appropriate for circuit-switched networks with dynamic routing.

Without dynamic routing, digital voice networks can be modeled using PD models based on load sharing (refer to Sections 3.4 and 9.1.3). Finally, it may be noted that local semi-permanent re-switching of the circuits around a failed trunk group is not done in any circuit-switched network implementation (for example because multiple link failures are typical, and the mechanism is rather hard to implement). Thus, the link protection/restoration models are not applicable to circuit-switched networks.

9.6.2 Backbone IP, MPLS, and ATM Networks

IP networks are another example (besides circuit-switched voice networks) of traffic networks and hence the unrestricted flow reconfiguration is a natural protection mechanism in IP networks, achievable using adaptively controlled packet routing tables. Thus, routing, flow, and capacity design for IP backbone networks running OSPF (or IS-IS) protocol can be addressed for modeling major failures by using formulation DR-U (9.3.1) with the modification that the flow induced by shortest-path routing due to the state-dependent link metric system $\boldsymbol{w}_s$ for state s, is reflected as $x_{dps}(\boldsymbol{w}_s)$, instead of simply as x_{dps}. For shortest-path routing, binary failure coefficients α_{es} should be assumed since otherwise (i.e., in the case of fractional α_{es}) the weight-based routing would not work properly (think why). Recall that the binary failure coefficient assumption can always be made as explained in Section 9.1.3 (refer to Figure 9.3). Also, packet traffic entering the network in a failure state can be throttled by means of admission control mechanisms applied in the edge routers, giving a way for controlling demand coefficients χ_{ds}. It may be noted that for transient link failures reloading a complete new link metric is often undesirable; in this case, the approach discussed earlier in Section 7.9 can be used, where temporarily failed links are assigned infinite weights.

As already mentioned first in Section 3.2, MPLS is a recent development [DR00] to control traffic for different service classes, for example, through the use of MPLS tunnel concept. Earlier, we have illustrated a network tunneling optimization model in Section 3.2. Here, we will consider several possible usages of MPLS networks and tunnels, and discuss appropriate use of various protection/restoration models.

Recall that end-to-end MPLS tunnels can be set up to carry demand volumes for different traffic demand types that require different quality of service; thus, MPLS networks can provide transport services through use of tunnels. Possible services considered for MPLS are IP-VPN (virtual private network) services, layer-2 VPN transport services, and so on. Regardless of the actual service, demand volumes can for example be given in Megabits per second (Mbps) (these volumes determine the capacity of the corresponding tunnels). Hence, the tunnel capacity does not need to be necessarily in integral units of Mbps; thus, we can use models where continuous flow variables are allowed. In effect, DVU can be assumed to be in Mbps while LCU can for example be given in Mbps with the use of module value M, e.g., 1 LCU= M = 155.52 Mbps; this results in having link capacity in integral values.

For MPLS networks providing transport services with single end-to-end (primary) tunnels for each demand node pair, which are set up using the LSP (label switched path) concept of MPLS, single back-up restoration can be considered. In many cases, a network provider might want to set up a back-up tunnel for survivability and restoration of traffic taking the primary tunnel. As a matter of fact, as of this writing, the MPLS Working Group of the Internet Engineering Task Force is exploring a concept called *Fast-Reroute* [PSA04] (see also [AN03]), where a back-up tunnel is to be set up for a working tunnel so that through a signaling mechanism a service can be restored on the back-up path very quickly. Clearly, either DR-F (9.3.6) or DR/CF/BR/CC/LIN/PR+FSBP (9.3.7) can be used to model the Fast-Reroute mechanism. Note that hot-standby path protection (refer to DR/CF/BR/CC/LIN/PP+HS (9.3.8)) can be applied instead of the single back-up path protection (with shared pool of protection capacity). Certainly, other path restoration models from Section 9.3 can be used for investigations of the impact of different PR mechanisms on the amount (and cost) of network capacity.

Another aspect to consider is when the end-to-end demand volumes are allowed to be tunneled over multiple parallel end-to-end tunnels (not only over one tunnel). If tunneling over multiple LSR paths is allowed, then for protection design, the restricted path restoration model DR-R (9.3.2) can be used since a non-affected tunnel is unlikely to be rearranged (for example, due to network management tunnel set up cost). Alternately, single back-up path restorations models are also appropriate here, especially the one with single, situation-independent restoration paths (model DR/CF/BR/CC/LIN/PR+FSBP (9.3.7)).

Note that in either of these cases, we first solve the basic model. If in the optimal solution, a path has positive normal flow, then this indicates that a basic tunnel with bandwidth equal to this flow amount would need to be set up and maintained in the network. The back-up tunnels calculated within the optimization model would be activated in failure situations when such a necessity (the loss of the corresponding protected basic tunnel) arises.

Yet another possibility in MPLS networks is to establish tunnels between pairs of nodes and treat them as links supporting IP demand flows (and perhaps also flows imposed by other networks). As a matter of fact, in such a case MPLS introduces a new layer of resources (links - tunnels, and nodes - LSR routers) between the IP network layer (and perhaps other parallel networks as frame-relay, Ethernet, and so on) and the transport network layer. If this is the case, the demand paths can traverse multiple tunnels, and one tunnel can support several end-to-end demand flow paths. The tunnels, in turn, are realized by means of their own (single) paths over the modular links. It can be assumed that when a set of tunnels are affected by a network failure, they can be restored individually in the surviving links capacity by means of the mechanisms described above for the end-to-end tunnel case (as Fast-Reroute). This would lead to two-layer restoration design models which are discussed in Section 12.2.

On the other hand, we can assume that MPLS tunnels are subject to failures and are not restored; instead the demand flows are restored individually in the surviving tunnels. For such hypothetical restoration mechanisms, all the models of Section 9.3 apply.

In addition to the default notion and usage of explicit paths in MPLS networks, MPLS allows for constraints-based routing [AMA+99], which is useful for QoS routing of heterogeneous calls/connections that require quality of service, for example, in terms of bandwidth guarantee. Here each link of an MLPS network can act as a traffic link (or tunnels can be set up to build traffic links) and connection paths can be composed of such links. For instance, a possible constraint to use in constraint-based routing is available link bandwidth that can be used for constructing and updating routing tables which contain paths with some acceptable bandwidth guarantee. Such paths configured through the use of routing tables are made up of multiple links for call/connection routing; see, for example, [SKV+02] for potential usage and benefit. In essence, this has similarity to dynamic routing circuit-switched voice networks with the exception that call routing can be carried over connection paths consisting of more than just two "links" and calls can be of heterogeneous bandwidth requirement. Thus, the discussion earlier in Section 9.6.1 regarding applicability of various protection/restoration models for circuit-switched voice networks usually holds here.

Lastly, we consider the case of backbone ATM networks. We will discuss two cases: virtual-path based ATM networks and PNNI-based ATM networks. A backbone core VP-based ATM network has similar properties as an MPLS network with end-to-end LSPs and acts primarily to provide transport services. Here, VPs are set up instead of tunnels. In ATM networks, VP demands for bandwidth can also be given in Mbps (DVU), similar to MPLS networks. Link capacities can be either 155 Mbps or 622 Mbps (as typically an ATM link is realized by means of a SONET/SDH path). Thus, LCU can be expressed in Mbps with module value of $M = 155$ or $M = 622$. For ATM networks, restoration models DR-U (9.3.1), DR-R (9.3.2), and DR-F (9.3.6) are basically applicable, especially the last one.

In a VP-based ATM network, a basic (working) VP can be provided with one pre-planned single failure-disjoint back-up (protection) VP with no bandwidth assigned to it during normal network operation condition (state). In the case, when the basic VP fails (in terms of the QoS requirements defined for it), the back-up VP is activated and an appropriate bandwidth is assigned along its route for the duration of the failure state. The approach, known as *guided restoration* [SO94a], is a trade-off between network resilience performance and protection capacity costs. Taking advantage of the flexibility of this scheme, networks can survive even failures not forseen in the design scenario, since a pre-planned solution can be dynamically modified on a local basis. This is the way the back-up path restoration mechanisms with shared protection are currently used in ATM core networks. Certainly, they can be properly modeled by the DR-F model (refer to [SO94b]).

For an ATM network equipped with PNNI routing [For96], call set up and routing come into the picture, and the network becomes a traffic network. In this case, affected calls will be rerouted around the failure depending on the availability of call-rerouting feature at ATM switches. From a protocol functionality point of view, PNNI does allow local call reroute (as opposed to dynamic call routing circuit-switched networks), in addition to an end-to-end reroute; however, this functionality has been rarely implemented in ATM switches by vendors due to complexity of implementation. Regardless, with a PNNI-capable ATM network (depending on the actual implementation available on switches), it can be possible to use either DR-U (9.3.1) or DR-R (9.3.2). Not only that, due to the local reroute functionality described in the PNNI protocol, at least from a capacity design point of view, link restoration models such as (9.2.1) or (9.2.3) can be used; certainly, this will depend on having this functionality available on a vendor's ATM switch product.

9.6.3 Optical Systems, SONET/SDH, and WDM Networks

For many years, optical systems have become dominant in telecommunication transport services. Historically, there have been three evolutionary stages in this regard: in the first stage, fiber systems were deployed with proprietary node terminal functionality; in the second stage, the SONET/SDH standards were developed—now SONET/SDH have been widely deployed; and in recent years, WDM technology has emerged. In Chapter 3, we have briefly discussed the SONET/SDH and WDM technologies and presented examples of protection design problems. Readers are directed to references [Muk97], [DGA+99], [Gro04], [RS02], and [Wu92] that discuss optical technologies in general and network design problems in particular.

A common protection mechanism in the optical technology supporting the SONET/SDH transmission systems is the 1+1 (or 1:1) hot-standby functionality (refer to Section 9.1.2) called automatic protection switching (APS) [Wu92]. APS can be activated between any two terminating nodes of an optical transmission system. For example, a 1:1 APS can restore a single fiber transmission system between two terminating nodes by switching the signal from the basic fiber to the protection fiber. If the protection fiber is a part of an optical cable which follows a path (conduit) which is physically diverse from the path (conduit) of the cable of the basic fiber, then we achieve protection against single optical cable cuts. Thus, for APS, the restoration capacity design model for hot-standby path protection DR/CF/BR/CC/LIN/PP+HS (9.3.8) is applicable in the fiber (physical) layer with physical distribution frames used as switches.

A DVU for the SONET/SDH system is typically VT-1.5/VC-12 or STS-3/VC-4, depending on the considered sub-layer. The link capacity is determined by the number of optical fibers activated between two end terminals as well as the termination capacity of a SONET/SDH transmission systems realized on the fibers. All such terminations have rates in multiples of OC-3/STM-1 units (or higher rate units). Thus, LCU can then be considered as an integral multiple of DVU, and LCU can also use OC-3/STM-1 as the base unit.

Typically link availability coefficients for transmission links in SONET/SDH (and WDM) networks are assumed to be binary (i.e., for link e and state s, α_{es} is either 1 or 0), as, roughly speaking, links (i.e., transmission lines) correspond to conduits. Also, single link failures are the most common case.

In most cases, the basic switching devices in the nodes of large SONET/SDH core networks are digital cross-connect systems (DCS) which are capable of switching STS-3/VC-4 (or even lower rate) signals and are used for establishing (and re-establishing) transmission paths. These actions are usually controlled manually from the network management center, in this way performing link or path restoration when such a necessity arises. Restoration uses the common pool of spare capacity; hence, the routing, flow, and capacity design models of Sections 9.2.1 and 9.3 apply here. Certainly, the most common solution in manual restoration is the single (situation-dependent) back-up link or path restoration as described in models DR/CF/BR/CC/LIN/LR+SBP (9.2.3), and DR-SD (9.3.5) (or DR-F (9.3.6)), respectively.

Automation of the re-establishment mechanisms using shared protection capacity, although technically feasible, is not common in today's SONET/SDH networks. The most technologically mature is automatic link protection with restoration time of the order from tens of milliseconds to seconds.

A popular use of SONET/SDH has been in building SONET (or SDH) rings either with uni-directional path-switched rings (UPSR) or with bi-directional line-switched rings (BLSR, refer to Section 3.6). Protection in UPSR rings is based on a simple version of the path protection principle (for example in the VT-1.5 layer in a OC-3 SONET ring, or in the VC-12 layer in a STM-1 SDH ring, refer to Tables 3.1 and 3.2 in Section 3.5)) and in fact it does not need any optimization model (dimensioning of UPSRs is trivial). On the other hand, protection in BLSR rings is a simple application of the link restoration mechanism (in the STS-3 layer in the OC-3 SONET ring, or in the VC-4 layer in a STM-1 SDH ring); the specific model (3.6.1) we presented in Section 3.6 for BLSR essentially captures the basic protection design problem of a single SONET/SDH ring. Capacity restoration time in rings is very short, below 50 ms.

WDM technology is based on using a set of different wavelengths (i.e., 80 wavelengths) in one optical fiber to realize a set of corresponding SONET/SDH transmission systems (typically OC-48/STM-16). WDM core networks use optical cross-connect switches that are capable of switching wavelengths (so called λ-switching) to form light-paths. Because demand volumes in WDM networks are routed using wavelength, the restoration models need to consider integral flows (as in the case of SONET/SDH). Today, restoration in WDM networks is typically performed manually using path restoration. Hence, optimization formulations associated with the single back-up restoration mechanism are applicable. We would like to point out that WDM networks with optical cross-connects that cannot perform wavelength conversion lead to specific restoration problems (refer to Section 10.6 for further discussion).

Finally, we can expect that in future optical networks (refer to ASON) automatic link/path protection/restoration mechanisms will be considered and most likely widely used, opening a way for new applications of the design models discussed in this chapter.

To end this section we wish to make an important remark that resource protection can be performed in different layers of a multi-layer network. For example, trunk groups of the circuit-switched traffic layer (or IP links of the IP network) can be 100% protected in the underlying transport layer, such as synchronous optical SONET/SDH network, and then the circuit-switched network (IP network) can be regarded as fully robust against failures. In such a case, however, restoration is performed in the transport network and the call (packet) flows simply do not see any failures (provided restoration of trunk groups is a matter of milliseconds). Similarly, links in the SONET/SDH layer can be protected in the underlying (physical) optical fiber layer by means of APS. This is a general rule: resources of a certain network layer can be protected in the neighboring lower resource layer. We will return to this issue in Chapter 12.

9.7 SUMMARY AND FURTHER READING

Restoration design problems in communication and computer networks have become profound in the last two decades, as the evolving network technologies made it available to protect and restore network resources (most of all link capacity) at different network layers against resource failures. With old technologies, such as cross-bar switching and plesiochronous digital hierarchy (PDH) transmission, the protection mechanisms were rather static and based mostly on the PD for trunk groups and hot-standby for transmission systems (Section 9.3.5). With these two mechanisms, the related restoration/protection design problems (discussed in Sections 9.3.1 and 9.3.5, respectively) were in fact not explicitly taken into account because shortest-path allocation was simply used for the design purpose. With the introduction of digital switching and SONET/SDH synchronous transmission with their intrinsic ability of reswitching demand flows (through dynamic adjusting of call routing tables and reswitching digital flows, respectively) in response to network components failures, the need for explicit consideration of restoration design problems at the planning/design stage became evident. Of course, the continuing evolution of network technology (ATM, IP, MPLS, and WDM) amplified this need, as the introduced powerful technological protection/restoration means must be effectively utilized; this can be made only by proper design of routing, flow, and capacity, taking into account the most important failure scenarios.

We have started this chapter with a general discussion of the restoration modeling issues, including modeling of failures states (situations) by means of the link availability coefficients and demand coefficients (Section 9.1.1), definitions of different types of protection capacity and protection/restoration mechanisms (Section 9.1.2), and an explanation of the simplest way of protection resources by flow diversity (Section 9.1.3).

Section 9.2 is devoted to link re-establishment, an important mechanism used for protecting capacity of links (such mechanisms are called, commonly and somewhat unambiguously, link protection). We distinguish between two basic types of link re-establishment. The first, active link capacity restoration, involves switching and signaling actions in the neighborhood of the failed link, and using shared protection capacity is treated by means of the relevant design problems in Section 9.2.1. The second simpler case is of the hot-standby type (Section 9.2.2). As discussed in Section 9.6.3, link protection is applicable with the SONET/SDH and WDM technologies.

Demand flow restoration is discussed in detail in Section 9.3. In this case the end-to-end demand flows are restored on individual paths, rather than the whole capacity of the failed links. Different cases are considered, from unrestricted flow reconfiguration (Section 9.3.1) applicable in digital telephone networks, through restricted reconfiguration (when unaffected flows are not moved, Section 9.3.2) applicable in ATM/VP and IP/MPLS, to single back-up path restoration (Sections 9.3.3 and 9.3.4) applicable in ATM/VP, and IP/MPLS, as well as in SONET/SDH, WDM, and future ASON networks.

Sections 9.2 and 9.3 specify a set of interesting (and challenging) design problems. Still, in Section 9.4, we present various extensions of the already discussed models, associated with such important elements of modeling, as non-linear and modular capacity (Sections 9.4.1 and 9.4.2), budget constraint (9.4.3), various routing restrictions as single-path routing (Section 9.4.4), and separation of the basic and protection capacity (Sections 9.4.5 and 9.4.6).

In Section 9.5 we deal with an important case when the basic capacity used to realize the normal network demand is already installed and the issue is to find optimal configuration of the protection capacity, on top of the given basic capacity. The cases of link capacity restoration and of flow restoration are considered in Sections 9.5.1 and 9.5.2, respectively.

Finally, in Section 9.6, we discuss where in the contemporary network technologies the considered re-establishment mechanisms and related design problems are applicable.

As you have surely noticed in reading this chapter, the number of possible multi-commodity flow problem formulations related to restoration design is enormous. A considerable number of them have been presented in the previous sections and many more could be formulated. We may safely say that the problems discussed in this chapter are among the most important and challenging multi-commodity flow problems in telecommunications. Many of the considered problems have been studied in the literature (not only related to telecommunications) and the particular formulations are spread over a very large number of papers and some monographs. In consequence, it is again difficult (as it was the case of the problems discussed in Chapter 4) to identify where and when exactly a particular problem was first considered. Nevertheless, even with a considerable risk of being sometimes wrong, we will try to survey problem formulations below.

The work by Stegleitz et al. [SWK69] is possibly the first published work on survivable network design. General discussion on the restoration problems can be found in such papers as [ACL94], [KDP94] and [MK95]. These problems are also discussed in the monograph [Wu92] and the recent book [Gro04]. A distributed scheme for implementation of shared protection is described in [San00].

The approach to failure and modular design problem modeling with the use of link availability coefficients (α_{es}) has been used in the paper of Gavish et al. [GTD+89], where unrestricted flow reconfiguration problems (refer to DR-U in Section 9.3.1) are considered (see [Med94b] for a multi-layer restoration design problem). Similar problems, such as admitting flow diversity in the normal state, are considered by Dahl and Stoer in [DS98], but with emphasis put on the single-element (link or node) failure scenarios. The restoration problem with restricted flow reconfiguration of the DR-R (Section 9.2.2) type is studied by Wessäly [Wes00]. The single back-up path flow restoration problems (Section 9.3.4), but for single-link failure scenarios, are considered in [CLH99], [GOK03], [Med91a], [SOT90], [VSH96], and many others. The five basic types of flow restoration problems treated in Section 9.3 are identified and discussed in [Pió97a]. An early paper on link protection problems (Section 9.2) is by Lindberg [Lin80]. These types of problems have been also treated in [HB94], [SNH90], and [VHS97]. Protection problems discussed in Section 9.5 are treated in such papers as [BL99], [KPNG02], [LNC00], [MS81b], [NPD03], [SNH90], [VHS97].

The ring protection concept for SONET/SDH can be used in a core optical network by considering the network composed of a set of rings where each ring connects a subset of nodes and the neighboring rings are interconnected via common nodes. While this concept can provide restoration in a short time, the overall network capacity for protection can in general be more costly than an equivalent protection design of a mesh-network. Recently, the concept of p-Cycles has been introduced [GS00] that has the benefit of ring restoration but yet is not as expensive as the multi-ring based solution. For further discussion, refer to [Gro04] and [SG04].

EXERCISES FOR CHAPTER 9

9.1. Specify the optimal bifurcated and non-bifurcated flows of DR-U for the network from Figure 9.4 considered in Example 9.4.

9.2. Show that the optimal solution of DR/CF/BR/CC/LIN/LR+BR (9.2.1) can be converted to a feasible solution of DR-U (9.3.1) with the same cost.

9.3. Formulate an extended version of DR-U (9.3.1) with the generalized diversity (refer to A/GD (4.2.2) in Section 4.2.1) assumed for the normal network operating state $s = 0$ (and only for the normal network operating state).

9.4. Derive the formula for the released capacity y''_e in DR-R (9.3.3).

9.5. *Formulate problem DR/CF/NBR/CC/LIN/PR+SDBP with forced situation-dependent single restoration path. (Hint: adjust formulation of DR/CF/BR/CC/LIN/PR+FSBP (9.3.7).)

9.6. Formulate versions of DR-U (9.3.1), DR-R (9.3.3) and DR-SD (9.3.5) for the case with separated normal and protection capacity (released capacity cannot be used for path restoration).

9.7. Find a simple network example with the optimal cost of DR/CF/BR/CC/LIN/LR+BR (9.2.1) less than the optimal cost of D+P/CF/BR/CC/LIN/LR+BR (9.4.12).

9.8. Consider a two-node network with two links and two demands between the two nodes. Suppose that $c_1 = 1, c_2 = n$ and $h_1 = 1, h_2 = n$, and that demand $d = 1$ uses only one path $\mathcal{P}_{11} = \{1\}$, and demand $d = 2$ uses only one path $\mathcal{P}_{21} = \{2\}$. What is the optimal solution of problem P/CF/BR/CC/LIN/LR+BR $\{PAC\}$ (9.5.2)? What percentage of the normal capacity $c_1 + c_2 = n + 1$ is not used in the resulting 100% network? (Hint: the percentage of the unused capacity is $100(n-1)/(n+1)\%$, hence the percentage of unused capacity tends to 100% as n tends to infinity!)

9.9. Write down a MIP formulation of P/CF/BR/CC/LIN/PR+SDBP with forced situation-dependent single restoration path. (Hint: adjust the formulation (9.5.6).)

9.10. Formulate problems analogous to P/CF/BR/CC/LIN/PR+UR $\{PAC\}$ (9.5.7) for the restricted reconfiguration, situation-dependent back-up paths, and single back-up paths re-establishment mechanisms.

CHAPTER 10

Application of Optimization Techniques for Protection and Restoration Design

In this chapter we will discuss applications of the optimization approaches described in Chapter 5 to the restoration design problems presented in Chapter 9. We concentrate on decomposition methods available in linear programming (LP), on mixed integer programming (MIP), as well as on stochastic meta-heuristics of simulated allocation (SAL), simulated annealing (SAN), and evolutionary algorithms (EA). This chapter is developed for readers who are interested in algorithmic details for restoration design problems; readers who are primarily interested in modeling aspects may skip this chapter.

The LP optimization framework has been already discussed in Sections 5.1 and 5.4, while the BB and BC methods have been presented in Section 5.2. The stochastic meta-heuristics, SAL, SAN, and EA have been described in Section 5.3 (in the context of normal network design). These methods have been already used for the design problems in Chapters 6 and 7.

We start this chapter by showing how the column generation technique of LP for path generation (PG) for candidate path lists can be applied to the flow restoration problems formulated in Section 9.3. Recall that column generation has been introduced in Section 5.4.2, and already used in Section 8.2.1. The method is important since the node-link formulation is not applicable to the cases with restricted flow reconfiguration, as for example the single back-up path restoration. Next, in Section 10.2, we apply the Lagrangian relaxation (LR) technique (Section 5.4.1) to the same set of problems. These applications are important as they can be used for the lower bound computations in the branch-and-cut (BC) approach for the MIP versions of the considered problems; also LR solutions can help to improve Benders' decomposition (BD) - the next technique which is described in Section 10.3. Applications of PG and DB are illustrated with numerical examples.

In Section 10.4 we discuss the MIP versions of the flow restoration models treated in Sections 10.1, 10.2, and 10.3. The problems considered in Section 10.4 involve modular links and as such are among the most challenging problems considered in the area of the multi-commodity network optimization. The basic approach here is BC (Section 5.2.2); we do not give description of the particular algorithms, rather make a survey of the literature where appropriate methods can be found.

Section 10.5 shows how to apply the basic stochastic meta-heuristics for the restoration problems. This is done in a fairly detailed way, as these applications are quite new and hard to find in other books. Selected numerical examples illustrate the applications. Section 10.6 is devoted to a particular application of some of the heuristic methods, namely to the wavelength assignment problem in WDM networks. The specific problems studied are described and a numerical study is presented. Finally, Section 10.7 gives a summary and suggests further reading.

10.1 PATH GENERATION

The LP versions of the problems formulated in Section 9.3 can be directly approached with standard LP solvers. It should be noted, however, that for large networks of, for example, 100 nodes, even most effective solvers may fail to deliver an optimal solution due to an excessive number of variables and constraints. One option can be to generate a limited set of pre-processed paths based on the knowledge about the network (or the network designer's knowledge) so that the number of variables is contained; another option is to generate a limited set of pre-processed paths using the K-shortest path method (Section C.3 of Appendix C) where the known link cost (ξ_e) can be used for generating the set of pre-processed paths. However, such a set of pre-processed paths cannot guarantee that the set contains the optimal paths for the original design problem. Thus, an LP technique called column generation applied to generate paths (on top of the pre-processed candidate paths) with the potential to identify and capture the optimal paths can be very useful; another advantage of such an approach is that the initial candidate path-lists can be very small, to start with, and they usually remain small until the optimum is found. Since the column generation technique is used for generating paths for network design problems, we refer to it as the path generation (PG) method (we will use the terms column generation and path generation interchangeably).

In this section we will demonstrate how to use the PG technique (described in Section 5.4.2) for the three selected problems from Section 9.3, namely DR/CF/BR/CC/LIN/PR+UR (9.3.1), DR/CF/BR/CC/LIN/PR+RR (9.3.2), and DR/CF/BR/CC/LIN/PR+FBP (9.3.6). Through this chapter, these problems will be referred to as DR-U, DR-R, and DR-F, respectively. While solving these link-path formulations, the column generation technique can be very helpful, especially for problem DR-F where it can be particularly difficult to define proper sets of pairs of normal/back-up paths in advance.

10.1.1 Unrestricted Reconfiguration

Application of the column generation technique to the unrestricted problem DR-U is fairly straightforward and most effective if we allow the use of different path lists in different situations (states), which is more natural than using the same sets of paths in all situations. The use of PG for a similar problem has been described in [DS98] and [Wes00].

LP: DR/CC/BR/CC/LIN/PR+UR/SDPL {DR-U} Link-Path Formulation
Problem DR/CF/BR/CC/LIN/PR+UR With Situation-Dependent Path Lists

indices

$e = 1, 2, \ldots, E$ links
$d = 1, 2, \ldots, D$ demands
$s = 1, 2, \ldots, S$ situations (or states)
$p = 1, 2, \ldots, P_{ds}$ candidate path list for demand d in situation s

constants

δ_{edps} = 1 if link e belongs to path p realizing demand d in situation s; 0, otherwise
h_d volume of demand d
χ_{ds} demand coefficient of demand d in situation s, $h_{ds} = \chi_{ds} h_d$
ξ_e marginal cost of link e
α_{es} fractional availability coefficient of link e in situation s ($0 \leq \alpha_{es} \leq 1$)

variables (continuous non-negative)

x_{dps} flow allocated to path p of demand d in situation s
y_e capacity of link e

objective

$$\text{minimize} \quad \boldsymbol{F} = \textstyle\sum_e \xi_e y_e \tag{10.1.1a}$$

constraints

$$\textstyle\sum_p x_{dps} = h_{ds}, \quad d = 1, 2, \ldots, D \quad s = 1, 2, \ldots, S \tag{10.1.1b}$$

$$\textstyle\sum_d \sum_p \delta_{edps} x_{dps} \leq \alpha_{es} y_e, \quad e = 1, 2, \ldots, E \quad s = 1, 2, \ldots, S. \tag{10.1.1c}$$

Note that states are labeled from 1 to S and, hence, the normal state is not distinguished. This is not necessary as the flows are configured in each situation from scratch, and the flow patterns in different situations do not influence each other. Recall that the above problem will be referred to as DR-U in the balance of this chapter.

To illustrate the PG method for DR-U we dualize constraints (10.1.1b) (dual variables $\boldsymbol{\lambda} = (\lambda_{ds} : d = 1, 2, \ldots, D, s = 1, 2, \ldots, S)$) and (10.1.1c) (dual variables $\boldsymbol{\pi} = (\pi_{es} : e = 1, 2, \ldots, E, s = 1, 2, \ldots, S)$, $\boldsymbol{\pi} \geq \mathbf{0}$), and construct the Lagrangian

$$\begin{aligned} L(\boldsymbol{x}, \boldsymbol{y}; \boldsymbol{\lambda}, \boldsymbol{\pi}) &= \textstyle\sum_e \xi_e y_e + \sum_d \sum_s \lambda_{ds}(h_{ds} - \sum_p x_{dps}) - \sum_e \sum_s \sum_d \sum_p \pi_{es} \delta_{edps} x_{dps} \\ &\quad - \textstyle\sum_e \sum_s \pi_{es} \alpha_{es} y_e \\ &= \textstyle\sum_d \sum_s \lambda_{ds} h_{ds} + \sum_s \sum_d \sum_p (\sum_e \delta_{edps} \pi_{es} - \lambda_{ds}) x_{dps} \\ &\quad + \textstyle\sum_e (\xi_e - \sum_s \alpha_{es} \pi_{es}) y_e. \end{aligned} \tag{10.1.2}$$

It follows that the maximum of the dual function

$$W(\boldsymbol{\lambda}, \boldsymbol{\pi}) = \min_{\boldsymbol{x}, \boldsymbol{y} \geq \mathbf{0}} L(\boldsymbol{x}, \boldsymbol{y}; \boldsymbol{\lambda}, \boldsymbol{\pi}) \tag{10.1.3}$$

is equal to

$$W(\boldsymbol{\lambda}^*, \boldsymbol{\pi}^*) = \max_{\boldsymbol{\pi} \geq \mathbf{0}, \boldsymbol{\lambda}} \sum_d \sum_s \lambda_{ds} h_{ds} \tag{10.1.4a}$$

and is attained in the subspace of multipliers (dual variables) defined by (Exercise 10.1):

$$\lambda_{ds} \leq \sum_e \delta_{edps} \pi_{es}, \qquad d = 1, 2, \ldots, D \quad s = 1, 2, \ldots, S \quad p = 1, 2, \ldots, P_{ds} \tag{10.1.4b}$$

$$\sum_s \alpha_{es} \pi_{es} \leq \xi_e, \quad e = 1, 2, \ldots, E \tag{10.1.4c}$$

$$\alpha_{es} = 0 \text{ implies } \pi_{es} = +\infty, \quad e = 1, 2, \ldots, E \quad s = 1, 2, \ldots, S \tag{10.1.4d}$$

$$\boldsymbol{\pi} \geq \mathbf{0}. \tag{10.1.4e}$$

An optimal solution (i.e., optimal dual variables $(\boldsymbol{\lambda}^*, \boldsymbol{\pi}^*)$) of the dual Problem (10.1.4) can be obtained by solving the primal Problem (10.1.1) with an LP solver or by the subgradient maximization method described in Section 10.2.1 (also see Section A.8 in Appendix A). We observe that

$$\sum_s \alpha_{es} \pi^*_{es} = \xi_e, \quad e = 1, 2, \ldots, E \tag{10.1.5a}$$

$$\lambda^*_{ds} = \min\{\sum_e \delta_{edps} \pi^*_{es} : p = 1, 2, \ldots, P_{ds}\}, \qquad d = 1, 2, \ldots, D \quad s = 1, 2, \ldots, S \tag{10.1.5b}$$

because from the viewpoint of maximization of the dual function the values of π^*_{es} and λ^*_{ds} must be as large as possible. Hence each λ^*_{ds} is the length of the shortest path of demand d in situation s for the link metrics equal to $\pi^*_{1s}, \pi^*_{2s}, \ldots, \pi^*_{Es}$ (10.1.4b). It can then be shown, in essentially the same way as in Section 5.4.2, that if a situation s and demand d exist for which a path shorter with respect to $(\pi^*_{1s}, \pi^*_{2s}, \ldots, \pi^*_{Es})$ than λ^*_{ds} (i.e., shorter than any path $\mathcal{P}_{dp}$, $p = 1, 2, \ldots, P_{ds}$) can be found, then including such a shortest path into the list of candidate paths will possibly improve the current optimal solution computed for the current path lists. Note that while looking for the shortest paths we eliminate totally failed links as, according to (10.1.4d), $\pi_{es} = +\infty$ if $\alpha_{es} = 0$.

To prove a proposition analogous to Proposition 5.1 from Section 5.4.2, we consider the perturbed problem in which the flow equal to ε realizing demand d' in situation s' is assigned in advance to a certain path $\mathcal{P}_{d'}$ which is not at the current path list (consisting of other $P_{d's'}$ paths). Hence, in the perturbed problem the demand volume $h_{d's'}$ is decreased by ε and the capacities of links e on path $\mathcal{P}_{d'}$ ($e \in \mathcal{P}_{d'}$) are equal to $y_e + \dfrac{\varepsilon}{\alpha_{es'}}$ (where $y_e \geq 0$ are variables) since at least capacity equal to ε must be available on each link on path $\mathcal{P}_{d'}$ in situation s' (we assume here that $\alpha_{es} > 0$ for all $e \in \mathcal{P}_{d'}$ as the considered path must be available in situation s'). Let $\psi_e = 1$ if $e \in \mathcal{P}_{d'}$ and $\psi_e = 0$ otherwise. Then the Lagrangian function L' of the perturbed problem is as follows:

$$\begin{aligned}
L'(\boldsymbol{x}, \boldsymbol{y}; \boldsymbol{\lambda}, \boldsymbol{\pi}) &= \textstyle\sum_e \xi_e (y_e + \psi_e \frac{\varepsilon}{\alpha_{es'}}) + \sum_d \sum_s \lambda_{ds}(h_{ds} - \sum_p x_{dps}) - \varepsilon\lambda_{d's'} \\
&\quad + \textstyle\sum_e \sum_{s \neq s'} \pi_{es} (\sum_d \sum_p \delta_{edps} x_{dps} - \alpha_{es}(y_e + \psi_e \frac{\varepsilon}{\alpha_{es'}})) \\
&\quad + \textstyle\sum_e \pi_{es'} (\sum_d \sum_p \delta_{edps'} x_{dps'} - \alpha_{es'} y_e) \qquad (10.1.6) \\
&= \textstyle\sum_e (\xi_e - \sum_s \alpha_{es}\pi_{es}) y_e + \sum_s \sum_d \sum_p (\sum_e \delta_{edps}\pi_{es} - \lambda_{ds}) x_{dps} \\
&\quad + \textstyle\sum_d \sum_s \lambda_{ds} h_{ds} + \sum_e \xi_e \psi_e \frac{\varepsilon}{\alpha_{es'}} - \varepsilon \lambda_{d's'} \\
&\quad - \textstyle\sum_e \sum_{s \neq s'} \alpha_{es} \pi_{es} \psi_e \frac{\varepsilon}{\alpha_{es'}}.
\end{aligned}$$

It follows that the dual to the perturbed problem reads:

$$\begin{aligned}
\textbf{\textit{maximize}} \quad & W'(\boldsymbol{\lambda}, \boldsymbol{\pi}) = \textstyle\sum_d \sum_s \lambda_{ds} h_{ds} + \sum_e \xi_e \psi_e \frac{\varepsilon}{\alpha_{es'}} - \varepsilon \lambda_{d's'} \\
& \quad - \textstyle\sum_e \sum_{s \neq s'} \alpha_{es} \pi_{es} \psi_e \frac{\varepsilon}{\alpha_{es'}} \qquad (10.1.7) \\
\textbf{\textit{subject to}} \quad & (10.1.4b) \text{ to } (10.1.4e).
\end{aligned}$$

Let $(\boldsymbol{\lambda}^*, \boldsymbol{\pi}^*)$ be an optimal solution of the above problem. Using (10.1.5) we have $\sum_s \alpha_{es}\pi^*_{es} = \xi_e$ for each link e and hence

$$\begin{aligned}
& \textstyle\sum_e \xi_e \frac{\psi_e}{\alpha_{es'}} - \sum_e \sum_{s \neq s'} \alpha_{es} \pi^*_{es} \frac{\psi_e}{\alpha_{es'}} \\
&= \textstyle\sum_e \psi_e \frac{\xi_e}{\alpha_{es'}} - \sum_e \psi_e \frac{(\xi_e - \alpha_{es'}\pi^*_{es'})}{\alpha_{es'}} = \sum_e \psi_e \pi^*_{es'}. \qquad (10.1.8)
\end{aligned}$$

We finally note that at the optimum

$$W'(\boldsymbol{\lambda}^*, \boldsymbol{\pi}^*) = W(\boldsymbol{\lambda}^*, \boldsymbol{\pi}^*) - \varepsilon(\lambda^*_{d's'} - \textstyle\sum_e \psi_e \pi^*_{es'}) \qquad (10.1.9)$$

where $W(\boldsymbol{\lambda}^*, \boldsymbol{\pi}^*)$ is the dual function (10.1.4) of the original (not perturbed) problem. Using relation (10.1.9) a proposition analogous to Proposition 5.1 can be easily proved (Exercise 10.2).

The above considerations lead to a PG algorithm for solving DR-U analogous to the algorithm given in Section 5.4.2. After each iteration new shortest paths for all demands d and all situations s for which such paths exist can be added simultaneously to the path lists (Exercise 10.3).

10.1.2 Restricted Reconfiguration

The problem considered in this section allows for the use of different candidate path lists in different situations and is a modified formulation of (9.3.3), referred to as DR-R for short.

***LP:* DR/CC/BR/CC/LIN/PR+RR/SDPL $\{$DR-R$\}$ Link-Path Formulation**
Problem DR/CF/BR/CC/LIN/PR+RR With Situation-Dependent Path Lists

indices

$e = 1, 2, \ldots, E$ links
$d = 1, 2, \ldots, D$ demands
$s = 0, 1, \ldots, S$ situations
$p = 1, 2, \ldots, P_{ds}$ allowable paths for flows realizing demand d in situation s

constants

δ_{edps} = 1 if link e belongs to path p realizing demand d in situations s; 0 otherwise
h_d volume of demand d
χ_{ds} demand coefficient of demand d in situation s, $h_{ds} = \chi_{ds} h_d$
ξ_e unit cost of link e
α_{es} binary availability coefficient of link e in situation s ($\alpha_{es} \in \{0, 1\}$)
θ_{dps} binary availability coefficient of the normal path (d, p) link in situation s ($\theta_{dps} = \prod_{\{e:\delta_{edp0}=1\}} \alpha_{es}$)

variables (all variables continuous non-negative)

x_{dp0} flow allocated to normal path p of demand d in the normal state
x_{dps} flow allocated to path p of demand d in situation s on top of the flow x_{dp0} for the normal state $s = 0$ $(s = 1, 2, \ldots, S)$
y_e capacity of link e

objective

$$\text{minimize } \boldsymbol{F} = \textstyle\sum_e \xi_e y_e \tag{10.1.10a}$$

constraints

$$\textstyle\sum_p x_{dp0} = h_d, \quad d = 1, 2, \ldots, D \tag{10.1.10b}$$

$$\textstyle\sum_d \sum_p \delta_{edp0} x_{dp0} \le y_e, \quad e = 1, 2, \ldots, E \tag{10.1.10c}$$

$$\textstyle\sum_p x_{dps} + \sum_p \theta_{dps} x_{dp0} \ge h_{ds}, \quad d = 1, 2, \ldots, D \quad s = 1, 2, \ldots, S \tag{10.1.10d}$$

$$\textstyle\sum_d \sum_p \delta_{edps} x_{dps} \le \alpha_{es}(y_e - \sum_d \sum_p \delta_{edp0} \theta_{dps} x_{dp0}), \quad e = 1, 2, \ldots, E \quad s = 1, 2, \ldots, S. \tag{10.1.10e}$$

In the rest of the discussion, we will assume that all the normal paths (d, p) that survive in a situation s ($\theta_{dps} = 1, s > 0$) are on the path lists of this situation. This (natural) assumption allows avoiding certain technical problems which would otherwise appear in the PG method (see the remark in the next to last paragraph at the end of this section) and the Benders' method (see the remark after the BD algorithm in Section 10.3.2).

Let us dualize constraints (10.1.10b) and (10.1.10d) using multipliers $\boldsymbol{\lambda} = (\lambda_{ds} : d = 1, 2, \ldots, D, s = 0, 1, \ldots, S)$ (note that $\lambda_{ds} \geq 0$ for $d = 1, 2, \ldots, D$, $s = 1, 2, \ldots, S$ and λ_{d0} are unconstrained in sign for $d = 1, 2, \ldots, D$), and constraints (10.1.10c) and (10.1.10e) using dual variables $\boldsymbol{\pi} = (\pi_{es} : e = 1, 2, \ldots, E, s = 0, 1, \ldots, S)$ (note that $\boldsymbol{\pi} \geq 0$). The resulting Lagrangian is as follows:

$$\begin{aligned} L(\boldsymbol{x}, \boldsymbol{y}; \boldsymbol{\lambda}, \boldsymbol{\pi}) &= \textstyle\sum_e \xi_e y_e + \sum_d \lambda_{d0}(h_{d0} - \sum_p x_{dp0}) + \sum_d \sum_{s>0} \lambda_{ds}(h_{ds} - \sum_p x_{dps}) \\ &\quad \textstyle - \sum_d \sum_{s>0} \lambda_{ds} \sum_p \theta_{dps} x_{dp0}) \\ &\quad \textstyle + \sum_e \pi_{e0}(\sum_d \sum_p \delta_{edp0} x_{dp0} - y_e) \\ &\quad \textstyle - \sum_e \sum_{s>0} \pi_{es}(\sum_d \sum_p \delta_{edps} x_{dps} - \alpha_{es} y_e \\ &\quad \textstyle + \alpha_{es} \sum_d \sum_p \delta_{edps} \theta_{dps} x_{dp0}) \\ &= \textstyle\sum_d \sum_s \lambda_{ds} h_{ds} + \sum_e (\xi_e - \sum_s \alpha_{es} \pi_{es}) y_e \\ &\quad \textstyle + \sum_d \sum_{s>0} \sum_p (\sum_e \delta_{edps} \pi_{es} - \lambda_{ds}) x_{dps} + \sum_d \sum_p \sum_e \delta_{edp0} \pi_{e0} x_{dp0} \\ &\quad \textstyle + \sum_d \sum_{s>0} \sum_p (\sum_e \alpha_{es} \delta_{edp0} \theta_{dps} \pi_{es} - \theta_{dps} \lambda_{ds} - \lambda_{d0}) x_{dp0}. \end{aligned} \tag{10.1.11}$$

It follows that the maximum of the dual function

$$W(\boldsymbol{\lambda}, \boldsymbol{\pi}) = \min_{\boldsymbol{x}, \boldsymbol{y} \geq 0} L(\boldsymbol{x}, \boldsymbol{y}; \boldsymbol{\lambda}, \boldsymbol{\pi}) \tag{10.1.12}$$

is equal to

$$W(\boldsymbol{\lambda}^*, \boldsymbol{\pi}^*) = \max_{\boldsymbol{\pi} \geq \mathbf{0}, \boldsymbol{\lambda} \in \boldsymbol{\Lambda}} \textstyle\sum_d \sum_s \lambda_{ds} h_{ds} \tag{10.1.13a}$$

and is attained in the subspace of multipliers (dual variables) defined by:

$$\lambda_{ds} \leq \textstyle\sum_e \delta_{edps} \pi_{es}, \qquad d = 1, 2, \ldots, D \quad s = 1, 2, \ldots, S \quad p = 1, 2, \ldots, P_{ds} \tag{10.1.13b}$$

$$\lambda_{d0} \leq \textstyle\sum_e \delta_{edp0} \pi_{e0} + \sum_{s>0} (\sum_e \alpha_{es} \delta_{edp0} \theta_{dps} \pi_{es} - \theta_{dps} \lambda_{ds}), \quad d = 1, 2, \ldots, D \quad p = 1, 2, \ldots, P_{d0} \tag{10.1.13c}$$

$$\textstyle\sum_s \alpha_{es} \pi_{es} \leq \xi_e, \quad e = 1, 2, \ldots, E \tag{10.1.13d}$$

$$\alpha_{es} = 0 \text{ implies } \pi_{es} = +\infty, \quad e = 1, 2, \ldots, E \quad s = 1, 2, \ldots, S \tag{10.1.13e}$$

$$\boldsymbol{\pi} \geq \mathbf{0}, \boldsymbol{\lambda} \in \boldsymbol{\Lambda}, \tag{10.1.13f}$$

where $\boldsymbol{\Lambda} = \{\lambda_{ds} : \lambda_{ds} \geq 0$ for $d = 1, 2, ..., D$, $s = 1, 2, ..., S$, λ_{d0} unconstrained in sign for $d = 1, 2, ..., D\}$.

As for DR-U, optimal multipliers $(\boldsymbol{\lambda}^*, \boldsymbol{\pi}^*)$ of the dual Problem (10.1.13) can be obtained by solving the primal Problem (10.1.10) with an LP solver or by the subgradient maximization method described in Section 10.2.2. We observe that

$$\textstyle\sum_s \alpha_{es}\pi^*_{es} = \xi_e, \quad e = 1,2,\ldots,E \tag{10.1.14a}$$

$$\lambda^*_{ds} \leq \textstyle\sum_e \delta_{edps}\pi^*_{es}, \quad d = 1,2,\ldots,D \quad s = 1,2,\ldots,S \quad p = 1,2,\ldots,P_{ds} \tag{10.1.14b}$$

$$\lambda^*_{d0} = \min\{\textstyle\sum_e \delta_{edp0}\pi^*_{e0} + \sum_{s\in S(d,p)}(\sum_e \delta_{edp0}\pi^*_{es} - \lambda^*_{ds}) : p = 1,2,\ldots,P_{d0}\}, \quad d = 1,2,\ldots,D \tag{10.1.14c}$$

where $S(d,p) = \{s : s > 0, \theta_{dps} = 1\}$. Let $(\boldsymbol{x}^*, \boldsymbol{y}^*)$ be a primal optimal solution forming a saddle point of the Lagrangian (10.1.11) together with $(\boldsymbol{\lambda}^*, \boldsymbol{\pi}^*)$. If for certain demand d' in certain situation s' the primal optimal flows $x^*_{d'p0}$ (in normal state) do not suffice to realize $h_{d's'}$, then it must be the case that

$$\lambda^*_{d's'} = \min\{\textstyle\sum_e \delta_{ed'ps'}\pi^*_{es'} : p = 1,2,\ldots,P_{ds}\} \tag{10.1.15}$$

since otherwise all primal optimal flows $x_{d'ps'}$ would have to be equal to 0 in order to minimize the Lagrangian for $(\boldsymbol{\lambda}^*, \boldsymbol{\pi}^*)$. Hence, (10.1.15) implies that for each such pair d' and s', $\lambda^*_{d's'}$ is the length of the shortest path of demand d' in situation s' for the link metrics $\pi^*_{1s'}, \pi^*_{2s'}, \ldots, \pi^*_{Es'}$.

The interpretation of λ^*_{d0} is different. Let d and p be fixed. Then the quantity

$$\begin{aligned}&\textstyle\sum_e \delta_{edp0}\pi^*_{e0} + \sum_{s\in S(d,p)}(\sum_e \delta_{edp0}\pi^*_{es} - \lambda^*_{ds}) \\ &\quad = \textstyle\sum_e \delta_{edp}(\sum_{s\in S(d,p)\cup\{0\}}\pi^*_{es}) - \sum_{s\in S(d,p)}\lambda^*_{ds}\end{aligned} \tag{10.1.16}$$

is the sum of the length of the normal path (d, p) in the normal state with respect to the link metrics in the normal state $\pi^*_{10}, \pi^*_{20}, \ldots, \pi^*_{E0}$ $(\sum_e \delta_{edp0}\pi^*_{e0})$, and of the differences, for all failure situations s $(s > 0)$ for which the considered path is working, of the length of this normal path in situation s with respect to the link metrics $\pi^*_{1s}, \pi^*_{2s}, \ldots, \pi^*_{Es}$ $(\sum_e \delta_{edps}\pi^*_{es})$ and the current length of the shortest available path in this situation (λ^*_{ds}). We shall refer to quantity (10.1.16) as the *generalized path length.*

There are two reasons for introducing new paths. First, it can be advantageous to introduce a new restoration path for demand d in situation s for which the normal flows are not sufficient to fulfill constraint (10.1.10d). Then, if there is a path $\mathcal{P}_{ds}$ in the network graph between the end nodes of demand d shorter (with respect to $(\pi^*_{1s}, \pi^*_{2s}, \ldots, \pi^*_{Es})$) than λ^*_{ds} then its introduction may improve the objective function (10.1.10a). Such a path can be found with a shortest path algorithm.

Second, it can be advantageous to introduce a new normal path for a demand d. If a path $\mathcal{P}_{d0}$ between the end nodes of demand d with the value of the generalized length (10.1.16) smaller than λ^*_{d0} exists, then introducing it into the list of candidate normal paths for demand d may also improve the currently optimal objective function (10.1.10a).

Finding a shortest path with respect to the generalized length (10.1.16) cannot be done by a direct application of a shortest path algorithm; therefore, some other algorithms have to be used. For instance, we may select a shortest path out of a large number of the predefined candidate paths. Observe that if the normal path (d,p) is given, then the link metrics

$$\pi'_e = \sum_{s\in S(d,p)\cup\{0\}} \pi^*_{es}, \quad e = 1,2,\ldots,E \tag{10.1.17}$$

are used to compute its length. Its generalized length (10.1.16) becomes the length with respect to metrics (10.1.17) minus the sum of the lengths of the shortest paths in all the situations from $S(d,p)$. Note that in the above formula, according to (10.1.13e), $\pi^*_{es} = +\infty$ if $\alpha_{es} = 0$.

Finally note that it is advantageous to keep the normal paths that are available in a particular non-normal state s on the candidate path list for situation s, i.e., to keep on the list of paths for situation s all the normal paths (d,p) with $\theta_{dps} = 1$ (refer to the assumption made earlier). This requirement will assure, according to (10.1.14b) and (10.1.14c) that $\sum_e \delta_{edp0}\pi^*_{es} \geq \lambda_{ds0}$ for all $s \in S(d,p)$, i.e., that the length of the normal path (d,p) is not smaller than the length of the shortest path in each situation $s \in S(d,p)$.

The above observations lead to a path generation algorithm for solving DR-R (10.1.10) analogous to the algorithm given in Section 5.4.2 (Exercise 10.4). After each iteration, new shortest paths (with respect to optimal multipliers $\boldsymbol{\pi}^*$) are added for all demands and all situations for which such paths exist. Note, however, one important difference in regard to the previous application to DR-U (and to problem A/PAP in Section 5.4.2). Now, the new shortest paths must be considered for the normal state since otherwise we may overlook the paths that can improve the solution. In other situations, the shortest path for demand d in situation s must be considered if it is shorter than the current value of λ^*_{ds}. Still, if this is not the case but the new shortest path is shorter than all the paths on the current candidate list for pair (d,s), then we add such a path to the list because it may become important in the next iterations.

10.1.3 Back-up Path Restoration

Application of the column generation technique to the back-up path restoration problems DR-SD (9.3.5) and DR-F (9.3.6) is unavoidable for large networks if the solution is to be based on a sufficiently wide scanning of the huge set of all allowable situation-disjoint pairs of the form: normal path/back-up (situation-dependent) path. Below we show how the column generation technique works for the latter problem, i.e., for problem DR-F. Problem DR-SD is left to the reader as Exercise 10.5.

We dualize constraints (9.3.6b) (dual variables $\boldsymbol{\lambda} = (\lambda_d : d = 1,2,\ldots,D)$) and (9.3.6c) (dual variables $\boldsymbol{\pi} = (\pi_{es} \geq 0 : e = 1,2,\ldots,E,\ s = 0,1,\ldots,S)$) and construct the Lagrangian:

$$\begin{aligned} L(\boldsymbol{x},\boldsymbol{y};\boldsymbol{\lambda},\boldsymbol{\pi}) &= \sum_e \xi_e y_e + \sum_d \lambda_d (h_d - \sum_p x_{dp0}) \\ &\quad + \sum_e\sum_s \pi_{es}(\sum_d\sum_p(\delta_{edp}\theta_{dps} + \beta_{edp}(1-\theta_{dps}))x_{dp0} - \alpha_{es}y_e) \\ &= \sum_d \lambda_d h_d + \sum_e(\xi_e - \sum_s \alpha_{es}\pi_{es})y_e \\ &\quad + \sum_s\sum_d(\sum_p\sum_e \pi_{es}(\delta_{edp}\theta_{dps} + \beta_{edp}(1-\theta_{dps})) - \lambda_d)x_{dp0}. \end{aligned} \tag{10.1.18}$$

It follows that the maximum of the dual function

$$W(\boldsymbol{\lambda}, \boldsymbol{\pi}) = \min_{\boldsymbol{x},\boldsymbol{y}\geq 0} L(\boldsymbol{x}, \boldsymbol{y}; \boldsymbol{\lambda}, \boldsymbol{\pi}) \tag{10.1.19}$$

is equal to

$$W(\boldsymbol{\lambda}^*, \boldsymbol{\pi}^*) = \max_{\boldsymbol{\pi}\geq \mathbf{0},\boldsymbol{\lambda}} \sum_d \lambda_d h_d \tag{10.1.20a}$$

and is attained in the subspace of multipliers (dual variables) defined by:

$$\lambda_d \leq \sum_s \sum_e \pi_{es}(\delta_{edp}\theta_{dps} + \beta_{edp}(1 - \theta_{dps})), \qquad d = 1, 2, \ldots, D \quad p = 1, 2, \ldots, P_d \tag{10.1.20b}$$

$$\sum_s \alpha_{es}\pi_{es} \leq \xi_e, \quad e = 1, 2, \ldots, E \tag{10.1.20c}$$

$$\alpha_{es} = 0 \text{ implies } \pi_{es} = +\infty, \quad e = 1, 2, \ldots, E \quad s = 0, 1, \ldots, S \tag{10.1.20d}$$

$$\boldsymbol{\pi} \geq \mathbf{0}. \tag{10.1.20e}$$

The solution of (10.1.20) yields optimal multipliers $(\boldsymbol{\lambda}^*, \boldsymbol{\pi}^*)$ (refer to Section 10.2.3). At the optimum the equalities

$$\sum_s \alpha_{es}\pi^*_{es} = \xi_e, \quad e = 1, 2, \ldots, E \tag{10.1.21a}$$

$$\lambda^*_d = \min\{\sum_s \sum_e \pi_{es}(\delta_{edp}\theta_{dps} + \beta_{edp}(1 - \theta_{dps})) : p = 1, 2, \ldots, P_d\}, \quad d = 1, 2, \ldots, D \tag{10.1.21b}$$

hold since all optimal π^*_{es} and λ^*_d must be as large as possible. Hence, each λ^*_d can be interpreted as the generalized length of the shortest pair of situation-disjoint normal and back-up paths of demand d for the link metrics equal to $\boldsymbol{\pi}^*$. Again, it can be shown that if a demand d for which a situation-disjoint pair of paths (d, p') shorter with respect to $\boldsymbol{\pi}^*$ than λ^*_d in the sense of the generalized path length measure can be found

$$\sum_s \sum_e \pi^*_{es}(\delta_{edp'}\theta_{dp's} + \beta_{edp'}(1 - \theta_{dp's})) \tag{10.1.22}$$

(i.e., shorter than any pair on the current list of candidate pairs $p = 1, 2, \ldots, P_d$), then including such a shortest pair to the current lists of candidate pairs may improve the current optimal solution. This observation leads to a column generation algorithm for solving DR-F analogous to the algorithm given in Section 5.4.2 (Exercise 10.6).

Numerically efficient computation of a shortest pair of situation disjoint paths is not a trivial problem. A somewhat simplified, yet effective solution would be to find, for each

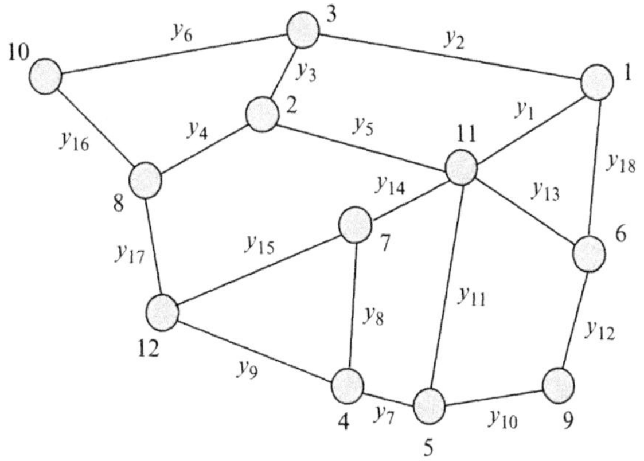

FIGURE 10.1 12-Node, 18-Link Network (Network-P)

fixed normal path $\mathcal{P}_{dp}$ from the current list $p = 1, 2, \ldots, P_d$, a path $\mathcal{Q}_{dp}$ such that the pair $(\mathcal{P}_{dp}, \mathcal{Q}_{dp})$ is the shortest pair among all possible paths $\mathcal{Q}_{dp}$ which are situation-disjoint with path $\mathcal{P}_{dp}$. Such a path $\mathcal{Q}_{dp}$ between the end nodes of demand d is found using a shortest path algorithm for the following set of link metrics dependent on (d, p):

$$\pi'_e = \textstyle\sum_{s:\theta_{dps}=0} \pi^*_{es}. \tag{10.1.23}$$

Note that, according to (10.1.20d), $\pi^*_{es} = +\infty$ if $\alpha_{es} = 0$. Of course, if $\theta_{dps} = 1$ for all $s \geq 1$, then the normal path $\mathcal{P}_{dp}$ does not need a back-up path. Note that in problem DR-SD, the shortest sequences of paths are found instead of the shortest pairs of paths.

10.1.4 Numerical Results

The network chosen here for the numerical results is depicted in Figure 10.1. This network (Network-P) consists of 12 nodes, 18 links, and 66 demand pairs; demand volumes are listed in Table 10.1.

We have considered all single-link non-simultaneous failure situations (i.e., 18 failure situations) in this example. In order to understand the impact of controlling the number of paths (path pairs) on the speed of convergence towards the optimal solution, we have considered three different path list updating policies:

- AF (Add-First): in the lexicographic order of demands, add the first path found (over all demands) for each situation s (or a path pair in the case of DR-F) to the path list of the corresponding demand whose length (generalized length) is shorter than that of λ_{ds} (λ_d in the case of DR-F).

TABLE 10.1 **Demand Volume: Network-P**

	2	3	4	5	6	7	8	9	10	11	12
1	10	11	13	13	16	7	19	10	6	13	14
2	0	3	21	19	21	14	32	14	5	68	32
3	0	0	27	21	25	17	35	14	3	107	24
4	0	0	0	11	21	15	51	21	19	84	40
5	0	0	0	0	13	20	35	5	18	74	28
6	0	0	0	0	0	16	34	4	9	30	18
7	0	0	0	0	0	0	21	14	12	4	15
8	0	0	0	0	0	0	0	28	47	129	14
9	0	0	0	0	0	0	0	0	7	61	13
10	0	0	0	0	0	0	0	0	0	24	19
11	0	0	0	0	0	0	0	0	0	0	97

- AA (Add-All): add all the paths found for all demands for each situation s (or all path pairs in the case of DR-F) to the path list of corresponding demands whose length (generalized length) is shorter than that of λ_{ds} (λ_d in the case of DR-F).
- AB (Add-Best): add all the best paths found (over all demands) for each situation s (or the best path pair in the case of DR-F) to the path list of corresponding demand whose length/generalized length is shortest among all the paths (path pairs) that have its length shorter than λ_{ds} (λ_d in the case of DR-F).

For problems DR-R and DR-F, since we have a more general notion of path length for the normal situation, it is non-trivial to compute paths based on the multipliers π. We overcome this by maintaining a large path pool computed initially from which paths are selected based on the shortest generalized length at each iteration. In this example, we have considered the size of path pool to be 12 and 15 for DR-R and DR-F, respectively. The results are presented in Table 10.2.

Of all the three updating policies, AB performs the best in terms of the number of flow variables that are eventually added to the problem in order to achieve a near-optimal solution. In this context, AF performs the worst due to the inherent bias towards the first choice of the path (path pair). In terms of the number of iterations and thus the convergence towards optimal solution, AA outperforms AB as well as AF. Among AB and AF policy, AF suffers from poor convergence. The convergence results are shown in Figures 10.2 to 10.4.

In DR-F, uniqueness of a path pair is assumed in terms of the pair and not individually. In other words, it is possible to have two path pairs for some demand such that those two pairs share either the same normal path or the same back-up path but not both. In fact, for this example, we have reported such information in Table 10.3.

TABLE 10.2 **Numerical Results for the 12-Node, 18-Link Network (Network-P)**

	DR-U			DR-R			DR-F		
y_e	AA	AB	AF	AA	AB	AF	AA	AB	AF
y_1	276.5	277	260	253.464	290	256	255	271.107	225.158
y_2	445	445	445	445	445	445	445	445	445
y_3	177	177	177	159.393	177	152	177	170.947	161.947
y_4	326	326	326	326	326	326	326	326	311.342
y_5	445	445	445	445	445	445	445	445	445
y_6	248	248	248	248	248	248	248	248	262.658
y_7	326	326	326	326	326	326	326	326	326
y_8	124	147	135	147	147	147	147	147	121.026
y_9	376	353	372	303.929	345.958	358.444	324.5	324.105	351.684
y_{10}	191	208	225	191	195	229	207.667	193.701	235.316
y_{11}	376	353	370	292.679	345.958	358.444	324.5	324.105	351.684
y_{12}	197	197	192	257.321	204.042	191.556	225.5	225.895	224.289
y_{13}	199	182	165	199	195	161	182.333	196.299	154.684
y_{14}	326	326	326	326	326	326	347.667	326	326
y_{15}	205	228	209	277.071	235.042	222.556	256.5	256.895	229.316
y_{16}	273	273	273	290.607	273	298	273	279.053	288.053
y_{17}	445	445	445	445	445	445	445	445	445
y_{18}	208.5	208	225	231.536	195	229	230	213.893	259.842
Cost	**5,164**	**5,164**	**5,164**	**5,164**	**5,164**	**5,164**	**5,164**	**5,164**	**5,164**
	1,254[a] 2,145[b]	1,254[a] 1,525[b]	1,254[a] 1,707[b]	1,254[a] 1,735[b]	1,254[a] 1,539[b]	1,254[a] 1,846[b]	66[c] 213[d]	66[c] 134[d]	66[c] 330[d]
No. Itr	16	72	127	5	51	96	4	69	265
t^* (secs)	0.69	1.37	2.52	0.62	1.9	3.87	0.15	0.78	3.48

[a] Total no. of paths in the candidate path lists in the first iteration.

[b] Total no. of paths in the candidate path lists in the final iteration.

[c] Total no. of situation-disjoint path pairs in the path lists in the first iteration.

[d] Total no. of situation-disjoint path pairs in the path lists in the final iteration.

* Time spent in the CPLEX solver.

10.2 LAGRANGIAN RELAXATION (LR) WITH SUBGRADIENT MAXIMIZATION

In Section 10.1 we have already introduced the Lagrangian functions for problems DR-U, DR-R, and DR-F as well as the corresponding dual problems (see Sections 10.1.1, 10.1.2,

TABLE 10.3 **Numerical Results Continued-DR-F Path-Pair Information**

	1/1	1/2	1/3	1/4	$1/n,\ n \geq 5$
AA	62	19	1	0	0
AB	72	15	0	0	0
AF	55	20	5	1	0

$1/n$ denotes the number of cases when one basic path is shared by n back-up paths.

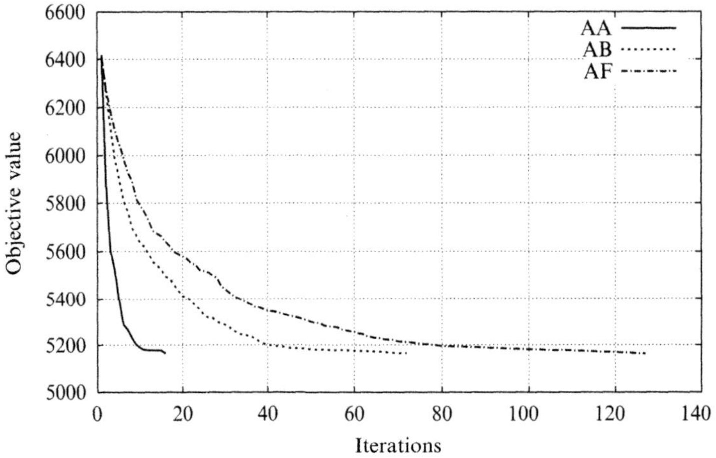

FIGURE 10.2 DR-U: Convergence of the Objective Function

and 10.1.3, respectively). The dual problems are LP problems and can be solved as such. Alternatively, they can be solved by subgradient optimization techniques which will be described in the subsequent sections.

The subgradient approach can be more effective numerically than the direct LP solution, especially for a large network and when very accurate solutions are not required. On the other hand, as will soon become clear, in general the dual optimal solution does not yield all the information about the corresponding primal optimal solution.

Numerical results illustrating the effectiveness of the LR and subgradient maximization technique for two-layer networks will be presented in Section 12.4.1.

10.2.1 Unrestricted Reconfiguration

To solve the dual to DR-U (9.3.1) it suffices to dualize only constraint (9.3.1c), using dual variables $\boldsymbol{\pi} = (\pi_{es} \geq 0 : e = 1, 2, \ldots, E,\ s = 1, 2, \ldots, S)$, and construct the Lagrangian:

$$\begin{aligned} L(\boldsymbol{x}, \boldsymbol{y}; \boldsymbol{\pi}) &= \textstyle\sum_e \xi_e y_e + \sum_e \sum_s \pi_{es} (\sum_d \sum_p \delta_{edps} x_{dps} - \alpha_{es} y_e) \\ &= \textstyle\sum_e (\xi_e - \sum_s \alpha_{es} \pi_{es}) y_e + \sum_s \sum_d \sum_p \sum_e \delta_{edp} \pi_{es} x_{dps}. \end{aligned} \tag{10.2.1}$$

The corresponding dual function is defined as

$$W(\boldsymbol{\pi}) = \min_{\boldsymbol{x} \in \boldsymbol{X}, \boldsymbol{y} \geq \boldsymbol{0}} L(\boldsymbol{x}, \boldsymbol{y}; \boldsymbol{\pi}) \tag{10.2.2}$$

where $\boldsymbol{X}$ is the set of all flow allocations $\boldsymbol{x} = (x_{dps} : d = 1, 2, \ldots, D, p = 1, 2, \ldots, P_d,$ $s = 1, 2, \ldots, S)$ satisfying (9.3.1b). The value of $W(\boldsymbol{\pi})$ is finite only for multipliers satisfying the inequalities

$$\textstyle\sum_s \alpha_{es} \pi_{es} \leq \xi_e, \quad e = 1, 2, \ldots, E \tag{10.2.3}$$

since if $\sum_s \alpha_{es} \pi_{es} > \xi_e$ for some e then $W(\boldsymbol{\pi}) = -\infty$. Assuming (10.2.3) we arrive at

$$W(\boldsymbol{\pi}) = \textstyle\sum_s \min_{\boldsymbol{x} \in \boldsymbol{X}} \sum_d \sum_p \sum_e \delta_{edp} \pi_{es} x_{dps}. \tag{10.2.4}$$

The minima in (10.2.4) are for all $s = 1, 2, \ldots, S$ attained for shortest path allocations $\boldsymbol{x}_s = (x_{dps} :\ d = 1, 2, \ldots, D,\ p = 1, 2, \ldots, P_d)$, with respect to the current multipliers $\boldsymbol{\pi}_s = (\pi_{es} :\ e = 1, 2, \ldots, E)$. For instance, such an allocation is obtained if for each pair (d, s) we choose a shortest path $p(d, s)$ and define

$$x_{dps} = \begin{cases} h_{ds} & \text{if } p = p(d, s) \\ 0 & \text{otherwise.} \end{cases} \tag{10.2.5}$$

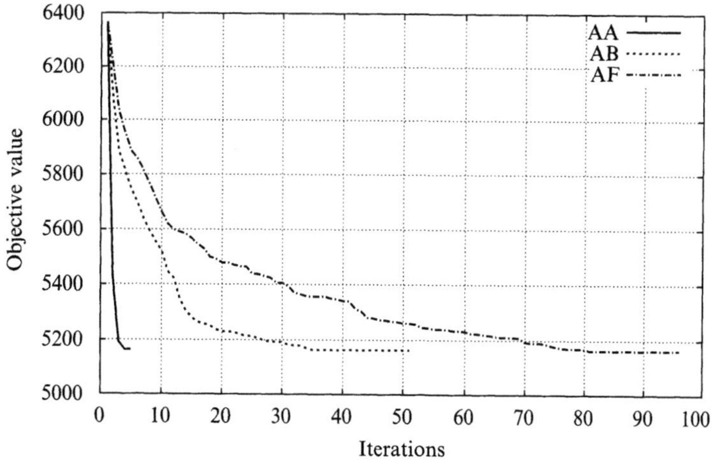

FIGURE 10.3 DR-R: Convergence of the Objective Function

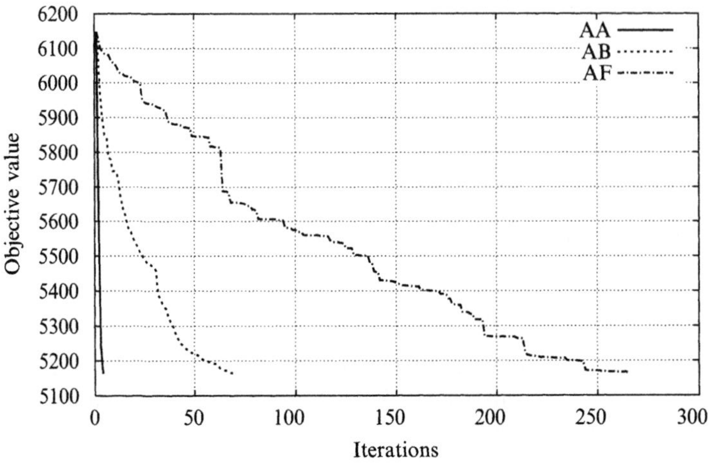

FIGURE 10.4 DR-F: Convergence of the Objective Function

Then

$$W(\boldsymbol{\pi}) = \sum_s \sum_d \sum_e \delta_{edp(d,s)} \pi_{es} h_{ds} = \sum_s \sum_d \lambda_{ds}(\boldsymbol{\pi}_s) h_{ds} \tag{10.2.6a}$$

where $\lambda_{ds}(\boldsymbol{\pi}_s) = \sum_e \delta_{edp(d,s)} \pi_{es}$ is the length of the (shortest) path $p(d, s)$. Also

$$W(\boldsymbol{\pi}) = \sum_s \sum_e \pi_{es} (\sum_d \delta_{edp(d,s)} h_{ds}) = \sum_s \sum_e \pi_{es} \underline{y}_{es}, \tag{10.2.6b}$$

where $\underline{y}_{es} = \sum_d \delta_{edp(d,s)} h_{ds}$ is the load of link e in situation s resulting from the dually optimal allocation $\boldsymbol{x}_s$ defined by (10.2.5). The corresponding subgradient (in general there are continuously many subgradients, each corresponding to one of the dual optimal flow allocation) of the dual function is given by the formula

$$\nabla W(\boldsymbol{\pi}) = (\sum_d \delta_{edp(d,s)} h_{ds} : e = 1, 2, \ldots, E, s = 1, 2, \ldots, S). \tag{10.2.7}$$

Hence, the subgradient (10.2.7) depends on the selected dual optimal flow allocations $\boldsymbol{x}_s$, $s = 1, 2, \ldots, S$ defined in (10.2.5). Note that the flows (10.2.5) are in general not primal optimal (for instance, because optimal flows in DR-U are, in general, bifurcated).

It is clear that from the viewpoint of the dual function maximization the values π_{es} should be as large as possible, so the inequalities in (10.2.3) can be substituted with equalities (note that this follows from the complementary slackness property as well) and the dual problem finally takes the form:

$$\begin{aligned} &\textbf{\textit{maximize}} \quad W(\boldsymbol{\pi}) = \sum_e \sum_s \pi_{es} (\sum_d \delta_{edp(d,s)} h_{ds}) \\ &\textbf{\textit{subject to}} \quad \sum_s \alpha_{es} \pi_{es} = \xi_e \quad e = 1, 2, \ldots, E \\ &\qquad\qquad\quad \boldsymbol{\pi} \geq \mathbf{0}. \end{aligned} \tag{10.2.8}$$

For a given feasible vector of multipliers $\boldsymbol{\pi}$, the value of dual function $W(\boldsymbol{\pi})$ and the link loads $\underline{y}_{es}$ are computed by selecting a shortest path $p(d, s)$ for each demand d and situation s. Alternatively, the shortest paths can be computed with a shortest path algorithm which corresponds to the node-link formulation of DR-U. Both methods are effective even for large networks.

The projection in Step 2 of Algorithm 10.1 is obtained in a way similar to that used in Section 5.5.2 (formulae (5.5.13) and (5.5.14)), see Exercise 10.7).

ALGORITHM 10.1 **Algorithm for Solving the Dual of DR-U**

Step 1: Let $S(e)$ be the set of situations for which link e is not totally failed ($S(e) = \{s : \alpha_{es} > 0\}$) and let $a(e) = \frac{\xi_e}{|S(e)|}$. Define the following initial multiplier vector $\pi^0 = (\pi^0_{es} : e = 1, 2, \ldots, E, \; s = 1, 2, \ldots, S)$:

$$\pi^0_{es} = \begin{cases} +\infty & \text{if } \alpha_{es} = 0 \\ \dfrac{a(e)}{\alpha_{es}} & \text{otherwise.} \end{cases} \tag{10.2.9}$$

Set iteration counter k to 0.

Step 2: Compute the shortest paths for all demands with respect to multipliers π^k. Let $p(d, s)$ be the corresponding shortest paths. Compute the objective function of the dual Problem (10.2.8) and the subgradient(10.2.7). Move along the subgradient direction according to the procedure described in Section 5.4.1. Project the resulting point π^k onto the constraint set of the Problem (10.2.8) and put π^k to be equal to its projection.

Step 3: Set $k := k + 1$. If

$$\left|W(\pi^k) - W(\pi^{k-1})\right| \le \varepsilon W(\pi^k) \tag{10.2.10}$$

then stop (π^k is close to optimal); otherwise go to Step 2.

Observe that after solving the dual Problem (10.2.8), the optimal multipliers π^* reveal the following information:

a) the primal minimal cost (9.3.1a): $F^* = W(\pi^*)$

b) the lists of candidate paths: for each situation s, these are all the shortest paths with respect to π^*_s.

Although the optimal primal flows are not known from the dual solution, the information yielded from π^* can be very useful. We can expect that the lists of candidate (shortest) paths (see b) above) are very short, containing one element in most cases. If there is only one path for demand d in situation s, for example path number $p(d, s)$, then the primal optimal flow is

$$x^*_{dps} = \begin{cases} h_{ds} & \text{if } p = p(d, s) \\ 0 & \text{otherwise.} \end{cases} \tag{10.2.11}$$

If the single candidate paths are the frequent case and for the remaining cases the lists are short, then the solution of the primal problem can be significantly more effective due to the reduction of the number of variables and constraints.

We will illustrate the effectiveness of the above algorithm for its multi-layer generalization in Section 12.4.1.

10.2.2 Restricted Reconfiguration

Consider the formulation DR-R (9.3.3). To solve the corresponding dual problem it is enough to dualize only constraints (9.3.3c) and (9.3.3g) using the dual variables $\boldsymbol{\pi} = (\pi_{es} \geq 0 : e = 1, 2, \ldots, E, s = 0, 1, \ldots, S)$. The resulting Lagrangian is as follows.

$$\begin{aligned} L(\boldsymbol{x}, \boldsymbol{y}; \boldsymbol{\pi}) &= \textstyle\sum_e \xi_e y_e + \sum_e \pi_{e0}(\sum_d \sum_p \delta_{edp0} x_{dp0} - y_e) \\ &\quad + \textstyle\sum_e \sum_{s>0} \pi_{es}(\sum_d \sum_p \delta_{edps} x_{dps} - \alpha_{es} y_e \\ &\quad + \alpha_{es} \textstyle\sum_d \sum_p \delta_{edp0} \theta_{dps} x_{dp0}) \\ &= \textstyle\sum_e (\xi_e - \sum_s \alpha_{es} \pi_{es}) y_e + \sum_{s>0} \sum_d \sum_p (\sum_e \delta_{edps} \pi_{es}) x_{dps} \\ &\quad + \textstyle\sum_{s \in S(d,p) \cup \{0\}} \sum_d \sum_p (\sum_e \pi_{es} \delta_{edp0}) x_{dp0} \end{aligned} \tag{10.2.12}$$

where $S(d,p) = \{s : s > 0, \theta_{dps} = 1\}$ and $\boldsymbol{x} \in \boldsymbol{X}$ where $\boldsymbol{x} = (x_{dps} : d = 1, 2, \ldots, D,\ p = 1, 2, \ldots, P_d,\ s = 0, 1, \ldots, S)$, and $\boldsymbol{X}$ is the set of all flow allocation vectors satisfying (9.3.3b), (9.3.3d), and (9.3.3e). The corresponding dual function is defined as

$$W(\boldsymbol{\pi}) = \min_{\boldsymbol{x} \in \boldsymbol{X}, \boldsymbol{y} \geq \boldsymbol{0}} L(\boldsymbol{x}, \boldsymbol{y}; \boldsymbol{\pi}). \tag{10.2.13}$$

The value of $W(\boldsymbol{\pi})$ is finite only for multipliers $\boldsymbol{\pi}$ satisfying the inequalities

$$\textstyle\sum_s \alpha_{es} \pi_{es} \leq \xi_e, \quad e = 1, 2, \ldots, E \tag{10.2.14}$$

and hence

$$\begin{aligned} W(\boldsymbol{\pi}) &= \textstyle\sum_{s>0} \min_{\boldsymbol{x} \in \boldsymbol{X}} \{\sum_d \sum_p (\sum_e \delta_{edps} \pi_{es}) x_{dps}\} \\ &\quad + \min_{\boldsymbol{x} \in \boldsymbol{X}} \{\textstyle\sum_d \sum_p (\sum_e \sum_{s \in S(d,p) \cup \{0\}} \pi_{es} \delta_{edp0}) x_{dp0}\}. \end{aligned} \tag{10.2.15}$$

For all s ($s = 0, 1, \ldots, S$) the minima in (10.2.15) are attained for allocations $\boldsymbol{x}_s = (x_{dps} : d = 1, 2, \ldots, D\ p = 1, 2, \ldots, P_d)$ shortest with respect to the current multipliers $\boldsymbol{\pi}_s = (\pi_{es} : e = 1, 2, \ldots, E)$ (in the normal state the generalized path length is considered). Such a shortest path allocation can be obtained in the following way:

a) For each pair (d, s) with $s > 0$ find a shortest path $p(d, s)$ with respect to $\pi_s = (\pi_{1s}, \pi_{2s}, \dots, \pi_{Es})$ (from a given list of candidate paths or by means of a shortest path algorithm). Let λ^*_{ds} be the length of $p(d, s)$.

b) For each demand d find a normal path $p(d, 0)$ with the minimal value of the generalized path length

$$\sum_e (\sum_{s \in S(d,p) \cup \{0\}} \pi^*_{es}) \delta_{edp0} - \sum_{s \in S(d,p)} \lambda^*_{ds} \tag{10.2.16}$$

(refer to (10.1.16)) out of the list of candidate normal paths for demand d and define

$$x_{dp(d,0)0} = \begin{cases} h_{d0} & \text{if } p = p(d,0) \\ 0 & \text{otherwise.} \end{cases} \tag{10.2.17}$$

c) For each pair (d, s) with $s > 0$ compute $h'_{ds} = \max\{h_{ds} - \theta_{dp(d,0)s} h_{d0}, 0\}$. If $h'_{ds} = 0$ then put $x_{dps} = 0$ for all $p = 1, 2, \dots, P_{ds}$, otherwise define

$$x_{dps} = \begin{cases} h'_{ds} & \text{if } p = p(d,s) \\ 0 & \text{otherwise.} \end{cases} \tag{10.2.18}$$

The allocation (10.2.17) and (10.2.18) minimizes the Lagrangian, hence

$$\begin{aligned} W(\pi) &= \sum_d \sum_{s>0} \sum_e \delta_{edp(d,s)s} \pi_{es} h'_{ds} + \sum_d \sum_e (\sum_{s \in S(d,p) \cup \{0\}} \pi_{es} \delta_{edp(d,0)0}) h_{d0} \\ &= \sum_e \pi_{e0} (\sum_d \delta_{edp(d,0)0} h_{d0}) + \sum_e \sum_{s>0} \pi_{es} \sum_d \delta_{edp(d,s)s} h'_{ds} \\ &\quad + \sum_e \sum_{s>0} \pi_{es} \sum_d (\delta_{edp(d,0)0} \theta_{dp(d,0)s} h_{d0}). \end{aligned} \tag{10.2.19}$$

The quantities in the brackets in (10.2.19) are the link loads $\underline{y}_{es}$ in the consecutive situations $s = 0, 1, \dots, S$, hence

$$W(\pi) = \sum_s \sum_e \pi_{es} \underline{y}_{es}, \tag{10.2.20a}$$

where

$$\begin{aligned} \underline{y}_{e0}(\pi) &= \sum_d \delta_{edp(d,0)0} h_{d0} \\ \underline{y}_{es}(\pi) &= \sum_d \delta_{edp(d,s)s} h'_{ds} + \delta_{edp(d,0)0} \theta_{dp(d,0)s} h_{d0}, \quad s = 1, 2, \dots, S. \end{aligned} \tag{10.2.20b}$$

The corresponding subgradient of the dual function is given by the formula

$$\nabla W(\pi) = (\underline{y}_{es}(\pi) : e = 1, 2, \dots E, s = 0, 1, \dots, S). \tag{10.2.21}$$

As stated in Section 10.2.1, the subgradient depends on the selected dual optimal allocation $\boldsymbol{x}_s, s = 0, 1, \dots, S$ (10.2.17) to (10.2.18). Note that the flows $\boldsymbol{x}_s$ are in general not primal optimal.

As before, from the viewpoint of the dual function maximization, the values of π should be as large as possible so the equalities can be assumed in (10.2.14) and the dual problem becomes:

$$\begin{aligned}&\textit{maximize} && W(\pi) = \sum_s \sum_e \pi_{es} \underline{y}_{es}(\pi)\\ &\textit{subject to} && \sum_s \alpha_{es}\pi_{es} = \xi_e, \quad e = 1, 2, \ldots, E, \quad \pi \geq 0.\end{aligned} \tag{10.2.22}$$

The subgradient optimization algorithm for solving the dual of DR-R is essentially the same as the algorithm for solving the dual of DR-U given in the previous section. As for DR-U, after solving the dual Problem (10.2.22), the optimal multipliers π^* yield the following information:

a) the primal minimal cost (9.3.3a): $F^* = W(\pi^*)$

b) the lists of candidate paths: for each situation $s > 0$ these are all the shortest paths with respect to π^*_s, and for $s = 0$ these are the paths with the shortest generalized length (10.2.16).

10.2.3 Back-up Path Restoration

Let us dualize constraint (9.3.6c) in DR-F (dual variables $\pi = (\pi_{es} \geq 0 : e = 1, 2, \ldots, E$ and $s = 0, 1, \ldots, S)$) and construct the Lagrangian:

$$\begin{aligned}L(x, y; \pi) &= \sum_e \xi_e y_e + \sum_e \sum_s \pi_{es}(\sum_d \sum_p (\delta_{edp}\theta_{dps}\\ &\quad +\beta_{edp}(1 - \theta_{dps}))x_{dp0} - \alpha_{es}y_e)\\ &= \sum_e (\xi_e - \sum_s \alpha_{es})y_e + \sum_s \sum_e \pi_{es} \sum_d \sum_p (\delta_{edp}\theta_{dps}\\ &\quad +\beta_{edp}(1 - \theta_{dps}))x_{dp0}.\end{aligned} \tag{10.2.23}$$

Proceeding in an analogous way as in the two previous sections the dual problem based on Lagrangian (10.2.23) reads:

$$\begin{aligned}&\textit{maximize} && W(\pi) = \sum_s \sum_e \pi_{es} \underline{y}_{es}(\pi)\\ &\textit{subject to} && \sum_s \alpha_{es}\pi_{es} = \xi_e \quad e = 1, 2, \ldots, E\\ &&& \pi \geq 0,\end{aligned} \tag{10.2.24}$$

where link loads $\underline{y}_{es}(\pi)$ are computed in the following way:

a) for each demand d find a shortest path $p(d)$ minimizing the generalized length

$$\sum_s \sum_e \pi^*_{es}(\delta_{edp}\theta_{dps} + \beta_{edp}(1 - \theta_{dps})) \tag{10.2.25}$$

among all paths $p = 1, 2, \ldots, P_d$

b) for each demand d define

$$x_{dp(d)0} = \begin{cases} h_d & \text{if } p = p(d)\\ 0 & \text{otherwise}\end{cases} \tag{10.2.26}$$

c) for each link e and situation s define

$$\underline{y}_{es}(\pi) = \sum_d \sum_p (\delta_{edp}\theta_{dps} + \beta_{edp}(1 - \theta_{dps}))x_{dp0}. \quad (10.2.27)$$

As before, the corresponding subgradient of the dual function is given by the formula

$$\nabla W(\pi) = (\underline{y}_{es}(\pi) : e = 1, 2, \ldots, E, s = 0, 1, \ldots, S). \quad (10.2.28)$$

The subgradient optimization algorithm for solving the dual (10.2.24) of DR-F is essentially the same as the algorithms for solving the dual of DR-U and of DR-R given in the previous sections. After solving the dual Problem (10.2.24), the optimal multipliers π^* yield the following information:

a) the primal minimal cost (9.3.6a): $\boldsymbol{F}^* = W(\pi^*)$

b) the lists of candidate pairs: these are all the shortest pairs with respect to π^*.

10.3 BENDERS' DECOMPOSITION

Robust design problems tend to have a very large number of variables and constraints for large networks. For instance, if we consider the flow restoration problem with unrestricted reconfiguration DR-U for a network with $M = 100$ nodes, $E = 500$ links, $D = 5000$ demands, $S = 500$ failure states, and $P_d = 10$ paths for each demand d, then the number of variables in the resulting link-path formulation (9.3.1) is around 2.5×10^7, and the number of constraints is around 2.5×10^6. These are really large numbers that can make the use of LP solvers impossible. In the previous two sections we have described two methods to reduce the actual number of variables and constraints in the robust design LP problems: PG and LR. The third of these kind of methods is BD (Section 5.4.3). Below we shall discuss applications of BD to DR-U and DR-R, as these two problems require large number of flow variables.

10.3.1 *Unrestricted Reconfiguration*

Consider problem DR-U from Section 10.1.1 (with a slight modification: situations are numbered from 0 to S). The idea of the presented application of BD is to first find only optimal link capacities $\boldsymbol{y}^*$ using an iterative procedure solving certain LP subproblems (the master problem involving only link capacities as optimization variables, and the tests involving only flow variables separately for each situation). After that the corresponding feasible flows can be found separately for every situation. The iterative procedure is based on the following proposition.

Let $\boldsymbol{y} = (y_1, y_2, \ldots, y_E)$ be a vector of link capacities. We shall call this vector *globally feasible* if it is sufficient to carry the assumed demand volumes in all situations $s = 0, 1, \ldots, S$.

PROPOSITION 10.1 *Link capacity vector y is globally feasible if and only if for each vector $\pi = (\pi_e \geq 0 : e = 1,2,\dots,E)$ and for each situation $s = 0,1,\dots,S$, the inequality*

$$\textstyle\sum_e \pi_e \alpha_{es} y_e \geq \sum_d \lambda_d(\pi) h_{ds} \qquad (10.3.1)$$

holds, where $\lambda_d(\pi)$ is the length of the shortest path for demand d with respect to link metrics π.

Proof:

By definition, a given vector y of link capacities is feasible if and only if for each situation s the allocation problem A/PAP(4.1.7), consisting in finding an allocation vector $x = (x_{dp} : d = 1,2,\dots,D, p = 1,2,\dots,P_{ds})$ satisfying the following constraints for fixed y:

$$\textstyle\sum_p x_{dp} = h_{ds}, \quad d = 1,2,\dots,D \qquad (10.3.2a)$$

$$\textstyle\sum_d \sum_p \delta_{edps} x_{dp} \leq \alpha_{es} y_e, \quad e = 1,2,\dots,E \qquad (10.3.2b)$$

$$\text{all } x_{dp} \text{ non-negative} \qquad (10.3.2c)$$

is feasible. The proof is implied by the properties of the problem dual to (10.3.2). Dualizing constraints (10.3.2a) (using dual variables $\lambda = (\lambda_{ds} : d = 1,2,\dots,D)$) and (10.3.2b) (using dual variables $\pi = (\pi_e \geq 0 : e = 1,2,\dots,E)$) and constructing the Lagrangian:

$$\begin{aligned} L(x;\pi,\lambda) &= \textstyle\sum_d \lambda_d (h_{ds} - \sum_p x_{dp}) + \sum_e \pi_e (\sum_d \sum_p \delta_{edps} x_{dp} - \alpha_{es} y_e) \\ &= \textstyle\sum_d \lambda_d h_{ds} - \sum_e \pi_e \alpha_{es} y_e + \sum_d \sum_p (\sum_e \delta_{edps} \pi_e - \lambda_d) x_{dp}. \end{aligned} \qquad (10.3.3)$$

The dual function is given by:

$$\begin{aligned} &W(\lambda,\pi) = \textstyle\sum_d \lambda_d h_{ds} - \sum_e \pi_e \alpha_{es} y_e \\ &\lambda_d \leq \textstyle\sum_e \delta_{edps} \pi_e, \quad d = 1,2,\dots,D \quad p = 1,2,\dots,P_{ds}. \end{aligned} \qquad (10.3.4)$$

Hence, when looking for optimal multipliers (λ^*, π^*) by maximizing the dual function 10.3.4, we can assume that

$$\lambda_d = \min\{\textstyle\sum_e \delta_{edps} \pi_e : p = 1,2,\dots,P_{ds}\}, \quad d = 1,2,\dots,D \qquad (10.3.5)$$

so for each d, $\lambda_d = \lambda_d(\pi)$ is the length of the shortest path with respect to π. If the primal Problem (10.3.2) is feasible then $W(\lambda^*, \pi^*) = 0$ as the primal problem has no objective function. In such a case

$$\begin{aligned} 0 &= W(\lambda^*, \pi^*) \\ &= \max\{W(\lambda,\pi) : \pi \geq 0, \lambda_d = \min\{\textstyle\sum_e \delta_{edps} \pi_e : p = 1,2,\dots,P_{ds}\}, \\ &\quad d = 1,2,\dots,D\} \geq \textstyle\sum_d \lambda_d(\pi) h_{ds} - \sum_e \pi_e \alpha_{es} y_e. \end{aligned} \qquad (10.3.6)$$

Hence, $\sum_e \pi_e \alpha_{es} y_e \geq \sum_d \lambda_d(\boldsymbol{\pi}) h_{ds}$ for all $\boldsymbol{\pi} \geq \mathbf{0}$.

To prove the inverse implication assume that for some $\boldsymbol{\pi} \geq \mathbf{0}$,

$\sum_e \pi_e \alpha_{es} y_e < \sum_d \lambda_d(\boldsymbol{\pi}) h_{ds}$.

Then

$$W(\boldsymbol{\lambda}(\boldsymbol{\pi}), \boldsymbol{\pi}) = \sum_d \lambda_d(\boldsymbol{\pi}) h_{ds} - \sum_e \pi_e \alpha_{es} y_e > 0. \tag{10.3.7}$$

But for any scalar $t > 0$ we have that $\boldsymbol{\lambda}(t\boldsymbol{\pi}) = t\boldsymbol{\lambda}(\boldsymbol{\pi})$ so

$$W(\boldsymbol{\lambda}(t\boldsymbol{\pi}), t\boldsymbol{\pi}) = tW(\boldsymbol{\lambda}(\boldsymbol{\pi}), \boldsymbol{\pi}) \tag{10.3.8}$$

and since $tW(\boldsymbol{\lambda}(\boldsymbol{\pi}), \boldsymbol{\pi})$ can be made arbitrary large, the primal problem is infeasible. ■

The BD algorithm for finding optimal link capacities for DR-U starts with some initial set Ω of inequalities for the variables $\boldsymbol{y}$. The main loop solves the *master problem* to obtain a new vector $\boldsymbol{y}$, performs the *feasibility tests* for the current vector $\boldsymbol{y}$ and updates set Ω with new inequalities generated by the tests. The cycle is repeated until the optimal solution is found.

ALGORITHM 10.2 BD Algorithm for DR-U

Step 1: Initialize Ω.

Step 2: Solve the master problem (in variables $\boldsymbol{y}$):

$$\begin{aligned} &\textbf{\textit{minimize}} \quad F = \textstyle\sum_e \xi_e y_e \\ &\textbf{\textit{subject to}} \quad \text{all inequalities from } \Omega \text{ and } \boldsymbol{y} \geq \mathbf{0}. \end{aligned} \tag{10.3.9}$$

Step 3: For each situation $s = 0, 1, \ldots, S$ perform the feasibility test by solving the problem (in variables $\boldsymbol{\pi}$ and $\boldsymbol{\lambda}$):

$$\begin{aligned} &\textbf{\textit{maximize}} \quad W(\boldsymbol{\lambda}, \boldsymbol{\pi}) = \textstyle\sum_d \lambda_d h_{ds} - \sum_e \pi_e \alpha_{es} y_e \\ &\textbf{\textit{subject to}} \quad \boldsymbol{\pi} \geq \mathbf{0} \\ &\qquad \textstyle\sum_e \pi_e = 1 \\ &\qquad \lambda_d \leq \textstyle\sum_e \delta_{edps} \pi_e, \quad d = 1, 2, \ldots, D \quad p = 1, 2, \ldots, P_{ds}. \end{aligned} \tag{10.3.10}$$

If for the optimal solution $W(\boldsymbol{\lambda}^*, \boldsymbol{\pi}^*)$ of (10.3.10) is greater than zero, then add the inequality

$$(\pi_1{}^* \alpha_{1s}) y_1 + (\pi_2{}^* \alpha_{2s}) y_2 + \ldots + (\pi_E{}^* \alpha_{Es}) y_E \geq \textstyle\sum_d \lambda_d{}^* h_{ds} \tag{10.3.11}$$

to the set of inequalities Ω of the master problem.

Step 4: If all the feasibility tests have been positive then stop: current $\boldsymbol{y}$ is globally feasible and optimal. Otherwise go to Step 2.

Observe that the feasibility test (10.3.10) in Step 3 involves additional constraint on the dual variables $\boldsymbol{\pi}$ (with respect to (10.3.4)). This constraint bounds the otherwise unbounded dual solution in the case when the primal problem is infeasible. Another interpretation of the test (10.3.10) is given in Exercise 10.8.

Note that in a special (but important) case when the demand volumes for each demand are equal in all situations (100% restoration: $h_{ds} \equiv h_d$), then, we can skip the inequalities for $s = 0$ in the set Ω as they are implied by the inequalities obtained for other situations and are never active.

Once the optimal link capacities $\boldsymbol{y}^*$ are found, the allocation Problem (10.3.2) is solved for each situation $s = 0, 1, \ldots, S$ in order to find the situation-dependent feasible (optimal) flow allocations.

Although the BD algorithm can be initialized with the empty set of inequalities ($\Omega = \emptyset$), a good starting set of inequalities can substantially speed up the algorithm by reducing the number of iterations. Such initial inequalities, for instance, can be derived from the "cut inequalities." Recall that a cut in a graph is the set of links between two sets $\boldsymbol{V}'$ and $\boldsymbol{V}''$ of nodes forming a partition of the set of nodes $\boldsymbol{V} = \{1, 2, \ldots, V\}$, i.e., $\boldsymbol{V}', \boldsymbol{V}'' \subset \boldsymbol{V}$ and $\boldsymbol{V}' \cup \boldsymbol{V}'' = \boldsymbol{V}$ and $\boldsymbol{V}' \cap \boldsymbol{V}'' = \emptyset$. If we take $\boldsymbol{V}' = \{v\}$ and $\pi_e^* = 1$ for each link e incident with node v, and $\pi_e^* = 0$ otherwise, then the corresponding inequality (10.3.11) will require that the total available capacity of links incident with the node is greater than or equal to the total demand generated at the node (that is, the total demand volume of the demands with v as one of the end nodes). Hence, initially, the set Ω can contain the cut inequalities corresponding to all nodes (generating demand) in all situations (Exercise 10.9).

Example 10.1 *Illustration of BD Algorithm for DR-U*

Consider the simple network shown in Figure 10.5. Assume $S = 2$ and let $s = 0$ denote the normal state, $s = 1$ denote the failure situation with link $e = 1$ totally failed and link $e = 2$ fully operational, and $s = 2$ denote the failure situation with link $e = 2$ totally failed and link $e = 1$ fully operational. Let $h_0 = 3$ be the normal demand volume for the demand between the two nodes, $h_1 = 1$ be the demand volume in situation $s = 1$, and $h_2 = 1$ be the demand volume in situation $s = 2$. In Step 2 we put $\Omega = \emptyset$. With this, the optimal solution of Step 2 results in $y_1 = y_2 = 0$. Next we perform the feasibility tests (Step 3).

For $s = 0$ we have to maximize $W(\lambda, \boldsymbol{\pi}) = 3\lambda - \pi_1 y_1 - \pi_2 y_2 = 3\lambda$ subject to $\pi_1 + \pi_2 = 1$, and $\lambda \leq \pi_1$ and $\lambda \leq \pi_2$. The maximization gives $\pi_1 = \pi_2 = \frac{1}{2}, \lambda = \frac{1}{2}$ and $W(\lambda, \boldsymbol{\pi}) = 1\frac{1}{2}$, and results in a new inequality added to Ω: $\frac{1}{2}y_1 + \frac{1}{2}y_2 \geq 1\frac{1}{2}$, i.e., $y_1 + y_2 \geq 3$. For $s = 1$ we maximize $W(\lambda, \boldsymbol{\pi}) = \lambda - \pi_1 y_1 - \pi_2 y_2 = \lambda$ subject to $\pi_1 + \pi_2 = 1$, and $\lambda \leq \pi_2$. The maximization yields $\pi_1 = 0, \pi_2 = 1, \lambda = 1$ and $W(\lambda, \boldsymbol{\pi}) = 1$, and results in a new inequality added to Ω: $y_2 \geq 1$. Similarly, for $s = 2$ we maximize $W(\lambda, \boldsymbol{\pi}) = \lambda - \pi_1 y_1 - \pi_2 y_2 = \lambda$ subject to $\pi_1 + \pi_2 = 1$, and $\lambda \leq \pi_2$. The maximization gives $\pi_1 = 1, \pi_2 = 0, \lambda = 1$ and $W(\lambda, \boldsymbol{\pi}) = 1$, and results in a new inequality added to Ω: $y_1 \geq 1$.

Now we come back to Step 2 and solve the master problem: minimize $\boldsymbol{F} = y_1 + 2y_2$ subject to $y_1 + y_2 \geq 3, y_1 \geq 1, y_2 \geq 1$. The result is $y_1 = 2$ and $y_2 = 1$, and this is the final solution.

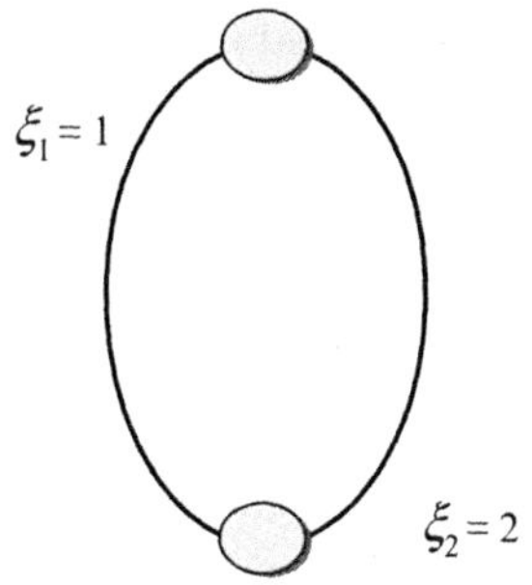

FIGURE 10.5 A Simple Network

The final optimization space for the master problem defined by the inequalities from set Ω and the non-negativity constraints $y \geq 0$ (not active) is illustrated in Figure 10.6.

Note that all the three inequalities in set Ω are of the cut type. They state that in each situation the total available capacity of the links (expressed in DVUs) in the minimal cut separating the nodes of the demand (there is only one such cut in the considered case) must not be less than the demand volume. In the general case most of the generated constraints (10.3.11) are of such a cut type; still, there can be other types of inequalities, as follows from Exercise 10.10. ●

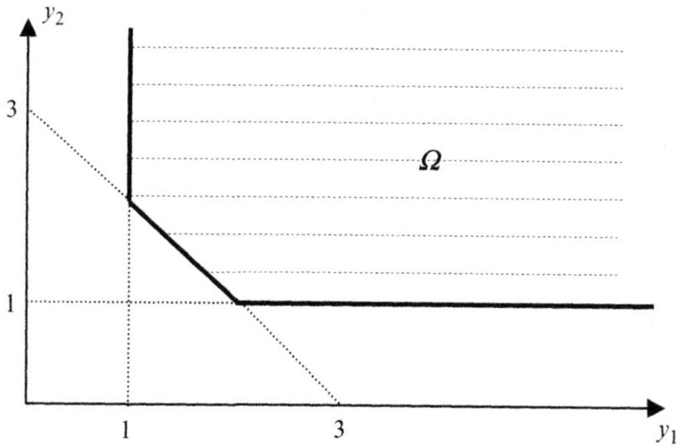

FIGURE 10.6 Final Optimization Space

A particularly powerful initial set of the inequalities can be generated using the dual solution of DR-U obtained by the method described below.

PROPOSITION 10.2 *Let $(\boldsymbol{x}^*, \boldsymbol{y}^*; \boldsymbol{\lambda}^*, \boldsymbol{\pi}^*)$ be a saddle point of the problem DR-U (i.e., a saddle point of Lagrangian (10.1.2)). Then*

$$\textstyle\sum_e \alpha_{es}\pi^*_{es}y^*_e = \sum_d \lambda^*_{ds}h_{ds}, \quad s = 0, 1, \ldots, S. \tag{10.3.12}$$

Proof:

Equality (10.3.12) follows from the fact that DR-U is a convex (linear) minimization problem, so the minimum of the primal problem is equal to the maximum of the dual problem (10.1.4). Hence,

$$\boldsymbol{F}^* = \textstyle\sum_e \xi_e y^*_e = \sum_s \sum_d \lambda^*_{ds}h_{ds} = W(\boldsymbol{\lambda}^*, \boldsymbol{\pi}^*). \tag{10.3.13}$$

Using equality (10.1.5a) we can further write that

$$\textstyle\sum_e \xi_e y^*_e = \sum_e (\sum_s \alpha_{es}\pi^*_{es})y^*_e = \sum_s (\sum_e \pi^*_{es}\alpha_{es}y^*_e) \geq \sum_s \sum_d \lambda^*_{ds}h_{ds}. \tag{10.3.14}$$

The last inequality in (10.3.14) follows from inequality (10.3.1) of Proposition 10.1, applied for each situation s. The inequality in (10.3.14) together with equality (10.3.13) implies property (10.3.12), since if for some situation s, $\sum_e \pi^*_{es}\alpha_{es}y^*_e$ were strictly greater than $\sum_d \boldsymbol{\lambda}^*_{ds}h_{ds}$, then 10.3.13 could not hold. ■

Thus, inequalities

$$(\pi^*_1\alpha_{1s})y^*_1 + (\pi^*_2\alpha_{2s})y^*_2 + \ldots + (\pi^*_E\alpha_{Es})y^*_E \geq \textstyle\sum_d \lambda^*_d h_{ds}, \; s = 0, 1, \ldots, S \tag{10.3.15}$$

can be used to initialize the set Ω. The power of (10.3.15) lies in the fact that these inequalities are really the equalities (10.3.12); using inequalities is just safer when the optimal multipliers can be found only approximately (which is the case for the LR subgradient maximization described in Section 10.2.1). Observe that the inequalities (10.3.15) are exactly the ones obtained with the BD algorithm in Example 10.1 starting from $\Omega = \emptyset$ (Exercise 10.11).

Another advantage from using the LR technique is that when the optimal multipliers $\boldsymbol{\pi}^*_s = (\pi^*_{1s}, \pi^*_{2s}, \ldots, \pi^*_{Es})$, $s = 0, 1, \ldots, S$, are known, then for each situation s the path lists for demands consisting of all the shortest paths with respect to $\boldsymbol{\pi}^*_s$ are sufficient for the feasibility tests of the BD algorithm, as the non-zero flows in the optimal solution of the original problem can be put only on such shortest paths. If the multipliers are known only approximately then the ε-shortest paths (i.e., the paths with lengths not greater than the length of the shortest path plus some $\varepsilon > 0$) can be used for the path lists.

To this end, observe that if the LR initialization is not used, then in order to get the proper path lists, the PG technique can be first used to solve, for each fixed s ($s = 0, 1, \ldots, S$), capacitated Problem (10.3.2) adjusted in the following way (refer to problem A/ALC (5.4.11) in Section 5.4.2):

$$\begin{aligned} \textbf{minimize} \quad & F(z) = \textstyle\sum_e z_e \\ \textbf{subject to} \quad & \textstyle\sum_p x_{dp} = h_{ds}, \quad d = 1,2,\ldots,D \\ & \textstyle\sum_d \sum_p \delta_{edps} x_{dp} \le \alpha_{es} y_e + z_e, \quad e = 1,2,\ldots,E \\ & \text{all } x_{dp} \text{ and } z_e \text{non-negative.} \end{aligned} \tag{10.3.16}$$

The feasibility test is positive if, and only if, the optimal solution is $\boldsymbol{z}^* = \mathbf{0}$. In any case (whether the feasibility test is positive or not), the path lists resulting from the first optimal solution encountered by PG should be formed (note that in the light of Exercise 5.15 the paths that are generated after reaching the optimal solution should not be included to the path lists) and used to solve the dual Problem (10.3.10) in order to produce a new valid inequality for the set Ω. The adjusted path lists should be used in the subsequent steps of the BD algorithm.

It should be pointed out that the feasibility tests (10.3.10) can be solved with the subgradient maximization techniques, as proposed (for a somewhat different problem) in [Min89]. Such a transformed feasibility test for situation s consists in solving the following problem:

$$\begin{aligned} \textbf{maximize} \quad & W_s(\boldsymbol{\pi}) = \textstyle\sum_e \pi_e(\underline{y}_e(\boldsymbol{\pi}) - \alpha_{es} y_e) \\ \textbf{subject to} \quad & \boldsymbol{\pi} \ge \mathbf{0} \\ & \textstyle\sum_e \pi_e = 1. \end{aligned} \tag{10.3.17}$$

In (10.3.17) link loads $\underline{y}_e(\boldsymbol{\pi})$ result from the allocation, for each demand d in each situation s, of the whole demanded volume h_{ds} to path $p(d)$, where $p(d)$ is a shortest path (with respect to link metrics $\boldsymbol{\pi} = (\pi_1, \pi_2, \ldots, \pi_E)$) on the candidate path list for demand d in situation s. Hence, the link load $\underline{y}_e(\boldsymbol{\pi})$ is given by

$$\underline{y}_e(\boldsymbol{\pi}) = \textstyle\sum_d \delta_{edp(d)s} h_{ds}. \tag{10.3.18}$$

Observe that for computing link loads (10.3.18) the path lists does not have to be given in advance—what is important is to have an effective method for computing a shortest path from a certain set of allowable paths, for instance, the set of all paths for demand d in situation s (then Dijkstra algorithm applies), or the set of all paths with at most n hops Then a modification of the Dijkstra algorithm (refer to Appendix C, Section C.2.2) can be effectively applied.

For each s ($s = 0, 1, \ldots, S$) the resulting subgradient of the dual function (10.3.17) is given by the formula:

$$\nabla W_s(\boldsymbol{\pi}) = (\underline{y}_e(\boldsymbol{\pi}) - \alpha_{es} y_e : e = 1,2,\ldots,E). \tag{10.3.19}$$

As already mentioned in Section 10.2.1, in the maximization process the projection of the current point onto the constraint set (10.3.17) is done with a formula analogous to formulae (5.5.13) and (5.5.14) given in Section 5.5.2 (Exercise 10.12). Examples of the performance of BD for DR-U are given in Section 10.3.3, and its generalized two-layer version is given in Section 12.4.2.

10.3.2 Restricted Reconfiguration

Application of BD to the restricted flow reconfiguration problem DR-R (10.1.10) is somewhat different because now the normal flow pattern influences the flow patterns in failure situations. Then the flow patterns in failure situations s (with $s > 0$) are independent of each other, provided the link capacities and the normal flow pattern are given. It follows that the iterative BD algorithm has to find not only the optimal link capacities $\boldsymbol{y}^*$ but also the optimal normal flow allocation $\boldsymbol{x}_0^*$.

Let $\boldsymbol{y} = (y_1, y_2, \ldots, y_E)$ be a vector of link capacities and $\boldsymbol{x}_0 = (x_{dp0} : d = 1,2,\ldots,D,\ p = 1,2,\ldots,P_{d0})$ a normal flow allocation vector. We shall call the pair $(\boldsymbol{y}, \boldsymbol{x}_0)$ *globally feasible* if it satisfies constraints (10.1.10b) to (10.1.10-c) and the capacity vector $\boldsymbol{y}$ is sufficient to carry the assumed demand volumes in all the remaining situations $s = 1,2,\ldots,S$ subject to constraints (10.1.10d) to (10.1.10e). For DR-R, the result analogous to Proposition 10.1 is as follows.

PROPOSITION 10.3 *Link capacity vector $\boldsymbol{y}$ and normal flow allocation vector $\boldsymbol{x}_0^*$ are globally feasible if and only if for each vector $\boldsymbol{\pi} = (\pi_e \geq 0 : \ e = 1,2,\ldots,E)$ and each situation $s = 1,2,\ldots,S$ the inequality*

$$\textstyle\sum_e \pi_e \alpha_{es}(y_e - \sum_d \sum_p \delta_{edp0}\theta_{dps}x_{dp0}) \geq \sum_d \lambda_d(\boldsymbol{\pi})h'_{ds} \qquad (10.3.20)$$

holds, where $\lambda_d(\boldsymbol{\pi})$ is the length of the shortest path for demand d with respect to link metrics $\boldsymbol{\pi}$ and $h'_{ds} = \max\{h_{ds} - \sum_p \theta_{dps}x_{dp0}, 0\}$.

The proof is left to the reader as an exercise (Exercise 10.13). For the BD algorithm we will assume that $\chi_{ds} \equiv 1$ (i.e., $h_{ds} \equiv h_d$ for $d = 1,2,\ldots,D$) in order to get rid of the technical problems introduced by the cases with $h_{ds} < \sum_p \theta_{dps}x_{dp0}$.

ALGORITHM 10.3 **BD Algorithm for DR-R**

Step 1: Initialize Ω.

Step 2: Solve the master problem (in variables $\boldsymbol{x}_0$ and $\boldsymbol{y}$):

minimize $\quad F = \sum_e \xi_e y_e$

subject to $\quad$ all inequalities from Ω and

$$\begin{aligned} &\textstyle\sum_p x_{dp0} = h_d, \quad d = 1,2,\ldots,D \\ &\textstyle\sum_d \sum_p \delta_{edp} x_{dp0} \leq y_e, \quad e = 1,2,\ldots,E \qquad (10.3.21) \\ &\boldsymbol{x}_0, \boldsymbol{y} \geq \boldsymbol{0}. \end{aligned}$$

Step 3: For each situation $s = 1,2,\ldots,S$ perform the feasibility test by solving the following problem (in variables $\boldsymbol{\pi}$ and $\boldsymbol{\lambda}$):

maximize $\quad W(\boldsymbol{\lambda}, \boldsymbol{\pi}) = \sum_d \lambda_d(h_d - \sum_p \theta_{dps}x_{dp0}) - \sum_e \pi_e \alpha_{es}(y_e - {}$
$\quad - \sum_d \sum_p \delta_{edp0}\theta_{dps}x_{dp0})$

subject to $\quad \boldsymbol{\pi} \geq \boldsymbol{0}, \boldsymbol{\lambda} \geq \boldsymbol{0}$

$$\begin{aligned} &\textstyle\sum_e \pi_e = 1 \\ &\textstyle\lambda_d \leq \sum_e \delta_{edps}\pi_e, \quad d = 1,2,\ldots,D \quad p = 1,2,\ldots,P_{ds}. \end{aligned} \qquad (10.3.22)$$

If for the optimal solution $(\boldsymbol{\lambda}^*, \boldsymbol{\pi}^*)$ of (10.3.22) it turns out that $W(\boldsymbol{\lambda}^*, \boldsymbol{\pi}^*) > 0$, then add the inequality

$$\begin{aligned}
\textstyle\sum_d \lambda_d^* h_d \;\le\; & (\pi_1^*\alpha_{1s})y_1 + (\pi_2^*\alpha_{2s})y_2 + \ldots + (\pi_E^*\alpha_{Es})y_E \\
& +(\lambda_1^* - \textstyle\sum_e \pi_e^*\alpha_{es}\delta_{e110})\theta_{11s}x_{110} + (\lambda_1^* - \sum_e \pi_e^*\alpha_{es}\delta_{e120})\theta_{12s}x_{120} \\
& + \ldots + (\lambda_1^* - \textstyle\sum_e \pi_e^*\alpha_{es}\delta_{e1P_{10}s})\theta_{1P_{10}s}x_{1P_{10}0} \\
& +(\lambda_2^* - \textstyle\sum_e \pi_e^*\alpha_{es}\delta_{e210})\theta_{21s}x_{210} + (\lambda_2^* - \sum_e \pi_e^*\alpha_{es}\delta_{e220})\theta_{22s}x_{220} \\
& + \ldots + (\lambda_2^* - \textstyle\sum_e \pi_e^*\alpha_{es}\delta_{e2P_{20}s})\theta_{2P_{20}s}x_{2P_{20}0} \\
& + \ldots \\
& +(\lambda_D^* - \textstyle\sum_e \pi_e^*\alpha_{es}\delta_{eD10})\theta_{D1s}x_{D10} + (\lambda_D^* \\
& - \textstyle\sum_e \pi_e^*\alpha_{es}\delta_{eD20})\theta_{D2s}x_{D20} \\
& + \ldots + (\lambda_D^* - \textstyle\sum_e \pi_e^*\alpha_{es}\delta_{eDP_{D0}s})\theta_{DP_{D0}s}x_{DP_{D0}0}
\end{aligned} \tag{10.3.23}$$

to the set of inequalities Ω of the master problem (in the inequalities (10.3.23) the summations over p are carried out for the normal path lists, i.e., $p = 1, 2, \ldots, P_{d0}$ for each d).

Step 4: If all the feasibility tests have been positive then stop: current $\boldsymbol{y}^*$ and $\boldsymbol{x}_0^*$ are globally feasible and optimal. Otherwise go to Step 2.

Observe that due to the assumption made for formulation (10.1.10) of DR-R (all normal paths surviving in a given situation are on the path lists for this situation), all the coefficients in front of the flows x_{dp0} in the inequalities (10.3.23) in Step 3 of Algorithm 10.3 are, due to (10.3.22), non-positive. Because of that, the inequalities on the values of $\boldsymbol{y}$ for the failure situations are, as could be expected, more demanding than their counterparts (10.3.11) for DR-U.

Once the optimal link capacities $\boldsymbol{y}^*$ and normal flows $\boldsymbol{x}_0^*$ are found, the appropriate allocation problems for separate situations $s = 1, 2, \ldots, S$ are solved in order to find the situation-dependent feasible (optimal) flow allocations.

As before, a powerful initial set of the inequalities for the set Ω can be generated using the dual solution of DR-R.

PROPOSITION 10.4 *Let $(\boldsymbol{x}^*, \boldsymbol{y}^*; \boldsymbol{\lambda}^*, \boldsymbol{\pi}^*)$ be a saddle point of the problem DR-R (i.e., a saddle point of Lagrangian (10.1.11)). Then*

$$\textstyle\sum_e (\pi_{es}^*\alpha_{es})y_e + \sum_d \sum_p (\lambda_{ds}^* - \sum_e \pi_{es}^*\alpha_{es}\delta_{edp0})\theta_{dps}x_{dp0} = \sum_d \lambda_{ds}^* h_d, \quad s = 1, 2, \ldots, S. \tag{10.3.24}$$

The proof is left as an exercise for the reader (Exercise 10.14). Note that as in the inequalities (10.3.23) of Step 3, in the equalities (10.3.24) the summations over p are carried out for the normal path lists. Hence, the inequalities

$$\textstyle\sum_e (\pi_{es}^*\alpha_{es})y_e + \sum_d \sum_p (\lambda_{ds}^* - \sum_e \pi_{es}^*\alpha_{es}\delta_{edp0})\theta_{dps}x_{dp0} \ge \sum_d \lambda_{ds}^* h_d \quad s = 1, 2, \ldots, S. \tag{10.3.25}$$

can be used to initialize the set Ω. The optimal multipliers can be found in an approximate way using the LR subgradient maximization technique described in Section 10.2.2.

As before, the feasibility tests can be solved with the subgradient maximization techniques. The dual versions of the tests are analogous to the tests (10.3.17) for DR-U. Exercises 10.15 and 10.16 illustrate applications of BD to protection problems involving restricted reconfiguration.

10.3.3 Numerical Results

Table 10.4 shows a rather fast increase of the number of variables and constraints in the LP formulations of problem DR-U as a function of the number of nodes V. The choices of V considered here are 10, 20, 30, 50, and 100 nodes. Our additional assumptions are average node degree (deg(v)) being 4, path list size (P_{ds}) being 5 paths for each demand in each situation, and only single-link failures.

The following tables contain results of numerical calculations for three network examples using CPLEX libraries version 7.1. All the computations have been run on a Sun Enterprise 450 (4 ×UltraSPARC 248 MHz). The first network is the standard 12-node example used throughout this book, considered in Section 10.1.4 for illustrating the PG technique (Figure 10.1). The network consists of 12 nodes, 18 links, 66 demands (refer to Table 10.1), and 507 allowable paths (all simple paths are considered). All the link unit costs are equal to 1 ($\xi_e \equiv 1$).

The first 18 rows of Table 10.5 show the optimal link capacities obtained for the five considered cases. As we see, all the cases exhibit different optimal capacity vectors $\boldsymbol{y}^*$ but the same optimal cost (F = 5164). The cost obtained by the direct solution of the primal problems (columns "Primal") and by BD (columns "BD") are always the same for the same problem (DR-U or DR-R). In this case, incidentally, the cost is the same for DR-U and DR-R, which is not always true (but, as shown in [OW03], the costs of resilient networks with different capacity-sharing mechanisms are, as a rule, very close to each other in practice). Already for this network, for DR-U the simplest version of BD (with set Ω initially empty) gives slightly shorter computation time than the direct approach (11 vs. 12 seconds). For DR-R (modified formulation (9.3.3)), the direct approach is much faster as compared to BD, especially when the set Ω is not initialized (column "BD" under DR-R). Note that the computation time of BD can be substantially decreased (three times in the considered case) when set Ω is initialized using the optimal dual variables (Step 1 in the BD algorithms). In column "BD/I", the results for such a case are shown, where the optimal dual multipliers were taken from the optimal dual solution corresponding to the optimal primal solution obtained by the simplex algorithm.

In Table 10.6 we show results for four network configurations. Column E = 18 corresponds to the case described in Table 10.5; column E = 18* corresponds to the same networks with different unit link costs given as

$$\boldsymbol{\xi} = (1.85, 3.4, 1, 1.45, 2.3, 2.9, 1, 1.6, 2.2, 1.5, 2.3, 1.4, 1.65, 1.25, 2.3, 1.55, 1.35, 1.7),$$

TABLE 10.4 **Number of Variables and Constraints in DR-U**

# nodes (V)	10	20	30	50	100
# demands (D)	45	190	435	1225	4950
# links (E)	20	40	60	100	200
# situations (S)	21	41	61	101	201
# constraints	1,365	9,430	30,195	133,825	1,035,150
# variables	4,745	38,990	132,735	618,725	4,974,850
size of memory	0.5 MB	26 MB	273 MB	5.5 GB	331 GB

TABLE 10.5 **Results for the 12-Node, 18-Link Network**

	DR-U		DR-R		
Link y_e (end nodes)	**Primal**	**BD**	**Primal**	**BD**	**BD/I**
y_1 (1,11)	288.72	209	245.66	220.56	213
y_2 (1,3)	445	445	445	445	445
y_3 (2,3)	177	177	167.54	173.35	173
y_4 (2,8)	326	326	326	322.35	322
y_5 (2,11)	445	445	445	445	445
y_6 (3,10)	248	248	248	251.65	252
y_7 (4,5)	326	326	326	326	326
y_8 (4,7)	146.84	103	147	145.13	147
y_9 (4,12)	331.16	387	359.66	346.78	367
y_{10} (5,9)	193.72	273	191.57	191	191
y_{11} (5,11)	330.24	387	359	360.87	359
y_{12} (6,9)	219.92	207	191	191	191
y_{13} (6,11)	196.28	117	198.43	199	199
y_{14} (7,11)	326	326	326	326	326
y_{15} (7,12)	249.84	194	221.34	216.28	214
y_{16} (8,10)	273	273	282.46	276.65	277
y_{17} (8,12)	445	445	445	445	445
y_{18} (1,6)	196.28	276	239.34	264.43	272
objective F	5164	5164	5164	5164	5164
# variables	9651	18/84*	9651	525/84*	525/84*
# constraints	1596	82/8**	10722	1439/226**	1095/117**
time [sec.]	12	11	17	2948	908

*number of variables in master problem/number of variables in test problems.
**total number of generated constraints for Ω/number of iterations for BD

TABLE 10.6 **Results for Three Networks**

		E = 18	E = 18*	E = 36	E = 46
DR-U/P/SM	objective ***F***	5,164	9,505.95	8,139.36	6,742.94
	# variables	9,651	9,651	18,055	36,424
	# constraints	1,596	1,596	6,364	12,032
	time [s]	12	14	301	1,680
DR-U/P/IPM	objective ***F***	5,164	9,505.95	8,139.36	–
	# variables	9,651	9,651	18,055	–
	# constraints	1,596	1,596	6,364	–
	time [s]	3	4	45	–
DR-U/BD	objective ***F***	5,164	9,505.95	8,139.36	6,742.94
	# variables	18/84*	18/84*	36/172	46/256*
	# constraints	82/8**	78/7**	320/15	1,461/84**
	time [s]	11	11	151	3,159
DR-R/P/SM	objective ***F***	5,164	9,513.81	8,801.09	7,353.37
	# variables	9,651	9,651	18,055	36,424
	# constraints	10,722	10,722	23,896	47,636
	time [s]	19	22	382	1,925
DR-R/P/IPM	objective ***F***	5,164	9,513.81	8,801.09	–
	# variables	9,651	9,651	18,055	–
	# constraints	10,722	10,722	23,896	–
	time [s]	42	46	453	–
DR-RM/P/SM	objective ***F***	5,164	9,513.81	8,801.09	7,353.37
	# variables	9,651	9,651	18,055	36,424
	# constraints	1,596	1,596	6,364	12,032
	time [s]	17	24	69	275
DR-RM/P/IPM	objective ***F***	5,164	9,513.81	8,801.09	–
	# variables	9,651	9,651	18,055	–
	# constraints	1,596	1,596	6,364	–
	time [s]	15	19	226	–

continues

and columns $E = 36$ and $E = 46$ correspond to a 36-link network and a 46-link network, respectively. In the table, DR-x/P/SM (where x = U or x = R; in the latter case, DR-R, formulation (9.3.2) is used) denotes the case of the primal problem solved directly by the simplex method, and DR-x/P/IPM denotes the case of the primal problem solved

TABLE 10.6 **Results for Three Networks** ***continued***

DR-RM/BD	objective ***F***	5,164	9,513.81	8,801.09	7,353.37
	# variables	525/84*	525/84*	523/172*	820/256*
	# constraints	1,439/226**	937/138**	771/48**	1022/48**
	time [s]	2,948	1,391	564	1,910
DR-RM/BD/I	objective ***F***	5,164	9,513.81	8,801.09	7,353.37
	# variables	525/84*	525/84*	523/172*	820/256*
	# constraints	1,095/117**	440/59**	584/32**	1257/61**
	time [s]	908	150	242	3,155

*number of variables in master problem/number of variables in test problems
**total number of generated constraints for Ω/number of iterations for BD

directly by the internal point method (IPM) of CPLEX, and DR-RM denotes DR-R in formulation (9.3.3). For BD the simplex algorithm was used (as in the case of Table 10.5). The table contains several interesting results. First of all, note that for DR-U, the IPM method is faster than the simplex method. For DR-R (formulation (9.3.2)), however, the opposite holds. For DR-RM, simplex is faster for the third case while slower for the first two cases. Also, there is no rule which formulation for DR-R ((9.3.2) or (9.3.3)) is better for the primal approach. This is because although formulation DR-R (9.3.2) has much more constraints than formulation DR-RM (9.3.3), the former has a much more sparse matrix of coefficients.

Finally, if we compare the results of BD for DR-RM, then we see that initialization of set Ω usually decreases substantially with the number of iterations (and the computation time); this is illustrated for DR-RM. Surprisingly, this is not the case for the last case (E = 46) where the initialization does not help (this issue requires further investigation).

10.4 MODULAR LINKS

In most communication applications it is required that links are of a modular capacity (see Problem (9.3.1) with constraint (9.3.1c) substituted with constraint (9.3.1d)). In the simplest modularity case, the capacity of each link is equal to a multiple of module M, i.e., the capacity of link e is equal to My_e for a non-negative integer y_e. This assumption changes the character of the considered restoration problems quite dramatically, as they become $\mathcal{NP}$-complete MIP problems. Hence, we have virtually no chance for exact solutions in the case of large networks, and we have to approach such cases in some other ways.

The first most obvious and simple approach is to solve the relaxed LP problem (dropping the integrality constraints for link capacities) directly (or with the help of the LP decomposition methods described in Sections 10.1-10.3) and round up the resulting optimal continuous link capacities to the next modular values. While not exact, this method is attractive from the network engineering point of view. The main reason for the appropriateness of rounding-up is that networks are designed with some degree of over-dimensioning, and here we are on the safe side. In fact, we can expect that the resulting over-dimensioning will in practice be quite proper. This is because the LP relaxation is already capable of finding the economical placement of the link capacities in the sense that the capacity is not placed where it is not effectively used. Certainly, the rounding-up approach is better the lower link modularity (LCU) is with respect to the demand volume unit (DVU).

The next step could be to apply one of the heuristic methods described in Section 10.5 to the initial rounded-up LP solution. Then in most cases we can end up with an improved modular solution, although perhaps not significantly improved. Observe that the meta-heuristics can be initialized with the relaxed/rounded LP solutions also when other binary/integer variables are involved, as in the case of the single back-up path protection problem (Section 10.5.1). Also note that for heuristic methods it is usually the case that the more binary/integer variables involved, the better for their effectiveness.

For small network examples the modular (and other) MIP formulations can be solved directly by means of BB using self-developed procedures or available MIP solvers (Section 5.2). The BB technique can be made more effective using BD (note that BD was initially devised for MIP problems; see [Ben62]). Compared to the BD algorithms presented in Sections 10.3.1 and 10.3.2, the only difference is that in the modular case the master problem becomes an integer programming problem (DR-U) or an MIP problem (DR-R), respectively. Note that the feasibility tests remain the same and are still LP problems. Of course, even with BD, the BB method used for solving the master problem can become excessively time- and memory-consuming, still, for moderate size networks, with up to 20 nodes, for example, it can be effectively applied ([TH00]).

Still, certainly, the biggest challenge is trying to exactly solve the modular restoration problems for large networks. Much work has been devoted to this issue, virtually all of them using the branch-and-cut (BC) approach. Below we summarize the work done for DR-U and DR-R, based on the results of Dahl and Stoer [DS98], [Sto92] and [Wes00], closely related to the work done by other researchers (see [AGW98], [BM01], [GMS95], [Gün99].

Using the BC framework, the BD approach can be maintained; still the "plain" BB approach must be substituted with more powerful methods for improved lower bound computations. Such computations can be based on LR (Section 5.4.1), still the most effective approach, as it appears from the literature, is based on generation *valid inequalities* (VI). VI are generated on top (or partly instead) of the BD inequalities, and try to take advantage of the special structure of the convex hull spanned over the vertices of the points of the solution space with integral link capacities ([BM01]). We will call such a convex hull *modular polyhedron* in the sequel. The form of VIs depends on the particular shape of the modular link dimensioning functions. For the step functions of the form (9.4.2) specified in Section 9.4.2, VIs are called "band inequalities" ([DS98],[Wes00]). In any case, the issue here is that we want the VIs to force the solutions of the relaxed LP problems involving VIs to stay at the facets of the modular polyhedron, not at the facets of the polyhedron of the relaxed original problem with the BD constraints only.

The numerical results presented in the [DS98] and [Wes00] suggest that the resulting BC approach can be in many cases effective, even for large networks. It is worth mentioning that the methods developed for DR-U can be applied for the normal design problem involving modular capacities, as presented in Section 4.3.1. Interestingly, for such a single-state case the BC methods perform worse than for the restoration problems with many failure situations. This fact is discussed and explained in Section 4 of [DS98], and is related to the connectivity of the resulting network graphs (and to the Steiner problem, which is not a surprise as the single-state modular problems and topological problems have much in common).

We deliberately do not go further into the description of the BC methods summarized above, as they are highly specialized and too difficult to follow in a book of this nature (theoretical background for the development of VIs involves deep results on the modular polyhedra defined above, refer to [BM01], [GMS91], and [SD94]).

We end this section with showing the results of applying CPLEX to the 12-node, 18-link network considered in Section 10.3.3. In the LP, MIP, and IP (integer programming) formulations of DR-U and DR-R we assume modularity $M = 63$ and the capacity constraints of the form

$$\textstyle\sum_d \sum_p \delta_{edps} x_{dps} \leq M \alpha_{es} y_e, \quad e = 1, 2, \ldots, E \quad s = 1, 2, \ldots, S \tag{10.4.1}$$

and

$$\textstyle\sum_d \sum_p \delta_{edp0} x_{dp0} \leq M y_e, \quad e = 1, 2, \ldots, E \tag{10.4.2a}$$

$$\textstyle\sum_d \sum_p \delta_{edps} x_{dps} \leq \alpha_{es} M(y_e - \sum_d \sum_p \delta_{edp0} \theta_{dps} x_{dp0}), \quad e = 1, 2, \ldots, E \quad s = 1, 2, \ldots, S \tag{10.4.2b}$$

for DR-U and (modified) DR-R, respectively. All of the results have been obtained on a Gateway Pentium III 800 MHz machine with CPLEX version 8.0.

In the formulations we have assumed uniform unit costs of one module on each link ($\xi_e \equiv 1$). In Table 10.7, we show results for D/SDP(4.1.1), DR-U (9.3.1), DR-R (9.3.2), and DR-RM (9.3.3) obtained by simplex (for the LP formulations) and by the MIP optimizer (MIP formulations and IP formulations). MIP formulations correspond to modular links and continuous flows, and integer programming formulations correspond to modular links and integral flows. We can see from the table that CPLEX is able to solve all of the problems in a reasonable time frame (except for the IP case for DR-RM). What is interesting is that in some cases solving the IP version is much faster than solving the MIP version. This is somewhat surprising, and shows that the path in the BB (and BC) tree leading to optimal solution can be quite tricky.

TABLE 10.7 **Results for Modular Dimensioning of the 12-Node Network**

		time	F	iterations	nodes
	LP	0.01 sec	55.89	0	0
D0	MIP	758.71 sec	59	2,550,522	305,736
	IP	276.59 sec	59	1,044,334	141,213
	LP	1.43 sec	81.97	504	0
DR-U	MIP	370.82 sec	88	234,435	7,734
	IP	409.12 sec	88	311,635	6,479
	LP	19.87 sec	81.97	5,777	0
DR-R	MIP	2 hr 40 min	88	2,264,327	11,336
	IP	2 hr 37 min	88	2,064,384	10,996
	LP	7.62 sec	81.97	6,766	0
DR-RM	MIP	4 hr 40 min	88	5,051,550	15,470
	IP	–	–	–	–

10.5 STOCHASTIC HEURISTIC METHODS

This section discusses applications of heuristic stochastic methods of SAL (Section 5.3.4), SAN (Section 5.3.2), and EA (Section 5.3.3) to restoration design with flow reallocation described in Section 9.3. The methods can be as well applied to the link capacity restoration mechanism (Section 9.2.1) and path diversity (PD) (Section 9.1.3), and to the other problems discussed in Chapter 9.

10.5.1 *Simulated Allocation (SAL)*

The SAL method has been introduced in Section 5.3.4 in application to a (normal) design problem with modular links. Then, applications of SAL to topological design (Section 6.3.5) and to shortest-path routing allocation (Section 7.4.2) have been presented, showing that this simple heuristic can be quite effective in the normal design applications. Below we will show how the method of SAL can be applied to robust design problems, in particular to problems DR/CF/BR/CC/LIN/PR+FSBP (Section 9.3.4) and P/CF/BR/CC/LIN/PR+FSBP (Section 9.5.2).

Single Back-up Path Flow Protection

First, consider problem DR/CF/BR/CC/LIN/PR+FSBP (9.3.6) with single back-up paths used for restoring the broken normal flows. In the following we consider an integral version of this problem, assuming that all flows and link capacities are integers, the link capacity module (one LCU) is equal to $M \geq 1$, and that the demand volume module (one DVU) is equal to 1 ($L = 1$). In the following we will use an equivalent formulation of DR/CF/BR/CC/LIN/PR+FSBP, which is somewhat different than the formulation from Section 9.3.4.

***IP:* DR/MF/BR/MC/LIN/PR+FSBP** **Link-Path Formulation**

Problem DR/CF/BR/CC/LIN/PR+FSBP with Integral Flows and Links

indices

$e = 1, 2, \ldots, E$ links
$d = 1, 2, \ldots, D$ demands
$s = 0, 1, \ldots, S$ situations
$p = 1, 2, \ldots, P_d$ normal paths allowable for flows realizing demand d
$q = 1, 2, \ldots, Q_{dp}$ back-up paths for normal path p of demand d (all paths q are situation disjoint with path p)

constants

δ_{edp} = 1 if link e belongs to normal path p realizing demand d; 0, otherwise
β_{edpq} = 1 if link e belongs to back-up path q protecting normal path p of demand d; 0, otherwise
h_d volume of demand d
ξ_e unit cost of link e
α_{es} binary availability coefficient of link e in situation s ($\alpha_{es} \in \{0, 1\}$)
θ_{dps} binary availability coefficient indicating whether normal path p realizing demand d available in situation s ($\theta_{dps} = \prod_{\{e:\delta_{edp}=1\}} \alpha_{es}$)

variables

x_{dp0} integer normal flow allocated to normal path p of demand d
u_{dpq} binary variable corresponding to flow x_{dp0} (u_{dpq} = 1 if back-up path q protects normal path p of demand d)
y_e integer capacity of link e

objective

$$\text{minimize } \boldsymbol{F} = \sum_e \xi_e y_e \tag{10.5.1a}$$

constraints

$$\sum_p x_{dp0} = h_d, \quad d = 1, 2, \ldots, D \tag{10.5.1b}$$

$$\sum_q u_{dpq} \leq 1, \quad d = 1, 2, \ldots, D \quad p = 1, 2, \ldots, P_d \tag{10.5.1c}$$

$$x_{dp0} \leq (\textstyle\sum_q u_{dpq}) h_d, \quad d = 1, 2, \ldots, D \quad p = 1, 2, \ldots, P_d \tag{10.5.1d}$$

$$\sum_d \sum_p \sum_q (\delta_{edp}\theta_{dps} + \beta_{edpq}(1 - \theta_{dps})) x_{dp0} u_{dpq} \leq \alpha_{es} M y_e, \quad e = 1, 2, \ldots, E \quad s = 0, 1, \ldots, S. \tag{10.5.1e}$$

For the purpose of SAL we will call a pair of vectors $(\boldsymbol{x}, \boldsymbol{u})$ where $\boldsymbol{x} = (x_{dp0} : d = 1,2,\ldots,D, p = 1,2,\ldots,P_d)$ and $\boldsymbol{u} = (u_{dpq} : d = 1,2,\ldots,D, p = 1,2,\ldots,P_d, q = 1,2,\ldots,Q_{dp})$ the allocation state if the vectors $\boldsymbol{x}$ and $\boldsymbol{u}$ satisfy the relaxed set of constraints:

$$\textstyle\sum_p x_{dp0} \le h_d, \quad d = 1,2,\ldots,D \tag{10.5.2a}$$

$$\textstyle\sum_q u_{dpq} \le 1, \quad d = 1,2,\ldots,D \quad p = 1,2,\ldots,P_d \tag{10.5.2b}$$

all x_{dp0} are non-negative integers, and all u_{dpq} are binary. (10.5.2c)

The inequality in (10.5.2b) reflects the fact that SAL works with incomplete allocation states, and the lack of constraint (10.5.1d) reflects that not all normal flows have to be protected (in certain hypothetical states). For any allocation state $(\boldsymbol{x}, \boldsymbol{u})$ the cost function for SAL is defined as

$$cost(\boldsymbol{x}, \boldsymbol{u}) = \textstyle\sum_e \xi_e y_e(\boldsymbol{x}, \boldsymbol{u}) \tag{10.5.3a}$$

where

$$\begin{aligned} y_e(\boldsymbol{x}, \boldsymbol{u}) \;=\; & \min\{z : \textstyle\sum_d \sum_p \sum_q (\delta_{edp}\theta_{dps} + \beta_{edpq}(1 - \theta_{dps}))u_{dpq}x_{dp0} \le \alpha_{es} M z, \\ & s = 0,1,\ldots,S; z - \text{integer}\}. \end{aligned} \tag{10.5.3b}$$

Let $H = \sum_d h_d$ be the total number of DVUs to be allocated, and $\underline{h}_d(\boldsymbol{x}) = \sum_p x_{dp0}$ be the number of DVUs allocated in state $\boldsymbol{x}$. Finally, let $|\boldsymbol{x}| = \sum_d \underline{h}_d(\boldsymbol{x})$ be the state height. In order to apply the SAL algorithm specified by the pseudo-code of Section 5.3.4 we change the state description from $(\boldsymbol{x})$ to $(\boldsymbol{x}, \boldsymbol{u})$ and define the two basic procedures *allocate* $(\boldsymbol{x}, \boldsymbol{u})$ and *disconnect* $(\boldsymbol{x}, \boldsymbol{u})$.

Procedure *allocate* $(\boldsymbol{x}, \boldsymbol{u})$: Roughly speaking, the procedure randomly draws one of the not currently allocated DVUs, and allocates it to one of the normal paths from the path list, i.e., increases the existing normal flow allocated to the chosen path by one DVU. At the same time the back-up path is selected, possibly different from the current back-up path used for the chosen normal one. Since the flow increase can increase the capacity of involved links, the selection is guided by the minimal increment of the cost function (10.5.3a). More precisely, assuming that $|\boldsymbol{x}| < H$ we draw a demand d' with probability Prob$\{\boldsymbol{x}; d'\}$ given by formula (5.3.7), and find a pair (p', q') $(1 \le p' \le P_{d'}, 1 \le q' \le Q_{d'p'})$ defining a pair of situation-disjoint paths (normal and back-up, respectively) from the path lists, minimizing the incremental cost of the network

$$cost(\boldsymbol{x}', \boldsymbol{u}') - cost(\boldsymbol{x}, \boldsymbol{u}''), \tag{10.5.4}$$

where

$$
\begin{aligned}
x'_{dp0} &= x_{dp0} + 1 && \text{for } d = d' \text{ and } p = p' \\
&= x_{dp0} && \text{for } d = d' \text{ and } p \neq p' \\
&= x_{dp0} && \text{for } d \neq d' \text{ and } p = 1, 2, \ldots, P_d \\
u'_{dpq} &= 1 && \text{for } d = d', p = p' \text{ and } q = q' \\
&= 0 && \text{for } d = d', p = p' \text{ and } q \neq q' \\
&= u_{dpq} && \text{for } d = d', p \neq p' \text{ and } q = 1, 2, \ldots, Q_{d'p} \\
&= u_{dpq} && \text{for } d \neq d', p = 1, 2, \ldots, P_d \text{ and} \\
& && q = 1, 2, \ldots, Q_{dp} \\
u''_{dpq} &= 0 && \text{for } d = d', p = p' \text{ and } q = 1, 2, \ldots, Q_{d'p'} \\
&= u_{dpq} && \text{for } d = d', p \neq p' \text{ and } q = 1, 2, \ldots, Q_{d'p} \\
&= u_{dpq} && \text{for } d \neq d', p = 1, 2, \ldots, P_d \text{ and} \\
& && q = 1, 2, \ldots, Q_{dp}.
\end{aligned}
\tag{10.5.5}
$$

Having found the desired pair (p', q'), the procedure allocates one new DVU of demand d' to this path pair, changing the state from $(\boldsymbol{x}, \boldsymbol{u})$ to $(\boldsymbol{x}', \boldsymbol{u}')$. In other words, procedure *allocate* looks for the best, from the incremental cost minimization viewpoint, pair of paths (p', q') to which the additional DVU should be assigned. It should be emphasized, that during this operation the back-up path q currently used for path p' (the one with $u_{dp'q} = 1$, if any) can be changed (to q'), if this is beneficial.

Procedure *disconnect* $(\boldsymbol{x}, \boldsymbol{u})$: The demand module for disconnection is chosen randomly, the corresponding flow decremented by 1, and the back-up path possibly changed if this is beneficial. Formally, assume that $|\boldsymbol{x}| > 0$ and draw a DVU to be disconnected by choosing a demand d' with probability Prob$\{\boldsymbol{x}; d'\}$ given by formula (5.3.9). Suppose that the chosen unit is assigned to pair (p', q') $(1 \leq p' \leq P_{d'}, 1 \leq q' \leq Q_{d'p'}, u_{dp'q'} = 1)$. Then we look for a back-up path q'' protecting the normal path $p' (1 \leq q'' \leq Q_{d'p'})$ such that the vectors $\boldsymbol{x}'$, $\boldsymbol{u}'$ and $\boldsymbol{u}''$ defined as follows:

$$
\begin{aligned}
x'_{dp0} &= x_{dp0} - 1 && \text{for } d = d' \text{ and } p = p' \\
&= x_{dp0} && \text{for } d = d' \text{ and } p \neq p' \\
&= x_{dp0} && \text{for } d \neq d' \text{ and } p = 1, 2, \ldots, P_d \\
u'_{dpq} &= 1 && \text{for } d = d', p = p' \text{ and } q = q'' \\
&= 0 && \text{for } d = d', p = p' \text{ and } q \neq q'' \\
&= u_{dpq} && \text{for } d = d', p \neq p' \text{ and } q = 1, 2, \ldots, Q_{d'p} \\
&= u_{dpq} && \text{for } d \neq d', p = 1, 2, \ldots, P_d \text{ and } q = 1, 2, \ldots, Q_{dp} \\
u''_{dpq} &= 0 && \text{for } d = d', p = p' \text{ and } q = 1, 2, \ldots, Q_{d'p'} \\
&= u_{dpq} && \text{for } d = d', p \neq p' \text{ and } q = 1, 2, \ldots, Q_{d'p} \\
&= u_{dpq} && \text{for } d \neq d', p = 1, 2, \ldots, P_d \text{ and } q = 1, 2, \ldots, Q_{dp}
\end{aligned}
\tag{10.5.6}
$$

minimize the incremental cost (10.5.4). Finally, we proceed to state $(\boldsymbol{x}', \boldsymbol{u}')$. (Observe that the current back-up path can be changed upon disconnection.)

It is easy to adapt the above procedures to single path allocation, i.e., when the entire demand volumes are assigned to single normal paths and also restored on single back-up paths (problem DR/CF/NBR/CC/LIN/PR+FSBP (9.4.10)). In such a case we can simply assume demand-dependent DVUs equal to the demanded volumes h_d (Exercise 10.17). Then the probability of choosing a demand for allocation or disconnection is proportional to its volume. In fact, SAL is more effective for the single path allocation case, both from the computation time and quality of solution viewpoints.

Dynamic Search for Back-up Path

When selecting a normal allocation path for demand d it is reasonable to use a predefined path list (static selection) composed of several short (in terms of number of hops) paths. The back-up paths, however, should be the shortest paths rather to incremental link costs, a notion discussed below. It follows that the back-up paths must be found dynamically since such metrics are state dependent.

When considering a normal path p for demand d for allocating a DVU, the protection, situation disjoint path q is found using some shortest path algorithm. The cost of allocating one additional DVU on a back-up path is the sum of the incremental costs of all the links forming the path. The notion of *incremental link cost*, used as the link metric for the shortest path algorithm is as follows.

Suppose that the allocation state is $(\boldsymbol{x}, \boldsymbol{u})$ and we wish to define the incremental link costs Δ_e for a fixed demand d' and its normal path p'. To do this we hypothetically modify state $(\boldsymbol{x}, \boldsymbol{u})$ by increasing flow $x_{d'p'0}$ by 1, setting $u_{d'p'q} = 0$ for all $q = 1, 2, \ldots, Q_{d'p'}$, and not changing other components of $\boldsymbol{x}$ and $\boldsymbol{u}$ (the modified state is denoted by $(\boldsymbol{x}', \boldsymbol{u}')$). This flow modification (increasing flow $x_{d'p'0}$ by 1 and making it unprotected for a while) will in general affect the link capacities and the network cost. Denote the set of indices of links that can be used for protecting path (d', p') with $E(d', p')$, i.e., $E(d', p') = \{e : \forall s > 0, \theta_{d'p's} = 0 \Rightarrow \alpha_{es} = 1\}$. The incremental link costs are finally defined as:

$$\begin{aligned}
\Delta_e &= +\infty \quad \text{if } e \notin E(d', p') \\
&= 0 \quad \text{if } e \in E(d', p') \text{ and} \\
&\qquad \textstyle\sum_d \sum_p \sum_q (\delta_{edp}\theta_{dps} + \beta_{edpq}(1 - \theta_{dps}))u'_{dpq}x'_{dp0} < My_e(\boldsymbol{x}', \boldsymbol{u}') \\
&= \xi_e \quad \text{if } e \in E(d', p') \text{ and} \\
&\qquad \textstyle\sum_d \sum_p \sum_q (\delta_{edp}\theta_{dps} + \beta_{edpq}(1 - \theta_{dps}))u'_{dpq}x'_{dp0} = My_e(\boldsymbol{x}', \boldsymbol{u}').
\end{aligned} \tag{10.5.7}$$

Hence, the incremental cost of link e is either $+\infty$ (if the link can fail simultaneously with path (d', p')), 0 if link e is under-loaded, and ξ_e if it is saturated in the hypothetical state $(\boldsymbol{x}', \boldsymbol{u}')$.

The allocation of a DVU for demand d'' consists in checking all normal paths from the normal path list of the demand, finding the best back-up path using the shortest path algorithm for the appropriate incremental link costs, and finally by choosing the best pair (p'', q'') and changing the current state $(\boldsymbol{x}, \boldsymbol{u})$ to $(\boldsymbol{x}'', \boldsymbol{u}'')$ in the following way:

$$\begin{aligned}
x''_{dp0} &= x_{dp0} + 1 \quad \text{for } d = d'' \text{ and } p = p'' \\
&= x_{dp0} \quad \text{for } d = d'' \text{ and } p \neq p'' \\
&= x_{dp0} \quad \text{for } d \neq d'' \text{ and } p = 1, 2, \ldots, P_d \\
u''_{dpq} &= 1 \quad \text{for } d = d'', p = p'' \text{ and } q = q'' \\
&= 0 \quad \text{for } d = d'', p = p'' \text{ and } q \neq q'' \\
&= u_{dpq} \quad \text{for } d \neq d'', p = 1, 2, \ldots, P_d \text{ and } q = 1, 2, \ldots, Q_{dp}.
\end{aligned} \tag{10.5.8}$$

For the disconnection the incremental link costs are defined in a similar way (for $x'_{dp0} = x_{dp0} - 1$ in this case).

Other Extensions

It can happen that there are more than one pair of paths with the same minimal incremental cost (10.5.4). Then a second order criterion can be applied, choosing, for instance, the pair of paths which maximize the total free capacity of links after allocation of DVU.

The effectiveness of SAL can often be improved through a modification consisting in adding to the incremental link cost Δ_e the term $a(|\boldsymbol{x}|)\sum_e \delta_{ed'p'}$, proportional to the length of the normal path measured as the number of its links. This favors selection of shorter paths. Factor $a(|\boldsymbol{x}|)$ of the additional cost should be a non-increasing function of the state height $|\boldsymbol{x}|$, tending to 0, as $|\boldsymbol{x}|$ tends to H, and should assume reasonably small values as compared with the link incremental costs Δ_e. Clearly, the idea of such a modification is to use short paths at the low allocation states, and to try to use the available non-occupied capacity of the last modules on the links in the states close to maximal.

Another possibility is to compute the network cost using non-modular capacity in low allocation states:

$$\begin{aligned} y_e(\boldsymbol{x}, \boldsymbol{u}) &= \max\{(\textstyle\sum_d \sum_p \sum_q (\delta_{edp}\theta_{dps} + \beta_{edpq}(1 - \theta_{dps}))u_{dpq}x_{dp0})/M : \\ & \quad s = 0, 1, \ldots, S\}. \end{aligned} \tag{10.5.9}$$

While allocating a DVU we can also select d in a way different from purely random, e.g., assuming that allocation of certain demands has a priority. Similarly, while disconnecting a DVU the choice can be different from random. For instance, often it is advantageous to increase the probability of choosing a DCU allocated to a long path, consuming capacity on many links.

As discussed in Section 5.3.4, still another improvement can be achieved by disconnecting in certain states more than one DVU. This can be done in e.g., maximal states (with $|\boldsymbol{x}| = H$), but not necessarily every time a maximal state is reached. Such an action is called a bulk disconnection, and it typically consists in disconnecting all normal flows allocated to links from a randomly selected set of links.

Also, learning allocation/disconnection rules can be considered with decisions depending on the so far generated trajectory of the allocation process. This gives a possibility of detecting, and in consequence avoiding, erroneous local allocation/disconnection decisions, not advantageous from the global point of view. Here methods from Tabu Search can be applied (see [GL97]).

Finally, SAL can be combined with Simulated Annealing (SAN, see Section 10.5.2) into one, so called greedy randomized adaptive search procedure (GRASP, see Section 5.3.6 and [FR95]). In such a combination SAL is used to generate maximal allocation states, and once a maximal state $(\boldsymbol{x}, \boldsymbol{u})$ is reached, a SAN-type procedure is activated to search the set of maximal allocation states around $(\boldsymbol{x}, \boldsymbol{u})$. A procedure of this type applied to topological design can be found in [Mys01].

Protection With Single Back-up Paths

Somewhat different SAL procedures can be used for the integer programming variant of the protection problem P/CF/BR/CC/LIN/PR+FSB (9.5.6). In this case the flow vector $\boldsymbol{x}$

is given and the issue is to find the binary back-up path allocation vector $\boldsymbol{u}$ satisfying constraints

$$\textstyle\sum_q u_{dpq} = 1, \quad d = 1,2,\ldots,D \quad p = 1,2,\ldots,P_d \tag{10.5.10a}$$

(recall that in P/CF/BR/CC/LIN/PR+FSBP it is assumed that $x_{dp0} > 0$ for all d and p which is why the strict equality must be assumed in (10.5.10a)) and minimizing the cost function

$$cost(\boldsymbol{u}) = \textstyle\sum_e \xi_e y_e(\boldsymbol{u}) \tag{10.5.10b}$$

where

$$\begin{aligned} y_e(\boldsymbol{u}) \;\; = \;\; & \min\{z : \textstyle\sum_d \sum_p \sum_q (\delta_{edp}\theta_{dps} + \beta_{edpq}(1 - \theta_{dps}))u_{dpq}x_{dp0} \le \\ & \alpha_{es}M(c_e + z), \quad s = 1,2,\ldots,S;\, z - \text{integer}\}. \end{aligned} \tag{10.5.10c}$$

The modification is as follows. Normal flow $x_{dp0} > 0$ is called *non-labeled* if $u_{dpq} = 0$ for all $q = 1,2,\ldots,Q_{dp}$ (at the initialization all flows are non-labeled, i.e., $\boldsymbol{u} = \boldsymbol{0}$). Procedure *allocate* $(\boldsymbol{u})$ draws one of the non-labeled normal flows, for example, flow x_{dp0} $(1 \le p \le P_d)$, and selects one of its allowable back-up paths, for example, path q $(1 \le q \le Q_{dp})$, minimizing the incremental network cost, and modifying the current state $\boldsymbol{u}$ by setting $u_{dpq} = 1$ (this makes flow x_{dp0} labeled). The probability of drawing a particular non-labeled flow is proportional to its value.

Procedure *disconnect* is even simpler: it draws a labeled normal flow x_{dp0} (with the probability proportional to its value) and simply disconnects its back-up flow on path q by setting $u_{dpq} = 0$.

Application of SAL to Other Problems

It should be clear to the reader how to modify procedures *allocate* and *disconnect* and apply them to problem (9.4.8) (Exercise 10.18) involving situation-dependent back-up paths. As described in [Pi697a], SAL can be also applied to DR-U and DR-R (and their respective protection counterparts, (9.5.4) and (9.5.5)). Another application of SAL (to a problem with the link capacity protection mechanism) is the subject of Exercise 10.19.

10.5.2 Simulated Annealing (SAN)

As already mentioned, SAN (Section 5.3.2) can be also used for DR/CF/NBR/CC/LIN/PR+FSBP. Contrary to SAL, SAN works with full allocation states $(\boldsymbol{x}, \boldsymbol{u})$, i.e., with the feasible solutions of (10.5.1). For the purpose of SAN, the neighborhood $\mathcal{N}(\boldsymbol{x}, \boldsymbol{u})$ of $(\boldsymbol{x}, \boldsymbol{u})$ can be defined in many ways. If we assume the static path case with fixed normal and back-up path lists, then one such neighborhood relation can be defined as follows. Two feasible states $(\boldsymbol{x}^1, \boldsymbol{u}^1)$ and $(\boldsymbol{x}^2, \boldsymbol{u}^2)$ are said to be the neighboring states if exactly one of the two following conditions holds:

1) there exists a demand d', and two different normal paths p' and p'' such that

$$\begin{aligned} x^1_{d'p'0} &= x^2_{dp''0} + 1 \\ x^1_{d'p''0} &= x^2_{dp'0} - 1 \\ x^1_{dp0} &= x^2_{dp0} && \text{for } (d,p) \neq (d',p') \text{ and } (d,p) \neq (d',p'') \\ u^1_{dpq} &= u^2_{dpq} && \text{for all } d = 1,2,\dots,D, p = 1,2,\dots,P_d, \\ & && q = 1,2,\dots,Q_{dp} \end{aligned} \tag{10.5.11}$$

2) there exists a demand d', one normal path p', and two different back-up paths q' and q'' for $p'(1 \le q', q'' \le Q_{d'p'})$ such that $x^1_{d'p'0}(= x^2_{dp''0}) > 0$ and

$$\begin{aligned} x^1_{dp0} &= x^2_{dp0} && \text{for all } d = 1,2\dots,D, p = 1,2,\dots,P_d \\ u^1_{d'p'q'} &= 1 \\ u^1_{d'p'q''} &= 0 \\ u^2_{d'p'q'} &= 0 \\ u^2_{d'p'q''} &= 1 \\ u^1_{dpq} &= u^2_{dpq} && \text{for all } d = 1,2,\dots,D, p = 1,2,\dots,P_d, \\ & && q = 1,2,\dots,Q_{dp} \text{ and } (d,p) \neq (d',p'). \end{aligned} \tag{10.5.12}$$

In other words, a neighboring state is obtained by shifting one DVU from one normal path to another, or by changing the back-up path for one normal path.

It is rather straightforward to generalize the above-defined neighborhood relation for other robust design problems (for an example, see Exercise 10.20).

10.5.3 *Evolutionary Algorithm (EA)*

In Section 5.3.3 we have presented a generic pseudo-code for EA (one of its many variants) and discussed its application to allocation problem A/SPA(4.2.4). As for SAL and SAN, we will show how to apply EA to DR/MF/BR/MC/LIN/PR+FSBP (10.5.1).

Any feasible solution of the considered problem is called a *chromosome*, and is composed of genes which define the internal structure of the solution—each *gene* corresponds to the flow pattern associated with one individual demand. In our case the gene corresponding to demand d is represented by two vectors $\boldsymbol{x}_d = (x_{d10}, x_{d20}, \dots, x_{dP_d0})$ and $\boldsymbol{u}_d = (u_{d11}, u_{d12}, \dots, u_{d1Q_{d1}}, u_{d21}, u_{d22}, \dots, u_{d2Q_{d2}}, \dots, u_{dP_d1}, u_{dP_d2}, \dots, u_{dP_dQ_{dP_d}})$. The crossover operation between two parent chromosomes $(\boldsymbol{x}^1, \boldsymbol{u}^1)$ and $(\boldsymbol{x}^2, \boldsymbol{u}^2)$ results in two offsprings with the consecutive genes taken from their parents at random; if the first offspring receives a gene $(\boldsymbol{x}^1_d, \boldsymbol{u}^1_d)$ from the first parent (this happens with probability $\frac{1}{2}$) then the second one gets the gene $(\boldsymbol{x}^2_d, \boldsymbol{u}^2_d)$ from the second parent.

There are two mutation operations, corresponding to the two types of neighbors defined in the previous section for SAN. Hence, the first mutation type consists of shifting a flow unit from one normal path to another, and the second type consists of changing the back-up path. As for the two previously described approaches, the crossover and mutation operations can be easily adapted for other robust design problems.

10.6 *SELECTED APPLICATION: WAVELENGTH ASSIGNMENT PROBLEM IN WDM NETWORKS

The goal of this section is two-fold. First, it formulates a set of optimization problems relevant for the design of optical WDM networks robust to failures, and encompassing demand routing, wavelength assignment (wavelength continuity is assumed), and link dimensioning. Two basic protection mechanisms are considered: path diversity (PD) and single back-up path (SBP) restoration. The design problems are formulated as integer programming problems. For small networks these problems can be solved directly with the BB approach available e.g., within CPLEX. As the considered problems are $\mathcal{NP}$-complete, for networks of realistic size heuristic methods are needed. Accordingly, the second goal of this section is to demonstrate how two stochastic heuristic approaches, namely SAN and SAL, perform for the specified problems. It is shown using two network configurations that the latter approach is superior to the former, and yields desirable close-to-optimal solutions in a reasonable time. The numerical results also show what extra spare capacity volume is required by the considered protection mechanisms. This can help in solving the tradeoff between the reconfiguration complexity and the extra link and node capacity cost. This section is based on the considerations of [PSG+00], developed further in [Gle02].

In this section we will use local notation for the considered problems.

10.6.1 Design Problems

Below we will specify several IP restoration design problems for the path diversity protection (PDP) and to single back-up-path protection (SBP) mechanisms.

***IP:* PDP** **Link-Path Formulation**

Path Diversity Protection

indices

$e = 1, 2, \ldots, E$	links
$d = 1, 2, \ldots, D$	demands
$s = 0, 1, \ldots, S$	situations
$p = 1, 2, \ldots, P_d$	paths allowable for flows realizing demand d
$c = 1, 2, \ldots, C$	colors (wavelengths) available on fibers

constants

δ_{edp}	= 1 if link e belongs to path p realizing demand d; 0 otherwise
h_{ds}	volume of demand d to be realized in situation s, expressed as the number of light paths
ξ_e	unit cost of link e
α_{es}	binary availability coefficient: = 0 if link e is failed in situation s; 1, otherwise ($\alpha_{e0} \equiv 1$, $\alpha_{es} \in \{0, 1\}$)
θ_{dps}	binary availability coefficient: = 0 if path p of demand d is failed in situation s; 1, otherwise ($\theta_{dps} = \prod_{\{e:\delta_{edp}=1\}} \alpha_{es}$)

variables

x_{dpc} flow (number of light-paths) realizing demand d in color c on path p (non-negative integer)

w_{ce} the number of times the color c is used on link e (non-negative integer, auxiliary)

y_e capacity of link e expressed in the number of fibers (non-negative integer)

objective

$$\text{minimize } \boldsymbol{C}(\boldsymbol{y}) = \textstyle\sum_e \xi_e y_e \tag{10.6.1a}$$

constraints

$$\textstyle\sum_p \theta_{dps} \sum_c x_{dpc} \geq h_{ds}, \quad d = 1, 2, \ldots, D \quad s = 0, 1, \ldots, S \tag{10.6.1b}$$

$$\textstyle\sum_d \sum_p \delta_{edp} x_{dpc} = w_{ce}, \quad c = 1, 2, \ldots, C \quad e = 1, 2, \ldots, E \tag{10.6.1c}$$

$$y_e \geq w_{ce}, \quad c = 1, 2, \ldots, C \quad e = 1, 2, \ldots, E. \tag{10.6.1d}$$

For example, $x_{dpc} = x_{121}$ specifies that x_{121} light-paths are used for demand $d = 1$ on its path $p = 2$ using the laser beam with color $c = 1$, and $x_{dpc} = x_{152}$ implies that x_{152} light-paths are used for demand $d = 1$ on its path $p = 5$ using the laser beam with $c = 2$.

***IP:* SBP** **Link-Path Formulation**

Single Back-up path Protection

indices

$e = 1, 2, \ldots, E$	links
$d = 1, 2, \ldots, D$	demands
$s = 0, 1, \ldots, S$	situations
$p = 1, 2, \ldots, P_d$	paths allowable for normal flows realizing demand d
$c = 1, 2, \ldots, C$	colors (wavelengths) available on fibers on normal path
$g = 1, 2, \ldots, C$	colors (wavelengths) available on fibers on back-up path
$k = 1, 2, \ldots, Q_{dp}$	back-up paths for protecting normal flow realizing demand d on path p (all paths k are situation disjoint with normal path p)

constants

δ_{edp} = 1 if link e belongs to normal path p of demand d; 0, otherwise

β_{edpk} = 1 if link e belongs to back-up path k protecting path p of demand d; 0, otherwise

h_{ds} volume of demand d to be realized in situation s, expressed as the number of light paths

ξ_e unit cost of link e

α_{es} binary availability coefficient: = 0 if link e is failed in situation s; 1, otherwise ($\alpha_{e0} \equiv 1$, $\alpha_{es} \in \{0,1\}$)

θ_{dps} binary availability coefficient: = 0 if path p of demand d is failed demand d; 1, otherwise

ω_{dpks} = 0 if back-up path k protecting path p of demand d is failed in situation s, 1, otherwise; ($\omega_{dpks} = \prod_{\{e:\beta_{edpk=1}\}} \alpha_{es}$; we require that for each s, d, p and k, $\theta_{dps} = 0$ implies $\omega_{dpks} = 1$, i.e., that the paths p and k are failure disjoint)

variables

x_{dpc} normal flow (number of light-paths) realizing demand d in color c on path p (non-negative integer)

z_{dpkcg} back-up flow on path k in color g protecting normal flow x_{dpc} on path p (non-negative integer)

u_{dpkcg} back-up flow allocation variable (binary)

w_{ces} the number of times the color c is used on link e in situation s (non-negative integer, auxiliary)

y_e capacity of link e expressed in the number of fibres (non-negative integer)

objective

$$\text{minimize } C(y) = \textstyle\sum_e \xi_e y_e \tag{10.6.2a}$$

constraints

$$\textstyle\sum_p \sum_c x_{dpc} \geq h_d, \quad d = 1, 2, \dots, D \tag{10.6.2b}$$
(full restoration assumed: $h_{ds} = h_d$, $s = 0, 1, \dots, S$)

$$\textstyle\sum_k \sum_g u_{dpkcg} = 1, \quad d = 1, 2, \dots, D \quad p = 1, 2, \dots, P_d \quad c = 1, 2, \dots, C \tag{10.6.2c}$$

$$z_{dpkcg} \leq u_{dpkcg} h_d, \quad d = 1, 2, \dots, D \quad p = 1, 2, \dots, P_d \quad k = 1, 2, \dots, Q_{dp} \quad c, g = 1, 2, \dots, C \tag{10.6.2d}$$

$$\textstyle\sum_k \sum_g z_{dpkcg} = x_{dpc}, \quad d = 1, 2, \dots, D \quad p = 1, 2, \dots, P_d \quad c = 1, 2, \dots, C \tag{10.6.2e}$$

$$\sum_d \sum_p (\theta_{dps}\delta_{edp}x_{dpc} + (1-\theta_{dps})\sum_k \sum_g \beta_{edpk} z_{dpkgc}) = w_{ces}, \quad c = 1,2,\ldots,C \quad e = 1,2,\ldots,E \quad s = 0,1,\ldots,S \tag{10.6.2f}$$

$$y_e \geq w_{ces}, \quad c = 1,2,\ldots,C \quad e = 1,2,\ldots,E \quad s = 0,1,\ldots,S. \tag{10.6.2g}$$

The rest of the design problems considered here can be obtained from PDP or SBP as follows.

ND: Normal Design. ND is identical with PDP with $S = 0$ (only normal state is considered).

SBP/FC: SBP with Fixed Colors. One additional constraint is added to SBP:

$$\sum_{g \neq c} u_{dpkcg} = 0, \quad d = 1,2,\ldots,D \quad p = 1,2,\ldots,P_d \quad k = 1,2,\ldots,Q_{dp} \quad c = 1,2,\ldots,C. \tag{10.6.3}$$

SBP/NC: SBP with Non-reusable Normal Capacity. Constraint (10.6.4) substitutes (10.6.2f):

$$\sum_d \sum_p (\delta_{edp}x_{dpc} + (1-\theta_{dps})\sum_k \sum_g \beta_{edpk} z_{dpkgc}) = w_{ces}, \quad c = 1,2,\ldots,C \quad e = 1,2,\ldots,E \quad s = 0,1,\ldots,S. \tag{10.6.4}$$

SBP/FC/NC: SBP with Fixed Colors and Non-reusable Normal Capacity. Constraint (10.6.3) is added to SBP and constraint (10.6.4) substitutes (10.6.2f).

Using binary variables we are able to consider, maintaining the IP formulation, the extended objective function (10.6.1a) taking into account the constant "link-opening" costs:

$$C(y) = \sum_e F_e(y_e), \quad F_e(y_e) = \xi_e y_e + \kappa_e \text{ for } y_e > 0, \text{ and } F_e(y_e) = 0 \text{ for } y_e = 0. \tag{10.6.5}$$

To achieve this, for each link e we introduce an additional binary variable σ_e and add the following (where K is a large number):

$$\textbf{objective:} \quad \text{minimize } C(y,\sigma) = \sum_e (\xi_e y_e + \kappa_e \sigma_e)$$
$$\textbf{additional constraint:} \quad y_e \leq \sigma_e K \quad e = 1,2,\ldots,E. \tag{10.6.6}$$

10.6.2 *Design Methods*

For solving the optimization problems specified in the previous section we have tried three optimization methods, one exact (BB/BC method available within CPLEX) and two stochastic heuristics (SAL and SAN). As the exact approaches are effective only for small networks, the heuristic methods have to be used for large networks.

TABLE 10.8 **Results for a Small Network**

	ND	PDP	SBP	SBP/NC	SBP/FC	SBP/FC/NC
Exact LP	640.28	918.40	885.63	885.63	885.63	885.63
Exact IP	645	1053	991	991	991	991
SAN	869	–	–	1523	–	–
SAL	645	–	–	1016	–	–

Applications of SAL and SAN to the considered problems follow essentially the lines described in Section 10.5.

Paths (path lists) considered by the algorithms are predefined; they can be calculated e.g., with the well-known techniques for finding a set of K-shortest paths (see Appendix C) (SDP) or a shortest set of K-disjoint paths (see Appendix C) (ND, PDP), depending on the problem.

We have performed some tests for the six design problems of Section 10.6.1 using a small network example with 5 nodes and 7 links. All node pairs are to be connected with 1 to 6 light-paths. Cost function (10.6.5) is used, with unit link costs ξ_e per fiber between 1 and 4, and the constant conduit (duct) costs κ_e - between 100 and 400 (the duct costs are 100 times greater than the fiber costs). Table 10.8 shows that, as expected, the PDP scheme is cost inefficient because it does not allow the restoration of the broken flows. The different SBP mechanisms are equivalent in terms of cost for this small network, but this is by no means a general property. Observe, that SAL is significantly better than SAN.

10.6.3 Numerical Results

Below we discuss results of the case studies performed to examine the methods described in Section 10.6.2 for the problems specified in Section 10.6.1. We have solved problems ND and SBP/NC for the cost function (10.6.5) on an HPJ7000/440MHz for the networks described in Table 10.9. For Network-D, two different demand patterns have been used. Each case has been run for 30 minutes for the number of wavelengths $C = 2, 4, 16$. For each case the stochastic algorithms have been run 3 times while the deterministic IP solver was run just once.

The results are presented in Tables 10.10 and 10.11. For SBP/NC, the CPLEX IP solver in many cases did not find a feasible solution before exceeding either the time limit of 30 minutes or the memory limit of 1 GB. In fact the IP solver did terminate with an optimal solution within 30 minutes only for some instances of problem ND (refer to Table 10.10). Observe that SAL usually produced results at least as good as SAN, and in most cases much better results were seen.

Figure 10.7 depicts a graph illustrating how the heuristic improvement proceeds; the specs at the top correspond to all SAN solutions. The three lines show the current best solution cost for the three considered methods. It can be seen that SAL reaches a sub-optimal result very quickly and then is not able to improve it.

TABLE 10.9 Optimal Costs for One ND Run for 30 min

Network	Nodes	Links	Average Duct Cost (κ_e)	Average Fiber Cost (ξ_e)	Demands
Network-P	12	18	182	1.82	66
Network-D	23	29	214	2.00	21

TABLE 10.10 Results for ND

			Simulated Allocation		Simulated Annealing		IP	
Network	**Volume**	**C**	**Average**	**Std.dev.**	**Average**	**Std.dev.**	**Result**	**Status**
Network-P	1695	2	5677.05	0.00	6373.45	8.45	5298.30	timeout
		4	3950.77	39.00	4881.27	19.26	3607.45	optimal
		16	2568.20	10.48	3812.05	7.47	2324.75	timeout
Network-D	63	2	2646.38	0.00	3377.25	172.56	2646.38	optimal
		4	2509.74	2.41	3309.88	135.87	2506.01	optimal
		16	2409.15	4.70	3401.67	211.04	2403.01	timeout
	844	2	6275.49	2.29	6947.73	1.76	6201.16	optimal
		4	4450.85	1.47	6030.99	1098.78	4377.68	optimal
		16	3085.53	3.32	5674.85	2.25	3010.46	optimal

TABLE 10.11 Results for SBP/NC

			Simulated Allocation		Simulated Annealing		IP	
Network	**Volume**	**C**	**Average**	**Std.dev.**	**Average**	**Std.dev.**	**Result**	**Status**
Network-P	1695	2	9299.78	51.10	8298.35	23.64	timeout	
		4	6376.07	19.92	5823.92	11.18	timeout	
		16	3998.87	5.72	4065.42	3.19	memout	
Network-D	63	2	5128.27	3.65	5444.97	0.33	5139.94	timeout
		4	4894.00	2.53	5221.27	1.50	5253.74	timeout
		16	4721.31	1.50	5070.91	2.61	timeout	
	844	2	14573.26	16.00	14514.11	3.95	14175.7	timeout
		4	9748.49	7.66	9860.28	5.38	timeout	
		16	6123.11	3.21	6377.99	1.56	memout	

10.6.4 Remarks

In this section we have formulated a set of integer programming design problems for wavelength routed optical networks robust to failures, with the robustness assured by either the path diversity (PD) or the single back-up path (SBP) protection mechanisms. The formulations encompass simultaneous design of demands routing, wavelengths assignment and link capacities, with the cost function taking into account the constant conduit costs.

For networks of practical size the exact solutions through the BB approach using LP cannot be achieved in a reasonable time and, hence, heuristic approaches must be applied. We have shown results for two such approaches: SAN and SAL. It is shown by numerical studies that SAL, in most cases, performs better than SAN and can be used for finding acceptable close-to-optimal solutions even for large networks when the exact approaches can fail to give even one feasible (integer) solution.

Note that without the wavelength continuity assumption, all the design problems considered in this section are identical with the corresponding generic problems considered in Chapter 9. Introducing the continuity assumption adds difficulty to the considered problems, as it requires many more integer variables.

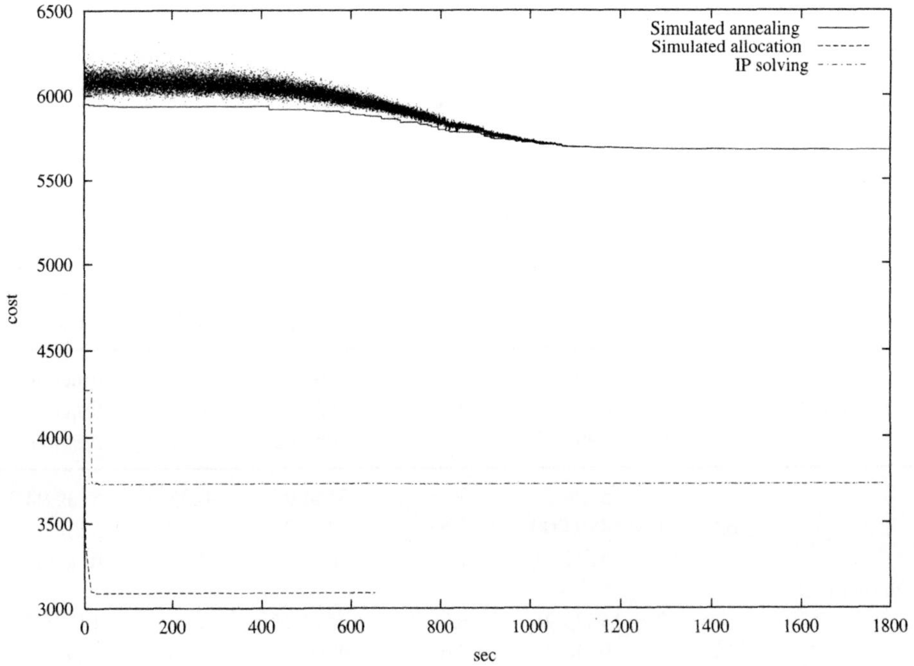

FIGURE 10.7 Current Cost during ND Optimization (Case: Network-D II/844 Lightpaths/C=16)

10.7 SUMMARY AND FURTHER READING

In Chapter 10 we have concentrated on the presentation of optimization approaches to the design problems in resilient networks involving flow restoration. The choice of these particular problems out of many possible models presented in Chapter 9 has been motivated by the relative difficulty (which coincides with the actual difficulty in the case of modular links) of the DR-type problems involving path restoration with respect to others, e.g., to problems involving the link restoration mechanisms. We have started with LP formulations and showed how to apply the LP decomposition methods which can be useful in solving large-scale network examples. In Section 10.4 we have addressed a very important case of modular links. Although we have not described any particular method, we have explained how the solution can be approached approximately and exactly by means of the BC method. Next, in Section 10.5, we have moved to heuristic methods and demonstrated their applicability to such difficult problems as e.g., flow restoration with modular links and single-path routing. Both the LP decompositions and heuristic methods are illustrated with numerical examples. Finally, in Section 10.6, we have shown a case study of the design of resilient optical networks without wave conversion, an important and difficult issue.

The LP decomposition methods of column generation (called PG in our context), LR, and BD have been explained in Section 5.4, and the appropriate further reading in these topics is suggested in Section 5.8. Here we note that applications of PG to similar problems are described in [DS98] and [Wes00]. It seems that the use of BD for DR-like problems was first suggested in [Min81] and then developed in [MS81b], [Min84], and [Min89]; also, see [KPNG02], [BL99], [PS01], [Szy02], and [TH00].

The BC approach to modular design with flow restoration was studied in papers such as [DS98], [Sto92], [Wes00], [AGW98], [BM01], [GMS95], [Gün99], and others. An excellent survey can be found in [Wes00]. Important heuristic methods especially developed for this purpose can be found in [Aga89], [GTD⁺89], [SNH90] and many others. The use of stochastic meta-heuristics for restoration design can be found, for example, in [CLH99], [CL02], [Pió97a], and [PSG⁺00].

EXERCISES FOR CHAPTER 10

10.1. Show that the set defined by (10.1.4b) to (10.1.4e) contains the optimal solution of the dual Problem (10.1.4) and that in this set the dual function is given by (10.1.4a).

10.2. Using formula (10.1.9) prove a proposition analogous to Proposition 5.1 from Section 5.4.2 for DR-U (10.1.1).

10.3. Formulate the PG algorithm for (10.1.1).

10.4. Formulate the PG algorithm for (10.1.10).

10.5. Derive the formulae underlying the path generation technique for (9.3.5) analogous to (10.1.18) to (10.1.22), and formulate the resulting PG algorithm.

10.6. Formulate the PG algorithm for (9.3.6).

10.7. Derive formulae for the projection in Step 2 of Algorithm 10.1 from Section 10.2.1.

10.8. Show that the feasibility test (10.3.10) is the dual to the following primal problem

$$\begin{aligned} &\textbf{\textit{minimize}} \quad z \\ &\textbf{\textit{subject to}} \quad \textstyle\sum_p x_{dp} = h_{ds}, \quad d = 1, 2, \dots, D \\ &\qquad \textstyle\sum_d \sum_p \delta_{edp} x_{dp} \le \alpha_{es} y_e + z, \quad e = 1, 2, \dots, E \\ &\qquad z \text{ is continuous and all } x_{dp} \text{ are continuous and non-negative.} \end{aligned} \tag{10.7.1}$$

10.9. Find the cut inequality corresponding to node $v = 1$ for the network in Figure 10.1 (the correspondence between link and node numbering is given in the first column of Table 10.5).

10.10. Assume that in situation s all links are fully available ($\alpha_{es} \equiv 1$) and that all multipliers π_e^* in inequality (10.3.11) are equal to 1. Does the resulting inequality represent "a cut inequality"? If not, what is the interpretation of this inequality? (Hint: note that in the considered case λ_d^* is the length of the shortest path for demand d in terms of number of hops.)

10.11. Solve dual to the problem considered in Example 10.1. Show that the resulting optimal multipliers $\boldsymbol{\pi}^*$ and λ^* define inequalities (10.3.15) which are exactly the ones obtained with the BD algorithm in Example 10.1 starting from $\Omega = \emptyset$.

10.12. Derive formulae for the projection of the current solution point onto set defined in (10.3.17).

10.13. Prove Proposition 10.3.

10.14. Prove Proposition 10.4.

10.15. Consider Problem (9.5.5)—a protection counterpart (normal link capacities $\boldsymbol{c}$ and normal flows $\boldsymbol{x}_0$ are given) of problem DR-R (9.3.3). Formulate the BD algorithm for this problem.

10.16. Consider another version of Problem (9.5.5) assuming that the normal link capacities $\boldsymbol{c}$ are given but not the normal flows. Write down the BD algorithm for this modification.

10.17. Define procedures *allocate* and *disconnect* for Problem (9.4.10).

10.18. Adapt procedures *allocate* and *disconnect* described in the first part of Section 10.5.1 for Problem (9.4.8).

10.19. Define procedures *allocate* and *disconnect* for Problem (9.2.3).

10.20. Define the neighborhood relation for the feasible solutions of (9.3.5) and (9.4.8).

CHAPTER 11

Multi-Hour and Multi–Time-Period Network Modeling and Design

There are two important classes of network design problems that will be discussed in this chapter: 1) multi–busy-hour, or multi-hour, and 2) multi–time-period, multi–planning-period, or simply multi-period.

Multi-hour refers to considering different traffic matrices at different times during the day. So far, in our discussion we have primarily considered a single demand volume matrix (which is based on traffic measurement and marketing input) to reflect the peak traffic during the day (except for consideration of multiple matrices due to failure states in Chapter 9). Multi–busy-hour behavior of the traffic is observed, especially when the network spans over multiple time zones and has different peaks for different demands at different times, i.e., non-coincidence of busy hours. For example, this happens in the continental U.S. due to multiple time zones. Consider telephone traffic at 8:00 am in the morning in the eastern time zone in the U.S. for east-coast cities such as New York, Boston, and Washington, DC. We can expect traffic to increase between east-coast cities (due to offices opening at 8:00 am), but we are unlikely to see much cross-country traffic to the west coast (where cities such as San Francisco, Seattle, and Los Angeles are located), or between cities in the west coast where the local time is 5:00 am in the Pacific time zone. This also suggests that routing that is either dynamic or at least changes with the time during the day can exploit the *unused* capacity in the network; e.g., a call, at around 8:00 am in the eastern time zone, between Boston and Washington, DC (both cities located in the east coast), can conceivably be routed via San Francisco (a city located in the west coast). In fact, exploiting non-coincidence of busy hours along with dynamic (time-dependent) routing, the first ever dynamic routing for the telephone network called *dynamic non-hierarchical routing (DNHR),* was deployed in the mid 1980s spanning the continental U.S.; furthermore, it was estimated that network design for the DNHR network was achievable at savings in the order of 16% compared to a network with (previously used) old hierarchical routing while providing the same grade-of-service [Ash97]. It may be noted that multi-hour design problems appear primarily for design of traffic or application services networks; note that a model was presented earlier in Section 3.4 for telephone networks.

There is yet another set of design problems where the time factor plays a role. Traditionally, this set of problems has been referred to as *network planning* or *capacity planning* problems arising in transport network design when considered over a planning period or a time horizon. For example, the entire planning period could be two years which is divided into three-month (quarterly) time periods, so there is *new* demand in each time period. Depending on the capabilities provided by the networking technology and the network management system, either new capacity can be added in each period or capacity can be added for the first time only after the elapse of, for example, three time periods. Furthermore, transport network routing done in one period may or may not be reconfigurable in a subsequent period—this would partly depend on reconfigurability cost. Thus, a goal could be to determine the optimal network cost over multiple periods. Note that multi-period problems also have multiple demand matrices. Unlike the multi-hour case, we now have actual *new* or *incremental* demand volumes in each period that need to be physically routed in the networks; such situations are common in transport networks.

In this chapter, we will discuss several models taking into account factors that are primarily applicable to multi-hour or multi-period modeling and design. In Section 11.1, we discuss capacity design for multi-hour traffic that covers network dimensioning (including multi-service case), computational results, and the meaning of multi-hour problem for the capacitated case. In Section 11.2, we present multi-period design models for transport networks (both the uncapacitated and the capacitated case), and show examples on how these models can be combined with models for protection and restoration design presented earlier in Chapter 9.

11.1 MULTI-HOUR DESIGN

In this section, we will present several variants of problems depending on the capabilities of the networking technology. First, we begin with an illustration to show the implication of explicitly considering multi-hour demand volume in the presence of unrestricted routing (and re-routing).

11.1.1 Illustration of Multi-Hour Dimensioning

First, we will discuss a design example by considering a three-node network with bi-directional traffic. Suppose we are given demand volumes for three different hours during the day which we will label as morning, afternoon, and evening; we will refer to this problem as the three-hour design problem. We will also use the term *time window* instead of *hour* since we do not necessarily mean every hour of a day. Clearly, in this example we have three time windows (not really hours). The demand volumes are given in Table 11.1.

There is an important point to note here about multi-hour traffic matrix. The demand volume for a particular time window (hour) is only for that window; it disappears and is *not* added to the next time window. Thus, this scenario is more applicable in traffic networks such as IP networks or circuit-switched networks (also, try to imagine road traffic which can have different traffic volume during the day). The question is: how much capacity is needed to satisfy the multi-hour demand volumes? This problem is somewhat similar to

TABLE 11.1 Data for Three-Hour Design Problem (Three-Node Network)

Demand Pair	Morning (M)	Afternoon (A)	Evening (E)
⟨1,2⟩	5	11	8
⟨1,3⟩	6	13	6
⟨2,3⟩	10	2	7

the network dimensioning problem illustrated through the four-node example discussed in Section 2.4; the main difference is that we need to address network dimensioning in the presence of multi-hour demand volumes.

To understand the multi-hour capacity design problem, we assume for our example that the link capacity variable is a continuous variable and the unit cost of capacity on each link is 1; thus, the total network cost is nothing but the total capacity required. In order to obtain the minimal capacity, a possibility is to consider the *peak* of demand volumes over all time periods, for each demand pair separately. Thus for ⟨1,2⟩, we have a demand volume of 11 (= $\max\{5, 11, 8\}$) (units); similarly, the peak demand volume are 13 and 10 for demand pairs ⟨1,3⟩ and ⟨2,3⟩, respectively. If we now just consider this maximum volume, then we have in essence a single busy hour, and can use the shortest path allocation rule (2.4.13) to determine the total capacity required; this works out to be 34 (= $11+13+10$) units.

Now consider explicitly the multi-hour demand volumes. In fact, we can show that the optimal network cost is less than compared to the cost obtained when just the single (max) hour demand matrix is considered. For this example, the optimal network cost is 27.5 (= 11.5 + 12.5 + 3.5) if we take into account that the flow allocation over different paths can be *different* from one time window to another. The associated optimal flow allocation over different paths is shown in Table 11.2. Note that flows are assumed to be fully rearrangeable regardless of the time of the day. We also see that the shortest path allocation rule (2.4.13), which is applicable in the case of single-demand matrix, does not apply to multi-hour design (we have also had a similar case when we discussed network failures, see Example 9.4).

We will now illustrate two variations of this design problem. We first consider the variation where the demand volume for a demand pair is *not* splittable over multiple paths during a time window. This means non-bifurcated routing, but with the flexibility that the non-bifurcated route chosen can be *different* from one time window to another for a particular demand pair—this can be referred to as the unsplittable rearrangeable configuration. A second variation is that rearrangeability of the non-bifurcated route is *not* allowed from one hour to the next. For both of these variations, the optimal solution is to route the demand volume for ⟨2,3⟩ via path 2-1-3 regardless of the time of the day (Figure 11.1); this is certainly a different solution than the splittable fully-rearrangeable case which we have already discussed. Now, we need 15 units of capacity on link 1-2 and 16 units on link 1-3,

TABLE 11.2 **Three-Node Network Solution: Multi-Hour Demand Volume (Fully Rearrangeable)**

Demand Pair	Route	Morning (M): flow	Afternoon (A): flow	Evening (E): flow
⟨1,2⟩	1-2	5.0	11.0	8.0
	1-3-2	—	—	—
⟨1,3⟩	1-3	6.0	12.5	6.0
	1-2-3	—	0.5	—
⟨2,3⟩	2-3	3.5	2.0	3.5
	2-1-3	6.5	—	3.5

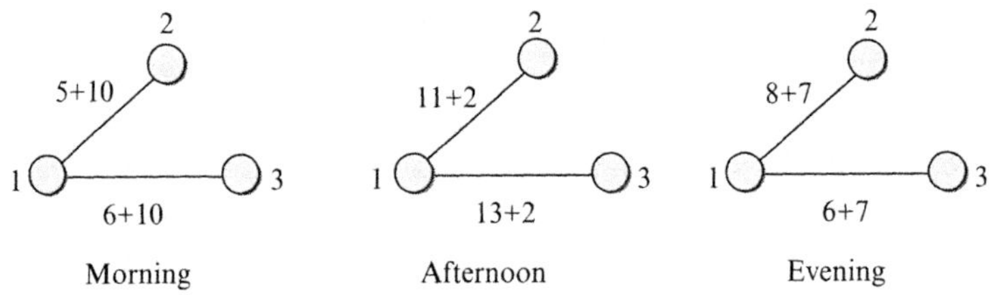

FIGURE 11.1 Three-Node Nonifurcated Solution

thus needing a total of 31 units to route all the traffic. It should be noted that for this example the optimal decision is the same for both variations (unsplittable+rearrangeable and unsplittable+nonrearrangeable), although the optimal solution for both variations may not be the same in general. Incidently, the case of unsplittable non-reconfigurable design with multi-hour traffic results in cheaper design than the case when the single maximum busy hour traffic was used for network design (which also *looks* like unsplittable non-reconfigurable).

The variations illustrated here give the impression that the case of splittable routing, with rearrangeability allowable for different time windows during the day, results in the most economical design. This advantage is noticeable only when the demand volumes between different pairs of nodes peak at different time windows during the day due to the non-coincidence of traffic busy hours (see Exercise 11.1).

11.1.2 Multi-Hour Dimensioning Models

We first consider the case where paths and flows are fully reconfigurable from one time window to another, and we want to consider modular link capacity variables (as opposed to the illustration in Figure 11.1 where the capacity variables were assumed to be continuous).

This model has multiple demand information than the equivalent single-hour modular design Problem (4.3.1). First, we have demand volumes (traffic) for different times of the day (busy hours); we use the new subscript t to denote time variability so that we can incorporate demand volumes which is dependent on time of the day. Since the flow amount and the path chosen can be different at different times during the day, the flow vector $\boldsymbol{x}$, need to reflect this as well. Finally, link capacity $\boldsymbol{y}$ needs to be considered across all time windows; i.e., capacity variables are *not* time-dependent. The entire model is presented below.

***MIP:* D/MH/ML** **Link-Path Formulation**

Modular Links, Multi-Hour, Rearrangeable

indices

$d = 1, 2, ..., D$ demands

$t = 1, 2, ..., T$ traffic busy hours

$p = 1, 2, ..., P_d$ candidate paths for demand d

$e = 1, 2, ..., E$ links

constants

δ_{edp} = 1, if link e belongs to path p realizing demand d; 0, otherwise

h_{dt} volume of demand d at time t

ξ_e cost of one capacity module on link e

M size of the link capacity module

variables

x_{dpt} flow allocated to path p of demand d at time t (continuous non-negative)

y_e capacity of link e expressed in number of modules (non-negative integer)

objective

$$\text{minimize } \boldsymbol{F} = \textstyle\sum_e \xi_e y_e \tag{11.1.1a}$$

constraints

$$\textstyle\sum_p x_{dpt} = h_{dt}, \quad d = 1, 2, ..., D \quad t = 1, 2, ..., T \tag{11.1.1b}$$

$$\textstyle\sum_d \sum_p \delta_{edp} x_{dpt} \le M y_e, \quad e = 1, 2, ..., E \quad t = 1, 2, ..., T. \tag{11.1.1c}$$

In (11.1.1b), we have a separate set of demand constraints for each hour t. The link load on the left-hand side (11.1.1c) is computed independently for each hour t, which must be satisfied by the capacity required for each link e regardless of the time of the day since the capacity constraint (11.1.1c) does in fact couple the flow variables x_{dt} over different hours. It may be noted that the set of candidate paths is assumed to be the same from one hour to another. If the set of candidate paths is different from one hour to another, then the time index t can be incorporated in the description of the set of paths; furthermore, the link-path indicator δ can reflect this change without requiring a major change in the representation of the above model.

It may also be noted that the case of the continuous capacity variable is easily addressed by relaxing the modularity requirement on the capacity variables (Exercises 11.2). As we know from our discussion of linear programming (LP) problems, the continuous case is

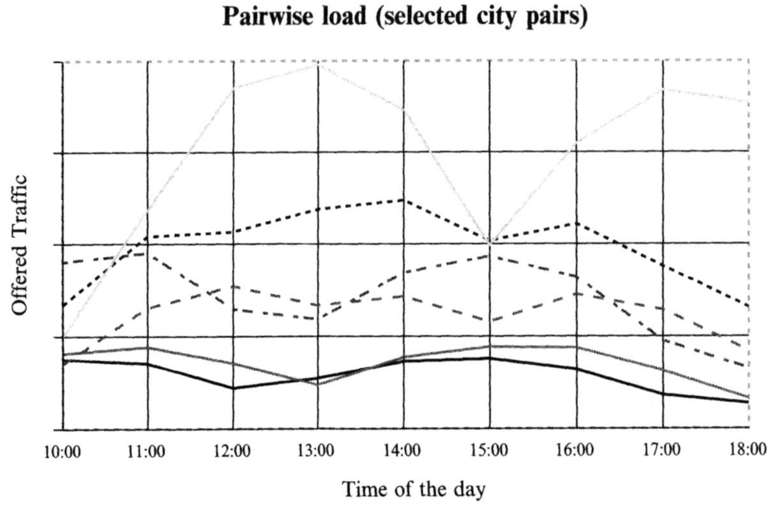

FIGURE 11.2 Traffic Variation for a Selected Set of City Pairs During the Day for a 10-Node Network Spanning Continental U.S. (Time is on Eastern Time Zone in U.S.)

much less time consuming (to solve) compared to the case where some variables, such as the capacity variables, take integer values (also see Chapter 10).

Compare this model with DR-U (9.3.1) (modular case) where we have incorporated failure situations (including normal) in restoration design for the unrestricted reconfiguration case. These two models are very similar (from a formulation point-of-view) with some differences. While the subscript s was used in (9.3.1) to reflect different failure situations (and the normal state), the subscript t is used in (11.1.1) to reflect traffic variation in different hours; also, parameter α_{es} was introduced in (9.3.1) to indicate availability of link capacity in a particular failure situation.

Note that demand volumes can vary significantly from one hour to another in the multi-hour case, especially due to non-coincidence of busy hours. See Figure 11.2 where we have shown the traffic volume variation from 10:00 in the morning to 18:00 in the evening (eastern time zone in U.S.) for a selected set of demand pairs of a 10-node traffic network. Note that some pairs have a dip around 15:00—these are for cities located in the pacific time zone where the local time is 12 noon (lunch hour).

On the other hand, it may be noted that the demand volume is at the maximum value in the normal state ($s = 0$) in (9.3.1); it can be at the same value or smaller (for partial restoration) for each of the failure states. From the viewpoint of the topology, there is also a difference since in (11.1.1) the entire topology is available in each hour while for DR-U. A subset of links is (partially) failed in a failure situation. We refer you to Example 9.4 where differences between failure and demand situations have been illustrated.

Another distinction between (9.3.1) and (11.1.1) is that while the unrestricted reconfiguration in case of failure is not necessarily realistic, a fully-reconfigurable multi-hour design approach has been used in practice, e.g., in the network design of DNHR networks [Ash97]. Thus, we briefly revisit a multi-hour model that can be used for network design of a dynamic routing circuit-switched network (Section 3.4); this particular model uses the notion of load sharing (i.e., arbitrarily splitting demand traffic) among paths and is not the same as the unified algorithm presented in [ACM81] for multi-hour design of DNHR networks. Recall that for circuit-switched networks, we need to address link blocking, as discussed in (3.4.1), using function $F_{et}(\cdot)$ which can be time-dependent to reflect a different grade-of-service (if required) at a different hour during the day. For completeness, we reproduce (3.4.3) below.

***MINP:* D/MH/ML/LS** **Link-Path Formulation**

Multi-Hour Design for Load Sharing with Modular Links

objective

$$\text{minimize } \boldsymbol{F} = \textstyle\sum_e \xi_e y_e \tag{11.1.2a}$$

constraints

$$\textstyle\sum_p x_{dpt} = h_{dt}, \quad d = 1, 2, ..., D \quad t = 1, 2, ..., T \tag{11.1.2b}$$

$$F_{et}(\textstyle\sum_d \sum_p \delta_{edp} x_{dpt}) \le M y_e, \quad e = 1, 2, ..., E \quad t = 1, 2, ..., T. \tag{11.1.2c}$$

Note that the assumption that flow variables are continuous for a load sharing-based network design model for dynamic routing circuit-switched networks is reasonable since demand volume h_{dt} reflects the offered load in *Erl*; this means that flow variables represent proportional allocation of the load that can take a certain path using the concept of load sharing (while minimizing the network cost). It is certainly possible to use the mixed integer programming (MIP) model (11.1.1) instead of (concave) non-linear integer programming formulation (11.1.2) for the network design of dynamic routing of circuit-switched networks based on load sharing; this would require a reinterpretation of demand volume from being given in offered load in (11.1.2) to carried load in (11.1.1) under acceptable quality of service guarantee and factoring in the basic bandwidth unit for each unit of carried load (for example, see [MG97]). The MIP model is particularly attractive when we take into consideration an important technological trend: due to deployment of digital signal rates of high modular capacity (refer to Table 1.1) at switch interfaces, capacity needed for traffic under an acceptable grade-of-service need no longer be approximated to the smallest capacity unit (e.g., DS0). Thus, for many current practical situations, the MIP formulation (11.1.1) can be more suitable for multi-hour design of dynamic routing networks instead of using models such as the non-linear concave programming model (11.1.2). Nevertheless, it is possible to use a piecewise linear approximation of concave dimensioning functions $F_{et}(\cdot)$ and transform Problem (11.1.2) to derive a different MIP formulation (see Exercise 11.3). However, in the remaining discussion, we will only consider models without any concave constraints.

We now return to formulation (11.1.1) and consider an important variation when demand volume for a demand is unsplittable over multiple paths (i.e., non-bifurcated routing) within a particular time window, but a different route may be chosen for the unsplittable flow from one time window to another. This has been illustrated in the three-node example in Section 11.1.1 (for the case of the link capacity variable being continuous). The general model is shown below by introducing the binary variable u for selection of a path within a particular time window.

***IP:* D/MH/ML/R/US** **Link-Path Formulation**

Modular Links, Multi-Hour, Rearrangeable, Unsplittable

variables

u_{dpt} binary variable corresponding to the flow allocated to path p of demand d at time t

y_e capacity of link e expressed in the number of modules (non-negative integer)

objective

$$\text{minimize } \boldsymbol{F} = \sum_e \xi_e y_e \tag{11.1.3a}$$

constraints

$$\sum_p u_{dpt} = 1, \quad d = 1, 2, ..., D \quad t = 1, 2, ..., T \tag{11.1.3b}$$

$$\sum_d h_{dt} \sum_p \delta_{edp} u_{dpt} \le M y_e, \quad e = 1, 2, ..., E \quad t = 1, 2, ..., T. \tag{11.1.3c}$$

A further restriction is when we assume that rearrangeability of a path is *not* allowed from one time window to another; that is, the selected route remains the same regardless of the time of the day. However, the capacity still needs to consider and reflect the demand volume variation from one hour to another.

***IP:* D/MH/ML/NR/US** **Link-Path Formulation**

Modular Links, Multi-Hour, Non-Rearrangeable, Unsplittable

variables

u_{dp} binary variable corresponding to the flow allocated to path p of demand d

y_e capacity of link e expressed in the number of modules (non-negative integer)

objective

$$\text{minimize } \boldsymbol{F} = \sum_e \xi_e y_e \tag{11.1.4a}$$

constraints

$$\sum_p u_{dp} = 1, \quad d = 1, 2, ..., D \tag{11.1.4b}$$

$$\sum_d h_{dt} \sum_p \delta_{edp} u_{dp} \le M y_e, \quad e = 1, 2, ..., E \quad t = 1, 2, ..., T. \tag{11.1.4c}$$

TABLE 11.3 **Multi-Hour Model Comparison**

	Model (11.1.1): Rearrangeable	Model (11.1.3): Rearrangeable, Unsplittable	Model (11.1.4): Non-Rearrangeable Unsplittable
Number of routing/ flow variables	$DT\bar{P}$ (continuous)	$DT\bar{P}$ (binary)	$D\bar{P}$ (binary)
Number of capacity variables	E (integer)	E (integer)	E (integer)
Number of constraints	$DT + ET$	$DT + ET$	$D + ET$

Note that by dropping the subscript t from path decision vector $\boldsymbol{u}$, we have easily tailored formulation (11.1.3) to (11.1.4) to address non-rearrangability. Note that model (11.1.4) is not the same as the case when only a single (busy-hour) traffic matrix for all hours is chosen. To see this, note that we actually consider the following demand volume

$$\hat{h}_d = \max\ \{h_{dt} : t = 1, 2, ..., T\},$$

which is *peak* of demand volume over time for each demand d, i.e., in essence, $\hat{h}_d$ corresponds to a single-maximum busy hour. In turn, for each $e(e = 1, 2, ..., E)$ and $t(t = 1, 2, ..., T)$, we have

$$\textstyle\sum_d h_{dt} \sum_p \delta_{edp} u_{dp} \leq \sum_d \hat{h}_d \sum_p \delta_{edp} u_{dp}.$$

Thus, the capacity on a link e due to the term on the left-hand side can be smaller than the capacity for the term on the right-hand side; this is true at least for some links while minimizing the total cost. Incidently, we have already illustrated the cost difference due to single busy-hour and multiple busy-hour demand matrix (without rearrangeability) in the example presented in Section 11.1.1.

Finally, note that while we discuss models (11.1.1) and (11.1.3) for traffic networks due to rearrangeability of traffic during the day, it is conceivable that these models can be suitable for (future) transport networks that incorporates demand dynamics during the day along with time-dependent reconfigurability (refer to Section 9.6).

Now consider the impact of problem size from the viewpoint of the number of variables and constraints. For models considered so far in this section, this information is shown in Table 11.3 assuming that the average number of candidate paths per demand is denoted by $\bar{P}$. Especially note that the introduction of the time factor increases the number of routing/flow variables as well as the number of constraints which in turn means that the ensuing problems are much larger in size. An important point to consider is how many busy-hour demand volume matrices to use in practice. This would depend on conducting statistical analysis to determine significance of variability of traffic so as to reduce the number of time windows from 24 hours in a day to a more manageable number. For example, in the network design of

DNHR circuit-switched networks, 24 hours of a weekday was aggregated to 10 busy-hour time windows ("load set periods") and for 24 hours of a weekend day to 5 load set periods [Ash97]. In fact, it was found that the total of 15 load set periods together for weekdays and weekends captured the load variability during the day and resulted in a cost-effective network design.

11.1.3 Multiple Services Case

In addition to multiple busy hours, we sometimes need to consider different service types in each busy-hour which share the same network capacity. This in fact adds another dimension to variants of network design problems considered in this book. For the purpose of network design modeling, service types can be voice, data, and video in an integrated network, or they can be different services that can be available to different groups of end customers. While we have not explicitly discussed the multi-service case so far in this book, the basic elements of considering this variation can be seen from models introduced in Chapter 4. In this section, we present some special cases.

There are two possibilities on how multiple services can be treated. If all services can fully share capacity, then different services can be collapsed into one service class for the purpose of design modeling. For example, if we have I service classes, then we have I traffic matrices for each busy hour, thus totaling $I \times T$ traffic matrices. Notice from Table 11.3 that this change would again impact the number of variables and constraints. Thus, a network (and technology) capable of considering full share among different services would allow the option of an aggregated demand volume for all services together (for each demand pair) instead of doing it separately for each service. Thus, a formulation such as the one given in (11.1.1) is applicable where multiple services can be collapsed/aggregated into a single-service class.

On the other hand, in many situations, services may not be combined while the capacity is shared among different services, or when different business units of a network provider require that the demand needed for each business unit be *marked* or provisioned separately for the purpose of network design (e.g., for ease of manageability as well as accountability). This is usually the case where for each service (and for each demand), a separate tunnel or a virtual path must be established, or when modular flows need to be considered to separate different services. The variation of formulation (11.1.3) can be applicable for the multi-service case. We introduce index i to reflect the service class dimension where the notion of tunneling is used for service class differentiation.

***IP:* D/MH/MH/ML/NS** **Link-Path Formulation**

Modular Links, Multi-Hour/Multi-Service, Rearrangeable, Unsplittable

indices

$d = 1, 2, ..., D$	demands
$i = 1, 2, ..., I$	services
$t = 1, 2, ..., T$	traffic hours
$p = 1, 2, ..., P_{dti}$	candidate paths for demand d in time t for service i
$e = 1, 2, ..., E$	links

constants

δ_{edpti} = 1, if link e belongs to path p realizing demand d for service type i in time window t; 0, otherwise
h_{dti} volume of demand d, service i at time t
ξ_e cost of one capacity module on link e
M size of the link capacity module

variables

u_{dpti} binary variable corresponding to the flow allocated to path p of service i for demand d at time t
y_e capacity of link e expressed in the number of modules (non-negative integer)

objective

$$\text{minimize } \boldsymbol{F} = \textstyle\sum_e \xi_e y_e \tag{11.1.5a}$$

constraints

$$\textstyle\sum_p u_{dpti} = 1, \quad i = 1, 2, ..., I \quad d = 1, 2, ..., D \quad t = 1, 2, ..., T \tag{11.1.5b}$$

$$\textstyle\sum_d \sum_i h_{dti} \sum_p \delta_{edpti} u_{dpti} \le M y_e, \quad e = 1, 2, ..., E \quad t = 1, 2, ..., T. \tag{11.1.5c}$$

It is possible that the set of candidate paths is the same for different time windows during the day and among different services for a particular demand pair (which can be reflected by changing P_{dti} to P_d); consequently, δ_{edpti} can be replaced by δ_{edp}. We have deliberately included the subscripts for the ease of readability of the formulation. It is also worthwhile to note that introduction of service class index i is not actually necessary *if* we redefine the meaning of demand d itself to uniquely identify a service *and* a demand pair (see Section 4.6.2 for a discussion on such interpretation and its implication on formulations such as (11.1.3)). Another variation is to consider modular flow allocation for different demands and services by drawing a parallel to the model presented in (4.2.11); this will be discussed later in this chapter since it is more appropriate in the context of multi-period than multi-hour.

11.1.4 Algorithmic Approaches

While commercial LP and MIP solvers can possibly be used for small to moderate size problems, more efficient approaches are desirable for large-scale problems. In Chapter 5 and further in Chapter 10, we have discussed several approaches for solving specialized large-scale problems. In this section, we will highlight two approaches for formulation (11.1.5); 1) Lagrangian-based dual-subgradient method and 2) evolutionary algorithm (EA). Certainly, other approaches discussed in Chapters 5 and 10 are applicable to several design models discussed so far in this chapter; the interested reader may want to pursue the understanding of various such algorithmic approaches (see Exercises 11.4 and 11.5).

Lagrangian-Relaxation (LR) based Dual Approach

Recall that in this approach the primal problem is transformed by relaxing constraints (or a subset of them) and then solved in the dual variable space (Section 5.4.1). For formulation

(11.1.5), we dualize with respect to (11.1.5c) by associating dual multipliers π_{et}. The Lagrangian is:

$$\begin{aligned} L(\boldsymbol{u}, \boldsymbol{y}; \boldsymbol{\pi}) &= \sum_e \xi_e y_e + \sum_e \sum_t \pi_{et} \left(\sum_d \sum_i h_{dti} \sum \delta_{edpti} u_{dpti} - M y_e \right) \\ &= \sum_e (\xi_e - M \sum_t \pi_{et}) y_e + \sum_t \sum_d \sum_i h_{dti} \sum_p \sum_e \pi_{et} \delta_{edpti} u_{dpti}. \end{aligned}$$

From the rearrangement shown above, it is easy to see that once dual multiplier $\boldsymbol{\pi}$ (≥ 0) is given, the Lagrangian can be decoupled into two separate subproblems, one involving $\boldsymbol{u}$ and the other involving $\boldsymbol{y}$. The dual problem is to maximize $W(\boldsymbol{\pi})$ over $\boldsymbol{\pi} \geq \mathbf{0}$, where $W(\boldsymbol{\pi}) = \min_{\boldsymbol{u},\boldsymbol{y}} L(\boldsymbol{u}, \boldsymbol{y}; \boldsymbol{\pi})$. Assume that we are currently at dual iteration k and the dual multiplier is denoted by $\boldsymbol{\pi}^k = (\pi^k_{et} : e = 1, 2, ..., E,\ t = 1, 2, ..., I)$. Then, at iteration k, for (part of) the last term in the expression associated with $\boldsymbol{u}$ in the Lagrangian, we can write:

$$\zeta_{dpti} = \sum_e \pi^k_{et} \delta_{edpti} \quad d = 1, 2, .., D \quad t = 1, 2, ..., T \quad i = 1, 2, ..., I \quad p = 1, 2, ..., P_{dti}. \tag{11.1.6}$$

Thus, dual multiplier $\boldsymbol{\pi}^k$ is the sole contributor to determining cost, ζ_{dpti}, of path p for each d, t, i (at iteration k); for clarity, we can indicate this dependency on $\boldsymbol{\pi}^k$ by using instead $\zeta_{dpti}(\boldsymbol{\pi}^k)$, i.e.,

$$\zeta_{dpti}(\boldsymbol{\pi}^k) = \sum_e \pi^k_{et} \delta_{edpti}$$

for each d, t, i, p. From constraint (11.1.5b), we can also see that the subproblem related to $\boldsymbol{u}$ can be further subdivided into decoupled subproblems for each d, t, i since there is no coupling (in terms of constraints) connecting d, t, i. That is, the *atomic* subproblem is

$$\begin{aligned} &\textbf{\textit{minimize}} \quad \sum_p \zeta_{dpti}(\boldsymbol{\pi}^k)\, u_{dpti} \\ &\textbf{\textit{subject to}} \quad \sum_p u_{dpti} = 1 \qquad (u_{dpti} \text{ binary}) \end{aligned} \tag{11.1.7}$$

for each d, t, i separately. This is easily solvable since for each atomic subproblem, we need to identify the path p for which the path cost $\zeta_{dpti}(\boldsymbol{\pi}^k)$ is the smallest and we set the corresponding u_{dpti} to 1, i.e., the shortest path (dictated by the current value of $\boldsymbol{\pi}^k$) for each d, t, i. We repeat this procedure for each d, t, i (for a given $\boldsymbol{\pi}^k$).

Furthermore, the subproblem related to $\boldsymbol{y}$ can also be subdivided into atomic subproblems for each link e:

$$\begin{aligned} &\textbf{\textit{minimize}} \quad (\xi_e - M \sum_t \pi^k_{et})\, y_e \\ &\textbf{\textit{subject to}} \quad y_e \geq 0. \end{aligned} \tag{11.1.8}$$

The solution for the above subproblem has a peculiarity since y_e is infinite (∞) if the condition $\xi_e < M \sum_t \pi^k_{ef}$ holds. In the actual implementation of the algorithm, a large value for y_e is sufficient to use as an upper bound (in place of infinity) to maintain the overall feasibility of the original (primal) Problem (11.1.5) (see Section 5.4.1). Recall that y_e is the capacity of link e, which is to be determined; at the same time, the value of y_e as the solution to subproblem (11.1.8) is not meant for the original problem, but only for this $\boldsymbol{\pi}$-dependent dual subproblem at iteration k.

Next, we need to determine a dual subgradient. If at iteration k for the dual problem, the path index that solves atomic subproblem (11.1.7) in $\boldsymbol{u}$ is denoted by $\hat{p}_k$ and the optimal y_e for the other subproblem (11.1.8) is denoted by $\hat{y}_e^k$, then a dual subgradient at iteration k is given by

$$\left.\frac{\partial W(\pi)}{\partial \pi_{et}}\right|_{\pi = \pi^k} = \sum_d \sum_i h_{dti} \delta_{ed\hat{p}_k ti} - M\hat{y}_e^k, \quad e = 1, 2, ..., E \quad t = 1, 2, ..., T.$$

The rest of of iterative steps in regard to updating the dual multiplier $\pi (\geq 0)$ is the same as discussed in Algorithm 5.8 in Section 5.4.1.

Evolutionary Approach

In the case of an evolutionary approach (refer to Section 5.3.3), we need to consider chromosome mapping of the candidate path list and a fitness function (which is to be maximized). Given a large positive number, Δ, we can use the following fitness function

$$\boldsymbol{F}(\boldsymbol{u}) = \Delta - \sum_e \xi_e \left\lceil \max_{t=1,2,..,T} \left\{ \sum_d \sum_i h_{dti} \sum_p \delta_{edpti} u_{dpti} \right\} \Big/ M \right\rceil \tag{11.1.9}$$

since this is nothing but another representation of the objective function given in (11.1.5a) combined with constraint (11.1.5c) (Exercise 11.6). Also note that with this transformation, we are left with only the set of flow variables $\boldsymbol{u}$, and that we are to maximize (11.1.9) given constraint (11.1.5b).

Note the binary route decision vector $\boldsymbol{u}$ corresponds to all the candidate paths. In regard to chromosome mapping, each candidate path can thus be given a bit value in the chromosome string. While this results in a string which is as long as the total number of candidate paths (over all of d, t, i), it also causes another problem. For example, two consecutive bits, due to mutation, can be both set to 1 during the evolution which may correspond to two paths for a specific d, t, i, which violates (11.1.5b). A better representation is to consider the set of *all* candidate paths for a specific d, t, i in a single pool. Suppose we have eight candidate paths for a specific d, t, i — they can be collectively represented using three bits (instead of eight bits) where each bit combination reflects the selection of a valid path that satisfies (11.1.5b). Note that this works best when the number of paths, P_d, in each candidate set of paths is a power of 2. If the number of candidate paths is other than a power of 2, then $\lceil \log_2 P_d \rceil$ bits can be used as long an artificially high penalty cost is assigned for the bit combination that is associated with a fictitious path. Alternately, mutation and cross-over process (see Section 5.3.3) should be such that it allows to filter out invalid combinations of paths.

11.1.5 *Computational Results*

Although we have presented several formulations so far in this chapter, we will present computational results only for formulation (11.1.5); we are then aligned with the discussion

TABLE 11.4 Size Information for Test Networks (All Have Three Busy Hours and Two Service Classes)

Network	No. of Nodes	No. of Demand Pairs	No. of Links	No. of Paths per Demand Pair	No. of Binary Variables	No. of Constraints
R7	7	21	14	6	756	210
R10	10	45	27	10	2,700	432
R15	15	105	33	15	9,450	828
A10	10	45	28	7	1,890	438
A12	12	66	25	7	2,772	546
A26	26	325	30	8	15,600	2,130
A50	50	1,225	82	8	58,800	7,842

on algorithmic approaches. We have considered seven different test networks (Figure 11.3, Table 11.4) each with two service classes and three busy hours. The first three test problems, R7, R10, and R15, are extracted from real networks, including the demand volume pattern at different times during the day for the first traffic type [Med94b]. Due to the non-availability of a measurement-based demand volume for the second traffic type, the demand volume was uniformly generated for the second traffic class from the volume for the first traffic class for these three problems. Preserving the traffic patterns for different hours, the demand volume is then translated to units in Mbps using an equivalent bandwidth approach (see, for example, [Med95]). The topologies for problem A10, A12, and A26 are drawn from the literature (for example, see [LY92]); the topology for the final test problem, A50, is a mixture of a process that included randomly generating a topology followed by manual intervention to provide connectivity. For the second set of test problems (i.e., A10, A12, A26, and A50), the traffic matrix for each service type and each busy hour is originally generated randomly from a uniform distribution which is then mapped to demand volumes in Mbps.

Link Cost Structure

The link modularity M for all test problems was assumed to be 155 to correspond to a 155-Mbps link capacity unit. The cost of one 155-Mbps module on a link consists of two components: 1) a termination cost and 2) a distance-based cost. We use 100 as the cost of each termination port (on each end) and 0.1 as the distance cost per mile. This means that we can write the modular link capacity cost of link e as $\xi_e = 2 \times 100 + 0.1 \times distance_e$, where $distance_e$ is the distance in miles for a 155-Mbps pipe for link e. Note that the termination cost is the dominant cost here which is realistic in most current networks; the dominance of termination cost over distance-based cost may not be true in future networks or certain types of networks. The advantage of breaking down a link capacity cost in this manner into two parts is that suitable termination and distance-based cost components can be used, as applicable in a particular network, *without* needing to change anything in formulation (11.1.5).

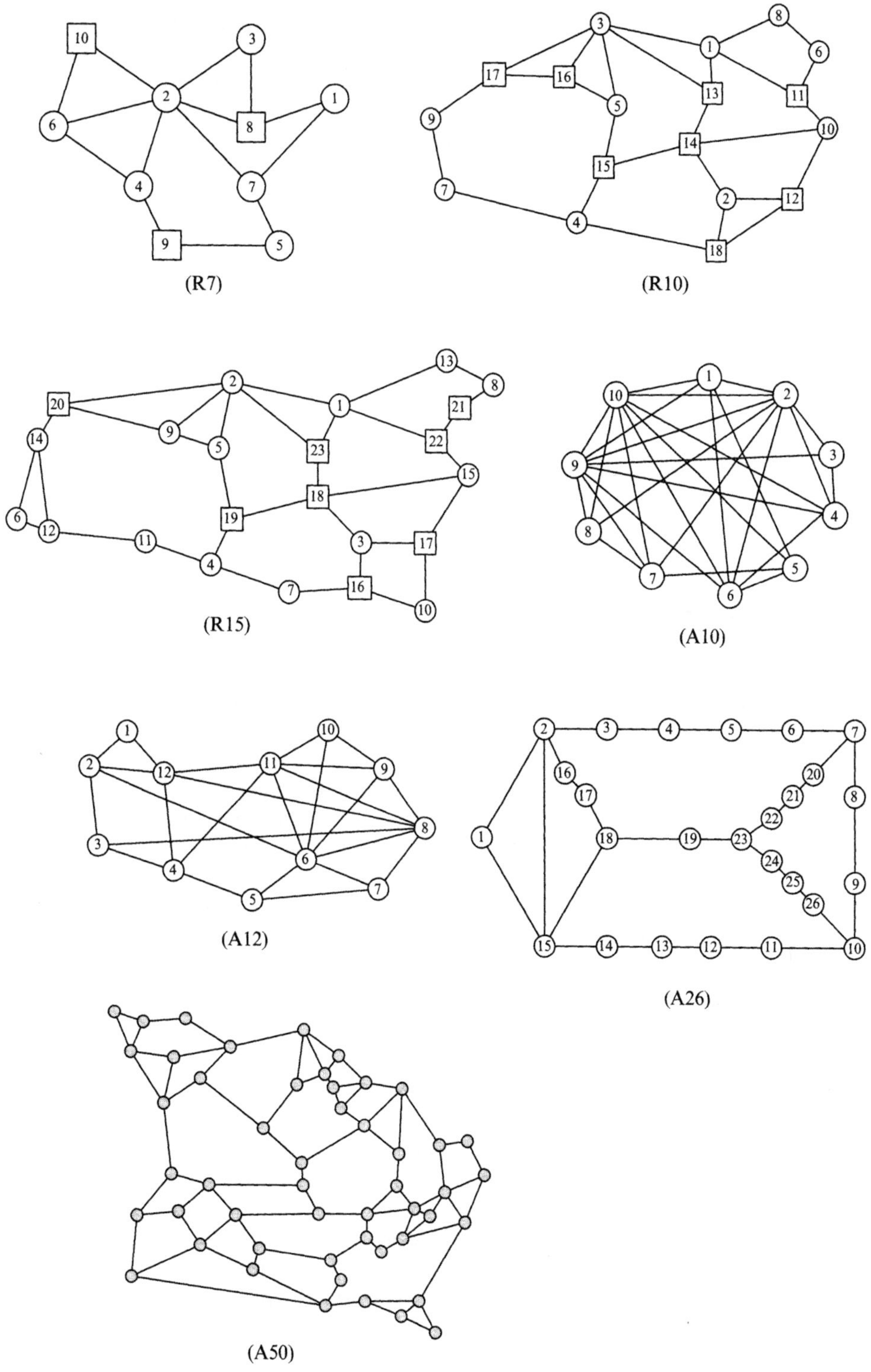

FIGURE 11.3 Topology of Test Networks

TABLE 11.5 Computation Time (Normalized to R7 with SGOPT) and Network Cost (Relative to Best Solution from Hybrid Approach)

	Computation Time			Relative Cost (in %)	
3-9	SGOPT	EA	CPLEX (LP-relaxed)	SGOPT	EA
R7	1.0	3.7	0.1	1.75	10.03
R10	7.0	13.0	0.3	0.77	4.80
R15	34.3	35.4	1.7	1.50	8.08
A10	2.6	8.5	0.2	6.83	-0.59
A12	4.3	13.2	0.5	0.40	8.27
A26	80.9	146.2	10.1	0.00	9.83
A50	451.7	788.2	336.0	0.00	5.48

Computation Time

First, we report our attempt to solve test problems using the CPLEX solver [CPL99]. The LP relaxation of Problem (11.1.5) is where all binary routing and capacity variables are relaxed to take continuous values (LP-relaxed). The MIP model relaxation (MIP-relaxed) is where routing variables were kept real while capacity variables took integral values. For both the MIP-relaxed version and the original formulation, a CPLEX MIP solver could solve only problem R7 and could not solve the other problems even after running for a significant amount time (see the number of variables and constraints for each test problem in Table 11.4). This does not mean to suggest any handicap of CPLEX, per se; this only points to the fact that some models are inherently hard to solve with a standard MIP solver, and that the development of specialized algorithms such as the ones presented here may be necessary. Needless to say, all test examples were solvable with CPLEX for the LP-relaxed version.

Comparing Results

We now discuss results using the Lagrangian-based dual subgradient optimization approach (SGOPT) and EA. We also tested a hybrid approach where the solution for SGOPT was included in the initial population in EA (for another approach called the generalized proximal point method and its associated results as well as other details, see [MT00b]). In Table 11.5, we give comparative information on the computation time as well as the total network cost. All of the time information has been normalized with respect to the computation time for solving R7 using SGOPT. The network cost has been similarly normalized for each test problem in regard to the lowest network cost obtained using the hybrid approach. First, we note that if we count both computation time and network cost, SGOPT is a successful approach. EA is more time-consuming than SGOPT; note that computation time for EA is for a specific set of parameters used for mutation and crossover strategies; altogether, 16 different strategies were run and the network cost for EA reflects the best cost.

An Interesting Observation

There is another reason to consider the hybrid approach. Recall the path cost given in (11.1.6). If the same set of candidate paths are used irrespective of service class, then subscript i from δ_{dpti} can be dropped. Note that dual multiplier, π^k_{et}, for link e is dependent on the time window, but not on service class. Thus, the path cost $\zeta_{dpti}(\boldsymbol{\pi}^k)$ is insensitive to service class differentiation in SGOPT, i.e.,

$$\zeta_{dt\breve{i}p}(\boldsymbol{\pi}^k) = \zeta_{dt\tilde{i}p}(\boldsymbol{\pi}^k) \quad \text{for } \breve{i} \neg \tilde{i}.$$

This means that the atomic subproblem (11.1.7) when solved for a specific d and t but for different i's cannot generate a solution $(\boldsymbol{u})$ where two different service classes for a demand pair in a particular time window can have different optimal routes. However, EA does not get stuck in this trap while it may not necessarily be effective in always obtaining the lowest cost. Thus, the hybrid approach provides a marriage between SGOPT and EA to avoid such traps.

How Much Improvement Over Shortest Path-Based Heuristic?

A heuristic approach for solving the problem considered here would be to use a distance-based shortest path heuristic to route the demand on a single path between origin and destination first, then separately for each hour, and finally taking the maximum capacity required on each link by using the maximum over all the hours subject to modularity requirement. We have made a comparison between this heuristic and the Lagrangian-based dual approach, SGOPT. We found that for problem R7, R10, and R15, the solution obtained from the shortest-path based heuristic is 19.51%, 6.27%, and 9.47% more costly than that of SGOPT.

A General Remark

While we found SGOPT to be in general better than EA (in terms of network cost), note that for A10, EA shows a negative percentage—this means that EA from a random initial population gave a *lower* cost than the cost from the hybrid approach where the solution of SGOPT was included in the initial population in EA; this also suggests that for EA more tweaking is necessary to get to a better solution. Note that this is also the test example for which SGOPT is the furthest away from the lowest cost solution. There was no specific cause found for this anomaly. This essentially indicates that it is often possible to find an example where a method may not work as well as others. Finally, the implication of the results on network cost should be understood only in the context of an actual practical design problem a network designer may encounter. In many cases, 3% to 5% from the best solution is still acceptable to a network designer, especially since the projected demand used for such analysis cannot completely avoid any forecasting error or missed projection.

Finally, we present a general remark about the duality gap. A common perception is that the duality gap is a good measure about the performance of an algorithm. However, this is not necessarily true for modular capacity design. To illustrate this point, consider a three-node network with a single-service class, a single-load hour (thus, we will ignore the subscripts d and s), and $M = 1$. Assume that the traffic demand is uniform for each node-pair and is given as $h_d = h$ ($d = 1, 2, 3$). We also set $\xi_e = 1$. We are only interested in the value of h in the range $0 < h \leq 2/3$. For the relaxed LP problem (i.e., allowing capacity variables to take real values), the minimum cost is $3h$ (i.e., capacity of h is assigned to each link); this is also the dual optimal cost. Now, assume that the capacity variables are integral. For the same demand set, we now need two of the three links to have one unit of capacity each, and the third link to be of zero capacity (since the demand for this end point can be routed over the other two links due to ample capacity availability); thus, the minimum optimal cost is 2 for this integer program. Note that this integer optimal cost is $\frac{100(2-3h)}{3h}\%$ greater than the relaxed LP optimal solution for h in the range $0 < h \leq 2/3$; this also gives the best duality gap possible for the integer program. If we use h to be 0.6, then the duality gap is already at 11.11%; on the other hand, if h is reduced to 0.1, the duality gap jumps to 566.67%! Thus, the duality gap is not always a good indicator of the quality of a solution, especially when the traffic demand is low compared to the modular capacity of a link.

11.1.6 Capacitated Case: Multi-Hour Routing

The capacitated case refers to the situation when the network already has capacity but multiple busy hours of demand needs to be considered for routing/flow optimization and/or virtual tunnel establishment and reconfiguration during capacity management cycle of network management. We first consider the case when the route/flow are rearrangeable from one hour to another, and suppose our goal is to minimize the routing cost. Thus, as a counterpart to the dimensioning Problem (11.1.1), we have the following model.

***LP:* A/MH/R** **Link-Path Formulation**

Multi-Hour, Rearrangeable, Capacitated

indices

$d = 1, 2, ..., D$ demands

$t = 1, 2, ..., T$ time of the day index

$p = 1, 2, ..., P_d$ candidate paths for demand d

$e = 1, 2, ..., E$ links

constants

δ_{edp} = 1, if link e belongs to path p realizing demand d; 0, otherwise

h_{dt} volume of demand d at time t

ζ_{dpt} unit routing cost on path p for demand d in time window t

c_e capacity of link e

variables

x_{dpt} flow allocated to path p of demand d at time t (continuous non-negative)

objective

$$\text{minimize } \boldsymbol{F} = \sum_d \sum_p \zeta_{dpt} x_{dpt} \tag{11.1.10a}$$

constraints

$$\sum_p x_{dpt} = h_{dt}, \quad d = 1, 2, ..., D \quad t = 1, 2, ..., T \tag{11.1.10b}$$

$$\sum_d \sum_p \delta_{edp} x_{dpt} \leq c_e, \quad e = 1, 2, ..., E \quad t = 1, 2, ..., T. \tag{11.1.10c}$$

In the above formulation, we assume that the problem is feasible (otherwise, we must add capacity as quickly as possible!). By closely inspecting the above model, it can be seen that due to rearrangeability, the routing optimization problem can be solved *separately* for *each* time window since there is no coupling constraints between time windows once the capacity is given. This is a simple but important point to note; thus it is not necessary to include summation over t in the objective (11.1.10a).

There is still a possibility where the capacitated problem is such that the network does not have enough capacity to carry the demand. This situation arises primarily in traffic networks, specifically in blocking networks, where not all traffic may be admitted. To ensure feasibility of the mathematical formulation, we are tempted to use

$$\sum_p x_{dpt} \leq h_{dt} \quad d = 1, 2, ..., D \quad t = 1, 2, ..., T$$

instead of (11.1.10b) in formulation (11.1.10). Note that this will result in the optimal solution where the allocation vector $\boldsymbol{x}$ is set to 0! This is because the function is minimized and the cost coefficients ζ_{dpt} are non-negative. Thus, in traffic networks where we have the scenario of all traffic not possibly being admitted, a more useful objective is to consider revenue maximization (for example, see [Cha89]). To make it more general, we discuss the revenue optimization case when multiple services are present. For each service type and for each demand, a separate unit revenue weight may be used. Furthermore, we need to take into account the bandwidth weight of each service type.

***LP:* A/MH/MS/RM** **Link-Path Formulation**

Time-Dependent Multi-Service Revenue Maximization

constants

- h_{dti} projected (goal) volume of demand d for service i at time t
- η_{dpi} unit revenue for demand d in time window t for service i
- L_i bandwidth unit for service i

variables

- x_{dpti} flow allocated to path p of demand d for service i at time t (continuous non-negative)

objective

$$\text{maximize } \boldsymbol{F} = \sum_d \sum_i \sum_p \eta_{dti} x_{dpti} \tag{11.1.11a}$$

constraints

$$\sum_p x_{dpti} \leq h_{dti}, \quad i = 1, 2, ..., I \quad d = 1, 2, ..., D \quad t = 1, 2, ..., T \tag{11.1.11b}$$

$$\sum_i L_i \sum_d \sum_p \delta_{edp} x_{dpti} \leq c_e, \quad e = 1, 2, ..., E \quad t = 1, 2, ..., T. \tag{11.1.11c}$$

Note that the overall goal is to maximize revenue where the unit revenue is service-dependent, but not path-dependent. Similar to (11.1.10), the revenue maximization model (11.1.11) can be solved independently for each time window to determine the best routing and flow for each window since there is no coupling constraints between time windows; thus summation over t is not necessary in the objective function. Since the unit revenue and the demand volume is time-dependent, the optimal route/flow realized for revenue maximization will vary from one hour to another. An important remark in regard to (11.1.11) is that fairness to a service and demand may also be an issue while maximizing total revenue (see Chapters 8 and 13). Thus, this aspect may need to be addressed as well.

Multi-hour capacitated scenario can be useful in other situations as well. Recall the case of shortest-path routing presented in Chapter 7 where we considered determination of an optimal link weight system for a given traffic demand and capacity. While the capacity is fixed, the traffic matrix is different at different hours during the day. If this variability from one hour to another is significantly different, then it may be desirable to consider a time-window–based traffic matrix. If this is the case, for each traffic matrix that corresponds to a particular time window, a link weight system can be generated that is *optimal* with respect to the objective/goal for the network; that is, the actual values of the optimal link weight system can be different for each time-dependent traffic matrix. In other words, the link weight system which is to be loaded to routers in the network can be different at different times during the course of a day, thus resulting in a dynamic or time-dependent link weight system. While this works conceptually, its applicability in a practical network should only be considered without causing any undue side effects.

11.2 MULTI-PERIOD DESIGN

Multi-period design (MPD) refers to network design problems that span over a time horizon in terms of weeks to months, and sometimes even to several years. In general, MPD models are primarily applicable in transport networks while multi-hour design discussed above is applicable in traffic networks (such as circuit-switched or IP networks). An important distinction between multi-period and multi-hour is the interpretation of demand volume. In the multi-hour case, demand volume changes from one hour to another and the demand for a prior hour disappears as a new demand surfaces. On the other hand, in the multi-period case, the demand volume for each time period is new, meaning that this volume is in *addition* to the demand volume that was present in prior periods; this newness of demand in a subsequent time period is sometimes better understood as *incremental* demand volume.

When we consider multiple periods, there are a few important issues to consider (besides the incremental demand volume): 1) the cost structure may change over time (e.g., due to economic discounting); 2) demand routed in one time window may have maintenance cost in a subsequent time window, and 3) the capacity expansion can happen over the entire time horizon. In this section, we consider a sampling of models that are related to these aspects.

11.2.1 Capacity Planning

Recall that an important aspect about MPD is that the demand volume given in each time period is new (incremental) demand volume. Any demand volume in a particular time period must be routed in that time unit using the available paths and capacity in that time period, i.e., rearrangeability is not allowed (later we will discuss the situation where this requirement is relaxed). Secondly, there can be two cost components: one for installing new capacity on a link, and the other for maintenance of the existing capacity already installed in prior periods. We will assume here that only one type of demand module is considered. Note that the models presented in this section can be extended to consider multiple modular units using extensions outlined in Section 4.3.1.

***MIP:* D/MPD/ML** **Link-Path Formulation**

MPD, Modular Links

indices

$d = 1, 2, ..., D$ demands

$t, \tau = 1, 2, ..., \mathcal{T}$ planning period ($\mathcal{T}$: time horizon)

$p = 1, 2, ..., P_{d\tau}$ candidate paths for demand d in period τ

$e = 1, 2, ..., E$ links

constants

$\delta_{edp\tau}$ = 1, if link e belongs to path p realizing demand d in time period τ; 0, otherwise

$h_{d\tau} (\geq 0)$ new (incremental) demand volume for demand d in period τ

$\xi'_{e\tau}$ installation cost of one capacity module on link e for period τ

$\xi''_{e\tau}$ maintenance cost of one capacity module on link e during period τ for capacity installed in prior time period(s)

M size of the link capacity module

variables

$x_{dp\tau}$ (non-negative) flow allocated to path p of demand d at time τ

$y_{e\tau}$ (new) capacity of link e expressed in the number of modules (non-negative integer) needed in time period τ

objective

$$\text{minimize } \boldsymbol{F} = \sum_{\tau} \sum_{e} \left(\xi'_{e\tau} y_{e\tau} + \xi''_{e\tau} \sum_{t<\tau} y_{et} \right) \tag{11.2.1a}$$

constraints

$$\sum_{p} x_{dp\tau} = h_{d\tau}, \quad d = 1, 2, ..., D \quad \tau = 1, 2, ..., \mathcal{T} \tag{11.2.1b}$$

$$\sum_{d} \sum_{p} \delta_{edp\tau} x_{dp\tau} \leq M y_{e\tau}, \quad e = 1, 2, ..., E \quad \tau = 1, 2, ..., \mathcal{T}. \tag{11.2.1c}$$

We need to make a couple of important remarks about the cost function. Note that it includes the link installation cost and the link maintenance cost. In large network planning and design, the link installation cost is considered under CapEx while the link maintainance cost is considered under OpEx. Recall that traditionally, CapEx and OpEx are considered under separate budgetary authorities and organizations within a network provider (Section 1.7). This model reflects above shows that it is sometimes necessary to consider two different budgetary considerations under a unified model to see the overall network cost, especially for multi-period problems.

Secondly, there is another way to represent the cost if we rearrange the terms using the following alternate interpretation of the link cost: if we install capacity in period τ, it will incur maintenance costs in *all* subsequent periods (including period τ) until the end of the planning horizon. Then, overall the link capacity $y_{e\tau}$ has the following unit cost:

$$\xi'_{e\tau} + \textstyle\sum_{t\geq\tau}\xi''_{e\tau}$$

Thus, the total cost, given in (11.2.1a), can be rewritten as:

$$\boldsymbol{F} = \textstyle\sum_{\tau}\sum_{e}\xi_{e\tau}y_{e\tau} \quad \text{where} \quad \xi_{e\tau} := \xi'_{e\tau} + \sum_{t\geq\tau}\xi''_{e\tau}. \tag{11.2.2}$$

The benefit of writing the cost function (11.2.2) in this format is that it is easy to see that the design problem, minimization of (11.2.2) subject to (11.2.1b) and (11.2.1c) (with non-negative variables), can actually be completely decoupled into $\mathcal{T}$-independent problems! Furthermore, the aggregated cost component, $\xi_{e\tau}$, provides a sense that although CapEx and OpEx cost components are needed to be considered for the entire planning horizon, for modeling purpose it is not *always* necessary to model them completely separately, at least for models such as (11.2.1).

The fact that the above model can be decoupled into $\mathcal{T}$-independent problems raises the question on whether multi-period modeling is necessary at all. We will now discuss two basic problems associated with formulation (11.2.1).

In the above model, we have assumed that the incremental demand is non-negative which reflects network growth over the planning horizon. It is certainly possible to imagine the case where installed demand volume from a previous period is no longer needed in a future period (negative growth in a network); for example, disconnection in a future period of circuits already installed in a previous period in the case of transport networks. As discussed in [LMS+89], a way to capture this effect is to have $h_{d\tau} < 0$ which would imply that previously routed demand volumes need to be altered and that we must allow $x_{dp\tau} < 0$ in the formulation! However, we need to ensure that the decrease is only on paths that have positive flows in prior periods. To do this, we need to replace the requirement that each flow ($x_{dp\tau}$) is non-negative, with the following condition

$$\textstyle\sum_{t\leq\tau}x_{dpt} \geq 0 \quad \tau = 1, 2, ..., \mathcal{T}$$

along with the understanding that path index p, in this case, refers to the exact same path from one time period to the next for the same demand d. The inclusion of this constraint in (11.2.1) implies that the modified design problem can *no* longer be naturally decoupled into $\mathcal{T}$-independent design problems! Although this new constraint satisfies feasibility, the restriction on demand routing (i.e., routing for any new incremental demand volume to be performed on a period-by-period basis) is no longer maintained; in other words, rearrangeability of routed demand volume from one period to the next is permitted. While this flexibility is good from a formulation point of view, the rearrangeability option may not be allowable/possible for many real transport networks.

For the rest of the discussion, we assume that the incremental demand volume is $h_{dt} \geq 0$ and that the rearrangement of routed demand from one period to the next is not allowable. Thus, we return to Problem (11.2.1) and the fact that this problem can still be decoupled into $\mathcal{T}$-independent single-period problems. Therefore, we will now discuss another important reason to consider multi-period modeling instead of using just multiple single-period design independently, one for each time period.

If you follow model (11.2.1) carefully, you will notice that this model does not necessarily generate optimal solutions from the standpoint of overall network capacity over the entire planning horizon. For example, from (11.2.1c), it is easy to see that due to modularity of capacity installed, *not* all capacity that was installed in the previous period may be completely depleted by routing of demand volume in that period. Thus, in actuality, there is a good chance that some *spare* capacity will be available from one time period to the next which can be used for realizing flows in future periods; this aspect is not considered explicitly in the above model. Thus, in reality, there is a natural coupling between periods in multi-period design.

To illustrate the effect of spare capacity from one period for use in future periods for flow routing, we denote $\underline{y}_{e\tau}$ as the link load on link e in period τ ($\tau = 1, 2, ..., \mathcal{T}$). Furthermore, we denote the spare capacity in DVU on link e in period τ by $\hat{y}_{e\tau} \geq 0$ ($\tau = 0, 1, 2, ..., \mathcal{T}$). Note that $\hat{y}_{e0}$ denotes any spare capacity available at the beginning of the entire planning cycle. Now at the end of time $\tau = 1$, any new, incremental demand volume must be satisfied using already-available capacity at the beginning of this period plus any new capacity added in this period; thus, we have the following link-load satisfiability condition for $\tau = 1$:

$$\underline{y}_{e1} \leq \hat{y}_{e0} + M y_{e1}, \quad e = 1, 2, ..., E.$$

Then, the spare capacity (if any) left at the end of period $\tau = 1$ is available in period $\tau = 2$; this spare capacity can be written as:

$$\hat{y}_{e1} = \hat{y}_{e0} + M y_{e1} - \underline{y}_{e1}, \quad e = 1, 2, ..., E.$$

Similarly, at the end of period $\tau = 2$, the link load satisfiability condition and the spare capacity can be written as:

$$\underline{y}_{e2} \leq \hat{y}_{e1} + M y_{e2}, \quad e = 1, 2, ..., E$$

$$\hat{y}_{e2} = \hat{y}_{e1} + M y_{e2} - \underline{y}_{e2}, \quad e = 1, 2, ..., E,$$

respectively. Generalizing, we have

$$\underline{y}_{e\tau} \leq \hat{y}_{e,\tau-1} + M y_{e\tau}, \quad e = 1, 2, ..., E \quad \tau = 1, 2, ..., T$$

$$\hat{y}_{e\tau} = \hat{y}_{e,\tau-1} + M y_{e\tau} - \underline{y}_{e\tau}, \quad e = 1, 2, ..., E \quad \tau = 1, 2, ..., T.$$

Essentially, we need to incorporate these two sets of relations into model (11.2.1) to account for reuse of spare capacity from one period to the next. Using substitution, we can rewrite spare capacity in period τ (for each link e) as:

$$\begin{aligned}
\hat{y}_{e\tau} &= \hat{y}_{e,\tau-1} + My_{e\tau} - \underline{y}_{e\tau} \\
&= \hat{y}_{e,\tau-2} + My_{e,\tau-1} - \underline{y}_{e,\tau-1} + My_{e\tau} - \underline{y}_{e\tau} \\
&= \hat{y}_{e,\tau-3} + My_{e,\tau-2} - \underline{y}_{e,\tau-2} + My_{e,\tau-1} - \underline{y}_{e,\tau-1} + My_{e\tau} - \underline{y}_{e\tau} \\
&\dots \\
&= \hat{y}_{e0} + My_{e\tau} - \underline{y}_{e\tau} + \textstyle\sum_{t=1}^{\tau-1}(My_{et} - \underline{y}_{et}).
\end{aligned}$$

Rearranging, we get

$$\underline{y}_{e\tau} + \hat{y}_{e\tau} = \hat{y}_{e0} + My_{e\tau} + \textstyle\sum_{t=1}^{\tau-1}(My_{et} - \underline{y}_{et}).$$

Since spare capacity is non-negative, we can arrive at the following inequality

$$\underline{y}_{e\tau} \leq \hat{y}_{e0} + My_{e\tau} + \textstyle\sum_{t=1}^{\tau-1}(My_{et} - \underline{y}_{et}).$$

Finally, if we denote the initial spare capacity as $\hat{y}_{e0} = My_{e0} - \underline{y}_{e0}$ for time $\tau = 0$, if there is any spare capacity available (and 0, otherwise), we have the following relation

$$\underline{y}_{e\tau} \leq My_{e\tau} + \textstyle\sum_{t<\tau}(My_{et} - \underline{y}_{et}).$$

This also shows that spare capacity variables do not need to be explicitly introduced in the model.

Another factor in transport network design is that sometimes it is possible to have a separate and explicit per-unit routing cost over the installed capacity in the same time period. By incorporating the routing cost and taking into account the spare capacity issue as discussed above, we arrive at the following model.

***MIP:* D/MPD/ML/CR** **Link-Path Formulation**

Modular Links, Multi-Time Period, Routing Cost, Capacity Reuse

constants (cost)

$\xi'_{e\tau}$ (installation) cost of one capacity module on link e for time period τ

$\xi''_{e\tau}$ (maintenance) cost of one capacity module on link e during time period τ for capacity installed in prior time period(s)

$\zeta_{dp\tau}$ unit routing cost on path p of demand d in time period τ

variables

$x_{dp\tau}$ (non-negative) flow allocated to path p of demand d at time τ

$\underline{y}_{e\tau}$ link flow on link e in time t due to routing of *new* demand for that time period

$y_{e\tau}$ (new) capacity of link e expressed in the number of modules (non-negative integer) needed in time period τ

objective

$$\text{minimize } \boldsymbol{F} = \textstyle\sum_\tau\sum_e \left(\xi'_{e\tau}y_{e\tau} + \xi''_{e\tau}\sum_{t<\tau}y_{et}\right) + \sum_\tau\sum_d\sum_p\zeta_{dp\tau}x_{dp\tau} \qquad (11.2.3a)$$

constraints

$$\sum_p x_{dp\tau} = h_{d\tau}, \quad d = 1,2,...,D \quad \tau = 1,2,...,\mathcal{T} \tag{11.2.3b}$$

$$\sum_d \sum_p \delta_{edp\tau} x_{dp\tau} = \underline{y}_{e\tau}, \quad e = 1,2,...,E \quad \tau = 1,2,...,\mathcal{T} \tag{11.2.3c}$$

$$\underline{y}_{e\tau} \le M y_{e\tau} + \sum_{t<\tau}(M y_{et} - \underline{y}_{et}), \quad e = 1,2,...,E \quad \tau = 1,2,...,\mathcal{T}. \tag{11.2.3d}$$

The astute reader may notice that the last relation (11.2.3d) can be rewritten as

$$0 \le \sum_{t\le\tau}(M y_{et} - \underline{y}_{et})$$

which is the same as

$$\sum_{t\le\tau} \underline{y}_{et} \le \sum_{t\le\tau} M y_{et}.$$

Now, replacing $\underline{y}_{et}$ using (11.2.3c), we arrive at

$$\sum_{t\le\tau} \sum_d \sum_p \delta_{edpt} x_{dpt} \le \sum_{t\le\tau} M y_{et} \quad e = 1,2,...,E \quad \tau = 1,2,...,\mathcal{T}. \tag{11.2.4}$$

We chose to keep the form (11.2.3d) in the above model since it shows the logical relation and progression over time between new capacity, spare capacity, and link load. Nevertheless, minimizing (11.2.3a) subject to (11.2.3b) and (11.2.4) is equivalent to the entire Problem (11.2.3) without needing to use the link load variable $\underline{y}_{et}$ at all. In any case, you might want to compare (11.2.4) with (11.2.1c) to see the difference between models (11.2.3) and (11.2.1) from another angle.

We conclude this section by presenting a multi-period design problem where rearrangeability of demand routing from one period to another is allowable. Thus, in each time period we need to consider demand volumes to be *cumulative* demand volumes up to and including that period. Due to rearrangeability the meaning of flow allocation $x_{dp\tau}$ changes as well. Thus, we have the following model.

***MIP:* D/MPRD/ML/RD** **Link-Path Formulation**

Multi-Period Rearrangeable Design

constants (cost)

- $h_{d\tau}(\ge 0)$ new (incremental) demand volume for demand d in period τ
- $\xi'_{e\tau}$ installation cost of one capacity module on link e for time period τ
- $\xi''_{e\tau}$ maintenance cost of one capacity model on link e during time period τ for capacity installed in prior time period(s)
- $\zeta_{dp\tau}$ unit routing cost on path p of *cumulative* demand volume for demand d in time period τ

variables

- $x_{dp\tau}$ (non-negative) flow allocated to path p for routing cumulative demand volume for demand d in period τ
- $y_{e\tau}$ (new) capacity of link e expressed in the number of modules (non-negative integer) needed in time period τ

objective

$$\text{minimize } \boldsymbol{F} = \sum_{\tau}\sum_{e}\left(\xi'_{e\tau}y_{e\tau} + \xi''_{e\tau}\sum_{t<\tau}y_{et}\right) + \sum_{\tau}\sum_{d}\sum_{p}\zeta_{dp\tau}x_{dp\tau} \tag{11.2.5a}$$

constraints

$$\sum_{p}x_{dp\tau} = \sum_{t\leq\tau}h_{dt}, \quad d = 1,2,...,D \quad \tau = 1,2,...,\mathcal{T} \tag{11.2.5b}$$

$$\sum_{d}\sum_{p}\delta_{edp\tau}x_{dp\tau} \leq \sum_{t\leq\tau}My_{et}, \quad e = 1,2,...,E \quad \tau = 1,2,...,\mathcal{T}. \tag{11.2.5c}$$

11.2.2 *Multi-Period Flow Routing Problem*

When a transport network has already installed capacity or demand projection on installed capacity over multiple time periods, we face the design problem of routing of multi-period transport demand in the network at a minimum cost; this is classically referred to as the *circuit routing* problem (see § 4.5 of [Rey83]), or *telecommunications loading* problem [LMS+89]. We will use the term *flow routing*. The projected demand can be caused by either re-forecasting or by actual new demand requests in future. The routing cost can have an economic discounting factor from one period to another; thus, discount factor is important to consider in routing cost. Again, as before we will use the demand volume in a period to mean new/incremental demand for that particular period. We again begin with the case when demand routing in a period cannot be re-routed in a subsequent period.

***LP:* A/MPD/FR** **Link-Path Formulation**

Multi-Period Flow Routing Problem

indices

$d = 1,2,...,D$ demands
$\tau = 1,2,...,\mathcal{T}$ time horizon
$p = 1,2,...,P_{d\tau}$ candidate paths for demand d in time period τ
$e = 1,2,...,E$ links

constants

$\delta_{edp\tau}$ = 1, if link e belongs to path p realizing demand d in time period τ; 0, otherwise
$h_{d\tau}$ volume of demand d at time τ
$\zeta_{dp\tau}$ (economic discounted) routing cost of one capacity module on path p for demand d in time period τ
$c_{e\tau}$ *new* capacity on link e in time period τ

variables

$x_{dp\tau}$ (non-negative) flow allocated to path p of demand d at time τ
$\underline{y}_{e\tau}$ link load on link e in time τ due to new demand in time τ

objective

$$\text{minimize } \boldsymbol{F} = \sum_{\tau}\sum_{d}\sum_{p}\zeta_{dp\tau}x_{dp\tau} \tag{11.2.6a}$$

constraints

$$\sum_p x_{dp\tau} = h_{d\tau}, \quad d = 1, 2, ..., D \quad \tau = 1, 2, ..., \mathcal{T} \tag{11.2.6b}$$

$$\sum_d \sum_p \delta_{edp\tau} x_{dp\tau} = \underline{y}_{e\tau}, \quad e = 1, 2, ..., E \quad \tau = 1, 2, ..., \mathcal{T} \tag{11.2.6c}$$

$$\underline{y}_{e\tau} \le c_{e\tau} + \sum_{t<\tau}(c_{et} - \underline{y}_{et}), \quad e = 1, 2, ..., E \quad \tau = 1, 2, ..., \mathcal{T}. \tag{11.2.6d}$$

Note the similarity between (11.2.6d) and (11.2.3d). There is another way to write the above model if we redefine the capacity in a period to mean the *cumulative* capacity up to and including that period. Thus, we can rewrite the above model without using the link load variable as follows.

LP: **A/MPD/FRM** — **Link-Path Formulation**

Multi-Time Period Flow Routing Problem—Modified

constants (modified)

$C_{e\tau}$ *cumulative* capacity on link e in period τ ($C_{e\tau} = \sum_{t\le\tau} c_{et}$)

variables

$x_{dp\tau}$ (non-negative) flow allocated to path p of demand d at time τ

objective

$$\text{minimize } \boldsymbol{F} = \sum_\tau \sum_d \sum_p \zeta_{dp\tau} x_{dp\tau} \tag{11.2.7a}$$

constraints

$$\sum_p x_{dp\tau} = h_{d\tau}, \quad d = 1, 2, ..., D \quad \tau = 1, 2, ..., \mathcal{T} \tag{11.2.7b}$$

$$\sum_{t\le\tau} \sum_d \sum_p \delta_{edpt} x_{dpt} \le C_{e\tau}, \quad e = 1, 2, ..., E \quad \tau = 1, 2, ..., \mathcal{T}. \tag{11.2.7c}$$

Note how t and τ are used (in subscripts) to satisfy link feasibility over time. Furthermore, it is also good to compare this model to the single-period model (4.1.7). A danger with either of the models, (11.2.6) and (11.2.7), is that the problem can be infeasible when trying to solve over the entire planning horizon since it is possible that there may not be capacity available in a future period to accommodate the demand. While in a single-period model feasibility it might be easy to catch (see (4.1.7)), this is rather hard to gauge over multiple time periods. Thus, the concept of introducing an artificial path variable (for each demand and period) with high cost is desirable to maintain the feasibility of the model (in the mathematical sense).

LP: A/MPD/FRM2 **Link-Path Formulation**

Multi-Time Period Flow Routing Problem—Modified 2

constants

$C_{e\tau}$ *cumulative* capacity on link e in time period τ

Δ a large positive penalty value

variables

$x_{dp\tau}$ (non-negative) flow allocated to path p of demand d at time τ

$\tilde{x}_{d\tau}$ (non-negative) flow on an artificial path for demand d at time τ

objective

$$\text{minimize } \boldsymbol{F} = \sum_\tau \sum_d \sum_p \zeta_{dp\tau} x_{dp\tau} + \sum_\tau \sum_d \Delta \tilde{x}_{d\tau} \tag{11.2.8a}$$

constraints

$$\sum_p x_{dp\tau} + \tilde{x}_{d\tau} = h_{d\tau}, \quad d = 1, 2, ..., D \quad \tau = 1, 2, ..., T \tag{11.2.8b}$$

$$\sum_{t \le \tau} \sum_d \sum_p \delta_{edtp} x_{dpt} \le C_{e\tau}, \quad e = 1, 2, ..., E \quad \tau = 1, 2, ..., T. \tag{11.2.8c}$$

Now $\tilde{x}_{d\tau} = h_{d\tau}$ ($d = 1, 2, ..., D$ and $\tau = 1, 2, ..., T$) is a feasible solution that satisfies the constraints in the above problem (certainly, at a very high artificial cost); if the network has enough capacity to satisfy all the demands, artificial variables $\tilde{x}_{d\tau}$ will take the value 0 in the final solution. If, on the other hand, some $\tilde{x}_{d\tau}$s are positive in the final solution, this then serves as an indicator that the network does not have enough capacity to route all the demands and models such as (11.2.3) need to be solved to determine any additional capacity needed (and where this is needed); also see model A/ALC (5.4.11) and the algorithmic discussion in regard to determining additional capacity for feasibility.

This leads to another conceivable situation that lies between (11.2.3) and (11.2.7). In a transport network, consider that we are interested in the planning horizon that spans 10 periods where in the first 3 periods no capacity can be added. This is certainly possible due to lag time in the installation process of new capacity. Interestingly, model (11.2.3) can be used for this situation with a slight twist. Suppose that $\hat{T}$ (where $\hat{T} < T$) is the period during the planning horizon such that no capacity can be installed prior to period $\hat{T}$. Then, we can use (11.2.3) with the following additional constraints

$$y_{e\tau} = 0 \qquad \tau = 1, 2, ..., \hat{T} - 1$$

to address the situation of not being able to add capacity prior to $\hat{T}$ while capacity can be added from $\hat{T}$ onwards.

We will now briefly discuss two additional cases: 1) flow routing done in a particular period can be disconnected in a future period, and 2) rearrangeability of flow routing is allowed from one period to another.

For the first case, we could have negative demand ($h_{d\tau} < 0$) in certain periods; this can be handled similar to our discussion earlier in Section 11.2.1 in the context of capacity planning.

For the second case, we need to redefine the demand flow constraint from (11.2.8b) to arrive at the following.

***LP:* A/MTPR** **Link-Path Formulation**

Multi-Time Period Rearrangeable Routing

constants

$C_{e\tau}$ *cumulative* capacity on link e in time period τ

Δ a large positive penalty value

variables

x_{dpt} (non-negative) total flow allocated to path p of demand d at time τ (including rearrangeable)

$\tilde{x}_{dt}$ (non-negative) flow on an artificial path for demand d at time τ

objective

$$\text{minimize } \boldsymbol{F} = \sum_\tau \sum_d \sum_p \zeta_{dp\tau} x_{dp\tau} + \sum_\tau \sum_d \Delta \tilde{x}_{d\tau} \quad (11.2.9a)$$

constraints

$$\sum_p x_{dp\tau} + \tilde{x}_{d\tau} = \sum_{t \le \tau} h_{dt}, \quad d = 1, 2, ..., D \quad \tau = 1, 2, ..., \mathcal{T} \quad (11.2.9b)$$

$$\sum_d \sum_p \delta_{ed\tau p} x_{dp\tau} \le C_{e\tau}, \quad e = 1, 2, ..., E \quad \tau = 1, 2, ..., \mathcal{T}. \quad (11.2.9c)$$

11.2.3 *Model Extensions*

As you can imagine there are a number of possible MPD extensions of various models we have presented throughout this book. For example, the models above can be easily extended to consider multiple facility module types; we have discussed this extension for a single period in Section 4.3.1 and, thus, such extensions for multiple periods have been left as an exercise (Exercise 11.7). Multi-period design can also include multiple service classes; this can be handled along the line already discussed for the multi-service with multi-hour design. Below we will highlight only a couple of important variations.

Integral Flows

In reality, most transport network planning and routing problems require integral, modular allocation of flows since demand are in modular units. Instead of showing this requirement for entire set of models covered in this section so far, we will show this extension only for one model, specifically for (11.2.8), using the integral flow concept described earlier in formulation (4.2.12).

***IP:* A/MPD/FRM3** **Link-Path Formulation**

Multi-Time Period Flow Routing Problem—Modified 3

constants

$L_{d\tau}$	demand module for demand d in period τ
$H_{d\tau}$	volume of demand d expressed as the number of demand modules for period τ
$C_{e\tau}$	*cumulative* capacity on link e in period τ
$\zeta_{dp\tau}$	routing cost of unit demand module for demand d in time τ on path p
Δ	a large positive penalty value

variables

$u_{dp\tau}$	(non-negative) integral flow allocated to path p of demand d at time τ
$\tilde{u}_{d\tau}$	(non-negative) integral flow on an artificial path for demand d at time τ

objective

$$\text{minimize } \boldsymbol{F} = \sum_{\tau}\sum_{d}\sum_{p}\left(\zeta_{dp\tau}u_{dp\tau}\right) + \sum_{\tau}\sum_{d}\Delta\tilde{u}_{d\tau} \qquad (11.2.10a)$$

constraints

$$\sum_{p}u_{dp\tau} + \tilde{u}_{d\tau} = H_{d\tau}, \quad d = 1,2,...,D \quad \tau = 1,2,...,\mathcal{T} \qquad (11.2.10b)$$

$$\sum_{t\leq\tau}\sum_{d}L_{d\tau}\sum_{p}\delta_{edtp}u_{dpt} \leq C_{e\tau}, \quad e = 1,2,...,E \quad \tau = 1,2,...,\mathcal{T}. \qquad (11.2.10c)$$

Protection Design

In Chapter 9, we have extensively discussed protection and restoration design of networks for resiliency. Here we will show just an example of network protection for the 1+1 protection mechanism (Section 9.1.2) of demand over multiple time periods. While protection can be modeled in many different ways, we will use a special method which was first described for fiber-network survivability in [Med91a].

Recall that so far we have used the term path in link-path formulation of the multi-commodity flow based models to mean a candidate path for a demand pair that uses a series of links in a sequence from origin to destination in the network. However, the notion of path can be generalized since an important requirement of link-path formulation, the pre-processed candidate lists of paths, can be applied in a different manner. This has been briefly discussed earlier in Section 4.6.2. Now, we will provide an illustration.

We will illustrate the notion of generalization of the path representation in link-path formulation through the 4-node example shown in Figure 11.4. Consider demand pair $\langle 1,2\rangle$. For this demand pair, we can construct a *cycle* that is given by 1-2-3-1 which consists of three links 1-2, 2-3, and 3-1. Note that this cycle is actually a link disjoint cycle; not only that, it can be thought of as consisting of two link-disjoint paths connecting demand pair $\langle 1,2\rangle$ with path 1-2 and path 1-3-2. Since these two paths have no links in common, one path can serve as back-up to the other for 1+1 end-to-end protection for demand pair $\langle 1,2\rangle$.

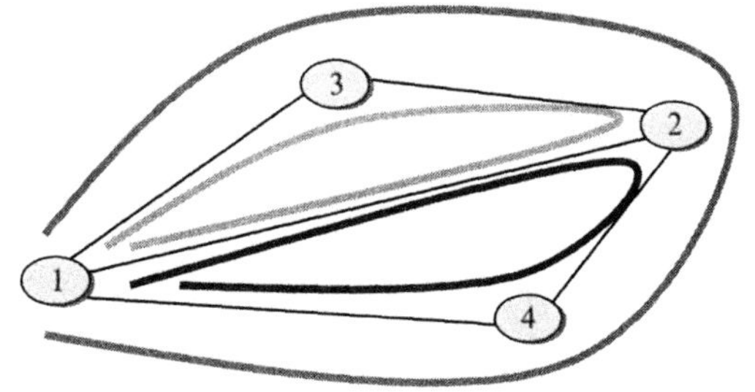

FIGURE 11.4 Set of Link-Disjoint Path Paths for Demand Pair $\langle 1,2 \rangle$ that Form Cycles

Altogether, demand pair $\langle 1,2 \rangle$ has three cycles that consist of link-disjoint route segments; they are: 1-2-3-1 (already discussed), 1-2-4-1, and 1-3-2-4-1. Thus, this list can be used as candidate cycles for demand pair $\langle 1,2 \rangle$ in place of a list of regular paths. Similarly, link-disjoint path pairs can be used to build a list of cycles for other demand pairs (see Section 9.3.4).

Now recall that for a link-path formulation, we need to feed the pre-processed candidate lists of paths; instead, we can now consider feeding the pre-processed candidate lists of cycles in place of candidate paths. Interestingly, this swap does not change anything in the formulation; it only changes the interpretation of the path as in link-path representation changes.

***IP:* D/MTP/MLR** **Link-Path Formulation**

Modular Links, Multi-Time Period, 1+1 Protection Routing

indices (modified)

$p = 1, 2, ..., P_{d\tau}$ candidate cycles (that are constructed by forming link-disjoint pair of paths) for demand d in time period τ

constants (cost)

$\xi_{e\tau}$ (installation) cost of one capacity module on link e for time period τ

$\xi'_{e\tau}$ (maintenance) cost of one capacity model on link e during time period τ for capacity installed in prior time period(s)

$\zeta_{dp\tau}$ unit routing cost on generalized path p of demand d in time period τ

$\delta_{edp\tau}$ = 1, if link e belongs to cycle p realizing demand d in time period τ; 0, otherwise

variables

$u_{dp\tau}$ binary decision variable associate with allocation of demand volumes to cylce p of demand d at time τ

$\underline{y}_{et}$ link flow on link e in time t due to routing of *new* demand for that time period

$y_{e\tau}$ (new) capacity of link e expressed in the number of modules (non-negative integer) needed in time period τ

objective

$$\text{minimize } \boldsymbol{F} = \textstyle\sum_\tau \sum_e \left(\xi_{e\tau} y_{e\tau} + \xi'_{e\tau} \sum_{t<\tau} y_{et}\right) + \sum_\tau \sum_d \sum_p \zeta_{dp\tau} x_{dp\tau} \qquad (11.2.11a)$$

constraints

$$\sum_p u_{dp\tau} = 1, \quad d = 1,2,...,D \quad \tau = 1,2,...,\mathcal{T} \tag{11.2.11b}$$

$$\sum_d h_{d\tau} \sum_p \delta_{edp\tau} u_{dp\tau} = \underline{y}_{e\tau}, \quad e = 1,2,...,E \quad \tau = 1,2,...,\mathcal{T} \tag{11.2.11c}$$

$$\underline{y}_{e\tau} \leq M y_{e\tau} + \sum_{t<\tau}(M y_{et} - \underline{y}_{et}), \quad e = 1,2,...,E \quad \tau = 1,2,...,\mathcal{T}. \tag{11.2.11d}$$

Again, there is no difference in the actual mathematical formulation between (11.2.3) and (11.2.11)! The only difference is how path index p is defined to represent cycles that consist of a pair of link-disjoint paths, instead of just paths in earlier context. There is another implicit requirement for the latter model—the network graph must be two-connected so that every demand pair has at least one cycle (consisting of a pair of link-disjoint paths).

11.2.4 Algorithmic Approaches

For multi-time period problems, various methods described throughout the book (in particular, see Chapters 5 and 10) can be applicable. For example, the multi-period design Problem (11.2.3) can be solved using the Lagrangian relaxation (LR) based dual approach (Section 5.4.1) by relaxing constraint (11.2.3d); see also Exercise 11.8.

In this part, we will consider two specific problems and describe different approaches. In particular, for the multi-period capacity expansion Problem (11.2.3), we will describe a dynamic programming approach, while for multi-period flow routing/allocation Problem (11.2.8), we will describe a hybrid approach that combines the flow deviation method and the gradient projection method.

11.2.5 Dynamic Programming

Here, we will illustrate a dynamic programming framework (Section 5.2.4) to solve (11.2.3). For simplicity of illustration, we will consider only the capacity expansion cost, no maintenance cost or routing cost, i.e.,

$$\begin{aligned}
&\xi''_{e\tau} = 0 && e = 1,2,...,E \quad \tau = 1,2,...,\mathcal{T} \\
&\zeta_{dp\tau} = 0 && d = 1,2,...,D \quad p = 1,2,...,P_d \quad \tau = 1,2,...,\mathcal{T}.
\end{aligned}$$

Thus, the multi-period Problem (11.2.3) with the above simplification can be thought of as a "pure" capacity expansion problem over multiple time periods given incremental demand in each time period.

In order to illustrate the dynamic programming approach, we need to use the following notations:

$Y_{e\tau}$	cumulative capacity on link e in time period τ
$\underline{Y}_{e\tau}$	cumulative flow on link e in time period τ; link flow vector at period τ is $\underline{\mathbf{Y}}_\tau = (\underline{Y}_{1\tau}, \underline{Y}_{2\tau}, ..., \underline{Y}_{E\tau})$
$\Lambda_\tau(\boldsymbol{y}_\tau)$	$= \sum_e \xi'_{e\tau} y_{e\tau} = \sum_e \xi'_{e\tau}(Y_{e\tau} - Y_{e,\tau-1})$, cost in period τ
$\mathbf{\Pi}_\tau$	policy $= (\underline{\mathbf{Y}}_t), t = 1, 2, ..., \tau$
$\mathcal{C}(\mathbf{\Pi}_\tau)$	cost of policy up to (and including) period τ, $\mathcal{C}(\mathbf{\Pi}_\tau) = \sum_{t \leq \tau} \Lambda_t$

The basic idea behind the dynamic programming approach is to consider that, given a policy up to a particular time period, we want to optimize capacity expansion in the next time period. First, denote

$$\psi(z) = \min\{\mathcal{C}(\mathbf{\Pi}_\tau) : \mathbf{\Pi}_\tau \text{ is a policy with } \underline{\mathbf{Y}}_\tau = z\}.$$

Thus, we need to solve the following functional equation, with variable $\boldsymbol{y}$ being feasible, as time progresses:

$$\psi(\underline{\mathbf{Y}}_\tau) = \min_{\boldsymbol{y}}\{\Lambda_\tau(\boldsymbol{y}) + \psi(\underline{\mathbf{Y}}_{\tau-1})\} \quad \tau = 1, 2, ..., \tau. \tag{11.2.12}$$

This looks like a recurrence relation; however, this is referred to as a functional equation since the same function appears on both sides. The approach above is also known as the forward dynamic programming approach.

While the above dynamic programming approach provides a nice framework, we need to keep in mind that at each stage, a large single-period problem needs to be solved which in itself can be time-consuming. This would then warrant the need to use some decomposition algorithms such as LR-based dual approach, Benders' decomposition (BD), and so on. Thus, if the decomposition approach is needed, then it might be worthwhile to use it over the entire multi-period problem, instead of using it for only one period. In other words, for this problem, the use of the dynamic programming approach may not necessarily be benefitial.

11.2.6 A Hybrid Method

In this section, we consider a hybrid solution approach for multi-period flow routing/allocation Problem (11.2.8). It may be noted that this is an LP problem; thus, a commercial solver may be used for solving the entire problem. Particularly, a commercial solver can be used if the number of links is about 50 to 200 (for example, see Table 10.4 for how the number of constraints and variables grow). However, if a problem has 5,000 links and this needed be considered over multiple time periods, the approach described below can be a worthwhile approach. Certainly, in such cases, approaches such as BD and LR-based dual approach, can also be applicable.

The method described below is a hybrid of the flow deviation approach and the gradient projection method to solve the multi-period flow routing/allocation Problem (11.2.8) (see

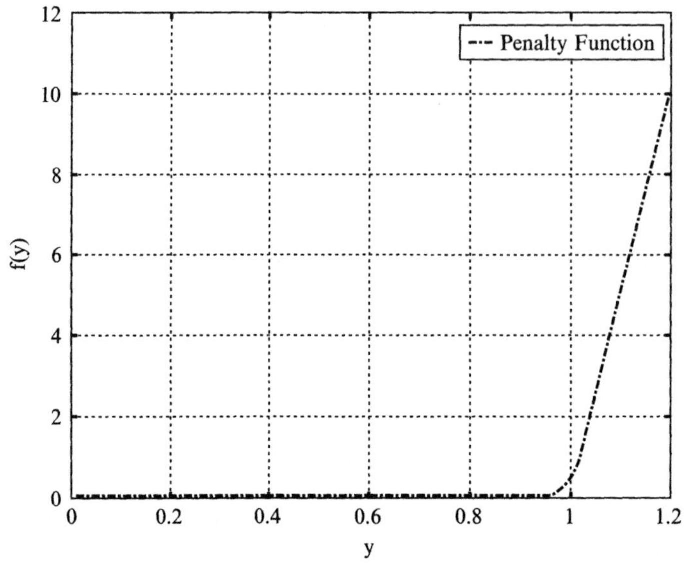

FIGURE 11.5 Penalty Function (shown for $C_{e\tau} \equiv 1, \Upsilon = 50, \sigma = 0.05$)

[LMS+89]). Note that this problem is referred to as the *loading* problem since a goal is to load or allocate as much demand as possible given that the network is capacitated. Recall that the flow deviation method and the gradient projection method have been described in Sections 5.5.1 and 5.5.2, respectively, for solving a convex programming problem with a convex objective function and linear constraints. To begin with, we need to convert (11.2.8) to a convex programming problem.

In order to do that, the first task is to add the set of coupling constraints (11.2.8c) to the objective function (11.2.8a) as a penalty term. Given a predefined small number $\sigma > 0$ and a large positive number Υ, the penalty term for (11.2.8c) can be written as

$$f_{e\tau}(\underline{y}_{e\tau}) = \begin{cases} 0 & \text{if } \underline{y}_{e\tau} - C_{e\tau} \leq -\sigma \\ \Upsilon(\underline{y}_{e\tau} - C_{e\tau} + \sigma)^2/(4\sigma) & \text{if } -\sigma \leq \underline{y}_{e\tau} - C_{e\tau} \leq \sigma \\ \Upsilon(\underline{y}_{e\tau} - C_{e\tau}) & \text{if } \underline{y}_{e\tau} - C_{e\tau} \geq \sigma. \end{cases} \tag{11.2.13}$$

where $\underline{y}_{e\tau} = \sum_{t\leq\tau}\sum_d\sum_p \delta_{edtp}x_{dpt}$ is the cumulative link-load for link e in period τ. In Figure 11.5, the penalty function is illustrated for one instance of e, τ. The penalty starts accruing within σ of the capacity; thus, it needs to be small enough so as not to drastically incur a huge penalty in this region.

The penalty function given in (11.2.13) is convex and differentiable everywhere. Then, the modified objective function (with penalty term incorporated in the objective) is the following convex function:

$$\phi(\boldsymbol{x}) = \sum_\tau\sum_d\sum_p \zeta_{dp\tau}x_{dp\tau} + \sum_\tau\sum_d \Delta\tilde{x}_{d\tau} + \sum_\tau\sum_e f_{e\tau}(\underline{y}_{e\tau}).$$

A comment is in order for the last two terms in the above objective function. There are two forms of penalty, one for the artificial path (second term) and one for the link violation constraints (third term). It can be argued that the second term may not be necessary. The issue here is that having these terms allows you to identify which demand is not satisfied; if only the third term is left, it is not easy to identify which demand was not met by the network. Regardless, the choice of the penalty constants for each of these two terms, Υ and Δ, needs to be done carefully to address the trade-off issue of not picking any artificial path at all (e.g., Δ is really large).

For convenience, in the rest of the discussion we will incorporate the artificial flow variable, $\tilde{x}_{d\tau}$, to be an additional path in the candidate path list which contribute only to the demand flow constraint, but not to the capacity constraint (since no real link is used for this path). With this augmentation, we write constraints (11.2.8b) compactly in matrix notation as $\boldsymbol{Ex} = \boldsymbol{h}$ where $\boldsymbol{E}$ has the following structure:

$$\boldsymbol{E} = \begin{bmatrix} 1\,1\,1\,1 & & & \\ & 1\,1\,1\,1\,1 & & \\ & & \cdots & \\ & & & 1\,1\,1 \end{bmatrix}.$$

Then, the modified problem of (11.2.8) is the following convex programming problem:

$$\begin{aligned} \textbf{\textit{minimize}} \quad & \phi(\boldsymbol{x}) \\ \textbf{\textit{subject to}} \quad & \boldsymbol{Ex} = \boldsymbol{h} \\ & \boldsymbol{x} \geq \boldsymbol{0}. \end{aligned} \tag{11.2.14}$$

We will now discuss how to use the hybrid approach to solve this problem. First, recall that at iteration k of the flow deviation algorithm (Algorithm 5.10), we need to solve the following linearized subproblem of (11.2.14):

$$\begin{aligned} \textbf{\textit{minimize}} \quad & \nabla\phi(\boldsymbol{x}^k)\,\boldsymbol{x} \\ \textbf{\textit{subject to}} \quad & \boldsymbol{Ex} = \boldsymbol{h} \\ & \boldsymbol{x} \geq \boldsymbol{0} \end{aligned} \tag{11.2.15}$$

where $\nabla\phi(\boldsymbol{x}^k)$ is the gradient of $\phi(\boldsymbol{x}^k)$ at iteration k. Due to the structure of matrix $\boldsymbol{E}$, this linearized problem is completely separable for each τ and d; the resulting atomic-level (linearized) subproblem with respect to each τ and d can be easily solved by finding the minimum first derivative length path, $\bar{p}(d,\tau)$, i.e., assign

$$x_{dp\tau} = \begin{cases} h_{d\tau} & \text{if } p = \bar{p}(d,\tau) \\ 0, & \text{otherwise.} \end{cases}$$

Collectively, this solution for the linearized subproblem will be denoted by $\bar{\boldsymbol{x}}$. In the case of the classical flow deviation algorithm, a new point $\boldsymbol{x}^{k+1}$ is derived using

$$\boldsymbol{x}^{k+1} = \boldsymbol{x}^k + \bar{\alpha}(\bar{\boldsymbol{x}} - \boldsymbol{x}^k) \tag{11.2.16}$$

where $\bar{\alpha}$ is the optimal step size from the following line search optimization

$$\phi(\boldsymbol{x}^k + \bar{\alpha}(\bar{\boldsymbol{x}} - \boldsymbol{x}^k)) = \min_{0 \le \alpha \le 1} \phi(\boldsymbol{x}^k + \alpha(\bar{\boldsymbol{x}} - \boldsymbol{x}^k)). \tag{11.2.17}$$

Note here that vector, $\bar{\boldsymbol{x}} - \boldsymbol{x}^k$, serves as the direction for taking the step size $\bar{\alpha}$. However, it is well known that this direction can zigzag from one iteration to the next since the first derivative length of the linearized problem takes an extreme point in the feasible region. Thus a modified approach called, the PARTAN (PARallel TANgent) extension ([FGS87], [LMS+89], [Him72]), can be used to avoid this zigzagging problem by considering the direction at iteration k to be the vector, $\bar{\boldsymbol{\omega}} - \boldsymbol{x}^{k-1}$, where

$$\bar{\boldsymbol{\omega}} = \boldsymbol{x}^k + \bar{\alpha}(\bar{\boldsymbol{x}} - \boldsymbol{x}^k). \tag{11.2.18}$$

Here, $\bar{\alpha}$ is the solution of (11.2.17). Now given this modified direction, a new step-size is chosen to be $\underline{\alpha}$ where

$$\boldsymbol{x}^{k+1} = \boldsymbol{x}^k + \underline{\alpha}(\bar{\boldsymbol{\omega}} - \boldsymbol{x}^{k-1}) \tag{11.2.19}$$

and where $\underline{\alpha}$ solves the one-dimensional search problem

$$\min_{0 \le \alpha \le \hat{\alpha}} \phi(\boldsymbol{x}^k + \alpha(\bar{\boldsymbol{w}} - \boldsymbol{x}^{k-1})). \tag{11.2.20}$$

In the above, the scalar, $\hat{\alpha}$, is the largest step-size without violating constraints, $\boldsymbol{E}\boldsymbol{x} = \boldsymbol{h}, \boldsymbol{x} \ge \boldsymbol{0}$. It is not hard to see that, indeed, the equality constraints are always satisfied (Exercise 11.9); thus, preserving non-negativity is all that is needed in order to determine $\hat{\alpha}$.

Another approach besides the flow deviation method for (11.2.14) is the gradient projection based approach which usually works well near the optimal solution. We will highlight the main parts of gradient projection which is relevant in our context.

At iteration k, define $\widetilde{\boldsymbol{E}}$ to be the matrix $\boldsymbol{E}$ deleting the columns for which the corresponding variables are zero at the current iteration, i.e., only active variables are considered. Similarly, consider the gradient $\widetilde{\nabla}\phi(\boldsymbol{x}^k)$ of $\phi(\boldsymbol{x})$ corresponding to only these active variables. Then, we define the direction vector, $\boldsymbol{d}^k$, to be

$$\boldsymbol{d}^k = -\left[\mathbf{I} - \widetilde{\boldsymbol{E}}^T(\widetilde{\boldsymbol{E}}\widetilde{\boldsymbol{E}}^T)^{-1}\widetilde{\boldsymbol{E}}\right]\widetilde{\nabla}\phi(\boldsymbol{x}^k). \tag{11.2.21}$$

where $\widetilde{\boldsymbol{E}}^T$ is the transpose of the matrix $\widetilde{\boldsymbol{E}}$, and $\boldsymbol{I}$ is the identity matrix. Now, we can determine $\boldsymbol{x}^{k+1}$ to be

$$\boldsymbol{x}^{k+1} = \boldsymbol{x}^k + \tilde{\alpha}\boldsymbol{d}^k \tag{11.2.22}$$

where step size $\tilde{\alpha}$ solves the one-dimensional search problem

$$\min_{0 \le \alpha \le \hat{\alpha}} \phi(\boldsymbol{x}^k + \alpha\boldsymbol{d}^k). \tag{11.2.23}$$

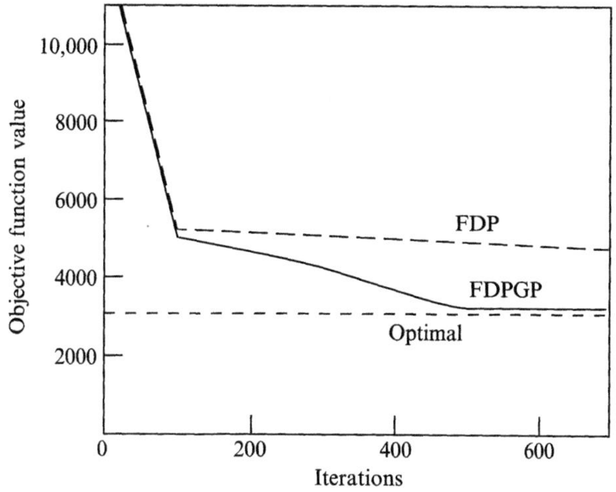

FIGURE 11.6 Comparison between FDP and FDPGP (From [LMS+89])

It may be noted that, in general, computing inverse of a matrix is not a trivial task. Fortunately, in this case, $\boldsymbol{E}$ is the demand-path matrix (corresponding to active variables) which is specially structured, decoupled for each demand and period. Thus, $\widetilde{\boldsymbol{E}}^T\widetilde{\boldsymbol{E}}$ is then a diagonal matrix and, thus, the inverse can be readily determined.

Both approaches described above have their own benefits: initial decent of flow deviation with PARTAN extension (FDP, for short) is fast, while the gradient projection (GP) approach works well near the solution, especially if the correct active set (i.e., flow variables that should be positive at optimal solution) is obtained. Thus, a hybrid approach, to be referred to as FDPGP (flow deviation with PARTAN extension and gradient projection), is to start with FDP at first, and then switch to GP for a push. So as not to be stuck on the wrong active set, the method switches back to FDP for a while and then takes again the projection step. If the correct active set is identified by the GP step, then FDP converges linearly. In Figure 11.6, the convergence behavior between FDP and FDPGP is shown (refer to [LMS+89]).

This hybrid method has been successfully used in practice to solve the multi-period telecommunication loading problem with thousands of link constraints where it was shown that the approach was able to do 5% to 7.5% more loading and at significant reduction in computation time compared to a previously used sequential heuristic [LMS+89]. It is worth noting that for this specially structured problem, the most time-consuming part was the repeated computation of the step size.

11.3 SUMMARY AND FURTHER READING

In this chapter, we have covered design models that take into account the time factor and its impact on temporal demand change. There are primarily two groups of problems: one for multi-hour design and one for multi-time period design.

TABLE 11.6 Trade-off: Normalized Cost of Multi-Hour/Single-Hour Design in the Presence of Different Number of Candidate Paths

# of Candidate Paths/ Per Demand Pair		3	7
R15	MuHr	98.00	96.68
	MaxBHr	102.60	100.00
A50	MuHr	72.29	71.79
	MaxBHr	102.45	100.00

Multi-hour design problems consider demand variation during the day and can be primarily applicable for traffic networks. This is especially beneficial when demand volumes peak at different times of the day for different parts of the network, i.e., non-coincidence of busy hours; this can happen if a network spans over multiple time zones. There are following implications of multi-hour design: 1) it increases the problem size for capacity design problems significantly due to consideration of the time factor, and 2) multi-hour design can result in a more cost-effective network compared to the case where the network demand is mapped into a single maximum busy-hour demand. Besides the demand volume variation that can occur during the day, it is important to understand where and how the multi-hour design may be applicable depending on the capability and the technology in place for the network. We have already illustrated through our computational results that designing networks with multi-hour traffic results in significant savings compared to designing the same network using a single-maximum busy-hour traffic. Note that there is another dimension to consider: most of the models presented in this chapter are based on link-path formulation which requires that pre-processed candidate lists of paths be provided. This also means a user can vary the number of candidate paths to include for a demand pair; intuitively, the larger the number of candidate paths, the better the savings in the networks.

An interesting trade-off question to ask is whether to use a larger number of candidate paths (per demand) in the design when a single-maximum busy-hour traffic matrix is considered, or to use less numbers of candidate paths (per demand) in the network design when multiple busy-hour traffic matrices are considered (certainly, we mean this only for networking technology where the multi-hour case is applicable). This trade-off was addressed in a series of studies presented in [Zho95] for formulation (11.1.1) assuming in addition that the capacity variables are continuous. From this work, we highlight two network examples: one where the traffic variation between hours during a day is not much (R7) and the other where the traffic variation between hours during a day is significant (A50) (note: network examples of R7 and A50 shown in Figure 11.3 used a different set of demand volumes.). In Table 11.6, the normalized network cost is shown for the case of multi-hour (with 3 traffic time windows during the day) considering 3 candidate paths per pair and 7 candidate paths per pair, and for the maximum busy hour also with the same number of paths (all cost normalized to the network cost for maximum busy hour with 7 candidate paths per pair). As we can see from Table 11.6, having a lower number of candidate paths but considering multiple busy-hour traffic matrix results in cheaper design compared to the case of higher number of paths but with just one maximum busy-hour traffic matrix; this difference can be significant if the traffic varies tremendously during the 24-hour period!

In the other class of design problems considered in this chapter, multi-time period design, *new* demand volumes over the time horizon are incorporated; we show how this influences network design modeling. The continuity of any spare capacity from one time period to the next need to be captured in any multi-time period models. From the viewpoint of the problem size, multi-period models have the same-size complexity as multi-hour design problems.

Multi-hour modeling for network design was apparently first addressed in [OP71]. Multi-hour capacity design model for dynamic routing circuit-switched networks was first discussed in [ACM81] (also see [AKK81] and [Ash97]). Girard's book [Gir90] provides extensive treatment on multi-hour circuit-switched networks with dynamic routing. Additional work on modeling and algorithms can be found for circuit-switched networks ([Eis77], [Els77], [Med94b], [MG97], [PW85], [Ros87]), IP networks ([Ben02]) and asynchronous transfer mode/broadband networks ([CMT97],[Cot99], [Med95], [MT00b]).

Multi-time period modeling for network design was reportedly first discussed in [Yag73]. Various models and algorithms for multi-period design has been addressed over the years; for example, see [DL92], [GADO01], [LMS+89], [Lus82], and [PD99]. A key approach to multi-period design is the dynamic programming approach. The literature on dynamic programming is rich; a brief summary can be found in [Den78]; the reader may consult books such as [Bel58], [BD62], and [Den82] for additional detail. Incidently, a dynamic programming case study of multi-year cable demand for a telephone company can be found in [Sha84, p.558]. We have also presented a hybrid approach for the loading problem based on combining the flow deviation algorithm (with PARTAN extension) and a projected gradient push. The literature on multi-period is very extensive in areas other than telecommunications such as production, operations, and inventory management. We direct the reader to [Gre97], [JM74], [KR87], and [KT81].

EXERCISES FOR CHAPTER 11

11.1. Consider the three-hour demand matrix in Table 11.7 and determine why the multi-hour design approach does not have any benefit over the single-busy hour case.

11.2. Extend formulation (11.1.1) to consider multiple and different types of modular capacity instead of just one. (Hint: see Section 4.3.1.)

11.3. Reformulate Problem (11.1.2) using incremental link cost functions according to (4.3.4) with the constraint incremental module $m_k \equiv M$ (with a concave envelope) instead of the concave dimensioning functions $F_{et}(\cdot)$ (you may skip the dependence on t).

TABLE 11.7 Multi-Hour Demand

Demand Pair	Hour-1	Hour-2	Hour-3
⟨1,2⟩	13	8	13
⟨1,3⟩	7	12	12
⟨2,3⟩	11	5	11

11.4. Develop a Lagrangian relaxation-based dual approach for (11.1.1).

11.5. Write the formulation similar to (11.1.5) when flows can be splittable, and discuss the applicability of Benders' decomposition approach (Section 10.3) to your model.

11.6. Show the equivalence between the transformed problem of maximizing (11.1.9) subject to constraints (11.1.5b) and the original Problem (11.1.5).

11.7. Extend formulation (11.2.9) to include multiple transport link module types.

11.8. For the integral flow multi-period Problem (11.2.10), develop a Lagrangian relaxation-based dual approach.

11.9. Show that the vector $\boldsymbol{x}^k + \alpha(\bar{\boldsymbol{w}} - \boldsymbol{x}^{k-1})$, where $\bar{w}$ is given by (11.2.18), satisfies $\boldsymbol{E}\boldsymbol{x} = \boldsymbol{h}$.

CHAPTER 12

Multi-Layer Networks: Modeling and Design

So far the discussion of the book has been concentrated on single-layer networks. In this chapter we will extend the presentation of Chapters 4 and 9 (problem formulations) and Chapters 5 and 10 (optimization methods), and proceed to networks composed of more than one layer of resources. Recall that examples of multi-layer modeling and its importance to the design of communication networks have already been addressed in Sections 2.8 and 3.7. In this chapter we will deal only with selected, most characteristic issues related to multi-layer network modeling; more comprehensive treatment of this subject would require a book on its own. We believe that this chapter will provide the reader with the essence of multi-layer network modeling, thus opening the way for his/her own developments in this type of problem.

We start with discussing networks composed of two layers of resources in the normal operating state (Section 12.1). We introduce models (formulations) of basic problems and briefly discuss methods for their resolution, using the approaches already known from Chapters 4 and 5. We then show how the basic formulations can be extended to more than two resource layers and discuss other extensions. The methods and resulting algorithms are generalizations of their single-layer counterparts; introducing more layers adds a new "dimension" to the optimization algorithms (refer to the generalization of the single-path allocation rule), corresponding to layer hierarchy.

In Section 12.2 we discuss optimization models for basic restoration design problems of reconfigurable two-layer networks robust to failures. In these models the lowermost layer links are subject to failures as this is the most important case in failure modeling. Three basic problems are discussed in detail, differing in the particular combination of layers that can be reconfigured. Extensions of the three basic models are explained and, finally, general optimization methods applicable for the multi-layer restoration problems are discussed.

Section 12.3 is devoted to an important case of mixed capacitated-uncapacitated problems for networks robust to failures, with fixed capacities of the lowermost layer links. In this section we additionally discuss several important issues related to multi-layer modeling and design, including failure and cost propagation and demand propagation and the resulting (natural) approach to multi-layer network design through iterative consideration of single-layer problems.

Section 12.4 presents applications of the decomposition methods of LR (with subgradient maximization), BD, and PG, to the most representative restoration design problems selected from Sections 12.1 and 12.2. We formulate detailed optimization algorithms and the underlying theoretical results. Although this section is sometimes rather complicated, it should give the reader a great deal of skill in using the presented, basic optimization methods. Numerical examples illustrating the methods discussed in Section 12.4 are shown in Section 12.5. Cost comparison illustrating the material of Section 12.3 is reported in Section 12.6.

The last large section of this chapter, Section 12.7, discusses an important class of design problems called *grooming*—a technique associated with traffic (demand) multiplexing in multi-layer transmission networks. We end the chapter with summary and suggested reading for the material presented in this chapter.

In this chapter we adopt a problem naming convention that uses the name $(L+1)$-layer network for a network composed of L resource layers numbered from 1 (the lowermost layer) to L. The uppermost $(L+1)$-th layer is added and used merely to represent the demand volume imposed on the network, to be realized jointly by all the lower (resource) layers. As you will notice that this convention helps to formulate the multi-layer problems since this makes it is easier for all of the objects (mainly links) appearing in the models. Note that with this convention all of the problems considered earlier in this book could be thought of as two-layer problems as they deal with one (selected) resource layer and the demand layer on top of it.

To describe the (unavoidably complex) abbreviation convention for the problems formulated in this chapter consider first the following example: D/2L/CF(1)-CF(2)/NBR(1)-BR(2)/MC(1)-CC(2)/LIN for a two resource-layer architecture. Here D stands (as usual) for normal design (i.e., for normal operating state), 2L denotes the problem with two layers of resources, CF(1) means continuous flows in layer 1 (lower layer), CF(2) continuous flows in layer 2 (upper layer), NBR(1) stands for non-bifurcated routing (as you may remember called also single-path or unsplittable flow routing) in lower layer, BR(2) for bifurcated (arbitrary) routing in layer 2 (upper layer), MC(1) means that layer 1 (lower layer) is dimensioned for modular capacity of links (and hence with integral link capacity variables), CC(2) means that layer 2 has continuous link capacity variables, and finally LIN denotes that the cost function is linear. To simplify this tedious explanation we will skip the distinction between layers if the same option is used in all of them. For instance, D/2L/CF/BR/CC/LIN means that the CF, BR and CC option is used in both layers of resources for flow allocation, for flow routing, and for link dimensioning, respectively. We note that for other types of problems the abbreviation may became shorter (e.g., for allocation problems A) or longer. The last case holds for restoration design problems (DR), as we have to specify what kind of protection/restoration is admitted in each resource layer (including the case with no protection). For instance, DR/2L/CF/BR/CC/LIN/LRU(1)-PRR(2) means a restoration (multi-state) 2-layer dimensioning problem with continuous flows (both layers) and bifurcated routing in the normal state (both layers), continuous capacities (both layers), and linear cost function. Then, LRU(1) stands for unrestricted link restoration in layer 1 and restricted path restoration in layer 2. Again, if the same protection mechanism is used in all layers then only one option will appear in the last position.

The list of options used in this chapter for the consecutive positions is as follows:

1. D (dimensioning for the normal state), A (allocation), M (mixed, e.g., capacitated in layer 1 and uncapacitated in layer 2 (upper layer)), DR (restoration design), MH (multi-hour design)
2. 2L, 3L, and so on , and ML (the last denotes the general multi-layer case)
3. LIN (linear cost), MOD (modular cost), CX (convex cost), CV (concave cost)
4. CF(ℓ) (continuous flows in layer ℓ), MF (modular)
5. BR(ℓ) (bifurcated routing in layer ℓ), NBR(ℓ) (non-bifurcated, i.e., single-path routing)
6. CC(ℓ) (continuous link capacity in layer ℓ), MC (modular)
7. NPR(ℓ) (no protection/restoration in layer ℓ), LRU(ℓ) (unrestricted link restoration), PRU(ℓ) (unrestricted path restoration), PRR(ℓ) (restricted path restoration), and others, as in Chapter 9.

Finally we mention that we will occasionally be adding a comment at the end of the abbreviation of a problem. The purpose of using such a comment is two-fold. First, it can indicate a modification of a previously formulated problem; for example, A/2L/CF/BR/CC {ALC} will denote the basic two-layer allocation problem A/2L/CF/BR/CC with augmented link capacities. Second, the comment will serve as a (short) acronym which can be used to denote the introduced problem instead of using its full abbreviation (which is typically quite long). For example, after introducing the abbreviation DR/2L/CF/BR/CC/LIN/PRU {TLDP} (which denotes a basic two-layer restoration design problem) we can use only 'TLDP' instead of the full abbreviation.

12.1 DESIGN OF MULTI-LAYER NETWORKS

In this section we will survey basic design problems for multi-layer networks. The discussion will not be as detailed as the one on the single-layer networks in Chapter 4. We hope that, with the knowledge of Chapter 4, the reader will not have difficulties in formulating the various extensions of the presented problems and selecting the appropriate solution methods when such a necessity arises.

12.1.1 Multi-Layer Technology-Related Example

Before we delve into modeling aspects, it is beneficial to illustrate multi-layer networks. Recall that in Section 1.6 in Chapter 1, we have briefly discussed multi-layer networks to illustrate how complex networks are intertwined due to deployment and role of different technologies (for example, see Figure 1.14).

A multi-layer network environment originally emerged in a traffic-transport layer setting where the traffic network consisted of the circuit-switched voice network and the transport network consisted of the underlying transmission facility network. In this architecture (see Figure 12.1), the circuit-switched voice network has telephone switches (SW) with

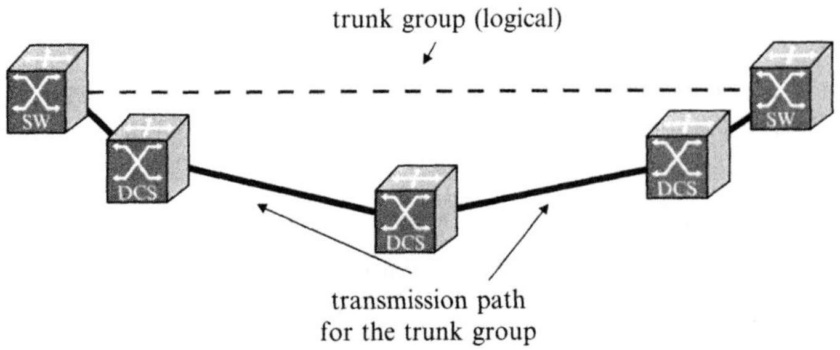

FIGURE 12.1 Two-Layer Technology Example: Circuit-Switched Voice Trunk Group over Transmission System

trunk group (inter-machine trunks) between switches. The trunk groups required between switches are physically cross-connected through digital cross-connect systems (DCS) in the transmission facility network as shown in Figure 12.1. That is, the *logical* trunk group is routed in the physical transmission network.

In recent years, multi-layer technology has evolved with many different multi-layering possibilities. For example, we consider here the case of IP over multi-protocol-label-switched (MPLS) over synchronous optical network (SONET) to illustrate a three-layer case. In this case user data traffic (packets) enters an IP network at an ingress router and leaves the network at an egress router. Now a link in the IP network is provided through MPLS routers where a label-switched path-based semi-permanent tunnel is set up over links in the MPLS networks. In turn, links for the MPLS networks are connected on the SONET network using SONET cross-connecting capability. This layered network architecture is shown in Figure 12.2.

The examples above are provided to give the reader some idea about how multi-layered networks occur in practice and as a pre-cursor for understanding network design models that encompass multiple layers. However, we do need to make a few general remarks. In a two-layer set-up, both traffic-transport layering and transport-over-transport layering are possible. For example, circuit-switched voice over DCS networks and IP over MPLS are traffic-transport layering examples. On the other hand, MPLS over SONET is a transport-over-transport two-layer example since the MPLS network provides the tunnel-based semi-permanent transport service, and SONET also provides semi-permanent transport service at a higher signal rate. Certainly, IP directly over SONET is possible with packet over SONET (PoS) technology in which case we have a traffic-transport two-layer example.

The models to be presented henceforth are mainly two-layer models. To keep the discussion at a general level, we will refer to the layers as the upper and the lower layer in a two-layer context. Thus, if we are referring to IP over SONET, then IP is the *upper* layer and SONET is the *lower* layer. Note that two layers here refer to two *resource* layers; external demand volume is what the upper layer needs to have capacity (resource) for. The general relation between demand volume and resource is discussed later in Section 12.1.4. For

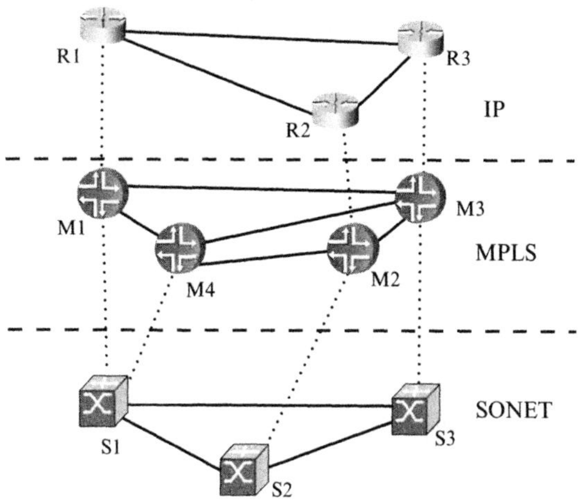

FIGURE 12.2 Three-Layer Technology Example: IP Over MPLS over SONET

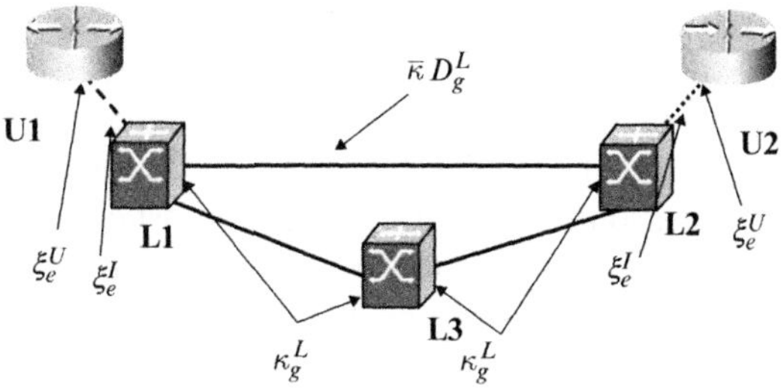

FIGURE 12.3 Cost Components

instance, for an IP network, the demand volume is the packet traffic estimate, for example, in Mbps. In models presented later, we will provide a brief discussion on the applicability of a model in regard to whether the model is for traffic-transport or transport-over-transport architecture; in addition, we will identify what specific technology/architecture a model is applicable for, even to the point where we will give models which could possibly be used with a future technological capability.

There is another important aspect we need to discuss in regard to multi-layer models, i.e., what may constitute a link cost. We will illustrate this through an example shown in Figure 12.3. For ease of understanding, we will index an upper layer link with e and a lower layer link with g. Note that on the left side of this figure, there is an upper layer node, U1, which is connected to a lower layer node, L1. The lower layer end node, L1, is then connected by a lower layer link to another lower layer end node on the right side (L2), or a transit lower layer node, L3. Finally, the lower layer node on the right side, L2, is connected to the upper layer node, U2.

The following different cost components are possible:

- ξ_e^U interface cost (cost of one line-card) for the upper layer end of the connection between an upper layer node and a lower layer node
- ξ_e^I interface cost of one line-card for the lower layer end of the connection between an upper layer node and a lower layer node
- κ_g^L interface cost for line-cards connected to transport end of node L1, and the same interface cost on the other side at node L2
- $\bar{\kappa}$ lower layer unit distance-based cost between L1 and L2
- $\mathcal{D}_g^L$ lower layer distance between nodes L1 and L2

Thus, an upper layer link cost for link e is as follows:

$$\xi_e = 2\xi_e^U + 2\xi_e^I. \tag{12.1.1a}$$

Similarly, a lower layer link cost for link g is:

$$\kappa_g = 2\kappa_g^L + \bar{\kappa}\mathcal{D}_g^L. \tag{12.1.1b}$$

The reader may wonder if there is any distance-based cost between upper layer and lower layer nodes (i.e., between U1 and L1, and between L2 and U2, identified with a dotted line). In most networks, the distance cost between an upper layer node and its corresponding lower layer "home" node can be ignored due to close proximity; in many cases, such nodes are physically located in the same building. Furthermore, note that any nodal device has an initial fixed cost, sometimes referred to as the *switch fabric* cost. In most cases, this cost can be ignored for dimensioning and allocation problems since the equipment is already in place. If the network design goal is to consider some equipment upgrade (more than just adding new line-cards), then the cost of new switch fabric needs to be considered, as well as for adding a new switch to an existing network. In general, design problems where the switch nodes and possible links are known, the dominant cost is the line-card cost and distance-dependent link cost.

12.1.2 Network Dimensioning Involving Two Resource Layers

Frequently, multi-layer network design problems involve two resource layers. These layers can appear in different combinations. In our context, we will consider two basic possibilities; in the first case, the upper layer represents a traffic network and the lower layer represents a transport network. In the second case, both layers perform transport functions and in fact represent two neighboring sublayers of the transport network. Recall our discussion in Section 1.3.3 regarding the difference between a traffic network and a transport network, and note that this discussion has relevance to multi-layer modeling. We consider a traffic network to be the one where the demand arrival is stochastic and the requests are short-lived (irrespective of their data rate); on the other hand, transport networks provide semi-permanent or permanent connections/circuits for requests at fixed data rates that are set up on a periodic basis.

We will present several models here and discuss their relevance to traffic and transport networks, and in particular to applicable technology. For ease of convenience, we will describe them as two-layer problems with upper and lower layers.

The following formulation is an extension of the single-layer design problem D/SDP (4.1.1), and is a formalized (and somewhat generalized) version of the description of the design problem described in Section 2.9 (this is a good time to revisit and refresh the contents of Section 2.9).

***LP:* D/2L/CF/BR/CC/LIN** **Link-Path Formulation**

Two-Layer Dimensioning (Continuous Case)

indices

$d = 1, 2, \dots, D$ demands

$p = 1, 2, \dots, P_d$ candidate paths in upper layer for flows realizing demand d

$e = 1, 2, \dots, E$ links of upper layer

$q = 1, 2, \dots, Q_e$ candidate paths in lower layer for flows realizing link e

$g = 1, 2, \dots, G$ links of lower layer

constants

h_d volume of demand d

δ_{edp} = 1 if link e of upper layer belongs to path p realizing demand d; 0, otherwise

ξ_e unit cost of link e of upper layer

γ_{geq} = 1 if link g of lower layer belongs to path q realizing link e of upper layer; 0, otherwise

κ_g unit cost of link g of lower layer

variables

x_{dp} (non-negative continuous) flow allocated to path p realizing volume of demand d

y_e (non-negative continuous) capacity of upper layer link e

z_{eq} (non-negative continuous) flow allocated to path q realizing capacity of link e

u_g (non-negative continuous) capacity of lower layer link g

objective

$$\text{minimize } \boldsymbol{F} = \sum_e \xi_e y_e + \sum_g \kappa_g u_g \tag{12.1.2a}$$

constraints

$$\sum_p x_{dp} = h_d, \quad d = 1, 2, \dots, D \tag{12.1.2b}$$

$$\sum_d \sum_p \delta_{edp} x_{dp} \le y_e, \quad e = 1, 2, \dots, E \tag{12.1.2c}$$

$$\sum_q z_{eq} = y_e, \quad e = 1, 2, \dots, E \tag{12.1.2d}$$

$$\sum_e \sum_q \gamma_{geq} z_{eq} \le u_g, \quad g = 1, 2, \dots, G. \tag{12.1.2e}$$

Note that in the formulation above all of the variables take continuous values. While continuity of variables (especially capacity variables) is not directly applicable in a majority of real networks, this model can serve as continuous relaxation for actual models, often used

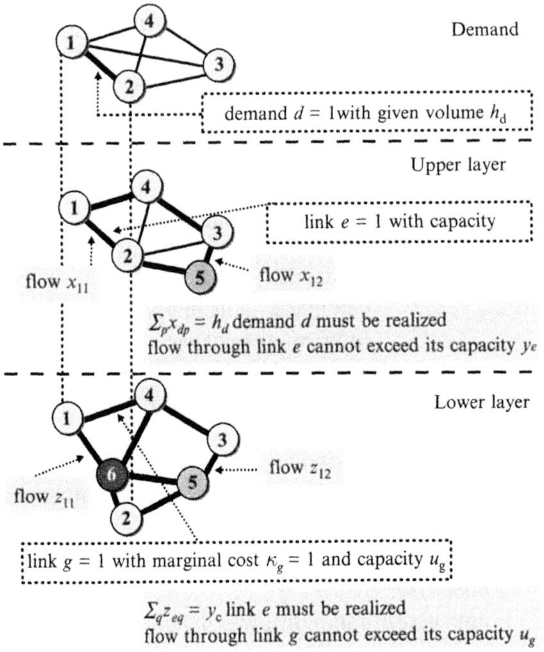

FIGURE 12.4 Two Resource Layer Network Example

in algorithm development and as approximations. In this sense, the continuous mode can be used for either traffic and transport network combination or for two adjacent transport network layers. As already mentioned in Section 2.9, in the problem above the shortest path allocation rule applies (see Exercise 12.1 and Section 12.1.4).

The important point to note about the above model is that the original demand h_d leads to determination of capacity of link in the upper layer (y_e) which in turn serves as the demand to be routed in the lower layer. Because of the routing in the lower layer, in turn, we need to determine capacity, u_g, in the lower layer links. Thus, because of original demand and the upper layer link capacity, there are two sets of demand-flow constraints (12.1.2b) and (12.1.2d), and because of routing in both upper and lower layers there are two sets of load-capacity constraints (12.1.2c and 12.1.2e). As you may remember from Section 2.4, the rule is that the capacity of links of the upper layer is realized by means of the path flows in the neighboring lower layer; this is expressed by the demand constraints. Also, both resource layers (upper and lower) are networks on their own sense, so the link capacity constraint must be obeyed in each of them. Finally, there are two cost components: one for link capacity in the upper layer and one for link capacity in the lower layer.

Note that although in the optimal solution to the linear programming (LP) Problem (12.1.2) all the constraints are binding, we have purposely used the weak inequalities in the capacity constraints, in order to maintain (almost) the same formulation in the case of integral (modular) flow and/or link variables (in the above case all variables are continuous).

Example 12.1

Problem D/2L/CF/BR/CC/LIN is illustrated in Figure 12.4 which shows that the volume h_1 of demand $d = 1$ between nodes 1 and 2 can be realized by means of two upper layer flows (direct flow x_{11} and flow x_{12} on path 1-4-3-5-2). Then the capacity of link $e = 1$ resulting from its load (the sum of all flows through the link) can be realized by means of two lower layer flows (flow z_{11} on path 1-6-2 and flow z_{12} on path 1-4-3-5-2). The resulting loads of the lower layer links determine their capacities. ●

The first generalization of the model above is to consider the case where the upper layer flow variables are continuous while the rest take integral values and the modularization of capacity is addressed.

***MIP:* D/2L/MF(1)-CF(2)/BR/MC/LIN** **Link-Path Formulation**

Two-Layer Dimensioning (Continuous/Integral Case)

constants

h_d	volume of demand d
δ_{edp}	= 1 if link e of upper layer belongs to path p realizing demand d; 0, otherwise
M	size of the link capacity module in upper layer
ξ_e	cost of one (M-module) capacity unit of link e of upper layer
γ_{geq}	= 1 if link g of lower layer belongs to path q realizing link e of upper layer; 0, otherwise
N	size of link capacity module in lower layer
κ_g	cost of one (N-module) capacity unit of link g of lower layer

variables

x_{dp}	(non-negative continuous) flow allocated to path p realizing volume of demand d
y_e	(non-negative integral) M-module capacity of upper layer link e
z_{eq}	(non-negative integral) flow allocated to path q realizing capacity of link e
u_g	(non-negative integral) N-module capacity of lower layer link g

objective

$$\text{minimize } \boldsymbol{F} = \textstyle\sum_e \xi_e y_e + \sum_g \kappa_g u_g \tag{12.1.3a}$$

constraints

$$\textstyle\sum_p x_{dp} = h_d, \quad d = 1, 2, \ldots, D \tag{12.1.3b}$$

$$\textstyle\sum_d \sum_p \delta_{edp} x_{dp} \le M y_e, \quad e = 1, 2, \ldots, E \tag{12.1.3c}$$

$$\textstyle\sum_q z_{eq} = y_e, \quad e = 1, 2, \ldots, E \tag{12.1.3d}$$

$$M \textstyle\sum_e \sum_q \gamma_{geq} z_{eq} \le N u_g, \quad g = 1, 2, \ldots, G. \tag{12.1.3e}$$

The above model is a good representation of a two-layer situation involving the traffic network (upper layer) and the adjacent transport network (lower layer). Most often, demand h_d for traffic networks can be routed (and modeled) using continuous flows for modeling purpose. On the other hand, link capacity at the upper layer can have modular values; this is where M and integral capacity variables y_e enter into the picture. Since the routing in the lower layer is on the transport network, the integrality of flows (z_{eq}) is often important. With our notion of traffic networks and transport networks, the model above is applicable for many real-world instances such as circuit-switched voice over DCS, circuit-switched OC-3 services over WDM and so on. The model above is also applicable for IP traffic in an intra-domain environment over SONET networks; however, this requires a modification of (12.1.3b) to capture flows induced by routing protocols, open shortest path first (OSPF) or intermediate system to intermediate system (IS-IS). Thus, (12.1.3b) would need to be re-written as

$$\sum_p x_{dp}(\boldsymbol{w}) = h_d, \quad d = 1, 2, \ldots, D \tag{12.1.4}$$

where $\boldsymbol{w}$ is the link metric system for using equal cost multi-path–based shortest path routing (refer to Chapter 7), and $x_{dp}(\boldsymbol{w})$ is the flow in upper layer on path p for demand d induced by the link metric system.

Having now discussed the IP network case, we are ready to provide an example of modular units M and N used in upper and lower layer, respectively. Typically, in IP networks the demand volumes are given in Mbps (demand volume units [DVUs]); the interface line-cards for IP network routers can, for example, be OC-3 rates (155 Mbps); then the link capacity variables for upper layer, y_e, are in number of OC-3 units, and $M = 155.52$ Mbps (link capacity units [LCUs] for upper layer). This upper layer capacity, y_e, is now demand in the lower layer; (DVU for lower layer is OC-3), which is now routed on the lower layer SONET network with OC-48 line cards interface units; thus, the lower layer capacity variables u_g are in OC-48 rates, and $N = 2,488.32$ Mbps (LCUs for the lower layer). Note that it is certainly possible to use $\hat{N} = M/N$ and replace (12.1.3e) by

$$\sum_e \sum_q \gamma_{geq} z_{eq} \le \hat{N} u_g, \quad g = 1, 2, \ldots, G.$$

For the IP over SONET example, this would mean that $\hat{N} = 16$. An advantage of using (12.1.3e) over the above inequality with $\hat{N}$ is that (12.1.3e) allows you to see the role of different data rates at different layers for multi-layer modeling.

Next we will discuss the case where the flow at the upper layer is required to be *integral* as well. This formulation is primarily for the case where we are considering two adjacent layers *both* providing transport layer functions. While we can essentially change the requirement on the upper layer flow variables x_{dp} in the model above to use only integral flows, a slightly different representation where we define demand h_d to include the modular data rate factor m of the upper layer DVU with integral flow requirement on the demand volume (and similarly for the lower layer) is presented below.

***IP:* D/2L/MF/BR/MC/LIN** **Link-Path Formulation**

Two-Layer Dimensioning (All Integral Case)

additional constants

m upper layer module for which DVUs are allocated

n lower layer module for which DVUs are allocated

variables (all non-negative integral)

x_{dp} flow allocated to path p realizing volume of demand d

y_e M-module capacity units of link e

z_{eq} flow allocated to path q realizing capacity of link e

u_g N-module capacity of lower layer link g

objective

$$\text{minimize } \boldsymbol{F} = \textstyle\sum_e \xi_e y_e + \sum_g \kappa_g u_g \tag{12.1.5a}$$

constraints

$$\textstyle\sum_p m x_{dp} = h_d, \quad d = 1, 2, \ldots, D \tag{12.1.5b}$$

$$\textstyle\sum_d \sum_p \delta_{edp} m x_{dp} \le M y_e, \quad e = 1, 2, \ldots, E \tag{12.1.5c}$$

$$\textstyle\sum_q n z_{eq} = y_e, \quad e = 1, 2, \ldots, E \tag{12.1.5d}$$

$$M \textstyle\sum_e \sum_q \gamma_{geq} n z_{eq} \le N u_g, \quad g = 1, 2, \ldots, G. \tag{12.1.5e}$$

Note how constraints in (12.1.2c), (12.1.2e), and (12.1.2f) are substituted here. In the above, M (upper layer) and N (lower layer) are link capacity modules; thus one LCU in the upper layer is equal to M/m DVUs, and one LCU in the lower layer is equal to N/n DVUs; besides, one DVU in the lower layer is equal to n LCUs in the upper layer.

In the two models above, we have considered only a single modular type link at each layer. However, in many real networks, each layer can have multiple different modular interfaces. A case in point is that if the upper layer is a circuit-switched voice network, then typically a switch in such networks can have interfaces of multiple different types, such as T1 and T3. Then, the multi-layer capacity determined in T1s and T3s will be routed in the transport network such as SONET which may itself have multiple different interface cards at OC-12, OC-48, and higher rates.

Thus, in the following model, we show generalization of (12.1.3) (i.e., continuous flow variables at the upper layer, rest of the variables all integral) in the presence of multiple modular interface units following the formulation presented in (4.3.3) for single-layer design; this model is again applicable in layering between a traffic network and the adjacent transport network.

***MIP:* D/2L/MF(1)-CF(2)/BR/MC/MOD (Link-Path) Formulation**
Two-Layer Dimensioning Problem (Integral Case With Multiple Modules)
additional indices
$j = 1, 2, ..., J$ interface types at upper layer
$k = 1, 2, ..., K$ interface types at lower layer

additional constants
M_j size of the link capacity module of type j in upper layer
ξ_{ej} cost of one capacity unit of module type M_j of link e of upper layer
N_k size of link capacity module of type k in lower layer
κ_{gk} cost of one capacity unit of module type N_k link g of lower layer

variables
x_{dp} (non-negative continuous) flow allocated to path p realizing volume of demand d
y_{ej} (non-negative integral) capacity units of upper link e for upper layer module type j
z_{ejq} (non-negative integral) flow allocated to path q realizing capacity of type j of link e
u_{gk} (non-negative integral) capacity of link g with lower layer module type k

objective

$$\text{minimize } \boldsymbol{F} = \sum_e \sum_j \xi_e y_{ej} + \sum_g \sum_q \kappa_{gk} u_{gk} \tag{12.1.6a}$$

constraints

$$\sum_p x_{dp} = h_d, \quad d = 1, 2, \ldots, D \tag{12.1.6b}$$

$$\sum_d \sum_p \delta_{edp} x_{dp} \leq \sum_j M_j y_{ej}, \quad e = 1, 2, \ldots, E \tag{12.1.6c}$$

$$\sum_q z_{ejq} = y_{ej}, \quad j = 1, 2, ..., J, \quad e = 1, 2, \ldots, E \tag{12.1.6d}$$

$$\sum_e \sum_j M_j \sum_q \gamma_{geq} z_{ejq} \leq \sum_k N_k u_{gk}, \quad g = 1, 2, \ldots, G. \tag{12.1.6e}$$

Recall that we have presented another formulation (refer to (4.3.4)) for the modular link capacity case in Section 4.3.1 of Chapter 4 (see Exercise 12.2).

12.1.3 Allocation Problems with Two Layers of Resources

The next generalization is the extension of the single-layer allocation problem A/PAP (4.1.7) for the case of two layers of resources. We first start with the case where all variables take continuous values.

LP: **A/2L/CF/BR/CC** **Link-Path Formulation**

Two-Layer Allocation Problem

indices

$d = 1, 2, \ldots, D$ demands

$p = 1, 2, \ldots, P_d$ candidate paths in upper layer for demand d

$e = 1, 2, \ldots, E$ links of upper layer

$q = 1, 2, \ldots, Q_e$ candidate paths in lower layer for flows realizing link e

$g = 1, 2, \ldots, G$ links of lower layer

constants

h_d volume of demand d

δ_{edp} = 1 if link e of upper layer belongs to path p realizing demand d; 0, otherwise

γ_{geq} = 1 if link g of lower layer belongs to path q realizing link e of upper layer; 0, otherwise

c_g capacity of lower layer link g

variables (all non-negative continuous)

x_{dp} flow allocated to path p realizing volume of demand d

y_e capacity of upper layer link e

z_{eq} flow allocated to path q realizing capacity of link e

constraints

$$\sum_p x_{dp} = h_d, \quad d = 1, 2, \ldots, D \tag{12.1.7a}$$

$$\sum_d \sum_p \delta_{edp} x_{dp} \le y_e, \quad e = 1, 2, \ldots, E \tag{12.1.7b}$$

$$\sum_q z_{eq} = y_e, \quad e = 1, 2, \ldots, E \tag{12.1.7c}$$

$$\sum_e \sum_q \gamma_{geq} z_{eq} \le c_g, \quad g = 1, 2, \ldots, G. \tag{12.1.7d}$$

Note that A/2L/CF/BR/CC is a LP problem with capacities of the lower layer links as fixed and the capacities of the upper layer links as variables. In the above formulation, the flow routing is unrestricted (i.e., bifurcated). Note that because this is an allocation problem, it may not be feasible if there is not enough capacity c_g. The following formulation introduces single-path (i.e., unsplittable, non-bifurcated) routing using appropriate binary variables (refer to Section 4.2.2).

MIP: **A/2L/CF/NBR/CC** **Link-Path Formulation**

Two-Layer Single-Path Allocation Problem

additional constant

C upper bound on the upper layer links capacities

variables

u_{dp} binary variable associated with path p realizing demand d

y_e (non-negative continuous) capacity of upper layer link e

r_{eq} binary variable associated with path q realizing link e

z_{eq} (non-negative continuous) flow allocated to path q realizing capacity of link e

constraints

$$\sum_p u_{dp} = 1, \quad d = 1, 2, \ldots, D \tag{12.1.8a}$$

$$\sum_d h_d \sum_p \delta_{edp} u_{dp} = y_e, \quad e = 1, 2, \ldots, E \tag{12.1.8b}$$

$$\sum_q z_{eq} = y_e, \quad e = 1, 2, \ldots, E \tag{12.1.8c}$$

$$\sum_q r_{eq} = 1, \quad e = 1, 2, \ldots, E \tag{12.1.8d}$$

$$z_{eq} \leq r_{eq} C, \quad e = 1, 2, \ldots, E \tag{12.1.8e}$$

$$\sum_e \sum_q \gamma_{geq} z_{eq} \leq c_g, \quad g = 1, 2, \ldots, G. \tag{12.1.8f}$$

In the above formulation, capacity bound C helps to connect between z_{eq} and r_{eq}. Next, we will consider the mixed problem, where lower link capacities are given but we add an objective function by including the upper layer link capacity cost and the lower layer flow routing cost. In this variant the capacity variables in the upper layer are integral (with modular capacity units), as well as the routing flow variables on the lower layer; however, the routing flow variables in the upper layer are continuous. This leads to the following formulation.

***MIP:* M/2L/MF(1)-CF(2)/BR/MC(2)/LIN** **Link-Path Formulation**

Two-Layer Mixed Dimensioning Allocation Problem

additional constants

- M size of the link capacity module in upper layer
- ξ_e cost of one (M-module) capacity unit of link e of upper layer
- ζ_{eq} unit routing cost in the lower layer

variables

- x_{dp} (non-negative continuous) flow allocated to path p realizing volume of demand d
- y_e (non-negative integral) capacity of upper layer link e
- z_{eq} (non-negative integral) flow allocated to path q realizing capacity of link e

objective

$$\text{minimize} \quad \sum_e \xi_e y_e + \sum_e \sum_q \zeta_{eq} z_{eq} \tag{12.1.9a}$$

constraints

$$\sum_p x_{dp} = h_d, \quad d = 1, 2, \ldots, D \tag{12.1.9b}$$

$$\sum_d \sum_p \delta_{edp} x_{dp} \leq M y_e, \quad e = 1, 2, \ldots, E \tag{12.1.9c}$$

$$\sum_q z_{eq} = y_e, \quad e = 1, 2, \dots, E \tag{12.1.9d}$$

$$\sum_e \sum_q \gamma_{geq} z_{eq} \le c_g, \quad g = 1, 2, \dots, G. \tag{12.1.9e}$$

The model above is important in the situation when the traffic network constitutes the upper layer and the transport network is considered for the lower layer. In such a case, the lower layer link capacities can be considered fixed from the viewpoint of the upper layer, since the lower layer is dimensioned in the management/planning cycle which is different (much longer) from the traffic network management/planning cycle.

As before, the above traffic network/transport network framework is applicable to various technological cases. For instance, when applied to IP over SONET with the intra-domain IP network running the OSPF/IS-IS protocol, we can take into consideration the link metric system $\boldsymbol{w}$, and in the demand flow constraints for the upper layer we use $\sum_p x_{dp}(\boldsymbol{w}) = h_d$ instead of (12.1.9b) in the above formulation.

Problems (12.1.2) and (12.1.7) use the link-path formulation; thus, the problem of using appropriate paths in the candidate path lists arises. Clearly, in the case of D/2L/CF/BR/CC/LIN, due to the applicability of the shortest-path allocation rule (refer to Section 12.1.4), this is not an issue since the proper paths and the resulting optimal solution can be found directly using a shortest-path algorithm (the candidate path lists are not explicitly required). In many instances, a pre-defined candidate path list can be used—such list can be based on a network designer's knowledge of a network, or using a k-shortest path algorithm with metric such as hop-count as link cost to determine the initial path list (see Appendix C). In the case of A/2L/CF/BR/CC, however, if the candidate paths lists are not predefined, then, in the LP case, the proper path lists may have to be found using the path generation technique (Section 5.4.2). Certainly, when all possible paths in the lower layer and in the upper layer are allowable, then, alternatively, the node-link formulation can be used. Note that the node-link formulation cannot be used in networks such as dynamic call routing networks where a path is limited to a maximum of two links [Ash97],[Gir90]. Recall that the node-link formulation assumes directed links; for undirected graphs this limitation can be overcome by introducing directed flows for undirected links, as explained in Section 4.6.1. The node link formulation is as follows.

***LP:* A/2L/CF/BR/CC** **Node-Link Formulation**

Two-Resource Layer Mixed Allocation Problem

indices

$d = 1, 2, \dots, D$	demands
$v' = 1, 2, \dots, V'$	nodes of upper layer (all nodes of upper layer are also nodes of lower layer)
$e = 1, 2, \dots, E$	links of upper layer
$v'' = 1, 2, \dots, V' + V''$	nodes of lower layer (first V' nodes of lower layer are the nodes of upper layer)
$g = 1, 2, \dots, G$	links of lower layer

constants

h_d volume of demand d
s_d source node (in upper layer) of demand d
t_d sink node (in upper layer) of demand d
$a_{ev'}$ = 1 if link e originates at node v'; 0, otherwise
$b_{ev'}$ = 1 if link e terminates in node v'; 0, otherwise
S_e source node (in lower layer) of link e
T_e sink node (in lower layer) of link e
$A_{gv''}$ = 1 if link g originates at node v''; 0, otherwise
$B_{gv''}$ = 1 if link g terminates in node v''; 0, otherwise
c_g capacity of lower layer link g

variables (all variables are continuous and non-negative)

x_{ed} flow realizing demand d allocated to link e
y_e capacity of link e
z_{ge} flow realizing link e allocated to link g

constraints

$$\sum_e a_{ev'} x_{ed} - \sum_e b_{ev'} x_{ed} = \begin{cases} h_d & \text{if } v' = s_d \\ 0 & \text{if } v' \neq s_d, t_d \\ -h_d & \text{if } v' = t_d, \\ & v' = 1, 2, \ldots, V' \quad d = 1, 2, \ldots, D \end{cases} \tag{12.1.10a}$$

$$\sum_d x_{ed} \leq y_e, \quad e = 1, 2, \ldots, E \tag{12.1.10b}$$

$$\sum_g A_{gv''} z_{ge} - \sum_g B_{gv''} z_{ge} = \begin{cases} y_e & \text{if } v'' = S_e \\ 0 & \text{if } v'' \neq S_e, T_e \\ -y_e & \text{if } v'' = T_e, \\ & v'' = 1, 2, \ldots, V' + V'' \\ & e = 1, 2, \ldots, E \end{cases} \tag{12.1.10c}$$

$$\sum_e z_{ge} \leq c_g, \quad g = 1, 2, \ldots, G. \tag{12.1.10d}$$

As we know the node-link formulation can be used in a mixed integer programming (MIP) version for forcing single-path routing (see Section 4.2.3 and Exercise 12.3). Observe that in some networks a hop limit may be imposed on the allowable paths (for instance, in the transport networks), making the node-link formulation less useful.

12.1.4 Extensions to More than Two Layers

In this section we will show how to generalize a two-layer problem to multiple layers. Consider a two-layer design problem and note that the upper layer (layer 2) link capacities, y_e, are in fact demand volumes for the lower layer (layer 1); this "intermediate" demand is realized in the lower layer by means of the appropriate flows, leading to determining the lower layer link capacities, u_g. Now suppose that we add one more layer below the lower layer. Then the current lower layer link capacities, u_g, become demand volumes for the new layer which have to be routed in the new layer and consequently, determining the capacities of the links in the new layer. As you can see, the process can be continued: the basic observation is that the link capacity to be determined in a particular layer becomes the demand volume for its neighboring lower layer. Thus, if we denote a link in layer ℓ by e^ℓ, then its capacity, $y^\ell_{e^\ell}$, is routed in the layer below, i.e., in layer $(\ell - 1)$, by means of flows $x^\ell_{e^\ell p^{\ell-1}}$, to determine the link capacities in layer $\ell - 1$, denoted by $y^{\ell-1}_{e^{\ell-1}}$.

Now, let us consider the upward direction. So far, for the two-layer models, we have used two subscripts: d for demand and e for link. If we now re-orient how to think about demand d, then we can consider a new "demand layer" to be just a layer above the current upper layer (or layer L in the general multi-layer case). This means that in layer L, we have demand volumes that are imposed on it by a (fictitious) layer $L + 1$ which is where the original demand d is given. That is, we can in effect think of the demand layer as layer $L+1$ just above the current uppermost layer L. Thus, instead of the relationship between h_d and y_e, we can equivalently consider the generic relationship $y^{\ell+1}_{e^{\ell+1}}$ and $y^\ell_{e^\ell}$ for a generic layer ℓ. However, note that we have $h_d = y^{L+1}_{e^{L+1}}$ for the top (demand) layer. Having determined the relation between two adjacent layers, we can write the link-path indicator for layer ℓ as $\delta^\ell_{e^\ell e^{\ell+1} p^\ell}$.

Finally, another way to examine this is to consider "links" in layer $L + 1$ as the demands imposed on the whole network. Then, in essence, we can consider the L-resource layer problem as $(L + 1)$-layer design problem. Obviously, this would mean that the two-resource layer problems presented earlier in this chapter are in effect three-layer problems. Also, what we have considered as single-layer problems are in essence two-layer problems. Incorporating the above discussions, we can provide the general formulation.

***LP:* D/ML/CF/BR/CC/LIN** **Link-Path Formulation**

Multi-Layer Design Problem

indices

$\ell = 1, 2, \ldots, L + 1$ layers (layer $L + 1$ is the artificial demand layer)

$e^\ell = 1, 2, \ldots, E^\ell$ links of layer ℓ, $\ell = 1, 2, \ldots, L + 1$
(links of layer $L+1$ are identified with demands, i.e., $E^{L+1} = D$)

$p^\ell = 1, 2, \ldots, P^\ell_{e^{\ell+1}}$ candidate paths in layer ℓ for flows realizing link $e^{\ell+1}$ of layer $\ell + 1$

constants

$y^{L+1}_{e^{L+1}}$ volume of demand (i.e., link of layer $L + 1$) e^{L+1}

$\delta_{e^\ell e^{\ell+1} p^\ell}$ = 1 if link e^ℓ of layer ℓ belongs to path p^ℓ realizing link $e^{\ell+1}$ of layer $\ell + 1$; 0, otherwise, $\ell = 1, 2, \ldots, L$

$\xi^\ell_{e^\ell}$ marginal cost of link e^ℓ of layer ℓ, $\ell = 1, 2, \ldots, L$

variables

$x^\ell_{e^{\ell+1} p^\ell}$ continuous non-negative flow of layer ℓ allocated to path p^ℓ realizing capacity of link $e^{\ell+1}$ of layer $\ell + 1$, $\ell = 1, 2, \ldots, L$

$y^\ell_{e^\ell}$ continuous non-negative capacity of link e^ℓ of layer ℓ, $\ell = 1, 2, \ldots, L$

objective

$$\text{minimize } \boldsymbol{F} = \textstyle\sum_{\ell=1}^{L} \sum_{e^\ell} \xi^\ell_{e^\ell} y^\ell_{e^\ell} \qquad (12.1.11a)$$

constraints

$$\sum_{p^\ell} x^\ell_{e^{\ell+1}p^\ell} = y^{\ell+1}_{e^{\ell+1}}, \quad e^{\ell+1} = 1, 2, \dots, E^{\ell+1} \quad \ell = 1, 2, \dots, L \tag{12.1.11b}$$

$$\sum_{e^{\ell+1}} \sum_{p^\ell} \delta^\ell_{e^\ell e^{\ell+1} p^\ell} x^\ell_{e^{\ell+1}p^\ell} = y^\ell_{e^\ell}, \quad e^\ell = 1, 2, \dots, E^\ell \quad \ell = 1, 2, \dots, L. \tag{12.1.11c}$$

As we already know from Sections 2.4 and 4.1.1 (single-layer) and from Section 2.9 (two-layer), the shortest-path allocation rule is applicable for $L = 1$ and $L = 2$. Below, we present the generalized shortest-path allocation rule (GSPAR) for the general multi-layer case.

ALGORITHM 12.1 **Generalized Shortest Path Allocation Rule (GSPAR)**

procedure $GSPAR$
begin
  set all flows in all resource layers ($\ell = 1, 2, \dots, L$) equal to 0;
  set $\zeta^1_{e^1} = \xi^1_{e^1}$ for all links e^1 of layer 1;
  for ℓ := 1 **to** $L - 1$ **do**
    for $e^{\ell+1}$:= 1 **to** $E^{\ell+1}$ **do** $\zeta^{\ell+1}_{e^{\ell+1}} := length\_shortest\_path(e^{\ell+1}, \zeta^\ell) + \xi^{\ell+1}_{e^{\ell+1}}$;
  for ℓ := L **downto** 1 **do**
    begin
      for $e^{\ell+1}$:= 1 **to** $E^{\ell+1}$ **do**
        begin
          $p(e^{\ell+1}, \ell) := shortest\_path(e^{\ell+1}, \zeta^\ell)$;
          $x^\ell_{e^{\ell+1}p(e^{\ell+1},l)} := y^{\ell+1}_{e^{\ell+1}}$
        end;
      for e^ℓ := 1 **to** E^ℓ **do** $y^\ell_{e^\ell} := \sum_{e^{\ell+1}} \delta^\ell_{e^\ell e^{\ell+1} p(e^{\ell+1},\ell)} y^{\ell+1}_{e^{\ell+1}}$
    end
end $\{procedure\}$

Observe that $\zeta^\ell = (\zeta^\ell_1, \zeta^\ell_2, \dots, \zeta^\ell_{E^\ell})$ denotes the vector of *cumulated* costs of links in layer ℓ ($\ell = 1, 2, \dots, L$), taking into account not only the layer-specific cost $\xi^\ell_{e^\ell}$ of link e^ℓ but also the costs of realizing the link in all the layers below layer ℓ. Function *length_shortest_path*($e^{\ell+1}, \zeta^\ell$) returns the length of the shortest path (of layer ℓ) on the routing list for link $e^{\ell+1}$ of layer $\ell+1$, with respect to costs ζ^ℓ, and function *shortest_path*($e^{\ell+1}, \zeta^\ell$) returns the number of the shortest path on the routing list for link $e^{\ell+1}$ of layer $\ell + 1$ with respect to costs ζ^ℓ.

As you can see, GSPAR consists of two phases. In the first phase (which can be called cost propagation), we go upwards and define the unit costs of links ($\zeta^\ell_{e^\ell}$) in the consecutive layers of resources. Once the costs for the all L layers are defined, we start the second phase (referred to as demand propagation), which considers the consecutive layers downwards the hierarchy, and for each layer: 1) realizes the link capacities of the neighboring upper layer on the appropriate shortest paths, and 2) computes the resulting link loads/capacities ($y^{\ell}_{e^{\ell}}$) in the currently considered layer ℓ.

As we already know for the single-layer case, GSPAR works only for the LP formulations of the design problems. Still, the procedure can be used for the case of the modular lower layer links, although only as an approximate method. In the modular case, GSPAR is initialized by defining the unit costs of the links of lower layer (unit cost is the cost of carrying one DVU on a link) as $\zeta^1_{e^1} = \xi^1_{e^1}/N$, where N is the lower layer links, module size (expressed in DVUs of lower layer), and $\xi^1_{e^1}$ is the unit cost of one such module for link e^1. After that, GSPAR is executed, resulting in the flow allocations for all layers and, ultimately, in loads $\underline{y}^1_{e^1}$ of the layer 1 links. Then we can either stop (adopting the values $y^1_{e^1} = \lceil \underline{y}^1_{e^1}/M \rceil$ as the modular capacities of the layer 1 links), or continue by repeating GSPAR with the unit costs $\zeta^1_{e^1}$ modified according to the formula $\zeta^1_{e^1} = y^1_{e^1}\xi^1_{e^1}/\underline{y}^1_{e^1}$. The idea behind such an iterative procedure is to promote these links of layer 1 which are better utilized and do not have excessive unused capacity which may occur as the result of modularity. This type of iterative generalization of GSPAR has been suggested in [GD98] and [Pió99].

An important issue that may have already been observed by a careful reader is that we have assumed that the demand imposed on the network has its origin only in the uppermost layer $L+1$ (especially introduced for this purpose to the hierarchy of layers). Although this kind of demand is very important, in practice, demands from other sources can be imposed directly on resource layers. For instance, a telephone/facility network operator deals with the demand imposed by the telephone traffic modeled in the way we have used so far; still the facility network can be used for other purposes, besides realizing the trunk groups for telephony. This extra demand can have its source, e.g., in the "leased line" service, a common way for small operators to create their own application networks on top of the large facility networks owned by others. This type of extension is easy to incorporate into the formulations we have used so far. For instance, in the case of two layers of resources (refer to problem D/2L/CF/BR/CC/LIN (12.1.2)) we would rewrite constraint (12.1.2d) as

$$\textstyle\sum_q z_{eq} = y_e + r_e, \qquad e = 1, 2, ..., E, \tag{12.1.2d'}$$

where r_e is the constant local demand volume between the end nodes of link e to be realized in layer 1. Of course, the local demand in general cannot occur exclusively between the nodes of the links e actually provided in layer 2—but this is not an issue—and can be easily taken into account by adding appropriate dummy layer 2 links, not used in the paths carrying flows in this layer.

Finally we observe that all the problems formulated in Sections 12.1.2 and 12.1.3 can be formulated in the multi-layer version similar to D/ML/CF/BR/CC/LIN (12.1.11) (see Exercise 12.4).

12.1.5 Optimization Methods for Multi-Layer Normal Design Problems

Multi-layer extensions of the normal design formulations considered in Chapter 4 are characterized by a larger number of variables and constraints, as well as by a greater variety of possible formulations, combining different routing/dimensioning features in different layers. The basic two-layer design LP problems, D/2L/CF/BR/CC/LIN (12.1.2) and its multi-layer extension D/ML/CF/BR/CC/LIN (12.1.11), can be solved by GSPAR. This is a desirable property, allowing for very fast approximate solutions of more complicated problems involving modular links. Basically, all other LP formulations for the normal-state design can be treated effectively by LP solvers, applying if necessary the path generation (PG) method for link-path formulations. An application of PG to problem A/2L/CF/BR/CC (12.1.7) is discussed in Section 12.4.3 (refer to Algorithm 12.5).

As already shown in Section 4.3.1, adding the requirement of integral (modular) link capacities in the single-layer case makes the design problems $\mathcal{NP}$-complete and, hence, difficult to solve exactly. Observe that if the modularity of the lower layer links is assumed then the multi-layer design problems become $\mathcal{NP}$-complete as well. Also, it is a general property of multi-layer communication (and computer) networks that when links of certain layer are modular, then the links of all the layers below are also modular. This makes all the considered modular problems $\mathcal{NP}$-complete. In addition, if the modularity requirement for the upper layer links is added to the formulation (12.1.7) (as in Problem (12.1.9)), then the resulting problem remains $\mathcal{NP}$-complete (although this remains to be shown; see Exercise 12.5). As discussed in Section 5.7.1, the basic (and practically only) exact method to deal with such $\mathcal{NP}$-complete MIP problems is the branch-and-cut (BC) approach, substantially advanced in the recent years for single-layer multi-commodity network design problems (refer to the discussion in Section 5.7.1). Certainly, application of BC to the multi-layer case poses additional problems as there are more variables and constraints involved in the solution of intermediate subproblems at the nodes of the branch-and-bound (BB) tree. Here, in some cases, the natural sequential decomposition method (that is solving the upper layer problem first and then solving the lower layer problem) can be a reasonable heuristic approach to decrease the number of variables and constraints simultaneously considered in the MIP problems. The design problems for multi-layer networks with modular capacity have not been systematically attacked yet, and only several papers (based on the BC approach) have been published. The recent paper [CMM03] discusses a BB approach (based on LR) to a multi-layer model involving simultaneous topological design, facility location, and modular dimensioning. The paper also discusses the previous work in this area including papers [CRC86] and [DV89] on modular design, and [BMM94a] and [BMM94b] on topological design. Other interesting recent papers on modular two-layer design are [BGLM03] and [LKG03].

Although the MIP approaches can in principle be generalized to the multi-layer cases, still for large networks a reasonable practical approach is to use the LP relaxation and then round off the resulting continuous values from the optimal LP solution to the integral values, using perhaps some enhancements for the rounding-off rules. We should also note that the case of modular links (and flows) can be treated in an approximate way by the iterative generalization of GSPAR, as mentioned at the end of Section 12.1.4 (refer to [Pió99]). A systematic approach of this type is given in a recent paper [MPCD03] (also see [GD98]).

Another type of $\mathcal{NP}$-complete problem is associated with the single-path (non-bifurcated, unsplittable) flow routing requirement (Section 4.2.2). This requirement for the two-layer case is illustrated through formulation A/2L/CF/BR/CC-NBR (12.1.8). So far the single-path routing multi-layer problems have not yet been addressed in the literature (except for the paper [BLM03]). One way to attack them is to extend methods for their single-layer counterparts discussed in Section 5.7.2.

It seems that the interest in multi-layer modeling and optimization algorithms for the MIP problems discussed above, especially for the two-layer case, will grow in the nearest future. This interest will be stimulated by the necessity of dealing with resilient next generation IP networks based on optical transport.

Certainly, for all of the above-discussed cases, heuristic methods can be applied, using the rounded-off LP solutions as the reference points. In Sections 5.3 and 10.5, we have already discussed selected applications of such heuristic methods as simulated annealing (SAN), evolutionary algorithms (EA) and simulated allocation (SAL) to the single-layer modular/single-path/restoration design problems. These methods can be quite well suited for such problems in the multi-layer cases, especially for the otherwise most difficult cases combining modularity with non-bifurcated flow routing.

12.2 MODELING OF MULTI-LAYER NETWORKS FOR RESTORATION DESIGN

In this section we will discuss restoration design problems that can arise in multi-layer networks. First we will describe three reference types of optimization problems for designing two-layer networks robust to failures (Sections 12.2.1 to 12.2.3), assuming (to simplify the presentation) the unrestricted path restoration mechanism in those layers where the flow reconfiguration is permitted. The three problems allow for flow reconfiguration in different combinations of resource layers: in both layers (upper and lower), only in the lower layer, and only in the upper layer. The reader will notice that the considered problems are generalizations of the single-layer restoration design problem with unrestricted flow reconfiguration (Problem (9.3.1)) formulated in Section 9.3.1. In Section 12.2.4 we will discuss some natural extensions of the previous formulations and, then, in Section 12.2.5, we will survey optimization methods for multi-layer restoration design.

All three multi-layer restoration designs are important problems from an applicability point-of-view. For example, consider IP over SONET. If IP routing does allow re-routing under a failure and SONET can provide reconfigurability, this can serve as an example of reconfigurability in both layers. If we consider dynamic routing circuit-switched voice networks over SONET where trunk routing is done statically, then flow reconfiguration is possible only in the upper layer. The final case is when the upper layer reconfigurability is not possible or disabled, but only the lower layer re-configurability is possible—an example is a private IP/VP network that is provided over a dynamic SONET-based transport network. Needless to say, other applicabilities can be easily conceived.

12.2.1 *The Case of Two Reconfigurable Layers*

We start with the LP problem of designing two-layer networks robust to failures, where flows of layers 1 and 2 are assumed to be reconfigurable and the reconfiguration is unrestricted.

It will soon become clear that this assumption implies that the capacities of the links of the upper layer are flexible and, hence, situation-dependent (network state-dependent). Links of the lower layer are not flexible: only a part or the entire normal capacity of a link can be lost in a failure state (situation).

Below, as in Chapters 9 to 11, we assume that there is a predefined list of S different states and that for each such state it is specified what part of capacity of each lower layer link g works ($\alpha_{gs}u_g$, where $0 \le \alpha_{gs} \le 1$ or $\alpha_{gs} \in \{0,1\}$) and what is the volume of each demand d ($\chi_{ds}h_d$, where $\chi_{ds} \ge 0$) to be actually realized. Besides, we also assume (binary) availability coefficients for nodes of upper layer, β_{vs}. Since in this section we are dealing only with the unrestricted flow reallocation problems, all of the states are treated equally. Hence, it is not necessary to distinguish $s = 0$ (denoting the normal state) and we will label the states with $s = 1, 2, \ldots, S$.

***LP:* DR/2L/CF/BR/CC/LIN/PRU** **Link-Path Formulation**

Two-Layer Restoration Dimensioning With Unrestricted Flow Reconfiguration in Both Layers

indices

$d = 1, 2, \ldots, D$	demands
$p = 1, 2, \ldots, P_d$	candidate paths in upper layer for flows realizing demand d
$e = 1, 2, \ldots, E$	links of upper layer
$q = 1, 2, \ldots, Q_e$	candidate paths in lower layer for flows realizing link e
$g = 1, 2, \ldots, G$	links of lower layer
$v = 1, 2, \ldots, V$	nodes of upper layer
$s = 1, 2, \ldots, S$	failure-demand states (situations) (including the normal state)

constants

h_d	volume of demand d
a_{ve}	= 1 if link e is incident with node v; 0, otherwise
δ_{edp}	= 1 if link e of upper layer belongs to path p realizing demand d; 0, otherwise
γ_{geq}	= 1 if link g of lower layer belongs to path q realizing link e of upper layer; 0, otherwise
ς_v	unit cost of the capacity of node v of upper layer (termination cost and switching cost)
κ_g	unit cost of link g of lower layer
χ_{ds}	demand coefficient of demand d in state s, $h_{ds} = \chi_{ds}h_d$
β_{vs}	binary availability coefficient of node v of upper layer in state s ($\beta_{vs} \in \{0,1\}$)
α_{gs}	fractional availability coefficient of link g of lower layer in state s ($0 \le \alpha_{gs} \le 1$)

variables (all variables are continuous and non-negative)

x_{dps}	flow allocated to path p of demand d in state s (state-dependent)
Y_v	capacity of node v of upper layer (state-independent)
y_{es}	capacity of link e in state s (state-dependent)
z_{eqs}	flow allocated to path q realizing capacity of link e in state s (state-dependent)
u_g	capacity of link g (state independent)

objective

$$\text{minimize } \boldsymbol{F} = \textstyle\sum_g \kappa_g u_g + \sum_v \varsigma_v Y_v \qquad (12.2.1a)$$

constraints

$$\sum_p x_{dps} = h_{ds}, \quad d = 1,2,\dots,D \quad s = 1,2,\dots,S \tag{12.2.1b}$$

$$\sum_d \sum_p \delta_{edp} x_{dps} \le y_{es}, \quad e = 1,2,\dots,E \quad s = 1,2,\dots,S \tag{12.2.1c}$$

$$\sum_e a_{ve} y_{es} \le \beta_{vs} Y_v, \quad v = 1,2,\dots,V \quad s = 1,2,\dots,S \tag{12.2.1d}$$

$$\sum_q z_{eqs} = y_{es}, \quad e = 1,2,\dots,E \quad s = 1,2,\dots,S \tag{12.2.1e}$$

$$\sum_e \sum_q \gamma_{geq} z_{eqs} \le \alpha_{gs} u_g, \quad g = 1,2,\dots,G \quad s = 1,2,\dots,S. \tag{12.2.1f}$$

The demand-flow constraints assure that the state-dependent demand volumes h_{ds} are realized by the state-dependent flows in the upper layer (constraint (12.2.1b)), and that the state-dependent demand imposed on the lower layer (specified by the upper layer link capacities y_{es}) is realized by the state-dependent lower layer flows (constraint (12.2.1e)). The load-capacity constraints (12.2.1c) and (12.2.1f) assure feasibility of flows in the upper layer and the lower layer, respectively, i.e., that the state-dependent loads of links do not exceed their capacities. Observe that although for any optimal solution to (12.2.1) (which is an LP problem) the equalities will hold in constraint (12.2.1c), this is not the case for constraint (12.2.1f). In the latter case, at the optimum, links are not in general saturated in all states. Constraint (12.2.1c) defines the capacity Y_v of each node v in the upper layer, expressed as the maximum (over all states) of the working link capacity connected to the node. Such defined node capacity is used in the cost function (12.2.1a). Note that, contrary to the normal design problem D/2L/CF/BR/CC/LIN (12.1.2), we cannot use the capacity of the upper layer links in the cost function, as this capacity is in fact "virtual" and is in general different in various situations. Also note that the failure of nodes of the upper layer is directly taken into account in the formulation (in constraint (12.2.1d)). For nodes of the lower layer, this is not necessary because here the node failures can be effectively modeled by the link failures (refer to the discussion in Section 9.1.1). Also, when a node which generates demand is affected in state s, then this can be taken into account by using appropriately defined demand coefficients χ_{ds}, $d = 1,2,\dots,D, s = 1,2,\dots,S$.

We wish to point out that even if the capacity of the upper layer nodes (Y_e) is skipped in the formulation, the resulting problem is still meaningful. This is clearly the case when the link capacity is the dominant cost factor in the network optimization problem, i.e., when the nodes are dimensioned independently (or assumed to be already installed).

Skipping capacity of the upper layer nodes leads to the following relatively simple LP formulation, referred in the rest of the discussion as the (simple) two-layer design problem (TLDP).

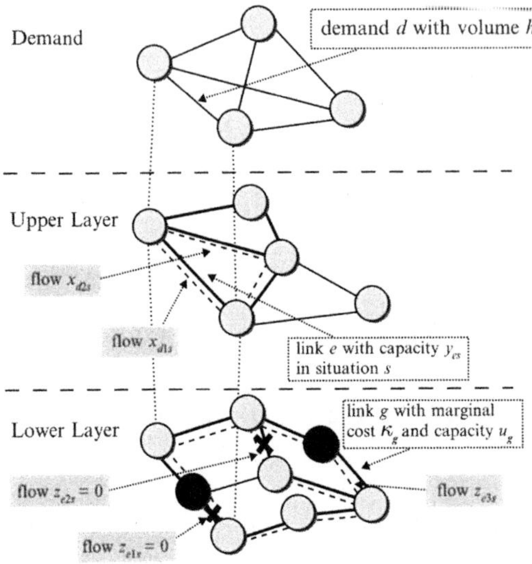

FIGURE 12.5 Two-Layer Networks with Failures

LP: DR/2L/CF/BR/CC/LIN/PRU {TLDP} **Link-Path Formulation**
Two-Layer Restoration Dimensioning With Unrestricted Flow Reconfiguration in Both Layers—Simple Case
objective

$$\text{minimize } \boldsymbol{F} = \sum_g \kappa_g u_g \tag{12.2.2a}$$

constraints

$$\sum_p x_{dps} = h_{ds}, \quad d = 1, 2, \dots, D \quad s = 1, 2, \dots, S \tag{12.2.2b}$$

$$\sum_d \sum_p \delta_{edp} x_{dps} \le y_{es}, \quad e = 1, 2, \dots, E \quad s = 1, 2, \dots, S \tag{12.2.2c}$$

$$\sum_q z_{eqs} = y_{es}, \quad e = 1, 2, \dots, E \quad s = 1, 2, \dots, S \tag{12.2.2d}$$

$$\sum_e \sum_q \gamma_{geq} z_{eqs} \le \alpha_{gs} u_g, \quad g = 1, 2, \dots, G \quad s = 1, 2, \dots, S. \tag{12.2.2e}$$

Problem TLDP is illustrated in Figure 12.5. As you can see, volume h_{ds} of demand d in state s can be realized by means of two flows, x_{d1s} and x_{d2s}, in the upper layer. In the considered situation two of the lower layer links completely fail, thus capacity y_{es} can be

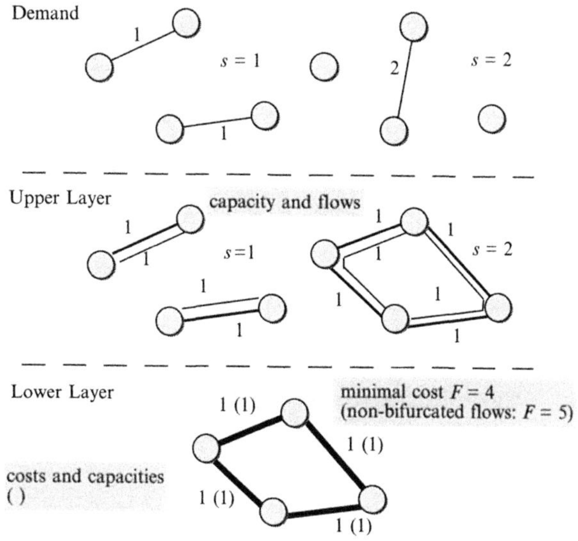

FIGURE 12.6 Necessarily Bifurcated Optimal Flows

realized only by flow z_{e3s} in the lower layer since the two remaining flows, z_{e1s} and z_{e2s}, use failed links.

Example 12.2

Figure 12.6 illustrates the fact (already discussed in Section 9.3.1 for the single-layer networks) that in general the optimal flows for the robust multi-layer problems are bifurcated (refer to Example 9.4 in Section 9.3.1). This implies that no simple shortest-path allocation rule, as GSPAR of Section 12.1.2, can apply. As illustrated by Exercise 12.6, an example analogous to that of Figure 2.9 in Section 2.10 can also be given for the two-layer network.●

In practice, modular link capacity, modular node capacity, and/or integer flows can be required in either one of the layers or in both layers. In the fully modular case, we introduce integral variables for the capacity of links and nodes in both layers, as well as for the path flows. In such a case we can explicitly introduce the availability coefficients for the nodes and use them in the formulation. This leads to the following, complicated, but quite general, formulation.

***IP:* DR/2L/MF/BR/MC/LIN/PRU** **Link-Path Formulation**
Two-Layer Restoration Dimensioning With Unrestricted Flow Reconfiguration in Both Layers—Modular Links and Flows
additional indices

$v' = 1, 2, \ldots, V'$	nodes of upper layer
$v'' = 1, 2, \ldots, V' + V''$	nodes of lower layer (first V' nodes are common for layer 1 and layer 2)

additional constants

$b_{v''g}$ = 1 if link g of lower layer is incident with node v''; 0, otherwise
M module of capacity of the upper layer nodes
m module of capacity of the upper layer links
N module of capacity of the lower layer nodes
n module of capacity of the lower layer links
$\psi_{v''}$ unit cost of the capacity of node v'' of lower layer (termination and switching cost)

variables (all variables are continuous and non-negative)

x_{dps} flow allocated to path p of demand d in state s
$Y_{v'}$ capacity of node v' of upper layer (state-independent)
y_{es} capacity of link e in state s (state-dependent)
z_{eqs} flow allocated to path q realizing capacity of link e in state s
$U_{v''}$ capacity of node v'' of lower layer (state-independent)
u_g capacity of link g

objective

$$\text{minimize } \boldsymbol{F} = \textstyle\sum_g \kappa_g u_g + \sum_{v''} \psi_{v''} U_{v''} + \sum_{v'} \varsigma_{v'} Y_{v'} \tag{12.2.3a}$$

constraints

$$\textstyle\sum_p x_{dps} = h_{ds}, \quad d = 1, 2, \ldots, D \quad s = 1, 2, \ldots, S \tag{12.2.3b}$$

$$\textstyle\sum_d \sum_p \delta_{edp} x_{dps} \leq m y_{es}, \quad e = 1, 2, \ldots, E \quad s = 1, 2, \ldots, S \tag{12.2.3c}$$

$$\textstyle\sum_e a_{v'e} y_{es} \leq M \beta_{v's} Y_{v'}, \quad v' = 1, 2, \ldots, V' \quad s = 1, 2, \ldots, S \tag{12.2.3d}$$

$$\textstyle\sum_q z_{eqs} = y_{es}, \quad e = 1, 2, \ldots, E \quad s = 1, 2, \ldots, S \tag{12.2.3e}$$

$$\textstyle\sum_e \sum_q \gamma_{geq} z_{eqs} \leq \alpha_{gs} u_g, \quad g = 1, 2, \ldots, G \quad s = 1, 2, \ldots, S. \tag{12.2.3f}$$

$$\textstyle\sum_g b_{v''g} u_g \leq N U_{v''}, \quad v'' = 1, 2, \ldots, V' + V'' \quad s = 1, 2, \ldots, S. \tag{12.2.3g}$$

The modular requirement for the link capacities of the lower layer makes the problem $\mathcal{NP}$-complete. Certainly, not all types of variables are required to be assumed as integers; for instance, in many applications flows in the upper layer are continuous (e.g., when demands represent IP traffic expressed in Mbps), leading to problem *MIP:* DR/2L/MF(1)-CF(2)/BR/MC/LIN/PRU. Note that typically the modularity requirement for the lower layer links is common to all such MIP formulations.

It should be clear to the reader that there are many potential variations of Problem (12.2.3). Besides relaxing particular integrality requirements, new problems can be formulated by assuming different routing and protection/restoration mechanisms. This observation is further discussed in Section 12.2.4 and holds for the rest of the problems considered in Sections 12.2.2 and 12.2.3 below.

12.2.2 *Restoration Involving Only Reconfiguration of Lower Layer*

The next generalization of the single-layer restoration Problem (9.3.1) is obtained when the upper layer (layer 2) is not rearrangeable and, hence, its flow and link capacities are the same in all states (are not state-dependent, as in the problems considered in the previous section). However, the (unrestricted) flow reconfiguration is allowed in the lower layer. The LP formulation is as follows.

***LP:* DR/2L/CF/BR/CC/LIN/PRU(1)-NPR(2) {LLDP} Link-Path Formulation**
Two-Layer Restoration Dimensioning With Unrestricted Flow Reconfiguration in the Lower Layer
additional constants
H_d $\max\{h_{ds},\ s = 1,2,\dots,S\}$ maximal value of demand d
variables (all variables are continuous and non-negative)
x_{dp} flow allocated to path p of demand d in all states
y_e capacity of link e in all states
z_{eqs} flow allocated to path q realizing capacity of link e in state s
u_g capacity of link g
objective

$$\text{minimize } \boldsymbol{F} = \textstyle\sum_g \kappa_g u_g \tag{12.2.4a}$$

constraints

$$\textstyle\sum_p x_{dp} = H_d, \quad d = 1,2,\dots,D \tag{12.2.4b}$$

$$\textstyle\sum_d \sum_p \delta_{edp} x_{dp} \le y_e, \quad e = 1,2,\dots,E \tag{12.2.4c}$$

$$\textstyle\sum_q z_{eqs} = y_e, \quad e = 1,2,\dots,E \quad s = 1,2,\dots,S \tag{12.2.4d}$$

$$\textstyle\sum_e \sum_q \gamma_{geq} z_{eqs} \le \alpha_{gs} u_g, \quad g = 1,2,\dots,G \quad s = 1,2,\dots,S. \tag{12.2.4e}$$

In the network configuration obtained as a solution to the above problem, flow and link capacities of the upper layer are fixed; in other words, the demands do not see that there are any failures because from their viewpoint, the links (of the upper layer) are perfectly reliable as it is entirely the duty of the lower layer flow restoration mechanism to deal with the lower layer link failures and make them invisible in the upper layer. A certain disadvantage of the considered reconfiguration restriction is that for each demand the same demand volume is realized in all states (refer to constraint (12.2.4b)) although this may be otherwise unnecessary. Observe that in the above formulation we needed to assume perfectly reliable nodes of the upper layer as we have no means to restore the flows in the upper layer. Note that for simplicity of the formulation we have skipped the cost of the upper layer nodes, although this can be easily added in the same way as in Problem (12.2.1). Similar to the interger programming formulation (12.2.3), we can add modular requirements on the link and node capacity in the above problem. Problem (12.2.4) will be abbreviated as lower-layer design problem (LLDP) in the sequel.

12.2.3 Restoration Involving Only Reconfiguration of Upper Layer

In the last problem of the considered series, the flow and link capacities of the upper layer are reconfigurable, while the flows of the lower layer are not. This time we assume binary link availability coefficients α_{gs} ($\alpha_{gs} \in \{0,1\}$) and define the lower layer path availability coefficients: $\theta_{eqs} = \prod_{\{g:\ \gamma_{geq}=1\}} \alpha_{gs}$ (θ_{eqs} equals 1 if path q realizing link e in layer 1 is available in state s; and 0, otherwise). Note that similar coefficients have already been used in the formulations of Section 9.3.2.

***LP:* DR/2L/CF/BR/CC/LIN/NPR(1)-PRU(2) {ULDP}** **Link-Path Formulation**
Two-Layer Restoration Dimensioning With Unrestricted Flow Reconfiguration in the Upper Layer

variables (all variables are continuous and non-negative)

- x_{dps} flow allocated to path p of demand d in state s
- y_{es} capacity of link e in state s
- z_{eq} flow allocated to path q realizing capacity of link e in all state
- u_g capacity of link g

objective

$$\text{minimize } \boldsymbol{F} = \textstyle\sum_g \kappa_g u_g \tag{12.2.5a}$$

constraints

$$\textstyle\sum_p x_{dp} = h_{ds}, \quad d = 1,2,\dots,D \quad s = 1,2,\dots,S \tag{12.2.5b}$$

$$\textstyle\sum_d \sum_p \delta_{edp} x_{dps} \le y_{es}, \quad e = 1,2,\dots,E \quad s = 1,2,\dots,S \tag{12.2.5c}$$

$$\textstyle\sum_q \theta_{eqs} z_{eq} \ge y_{es}, \quad e = 1,2,\dots,E \quad s = 1,2,\dots,S \tag{12.2.5d}$$

$$\textstyle\sum_e \sum_q \gamma_{geq} z_{eq} \le u_g, \quad g = 1,2,\dots,G. \tag{12.2.5e}$$

Note that y_{es} is the capacity of link e of upper layer that survives the failures of lower layer link assumed for state s. Remarks made at the end of Section 12.2.2 apply to Problem (12.2.5) as well. Problem (12.2.5) will be henceforth referred to as ULDP (upper layer design problem).

12.2.4 Extensions

The set of problems and methods considered in Sections 12.2.1 to 12.2.3 can be extended in many ways. Extensions of the restoration design formulations involving two layers of resources to more layers is quite straightforward (as for the normal design problems considered in Section 12.1.2). In the case of L layers of resources (plus one demand layer) we potentially have 2^L different basic design problems, each corresponding to a particular subset of reconfigurable layers, including the already considered $(L + 1)$-layer normal design Problem (12.1.11) with no reconfiguration.

The unrestricted path restoration mechanism assumed in the three basic two-layer problem types allows for the full flow reconfiguration (from scratch) for a new failure state. Such a path protection mechanism can be applied in some cases, but in practice, as we already know from Chapter 9, the protection/reconfiguration mechanisms are further restricted. As in the single-layer case, the formulations can be extended to the problems involving flow restoration mechanisms which do not move unaffected normal flows in a failure state, such as restricted flow reconfiguration or back-up path restoration considered in Section 9.3.

Flow restoration in a layer can be further limited when only the link capacity restoration is allowed through the link protection mechanism as described in Section 9.2. For example, we can consider link protection and single back-up path restoration mechanisms for the upper layer and the lower layer, respectively. Such a problem may naturally arise in IP/MPLS networks (upper layer) with the SONET transport lower layer (refer to Section 3.5), because link protection can be used in SONET networks, while the single backup-path restoration can be considered for the IP/MPLS solutions. The appropriate formulation is left to the reader as exercise (Exercise 12.7) where the reader is asked to formulate a somewhat tricky problem *MIP:* DR/2L/MF(1)- CF(2)/BR(1)-NBR(2)/MC/LIN/LRU(1)-SBP(2). Other problem variations are the subject of Exercises 12.8 and 12.9.

In general, if we consider the case of not using any restoration as also a (trivial) restoration mechanism, then we can formulate a restoration problem corresponding to any combination of restoration mechanisms used in each of L resource layers. Of course, the question of whether a particular combination is technologically meaningful is another issue. What we point out is that, at least theoretically, we can formulate any arising problem in the discussed framework.

As for the single-layer design problems discussed in Section 4.3, we may consider other cost and dimensioning functions in the multi-layer formulations. First of all, we may use multi-modular cost functions as in Problems (12.1.6) and (4.3.4). We may also use $\boldsymbol{F} = \sum_g F_g(u_g)$ instead of (12.2.2a) and assume that functions $F_g(\cdot)$ are differentiable and concave. Another even more important problem involving concave functions appears when the dimensioning functions (translating link load to link capacity) in one or more layers are not linear. For instance, consider Problem (12.2.2) with constraint (12.2.2c) substituted with $f_e(\sum_d \sum_p \delta_{edp} x_{dps}) \leq y_{es}$, i.e., when the capacity of a link in the upper layer is concave with respect to its load. This is in fact an important case (think of the digital telephone trunk groups as links of the upper layer; refer to Section 3.4 and 11.1.1).

In Section 12.4, we will discuss the selected optimization methods for the problems formulated in Sections 12.2.1 to 12.2.3.

12.2.5 Optimization Methods for Multi-Layer Restoration Design

The LP formulations for multi-layer restoration design can be effectively treated with solvers when aided with appropriate decomposition methods. This issue is discussed in detail in Section 12.4 where the applications of LR, BD, and PG for multi (two)-layer restoration design are presented in detail, especially for two-layer case.

As we already know from Section 10.4, adding the requirement of integral (modular) link capacities makes the restoration single-layer design problems $\mathcal{NP}$-complete and, hence, difficult (and for large instances, even impossible) to solve exactly. Of course, this issue becomes more profound in the multi-layer case because more types of variables (e.g., as link capacities in the upper layer and the flows in the lower layer in the two-layer case) can assume modular values and, hence, the resulting MIP problems get substantially larger in terms of the number of all variables and constraints. As in the case of the normal-state design (Section 12.1.5), the restoration design problems for multi-layer networks with modular capacity have not been systematically attacked yet, although the papers based on the BC approach (what else!) have started to appear ([BGLM03]). It is our conviction that as for the normal-state design discussed in Section 12.1.5, in the nearest future the development of optimization algorithms for the multi-layer restoration design, especially for the two-layer case, will become central to the theory of multi-commodity network optimization.

As already discussed for the single-layer case in Section 10.5, the BD technique is very useful in dealing with modular lower layer links. For example, in TLDP (12.2.2) the master interger programming problem involves only integer variables associated with the lower layer link capacities and, hence, can be treated within the BC framework essentially in the same way as its single-layer counterpart considered in Section 10.3.1. For LLDP (12.2.4) and ULDP (12.2.5), the corresponding master problems contain additional continuous variables. Observe that for ULDP (12.2.5), the master problem must be reformulated in order to consider the integral lower layer link capacities explicitly (see Exercise 12.10).

It should be noted that the three LP formulations considered earlier in this section, although sometimes difficult to solve, are in a sense simple, as they contain the minimum number of variables and constraints. More difficult problems arise when such limitations as, e.g., the rule "non-affected flows are not reconfigured" or when the single-path routing is assumed. In the latter case the LP problems become MIP problems and they need to be solved accordingly, either through BC or through heuristic methods.

As usual, heuristic methods can be applied to the class of MIP problems considered in this section. As you already know from Section 10.5, the more "integrality" in terms of routing, flows, and link capacities is involved in the problem formulation, the more effective the heuristics become. For this reason it may be quite efficient to apply simple heuristics, for instance, as SAL (see Section 10.5.1), SAN (Section 10.5.2), or EA (Section 10.5.3), e.g., to a restoration problem with non-bifurcated routing, single back-up paths, and modular link capacities (i.e., to problem DR/2L/MF/NBR/MC/LIN/SBP). However, we are not aiming at discussing any particular application here and ask the reader to solve Exercise 12.11 in order to gain some insight into such an approach.

Finally, we note that all the remarks made in Section 12.1.5 on the usefulness of the rounded-off LP approximate solutions are valid for the multi-layer restoration design.

12.3 MULTI-LAYER DESIGN WITH MULTI-HOUR TRAFFIC

In Chapter 11, we have discussed multi-hour traffic demand models for single-layer networks. As illustrated in that chapter, multi-hour traffic models have been used for dynamic routing telephone networks for more than two decades. In essence, multi-hour models are used to take advantage of the non-coincidence of busy hours. In this section, we will consider two resource layers problems where the upper layer is a traffic network with multi-hour traffic and the lower layer is a transport network. For instance, a dynamic routing circuit-switched voice network is an example of a traffic network where multi-hour traffic has been considered for network design; such networks are provided over a digital cross-connect network. It is known that link dimensioning can involve concave functions for such traffic networks. However, as discussed in Chapter 11, linear models can be used if demand approximation takes into account grade-of-service requirements, especially when the network is required to be designed for large-size modular capacity. In this section, we will continue to follow the same principle for multi-hour traffic. Furthermore, we present our framework in such a way that these models can be used for any traffic network with multi-hour traffic, not necessarily limited to dynamic routing circuit-switched voice networks.

We will cover two classes of multi-layer design problems. In Section 12.3.1, we will consider mixed design with multi-hour traffic (without and with restoration), while in Section 12.3.2, we consider multi-layer dimensioning in the presence of multiple services with multi-hour traffic. Certainly, as you can imagine, others combinations are possible based on various models we have presented so far in this chapter.

12.3.1 *Mixed Two-Resource Layer Design with Multi-Hour Traffic and Restoration*

In this section, we will consider mixed design with the traffic and transport network layer together. The traffic network uses multi-hour traffic demand and allow some form of dynamic (time-dependent) traffic routing. Our goal is to determine capacity in the traffic (upper) layer while meeting lower layer capacity constraint as well as diversity constraints. Note that in the following model, we have introduced the diversity factor initially discussed in formulation (4.2.1) in Chapter 4; note that diversity could have been considered in most of the models discussed so far in this chapter. We take this opportunity to introduce the diversity factor which can place a critical factor in mixed design. Furthermore, the following model extends (12.1.9).

***LP:* MH/2L/CF/BR/CC/LIN/PD(1)-PRU(2)** **Link-Path Formulation**
Two-Layer Mixed Design with Multi-Hour Traffic
indices

$d = 1, 2, \ldots, D$	demands
$p = 1, 2, \ldots, P_d$	candidate paths in upper layer for flows realizing demand d
$e = 1, 2, \ldots, E$	links of upper layer
$q = 1, 2, \ldots, Q_e$	candidate paths in lower layer for flows realizing link e
$g = 1, 2, \ldots, G$	links of lower layer
$t = 1, 2, \ldots T$	traffic busy hours

constants

h_{dt} volume of demand d at time t

δ_{edp} = 1 if link e of upper layer belongs to path p realizing demand d; 0, otherwise

ξ_e cost of one capacity unit of link e of upper layer

γ_{geq} = 1 if link g of lower layer belongs to path q realizing link e of upper layer; 0, otherwise

ζ_{eq} routing cost on lower layer path q for upper layer link e

ϑ_e diversity factor in lower layer for for link e capacity ($0 < \vartheta_e \leq 1$)

c_g capacity of lower layer link g

variables

x_{dpt} (non-negative continuous) flow allocated to path p realizing volume of demand d in time t

y_e (non-negative continuous) flow on link e in state s

z_{eq} (non-negative continuous) flow allocated to path q

objective

$$\text{minimize } \boldsymbol{F} = \sum_e \xi_e y_e + \sum_e \sum_q \zeta_{eq} z_{eq} \qquad (12.3.1a)$$

constraints

$$\sum_p x_{dpt} = h_{dt}, \quad d = 1, 2, \ldots, D \quad t = 1, 2, \ldots, T \qquad (12.3.1b)$$

$$\sum_d \sum_p \delta_{edp} x_{dpt} \leq y_e, \quad e = 1, 2, \ldots, E \quad t = 1, 2, \ldots, T \qquad (12.3.1c)$$

$$\sum_q z_{eq} = y_e, \quad e = 1, 2, \ldots, E \qquad (12.3.1d)$$

$$\sum_e \sum_q \gamma_{geq} z_{eq} \leq c_g, \quad g = 1, 2, \ldots, G \qquad (12.3.1e)$$

$$z_{eq} \leq \vartheta_e y_e, \quad e = 1, 2, \ldots, E \quad q = 1, 2, ..., Q_e. \qquad (12.3.1f)$$

In this model, (12.3.1b) captures demand flow requirement for demand d in time t. The relation (12.3.1c) addresses that the upper layer link capacity is to be determined in such a way that this can satisfy the link flow demand over all time t. Then, in the lower layer network, the link capacity y_e is to be routed on the lower layer paths, i.e., to satisfy demand flow requirement in the lower layer (refer to (12.3.1d)), while satisfying the lower layer capacity requirement (refer to (12.3.1e).

It may be noted that capacity modularity can be easily considered for upper layer link capacity in the above model, i.e., replace y_e by My_e, and then accordingly redefine the relevant variables. For example, when a single-hour traffic/demand volume matrix is considered, this model is as presented (12.1.9) with the additional requirement on diversity as shown in (12.3.1f).

The model above can be used for dynamic call routing circuit-switched voice networks (considered as traffic networks) which is provided over a transport network such as DCS or SONET networks where the capacity is already given. Note that in the case of dynamic call routing networks, h_{dt} would refer to a desirable load to be carried that meet quality-of-service requirements which is mapped into equivalent *virtual* demand in trunk units such as DS0s (see Section 11.1.2 in Chapter 11). Thus, flow variables x_{dpt} reflect the proportion of this demand that is allocated to path p in time t, which is in essence proportion of call traffic carried on different paths. It may be noted that most dynamic call routing schemes allow a path to be of a maximum of two links [Ash97], [Gir90]. The advantage of the link-path formulation as given above is that a candidate path list can be generated for the upper layer that consists of paths with a maximum of two links.

The model above can also be considered for IP networks, if we bring in the link metric system $\boldsymbol{w}$ to address for shortest-path routing–based induced flows. While currently IP networks do not use time-dependent change in the link metric system, it can be appropriate in IP networks with high traffic variability during the day to reflect time-dependent nature of traffic. In such a case, it would be more appropriate to consider the time-dependent link metric vector $\boldsymbol{w}^t$, instead of a single link-metric system. However, this does not mean that $\boldsymbol{w}^t$ changes the instant there is change in traffic; rather, the dependability of temporal indicator t is to reflect that the link metric system may be changed periodically (during the day). To reflect the time-dependent link metric system $\boldsymbol{w}^t$ in an IP network environment, we can replace (12.3.1b) with

$$\sum_p x_{dpt}(\boldsymbol{w}^t) = h_{dt}, \quad d = 1, 2, \ldots, D \quad t = 1, 2, \ldots, T.$$

Next, we discuss two traffic/transport layer mixed protection design with capacity determination in the upper layer and routing determination in the lower layer with the assumption that the capacity in the lower layer is given. Furthermore, we assume that time-dependent variability of traffic is allowed in the network along with dynamic routing as in the above model. Again, this is, for example, the case when the traffic network is a dynamic routing circuit-switched voice network where traffic is given to be time-dependent (to reflect for non-coincidence of busy-hour traffic).

We want to consider this problem for failure states that arise from the failure of a lower layer link. In this model, we assume that the lower layer link failure parameter, $\alpha_{gs} (0 \leq \alpha_{gs} \leq 1)$ for failure of lower layer link g in state s. Now, if link g in the lower layer is considered as a failure state, this can then affect multiple upper layer links e; the actual effect and the level of effect really depend on the flow allocation in the lower layer subject to diversity requirement. In the following, we will use $s = 0$ to denote the normal state of the network, while $s = 1, 2, ..., S$ to denote different failures states such as non-simultaneous failure of each transport network link (one at a time).

We first present the model and then we will explain the specifics in more details.

***LP:* MMH/2L/CF/BR/CC/LIN/PRU** {Path Diversity} **Link-Path Formulation**
Two-Layer Mixed Restoration Design With Multi-Hour Traffic
additional indices

$s = 0, 1, \ldots, S$ states (normal state $s = 0$ plus failure states)

constants (additional, or changed)

h_{dt} volume of demand d at time t
χ_{dts} traffic restoration objective in state s for demand d in time t
h_{dts} (restoration) volume of demand d at time t in state s, $h_{dts} = \chi_{dts} h_{dt}$
ζ_{eq} routing cost on lower layer path q for upper layer link e
ϑ_{es} diversity factor ($0 \leq \vartheta_{es} \leq 1$) for link e in state s
c_g capacity of lower layer link g
α_{gs} indicator for lower layer link status ($0 \leq \alpha_{gs} \leq 1$)

variables

x_{dpts} (non-negative continuous) flow allocated to path p realizing volume of demand d in time t in state s
y_{es} (non-negative continuous) flow on link e in state s
y_e (non-negative continuous) overall link capacity on link e
z_{eqs} (non-negative continuous) flow allocated to path q realizing capacity of link e in state s
z_{eq} (non-negative continuous) maximum flow allocated to path q realizing capacity of link e

objective

$$\text{minimize } \boldsymbol{F} = \textstyle\sum_e \xi_e y_e + \sum_e \sum_q \zeta_{eq} z_{eq} \tag{12.3.2a}$$

constraints

$$\textstyle\sum_p x_{dpts} = h_{dts}, \quad d = 1, 2, \ldots, D \quad t = 1, 2, \ldots, T \quad s = 0, 1, \ldots, S \tag{12.3.2b}$$

$$\textstyle\sum_d \sum_p \delta_{edp} x_{dpts} \leq y_{es}, \quad e = 1, 2, \ldots, E \quad t = 1, 2, \ldots, T \quad s = 0, 1, \ldots, S \tag{12.3.2c}$$

$$y_{es} \leq y_e, \quad e = 1, 2, \ldots, E \quad s = 0, 1, \ldots, S \tag{12.3.2d}$$

$$\textstyle\sum_q z_{eqs} = y_{es}, \quad e = 1, 2, \ldots, E \quad s = 0, 1, \ldots, S \tag{12.3.2e}$$

$$z_{eqs} \leq \vartheta_{es} y_{es}, \quad e = 1, 2, \ldots, E \quad s = 0, 1, \ldots, S \tag{12.3.2f}$$

$$\textstyle\sum_e \sum_q \gamma_{geq} z_{eqs} \leq \alpha_{gs} c_g, \quad g = 1, 2, \ldots, G \quad s = 0, 1, \ldots, S \tag{12.3.2g}$$

$$z_{eqs} \leq z_{eq}, \quad e = 1, 2, \ldots, E \quad q = 1, 2, \ldots, Q_e. \tag{12.3.2h}$$

First, note that upper layer state (situation)-dependent link capacities y_{es} and lower layer state-dependent flows z_{eqs} serve as variables expressing link/flow requirement necessary for each failure state. Now consider (12.3.2g) which is lower layer capacity constraint subject to failure state s. Note that when $\alpha_{gs} = 0$ we refer to complete failure of link g and then, for a specific failure state s when lower layer link g is unavailable (essentially, this means that $c_g = 0$ temporarily for this failure state), we automatically avoid putting any flow on the corresponding lower layer path flow variables (z_{eqs}). In other words, the capacity required for the upper layer on link e in state s, y_{es}, would need to be routed around the failure in the lower layer. Recall that this point has been mentioned earlier in Sections 2.8 and 9.1.1 with the discussion of failure states.

The main objective is to determine variables y_e and z_{eq} which appear in the cost function; note that y_e and z_{eq} are the maximum over all states s with regard to y_{es} and z_{eqs}, respectively (see constraints (12.3.2d) and (12.3.2h)). Furthermore, with (12.3.2f), diversity of flow on the lower layer paths can be enforced so that no-single failure can wipe out all the link capacity of an upper layer link for the normal (no failure) state $s = 0$, i.e., most importantly, $z_{eq0} \leq \vartheta_{e0} y_{e0}$ (note that for generality, we have included the diversity requirement for all failure states $s = 1, 2, \ldots, S$; if not required, this can be ignored).

Now, we discuss (12.3.2b) which refers to demand flow for traffic volume h_{dts}. As we have noted, the amount to be carried can be based on a restoration objective χ_{dts} for a particular time t and state s. χ_{dts} can be used as a different level of objective depending on demand, time, or failure state.

Another important aspect to note regarding model (12.3.2) is that since the capacity is limited in the lower layer, it is possible that the transport network may not have enough capacity to carry the demand requirement of the upper layer for all failure states. Thus, in practice, it is a good idea to add an artificial variable, $\hat{z}_{es}$ for each state s with the lower layer paths for flow variables z_{eqs} (as an artificial path), with an artificial cost. Thus, (12.3.2e) changes to $\sum_q z_{eqs} + \hat{z}_{es} = y_{es}$. Furthermore, a high cost, $\widehat{C}$, is added for this artificial path in the objective function; i.e., the term $\sum_e \sum_s \widehat{C} \hat{z}_{es}$ is added to the objective function (12.3.2a). Note that a positive flow on this artificial path also means that some of upper layer link capacity y_{es} which needed cannot be fulfilled by the current network link capacity. Thus, this model can also aid in determination of capacity expansion in the transport networks for two-layer model, if such an artificial variable is introduced.

12.3.2 Multi-Layer Design Problems With Multi-Hour, Multi-Service Traffic

In the previous section, we have introduced multi-layer mixed design for multi-hour traffic. However, there is another dimension we can consider with different service classes for each demand. Note that we have introduced service class aspects earlier in Chapter 4 (from a modeling point of view), and in Chapter 11. In this section, we consider the service class as another dimension and show how certain multi-layer designs are in fact beneficial in the presence of multi-service class traffic.

In the first model, we assume the flow determination in the lower layer to be static while the upper layer has multi-hour, multi-service class traffic. This is a natural extension of the single-hour, single-service class model presented earlier in (12.1.3).

MIP: DMH/2L/CF/BR/MC/LIN/NPR(1)-PRU(2) **Link-Path Formulation**
Two-Layer Network Dimensioning With Multi-Service and Multi-Hour Traffic

indices

$d = 1, 2, \ldots, D$	demands
$p = 1, 2, \ldots, P_d$	candidate paths in upper layer for flows realizing demand d
$e = 1, 2, \ldots, E$	links of upper layer
$q = 1, 2, \ldots, Q_e$	candidate paths in lower layer for flows realizing link e
$g = 1, 2, \ldots, G$	links of lower layer
$t = 1, 2, \ldots T$	traffic busy hours
$i = 1, 2, \ldots, I$	service classes

constants

h_{dti}	volume of demand d at time t for service class i
δ_{edpti}	= 1 if link e of upper layer belongs to path p realizing demand d at time t for service class i; 0, otherwise
M	size of the link capacity module in upper layer
ξ_e	cost of one (M-module) capacity unit of link e of upper layer
γ_{geiq}	= 1 if link g of lower layer belongs to path q for service class i on upper layer tunneling link e; 0, otherwise
N	size of link capacity module in lower layer
κ_g	cost of one (N-module) capacity unit of link g of lower Layer

variables

x_{dpti}	(non-negative continuous) flow allocated to path p realizing volume of demand d in time t for service class i
y_{ei}	(non-negative continuous) tunnel flow on link e for service class i
y_e	(non-negative integral) capacity on link e
z_{eiq}	(non-negative continuous) flow allocated to path q realizing tunnel capacity of service i on link e
u_g	(non-negative integral) capacity of link g

objective

$$\text{minimize } \boldsymbol{F} = \sum_e \xi_e y_e + \sum_g \kappa_g u_g \tag{12.3.3a}$$

constraints

$$\sum_p x_{dpti} = h_{dti}, \quad d = 1, 2, \ldots, D \quad i = 1, 2, \ldots, I \quad t = 1, 2, \ldots, T \tag{12.3.3b}$$

$$\sum_d \sum_p \delta_{edpti} x_{dpti} \le y_{ei}, \quad e = 1, 2, \ldots, E \quad i = 1, 2, \ldots, I \quad t = 1, 2, \ldots, T \tag{12.3.3c}$$

$$\sum_i y_{ei} \le M y_e, \quad e = 1, 2, \ldots, E \tag{12.3.3d}$$

$$\sum_q z_{eiq} = y_{ei}, \quad e = 1, 2, \ldots, E \quad i = 1, 2, \ldots, I \tag{12.3.3e}$$

$$\sum_e \sum_i \sum_q \gamma_{geiq} z_{eiq} \le N u_g, \quad g = 1, 2, \dots, G. \qquad (12.3.3f)$$

The following model is another time-dependent two-resource layer model, where upper layer flows can change over time based on time-dependent demand volume, thus requiring time-dependent link configuration; such link configurations are usually done more in terms of semi-permanent tunnels. The link capacity of the upper layer link (tunnels) being time-dependent influences the time dependent routing in the lower layer. On the other hand, to support the tunneling activities, the upper layer nodes must have interface modules in terms of capacity to handle this variability. The overall goal is to minimize modular network capacity (upper and lower layer).

***MIP:* DMH/2L/CF/BR/MC/LIN/PRU** **Link-Path Formulation**

Two-Layer Dynamically Reconfigurable Network Dimensioning

variables

- x_{dpti} (non-negative continuous) flow allocated to path p realizing volume of demand d in time t for service class i
- y_{eit} (non-negative continuous) tunnel flow on link e in time t for service class i
- y_e (non-negative integral) capacity on link e
- z_{eiqt} (non-negative continuous) flow allocated to path q realizing tunnel capacity of service i on link e in time t
- u_g (non-negative integral) capacity of link g

objective

$$\text{minimize } \boldsymbol{F} = \sum_e \xi_e y_e + \sum_g \kappa_g u_g \qquad (12.3.4a)$$

constraints

$$\sum_p x_{dpti} = h_{dti}, \quad d = 1, 2, \dots, D \quad i = 1, 2, \dots, I \quad t = 1, 2, \dots, T \qquad (12.3.4b)$$

$$\sum_d \sum_p \delta_{edpti} x_{dpti} = y_{eit}, \quad e = 1, 2, \dots, E \quad i = 1, 2, \dots, I \quad t = 1, 2, \dots, T \qquad (12.3.4c)$$

$$\sum_i y_{eit} \le M y_e, \quad e = 1, 2, \dots, E \quad t = 1, 2, \dots, T \qquad (12.3.4d)$$

$$\sum_q z_{eiqt} = y_{eit}, \quad e = 1, 2, \dots, E \quad i = 1, 2, \dots, I \quad t = 1, 2, \dots, T \qquad (12.3.4e)$$

$$\sum_e \sum_i \sum_q \gamma_{geiq} z_{eiqt} \le N u_g, \quad g = 1, 2, \dots, G \quad t = 1, 2, \dots, T. \qquad (12.3.4f)$$

Note that (12.3.4) is different from the failure state dependent model (with subscript s) which were discussed in Section 12.2, while from a formulation point-of-view they both look similar and, in fact, are the same model in some cases.

The model above is subtle in the way it handles upper and lower layer time-dependent variability of demand requirements. Note that (12.3.4b) and (12.3.4c) are standard extensions of demand-flow and capacity constraints by incorporating the time-dependent indicator t. Note that y_{et} reflects upper layer capacity required on link e at time t. For reconfigurability, we are required to route this time-dependent quantity in the lower layer—this is reflected in (12.3.4e), for which we need lower layer modular capacity u_g as shown in (12.3.4f). The subtle constraint to note is (12.3.4d)—this constraint signifies that the time dependent upper layer link requirement y_{et} can be provided only if the upper layer modular link capacity (rather interface/line-card) is available.

The discussion above also lends well to the fact that model (12.3.4) is applicable in an upper-layer environment where the upper layer is for traffic networks and the lower layer is for transport networks; for example, multi-service circuit-switched (multi-rate) based traffic networks with dynamic routing, and the lower layer is a DCS. Another applicability scenario is that the traffic network is an IP network either with *integrated services (int-serv)* [BCS94] or *differentiated services (diff-serv)* [NJZ99] capability—thus, multiple service classes can be offered with different quality of service requirements where the demand volume is available for multiple traffic hours. Note that this would require quality-of-service–based routing in the Internet (for example, see [AKW+99] and [CNRS98]). For example, an MPLS network can be established with time-dependent tunneling set up and adjustment to support for multiple services [Bla00], [FL03]. An application for broadband networks has been presented earlier in [ML97].

There is a mixed model counterpart to (12.3.4) where the capacity in the lower layer link g is already given as c_g. In this case, we only need to replace (12.3.4f) by the following capacity constraint:

$$\sum_e \sum_q \gamma_{geq} z_{eqt} \leq c_g, \quad g = 1, 2, \ldots, G \quad t = 1, 2, \ldots, T. \tag{12.3.5}$$

There is yet another version of (12.3.4) which uses the capacities of the nodes of layer 2 instead of the capacities of links of layer 2. In this modification we use variables Y_v instead of variables y_e and replace constraint (12.3.4d) with

$$\sum_i \sum_e a_{ve} y_{eit} \leq \bar{m} Y_v, \qquad v = 1, 2, \ldots, V \quad t = 1, 2, \ldots, T \tag{12.3.6}$$

where a_{ve} are appropriate incidence coefficients (refer to TLDP DR/2L/CF/BR/CC/LIN/PRU (12.2.1)) and m is the node modularity. The introduced modification allows for full flexibility of the upper layer link capacity reconfiguration within the available node capacities; note that in the original Problem (12.3.4) this flexibility was restricted by the total link capacities y_e. As done in (12.2.1a), the cost function in (12.3.4) needs to reflect cost due to node capacity Y_v.

12.3.3 Multi-Layer Design Through Layer Separation

Clearly, the multi-layer restoration design formulations presented so far in this chapter are generalizations of their single-layer counterparts. It is important to realize, however, that there is a strong relationship between the two types of problems, making the single-layer problems sufficient for the multi-layer design. As multiple layers of resources are the reality in the communication and computer networks, the operators must handle multi-layer resource hierarchy in the network management cycle. In fact, the common way to do this is to decompose the network into separate layers with their own demands and costs, and to design each layer separately, sometimes within an iterative process.

Such a layer-decomposition approach is best illustrated by GSPAR (discussed in Section 12.1.4) for the pure multi-layer capacity design problem (for the continuous variable case) considered in (12.1.11). Recall that in its simplest form the procedure is not iterative and consists of two phases. In the first phase (which can be called cost propagation), we move upwards, starting from lower layer, and define the unit costs of links ($\zeta_{e\ell}^{\ell}$) in the consecutive L layers of resources. Once the link costs for the consecutive layers are defined, we start the second phase (demand propagation), which considers the consecutive layers downwards on the hierarchy, starting from layer L. For each layer ℓ, the second phase 1) realizes the link capacities of the neighboring upper layer $\ell + 1$ on the selected shortest paths in layer ℓ, and 2) computes the resulting link loads/capacities ($y_{e\ell}^{\ell}$). Later, we will present another example of the layered-decomposition approach (see Algorithm 12.6 in Section 12.6.1 for Problem (12.3.2)).

It should be noted that in practice the design based on such a layer-separation is natural in the multi-layer environment (and even necessary) in the (common) case when different resource layers belong to different operators/providers. Moreover, even when the entire network (and, hence, all its resource layers) belong to the same company, it is a common practice that different layers are controlled/operated by independent units which act as independent operators. For instance, consider an IP network provider who uses the transport infrastructure belonging to an independent operator of an optical network. The IP network provider will design their (single-layer) network on the basis of the forecasted demand volumes generated by their potential users and of the bandwidth unit costs negotiated with the transport network operator, expressed, e.g., in the cost rates (in $) per unit bandwidth per month. A particular design of the IP network adopted by its operator will result in the bandwidth orders for the transport network. In turn, the transport provider will design their network using the estimates of the equipment purchase/exploitation costs, and the demand volumes implied by the orders of all of their clients such as IP providers, (possibly) telephone network operators, leased lines, and so on. The transport network design will eventually result in the cost rates for the link bandwidth offered to the IP operator. This process of ordering/pricing can be made in an iterative way, on, for example, monthly re-negotiation basis.

Observe, that in the case of layer separation, the layer operator can in general have a choice of either buying (in fact, leasing) the unprotected (and, hence, cheaper) capacity for their links, or buying the protected (more expensive) link capacity from his supplier. Then effective restoration (capacity dimensioning) design methods for the single-layer case can become important, as they can give a credible base for deciding for which links it is beneficial to lease protected capacity, and for which unprotected capacity will be a better option. Note that for the restoration design in their layer, the operator must have the knowledge of how the failures propagate to their layer from the lower layers of the telecommunication resource infrastructure, i.e., they must be aware of the topology of the lower layers and the kind of diversity applied there.

12.3.4 Failure Propagation

Failure and demand variation modeling in multi-layer networks deserves special attention as it influences the failure and demand models used for the single-layer design. As we will see later, in general the single-layer failure models should be derived through the multi-layer considerations. If this is not the case (and this is unfortunately quite a common practice) the considered failure models can be improper and misleading.

Consider a multi-layer network with the links of layer 1 composed of conduits (ducts) filled with optical fibers. When such a duct is for some reason devastated at some spot, all of its fibers may be cut, leading to a major failure in the network. This failure is seen as the total failure of a single link in the lower layer. In fact, it is quite unlikely (except for catastrophic situations when nothing will help!) that there will be another failure like this in the near future. Hence, for modeling network resilience, we may safely assume only single failures of links in the list of states. If such total cuts ($\alpha_{es} = 0$) are taken into account in the failure scenario for the restoration design, then, usually, there is no use to take partial cuts ($0 < \alpha_{es} < 1$) into account, especially when full resource reconfiguration is assumed, as their impact on the network is negligible as compared with the total failures. To summarize, in lower layer we may assume the scenario of single, total failures of links and use it for the restoration design.

If we move to the next upper layer then we immediately see that the single-failure scenario may no longer be valid. For instance, assume that the capacities of links in the upper layer are realized under the path diversity assumption (refer to Problem (12.3.2)), using three link-disjoint paths for each link to equally split its capacity. Then the failure of one duct in the lower layer will be seen in the upper layer as a simultaneous failure of $\frac{1}{3}$ of the capacity for a certain subset of (several) links (for the links whose non-zero flows use the failed duct in lower layer). Thus, if we were to design upper layer separately, then we would have to assume this type of partial, simultaneous link failure. We wish to emphasize at this point that many works mistakenly assume the former failure scenario, applicable for lower network layers, when considering upper network layers (e.g., trunk group layer in the telephone network or the packet layer in the IP network).

As you may have noticed, we do not assume single-link failures in our design problem formulations unless necessary; thus, our framework automatically allows us to consider multiple simultaneous link failures. Indeed, single-link failure assumption is important in the link protection mechanism; refer to Section 9.2. However, from a modeling viewpoint, partial failures (with $0 < \alpha_{es} < 1$) do pose difficulty. The reason is that the restricted flow reconfiguration models (Section 9.3.2) require binary failure coefficients, since we need to know which flows are broken in a particular situation. Thus, for the combination of certain restoration mechanisms and partial link failures, a special modeling approach must be used.

As already discussed in Section 9.1.1, the proper modeling in the considered case is to use multi-graphs (with multi-links) to represent network topology. In such a representation, each "normal" link in the single-layer network can be represented by a set of parallel links, each with its own unit cost reflecting the unique path that is used by the link in the lower layer. Of course, this modeling approach may lead to a substantial increase in the number of links (by a factor of 3, for example) leading to the explosion of the admissible paths. Still, using the PG method we can keep the number of flow variables on an acceptable level and be able to cope with even large networks.

Another issue is modeling of the node failures. The total failure of a node (i.e., the failure of the node in all the layers in which the node is present) can be modeled as the simultaneous total failure of all the lower layer links incident with the considered node. Note that this is sufficient—the node in question, for example node v, and all its incident links will not carry any demand in any layer in each failure state $s(v)$ when node v is failed (this will be assured by the constraints in problem formulations). Notice that instead of failing all the links incident to node v, we may as well split the node, and fail only the introduced internal link $e(v)$, leaving the true links unaffected. You may also note that when node v appears in the uppermost demand layer, the demand volume generated by this node must be cancelled in each state $s(v)$, by setting the appropriate demand coefficients $\chi_{ds(v)}$ to 0.

A slightly more complicated modeling effort is required when (a part of) node v fails only in a certain layer ℓ. For instance, it may happen that an IP router fails (e.g., for software reasons) but its optical part survives the failure. Then, it is reasonable to assume that the node fails also in all the layers above ℓ (in which it is present) and in effect we should eliminate node v from all the layers upwards, starting from layer ℓ. This again can be done by assuming total failures of all links in layer ℓ which are incident with node v. This can be done by introducing binary failure coefficients for the links of layer ℓ (α^{ℓ}_{es}) and using them in the capacity constraints for layer ℓ. Of course, if the total node failures are included into the failure scenario, then the partial failures are less important and may be in most cases neglected. Observe that for modeling a failure of the entire node in a particular layer we can alternatively introduce the node capacity variable Y^{ℓ}_{v} and the node availability coefficient β^{ℓ}_{vs}, and use constraints similar to (12.2.1d) for the appropriate layer.

12.4 APPLICATION OF DECOMPOSITION METHODS FOR TWO-LAYER DESIGN

The main purpose of using the decomposition methods is to decrease the size of the LP problems treated by the LP solver. In the case of the multi-layer restoration design the number of flow variables of the primal formulations can be excessive for networks of realistic size, e.g., for networks with 100 nodes in the lower layer. The decomposition helps to overcome this problem. The use of primal LP formulations provide proper results only when the number of constraints and variables is manageable; in the case of large networks the available computer resources can be easily exceeded, and numerical errors can appear.

In this section we will discuss the selected two-layer applications of the decomposition methods used in Chapter 10 for the single-layer restoration design problems. As we will see, the methods do extend to the two-layer case, but their applications become more tedious.

For this discussion we will use the two-layer formulations presented in Section 12.2. We will start by discussing LR (Section 12.4.1) and BD (Section 12.4.2) for the LP versions of the two-layer restoration problems. In Section 12.4.3, we will show how to apply the PG method for augmenting the candidate path lists for allocation Problem (12.1.7) formulated in Section 12.1.3.

12.4.1 LR With Subgradient Maximization of the Dual Function

The LR technique has been described in Section 5.4.1 and applied to the single-layer restoration design in Section 10.2. Now we will apply it to the three LP problems dealt with in Sections 12.2.1 to 12.2.3.

Problem TLDP (12.2.2)
The LR technique applied to Problem (12.2.2) (and to two other problems considered below) allows for a relatively simple decomposed computational algorithm for solving the dual problem. In LR, the computation of the dual function is split into S separate subproblems, each involving only the shortest path computations, performed separately for each failure state. Construct the Lagrangian function by relaxing constraints (12.2.2d) and (12.2.2e):

$$\begin{aligned} L(\boldsymbol{y},\boldsymbol{x},\boldsymbol{u},\boldsymbol{z};\boldsymbol{\lambda},\boldsymbol{\pi}) &= \textstyle\sum_g \kappa_g u_g + \sum_e \sum_s \lambda_{es}(y_{es} - \sum_q z_{eqs}) \\ &\quad + \textstyle\sum_g \sum_s \pi_{gs}(\sum_e \sum_q \gamma_{geq} z_{eqs} - \alpha_{gs} u_g) \\ &= \textstyle\sum_g (\kappa_g - \sum_s \alpha_{gs}\pi_{gs}) u_g + \sum_e \sum_s \lambda_{es} y_{es} \\ &\quad + \textstyle\sum_e \sum_q \sum_s (\sum_g \pi_{gs}\gamma_{geq} - \lambda_{es}) z_{eqs}. \end{aligned} \tag{12.4.1}$$

where $\boldsymbol{\lambda} = (\lambda_{es} : e = 1, 2, \ldots, E, s = 1, 2, \ldots, S)$ and $\boldsymbol{\pi} = (\pi_{gs} \geq 0 : g = 1, 2, \ldots, G, s = 1, 2, \ldots, S)$ are the multipliers corresponding to (12.2.2d) and (12.2.2e), respectively. It is easy to see (Exercise 12.12) that the dual function resulting from (12.4.1) is as follows:

$$W(\boldsymbol{\lambda}, \boldsymbol{\pi}) = W_1(\boldsymbol{\pi}) + W_2(\boldsymbol{\lambda}) + W_3(\boldsymbol{\lambda}\boldsymbol{\pi}), \tag{12.4.2}$$

where

$$W_1(\boldsymbol{\pi}) = \min\{\textstyle\sum_g (\kappa_g - \sum_s \alpha_{gs}\pi_{gs}) u_g : \boldsymbol{u} \geq \boldsymbol{0}\} \tag{12.4.3a}$$

$$W_2(\boldsymbol{\lambda}) = \textstyle\sum_s \min\{\sum_e \lambda_{es} y_{es} : (\boldsymbol{y}, \boldsymbol{x}) \in X_s\} \tag{12.4.3b}$$

$$W_3(\boldsymbol{\lambda}, \boldsymbol{\pi}) = \min\{\textstyle\sum_e \sum_q \sum_s (\sum_g \pi_{gs}\gamma_{geq} - \lambda_{es}) z_{eqs} : \boldsymbol{z} \geq \boldsymbol{0}\} \tag{12.4.3c}$$

and for a given s, X_s is the set of points satisfying constraints (12.2.2b) and (12.2.2c), and the non-negativity constraints on the variables. The value of $W_1(\boldsymbol{\pi})$ is equal either to 0 or to $-\infty$, and $W_1(\boldsymbol{\pi}) = 0$ if and only if

$$\begin{aligned} &\textstyle\sum_s \alpha_{gs}\pi_{gs} \leq \kappa_g, && g = 1, 2, \ldots, G \\ &\pi_{gs} \geq 0, \quad g = 1, 2, \ldots, G && s = 1, 2, \ldots, S. \end{aligned} \tag{12.4.4}$$

Similarly, the value of $W_3(\boldsymbol{\lambda}, \boldsymbol{\pi})$ is either equal to 0 or to $-\infty$, and $W_3(\boldsymbol{\lambda}, \boldsymbol{\pi}) = 0$ if and only if

$$\lambda_{es} \le \textstyle\sum_g \pi_{gs}\gamma_{geq}, \quad s = 1,2,\dots,S \quad e = 1,2,\dots,E \quad q = 1,2,\dots,Q_e. \tag{12.4.5}$$

Thus, the following problem is the dual to the considered primal Problem (12.2.2):

$$\textbf{\textit{DP1:}} \quad \textbf{\textit{maximize}} \quad W(\boldsymbol{\lambda}, \boldsymbol{\pi}) \quad \textbf{\textit{subject to}} \quad \text{(12.4.4) and (12.4.5)}, \tag{12.4.6}$$

and equivalently

$$\textbf{\textit{DP1:}} \quad \textbf{\textit{maximize}} \quad V(\boldsymbol{\pi}) = W(\lambda(\boldsymbol{\pi}), \boldsymbol{\pi}) \qquad \textbf{\textit{subject to}} \quad \boldsymbol{\pi} \in \boldsymbol{\Pi}, \tag{12.4.7a}$$

where

$$\begin{aligned} \boldsymbol{\Pi} \;=\; \{\boldsymbol{\pi} \ge \mathbf{0} : \textstyle\sum_s \alpha_{gs}\pi_{gs} = \kappa_g, g = 1,2,\dots,G; \\ \alpha_{gs} = 0 \Rightarrow \pi_{gs} = +\infty, g = 1,2,\dots,G, s = 1,2,\dots,S\} \end{aligned} \tag{12.4.7b}$$

$$\begin{aligned} \lambda_{es}(\boldsymbol{\pi}) = \min\{\textstyle\sum_g \pi_{gs}\gamma_{geq}, q = 1,2,\dots,Q_e\}, \\ s = 1,2,\dots,S \quad e = 1,2,\dots,E. \end{aligned} \tag{12.4.7c}$$

Condition $\alpha_{gs} = 0 \Rightarrow \pi_{gs} = +\infty$ in (12.4.7b)) can be introduced because for $\alpha_{gs} = 0$ the infinite multipliers are optimal in the dual solution (in effect they force the primal solution to avoid using paths with totally failed links). The inequalities in (12.4.4) can be substituted with the equalities $\sum_s \alpha_{gs}\pi_{gs} = \kappa_g$ ($g = 1,2,\dots,G$) because the maximum of the dual function is equal to the maximum of (12.4.3b); this maximum is attained, due to (12.4.5), for multipliers π_{gs} as large as possible.

For a given $\boldsymbol{\pi}$, the value of dual function $V(\boldsymbol{\pi})$ is obtained as follows. For a fixed state s, each demand d is realized by arbitrarily splitting its demand volume h_{ds} (by means of flows x_{dps}) among its shortest paths with respect to the weights $\lambda_{es}(\boldsymbol{\pi}), e = 1,2,\dots,E$. Any such splitting will minimize the Lagrangian function (12.4.1); in particular, the entire demand can be realized on only one of its shortest paths. After realizing all demands d, the resulting capacities $y_{es}, e = 1,2,\dots,E$ are computed according to (12.2.2c). The same procedure is repeated, separately for each s, in order to realize links of the upper layer in the lower layer: for each link e its capacity y_{es} is arbitrarily split (using flows z_{eqs}) among its shortest paths with respect to the weights $\pi_{gs}, g = 1,2,\dots,G$. Finally, the loads $\underline{u}_{gs}$ on all links g result from the left-hand side of (12.2.2e).

Note that the value of the dual function $V(\boldsymbol{\pi})$ and its subgradient $\nabla V(\boldsymbol{\pi})$ corresponding to the selected flows defined in the above way can be written in the form:

$$\begin{aligned} V(\boldsymbol{\pi}) \;&=\; \textstyle\sum_s \sum_g \pi_{gs}\underline{u}_{gs} \\ \nabla V(\boldsymbol{\pi}) \;&=\; (\underline{u}_{gs} : g = 1,2,\dots,G, s = 1,2,\dots,S). \end{aligned} \tag{12.4.8}$$

$V(\boldsymbol{\pi})$, as the dual function is concave (see Section A.5), and in the studied case it is linear piecewise. To solve (approximately) the dual problem **DP1** (12.4.7) the subgradient maximization is used. The maximization procedure (one of its versions is given in Section

5.4.1, also see Section 2 of [HWC74]; for the theoretical background refer to Sections A.8 and A.9 in Appendix A) starts with some initial vector of multipliers $\boldsymbol{\pi}^0 \in \boldsymbol{\Pi}$ and in each iteration tries to increase the dual function along the direction determined by a subgradient computed according to (12.4.8). Hence, the procedure constructs the sequence of points $(\boldsymbol{\pi}^n)$:

$$\boldsymbol{\pi}^{n+1} = P_{\boldsymbol{\Pi}}(\boldsymbol{\pi}^n + t_n \nabla V(\boldsymbol{\pi}^n)), t_n = \varphi_n \frac{(\widehat{V} - V(\boldsymbol{\pi}^n))}{\| \nabla V(\boldsymbol{\pi}^n) \|^2}, \quad n = 0, 1, \dots \tag{12.4.9}$$

where t_n is the sequence of positive real numbers, called step sizes, and $\| \cdot \|$ denotes the Euclidian norm. In (12.4.9) we assume $\widehat{V} \geq \max_{\boldsymbol{\pi} \in \boldsymbol{\Pi}} V(\boldsymbol{\pi})$ and $\rho < \varphi_n \leq 2$ for some fixed $\varphi > 0$, $\varphi_n \to 0$ as $n \to \infty$ (for details see Section 5.4.1 and pages 66–68 in [HWC74]). Here, $P_{\boldsymbol{\Pi}}$ is the operator projecting Euclidian space $\Re^{GS}$ onto $\boldsymbol{\Pi}$ (i.e., for any $\boldsymbol{\pi} \in \Re^{GS}$, $P_{\boldsymbol{\Pi}}(\boldsymbol{\pi})$ is the unique point in $\boldsymbol{\Pi}$ nearest to $\boldsymbol{\pi}$).

Observe that projection $P_{\boldsymbol{\Pi}}(\cdot)$ can be made in an efficient and explicit way using the appropriately modified formulae (5.5.13) to (5.5.14) given in Section 5.5.2 (also see Exercise 5.21 and Section 5 in [HWC74]). The modification is required because conditions (12.4.7b) defining set $\boldsymbol{\Pi}$ are somewhat different from constraint (5.5.11) (and from constraint (5.6) in [HWC74]). Note that the computation of the dual function and its subgradient is fast and requires finding the total of $S \times (D + E)$ shortest paths.

For the vector of optimal multipliers $\boldsymbol{\pi}^*$ resulting from the subgradient maximization of the dual function $V(\boldsymbol{\pi})$ the vectors $(\boldsymbol{\lambda}^*, \boldsymbol{\pi}^*)$ and $(\boldsymbol{y}^*, \boldsymbol{x}^*, \boldsymbol{u}^*, \boldsymbol{z}^*)$, where the latter is any optimal primal solution of TLDP, form a saddle point of the Lagrangian function (12.4.1). Unfortunately, the optimal dual solution $\boldsymbol{\pi}^*$ does not reveal any such optimal primal solution $(\boldsymbol{y}^*, \boldsymbol{x}^*, \boldsymbol{u}^*, \boldsymbol{z}^*)$. In general, the flows used to minimize Lagrangian (12.4.1) for optimal $(\boldsymbol{\lambda}^*, \boldsymbol{\pi}^*)$ are not primal optimal. To see this, note, for instance, that (as shown in Example 12.2) optimal primal flows $\boldsymbol{x}^*$ and $\boldsymbol{z}^*$ are in general bifurcated, i.e., split up into more than one path, although the flows minimizing the Lagrangian can be always made non-bifurcated.

Still, an optimal dual solution yields important and useful information. What we do know from such a solution $(\boldsymbol{\lambda}^*, \boldsymbol{\pi}^*)$ are the sets of paths which can be used by non-zero primal optimal flows in layers 1 and 2. These are, by the complementary slackness property, the shortest paths with respect to $\boldsymbol{\pi}^*$ in lower layer (refer to (12.4.5), and with respect to $\boldsymbol{\lambda}^*$ in upper layer (this is not shown explicitly; see Exercise 12.13). Moreover, we obtain the optimal value of the cost function (12.2.2a) which is equal to $V(\boldsymbol{\pi}^*)$. Observe that this information is sufficient for obtaining an approximate solution for the original primal problem. We may simply use the non-bifurcated flows $\boldsymbol{x}$ and $\boldsymbol{z}$ (or any feasible flow pattern assigned to the shortest paths) minimizing the Lagrangian for optimal multipliers $(\boldsymbol{\lambda}^*, \boldsymbol{\pi}^*)$ to define suboptimal capacities of the lower layer links as:

$$u_g = \max\{\underline{u}_g(\boldsymbol{z}_s) = \textstyle\sum_e \sum_q \gamma_{geq} z_{eqs} : \ s = 1, 2, \dots, S\}, \quad g = 1, 2, \dots, G. \tag{12.4.10}$$

Since we know that the value of the optimal primal cost (12.2.2a) is equal to $V(\boldsymbol{\pi}^*)$, we can see whether the cost of the so defined solution $\boldsymbol{F} = \sum_g \kappa_g u_g$ is acceptable. This procedure is nothing else but an application of GSPAR described in Section 12.1.4, separately for each state.

As will be explained in Section 12.4.2, the optimal multipliers resulting from LR can be used for effectively initializing the BD algorithm.

Finally, observe that the LR technique can be easily generalized to more than two layers. For instance, if one more reconfigurable layer is added above the upper layer (leading to problem type: DR/3L/CF/BR/CC/LIN/PRU), then the vector of multipliers $\boldsymbol{\mu}$ to be used as links' weights in the new layer is defined using $\boldsymbol{\lambda}$ instead of $\boldsymbol{\pi}$ in (12.4.5):

$$\mu_{ds} \leq \sum_g \lambda_{es}\delta_{edp}, \quad s = 1, 2, ..., S \quad d = 1, 2, ..., D \quad p = 1, 2, ..., P_d. \qquad (12.4.11)$$

The computation of the dual function of the resulting three-layer restoration problem with unlimited flow reconfiguration in all layers and its subgradients is carried out analogously (see Exercise 12.14). Note that when LR for the extended problem is solved, then an approximate solution based on the non-bifurcated shortest-path flow allocation in all resource layers can be easily found (using GSPAR).

Problem LLDP (12.2.4)

The case of LLDP is simpler as compared with TLDP. Indeed, the computation of the dual function $V(\boldsymbol{\pi})$ is easier, since instead of (12.4.3b) we have a simpler minimization problem:

$$W_2(\boldsymbol{\lambda}) = \min\{\sum_e(\sum_s \lambda_{es})y_e : (\boldsymbol{y}, \boldsymbol{x}) \in X\} \qquad (12.4.12)$$

with the constraint set X defined by (12.2.4b), (12.2.4c), and the non-negativity constraints. Hence, the dual problem **DP2** for LLDP is obtained from the dual **DP1** for TLDP by using (12.4.12) instead of (12.4.3b). As you may notice (Exercise 12.15) for the given vector $\boldsymbol{\lambda}$ of dual variables, the point $(\boldsymbol{y}, \boldsymbol{x})$ minimizing the right-hand side of (12.4.12) can be computed by first allocating the whole demand volume H_d for each demand d to one of its shortest paths with respect to the link weights λ_e (where $\lambda_e = \sum_s \lambda_{es}$, $e = 1, 2, ..., E$), and then by computing the link capacities as the resulting link loads.

Besides the simplified computation of the value of the dual function, the subgradient maximization algorithm for solving **DP2** is essentially the same as for **DP1**; we ask you to solve Exercise 12.16 to see the details. The computation of the dual function and one of its subgradient requires finding the total of $D + (S \times E)$ shortest paths.

Problem ULDP (12.2.5)

In this case we dualize constraint (12.2.5d) and substitute $\sum_e \sum_q \gamma_{geq} z_{eq}$ for u_g, forming the Lagrangian function:

$$\begin{aligned} L(\boldsymbol{y}, \boldsymbol{x}, \boldsymbol{u}, \boldsymbol{z}; \boldsymbol{\sigma}) &= \sum_g \kappa_g u_g + \sum_e \sum_s \sigma_{es}(y_{es} - \sum_q \theta_{eqs} z_{eq}) \\ &= \sum_e \sum_s \sigma_{es} y_{es} + \sum_e \sum_q (\sum_g \kappa_g \gamma_{geq} - \sum_s \theta_{eqs} \sigma_{es}) z_{eq}. \end{aligned} \qquad (12.4.13)$$

where $\boldsymbol{\sigma} = (\sigma_{es} \geq 0 : \; e = 1, 2, ..., E, \; s = 1, 2, ..., S)$ are the appropriate Lagrange multipliers. Then it can be shown that the corresponding dual problem reads:

$$\textbf{\textit{DP3:}} \quad \textbf{\textit{maximize}} \quad V(\boldsymbol{\sigma}) \tag{12.4.14a}$$

$$\textbf{\textit{subject to}} \quad \boldsymbol{\sigma} \geq \mathbf{0} \tag{12.4.14b}$$

$$\textstyle\sum_s \theta_{eqs}\sigma_{es} \leq \sum_g \kappa_g \gamma_{geq}. \tag{12.4.14c}$$

The dual function (12.4.14a) is defined by

$$V(\boldsymbol{\sigma}) = \min\{\textstyle\sum_s \sum_e \sigma_{es} y_{es} : \; (\boldsymbol{y}, \boldsymbol{x}) \in X_s\} \tag{12.4.15}$$

and for a given s, X_s is the set of points satisfying constraints (12.2.5b), (12.2.5c), and the non-negativity constraints for the variables. If for a certain link e all of its paths $q = 1, 2, \ldots, Q_e$ are failed in state s ($\theta_{eqs} = 0$ for all q) then multiplier σ_{es} does not appear in the system of inequalities (12.4.14) and we can put $\sigma_{es} = +\infty$.

In order to find the maximum of the dual function we again use the subgradient maximization technique. To obtain the subgradient $\nabla V(\boldsymbol{\sigma})$ we find, for each s and d, a shortest path $p(d, s)$ with respect to $(\sigma_{1s}, \sigma_{2s}, ..., \sigma_{Es})$ and compute link capacities $y_{es}(\boldsymbol{\sigma}) = \sum_d \delta_{edp(d,s)} h_{ds}$ for $e = 1, 2, ..., E$. Then we compute the corresponding subgradient of the dual function:

$$\nabla V(\boldsymbol{\sigma}) = (y_{es}(\boldsymbol{\sigma}) : \; e = 1, 2, ..., E \; s = 1, 2, ..., S). \tag{12.4.16}$$

Any optimal dual solution $\boldsymbol{\sigma}^*$ determines admissible primal paths in layers 1 and 2. In layer 1 the optimal primal flows $\boldsymbol{z}^*$ have the complementary slackness property: if $\sum_s \delta_{eqs}\sigma^*_{es} < \sum_g \kappa_g \gamma_{geq}$ then $z^*_{eq} = 0$. Similarly, optimal non-zero primal flows x^*_{dps} for state s can be realized only on the shortest paths with respect to weights σ^*_{es} ($e = 1, 2, ..., E$).

In the case of ULDP, the projection $P(\boldsymbol{\sigma})$ of the vector of multipliers $\boldsymbol{\sigma}$ onto set (12.4.14b) to (12.4.14c) is more complicated than for TLDP and for LLDP. It requires solving the following quadratic problem (where σ'_{es} are variables and σ_{es} are constants):

$$\textbf{\textit{minimize}} \quad \textstyle\sum_e \sum_s (\sigma_{es} - \sigma'_{es})^2 \tag{12.4.17a}$$

$$\textbf{\textit{subject to}} \quad \textstyle\sum_s \theta_{eqs}\sigma'_{es} \leq \sum_g \kappa_g \gamma_{geq} \qquad q = 1, 2, \ldots, Q_e \tag{12.4.17b}$$

$$\sigma'_{es} \geq 0 \qquad s = 1, 2, \ldots, S. \tag{12.4.17c}$$

Problem (12.4.17) can be solved be using quadratic programming solvers (refer to [CPL99] and [XM]). The computation of the dual function and its subgradient requires finding the total of $(S \times D) + E$ shortest paths.

12.4.2 Benders' Decomposition

Now we will discuss the application of the BD method (see Section 5.4.3) to all three two-layer problems considered in Section 12.4.1. This application extends the BD approach used for problems DR-U and DR-R in Section10.3. This time, however, to simplify the formulation we will not assume situation-dependent routing lists as in Problem (10.1.1) (such routing lists can be easily introduced in layers 1 and 2).

Problem TLDP (12.2.2)

We start with two basic facts—generalizations of Propositions 10.1 and 10.2 from Section 10.3.1.

PROPOSITION 12.1 *A vector $\boldsymbol{u}$ of the lower layer link capacities is feasible for TLDP (is sufficient to realize the demands in all states) if and only if for any vector $\boldsymbol{\eta} = (\eta_g \geq 0 : g = 1, 2, \ldots, G)$ the following condition holds:*

$$\textstyle\sum_g \alpha_{gs} \eta_g u_g \geq F_s(\boldsymbol{\eta}), \quad s = 1, 2, \ldots, S, \tag{12.4.18}$$

where $F_s(\boldsymbol{\eta})$, for a fixed state s, is the optimal objective of the following minimization problem:

$$\begin{aligned}
&\textit{minimize} && \textstyle\sum_g \eta_g \underline{u}_{gs} && (12.4.19a)\\
&\textit{subject to} && \boldsymbol{x}, \boldsymbol{y}, \boldsymbol{z}, \underline{\boldsymbol{u}} \text{ continuous and non-negative} && (12.4.19b)\\
& && \textstyle\sum_p x_{dps} = h_{ds}, \quad d = 1, 2, \ldots, D && (12.4.19c)\\
& && \textstyle\sum_d \sum_p \delta_{edp} x_{dps} = y_{es}, \quad e = 1, 2, \ldots, E && (12.4.19d)\\
& && \textstyle\sum_q z_{eqs} = y_{es}, \quad e = 1, 2, \ldots, E && (12.4.19e)\\
& && \textstyle\sum_e \sum_q \gamma_{geq} z_{eqs} = \underline{u}_{gs}, \quad g = 1, 2, \ldots, G. && (12.4.19f)
\end{aligned}$$

The proof of the Proposition 12.4.19, based on the dual theory, can be found in [PS01] (it is a straightforward extension of the proof in Proposition 10.1; see Exercise 12.17). A solution to the minimization Problem (12.4.19) can be found by first allocating all demands to their shortest paths in the upper layer, and then by realizing the resulting link capacities, y_{es}, on their shortest paths (with respect to link weights $\boldsymbol{\eta}$) in the lower layer. More precisely, for each upper layer link e we first define its metric as

$$\lambda_e = \lambda_e(\boldsymbol{\eta}) = \min\{\textstyle\sum_g \eta_g \gamma_{geq}, q = 1, 2, \ldots, Q_e\} \tag{12.4.20}$$

and allocate, for each demand d, the whole demand volume h_{ds} to (one of) its shortest paths with respect to λ_e. Then, for each link $e = 1, 2, \ldots, E$, the capacity y_{es} (computed according to (12.4.19d) for the just-found middle layer flows $\boldsymbol{x}$) is allocated to its shortest path (according to $\boldsymbol{\eta}$) in the lower layer. This will result in a vector of $\underline{u}_{gs}$ minimizing (12.4.19).

PROPOSITION 12.2 *Let $\boldsymbol{\pi}^* = (\pi^*_{gs} \geq 0 : g = 1, 2, \ldots, G, s = 1, 2, \ldots, S)$ be the set of optimal multipliers corresponding to constraints (12.2.2e), solving (12.4.7), the dual to TLDP:*

$$\textit{maximize} \quad V(\boldsymbol{\pi}) = \textstyle\sum_s F_s(\boldsymbol{\pi}_s) \quad \textit{subject to} \quad \boldsymbol{\pi} \in \boldsymbol{\Pi}, \tag{12.4.21}$$

where set $\boldsymbol{\Pi}$ is defined by (12.4.7b).

Then for each primal optimal solution $(\boldsymbol{x}^*, \boldsymbol{y}^*, \boldsymbol{z}^*, \boldsymbol{u}^*)$ it holds that:

1) vector $\boldsymbol{u}^* = (u^*_g : g = 1, 2, \ldots, G)$ of the lower-layer link capacities satisfies the set of equations

$$\begin{aligned}
&\textstyle\sum_g \alpha_{gs} \pi^*_{gs} w^*_g = F_s(\boldsymbol{\pi}^*_s),\\
&s = 1, 2, \ldots, S \text{ where } \boldsymbol{\pi}^*_s = (\pi^*_{gs} : g = 1, 2, \ldots, G)
\end{aligned} \tag{12.4.22}$$

2) *if an upper-layer path p realizing demand d is not a shortest path with respect to* $\lambda_{es} = \lambda_e(\boldsymbol{\pi}_s^*)$ *defined by (12.4.20) then* $x_{dps} = 0$ *(i.e., primal optimal flows* $\boldsymbol{x}^*$ *are realized on the shortest paths with respect to* $\lambda_e(\boldsymbol{\pi}_s^*)$*)*

3) *if a lower-layer path q realizing capacity* y_{es}^* *is not a shortest path with respect to* $\boldsymbol{\pi}_s^*$ *then* $z_{eqs} = 0$ *(i.e., primal optimal flows* $\boldsymbol{z}^*$ *are realized on the shortest paths with respect to* $\boldsymbol{\pi}_s^*$*).*

Proof:

Property 1) follows from the fact that TLDP is a linear (convex) minimization problem, hence, the minimum of the primal problem is equal to the maximum of the dual problem, therefore,

$$\boldsymbol{F}^* = \sum_g \kappa_g u_g^* = \sum_s F_s(\boldsymbol{\pi}_s^*) = V^*. \tag{12.4.23}$$

Using the definition of set $\boldsymbol{\Pi}$, we may further write

$$\sum_g \eta_g u_g^* = \sum_g (\sum_s \alpha_{gs} \pi_{gs}^*) u_g^* = \sum_s (\sum_g \alpha_{gs} \pi_{gs}^* u_g^*) \geq \sum_s F_s(\pi_s^*). \tag{12.4.24}$$

The last inequality in (12.4.24) follows from Proposition 12.1; together with (12.4.23) it implies property 1), since if for some state s, $\sum_s \alpha_{gs} \pi_{gs}^* u_g^*$ would be strictly greater than $\sum_s F_s(\boldsymbol{\pi}_s^*)$ then (12.4.22) could not hold.

Properties 2) and 3) state that for any optimal primal solution, in each situation all non-zero flows $\boldsymbol{z}^*$ can be assigned only to the lower-layer paths shortest with respect to $\boldsymbol{\pi}^*$, and all non-zero flows $\boldsymbol{x}^*$ can be assigned only to the upper-layer paths shortest with respect to $\boldsymbol{\lambda}(\boldsymbol{\pi}^*)$. This follows from the complementary slackness property of the saddle point $(\boldsymbol{x}^*, \boldsymbol{y}^*, \boldsymbol{z}^*, \boldsymbol{u}^*; \boldsymbol{\lambda}(\boldsymbol{\pi}^*), \boldsymbol{\pi}^*)$ (recall that for LP problems every optimal primal solution and every optimal dual solution form a saddle point of the Lagrangian, refer to Section A.7). Hence, in Step 3 of the BD Algorithm 12.2 it is sufficient to use only the above-described shortest paths; this allows for a considerable reduction of the computation times. ■

ALGORITHM 12.2 **Benders' Decomposition for TLDP**

Step 0: **Initialization**

To find the initial set of constraints on variables $\boldsymbol{u}$, the dual Problem (12.4.21) is solved using the subgradient maximization procedure. The solution, i.e., the vector of optimal multipliers $\boldsymbol{\pi}^*$, defines the initial constraint set Ω:

$$\sum_g \alpha_{gs} \pi_{gs}^* u_g \geq F_s(\boldsymbol{\pi}_s^*), \quad s = 1, 2, \ldots, S. \tag{12.4.25}$$

(The optimal multipliers can be also used for predefining candidate path lists in the lower layer and the upper layer for all situations to be used in the feasibility tests of Step 2.)

Step 1: **Master problem: finding new current u**
The following LP problem is solved yielding new estimates for u:

$$\begin{aligned} &\textit{minimize} \quad F(u) = \textstyle\sum_g \kappa_g u_g \text{ over } u \\ &\textit{subject to} \quad \text{all inequalities from } \Omega \text{ and } u \geq 0. \end{aligned} \tag{12.4.26}$$

Step 2: **Feasibility tests: testing current u for feasibility**
The feasibility tests are performed for the current u obtained in Step 1; separately for each state s ($s = 1, 2, \ldots, S$) the following optimization problem is solved:

$$\begin{aligned} &\textit{maximize} \quad P_s(\eta) = F_s(\eta) - \textstyle\sum_g \alpha_{gs}\eta_g u_g \\ &\textit{subject to} \quad \textstyle\sum_g \eta_g = 1 \text{ and } \eta = (\eta_1, \eta_2, \ldots, \eta_G) \geq 0. \end{aligned} \tag{12.4.27}$$

Let η^* be an optimal solution of (12.4.27). If $P_s(\eta^*) \leq 0$ for all s, the BD procedure terminates (current u is feasible and primal optimal). Otherwise, u is not feasible and for all those s for which $P_s(\eta^*) > 0$, the violated constraints $\sum_g \alpha_{gs}\eta_g^* u_g \geq F_s(\eta)$ are added to the constraint set Ω, and Step 1 is repeated.

Note that in condition (12.4.25) needed in Algorithm 12.2, we use inequalities instead of equalities following Property 1) of Proposition 12.2 because in general we are able to obtain only approximate values for optimal multipliers π^* from the subgradient maximization in Step 0. Nevertheless, the initial set of inequalities is rather powerful and substantially reduces the number of iterations in the BD scheme. Observe also that the maximization Problem (12.4.27) is not an LP problem. It can be solved using subgradient maximization, as shown above in Section 12.4.1. Still, having the sets of optimal paths resulting from Step 0 in hand (refer to Property 2) and Property 3) of Proposition 12.2), or using the PG technique, we can use the following LP link-path formulation instead of (12.4.27):

$$\begin{aligned} &\textit{maximize} \quad P_s(\eta) = \textstyle\sum_d \mu_d h_{ds} - \sum_g \alpha_{gs}\eta_g u_g \\ &\textit{subject to} \quad \textstyle\sum_g \eta_g = 1, \;\; \eta = (\eta_1, \eta_2, \ldots, \eta_G) \geq 0 \\ &\qquad \lambda_e \leq \textstyle\sum_g \eta_g \gamma_{geq}, \quad e = 1, 2, \ldots, E \quad q = 1, 2, \ldots, Q_e \\ &\qquad \mu_d \leq \textstyle\sum_e \lambda_e \delta_{edp}, \quad d = 1, 2, \ldots, D \quad p = 1, 2, \ldots, P_d. \end{aligned} \tag{12.4.28}$$

Steps 1 and 2 are repeated until the current u passes all the feasibility tests. Then the so-obtained link capacities u^* are primal optimal, and the corresponding middle- and lower-layer optimal flows can be found separately for each state s by solving an appropriate LP allocation problem.

Problem LLDP (12.2.4)

In LLDP the flow and link capacities in the middle layer are fixed and are not situation-dependent, making (somewhat unexpectedly) the use of BD more difficult than for TLDP. This time not only the capacities $\boldsymbol{u} = (u_1, u_2, ..., u_G)$ of the lower-layer links but also the capacities $\boldsymbol{y} = (y_1, y_2, ..., y_E)$ of the upper-layer links impose dependence among the situation-dependent lower layer flows $\boldsymbol{z}$. Hence, both $\boldsymbol{y}$ and $\boldsymbol{u}$ must be the variables of the master problem in BD, and the inequalities of the constraint set Ω must be adjusted accordingly.

PROPOSITION 12.3 *A pair of vectors $(\boldsymbol{y}, \boldsymbol{u})$ is feasible for LLDP if and only if for any vectors $\boldsymbol{\tau} = (\tau_e \geq 0 : e = 1, 2, ..., E)$ and $\boldsymbol{\eta} = (\eta_g \geq 0 : g = 1, 2, ..., G)$ the following conditions hold:*

$$\textstyle\sum_e \tau_e y_e \geq R(\boldsymbol{\tau}) \qquad (12.4.29a)$$

$$\textstyle\sum_g \alpha_{gs} \eta_g u_g \geq Q(\boldsymbol{\eta}; \boldsymbol{y}) \text{ for } s = 1, 2, ..., S, \qquad (12.4.29b)$$

where

$$R(\boldsymbol{\tau}) = \textstyle\sum_d \mu_d H_d \text{ and } \mu_d = \min\{\sum_e \tau_e \delta_{edp} : p = 1, 2, ..., P_d\} \text{ for } d = 1, 2, ..., D \qquad (12.4.30a)$$

$$Q(\boldsymbol{\eta}; \boldsymbol{y}) = \textstyle\sum_e \lambda_e y_e \text{ and } \lambda_e = \min\{\sum_g \eta_g \gamma_{geq} : q = 1, 2, ..., Q_e\} \text{ for } e = 1, 2, ..., E. \qquad (12.4.30b)$$

The proof of Proposition 12.3 is analogous to the proof of Proposition 12.1 (see Exercise 12.18). Note that equalities (12.4.30) imply that the values $R(\boldsymbol{\tau})$ and $Q(\boldsymbol{\eta}; \boldsymbol{y})$ can be found by allocating flows realizing the demand volumes H_d to their shortest paths with respect to $\boldsymbol{\tau}$ (layer 2) and to $\boldsymbol{\eta}$ (layer 1), respectively, and by calculating the costs $\sum_e \tau_e \underline{y}_e$ and $\sum_g \eta_g \underline{u}_g$ induced by the resulting link load.

PROPOSITION 12.4 *Let $\boldsymbol{\pi}^* = (\pi^*_{gs} : g = 1, 2, ..., G, \ s = 1, 2, ..., S)$ be the set of optimal multipliers corresponding to constraint (12.2.4e) solving the following problem dual to LLDP:*

$$\textbf{\textit{maximize}} \quad V(\boldsymbol{\pi}) = \textstyle\sum_s F_s(\boldsymbol{\pi}) \quad \textbf{\textit{subject to}} \quad \boldsymbol{\pi} \in \boldsymbol{\Pi}, \qquad (12.4.31)$$

where $\boldsymbol{\Pi}$ is defined by (12.4.7b) and $F_s(\boldsymbol{\pi})$ is computed by allocating, for each demand d, the entire demand volume H_d to one of its shortest path in the middle layer with respect to the link metrics

$$\lambda^*_e = \textstyle\sum_s \lambda^*_{es}, \text{ where } \lambda^*_{es} = \min\{\sum_g \pi^*_{gs} \gamma_{geq} : q = 1, 2, ..., Q_e\}, \quad e = 1, 2, ..., E, \qquad (12.4.32)$$

and then by allocating the resulting loads, $\underline{y}_e$, of the middle layer links to their shortest paths in the lower layer with respect to $\boldsymbol{\pi}^*_s = (\pi^*_{gs} : g = 1, 2, ..., G)$, and finally by calculating

$F_s(\boldsymbol{\pi}) = \sum_g \pi^*_{gs} \underline{u}_{gs}$ for the resulting loads $\underline{u}_{gs}$ of the lower layer links. Then for each primal optimal solution $(\boldsymbol{x}^*, \boldsymbol{y}^*, \boldsymbol{z}^*, \boldsymbol{u}^*)$ it holds that:

1) *vector $\boldsymbol{y}^* = (y^*_e : e = 1, 2, ..., E)$ of the layer 2 link capacities satisfies the equation*

$$\textstyle\sum_e \lambda^*_e y^*_e = R(\boldsymbol{\lambda}^*) \quad (\boldsymbol{\lambda}^* \text{ is defined by (12.4.32)}) \tag{12.4.33}$$

2) *vector $\boldsymbol{u}^* = (u^*_g : g = 1, 2, ..., G)$ of the layer 1 link capacities satisfies the set of equations*

$$\textstyle\sum_g \alpha_{gs} \pi^*_{gs} u^*_g = Q(\boldsymbol{\pi}^*_s; \boldsymbol{y}^*), \quad s = 1, 2, ..., S \tag{12.4.34}$$

3) *if a layer 2 path p realizing demand d is not a shortest path with respect to $\boldsymbol{\lambda}^*$ defined by (12.4.32) then $x_{dp} = 0$ (i.e., primal optimal flows $\boldsymbol{x}^*$ are realized only on the shortest paths)*
4) *if a lower-layer path q realizing capacity y^*_e is not a shortest path with respect to $\boldsymbol{\pi}^*_s$ then $z^*_{eqs} = 0$ (i.e., primal optimal flows $\boldsymbol{z}^*$ are realized only on the shortest paths).*

The proof of Proposition 12.4 is similar to that of Proposition 12.2 and is omitted here (see Exercise 12.18).

ALGORITHM 12.3 Benders' decomposition for LLDP

Step 0: **Initialization**
The initial set $\Omega$of constraints on $\boldsymbol{y}$ and $\boldsymbol{u}$ consists of (12.2.4b), (12.2.4c) and

$$\textstyle\sum_g \alpha_{gs} \pi^*_{gs} u_g \geq Q(\boldsymbol{\pi}^*_s; \boldsymbol{y}), \quad s = 1, 2, ..., S, \tag{12.4.35}$$

where the multipliers π^*_{gs} solve the dual Problem (12.4.31).

(The optimal multipliers can be also used for predefining candidate path lists in layer 1 and layer 2 for all situations to be used in the feasibility tests of Step 2.)

Step 1: **Master problem: finding new current $\boldsymbol{u}$**
The following LP problem is solved yielding new estimates for $(\boldsymbol{y}, \boldsymbol{u})$:

minimize $\quad F(\boldsymbol{u}) = \sum_g \kappa_g u_g$ over $\boldsymbol{x}, \boldsymbol{y}$ and $\boldsymbol{u}$ (12.4.36a)

subject to $\quad$ all inequalities in $\Omega$and $\boldsymbol{y}, \boldsymbol{u} \geq \mathbf{0}$. (12.4.36b)

Step 2: **Feasibility tests: testing current $\boldsymbol{y}$ and $\boldsymbol{u}$ for feasibility**

The feasibility tests are performed for the current $(\boldsymbol{y}, \boldsymbol{u})$ obtained in Step 1; separately for each state s $(s = 1, 2, ..., S)$ the following optimization problem is solved:

$$\textbf{\textit{maximize}} \quad P_s(\boldsymbol{\eta}) = Q(\boldsymbol{\eta}; \boldsymbol{y}) - \textstyle\sum_g \alpha_{gs}\eta_g u_g \qquad (12.4.37a)$$

$$\textbf{\textit{subject to}} \quad \textstyle\sum_g \eta_g = 1 \text{ and } \boldsymbol{\eta} = (\eta_1, \eta_2, ..., \eta_G) \geq \mathbf{0} \qquad (12.4.37b)$$

Let $\boldsymbol{\eta}^*$ be an optimal solution of 12.4.37. If $P_s(\boldsymbol{\eta}^*) \leq 0$ for all states s, the procedure terminates (current $\boldsymbol{y}$ and $\boldsymbol{u}$ are feasible and primal optimal). Otherwise, the pair $(\boldsymbol{y}, \boldsymbol{u})$ is not feasible and for all these s for which $P_s(\boldsymbol{\eta}^*) > 0$, the violated constraints $\sum_g \alpha_{gs}\eta_g^* u_g \geq Q(\boldsymbol{\eta}; \boldsymbol{y})$ are added to the constraint set Ω, and Step 1 is repeated.

For Algorithm 12.3 remarks similar to those made after the BD procedure for TLDP apply. In particular, the following LP can be used instead of (12.4.37):

$$\textbf{\textit{maximize}} \quad P_s(\boldsymbol{\eta}) = \textstyle\sum_e \lambda_e y_e - \sum_g \alpha_{gs}\eta_g u_g \qquad (12.4.38a)$$

$$\textbf{\textit{subject to}} \quad \textstyle\sum_g \eta_g = 1 \text{ and } \boldsymbol{\eta} = (\eta_1, \eta_2, ..., \eta_G) \geq \mathbf{0}, \qquad (12.4.38b)$$

$$\lambda_e \leq \textstyle\sum_g \eta_g \gamma_{geq}, \quad e = 1, 2, ..., E \quad q = 1, 2, ..., Q_e. \qquad (12.4.38c)$$

Note also that instead of the constraints (12.2.4b) and (12.2.4c) we could alternatively use in the inequalities derived from (12.4.30a) and (12.4.33).

Problem ULDP (12.2.5)

In ULDP there is the variable $\boldsymbol{z}$ (normal lower-layer flows) that couples the variables of the middle layer ($\boldsymbol{x}_s$ and $\boldsymbol{y}_s$; refer to constraints (12.2.5c) and (12.2.5d)) in different failure states and, hence, optimal primal flow $\boldsymbol{z}$ should be found by means of the BD scheme rather than primal optimal capacity $\boldsymbol{u}$.

PROPOSITION 12.5 *The layer 1 flow vector $\boldsymbol{z} = (z_{eq} : e = 1, 2, ..., E, \ q = 1, 2, ..., Q_e)$ is feasible if and only if for any vector $\boldsymbol{\tau} = (\tau_e \geq 0 : e = 1, 2, ..., E)$ the following condition holds:*

$$\textstyle\sum_e \tau_e (\sum_q \theta_{eqs} z_{eq}) \geq T_s(\boldsymbol{\tau}) \text{ for } s = 1, 2, ..., S, \qquad (12.4.39)$$

where $T_s(\boldsymbol{\tau})$, for each state s, is the solution of the following minimization problem:

$$\textbf{\textit{minimize}} \quad \textstyle\sum_e \tau_e y_{es} \text{ over } \boldsymbol{x}_s \geq \mathbf{0} \text{ and } \boldsymbol{y}_s \geq \mathbf{0} \qquad (12.4.40)$$

$$\textbf{\textit{subject to}} \quad (12.2.5b) \text{ to } (12.2.5c).$$

Proof:

Consider the set of allocation problems corresponding to states $s = 1, 2, ..., S$ obtained from ULDP by fixing the layer 1 flow $\boldsymbol{z}$. In each problem, the objective function is equal to 0 and we are to find flows $\boldsymbol{x}_s = (x_{dps} : d = 1,2,...,D, p = 1,2,...,P_d)$ and capacities $\boldsymbol{y}_s = (y_{es} : e = 1,2,...,E)$ realizing the demand volumes h_{ds} assumed for state s. For each of the problems, the Lagrangian is defined as:

$$L_s(\boldsymbol{x}_s, \boldsymbol{y}_s; \boldsymbol{\tau}) = \sum_e \tau_e(y_{es} - \sum_q \theta_{eqs} z_{eq}) = \sum_e \tau_e y_{es} - \sum_e \tau_e(\sum_q \theta_{eqs} z_{eq}). \tag{12.4.41}$$

Hence, for fixed $\boldsymbol{\tau}$, the dual function is equal to

$$W_s(\boldsymbol{\tau}) = T_s(\boldsymbol{\tau}) - \sum_e \tau_e(\sum_q \theta_{eqs} z_{eq}) \tag{12.4.42}$$

and the dual problem becomes

$$\textbf{\textit{maximize}}\ W_s(\boldsymbol{\tau}) \quad \textbf{\textit{subject to}} \quad \boldsymbol{\tau} \geq \mathbf{0}. \tag{12.4.43}$$

Thus, if for some $\boldsymbol{\tau} \geq \mathbf{0}$, $W_s(\boldsymbol{\tau}) > 0$ then the dual function can be made arbitrarily large by multiplying all elements of $\boldsymbol{\tau}$ by an appropriate positive constant. This would imply that the allocation problem for the considered state s is infeasible. Conversely, if (12.4.39) holds then all the considered allocation problems are feasible (maximum of the dual function is 0 for all s). ■

The problem dual to (12.2.5) can be written as:

$$\textbf{\textit{maximize}}\ W(\boldsymbol{\sigma}) = \sum_s T_s(\boldsymbol{\sigma}_s) \tag{12.4.44a}$$

$$\textbf{\textit{subject to}}\ \boldsymbol{\sigma} \geq \mathbf{0}$$

$$\sum_s \theta_{eqs}\sigma_{es} \leq \sum_g \kappa_g \gamma_{geq}, \quad q = 1,2,...,Q_e \quad e = 1,2,...,E, \tag{12.4.44b}$$

where $\boldsymbol{\sigma}_s = (\sigma_{1s}, \sigma_{2s}, ..., \sigma_{Es})$ and $\boldsymbol{\sigma} = (\boldsymbol{\sigma}_s : s = 1,2,...,S)$ are Lagrange multipliers corresponding to (12.2.5d).

PROPOSITION 12.6 *Let $\boldsymbol{\sigma}^*$ be a vector of optimal multipliers maximizing (12.4.44a). Then for each primal optimal solution $(\boldsymbol{x}^*, \boldsymbol{y}^*, \boldsymbol{z}^*, \boldsymbol{u}^*)$ it holds that:*

1) vector $\boldsymbol{z}^* = (z^*_{eq} : e = 1,2,...,E, q = 1,2,...,Q_e)$ satisfies the set of equations:

$$\sum_e \sum_q (\sum_g \kappa_g \gamma_{geq}) z^*_{eq} = T_s(\boldsymbol{\sigma}^*_s), \quad s = 1,2,...,S \tag{12.4.45}$$

2) flow z^*_{eq} can be non-zero only if for $\boldsymbol{\sigma}^*$ inequality (12.4.44b) becomes equality

3) all non-zero flows in $\boldsymbol{x}^*$ are allocated only to the layer 2 paths shortest with respect to the weights $\boldsymbol{\sigma}^*$.

The proof of Proposition 12.6 is left as an exercise (Exercise 12.20).

ALGORITHM 12.4 Benders' Decomposition for ULDP

Step 0: **Initialization**
The dual Problem (12.4.44) is solved; the resulting optimal multipliers $\boldsymbol{\sigma}^*$ define the initial constraint set Ω for primal optimal flows $\boldsymbol{z}$:

$$\textstyle\sum_e \sigma^*_{es}(\sum_q \theta_{eqs} z_{eq}) \geq T_s(\boldsymbol{\sigma}^*_s) \qquad s = 1, 2, ..., S \qquad (12.4.46a)$$

$$z_{eq} = 0 \text{ if } \textstyle\sum_s \theta_{eqs}\sigma_{es} < \sum_g \kappa_g \gamma_{geq} \qquad e = 1, 2, ..., E$$

$$q = 1, 2, ..., Q_e. \qquad (12.4.46b)$$

(The optimal multipliers can be also used for predefining candidate path lists in layer 1 and layer 2 for all states to be used in the feasibility tests of Step 2.)

Step 1: **Master problem: finding new current $\boldsymbol{z}$**
The following LP task is solved yielding new estimates for $\boldsymbol{z}$:

$$\textbf{\textit{minimize}} \;\; F(\boldsymbol{z}) = \textstyle\sum_g \kappa_g (\sum_e \sum_q \gamma_{geq} z_{eq}) \qquad (12.4.47a)$$

$$\textbf{\textit{subject to}} \;\; \text{all inequalities in } \Omega \text{ and } \boldsymbol{z} \geq \mathbf{0}. \qquad (12.4.47b)$$

Step 2: **Feasibility tests: testing current $\boldsymbol{z}$ for feasibility**
The feasibility tests are performed for the current $\boldsymbol{z}$ obtained in Step 1; separately for each state s ($s = 1, 2, ..., S$) the following optimization problem is solved:

$$\textbf{\textit{maximize}} \;\; P_s(\boldsymbol{\tau}) = T_s(\boldsymbol{\tau}) - \textstyle\sum_e \tau_e (\sum_q \theta_{eqs} z_{eq}) \qquad (12.4.48a)$$

$$\textbf{\textit{subject to}} \;\; \textstyle\sum_s \tau_e = 1 \text{ and } \boldsymbol{\tau} = (\tau_1, \tau_2, ..., \tau_E) \geq \mathbf{0}. \qquad (12.4.48b)$$

Let $P^*_s = P_s(\boldsymbol{\tau}^*)$ be an optimal solution for (12.4.48). If for all s, $P^*_s \leq 0$ then the current $\boldsymbol{z}$ is feasible and primal optimal, and the procedure terminates. Otherwise, $\boldsymbol{z}$ is not feasible and the violated constraints $\sum_e \tau^*_e (\sum_q \theta_{eqs} z_{eq}) \geq T_s(\boldsymbol{\tau}^*)$ are added to the constraint set Ω for all those s for which $P_s(\boldsymbol{\tau}^*) > 0$, and Step 1 is repeated.

As for TLDP (12.2.2) and LLDP (12.2.4), we can use the LP formulation for solving (12.4.48):

$$\textbf{\textit{maximize}} \;\; P_s(\boldsymbol{\tau}) = \textstyle\sum_d \eta_d h_{ds} - \sum_e \tau_e (\sum_q \theta_{eqs} z_{eq}) \qquad (12.4.49a)$$

$$\textbf{\textit{subject to}} \;\; \textstyle\sum_s \tau_e = 1, \;\; \boldsymbol{\tau} = (\tau_1, \tau_2, ..., \tau_E) \geq \mathbf{0} \text{ and}$$

$$\eta_d \leq \textstyle\sum_e \tau_e \delta_{edp} \qquad d = 1, 2, ..., D, \quad p = 1, 2, ..., P_d, \qquad (12.4.49b)$$

where the set of paths is limited to the set specified by Property 3 of Proposition 12.6.

12.4.3 Path Generation

Below we will describe in detail an application of the PG technique to the two-layer allocation problem A/2L/CF/BR/CC (12.1.7). Recall that the PG technique for candidate path lists augmentation was introduced in Section 5.4.2, and used in Section 10.1 for single-layer restoration design problems.

We start with introducing auxiliary variables $r_g,\ g = 1, 2, \dots, G$ (analogous to variables $z_e,\ e = 1, 2, \dots, E$ in problem A/ALC (5.4.11)), and consider the following problem.

***LP:* A/2L/CF/BR/CC {ALC}** **Link-Path Formulation**

Two-Layer Allocation Problem With Augmented Link Capacities

indices

$d = 1, 2, \dots, D$ demands

$p = 1, 2, \dots, P_d$ candidate paths in upper layer for flows realizing demand d

$e = 1, 2, \dots, E$ links of upper layer

$q = 1, 2, \dots, Q_e$ candidate paths in lower layer for flows realizing link e

$g = 1, 2, \dots, G$ links of lower layer

constants

h_d volume of demand d

δ_{edp} = 1 if link e of upper layer belongs to path p realizing demand d; 0, otherwise

γ_{geq} = 1 if link g of lower layer belongs to path q realizing link e of upper layer; 0, otherwise

c_g capacity of link g of lower layer

variables

x_{dp} continuous flow allocated to path p realizing volume of demand d

z_{eq} continuous flow allocated to path q realizing capacity of link e

r_g auxiliary non-negative continuous variables

objective

$$\text{minimize } \boldsymbol{F}(\boldsymbol{r}) = \textstyle\sum_g r_g \qquad (12.4.50a)$$

constraints

$$\textstyle\sum_p x_{dp} = h_d, \quad d = 1, 2, \dots, D \qquad (12.4.50b)$$

$$\textstyle\sum_d \sum_p \delta_{edp} x_{dp} = \sum_q z_{eq}, \quad e = 1, 2, \dots, E \qquad (12.4.50c)$$

$$\textstyle\sum_e \sum_q \gamma_{geq} z_{eq} \le c_g + r_g, \quad g = 1, 2, \dots, G. \qquad (12.4.50d)$$

In the sequel we will refer to Problem (12.4.50) as A{ALC}. The following algorithm for the considered two-layer allocation problem is an extension of Algorithm 5.9 formulated in Section 5.4.2, with a new dimension imposed by the presence of the second layer. Below, we will summarize the basic results and the PG algorithm for the augmented problem.

Let $\boldsymbol{\mu} = (\mu_1, \mu_2, \ldots, \mu_D)$ and $\boldsymbol{\lambda} = (\lambda_1, \lambda_2, \ldots, \lambda_E)$ be the vectors of the dual variables (with unconstrained signs) corresponding to constraints (12.4.50b) and (12.4.50c), respectively. Further, let $\boldsymbol{\pi} = (\pi_1, \pi_2, \ldots, \pi_G)$, $\boldsymbol{\pi} \geq \mathbf{0}$ be the vector of dual variables corresponding to constraint (12.4.50d). The Lagrangian function for A{ALC} is as follows:

$$\begin{aligned} L(\boldsymbol{x}, \boldsymbol{z}, \boldsymbol{r}; \boldsymbol{\mu}, \boldsymbol{\lambda}, \boldsymbol{\pi}) &= \textstyle\sum_g r_g + \sum_d \mu_d (h_d - \sum_p x_{dp}) + \sum_e \lambda_e (\sum_d \sum_p \delta_{edp} x_{dp} - \sum_q z_{eq}) \\ &\quad + \textstyle\sum_g \pi_g (\sum_e \sum_q \gamma_{geq} z_{eq} - c_g - r_g) \\ &= \textstyle\sum_d \mu_d h_d - \sum_g \pi_g c_g + \sum_g (1 - \pi_g) r_g \\ &\quad + \textstyle\sum_d \sum_p (\sum_e \delta_{edp} \lambda_e - \mu_d) x_{dp} + \sum_e \sum_q (\sum_g \gamma_{geq} \pi_g - \lambda_e) z_{eq}. \end{aligned} \tag{12.4.51}$$

The dual function of Problem (12.4.50) is given by the formula:

$$W(\boldsymbol{\mu}, \boldsymbol{\lambda}, \boldsymbol{\pi}) = \min_{\boldsymbol{x}, \boldsymbol{z}, \boldsymbol{r} \geq \mathbf{0}} L(\boldsymbol{x}, \boldsymbol{z}, \boldsymbol{r}; \boldsymbol{\mu}, \boldsymbol{\lambda}, \boldsymbol{\pi}) \quad \text{for } \boldsymbol{\pi} \geq \mathbf{0}. \tag{12.4.52}$$

Hence, the dual problem to A{ALC} is as follows

$$\begin{aligned} &\textbf{\textit{maximize}} \quad W(\boldsymbol{\mu}, \boldsymbol{\lambda}, \boldsymbol{\pi}) = \textstyle\sum_d h_d \mu_d - \sum_g c_g \pi_g \\ &\textbf{\textit{subject to}} \quad 0 \leq \pi_g \leq 1, \quad g = 1, 2, \ldots, G \\ &\qquad \mu_d \leq \textstyle\sum_e \delta_{edp} \lambda_e, \quad d = 1, 2, \ldots, D \quad p = 1, 2, \ldots, P_d \\ &\qquad \lambda_e \leq \textstyle\sum_g \gamma_{geq} \pi_g, \quad e = 1, 2, \ldots, D \quad q = 1, 2, \ldots, Q_e. \end{aligned} \tag{12.4.53}$$

The correctness of the above formulation follows from the fact that outside the set defined by constraints of (12.4.53) the dual function $W(\boldsymbol{\mu}, \boldsymbol{\lambda}, \boldsymbol{\pi})$ is equal to $-\infty$. The constraints also imply that for any optimal solution $(\boldsymbol{\mu}^*, \boldsymbol{\lambda}^*, \boldsymbol{\pi}^*)$ of (12.4.53), λ_e^* is equal to the length of the shortest path on the routing list of link e (with respect to weights $\boldsymbol{\pi}^*$), and μ_d^* is equal to the length of the shortest path on the routing list of demand d (with respect to weights $\boldsymbol{\lambda}^*$).

PROPOSITION 12.7 *(**Sufficient Condition for Optimality**). Suppose $(\boldsymbol{x}^*, \boldsymbol{z}^*, \boldsymbol{r}^*; \boldsymbol{\mu}^*, \boldsymbol{\lambda}^*, \boldsymbol{\pi}^*)$ is a saddle point of a restricted problem A{ALC} with a given fixed set of (restricted) routing lists in both layers. Let $\mathcal{Q}_e$ be a shortest path for link e (among all allowable paths in the lower layer) with respect to (optimal) multipliers $\boldsymbol{\pi}^*$, and let $\varsigma_e(\boldsymbol{\pi}^*)$ denote the length of $\mathcal{Q}_e$. Similarly, let $\mathcal{P}_d$ be the shortest path for demand d (among all allowable paths in the upper layer) with respect to the weights $\boldsymbol{\varsigma}^* = (\varsigma_1(\boldsymbol{\pi}^*), \varsigma_2(\boldsymbol{\pi}^*), \ldots, \varsigma_E(\boldsymbol{\pi}^*))$ and let $\zeta_d(\boldsymbol{\varsigma}^*)$ denote the length of $\mathcal{P}_d$. If for all d, $\zeta_d(\boldsymbol{\varsigma}^*) = \mu_d^*$ (i.e., for each d its routing list already contains a path with the shortest possible length for the given vector $\boldsymbol{\varsigma}^*$) then the primal solution $(\boldsymbol{x}^*, \boldsymbol{z}^*, \boldsymbol{r}^*)$ of A{ALC} is optimal in the wider sense (that is when all allowable paths are on the routing lists).*

Proof:

The proof of Proposition 12.7 is essentially the same as the proof of the first part of Proposition 5.1 It consists in showing that the dual function $V(\boldsymbol{\mu}, \boldsymbol{\lambda}, \boldsymbol{\pi})$ of the maximal instance of the problem (i.e., A{ALC} with maximal routing lists in *both* layers) assumes its maximum at $(\boldsymbol{\mu}^*, \boldsymbol{\lambda}^*, \boldsymbol{\pi}^*)$. Observe that for some e, λ_e^* can be greater than $\varsigma_e(\boldsymbol{\pi}^*)$; in such a case, however, link e does not appear in any of the shortest paths of the upper layer. We omit the details here and ask the reader to complete the proof (Exercise 12.21). ■

Steming from Proposition 12.7, in order to see when an improvement of the primal objective (12.4.50a) of the considered restricted instance of problem A{ALC} is possible, it is sufficient to consider the following three cases.

Case 1. Suppose that there exists a demand d' and an allowable upper layer path $P_{d'}$ outside the current routing list for d' such that the length $\zeta_{d'}(\boldsymbol{\lambda}^*)$ of path $P_{d'}$ with respect to $\boldsymbol{\lambda}^*$ is strictly less than $\mu^*_{d'}$. Then, adding path $P_{d'}$ to the routing list of demand d' can result in decreasing the optimal value of (12.4.50a).

Following the lines of the proof of the second part of Proposition 5.1 we fix a (sufficiently) small positive ε and define the perturbed problem A{ALC}* by introducing the following two modifications of the original problem:

$$\begin{aligned} h_{d'} &:= h_{d'} - \varepsilon \\ c_g &:= c_g - \textstyle\sum_{e\in P_{d'}} \psi_{eg}\varepsilon, \quad g = 1, 2, \ldots, G. \end{aligned} \tag{12.4.54}$$

The binary incidence coefficients ψ_{eg} are defined as follows. Let $\mathcal{Q}_e$, for each $e \in \mathcal{P}_{d'}$, denote one selected lower layer path realizing link e ($\mathcal{Q}_e$ is identified by the pair (e, q), $1 \le q \le Q_e$) with non-zero flow in $\boldsymbol{z}^*$ ($z^*_{eq} > 0$). Then $\psi_{eg} = 1$ if, and only if, $g \in \mathcal{Q}_e$. Note that $\mathcal{Q}_e$ is necessarily one of the shortest paths, with respect to $\boldsymbol{\pi}^*$, on the routing list of link e. The perturbed problem corresponds to the situation when flow $x = \varepsilon$ realizing demand d' is assigned in advance to path $\mathcal{P}_{d'}$, and for each link $e \in \mathcal{P}_{d'}$ the fraction of capacity equal to $z = \varepsilon$ is assigned to one of its shortest path (with respect to $\boldsymbol{\pi}^*$) in the lower layer. The dual function of the perturbed problem is equal to $-\infty$ outside the set defined by the constraint of (12.4.53), and equal to

$$\begin{aligned} W^*(\boldsymbol{\mu}, \boldsymbol{\lambda}, \boldsymbol{\pi}) &= \textstyle\sum_d h_d\mu_d - \sum_g c_g\pi_g - \mu_{d'}\varepsilon + \sum_g \sum_{e\in P_{d'}} \psi_{eg}\pi_g\varepsilon \\ &= W(\boldsymbol{\mu}, \boldsymbol{\lambda}, \boldsymbol{\pi}) - \varepsilon(\mu_{d'} - \textstyle\sum_{e\in P_{d'}} \sum_g \psi_{eg}\pi_g) \end{aligned} \tag{12.4.55}$$

inside this set. Now observe that $\sum_{e\in P_{d'}} \sum_g \psi_{eg}\pi^*_g$ is equal to the length of path $\mathcal{P}_{d'}$, i.e., equal to $\zeta_{d'}(\boldsymbol{\lambda}^*)$. Hence,

$$W^*(\boldsymbol{\mu}^*, \boldsymbol{\lambda}^*, \boldsymbol{\pi}^*) = W(\boldsymbol{\mu}^*, \boldsymbol{\lambda}^*, \boldsymbol{\pi}^*) - \sigma\varepsilon \tag{12.4.56}$$

where

$$\sigma = \mu^*_{d'} - \zeta_{d'}(\boldsymbol{\lambda}^*). \tag{12.4.57}$$

Hence, if for some $\varepsilon > 0$, dual variables $\boldsymbol{\mu}^*, \boldsymbol{\lambda}^*$, and $\boldsymbol{\pi}^*$ exist that are optimal for both considered problems A{ALC} and A{ALC}*, then introducing path $\mathcal{P}_{d'}$ to the routing list of demand d' and assigning flow $x = \varepsilon$ to it will decrease the primal objective function by

$\sigma\varepsilon$. As mentioned in the proof of Proposition 5.1, this is the case when both problems have the same optimal base. ■

Case 2. Suppose that for each demand d one of its shortest paths (in the upper layer) with respect to the weights $\boldsymbol{\lambda}^*$ is already on its routing list (i.e., $\mu^*_{d'} = \zeta_{d'}(\boldsymbol{\lambda}^*)$). Assume that a demand d' exists as well as an upper layer path $\mathcal{P}_{d'}$ on the routing list of demand d' and a non-empty subset $R \subseteq \mathcal{P}_{d'}$ such that for each link $e \in R$ a path $\mathcal{Q}_e$ exists in the lower layer resulting in: $\mathcal{Q}_e$ is allowable for link e, $\mathcal{Q}_e$ is not on its routing list, $\mathcal{Q}_e$ is the shortest allowable path (in terms of the weights $\boldsymbol{\pi}^*$) for link e, and $\mathcal{Q}_e$ is shorter than all the paths on its list (i.e., $|\mathcal{Q}_e| = \varsigma_e(\boldsymbol{\pi}^*) < \lambda^*_e$), where $|\cdot|$ denotes the path length. Then, using paths $\mathcal{Q}_e$ for realizing links $e \in R$ would reduce the length of path $\mathcal{P}_{d'}$:

$$|\mathcal{P}_{d'}| = \textstyle\sum_{e \in \mathcal{P}_{d'}} \varsigma_e(\boldsymbol{\pi}^*) < \mu^*_{d'}. \qquad (12.4.58)$$

This can result in decreasing the optimal value of (12.4.50a).

Let $\psi_{eg} = 1$ for $e \in \mathcal{P}_{d'}$ and $g \in \mathcal{Q}_e$, and $\psi_{eg} = 0$ otherwise and define the perturbed problem A{ALC}* by introducing modifications (12.4.54). The rest of the proof is the same as in Case 1. Observe that although the portion $x = \varepsilon$ of the volume of demand d' is routed on path $\mathcal{P}_{d'}$ and consequently on paths $\mathcal{Q}_e$, $e \in \mathcal{P}_{d'}$ (some of which are not on the lower layer routing lists), the flows solving the perturbed problem use only the lower layer paths on the restricted routing lists. ■

Case 3. Suppose that Cases 1 and 2 do not apply. Assume that a demand d' exists as well as an upper layer path $\mathcal{P}_{d'}$ outside the routing list of demand d and a non-empty subset $R \subseteq \mathcal{P}_{d'}$ such that for each link $e \in R$ a path $\mathcal{Q}_e$ exists in the lower layer resulting in: $\mathcal{Q}_e$ is allowable for link e, $\mathcal{Q}_e$ is not on its routing list, $\mathcal{Q}_e$ is the shortest allowable path (in terms of the weights $\boldsymbol{\pi}^*$) for link e, and $\mathcal{Q}_e$ is shorter than all the paths on its list (i.e., $|\mathcal{Q}_e| = \varsigma_e(\boldsymbol{\pi}^*) < \lambda^*_e$). Finally suppose that the length of path $\mathcal{P}_{d'}$, $|\mathcal{P}_{d'}| = \sum_{e \in \mathcal{P}_{d'}} \varsigma_e(\boldsymbol{\pi}^*)$, is less than $\mu^*_{d'}$. Then, adding path $\mathcal{P}_{d'}$ to the routing list of demand d can result in decreasing the optimal value of (12.4.50a). The proof is analogous to that of Case 2. ■

The above considered cases exhaust all the possibilities of improving the primal objective. Cases 1 to 3 and Proposition 12.7 suggest an iterative PG Algorithm 12.5 for augmenting the routing lists, analogous to Algorithm 5.9 described in Section 5.4.2.

ALGORITHM 12.5 **Path Generation Algorithm to Solve A{ALC}**

Step 0: Assume initial (short) routing lists of candidate paths and form the initial instance of A{ALC}.

Step 1: Solve A{ALC} (using the solution of the previously solved task as the starting point, provided Step 1 is entered from Step 2). Let $(\boldsymbol{x}^*, \boldsymbol{z}^*, \boldsymbol{r}^*)$ be the solution of the current problem. If $\boldsymbol{F}(\boldsymbol{r}^*) = 0$ $(\boldsymbol{r}^* = 0)$ then the optimal solution in the wider sense is found and the algorithm terminates.

Step 2: Let $(\boldsymbol{x}^*, \boldsymbol{z}^*, \boldsymbol{r}^*; \boldsymbol{\mu}^*, \boldsymbol{\lambda}^*, \boldsymbol{\pi}^*)$ be a saddle point of the problem. Using the optimal multipliers $\boldsymbol{\pi}^*$ as link weights, run a shortest path algorithm to determine a shortest allowable path $\mathcal{Q}_e$ in lower layer (with respect to multipliers $\boldsymbol{\pi}^*$) for each link e of upper layer. Let $\boldsymbol{\varsigma}^* = (\varsigma_1(\boldsymbol{\pi}^*), \varsigma_2(\boldsymbol{\pi}^*), \ldots, \varsigma_E(\boldsymbol{\pi}^*))$ denote the vector of the lengths of the resulting shortest paths. Now determine a shortest allowable path $\mathcal{P}_d$ in the upper layer (with respect to weights $\boldsymbol{\varsigma}^*$) for each demand d and let $\zeta_d(\boldsymbol{\varsigma}^*)$ denote the length of $\mathcal{P}_d$. If $\zeta_d(\boldsymbol{\varsigma}^*) = \mu_d^*$ for every demand d then the solution of A{ALC} is optimal in the wider sense and the algorithm terminates. Otherwise, form a new instance of A{ALC} by adding shortest path $\mathcal{Q}_e$ to the current routing list of each link e with $\varsigma_e(\boldsymbol{\pi}^*) < \lambda_e^*$, and shortest path $\mathcal{P}_d$ to the current routing list of each demand d with $\zeta_d(\boldsymbol{\varsigma}^*) < \mu_d^*$. Go to Step 1.

12.5 NUMERICAL RESULTS

The problem of an excessive number of variables and constraints in the LP formulations for restoration design has been already addressed in Section 10.3.3, where Table 10.4 shows how the number of variables and constraints increases with the number of nodes for the single-layer case. To illustrate this issue for two-layer networks, consider problem TLDP (12.2.2) and assume that the number of nodes in each layer is equal to $V = 100$. Then, for instance, we can consider $D \approx 10000$, $E \approx 5000$, $G \approx 1000$ (the layers get less connected as we go downwards in the layer hierarchy), and $S \approx 1000$. Then, assuming $P_d = 10$ and $Q_e = 5$ (on the average), we find that the considered problem requires the following number of variables of each type:

- upper layer flows $\boldsymbol{x} : \sim 10^8$ $(D \times P_d \times S)$
- upper layer link capacities $\boldsymbol{y} : \sim 0.5 \times 10^7$ $(E \times S)$ (auxiliary variables)
- lower layer flows $\boldsymbol{z} : \sim 2.5 \times 10^7 (E \times Q_e \times S)$
- lower layer link capacities $\boldsymbol{u} : \sim 10^2$ (G).

After eliminating auxiliary variables $\boldsymbol{y}$, the total number of variables is roughly 1.25×10^8. The total number of constraints (after eliminating $\boldsymbol{y}$) is roughly 1.6×10^7 $((D + E + G) \times S)$. It follows that even for the LP formulations, decomposition methods have to be used, since the number of variables and constraints become very large (the same also holds for the two remaining problems to be considered). Note that in the decomposition methods of LR, BD, and PG, we deal with the decomposed problems corresponding to individual failure states s, which are roughly two orders of magnitude (S) less than the original primal LP formulations and, hence, perfectly tractable by the contemporary LP solvers.

Below we will illustrate the applications of LR and BD to two-layer networks, using the three LP formulations considered in Sections 12.4.1 to 12.4.2. We will use network examples

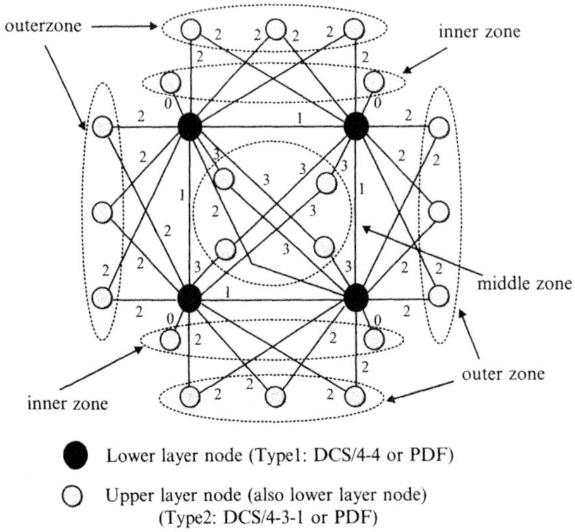

FIGURE 12.7 Network Structure

TABLE 12.1 Demand Matrix Expressed in Circuits

	Inner Zone	Middle Zone	Outer Zone
Inner Zone	90 (120)	90	60
Middle Zone	90	30 (120)	60
Outer Zone	60	60	30 (120)

derived from a model of the upper layers of the integrated digital network composed of the circuit group layer (demand layer), VC-12 layer (upper layer), and VC-4 layer (lower layer). The reader is referred to Sections 3.4 and 3.5 and Tables 3.1 and 3.2 for the modeling details.

The network to be considered is depicted in Figure 12.7. The set of nodes of the upper layer is composed of $V = 20$ nodes of type 2, representing digital cross-connects 4-3-1 (DCS/4-3-1), which are capable of switching VC-12 as well as VC-4 containers (digital streams). Note that the type 2 nodes are also nodes of the lower layer. Nodes of type 1 represent digital cross-connects 4-4 (DCS/4-4) and can switch only VC-4 containers. There are $W = 4$ of such nodes, so the lower layer is composed of 24 nodes (all nodes of type 1 and type 2). Demand volume is expressed in 64 kbps digital circuits between undirected pairs of the type 2. The demand volume between pairs of nodes is given in Table 12.1, and depends on the particular zones the nodes belong to (the zones are depicted in Figure 12.7). The number (120) in parantheses is the demand between nodes of the same zone.

TABLE 12.2 **Optimal Network Cost for the Two-Layer Design**

	Fixed Paths	Dynamic Paths
TLDP	11 250, 12 232 (11 291)	10 490, 12 181
LLDP	11 747, 11 951 (11 751)	10 754, 12 039
ULDP	10 950, 11 723 (11 295)	10 799, 11 725
ULDP′	11 019, 11 724 (11 301)	–

The graph of the lower layer is composed of $G = 43$ links. The graph of the upper layer is almost identical with the graph of the lower layer; it is obtained from the latter by replacing the four type 1 nodes by their subordinate nodes of type 2 (the four nodes of type 2 in the inner zones) and skipping the links of length 0. One DVU in the upper layer is equal to one circuit, while one LCU in the upper layer is equal to one VC-12 and realizes 30 circuits. DVUs of the lower layer are equal to LCUs of the upper layer. Finally, one LCU in the lower layer is equal to VC-4 and realizes 63 DVUs (as one VC-4 container can carry 63 VC-12 containers). Since we are considering only the linear program, for the problem formulations all of the DVUs and LCUs are translated into the DVUs of the upper layer, i.e., 64 Kbps circuits.

The failure model assumes that 37 out of 43 lower-layer links are subject to failures (the four internal links of length 0 are not subject to failures). Links are fully operative or fully failed ($\alpha_{gs} \in \{0, 1\}$) and only one link can fail at a time. This results in 38 states (normal state and 37 single-link failure states). The demand is the same for all states ($\chi_{ds} \equiv 1$).

There are three cost factors of the unit cost (i.e., the cost per one circuit realized on the link) for each link of the lower layer: $a_{LT} = 0.025$ per circuit termination at the line termination module, $a_R = 0.025$ per one circuit traversing a regenerator (regenerators are placed every 50 km), and the length-dependent factor $a_L = 0.078$ per 100 km per one circuit. Thus, the unit cost of link g in the lower layer is given by $\kappa_g = a_L \times l_g + 2 \times a_{LT} + (\lceil \frac{l_g}{50} \rceil - 1) \times a_R$, where l_g denotes the geographical length of the link expressed in kilometers.

In the case when candidate path lists are fixed (the fixed paths case in Table 12.2) the paths in both layers are pre-processed and each routing list contains 3 to 10 paths (915 paths in total in each layer). The dynamic paths case in Table 12.2 refers to the case when in LR the shortest upper-layer paths are found by the Dijkstra algorithm to find the flow allocations minimizing the Lagrangian, while the lower-layer paths are fixed as in the fixed paths case. In the upper layer, the paths can traverse any node (of type 2); in the lower layer, however, only nodes of type 1 are used as transit nodes and nodes of type 2 are only the end nodes in the paths.

Lagrangian Relaxation

Table 12.2 shows the results for application of the LR technique to problems TLDP, LLDP and ULDP formulated for the network described above, based on the study presented in

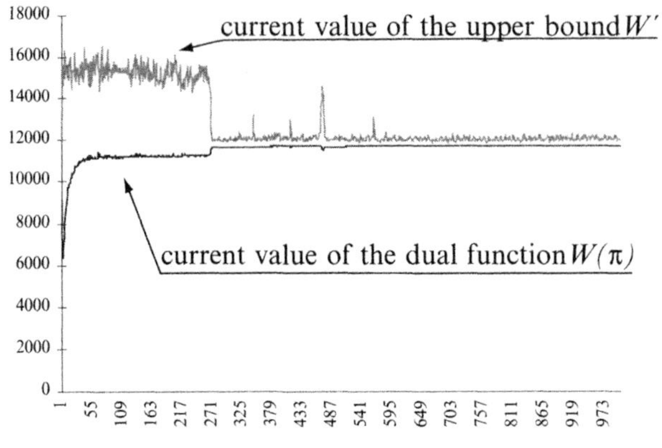

FIGURE 12.8 Subgradient Maximization for LLRP

[PS99]. In the two main columns, the first value is the lower bound of the cost function $\boldsymbol{F} = \sum_g \kappa_g u_g$ obtained through dual function maximization. The second value is the upper bound obtained by realizing all of the flows on the randomly chosen shortest paths (with respect to the optimal dual multipliers). The value in parentheses is the optimal primal cost obtained by CPLEX. Additionally, we have considered the variation, DR/2L/CF/BR/CC/LIN/NPR(1)-PRR(2), of ULDP, denoted by ULDP′, with the restricted flow reconfiguration in the upper layer: normal flows of the upper layer not affected by the failure are preserved (refer to problem DR-R (9.3.2) in Section 9.3.2).

For all the cases reported in Table 12.2, 1,000 steps of the subgradient maximization algorithm were performed in order to maximize the dual function. If there was no increase during the 50 consecutive iterations, parameter φ_n (refer to 12.4.9) was halved. Figure 12.8 illustrates a typical curve followed during the maximization of the dual function. Note that the maximum is reached practically after 400 iterations.

For TLDP the computation time for LR was 5 minutes (on a Sun Sparc 160 MHz computer) for fixed paths and around 60 minutes for dynamic paths. Direct computation for solving the primal LP formulations (using CPLEX) takes time comparable with the dynamic path case (around 60 minutes for TLDP and fixed paths—the exact results obtained by CPLEX are given in paratheses in the fixed paths column of Table 12.2). Note that the estimated minimum obtained from the optimization is rather close to the actual minimum (within 1% to 2%). In some cases, the upper bound also closely approximates the actual minimum, and the corresponding (easily obtainable) solution can be used as a good approximation of the optimal solution.

The use of dynamic paths instead of fixed paths can substantially improve the solution, by 8% to 10% for TLDP and LLDP (for ULDP the decrease is smaller, only of 1.5%). However, as already mentioned, the use of dynamic paths can substantially increase the computation time. It is also interesting to note that restricting the flow reconfiguration only to those flows which are affected, increases the link capacity cost only by around 1%. This indicates that a more practical protection mechanism PRR assumed for ULDP′ is practically as good as the most capacity-effective, non-restricted flow restoration mechanism PRU.

Benders' Decomposition

Table 12.3 shows the results of the BD method obtained by means of CPLEX on a Sun Sparc II 250MHz computer (the results are taken from [PS01]). In each case the first column (LP) shows the results for the direct use of LP, the second (BD) for BD without initialization of the set of the master problem constraints via the LR approach, the third (BD+D) for BD with initialization of Ω, and the fourth (BD+D/P) for BD with initialization of Ω and the candidate path lists composed of the shortest paths with respect to optimal multipliers computed via LR. We note that the candidate path lists for the computations reported in the first three columns contain many more paths than necessary to reach the cost minimum. In the fourth computation, however, the lists are limited only to the necessary set of paths, i.e., the shortest paths with respect to (sub)optimal multipliers found in Step 0. The difference between the total number of the paths on the routing lists and the number of the necessary paths is given in the "removed paths" row. Observe that in all the considered cases the initialization of set Ω reduces the execution time of the subsequent BD procedure. Further reduction is achieved when only the shortest paths resulting from LR (Step 0 of the BD algorithm) are used.

It should be emphasized that the initial Step 0 can be important for the effectiveness of the BD algorithms described in Section 12.4.2 for two reasons. First, the optimal multipliers obtained with LR by the maximization of the dual function (during this maximization the paths are generated with the shortest path algorithm) specify the short lists of candidate paths which are sufficient for performing valid feasibility tests in Step 2. Without the dual optimization of Step 0, the sets of paths would either have to be predefined and the PG technique used for the tests, or the node-link formulations of the feasibility tests would have to be used. As we know, both options have their drawbacks. On the other hand, the difficulty of the subgradient maximization of the dual function is that it does not yield exact values of optimal multipliers. However, this can be overcome by considering sets of shortest paths (for each demand d and each state s all the paths of the length within ε of the length of the shortest path are put on the routing list for d and s). The second advantage of performing Step 0 is that it specifies the initial set of inequalities for set Ω. Such an initial set is powerful as it in fact contains active inequalities (assuming that exact optimal multipliers are known). Also, the initial set contains typically some 40% of the inequalities that are actually required to solve the considered problems with BD.

Table 12.3 also reveals the importance of the initial step (consisting in solving the dual problem by LR) of BD. The third row shows the computation time split into two factors: the time spent in Steps 2 and 3, and (plus) the time spent in Step 0, for the three cases: (1) without executing Step 0, (2) with Step 0, and (3) with Step 0 and the resulting limited routing lists. Table 12.3 suggests that the role of Step 0 can be significant for large networks, since Step 0 is executed only once and considerably decreases the computation time of the remaining BD computations (this latter time is dominant for large networks).

The profits of using BD for the two-layer restoration design problems are further illustrated in Table 12.4 which shows the execution times (on a Sun Sparc II 250-MHz computer) for three-network configurations (including the 43-link configuration discussed in details above). The original (primal) non-decomposed LLDP and ULDP problems, as well as the appropriate BD subproblems have been solved by means of CPLEX. The direct solution of the problems is profitable for small networks (refer to the 18-link network for both problems and the 43-link network for LLDP). For large networks, however, the gain from using BD

TABLE 12.3 **Results for 43-Link Network**

	TLDP				**LLDP**				**ULDP**			
Method	LP	BD	BD+D	BD+D/P	LP	BD	BD+D	BD+D/P	LP	BD	BD+D	BD+D/P
Total cost	11 291	11 291	11 291	11 291	11 751	11 751	11 751	11 751	11 295	11 295	11 295	11 295
Time [s]	620	743+0	731+992	554+992	20	162+0	129+61	117+61	1056	675+0	565+372	328+372
Initial $\lvert\Omega\rvert$	—	0	43	43	—	0	43	43	—	0	43	43
Final $\lvert\Omega\rvert$	—	448	468	471	—	840	549	462	—	857	501	479
Removed paths	—	—	—	286	—	—	—	526	—	—	—	13 011
BD iterations	—	13	2	1	—	20	15	14	—	32	27	21

TABLE 12.4 **Execution Times for LLDP and ULDP [s]**

Number of links	18	43	53
Original LLDP	8	20	9820
Benders LLDP	48	162	837
Original ULDP	35	1056	13157
Benders ULDP	51	675	9241

can be significant. For the 43-link network and ULDP the gain of 50% of the execution time is observed, while for the 53-link network and LLDP the gain is $> 90\%$ (for the 53-link network and ULDP the gain is $> 30\%$).

12.6 COST COMPARISON

In this section, we present two different types of network cost comparison for the models presented in Sections 12.3.1 and 12.3.2.

12.6.1 *Diversity and Restoration (with Multi-Hour Traffic)*

Recall that in Section 12.3.1, we have presented MH/2L/CF/BR/CC/LIN/PD(1)-PRU(2) (12.3.1) for multi-hour traffic incorporating diversity requirement at the lower layer; this model is then followed by MMH/2L/CF/BR/CC/LIN/PRU {Path Diversity} (12.3.2) where network restoration objective is considered to address for robustness. We will now discuss two aspects in regard to these models: 1) the algorithmic approaches and 2) how these models can be useful in understanding trade-off in a network and their relation to network performance.

It may be noted that decomposition algorithms presented earlier in Section 12.4.1 can be applicable with suitable modifications for multi-layer design with multi-hour traffic. Furthermore, the LR-based dual approach has been described for multi-hour traffic in Section 11.1.4. For example, the LR based dual algorithm can be applied to Problem (12.3.1) by dualizing with respect to constraints (12.3.1c) and (12.3.1d), as described earlier in this chapter in Section 12.4.1; see also Section 5.4.1. The reader is asked to develop and implement these approaches (Exercises 12.22 and 12.23).

However, there is a natural decomposition that can be performed similar to the discussion presented in Section 12.3.3. For example, consider model (12.3.1). An approach would be to first solve the upper-layer multi-hour traffic-based capacity design problem to determine y_e; this is then given to the lower-layer flow allocation problem (with diversity constraint) as a "fixed" demand to be solved independently from the upper-layer problem—this approach can be called a sequential natural decomposition approach.

In the case of Problem (12.3.2), we also have failure states in addition to the normal state. We will now describe a heuristic for Problem (12.3.2). Specifically, our primary interest here is to consider non-simultaneous failure of each transport network link, and to consider the binary failure states, i.e., $\alpha_{gs} \in \{0, 1\}$. For Problem (12.3.2), a natural state-based decomposition heuristic established by considering each state separately is given in Algorithm 12.6 (see [Med94b] for details). In order to understand this algorithm, we need to define the following two subproblems for a generic state s:

$$\begin{array}{llll} \textbf{\textit{minimize}} & \sum_e \xi_e y_{es} & & \\ \textbf{\textit{subject to}} & \sum_p x_{dpts} = h_{dts}, & d = 1, 2, ..., D & t = 1, 2, ...T \\ & \sum_d \sum_p \delta_{edp} x_{dpts} \leq y'_{es} + y_{es}, & e = 1, 2, ..., E & t = 1, 2, ..., T \\ & x_{dtps} \geq 0, y_{es} \geq 0. & & \end{array} \quad (12.6.1)$$

$$\begin{array}{lll} \textbf{\textit{minimize}} & \sum_e \zeta_{eq} z_{eqs} & \\ \textbf{\textit{subject to}} & \sum_q z_{eqs} = \hat{y}_{es}, & e = 1, 2, ..., S \\ & \sum_e \sum_q \gamma_{geq} z_{eqs} \leq \alpha_{es} \hat{c}_g, & g = 1, 2, ..., G \\ & z_{eqs} \geq 0. & \end{array} \quad (12.6.2)$$

We will denote the solution at each state s for the upper-layer Problem (12.6.1) by $\hat{y}_{es}$; once this is solved, the lower-layer allocation Problem (12.6.2) uses $\hat{y}_{es}$ as demand, and the solution is denoted by $\hat{z}_{eqs}$. The available capacity on the lower-layer link in state s is denoted by $\hat{c}_g$. Furthermore, θ'_{eqs} denotes 1 if the path q realizing link e in state s is *not* available (0, otherwise).

We now discuss trade-off studies that can be performed using models (12.3.1) and (12.3.2). Consider first the mixed design model (12.3.1) for the normal state. Suppose we want to include some network robustness to address for failures, but not necessarily additional capacity in the upper layer. Recall that we have included diversity requirement for flow allocation in lower layer for upper layer capacity requirement—this requirement can be used here to provide some level of robustness. The question is where and how this may be helpful. Consider for a moment that there is infinite capacity in the lower layer, i.e., $c_g = \infty$, for $g = 1, 2, ..., G$. By the generalized shortest-path allocation rule, we would then know that for any capacity required for the upper layer y_e, the demand flow will be on the shortest path in the lower layer. In most practical networks, capacity can be abundant in the lower layer (at least on significant number of lower layer links) so that most demands can still be routed on the shortest path. Essentially, what this means is that if a link along such shortest paths (for upper layer capacity) is disrupted due to a complete failure in the lower layer (i.e., $\alpha_{gs} = 0$), then the corresponding y_e will be 0. Now, if the upper layer for the traffic network is essentially fully-connected, then many links for demand pairs can be completely affected. This then has significant impact on the overall network. On the other hand, if diversity is provided in the lower layer (using the parameter ϑ_{es}), then no lower-layer path would carry upper-layer capacity y_e by more than a certain percentage (as dictated by ϑ_{es}); this means that flows will be allocated to at least two lower layer paths (shortest and next shortest) if $\frac{1}{2} \leq \vartheta_{es} \leq 1$, and more paths if $\vartheta_{es} < \frac{1}{2}$. Thus, a complete failure of a lower-layer link g would result in only a partial loss of upper-layer capacity y_e. In many cases, this is more desirable than having a complete loss of an upper layer link.

ALGORITHM 12.6 Natural State-Based Heuristic for MMH/2L/CF/BR/CC/LIN/PRU {Path Diversity} (12.3.2)

Step 1a: Set $y'_{eD} = 0, e = 1, 2, \ldots, E$. Solve the upper-layer multi-hour design Problem (12.6.1) for state $s = 0$ to determine $\hat{y}_{e0}$, $e = 1, 2, ..., E$. Set $y'_e = \hat{y}_{e0}$, for each $e = 1, 2, ..., E$; $\widehat{C}_g = c_g$ for $g = 1, 2, \ldots, G$.

Step 1b: Given $\hat{y}_{e0}$ as demand for the lower-layer problem, solve the lower-layer flow allocation Problem (12.6.2) to determine $\hat{z}_{eq0}$, for state $s = 0$. Determine the lower-layer link flow induced by solution $\hat{z}_{eq0}$ to be $\hat{u}_g, g = 1, 2, ..., G$. Set $z'_{eq} = \hat{z}_{eq0}$. Set $\hat{c}_g = c_g - \sum_e \sum_q \gamma_{geq} \hat{z}_{eq0}, \quad g = 1, 2, ..., G$.

Step 2: Organize failure states corresponding to lower-layer links sorted by highest link flow to lowest link flow (i.e., cost $\hat{u}_g$).

Step 3: For each failure state $s = 1, 2, ..., S$, do the following:

(3a) identify transport network link $g = s$

(3b) $y'_{es} = y'_e - \sum_q \theta'_{eqs} z'_{eq}, \quad e = 1, 2, ..., E$

(3c) solve upper-layer Problem (12.6.1) to determine $\hat{y}_{es}$

(3d) given $\hat{y}_{es}$, solve lower-layer flow allocation Problem (12.6.2) to determine $\hat{z}_{eqs}$

(3e) update: $y'_e = y'_e + \hat{y}_{es}, \quad e = 1, 2, ..., E, e \neq s$

(3f) update: $z'_{eq} = z'_{eq} + \hat{z}_{eqs}, \quad e = 1, 2, ..., E \quad q = 1, 2, ..., Q_e$

(3g) update: $\hat{c}_g = \hat{c}_g - \sum_e \sum_q \gamma_{geq} \hat{z}_{eqs}, \quad g = 1, 2, ..., G.$

We may, however, need to be alert to the fact that, introduction of diversity in the lower layer can result in affecting multiple upper-layer link e, than is likely to be the case when there is no lower-layer diversity. This trade-off needs to be understood as well.

Another aspect of robustness to consider is if we do want to provide upper-layer capacity to address for failure, in addition to lower-layer diversity. For this purpose, we can use model (12.3.2). An important way to use this model is to consider different traffic restoration objectives for normal state and failure through use of χ_{dts} (regardless of time and demand pair). Note that the term traffic restoration objective is more meaningful here than the term network restoration objective. This would result in different network cost depending on the level of traffic restoration objective.

Finally, we wish to discuss the role of multi-hour traffic and network restoration. Recall that multi-hour traffic models are useful for dynamic call routing circuit-switched voice networks ([Ash97] and [Gir90]). Our discussion here will be specifically for using a dynamic call routing environment with a fully-interconnected (mesh) traffic network where a maximum of two traffic link paths are used for call connections. For additional details, the reader is directed to [Med94b].

Note that dynamic call routing has a natural tendency to route calls around a failure. How much and what the call routing can do depend on if the underlying transport network

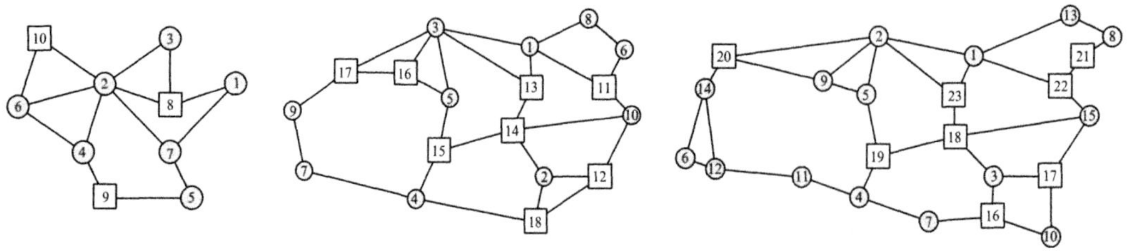

FIGURE 12.9 Example Networks (EN-1, EN-2, EN-3)

TABLE 12.5 **Increase in Trunking and Network Cost to Provide Diversity and/or Restoration over Baseline Cost**

Network	Cost of Diversity (over baseline, in %)	Additional Capacity (over baseline, %)	Restoration Design Cost (over baseline, %)
EN-1	12.02	18.06	31.77
EN-2	12.82	9.78	25.24
EN-3	13.38	15.41	36.25

has diversity requirement, and whether the call routing network has a protection capacity for some failure restoration objective, and interestingly, also the time of the actual failure. First, in Table 12.5 consider network costs for three example networks for the given transport network topologies; note that the traffic network is fully-interconnected. Using the baseline network for carrying normal traffic load with a normal grade-of-service objective of 1% and no diversity on flow allocation in the lower layer, we see that incorporation of diversity can incur (without any additional upper-layer link capacity) about 13% increase in network cost. If a 50% traffic restoration objective for affected traffic under any failure state is required and assuming a single-link transport network failure at a time, we require an additional capacity in the order of 10% to 18% while incurring a cost over 25% (over baseline cost).

While the network cost is only one aspect, we now discuss the impact of a failure on the network knowing that dynamic call routing can still move some traffic around the failure. There are two aspects to understand: 1) the severity of a failure and 2) its relation to network performance in the event of a major link failure (and the time of failure). For illustration, consider the example network EN-2 with 10 traffic nodes and 18 transport nodes (the network in the middle in Figure 12.9). We consider two major transport link failures, 1-3 and 4-15, each independently (see Table 12.6). We can see from the failure of 4-15 that it affects 12 (out of a maximum possible 45) trunk groups in the baseline case, but increases to 23 when lower-layer diversity is introduced. For the restoration design option, additional trunks are also affected. In any case, consideration of failure seems to give the impression that introduction of diversity causes more trunk groups as well as trunks to be

TABLE 12.6 **Number of Trunk Groups (TG) Affected and Trunks (tk) Lost Due to a Failure for Network EN-2; also, Total Capacity and Number of Trunk Groups under Regular Case**

	Baseline		With Diversity		Restoration Design	
Transport Link	**TG**	**tk**	**TG**	**tk**	**TG**	**tk**
4–15	12	977	23	1,006	23	1,101
1–3	18	1,313	20	716	21	813
all	45	3,863	45	3,863	45	4,242

affected. However, when we consider a different transport link failure (1-3), then we find out that a similar number of trunk groups are affected; but in terms of capacity, less trunks are affected with diversity compared to the baseline case.

However, to understand the actual effect of a failure and complete this discussion, call-routing simulation is required in addition to cost and capacity comparison; summary results from simulation are shown in Table 12.7 by listing network call blocking (see [Med94b] for details). Note that we show the blocking results for network blocking performance for three different traffic busy hours (had the failure occurred during any of these busy hours). When comparing with Table 12.6, we see that although more capacity is affected when diversity is introduced for failure of transport link 4-15 compared to the baseline, we see the network blocking is *less* than compared to the baseline case. Furthermore, depending on the time of the failure and associated network traffic, dynamic call routing can bring the network down to 10% blocking when transport diversity is presented, and further down to 5% blocking when the network has upper layer restoration capacity. An important lesson to learn here is that network design models can be used to determine network cost for diversity and restoration; however, in some cases additional simulation is required for the dynamics within the traffic network to fully understand how capacity can be better exploited by the traffic network to improve network performance. It may be noted that restoration capacity in the upper layer is usable under the normal condition meaning that any sudden traffic surge can take advantage of this capacity as well.

Finally, quality-of-service–based routing in the Internet ([CNRS98]) is a recent concept; it can have a dynamic routing capability, similar to dynamic call routing in circuit-switched networks. Thus, the above result can be applicable, and this discussion can be beneficial to those who are interested in robust design of QoS routing networks.

12.6.2 *Gain With Dynamic Transport Over Static Transport (with Multi-Service, Multi-Hour Traffic)*

In this section, we will discuss the benefit of dynamic transport taking into account cost structure using models (12.2.3) and (12.2.4), presented in Section 12.3.2. Both of these models take into account multiple services for each demand (or traffic node pairs) in addi-

TABLE 12.7 **Average Network Blocking due to Failure (for EN-2)**

Transport-Link	Traffic Load Hour	Baseline	Diversity	Restoration Design
	1	19.72	10.36	5.46
4–15	2	28.57	25.33	19.93
	3	28.20	24.57	19.43
	1	37.29	14.91	10.81
1–3	2	35.30	14.48	11.05
	3	36.44	18.05	15.00

tion to multi-busy hour traffic profiling. A general comment about these two models is that due to link capacity taking integral values, they are difficult to solve and are $\mathcal{NP}$-complete. In this regard, remarks made in Section 12.2.5 are relevant here.

In general, we note that (12.3.3) and (12.3.4) are MIP problems. In Section 5.4.1, we have described how MIP problems can be solved using the LR-based dual approach; this is further discussed for multi-hour design problems in Section 11.1.4. Thus, we can develop a LR-based dual approach for each of the models (Exercise 12.24). As in the last illustration, a sequential decomposition approach can be applied to Problem (12.3.3) (see [ML97]). In this case, we need to take into account the presence of multiple services. Thus, in the upper layer, using multi-hour traffic separately for *each* service, the upper layer capacity need, y_{ei}, is first determined for each service. This is then routed in the lower layer for each service—the sum of lower-layer capacity for each service is than modularized to determine lower-layer capacity u_g. For Problem (12.3.4), the sequential approach can be taken with a slight twist. The upper-layer capacity need for each service in each time, y_{eit}, is separately recorded which is then routed in the lower layer subject to modularity requirement. A general comment here is that generalized shortest path allocation is not applicable since the variables are not all continuous.

It is important to note the major difference between the first and the second model. In the first model, the modular capacity needed for upper layer y_e (for all services and to address for multi-hour traffic) is statically routed in the lower layer for each service class to determine the lower layer modular capacity u_g in such a way that the total network cost is minimized. On the other hand, in the second model (12.3.4), we allow for capacity, y_{eit}, for each service i and each time window t to be allocated in a time-dependent manner in the lower layer—in essence, the network allows semi-permanent dynamic (time-dependent) transport capability in the lower layer to accommodate for time-varying traffic. An important point to note here is that different services for the same demand pair may not have the same busy-hour and, thus, allow for better packing in the lower layer.

In determining the benefit of dynamic transport over traffic transport, we also show how the cost model presented earlier in (12.1.1) can be beneficial. In many cases, since the line cards and equipment can be from different vendors, and there may be anticipated

TABLE 12.8 **Increase in Cost of Static Transport over Dynamic Transport (in %) for Multi-Hour Traffic, for Different Combinations of Cost Parameters**

$\{\xi^U + \xi^I, \kappa^L, \bar{\kappa}\}$	EN-1	EN-2	EN-3
{100,50,1}	10.39%	27.89%	28.21%
{100,75,1}	12.49%	28.06%	28.90%
{100,50,0.1}	15.09%	20.32%	22.96%

change in cost components, network designers like to do 'what-if' studies. In Table 12.8, we show such a study with varying value of cost components, discussed earlier in (12.1.1). For this specific study, three networks shown earlier in Figure 12.9 are used, this time with multiple services. The modular capacity of only one type is used in both the upper and lower layer. From Table 12.8, we see that dynamic transport can generate savings as low as 10% to as high as 30%—the actual savings depend not only on the network but also on different values of cost components. From a model point of view, having an independent structural model for cost components as in (12.1.1) allow us to use the same general models (12.3.3) and (12.3.4); that is, no change is necessary in the formulation or algorithm to understand the impact of changes in cost structure.

12.7 GROOMING/MULTIPLEX BUNDLING

Grooming is a generic term used for packing low-rate signals into higher-rate signals. Multiplex Bundling is another term used for the same purpose, although the latter term is usually used to further imply grooming within the context of network optimization, i.e., minimization of network resources. Grooming is a very important functionality faced by network providers on a daily basis for their transport networks. Because signal packing to higher rate is involved, grooming problems are inherently multi-layer problems, but only for within transport networks and generally within the operation of a particular network provider.

There are many ways grooming problems are important. In particular, economy of scale for transport networks dictates that signals must be transported at high rates, assuming that one can achieve high utilization on the links. Grooming allows high utilization by efficiently packing these high-speed links with low rate signals. In many cases, the complexity of grooming is that these functionalities needed to be added a pair of nodes at a time. Secondly, due to the long transmission facilities in a cross-country network, the decision on where to put grooming functionalities along the way from one end to the other is a difficult combinatorial problem. Furthermore, grooming problems can become more complicated when looking at multi-time period problems. This is further complicated because, in practice, rearranging low speed signals within high speed links is a difficult or prohibitively expensive network management problem from one time period to another.

In any case, we will illustrate grooming through examples, consider a few special cases, and then go to the general problem.

12.7.1 Illustration of Multi-Layer in the Presence of Grooming

First we will illustrate a few grooming examples in a cross-connect transport network. They illustrate the traditional network design problems for point-to-point pre-SONET systems (also called SONET linear systems) environment. The multi-layer design problem still valid in the context of some DS1/DS3 (or STS-1)/OC-48 contexts where traditional DCSs are used. Fortunately, a lot of stride has been made with SONET transmission. In fact with the newly emerged Virtual Concatenation (VCAT) standard from ITU-T, one can define an arbitrary number of STS-1s scattered across various links and channels into a VCAT group (e.g., STS-7v).

Consider a linear network with three nodes as shown in Figure 12.10. Between each node pair, assume that there are 5 OC-3 demands. We can place OC-3/OC-48 multiplexer in pairs to transport the demand. Thus, since an OC-48 holds 16 OC-3s, we need *three* OC-3/OC-48 multiplex system, one between node 1 and 2, another between 1 and 3, and the third one between 2 and 3. However, suppose an OC-48 signal can de-multiplex to OC-3 at node 2, and multiplex back up to OC-48. Since an OC-48 has spare capacity (due to only 5 OC-3 demands for each pair), we can take advantage of this demux-mux functionality at node 2. Thus, we can route both 5 units of demand in OC-3s for node pairs $\langle 1,2\rangle$ and $\langle 1,3\rangle$ on an OC-48 link between nodes 1 and 2 since they can fit in one OC-48 system. While the demand for demand pair $\langle 1,2\rangle$ will terminate at node 2, the demand for demand pair $\langle 1,3\rangle$ will be de-multiplexed to OC-3, and then multiplexed back on to the OC-3/OC-48 multiplex system on the link 2-3 at OC-48 level, along with the demand for the demand pair $\langle 2,3\rangle$. Thus, we can see that with this setup, we end up needing just two OC-3/OC-48 multiplexed systems, instead of three OC-3/OC-48 multiplex systems. Certainly, you want to do that if the demux-mux functionality introduced at node 2 is cheaper in cost. Astute readers may notice that in fact we are considering links at both OC-3 level and OC-48 level (if multiplexed up)—in this example no OC-3 links are used.

Our second example is somewhat different. We again consider a three-node network where we have spare capacity in the OC-3/OC-48 multiplexed (link) system between nodes 1 and 3 (Figure 12.11). Similarly, there is spare capacity in the OC-3/OC-48 multiplexed (link) system between node 2 and 3. Suppose now in the next time period, we have a new, incremental demand only for node pair $\langle 1,2\rangle$. Certainly, one possibility is to do a new capacity expansion with a multiplexed link between nodes 1 and 2 to accommodate this demand. On the other hand, if there are sufficient spare capacity on the multiplexed system between nodes 1 and 3, and between nodes 2 and 3, then the new, incremental demand between nodes 1 and 2 can be routed on the multiplexed system between 1 and 3, demultiplex at node 3 and multiplex back up on the multiplexed system between nodes 2 and 3. You may notice that the actual bandwidth is routed in a round about way from node 1 to 3 and then back on 3 to 2! This is a common phenomenon in multi-layered transport networks and is referred to as *backhaul*; often, the physical capacity for backhaul rides on the same conduit. Generally, the more transport layers, the higher the tendency for demands

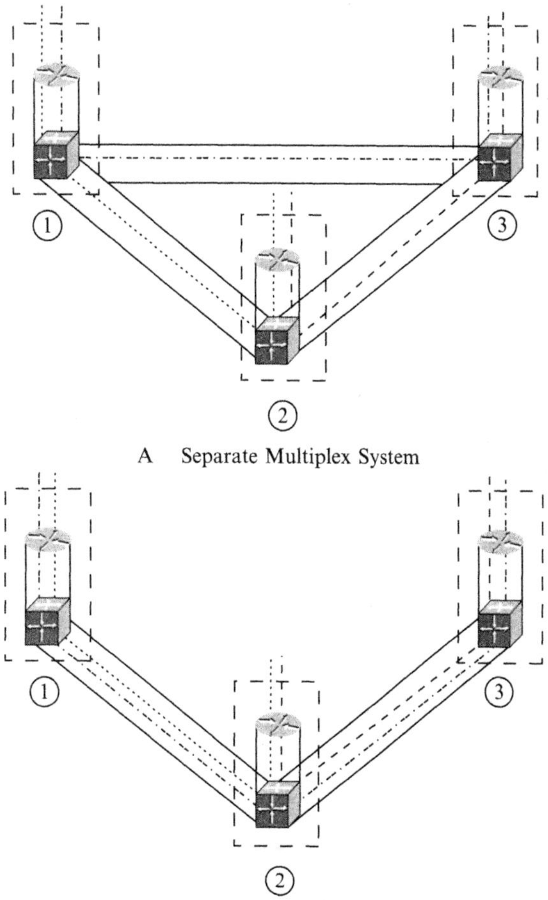

A Separate Multiplex System

B Demux-Mux at this Node

FIGURE 12.10 3-Node Multiplexed System

to re-traverse (backhaul) the links of the bottom layer. In many instances, backhauling is cheaper than doing new capacity expansion—again, this depends on cost components of various pieces.

A third problem adds another level of complexity when there are external demands also at other rates, for example, OC-12 between these nodes. Thus, at a node, there can be a two-level multiplexer as shown in Figure 12.12. Thus, a design trade-off can be between where and how such systems may be used so that the overall cost is minimized.

Note that all the above examples are applicable in a cross-connect mesh networks, especially with pair-based multiplexing and de-multiplexing. SONET ring networks (refer to Section 3.6) are, however, different. Add-drop multiplexers can multiplex low rate signals (called tributaries) entering or leaving a node without (in effect) de-multiplexing the entire high rate signal. That is, no pair-based grooming is needed. In fact, in this case, formulation (3.6.1) is applicable.

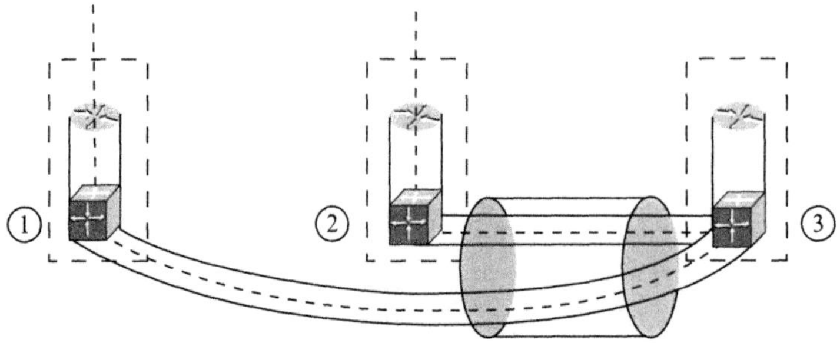

FIGURE 12.11 Backhauling in a Network

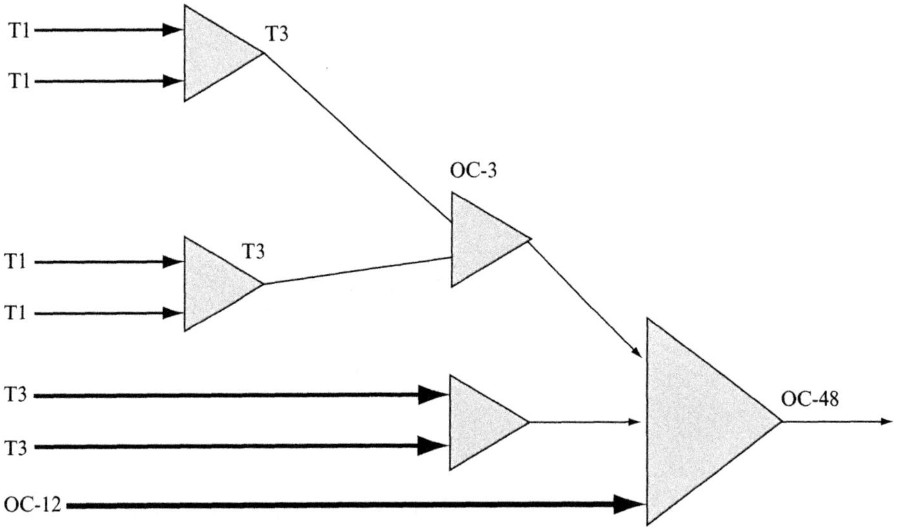

FIGURE 12.12 Multi-Level Multiplexer at a Node

12.7.2 Special Cases when Grooming Nodes are Known

We will discuss several special cases where either grooming nodes are known ahead of time or possible locations are known. In some cases, this can simplify the overall problem.

Express (End-To-End) Grooming

Express grooming refers to grooming/multiplexing at the end points. In this approach, each path from source to destination acts as a link for the purpose of design, although such a path may be routed over a series of lower layer links. Because of end to end grooming, for the purpose of network design, the demand can be routed on the shortest path made up of lower layer links. This path itself then form a link for end-to-end grooming.

Grooming and De-multiplexing at Each Node

If grooming and de-multiplexing is possible at each node, then each node looks more like a cross-connect node with modular capacity on links connecting two adjacent nodes. In this case, the problem takes the following simpler form in a single-layer design:

***IP:* GD/1L/MF/BR/MC/LIN** **Link-Path Formulation**

Grooming and De-multiplexing at each node (all integral case)

indices

$d = 1, 2, \ldots, D$ demands

$p = 1, 2, \ldots, P_d$ candidate paths in upper layer for flows realizing demand d

$e = 1, 2, \ldots, E$ links of upper layer

constants

h_d volume of demand d

δ_{edp} = 1 if link e of upper layer belongs to path p realizing demand d; 0, otherwise

ξ_e unit cost of link e of upper layer

m module for which DVUs are allocated

M module units of the link capacity

variables (all non-negative integral)

x_{dp} flow allocated to path p realizing volume of demand d

y_e M-module capacity units of link e

objective

$$\text{minimize } \boldsymbol{F} = \textstyle\sum_e \xi_e y_e \quad (12.7.1a)$$

constraints

$$\textstyle\sum_p m x_{dp} = h_d, \quad d = 1, 2, \ldots, D \quad (12.7.1b)$$

$$\textstyle\sum_d \sum_p \delta_{edp} m x_{dp} \le M y_e, \quad e = 1, 2, \ldots, E. \quad (12.7.1c)$$

Regional Grooming

In the regional grooming concept, there are certain selected nodes in a network that can be grooming nodes, typically spread out by geographical locations (see Figure 12.13).

Here for the purpose of regional grooming (as shown in Figure 12.13), the demand between two end nodes may have multiple different ways to be routed through possible regional grooming nodes. In this case, links such as the one from one end to nearest grooming site may have a level of multiplexing, while the regional grooming links may have another level (higher level) of multiplexing. In fact, non-regional grooming links do multiplexing at smaller signal rates. Note that grooming only takes places at a node where a non-regional link is incident on a regional link.

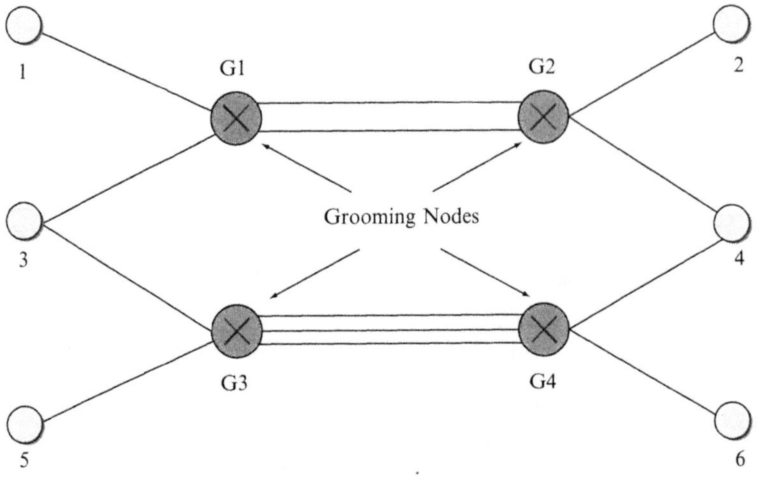

FIGURE 12.13 Regional Grooming

IP: GD/2L/MF/BR/MC/LIN/R **Link-Path Formulation**

Regional Grooming (all integral case)

indices

$e = 1, 2, ..., E$ links for non-regional grooming links

$g = 1, 2, ..., G$ regional grooming links

constants

h_d volume of demand d

δ_{edp} = 1 if link e belongs to path p realizing demand d; 0, otherwise

m module for which DVUs are allocated

ξ_e M-module capacity units cost of non-regional link e'

κ_g N-module capacity units cost of regional link g

a_{eg} = 1 if non-regional link e is incident on regional link g; 0, otherwise

M module of capacity of regional link

N module of capacity of non-regional link

variables (all non-negative integral)

x_{dp} flow allocated to path p realizing volume of demand d

y_e M-module capacity units of non-regional link e

u_g N-module capacity units of regional link g

objective

$$\text{minimize } \boldsymbol{F} = \textstyle\sum_e \xi_e y_e + \sum_g \kappa_g u_g \tag{12.7.2a}$$

constraints

$$\textstyle\sum_p m x_{dp} = h_d, \quad d = 1, 2, \ldots, D \tag{12.7.2b}$$

$$\sum_d \sum_p \delta_{edp} m x_{dp} \leq M y_e, \quad e = 1, 2, \ldots, E \tag{12.7.2c}$$

$$\sum_e a_{eg} M y_e \leq N u_g, \quad g = 1, 2, \ldots, G. \tag{12.7.2d}$$

12.7.3 A General Two Layer Formulation

Now, we will discuss a general two-layer formulation following the work by [Dov91a]. In this case, we will consider pair-based multiplexer-demultiplexers as well as demand at both layers within a transport network. This model also assumes that there is initial spare capacity in the network. We will mark the layers by lower and upper layer. Demand enters the network externally at either of the two layers. This demand is routed onto links of the network. To take advantage of transmission economies of scale, the network is considered to have two different types of links: a transmission link (of various media sizes) and a multiplexed link. A transmission link transmits directly at its defined rate over media such as fiber or coax. A "multiplex link" is a logical multiplex system that is created for multiplex grooming/bundling purposes. In the general multi-layer context, a multiplex link becomes a demand for higher layers that must eventually be routed over a transmission link (in the two-layer model, any multiplex link can route only over transmission links). Going through the hierarchy, all demands must eventually be routed over a transmission link.

IP: GD/2L/MF/BR/MC/LIN **Node-Link Formulation**

Two-Layer Grooming Design

indices

$v = 1, 2, \ldots, V$ nodes
$\ell = 1, 2$ layers
$e = 1, 2, \ldots, E_\ell$ transmission link at layer ℓ
$f = 1, 2, \ldots, F$ multiplexed links
$j = 1, 2, \ldots, J_\ell$ transmission Sizes at level ℓ
$d = 1, 2, \ldots, D_\ell$ demands at each level ℓ

constants

$\phi_{\ell j}$ number of layer ℓ signals provided by one unit of transmission size $\psi_{j\ell}$
μ number of lower layer signals multiplexed by an upper layer signal
$\hat{c}_f$ initial spare capacity on multiplexed link f
$\bar{c}_{e\ell}$ initial spare capacity on transmission links e at layer ℓ
ξ_f cost of one multiplexed system on multiplexed link f
$\eta_{ej\ell}$ cost of one unit of transmission size $\psi_{j\ell}$ on transmission link e at layer ℓ
$h_{d\ell}$ external demand d in units of layer ℓ signals
a_{vf} node-multiplex link incidence indicator—1 if node v is incident on multiplex link f; 0, otherwise
$b_{ve\ell}$ node-transmission link incidence indicator—1 if node v is incident on transmission link e in layer ℓ

variables

y_f number of multiplexed systems on multiplexed link f

$z_{ej\ell}$ number of units of transmission size $\psi_{j\ell}$ on the transmission link e at level ℓ

r_{fd} binary (routing) variable: 1, if demand d at lower level is routed over multiplexed link f; 0, otherwise

$R_{ed\ell}$ binary (routing) variable: 1 if demand d aggregated up to level ℓ is routed over transmission link e at level ℓ; 0, otherwise (here, demand d can be multiplexed link f for internal demand)

$w_{vd\ell}$ binary artificial variable for demand d at level ℓ that forces routing integrity at intermediate node v for the routing variables r_{fd} and $R_{ed\ell}$

objective

$$\text{minimize } \sum_{f=1}^{F} \xi_f y_f + \sum_{\ell=1}^{2} \sum_{e=1}^{E_\ell} \sum_{j=1}^{J_\ell} \eta_{ej\ell} z_{ej\ell} \tag{12.7.3a}$$

constraints

$$\sum_{f=1}^{F} a_{vf} r_{fd} + \sum_{e=1}^{E_1} b_{ve1} R_{ed1} = \begin{cases} 1 & \text{if either of the endpoints of demand } d \text{ at lower layer is } v \\ 2w_{vd1} & \text{otherwise} \end{cases}$$
$$d = 1, 2, \ldots D_1 \quad v = 1, 2, \ldots, V \tag{12.7.3b}$$

$$\sum_{e=1}^{E_2} b_{ve2} R_{ed2} = \begin{cases} 1 & \text{if either of the endpoints of demand } d \text{ at upper layer is } v \\ 2w_{vd2} & \text{otherwise } d = 1, 2, \ldots D_2 \quad v = 1, 2, \ldots, V \end{cases} \tag{12.7.3c}$$

$$\sum_{d=1}^{D_1} h_{d1} r_{fd} \le \mu y_f + \hat{c}_f, \quad f = 1, 2, \ldots, F \tag{12.7.3d}$$

$$\sum_{d=1}^{D_1} h_{d1} R_{ed1} \le \sum_{j=1}^{J_1} \phi_{1j} z_{ej1} + \bar{c}_{e1}, \quad e = 1, 2, \ldots, E_1 \tag{12.7.3e}$$

$$\sum_{f=1}^{F} y_f R_{ef2} + \sum_{d=1}^{D_2} h_{d2} R_{ed2} \le \sum_{j=1}^{J_2} \phi_{2j} z_{ej2} + \bar{c}_{e2}, \quad e = 1, 2, \ldots, E_2 \tag{12.7.3f}$$

$$w_{vf\ell} \le y_f \text{ or } h_{d\ell}, \quad \ell = 1, 2. \quad d = 1, 2, \ldots, D_\ell \tag{12.7.3g}$$

$$r_{fd} \le y_f \text{ or } h_{d1}, \quad d = 1, 2, \ldots, D_1 \tag{12.7.3h}$$

$$h_{d\ell}, y_f, z_{ej\ell} \ge 0 \text{ and integer.} \tag{12.7.3i}$$

The first five sets of constraints require some elaboration.

Constraints (12.7.3b) enforce that the routes are set properly at layer 1 (lower layer). On the left hand side, we have all the possible ways of a demand d at lower layer to enter or exit a node v. If vertex v is the source or destination node of demand d, then the sum will be 1, otherwise it is equal to $2w_{vd}$. Variable w_{vd} captures whether the demand at lower layer travel through the node v. If the demand does not transit through node v, w_{vd} is 0. If they indeed travel then the sum of flows will be 2.

Constraints (12.7.3c) force the same routing restriction at layer 2 (upper layer). Observe that at the upper layer, there are no multiplex links and hence routes need to be constructed only using transmission links.

Constraints (12.7.3d) compare the flow allocated and the capacity assigned to multiplex link f. Observe that multiplex links are only present at the lower layer and hence we do not have variable ℓ in the formulation. On the left hand side we have the incoming demand from the lower layer which is carried over multiplex link f. On the right hand side, we sum the current spare capacity on the multiplex link f and the possible new multiplex system which needs to be added to carry the demand volume. If we are willing to add another multiplex system ($y_f = 1$), we can have μ more lower layer signals carried over the multiplexed link f.

Constraints (12.7.3e) compare the flow allocated and the capacity assigned to transmission link e at the lower layer. On the left hand side, we have the external demand at the lower layer routed over the transmission link e at lower layer. For such a flow to be carried, on the right hand side we find the required capacity for the link e at the lower layer. The total capacity on the transmission link e at the lower layer is the sum of already existing capacity ($\bar{c}_{e\ell}$) and the z_{ej1} additional units (e.g., cables of a particular size or wavelengths for WDM) of types j that need to be installed so as to carry the total flow. Observe that each additional unit of type j carries ϕ_{1j} lower layer signals.

Constraints (12.7.3f) compare the flow allocated and the capacity assigned to transmission link e at the upper layer. On the left hand side, we have two types of demands that need to be carried. First are the demands which were from lower layer but they were routed over the multiplex link f and hence need to be carried by the transmission links of the upper layer. R_{ef2} captures whether such a multiplex link has been activated and y_f gives the number of upper layer signals that will be required. Second are the demands entering at the upper layer, which are carried by the transmission links of the upper layer. Since the problem has only two layers, all the newly entering demands will have to be carried by transmission links at the upper layer only. These total upper layer signals need to carried by the total capacity of the upper layer transmission link e. The currently available spare can be used without additional cost but after that new z_{ej2} media units of type j need to be added to transmission link e at upper layer. Each media units of type j carries ϕ_{2j} upper layer signals.

It may be noted that the above problem can be extended to consider more than two layers (including multiplex bundling by skipping intermediate layers) as well as for multiple time periods; see for example, [Dov91a].

It may further be noted that demand may incur a cost to route over links that is associated on a unit basis with the demand, i.e., not only in the cost of the transmission or multiplexed links, but also a low speed, high speed line card cost model, such as a WDM or ADM terminal. For example, in WDM, the transmission link costs would capture the WDM multiplexers (muxes), while a unit charge would be needed to capture the cost of doing optical-to-electronic-to-optical (O/E/O) conversion at each node. This was not addressed in the original model in [Dov91a] because at that time multiplexers de-multiplexed *every* lower rate signal and provided terminations for all of them, whereas in today's multiplexers you only need cards for those signals you terminate. Thus, this aspect needs to be addressed for modern day systems.

12.7.4 Remark

Grooming or multiplex bundling inherently connects more than one layer within the transport network and thus falls under the class of multi-layer problems. In general, the grooming problems do differ from multi-layer problems discussed earlier in this chapter. For example, grooming node locations may be specially marked; external demand occurs at grooming nodes at different layers; multiplex systems are deployed in pairs, and so on. Special cases of the problem can be specifically formulated as illustrated above; such formulations can be solved using techniques discussed earlier in this book. The general problem is however intractable. A common heuristic to solve the general problem is to do routing of demand first, and then independently consider where to put multiplex systems (given the routed demands). The decision of putting multiplex systems (for example, in pairs) can itself be a combinatorial optimization problem; for such problems, approaches such as simulated annealing can be employed. See [BHLM94], [Dov86], [Lin86], [LM93], [WB02], [WCB91], and [Wes02] for additional work on multiplex bundling.

12.8 SUMMARY AND FURTHER READING

In this chapter, we have presented models, algorithms, and results for multi-layer network design, including protection and restoration issues. In many ways, this chapter captures and extends various models presented in Chapters 4, 9, 10, and 11.

A critical issue about multi-layer networks is to understand the basic concept that the link capacity from an upper layer becomes the demand for the layer immediate below it. The general rule is that the link capacities of layer $\ell + 1$ are realized by means of flows routed in layer ℓ; these flows are formed along the paths of layer ℓ using the multiplexing–de-multiplexing mechanisms between the two layers (applied at the end nodes of the paths), and through the switching mechanism of layer ℓ (applied in the intermediate nodes of the paths). Following these rules, in Section 12.1 we have presented models for network design of multi-layer networks for the normal operating state. We have first illustrated this through technology examples in Section 12.1.1, including the description of basic cost components. With this as the basic premise, we present models for dimensioning of two-layer networks for the normal operating state (Section 12.1.2), as well as for mixed design that include dimensioning in one layer and allocation in another layer (Section 12.1.3). While doing so, we have identified and shown models when certain variables take integral values, and also when unsplittable routing is present. We have also made a point to discuss which models are applicable for two-layer architecture consisting of traffic and transport layers, and the models that are more suitable for transport over transport (e.g., MPLS tunnels over SONET, or between different sub-layers of SONET/SDH hierarchy when used as semi-permanent or permanent connections). In Section 12.1.4, we then give a general multi-layer dimensioning model and discuss why the demand in the top layer can be considered as another layer with logical link capacity, and that the L-resource layer problem can also be thought of as $(L + 1)$-layer design problem. Furthermore, we also present GSPAR, extending the single-layer case (2.4.13) and its two-layer counterpart described in Section 2.9 (see Chapter 2). We conclude with Section 12.1.5, which provides a summary on the solvability of the optimization models presented in Section 12.1.

In Section 12.2, we take another step in multi-layer modeling by considering resilience (recall that we have presented restoration design models for the single-layer case in Chapter 9). When it comes to restoration design in a two-layer setting, it is possible to do restoration in one or the other layer or both. For example, consider IP over SONET networks, where IP flows can be re-routed if a failure-dependent link metric system is used, and the SONET network has re-configurability through the cross-connect systems. By presenting different models, we show how one model differs from another depending on the restorable capability of one layer over another. The first three sections (12.2.1 to 12.2.3) address problems, both in LP and MIP versions, for three different combinations of reconfigurable (dynamic) layers. Extensions of the basic formulations are discussed in Section 12.2.4. We conclude this section by presenting a general discussion on optimization methods applicable for solving the models presented earlier in Section 12.2.

In Section 12.3, we took yet another step to incorporate multi-hour traffic; recall that we have presented multi-hour network design in Chapter 11. Given the modeling framework presented in Sections 12.1 and 12.2, we show how to incorporate multi-hour traffic in a mixed design environment, first without restoration and then with restoration capacity; we have also shown how the diversity factor, first discussed in Section 4.2.1, can be incorporated into these models (note that diversity can be similarly added to models discussed in Sections 12.1 and 12.2). We then provide an altogether different extension with multi-hour traffic by incorporating multiple services as well as both static and dynamic transport in a two-layer setting.

In Section 12.4, we move on to present algorithmic approaches and numerical results. As you can imagine, it is not possible to discuss algorithms for every model presented so far in this chapter. Thus, we select a set of specific models and show how methods discussed earlier in Chapters 5 and 10 are applicable. In particular, in Sections 12.4.1 to 12.4.3 we describe LP decomposition methods in application to the basic two-layer restoration design LP formulations introduced in Section 12.2. These sections, based on papers [PS98], [PS99], [PS00], [PS01], show how LR, BD and PG can be used for the two- and multi-layer modeling to decrease the number of variables and constraints in the underlying LP problems. It is worth mentioning that a natural decomposition heuristic, first discussed in [Med94b] for multi-layer traffic + transport restoration design model (12.3.2), is described in Section 12.6. Furthermore, in Sections 12.5 and 12.6, we show numerical results illustrating the introduced methods for solving selected two-layer problems introduced in Sections 12.2 and 12.3. We present two forms of numerical results: (1) performance of algorithms, and (2) how different cost comparisons can be done using various models presented in this chapter.

Historically, the first important instance of multi-layer networking goes back to the development of the circuit-switched voice network as the traffic network, and the transmission system (for circuit routing of the link capacity, i.e., trunk-groups, for circuit-switched voice) with rates such as T1 and T3 as the transport network, thus forming a traffic-transport layering architecture. That is, in summary, this combination of circuit-switched voice traffic networks over transport networks is the first example of multi-layered networks.

While this relationship has been known and has been in use for several decades (see [Rap64], [Rap65], [Rap67], and [Rey83]), integrated network modeling and design considering both of these networks together was not considered initially. In earnest, it can be said that the need was not as great when the transmission system was made of co-axial cables which is inherently physically diverse. The need became much more pronounced when the transmission network started to move from the PDH systems based on co-axial cables to fiber-based SDH/SONET systems in the late 1980s. The immediate effect was that the transmission network becomes sparse, with links composed of fibers of enormous capacity, capable of carrying many trunk groups between distant switching nodes. The downside of this was that a single fiber cut could affect multiple trunk groups in the circuit-switched voice networks (this was illustrated in Section 12.6).

Essentially, the need to understand the impact of a major failure of a transport network on the traffic network has given rise to early work on modeling of multi-layer (mostly two-layer) survivable networks in a traffic-transport setting and what types of restoration approaches to be considered ([ACM91], [Med89] and [MS93]) while taking into account the lower-layer topology. The work presented in [Med94b] (with a preliminary version in [Med92]) is perhaps the first paper where a two-layer joint formulation was presented for the traffic-transport layer dependency; in addition, this work also addressed how to consider failure states as well as multi-hour traffic in the same framework, and how to consider trade-offs such as diversity. Work by [ACL94], [KDP95], and [MK95] has also considered the multi-layer issue and impact, as well as failure and restoration.

Several independent early works on multi-layer modeling deserve special mention. A generic framework for modeling multi-commodity networks with multiple resource layers can be found in [LJPS90]. In parallel, independently, multi-commodity flow modeling sub-layers of the transport multiplex hierarchy has been described first in [SDD89], followed by the work presented in [Dov91a] and in [Dov91b]. It should be noted that these models are in a way abstractions of the strict modeling approach recommended for the SDH networks in the ITU Recommendation G.803 [ITU94].

Somewhat parallel to the above development on traffic network–transport network layering, there have been several works related to the the multi-layer concept within the transport network that paved the way for early work on multi-layer modeling. This primarily arose due to multiplexing of one demand unit to another, e.g., originally from multiplexing of demands in T1 to demands in T3. Several works have discussed the multiplexing problems in the mid 1980's; for example, see [Dov86], [Lin86], [Lus84], and [Tsa86]. Note that none of these works consider restoration design. However, it may be noted that the need for a multi-layer that is induced by multiplex bundling has been recognized in [Rey83] and some early work on transport network planning, especially over multiple time periods, have been presented in [Yag73] and [Zad74]. Multiplex bundling (grooming) has received considerable attention in the past decade; for example, see [BHLM94], [LM93], [WB02], [WCB91], and [Wes02].

Multi-layering with traffic-transport combination has been further considered in the works of [DGA$^+$99], [GSPD98], [GS98], and others. The number of papers in this area has grown significantly in the last few years due to the deployment consideration of IP over WDM; for example, see [FV00] and [VCD$^+$01]. For a more general framework, see [LTC$^+$01], [LT01], [MCG$^+$02], and [CMD$^+$02]. Similarly, for a recent work on the problems that fit the transport over transport multi-layering (MPLS over SONET) see [DY01]; for ultra-long haul transmission system, see [Wes02].

Optimization models and methods for solving two-layer problems for normal operating state have been considered in several papers already discussed in Section 12.1.5 ([BGLM03], [BLM03], [BMM94a], [BMM94b], [CMM03], [CRC86], [DV89], [GD98], [LKG03], [MPCD03], and [Pió99]). Two other papers dealing with this issue are [FBA$^+$95], where a mixed allocation two-layer problem is considered, and [KKP99], where a concave dimensioning function is assumed. Restoration design optimization models for multi-layer (mainly two-layer) networks (often referred to as survivable multi-layer networks) have been considered in several papers ([AN03], [BGLM03], [GSPD98], [LBC03], [Med94b], [MK95], [MSG03], [ZOM03]). It is important to note that multi-layer restoration design often requires network management coordination between layers; interested readers are directed to work, such as [MJR$^+$01], [ZM03].

It is most likely that in the future the development of optimization algorithms for multi-layer networks, especially for the two-layer case, will become central to the application of the multi-commodity networks theory. It seems to be only a matter of time before the branch-and-cut approach (refer to Section 10.4), will be efficiently extended to multi-layer restoration design. Besides the emerging technological applications in the next generation network, the development will be stimulated by the fact that the considered problems are attractive and interesting from the theoretical viewpoint, and are a natural field for extending the results for the single-layer case.

EXERCISES FOR CHAPTER 12

12.1. *Formulate the dual to problem D/2L/CF/BR/CC/LIN (12.1.2) (with only the second term in the objective function) by dualizing constraints (12.1.2b) to (12.1.2e) and show that the shortest-path allocation rule indeed yields optimal primal solutions.

12.2. Formulate the modular two-layer design problem analogous to (12.1.6) with modular link capacity in layer 1 given by formula (4.3.4) (refer to Section 4.3.1 of Chapter 4). Use only one value, M, for the module of the capacity of layer 2 links ($J = 1$).

12.3. Add the single-path routing requirement for both layers in the formulation of Problem (12.1.10).

12.4. Formulate problem A/3L/CF/BR(1)-BR(2)-NBR(3)/MC.

12.5. **Prove $\mathcal{NP}$-completeness of problem A/2L/MF(1)-CF(2)/BR/MC (i.e., of Problem (12.1.7) with integral capacity in layer 2 and integral flow in layer 1).

12.6. Give an example of an instance of TLDP (12.2.2), where optimal flows in layer 1 are always bifurcated.

12.7. *Formulate problem DR/2L/MF(1)-CF(2)/BR(1)-NBR(2)/MC/LIN/LRU(1)-SBP(2).

12.8. *Formulate problem DR/2L/CF/BR/CC/LIN/PRR(1)-NPR(2) corresponding to a two-layer network with reconfigurable layer 1 (only) where the restricted flow reconfiguration mechanism is assumed (as in Problem (9.3.2)). Show how the LR technique can be applied in order to find optimal multipliers and resulting shortest paths. Finally, write down the shortest-path allocation procedure for finding approximate solutions of the problem.

12.9. *Formulate problem DR/2L/CF/BR/CC/LIN/NPR(1)-PRR(2) corresponding to a two-layer network with reconfigurable layer 2 (only) where the restricted flow reconfiguration mechanism is assumed (as in Problem (9.3.2)). Show how the LR technique can be applied in order to find optimal multipliers and resulting shortest paths. Finally, write down the shortest-path allocation procedure for finding approximate solutions of the problem.

12.10. *Formulate the BD algorithm for ULDP (12.2.5) with integral link capacities in layer 1.

12.11. *Write down the SAL algorithm for DR/2L/MF/NBR/MC/LIN/SBP.

12.12. Derive formulae (12.4.2) to (12.4.3) for the dual function of TLDP.

12.13. *Show that in TLDP the optimal non-zero flows in layer 2 can be assigned only to the paths shortest with respect to $\boldsymbol{\lambda}^*$. (Hint: dualize all constraints in TLDP and use the complementary slackness property.)

12.14. What is a simple way of computing the value of the dual function and its subgradients for the three-layer extension of TLDP for given values of multipliers π? How does this method extend to any number of layers?

12.15. How do we compute the dual function and its subgradients for LLDP?

12.16. Write the subgradient maximization algorithm for the dual function for LLDP.

12.17. *Prove Proposition 12.1.

12.18. *Prove Proposition 12.2.

12.19. *Prove Proposition 12.3.

12.20. *Prove Proposition 12.6.

12.21. Complete the proof of Proposition 12.7.

12.22. Consider formulation (12.3.1). Develop and implement the LR based dual algorithm by relaxing constraints (12.3.1c) and (12.3.1d). Determine if there is any advantage of relaxation other constraints in lieu of these constraints. (Hint: consult Section 12.4.1 in considering this approach.)

12.23. Consider formulation (12.3.2). Develop a LR-based dual algorithm (refer to Section 12.4.1) by considering a suitable set of constraints to relax.

12.24. For model (12.3.3), develop a LR-based dual algorithm (refer to Section 12.4.1) by considering a suitable set of constraints to relax. Apply the same approach to model 12.3.4.

CHAPTER 13

Restoration Design of Single- and Multi-Layer Fair Networks

In this chapter we will extend the considerations of Chapter 8 along the lines of Chapters 9, 10, and 12, and discuss restoration design problems and algorithms for fair networks robust to failures, for both the single-layer and the multi-layer cases. We will proceed in a way somewhat different than in Chapters 9, 10, and 12. Instead of minimizing the cost function we will use the budget constraint and maximize the network revenue in individual failure situations.

The presentation will be concentrated on the proportionally fair (PF) networks, still, as will be discussed, the considerations can be extended to cover the Max-Min Fair (MMF) demand volume allocation rule. The considered problems involving fairness in the demand volume allocation can be regarded as generalizations of the classical restoration design problems discussed in Chapters 9 and 12. Still, as you will soon notice, these generalizations are quite peculiar. Namely, if we consider PF to be assured for the demand volume allocation in particular failure situations, then it appears that the (logarithmic) revenues distributed (within the assumed budget) over the situations should follow the MMF principle. This makes the considered problem quite original and different from what we are accustomed to. In fact, this chapter contains original, non-classical material, and may be omitted during the first reading of this book.

In Section 13.1, we consider single-layer restoration problems and present basic theories and algorithms for fair network restoration design, which at the same time underlay the ideas of the algorithms for the MMF routing optimization given in Section 8.2.1. The introduced approach is illustrated with numerical examples. In Section 13.2, we show how the already familiar approaches of Benders' decomposition (BD) and path generation (PG) for candidate path lists augmentation can be applied to the problems considered in Section 13.1. Section 13.3 extends the discussion to multi-layer networks. The three basic two-layer cases studied in Section 13.3 correspond to the three problems studied in Section 12.2. Numerical results are also provided. Different variations of the problems considered earlier in this chapter are briefly discussed in Section 13.4, for instance, the case with MMF used instead of PF for the situation-dependent demand volume allocation. A summary and suggestions for further reading conclude this chapter.

Finally, we note that unless stated explicitly otherwise, all variables used in the problem formulations of this chapter are continuous and non-negative.

13.1 RESTORATION DESIGN OF SINGLE-LAYER PF NETWORKS

We start the presentation with a generalization of the single-state PF design problem D/PF/BCUF (8.3.2) from Section 8.3.2.

13.1.1 Problem Formulation and Iterative Solution

Consider the following restoration design problem.

***LMX:* DR/PF/PR+UR** **Link-Path Formulation**

Path Restoration with Unrestricted Flow Reconfiguration

indices

- $d = 1, 2, \ldots, D$ demands
- $p = 1, 2, \ldots, P_d$ candidate paths for demand d
- $e = 1, 2, \ldots, E$ links
- $s = 1, 2, \ldots, S$ situations (normal state is not distinguished)

constants

- δ_{ed} = 1 if link e belongs to the fixed path of demand d; 0, otherwise
- r_{ds} revenue from demand d in situation s
- ξ_e unit cost of link e
- α_{es} fractional availability coefficient of link e in situation s ($0 \le \alpha_{es} \le 1$)
- B assumed budget

variables

- y_e capacity of link e
- x_{dps} flow allocated to path p of demand d in situation s
- X_{ds} total flow allocated to demand d in situation s
  $\boldsymbol{X} = (\boldsymbol{X}_0, \boldsymbol{X}_1, \ldots, \boldsymbol{X}_S)$, $\boldsymbol{X}_s = (X_{ds} : d = 1, 2, \ldots, D)$ for $s = 1, 2, \ldots, S$
- R_s logarithmic revenue in situation s, $\boldsymbol{R} = (R_1, R_2, \ldots, R_S)$
- $\boldsymbol{R}$ vector $\boldsymbol{R} = (R_1, R_2, \ldots, R_S)$ of the revenues sorted in the non-decreasing order

objective

$$\text{maximize lexicographically } [\boldsymbol{R}] \tag{13.1.1a}$$

constraints

$$\textstyle\sum_e \xi_e y_e \le B \tag{13.1.1b}$$

$$\textstyle\sum_d \sum_p \delta_{edp} x_{dps} \le \alpha_{es} y_e, \qquad e = 1, 2, \ldots, E \tag{13.1.1c}$$

$$X_{ds} = \textstyle\sum_p x_{dps}, \qquad d = 1, 2, \ldots, D \quad s = 1, 2, \ldots, S \tag{13.1.1d}$$

$$R_s \le \textstyle\sum_d r_{ds} \log X_{ds}, \qquad s = 1, 2, \ldots, S. \tag{13.1.1e}$$

In essence, the formulated problem assures: 1) PF among demands in every situation, and 2) MMF among revenues over all situations. Recall that a vector $(a_1, a_2, \ldots, a_S)$ is lexicographically greater than vector $(b_1, b_2, \ldots, b_S)$ if and only if s' $(0 \leq s' < S)$ exists, such that $a_s = b_s$ for $s = 1, 2, \ldots, s'$ and $a_{s'+1} > b_{s'+1}$. Since the flows are reconfigured from scratch, the normal state $s = 0$ is not important in the following considerations, and the situations are labeled from 1 to S. Problem (13.1.1) is not a mathematical program since it involves lexicographical maximization of a vector rather than maximization of a given objective function. Thus, as for the MMF allocation problem A/MMF/FLMP (8.2.1) from Section 8.2.1, an iterative procedure is required to solve DR/PF/PR+UR. The procedure is given in the next paragraph.

The considered problem can be extended by introducing the bounds on the total flows in different failure situations. Then the following constraints are added:

$$h_{ds} \leq X_{ds} \leq H_{ds} \quad d = 1, 2, \ldots, D \quad s = 1, 2, \ldots, S \tag{13.1.1f}$$

where h_{ds} and H_{ds} are given constants.

The iterative solution of Problem (13.1.1) is similar to Algorithm 8.3 studied in Section 8.2.1 and starts with solving the following convex programming (CXP) problem.

***CXP:* DR/PF/PR+UR {FS}** **Link-Path Formulation**
First Step of DR/PF/PR+UR
additional variable

t auxiliary continuous variable (with unlimited sign)

objective

$$\text{maximize } t \tag{13.1.2a}$$

constraints

$$\textstyle\sum_e \xi_e y_e \leq B \tag{13.1.2b}$$

$$\textstyle\sum_d \sum_p \delta_{edp} x_{dps} \leq \alpha_{es} y_e, \quad e = 1, 2, \ldots, E \tag{13.1.2c}$$

$$X_{ds} = \textstyle\sum_p x_{dps}, \quad d = 1, 2, \ldots, D \quad s = 1, 2, \ldots, S \tag{13.1.2d}$$

$$R_s \leq \textstyle\sum_d r_{ds} \log X_{ds}, \quad s = 1, 2, \ldots, S \tag{13.1.2e}$$

$$t - R_s \leq 0, \quad s = 1, 2, \ldots, S. \tag{13.1.2f}$$

Recall that constraint (13.1.2f) together with objective (13.1.2a) assures the desired objective of maximizing the minimal R_s (minimum taken over $s = 1, 2, \ldots, S$), so the unique solution t^* of (13.1.2) is the first entry of the optimal vector $[\boldsymbol{R}^*]$ solving the original Problem (13.1.1). The full procedure for solving DR/PF/PR+UR is given by Algorithm 13.1.

ALGORITHM 13.1 Solving DR/PF/PR+UR

Step 0: Solve CXP (13.1.2) and let $(t^*, \boldsymbol{x}^*, \boldsymbol{X}^*, \boldsymbol{R}^*, \boldsymbol{y}^*)$ be the optimal solution of CXP (13.1.2). Put $n := 0,\ Z_0 := \emptyset\ Z_1 := \{1, 2, \dots, S\}$, and $t_s := t^*$ for each $s \in Z_1$.

Step 1: Put $n := n+1$. Start considering situations $s' \in Z_1$ one by one, checking whether the total revenue $R^*_{s'}$ can be made greater than t^*, without decreasing the already found maximal revenues t_s for all other situations s. The check is performed by the following *non-blocking test* (called NBT1, as in Section 8.2.1):

$$
\begin{aligned}
&\textbf{\textit{maximize}} \quad R_{s'} = \textstyle\sum_d r_{ds'} \log X_{ds'} && && (13.1.3a)\\
&\textbf{\textit{subject to}} \quad \textstyle\sum_e \xi_e y_e \le B && && (13.1.3b)\\
&\textstyle\sum_d \sum_p \delta_{edp} x_{dps} \le \alpha_{es} y_e, && e = 1, 2, \dots, E && (13.1.3c)\\
&X_{ds} = \textstyle\sum_p x_{dps}, && d = 1, 2, \dots, D && \\
& && s = 1, 2, \dots, S && (13.1.3d)\\
&t_s \le \textstyle\sum_d r_{ds} \log X_{ds}, && s = 1, 2, \dots, S. && (13.1.3e)
\end{aligned}
$$

If there are no blocking situations in Z_1 (situation $s \in Z_1$ is blocking if R_s cannot be further increased) then go to Step 2. Otherwise, when the first blocking situation, say situation s, is detected, then add s to set Z_0 and delete it from set Z_1 ($Z_0 := Z_0 \cup \{s\},\ Z_1 := Z_1 \backslash \{s\}$). If $Z_1 = \emptyset$ then stop (vector $\boldsymbol{R}^* = (R^*_1, R^*_2, \dots, R^*_S) = (t_1, t_2, \dots, t_S)$ is the solution of Problem (13.1.1)); else proceed to Step 2.
{Set Z_0 is the current set of blocking situations. Those situations $s \in Z_1$, for which $R^*_s > t^*$ (the revenue resulting from the optimal solution of Step 0 or Step 2 is greater than t^*) are not tested, as this means that they are non-blocking.}

Step 2: Solve the following CXP to improve the currently best revenues:

$$
\begin{aligned}
&\textbf{\textit{maximize}} \quad t && && (13.1.4a)\\
&\textbf{\textit{subject to}} \quad \textstyle\sum_e \xi_e y_e \le B && && (13.1.4b)\\
&\textstyle\sum_d \sum_p \delta_{edp} x_{dps} \le \alpha_{es} y_e, && e = 1, 2, \dots, E && (13.1.4c)\\
&X_{ds} = \textstyle\sum_p x_{dps}, && d = 1, 2, \dots, D && \\
& && s = 1, 2, \dots, S && (13.1.4d)\\
&t_s \le \textstyle\sum_d r_{ds} \log X_{ds}, && s \in Z_0,\ t_s - \text{constants} && (13.1.4e)\\
&t \le \textstyle\sum_d r_{ds} \log X_{ds}, && s \in Z_1. && (13.1.4f)
\end{aligned}
$$

Step 3: Let $(t^*, \boldsymbol{x}^*, \boldsymbol{X}^*, \boldsymbol{R}^*, \boldsymbol{y}^*)$ be the optimal solution of CXP (13.1.4). Put $t_s := t^*$ for each $s \in Z_1$ and go to Step 1.
{Note that it may happen that the optimal solution of (13.1.4) will not increase current t^* because there may be more blocking situations besides the one detected in Step 1.}

Notice that multiple solving of test (13.1.3) in Step 1 can be too time-consuming for large networks and hence, a more efficient test is required for Step 1. Such tests are described in the next section.

13.1.2 Algorithm With Dual Non-Blocking Tests

In this section we will formulate an improved version of Algorithm 13.1 based on the dual non-blocking tests, analogous to tests NBT3 used in Algorithm 8.4 of Section 8.2.1. Consider Problem (13.1.2) solved in Step 0 of Algorithm 13.1. Let $\boldsymbol{A}$ be the set of all feasible solutions $\boldsymbol{a} = (t, \boldsymbol{x}, \boldsymbol{X}, \boldsymbol{R}, \boldsymbol{y})$ defined by constraints (13.1.2b) to (13.1.2f) and $\boldsymbol{x} \geq \boldsymbol{0}$. Further, let t^* denote the optimal value of the primal function (13.1.2a), and $\boldsymbol{A}^* \subseteq \boldsymbol{A}$ denote the (convex) set of all optimal solutions of the considered problem. Finally, let $\boldsymbol{B}$ denote the set of the blocking situations with respect to t^*, i.e., the situations with the property

$$s \in \boldsymbol{B} \text{ if and only if } R_s(\boldsymbol{a}) = t^* \text{ for all } \boldsymbol{a} \in \boldsymbol{A}^*, \tag{13.1.5}$$

where $R_s(\boldsymbol{a})$ denotes revenue R_s for $\boldsymbol{a} = (t, \boldsymbol{x}, \boldsymbol{X}, \boldsymbol{R}, \text{y})$ where $\boldsymbol{R} = (R_1, R_2, \ldots, R_S)$. Note that due to the convexity of the set $\boldsymbol{A}^*$ an optimal solution $\boldsymbol{a}^* \in \boldsymbol{A}^*$ exists such that (see Exercise 13.1)

$$R_s(\boldsymbol{a}^*) = t^* \text{ for all } s \in \boldsymbol{B} \text{ and } R_s(\boldsymbol{a}^*) > t^* \text{ for all } s \notin \boldsymbol{B}. \tag{13.1.6}$$

PROPOSITION 13.1 *Let $\boldsymbol{\lambda}^* = (\lambda_1^*, \lambda_2^*, \ldots, \lambda_S^*)$ be the vector of optimal dual variables corresponding to constraint (13.1.2f). Then for $s = 1, 2, \ldots, S$ the following implication holds:*

$$\text{if } \lambda_s^* > 0 \text{ then } s \in \boldsymbol{B}. \tag{13.1.7}$$

Proof:

Let us dualize constraint (13.1.2f), and form the Lagrangian

$$\begin{aligned} L(\boldsymbol{a}; \boldsymbol{\lambda}) &= t - \textstyle\sum_s \lambda_s (t - R_s(\boldsymbol{a})) = t - \sum_s \lambda_s (t - \sum_d r_{ds} \log X_{ds}) \\ &= t(1 - \textstyle\sum_s \lambda_s) + \sum_s \lambda_s \sum_d r_{ds} \log X_{ds} \end{aligned} \tag{13.1.8}$$

and the dual function

$$W(\boldsymbol{\lambda}) = \max\nolimits_{\boldsymbol{a} \in \underline{\boldsymbol{A}}} L(\boldsymbol{a}; \boldsymbol{\lambda}),\ \lambda_s \geq 0, \quad s = 1, 2, \ldots, S, \tag{13.1.9}$$

where $\underline{\boldsymbol{A}}$ is the set of all points $\boldsymbol{a} = (t, \boldsymbol{x}, \boldsymbol{X}, \boldsymbol{R}, \boldsymbol{y})$ defined by constraints (13.1.2b to 13.1.2e) and $\boldsymbol{x} \geq \boldsymbol{0}$. Note that in the present case we are maximizing the Lagrangian (instead of minimizing, as it was usually the case before) because now the primal problem involves maximization (not minimization) of the objective function; also the dual problem involves minimization of the dual function. Since we are considering a convex optimization problem, any vector of the optimal dual variables (multipliers) $\boldsymbol{\lambda}^*$ satisfies the following equality

$$W(\boldsymbol{\lambda}^*) = \min_{\boldsymbol{\lambda}\geq \mathbf{0}} W(\boldsymbol{\lambda}) = t^*. \tag{13.1.10}$$

It follows that the set Λ in which the dual function assumes its minimum can be limited to

$$\Lambda = \{\boldsymbol{\lambda} : \textstyle\sum_s \lambda_s = 1,\ \lambda_s \geq 0,\ s = 1, 2, \ldots, S\}, \tag{13.1.11}$$

because if $\sum_s \lambda_s \neq 1$ then $W(\boldsymbol{\lambda})$ can be made infinitely large by letting $t \to -\infty$ or $t \to +\infty$ if $\sum_s \lambda_s > 1$ or $\sum_s \lambda_s < 1$, respectively. Hence, as we are interested in the minimization of the dual function, we may restrict the domain of (13.1.9) and transform it into the form:

$$W(\boldsymbol{\lambda}) = \max_{\boldsymbol{a}\in\underline{\boldsymbol{A}}} \textstyle\sum_s \lambda_s R_s(\boldsymbol{a}),\ \boldsymbol{\lambda} \in \Lambda. \tag{13.1.12}$$

Now let $\boldsymbol{\lambda}^*$ be a vector of optimal multipliers. Then

$$t^* = W(\boldsymbol{\lambda}^*) = L(\boldsymbol{a}^*; \boldsymbol{\lambda}^*) = \max_{\boldsymbol{a}\in\underline{\boldsymbol{A}}} L(\boldsymbol{a}; \boldsymbol{\lambda}^*) = \max_{\boldsymbol{a}\in\boldsymbol{A}^*} L(\boldsymbol{a}; \boldsymbol{\lambda}^*) \tag{13.1.13}$$

so that for some $\boldsymbol{a}^* \in \boldsymbol{A}^*$

$$\textstyle\sum_s \lambda_s^* R_s(\boldsymbol{a}^*) = t^*. \tag{13.1.14}$$

Since $\sum_s \lambda_s = 1$, equality (13.1.14) implies that $R_s(\boldsymbol{a}^*) = t^*$ for all s such that $\lambda_s > 0$. Otherwise the sharp inequality $\sum_s \lambda_s^* R_s(\boldsymbol{a}^*) > t^*$ would hold, since inequalities $\sum_s \lambda_s^* R_s(\boldsymbol{a}^*) \geq t^*$ $(s = 1, 2, \ldots, S)$ hold for any optimal solution. This in fact implies that λ_s^* cannot be positive if s is a non-blocking situation. Indeed, let us assume additionally that $\boldsymbol{a}^*$ is an optimal solution with property (13.1.6). Then it is clear that if $\boldsymbol{\lambda}^* \in \Lambda$ and a situation $s \notin \boldsymbol{B}$ with $\lambda_s^* > 0$ existed, it would hold that

$$\textstyle\sum_s \lambda_s^* R_s(\boldsymbol{a}^*) > t^*. \tag{13.1.15}$$

which would be a contradiction. Hence,

$$\text{if } s \notin \boldsymbol{B} \text{ then } \lambda_s^* = 0 \tag{13.1.16}$$

and this completes the proof. ■

In the next section we will show that the inverse implication is not always true, i.e. in general $\lambda_s^* = 0$ does not imply that situation s is non-blocking. Still, Proposition 13.1 implies a modification of Algorithm 13.1, given by Algorithm 13.2.

ALGORITHM 13.2 Improved Algorithm for DR/PF/PR+UR

Step 0: Solve CXP (13.1.2) and let t^* be the optimal value of (13.1.2a). Put $n := 0$, $Z_0 := \emptyset$, $Z_1 := \{1, 2, \ldots, S\}$ and $t_s = t^*$ for each $s \in Z_1$. Let λ_s^*, $s \in Z_1$ be optimal dual variables corresponding to constraint (13.1.2f).

Step 1: Put $n := n + 1$, $Z_0 := Z_0 \cup \{s \in Z_1 : \lambda_s^0 > 0\}$ and $Z_1 = \{s \in Z_1 : \lambda_s^* = 0\}$. If $Z_1 = \emptyset$ then stop (the vector $\boldsymbol{R} = (t_1, t_2, \ldots, t_S)$ is the solution of Problem (13.1.1)); otherwise proceed to Step 2.

Step 2: Solve CXP (13.1.4). Let t^* be the optimal value of (13.1.4a). Let λ_s^*, $s \in Z_1$ be the optimal dual variables corresponding to constraint (13.1.4f). Put $t_s = t^*$ for each $s \in Z_1$. Go to Step 1.

If optimal t^* in Step 2 happens to be strictly greater than the optimal solution obtained in the previous iteration, then all situations s in set Z_1 are non-blocking. If not, then one or more situations in set Z_1 are blocking (they are "false" non-blocking situations) and t^* cannot be increased. Still, among the newly obtained optimal dual variables λ_s^* for $s \in Z_1$, at least one with $\lambda_s^* > 0$ will appear, and hence, at least one new blocking situation will be detected. This follows from the fact that in the optimal dual solution of (13.1.4), the dual variables corresponding to (13.1.4f), λ_s^*, have the property defined in (13.1.11) (see Exercise 13.2):

$$\sum_{s \in Z_1} \lambda_s^* = 1 \text{ and } \lambda_s^* \geq 0 \text{ for } s \in Z_1. \tag{13.1.17}$$

13.1.3 *Regular Sets of Blocking Situations

Below we will establish a necessary and sufficient condition for the inverse implication in Proposition 13.1. Consider again Problem (13.1.2) and the corresponding set $\boldsymbol{B}$ of blocking situations with respect to t^*.

DEFINITION 13.1 *Set $\boldsymbol{B}$ is called* regular *if it has the following property: when any proper subset $\boldsymbol{B}_0$ of $\boldsymbol{B}$ is removed from the formulation of Problem (13.1.2) then in the resulting reduced optimization problem at least one situation $s \in \boldsymbol{B} \backslash \boldsymbol{B}_0$ becomes non-blocking with respect to t^*.*

In other words, if we arbitrarily decrease the set of blocking situations **B**, then the revenue for at least one of the remaining situations can be increased without decreasing the revenue of the remaining situations.

Example 13.1 *Irregular and regular sets of blocking situations.*
Consider the simple network depicted in Figure 13.1. There are two nodes, two links, and one demand. We assume normal state $s = 0$ and two failure situations ($S = 2$) modeling the complete failures of the individual links (situation s corresponds to the failure of link

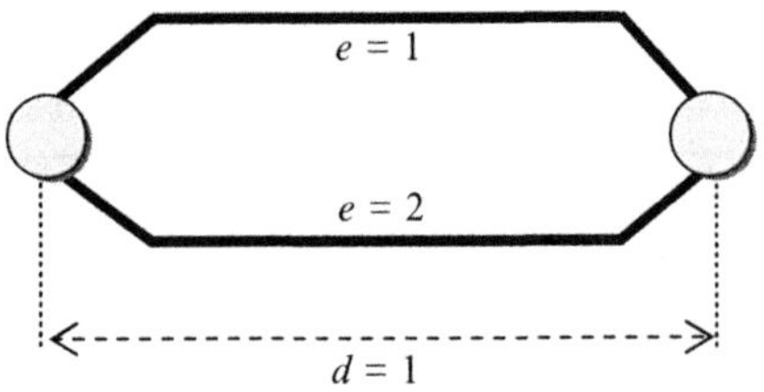

FIGURE 13.1 Two-Link Network

$e = s$). The revenue coefficient r_{1s} is equal to 1 for each situation and the link unit costs are equal to $1: \ \xi_1 = \xi_2 = 1$; budget B is equal to 2. The optimal solution of Problem (13.1.2) for the considered network assigns capacity $y_e^* = 1$ to each link, resulting in the optimal revenues: $\log 1 \le R_0^* \le \log 2, \ R_1^* = R_2^* = \log 1 = 0$. Situation $s = 0$ is clearly non-blocking while situations $s = 1$ and $s = 2$ are blocking. The set of blocking situations $\boldsymbol{B} = \{1, 2\}$ is regular because if we delete any one of its situations, for example, situation $s = 2$, then we arrive at the modified problem for which the optimal solution consists in assigning capacity 2 to link $e = 2$ ($y_2^* = 2$), and we then can further increase revenue R_1^* to $\log 2$.

Now, consider the network depicted in Figure 13.2 with three nodes, three links, and one demand. We have the normal state $s = 0$ and three failure situations ($S = 3$) modeling the individual complete failure of the links (situation s corresponds to the failure of link $e = s$). The revenue coefficient r_{1s} is equal to 1 for each situation and the link unit costs are $\xi_1 = \xi_2 = 1, \ \xi_3 = 2$; budget B is equal to 4. The optimal primal solution for the considered network also assigns capacity $y_e^* = 1$ to each link, resulting in the optimal revenues: $\log 1 \le R_0^* \le \log 2, \ R_1^* = R_2^* = R_3^* = \log 1 = 0$. Now situations $\boldsymbol{B} = \{1, 2, 3\}$ are blocking, and set $\boldsymbol{B}$ is irregular. If we delete one of situations $s = 1$ or $s = 2$, then we will not be able to increase the revenue in the remaining blocking situations. For instance, if we delete situation $s = 2$ from the formulation of Problem (13.1.2), then the above solution of the original problem is still the optimal solution of the modified problem, so we cannot increase the revenue in any of situations $s = 1$ and $s = 3$. ●

PROPOSITION 13.2 *If* $\boldsymbol{B}$ *is regular then for any optimal vector of optimal dual variables* $\boldsymbol{\lambda}^* = (\lambda_0^*, \lambda_1^*, \dots, \lambda_S^*)$ *corresponding to constraint (13.1.2f) the following equivalence is satisfied*

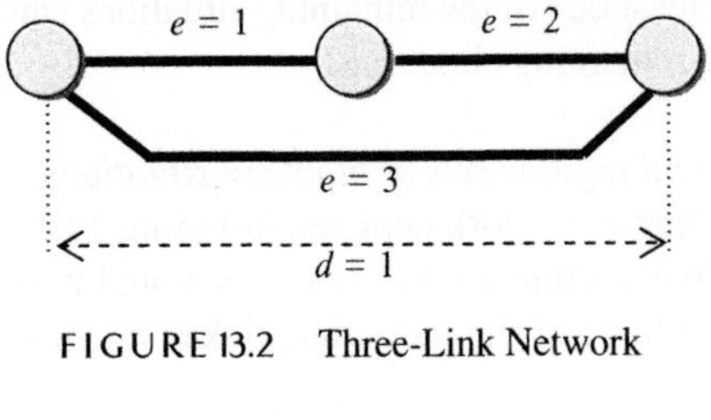

FIGURE 13.2 Three-Link Network

$$s \in \boldsymbol{B} \text{ if and only if } \lambda_s^* > 0, \quad s = 1, 2, \ldots, S. \tag{13.1.18}$$

Proof:

Implication $\lambda_s^* > 0 \Rightarrow s \in \boldsymbol{B}$ has already been proved in Proposition 13.1. To prove the inverse implication notice that (13.1.16) implies that from the viewpoint of the dual problem (i.e., minimization of the dual function), the non-blocking situations (i.e., situations not in $\boldsymbol{B}$) are not important because $W(\boldsymbol{\lambda}^*) = \sum_{s \in \boldsymbol{B}} \lambda_s^* R_s(\boldsymbol{a}^*)$ since for any optimal dual solution $\boldsymbol{\lambda}^*$, $\lambda_s^* = 0$ for all $s \notin \boldsymbol{B}$. In other words, the primal Problem (13.1.2) reduced to the situations from set $\boldsymbol{B}$, and the original problem which takes into account all situations $s \in \{1, 2, \ldots, S\}$, are identical in terms of the dual problem. The dual problem, common to both problems, original and reduced, is given by:

$$\textbf{\textit{maximize}} \quad W(\boldsymbol{\lambda}) = \max_{\boldsymbol{a} \in \underline{\boldsymbol{A}}} \textstyle\sum_{s \in \boldsymbol{B}} \lambda_s R_s(\boldsymbol{a}) \tag{13.1.19a}$$

$$\textbf{\textit{subject to}} \quad \boldsymbol{\lambda} \in \Lambda(\boldsymbol{B}),\ \Lambda(\boldsymbol{B}) = \{(\lambda_s,\ s \in \boldsymbol{B}) : \textstyle\sum_{s \in \boldsymbol{B}} \lambda_s = 1,\ \lambda_s \geq 0,\ s \in \boldsymbol{B}\}. \tag{13.1.19b}$$

Now suppose that $\lambda_s^* = 0$ for some $s' \in \boldsymbol{B}$ and some optimal dual solution $\boldsymbol{\lambda}^* \in \Lambda(\boldsymbol{B})$. For finding the minimum of the dual function, this assumption allows for the following additional restriction of the dual problem:

$$\textbf{\textit{maximize}} \quad W(\boldsymbol{\lambda}) = \max_{\boldsymbol{a} \in \underline{\boldsymbol{A}}} \textstyle\sum_{s \in \boldsymbol{B} \setminus \{s'\}} \lambda_s R_s(\boldsymbol{a}) \tag{13.1.20a}$$

$$\textbf{\textit{subject to}} \quad \boldsymbol{\lambda} \in \Lambda(\boldsymbol{B}),\ \lambda_{s'} = 0. \tag{13.1.20b}$$

Clearly, (13.1.20) is the dual problem of the primal optimization Problem (13.1.2) further reduced by deleting situation s' from the list of blocking situations. Since $\boldsymbol{B}$ is regular, one of the situations in the set $\boldsymbol{B} \setminus \{s'\}$, for example, situation s'', becomes non-blocking with respect to t^* which means that in the problem reduced to set $\boldsymbol{B} \setminus \{s'\}$, the set of blocking situations is a subset of $\boldsymbol{B} \setminus \{s', s''\}$. This in turn implies that in the new problem we have $\lambda_{s''}^* = 0$ for any optimal $\boldsymbol{\lambda}^*$, and we can further modify the dual problem arriving at:

$$\textbf{\textit{maximize}} \quad W(\boldsymbol{\lambda}) = \max_{\boldsymbol{a} \in \underline{\boldsymbol{A}}} \textstyle\sum_{s \in \boldsymbol{B} \setminus \{s', s''\}} \lambda_s R_s(\boldsymbol{a}) \tag{13.1.21a}$$

$$\textbf{\textit{subject to}} \quad \boldsymbol{\lambda} \in \Lambda(\boldsymbol{B}),\ \lambda_{s'} = \lambda_{s''} = 0. \tag{13.1.21b}$$

Continuing the above procedure of reducing the (regular) set $\boldsymbol{B}$ we will eventually reach the empty set of blocking situations, contradicting the assumption that $\sum_{s \in \boldsymbol{B}} \lambda_s^* = 1$. ■

COROLLARY 13.1 *The proof of Proposition 13.2 implies that the assumption "$\boldsymbol{B}$ is regular" is quite strong, as it is equivalent to the following property:*

If any proper subset B_0 of B is removed from the formulation of the original problem then the solution of the resulting reduced optimization problem, t_R^*, is strictly greater than the solution, t^*, of the original problem, i.e., $t_R^* > t^*$. In other words, in the reduced problem, *all of the situations* (i.e., the situations in the set $B \backslash B_0$) are non-blocking with respect to t^*.

PROPOSITION 13.3 *The assumption that B is regular (implying that the property of Corollary 13.1 holds) is also the necessary condition for equivalence (13.1.18). Hence, regularity of B is the necessary and sufficient condition for equivalence (13.1.18).*

Proof:

Due to Proposition 13.1, it suffices to show that if $s \in B$ and an optimal dual solution λ^* with $\lambda_s^* = 0$ exists, then a proper subset B_0 of B also exists, such that its removal from the formulation of Problem (13.1.2) results in the reduced optimization problem for which all situations $s \in B \backslash B_0$ are still blocking with respect to t^* (this, by Corollary 13.1, implies that B is irregular).

Such a set can be constructed as follows. Put $B_0 = \{s\}$. If B_0 does have the desired property then B is not regular, and we are done. Otherwise, the blocking set $B \backslash B_0$ of the reduced problem (without set B_0) contains a non-blocking situation, for example, situation s'. Hence, by the argument used in the proof of Proposition 13.2, an optimal solution λ^* of the dual to the original problem exists with $\lambda_s^* = \lambda_{s'}^* = 0$ and we put $B_0 = \{s, s'\}$. If B_0 does have the desired property then again we are done. Otherwise we continue the construction and include a new non-blocking situation $s'' \in B \backslash B_0$ to the set B_0, until either we arrive at a non-empty set $B \backslash B_0$ of blocking situations or B_0 becomes equal to B, which cannot happen since it would imply that $\sum_{s \in B} \lambda_s^* = 0$. ■

Note that if set Z_0 modified in Step 1 of Algorithm 13.2 is regular, then in Step 2 the optimal value t^* will necessarily be increased with respect to the previous one. The non-blocking tests of Step 1 are referred to as NBT3 (refer to Section 8.2.1). The property of regularity specified in Definition 13.1 gives the necessary and sufficient condition for the required (nice) behavior of the optimal multipliers λ^* leading to the increase of t^* in each iteration. The following example shows that this property can be essential.

Example 13.2 *Network with irregular set of blocking situations.*

Consider again problem DR/PF/PR+UR for the network depicted in Figure 13.2 from Example 13.1. Recall that any optimal primal solution for the considered network assigns one capacity unit to each link and results in optimal revenues: $\log 1 \le R_0^* \le \log 2$, $R_1^* = R_2^* = R_3^* = \log 1 = 0$.

The solution obtained after Step 1 gives $t^* = 0$. The structure of the problem implies that in any solution $a \in A$ the equality $R_1(a) = R_2(a) = \log X_1$ holds where X_1 is the flow allocated to path $\{1, 2\}$ in situation $s = 3$. Let X_2 be the flow allocated to path $\{3\}$ in situations $s = 1$ and $s = 2$. Then, due to the budget constraint, $X_1 + X_2 = 2$, and the Lagrangian (13.1.8) becomes equal to $L(a; \lambda) = \lambda_0 \log 2 + (\lambda_1 + \lambda_2)\log(2 - X) + \lambda_3 \log X$. Since the normal state ($s = 0$) is non-blocking we put $\lambda_0 = 0$; by computing the derivative of the Lagrangian (using the fact that $\lambda_1 + \lambda_2 + \lambda_3 = 1$) we find that its maximum is attained at the point $X = 2\lambda_3$ for any given λ_3, $0 \le \lambda_3 \le 1$. Hence, the dual function is in fact a scalar function equal to $W(\lambda) = (1 - \lambda)\log(2 - 2\lambda) + \lambda \log 2\lambda$, $0 \le \lambda \le 1$. The minimum of $W(\lambda)$ is attained for $\lambda = \frac{1}{2}$, implying that $\lambda_0^* = 0$, $\lambda_3^* = \frac{1}{2}$ and $\lambda_1^* + \lambda_2^* = \frac{1}{2}$. Thus, for instance, $\lambda^* = (0, 0, \frac{1}{2}, \frac{1}{2})$ is a vector of optimal multipliers with the corresponding optimal primal solution $X_1^* = X_2^* = 1$ (this primal solution is unique). So although $s = 1$ is a blocking situation ($1 \in \boldsymbol{B}$) with respect to $t^* = 0$, its optimal multiplier can be equal to 0, so it can appear as a "false" non-blocking situation in the set Z_1 of Step 1. Of course, with such a false non-blocking situation, the subsequent solution of Step 3 will not indicate any improvement over t^* although such an improvement, $t = \log 2$, is possible. (For derivations, see Exercise 13.4.)

The presented difficulty arises because in the considered network set $\boldsymbol{B}$ is not regular: deleting the blocking situation $s = 1$ from the list of situations does not make any of the remaining blocking situations ($s = 2$ and $s = 3$) non-blocking. This is also true for situation $s = 2$ (symmetric to $s = 1$), but not for situation $s = 3$, since deleting $s = 3$ makes situations $s = 1$ and $s = 2$ non-blocking, allowing for increasing t^* from 0 to $\log 2$. Of course, if we combine situations $s = 1$ and $s = 2$ and treat them as one situation with the simultaneous failures of links $e = 1$ and $e = 2$, then the discussed degeneracy will vanish. ●

13.1.4 Numerical Results

Note that it would be rather difficult to find optimal multipliers for the convex problems considered in Section 13.1.2. However, transformation of these problems to their approximative linear programming (LP) counterparts using a piecewise linear approximation of the logarithmic function (cf. Section 4.3.2) makes it feasible, since the values of optimal dual variables are available from the LP solvers. Below we shall present results for such LP approximations, using the following approximation $G(x)$ of the logarithmic function $log x$ (cf. 4.3.11):

$$G(x) = \min\{g_k x + f_k : k = 1, 2, \dots, K\}. \tag{13.1.22}$$

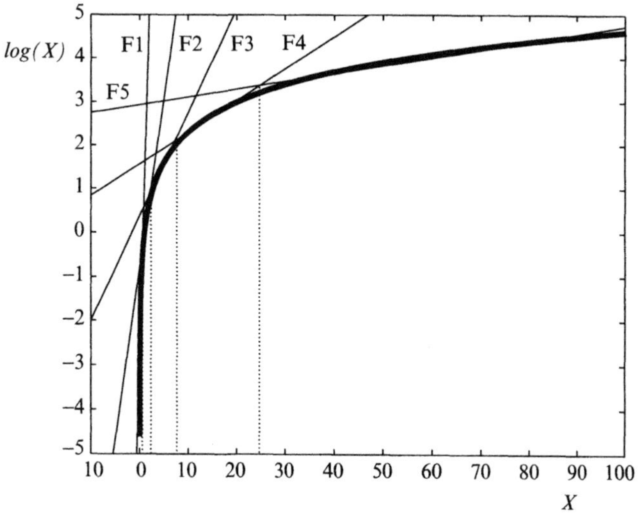

FIGURE 13.3 Approximation of log X

The consecutive pairs of coefficients (g_k, f_k) of the five ($K = 5$) linear pieces actually used for the approximation are as follows (refer to Figure 13.3):

(3.9805, −2.7170), (0.7774, −0.7910), (0.2380, 0.3761), (0.0731, 1.5649), (0.0180, 2.9318).

The linear approximation consists in introducing one auxiliary variable and a set of K constraints corresponding to the linear pieces of approximation (13.1.22) for each occurrence of the logarithmic function. In order to approximate problem DR/PF/PR+UR {FS}, new variables z_{ds} are introduced, resulting in the following approximation.

***LP:* DR/PF/PR+UR {FS-LA}** **Link-Path Formulation**
Linear Approximation of DR/PF/PR+UR {FS}
additional variables

z_{ds} approximation of $\log X_{ds}$ (continuous)

objective

maximize t (13.1.23a)

constraints

$\sum_e \xi_e y_e \le B$ (13.1.23b)

$\sum_d \sum_p \delta_{edp} x_{dps} \le \alpha_{es} y_e,$ $e = 1, 2, \ldots, E$ $s = 1, 2, \ldots, S$ (13.1.23c)

$X_{ds} = \sum_p x_{dps},$ $d = 1, 2, \ldots, D$ $s = 1, 2, \ldots, S$ (13.1.23d)

$z_{ds} \le g_k X_{ds} + f_k,$ $d = 1, 2, \ldots, D$ $s = 1, 2, \ldots, S$ $k = 1, 2, \ldots, K$ (13.1.23e)

$t \le \sum_d r_{ds} z_{ds},$ $s = 1, 2, \ldots, S.$ (13.1.23f)

Problem (13.1.4) in Algorithm 13.1 can be modified analogously, and the upper and lower bounds on the total flows X_{ds} ($d = 1, 2, \ldots, D,\ s = 1, 2, \ldots, S$) can be added to the LP formulations. In fact, using the LP approximations of the considered convex optimization problems is advantageous since the convex programming methods described in Section 5.5 are not applicable as they assume linear constraints, which is not the case for the constraints involving the logarithmic function. Also, from the network engineering point-of-view the use of approximations practically does not introduce any error.

Below we illustrate the algorithms introduced in the previous sections, i.e., Algorithm 13.1 (referred to as the basic algorithm in the sequel) and Algorithm 13.2 (referred to as the modified algorithm). We will use three network configurations depicted in Figure 13.4 and summarized in Table 13.1.

For each network we admit only single-link failures and label the situations starting from 0; hence, situation $s = 0$ denotes the normal state, while for each situation $s = 1, 2, \ldots, S$ ($S = E$), link $e = s$ totally fails. For N_3 and N_5, we assume $B = 1000$, and all link-unit costs and all demand revenues equal to 1 ($\xi_e \equiv 1$ and $r_{ds} \equiv 1$). For N_{12} we also assume $B = 1000$ and all demand revenues equal to 1. Further details about the input data are given in Tables 13.2 and 13.3. No bounds on the total flows assigned to demands are imposed.

TABLE 13.1 **Considered Networks**

code	# nodes	# links	# demands	# paths per demand	# failure situations
N_3	3	3	3	2	4
N_5	5	7	10	2-3	8
N_{12}	12	18	66	6-13	19

TABLE 13.2 **Demands and Paths for Network N_3**

Demand Nodes		$d = 1$ 1-2	$d = 2$ 1-3	$d = 3$ 2-3
Links (e)	$p = 1$	1	2	3
	$p = 2$	2,3	1,3	1,2

TABLE 13.3 **Link Marginal Costs for Network N_{12}**

e	1	2	3	4	5	6	7	8	9
ξ_e	1.85	3.4	1	1.45	2.3	2.9	1	1.6	2.2
e	10	11	12	13	14	15	16	17	18
ξ_e	1.5	2.3	1.4	1.65	1.25	2.3	1.55	1.35	1.7

TABLE 13.4 **Software Implementations of the Algorithms**

Variant	Programming environment	Solver
C++	Microsoft Visual C++ 6.0; Callable CPLEX libraries	CPLEX 7.5.0
AMPL	AMPL ver. 20010215	CPLEX 7.5.0
Matlab[a]	MATLAB 6.1	MATLAB Optimization toolbox

[a]Used only for the basic algorithm.

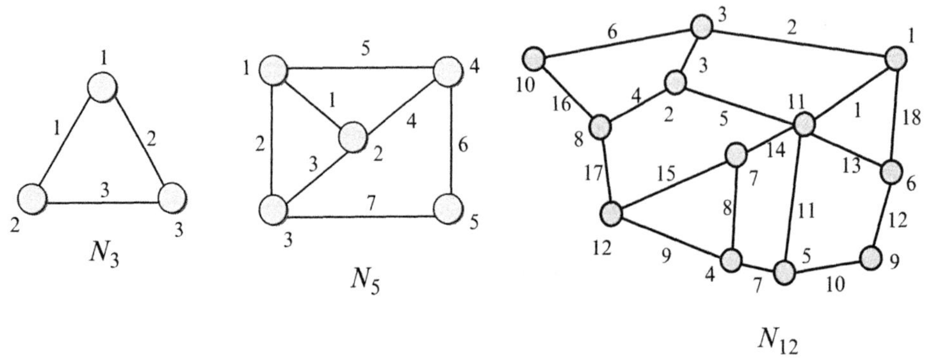

FIGURE 13.4 Considered Networks

TABLE 13.5 **Execution Times and Memory Requirements**

	Execution times (seconds)				
Reference code	**Implementations of basic algorithm**			**Implementations of modified algorithm**	
	C++	**AMPL**	**Matlab**	**C++**	**AMPL**
N_3	< 1	2	4	< 1	< 1
N_5	< 1	3	12	< 1	2
N_{12}	3859	390	6.4e4	179	325
Max. memory req. (MB)	16.8	28.3	83	18.6	27.3

For all of the three considered network examples we have applied both algorithms: Algorithm 13.1 with straightforward blocking tests NBT1, and its modified version, Algorithm 13.2, with the dual blocking tests NBT3. Both algorithms have been implemented in three variants described in Table 13.4 on the same hardware (Dell Precision 220 PC with Intel Pentium III-1GHz CPU, 260 MB RAM, Quantum Atlas 10K2-TY092L SCSI HDD under Windows 2000 Pro SP2 OS). The C++ and AMPL implementations use the simplex method (the C++ implementation uses CPLEX callable library), while with Matlab an interior point method LP solver is applied.

The execution times are given in Table 13.5 illustrating the time savings from the modified algorithm. Tables 13.6 and 13.7 show detailed solutions for N_3 and N_{12} obtained with the C++ implementation. In Table 13.6 only non-zero flows are listed and empty fields indicate that the corresponding entities are not changed with respect to the previous step. Final results are shown in the column of the table where they appear for

TABLE 13.6 **Numerical Results for the Basic and the Modified Algorithms Applied to N_3**

n	0	1		2
Instant	**After Step 0**	**After Step 1**	**After Steps 2 & 3**	**After Step 1**
t^*	20.35		26.8	
t_s	$t_s = 20.35$, $s = 0, 1, 2, 3$		$t_0 = 26.8$, $t_s = 20.35, s = 1, 2, 3$	
R_s	$R_s = 20.35$, $s = 0, 1, 2, 3$	$R_{0'} = 26.80$, $R_{s'} = 20.35$, $s' = 1, 2, 3$	$R_0 = 26.8$, $R_s = 20.35, s = 1, 2, 3$	$R_{0'} = 26.8$
y	$y_1 = y_2 = y_3 = 333.33$		$y_1 = y_2 = y_3 = 333.33$	
x_{dps}	$x_{110} = 24.81$ $x_{210} = 24.81$ $x_{310} = 283.72$ $x_{320} = 308.53$ $x_{121} = 24.81$ $x_{211} = 308.53$ $x_{311} = 308.53$ $x_{112} = 308.53$ $x_{222} = 24.81$ $x_{312} = 308.53$ $x_{113} = 308.53$ $x_{213} = 308.53$ $x_{323} = 24.81$		$x_{110} = 333.33$ $x_{210} = 333.33$ $x_{310} = 333.33$ $x_{121} = 24.81$ $x_{211} = 308.53$ $x_{311} = 308.53$ $x_{112} = 308.53$ $x_{222} = 24.81$ $x_{312} = 308.53$ $x_{113} = 308.53$ $x_{213} = 308.53$ $x_{323} = 24.81$	
Z_1	$s = 0, 1, 2, 3$	$s = 0$		$\emptyset$
Z_0	$\emptyset$	$s = 1, 2, 3$		$s = 0, 1, 2, 3$
λ_s	For constraint (13.1.2f): $\lambda_0 = 0$, $\lambda_1 = \lambda_2 = \lambda_3 = 0.33$		For constraint (13.1.4f): $\lambda_0 = 1$	

the last time. The quantities $R_{s'}$ are the outcomes of the NBT1 tests and are relevant only for the basic algorithm, while λ_s are relevant only for the modified version with the NBT3 tests. Table 13.7 shows the results obtained for N_{12} (the flows are not presented because of their excessive number). Both algorithms required 15 iterations to find the final solution.

In the second experiment for N_{12}, another failure scenario is assumed (the rest of the input data does not change). The failed links in the considered 19 failure situations are listed in Table 13.8. For the new scenario the case without bounds exhibits some total flows X_{ds} less than 1. To see the effect of the bounds, two cases with the lower bound (LB) imposed on all total flows in all situations, equal to 1 and to $1\frac{1}{2}$, together with the unbounded case,

TABLE 13.7 Selected Results and Parameters for Network N_{12}

n	t^*	s	R_s					e	y_e
			n						
			0	1	2	14	15		
0	91.62	0	91.62	92.15	92.32	97.83	101.64	1	25.89
1	92.15	1	91.62	92.15	92.32	96.22	96.22	2	33.32
2	92.32	2	91.62	92.18	92.32	92.33	92.33	3	42.54
3	92.33	3	91.62	92.15	92.32	93.96	93.96	4	49.76
4	93.11	4	91.62	91.62	91.62	91.62	91.62	5	40.46
5	93.56	5	91.62	91.62	91.62	91.62	91.62	6	13.70
6	93.96	6	91.62	92.15	92.32	97.37	97.37	7	54.97
7	94.06	7	91.62	92.15	92.15	92.15	92.15	8	27.97
8	94.27	8	91.62	92.15	92.32	95.93	95.93	9	22.43
9	95.93	9	91.62	92.15	92.32	94.27	94.27	10	31.64
10	96.22	10	91.62	92.15	92.32	93.56	93.56	11	16.55
11	96.26	11	91.62	92.15	92.32	97.83	97.83	12	38.13
12	96.68	12	91.62	92.15	92.32	93.11	93.11	13	22.43
13	97.37	13	91.62	92.15	92.32	96.68	96.68	14	55.60
14	97.83	14	91.62	91.62	91.62	91.62	91.62	15	22.24
15	101.64	15	91.62	92.15	92.32	96.26	96.26	16	25.24
		16	91.62	92.15	92.32	92.32	92.32	17	40.45
		17	91.62	91.62	91.62	91.62	91.62	18	29.56
		18	91.62	92.15	92.32	94.06	94.06		

TABLE 13.8 The Second Failure Scenario

Situation	0	1	2	3	4	5	6	7	8	9
Failed links	-	5,16	8,12	6,15	3,8	11,15	6,11	3,5	2,17	4,14
Situation	10	11	12	13	14	15	16	17	18	
Failed links	11,13	2,16	7,10	2,7	17,18	1,17	7,18	6,13	1,9	

are shown in Figure 13.5. The resulting ordered revenue vectors become, as expected, lexicographically smaller with the increase of the lower bound, still the differences are negligible. The average revenues over all of the situations are 86.58, 86.46, and 86.44 for lower bound equal to 0, 1, and $\frac{1}{2}$, respectively. Although after the final iteration, revenues R_s for different situations can differ only by a small number, the actual flow differences can still be significant, since such revenues are logarithmically related to the aggregated flows.

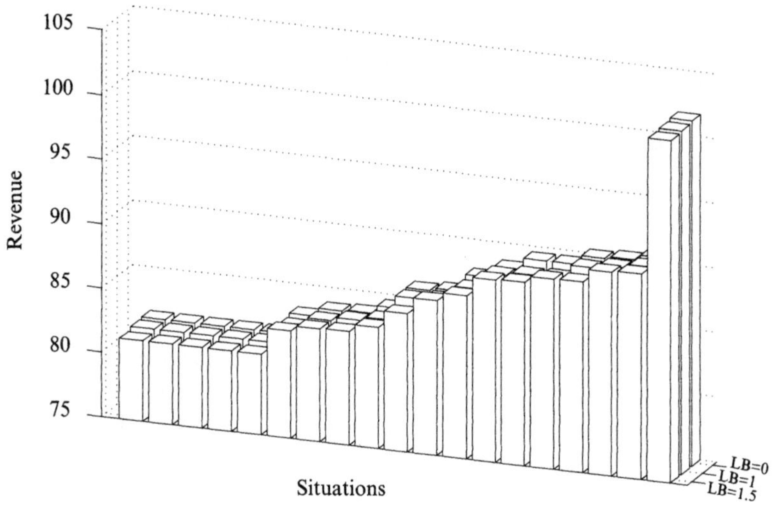

FIGURE 13.5 Revenue Vectors for N_{12} with Lower Bound (LB)

Applying the algorithms to larger networks will increase the superiority of the modified algorithm over the basic version, since the dual variable approach does not require the computationally exhaustive Step 1. This tendency can already be observed in Table 13.5 showing the execution time gain achieved with the modified algorithm.

13.2 DECOMPOSITION METHODS FOR THE SINGLE-LAYER RESTORATION PROBLEMS

In this section we will show how to apply BD and PG to the subproblems associated with problem DR/PF/PR+UR (13.1.1) studied in Section 13.1.

13.2.1 Benders' Decomposition

A natural question is whether the BD approach (refer to Sections 5.4.3 and 10.3) can help in solving problem DR/PF/PR+UR stated at the beginning of Section 13.1.1. The answer is, as expected, yes. BD can be applied to the linear approximation DR/PF/PR+UR {FS-LA} (13.1.23) of Problem (13.1.2), as well as for the analogous linear approximations of Problems (13.1.3) and (13.1.4) used in Algorithms 13.1 and 13.2.

For DR/PF/PR+UR {FS-LA}, the master problem involves variables t and $\boldsymbol{y}$ which couple the flow variables $\boldsymbol{x}$ and $\boldsymbol{z}$, and is as follows.

Master Problem

maximize	t	(13.2.1a)
subject to	(13.1.23b), $\boldsymbol{y} \geq \mathbf{0}$ and all inequalities from Ω	(13.2.1b)

To see how the inequalities for variables t and $\boldsymbol{y}$ in set Ω are generated suppose that t and $\boldsymbol{y}$ are given, and for each situation s consider the following problem with variables w, $\boldsymbol{x}$ and $\boldsymbol{z}$:

$$\textbf{minimize} \quad w \tag{13.2.2a}$$

$$\textbf{subject to} \quad \textstyle\sum_d \sum_p \delta_{edp} x_{dp} \leq \alpha_{es} y_e + w, \qquad e = 1, 2, \ldots, E \tag{13.2.2b}$$

$$z_d \leq g_k(\textstyle\sum_p x_{dp}) + f_k, \qquad d = 1, 2, \ldots, D, \quad k = 1, 2, \ldots, K \tag{13.2.2c}$$

$$t \leq \textstyle\sum_d r_{ds} z_d. \tag{13.2.2d}$$

Of course, the optimal solution $w^*(t, \boldsymbol{y})$ of the above problem is positive if and only if the current fixed link capacities $\boldsymbol{y}$ are not sufficient to realize revenue not less than the current fixed t for situation s (Problem (13.2.2) is always feasible). The dual problem to (13.2.2), which constitutes the feasibility test for situation s, is as follows (see Exercise 13.5).

Feasibility Test for Situation s

$$\textbf{maximize} \quad w(t, \boldsymbol{y}) = \lambda t - \textstyle\sum_e \pi_e \alpha_{es} y_e - \sum_d \sum_k \sigma_{dk} f_k \tag{13.2.3a}$$

$$\textbf{subject to} \quad \lambda \geq 0, \ \boldsymbol{\sigma} \geq \mathbf{0}, \ \boldsymbol{\pi} \geq \mathbf{0} \text{ and} \tag{13.2.3b}$$

$$\lambda r_{ds} = \textstyle\sum_k \sigma_{dk}, \qquad d = 1, 2, \ldots, D \tag{13.2.3c}$$

$$\textstyle\sum_k \sigma_{dk} g_k \leq \sum_e \delta_{edp} \pi_e, \qquad d = 1, 2, \ldots, D, \quad p = 1, 2, \ldots, P_d \tag{13.2.3d}$$

$$\textstyle\sum_e \pi_e = 1. \tag{13.2.3e}$$

If, after solving Problem (13.2.3), the optimal value $w^*(t, \boldsymbol{y})$ of (13.2.3a) is less equal 0, then the current values of t and $\boldsymbol{y}$ are feasible for situation s. Otherwise, a new inequality for t and $\boldsymbol{y}$ is added to set Ω using the values of optimal dual variables λ^*, $\boldsymbol{\pi}^*$, and $\boldsymbol{\sigma}^*$, corresponding to constraints (13.2.2d), (13.2.2b), and (13.2.2c), respectively:

$$\lambda^* t - \textstyle\sum_e \pi_e^* \alpha_{es} y_e - \sum_d \sum_k \sigma_{dk}^* f_k \leq 0. \tag{13.2.4}$$

The BD algorithm is very much the same as the one given in Section 10.3.1 for DR-U. As in the BD applications of Section 10.3, the set Ω can be made initially empty or can be initially filled with the inequalities (13.2.4) obtained for each situation s from the (sub)optimal values of multipliers λ^*, $\boldsymbol{\sigma}_s^* = (\sigma_{dks}^* : d = 1, 2, \ldots, D, \ k = 1, 2, \ldots, K)$ and $\boldsymbol{\pi}_s^* = (\pi_{es}^* : e = 1, 2, \ldots, E)$ resulting from solving the full dual problem to (13.1.23) by subgradient maximization of the dual function.

13.2.2 Path Generation

The PG method can be applied to the LP approximation (13.1.23) and to the remaining problems used in the iterative solution of the basic Problem (13.1.1). Rewriting the constraints (13.1.23b) to (13.1.23f) as

$$\sum_e \xi_e y_e = B \tag{13.2.5a}$$

$$\sum_d \sum_p \delta_{edp} x_{dps} \le \alpha_{es} y_e, \quad e = 1,2,\dots,E \quad s = 1,2,\dots,S \tag{13.2.5b}$$

$$z_{ds} \le g_k(\textstyle\sum_p x_{dps}) + f_k, \quad d = 1,2,\dots,D \quad s = 1,2,\dots,E \quad k = 1,2,\dots,K \tag{13.2.5c}$$

$$t \le \sum_d r_{ds} z_{ds}, \quad s = 1,2,\dots,S \tag{13.2.5d}$$

and introducing dual variables ω, $\boldsymbol{\pi} = (\pi_{es}, e = 1,2,\dots,E,\ s = 1,2,\dots,S)$, $\boldsymbol{\sigma} = (\sigma_{dsk},\ d = 1,2,\dots,D,\ s = 1,2,\dots,S,\ k = 1,2,\dots,K)$, $\boldsymbol{\lambda} = (\lambda_1, \lambda_2, \dots, \lambda_S)$ for constraints (13.2.5a), (13.2.5b), (13.2.5c), and (13.2.5d), respectively, we arrive at the following problem dual to DR/PF/PR+UR {FS-LA} (13.1.23) (see Exercise 13.6):

minimize $\quad W(\omega, \boldsymbol{\sigma}, \boldsymbol{\lambda}, \boldsymbol{\pi}) = \omega B + \sum_k (\sum_d \sum_s \sigma_{dsk}) f_k \quad$ (13.2.6a)

subject to $\quad \omega$ unconstrained in sign, $\boldsymbol{\pi}, \boldsymbol{\sigma}, \boldsymbol{\lambda} \ge \mathbf{0} \quad$ (13.2.6b)

$$\sum_s \lambda_s = 1 \tag{13.2.6c}$$

$$\lambda_s r_{ds} = \sum_k \sigma_{dsk}, \quad d = 1,2,\dots,D \quad s = 1,2,\dots,S \tag{13.2.6d}$$

$$\sum_k \sigma_{dsk} g_k \le \sum_e \pi_{es} \delta_{edp}, \quad d = 1,2,\dots,D \quad p = 1,2,\dots,P_d \quad s = 1,2,\dots,S \tag{13.2.6e}$$

$$\sum_s \alpha_{es} \pi_{es} \le \omega \xi_e, \quad e = 1,2,\dots,E. \tag{13.2.6f}$$

Assume that the dual Problem (13.2.6) is bounded from below (the necessary condition for this reads: for each demand d and each situation s at least one available path exists, i.e., at least one path (d,p) on the routing list for demand d exists such that $\alpha_{es} > 0$ for each $\delta_{edp} = 1$. Let $(\omega^*, \boldsymbol{\pi}^*, \boldsymbol{\lambda}^*, \boldsymbol{\sigma}^*)$ be any optimal solution of the dual problem and let $\varphi^*_{ds} = \sum_k \sigma^*_{dsk} g_k$. Then, for each d and s, the left-hand side of (13.2.6e) must be equal to $\sum_e \pi^*_{es} \delta_{edp}$ for some p, $1 \le p \le P_d$, i.e.,

$$\varphi^*_{ds} = \min\{\textstyle\sum_e \pi^*_{es} \delta_{edp} : p = 1,2,\dots,P_d\}. \tag{13.2.7}$$

In other words, φ^*_{ds} is the length of the shortest path for demand d in situation s with respect to optimal multipliers $\boldsymbol{\pi}^*_s = (\pi^*_{1s}, \pi^*_{2s}, \dots, \pi^*_{Es})$. The last statement follows from the complementary slackness property, which in this case states that any positive primal optimal flow x^*_{dps} can be assigned only to path (d,p) with $\varphi^*_{ds} = \sum_e \pi^*_{es} \delta_{edp}$. Observe that to assure equality (13.2.7) for all d and s we have to assume that for any optimal primal solution at least one flow x^*_{dps} is positive (this may not be the case if the approximation of the logarithm function is not steep enough at its first linear piece, i.e., when g_1 is not large enough).

Equality (13.2.7) forms the base for the PG algorithm for the considered problem. The algorithm is essentially the same as for the problem DR-U from Section 10.1.1, with λ^*_{ds} substituted with φ^*_{ds}.

13.3 DESIGN OF RESILIENT TWO-LAYER PF NETWORKS

In this section we will discuss three design problems for two-layer robust networks. We will focus on the unrestricted flow restoration cases applied in either one of the two layers or in both layers. The problems differ by the reconfiguration options in the case of link failures. The solution algorithms are extensions of the algorithm devised for the single layer problem DR/PF/PR+UR (13.1.1). All three reconfiguration options assure fair allocation of resources for a network robust to failures. The three problems are the fair network counterparts of the multi-commodity problems considered in Section 12.2.

13.3.1 *Three Basic Problems for Unrestricted Flow Restoration*

In this section we will formulate two-layer robust design problems involving the PF and MMF principles. The considered networks are assumed to be composed of two layers of resources: layer 1 (lower layer) and layer 2 (upper layer), and the auxiliary demand layer used for the demand specification. The three consecutive problems assume flow restoration in the lower, upper, and in both resource layers, respectively, and, hence, they correspond to the basic two-layer problems presented in Section 12.2. All of the three problems assure PF bandwidth allocation among the demands. Besides, the two latter problems also assure MMF total revenues among the failure situations. Therefore, we may say that the resulting solutions indicate "two-dimensional" fairness.

***CXP:* DR/2L/PRU(1)-NPR(2)** **Link-Path Formulation**
Flow Reconfiguration Only in Layer 1

indices

$d = 1, 2, \ldots, D$	demands
$p = 1, 2, \ldots, P_d$	candidate paths of layer 2 for demand d
$e = 1, 2, \ldots, E$	links of layer 2
$q = 1, 2, \ldots, Q_e$	candidate paths of layer 1 for link e
$g = 1, 2, \ldots, G$	links of layer 1
$s = 1, 2, \ldots, S$	situations (normal state is not distinguished)

constants

r_d	revenue from demand d
$h_d,\ H_d$	lower and upper bound, respectively, for total flow of demand d
δ_{edp}	= 1 if link e belongs to path p realizing demand d, 0 otherwise
γ_{geq}	= 1 if link g belongs to path q realizing link e, 0 otherwise
ξ_g	unit cost of link g
α_{gs}	fractional availability coefficient of link g in situation s ($0 \le \alpha_{gs} \le 1$)
B	assumed budget

variables

x_{dp}	flow allocated to path p of demand d
X_d	total flow allocated to demand d, $\boldsymbol{X} = (X_1, X_2, \ldots, X_D)$
y_e	capacity of link e
z_{eqs}	flow allocated to path q of link e in situation s
u_g	capacity of link g

objective

$$\text{maximize } \boldsymbol{F} = \textstyle\sum_d r_d \log X_d \tag{13.3.1a}$$

constraints

$$\textstyle\sum_g \xi_g u_g \leq B \tag{13.3.1b}$$
$$\textstyle\sum_p x_{dp} = X_d, \quad d = 1, 2, \ldots, D \tag{13.3.1c}$$
$$h_d \leq X_d \leq H_d, \quad d = 1, 2, \ldots, D \tag{13.3.1d}$$
$$\textstyle\sum_d \sum_p \delta_{edp} x_{dp} = y_e, \quad s = 1, 2, \ldots, S \tag{13.3.1e}$$
$$\textstyle\sum_q z_{eqs} = y_e, \quad e = 1, 2, \ldots, E \quad s = 1, 2, \ldots, S \tag{13.3.1f}$$
$$\textstyle\sum_e \sum_q \gamma_{geq} z_{eqs} \leq \alpha_{gs} u_g, \quad g = 1, 2, \ldots, G \quad s = 1, 2, \ldots, S. \tag{13.3.1g}$$

Note that in this particular case the revenue is not situation-dependent as the upper-layer link capacities are the same in all situations. Problem DR/2L/PRU(1)-NPR(2) is a convex mathematical programming problem that can be effectively approximated with a LP, using a piecewise linear approximation of the logarithmic function discussed in Section 13.1.4 (refer to Problem (13.1.23)).

The next problem admits reconfiguration only in Layer 2.

LXM: **DR/2L/NPR(1)-PRU(2)** **Link-Path Formulation**
Flow Reconfiguration Only in Layer 2
additional constants

r_{ds}	revenue from demand d in situation s
h_{ds}, H_{ds}	lower and upper bound, respectively, for total flow of demand d in situation s
α_{gs}	binary availability coefficient of link g in situation s ($\alpha_{gs} \in \{0, 1\}$)
θ_{eqs}	binary availability coefficient of path q realizing link e in situation s, $\theta_{eqs} = \prod_{\{g:\gamma_{geq}=1\}} \alpha_{gs}$

variables

x_{dps}	flow allocated to path p of demand d in situation s
X_{ds}	total flow allocated to demand d in situation s, $\boldsymbol{X} = (\boldsymbol{X}_1, \boldsymbol{X}_2, \ldots, \boldsymbol{X}_S)$, $\boldsymbol{X}_s = (X_{1s}, X_{2s}, \ldots, X_{Ds})$ for $s = 1, 2, \ldots, S$
y_{es}	capacity of link e in situation s
z_{eq}	flow allocated to path q of link e
u_g	capacity of link g
R_s	logarithmic revenue in situation s, $\boldsymbol{R} = (R_1, R_2, \ldots, R_S)$
$[\boldsymbol{R}]$	vector $\boldsymbol{R} = (R_1, R_2, \ldots, R_S)$ of the revenues sorted in the non-decreasing order

objective

$$\text{maximize lexicographically } [\boldsymbol{R}] \tag{13.3.2a}$$

constraints

$\sum_g \xi_g u_g \leq B$ (13.3.2b)

$\sum_p x_{dps} = X_{ds},\quad d = 1, 2, \dots, D \quad s = 1, 2, \dots, S$ (13.3.2c)

$h_{ds} \leq X_{ds} \leq H_{ds},\quad d = 1, 2, \dots, D \quad s = 1, 2, \dots, S$ (13.3.2d)

$\sum_d \sum_p \delta_{edp} x_{dps} = y_{es},\quad e = 1, 2, \dots, E \quad s = 1, 2, \dots, S$ (13.3.2e)

$\sum_q \theta_{eqs} z_{eq} \geq y_{es},\quad e = 1, 2, \dots, E \quad s = 1, 2, \dots, S$ (13.3.2f)

$\sum_e \sum_q \gamma_{geq} z_{eq} = u_g,\quad g = 1, 2, \dots, G$ (13.3.2g)

$R_s \leq \sum_d r_{ds} \log X_{ds},\quad s = 1, 2, \dots, S.$ (13.3.2h)

In the problem above the link capacities in the upper layer are situation-dependent as well as the revenues. Finally, let us consider the problem with reconfiguration mechanisms in both resource layers.

***LXM:* DR/2L/PRU(1)-PRU(2)** **Link-Path Formulation**

Flow Reconfiguration in Layers 1 and 2

variables

x_{dps} flow allocated to path p of demand d in situation s

X_{ds} total flow allocated to demand d in situation s, $\boldsymbol{X} = (\boldsymbol{X}_1, \boldsymbol{X}_2, \dots, \boldsymbol{X}_S)$, $\boldsymbol{X}_s = (X_{1s}, X_{2s}, \dots, X_{Ds})$ for $s = 1, 2, \dots, S$

y_{es} capacity of link e in situation s

z_{eqs} flow allocated to path q of link e in situation s

u_g capacity of link g

R_s logarithmic revenue in situation s, $\boldsymbol{R} = (R_1, R_2, \dots, R_S)$

$[\boldsymbol{R}]$ vector $\boldsymbol{R} = (R_1, R_2, \dots, R_S)$ of the revenues sorted in the non-decreasing order

objective

maximize lexicographically $[\boldsymbol{R}]$ (13.3.3a)

constraints

$\sum_g \xi_g u_g \leq B$ (13.3.3b)

$\sum_p x_{dps} = X_{ds},\quad d = 1, 2, \dots, D \quad s = 1, 2, \dots, S$ (13.3.3c)

$h_{ds} \leq X_{ds} \leq H_{ds},\quad d = 1, 2, \dots, D \quad s = 1, 2, \dots, S$ (13.3.3d)

$\sum_d \sum_p \delta_{edp} x_{dps} = y_{es},\quad e = 1, 2, \dots, E \quad s = 1, 2, \dots, S$ (13.3.3e)

$\sum_q z_{eqs} = y_{es},\quad e = 1, 2, \dots, E \quad s = 1, 2, \dots, S$ (13.3.3f)

$\sum_e \sum_q \gamma_{geq} z_{eqs} \leq \alpha_{gs} u_g,\quad g = 1, 2, \dots, G \quad s = 1, 2, \dots, S$ (13.3.3g)

$R_s \leq \sum_d r_{ds} \log X_{ds},\quad s = 1, 2, \dots, S.$ (13.3.3h)

Above, the link capacities in the upper layer and the revenues are again situation-dependent.

As the single-layer problem DR/PF/PR+UR (13.1.1), problems DR/2L/NPR(1)-PRU(2) and DR/2L/PRU(1)-PRU(2) are not mathematical programs, and must be solved iteratively. The appropriate algorithms are strictly analogous to Algorithms 13.1 and 13.2. To see how the latter algorithm can be adjusted for DR/2L/PRU(1)-PRU(2), below we formulate a counterpart of Problem (13.1.2) used in the initial step of the iterative algorithm for solving DR/2L/PRU(1)-PRU(2).

***CXP:* DR/2L/PRU(1)-PRU(2) {FS}** **Link-Path Formulation**
First Step of DR/2L/PRU(1)-PRU(2)
additional variable

t continuous variable with unlimited sign

objective

$$\text{maximize } t \tag{13.3.4a}$$

constraints

$$\textstyle\sum_g \xi_g u_g \le B \tag{13.3.4b}$$
$$\textstyle\sum_p x_{dps} = X_{ds} \qquad d = 1,2,\ldots,D \quad s = 1,2,\ldots,S \tag{13.3.4c}$$
$$h_{ds} \le X_{ds} \le H_{ds} \qquad d = 1,2,\ldots,D \quad s = 1,2,\ldots,S \tag{13.3.4d}$$
$$t \le \textstyle\sum_d r_{ds} \log X_{ds} \qquad s = 1,2,\ldots,S \tag{13.3.4e}$$
$$\textstyle\sum_d \sum_p \delta_{edp} x_{dps} = y_{es} \qquad e = 1,2,\ldots,E \quad s = 1,2,\ldots,S \tag{13.3.4f}$$
$$\textstyle\sum_q z_{eqs} = y_{es} \qquad e = 1,2,\ldots,E \quad s = 1,2,\ldots,S \tag{13.3.4g}$$
$$\textstyle\sum_e \sum_q \gamma_{geq} z_{eqs} \le \alpha_{gs} u_g \qquad g = 1,2,\ldots,G \quad s = 1,2,\ldots,S. \tag{13.3.4h}$$

The rest of the problems used in the algorithms of Sections 13.1.1 and 13.1.2 can be adjusted analogously (see Exercises 13.7 and 13.8).

13.3.2 *Numerical Examples*

In this section we will illustrate the performance of the MMF algorithms, presented in Section 13.1 for the single-layer case, to the three two-layer problems formulated in Section 13.3.1. The three problems DR/2L/PRU(1)-NPR(2), DR/2L/NPR(1)-PRU(2), and DR/2L/PRU(1)-PRU(2), from (13.3.1), (13.3.2), and (13.3.3), respectively will be referred to as RLL, RUL, and RBL, respectively, in the balance of this section. Below we will present two numerical examples for two different networks: mid-size (N_{12}) and large (N_{41}). The networks are presented in Table 13.9; the corresponding network topologies of both layers for the two networks are shown in Figures 13.6 to 13.9.

The link costs for networks N_{12} and N_{41} are given in the Tables 13.10 and 13.11, respectively. Failure situations have been generated according to the following rule: in situation $s = 1$ (called the normal state) all links are fully available. In each of the remaining situations two randomly selected links are assumed to fail entirely, so that their link availability coefficients α_{gs} are equal to 0 (the coefficients for the remaining links are equal

TABLE 13.9 **Networks Used for Experiments**

Ref. Code	Layer	# Nodes	# Links	# Paths per Demand	# Demands	# Failure Situations
N_{12}	2	12	22	6-14	66	-
	1	12	18	2-3	22	19
N_{41}	2	21	37	6	209	-
	1	41	72	3	37	21

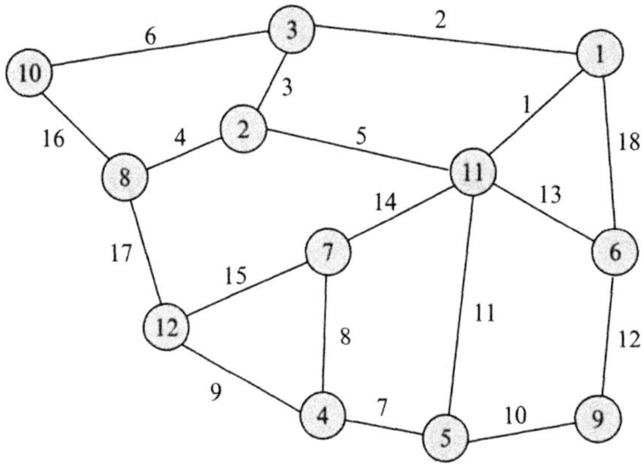

FIGURE 13.6 Topology of the Lower Layer Network for N_{12}

to 1). It has been assured that the situations are unique and that they do not result in disjoint graphs. The pairs of links that fail in each situation are given in Tables 13.12 and 13.13. For network N_{12} the number of predefined situations is $S = 19$, and for network N_{41} it is $S = 22$. In all experiments all revenue coefficients w_{ds} have been set to 1 and budget B to $1,000,000$.

We start with comparing the three reconfiguration options in the unbounded case (when X_d or X_{ds} could take any value between 0 and $+\infty$) and the bounded case (when X_d or X_{ds} could be assigned any values from the intervals $h_d \leq X_d \leq H_d$ or $h_{ds} \leq X_{ds} \leq H_{ds}$, respectively). Certainly, imposing upper bounds H_{ds} limits the total flows X_{ds} at a certain value, although otherwise, if allowed by the budget, it would be possible to increase them above the limit. In this way the resulting vectors of revenues are lexicographically smaller than in the unbounded case. Imposing lower bounds is more

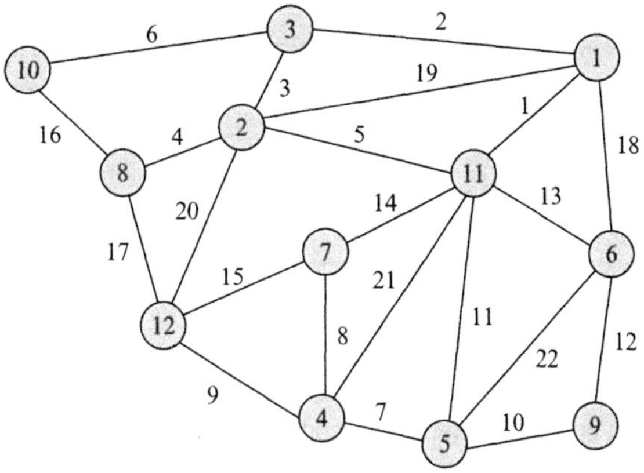

FIGURE 13.7 Topology of the Upper Layer Network for N_{12}

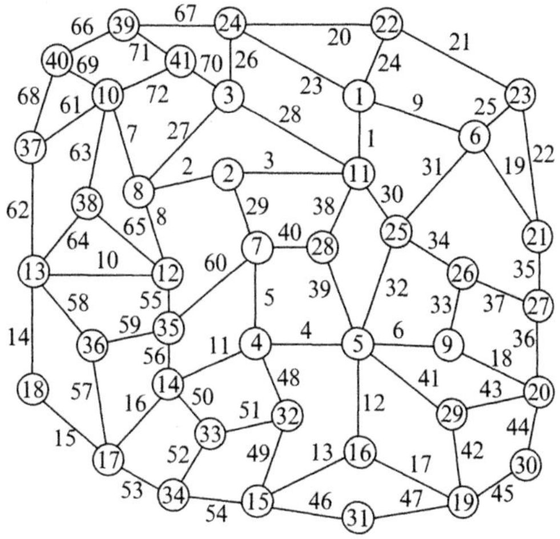

FIGURE 13.8 Topology of the Lower Layer Network for N_{41}

interesting, because it usually results in a different flow allocation scheme. Therefore, only the results for the unbounded case and with lower bounds ($LB = 1000$ for N_{12} and $LB = 10$ for N_{41}) are given. The upper bound in the experiments was always set to $+\infty$.

The revenue for problem RLL is not situation-dependent, so for different situations it is the same and equal to 6007.04 (in the unbounded case) for network N_{12} and 2072.19 for network N_{41}. Revenues of RUL and RBL are situation-dependent. Figures 13.10 and 13.11 illustrate lexicographically ordered revenue vectors for the three reconfiguration options in the unbounded case for networks N_{12} and N_{41}, respectively. Because of the lexicographical ordering, the numbering of situations does not in general coincide for different

TABLE 13.10 **Link Marginal Costs for Network N_{12}**

g	1	2	3	4	5	6	7	8	9
c_g	1.85	3.4	1	1.45	2.3	2.9	1	1.6	2.2
g	10	11	12	13	14	15	16	17	18
c_g	1.5	2.3	1.4	1.65	1.25	2.3	1.55	1.35	1.7

reconfiguration options (therefore, the situations are not numbered in the figures). As illustrated, revenue vectors for RUL and RBL are almost the same for network N_{12}, while for N_{41}, RBL is clearly better. It should be noted, that for N_{12} the differences between revenue vectors for RUL and RBL are negligible (the elements of the two vectors differ only at the 13th to 14th significant position). Of course, the vector for RBL is still lexicographically (marginally) bigger than for RUL, since any feasible solution of RUL is also a feasible solution of RBL. This similarity of RUL and RBL for N_{12} can be explained by very similar network topologies of the upper and lower layers. Network N_{41} with different layer topologies shows superiority of RBL.

For the bounded case (LB = 1000 for N_{12}, and LB = 10 for N_{41}), as it can be seen from the Figures 13.12 and 13.13, the situation is the same as in the unbounded case. The lexicographically ordered revenue vector for RBL is as usual greater than the one for RUL. In this case, the difference is non-negligible for both N_{41} and N_{12}, as it can be seen from the revenue values for N_{12}:

$$[\boldsymbol{R}]^{RBL} = (9078.90, 9078.90, 9078.90, \ldots, 11592.75) >$$

$$[\boldsymbol{R}]^{RUL} = (9069.50, 9069.50, 9069.50, \ldots, 11581.00).$$

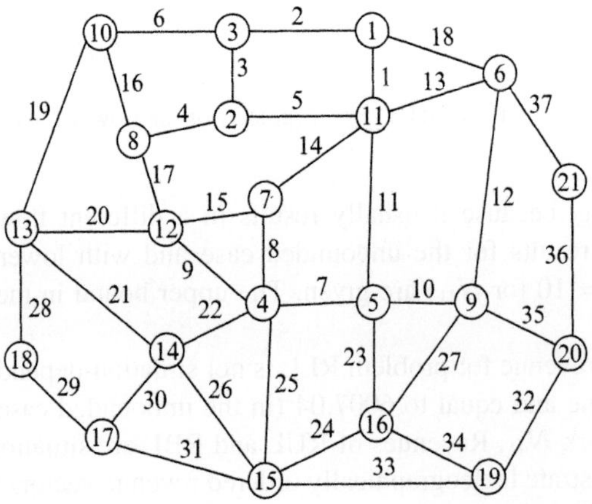

FIGURE 13.9 Topology of the Upper Layer Network for N_{41}

TABLE 13.11 **Link Marginal Costs for Network N_{41}**

g	1	2	3	4	5	6	7	8	9
c_g	7.8	9.4	13.7	10.6	9.7	9.3	10.1	8.9	12.9
g	10	11	12	13	14	15	16	17	18
c_g	14.2	10.2	11.1	11.8	11.9	10.7	9.9	12.2	10.9
g	19	20	21	22	23	24	25	26	27
c_g	12.0	16.4	15.6	14.6	15.2	7.8	6.6	7.3	13.5
g	28	29	30	31	32	33	34	35	36
c_g	15.5	8.1	6.9	12.6	12.0	7.3	8.3	7.1	8.7
g	37	38	39	40	41	42	43	44	45
c_g	8.5	8.3	10.3	6.9	12.1	9.2	9.7	7.8	7.8
g	46	47	48	49	50	51	52	53	54
c_g	10.7	11.1	8.3	9.3	6.8	8.2	7.6	7.7	8.9
g	55	56	57	58	59	60	61	62	63
c_g	5.7	5.7	11.7	9.7	8.2	12.5	9.9	12.5	11.4
g	64	65	66	67	68	69	70	71	72
c_g	8.8	10.9	8.1	11.2	9.3	6.4	6.2	7.0	8.3

TABLE 13.12 **Links that Fail in Each Situation for Network N_{12}**

g	1	2	3	4	5	6	7	8	9	10
s	-	5,16	8,12	6,15	3,8	11,15	6,11	3,5	2,17	4,14
g	11	12	13	14	15	16	17	18	19	
s	11,13	2,16	7,10	2,7	17,18	1,17	7,18	6,13	1,9	

In this case, revenue values for RBL are significantly higher than for RUL, because the former has more flexibility in reconfiguration (reconfiguration is allowed in both layers) which is apparently useful under the lower bound constraints. It can also be seen from the figures, that revenue values for the bounded case are, as expected, smaller than in the unbounded case.

The two examples considered above (N_{12} and N_{41}) show that RBL is superior to RUL when topologies of the layers are substantially different (N_{41}). RBL and RUL are almost equally good for networks with similar topology of their layers (N_{12}). RBL also performs significantly better than RUL when high lower bounds are imposed. It is also interesting, that in the case of N_{12}, the highest value in the revenue vector (in the unbounded case)

TABLE 13.13 Links that Fail in Each Situation for Network N_{41}

g	1	2	3	4	5	6	7	8	9	10	11
s	-	8,15	9,11	17,55	19,5	33,3	23,4	61,31	12,63	38,2	17,8
g	12	13	14	15	16	17	18	19	20	21	22
s	13,16	19,6	48,53	40,5	31,51	49,11	60,16	30,39	14,2	8,70	10,1

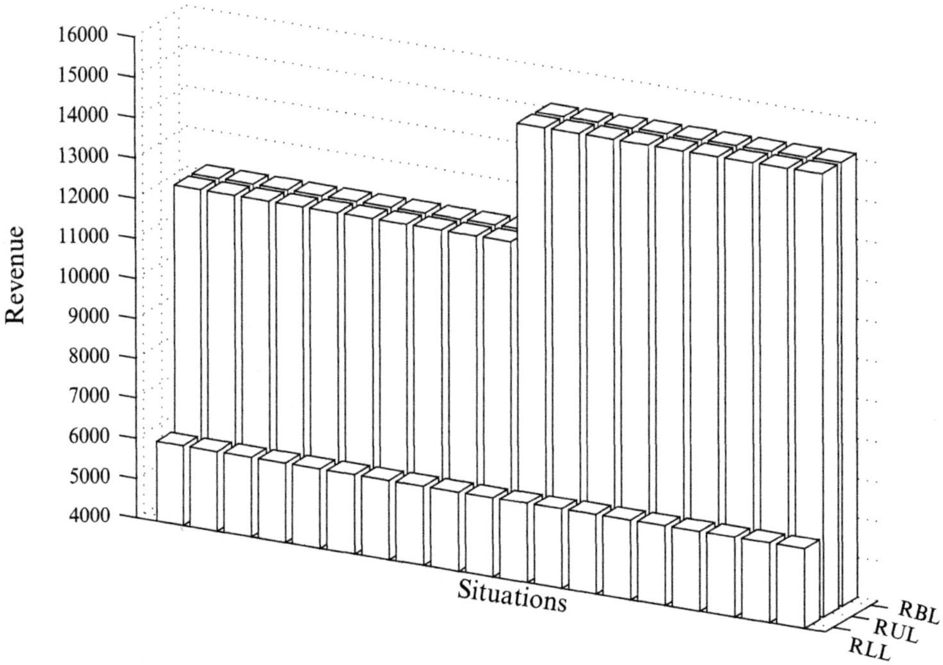

FIGURE 13.10 Revenue Values for RLL, RUL and RBL in the Unbounded Case (N_{12})

has been attained for RUL. Both RUL and RBL perform much better than RLL. These observations favor the RUL option for the networks with similar topologies of the layers, as it is considerably simpler than RBL. For the networks with different topologies of the layers, however, RBL can be significantly better than RUL.

13.3.3 Decomposition Methods for Two-Layer Networks

The two-layer problems that are convex mathematical programs can be linearized and treated by decomposition methods of LP such as LR with subgradient maximization of the dual function, BD, and PG. These are: Problem (13.3.1), Problem (13.3.4), and analogous problems that are required in the iterative algorithms for solving Problems (13.3.2) and (13.3.3). These methods can be applied using the approaches described in Section 13.2 for

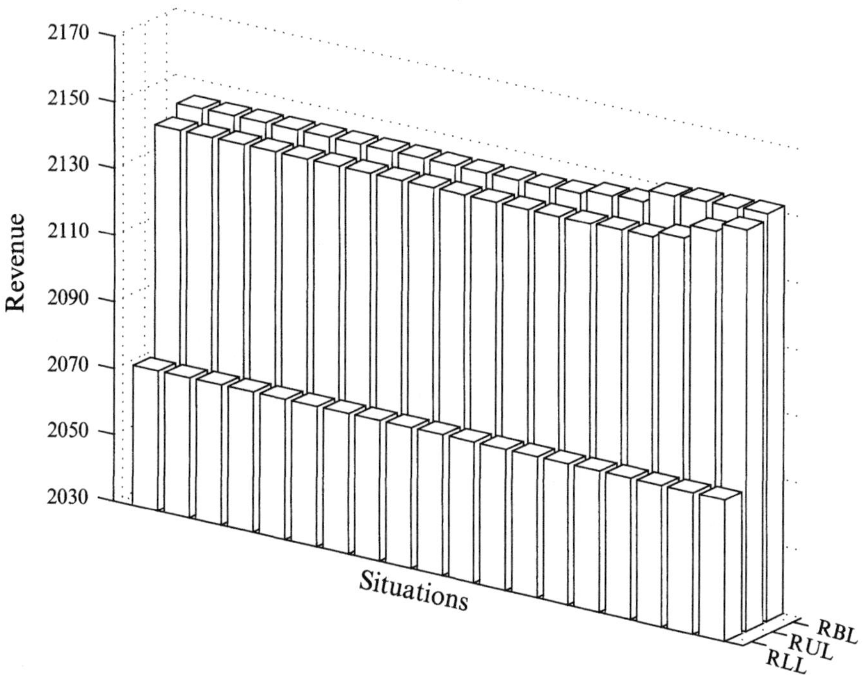

FIGURE 13.11 Revenue Values for RLL, RUL and RBL in the Unbounded Case (N_{41})

the single-layer PF network restoration problems, and in Section 12.4 for the two-layer restoration problems.

13.4 EXTENSIONS

Observe that in all the problems considered in this chapter, PF revenue maximization in each of the individual situations can be substituted with the MMF requirement of lexicographic maximization of the vector of total flows allocated to demands. Such an assumption will result in "doubly" MMF problems (see Exercise 13.9).

As for classical design problems described in Chapters 10 and 12, various other extensions of the single- and multi-layer robust design problems can be considered for fair networks. The first important set of extensions involves modular links. When modular links (refer to Section 4.3.1 in Chapter 4) are assumed (for the two-layer problems the links are typically modular in the lower layer) then the problems considered in Sections 13.1 and 13.3 become MIP problems (provided the piecewise linear approximation of the logarithmic function is used) and can be treated by the branch-and-bound (and branch-and-cut) approach (refer to Section 5.2).

The next group of extensions is associated with reconfiguration mechanisms. Besides unrestricted flow reconfiguration other flow restoration mechanisms such as restricted flow

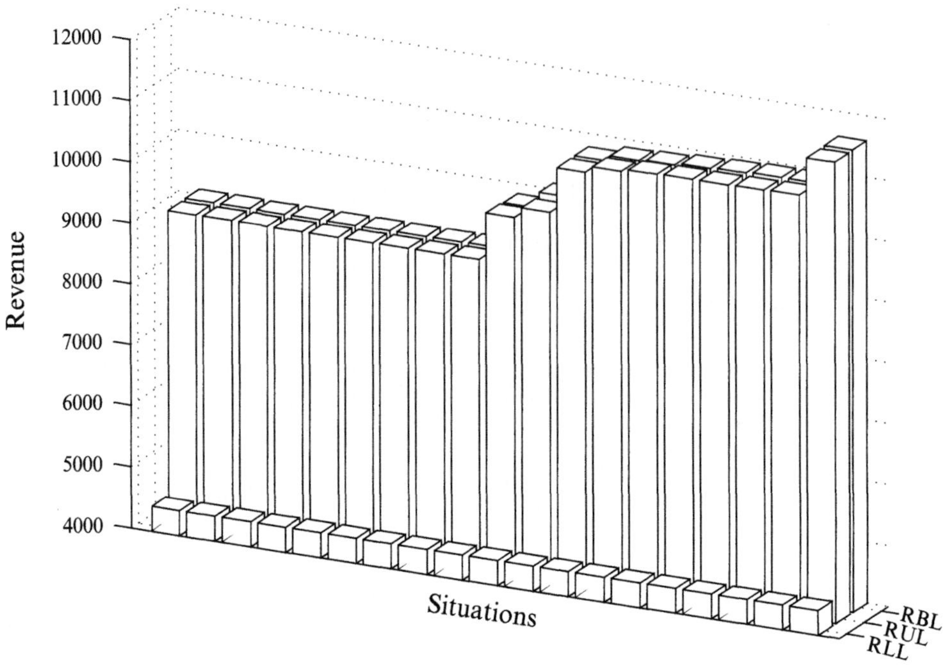

FIGURE 13.12 Revenue Values for RLL, RUL, and RBL when $LB = 1000$ (N_{12})

reconfiguration, flow restoration with situation-dependent back-up paths, and flow restoration with fixed single back-up paths can be considered (Section 9.3). Also, link protection mechanism (Section 9.2) can be assumed. Finally, single-path flow allocation and other routing restrictions can be added (Section 9.4.4). Of course different combinations of the above described extensions are possible and we hope that at this (final) stage of the book the reader can easily formulate some interesting cases (for examples see Exercises 13.10 and 13.11).

13.5 SUMMARY AND FURTHER READING

In this chapter we have discussed extensions of the classical restoration design problems for single- and two-layer networks involving PF allocation of demand volumes. In Section 13.1, a basic single-layer problem is introduced together with efficient iterative algorithms, illustrated with numerical examples. The propositions proved in this section are applicable for the problems from Section 8.2. Section 13.2 discusses the applicability of the basic decomposition techniques (BD and PG) for the problems introduced in Section 13.1. In Section 13.3, the PF models are extended to the two-layer problems and the appropriate solution algorithms are illustrated with the results of a numerical study. Finally, Section 13.4 discusses some extensions of the previously formulated problems.

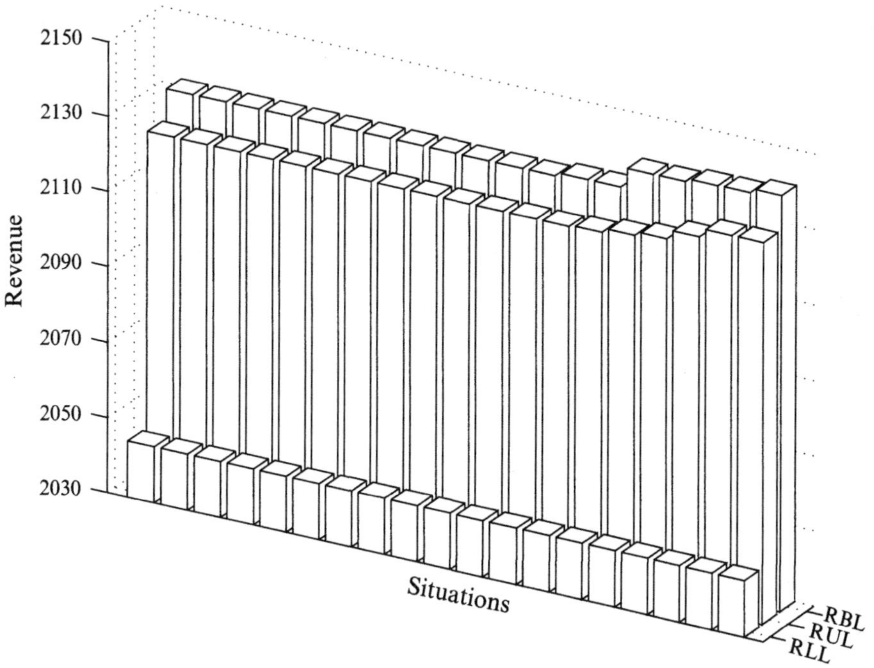

FIGURE 13.13 Revenue Values for RLL, RUL, and RBL when $LB = 10$ (N_{41})

Chapter 13 is based on original work described in papers [PKNM02] (Section 13.1) and [KPN03] (Section 13.3). The PF and MMF fundamentals on which this chapter is based are the same as those discussed in Chapter 8.

EXERCISES FOR CHAPTER 13

13.1. Construct an optimal solution $\boldsymbol{a}^* \in \boldsymbol{A}^*$ satisfying property (13.1.6).

13.2. Derive formula (13.1.17) $\sum_{d \in Z_1} \lambda_s^* = 1$ for the dual problem of (13.1.4), where optimal dual variables λ_s^* correspond to constraint (13.1.4f).

13.3. **Prove Proposition 8.3, Section 8.2.1, Chapter 8. (Hint: see the proof of Propositions 13.1 and 13.2.)

13.4. Derive the numerical results of Example 13.2.

13.5. Write down the Lagrangian for Problem (13.2.2) and then derive the dual Problem (13.2.3).

13.6. Derive dual Problem (13.2.6).

13.7. Formulate a counterpart of Problem (13.1.2) for DR/2L/NPR(1)-PRU(2).

13.8. Formulate a counterpart of Problem (13.1.4) for DR/2L/PRU(1)-PRU(2).

13.9. Use the lexicographical maximization of the overall demand allocation vector $\boldsymbol{X} = (X_{ds},\ d = 1,2,\dots,D,\ s = 1,2,\dots,S)$ to formulate an MMF counterpart of Problem (13.1.1).

13.10. Write down problem DR/2L/PRU(1)-NPR(2) (13.3.1) in node-link formulation used for both layers.

13.11. Write down problem DR/2L/PRU(1)-NPR(2) (13.3.1) in path-link formulation assuming restricted flow reconfiguration as in problem DR/CF/BR/CC/LIN/PR+RR (9.3.2) in Section 9.3.2.

APPENDIX A

Optimization Theory Refresher

A.1 BASIC NOTIONS

Optimization problems studied in this book are generally called static and belong to the theory called static optimization (in contrast to dynamic optimization). In the field of operations research, such problems are commonly referred to as *mathematical programming problems*, or simply *mathematical programs*. The general form of such problems is as follows:

$$\textbf{\textit{minimize}} \quad F(\boldsymbol{x}) \tag{A.1.1a}$$

$$\textbf{\textit{subject to}} \quad \boldsymbol{x} \in S \tag{A.1.1b}$$

where $F(\boldsymbol{x})$ is a given, real-valued objective function, $F : S \rightarrow \Re$, and S is a given *(feasible) solution set* (also called *optimization space*). Any point $\boldsymbol{x} \in S$ is called a (feasible) solution. For the purpose of this book, it is assumed that S is a subset (possibly finite) of the n-dimensional Euclidean space $\Re^n (S \subseteq \Re^n)$; hence, each point $\boldsymbol{x}$ is a n-vector $\boldsymbol{x} = (x_1, x_2, ..., x_n)$. If S is the empty set ($S = \emptyset$) then Problem (A.1.1) is *infeasible*.
Let $B(\boldsymbol{x}, \varepsilon) = \{\boldsymbol{y} : \|\boldsymbol{x} - \boldsymbol{y}\| < \varepsilon\}$ be the (open) ball of radius ε around point $\boldsymbol{x}$. Following [Min86], we now introduce the basic set of definitions of interest. Point $\boldsymbol{x}$ is an *interior point* of S, $\boldsymbol{x} \in int(S)$, if $B(\boldsymbol{x}, \varepsilon) \subseteq S$ for some $\varepsilon > 0$. Set S is *open* if $S = int(S)$, i.e., when each point is the interior point. A point $\boldsymbol{x}$ is a *cluster point* of set S if for any $\varepsilon > 0$, $B(\boldsymbol{x}, \varepsilon) \cap S \neq \emptyset$. The set of all cluster points of S is called the *closure* of set S. Set S is *closed* when it is equal to its closure. Set S is bounded if it is contained in ball $B(\boldsymbol{x}, r)$ for some finite radius r. A set is *compact* if it is closed and bounded. An example of a compact set is the n-dimensional unit cube $[0, 1]^n = \{\boldsymbol{x} \in \Re^n : 0 \leq x_i \leq 1, i = 1, 2, \ldots, n\}$. Note that any finite set of points is compact; if S is finite, Problem A.1.1 is called a *combinatorial*, or a *discrete optimization problem* (in fact a discrete problem can have infinite but countable solution space). Note that if F is continuous on S and S is compact, then, by the classical Weierstrass theorem, the objective function assumes its *global minimum* (and maximum for that matter) at some point $\boldsymbol{x}^* \in S$, which means that

$$\forall\, \boldsymbol{x} \in S, F(\boldsymbol{x}^*) \leq F(\boldsymbol{x}). \tag{A.1.2}$$

S is called a *convex set* if for all points $\boldsymbol{x}, \boldsymbol{y} \in S$, the whole segment joining $\boldsymbol{x}$ and $\boldsymbol{y}$ belongs to S, i.e., when $\{\alpha\boldsymbol{x} + (1 - \alpha)\boldsymbol{y} :\ 0 \leq \alpha \leq 1\} \subseteq S$. Hence, if a convex set contains at least two points, then it contains infinitely many (a continuum of) points. An example of an infinite convex set is the n-dimensional (closed) unit cube $[0, 1]^n$ or the (open) unit ball $B(\boldsymbol{x}, 1)$.

A real-valued function f defined on a convex set S is called a *convex function* if

$$\forall\, \boldsymbol{x}, \boldsymbol{y} \in S, \forall\, \alpha \in [0,1],\ f(\alpha \boldsymbol{x} + (1-\alpha)\boldsymbol{y}) \leq \alpha f(\boldsymbol{x}) + (1-\alpha) f(\boldsymbol{y}). \tag{A.1.3}$$

If in (A.1.3) the strict inequality holds for all $\alpha \notin \{0,1\}$, then f is *strictly convex*. Function f is (strictly) *concave* if the opposite inequality holds in (A.1.3). Note that f is (strictly) convex if and only if $-f$ is (strictly) concave. From the optimization theory viewpoint, convex sets and functions have many important unique properties making the convex optimization problems easier to solve than the non-convex ones. The properties of convex sets and functions are discussed in every optimization handbook (see [BSS93], [Ber95], [Las70], [Min86], [Roc70], and [Zan69]). One of these properties states that a convex function on an open convex set is always continuous, and another that the set $\{\boldsymbol{x} \in S :\ f(\boldsymbol{x}) \leq a\}$ is convex for any scalar a. We also mention that the intersection of a family of convex sets is also convex.

Problem (A.1.1) is a *convex optimization problem* if both function F and set S are convex. If S is also compact then, as we already know, a global minimum $\boldsymbol{x}^* \in S$ exists. Moreover, every *local minimum* of a convex problem is also a global minimum, and the set of all global minima of a convex problem is convex itself. (Recall that point $\boldsymbol{x}^* \in S$ is called a local minimum if (A.1.2) holds for all $\boldsymbol{x}$ in some neighborhood of $\boldsymbol{x}^*$, i.e., in some open ball around $\boldsymbol{x}^*$.) If the objective function is strictly convex then the global minimum $\boldsymbol{x}^*$ is unique. If an optimization problem is not convex then in general it can have local minima which are not global minima.

In the rest of this discussion (and in the book), convex optimization problems (CXP) will be called *convex programs*, in short. Note that Problem (A.1.1) can be equivalently written as

$$\textbf{\textit{maximize}} \quad -F(\boldsymbol{x}) \tag{A.1.4a}$$

$$\textbf{\textit{subject to}} \quad \boldsymbol{x} \in S \tag{A.1.4b}$$

hence, maximization of a concave function over a convex set is also a CXP.

Finally, we may sometimes face an optimization problem with conflicting objectives which need to be simultaneously minimized. For example, consider m different objectives $F_1(\boldsymbol{x}), F_2(\boldsymbol{x}), \ldots, F_m(\boldsymbol{x})$ for $\boldsymbol{x} \in S$. Then, a vector $\boldsymbol{x}^* \in S$ is set to be *Pareto optimal* if no $\boldsymbol{x} \in S$ exists such that $F_i(\boldsymbol{x}) \leq F_i(\boldsymbol{x}^*)$ for $i = 1, 2, \ldots, m$ with $F_i(\boldsymbol{x}) < F_i(\boldsymbol{x}^*)$ for at least one i. Thus, the knowledge of the set of all Pareto optimal solutions is clearly useful in solving multi-criteria optimization problems; for the discussion of the multi-criteria optimization see the classical book [SNT85] and a recent survey [WW00].

A.2 KARUSH-KUHN-TUCKER (KKT) OPTIMALITY CONDITIONS

It is well known that if function F is differentiable at point $\boldsymbol{x}^* \in int(S)$ (i.e., it has continuous partial derivatives in some open ball around $\boldsymbol{x}^*$) and point $\boldsymbol{x}^*$ is a local minimum, then $\nabla F(\boldsymbol{x}^*) = \mathbf{0}$, where $\nabla F(\boldsymbol{x})$ is the gradient of F, i.e., the vector of partial derivatives:

$$\nabla F(\boldsymbol{x}) = (\frac{\partial F(\boldsymbol{x})}{\partial x_1}, \frac{\partial F(\boldsymbol{x})}{\partial x_2}, \ldots, \frac{\partial F(\boldsymbol{x})}{\partial x_n}). \tag{A.2.1}$$

A sufficient condition for the local optimality is positive semi-definiteness of the Hessian (square matrix of the second order partial derivatives) of F, as demonstrated in every standard handbook of calculus or optimization. If function F is convex then any such interior local minimum $\boldsymbol{x}^*$ is also the global minimum. In fact, for the constrained optimization Problem (A.1.1) with compact optimization space S, local minima are frequently attained at the border of S, i.e., for points $\boldsymbol{x} \in S \setminus int(S)$. Thus, a natural question arises on how such border local minima are characterized. The answer is given by the famous KKT conditions (see [BSS93], [Ber95], [Las70], [Min86], [Roc70], and [Zan69]).

Suppose that the optimization space S is determined by the following constraints:

$x \in S$ if and only if

$$h_i(\boldsymbol{x}) = 0 \qquad i = 1, 2, \ldots, k \tag{A.2.2a}$$

$$g_j(\boldsymbol{x}) \leq 0 \qquad j = 1, 2, \ldots, m. \tag{A.2.2b}$$

Further, assume that all functions $h_i(\boldsymbol{x})$ and $g_j(\boldsymbol{x})$ are differentiable. Let $\boldsymbol{x}^* \in S$ be a local minimum and let $J(\boldsymbol{x}^*) = \{j : g_j(\boldsymbol{x}^*) = 0\}$ be the set of active inequality constraints at point $\boldsymbol{x}^*$. Then *multipliers* $\boldsymbol{\mu} = (\mu_1, \mu_2, \ldots, \mu_k)$ of unconstrained sign and non-negative *multipliers* $\boldsymbol{\lambda} = (\lambda_1, \lambda_2, \ldots, \lambda_m)$ exist such that

$$1) \qquad \lambda_j = 0 \;\text{ for }\; j \notin J(\boldsymbol{x}^*) \tag{A.2.3a}$$

$$2) \qquad \nabla F(\boldsymbol{x}^*) = -\textstyle\sum_i \mu_i \nabla h_i(\boldsymbol{x}^*) - \sum_{j \in J(\boldsymbol{x}^*)} \lambda_j \nabla g_j(\boldsymbol{x}^*). \tag{A.2.3b}$$

Note that condition (1) can be equivalently written as

$$1) \qquad \lambda_j g_j(\boldsymbol{x}^*) = 0 \qquad j = 1, 2, \ldots, m. \tag{A.2.3a$'$}$$

For the problems involving only the equality constraints ($k > 0$ and $m = 0$), the optimality condition (A.2.3b) was found by J. L. Langrange in the 18th century (coefficients $\mu_1, \mu_2, \ldots, \mu_k$ are called Lagrange multipliers). In general, the KKT conditions say that the gradient of the objective function is a linear combination of the minus gradients of active constraints (sometimes we say that the gradient of the objective function is contained in the convex cone formed by the minus gradients of active constraints). This in fact is equivalent to the property that the projection of $-\nabla F(\boldsymbol{x}^*)$ onto set S is the zero vector.

Some difficulty with the KKT conditions may arise when point $\boldsymbol{x}^*$ is *not regular*, i.e., when the set of the gradients of all active constraints, i.e., $\nabla h_i(\boldsymbol{x}^*)$ for $i = 1, 2, \ldots, k$, and $\nabla g_j(\boldsymbol{x}^*)$ for $j \in J(\boldsymbol{x}^*)$ is *linearly dependent*. It may happen that such an irregular point $\boldsymbol{x}^*$ is a local minimum and the KKT conditions are *not* satisfied. Fortunately, in the case of a convex objective function and *linear* constraints (A.2.2), the KKT conditions are always satisfied in a local minimum $\boldsymbol{x}^*$, whether it is regular or not (see Section 3.4 in [Ber95]). (The constraints are linear if they are of the form

$$a_1x_1 + a_2x_2 + \ldots + a_nx_n = b \quad \text{or} \quad a_1x_1 + a_2x_2 + \ldots + a_nx_n \leq b \tag{A.2.4}$$

for some scalars $a_1, a_2, \ldots, a_n$, and b.) This is a very important fact since the majority of the multi-commodity flow problems (most of this book is in fact about such problems) do have linearly dependent constraint gradients, and all of the constraints are still linear (as the typical demand and capacity constraints used in the problem formulations throughout this book).

If the objective function $F(\boldsymbol{x})$ is convex and constraint (A.2.2) is linear, then the KKT conditions are also sufficient, i.e., point $\boldsymbol{x}^* \in S$ is the global minimum if and only if $\boldsymbol{x}^*$ satisfies the KKT conditions. For a general convex problem when $\boldsymbol{x}^*$ is a regular point, then the KKT conditions are sufficient for $\boldsymbol{x}^* \in S$ to be a global minimum. In fact, a weaker condition is sufficient: if a feasible point $\boldsymbol{x} \in S$ exists for which $g_j(\boldsymbol{x}) < 0, j = 1, 2, \ldots, m$ then the KKT conditions are also sufficient for $\boldsymbol{x}^* \in S$ to be a global minimum [Zan69].

A.3 INTERPRETATION OF THE LAGRANGE MULTIPLIERS IN THE KKT CONDITIONS

There is a nice interpretation of the KKT multipliers at the regular points. Consider a *perturbed* problem

$$\begin{aligned} &\textbf{\textit{minimize}} && F(\boldsymbol{x}) && && \text{(A.3.1)} \\ &\textbf{\textit{subject to}} && h_i(\boldsymbol{x}) = \delta_i && i = 1, 2, \ldots, k \\ & && g_j(\boldsymbol{x}) \leq \varepsilon_j && j = 1, 2, \ldots, m \end{aligned}$$

and let $\boldsymbol{x}^*(\boldsymbol{\delta}, \boldsymbol{\varepsilon})$ be a regular local minimum of this perturbed problem, where $\boldsymbol{\delta} = (\delta_1, \delta_2, \ldots, \delta_k)$ and $\boldsymbol{\varepsilon} = (\varepsilon_1, \varepsilon_2, \ldots, \varepsilon_m)$. Suppose that $f(\boldsymbol{\delta}, \boldsymbol{\varepsilon}) = F(\boldsymbol{x}^*(\boldsymbol{\delta}, \boldsymbol{\varepsilon}))$ is the function determining the value of the local minimum of the perturbed problem in the neighborhood of $\boldsymbol{x}^*(\mathbf{0}, \mathbf{0})$, a local minimum of the original, non-perturbed problem. Then (refer to [BC99]):

$$\begin{aligned} &\frac{\partial f(\boldsymbol{\delta}, \boldsymbol{\varepsilon})}{\partial \delta_i} = -\mu_i && i = 1, 2, \ldots, k && \text{(A.3.2)} \\ &\frac{\partial f(\boldsymbol{\delta}, \boldsymbol{\varepsilon})}{\partial \varepsilon_j} = -\lambda_j && i = 1, 2, \ldots, k. \end{aligned}$$

This means that at the local minimum, the Lagrange multipliers measure the sensitivity of the minimum of the objective function to the right-hand side of the constraints. The sensitivity interpretation shows why the multiplier λ_j corresponding to an inequality constraint must be non-negative: when ε_j is made positive the optimization space of the perturbed problem gets larger so the minimum of the objective function can only decrease.

Unfortunately, when the local minimum is not regular then the vectors $(\boldsymbol{\mu}, \boldsymbol{\lambda})$ define one of continuously many subgradients (see Section A.8 below) of the sensitivity function $f(\boldsymbol{\delta}, \boldsymbol{\varepsilon})$ at point $(\mathbf{0}, \mathbf{0})$ [Roc70]. You will find many examples for such a situation in this book.

A.4 NUMERICAL METHODS FOR FINDING MINIMA OF DIFFERENTIABLE PROBLEMS

Consider a special case of *unconstrained problem* with $S = \Re^n$. Then if $F(\boldsymbol{x}') = c$ for some point $\boldsymbol{x}'$ and $\nabla F(\boldsymbol{x}') \neq 0$ then $\boldsymbol{x}'$ is not a minimum since any move in direction $-\nabla F(\boldsymbol{x}')$ will decrease the objective function. In fact, $-\nabla F(\boldsymbol{x}')$ is the direction of the steepest descent of function $F(\boldsymbol{x})$ at point $\boldsymbol{x}$. This property follows from the well-known fact that the directional derivative $\nabla F(\boldsymbol{x}'; \boldsymbol{d}))$ of function F at point $\boldsymbol{x}'$ in direction $\boldsymbol{d} \in \Re^n$ (i.e., the right derivative $f'(0^+)$ of the one-variable function $f(\alpha) = F(\boldsymbol{x} + \alpha\boldsymbol{d}))$ is equal to the scalar product $\nabla F(\boldsymbol{x}') \times \boldsymbol{d}$. We also note that the gradient, $\nabla F(\boldsymbol{x}')$, is orthogonal to the contour $\{\boldsymbol{x} : F(\boldsymbol{x}) = c\}$ of the objective function at point $\boldsymbol{x}'$. This observation provides the basis for the *steepest descent algorithm* of finding a local (global in the case of convex F) minimum of the unconstrained problem. Such an algorithm starts at some point $\boldsymbol{x}^0$ and performs one-directional minimization of the scalar function

$$f(\alpha) = F(\boldsymbol{x}^0 - \alpha\nabla F(\boldsymbol{x}^0)), \quad \alpha \geq 0 \tag{A.4.1}$$

to find its minimum α^0 for $0 \leq \alpha^0 < +\infty$. Then the next point $\boldsymbol{x}^1 = \boldsymbol{x}^0 - \alpha^0\nabla F(\boldsymbol{x}^0)$ is considered, and the procedure repeated until a minimum of $F(\boldsymbol{x})$ is found (usually only approximately). The steepest descent algorithms suffer from the zig-zagging effect that slows down the convergence of the algorithm in the neighborhood of the minimum. The zig-zagging is caused by the orthogonality of the consecutive directions of the one-dimensional search (directions $\nabla F(\boldsymbol{x}^i)$ and $\nabla F(\boldsymbol{x}^{i+1})$ are orthogonal, i.e., $\nabla F(\boldsymbol{x}^i) \times \nabla F(\boldsymbol{x}^{i+1}) = 0$, for $i = 0, 1, \ldots$). There are several ways to avoid zig-zagging and hence speed up the convergence of the algorithm; for instance, the accelerated steepest descent method or the conjugate directions method can be applied (refer to Section 4.2 in [Min86]).

If the optimization problem is constrained, then the steepest descent approach has to be modified because for a boundary point $\boldsymbol{x}^0 \in S \backslash int(S)$ the direction $-\nabla F(\boldsymbol{x}^0)$ may not be feasible. This can happen because any infinitesimal move from $\boldsymbol{x}^0$ along $-\nabla F(\boldsymbol{x}^0)$ may lead outside set S. (More precisely, $\underline{\alpha} > 0$ may exist such that $f(\alpha) \notin S$ for all α, $0 \leq \alpha \leq \underline{\alpha}$.) In fact, the KKT conditions state that $\underline{\alpha} > 0$ exists such that for any $0 \leq \alpha \leq \underline{\alpha}$ the projection of point $\boldsymbol{y}(\alpha) = \boldsymbol{x}^0 - \alpha\nabla F(\boldsymbol{x}^0)$ onto set S (for set S given by (A.2.2)) is equal to $\boldsymbol{x}^0$, which in turn means that at point $\boldsymbol{x}^0$ there is no feasible direction improving (decreasing) the objective function. However, if the KKT conditions are not satisfied (and $\boldsymbol{x}^0 \in S \setminus int(S)$ is regular) then a feasible improvement direction at point $\boldsymbol{x}^0$ exists, so we may move along this direction, improving the objective function, and not leaving optimization space S. For constrained problems, the descent direction methods depend on the type of constraints. For the general linear constraints case, the Rosen gradient projection method is applicable (see [Ros60], Section 5.3.3 in [Min86], and Section 5.7 in [BG92]). For the special type of the demand-like linear constraints, the Frank-Wolfe reduced gradient method can be applied (refer to Section 5.3.4 in [Min86] and Section 5.6 in [BG92]). These two methods are discussed in Section 5.5 of Chapter 5.

A.5 DUALITY

Consider the optimization problem (P) with additional constraint $\boldsymbol{x} \in X$ on top of constraint (A.2.2):

$$\textbf{\textit{minimize}} \quad F(\boldsymbol{x}) \tag{A.5.1a}$$

$$\textbf{\textit{subject to}} \quad h_i(\boldsymbol{x}) = 0 \qquad i = 1, 2, \ldots, k \tag{A.5.1b}$$

$$g_j(\boldsymbol{x}) \leq 0 \qquad j = 1, 2, \ldots, m \tag{A.5.1c}$$

$$\boldsymbol{x} \in X. \tag{A.5.1d}$$

The *dual problem* (D) to (A.5.1) (Problem (A.5.1)) is called the *primal problem* in this context is constructed as follows. First, the *Lagrangian function*

$$L(\boldsymbol{x}; \boldsymbol{\mu}, \boldsymbol{\lambda}) = F(\boldsymbol{x}) + \textstyle\sum_i \mu_i h_i(\boldsymbol{x}) + \sum_j \lambda_j g_j(\boldsymbol{x}), \quad \boldsymbol{x} \in X, \ \boldsymbol{\mu} \text{ unconstrained in sign, } \boldsymbol{\lambda} \geq \mathbf{0}. \tag{A.5.2}$$

is formed, and then the dual function

$$W(\boldsymbol{\mu}, \boldsymbol{\lambda}) = \min_{\boldsymbol{x} \in X} L(\mathbf{x}; \boldsymbol{\mu}, \boldsymbol{\lambda}), \quad \boldsymbol{\mu} \text{ unconstrained in sign, } \boldsymbol{\lambda} \geq 0. \tag{A.5.3}$$

is defined. Finally, dual (D) is formulated as:

$$\textbf{\textit{maximize}} \quad W(\boldsymbol{\mu}, \boldsymbol{\lambda}) \tag{A.5.4a}$$

$$\textbf{\textit{subject to}} \quad \boldsymbol{\mu} \text{ unconstrained in sign, } \boldsymbol{\lambda} \geq 0 \tag{A.5.4b}$$

It should be noted that for certain values of *dual variables* $(\boldsymbol{\mu}, \boldsymbol{\lambda})$, Lagrangian $L(\boldsymbol{x}; \boldsymbol{\mu}, \boldsymbol{\lambda})$ may be unbounded from below even for continuous functions F, h_i, and g_j and, hence, it may happen that $W(\boldsymbol{\mu}, \boldsymbol{\lambda}) = -\infty$. Thus, to exclude this, we may define the domain of the dual function as

$$Dom(W) = \{(\boldsymbol{\mu}, \boldsymbol{\lambda}) : \boldsymbol{\mu} \in \Re^k, \boldsymbol{\lambda} \in \Re^m, \boldsymbol{\lambda} \geq \mathbf{0}, \min_{\boldsymbol{x} \in X} L(\boldsymbol{x}; \boldsymbol{\mu}, \boldsymbol{\lambda}) > -\infty\}.$$

If all functions F, h_i, and g_j are continuous, and X is compact, then the $W(\boldsymbol{\mu}, \boldsymbol{\lambda})$ is a concave function with the full domain $Dom(W) = \{(\boldsymbol{\mu}, \boldsymbol{\lambda}) : \boldsymbol{\mu} \in \Re^k, \ \boldsymbol{\lambda} \in \Re^m, \ \boldsymbol{\lambda} \geq \mathbf{0}\}$ (see Section 6.2 in [Min86]). However, in general $Dom(W)$ may not be convex and may even be empty.

Let $\boldsymbol{x}^*$ and $(\boldsymbol{\mu}^*, \boldsymbol{\lambda}^*)$ be the solutions (global optima) of (P) and (D), respectively. The *weak duality theorem* states that:

$$F(\boldsymbol{x}^*) \geq W(\boldsymbol{\mu}^*, \boldsymbol{\lambda}^*) \tag{A.5.5}$$

so the optimal dual objective is always a lower bound of the optimal primal objective. In general, the strict inequality can hold in (A.5.5), and then the difference $F(\boldsymbol{x}^*) - W(\boldsymbol{\mu}^*, \boldsymbol{\lambda}^*) \geq 0$ is called the *duality gap*. One of the most important results of the (static) optimization theory states, between other facts, that for CXPs, the duality gap is equal to 0 (so the optimal dual objective is equal to the optimal primal objective), as we will see in the next section. For non-convex problems the duality gap is in general positive and can be even infinite.

Observe that (A.5.5) implies that if the dual is unbounded ($W(\boldsymbol{\mu}, \boldsymbol{\lambda})$ can be made arbitrarily large) then the primal is infeasible.

A.6 DUALITY FOR CONVEX PROGRAMS

Suppose that Problem (A.5.1) is convex, which means that set X, function F, and all functions g_j are convex, and functions h_i ($i = 1, 2, \ldots, k$) are linear. (Note that the last, strange at first sight, requirement appears because the set $\{\boldsymbol{x} : h_i(\boldsymbol{x}) = 0\}$ is convex if and only if h_i

is linear.) Let $\boldsymbol{x}^*$ and $(\boldsymbol{\mu}^*, \boldsymbol{\lambda}^*)$ be the optimal primal and dual solutions, respectively. Then the following basic relationships between the primal problem (P) and the dual problem (D) hold.

Fact 1: The dual function $W(\boldsymbol{\mu}, \boldsymbol{\lambda})$ is concave and its domain, $Dom(W)$, is convex. Hence, the dual of a CXP is also a CXP.

Fact 2: If both primal and dual are feasible then $F(\boldsymbol{x}^*) = W(\boldsymbol{\mu}^*, \boldsymbol{\lambda}^*)$.

Fact 3: If primal is unbounded (from below) then dual is infeasible; conversely, if dual is unbounded (from above) then primal is infeasible.

Fact 4: For each optimal dual solution $(\boldsymbol{\mu}^*, \boldsymbol{\lambda}^*)$ an optimal primal solution $\boldsymbol{x}^*$ exists, and conversely, for each optimal primal solution $\boldsymbol{x}^*$ an optimal dual solution $(\boldsymbol{\mu}^*, \boldsymbol{\lambda}^*)$ exists such that

$$W(\boldsymbol{\mu}^*, \boldsymbol{\lambda}^*) = L(\boldsymbol{x}^*; \boldsymbol{\mu}^*, \boldsymbol{\lambda}^*),$$

i.e., $\boldsymbol{x}^* = \arg\min_{\boldsymbol{x}\in X} F(\boldsymbol{x}) + \sum_i \mu_i^* h_i(\boldsymbol{x}) + \sum_j \lambda_j^* g_j(\boldsymbol{x})$.

The last property states that $(\boldsymbol{x}^*; \boldsymbol{\mu}^*, \boldsymbol{\lambda}^*)$ forms a *saddle point* of the Lagrangian, i.e.,

$$L(\boldsymbol{x}^*; \boldsymbol{\mu}^*, \boldsymbol{\lambda}^*) \leq L(\boldsymbol{x}; \boldsymbol{\mu}^*, \boldsymbol{\lambda}^*) \text{ for all } \boldsymbol{x} \in X$$
$$L(\boldsymbol{x}^*; \boldsymbol{\mu}^*, \boldsymbol{\lambda}^*) \geq L(\boldsymbol{x}^*; \boldsymbol{\mu}, \boldsymbol{\lambda}) \text{ for all } \boldsymbol{\lambda} \geq \boldsymbol{0} \text{ and all } \boldsymbol{\mu}.$$

We wish to emphasize here the fact that $\boldsymbol{x}' \in X$ and $\boldsymbol{x}' = \arg\min_{\boldsymbol{x}\in X} L(\boldsymbol{x}; \boldsymbol{\mu}^*, \boldsymbol{\lambda}^*)$ for some dually optimal $(\boldsymbol{\mu}^*, \boldsymbol{\lambda}^*)$ does not imply that $\boldsymbol{x}'$ is primal feasible and, hence, that $L(\boldsymbol{x}'; \boldsymbol{\mu}^*, \boldsymbol{\lambda}^*)$ is a saddle point. Moreover, even if it happens that $\boldsymbol{x}'$ is primal feasible then $\boldsymbol{x}'$ may not be primal optimal. In consequence, the knowledge of the optimal dual solution does not automatically yield an optimal primal solution, although in some cases it may be possible .

A.7 DUALITY FOR CONVEX OBJECTIVE AND LINEAR CONSTRAINTS

Suppose that constraint (A.2.2) is linear and that the objective function F is convex. Let $I \subseteq \{1, 2, \ldots, k\}$ and $J \subseteq \{1, 2, \ldots, m\}$ be two arbitrary subsets of the equality and inequality index sets, respectively. Also let X be the set specified by the following constraints:

$$h_i(\boldsymbol{x}) = 0 \qquad i \in I' = \{1, 2, \ldots, k\} \backslash I \tag{A.7.1a}$$
$$g_j(\boldsymbol{x}) \leq 0 \qquad j \in J' = \{1, 2, \ldots, m\} \backslash J. \tag{A.7.1b}$$

Consider the following primal problem (P):

$$\textbf{\textit{minimize}} \quad F(\boldsymbol{x}) \tag{A.7.2a}$$
$$\textbf{\textit{subject to}} \quad h_i(\boldsymbol{x}) = 0 \qquad i \in I \tag{A.7.2b}$$
$$g_j(\boldsymbol{x}) \leq 0 \qquad j \in J \tag{A.7.2c}$$
$$\boldsymbol{x} \in X \tag{A.7.2d}$$

and its dual (D):

$$\textbf{\textit{maximize}} \quad W(\boldsymbol{\mu}, \boldsymbol{\lambda}) \tag{A.7.3a}$$
$$\textbf{\textit{subject to}} \quad \boldsymbol{\mu} \in \Re^{|I|}, \ \boldsymbol{\lambda} \in \Re^{|J|}, \ \boldsymbol{\lambda} \geq \boldsymbol{0} \tag{A.7.3b}$$

where

$$L(\boldsymbol{x};\boldsymbol{\mu},\boldsymbol{\lambda}) = F(\boldsymbol{x}) + \sum_{i\in I}\mu_i h_i(\boldsymbol{x}) + \sum_{j\in J}\lambda_j g_j(\boldsymbol{x}),$$
$$\boldsymbol{x}\in X, \boldsymbol{\mu}\in\Re^{|I|}, \boldsymbol{\lambda}\in\Re^{|J|}, \boldsymbol{\lambda}\geq \mathbf{0} \tag{A.7.4}$$

and

$$W(\boldsymbol{\mu},\boldsymbol{\lambda}) = \min_{\boldsymbol{x}\in X} L(\boldsymbol{x};\boldsymbol{\mu},\boldsymbol{\lambda}). \tag{A.7.5}$$

Let $\boldsymbol{x}^*$ be *any* feasible solution of (P), and let $(\boldsymbol{\mu}^*, \boldsymbol{\lambda}^*)$ be *any* feasible solution of (D).Then the following properties hold (refer to Section 3.4 of [Ber95]):

Fact 5: Let $\boldsymbol{x}^*$ be an optimal primal solution and let $\boldsymbol{\mu}\in\Re^k$, $\boldsymbol{\lambda}\in\Re^m$, $(\boldsymbol{\lambda}\geq\mathbf{0})$ be the Lagrangian multipliers satisfying the KKT conditions (A.2.3) for the considered problem. Then the vectors $\boldsymbol{\mu}^* = (\mu_i,\ i\in I)$ and $\boldsymbol{\lambda}^* = (\lambda_j,\ j\in J)$ are the optimal dual vectors solving problem (D) (A.7.3). Conversely, if $\boldsymbol{\mu}^* = (\mu_i,\ i\in I)$ and $\boldsymbol{\lambda}^* = (\lambda_j,\ j\in J)$ are dually optimal, then they are a subset of one of the sets of the KKT multipliers for every primal optimal $\boldsymbol{x}^*$.

An important implication of Fact 5 is *complementary slackness* property: if for some primal optimal $\boldsymbol{x}^*$, inequality constraint $j\in J$ is not binding ($g_j(\boldsymbol{x}^*) < 0$), then every optimal dual variable λ_j^* is equal to 0.

Fact 6: Point $\boldsymbol{x}^*$ is primal optimal and $(\boldsymbol{\mu}^*, \boldsymbol{\lambda}^*)$ is dually optimal if and only if

$$F(\boldsymbol{x}^*) = L(\boldsymbol{x}^*;\boldsymbol{\mu}^*,\boldsymbol{\lambda}^*) = W(\boldsymbol{\mu}^*,\boldsymbol{\lambda}^*). \tag{A.7.6}$$

Observe in particular that Fact 6 implies a very important (and not obvious) property: any optimal primal solution and any optimal dual solution form a saddle point of the Lagrangian function of problem (P).

A.8 SUBGRADIENT MAXIMIZATION OF THE DUAL FUNCTION

Consider optimization problem of the form (A.5.1) where $k = 0$, all functions F, g_j are continuous, and set X is compact. The presentation of this and the next section is based on Chapter 6 of [Sha79]. The corresponding Lagrangian and the dual function are as follows:

$$L(\boldsymbol{x};\boldsymbol{\lambda}) = F(\boldsymbol{x}) + \sum_j \lambda_j g_j(\boldsymbol{x}) \tag{A.8.1}$$
$$W(\boldsymbol{\lambda}) = \min_{\boldsymbol{x}\in X} L(\boldsymbol{x};\boldsymbol{\lambda}), \tag{A.8.2}$$

where $\boldsymbol{\lambda}\in\Re^m$ and $\boldsymbol{\lambda}\geq\mathbf{0}$. We note that with the current assumptions, $W(\boldsymbol{\lambda})$ is a concave (and hence continuous) function for all $\boldsymbol{\lambda}\in\Re^m$ and $\boldsymbol{\lambda}\geq\mathbf{0}$. What is important now is that the computation of the value of the dual function for a given $\boldsymbol{\lambda}$ consists in solving another optimization problem, namely:

$$\textbf{\textit{minimize}} \quad F(\boldsymbol{x}) + \sum_j \lambda_j g_j(\boldsymbol{x}) \tag{A.8.3a}$$
$$\textbf{\textit{subject to}} \quad \boldsymbol{x}\in X. \tag{A.8.3b}$$

In general the solution of such a problem is not unique, so if we take two different optimal solutions $\boldsymbol{x}'$ and $\boldsymbol{x}''$ of (A.8.3), then we arrive at

$$W(\boldsymbol{\lambda}) = F(\boldsymbol{x}') + \sum_j \lambda_j g_j(\boldsymbol{x}') = F(\boldsymbol{x}'') + \sum_j \lambda_j g_j(\boldsymbol{x}''), \tag{A.8.4}$$

and if we try to differentiate $W(\boldsymbol{\lambda})$ with respect to the dual variables, then we see that

$$\frac{\partial W(\boldsymbol{\lambda})}{\partial \lambda_j} = g_j(\boldsymbol{x}') \quad \text{and} \quad \frac{\partial W(\boldsymbol{\lambda})}{\partial \lambda_j} = g_j(\boldsymbol{x}''). \tag{A.8.5}$$

This shows that the partial derivatives of $W(\boldsymbol{\lambda})$ simply do not exist! This in fact is the case; it happens that in the considered case the dual function is concave but not differentiable everywhere: it is not differentiable when (A.8.3) does not have the unique solution. Thus, a natural question arises (especially for a reader not familiar with non-differentiable analysis): what is the interpretation of the quantities $g_j(\boldsymbol{x}')$ and $g_j(\boldsymbol{x}'')$? The answer is that these quantities define *subgradients* of the dual function.

In general, $\boldsymbol{s} \in \Re^m$ is a subgradient of a concave function $w(\boldsymbol{y})$, $\boldsymbol{y} \in \Re^m$ at point $\underline{\boldsymbol{y}} \in \Re^m$ if

$$\forall\, \boldsymbol{y} \in \Re^m, \quad w(\boldsymbol{y}) \leq w(\underline{\boldsymbol{y}}) + (\boldsymbol{y} - \underline{\boldsymbol{y}}) \times s. \tag{A.8.6}$$

If the subgradient $\boldsymbol{s} = (s_1, s_2, \ldots, s_m)$ of w at $\underline{\mathbf{y}}$ is unique, then $\boldsymbol{s}$ is the gradient of w at $\underline{\boldsymbol{y}}$, i.e., $\boldsymbol{s} = \nabla w(\underline{\boldsymbol{y}})$. (Sometimes, for simplicity, we will use the same notation for a gradient and a subgradient.) Otherwise, the set of subgradients at a given point $\boldsymbol{y}$ is infinite since any convex combination of subgradients is also a subgradient. The set of all subgradients of function w at point $\boldsymbol{y}$ is called the *subdifferential* (generalization of the gradient), and denoted by $\partial w(\boldsymbol{y})$). The subdifferential is a non-empty closed, convex subset of $\Re^m$.

Consider a general unconstrained optimization problem

$$\textbf{maximize} \;\; w(\boldsymbol{y}), \quad \boldsymbol{y} \in \Re^m, \tag{A.8.7}$$

for a concave, real-valued function w. The two basic facts underlying algorithms of ascent directions for maximizing function w are as follows:

Fact 7: For any subgradient $\boldsymbol{s}$ of function w at point $\underline{\boldsymbol{y}}$ the set $\{\boldsymbol{y} : (\boldsymbol{y} - \underline{\boldsymbol{y}}) \times \boldsymbol{s} \geq 0\}$ contains all optimal solutions of Problem (A.8.7); this means that any subgradient points into a half space containing all optimal solutions.

Fact 8: The directional derivative at point $\underline{\boldsymbol{y}}$ in direction $\boldsymbol{d} \in \Re^m$, $\nabla w(\underline{\boldsymbol{y}}; \boldsymbol{d})$, is given by

$$\nabla w(\underline{\boldsymbol{y}}; \boldsymbol{d}) = \min_{\boldsymbol{s} \in \partial w(\underline{\boldsymbol{y}})} \boldsymbol{s} \times \boldsymbol{d}. \tag{A.8.8}$$

Since w is concave, point $\underline{\boldsymbol{y}}$ is a (global) maximum if and only if $\nabla w(\underline{\boldsymbol{y}}; \boldsymbol{d}) \leq 0$ for all directions $\boldsymbol{d}$. This can be formally expressed in the following way.

Fact 9: The solution $\boldsymbol{y}$ is optimal for (A.8.7) if and only if

$$\begin{aligned}&\max_d \min_{\boldsymbol{s}\in\partial w(\underline{\boldsymbol{y}})} \boldsymbol{s} \times \boldsymbol{d} = 0\\ &\text{over } \boldsymbol{d} = (d_1, d_2, \ldots, d_m),\ -1 \le d_i \le 1,\ i = 1, 2, \ldots, m,\end{aligned} \tag{A.8.9}$$

i.e., if and only if $\mathbf{0} \in \partial w(\underline{\boldsymbol{y}})$.

Unlike the differentiable case discussed in the beginning of Section A.4, an infinitesimal move along the direction equal to a non-zero subgradient s may not increase the objective function (although it will not decrease it, due to (A.8.6)). We may expect that in most cases a move along a subgradient will increase the objective. Hence, even if in general subgradients are not the steepest ascent directions, we can use them as the search directions in the ascent-direction algorithms similar to those described in the beginning of Section A.4. Note that in the currently considered case we assume $\boldsymbol{y} \ge \mathbf{0}$, so if at the current optimization point $\boldsymbol{y}^i$ we have $\boldsymbol{s} \in \partial w(\boldsymbol{y})$, $y^i_l = 0$, and $s_l < 0$, then we have to set s_l to 0, in order to make $\boldsymbol{s}$ a feasible direction and not to leave the optimization space $S = \{\boldsymbol{y} \in \Re^m : \boldsymbol{y} \ge \mathbf{0}\}$. (The projection of point $\boldsymbol{y}^i + \boldsymbol{s}$ on S is equal to $\boldsymbol{y}^i + \boldsymbol{s}^+$, where $\boldsymbol{s}^+ = (s^+_1, s^+_2, \ldots, s^+_m)$ and $s^+_l = \max\{s_l, 0\}$.)

Returning to function $W(\boldsymbol{\lambda})$ (A.8.4), we already know that each vector $g(\boldsymbol{x}) = (g_1(\boldsymbol{x}), g_2(\boldsymbol{x}), \ldots, g_m(\boldsymbol{x})) \in \Re^m$ such that $\boldsymbol{x} \in X$ minimizes (A.8.3a) is a subgradient, so that

$$\partial W(\boldsymbol{\lambda}) \supseteq \{g(\boldsymbol{x}) : \boldsymbol{x} \in X,\ \boldsymbol{x} \text{ minimizes (A.8.3a)}\}. \tag{A.8.10}$$

To be precise, $\partial W(\boldsymbol{\mu}, \boldsymbol{\lambda})$ is the convex hull of the set on the right-hand side of (A.8.10).

A.9 SUBGRADIENT MAXIMIZATION OF THE DUAL FUNCTION OF LINEAR PROGRAMMING PROBLEMS

In this section we will consider *linear programming* (LP) *problems*, i.e., optimization problems of the form:

$$\textbf{\textit{minimize}} \quad c_1x_1 + c_2x_2 + \ldots + c_nx_n \tag{A.9.1a}$$

$$\textbf{\textit{subject to}} \quad a_{j1}x_1 + a_{j2}x_2 + \ldots + a_{jn}x_n \le b_j, \quad j = 1, 2, \ldots, m. \tag{A.9.1b}$$

Above, we do not consider equality constraint $h_j(\boldsymbol{x}) = d_i$, since each such equality can be substituted with two inequalities $h_j(\boldsymbol{x}) \le d_i$ and $-h_j(\boldsymbol{x}) \le -d_i$. To be consistent with the notation of the previous section we impose the set of k linear constraints determining set X:

$$e_{i1}x_1 + e_{i2}x_2 + \ldots + e_{in}x_n \le p_j, \quad i = 1, 2, \ldots, k, \tag{A.9.1c}$$

i.e., $\boldsymbol{x} \in X$ if and only if $\boldsymbol{x}$ fulfils all inequalities in (A.9.1c). Note that below we do not assume the compactness of set S.

In the matrix form the considered problem (P) reads:

$$\textbf{\textit{minimize}} \quad \boldsymbol{cx} \tag{A.9.2a}$$

$$\textbf{\textit{subject to}} \quad \boldsymbol{Ax} \leq \boldsymbol{b} \tag{A.9.2b}$$

$$\boldsymbol{x} \in X \tag{A.9.2c}$$

where $\boldsymbol{c} = (c_1, c_2, \ldots, c_n)$, $\boldsymbol{A} = [a_{jl}]$ $j = 1, 2, \ldots, m$, $l = 1, 2, \ldots, n$, and $\boldsymbol{b} = (b_1, b_2, \ldots, b_n)$.

LP problems play a central role in this book (and generally in the theory of multi-commodity flow networks), and many of the considered decomposition methods for LP problems are based on the properties and/or solutions of their dual problems. One such decomposition is called Lagrangian relaxation (LR) and consists in solving the problem dual to the given LP problem. This approach can be effective because the dual problem is frequently substantially easier to solve than the primal one (especially when we deal with large-scale problems). In this section, we present basic results underlying the LR technique combined with subgradient maximization of the dual function.

The Lagrangian and the dual function of the considered problem are as follows:

$$\begin{aligned} L(\boldsymbol{x}; \boldsymbol{\lambda}) &= \boldsymbol{cx} + \textstyle\sum_j \lambda_j g_j(\boldsymbol{x}) = \sum_l c_l x_l \\ &\quad + \textstyle\sum_j \lambda_j (a_{j1}x_1 + a_{j2}x_2 + \ldots + a_{jn}x_n - b_j) \\ &= -\textstyle\sum_j \lambda_j b_j + \sum_l (c_l + \sum_j \lambda_j a_{jl}) x_l \end{aligned} \tag{A.9.3}$$

$$W(\boldsymbol{\lambda}) = \min_{\boldsymbol{x} \in X} L(\mathbf{x}; \boldsymbol{\lambda}), \tag{A.9.4}$$

where $\boldsymbol{\lambda} \in \Re^m$ and $\boldsymbol{\lambda} \geq \mathbf{0}$. Hence, computation of the value of the dual function for a given $\boldsymbol{\lambda}$ consists in solving another LP, namely:

$$\textbf{\textit{minimize}} \quad \textstyle\sum_l (c_l + \sum_j \lambda_j a_{jl}) x_l \tag{A.9.5a}$$

$$\textbf{\textit{subject to}} \quad \boldsymbol{x} \in X \tag{A.9.5b}$$

Note that, as already mentioned in Section A.8, for some dual variable $\boldsymbol{\lambda}$ the solution of the resulting LP problem (A.9.5a) can be unbounded. This is the case, e.g., when the condition $\boldsymbol{x} \in X$ does not put any upper bound on some primal variable x_l; then, additionally, the constraint $c_l + \sum_j \lambda_j a_{jl} \geq 0$ on dual variables must be introduced to the dual problem (otherwise $W(\boldsymbol{\lambda})$ could be made arbitrarily small). So in general, the dual problem, (D), is a non-differentiable optimization problem with linear constraints of the form:

$$\textbf{\textit{maximize}} \quad W(\boldsymbol{\lambda}) \tag{A.9.6a}$$

$$\textbf{\textit{subject to}} \quad \boldsymbol{T\lambda} \leq \boldsymbol{q} \tag{A.9.6b}$$

$$\boldsymbol{\lambda} \geq \mathbf{0} \tag{A.9.6c}$$

for some matrix $\boldsymbol{T}$ with m columns and k rows, and a corresponding k-vector $\boldsymbol{q}$. For A.9.6, the generalization of Fact 9 is as follows (refer to Section 6.2 in [Sha79]). Consider a feasible solution $\underline{\boldsymbol{\lambda}}$ of (A.9.6). A direction $\boldsymbol{d} \neq 0$ is a feasible direction at $\underline{\boldsymbol{\lambda}}$ if $\underline{\boldsymbol{\lambda}} + \alpha \boldsymbol{d}$ is feasible for some $\alpha > 0$. Let $I(\underline{\lambda}) = \{i : t_{i1}\underline{\lambda}_1 + t_{i2}\underline{\lambda}_2 + \ldots + t_{im}\underline{\lambda}_m = q_i\}$ be the set of indices of the active constraints in (A.9.6b), and let $J(\underline{\lambda}) = \{j : \underline{\lambda}_j = 0\}$. The feasible directions from $\underline{\lambda}$ are those $\boldsymbol{d} \in \Re^m$ which satisfy $t_{i1}d_1 + t_{i2}d_2 + \ldots + t_{im}d_m \leq 0$ for $i \in I(\underline{\lambda})$, and $d_j \geq 0$ for $j \in J(\underline{\lambda})$. Hence, the following holds:

Fact 10: The solution $\underline{\lambda}$ is optimal for (A.9.6) if and only if

$$\max_{\mathbf{d}} \min_{\boldsymbol{s} \in \partial w(\underline{\boldsymbol{y}})} \boldsymbol{s} \times \boldsymbol{d} = 0 \quad \text{(A.9.7a)}$$

over all $\boldsymbol{d} = (d_1, d_2, \ldots, d_m)$ such that

$$0 \leq d_j \leq 1, \quad j \in J(\underline{\lambda}) \quad \text{(A.9.7b)}$$

$$-1 \leq d_j \leq 1, \quad j \in \{1, 2, \ldots, m\} - J(\underline{\lambda}) \quad \text{(A.9.7c)}$$

$$t_{i1}d_1 + t_{i2}d_2 + \ldots + t_{im}d_m \leq 0, \quad i \in I(\underline{\lambda}). \quad \text{(A.9.7d)}$$

If $\boldsymbol{x} \in X$ is a solution of (A.9.5a) for a given $\boldsymbol{\lambda}$, then $\boldsymbol{s} = (\boldsymbol{Ax} - \boldsymbol{b})^T$ is a subgradient of $W(\boldsymbol{\lambda})$, and we may try to increase the value of the dual function by making a move along s and then to project the resulting point back onto the set defined by (A.9.6b) to (A.9.6c). Subgradient maximization algorithms for solving problems of the form of (A.9.6) are discussed in Section 6.3 of [HWC74], [Sha79], and [Sho85].

APPENDIX B

Introduction to Complexity Theory and $\mathcal{NP}$-Completeness

Appie van de Liefvoort
University of Missouri–Kansas City

B.1 INTRODUCTION

It has been said that there are at least two ways to catch a fly: with honey and with vinegar. However, one of these methods is much more effective in catching a fly. Such is the story of most problems: there are several methods or algorithms for their solution and some algorithms are more efficient than others. There are a number of problems, however, where the choice of algorithm does not seem to matter much: the worst case time complexity is terrible, no matter how you turn it. This is the focus of this appendix.

In keeping with this book we use the following terminology. By the *problem*, we mean problem formulation, i.e., the problem statement using parameters to denote appropriate constants. *Instance of the problem* (instance in short) refers to the particular formulation with all the parameters (constants) substituted with their actual values; for example, the instance of an linear programming (LP) problem can be written into a file and submitted directly to an LP solver. For any problem instance, we have its *solution space* and (feasible optimal) *solutions*. *Size of the problem instance*, n, should be understood intuitively; observe, however, that in general the size may depend not only on the number of variables and constraints, but also on the numerical values of the bounds used in the formulation (e.g., as the knapsack size in the knapsack problem).

Informally, the problems to be considered fall into two categories: those for which there are algorithms that always solve the problem in reasonable time, and those for which there is no such guarantee. For instance, consider an array of $2n$ integers. A problem that can be solved in reasonable time is: "Is this particular input such that the sum of the first n integers is equal the sum of the last n integers?," whereas the question "Is there a particular permutation such that the sum of the first n integers is equal to the sum of the last n integers?" is much harder to answer. Notice that verifying that the sum of the first n integers is equal to the sum of the last n integers can be done in linear time, which is of course polynomial.

Often the problem can be reformulated as: "Does a particular instance of the problem have property X?" or "Is there a solution in the solution space of a particular instance that has property X?" It is assumed that checking whether or not an instance has the property can be done by an algorithm with a worst case asymptotic time complexity that is bounded above by a polynomial. (The term "time complexity" in this appendix will refer to the worst case.) Thus, the first category of problems has a polynomial time complexity, whereas the second needs to search for a solution in the solution space of the considered instance, and has a time complexity depending in general on the size of this solution space. If this size is exponential with the problem (instance) size, then any algorithm based on brute-force checking of all possibilities will have a time complexity that is at least exponential. At the same time it appears that such an exhaustive search can be avoided by using a smart algorithm.

The purpose of this appendix is not to give a thorough and complete introduction to complexity theory, but rather to develop an appreciation and intuition for the direction taken. For a more detailed and rigorous presentation, see references [GJ79], [RND77], and [Wil86].

B.2 COMPLEXITY OF A PROBLEM

Complexity theory addresses problems and the algorithms that solve them. The theory must be very carefully built since it must be valid for all problems and algorithms, whether or not these problems or algorithms have already been identified or are yet to be discovered.

The complexity of a problem is based on the notion of complexity of an algorithm, which is defined when the problem size n is so large that it approaches the asymptotic neighborhood of infinity. (Note that for brevity we often say "problem size" instead of "problem instance size.") Thus, the time complexity $T(n)$ is said to be in $O(f(n))$, $T(n) = O(f(n))$, for some function $f(n)$ if there is a natural number N_0 and a positive constant c_1 such that if the problem size n is larger than N_0, $n \geq N_0$, then $T(n) \leq c_1 \cdot f(n)$. Similarly, the time complexity $T(n)$ is said to be in $\Theta(f(n))$, $T(n) = \Theta(f(n))$, for some function $f(n)$ if there is a natural number N_0 and two positive constants c_2 and c_3 such that if the problem size n is larger than N_0, $n \geq N_0$, then $c_2 \cdot f(n) \leq T(n) \leq c_3 \cdot f(n)$. Finally, the time complexity of an algorithm $T(n)$ is said to be in $\Omega(f(n))$, $T(n) = \Omega(f(n))$, if there is a natural number N_0 and one positive constant c_4 such that if the problem size n is larger than N_0, $n \geq N_0$, then $c_4 \cdot f(n) \leq T(n)$. Notice that $T(n) = \Theta(f(n)) \iff T(n) = O(f(n))$ *and* $T(n) = \Omega(f(n))$.

The notion of the *complexity of a problem* is defined in a similar manner: a problem of size n is *linear* if there is an algorithm A that solves the problem, and the time complexity in the worst case for this algorithm is $T_A^W(n) = O(n)$ *and* if any algorithm B that also solves the problem (already discovered or yet to be discovered) has a complexity $T_B^W(n) = \Omega(n)$. Similarly, a problem of size n is quadratic if $T_A^W(n) = O(n^2)$ *and* $T_B^W(n) = \Omega(n^2)$ for every other algorithm also solving the problem. Thus, selection from n elements is a linear problem, sorting n elements is an $n \log n$ problem, the (standard) towers of Hanoi with n rings is exponential, and so on. The disadvantage of such a classification is that there are many problems that are not classified yet. Take for instance the 0-1 knapsack problem or the travelling salesman problem (find a tour of smallest total weight in a graph with integer edge weights that visits every node exactly once). There are algorithms that solve these problems in an exponential amount of time, but the lower bound theory only demands "at least polynomial." Such problems are said to have an algorithmic gap and the complexity theory attempts to close this gap; either by developing faster algorithms or by providing a higher lower bound.

B.3 DETERMINISTIC AND NON-DETERMINISTIC MACHINES

As already mentioned, the complexity theory addresses problems and algorithms (both known algorithms as well as those that have yet to be discovered) that solve them. The only common framework for these algorithms are the machines that run them. Again, machines that have been built already and are operational, as well as machines that have yet to be designed and built. Therefore, the theory must be based on the same theoretical foundation upon which all current machines are built: the deterministic machine, where each next step is completely determined by the current internal state of the machine and the content of the cell on the tape at the location of the R/W head. This deterministic machine is reviewed below and extended to include non-deterministic behavior.

The theory is presented for *decision* problems. These are problems for which the solution is a **yes/no** answer, such as "is this array sorted?" and "is element x at location $A[123]$?" The collection of decision problems will be denoted as $\mathcal{D}$, and a single-decision problem will be denoted as a $\mathcal{D}$-problem (or just as a problem if it is clear from the context). Note that all optimization problems have a version that is a decision problem, such as "is there a path from A to B whose total cost is less than K?" At the same time, an optimization problem can often be solved by solving a sequence of decision problems, such as **begin** $k := 1$; **while** *solveDecisionProblem*(k) **do** $k := k + 1$ **end**.

The following definitions of a deterministic and a non-deterministic machine are somewhat loose, but suffice for the current presentation. A *deterministic machine*

1) can read and write on a (double-sided) infinite tape,
2) can scan one cell on the tape at any one time,
3) can make a finite number of operations on the tape (e.g., write 0/1),
4) can move either to the left or to the right on the tape,
5) has a program inside that tells the machine precisely (i.e., deterministically) where to go and what to do next. In particular, there is only one thing to do, and it is well defined.

Every currently existing computer is a realization of such a deterministic machine. These are extended to a *non-deterministic machine*, which has the identical capabilities as 1), 2), 3), and 4) above. Furthermore, capability 5) is replaced and three others are added. Thus, in addition to capabilities 1), 2), 3), and 4), a *non-deterministic machine*

5′) has a program inside that *sometimes* tells the machine precisely where to go and what to do next (the deterministic part). At *other times* there are a finite number (say n) of places to go to and/or things to do next. At these times, the machine instantly, and with no computational cost, clones itself into n machines, and continues each cloned version with a different choice. We will write `choice(`S`)` for these steps, with S indicating the possible choices.

6) There is no communication between these cloned versions.
7) If a cloned version realizes that it cannot solve the problem, it executes the statement `failure`, which causes it to cease operations, without interrupting the other cloned versions. The `failure` statement carries an $O(1)$ (i.e., bounded by a constant) computational cost.
8) If a cloned version realizes that it can solve the problem successfully, it executes the statement `success`, which causes a **yes** to be printed and causes all other cloned versions to cease operations (with failure). The `success` statement also carries an $O(1)$ computational cost.

An algorithm for a (non-)deterministic machine is referred to as a (non-)deterministic algorithm. A number of remarks are appropriate.

Remark B.1

All existing computers are realizations of the deterministic machine, and non-deterministic machines are not (yet?) realized, even after many years of trying and billions of research dollars. ♦

Remark B.2

A non-deterministic algorithm *solves* a problem if the algorithm executes the `success` statement, in other words that the **yes** has been printed (and a solution has been generated). An algorithm cannot solve the problem if none of the clones can execute a `success` statement, and a **yes** cannot be generated. The non-deterministic algorithm cannot decide between **yes** and **no**, it can only generate **yes** when appropriate. This appears to be a playing with words, but the difference is very real: the algorithm can report only a positive result by executing the `success` statement. Thus, as soon as there is a single clone that finds it can solve the problem, all other clones cease their operation. Negative results cannot be reported, because it would imply that clones can communicate somehow, or that there is a "master" that keeps track of the number of clones that died with failure. (The cloning is similar to the `fork` construct in a UNIX-like language, but in our developments, there is no `join` construct.) ♦

Remark B.3

Refer to capability 7) of a non-deterministic machine: "if a cloned version realizes that it cannot solve the problem, it executes the statement `failure`, which causes it to cease operations, without interrupting the other cloned versions." Thus, negative results cannot be reported in this set-up, because there is no "master" that can keep track of the number of clones that "failed." If negative results need to be acknowledged and reported, then the complement of the problem needs to be defined. This is the start of "co-$\mathcal{NP}$" theory, which is not addressed in this appendix. ♦

There is no difference between deterministic and non-deterministic machines as far as the set of problems they each can solve. Define

$$\mathcal{C}_{\mathcal{D}} = \{p \in \mathcal{D} : \text{there is a deterministic algorithm A that solves } p\}.$$

and similarly

$$\mathcal{C}_{\mathcal{ND}} = \{p \in \mathcal{D} : \text{there is a non-deterministic algorithm A that solves } p\}.$$

Notice that a non-deterministic machine with only deterministic steps is in essence a deterministic machine, so that $\mathcal{C}_{\mathcal{D}} \subseteq \mathcal{C}_{\mathcal{ND}}$. The reverse is also true: $\mathcal{C}_{\mathcal{N}D} \subseteq \mathcal{C}_{\mathcal{D}}$. Consider the execution path of a non-deterministic machine. At each deterministic step, there is precisely one thing to do next, so there is only one operation following the current one on the execution path. At each non-deterministic step, there is more than one, but a finitely bounded number of possible operations on the execution path. So the execution path of a non-deterministic algorithm for all clones concurrently can be envisioned as a general tree, where each node has a finite number of children. A deterministic algorithm can now be written that mimics a level-order traversal (=breath first search) of this general execution tree. Thus, $\mathcal{C}_{\mathcal{D}} = \mathcal{C}_{\mathcal{ND}}$. This means that every problem that can be solved on a non-deterministic machine can also be solved on a deterministic machine. Therefore, there is no difference between these two machines when considering the kinds of problems it can solve. Rather the difference is in the time it might need to execute them.

B.4 THE CLASSES OF PROBLEMS KNOWN AS $\mathcal{P}$ AND $\mathcal{NP}$

Now define the collection of problems that can be solved in polynomial time. For a deterministic machine this set is denoted as $\mathcal{P}$ and referred to as (deterministic) polynomial algorithms:

$$\mathcal{P} = \left\{ p \in \mathcal{C}_{\mathcal{D}} : \begin{array}{l} \text{there is a deterministic algorithm } A \text{ that solves } p, \\ \text{with } T_A^W(n) = O(n^k) \text{ for some integer } k > 0 \end{array} \right\}$$

and for a non-deterministic machine, this set is denoted as $\mathcal{NP}$ and referred to as the non-deterministic polynomial algorithms:

$$\mathcal{NP} = \left\{ p \in \mathcal{C}_{\mathcal{ND}} : \begin{array}{l} \text{there is a non-deterministic algorithm A that solves } p, \\ \text{with } T_A^W(n) = O(n^k) \text{ for some integer } k > 0 \end{array} \right\}.$$

Thus, if a problem p is in the set $\mathcal{P}$, $p \in \mathcal{P}$, then there is a deterministic algorithm that solves p and the length of its execution path is (bounded by a) polynomial. Similarly, if a problem p is in the set $\mathcal{NP}$, $p \in \mathcal{NP}$, then there is a non-deterministic algorithm that solves p and the execution tree has an accepting node whose depth is (bounded by a) polynomial. Again, it is easy to see that $\mathcal{P} \subseteq \mathcal{NP}$. The reverse inclusion, $\mathcal{NP} \subseteq \mathcal{P}$, however, is as yet an open question, the most famous open question in computer science. There are a few observations to be made.

Remark B.4

If a problem p is in $\mathcal{P}$, that means it can be solved on a deterministic machine in polynomial time. That also means, that it can be done on a non-deterministic machine in polynomial time. This does not imply that it can be done faster on a non-deterministic machine, nor does it exclude this possibility. Consider, for example, the problems "is the sum of all n elements in a set equal to K?" and "Is there an element x in this set?." ♦

Remark B.5

Similarly, if problem p is in $\mathcal{N}P$, it can be solved on a non-deterministic machine in polynomial time. That also means that it can be done on a deterministic machine in exponential time by using a level-order traversal of the execution tree. This does not imply that a deterministic algorithm must take exponential time, because it just might be that there is also a deterministic algorithm that solves p in polynomial time. The same two problems can be used as examples here. ♦

B.5 REDUCIBILITY RELATION BETWEEN PROBLEMS

Suppose you want to tackle the open question $\mathcal{P} = \mathcal{NP}$? If you believe it is true, you could take a problem $p \in \mathcal{NP}$ and find a polynomially bounded deterministic algorithm that solves it. But you must do this for *all* problems in $\mathcal{NP}$, both for problems that are currently already identified as well as problems that have yet to be discovered. So where would you start so that you can be successful? You could try to identify a "difficult" problem that is still in $\mathcal{NP}$, in fact, you may want one that is "most difficult". These "most difficult" problems are known as $\mathcal{NP}$*-complete* problems ($\mathcal{NPC}$) (see below for more formal introduction), and each $\mathcal{NPC}$ problem represents in some sense "all $\mathcal{NP}$ problems together." You (as well as all other researchers) could focus all your energies on any one of these $\mathcal{NPC}$ problems. Let q be such an $\mathcal{NPC}$ problem. Now, if a deterministic algorithm can be found that solves q in polynomial time, then $\mathcal{P} = \mathcal{NP}$. On the other hand, if it can be shown that the lower bound for q is exponential, then $\mathcal{P} \neq \mathcal{NP}$. Introduce now the notion of (polynomial) *reducibility* which will define a relation between problems p and q, similar to the relation $x \leq y$ between numbers x and y, and similar to the relation $T = O(f)$ between time complexity functions T and f.

Let $p, q \in \mathcal{C}_{\mathcal{ND}}$. Problem p *(polynomially) reduces* to problem q, denoted as $p \propto q$, if there is a deterministic, polynomial time algorithm A that transforms any instance of p into an instance of q, such that the result of any algorithm that solves q is consistent with the result of any algorithm solving p operating on the original instance. Another way to describe this is as follows. Suppose there are non-deterministic algorithms A_p and A_q that solve problems p and q, respectively. Suppose that there is a deterministic, polynomial time algorithm A_T that intercepts the input for algorithm A_p and transforms this input into an input for algorithm A_q. When this transformed input is given as input to algorithm A_q, then the output of A_q is indistinguishable from the output of algorithm A_p working on the original input I_p, symbolically: $A_q(A_T(I_p)) \equiv A_p(I_p)$, and in words: A_q working on $A_T(I_p)$ results in **yes** if and only if A_p working on I_p results in **yes**.

At first glance, this notion of "reducibility" appears rather awkward, and so it is. It defines a binary relationship between problems p and q, without resorting to any algorithms that solve these problems. The relationship $p \propto q$ indicates intuitively something like: "problem p is a special case of problem q," or "problem p is more general than problem q," as long as it is understood that there is a polynomial time algorithm involved in showing such specialization/generalization. This is a very common way to solve everyday problems. Suppose you need to find the median of a set of natural numbers, then you could first sort these numbers and find the middle. You have transformed a selection problem into a sorting problem. You have reduced a $\Theta(n)$ time problem to an $\Theta(n \log n)$ time problem. It is an interesting exercise to realize that any problem in $\mathcal{P}$ reduces to any other problem in $\mathcal{P}$. Notice it is true that the problems "Is there a minimum spanning tree with total cost $\leq M$?" and "Is $5 < 8$?" are equivalent problems. A beginning programmer (and many experienced ones) might not want to agree.

B.6 THE CLASS OF $\mathcal{NP}$-COMPLETE PROBLEMS

The notion of $\mathcal{NPC}$ can now be introduced formally. A problem p is said to be $\mathcal{NP}$-complete, if: 1) $p \in \mathcal{NP}$, and 2) all other problems in $\mathcal{NP}$ reduce to problem p, that is, for all $r \in \mathcal{NP}$ it is **true** that $r \propto p$.

Even though the definition is short and its intent is fairly clear, it is hard to identify the very first problem to be $\mathcal{NPC}$, because *all other* $\mathcal{NP}$ problems must reduce to this first problem. It is simply impossible to exhaustively reduce all $\mathcal{NP}$ problems that have been identified as well as all $\mathcal{NP}$ problems that have yet to be discovered. S. A. Cook, however, considered the non-deterministic machine when a non-deterministic algorithm operates on it for a polynomial time to solve an instance of any $\mathcal{NP}$ problem. He realized that this working can be represented as Boolean expressions, and that a **yes** is reached if all the variables in these expressions take the correct values. In other words, he realized that the machine always solves a specialized instance of the so-called *satisfiability problem (SAT)* (see below).

For any other problem suspected of being $\mathcal{NPC}$, the proof is usually quite different and is based on the transitivity of the reducibility relation; a problem r is $\mathcal{NPC}$ if 1) $r \in \mathcal{NP}$ and 2) one other problem p can be found in $\mathcal{NPC}$ such that this other problem reduces to r, that is, for a certain $p \in \mathcal{NPC}$ it is true that $p \propto r$.

It is clear how the open question $\mathcal{P} = \mathcal{NP}$? could be addressed, as the $\mathcal{NPC}$ problems are the best candidates for *not* being in $\mathcal{P}$. Thus:

1. Find as many problems as possible that are all equivalent to SAT.
2. For any of these problems, try to show it is in $\mathcal{P}$ (and thus concluding that $\mathcal{P} = \mathcal{NP}$), or is not in $\mathcal{P}$, (and thus concluding that $\mathcal{P} \neq \mathcal{NP}$).

B.7 THE SATISFIABILITY PROBLEM AND COOK'S THEOREM

The SAT is a decision problem that is solved when the values **true** or **false** can be assigned to Boolean variables $x_1, x_2, \ldots x_n$, so that the value of a Boolean expression in conjuctive normal form (CNF) in these n variables becomes **true**. The CNF (also called product-of-sums) of a Boolean function is the conjunction (**and**s) of clauses (also called maxterms), where each clause consists of disjunctions (**or**s) in which each variable or its negation, but not both, appears only once. Thus, if there is a valuation of the variables so that the CNF expression becomes **true**, then *all* clauses must be satisfied. Every Boolean formula which is not a tautology has an equivalent CNF which is unique (except for the ordering of the clauses in the conjunctions, and except for the ordering of the literals inside the clauses; a literal is either the variable, or its negation.)

Suppose you start with any Boolean expression f; then converting f to its CNF $F(f)$ can be done mechanically. This CNF $F(f)$ is by no means simpler, shorter, or faster to evaluate than the original expression f. The advantage of the CNF form is that there is only one expression in CNF form, whereas there are an infinite number of other Boolean expression also equivalent to f. Thus, if two expressions f and g are given, and you wish to determine if these are equivalent to each other, then it may be easier to convert them first to their CNFs and compare the CNFs, rather then trying to reduce one Boolean form to the other using the Boolean operations.

THEOREM B.1 *Every problem in $\mathcal{NP}$ reduces to the* **CNF-SAT** *(S. A. Cook [Coo71]).*
The formal proof is long, but ingenious. It is based on the observation that as soon as a problem p is identified as being in $\mathcal{NP}$, $p \in \mathcal{NP}$, then a non-deterministic algorithm exists that runs in polynomial time and returns a **yes**. So the only facts known about the problem is that that there is a sequence of instructions for a non-deterministic machine, whose length is bounded by a polynomial. By describing all initial conditions, program transitions, and program actions as Boolean expressions, a transformation from this instruction sequence to the **CNF-SAT** can be constructed. This effectively simulates the machine while it executes the program that solves p, and this suffices to show that $p \propto$ **CNF-SAT**. For more detailed proofs, see [HSR97], [RND77], and [Wil86].

After Cook's result, the area of $\mathcal{NPC}$ research started in earnest as proving problems to be in $\mathcal{NPC}$ became a lot easier. R. M. Karp showed a diverse number of problems to be in $\mathcal{NPC}$ ([Kar72] and [Kar75]), and M. Garey and D. Johnson gave a complete reference on the area in 1979 ([GJ79]). Since then, thousands of problems have been identified as being in $\mathcal{NPC}$, including the problem considered in Section 7.10 in this book.

B.8 NETWORK FLOW PROBLEMS

Consider now a graph G, with each edge $e = (i, j)$ having an associated capacity or cost $c(e)$, and with a starting or source node S and a sink node or terminal T. A network flow problem is to determine the maximal flow that can be routed from S to T. Special cases are recognized if the flows and capacities are all equal (the $0 - 1$ flow problems, or the "simple" flow problems), or are all integer multiples of a basic unit (the integer flow problems). Furthermore, in communication networks, there are D, $D > 1$, source-destination (demand) pairs over which route selection needs to connect the D sources with their destinations, and these are known as multi-commodity flow problems. They first appeared in the $\mathcal{NPC}$ literature in the paper by R. M. Karp ([Kar72]), who credits D. Knuth for showing that the discrete multi-commodity flow problem is in $\mathcal{NPC}$, (the paths need to be node-disjoint in this case). This result is strengthened by S. Even et al. ([EIS76], and [Eve79]) where it is shown that, even with $D = 2$ and even with all edge capacities equal to either 0 or 1, this simple two-commodity integer flow problem is in $\mathcal{NPC}$. This is shown for both directed graph (problem **D2CIF**), and an undirected graph (problem **U2CIF**). In this appendix, we will follow [EIS76, Eve79], and illustrate how the **CNF-SAT** reduces to the **D2CIF**, which in turn reduces to the **U2CIF**, thereby showing them both to be in $\mathcal{NPC}$.

First, define a single-commodity flow by a flow function $f(e)$ such that $f(e) \in \{0, 1\}$, $f(e) \leq c(e)$, and such that each flow is conserved at each node: for each node v, the sum of the flows into v must be equal to the sum of the flows out of v (except for source S and terminal T). Finally, the total flow F is the net difference between the total flow out of S and the flow into S (note that this difference is at the same time equal to the difference of the total flow into T and the total flow out of T). In a two-commodity flow, there are two such flows, f_1 and f_2, with the additional requirement that $f_1(e) + f_2(e) \leq c(e)$.

B.8.1 The D2CIF problem

The **D2CIF** problem can now be stated. Given is a directed graph $G(V, E)$ with capacity $c(e) \in \{0, 1\}$ for edge $e \in E$, four special nodes (all in V): sources S_1 and S_2 and terminals T_1 and T_2, and requirements R_1 and R_2 as positive integers. The **D2CIF** problem is a decision problem asking whether two-commodity flows, flow f_1 from S_1 to T_1, and f_2 from S_2 to T_2 exist, such that the total flow $F_1 \geq R_1$ and the total flow $F_2 \geq R_2$.

PROPOSITION B.1 CNF-SAT $\propto$ D2CIF.

Proof:

In order to show this, we will design a deterministic, polynomial time algorithm A that transforms any instance of **CNF-SAT** into an instance of **D2CIF**, such that the result of any algorithm that solves the resulting **D2CIF** instance is consistent with the result of any algorithm that solves the original **CNF-SAT** instance. There is no need to design an algorithm to solve either problem; it suffices to show that **CNF-SAT** is a special case of **D2CIF** by transforming (reducing) a CNF expression into a network. Thus, let a CNF expression be given and assume it consists of the n variables $\{x_1, x_2, \ldots, x_n\}$ and, thus, $2n$ literals $\{x_1, x_2, \ldots, x_n, \bar{x}_1, \bar{x}_2, \ldots \bar{x}_n\}$, which are incorporated in m clauses $C_1, C_2, \ldots, C_m$.

Remember that **CNF-SAT** is **true** if there is a consistent assignment of **true/false** values to the variables (and thus an assignment of **false/true** values to their complements), such that there is at least one literal assigned **true** in all the m clauses. The network that will be constructed mimics exactly these requirements: if there is a flow from S_1 to T_1 with total flow $F_1 = 1$, then the assignment is consistent, and if there is a flow from S_2 to T_2 with total flow $F_2 = m$ then all m clauses have at least one literal that is **true**.

The construction of the network is as follows: if variable x_i appears in clause C_j, then introduce a node $v(i, j)$, and if the $\bar{x}_i$ appears in clause C_j, then introduce node $\bar{v}(i, j)$. If variable x_i is consistent, then all instances of x_i (and of $\bar{x}_i$) have the same **true/false** assignment, which means that all $v(i, j)$ should be assigned the same value for clauses C_j

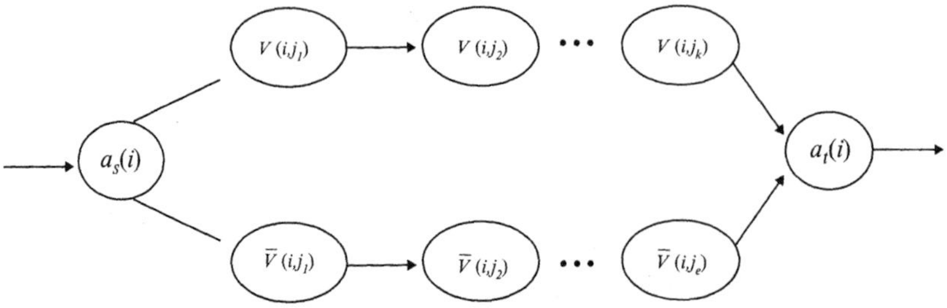

FIGURE B.1 The lobe L_i for variable x_i and its literal $\bar{x}_i$

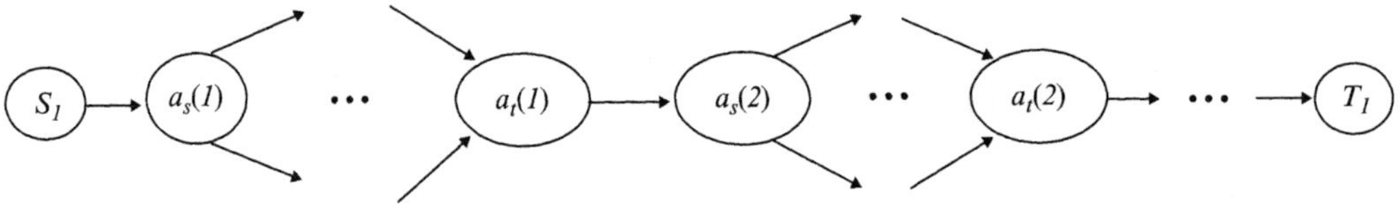

FIGURE B.2 Chaining the lobes

in which the literal x_i appears. Thus, for each fixed i, construct a path from the first existing $v(i, j)$, to the next existing $v(i, j)$, and so on. (With the first existing $v(i, j)$ we mean the clause C_j of smallest index j in which the literal x_i appears, and so on.) The same is done for the $\bar{v}(i, j)$ nodes. Now for each variable introduce a node $a_s(i)$ that allows a choice of assignment between **true/false** values for all $v(i, j)$ nodes together or all $\bar{v}(i, j)$ nodes together, and introduce a node $a_t(i)$ that allows the choice for the next variable x_{i+1} to made independent of the choice for the current variable x_i. Connect $a_s(i)$ to the first existing $v(i, j)$ and the first existing $\bar{v}(i, j)$, and connect the last existing $v(i, j)$ to $a_t(i)$ and the last existing $\bar{v}(i, j)$ to $a_t(i)$. The resulting construct from $a_s(i)$ to $a_t(i)$ through one of two straight pathways is called a *lobe* L_i, with first node $a_s(i)$ and last node $a_t(i)$ (Figure B.1). To allow choices to be made for all variables, connect S_1 to the first node $a_s(1)$ in the first lobe, connect the last node $a_t(1)$ of the first lobe to the first node $a_s(2)$ of the second lobe, connect $a_t(2)$ to $a_s(3)$, and so on, and connect $a_t(n)$ to T_1. The resulting network from S_1 to T_1 has indeed n independent assignment nodes $a_s(1), a_s(2) \ldots a_s(n)$, and there are indeed 2^n possible paths from S_1 to T_1. Since all capacities are one, the flow through this path is $F_1 = 1$ (Figure B.2).

Next, consider the clauses. Each clause must have at least one literal that is assigned **true**. Introduce nodes $b_s(1), b_s(2), \ldots b_s(m)$ and nodes $b_t(1), b_t(2), \ldots b_t(m)$ (one b_s-node and one b_t-node for each clause). Now connect S_2 to all the b_s-nodes, and connect each $b_s(j)$ to all the existing $v(i, j)$s and all the existing $\bar{v}(i, j)$s (now keeping j fixed). Notice, that there is at most one connection from a $b_s(j)$ node to a literal inside lobe i. Furthermore, connect all the existing $v(i, j)$s and all the existing $\bar{v}(i, j)$s (again keeping j fixed) to the $b_t(j)$ nodes (again, only one connection from lobe i to $b_t(j)$). These $b_t(j)$ nodes are in turn connected to the T_2 node. Notice, that every path from S_2 to T_2 has a length of exactly 4. The role of the b_s nodes is that of choice: for the expression to be **true**, each clause must

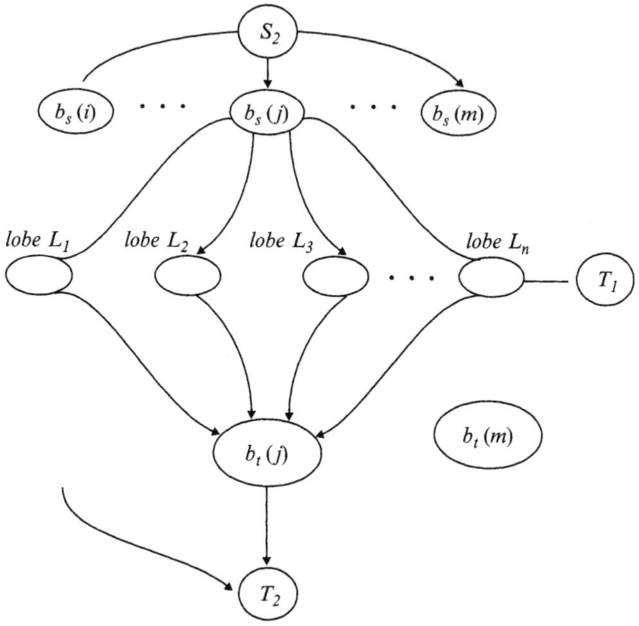

FIGURE B.3 Clause Selection

have at least one **true** literal. The $b_s(j)$ nodes reflect the choice of which literal to choose in clause C_j (Figure B.3). If there is a flow from S_2 to T_2 with a total flow of $F_2 = m$, then this is only possible by having m individual flows going through each $b_s(j)$ node, each flow starting at S_2 and ending at T_2. This reflects the need to have *all* clauses resulting in at least one literal that is **true**.

The constructed network is almost correct: every consistent assignment can be affected by a flow f_1 from S_1 to T_1 with requirement $F_1 \geq 1$. This consistency is not yet enforced by the clauses: each clause can still find a path independent of what other clauses do, and indeed independent of what the first flow does. Imagine that all the nodes on the path of the first flow are colored **RED**, and that all other nodes are **GREEN**. To enforce consistency among the clauses, it is now dictated that all of the nodes in all paths from S_2 to T_2 are all **GREEN**. This would make a network such that the resulting solution to the **D2CIF** problem is indeed consistent with a solution to the **CNF-SAT** problem. However, nodes do not have colors in the setting of a flow problem, so the notion of color needs to be replaced by the notion of capacity: replace each and every existing $v(i, j)$ by two nodes $v_s(i, j)$ and $v_t(i, j)$ that are connected with a link of capacity 1. All links that would end at $v(i, j)$ will now end at $v_s(i, j)$, and each link that would start at $v(i, j)$ will now start at $v_t(i, j)$ (Figure B.4). Do the same for the $\bar{v}(i, j)$: replace them by a pair of nodes $\bar{v}_s(i, j)$ and $\bar{v}_t(i, j)$, and connect them similarly. This effectively creates a bottleneck pipe, which enforces consistency: assign the value **false** to the nodes on the path taken by the flow from S_1 to T_1.

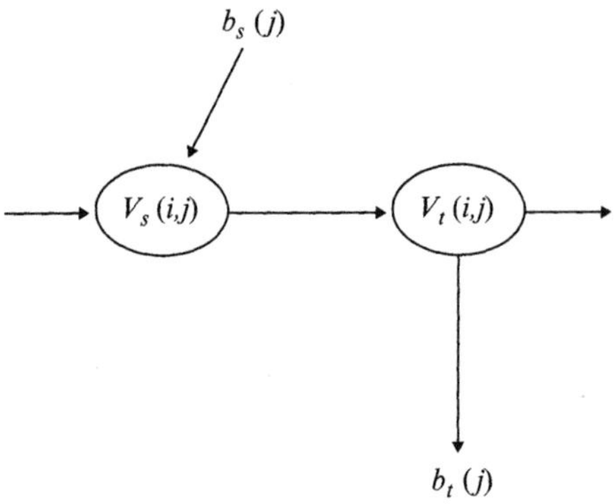

FIGURE B.4 Constrain

For the graph that has been carefully constructed, it can now be observed that if a flow f_1 exists from S_1 to T_1 with requirement $R_1 = 1$, and if at the same time a flow f_2 exists from S_2 to T_2 with requirement $R_1 = m$, then this also means that a compatible assignment of the Boolean variables x_i can be made such that there is at least one **true** value assigned for each clause C_j. ■

B.8.2 *The U2CIF Problem*

The definition for a flow in an *un*directed graph must be slightly adjusted from that in a directed network. In the undirected case, an edge $e = \{u, v\}$ can carry a flow in either direction, as long as $f(u \to v) = -f(v \to u)$. The other conditions for a function to become a flow are the same: no conservation of flow inside a node, total flow $F = \sum f(s \to x)$, and $|f(u \to v)| < c(u \to v)$.

PROPOSITION B.2 D2CIF $\propto$ U2CIF.

Proof:

Again, we need to design a deterministic, polynomial time algorithm A that transforms any instance of **D2CIF** into an instance of **U2CIF**, such that the result of any algorithm that solves **U2CIF** is consistent with result of any algorithm solving **D2CIF** operating on the original instance. There is no need to design an algorithm to solve either algorithm; it suffices to show that **D2CIF** is a special case of **U2CIF** by transforming a directed graph into an undirected graph.

First, suppose the input to the **D2CIF** problem is given: a directed graph $G = (V, E)$ with $0 - 1$ capacities, sources and terminals S_1, S_2, T_1, and T_2, and requirements R_1 and R_2. Before constructing an undirected graph with the desired properties, adjust this directed graph first to a directed graph $G' = (V', E')$, through the introduction of four new nodes to the given original directed graph $G = (V, E)$: S_1^+, S_2^+, T_1^+, and T_2^+, which are connected as follows: S_i^+ is connected to S_i using R_i parallel edges, and T_i is connected to T_i^+, also

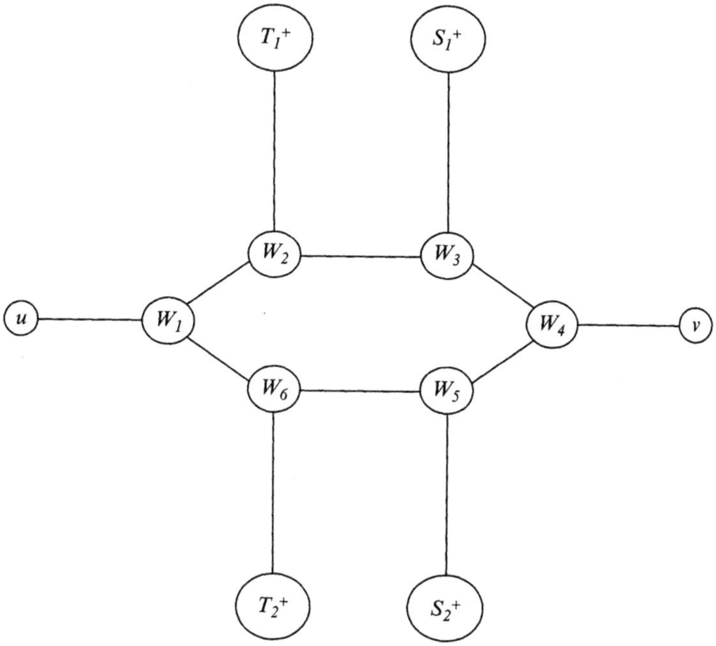

FIGURE B.5 Substructure in undirected graph for each node pair (u, v)

using R_i parallel edges. Thus, a new directed graph is constructed: $G' = (V', E')$. Now, construct an undirected graph $G^u = (V^u, E^u)$ as follows: for each node $v \in V'$, add a node $v \in V^u$. Also, for each edge $e = (u, v) \in E'$, add six nodes $w_1, w_2, w_3, w_4, w_5, w_6$ to V^u. (These nodes depend on the node-pair (u, v), but this dependency is not shown for clarity.) These nodes are connected in a circle as follows: connect w_1 and w_2, w_2 and w_3, w_3 and w_4, w_4 and w_5, w_5 and w_6, w_6 and w_1. Furthermore, connect w_1 and u, w_2 and T_1^+, w_3 and S_1^+, w_4 and v, w_5 and S_2^+, w_6 and T_2^+ (Figure B.5).

Finally, define $R_i^+ = R_i + |E'|$. The construction of the input to the *undirected* **U2CIF** from the input to *directed* **D2CIF** is somewhat easier than before, but showing that the solutions are equivalent is a little harder. First assume that the requirement for the **D2CIF** problem can be met. Now for each $e = (u, v) \in E'$ there is a flow from S_1^+ to w_3, to w_2, and to T_1^+. Similarly, there is a flow from S_2^+ to w_5, to w_6, and to T_2^+. Now, if $(u, v) \in E'$ is used in flow f_1 in the solution to the `simple` **D2CIF** problem, then replace the single flow from S_1^+ to w_3, to w_2, and to T_1^+ by the two flows: u to w_1, to w_2, and to T_1^+, and a flow from S_1^+ to w_3, to w_4, to v. (An edge used for flow f_2 is treated similarly.) ■

B.9 FINAL REMARKS

Remark B.6

The question of whether $\mathcal{NP} \subseteq \mathcal{P}$ is still an open-research dilemma that many scientists have attempted to solve. They have not answered the basic question as far as we know, but they have discovered many other interesting things along the way or found many parallels with other open questions in science. In a way, $\mathcal{NPC}$ theory is only the beginning, as more and more groups of problems are classified into what is called a "polynomial hierarchy" of classes of problems. These are fairly easy to construct by placing the words "for all instances, there exist a . . . " in front of a problem already defined. For instance, the polynomial problem "Is this a Hamiltonian Circuit?" can be considered at level 0, and the $\mathcal{NPC}$ problem "Does a Hamiltonian Circuit exist?" is at level 1. A level 2 problem could be: "For all the ways that half the edges can be removed, does a Hamiltonian Circuit always exist?" And an example for a level 3 problem: "For all the ways that half the edges can be removed, can we always restore half of the removed edges so that a Hamiltonian Circuit exists?" Definitions like $\mathcal{NP} - Hard$, co-$\mathcal{NP}$, and co-$\mathcal{NPC}$ have been introduced, just like notions of "generable," "recursively enumerable," or "decidability" are important to show that one can never conclude that a seemingly runaway program has stopped making useful computations (halting problem). ♦

Remark B.7

What should you do if the problem you need to solve is $\mathcal{N}PC$? If you are very lucky, it just may be that the particular problem size you have to deal with is not yet in the asymptotic neighborhood, or the particular inputs that will be given to you are not the "worst-case" kind, so *your* worst case may be very acceptable. Also, there may be special properties in *your* situation that you can capitalize on to reduce the worst case complexity. Otherwise you might be able to use randomization or probabilistic algorithms to effect acceptable behavior. If these approaches fail, you will have to use approximation algorithms or suboptimal solutions based on heuristics or based on a limited number of steps in branch-and-bound, pruning, backtracking, and others. These can perhaps be combined with parallel machines for additional speed-up. ♦

Remark B.8

The word "reducibility" has the connotation of "simplification," and implies "cheaper." There are other words that may have been better choices, like "embedded," "more general," "weaker" (in the mathematical sense), "more powerful" (in the sense that it can solve at least two problems), or simply "transformable" which is used by many authors at the suggestion of D. Knuth. Furthermore, it should be mentioned that there are several, slightly differing definitions of reducibility introduced in the literature. ♦

Remark B.9

For a continuously updated catalog for $\mathcal{NP}$ optimization problems, see [CK]. ♦

Remark B.10

This appendix is based on lecture notes made throughout the many years of teaching a first-year graduate course on 'Design and Analysis of Algorithms' at the University of Missouri–Kansas City. As such, the inspiration has come from many different sources, the main ones have been referenced in this appendix. Any omissions are not intentional. ♦

APPENDIX C

Shortest-Path Algorithms

C.1 INTRODUCTION AND BASIC NOTIONS

Algorithms for the basic problem of finding the shortest path $\mathcal{P}$ between vertices in a graph with edges of non-negative weights are well known, especially the Dijkstra's algorithm. Still, more sophisticated algorithms solving certain modifications of the basic problem, important for this book, are not so widespread. Therefore, in this appendix, we present a selected set of algorithms useful for computing sets of shortest paths with certain desirable properties. These algorithms are needed for generating candidate path lists for the network design problems in link-path formulation used extensively throughout the book. We will start with presenting Dijkstra's algorithm for the basic problem (Section A.2.1), and its variant taking into account the hop-limit imposed on the shortest paths (Section A.2.2). Then, in Section A.2.3, we modify the classical Dijkstra's approach to cover the case of negative edge weights, and present an alternative solution called the breadth-first-search (BFS) algorithm. In Section A.3, we show how to solve the problem of finding K-shortest paths (Section A.3.1) and the problem of finding all optimal paths, i.e., the set of all different paths with the same, shortest length (Section A.3.2). Finally, we discuss the problem of finding the shortest sets of K edge-disjoint paths (Section A.4.1) between two given vertices, and the analogous problem of finding the shortest sets of K vertex-disjoint paths (Section A.4.2).

We consider a (network) graph $\mathcal{G} =(\mathcal{V}, \mathcal{E})$, where $\mathcal{V}$ is the set of vertices (called nodes in the communication network context) denoted by v, w, s, t, and $\mathcal{E}$ is the set of edges (links) denoted by e, f. Let V and E denote the number of elements in sets $\mathcal{V}$ and $\mathcal{E}$, respectively. There are three basic types of graphs considered in this appendix: undirected, directed, and mixed graphs. In an undirected graph, the direction of edges is not important and, hence, all edges are undirected and each edge e can be identified with a set of two vertices (an undirected pair of vertices), i.e., $e = \{v, w\}$; in the directed graph, all edges are directed (and called arcs) and can be identified with ordered pairs of different vertices, i.e., $e = (v, w)$; note that arc (v, w) is different from arc (w, v). Directed arc (v, w) is also denoted by $v \rightarrow w$. On the other hand, undirected edge $\{v, w\}$ is denoted by v-w. In a mixed graph both types of edges can occur but only one type of edge can connect a pair of vertices (either an undirected edge or one or two arcs). In the rest of this appendix, we will assume undirected graphs, unless stated explicitly otherwise.

To explain the basic concepts we will use an example of the undirected graph depicted in Figure C.1. We have $\mathcal{V} = \{A, B, C, D, E, Z\}$ as the set of vertices and $\mathcal{E} = \{1, 2, 3, 4, 5, 6, 7, 8, 9, 10\}$ as the set of edges. Every edge e has an attribute, called

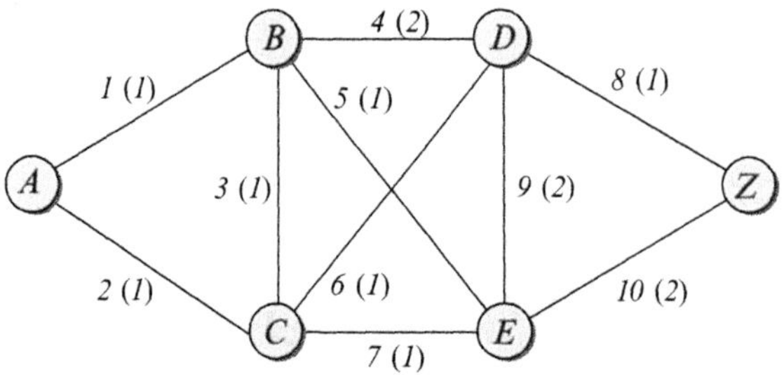

FIGURE C.1 A Sample Graph with Edge Weights

weight denoted by ℓ_e, used for evaluating the length of paths between the vertices. In Figure C.1, along with the number identifying the edge, the corresponding edge weight (ℓ_e) is given in parantheses. Two vertices are said to be neighbors when they have an edge connecting them. A set of all neighbors of a fixed vertex v is denoted by $\mathcal{N}(v)$; for example $\mathcal{N}(A) = \{B, C\}$. A (simple) path $\mathcal{P}$ from source vertex s to destination vertex t is a sequence of vertices of the form $\langle v_1, v_2, ..., v_n \rangle$ where $n \geq 2$, $v_1 = s$, $v_n = t$, all vertices are different and for each $i = 1, 2, ..., n-1$ the unordered pair $e = \{v_i, v_{i+1}\}$ is an edge, i.e., an element of $\mathcal{E}$. In the directed case, the last requirement should be substituted with: for each $i = 1, 2, ..., n-1$ the ordered pair $e = (v_i, v_{i+1})$ is an arc. For example, $\mathcal{P} = \langle A, B, D, Z \rangle$ is path from source $s = A$ to destination $t = Z$. Of course, in the undirected case, the reverse sequence $\langle v_n, v_{n-1}, ..., v_1 \rangle$ is a path from source Z to destination A. The example path $\mathcal{P}$ has $\{1, 4, 8\}$ as the set of its edges. The set of edges of path $\mathcal{P}$ will be denoted by $\hat{\mathcal{P}}$, so in our example $\hat{\mathcal{P}} = \{1, 4, 8\}$. The *length* $|\mathcal{P}|$ of path $\mathcal{P}$ is defined as the sum of the weights of all the edges forming the path: $|\mathcal{P}| = \sum_{e \in \hat{\mathcal{P}}} \ell_e$. In our example we have $|\mathcal{P}| = 1 + 2 + 1 = 4$. Finally, we note that instead of ℓ_e we will write ℓ_{vw} when $e = \{v, w\}$ or $e = (v, w)$.

C.2 BASIC SHORTEST-PATH PROBLEM

The basic problem of finding the shortest path can be expressed as: *given a source s and destination t, find the path which has the minimum length among all possible paths connecting s to t.*

Several shortest-path algorithms can be found in the literature. Probably the best known is the algorithm discovered by E. W. Dijkstra ([Dij59]). In fact, the algorithm is well suited for solving a more general problem of finding the shortest path from a fixed source s to all other vertices in the graph. Dijkstra's algorithm is applicable for graphs with non-negative weights. However, a minor modification can make it applicable for graphs with negative weights as well, provided the graphs do not contain negative cycles.

Another popular algorithm for computing shortest paths from a source to all the other vertices is the Bellman-Ford algorithm ([BG92]). It is applicable also when edges have negative weights (negative cycles are not allowed). The two algorithms differ in the network element on which they iterate. Dijkstra's algorithm iterates on the length of the path (updates it in every iteration) whereas Bellman-Ford's algorithm iterates on the number of edges in the path.

Another relevant problem is to find shortest paths between all pairs of vertices. Of course, using the aforementioned algorithms in a repetitive manner we can achieve this. However, there are other (faster) algorithms specialized for such a variant. The most well known is the Floyd-Warshall algorithm ([Che90],[BG92]). This algorithm assumes arbitrary edge weights, but as usual the negative cycles are forbidden. It iterates on the set of vertices that are allowed to be used as intermediate vertices in the paths.

C.2.1 Dijkstra's Algorithm for Non-Negative Weights

Dijkstra's original algorithm described below solves the basic shortest-path problem for undirected graphs where all weights are non-negative (like in our example network). It is a straightforward exercise to adapt the algorithm to solve the shortest-path problem in directed graphs. The algorithm, written in the form of a procedure in a Pascal-like pseudo-code, is referred to as Algorithm C.1. The procedure returns the shortest path, $\mathcal{P}$, from source s to destination t in graph $\mathcal{G}$.

ALGORITHM C.1 Shortest-Path Algorithm due to Dijkstra (SPD)

procedure $SPD(\mathcal{G}, s, t)$
  $\mathcal{S} := \emptyset;\ L(s) := 0;$
  for $v \in \mathcal{V} \setminus \{s\}$ **do** $L(v) := \infty;$
  while $t \notin \mathcal{S}$ **do** { **while** $|\mathcal{S}| < V$ **do** }
    begin
      $v := \text{argmin}\{L(v) :\ v \in \mathcal{S}'\};$ { $\mathcal{S}' = \mathcal{V} \setminus \mathcal{S}$ }
      $\mathcal{S} := \mathcal{S} \cup \{v\};$
      for $w \in \mathcal{N}(v) \cap \mathcal{S}'$ **do**
        if $L(w) > L(v) + \ell_{vw}$ **then**
          begin $L(w) := L(v) + \ell_{vw};\ P(w) := v$ **end**
    end;
  $\mathcal{P} := \langle t \rangle; v := t;$
  repeat
    $v := P(v);$
    $\mathcal{P} := v \oplus \mathcal{P}$
  until $v = s;$
  $SPD := \mathcal{P}$
end {*procedure*}

The algorithm uses vectors L and P and the set of *labeled* vertices $\mathcal{S}$. Each entry $L(v)$ contains the distance measured from s to v along the current shortest path, while each entry $P(v)$ contains the *parent* of vertex v, i.e., the vertex from which vertex v has been reached

TABLE C.1 Execution of SPD for Example Network

Step 0:	$S := \emptyset$	$L(A) := 0$	$P(A) := A$
Step 1:	$S := S \cup \{A\}$	$L(B) := 1,\ L(C) := 1$	$P(B) := A,\ P(C) := A$
Step 2:	$S := S \cup \{B\}$	$L(D) := 3,\ L(E) := 2$	$P(D) := B,\ P(E) := B$
Step 3:	$S := S \cup \{C\}$	$L(D) := 2$	$P(D) := C$
Step 4:	$S := S \cup \{D\}$	$L(Z) := 3$	$P(Z) := D$
Step 5:	$S := S \cup \{E\}$		
Step 6:	$S := S \cup \{Z\}$		

(labeled) during the construction of the shortest path. Vector P is used at the last stage of the procedure to restore the constructed shortest path ($\oplus$ is the concatenation operator). Upon completion, $L(t)$ is equal to the length of the shortest path, $\mathcal{P}$, from s to t.

Note that when we need to find the shortest path from s to every other vertex of the graph, this algorithm should be modified by replacing the condition in the **while** statement with the one given as a comment in the same line.

In Dijkstra's Algorithm C.1, the total number of vertices which need to be examined (in the worst case) is $V(V-1)$. Hence, the complexity of the algorithm is $O(V^2)$ (see [Bha99], and [Che90]). More sophisticated implementations, using advanced data structures, can decrease the complexity to $O(E + Vlog(V))$.

Table C.1 illustrates the way vectors L and P are adjusted in the consecutive steps of SPD run for source A and destination Z in the graph of Figure C.1. Note that the algorithm stops when the destination node Z becomes labeled (i.e., joins set S).

It is possible to generate information about multiple shortest paths, if they exist, with a slight modification in Algorithm C.1. If the condition, $L(w) > L(v) + \ell_{vw}$, is changed to $L(w) \geq L(v) + \ell_{vw}$, then the satisfaction of the **if** condition allows information about additional shortest paths to be captured; in order to do that, additional arrays are required to store relevant information.

C.2.2 *Shortest Paths With a Hop Limit*

A variant of the basic shortest-path problem that can be solved by adjusting Dijkstra's algorithm is to find a shortest path (in terms of weights ℓ_e) from s to each other node within the set of all paths with not more than n hops (i.e., edges). The variant presented below as Algorithm C.2, based on the algorithm published in Section 4.4.3 of [Wes00], finds the shortest paths with at most n hops from source s to all other nodes and returns such a path from s to a chosen node t.

For this variant, instead of the distance vector L and the predecessor vector P, we need to use sets of distance and predecessor vectors, L_i and P_i ($i = 1, 2, ..., n$), where $L_i(v)$ stores the length of the currently shortest path from s to v with at most i hops, and $P_i(v)$ stores the predecessor of vertex v on the currently shortest path with at most i hops. Also, instead of the set $\mathcal{S}$ of labeled vertices, for each $i = 1, 2, ..., n$ we introduce set $\mathcal{S}_i$ of the vertices labeled at level i, i.e., the set of vertices to which the shortest path with exactly i nodes has been found. Finally, the algorithm makes use of another set, $\mathcal{R}$, defined as the set of all pairs (v, i) (where v is unlabeled at level i and $1 \leq i \leq n$) such that $L_i(v) < \infty$ and vertex v can be reached from source s in exactly i hops, using only labeled intermediate vertices.

Computational complexity of the considered variant is at most n times greater than the complexity of the original algorithm and hence it is not greater than $O(n \times V^2)$.

ALGORITHM C.2 **Shortest-Path with Limited Number of Hops (SPDLH)**

---

procedure $SPDLH(\mathcal{G}, s, t, n)$
  $\mathcal{R} := \{(v, 1): v \in \mathcal{N}(s)\}$; **for** $i := 1$ **to** n **do** $\mathcal{S}_i := \{s\}$;
  for $v \in \mathcal{V} \setminus (\mathcal{N}(s) \cup \{s\})$ **do**
    for $i := 1$ **to** n **do** $L_i(v) := \infty$;
  for $v \in \mathcal{N}(s)$ **do**
    for $i := 1$ **to** n **do**
      begin $L_i(v) := \ell_{sv}$; $P_i(v) := s$ **end**;
  while $\mathcal{R} \neq \emptyset$ **do**
    begin
      find $(v, i) \in \mathcal{R}$ such that:
      (1) $\forall (w, j) \in \mathcal{R}, \ L_i(v) \leq L_j(w)$
      (2) $\forall (w, j) \in \mathcal{R}, \ L_i(v) = L_j(w) \Rightarrow j \geq i$;
      $\mathcal{S}_i := \mathcal{S}_i \cup \{v\}$; $\mathcal{R} := \mathcal{R} \setminus \{(v, i)\}$;
      if $i < n$ **then**
        for $w \in \mathcal{N}(v) \cap (\mathcal{S}_{i+1})'$ **do** $\{ (\mathcal{S}_{i+1})' = \mathcal{V} \setminus \mathcal{S}_{i+1} \}$
          begin
            if $L_{i+1}(w) > L_i(v) + \ell_{vw}$ **then** $\mathcal{R} := \mathcal{R} \cup \{(w, i+1)\}$;
            for $j := i + 1$ **to** n **do**
              if $L_j(w) > L_{j-1}(v) + \ell_{vw}$ **then**
                begin $L_j(w) := L_{j-1}(v) + \ell_{vw}$; $P_j(w) := v$ **end**
          end;
    end;
  $\mathcal{P} := \langle t \rangle$; $v := t$; $i := n$;
  repeat
    $v := P_i(v)$;
    $\mathcal{P} := v \oplus \mathcal{P}$;
    $i := i - 1$
  until $v = s$;
  $SPDLH := \mathcal{P}$
end {*procedure*}

C.2.3 Negative Weights

Now we consider a graph with some edges with negative weights ℓ_e, assuming that there are no negative cycles. It is easy to see that the original Dijkstra algorithm can fail in this case. However, Algorithm C.3, which is a variant of Algorithm C.1, addresses the issue of negative weights. The modified algorithm checks *all* the neighbors of vertex v under consideration, not only the unlabeled ones that are in set $\mathcal{S}'$ (complementary to the set $\mathcal{S}$ of labeled vertices). Then the updated vertices which have been currently labeled are deleted from $\mathcal{S}$ and become unlabeled. Observe, that even if we wish to find only the shortest path from s to t, we need to find the whole tree of the shortest paths from s to all other vertices.

ALGORITHM C.3 **Modified Dijkstra's Shortest-Path Algorithm SPDM**

```
procedure SPDM(G, s, t)
    S := ∅; L(s) := 0;
    for v ∈ V \ {s} do L(v) := ∞;
    while |S| < V do
        begin
            v := arg min{L(v) : v ∈ S'};                { S' = V \ S }
            S := S ∪ {v};
            for w ∈ N(v) do
                if L(w) > L(v) + ℓ_vw then
                    begin L(w) := L(v) + ℓ_vw; P(w) := v; S' := S' ∪ {w} end
        end;
    P := ⟨t⟩; v := t;
    repeat
        v := P(v);
        P := v ⊕ P
    until v = s;
    SPDM := P
end {procedure}
```

Another well-known algorithm that works with negative weights is the BFS algorithm (see [Bha99] and [Che90]), presented here as Algorithm C.4. In BFS, set $\mathcal{S}$ has a different interpretation than in the Dijkstra's algorithm. Now set $\mathcal{S}$ stores those vertices v which have been labeled (i.e., whose distance from s, $L(v)$, has changed) in the previous iteration, and instead of trying to label the neighboring nodes from one single "permanently" labeled node v, we try to label the neighbors from all vertices in $\mathcal{S}$.

Table C.2 shows how vectors L and P are adjusted by BFS while finding the shortest path for source A and destination Z in the graph from Figure C.1. Note that the algorithm stops when set $\mathcal{S}$ becomes empty.

TABLE C.2 BFS Execution for Example Network

Step 0:	$\mathcal{S} := \{A\}$	$L(A) := 0$	$P(A) := A$
Step 1:	$\mathcal{S} := \{A\}$	$L(B) := 1,\ L(C) := 1$	$P(B) := A,\ P(C) := A$
Step 2:	$\mathcal{S} := \{B, C\}$	$L(D) := 3,\ L(E) := 2$	$P(D) := B,\ P(E) := B$
Step 3:	$\mathcal{S} := \{B, C\}$	$L(D) := 2$	$P(D) := C$
Step 4:	$\mathcal{S} := \{D, E\}$	$L(Z) := 3$	$P(Z) := D$
Step 5:	$\mathcal{S} := \emptyset$		

ALGORITHM C.4 BFS Shortest-Path Algorithm

procedure $BFS(\mathcal{G}, s, t)$
  $\mathcal{S} := \{s\};\ L(s) := 0;$
  for $v \in \mathcal{V} \setminus \{s\}$ **do** $L(v) := \infty;$
  while $\mathcal{S} \neq \emptyset$ **do**
    begin
      $\mathcal{T} := \emptyset;$
      for $v \in \mathcal{S}$ **do**
        for $w \in \mathcal{N}(v)$ **do**
          if $L(w) > L(v) + \ell_{vw}$ **and** $L(t) > L(v) + \ell_{vw}$ **then**
            begin
              $L(w) := L(v) + \ell_{vw};\ P(w) := v;\ \mathcal{T} := \mathcal{T} \cup \{w\}$
            end;
      $\mathcal{S} := \mathcal{T} \setminus (\mathcal{T} \cap \{t\})$
    end;
  $\mathcal{P} := \langle t \rangle; v := t;$
  repeat
    $v := P(v);$
    $\mathcal{P} := v \oplus \mathcal{P}$
  until $v = s;$
  $BFS := \mathcal{P}$
end {*procedure*}

For non-negative weights, the complexity of BFS is $O(V + E)$ and, hence, as discussed in [Bha99], the BFS algorithm is better suited for sparse graphs than Dijkstra's algorithm (and the modified Dijkstra's algorithm in the case of negative weights). Still, the worst case complexity of the two algorithms is the same ($O(V^2)$). An important feature of BFS is that it always finds the shortest path with the minimum number of hops (when more than one shortest path exists).

C.3 K-SHORTEST PATHS AND ALL OPTIMAL PATHS

In this section we will consider two problems involving finding sets of shortest paths. The first of them is to find a set of K-shortest paths from source s to destination t, while the second requires finding all optimal paths, i.e., all paths from s to t with the same shortest length. In both cases, we assume non-negative weights. However, since we admit zero weights, the graph may contain cycles of zero length; such cycles can not appear in our paths, thus we must be careful and make sure that the generated paths are simple (i.e., contain no cycles).

C.3.1 K-Shortest Paths

The K-shortest-paths problem is as follows: *given graph $\mathcal{G}$ with non-negative link weights, source s and destination t, determine the shortest path, then the second shortest path, and so on, until the K-th shortest path.* The procedure solving this problem is described as Algorithm C.5. The presented version is based on [McC73] and [PCC03], and follows the original idea of [Yen71]. The procedure returns the set of K-shortest paths $\mathcal{K} = \{\mathcal{P}_1, \mathcal{P}_2, ..., \mathcal{P}_K\}$.

For $K = 1$ the algorithm finds the single shortest path and stops. Otherwise, in order to find each of the next shortest paths beyond the first one, a fairly sophisticated procedure is applied. The procedure makes use of an auxiliary set $\mathcal{S}$, composed of pairs of the form $(\mathcal{Q}, v)$, where $\mathcal{Q}$ is a path from s to t and $v \in \hat{\mathcal{Q}}$, which is then used to adjust the set $\mathcal{X}$ of candidate shortest paths. In the algorithm, $\ominus$ denotes the operator opposite to the concatenation operator $\oplus$. Also, $sub_{\mathcal{Q}}(v, w)$, where $v, w \in \hat{\mathcal{Q}}$, denotes the sub-path of $\mathcal{Q}$ from node v to node w (provided v appears earlier than w).

The procedure uses the shortest path $\mathcal{P}$ added to set $\mathcal{K}$ in the previous iteration to adjust the set of *candidate paths* $\mathcal{X}$. Finally, after doing this, it finds the shortest path in this set (using function $shortest(\mathcal{X})$), and adds it, as the consecutive shortest path, to set $\mathcal{K}$.

Set $\mathcal{X}$ is adjusted in the following way. First we use function $GetDeviationVertex$ $(\mathcal{S}, \mathcal{P})$ to find the unique pair of the form $(\mathcal{P}, w)$ in set $\mathcal{S}$ and the corresponding deviation vertex w associated with path $\mathcal{P}$. Then we consider all the consecutive vertices (except destination t) in the sub-path $sub_{\mathcal{P}}(w, t)$ (they are called *deviation vertices*). For each such vertex v we find the shortest path from source v to destination t, referred to as the *deviation path*, and concatenate this path with the sub-path of $\mathcal{P}$, $sub_{\mathcal{P}}(s, v)$, starting in s and terminating in v, to form path $\mathcal{Q}$ from s to t. Path $\mathcal{Q}$ is then added to set $\mathcal{X}$. In order to assure that path $\mathcal{Q}$ has not already been generated before running the Dijkstra algorithm, we need to modify the graph, by removing certain nodes and edges, using function $DisableVerticesAndEdges$. This function removes all vertices forming the sequence $sub_{\mathcal{P}}(s, v) \ominus v$ from graph $\mathcal{G}$, together with all edges incident to the deleted vertices. Note that this also assures that the newly constructed path $\mathcal{Q}$ is simple. Additionally, for each previously found shortest path $\mathcal{P}'$ $\in \mathcal{K} \cup \{\mathcal{P}\}$ with the property: $sub_{\mathcal{P}}(s, v) = sub_{\mathcal{P}'}(s, v)$, we remove its edge outgoing from vertex v towards t. After finding path $\mathcal{Q}$ for each deviation vertex v we add pair $(\mathcal{Q}, v)$ to set $\mathcal{S}$.

ALGORITHM C.5 K-Shortest-Path Algorithm

```
procedure K-SP(𝒢, s, t, K)
    k := 1;
    𝒫 := SPD(𝒢, s, t);
    𝒮 := {(𝒫, s)};                    {𝒮: set of pairs (path, deviation vertex)}
    𝒳 := {𝒫};
    𝒦 := {𝒫};
    while k < K and 𝒳 ≠ ∅ do
        begin
            𝒳 := 𝒳 \ {𝒫};
            w := GetDeviationVertex(𝒮, 𝒫);
            for v ∈ ⟨sub_𝒫(w, t) ⊖ {t}⟩ do
                begin
                    𝒢' := DisableVerticesAndEdges(𝒢, s, v, 𝒦, 𝒫);
                    𝒬 := sub_𝒫(s, v) ⊕ SPD(𝒢', v, t);
                    𝒳 := 𝒳 ∪ {𝒬};
                    𝒮 := 𝒮 ∪ {(𝒬, v)}
                end;
            𝒫 := shortest(𝒳);
            𝒦 := 𝒦 ∪ {𝒫};
            k := k + 1
        end
end {procedure}
```

Table C.3 shows how the sets $\mathcal{S}, \mathcal{X}, \mathcal{K}$ and variable path $\mathcal{P}$ are changing while searching for $K = 3$ shortest paths from A to Z in the graph depicted in Figure C.2. Sets $\mathcal{D}^{\mathcal{E}}$ and $\mathcal{D}^{\mathcal{V}}$ denote the sets of edges and vertices, respectively, disabled by procedure $DisableVerticesAndEdges$.

C.3.2 *All Optimal Paths*

Let the length of the shortest path between s and t be equal to p and consider the problem of finding all paths $\mathcal{P}$ from s to t with $|\mathcal{P}| = p$ in a given graph with non-negative edge weights. As you may notice, Algorithm C.5 for finding K-shortest paths can be easily applied for this purpose. This is due to the property that at the end of each iteration, the algorithm adds one path to the current set $\mathcal{K} = \{\mathcal{P}_1, P_2, ..., P_k\}$ of already found k shortest paths. Thus, to find all (and only) optimal paths, we just stop the algorithm when the first path longer than path $\mathcal{P}_1$ is found.

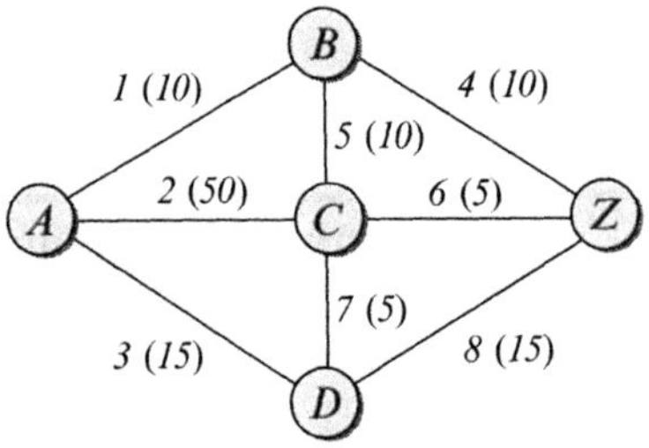

FIGURE C.2 A Sample Network Graph

TABLE C.3 Example Execution of K-SP

Step 0:	$\mathcal{Q}_1 := \langle A, B, Z\rangle$, $\lvert\mathcal{Q}_1\rvert = 20$, $\mathcal{Q}_1$ equals $\mathcal{P}$	
	$\mathcal{S} := \{(\mathcal{Q}_1, A)\}$, $\mathcal{X} := \{\mathcal{Q}_1\}$, $\mathcal{K} := \{\mathcal{Q}_1\}$	$\mathcal{P}^1 := \mathcal{Q}_1$
Step 1:	$\mathcal{X} := \mathcal{X} \setminus \{\mathcal{P}^1\}$,	
1.1:	$v = A$, $\mathcal{D}^{\mathcal{E}} = \{1\}$, $\mathcal{D}^{\mathcal{V}} = \emptyset$; $\mathcal{Q}_2 = \langle A, D, C, Z\rangle$, $\lvert\mathcal{Q}_2\rvert = 25$,	
1.2:	$v = B$, $\mathcal{D}^{\mathcal{E}} = \{1, 2, 3, 4\}$, $\mathcal{D}^{\mathcal{V}} = \{A\}$, $\mathcal{Q}_3 = \langle A, B, C, Z\rangle$, $\lvert\mathcal{Q}_3\rvert = 25$	
	$\mathcal{S} = \{(\mathcal{Q}_1, A), (\mathcal{Q}_2, A), (\mathcal{Q}_3, B)\}$, $\mathcal{X} = \{\mathcal{Q}_2, \mathcal{Q}_3\}$, $\mathcal{K} = \{\mathcal{P}^1, \mathcal{P}^2\}$	$\mathcal{P}^2 := \mathcal{Q}_2$
Step 2:	$\mathcal{X} := \mathcal{X} \setminus \{\mathcal{P}^2\}$,	
2.1:	$v = A$, $\mathcal{D}^{\mathcal{E}} = \{1, 3\}$, $\mathcal{D}^{\mathcal{V}} = \emptyset$, $\mathcal{Q}_4 = \langle A, C, Z\rangle$, $\lvert\mathcal{Q}_4\rvert = 55$,	
2.2:	$v = D$, $\mathcal{D}^{\mathcal{E}} = \{1, 2, 3, 7\}$, $\mathcal{D}^{\mathcal{V}} = \{A\}$, $\mathcal{Q}_5 = \langle A, D, Z\rangle$, $\lvert\mathcal{Q}_5\rvert = 30$	
2.3:	$v = C$, $\mathcal{D}^{\mathcal{E}} = \{1, 2, 3, 7, 8, 6\}$, $\mathcal{D}^{\mathcal{V}} = \{A, D\}$,	
	$\mathcal{Q}_6 = \langle A, D, C, B, Z\rangle$, $\lvert\mathcal{Q}_6\rvert = 40$	
	$\mathcal{S} = \{(\mathcal{Q}_1, A), (\mathcal{Q}_2, A), (\mathcal{Q}_3, B), (\mathcal{Q}_4, A), (\mathcal{Q}_5, D), (\mathcal{Q}_6, C)\}$,	
	$\mathcal{X} = \{\mathcal{Q}_3, \mathcal{Q}_4, \mathcal{Q}_5, \mathcal{Q}_6\}$, $\mathcal{K} = \{\mathcal{P}^1, \mathcal{P}^2, \mathcal{P}^3\}$	$\mathcal{P}^3 := \mathcal{Q}_3$

C.4 SHORTEST SETS OF DISJOINT PATHS

In this section, following [Bha99], we will discuss algorithms for finding a shortest set of K mutually disjoint paths between s and t, either edge-disjoint or vertex-disjoint. By the length of a *set of paths*, $\{\mathcal{P}_1, \mathcal{P}_2, \ldots, \mathcal{P}_K\}$, we understand the sum of the weights of all edges appearing in all these paths, i.e., $\sum_{e\in\hat{\mathcal{P}}_1\cup\hat{\mathcal{P}}_2\cup\ldots\cup\hat{\mathcal{P}}_K} K\ell_e$. We will first illustrate how to do this for a shortest pair of disjoint paths, and then show how the procedure for two paths can be extended to the case $K > 2$.

C.4.1 Shortest Sets of Edge-Disjoint Paths

We start with the problem of finding a shortest pair of edge-disjoint paths. Observe first, that the problem cannot be solved by a direct iterative application of the shortest-path algorithm, i.e., by finding a shortest path, then removing its edges from the graph, and finding

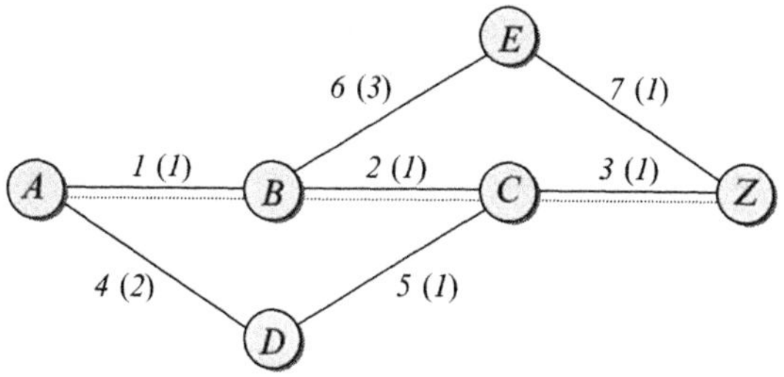

FIGURE C.3 Example Graph with the Shortest Path (Dashed Line) from A to Z of Length = 3

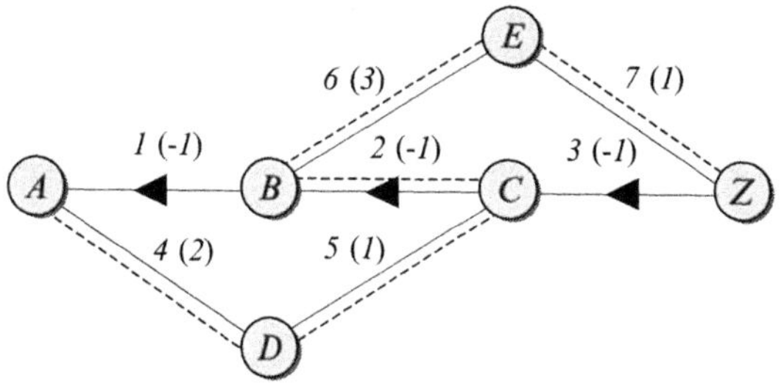

FIGURE C.4 Shortest Path is $\langle A, D, C, B, E, Z \rangle$ of Length = 6

the shortest path in the modified graph. This issue is illustrated in Figure C.3 for finding a shortest pair of edge-disjoint paths from A to Z. Following the naive procedure, after removing the shortest path $\mathcal{P}_1 = \langle A, B, C, Z \rangle$ (marked with the dashed line) the graph becomes disconnected; thus we are not able to find the solution consisting of $\mathcal{P}_2 = \langle A, B, E, Z \rangle$ and $\mathcal{P}_3 = \langle A, D, C, Z \rangle$. The proper algorithm for solving this problem, Algorithm C.6, is taken from [Bha99] (also see [Suu74]). We present this algorithm rather informally and illustrate it for source A and destination Z in the graph of Figure C.3, using Figures C.4 to C.6.

ALGORITHM C.6 Shortest Pair of Edge-Disjoint Paths

1. Find the shortest path $\mathcal{P}$ between A and Z, using one of the shortest-path algorithms, e.g., SPD or BFS ($\mathcal{P} = \langle A, B, C, Z \rangle$ in Figure C.3).
2. Replace each edge on the shortest path $\mathcal{P}$ by a single arc directed towards the source vertex A; make the weight of each such arc negative.
3. Run SPDM (or BFS) to find the shortest path $\mathcal{Q}$ from A to Z in the modified mixed graph with undirected edges and directed arcs ($\mathcal{Q} = \langle A, D, C, B, E, Z \rangle$ in Figure C.4).

4. Transform the modified graph back to the original one, and erase all the interlacing edges on paths $\mathcal{P}$ and $\mathcal{Q}$ (refer to Figure C.5) and all the edges which do not belong to any of these two paths. The remaining edges, i.e., the set of edges $(\hat{\mathcal{P}} \cup \hat{\mathcal{Q}}) \setminus (\hat{\mathcal{P}} \cap \hat{\mathcal{Q}})$, form altogether the required shortest pair of paths (refer to Figure C.6).

When more than two disjoint paths are required then the procedure of Algorithm C.6 is iterated. Let $\mathcal{H}_2 = (\hat{\mathcal{P}} \cup \hat{\mathcal{Q}}) \setminus (\hat{\mathcal{P}} \cap \hat{\mathcal{Q}})$ be the set of edges forming the shortest pair of edge-disjoint paths. To obtain the shortest set of three edge-disjoint paths ($K = 3$) we return to Step 2 and replace each edge in $\mathcal{H}_2$ by an arc directed towards source A with the negated weight. Then we again run SPDM or BFS on the modified graph to find the shortest path $\mathcal{Q}$ form A to Z. As the result we will obtain three shortest disjoint paths with the set of links $\mathcal{H}_3$ equal to $(\mathcal{H}_2 \cup \hat{\mathcal{Q}}) \setminus (\mathcal{H}_2 \cap \hat{\mathcal{Q}})$. To obtain the shortest set of four disjoint paths, we iterate the process with set $\mathcal{H}_3$ instead of $\mathcal{H}_2$, obtaining $\mathcal{H}_4$, and so on.

C.4.2 Shortest Sets of Vertex-Disjoint Paths

The vertex-disjoint shortest-path pair problem can be specified as: *given a graph $\mathcal{G}$, find a shortest pair of paths from source s to destination t with no common intermediate vertices (only source and destination are common to the two paths).* The algorithm presented as Algorithm C.7 is derived from [Bha99].

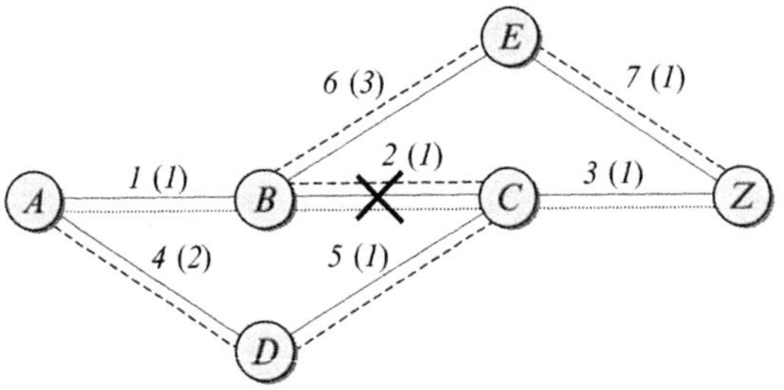

FIGURE C.5 Removing of an Interlacing Edge (B, C)

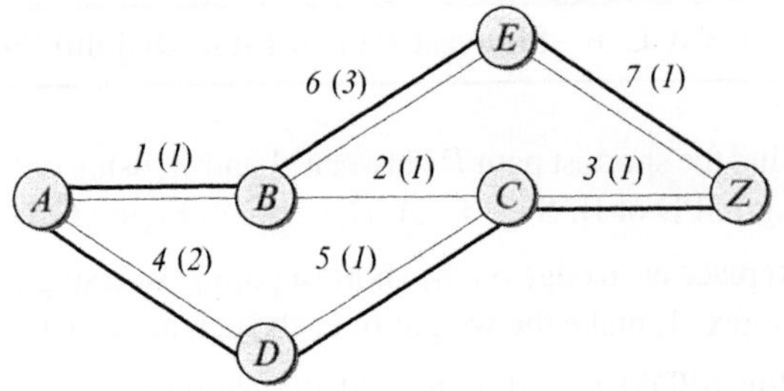

FIGURE C.6 The Shortest Pair of Edge-Disjoined Paths (Solid Lines)

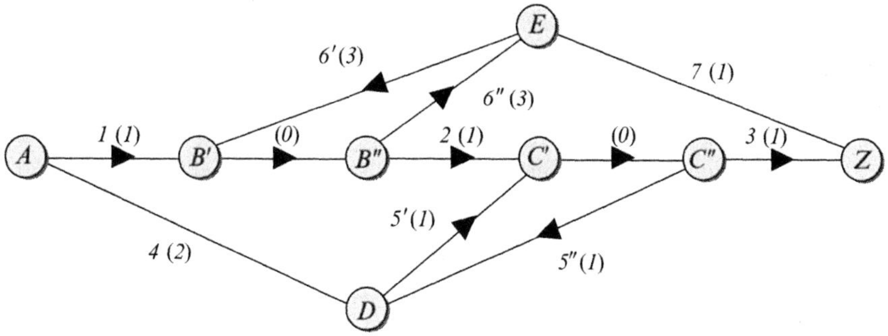

FIGURE C.7 Modified Graph with Directed Edges and Splitted Vertices

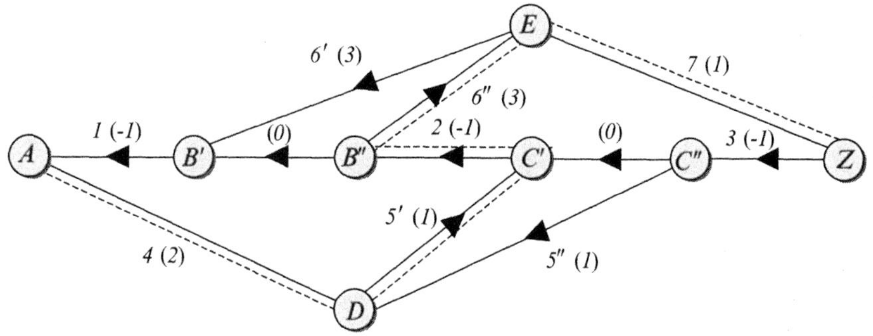

FIGURE C.8 Shortest Path is $\langle A, D, C', B'', E, Z\rangle$ of Length = 6

ALGORITHM C.7 Shortest Pair of Vertex-Disjoint Paths

1. Find the shortest path $\mathcal{P}$ between A and Z, using one of the shortest path algorithms, e.g., SPD or BFS ($\mathcal{P} = \langle A, B, C, Z\rangle$ in Figure C.3).
2. Replace each edge on the shortest path $\mathcal{P}$ by a single arc directed towards the destination vertex Z.
3. Split each intermediate vertex v on the shortest path $\mathcal{P}$ into two co-located sub-vertices v' and v'' joined by an arc of zero weight directed towards the destination vertex. For each intermediate vertex v on path $\mathcal{P}$ replace each edge not in $\hat{\mathcal{P}}$ and connected to v, by two oppositely directed arcs (of weight equal to the weight of the original edge); let one arc terminate in v' and the other originate in v'', so that the three arcs (the arc from v' to v'', the arc to v' and the arc from v'') form a cycle (refer to Figure C.7).
4. Reverse the direction of the arcs on the shortest path and negate the weight of each such arc.

5. Run SPDM (or BFS) to find the shortest path $\mathcal{Q}$ from A to Z in the modified mixed graph with undirected edges and directed arcs ($\mathcal{Q} = \langle A, D, C', B'', E, Z\rangle$ in Figure C.8).
6. Transform the modified graph back to the original one, and erase all the interlacing edges on paths $\mathcal{P}$ and $\mathcal{Q}$ (refer to Figure C.9) and all the edges which do not belong to any of these two paths. The remaining edges, i.e., the set of edges $(\hat{\mathcal{P}} \cup \hat{\mathcal{Q}}) \setminus (\hat{\mathcal{P}} \cap \hat{\mathcal{Q}})$, form altogether the required shortest pair of paths (refer to Figure C.10).

The generalization of Algorithm C.7 to the case $K > 2$ is straightforward and goes along the same lines as the the generalization of Algorithm C.6.

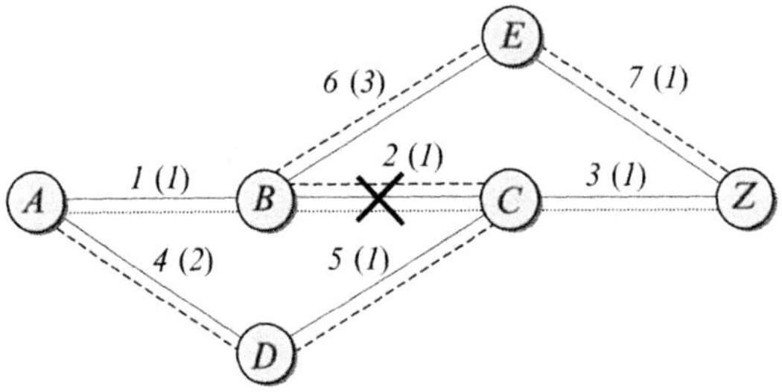

FIGURE C.9 Removing of an Interlacing Edge (B, C)

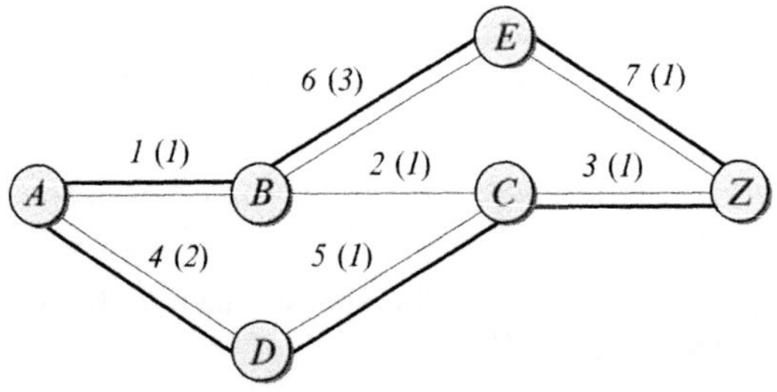

FIGURE C.10 The Shortest Pair of Vertex-Disjoined Paths (Solid Lines)

APPENDIX D

Using LP/MIP Packages

D.1 SOLVING LINEAR PROGRAMMING PROBLEMS USING MAPLE, MATLAB, AND CPLEX

Consider a network with two nodes and a demand of 10 units between them; the network is connected by two parallel paths (links) where capacity of one link is 10 while the other one is 15 (Figure D.1). The problem is to minimize the maximum utilization (or load-balance flows). If we denote the flows on two paths by x_1 and x_2, then the utilization of the first path is $x_1/10$ while that of the second path is $x_2/15$. Then, the optimization problem can be written as:

$$
\begin{array}{lllll}
\textbf{\textit{minimize}} & \max\{x_1/10, x_2/15\} & & & \\
\textbf{\textit{subject to}} & x_1 + x_2 & = & 10 & \\
 & x_1, x_2 & \geq & 0. &
\end{array}
\tag{D.1.1}
$$

By introducing the auxiliary variable r, the above problem can be written as the following linear programming (LP) problem:

$$
\begin{array}{llll}
\textbf{\textit{minimize}} & r & & \\
\textbf{\textit{subject to}} & x_1 + x_2 & = & 10 \\
 & x_1/10 & \leq & r \\
 & x_2/15 & \leq & r \\
 & x_1, x_2 & \geq & 0.
\end{array}
\tag{D.1.2}
$$

We will illustrate how to use Maple (version 8.0), Matlab (version 6.1), and CPLEX (version 8.0) to solve this example.

Maple

In Maple [Map], Problem (D.1.2) can be solved using Maple's implementation of the simplex method. In order to do that, first simplex must be invoked with the command, `with(simplex)`. The constraints are provided as a set. Maple provides the built-in definition `NONNEGATIVE` to indicate that the variables are non-negative. Note that for the above problem, it is not necessary to indicate non-negativity for r; however, we will use it in our illustration. The form of the problem followed by execution of the `minimize` command in Maple is shown below (where > is the command prompt):

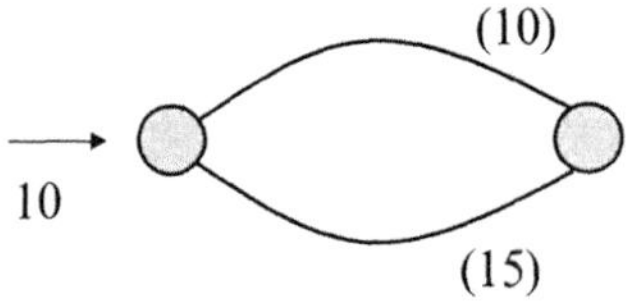

FIGURE D.1 Two-Node Network

```
> with(simplex):
> constraints := { x1 + x2 = 10, x1 / 10 <=  r,
    x2 / 15 <= r}:
> obj := r:
> minimize(obj,constraints,NONNEGATIVE);

                        {x1 = 4, x2 = 6, r = 2/5}
```

The manual page for solving LP problem can be found by searching for "simplex" in 'Topic Search' under the 'Help' menu.

Matlab

Now, we will illustrate how to solve the same problem using Matlab [MAT]. In case of Matlab, the routing `linprog` can be used for solving LP problems. The formulation which needs to be fed is a bit different since Matlab classifies the equality and inequality constraints separately using matrices and vectors, and all variables need to be on the left-hand side. For clarity, we first re-write the problem as we would want it to "look like" in Matlab:

$$
\begin{array}{lrcl}
\textbf{\textit{minimize}} & 0x_1 + 0x_2 + r & & \\
\textbf{\textit{subject to}} & x_1 + 0x_2 - 10r & \leq & 0 \\
& 0x_1 + x_2 - 15r & \leq & 0 \\
& x_1 + x_2 + 0r & = & 10 \\
& x_1, x_2 & \geq & 0.
\end{array}
\tag{D.1.3}
$$

Now, in Matlab, the problem can be entered at the prompt » and solved as follows:

```
>> obj = [ 0; 0; 1];
>> A = [1  0 -10
        0  1 -15];
>> b =   [ 0; 0];
>> Aeq = [ 1 1 0];
>> beq = [ 10 ];
>> lb = zeros(3,1);
>> [x,objval] = linprog(obj,A,b,Aeq,beq,lb)
Optimization terminated successfully.
```

```
 x =
    4.0000
    6.0000
    0.4000
objval =
    0.4000
```

Note that the second and the third arguments in `linprog` are for the matrix associated with "less than" equal to constraints and the corresponding right-hand side vector. The fourth and the fifth arguments are for the matrix associated with the equality constraints and the corresponding right-hand side vector. The fifth argument is the lower bound on the variables used to indicate that the variables are to be treated as non-negative. The first argument in the output is always the vector of variables that returns the solution. Note that, in our case, the third component of `x` for variable r. When a problem does not have any equality constraints, then they can be left empty as in

```
linprog(obj,A,b, [] , [] ,lb)
```

Matlab does allow you to find the dual multipliers in output

```
[x,objval,exitflag,output,lambda] =
                                    linprog(obj,A,b,Aeq,beq,lb)
```

where the last argument 'lambda' is to print the dual multipliers. The other two flags, 'exitflag' and 'output', describe the exit condition and information about optimization (such as number of iterations), respectively.

Finally, it may be noted that Matlab assumes that the problem provided is a minimization problem. Thus, if you have a maximization problem, then `obj` must be accordingly adjusted.

CPLEX

Now we will illustrate the same problem using CPLEX [CPL99]. First note that in CPLEX, Problem (D.1.2) can be given almost exactly how the original problem was described except for some caveats: 1) variables should be all on the left-hand side, and 2) no "divide by" entry such as `x1/10` which was done in Matlab is allowed. However, unlike Matlab, the product `*` is not required. A nice feature in CPLEX is that you can give a name for each constraint (dual multiplier). Thus, the CPLEX formulation looks like

```
Minimize
  r
Subject to
  demandflow: x1 + x2 = 10
  link1utilization: x1  -10 r <= 0
  link2utilization: x2  -15 r <= 0
End
```

If the above model is saved in a file, say, `load-balance.lp`, then in CPLEX, it can be invoked at the command prompt `CPLEX>` as follows:

```
CPLEX> read load-balance.lp
CPLEX> optimize
```

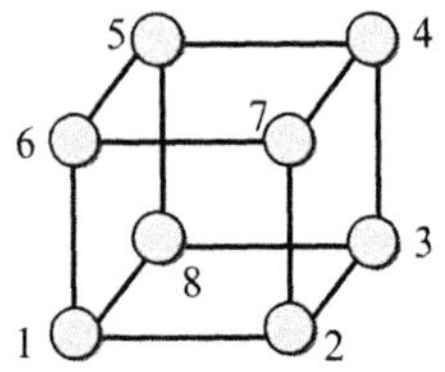

FIGURE D.2 Cube Network

```
CPLEX> display solution variables -
Variable Name              Solution Value
r                                0.400000
x1                               4.000000
x2                               6.000000
```

Note that in CPLEX, it is not necessary to indicate that the variables are non-negative. The dual solutions can be displayed by using

```
CPLEX> display solution  dual -
Constraint Name                Dual Price
demandflow                       0.040000
link1utilization                -0.040000
link2utilization                -0.040000
```

It may be noted that both Maple and Matlab also allow the use of a file to store the problem first, instead of typing the entire problem on the command line.

D.2 SOLVING (MIXED) INTEGER PROGRAMMING PROBLEMS USING CPLEX

It may be noted that Maple and Matlab cannot be used for solving problem where some or all variables take integral values. In this section, we will consider the cube network (Figure D.2), which has been considered in Chapter 9. In this case, the edges have 3 units of demand, and modular capacity is in 10 units with unit cost each. The capacity variables y is required to take integer values. They are explicitly listed as `Integer`, right before the statement `End` in the problem set-up. In the formulation listed below, we assume that each demand pair is fed with three pre-processed candidate path lists. For clarity, variables are numbered in such a way that it is easy to identify how the path is traversing from source of demand to the destination.

```
minimize
   y_12 + y_16 + y_18 + y_23 + y_27 + y_34 + y_38 + y_45
        + y_47 + y_56 + y_58 + y_67
subject to
d12:  x_1_2 + x_1_8_3_2 + x_1_6_7_2 = 3
d16:  x_1_6 + x_1_2_7_6 + x_1_8_5_6 = 3
d18:  x_1_8 + x_1_2_3_8 + x_1_6_5_8 = 3
d23:  x_2_3 + x_2_7_4_3 + x_2_1_8_3 = 3
```

```
d27:  x_2_7 + x_2_1_6_7 + x_2_3_4_7 = 3
d34:  x_3_4 + x_3_2_7_4 + x_3_8_5_4 = 3
d38:  x_3_8 + x_3_2_1_8 + x_3_4_5_8 = 3
d45:  x_4_5 + x_4_3_8_5 + x_4_7_6_5 = 3
d47:  x_4_7 + x_4_5_6_7 + x_4_3_2_7 = 3
d56:  x_5_6 + x_5_4_7_6 + x_5_8_1_6 = 3
d58:  x_5_8 + x_5_6_1_8 + x_5_4_3_8 = 3
d67:  x_6_7 + x_6_5_4_7 + x_6_1_2_7 = 3

l12:  x_1_2 + x_3_2_1_8 + x_6_1_2_7 + x_1_2_7_6 + x_1_2_3_8
    + x_2_1_6_7 + x_2_1_8_3 - 10 y_12 <= 0
l16:  x_1_6 + x_5_6_1_8 + x_2_1_6_7 + x_1_6_5_8 + x_1_6_7_2
    + x_5_8_1_6 + x_6_1_2_7 - 10 y_16 <= 0
l18:  x_1_8 + x_5_8_1_6 + x_2_1_8_3 + x_1_8_3_2 + x_1_8_5_6
    + x_5_6_1_8 + x_3_2_1_8 - 10 y_18 <= 0

l23:  x_2_3 + x_1_2_3_8 + x_4_3_2_7 + x_2_3_4_7 + x_1_8_3_2
    + x_3_2_7_4 + x_3_2_1_8 - 10 y_23 <= 0
l27:  x_2_7 + x_3_2_7_4 + x_1_2_7_6 + x_1_6_7_2 + x_2_7_4_3
    + x_6_1_2_7 + x_4_3_2_7 - 10 y_27 <= 0

l34:  x_3_4 + x_2_3_4_7 + x_5_4_3_8 + x_3_4_5_8 + x_2_7_4_3
    + x_4_3_8_5 + x_4_3_2_7 - 10 y_34 <= 0
l38:  x_3_8 + x_1_8_3_2 + x_4_3_8_5 + x_3_8_5_4 + x_2_1_8_3
    + x_5_4_3_8 + x_1_2_3_8 - 10 y_38 <= 0

l45:  x_4_5 + x_3_4_5_8 + x_6_5_4_7 + x_4_5_6_7 + x_3_8_5_4
    + x_5_4_7_6 + x_5_4_3_8 - 10 y_45 <= 0
l47:  x_4_7 + x_5_4_7_6 + x_2_7_4_3 + x_4_7_6_5 + x_3_2_7_4
    + x_6_5_4_7 + x_2_3_4_7 - 10 y_47 <= 0

l56:  x_5_6 + x_4_5_6_7 + x_1_6_5_8 + x_4_7_6_5 + x_5_6_1_8
    + x_1_8_5_6 + x_6_5_4_7 - 10 y_56 <= 0
l58:  x_5_8 + x_1_8_5_6 + x_3_8_5_4 + x_1_6_5_8 + x_3_4_5_8
    + x_4_3_8_5 + x_5_8_1_6 - 10 y_58 <= 0

l67:  x_6_7 + x_1_6_7_2 + x_4_7_6_5 + x_1_2_7_6 + x_4_5_6_7
    + x_2_1_6_7 + x_5_4_7_6 - 10 y_67 <= 0

Bounds
   0 <= y_12  <= 10
   0 <= y_16  <= 10
   0 <= y_18  <= 10
   0 <= y_23  <= 10
```

```
   0 <= y_27  <= 10
   0 <= y_34  <= 10
   0 <= y_38  <= 10
   0 <= y_45  <= 10
   0 <= y_47  <= 10
   0 <= y_56  <= 10
   0 <= y_58  <= 10
   0 <= y_67  <= 10
Integer
   y_12  y_16  y_18  y_23  y_27  y_34  y_38  y_45  y_47
   y_56  y_58  y_67
End
```

In the above description, besides declaring the capacity variables as integer, it is necessary to provide an upper bound is necessary. Without the bound, CPLEX assumes the integer variables to be binary variables. If now the routing variable, x, needs to be integer as well, then it needs to be declared under `Integer`. Similarly, if we want to solve the above problem for continuous capacity variables, then declaration with `Integer` can be removed. Finally, a nifty feature in CPLEX is that you can create a file with other comments/documentation before the declaration `minimize` and after the declaration `End` which CPLEX will ignore. Thus, to run the above model for continuous capacity variables, move `End` up to and list it before `Integer` declaration (without completely deleting `Integer` declaration from the file).

D.3 MODELING USING AMPL

AMPL [FGK02] is a powerful mathematical programming modeling language. The model can be set up almost exactly as the actual formulation. AMPL invokes separate linear or nonlinear programming solvers, such as CPLEX or MINOS [MS], to solve problems.

Consider the following model which generalizes (D.1.2) and the goal is to find flows x_{dp} and r:

$$
\begin{aligned}
&\textbf{\textit{minimize}} && r \\
&\textbf{\textit{subject to}} && \textstyle\sum_{p=1}^{P_d} x_{dp} = h_d && d = 1, 2, ..., D \\
& && \textstyle\sum_{d=1}^{D} \sum_{p=1}^{P_d} \delta_{edp} x_{dp} \le c_e r && e = 1, 2, ..., E \\
& && x_{dp}, r \text{ continuous, non-negative.}
\end{aligned}
\qquad \text{(D.3.1)}
$$

In AMPL, the above model can be written as follows:

```
# ***********************************************************
# This model captures the formulation presented above #
# ***********************************************************
# Required number of constants to understand the given
# network and its #// dimensions
```

```
param D  > 0 integer;
param E  > 0 integer;
param N  > 0 integer;
param Pd > 0 integer;
#//############################################################
set Nodes         := 1..N;
set link_nos      := 1..E;
set demand_nos    := 1..D;
set route_nos     := 1..Pd;


#Generation of links
param link_src {link_nos} within Nodes;
param link_dest {link_nos} within Nodes;
param link_capacity {link_nos} >= 0 integer;


#Generation of Demands
param demand_src {demand_nos} within Nodes;
param demand_dest {demand_nos} within Nodes;

#Generation of Routes
set Routes{demand_nos,route_nos} within link_nos;

param h {demand_nos} >= 0 integer;
##############################################################
#Generation of the variables required for optimization
#formulation
##############################################################
param delta {e in link_nos, d in demand_nos, p in route_nos}
        = if e in Routes[d,p] then 1 else 0;
##############################################################
#Variables for the problem
##############################################################
var x {d in demand_nos, p in route_nos} >= 0; var r >= 0;
##############################################################
#Objective function- Maximize the Throughput
##############################################################
minimize MaxLinkUtil: r;
##############################################################
#Constraints
##############################################################
subj to all_demands {d in demand_nos}:
    sum{p in route_nos} x[d,p] = h[d];
```

```
subj to capacity_constraints {e in link_nos}:
    sum{d in demand_nos} ( sum{p in route_nos} (delta[e,d,p]
            *x[d,p]))
            - link_capacity[e]*r <= 0;

############################################################
```

It is worth commenting that sets are not restricted to sequences of integers, but in general can contain arbitrary strings (and numbers). Also note that in some older versions of AMPL, ":=" is used (instead of "=") where `delta` is defined.

As you can see, the nice feature of AMPL is that the problem formulation is kept essentially the same. On the other hand, in the case of CPLEX, each constraint is required to be explicitly listed as we have illustrated in the previous section.

Test data for a three-node problem with two demands is given below.

```
data;
param D  := 2;
param E  := 3;
param N  := 3;
param Pd := 2;


param: link_src    link_dest   link_capacity    :
    1       1           2          20
    2       2           3          10
    3       3           1          10        ;

param: demand_src    demand_dest    h         :=
    1       1             2         12
    2       2             3         10        ;

set Routes[1,1] := 1;
set Routes[1,2] := 2 3;
set Routes[2,1] := 2;
set Routes[2,2] := 1 3;

end;
```

D.4 FINAL REMARK

Thus, many design problems can be solved using tools such as Matlab, Maple, CPLEX, and AMPL. These are only a sampling of the tools available. There are other tools that can be used, such as, Lindo, MINOS, XPRESS-LP, and lp_solve. There are also add-on LP solvers available for Microsoft Excel that can solve reasonable size problems. A good survey about linear programming software can be found in [Fou03].

LIST OF ACRONYMS

ADM	Add-Drop Multiplexer
APS	Automatic Protection Switching
ARPA	Advanced Research Project Agency
AS	Autonomous System
ASON	Automatically Switched Optical Network
ATM	Asynchronous Transfer Mode
BB	Branch-and-Bound
BC	Branch-and-Cut
BD	Benders' Decomposition
BLSR	Bi-directional Line-Switched Ring
CAPEX	Capital Expenditure
CPLA	Candidate Path List Augmentation
DAR	Dynamic Alternate Routing
DCR	Dynamically Controlled Routing
DCS	Digital Cross-connect Systems
DNHR	Dynamic Non-hierarchical Routing
DP	Dynamic Programming
DS-n	Digital Signal-n
DVU	Demand Volume Unit
DXC	Digital Cross-Connect Systems
EA	Evolutionary Algorithm
ECMP	Equal Cost Multi-Path
FD	Flow Deviation
Gbps	Gigabits per Second
GD	Greedy Descent
GoS	Grade-of-Service
GP	Gradient Projection
GRASP	Greedy Randomized Adaptive Search Procedure
GSPAR	Generalized Shortest Path Allocation Rule
IP	Internet Protocol
IP	Integer Programming
IPM	Interior Point Method
IS-IS	Intermediate System-to-Intermediate System
ISP	Internet Service Provider
KB	Kilo-bytes
LCU	Link Capacity Unit
LDP	Label Distribution Protocol
LER	Label Edge Router
LP	Linear Programming
LP	Link Protection
LR	Lagrangian Relaxation
LR	Link Restoration
LSP	Label Switched Path
LSR	Label Switch Router
Mbps	Megabits per Second
MFDLP	Minimum First Derivative Length Path
MIP	Mixed-Integer Programming
MMF	Max-Min Fairness
MPLS	Multi-Protocol Label Switching
NDP	Network Design Problem
NP	Non-deterministic Polynomial
NPC	Non-deterministic Polynomial-Complete
OC-n	Optical Carrier-n
OPEX	Operational Expenditure
OSPF	Open Shortest Path First
OTN	Optical Transport Network
OXC	Optical Cross-connects
PD	Path Diversity
PDF	Physical Distribution Frame
PDH	Plesiochronous Digital Hierarchy
PF	Proportional Fairness
PG	Path Generation
PNNI	Private (Public) Network-to-Network Interface

PoP	Point-of-Presence
PoS	Packet over SONET
PP	Path Protection
PR	Path Restoration
QoS	Qualiy-of-Service
RSVP	ReSource reserVation Protocol
RTNR	Real-Time Network Routing
SAL	Simulated Allocation
SAN	Simulated Annealing
SDH	Synchronous Digital Hierarchy
SONET	Synchronous Optical Network
SPA	Single Path Allocation
SPR	Shortest-Path Routing
STM	Synchronous Transfer Mode
STS	Synchronous Transfer Signal
TCP	Transmission Control Protocol
TCP/IP	Transmission Control Protocol/Internet Protocol
TS	Tabu Search
UPSR	Uni-directional Path-Switched Ring
VC	Virtual Circuit
VC	Virtual Container
VCAT	Virtual Concatenation
VI	Valid Inequalities
VP	Virtual Path
VPN	Virtual Private Network
VT	Virtual Tributary
WDM	Wavelength Division Multiplexing

SOLUTIONS TO SELECTED EXERCISES

Solution to 2.1

Link path formulation in link-demand-path identifier based notation

When $\hat{h}_{13} = 0$ in (2.1.1), then the paths for this demand do not need to be considered. Thus, the formulation is:

minimize

$$\boldsymbol{F} = x_{11} + 2x_{12} + x_{21} + 2x_{22}$$

subject to (constraints)

$$\begin{aligned}
&x_{11} + x_{12} = 5\\
&x_{21} + x_{22} = 8\\
&x_{11} + x_{22} \leq 10\\
&x_{12} + x_{22} \leq 10\\
&x_{12} + x_{21} \leq 15\\
&x_{11}, x_{12}, x_{21}, x_{22} \geq 0.
\end{aligned}$$

Solution to 2.5

3-node formulation

minimize

$$\boldsymbol{F} = y_1 + y_2 + y_3$$

subject to

$$\begin{aligned}
&x_{11} + x_{12} = h_1\\
&x_{21} + x_{22} = h_2\\
&x_{31} + x_{32} = h_3\\
&x_{11} + x_{22} + x_{32} \leq y_1\\
&x_{12} + x_{21} + x_{32} \leq y_2\\
&x_{12} + x_{22} + x_{31} \leq y_3\\
&x_{11}, x_{12}, x_{21}, x_{22}, x_{31}, x_{32}, y_1, y_2, y_3 \geq 0.
\end{aligned}$$

Solution to 2.6

Link weight system

For this set of capacity and demand, there is no weight system that induces feasible flow in this network. On the other hand, feasible flow is possible (but without any weight system).

Solution to 3.2

ATM design for a three-node network

minimize

$$F = y_1 + y_2 + y_3$$

subject to

$$x_{11} + x_{12} = 0.3$$
$$x_{21} + x_{22} = 0.3$$
$$x_{31} + x_{32} = 0.3$$
$$x_{11} + x_{22} + x_{32} \leq 1.54\, y_1$$
$$x_{12} + x_{21} + x_{32} \leq 1.54\, y_2$$
$$x_{12} + x_{22} + x_{31} \leq 1.54\, y_3$$
$$x_{11}, x_{12}, x_{21}, x_{22}, x_{31}, x_{32}, y_1, y_2, y_3 \geq 0$$
y_1, y_2, y_3 non-negative integer.

Solution to 3.3

Two-busy hour design formulation

We introduce a third index to identify two time-periods.

minimize

$$F = 2y_1 + y_2 + y_3 + 3y_4 + y_5$$

subject to

$$x_{111} = 15$$
$$x_{211} + x_{221} = 20$$
$$x_{311} + x_{321} = 10$$
$$x_{112} = 20$$
$$x_{212} + x_{222} = 5$$
$$x_{312} + x_{322} = 15$$
$$x_{311} \leq y_1$$
$$x_{111} + x_{321} \leq y_2$$

$x_{221} + x_{321} \leq y_3$
$x_{111} + x_{221} \leq y_4$
$x_{211} \leq y_5$
$x_{312} \leq y_1$
$x_{112} + x_{322} \leq y_2$
$x_{222} + x_{322} \leq y_3$
$x_{112} + x_{222} \leq y_4$
$x_{212} \leq y_5$
$x_{111}, x_{211}, x_{221}, x_{311}, x_{321}, x_{112}, x_{212}, x_{222}, x_{312}, x_{322} \geq 0$
$y_1, y_2, y_3, y_4, y_5 \geq 0.$

Solution to 3.4

General multi-hour design formulation

minimize

$$F = \sum_e \xi_e y_e$$

subject to

$$\sum_p x_{dpt} = h_{dt}, \quad d = 1, 2, ..., D \quad t = 1, 2, ..., T$$
$$\sum_d \sum_p \delta_{edpt} x_{dpt} \leq y_e, \quad e = 1, 2, ..., E \quad t = 1, 2, ..., T$$
$$\boldsymbol{x} \geq \mathbf{0}, \boldsymbol{y} \geq \mathbf{0}.$$

Solution to 4.3

Node-link formulation for A/PAP

MIP: **A/PAP (directed graph)** **Node-Link Formulation**

indices
- $d = 1, 2, ..., D$ demands
- $e = 1, 2, ..., E$ links (arcs)
- $v = 1, 2, ..., V$ nodes

constants
- h_d volume of demand d
- s_d source node of demand d
- t_d sink node of demand d
- c_e capacity of link e
- a_{ev} = 1 if link e originates at node v; 0, otherwise
- b_{ev} = 1 if link e terminates at node v; 0, otherwise

variables
- x_{ed} flow allocated to link e for demand d

constraints

$$\sum_e a_{ev} x_{ed} - \sum_e b_{ev} x_{ed} = \begin{cases} h_d, & \text{if } v = s_d \\ 0, & \text{if } v \neq s_d, t_d, \\ -h_d, & \text{if } v = t_d \end{cases} \quad v = 1, 2, ..., V \quad d = 1, 2, ..., D$$

$$\sum_d x_{ed} \le c_e, \quad e = 1, 2, ..., E.$$

This formulation can be extended to undirected graphs by using two oppositely directed flows for each link.

Solution to 4.5

Maximum split

***IP:* A/PAP (maximum split)** **Link-Path Formulation**

indices

$d = 1, 2, ..., D$ demands
$e = 1, 2, ..., E$ links
$p = 1, 2, ..., P_d$ candidate paths for demand d

constants

δ_{edp} = 1 if link e belongs to path p realizing demand d; 0, otherwise
h_d volume of demand d
c_e capacity of link e

variables

u_{dp} binary variable corresponding to flow allocated to path p of demand d
k the number of paths into which demand volume h_d is split

objective

maximize $\boldsymbol{F} = k$

constraints

$$\sum_p u_{dp} = k, \quad d = 1, 2, ..., D$$

$$\sum_d \sum_p \delta_{edp} u_{dp} h_d \le c_e k, \quad e = 1, 2, ..., E.$$

Note that the last relation is really $\sum_d \sum_p \delta_{edp} u_{dp} (h_d / k) \le c_e$ which would be in a non-linear form (due to division by variable k)—this can be easily changed to a linear relation as shown above.

Is it possible to write down this problem in the node-link formulation?

Solution to 4.8

Consider the MPLS tunnel model (3.2.1) presented in Section 3.2. Use this formulation as a guideline to formulate the allocation model.

Solution to 4.12

Convexity

In order to show that $f(0) = 0$ and $f(x) \geq 0$ for $x \geq 0$ is sufficient for a convex function $f(x)$ to be non-decreasing in $[0, \infty)$ suppose that x_1 and x_2 are two points such that $0 < x_1 < x_2$. Consider the convexity requirements for the points $x = 0$ and $x = x_2$, i.e.,

$$\alpha f(0) + (1-\alpha) f(x_2) \geq f(\alpha \cdot 0 + (1-\alpha) x_2).$$

Simplifying, we get:

$$(1-\alpha) f(x_2) \geq f((1-\alpha) x_2)$$

Clearly, we find an α such that $x_1 = (1-\alpha)x_2$, thus, we have

$$f(x_2) \geq (1-\alpha) f(x_2) \geq f(x_1).$$

Solution to 5.3

Telecommunication example

Let x_1 be the number of first medium and x_2 be the number of second medium. Then the T1-bandwidth maximization problem can be written as:

$$\begin{array}{lrcl} \textbf{\textit{maximize}} & 3x_1 + 5x_2 & & \\ \textbf{\textit{subject to}} & 8x_1 + 4x_2 & \leq & 4800 \\ & 10x_1 + 70x_2 & \leq & 38500 \\ & x_1 & \leq & 500 \\ & x_1, x_2 & \geq & 0. \end{array}$$

The optimal solution is $(x_1^*, x_2^*) = (350, 500)$.

Solution to 5.15

A "Nasty" Example for PG

The optimal solution of A/ALC consists in assigning all demand volumes to their direct one-link paths, leading to the optimal primal objective $\boldsymbol{F}^* = 2$. If we start Algorithm 5.9

with the routing list for demand $d = 1$ consisting of only one (direct) path $\mathcal{P}_1$, then we will immediately get the optimal solution. However, if we do not know this and continue to apply the algorithm, then it can happen that we will be forced to check all the allowable two-link paths for demand 1 before the algorithm terminates. This is caused by the degenerate basic variables in the optimal solutions of the consecutive instances of the considered LP problems.

If for the first problem (with only path $\mathcal{P}_1$ on the routing list of demand $d = 1$) the slack variables s_e (equal to 0) associated with constraints (5.4.11c) for $e > 1$ are in the basic optimal solution, then we get $\pi_e^* = \lambda_e^* = 0$ for $e > 1$, and $\pi_1^* = \lambda_1^* = 1$. Hence, a new path, for example, path $\mathcal{P}_2$, will be generated and added to the routing list of demand $d = 1$, since it has length $\zeta_1(\boldsymbol{\pi}^*) = 0 < \lambda_1^* = 1$. In the next step, the optimal basis will be changed, resulting in a new basic solution with the same $\boldsymbol{F}^*$ (equal to 2) and with the corresponding optimal dual solution $\pi_1^* = \pi_2^* = 1$ and $\pi_e^* = 0$ for $e > 2$. In the consecutive step, path $\mathcal{P}_3$ will be added, and so on, until all the paths for $d = 1$ will be examined. Finally, after examining all the paths available for demand $d = 1$ we arrive at the full instance of problem A/ALC with the optimal dual solution $\pi_1^* = \pi_2^* = \pi_4^* = \ldots = \pi^*{}_{2M-2} = 1$, $\pi_3^* = \pi_5^* = \ldots = \pi_{2M-1}^* = 0$, and $\lambda_d^* = 1$ for all d ($d = 1, 2, \ldots, 2M - 1$). Notice that the stopping criterion based on (5.4.17) is fulfilled only for this final instance of the considered problem: $\boldsymbol{F}(\boldsymbol{z}^*) = W(\boldsymbol{\pi}^*, \zeta_d(\boldsymbol{\pi}^*)) = 2$. For all the intermediate instances, we have $\boldsymbol{F}(\boldsymbol{z}^*) = 2$ and $W(\boldsymbol{\pi}^*, \zeta_d(\boldsymbol{\pi}^*)) = -10$.

Note that the disadvantageous situation shown in this example can be avoided by solving the following dual LP problem of maximizing the values of optimal $\boldsymbol{\pi}$ multipliers at the beginning of Step 2:

maximize	$G(\boldsymbol{\pi}) = \sum_e \pi_e$		
subject to	$\sum_d h_d \lambda_d - \sum_e c_e \pi_e = 2$	(because $\boldsymbol{F}^* = 2$)	
	$\lambda_d \leq \sum_e \delta_{edp} \pi_e$	$d = 1, 2, \ldots, D$	$p = 1, 2, \ldots, P_d$
	$0 \leq \pi_e \leq 1$	$e = 1, 2, \ldots, E$	
	$z_e^* > 0 \Rightarrow \pi_e = 1$	$e = 1, 2, \ldots, E$	(these π_e:s are fixed)
	$s_e^* > 0 \Rightarrow \pi_e = 0$	$e = 1, 2, \ldots, E$	(these π_e:s are fixed)
	λ_d and $\pi_e \geq 0$ are variables.		

The first constraint assures that solutions to the above problem are optimal dual variables for the considered instance of problem A/ALC. The (unique) solution of this problem will set all π_e:s equal to 1 and make the algorithm terminate after one iteration (instead of M). Observe that using this solution makes sense as for the considered LP problem any primal solution and any dual optimal solutions form a saddle point (this is true for all LP problems, refer to Section A.7 of Appendix A) so the assumptions of Proposition 5.1 are satisfied.

To end this example we observe that if the capacity of the last two links ($e = 2M-2$ and $e = 2M - 1$) is increased from 10 to 12 (not altering the rest of the data) then the feasible solution (with all links saturated) of the original pure allocation problem A/PAP will be eventually found by the CPLA algorithm; this will also be achieved in the last iteration, after examining the last allowable path $\mathcal{P}_M = \{2M - 2, 2M - 1\}$ for $d = 1$ by assigning flow $x_{1M} = 2$ to it, and flow $x_{11} = 10$ to path $\mathcal{P}_1$.

Solution to 5.17

Proof of the fact from Example 4.3

Assign the entire demand volume of each demand d to one of its shortest paths with respect to the number of links. If in the resulting (non-bifurcated) solution all links are saturated (i.e. $\sum_d \sum_p \delta_{edp} x_{dp} \geq c_e$ *for* $e = 1, 2, ..., E$*) and at least one link is overloaded (i.e.,* $\sum_d \sum_p \delta_{edp} x_{dp} > c_e$ *for some e), then A/PAP is infeasible.*

Proof:

The considered flow allocation is by assumption non-bifurcated and therefore it is trivially the unique feasible (hence optimal) solution of the instance of A/ALC (5.4.11) with the list of allowable paths, for each demand d, reduced to the selected shortest (with respect to the number of links) path ($P_d = 1$). Now consider the multipliers $\pi_e = 1$ for $e = 1, 2, ..., E$, and $\lambda_d = \sum_e \pi_e \delta_{ed1}$ for $d = 1, 2, ..., D$. These multipliers are obviously optimal since the corresponding value of the dual function $W(\boldsymbol{\pi}, \boldsymbol{\lambda}) = \sum_d \lambda_d h_d - \sum_e \pi_e c_e$ is equal to $\sum_e z_e$—the minimum of the primal function for the restricted problems (z_e are of course unique). This means that for no demand there exists a path shorter than the currently used one because the single allowable paths are by assumption the shortest paths with respect to the unit weights. Hence, by Proposition 5.1, the solution cannot be improved by adding new paths. But since we have assumed that at least one link is overloaded the solution is infeasible. ■

Solution to 6.1

Location Example

For SS7 node location design formulation, the only change that is needed is to modify (6.1.1b) in the following way:

$$\sum_j u_{ij} = 2, \qquad i = 1, 2, ..., N.$$

Solution to 7.1

Diamond Network

For demand volume h, with hop-count metric, the average delay in the original network would be minimum if we use the ECMP rule (i.e., split load equally among the two paths), and is given by $\frac{1}{h}\frac{4 \cdot h/2}{(100 - h/2)}$. In the upgraded network, the traffic would take the direct link path; thus, the delay is $\frac{1}{h}\frac{h}{100-h}$. Since, we want the delay in the upgraded network to be less, we require

$$\frac{4 \cdot h/2}{(100 - h/2)} > \frac{h}{100 - h}.$$

Simplifying, we get $h < 66\frac{2}{3}$.

Solution to 7.15

Use of piece-wise linear function for the Transient Failure case

First consider model (7.1.11) and compare with (7.9.1). In the former model, the term r_e was per link since the objective was to minimize sum of link congestions. In this case, we need a set of inequalities (due to the Fortz-Thorup function) for link maximization in normal state, e.g. one of them would be

$$r \geq 5,000\, \underline{y}_{e0} - \frac{16,318}{3} c_e$$

where $\underline{y}_{e0} = \sum_d \sum_p \delta_{edp} x_{dp0}(\boldsymbol{w})$, and assuming $\gamma_e = 1$. Similarly, for a failure state s, we need another similar set, one of which would be

$$\bar{r} \geq 5,000\, \underline{y}_{es} - \frac{16,318}{3} \alpha_{es} c_e.$$

Solution to 8.5

Non-Blocking Test NBT2

The following non-blocking test, referred to as NBT2, is based on the simplex tableau and can be found in a more precise form in [Beh81]. Note that while solving NBT1 we in fact are not interested in finding the maximum of (8.2.3a), but only in checking whether the initial value $X_d = t^*$ of (8.2.3a) can be increased. This can be done directly by examining the simplex tableau corresponding to the final solution of Step 0 (or Step 2) of Algorithm 8.3. We just have to examine the slack variable s_d associated with the constraint in (8.2.2c) (or (8.2.4c)) corresponding to the currently tested demand $d \in Z_1$. NBT2 is based on the following procedure.

- If the slack variable s_d is positive (and hence it is a basic variable) then X_d can be (obviously) increased.
- If the slack variable s_d is a degenerate basic variable (equal to 0) then one transformation of the tableau is performed. The last row of the tableau (corresponding to the objective function) is substituted with a row induced by the new objective

  maximize s_d

which is equivalent to (8.2.3a) because according to the adjusted constraint (8.2.3c)

$$t^* + s_d = X_d$$

(note that $t_d = t^*$ for the considered demand d) any increase of s_d results in the same increase of X_d. The new row contains zeros in all columns except for the column corresponding to the considered variable s_d - the element in this column is equal to 1. This "1" has to be transformed into "0", resulting in possibly many non-zero elements appearing in the columns of the non-basic variables. If there are no positive elements, then the considered demand is blocking. Otherwise, one step (or sometimes more steps - see the next case) of the simplex algorithm will (quickly) reveal whether s_d can be increased and hence whether demand d is really non-blocking.

- If the slack variable s_d is non-basic (and hence equal to 0) then its relative cost factor with respect to the above objective function is equal to 1, and all the rest of the relative cost factors equal to 0. Hence, according to the simplex algorithm we try to increase the value of of the objective by introducing s_d to the basis. If for each degenerate basic variable the corresponding coefficient a_{ij} in the tableau (where i is the index of the degenerate basic variable, and j is the index of the considered slack variable) is non-positive then s_d can be increased and hence demand d is non-blocking. Otherwise we introduce s_d to the basic solution (replacing one of the degenerate basic variables, which becomes non-basic) without increasing the objective and continue the simplex steps; this will (quickly) reveal whether or not s_d can be really increased.

NBT2 can be useful if we have direct access to the simplex tableau from the procedure implementing Algorithm 8.3, and if we can perform the simplex steps one by one.

Solution to 8.7

Proof of Proposition 8.5

Proof:

Let $V(\boldsymbol{\lambda}, \boldsymbol{\pi})$ be the dual function of the maximal problem for AMMF, i.e. the instance of problem AMMF with maximal candidate path lists (containing all possible allowable paths). Dual functions $V(\boldsymbol{\lambda}, \boldsymbol{\pi})$ and $W(\boldsymbol{\lambda}, \boldsymbol{\pi})$ (function $W(\boldsymbol{\lambda}, \boldsymbol{\pi})$ is the dual function of the considered restricted problem with limited routing lists) are defined by formula (8.2.9a), and differ only by the domains $Dom(V)$ and $Dom(W)$, respectively (for the definition of the domain of the dual function see Section A.5 of Appendix A). $Dom(V)$ is a subset of $Dom(W)$, $Dom(V) \subseteq Dom(W)$, as both domains are determined by constraints (8.2.9b) to (8.2.9d), and $Dom(V)$ is determined by constraints (8.2.9c) for all allowable paths, not only for the paths on the candidate path lists, as in the case of $Dom(W)$.

Consider the dual vectors $\boldsymbol{\lambda}^0$ and $\boldsymbol{\pi}^0$ of the saddle point of the restricted problem, $(\boldsymbol{\lambda}^0, \boldsymbol{\pi}^0) \in Dom(W)$. If $\lambda_d^0 = \zeta_d(\boldsymbol{\pi}^0)$ for $d = 1, 2, \ldots, D$, then also $(\boldsymbol{\lambda}^0, \boldsymbol{\pi}^0) \in Dom(V)$ and this implies that the optimal multipliers $(\boldsymbol{\lambda}^0, \boldsymbol{\pi}^0)$ of the restricted problem also maximize the dual function of the maximal problem. (Of course, the maximum of $V(\boldsymbol{\lambda}^0, \boldsymbol{\pi}^0)$ cannot be greater than the maximum of $W(\boldsymbol{\lambda}^0, \boldsymbol{\pi}^0)$ because $Dom(V) \subseteq Dom(W)$.) Hence, the primal solution $(t^0, \boldsymbol{x}^0)$ is optimal in the wider sense, proving the first part of the proposition.

Now suppose that for some demand $d' \in Z$ (it doesn't matter if $d' \in Z_0$ or $d' \in Z_1$) the length $\zeta_{d'}(\boldsymbol{\pi}^0)$ of path $\mathcal{P}_{d'}$ is strictly smaller than $\lambda^0_{d'}$, and consider a new problem, AMMF*, obtained for some fixed $\varepsilon > 0$ from the original restricted problem AMMF by the following two modifications:

$$t \leq \textstyle\sum_j x_{d'j} + \varepsilon$$
$$c_e := c_e - \psi_e \varepsilon \quad e = 1, 2, \ldots, E$$

where for each e, $\psi_e = 1$ if link e belongs to path $\mathcal{P}_{d'}$, and $\psi_e = 0$ otherwise. In other words, problem AMMF* is obtained from AMMF by assigning fixed flow $x = \varepsilon$ realizing demand d' to path $\mathcal{P}_{d'}$. It is easy to show that the relation between the dual function $W(\boldsymbol{\lambda}, \boldsymbol{\pi})$ of AMMF and the dual function $W^*(\boldsymbol{\lambda}, \boldsymbol{\pi})$ of AMMF* is as follows:

$$Dom(W^*) = Dom(W)$$
$$W^*(\boldsymbol{\lambda}, \boldsymbol{\pi}) = W(\boldsymbol{\lambda}, \boldsymbol{\pi}) - \sigma\varepsilon$$

where $\sigma = \lambda_{d'} - \zeta_{d'}(\boldsymbol{\pi})$.

This means that if for some $\varepsilon > 0$ dual variables $(\boldsymbol{\lambda}^0, \boldsymbol{\pi}^0)$ are optimal for both AMMF and AMMF*, then introducing path $\mathcal{P}_{d'}$ to the routing list of demand d' and assigning flow $x = \varepsilon$ to it, will decrease the primal objective function by $\sigma^0\varepsilon$, where $\sigma^0 = \lambda^0_d - \zeta_{d'}(\boldsymbol{\pi}^0)$. This is for instance the case when $(t^0, \boldsymbol{x}^0)$ is an optimal basic simplex solution of AMMF, $(\boldsymbol{\lambda}^0, \boldsymbol{\pi}^0)$ are the corresponding optimal simplex multipliers, and AMMF* has the same optimal simplex basis as AMMF. It can happen, however, that the optimal basis corresponding to $(t^0, \boldsymbol{x}^0)$ may not be optimal for AMMF* for all $\varepsilon > 0$ in some neighborhood of $\varepsilon = 0$; then using path $\mathcal{P}_{d'}$ may not decrease the objective function $-t$ in (8.2.5a). ■

Solution to 8.8

Candidate path lists augmentation for Problem AMMF (8.2.5)

Step 0: Assume initial (short) lists of allowable paths and form the initial instance of Problem (8.2.5).

Step 1: Solve (8.2.5) (using the basic solution of the previously solved problem as the starting point, provided Step 1 is entered from Step 3).

Step 2: Let $(t^0, \boldsymbol{x}^0; \boldsymbol{\lambda}^0, \boldsymbol{\pi}^0)$ be a saddle point of the problem. Using the optimal multipliers $\boldsymbol{\pi}^0$ as link weights, run a shortest path algorithm to determine a shortest path for each demand d.

Step 3: If for no demand d there exists a path with the length shorter than λ^0_d then the solution of (8.2.5) is optimal in the wider sense so the procedure terminates. If such paths exist, then form a new instance of (8.2.5) by adding these paths to the lists of allowable paths. Go to Step 1.

Solution to 9.8

Ineffective capacity protection

The reader is first asked to draw the considered network with two nodes, two parallel links between these two nodes, and with two parallel demands. Recall that the capacities of the two links are $c_1 = 1$ and $c_2 = n$, and that the two demand volumes are $h_1 = 1$ and $h_2 = n$. We assume that demand $d = 1$ uses only one path: $\mathcal{P}_{11} = \{1\}$, and demand $d = 2$ also uses only one path: $\mathcal{P}_{21} = \{2\}$. We also assume that each of the two links can totally fail at a time.

It is then clear that when "large" link $e = 2$ fails then the two demands must share the surviving capacity $c_1 = 1$. This share must be in proportion to the normal demand volumes and hence the demands actually realized when link $e = 2$ fails are $h'_1 = 1/(n+1)$ and $h'_2 = n/(n+1)$. So in fact when we strictly require 100% protection of demand volumes we have to reduce them (dramatically) from $h_1 = 1$ and $h_2 = n$ to $h'_1 = 1/(n+1)$ and $h'_2 = n/(n+1)$.

To realize these reduced demand volumes in the situation when link $e = 1$ fails we need 1 LCU on the second link. This means that the actually used capacity is equal to 2 LCU. Thus, the unused capacity is equal to $n - 1$ LCU and the percentage of the unused capacity is equal to $100(n-1)/(n+1)\%$, i.e., almost to 100% for large n.

Although this example is quite impractical, it illustrates the problem of unused capacity which appears when we introduce protection into the unprotected network. On the other hand, we should have in mind the fact that not all demand *must be* protected and then the whole surviving capacity can be in fact always used.

Solution to 10.9

Cut inequality

To find the cut inequality corresponding to node $v = 1$ for the network in Figure 10.1 we use the data in Tables 10.1 and 10.5. The inequality is as follows:

$$y_1 + y_2 + y_{18} \geq 40.$$

Solution to 10.10

Non-cut inequality

In the considered case inequality (10.3.11) takes the form:

$$\textstyle\sum_e y_e \geq \sum_d \lambda_d^* h_d$$

where λ_d^* is the length of the shortest path for demand d in terms of number of hops. If we assume that $p(d)$ is the number of such a shortest path for demand d then we may rewrite the above inequality as:

$$\sum_e (\sum_d \delta_{edp(d)} h_d) \leq \sum_e y_e$$

where $\underline{y}_e = \sum_d \delta_{edp(d)} h_d$ is the load of link e resulting from the allocation of demand volumes on paths $p(d)$. Hence, the first inequality expresses the fact that any of the shortest path allocations cannot produce the total link load greater than the total link capacity. This inequality is not the cut-type inequality.

Note that the above inequality is different than the system of inequalities considered in Example 4.3 and Exercise 5.17. This system when applied as a necessary condition for feasibility of the capacity vector $\boldsymbol{y} = (y_1, y_2, ..., y_E)$ would require that

$$\sum_d \delta_{edp(d)} h_d \geq y_e \qquad e = 1, 2, ..., E$$

and $\sum_d \delta_{edp(d)} h_d > y_e$ for at least one e cannot happen.

Solution to 11.8

Lagrangian relaxation

We will highlight here the main parts that are relevant in the development of the LR-based dual approach. For Problem (11.2.10), consider LR with respect to constraint (11.2.10c) to arrive at the Lagrangian:

$$\begin{aligned} L(\boldsymbol{u}, \boldsymbol{\pi}) &= \sum_\tau \sum_d \sum_p \left(\zeta_{dp\tau} u_{dp\tau} \right) + \sum_\tau \sum_d \Delta \tilde{u}_{d\tau} \\ &\quad + \sum_\tau \sum_e \pi_{e\tau} (\sum_{t \leq \tau} \sum_d L_{d\tau} \sum_p \delta_{edtp} u_{dpt} - C_{e\tau}). \end{aligned}$$

The dual function $W(\boldsymbol{\pi}) = \min_u L(\boldsymbol{u}, \boldsymbol{\pi})$. In order to compute $W(\boldsymbol{\pi})$ at dual iteration, and for given,$\boldsymbol{\pi}$, we need to solve the following simple integer programming problem that is separable for each τ and d:

$$\begin{aligned} \textbf{\textit{minimize}}_{\boldsymbol{u}} \quad & \sum_\tau \sum_d \sum_p \left(\zeta_{dp\tau} u_{dp\tau} + L_{d\tau} (\sum_{t \leq \tau} \pi_{et}) \delta_{ed\tau p} \right) u_{dp\tau} + \sum_\tau \sum_d \Delta \tilde{u}_{d\tau} \\ \textbf{\textit{subject to}} \quad & \sum_p u_{dp\tau} + \tilde{u}_{d\tau} = H_{d\tau} \\ & \boldsymbol{u} \geq \mathbf{0} \text{ and integer.} \end{aligned}$$

If $\bar{\boldsymbol{u}}$ is such a solution, then a sub-gradient is given by

$$\frac{\partial W}{\partial \pi_{e\tau}} = \sum_{t \leq \tau} \sum_d L_{d\tau} \sum_p \delta_{edtp} \bar{u}_{dpt} - C_{e\tau}.$$

Solution to 12.3

Two-layer mixed design with non-bifurcated flow

Consider the modification of Problem (12.1.10) where non-bifurcated routing is required in the upper layer. We introduce u_{ed} as the binary variables for the upper layer. For lower layer, let $\hat{z}_{ge}$ be binary variables for upper layer demand e using the lower layer link g. Then, the problem can be formulated as:

$$\sum_e a_{ev'} u_{ed} - \sum_e b_{ev'} u_{ed} = \begin{cases} 1 & \text{if } v' = s_d \\ 0 & \text{if } v' \neq s_d, t_d \\ -1 & \text{if } v' = t_d, \quad v' = 1, 2, \dots, V' \quad d = 1, 2, \dots, D \end{cases}$$

$$\sum_d h_d u_{ed} \leq y_e, \quad e = 1, 2, \dots, E$$

$$\sum_g A_{gv''} \hat{z}_{ge} - \sum_g B_{gv''} \hat{z}_{ge} = \begin{cases} 1 & \text{if } v'' = S_e \\ 0 & \text{if } v'' \neq S_e, T_e \\ -1 & \text{if } v'' = T_e, \quad v'' = 1, 2, \dots, V' + V'' \\ & \qquad e = 1, 2, \dots, E \end{cases}$$

$$\sum_e y_e \hat{z}_{ge} \leq c_g, \quad g = 1, 2, \dots, G.$$

Note that this is a non-linear formulation due to the product term $y_e \hat{z}_{ge}$ resulting in a mixed-integer non-linear programming problem.

The product term in the above formulation can be easily avoided. To show this, we keep the meaning of z_{ge} as in the original problem (12.1.10). Let H be a large number. We now introduce the following binary variables:

- $\bar{r}_{gv''e}$ binary variable associated with lower link g, lower layer node v'', and upper layer demand e
- $\underline{r}_{gv''e}$ binary variable associated with lower link g, lower layer node v'', and upper layer demand e

Then the last two sets of constraints (out of the four sets of constraints) in the above formulation can be replaced by the following six sets of constraints to obtain a mixed-integer (linear) programming formulation for the two-layer mixed design with non-bifurcated flow in both layers.

$$\sum_g A_{gv''} z_{ge} - \sum_g B_{gv''} z_{ge} = \begin{cases} y_e & \text{if } v'' = S_e \\ 0 & \text{if } v'' \neq S_e, T_e \\ -y_e & \text{if } v'' = T_e, \quad v'' = 1, 2, \dots, V' + V'' \\ & \qquad e = 1, 2, \dots, E \end{cases}$$

$$\sum_g A_{gv''} \bar{r}_{gv''e} = 1, \quad v'' = 1, 2, \dots, V'' \quad e = 1, 2, \dots, E$$

$$\sum_g B_{gv''} \underline{r}_{gv''e} = 1, \quad v'' = 1, 2, \dots, V'' \quad e = 1, 2, \dots, E$$

$$A_{gv''} z_{ge} \leq H A_{gv''} \bar{r}_{gv''e} \quad g = 1, 2, ..., G \quad v'' = 1, 2, ..., V'' \quad e = 1, 2, ..., E$$

$$B_{gv''} z_{ge} \leq H B_{gv''} \underline{r}_{gv''e} \quad g = 1, 2, ..., G \quad v'' = 1, 2, ..., V'' \quad e = 1, 2, ..., E$$

$$\textstyle\sum_e z_{ge} \leq c_g, \quad g = 1, 2, \ldots, G.$$

A good additional exercise would be determine additional number of variables and constraints needed with the mixed-integer linear programming formulation over the mixed-integer non-linear programming formulation.

Solution to 12.6

Two-layer network with bifurcated optimal flows

Consider the two-node, three-link network from Figure 2.10. Assume now that this network is the lower layer of the two-layer network with the upper layer composed of just one link $e = 1$. We change the labeling of links in the lower layer to $g = 1, 2, 3$ and leave the rest of notation unchanged. The instance of TLDP for this network is as follows:

$$\begin{array}{lllll}
\textbf{\textit{minimize}} & F = u_1 + u_2 + u_3 & & & \\
\textbf{\textit{subject to}} & x_{11s} = 3 & & & s = 0, 1, 2, 3 \\
& y_{1s} = 3 & & & s = 0, 1, 2, 3 \\
& z_{11s} + z_{12s} + z_{13s} = y_{1s} & & & s = 0, 1, 2, 3 \\
& z_{110} \leq u_1, & z_{120} \leq u_2, & z_{130} \leq u_3 & \\
& z_{111} \leq 0, & z_{121} \leq u_2, & z_{131} \leq u_3 & \\
& z_{112} \leq u_1, & z_{122} \leq 0, & z_{132} \leq u_3 & \\
& z_{113} \leq u_1, & z_{123} \leq u_2, & z_{133} \leq 0 & \\
& \text{all variables continuous and non-negative.} & & &
\end{array}$$

Now you can check that any optimal solution must always have bifurcated lower-layer flows.

Solution to 13.4

Maximization of Lagrangian in Example 13.2

One of the results not derived in Example 13.2 is the formula for the maximum of the Lagrangian. Assuming $\lambda_0 = 0$, the Lagrangian can be written as:

$$L(x; \lambda_1, \lambda_2, \lambda_3) = (\lambda_1 + \lambda_2) \log(2 - x) + \lambda_3 \log x.$$

The domain of the Lagrangian is given by the following conditions:

$$0 \leq x \leq 2, \lambda_1 + \lambda_2 + \lambda_3 = 1, \lambda_1 \geq 0, \lambda_2 \geq 0, \lambda_3 \geq 0.$$

Now we find that for any fixed $\boldsymbol{\lambda}$ the derivative of $L(x; \lambda_1, \lambda_2, \lambda_3)$ with respect to x is equal to

$$dL(x; \lambda_1, \lambda_2, \lambda_3)/dx = -(\lambda_1 + \lambda_2)/(2 - x) + \lambda_3/x.$$

Putting $dL(x; \lambda_1, \lambda_2, \lambda_3)/dx$ equal to 0 we obtain:

$$x\lambda_1 + x\lambda_2 + x\lambda_3 = 2\lambda_3$$

which (using the assumption $\lambda_1+\lambda_2+\lambda_3 = 1$) means that $x = 2\lambda_3$ is the only stationary point and the global maximum of the Lagrangian in interval $[0, 2]$ for any given λ_3, $0 \leq \lambda_3 \leq 1$.

The reader is now asked to continue and compute the minimum of the dual function $W(\lambda)$ for $0 \leq \lambda \leq 1$.

BIBLIOGRAPHY

[AC96] A. Arulambalam and X. Q. Chen. Allocating fair rates for available bit rate service in ATM networks. *IEEE Communications Magazine*, 34(11):92–100, November 1996.

[ACE⁺02] D. Awduche, A. Chiu, A. Elwalid, I. Widjaja, and X. Xiao. Overview and principles of Internet traffic engineering. *Internet RFC 3272*, May 2002. http://www.ietf.org/rfc/rfc3272.txt.

[ACL94] G. R. Ash, K. K. Chan, and J.-F. Labourdette. Analysis and design of fully shared networks. In *Proc. 14th International Teletraffic Congress (ITC14)*, Antibes, France, June 1994.

[ACM81] G. R. Ash, R. H. Cardwell, and R. P. Murray. Design and optimization of networks with dynamic routing. *Bell System Technical Journal*, 60:1787–1820, 1981.

[ACM91] G. R. Ash, F. Chang, and D. Medhi. Robust traffic design for dynamic routing networks. In *Proc. IEEE Conference on Computer Communications (INFOCOM'91)*, pages 508–514, Bal Harbour, Florida, April 1991.

[AFPR93] C. A. Anderson, F. Fraughnaugh, M. Parker, and J. Ryan. Path assignment for call routing: An application of tabu search. *Annals of Operations Research*, 41:301–312, 1993.

[AG99] A. Altman and J. Gondzio. Regularized symmetric indefinite systems in interior point methods for linear and quadratic optimization. *Optimization Methods and Software*, 11-12:275–302, 1999.

[Aga89] Y. Agarwal. An algorithm for designing survivable networks. *AT&T Technical Journal*, 68(3):64–76, May/June 1989.

[AGMX96] E. D. Andersen, J. Gondzio, C. Mészáros, and X. Xu. Implementation of interior point methods for large scale linear programming. In T. Terlaky, editor, *Interior Point Methods in Mathematical Programming*, pages 189–252. Kluwer Academic Publishers, 1996.

[AGW98] D. Alevras, M. Grötschel, and R. Wessäly. Cost-efficient network synthesis from leased lines. *Annual of Operations Research*, 76:1–20, 1998.

[AK01] J. Arabas and S. Kozdrowski. Applying and evolutionary algorithm to telecommunication network design. *IEEE Transactions on Evolutionary Computation*, 5(4):309–322, 2001.

[AKK81] G. R. Ash, A. H. Kafker, and K. Krishnan. Servicing and real-time control of networks with dynamic routing. *Bell System Technical Journal*, 60:1821–1845, 1981.

[AKW⁺99] G. Apostolopoulos, S. Kama, D. Williams, R. Guerin, A. Orda, and T. Przygienda. QoS routing mechanisms and OSPF extensions. *Internet RFC 2676*, August 1999. http://www.ietf.org/rfc/rfc2676.txt.

[AL97] E. Aarts and J. K. Lenstra. *Local Search in Combinatorial Optimization*. John Wiley & Sons, 1997.

[Alt94] K. Altinkemer. Topological design of ring networks. *Computers and Operations Research*, 21:421–431, 1994.

[AMA+99] D. Awduche, J. Malcolm, J. Agogbua, M. O'Dell, and J. McManus. Requirements for traffic engineering over MPLS. *Internet RFC 2702*, September 1999. http://www.ietf.org/rfc/rfc2702.txt.

[AMO93] R. K. Ahuja, T. L. Magnanti, and J. B. Orlin. *Network Flows: Theory, Algorithms, and Applications*. Prentice Hall, 1993.

[AN03] R. Aubin and H. Nasrallah. MPLS fast reroute and optical mesh protection: A comparative analysis of the capacity required for packet link protection. In *Proc. Design of Reliable Communication Networks (DRCN'2003)*, pages 349–355, Banff, Canada, 2003.

[Ash97] G. R. Ash. *Dynamic Routing in Telecommunication Networks*. McGraw-Hill, 1997.

[Ass78] A. A. Assad. Multicommodity network flows: A survey. *Networks*, 8:37–91, 1978.

[AV03] F. Alvelos and J. M. Valério de Carvalho. Comparing branch-and-price algorithms for the unsplittable multicommodity flow problem. In *Proc. International Network Optimization Conference (INOC'2003)*, pages 7–12, 2003.

[AY92] K. Altinkemer and Z. Yu. Topological design of wide area communication networks. *Annals of Operations Research*, 36:365–382, 1992.

[Bal89] A. Balakrishnan. A dual-ascent procedure for large-scale uncapacitated network design. *Operations Research*, 37(5):716–740, 1989.

[Bar64] P. Baran. On distributed communication networks. *IEEE Trans. on Communications Systems*, CS-12:1–9, 1964.

[BB96] G. Brassard and P. Bratley. *Fundamentals of Algorithmics*. Prentice-Hall, 1996.

[BB03] M. Belaidouni and W. Ben-Ameur. Super-additive approach to solve the minimum cost single path routing problem: Preliminary results. In *Proc. International Network Optimization Conference (INOC'2003)*, pages 67–71, 2003.

[BBD98] G. Bannock, R. E. Baxter, and E. Davies. *The Penguin Dictionary of Economics*. Penguin, 1998.

[BBM00] M. Baıou, F. Barahona, and A. R. Mahjoub. Separation of partition inequalities. *Mathematics of Operations Research*, 25(2):243–254, May 2000.

[BBP00] L. Bahiense, F. Bahona, and O. Porto. Solving steiner tree problems in graphs with Lagrangian relaxation. Technical report, IBM, 2000. Research Report, RC 21846(98327).

[BC99] A. D. Belegundu and T. R. Chandrupatla. *Optimization Concepts and Applications in Engineering*. Prentice-Hall, 1999.

[BCC93] E. Balas, S. Ceria, and G. Cornuejols. A lift-and-project cutting plane algorithm for mixed 0-1 programs. *Mathematical Programming*, 58:295–324, 1993.

[BCC96] E. Balas, S. Ceria, and G. Cornuejols. Mixed 0-1 programming by lift-and-project in a branch-and-cut framework. *Management Science*, 42:1229–1246, September 1996.

[BCS94] R. Braden, D. Clark, and S. Shenker. Integrated services in the Internet architecture: an overview. *Internet RFC 1633*, June 1994. http://www.ietf.org/rfc/rfc1633.txt.

[BD62] R. E. Bellman and S. E. Dreyfus. *Applied Dynamic Programming*. Princeton University Press, 1962.

[Bea79] E. M. L. Beale. *Branch and Bound Methods for Mathematical Programming Systems*. North-Holland, 1979. In P. L. Hammer, E. L. Johnson, B. H. Korte (eds), Annals of Discrete Mathematics 5: Discrete Optimization.

[Beh81] F. Behringer. A simplex based algorithm for the lexicographically extended linear max-min problem. *European Journal of Operational Research*, 7:274–283, 1981.

[Beh86] F. Behringer. Linear multi-objective maximum optimization and some Pareto and lexmaxmin extensions. *OR Spektrum*, 8:25–32, 1986.

[Bel57] R. Bellman. *Dynamic Programming*. Princeton University Press, 1957.

[Bel58] R. Bellman. On a routing problem. *Quarterly of Applied Mathematics*, 16(1):87–90, 1958.

[Bel91] J. Bellamy. *Digital Telephony—2nd Edition*. Wiley-Interscience, 1991.

[Ben62] J. F. Benders. Partitioning procedures for solving mixed variable programming problems. *Numerische Mathematik*, 4:238–252, 1962.

[Ben02] W. Ben-Ameur. Multi-hour design of survivable classical IP networks. *International Journal of Communication Systems*, 15:553–572, 2002.

[Ber95] D. P. Bertsekas. *Nonlinear Programming*. Athena Scientific, 1995.

[Ber98] D. P. Bertsekas. *Network Optimization: Continuous and Discrete Models*. Athena Scientific, 1998.

[Ber01] D. Bertsekas. *Dynamic Programming and Optimal Control (2nd Edition)*. Athena, 2001.

[BF77] R. G. Boorstyn and H. Frank. Large scale network topological optimization. *IEEE Trans. Communication*, COM-25:29–47, 1977.

[BFW73] D. E. Boyce, A. Farhi, and R. Weischedel. Optimal network problem: a branch and bound algorithm. *Environment Planning*, 5:519–533, 1973.

[BG92] D. Bertsekas and R. Gallager. *Data Networks—2nd Edition*. Prentice Hall, 1992.

[BG93] D.J. Bertsimas and M. X. Goemans. Survivable networks, linear programming relaxations and the parsimonious property. *Mathematical Programming*, 60(2):145–166, 1993.

[BG96] D. Bienstock and O. Günlük. Capacitated network design: Polyhedral structure and computation. *ORSA J. on Computing*, 8:243–260, 1996.

[BGG+71] M. Benichou, J.M. Gauthier, P. Girodet, G. Hentges, G. Ribiere, and D. Vincent. Experiments in mixed integer programming. *Mathematical Programming*, 1:76–94, 1971.

[BGL00] W. Ben-Ameur, E. Gourdin, and B. Liau. Internet routing and topology problems. In *Proc. International Workshop on Design of Reliable Communication Networks (DRCN'2000)*, Munich, Germany, 2000.

[BGLM00a] W. Ben-Ameur, E. Gourdin, B. Liau, and N. Michel. Dimensioning of Internet networks. In *Proc. International Workshop on Design of Reliable Communication Networks (DRCN'2000)*, Munich, Germany, 2000.

[BGLM00b] W. Ben-Ameur, E. Gourdin, B. Liau, and N. Michel. Optimizing administrative weights for efficient single path routing. In *Proc. Networks'2000*, Toronto, Canada, 2000.

[BGLM03] S. Borne, E. Gourdin, B. Liau, and Ali R. Mahjoub. Design of survivable IP-over-optical networks. In *Proc. International Network Optimization Conference (INOC'2003)*, pages 114–118, 2003.

[BH75] L. T. M. Berry and R. J. Harris. The gradient projection vector for multicommodity network problems. *Australian Telecommunications Research*, 9(1):18–27, 1975.

[BH93] S. C. Boyd and T. Hao. An integer polytope related to the design of survivable communication networks. *SIAM Journal on Discrete Mathematics*, 6(4):612–630, 1993.

[Bha99] R. Bhandari. *Survivable Networks—Algorithms for Diverse Routing*. Kluwer, 1999.

[BHLM94] J. Bradley, J. Harati, W.-J. Li, and K. T. Medhi. Multiplex optimization bundler (MOB) design. *AT&T Bell Laboratories—Technical Memorandum*, April 1994.

[BHV00] C. Barnhart, C. A. Hane, and P. H. Vance. Using branch-and-price-and-cut to solve origin-destination integer multicommodity flow problems. *Operations Research*, 48:318–326, 2000.

[BJN+98] C. Barnhart, E. L. Johnson, G. L. Nemhauser, M. W. P. Savelsbergh, and P. H. Vance. Branch-and-price: column generation for solving huge integer programs. *Operations Research*, 48:316–329, 1998.

[BJS90] M. S. Bazaraa, J. J. Jarvis, and H. D. Sherali. *Linear Programming and Network Flows (2nd Edition)*. John Wiley & Sons, 1990.

[BL94] R. Brandstrom and P. Lindberg. Using successive smooth approximation in optimization of sdh networks. In *Proc. 7th International Telecommunication Network Planning Symposium, NETWORKS'94, Budapest*, pages 1–6, 1994.

[BL99] W. Ben-Ameur and B. Liau. Design a reliable telephone network. In *Proc. IFIP Workshop on Traffic Management*. Montreal, 1999.

[Bla00] D. Black. Differentiated services and tunnels. *Internet RFC 2983*, October 2000. http://www.ietf.org/rfc/rfc2983.txt.

[BLM03] S. Bertrand, A. Laugier, and P. Mahey. A framework for the design of multi-protocol networks with encapsulation. In *Proc. International Network Optimization Conference (INOC'2003)*, pages 89–94, 2003.

[BM01] C. Bienstock and G. Muratore. Strong inequalities for capacitated survivable network design problems. *Mathematical Programming*, 89:127–147, 2001.

[BMLG01] W. Ben-Ameur, N. Michel, B. Liau, and E. Gourdin. Routing strategies for IP networks. *Telektronikk*, pages 145–158, March 2, 2001.

[BMM94a] A. Balakrishnan, T.L. Magnanti, and P. Mirchandani. A dual-based algorithm for multi-level network design. *Management Science*, 40(7):567–581, 1994.

[BMM94b] A. Balakrishnan, T.L. Magnanti, and P. Mirchandani. Modeling and heuristic worst-case performance analysis of two-level network design problem. *Management Science*, 40(7):846–867, 1994.

[BMMN95a] M. O. Ball, T. L. Magnanti, C. L. Monma, and G. L. Nemhauser, editors. *Handbooks in Operations Research and Management Science, 7: Network Models*. North-Holland, 1995.

[BMMN95b] M. O. Ball, T. L. Magnanti, C. L. Monmaand, and G. L. Nemhauser, editors. *Handbooks in Operations Research and Management Science, 8: Network Routing.* North-Holland, 1995.

[BMSV04] A. Bosco, E. Manconi, R. Sabella, and L. Valentini. An innovative solution for dynamic bandwidth engineering in IP/MPLS networks with QoS support. *Photonic Network Communications*, 7(1):37–42, 2004.

[BMW56] M. Beckmann, C. B. McGuire, and C. B. Winsten. *Studies in the Economics of Transportation.* Yale University Press, 1956.

[Bof89] T. B. Boffey. Location problems arising in computer networks. *Journal of the Operational Research Society*, 40:347–354, 1989.

[Bou00] J. Y. Le Boudec. Rate adaptation, congestion control and fairness: A tutorial. http://ica1www.epfl.ch/PS_files/LEB3132.pdf, 2000.

[BP89] M. Bern and P. Plassmann. The Steiner problem with edge lengths 1 and 2. *Information Processing Letters*, 32:171–176, 1989.

[BR91] R. E. Burkard and F. Rendl. Lexicographic bottleneck problems. *Operations Research Letters*, 10:303–308, 1991.

[Bra68] D. Braess. Uber ein paradoxon der verkehrsplanung. *Unternehmensforschung*, 12:258–268, 1968.

[BRT88] D. E. Bell, H. Raiffa, and A. Tversky. *Decision Making: Descriptive, Normative and Prescriptive Interactions.* Cambridge University Press, 1988.

[BS01] D. Bienstock and I. Saniee. ATM network design: Traffic models and optimization-based heuristics. *Telecommunication Systems*, 16:399–421, 2001.

[BSS93] M. S. Bazaraa, H. D. Sherali, and C. M. Shetty. *Nonlinear Programming: Theory and Algorithms (2nd Edition).* John Wiley & Sons, 1993.

[BT92] D. Burton and Ph. L. Toint. On an instance of the inverse shortest paths problem. *Mathematical Programming*, 53:45–62, 1992.

[CA95] L. W. Clarke and G. Anandalingam. A bootstrap heuristic for designing minimum cost survivable networks. *Computers Ops Res.*, 22:921–934, 1995.

[Cah98] R. Cahn. *Wide Area Network Design: Concepts and Tools for Optimization.* Morgan Kaufmann Publishers, 1998.

[Cal90] R. Callon. Use of OSI IS-IS for routing in TCP/IP and dual environments. *Internet RFC 1195*, December 1990. http://www.ietf.org/rfc/rfc1195.txt.

[Cam94] J. F. Campbell. A survey of network hub location. *Studies in Locational Analysis*, 6:31–49, 1994.

[Cas03] J. Castro. Solving difficult multicommodity problems with a specialized interior-point algorithm. *Annals of Operations Research*, 124:35–48, 2003.

[CCJ95] A. Charny, D. Clark, and R. Jain. Congestion control with explicit rate indication. In *Proc. International Conference on Communication (ICC'95)*, 1995.

[CCPS98] W. J. Cook, W. H. Cunningham, W. R. Pulleyblank, and A. Schrijver. *Combinatorial Optimization.* John Wiley & Sons, 1998.

[CDPP02] A. Chabrier, E. Danna, C. Le Pape, and L. Perron. Solving a network design problem. Technical report, ILOG, 2002. Technical Report Number 02-005.

[CDZ97] K. Calvert, M. Doar, and E. Zegura. Modeling Internet topology. *IEEE Communications Magazine*, 35(6):160–163, June 1997.

[CFG01] T. G. Crainic, A. Frangioni, and B. Gendron. Bundle-based relaxation methods for multicommodity capacitated fixed charge network design. *Discrete Applied Mathematics*, 112:73–99, 2001.

[CG74] D. G. Cantor and M. Gerla. Optimal routing in a packet switched computer network. *IEEE Trans Comput.*, C-23:1062–1069, 1974.

[CG93] S.-G. Chang and B. Gavish. Telecommunications network topological design and capacity expansion: Formulations and algorithms. *Telecommunications Systems*, 1:99–131, 1993.

[Cha89] F. Chang. Routing-sequence optimization for circuit-switched networks. *AT&T Technical Journal*, 68(3):57–63, May/June 1989.

[Che90] W. K. Chen. *Theory of Nets: Flows in Networks*. John Wiley & Sons, 1990.

[CHG00] T. Cinkler, T. Henk, and G. Gordos. Stochastic algorithms for design of thrifty single-failure-protected networks. In *Proc. Design of Reliable Communication Networks (DRCN 2000), Munich*, 2000.

[Chv83] V. Chvátal. *Linear Programming*. W. H. Freeman, 1983.

[CJ89] D. M. Chiu and R. Jain. Analysis of the increase and decrease algorithms for congestion avoidance in computer networks. *Computer Networks and ISDN Systems*, 17:1–14, 1989.

[CK] P. Crescenzi and V. Kann. (ed.) a compendium of NP optimization problems. http://www.nada.kth.se/∼viggo/problemlist/compendium.html.

[CL99] T. Cinkler and C. P. Larsen. Integer linear programming (ILP) formulation of the optimal light-path configuration problem in wavelength-routing WDM networks. In *ONDM'99, Paris*, 1999.

[CL02] T. Cinkler and P. Laborczi. Joint routing and bandwidth allocation for protected elastic traffic. In *Proc. 10th International Telecommunication Network Planning Symposium, NETWORKS'2002, Munich*, 2002.

[CLH99] T. Cinkler, P. Laborczi, and A. Horvath. Protection through thrifty configuration. In *Proc. 16th International Teletraffic Congress (ITC16)*, pages 975–987, Edinburgh, Scotland, 1999.

[CLV+91] B. A. Coan, W. E. Leland, M. P. Vecchi, A. Weinrib, and L. T. Wu. Using distributed topology update and preplanned configurations to achieve trunk network survivability. *IEEE Trans. on Reliability*, 40(4):404–416, 1991.

[CM98] H. I. Calvete and P. M. Mateo. Lexicographic optimization in generalised network flow problems. *Journal of the Operational Research Society*, 49:519–529, 1998.

[CMD+02] D. Colle, S. De Maesschalck, C. Develder, P. Van Heuven, A. Groebbens, J. Cheyns, I. Lievens, M. Pickavet, P. Lagasse, and P. Demeester. Data-centric optical networks and their survivability. *IEEE Journal on Selected Areas in Communications*, 20(1):6–20, 2002.

[CMLF00] T. Cinkler, D. Marx, C. P. Larsen, and D. Fogaras. Heuristic algorithms for joint configuration of the optical and electrical layer in multi-hop wavelength routing networks. In *Proc. IEEE Conference on Computer Communications (INFOCOM'2000), Tel Aviv*, pages 1000–1009, 2000.

[CMM03] F. R. B. Cruz, G. R. Mateus, and J. Macgregor-Smith. A branch-and-bound algorithm to solve a multi-level network optimization problem. *Journal of Mathematical Modelling and Algorithms*, 2:37–56, 2003.

[CMS96] S. Chamberland, O. Marcotte, and B. Sansò. On the joint topological, dimensioning and location problem for broadband networks. *Proc. International IEEE/IFIP Conference on Broadband Communication*, pages 525–536, 1996.

[CMT97] R. Cotter, D. Medhi, and D. Tipper. Traffic backlog and impact on network dimensioning for survivability for wide-area VP-based ATM networks. In *Proc. 15th International Teletraffic Congress (ITC15)*, pages 691–700, Washington, D.C., June 1997.

[CMT98] K. C. Claffy, G. Miller, and K. Thompson. The nature of the beast: Recent traffic measurements from an Internet backbone. In *Proc. INET'98*, 1998.

[CMW89] R. H. Cardwell, C. L. Monma, and T.-H. Wu. Computer aided design procedures for survivable fiber optic telephone networks. *IEEE Journal on Selected Areas in Communications*, 7:1188–1197, 1989.

[CNRS98] E. Crawley, R. Nair, B. Rajagopalan, and H. Sandick. A framework for QoS-based routing in the Internet. *Internet RFC 2386*, August 1998. http://www.ietf.org/rfc/rfc2386.txt.

[Com00] D. Comer. *Internetworking With TCP/IP, Volume 1: Principles Protocols, and Architecture, 4th edition*. Prentice Hall, 2000.

[Coo71] S. A. Cook. The complexity of theorem proving procedures. In *Proc. Third Annual ACM Symposium on the Theory of Computing*, pages 151–158, 1971.

[Cot99] R. E. Cotter. *Network and Protocol Design for Survivable Wide-Area ATM-based Virtual Networks*. PhD thesis, University of Missouri–Kansas City, 1999.

[CP02] T. Cinkler and M. Pióro. Impact of shared protection strategies on network design. In *Proc. 10th International Telecommunication Network Planning Symposium, NETWORKS 2002, Munich*, 2002.

[CPL99] CPLEX. *CPLEX User's Manual*. ILOG, 1999.

[CRC86] J. R. Current, C. S. ReVelle, and J. L. Cohon. The hierarchical network design problem. *European Journal on Operation Research*, 27:57–66, 1986.

[CS87] C. Clark and J. Strand. Application of Karmarkar's algorithm and expert system technology to transmission network planning. In *Proc. IEEE Global Communications Conference (GLOBECOM'87)*, pages 1058–1061, 1987.

[CS99] S. Chamberland and B. Sansò. Update of two-level networks with modular switches. In *Proc. 16th International Teletraffic Congress (ITC16)*, pages 1009–1018, Edinburgh, Scotland, 1999.

[DA91] A. Dekkers and E. Aarts. Global optimization and simulated annealing. *Mathematical Programming*, 50:367–393, 1991.

[Dal20] H. Dalton. The measurements of the inequality of incomes. *Econom. J*, 30:348–361, 1920.

[Dan63] G. B. Dantzig. *Linear Programming and Extensions*. Princeton University Press, 1963.

[DD76] H. Direlton and R. W. Donaldson. Topological design of teleprocessing networks using linear regression clustering. *IEEE Trans. Communications*, COM-24:1152–1159, 1976.

[Den78] E. V. Denardo. Dynamic programming. In J. J. Moder and S. E. Elmaghraby, editors, *Handbook of Operations Research: Foundations and Fundamentals (Vol. 1)*, pages 586–606. Van Nostrand Reinhold, 1978.

[Den82] E. V. Denardo. *Dynamic Programming: Models and Applications*. Prentice-Hall, 1982.

[Dev99] K. Devlin. *Mathematics: The New Golden Age*. Columbia University Press, 1999.

[DF79] R. Dionne and M. Florian. Exact and approximate algorithms for optimal network. *Networks*, 9:37–59, 1979.

[DGA+99] P. Demeester, M. Gryseels, A. Autenrieth, C. Brianza, L. Castagna, G. Signorelli, R. Clemente, M. Ravaera, A. Jajszczyk, D. Janukowicz, K. Van Doorselaere, and Y. Harada. Resilience in multilayer networks. *IEEE Communications Magazine*, 37(8):70–75, 1999.

[DGG98] Y. Dinitz, N. Garg, and M. Goemans. On single-source unsplittable flow problem. In *Proc. 39th IEEE FOCS*, 1998.

[Dia03] R. A. Dias. Implementing traffic engineering in MPLS-based IP networks with Lagrangean relaxation. In *Proc. 8th. International Symposium on Computers and Communications (ISCC'2003)*, pages 373–378, 2003.

[Dij59] E. Dijkstra. A note on two problems in connection with graphs. *Numerische Mathe-matik*, 1:269–271, 1959.

[DL77] S. E. Dreyfus and A. M. Law. *The Art and Theory of Dynamic Programming*. Academic Press, 1977.

[DL92] A. Dutta and J.-I. Lim. A multiperiod capacity planning model for backbone computer communication networks. *Operations Research*, 40:689–705, 1992.

[dMe99] G. de Marchis and R. Sabella (ed.). *Optical Networks Design and Modeling*. Kluwer Academic Publisher, 1999.

[DML94] R. D. Doverspike, J. A. Morgan, and W. Leland. Network design sensitivity studies for use of digital cross-connect systems in survivable network architectures. *IEEE Journal on Selected Areas in Communications*, 12(1):69–78, 1994.

[Dov] R. D. Doverspike. Evolution of layered telecommunications transport networks. *(Presentation Slides)*.

[Dov86] R. D. Doverspike. Multiplex bundling algorithms for the network planning system. In *Proc. 3rd International Network Planning Symposium, NETWORKS'86*, pages 29–32, 1986.

[Dov91a] R. D. Doverspike. Algorithms for multiplex bundling in a telecommunications network. *Operations Research*, 39(6):925–944, 1991.

[Dov91b] R. D. Doverspike. A multi-layered model for survivability in intra-LATA transport networks. In *Proc. IEEE Global Communications Conference (GLOBECOM'91)*, pages 2025–2031, 1991.

[DR00] B. Davie and Y. Rekhter. *MPLS Technology and Applications*. Morgan Kaufmann Publishers, 2000.

[Dre99] S. E. Dreyfus. An appraisal of some shortest-path algorithms. *Operations Research*, 17:395–412, 1999.

[DRS95] R. S. Dighe, Q. Ren, and B. Sengupta. A link based alternative routing scheme for network restoration under failure. In *Proc. IEEE Global Communications Conference (GLOBECOM'95)*, pages 2118–2123, 1995.

[DS98] G. Dahl and M. Stoer. A cutting plane algorithm for multicommodity survivable network design problems. *INFORMS Journal on Computing*, 10:1–11, 1998.

[DT97] G. B. Dantzig and M. N. Thapa. *Linear Programming 2: Theory and Extensions*. Springer, 1997.

[Dut94] A. Dutta. Capacity planning of private networks using DCS under multi-busy hour traffic. *IEEE Trans. on Communications*, 42:2371–2374, 1994.

[DV89] C. W. Duin and A. Volgenant. Reducing the hierarchical network design problem. *Europ. J. Oper. Res.*, 39, 1989.

[DW60] G. B. Dantzig and P. Wolfe. The decomposition algorithm for linear programming. *Operations Research*, 8:101–111, 1960.

[DW94] R. D. Doverspike and B. Wilson. Comparison of capacity efficiency of DCS network restoration routing techniques. *Journal of Network and System Management*, 2:95–124, 1994.

[DY01] R. D. Doverspike and J. Yates. Challenges for MPLS in optical network restoration. *IEEE Communications Magazine*, 39(2):89–96, February 2001.

[Dzi97] Z. Dziong. *ATM Network Resource Management*. McGraw-Hill, 1997.

[Ehr98] M. Ehrgott. Discrete decision problems, multiple criteria optimization classes and lexicographic max-ordering. *Springer Verlag*, pages 31–44, 1998. In T. J. Stewart, R. C. van den Honert (eds), Trends in Multicriteria Decision Making.

[EIS76] S. Even, A. Itai, and A. Shamir. On the complexity of timetable and multicommodity flow problems. *SIAM J. Computing*, 5:691–703, 1976.

[Eis77] M. Eisenberg. Engineering traffic networks for more than one busy hour. *Bell Systems Technical Journal*, 56:1–20, 1977.

[Els77] W. B. Elsner. A decent algorithm for the multi-hour sizing of traffic networks. *Bell Systems Technical Journal*, 56:1405–1429, 1977.

[Epp94] D. Eppstein. Finding the k shortest paths. In *Proc. 35th IEEE Symposium on Foundations of Computer Science*, pages 154–165, 1994.

[ERP02] M. Ericsson, M. G. C. Resende, and P. M. Pardalos. A genetic algorithm for the weight setting problem in OSPF routing. *Journal of Combinatorial Optimization*, 6(3):229–333, 2002.

[Eve79] S. Even. *Graph Algorithms*. Computer Science Press, New York, 1979.

[FBA$^+$95] A. Faragó, S. Blaabjerg, L. Ast, G. Gordos, and T. Henk. A new degree of freedom in ATM network dimensioning: Optimization the logical configuration. *IEEE Journal on Selected Areas in Communications*, 13(7):1199–1206, 1995.

[FC72] H. Frank and W. Chow. Topological optimization of computer networks. *Proceedings of the IEEE*, 60:1385–1397, 1972.

[FCHM96] A. Faragó, T. Cinkler, V. T. Hai, and S. Malomsoky. Joint planning of the physical and logical configuration of ATM networks. In *Networks'96, Sidney*, 1996.

[FCR+98] A. Farágo, T. Cinkler, S. Rácz, G. Gordos, Á. Horváth, and P. Laborczi. Virtual path layout design. In *Proc. 9th International Telecommunication Network Planning Symposium, NETWORKS'98, Sorento, Italy*, 1998.

[Fel68] W. Feller. *An Introduction to Probability Theory and Its Applications, Volume 1—3rd Edition.* John Wiley & Sons, 1968.

[FF58] L. R. Ford and D. R. Fulkerson. A suggested computation for maximal multicommodity network flows. *Management Science*, 5:97–101, 1958.

[FF62] L. R. Ford and D. R. Fulkerson. *Flows in Networks.* Princeton University Press, 1962.

[FF71] H. Frank and I. T. Frisch. *Communication, Transmission, and Transportation Networks.* Addison-Wesley, 1971.

[FGK73] L. Fratta, M. Gerla, and L. Kleinrock. The flow deviation method: An approach to store-and-forward communication network design. *Networks*, 3:97–133, 1973.

[FGK02] R. Fourer, D. M. Gay, and B. W. Kernighan. *AMPL: A Modeling Language for Mathematical Programming.* Duxbury Press / Brooks/Cole Publishing Company, 2002.

[FGL+00] A. Feldmann, A. Greenberg, C. Lund, N. Reingold, J. Rexford, and F. True. Deriving traffic demands for operational IP networks: Methodology and experience. In *Proc. ACM SIGCOMM'2000*, 2000.

[FGS87] M. Florian, J. Guélat, and H. Spiess. An efficient implementation of the PARTAN variant of the linear approximation for the network equilibrium problem. *Networks*, 17:319–339, 1987.

[FL03] F. Le Faucheur and W. Lai. Requirements for support of differentiated services-aware MPLS traffic engineering. *Internet RFC 3564*, July 2003. http://www.ietf.org/rfc/rfc3564.txt.

[FMP02] G. Fodor, G. Malicsko, and M. Pióro. Link capacity dimensioning and path optimization for networks supporting elastic services. In *Proc. International Conference on Communications (ICC'02)*, New York, 2002.

[FMPS01] G. Fodor, G. Malicsko, M. Pióro, and T. Szymanski. Path optimization for elastic traffic under fairness constraints. In *Proc. 17th International Teletraffic Congress (ITC17)*, Salvador de Bahia, Brazil, 2001.

[For96] ATM Forum. Private Network-Network Interface specification, version 1, af-pnni-0055.000. March 1996.

[Fou03] R. Fourer. 2003 software survey: Linear programming. *ORMS Today*, 30(6):34–43, December 2003.

[FPS+00] G. Fodor, M. Pióro, A. Szentesi, G. Malicsko, and T. Cinkler. Dimensioning and optimization of multi-rate networks supporting elastic traffic. Technical report, Ericsson Research, 2000. Technical Report T/N-00: 140.

[FR95] T. A. Feo and M. G. C. Resende. Greedy randomized adaptive search procedures. *Journal of Global Optimization*, 6:109–133, 1995.

[FSS98] A. Farago, A. Szentesi, and B. Szviatovszki. Allocation of administrative weights in PNNI. In *Proc. Networks'98*, pages 621–625, Sorrento, Italy, 1998.

[FT00] B. Fortz and M. Thorup. Internet traffic engineering by optimizing OSPF weights. In *Proc. IEEE Conference on Computer Communications (INFOCOM'2000)*, pages 519–528, 2000.

[FT02] B. Fortz and M. Thorup. Optimizing OSPF/IS-IS weights in a changing world. *IEEE Journal on Selected Areas in Communications*, 20:756–767, May 2002.

[FV00] A. Fumagalli and L. Valcarenghi. IP restoration vs. WDM protection: Is there an optimal choice? *IEEE Network*, 14(6):34–41, November 2000.

[FW56] M. Frank and P. Wolfe. An algorithm for quadratic programming. *Naval Research Logistics Quarterly*, 3:149–154, 1956.

[GADO01] N. Geary, A. Antonopoulos, E. Drakopoulos, and J. O'Reilly. Analysis of optimisation issues in multi-period DWDM network planning. In *Proc. IEEE Conference on Computer Communications (INFOCOM'2001)*, pages 152–158, 2001.

[GAdV03] L. Gouveia, P. Amaro, A. F. de Sousa, and R. Valadas. MPLS over WDM network design with packet level QoS constraints based on ILP models. In *Proc. IEEE Conference on Computer Communications (INFOCOM'2003)*, pages 576–586, San Francisco, USA, 2003.

[Gal77] R. G. Gallager. A minimum delay routing algorithm using distributed computation. *IEEE Trans. Comm.*, COM-25:73–85, 1977.

[Gas90] S. Gass. *An Illustrated Guide to Linear Programming*. Dover, 1990.

[Gav82] B. Gavish. Topological design of centralized computer networks: Formulations and algorithms. *Networks*, 12:355–377, 1982.

[Gav91] B. Gavish. Topological design of telecommunication networks—local access design methods. *Annals of Operations Research*, 33:17–71, 1991.

[GCM+03] A. Groebbens, D. Colle, S. De Maesschalck, M. Pickavet, and P. Demeester. Logical topology optimisation for dynamic multi-layer recovery schemes. In *Proc. Design of Reliable Communication Networks (DRCN'2003)*, pages 47–52, Banff, Canada, 2003.

[GD98] M. Gryseels and P. Demeester. A multi-layer planning approach for hybrid SDH-based ATM network. In *Proc. 6th ICTS*, 1998.

[GDC+02] W. Grover, J. Doucette, M. Clouqueur, D. Leung, and D. Stamatelakis. New options and insights for survivable transport networks. *IEEE Journal on Selected Areas in Communications*, 20(1):42–49, January 2002.

[Gef01] J. Geffard. A solution method for singly routing traffic demand in telecommunication networks. *Annales des Telecommunicationes*, 56(3-4):140–149, 2001.

[Geo74] A. M. Geoffrion. Lagrangean relaxation for integer programming. *Mathematical Programming Study*, 2:82–114, 1974.

[GGFS01] L. Georgiadis, P. Georgatsos, K. Floros, and S. Sartzetakis. Lexicographically optimal balanced networks. pages 689–698, 2001.

[GH61] R. E. Gomory and T. C. Hu. Multiterminal network flows. *SIAM J. Applied Math.*, 9:551–570, 1961.

[Gib85] A. Gibbons. *Algorithmic Graph Theory*. Cambridge University Press, Cambridge, UK, 1985.

[Gir90] A. Girard. *Routing and Dimensioning in Circuit-Switched Networks*. Addison-Wesley, Reading, MA, 1990.

[GJ79] M. R. Garey and D. R. Johnson. *Computers and Intractability: A Guide to the Theory of NP-Completeness.* W H Freeman & Co, 1979.

[GK77] M. Gerla and L. Kleinrock. On the topological design of distributed computer networks. *IEEE Trans. Communication*, COM-25:48–60, 1977.

[GKM99] V. Gabrel, A. Knippel, and M. Minoux. Exact solution of multicommodity network optimization problems with general step cost functions. *Operations Research Letters*, 25:15–23, 1999.

[GKM03] V. Gabrel, A. Knippel, and M. Minoux. A comparison of heuristics for the discrete cost multicommodity network optimization problem. *Journal of Heuristics*, 9:429–445, 2003.

[GL93] F. Glover and M. Laguna. Tabu search. In C. R. Reeves, editor, *Modern Heuristic Techniques for Combinatorial Problems*, pages 70–150. Blackwell Scientific Publications, 1993.

[GL97] F. Glover and M. Laguna. *Tabu Search.* Kluwer Academic Publisher, 1997.

[Gle02] A. Glenstrup. *Optimised Design and Analysis of All-Optical Networks.* PhD thesis, Research Center COM, Technical University of Denmark, 2002.

[GLL86] A. Girard, P. D. Lansard, and B. Liau. A multi-hour ECCS theory and applicationsIn *Proc. 3rd International Network Planning Symposium, NETWORKS'86*, volume 3, pages 78–84, 1986.

[Glo86] F. Glover. Future paths for integer programming and links to artificial intelligence. *Computers and Operations Research*, 13:533–549, 1986.

[Glo89] F. Glover. Tabu search—Part I. *ORSA Journal on Computing*, 1:190–206, 1989.

[Glo90] F. Glover. Tabu search—Part II. *ORSA Journal on Computing*, 2:4–32, 1990.

[Glo94] F. Glover. Tabu search fundamentals and uses. Technical report, University of Colorado at Boulder, 1994.

[GLY02] E. Gourdin, M. Labbe, and H. Yaman. Telecommunication and location. In Z. Drezner and H.W. Hamacher, editors, *Facility Location: Applications and Theory*, pages 275–305. Springer-Verlag, 2002.

[GM84] M. Gondran and M. Minoux. *Graphs and Algorithms.* John Wiley and Sons, 1984.

[GMS⁺86] P. E. Gill, W. Murray, M. A. Sanders, J. A. Tomlin, and M. H. Wright. On projected newton barrier methods for linear programming and an equivalence to Karmarkar's projective method. *Mathematical Programming*, 36:183–209, 1986.

[GMS91] M. Grotschel, C. Monma, and M. Stoer. Polyhedral approaches to network survivability. In F. Hwang F. Roberts and C. Monma, editors, *Reliability of computer and Communication Networks*, volume 5 of *Series Discrete Mathematics and Computer Science*, pages 121–141. AMS/ACM, 1991.

[GMS92a] M. Grotschel, C. Monma, and M. Stoer. Computational results with a cutting plane algorithm for designing communication networks with low-connectivity constraints. *Operations Research*, 40(2):309–330, 1992.

[GMS92b] M. Grotschel, C. Monma, and M. Stoer. Facets for polyhedra arising in the design of communication networks with low-connectivity constraints. *SIAM Journal on Optimization*, 2(3):474–504, August 1992.

[GMS95] M. Grötschel, C. Monma, and M. Stoer. *Network Models*, volume 7 of *Handbooks in Operations Research and Management Science*, chapter 10 : Design of Survivable Networks, pages 617–672. Elsevier, North-Holland, Amsterdam, 1995. M.O. Ball, T.L. Magnanti, C.L. Monma, G.L. Nemhauser (Eds.).

[GNS98] Z. Gu, G. L. Nemhauser, and M. W. P. Savelsbergh. Cover inequalities for 0-1 linear programs: computation. *INFORMS Journal on Computing*, 10:427–437, 1998.

[GNS99] Z. Gu, G. L. Nemhauser, and M. W. P. Savelsbergh. Cover inequalities for 0-1 linear programs: complexity. *INFORMS Journal on Computing*, 11:117–123, 1999.

[GOK03] B. G abor, D. Orincsay, and A. Kern. Surviving multiple network failures using shared backup path protection. In *HSN'03, Budapest*, 2003.

[Gol67] A. A. Goldstein. *Constructive Real Analysis*. Harper and Row, 1967.

[Gol89] D. E. Goldberg. *Genetic Algorithms in Search, Optimization, and Machine Learning*. Addison Wesley, 1989.

[Gom60] R. E. Gomory. An algorithm for the mixed integer problem. RM-2597, 1960.

[Gom63] R. E. Gomory. An algorithm for integer solutions to integer programs. In R. L. Graves and P. Wolfe, editors, *Recent Advances in Mathematical Programming*, pages 269–302. 1963.

[Gon95] J. Gondzio. HOPDM (version 2.12)—a fast LP solver based on a primal-dual interior point method. *European Journal of Operational Research*, 85:221–225, 1995.

[Gon96] J. Gondzio. Multiple centrality corrections in a primal-dual method for linear programming. *Computational Optimization and Applications*, 6:137–156, 1996.

[Gou01] E. Gourdin. Optimizing Internet networks. *ORMS Today*, 28(2):48–49, April 2001.

[GPS+00] P. Gajowniczek, M. Pióro, A. Szentesi, J. Harmatos, and A. Jüttner. Solving an OSPF routing problem with simulated allocation. In *Proc. 1st Polish-German Teletraffic Symposium*, pages 177–184, Dresden, Germany, 2000.

[GR00a] O. Gerstel and R. Ramaswami. Optical layer survivability: A services perspective. *IEEE Communications Magazine*, 38(3):104–113, March 2000.

[GR00b] O. Gerstel and R. Ramaswami. Optical layer survivability: An implementation perspective. *IEEE Journal on Selected Areas in Communications*, 18(10):1885–1899, October 2000.

[Gre97] J. H. Greene. *Production and Inventory Control Handbook*. McGraw Hill, 1997.

[Gro87] W. D. Grover. The selhealing network: A fast distributed restoration techniques for networks with digital cross-connect machines. In *Proc. IEEE Global Communications Conference (GLOBECOM'87)*, 1987.

[Gro99] W. D. Grover. High availability path design in optical ring-based networks. *IEEE/ACM Trans. on Networking*, 7:558–574, 1999.

[Gro04] W. D. Grover. *Mesh-based Survivable Networks: Options and Strategies for Optical, MPLS, SONET and ATM Networking*. Prentice Hall, 2004.

[GS98] A. Girard and B. Sansò. Multicommodity flow models, failure propagation and reliable network design. *IEEE/ACM Transactions on Networking*, 6:82–93, 1998.

[GS00] W. Grover and D. Stametaelakis. Bridging the ring-mesh dichotomy with p-cycles. In *Proc. Design of Reliable Communication Networks (DRCN'2000), Munich*, pages 92–104, 2000.

[GSPD98] M. Gryseels, K. Struyve, M. Pickavet, and P. Demeester. Survivability design in multilayer transport networks. In *Proc. 6th ICTS*, 1998.

[GSS96] M. Gendraeu, B. Sansò, and D. A. Stanford. Optimizing routing in packet-switched networks with non-poisson offered traffic. *Telecommunication Systems*, 5:323–340, 1996.

[GSTC02] C. Gáspár, S. Szentes, J. Tapolcai, and T. Cinkler. Approximative algorithms for configuration of multi-layer networks with protection. In *Proc. Design of Reliable Communication Networks (DRCN'2002), Budapest*, 2002.

[GT96] J. Gondzio and T. Terlaky. A computational view of interior point methods for large scale linear programming. In J. Beasley, editor, *Advances in Linear and Integer Programming*, pages 103–144. Oxford University Press, Oxford, England, 1996.

[GTD+89] B. Gavish, P. Trudeau, M. Dror, M. Gendreau, and L. Mason. Fiber optic circuit network design under reliability constraints. *IEEE Journal on Selected Areas in Communications*, 7(8):1181–1187, 1989.

[Gun99] O. Gunluk. A branch-and-cut algorithm for capacitated network design. *Mathematical Programming*, 86 (A):17–39, 1999.

[Had64] G. Hadley. *Nonlinear and Dynamic Programming*. Addison-Wesley, 1964.

[Hag] J. Hagstrom. Braess's paradox—web-site. http://tigger.uic.edu/ hagstrom/Research/Braess/index.html.

[Han86] P. Hansen. The steepest ascent mildest descent heuristic for combinatorial optimization. In *Proc. Congress of Numerical Methods in Combinatorial Optimization*, Capri, Italy, 1986.

[Har76] R. J. Harris. The modified reduced gradient method for optimally dimensioning telephone networks. *Australian Telecommunication Research*, 10, 1976.

[HB94] M. Herzberg and S. J. Bye. Spare-capacity assignment in survivable networks for multi-link and node failures with hop limits. In *Proc. IEEE Global Communications Conference (GLOBECOM'94)*, pages 1601–1606, 1994.

[HBCN97] E. J. Hernandez-Valencia, L. Benmohamed, S. Chong, and R. Nagarajan. Rate control algorithms for the ATM ABR service. *European Transactions on Telecommunications*, 8:7–20, 1997.

[HBU95] M. Herzberg, S. J. Bye, and A. Utano. The hop-limit approach for spare-capacity assignment in survivable networks. *IEEE/ACM Transactions on Networking*, 3:775–784, 1995.

[HH98] K. Holmberg and J. Hellstrand. Solving the uncapacitated network design problem by a Lagrangian heuristic and branch-and-bound. *Operations Research*, 46(2):247–259, 1998.

[Him72] D. M. Himmelblau. *Applied Nonlinear Programming*. McGraw-Hill, 1972.

[HLP29] G. H. Hardy, J. E. Littlewood, and G. Polya. Some simple inequalities satisfied by convex functions. *Messager Math*, 58:145–152, 1929.

[HLP52] G. H. Hardy, J. E. Littlewood, and G. Polya. *Inequalities*. Cambridge University Press, 1952.

[Hoa73] H. H. Hoang. A computational approach to the selection of an optimal network. *Management Science*, 19:488–498, 1973.

[HSR97] E. Horowitz, S. Sahni, and S. Rajasekaran. *Computer Algorithms/C++*. Computer Science Press, New York, 1997.

[HTP97] Y. T. Hou, H. H-Y. Tzeng, and S. S. Panwar. A simple ABR switch algorithm for the weighted max-min fairness policy. *IEEE ATM Workshop*, 97, 1997.

[HTP98] Y. T. Hou, H. H-Y. Tzeng, and S. S. Panwar. A generic weight-based network bandwidth sharing policy for ATM ABR service. In *Proc. IEEE International Conference on Communications (ICC'98)*, pages 1492–1499, 1998.

[Hu74] T. C. Hu. Optimum communication spanning trees. *SIAM J. Comput.*, 3:188–195, 1974.

[HU96] M. Herzberg and A. Utano. Optimal assignment of spare capacity to back-up VPs in survivable ATM networks. In *Networks'96, Sydney*, 1996.

[Hui00] C. Huitemma. *Routing in the Internet—2nd Edition*. Prentice-Hall, 2000.

[HWC74] M. Held, P. Wolfe, and H. Crowder. Validation of sub-gradient optimization. *Mathematical Programming*, 6:62–88, 1974.

[HY] K. Holmberg and D. Yuan. Optimization of Internet protocol network design and routing. *Networks*. (accepted for publication).

[HY98] K. Holmberg and D. Yuan. A Lagrangian approach to network design problems. *International Transactions in Operational Research*, 5:529–539, 1998.

[HY00] K. Holmberg and D. Yuan. A Lagrangian heuristic based branch-and-bound approach for the capacitated network design problem. *Operations Research*, 48:461–481, 2000.

[IMG98] R. R. Iraschko, M. MacGregor, and W. D. Grover. Optimal capacity placement for path restoration in STM or ATM mesh survivable networks. *IEEE/ACM Trans. on Networking*, 6:325–336, 1998.

[ISO90] ISO. Intermediate system to intermediate system routing information exchange protocol for use in conjunction with the protocol for providing the connectionless-mode network service (iso 8473). *ISO/IEC 10589*, February 1990. (also see Reference [Ora90]).

[ISS03] P. Iovanna, M. Settembre, and R. Sabella. A traffic engineering system for multi-layer networks based on the GMPLS paradigm. *IEEE Network*, 17(2):28–37, 2003.

[ITU94] *Architecture of Transport Networks Based on the SDH*. Recommendation G.803 ITU-C, 1994.

[Jac88] V. Jacobson. Congestion avoidance and control. In *Proc. SIGCOMM'88*, pages 314–329, 1988.

[Jaf81] J. Jaffe. Bottleneck flow control. *IEEE Transactions on Communications*, 29:954–962, 1981.

[JAMS89] D. S. Johnson, C. R. Aragon, L. A. McGeoch, and C. Schevon. Optimization by simulated annealing: An experimental evaluation. *Operations Research*, 37:865–892, 1989.

[Jen88] C.-Y. Jeng. An idealized model for understanding impact of key network parameters on airline routing. *Transportation Research Record*, 1158:5–13, 1988.

[Jer73] R. G. Jeroslow. The simplex algorithm with the pivot rule of maximizing criterion improvement. *Discrete Mathematics*, 4:367–378, 1973.

[JGL99] A. De Jongh, M. Gendreau, and M. Labbe. Finding disjoint routes in telecommunications networks with two technologies. *Operations Research*, 47:81–92, January 1999.

[JJU02] L. Jereb, T. Jakab, and F. Unghváry. Availability analysis of multi-layer optical networks. *Optical Networks*, 3:84–95, 2002.

[JLFP93] K. L. Jones, I. J. Lustig, J. M. Farvolden, and W. B. Powell. Multicommodity network flows: The impact of formulation on decomposition. *Mathematical Programming*, 62:95–117, 1993.

[JLK78] D. S. Johnson, J. K. Lenstra, and A. H. G. Rinnoy Kan. The complexity of the network design problem. *Networks*, 8:279–285, 1978.

[JM] V. Jiménez and A. Marzal. Algorithms for computing the k shortest paths. web-site: http://terra.act.uji.es/REA/ and http://www.mat.uc.pt/ eqvm/OPP/KSPP/KSPP.html.

[JM74] L. A. Johnson and D. C. Montgomery. *Operations Research in Production Planning, Scheduling, and Inventory Control.* John Wiley & Sons, 1974.

[JM99] V. M. Jiménez and A. Marzal. Computing the k shortest paths: A new algorithm and an experimental comparison. In *Proc. 3rd Annual Workshop on Algorithmic Engineering, London*, 1999.

[JOF04] A. Juttner, A. Orbán, and Z. Fiala. Two new algorithms for UMTS access network topology design. *European Journal of Operational Research*, 2004. accepted.

[JOK03] B. G. Józsa, D. Orincsay, and A. Kern. Surviving multiple network failures using shared backup path protection. In *Proc. High Speed Networks (HSN'2003), Budapest*, 2003.

[JSHP00] A. Juttner, A. Szentesi, J. Harmatos, and M. Pióro. On solvability of an OSPF routing problem. In *Proc. 15th Nordic Teletraffic Seminar*, Lund, Sweden, 2000.

[JSMR01] A. Juttner, B. Szviatovszki, I. Mécs, and Z. Rajkó. Lagrange relaxation based method for the QoS routing problem. In *Proc. IEEE Conference on Computer Communications (INFOCOM'2001)*, pages 859–868, April 2001.

[JUJ01] L. Jereb, F. Unghváry, and T. Jakab. A methodology for reliability analysis of multi-layer communication networks. *Optical Networks Magazine*, 2:42–51, 2001.

[KAK89] J. Korst, E. H. Aarts, and A. Korst. *Simulated Annealing and Boltzman Machines: A Stochastic Approach to Combinatorial Optimization and Neural Computing.* John Wiley & Sons, 1989.

[Kar72] R. M. Karp. Reducibility among combinatorial problems. In R. E. Miller and J. W. Thatcher, editors, *Complexity of Computer Communications*, pages 85–103. Plenum Press, 1972.

[Kar75] R. M. Karp. On the computational complexity of combinatorial problems. *Networks*, 5:45–68, 1975.

[Kar84] N. Karmarkar. A new polynomial-time algorithm for linear programming. *Combinatorica*, 4:373–395, 1984.

[KDP94] K. R. Krishnan, R. D. Doverspike, and C. D. Pack. Unified models of survivability for multi-technology networks. In *Proc. 14th International Teletraffic Congress (ITC14)*, Antibes, France, June 1994.

[KDP95] K. R. Krishnan, R. D. Doverspike, and C. D. Pack. Improved survivability with multi-layer dynamic routing. *IEEE Communications Magazine*, 33(7):62–68, July 1995.

[Kel97] F. P. Kelly. Charge and rate control for elastic traffic. *European Transactions on Telecommunications*, 8:33–37, 1997.

[Kel03] F. P. Kelly. Fairness and stability of end-to-end congestion control. *European Journal of Control*, 9:159–176, 2003.

[Ken78] J. L. Kennington. A survey of linear cost multi-commodity network flow problems. *Operations Research*, 26:209–236, 1978.

[Ker92] A. Kershenbaum. *Telecommunications Network Design Algorithms*. McGraw Hill, 1992.

[KG85] A. Kanafani and A. A. Ghobrial. Airline hubbing—some implications for airport economics. *Transportation Research*, 19A:15–27, 1985.

[KGV83] S. Kirkpatrick, C. D. Gelatt, and M. P. Vecchi. Optimization by simulated annealing. *Science*, 220(4598):671–680, May 1983.

[KH63] A. A. Kuehn and M. J. Hamburger. A heuristic program for locating warehouses. *Management Science*, 9:643–666, 1963.

[KH80] J. L. Kennington and R. V. Helgason. *Algorithms for Network Programming*. Wiley-Interscience, 1980.

[Kha79] L. Khachian. A polynomial algorithm for linear programming. *Soviet Mathematics Doklady*, 20:191–194, 1979.

[Kiw97] K. Kiwiel. Efficiency of the analytic center cutting plane method for convex minimization. *SIAM Journal on Optimization*, 7:336–346, 1997.

[KJ56] R. E. Kalaba and M. L. Juncosa. Optimal design and utilization of communication networks. *Management Science*, 3(1):33–44, October 1956.

[KKP99] P. Karas, S. Kozdrowski, and M. Pióro. Doubly iterative algorithm for multi-layer network design. *Digital Telecommunications - Technologies and Services*, 2(3/4):116–128, 1999. (In Polish; the first version of this paper appeared in English Proc. 6th Polish Teletraffic Symposium).

[KKY03] D. Katz, K. Kompella, and D. Yeung. Traffic engineering (TE) extensions to OSPF version 2. *Internet RFC 3630*, September 2003. http://www.ietf.org/rfc/rfc3630.txt.

[KL86] J. Klincewicz and H. Luss. A Lagrangian relaxation heuristic for capacitated facility location with single-source constraints. *Journal of the Operational Research Society*, 37:495–500, 1986.

[Kle] L. Kleinrock. The day the infant Internet uttered its first words. web-site: http://www.lk.cs.ucla.edu/LK/Inet/1stmesg.html.

[Kle96] J. Kleinberg. Single-source unsplittable flow. In *Proc. 37th IEEE FOCS*, 1996.

[Kli98] J. Klincewicz. Hub location in backbone/tributary network design: A review. *Location Science*, 6:307–335, 1998.

[KLS92] R. S. Klein, H. Luss, and D. R. Smith. A lexicographical minmax algorithm for multiperiod resource allocation. *Mathematical Programming*, 55:213–234, 1992.

[KM02] H. Kerivin and A.R. Mahjoub. Separation of partition inequalities for the $(1, 2)$-survivable network design problem. *Op. Research Letters*, 30:265–268, 2002.

[KMN02] H. Kerivin, A. R. Mahjoub, and C. Nocq. $(1, 2)$-survivable networks: Facets and branch-and-cut. to appear in The Sharpest Cut, MPS-SIAM Series in Optimization, 2002.

[KMT97] F. P. Kelly, A. K. Mauloo, and D. H. K. Tan. Rate control for communication networks: Shadow prices, proportional fairness and stability. *Journal of the Operations Research Society*, 49:2006–2017, 1997.

[Kni24] F. H. Knight. Some fallacies in the interpretation of social cost. *Quarterly Journal of Economics*, 38:582–606, 1924.

[Kni01] A. Knippel. *Modèls et Algorithmes de Multiflots à Coût discontinu pour l'Optimisation de Réseaux de Télécommunications*. PhD thesis, L'UNIVERSITE PARIS 6, 2001.

[KNP03] H. Kerivin, D. Nace, and T.-T.-L. Pham. Models for the capacitated survivable network design problem. In *Proc. International Network Optimization Conference (INOC'2003)*, 2003.

[KO99] M. M. Kostrewa and W. Ogryczak. Linear optimization with multiple equitable criteria. *RAIRO Operations Research*, pages 275–297, 1999.

[KP00] P. Karas and M. Pióro. Optimisation problems related to the assignment of administrative weights in the IP networks' routing protocols. In *Proc. 1st Polish-German Teletraffic Symposium (PGTS'2000)*, pages 185–192, 2000.

[KPF98] J. Kennington, M. Petkova, and F. Fahim. Multiplex bundling problem in SONET networks. Technical report, Southern Methodist University, January 1998. 97-CSE-20.

[KPN03] E. Kubilinskas, M. Pióro, and P. Nilsson. Design models for multi-layer next generation Internet core networks carrying elastic traffic. In *Proc. 4th International Workshop on the Design of Reliable Communication Networks (DRCN'2003)*, Banff, Canada, 2003.

[KPNG02] H. Kerivin, T.-T.-L. Pham, D. Nace, and J. Geffard. Design of survivable networks with single facility. In *Proc. ECUMN'02*, 2002.

[KR87] L. J. Krajewski and L. P. Ritzman. *Operations Management: Strategy and Analysis*. Addison-Wesley, 1987.

[KR02] J. Kurose and K. Ross. *Computer Networking: A Top-Down Approach Featuring the Internet: 2nd Edition*. Addison-Wesley, 2002.

[KRT99] J. Kleinberg, Y. Rabani, and E. Tardos. Fairness in routing and load balancing. In *Proc. 40th Annual IEEE Symposium on the Foundations of Computer Science*, 1999.

[Kru56] J. B. Kruskal. On the shotest spanning tree of a graph and the traveling salesman problem. *Proc. American Mathematical Monthly*, 7:48–50, 1956.

[KS97] S. Kolliopoulos and C. Stein. Improved algorithms for unsplittable flow problems. In *Proc. 38th IEEE FOCS*, 1997.

[KS99] S. G. Kolliopoulos and C. Stein. Experimental evaluation of approximation algorithms for single-source unsplittable flow. In *Proc. 7th International Integer Programming and Combinatorial Optimization Conference, Lecture Notes in Computer Science*, pages 328–344. Springer-Verlag, 1999.

[KSPM03] B. Krithikaivasan, S. Srivastava, M. Pióro, and D. Medhi. Backup path restoration design using path generation technique. In *Proc. 4th International Workshop on Design of Reliable Communication Networks (DRCN 2003)*, pages 77–84, Banff, Canada, 2003.

[KST01a] K. Kar, S. Sarkar, and L. Tassiulas. Optimization based rate control for multipath sessions. In *Proc. 17th International Teletraffic Congress (ITC17)*, Salvador de Bahia, Brazil, 2001.

[KST01b] K. Kar, S. Sarkar, and L. Tassiulas. A simple rate control algorithm for maximizing total user utility. In *Proc. IEEE Conference on Computer Communications (INFOCOM'2001)*, pages 133–141, 2001.

[KT81] L. J. Krajewski and H. E. Thompson. *Management Science: Quantitative Methods in Context*. John Wiley & Sons, 1981.

[KZ89] A. Khanna and J. Zinky. The revised ARPAnet routing metric. In *Proc. ACM SIGCOMM'1989*, pages 45–56, 1989.

[Lab91] J.-F. P. Labourdette. *Rearrangeability Techniques for Multihop Lightwave Networks and Applications to Distributed ATM Switching Systems*. PhD thesis, Columbia University, 1991.

[Las70] L. Lasdon. *Optimization Theory for Large Systems*. MacMillan, 1970.

[Law76] E. L. Lawler. *Combinatorial Optimization: Networks and Metroids*. Holt, Rinehart, and Winston, 1976.

[LBC03] J.-F. Labourdette, E. Bouillet, and S. Chaudhuri. Role of optical network and spare router strategy in resilient IP backbone architecture. In *Proc. 4th International Workshop on Design of Reliable Communication Networks (DRCN 2003)*, pages 244–253, Banff, Canada, 2003.

[LD02] M. E. Lübbecke and J. Desrosiers. *Selected topics in column generation*. Les Cahiers de GERAD G-2002-64, 2002.

[Lee93] C. Y. Lee. An algorithm for the design of multitype concentrator networks. *Journal of the Operational Research Society*, 44:471–482, 1993.

[Lev93] H. Levy. Stochastic dominance and expected utility: Survey and analysis. *Management Science*, 38:1993, 555–593.

[LG93] M. Laguna and F. Glover. Bandwidth packing: A tabu search approach. *Management Science*, 39:492–500, 1993.

[LGM98] Z. Liu, Y. Gu, and D. Medhi. On optimal location of switches/routers and interconnection. Technical report, University of Missouri-Kansas City, November 1998.

[Lin80] P. Lindberg. Optimization of a standby protection network. In *Networks'80*, 1980.

[Lin86] P. Lindberg. Optimization of a multiplexed transmission network under resilience constraints. In *Proc. 3rd International Network Planning Symposium, NETWORKS'86*, pages 33–36, 1986.

[LJPS90] J. Lubacz, M. Jarociński, M. Pióro, and O. Soto. On the ATM network architecture and routing principles. In *ITC Specialists' Seminar*, Morristown, New Jersey, USA, 1990.

[LKG03] B. Lardeux, A. Knippel, and J. Geffard. Efficient algorithms for solving the 2-layered network design problem. In *Proc. International Network Optimization Conference (INOC'2003)*, pages 367–373, 2003.

[LM93] W.-J. Li and K. T. Medhi. Multiplexing planning by simulated annealing. *AT&T Bell Laboratories—Technical Memorandum*, September 1993.

[LM02] W. Lai and D. McDysan (eds.). Network hierarchy and multi-layer survivability. *Internet RFC 3386*, November 2002. http://www.ietf.org/rfc/rfc3386.txt.

[LMS+89] D. N. Lee, K. T. Medhi, J. L. Strand, R. G. Cox, and S. Chen. Solving large telecommunications network loading problems. *AT&T Technical Journal*, 68(3):48–56, May/June 1989.

[LN94] L. J. LeBlanc and S. Narasimhan. Topological design of metropolitan area networks. *Computer Networks and ISDN Systems*, 26:1235–1248, 1994.

[LN98] P. J. Lederer and R. S. Nambimadom. Airline network design. *Operations Research*, 46:785–804, 1998.

[LNC00] J.-L. Lutton, D. Nace, and J. Carlier. Assigning spare capacities in mesh survivable networks. *Telecommunication Systems*, 13:441–451, 2000.

[LORS01] D. H. Lorenz, A. Orda, D. Raz, and Y. Shavitt. How good can IP routing be? Technical report, May 2001.

[LP79] A. H. Land and S. Powell. *Computer Codes for Problems of Integer Programming*. North-Holland, 1979. In P.L. Hammer, E.L. Johnson, B.H. Korte (eds) Annals of Discrete Mathematics 5: Discrete Optimization.

[LP95] J.-L. Lutton and E. Philippart. A simulated annealing algorithm for the computation of marginal costs of telecommunication links. In *Proc. Metaheuristics International Conference*, Breckenridge-Colorado, USA, 1995.

[LT01] J. Lubacz and A. Tomaszewski. A systematic approach to network planning. In *Proc. 17th International Teletraffic Congress (ITC17)*, pages 605–615, Salvador de Bahia, Brazil, 2001.

[LTC+01] K. Long, R. Tucker, S. Cheng, J. Ma, and R. Zhang. A new approach to multi-layer network survivability: strategies, model and algorithm. *Journal of High Speed Networks*, 10(2):127–134, 2001.

[LTS01] Y. Liu, D. Tipper, and P. Sinpongwutikorn. Approximating optimal spare capacity allocation by successive survivable routing. In *Proc. IEEE Conference on Computer Communication (INFOCOM'2001)*, pages 699–798, Anchorage, Alaska, USA, April 2001.

[Lus82] H. Luss. Operations research and capacity expansion problems; a survey. *Operations Research*, 30:907–947, 1982.

[Lus84] H. Luss. A capacity expansion model with application to multiplexing in communication networks. *IEEE Trans. on Systems, Man and Cybernatics*, 14:419–423, 1984.

[Lus99] H. Luss. On equitable resource allocation problems: A lexicographical minimax approach. *Operations Research*, 47:361–378, 1999.

[LV01] H. Luss and A. Vakhutinsky. A resource allocation approach for the generation of service-dependent demand matrices for communication networks. *Telecommunication Systems*, 17:413–433, 2001.

[LY92] F. Y. S. Lin and J. R. Yee. A new multiplier adjustment procedure for the distributed computation of routing assignments in virtual circuit data networks. *ORSA Journal on Computing*, 4:250–266, 1992.

[MA87] R. D. C. Monteneiro and I. Adler. Interior path following primal-dual algorithms—Part I: Linear programming. Technical report, Dept. of Industrial Engineering and Operations Research, University of California, Berkeley, CA, 1987.

[Map] Maple. *Maple User's Manual*.

[Mar] E. Martins. k-th shortest path problem. http://www.mat.uc.pt/ eqvm/OPP/KSPP/KSPP.html.

[Mar70] J. D. Marchland. Braess's paradox of traffic flow. *Transportation Research*, 4:391–394, 1970.

[Mar03] I. Maros. *Computational Techniques of the Simplex Method.* Kluwer, 2003.

[Mas85] L. G. Mason. Equilibrium flows, routing patterns and algorithms for store-and-forward networks. *Large Scale Systems*, 8:187–209, 1985.

[MAT] The MATH WORKS Inc. *MATLAB Users's Guide.*

[McC73] C. J. McCallum. An algorithm for finding the k shortest paths in a network. *Bell Laboratories Technical Memorandum*, 1973.

[McC03] J. McCabe. *Network Analysis, Architecture and Design (Second Edition).* Morgan Kaufmann Publishers, 2003.

[MCG+02] S. De Maesschalck, D. Colle, A. Groebbens, C. Develder, I. Lievens, P. Lagasse, M. Pickavet, P. Demeester, F. Saluta, and M. Quagliotti. Intelligent optical networking for multilayer survivability. *IEEE Communications Magazine*, 40(1):42–49, 2002.

[Med89] D. Medhi. Traffic restoration design for self-healing networks. *AT&T Bell Laboratories—Technical Memorandum*, 1989.

[Med91a] D. Medhi. Diverse routing for survivability in a fiber-based sparse network. In *Proc. IEEE International Conference on Communication (ICC'91)*, pages 672–676, Denver, Colorado, June 1991.

[Med91b] D. Medhi. Network dimensioning for a multi-service integrated digital network with dynamic routing. In *Proc. ACM/IEEE-CS Symposium on Applied Computing (SAC'91)*, pages 30–36, Kansas City, Missouri, USA, April 1991.

[Med92] D. Medhi. A unified framework for survivable telecommunications network design. In *Proc. IEEE International Conference on Communications (ICC'92)*, pages 411–415, Chicago, Illinois, June 1992.

[Med94a] D. Medhi. Bundle-based decomposition for structured large-scale convex optimization problems: Error estimate and application to block-angular linear programs. *Mathematical Programming*, 66:79–101, 1994.

[Med94b] D. Medhi. A unified approach to network survivability for teletraffic networks: Models, algorithms and analysis. *IEEE Trans. on Communications*, 42:534–548, 1994.

[Med95] D. Medhi. Multi-hour, multi-traffic class network design for virtual path-based dynamically reconfigurable wide-area ATM networks. *IEEE/ACM Trans. on Networking*, 3:809–818, 1995.

[Med97] D. Medhi. Models for network design, servicing and monitoring of ATM networks based on the virtual path concept. *Computer Networks and ISDN Systems*, 29(3):373–386, 1997.

[Med99] D. Medhi. Network reliability and fault tolerance (invited paper). In J. G. Webster, editor, *Wiley Encyclopedia of Electrical and Electronics Engineering*, volume 14, pages 213–218. John Wiley & Sons, 1999.

[Med02] J. Medhi. *Stochastic Models in Queueing Theory—2nd Edition.* Academic Press, 2002.

[Meg74] N. Megiddo. Optimal flows in networks with multiple sources and sinks. *Mathematical Programming*, 7:97–107, 1974.

[MG97] D. Medhi and S. Guptan. Network dimensioning and performance of multi-service, multi-rate loss networks with dynamic routing. *IEEE/ACM Trans. on Networking*, 5:944–957, 1997.

[MGR97] M. H. MacGregor, W. D. Grover, and K. Ryhorchuk. Optimal spare capacity preconfiguration for faster restoration of mesh networks. *Journal of Network and Systems Management*, 5:159–171, 1997.

[Mic96] Z. Michalewicz. *Genetic Algorithms + Data Structures = Evolution Programs*. Springer, III edition, 1996.

[Min81] M. Minoux. Optimal synthesis of a network with non-simultaneous multicommodity flow requirements. In P. Hansen, editor, *Studies in Graphs and Discrete Programming*, pages 269–277. North-Holland, 1981.

[Min84] M. Minoux. Subgradient optimization and Benders decomposition for large scale programming. In R. W. Cottle amd M. L. Kelmanson and B. Korte, editors, *Mathematical Programming*, pages 271–288. North-Holland, 1984.

[Min86] M. Minoux. *Mathematical Programming: Theory and Algorithms*. John Wiley & Sons, 1986.

[Min89] M. Minoux. Network synthesis and optimum network design problems: Models, solution methods and applications. *Networks*, 19:313–360, 1989.

[Min93] D. Minoli. *Broadband Network Analysis and Design*. Artech House, 1993.

[Min01] M. Minoux. Discrete cost multicommodity network optimization problems and exact solution methods. *Annals of Operations Research*, 106:19–46, 2001.

[MJR+01] D. Medhi, S. Jain, D. Shenoy Ramam, S. R. Thirumalasetty, M. Saddi, and F. Summa. A network management framework for multi-layered network survivability: An overview. In *Proc. IEEE/IFIP Conference on Integrated Network Management (IM'2001)*, pages 293–296, Seattle, WA, May 2001.

[MK95] D. Medhi and R. Khurana. Optimization and performance of network restoration schemes for wide-area teletraffic networks. *Journal of Network and Systems Management*, 3(3):265–294, 1995.

[MK00] E. Mulyana and U. Killat. Load balancing in IP networks by optimizing link weights. In *Proc. 2nd Polish-German Teletraffic Symposium (PGTS'2002)*, Gdansk, Poland, 2000.

[ML97] D. Medhi and C.-T. Lu. Dimensioning and computational results for wide-area broadband networks with two-level dynamic routing. *IEICE Trans. on Communications*, E80-B(2):273–281, 1997.

[MM95] T. L. Magnanti and P. Mirchandani. Modeling and solving the two-facility network loading problem. *Operations Research Letters*, 43(1):142–157, 1995.

[MMD91] R. Mazumdar, L. G. Mason, and C. Douligeris. Fairness in network optimal flow control: optimality of product forms. *IEEE Trans on Commun.*, 39:775–782, 1991.

[MMR96] D. Mitra, J. A. Morrison, and K. G. Ramakrishnan. ATM network design and optimization: A multi-rate loss network framework. *IEEE/ACM Trans. on Networking*, 4:531–543, 1996.

[MO79] A. W. Marshall and I. Olkin. *Inequalities: Theory of Majorization and Its Implications*. Academic Press, 1979.

[MO92] E. Marchi and J. A. Oviedo. Lexicographic optimality in the multi-objective linear programming: the nucleolar solution. *European Journal of Operational Research*, 57:355–359, 1992.

[MOY96] A. Mayer, Y. Ofek, and M. Yung. Approximating Max-Min fair rates via distributed local scheduling with partial information. In *Proc. IEEE Conference on Computer Communications (INFOCOM'96)*, pages 928–936, 1996.

[Moy98a] J. Moy. *OSPF: Anatomy of An Internet Routing Protocol*. Addison-Wesley, 1998.

[Moy98b] J. Moy. OSPF version 2. *Internt RFC 2328*, 1998. http://www.ietf.org/rfc/rfc2328.txt.

[MPCD03] S. De Maesschalck, M. Pickavet, D. Colle, and P. Demeester. On the optimization of the feedback loop for solving the multi-layer traffic grooming problem. In *Proc. International Network Optimization Conference (INOC'2003)*, pages 195–200, 2003.

[MR99] L. Massouli and J. W. Roberts. Bandwidth sharing: Objectives and algorithms. In *Proc. IEEE Conference on Computer Communications (INFOCOM'99)*, pages 1395–1403, 1999.

[MS] B. A. Murtagh and M. A. Saunders. *MINOS User's Guide*. http://www.sbsi-sol-optimize.com/manuals/Minos%20Manual.pdf.

[MS81a] M. Minoux and J. Y. Serrault. Subgradient optimization and large scale programming: an application to optimum multicommodity network synthesis with security constraints. *R.A.I.R.O. Operations Research*, 15(2), 1981.

[MS81b] M. Minoux and J.-Y. Serreault. Synthese optimal d'un reseau de telecommunication avec contraintes de securite. *Annales des Telecommunications*, 36(3-4):211–230, 1981.

[MS89] C. L. Monma and D. F. Shallcross. Methods for designing communications networks with certain two-connected survivability constraints. *Operations Research*, 37:531–541, 1989.

[MS93] D. Medhi and S. Sankarappan. Impact of a transmission facility link failure on dynamic call routing circuit-switched networks under various circuit layout policies. *Journal of Network and Systems Management*, 1:143–169, 1993.

[MS94] M. T. Marsh and D. A. Shilling. Equity measurement in facility location analysis: A review and framework. *European Journal of Operational Research*, 74:1–17, 1994.

[MS01] K. T. Medhi and J. L. Strand. Ultra-long haul DWDM: tool support for economic studies. In *Proc. Optical Fiber Communication Conference (OFC'2001)*, March 2001.

[MSG03] F. Mobiot, B. Sanso, and A. Girard. A method for the integrated design of reliable GMPLS networks. In *Proc. Design of Reliable Communication Networks (DRCN'2003)*, pages 53–60, Banff, Canada, 2003.

[MSS00] A. Magi, A. Szentesi, and B. Szviatovszki. Analysis of link cost functions for PNNI routing. *Computer Networks*, 34(1):181–197, July 2000.

[MT97] D. Medhi and D. Tipper. Towards fault recovery and management in communication networks. *Journal of Network and Systems Management*, 5(2):101–104, June 1997.

[MT00a] D. Medhi and D. Tipper. Multi-layered network survivability—models, analysis, architecture, framework and implementation: An overview. In *Proc. DARPA Information Survivability Conference and Exposition (DISCEX'2000)*, volume I, pages 173–186, Hilton Head Island, South Carolina, USA, January 2000.

[MT00b] D. Medhi and D. Tipper. Some approaches to solving a multi-hour broadband network capacity design problem with single-path routing. *Telecommunication Systems*, 13:269–291, 2000.

[Muh92] H. Muhlenbeim. How genetic algorithms really work: Mutation and hill climbing. In R. Manner and B. Manderick, editors, *Proc. Parallel Problem Solving from Nature*. North Holland, 1992.

[Muk97] B. Mukherjee. *Optical Communication Networks*. McGraw Hill, 1997.

[Mur81] B. A. Murtagh. *Advanced Linear Programming: Computation and Practice*. McGraw-Hill, 1981.

[Mur83] K. Murty. *Linear Programming*. Wiley, 1983.

[MW00] J. Mo and J. Warland. Fair end-to-end window-based congestion control. *IEEE/ACM Trans. on Networking*, 8(5):556–567, 2000.

[Mys01] A. Myslek. Greedy randomised adaptive search procedures (GRASP) for topological design. In *Proc. 8th Polish Teletraffic Symposium (PSRT'2001)*, pages 135–146, Zakopane, Poland, 2001.

[Nac02] D. Nace. A linear programming based approach for computing optimal fair splittable routing. In *Proc. 7th IEEE International Symposium on Computer and Communications (ISCC'2002)*, 2002.

[Nas50a] J. F. Nash, Jr. Equilibrium points in n-person games. *Proc. National Academy of Sciences*, 36:48–49, 1950.

[Nas50b] J. F. Nash, Jr. Non-cooperative games. PhD thesis, mathematics department, Princeton University, 1950.

[Naz87] J. L. Nazareth. *Computer Solutions for Linear Programs*. Oxford University Press, 1987.

[NDGL03] D. Nace, L. N. Doan, E. Gourdin, and B. Liau. The fair multi-commodity flow problem: Results and applications on telecommunications networks. Technical Report, 2003.

[Nem67] G. L. Nemhauser. *Introduction to Dynamic Programming*. John Wiley & Sons, 1967.

[NJZ99] K. Nichols, V. Jacobson, and L. Zhang. A two-bit differentiated services architecture for the Internet. *Internet RFC 2638*, July 1999. http://www.ietf.org/rfc/rfc2638.txt.

[NP92] S. Narasimhan and H. Pirkul. Hierarchical concentrator location problem. *Computer Communication*, 15:185–191, 1992.

[NP02] P. Nilsson and M. Pióro. Solving dimensioning tasks for proportionally fair networks carrying elastic traffic. In *Proc. Performance 2002*, 2002.

[NPD03] P. Nilsson, M. Pióro, and Z. Dziong. Link protection within an existing backbone network. In *Proc. International Network Optimization Conference (INOC)*, 2003.

[NSB$^+$02] A. Nucci, B. Schroeder, S. Bhattacharyya, N. Taft, and C. Diot. IGP link weight assignment for transient link failures. In *Technical Report TR02-ATL-071000, Sprint ATL*, 2002. (extended version of Reference [NSB$^+$03]).

[NSB$^+$03] A. Nucci, B. Schroeder, S. Bhattacharyya, N. Taft, and C. Diot. IGP link weight assignment for transient link failures. In *Proc. 18th International Teletraffic Congress (ITC18)*, pages 321–330, Berlin, Germany, September 2003.

[NW88] G. L. Nemhauser and L. A. Wolsey. *Integer and Combinatorial Optimization*. John Wiley & Sons, 1988.

[Ogr97] W. Ogryczak. On the lexicographical minmax approach to location problems. *European Journal of Operational Research*, 100:566–587, 1997.

[Oğu02] O. Oğuz. Generalized column generation for linear programming. *Management Science*, 48(3):444–452, 2002.

[OH68] W. Orchard-Hays. *Advanced Linear Programming Computing Techniques*. McGraw-Hill, 1968.

[OL96] I. H. Osman and G. Laporte. Metaheuristics: A bibliography. *Annals of Operations Research*, 63:513–628, 1996.

[OM94] M. E. O'Kelly and H. J. Miller. The hub network design problem: A review and synthesis. *Journal of Transport Geography*, 2:31–40, 1994.

[OP71] W. Oettli and W. Prager. Optimal and suboptimal capacity allocation in communication networks. *Journal of Optimization Theory and Applications*, 8:396–411, 1971.

[Ora90] D. Oran. OSI IS-IS intra-domain routing protocol. *Internt RFC 1142*, February 1990. http://www.ietf.org/rfc/rfc1142.txt (re-publication of Reference [ISO90]).

[OS03] W. Ogryczak and T. Sliwinski. On solving linear programs with ordered weighted averaging objective. *European Journal of Operational Research*, 148:80–91, 2003.

[OW03] S. Orlowski and R. Wessäly. Comparing restoration concept using optimal network configurations with integrated hardware and routing decisions. In *Proc. Design of Reliable Communication Networks (DRCN'2003)*, Banff, Canada, 2003.

[OZ96] W. Ogryczak and K. Zorychta. Modular optimizer for mixed integer programming MOMIP (version 2.3. working paper). Technical report, IIASA, Austria, 1996.

[Pad91] M. Padberg. *Linear Optimization and Extensions*. Springer-Verlag, 1991.

[PCC03] M. M. B. Pascoal, V. Captivo, and J. C. N. Climaco. An algorithm for ranking quickest simple paths. *Computers & Operations Research*, 2003.

[PD99] M. Pickavet and P. Demeester. Long-term planning of WDM networks: A comparison between single-period and multi-period techniques. *Photonic Network Communications*, 1(4):331–346, December 1999.

[PD03] L. Peterson and B. Davie. *Computer Networks—A Systems Approach, 3rd Edition*. Morgan Kaufmann Publishers, 2003.

[Per01] H. G. Perros. *An Introduction to ATM Networks*. John Wiley & Sons, 2001.

[PG97] M. Pióro and P. Gajowniczek. Solving multicommodity integral flow problems by simulated allocation. *Telecommunication Systems*, 7:17–28, 1997.

[Pig12] A. C. Pigou. *Wealth and Welfare*. Macmillan, 1912.

[Pió97a] M. Pióro. Robust design problems in telecommunication networks. In *Proc. 15th International Teletraffic Congress (ITC15)*. Washington, D.C., 1997.

[Pió97b] M. Pióro. Simulation approach to the optimization of multicommodity integral flow networks. In *Proc. International Conference on Optimization and Simulation*, Singapore, 1997.

[Pió99] M. Pióro. ATM network design. technical report p10352-1, swap project. Technical report, Lund University, 1999.

[Pir87] H. Pirkul. Efficient algorithms for the capacitated concentrator location problem. *Computers and Operations Research*, 14:197–208, 1987.

[PJH⁺01] M. Pióro, A. Juttner, J. Harmatos, A. Szentesi, P. Gajowniczek, and A. Myslek. Topological design of telecommunication networks. In *Proc. 17th International Teletraffic Congress (ITC17)*, pages 629–642, Salvador de Bahia, Brazil, 2001.

[PK96] K. Park and S. Kang. An integer programming approach to the bandwidth packing problem. *Management Science*, 42:1277–1291, 1996.

[PKL03] S. Park, D. Kim, and K. Lee. An integer programming approach to the path selection problems. In *Proc. International Network Optimization Conference (INOC'2003)*, pages 448–453, 2003.

[PKNM02] M. Pióro, E. Kubilinskas, P. Nilsson, and M. Matuszewski. Robust dimensioning of proportionally fair networks. In *Proc. 2nd Polish-German Teletraffic Symposium (PGTS'2002)*, Gdansk, Poland, 2002.

[PMF02] M. Pióro, G. Malicsko, and G. Fodor. Optimal link capacity dimensioning in proportionally fair networks. In *Proc. Networking'2002*, 2002.

[PMJ⁺01] M. Pióro, A. Myslek, A. Juttner, J. Harmatos, and A. Szentesi. Topological design of MPLS networks. In *Proc. IEEE Global Communications Conference (GLOBECOM'2001)*, volume 1, pages 12–16, 2001.

[PNKF03] M. Pióro, P. Nilsson, E. Kubilinskas, and G. Fodor. On efficient max-min fair routing algorithms. In *Proc. 8th IEEE International Symposium on Computer and Communications (ISCC'2003)*, 2003.

[Pop89] J. W. Popper, III . Restoration of fiber networks: a comparison of ring versus route diversity. In *Proc. IEEE Southeastcon'89*, pages 609–613, April 1989.

[PR94] M. Parker and J. Ryan. A column generation algorithm for bandwidth packing. *Telecommunication Systems*, 2:185–195, 1994.

[PS98] M. Pióro and M. Szcześniak. Lagrangean relaxation in the design of multi-layer robust multicommodity flow networks. In *Proc. 5th Polish Teletraffic Symposium*, Warsaw, Poland, 1998.

[PS99] M. Pióro and M. Szcześniak. Design of multi-layer robust telecommunication networks: Cost analysis of protection mechanisms using Lagrangean relaxation. In *Proc. 16th International Teletraffic Congress (ITC16)*, pages 989–998. Edinburgh, Scotland, 1999.

[PS00] M. Pióro and M. Szcześniak. Application of the dual Benders decomposition approach to the design of multi-layer robust telecommunication networks. In *Proc. Design of Reliable Communication Networks (DRCN'2000)*, Munich, Germany, 2000.

[PS01] M. Pióro and T. Szymanski. Basic reconfiguration options in multi-layer robust telecommunication networks. In *Proc. 17th International Teletraffic Congress (ITC17)*, pages 271–284, Salvador de Bahia, Brazil, 2001.

[PSA04] P. Pan, G. Swallow, and A. Atlas (eds.). Fast reroute extensions to RSVP-TE for LSP tunnels. Internet Drafts, 2004.

[PSG⁺00] M. Pióro, T. Stidsen, A. Glenstrup, Ch. Fender, and H. Chriastiansen. Design problems in robust optical networks. In *Networks 2000*, 2000.

[PSH+02] M. Pióro, A. Szentesi, J. Harmatos, A. Jüttner, P. Gajowniczek, and S. Kozdrowski. On OSPF related network optimization problems. *Performance Evaluation*, 48:201–223, 2002. (A preliminary version of this paper appeared in the proc. IFIP ATM IP 2000, Ilkley, England, July 2000).

[PT92] J. A. M. Potters and S. H. Tijs. The nucleous of s matrix game and other nucleoli. *Mathematics of Operations Research*, 17:164–174, 1992.

[PW85] M. Pióro and B. Wallström. Multi-hour optimization of non-hierarchical circuit-switched communication networks with sequential routing. *Proc. 11th International Teletraffic Congress (ITC11)*, pages 788–794, 1985.

[PW00] K. Park and W. Willinger (ed.). *Self-Similar Network Traffic and Performance Evaluation*. Wiley-Interscience, 2000.

[Rap64] Y. Rapp. Planning of a junction network in a multi-exchange area I. *General Principles Ericsson Tech.*, 20(1):77–130, 1964.

[Rap65] Y. Rapp. Planning of a junction network in a multi-exchange area II. *Extensions of the Principles and Applications. Ericsson Tech.*, 21(2):187–240, 1965.

[Rap67] Y. Rapp. Planning of a junction network in a multi-exchange area III. In *Proc. 5th International Teletraffic Congress (ITC5)*, New York, 1967.

[Raw69] M. R. Rawls. A column generation scheme for the deterministic multicommodity warehousing model with cash liquidity constraints. 1969. CORE Discussion No. 6902,ICMP.

[Raw71] J. Rawls. *The Theory of Justice*. Harvard University Press, Cambridge, 1971.

[Rey83] R. F. Rey. *(ed.) Engineering and Operations in the Bell System— 2nd Edition*. AT&T Bell Laboratories, Murray Hill, New Jersey, 1983.

[RJ03] G. N. Rouskas and L. E. Jackson. Optimal granularity of mpls tunnels. In *Proc. 18th. International Teletraffic Congress (ITC18)*, pages 1–10, Berlin, Germany, 2003.

[RK03] A. Rosenberg and S. Kemp. *CDMA Capacity and Quality Optimization*. McGraw-Hill, New York, 2003.

[RM01] U. Ranadive and D. Medhi. Some observations on the effect of route fluctuation and network link failure on TCP. In *Proc. 10th IEEE International Conference on Computer Communications and Networks (ICCCN'01)*, pages 460–467, Scottsdale, AZ, October 2001.

[RND77] E. M. Reingold, J. Nievergelt, and N. Deo. *Combinatorial Algorithms*. Prentice Hall, New Jersey, 1977.

[Rob72] S. M. Robinson. A quadratically-convergent algorithm for general nonlinear programming problems. *Mathematical Programming*, 7:145–156, 1972.

[Rob87] S. M. Robinson. Convex programming (invited essay). In *The New Palgrave: A Dictionary of Economics (J. Eatwell, M. Milgate, P. Newman, eds.)*, volume 1, pages 647–659. Macmillan, 1987.

[Roc70] R. T. Rockafellar. *Convex Analysis*. Princeton University Press, 1970.

[Ros60] J. B. Rosen. The gradient projection method for nonlinear programming: Part I, linear constraints. *SIAM Journal*, 8:181–217, 1960.

[Ros87] E. Rosenberg. A nonlinear programming heuristic for computing optimal link capacities in a multi-hour alternate routing communication network. *Operations Research*, 35:354–367, 1987.

[Ros94] E. Rosenberg. Designing multi-hour hierarchical communications networks with fixed charge and piecewise linear costs. *Telecommunication Systems*, 13(2), 1994.

[Ros01] E. Rosenberg. Dual ascent for uncapacitated telecommunication network design with access, backbone and switch costs. *Telecommunication Systems*, 16:423–435, 2001.

[Ros03a] K. Rosen. *Discrete Mathematics and Its Applications, 5th Edition.* McGraw Hill, 2003.

[Ros03b] A. Rosenberg. Private communication (in regard to feasibility of long, non-stop flights), 2003. email of June 8, 2003.

[RR01] K. G. Ramakrishnan and M. A. Rodrigues. Optimal routing in shortest-path data networks. *Bell Labs Technical Journal*, 6(1):117–138, 2001.

[RS02] R. Ramaswami and K. N. Sivarajan. *Optical Networks: A Practical Perspective (2nd Edition).* Morgan Kaufmann Publishers, 2002.

[RT02] T. Roughgarden and E. Tardos. How bad is selfish routing? *Journal of the ACM*, 49(2):236–259, March 2002. (A preliminary version of this paper appeared in Proceedings of the 41st Annual IEEE Symposium on Foundations of Computer Science, November 2000).

[RTB67] J. Reed, R. Toombs, and N. A. Barricelli. Simulation of biological evolution and machine learning. *Journal of Theoretical Biology*, 17:319–342, 1967.

[RTV97] C. Roos, T. Terlaky, and J.P. Vial. *Theory and Algorithms for Linear Optimization: An Interior Point Approach.* John Wiley & Sons, 1997.

[Rus02] T. Russell. *Signaling System # 7 (Fourth Edition).* McGraw-Hill, 2002.

[Sai67] R. Saigal. *Multicommodity Flow in Directed Networks.* PhD thesis, Stanford University, 1967.

[Sal94] M. J. Saltzman. Mixed-integer programming. *ORMS Today*, pages 42–51, April 1994.

[San00] I. Saniee. A distributed scheme for implementation of shared protection in optical meshes. Technical report, Bell Laboratories, December 2000.

[SAPM03] S. Srivastava, G. Agrawal, M. Pióro, and D. Medhi. Determining feasible weight system under various objectives for OSPF networks. Technical report, University of Missouri-Kansas City, September 2003.

[Sat96] K.-I. Sato. *Advances in Transport Network Technologies - Photonic Networks, ATM, and SDH.* Artech House, 1996.

[Sch77] M. Schwartz. *Computer-Communication Network Design and Analysis.* Prentice Hall, 1977.

[Sco69] A. J. Scott. The optimal network problem: Some computational procedures. *Trans. Res.*, 3:201–210, 1969.

[SD94] M. Stoer and G. Dahl. A polyhedral approach to multicommodity network design. *Numerische Mathematik*, 68:149–167, 1994.

[SDD89] S. Sen, R. D. Doverspike, and M. S. Dunatunga. Unified facilities optimizer. Technical report, University of Arizona, Department of Systems and Industrial Engineering, January 1989.

[Sen73] A. Sen. *On Economic Inequality*. Clarendon Press, Oxford, 1973.

[SG04] A. Sack and W. Grover. Hamiltonian p-cycles for fiber-level protection in homogeneous and semi-homogeneous optical networks. *IEEE Networks*, 18(2):49–56, 2004.

[Sha79] J. E. Shapiro. *Mathematical Programming: Structures and Algorithms*. John Wiley & Sons, 1979.

[Sha84] R. D. Shapiro. *Optimization Models for Planning and Allocation: Text and Cases in Mathematical Programming*. John Wiley & Sons, 1984.

[Sha90] R. L. Sharma. *Network Topology Optimization*. John Wiley & Sons, 1990.

[Sho85] N. Z. Shor. *Minimization Methods for Nondifferentiable Functions*. Springer-Verlag, 1985.

[SHSO93] M. Slomiński, S. Hasegawa, H. Sakauchi, and H. Okazaki. Multi-ring approach for ATM-VP networks survivability. In *Proc. IEEE International Conference on Communications (ICC'93), Geneva, Switzerland*, pages 245–249, 1993.

[Sin99] M. Sinclair. Evolutionary telecommunications: A summary. In A. Wu, editor, *Proc. 1999 Genetic and Evolutionary Computation Conference*. Morgan Kaufmann Publishers, 1999.

[SIOD04] R. Sabella, P. Iovanna, G. Oriolo, and P. D'Aprile. Routing and grooming of data flows into lightpaths in new generation network based on the GMPLS paradigm. *Photonic Network Communications*, 7(2):131–144, 2004.

[Ski97] S. Skiena. *The Algorithm Design Manual*. Springer Verlag, New York, 1997.

[SKMP03] S. Srivastava, B. Krithikaivasan, D. Medhi, and M. Pióro. Traffic engineering in the presence of tunneling and diversity constraints: Formulation and Lagrangian decomposition approach. In *Proc. 18th International Teletraffic Congress (ITC18)*, pages 461–470, Berlin, Germany, 2003.

[SKV+02] S. Srivastava, B. Krithikaivasan, V. Venkatachalam, C. Beard, D. Medhi, A. van de Liefvoort, W. Alanqar, and A. Nagarajan. A case study on evaluating the benefits of MPLS traffic engineering through constraint-based routing and network controls. In *Proc. IEEE International Conference on Communications (ICC'2002), New York, NY*, pages 2437–2442, 2002.

[SNH90] H. Sakauchi, Y. Nashimura, and S. Hasegawa. A self-healing network with an economical spare-channel assignment. In *IEEE Global Communications Conference (GLOBECOM'90)*, 1990.

[SNT85] Y. Sawaragi, H. Nakayama, and T. Tanino. *Theory of Multiobjective Optimization*. Academic Press, 1985.

[SO94a] M. Slomiński and H. Okazaki. Guided restoration of ATM cross-connect networks. In *Proc. IEEE International Conference on Communications (ICC'94), New Orleans, USA*, pages 446–470, 1994.

[SO94b] M. Slomiński and H. Okazaki. Planning survivability in ATM networks. In *Proc. 7th International Telecommunication Network Planning Symposium, NETWORKS'94, Budapest*, pages 65–70, 1994.

[SOT90] K.-I. Sato, S. Ohta, and I. Tokizawa. Broad-band ATM network architecture based on virtual paths. *IEEE Trans. on Comm.*, 38:1212–1222, 1990.

[Sri93] R. Sridharan. A Lagrangian heuristic for the capacitated plant location problem with single-source constraints. *European Journal of Operations Research*, 66:305–312, 1993.

[SSO+03] R. Sabella, M. Settembre, G. Oriolo, F. Razza, F. Ferlito, and G. Conte. A multi-layer solution for path provisioning in new-generation optical/MPLS networks. *IEEE Journal on Lightwave Technology*, 21(5):1141–1155, 2003.

[ST84] J. W. Suurballe and R. E. Tarjan. A quick method for finding shortest pairs of disjoint paths. *Networks*, 14:325–336, 1984.

[STM99] A. Srikitja, D. Tipper, and D. Medhi. On providing survivable services in the next generation Internet. In *Proc. IEEE MILCOM'99*, pages 902–907, Atlantic City, NJ, October 1999.

[Sto92] M. Stoer. *Design of Survivable Networks*, volume 1532. Springer-Verlag, 1992.

[Suu74] J. W. Suurballe. Disjoint paths in a network. *Networks*, 4:125–145, 1974.

[SWK69] K. Steiglitz, P. Weiner, and D. J. Kleitman. The design of minimum-cost survivable networks. *IEEE Trans. Circuit Theory*, 16(4):455–460, November 1969.

[SWY03] Y. Song, A. Wool, and B. Yener. Combinatorial design of multi-ring networks with combined routing and flow control. *Computer Networks*, 3(3):247–267, 2003.

[Sys66] R. Syski. *Introduction to Congestion Theory in Telephone Systems*. Elsevier, 1966.

[Szy02] T. Szymański. Application of Benders decomposition to the design of robust telecommunication networks with constrained reconfiguration. In *Proc. 2nd Polish-German Teletraffic Symposium (PGTS'2000)*, Dresden, Germany, 2002.

[Tan03] A. Tanenbaum. *Computer Networks—Fourth Edition*. Prentice Hall, 2003.

[TCR03] J. Tapolcai, T. Cinkler, and A. Recski. On-line routing algorithms with shared protection in WDM networks. In *IFIP ONDM 2003, Budapest*, 2003.

[Ter01] T. Terlaky. An easy way to teach interior point methods. *European Journal of Operational Research*, 130:1–19, 2001.

[TH00] A. Tomaszewski and N. Le Huang. Design of transport networks with multicast communications. In *Proc. 2nd Polish-German Teletraffic Symposium (PGTS'2002)*, Gdansk, Poland, 2000.

[Tom66] J. A. Tomlin. Minimum cost multicommodity network flows. *Operations Research*, 14:45–51, 1966.

[Tom70] J. A. Tomlin. Branch and bound methods for integer and nonconvex programming. In J. Abbie, editor, *Integer and Nonlinear Programming*, pages 437–450. North-Holland, 1970.

[Tom00] A. Tomaszewski. Private communication. August 2000.

[Tom02] A. Tomaszewski. A polynomial algorithm for solving a general mx-min fairness problem. In *Proc. 2nd Polish-German Teletraffic Symposium (PGTS'2002)*, Gdansk, Poland, 2002.

[Top88] D. Topkis. A k shortest path algorithm for adaptive routing in communication networks. *IEEE Transactions on Communications*, 36(7), July 1988.

[Tow88] D. M. Tow. Network management—recent advances and future trends. *IEEE Journal of Sel. Areas. in Comm.*, 6(4):732–741, 1988.

[TPB01] T. Tuyet, L. Pham, and W. Ben-Ameur. Design of survivable networks based on end-to-end rerouting. In *Proc. Workshop on Design of Reliable Communication Networks (DRCN'01), Budapest*, 2001.

[Tsa86] Y. K. Tsai. Inter-office transmission network planning with the network planning system (NPS). In *Proc. IEEE Global Communications Conference (GLOBECOM'86)*, pages 25.6.1–25.6.5, 1986.

[TW93] J. A. Tomlin and J. S. Welch. Mathematical programming systems. In E. Coffman and J.K. Lenstra, editors, *Handbook of Operations Research and Management Science: Computation*. North-Holland, 1993.

[Van98] R. J. Vanderbei. *Linear Programming: Foundations and Extensions (2nd Edition)*. Kluwer Academic Publishers, 1998.

[VCD⁺01] K. Vinodkrishnan, N. Chandhok, A. Durresi, R. Jain, R. Jagannathan, and S. Seetharaman. Survivability in IP over WDM networks. *Journal of High Speed Networks*, 10(2):79–90, 2001.

[VHS97] P. A. Veitch, I. Hawker, and D. G. Smith. Enhancing the self-healing capability of statically protected ATM networks. In D. Kouvatsos, editor, *ATM Networks Performance Modelling and Analysis, Volume 3*. Chapman & Hall, 1997.

[VPD04] J.-P. Vasseur, M. Pickavet, and P. Demeester. *Network Recovery: Protection and Restoration of Optical, SONET-SDH, IP, and MPLS*. Morgan Kaufmann Publishers, 2004.

[VSH96] R. A. Veitch, D. G. Smith, and I. Hawker. A comparison of pre-planned techniques for virtual path restoration. In D. D. Kouvatsos, editor, *Performance Modelling and Evaluation of ATM Networks*. Chapman & Hall, 1996.

[War52] J. G. Wardrop. Some theoretical aspects of road traffic research. *Proc. Inst of Civil Engineers, Part-2*, 1(2):325–378, 1952.

[Was91] O. J. Wasem. An algorithm for designing rings for survivable fiber networks. *IEEE Trans. on Reliability*, 40:428–432, 1991.

[WB02] J. Weston-Dawkes and S. Baroni. Mesh network grooming and restoration optimized for optical bypass. In *Proc. 2002 National Fiber Optic Engineers Conference*, pages 1438–1449, 2002.

[WCB91] T.-H. Wu, R. H. Cardwell, and M. Broyden. A multi-period design model for survivable network architecture selection for SONET interoffice networks. *IEEE Trans. on Reliability*, 40:417–427, October 1991.

[Wes00] R. Wessäly. *Dimensioning Survivable Capacitated NETworks*. Cuvillier Verlag Gottingen, 2000.

[Wes02] J. Weston-Dawkes. ULH-optimized grooming in optical mesh networks. In *Proc. Optical Fiber Communication Conference (OFC'2002)*, pages 784–786, March 2002.

[Wil86] H. Wilf. *Algorithms and Complexity*. Prentice Hall, New Jersey, 1986.

[Wil93] H. P. Williams. *Model Building in Mathematical Programming - Third Edition Revised*. John Wiles & Sons, Chichester, England, 1993.

[Wil01] W. E. Wilhelm. A technical review of column generation in integer programming. *Optimization and Engineering*, 2:159–200, 2001.

[Wol62] P. Wolfe. The reduced-gradient method. unpublished manuscript, RAND Corporation, 1962.

[Wol89] L. A. Wolsey. Strong formulations for mixed integer programming: A survey. *Mathematical Programming*, 45:173–191, 1989.

[Wol98] L. A. Wolsey. *Integer Programming.* John Wiley & Sons, 1998.

[Wol03] L. A. Wolsey. Strong formulations for mixed integer programs: Valid inequalities and extended forumulations. *Mathematical Programming Series B*, 97(1-2):423–447, 2003.

[WP98] W. Willinger and V. Paxson. Where mathematics meets the Internet. *Notices of the American Mathematical Society*, 45(8):961–970, August 1998.

[WTE96] W. Willinger, M. S. Taqqu, and A. Erramilli. A bibliographical guide to self-similar traffic and performance modeling for high-speed networks. In *Stochastic Networks: Theory and Applications (F. P. Kelly, S. Zachary and I Ziedins, eds.)*, pages 339–366. Clarendon Press, Oxford, 1996.

[WTJM97] W.-P. Wang, D. Tipper, B. Jæger, and D. Medhi. Fault recovery routing in wide area packet networks. In *Proc. 15th International Teletraffic Congress (ITC15)*, pages 1077–1086, Washington, DC, June 1997.

[Wu92] T.-H. Wu. *Fiber Network Service Survivability.* Artech House, 1992.

[WW00] J. Wessels and A. P. Wierzbicki. Model-based decision support. In A. P. Wierzbicki, M. Makowski, and J. Wessels, editors, *Model-Based Decision Support Methodology with Environmental Applications*, pages 9–28. Kluwer Academic Publishers, 2000.

[WWC94] O. J. Wasem, T.-H. Wu, and R. H. Cardwell. Survivable SONET networks—design methodology. *IEEE Journal on Selected Areas in Communications*, 12:205–212, 1994.

[WWZ01] Y. Wang, Z. Wang, and L. Zhang. Internet traffic engineering without full mesh overlaying. In *Proc. IEEE Conference on Computer Communications (INFOCOM'2001)*, pages 565–571, New York, USA, 2001.

[XM] XPRESS-MP. *XPRESS-MP Software.* http://www.dashoptimization.com/.

[Yag71] B. Yaged. Minimum cost routing for static network models. *Networks*, 1:139–172, 1971.

[Yag73] B. Yaged. Minimum cost routing for dynamic network models. *Networks*, 3:193–224, 1973.

[Yen71] J. Y. Yen. Finding the k shortest loopless paths in a network. *Management Science*, 17:712–716, 1971.

[YH88] C. H. Yaag and S. Hasegawa. FITNESS: Failure immunization technology for network services survivability. In *Proc. IEEE Global Communications Conference (GLOBECOM'88)*, 1988.

[YL92] J. R. Yee and F. Y. S. Lin. A routing algorithm for virtual circuit data networks with multiple sessions per O-D pair. *Networks*, 22:185–208, 1992.

[You94] H. P. Young. *Equity in Theory and Practice.* Princeton University Press, 1994.

[YOY97] B. Yener, Y. Ofek, and M. Yung. Combinatorial design of congestion free networks. *IEEE/ACM Trans. on Networking*, 5:989–1000, 1997.

[Yua03] D. Yuan. A bi-criteria optimization approach for robust OSPF routing. In *Proc. IEEE Workshop on IP Operations and Management (IPOM'2003)*, pages 91–98, Kansas City, USA, October 2003.

[YW02] Y. Yang and J. Wang. Routing permutations with link-disjoint and node-disjoint paths in a class of self-routable networks. In *IEEE International Conference on Parallel Processing (ICPP'02), Vancouver*, pages 154–165, 2002.

[Zad73] N. Zadeh. On building minimum cost communication networks. *Networks*, 3:315–331, 1973.

[Zad74] N. Zadeh. On building minimum cost communication networks over time. *Networks*, 4:19–34, 1974.

[Zan69] W. Zangwill. *Nonlinear Programming: A Unified Approach*. Prentice-Hall, 1969.

[ZCB96] E. Zegura, K. Calvert, and S. Bhattacharjee. How to model an Internetwork. In *Proc. IEEE Conference on Computer Communication (INFOCOM'1996)*, pages 594–602, 1996.

[Zho95] J. Zhou. Experience with a decomposition algorithm for solving a multi-hour computer communication network design problem with multi-path routing. MS thesis in computer science, University of Missouri–Kansas City, June 1995.

[ZM03] J. Zupan and D. Medhi. An alarm management approach in the management of multi-layered networks. In *Proc. 3rd IEEE Workshop on IP Operations and Management(IPOM'2003)*, pages 77–84, October 2003.

[ZO81] K. Zorychta and W. Ogryczak. *Linear and Integer Programming*. WNT Warsaw, 1981. in polish.

[ZOM03] H. Zang, C. Ou, and B. Mukherjee. Path-protection routing and wavelength assignment in WDM mesh networks under duct-layer constraints. *IEEE/ACM Trans. on Networking*, 11:248–258, 2003.

[ZS03] Y. Zhou and H. Sethu. On achieving fairness in the joint allocation of processing and bandwidth resources. In *Proc. 11th IEEE International Workshop on Quality of Service (IWQoS'2003)*, pages 97–114, 2003.

INDEX

C

E

O

Q

R

W